AF788716

Preface

This Advance Legislative Service is provided as part of the annual supplement service to all subscribers to the Tennessee Code Annotated. Depending upon the availability of acts, pamphlets will be issued at approximately monthly intervals.

The acts are reproduced as received by the publisher, and no corrections or editorial changes have been made.

This pamphlet contains a summary of public acts passed during the 2013 Regular Session of the Tennessee General Assembly, the text of these acts, a cumulative table of Tennessee Code Annotated sections which have been amended, repealed, transferred, or added, a table of effective dates, and a cumulative index. The text of acts also contains marginal notes of code sections amended, repealed, transferred, or added, and marginal notes of effective dates. Tennessee Code Annotated section numbers and subsection and subdivision designations are subject to change by the Tennessee Code Commission pursuant to T.C.A. § 1-1-108. Section numbers not assigned by the General Assembly are identified by an asterisk in the Table of Sections Affected. In instances where the effective date could not be determined because it is dependent upon some future contingency, an asterisk and footnote have been inserted explaining the contingency.

This pamphlet does not contain notes to recent cases, Attorney General opinions or law review annotations, or Tennessee Code Annotated section corrections or compiler or code commission notes. For this information, please refer to the Advance Code Service.

Please note that any law requiring the expenditure of state funds may be null and void under Tennessee Constitution Art. II, § 24, as amended in 1978, unless the first-year funding is approved in the year in which the act is passed.

The publisher has prepared the following aids:

July 2013 LexisNexis

Summary of 2013 Acts

T.C.A. Sec.	Action	Ch. No.	Bill No.	Sec. No.	Eff. Date	Pamphlet No.
1-1-108	Amended	236	sb1218	34	4-19-2013	2
1-2-114	Amended	1	sb0034	1	3-7-2013	1
1-3-120	Added	124	sb0461	1	4-12-2013	1
2-1-112	Amended	146	sb0873	1-3	4-12-2013	1
2-2-109	Amended	179	sb0127	2	7-1-2013	2
2-2-109	Amended	231	sb0906	1	7-1-2013	2
2-2-111	Amended	231	sb0906	2	7-1-2013	2
2-2-140	Amended	236	sb1218	65	4-19-2013	2
2-3-107	Amended	231	sb0906	3	7-1-2013	2
2-3-308	Amended	236	sb1218	65	4-19-2013	2
2-4-102	Amended	231	sb0906	4	7-1-2013	2
2-5-151	Amended	231	sb0906	5	7-1-2013	2
2-5-208	Amended	231	sb0906	6	7-1-2013	2
2-5-211	Amended	179	sb0127	3	7-1-2013	2
2-6-201	Amended	231	sb0906	7	7-1-2013	2
2-6-401	Amended	231	sb0906	8	7-1-2013	2
2-7-112	Amended	178	sb0125	1-3	4-23-2013	2
2-7-112	Amended	231	sb0906	9	7-1-2013	2
2-8-101	Amended	179	sb0127	1	7-1-2013	2
2-8-111	Amended	449	sb0026	1	7-1-2013	2
2-10-101	Amended	231	sb0906	10	7-1-2013	2
2-12-116	Amended	268	sb0626	1, 6	4-25-2013	2
2-12-201	Amended	268	sb0626	2, 3	4-25-2013	2
2-12-202	Amended	268	sb0626	4, 5	4-25-2013	2
3-1-106	Amended	241	hb0080	1-4	11-4-2014	2
3-2-107	Amended	446	sb0116	1	5-16-2013	2
3-9-101	Amended	236	sb1218	93	4-19-2013	2
3-12-109	Added*	475	sb0595	1	7-1-2013	2
3-17-103	Amended	109	sb0418	1-5	4-8-2013	1
3-17-108	Amended	236	sb1218	64	4-19-2013	2
4-1-333	Added*	152	sb0071	1	4-16-2013	1
4-1-412	Added	75	hb0553	2	4-1-2013	1
4-3-717	Amended	71	hb0149	1	4-2-2013	1
4-3-727	Amended	252	hb0809	5	4-19-2013	2
4-3-731	Added*	267	sb0605	1	7-1-2013	2
4-3-737	Amended	236	sb1218	12	4-19-2013	2
4-3-738	Added*	299	sb0806	1	4-29-2013	2

*Section number(s) not assigned by General Assembly

T.C.A. Sec.	Action	Ch. No.	Bill No.	Sec. No.	Eff. Date	Pamphlet No.
4-3-1003	Amended	454	sb0501	41	5-16-2013	2
4-3-1006	Amended	454	sb0501	25, 29	5-16-2013	2
4-3-1011	Amended	454	sb0501	10-12	5-16-2013	2
4-3-1011	Transferred to 9-4-5117	454	sb0501	13	5-16-2013	2
4-3-1012	Amended	236	sb1218	3	4-19-2013	2
4-3-1013	Amended	236	sb1218	49	4-19-2013	2
4-3-1018	Amended	236	sb1218	3	4-19-2013	2
4-3-1021	Added*	408	sb0063	1	5-14-2013	2
4-3-1104	Amended	207	sb0902	10	4-23-2013	2
4-3-1105	Amended	236	sb1218	3	4-19-2013	2
4-3-1105	Amended	454	sb0501	26	5-16-2013	2
4-3-1109	Amended	236	sb1218	4	4-19-2013	2
4-3-1109	Amended	423	sb0852	2	5-16-2013	2
4-3-1304	Amended	122	sb0493	2, 4, 6	7-1-2013	1
4-3-1405	Amended	473	sb0643	8	7-1-2013	2
4-3-1408	Amended	289	sb0200	1	4-29-2013	2
4-3-1409	Added	289	sb0200	2	4-29-2013	2
4-3-1422	Amended	448	sb0105	1	5-16-2013	2
4-3-2010	Amended	308	sb0521	19	7-1-2013	2
4-3-2018	Added*	184	sb0187	1	4-23-2013	2
4-3-2203	Amended	132	sb0331	3	4-12-2013	1
4-3-2205	Repealed	132	sb0331	4	4-12-2013	1
4-3-2303	Amended	236	sb1218	89	4-19-2013	2
4-3-2305	Amended	236	sb1218	88	4-19-2013	2
4-3-2305	Amended	308	sb0521	20	7-1-2013	2
4-3-2308	Repealed	308	sb0521	21	7-1-2013	2
4-3-2311	Amended	236	sb1218	88, 90	4-19-2013	2
4-3-2403	Amended	170	hb1035	19	4-16-2013	2
4-3-3001–4-3-3005	Added	464	sb1036	1	7-1-2013	2
4-3-5301–4-3-5305	Repealed	199	sb0770	1	4-23-2013	2
4-3-5301–4-3-5305	Repealed	454	sb0501	42	5-16-2013	2
4-4-101	Amended	454	sb0501	32	5-16-2013	2
4-4-119	Repealed	243	hb0155	2	4-19-2013	2
4-7-119	Obsolete	308	sb0521	18	7-1-2013	2
4-10-112	Amended	236	sb1218	13	4-19-2013	2
4-11-112	Added	248	hb0301	2	4-19-2013	2

*Section number(s) not assigned by General Assembly

T.C.A. Sec.	Action	Ch. No.	Bill No.	Sec. No.	Eff. Date	Pamphlet No.
4-11-401	Added*	290	sb0009	2	6-28-2014	2
4-11-402	Added*	290	sb0009	3	6-28-2014	2
4-11-403	Added*	290	sb0009	4	6-28-2014	2
4-11-404	Added*	290	sb0009	5	6-28-2014	2
4-11-405	Added*	290	sb0009	6	6-28-2014	2
4-14-109	Amended	252	hb0809	4	4-19-2013	2
4-14-303	Amended	252	hb0809	3	4-19-2013	2
4-15-104	Amended	363	hb1268	1	5-13-2013	2
4-16-101	Amended	21	sb0080	1, 3	3-20-2013	1
4-17-401–4-17-415	Repealed	198	sb0769	2	4-23-2013	2
4-20-301	Amended	478	sb0439	1	5-20-2013	2
4-22-101	Amended	228	sb0578	1, 2	4-19-2013	2
4-22-101	Amended	423	sb0852	3, 6	5-16-2013	2
4-22-103	Amended	236	sb1218	5	4-19-2013	2
4-22-103	Repealed	48	sb0081	1	3-26-2013	1
4-24-112	Amended	310	sb0453	1	4-29-2013	2
4-25-107	Amended	236	sb1218	70	4-19-2013	2
4-26-105	Amended	236	sb1218	14	4-19-2013	2
4-29-233	Amended	52	sb0305	1	3-26-2013	1
4-29-233	Amended	76	hb0747	1	4-1-2013	1
4-29-233	Amended	82	hb0793	1	4-1-2013	1
4-29-233	Amended	126	sb0369	1	4-12-2013	1
4-29-233	Amended	134	sb0304	1	4-12-2013	1
4-29-234	Amended	6	sb0307	1	3-7-2013	1
4-29-234	Amended	7	sb0335	1	3-7-2013	1
4-29-234	Amended	8	sb0340	1	3-7-2013	1
4-29-234	Amended	9	sb0341	1	3-7-2013	1
4-29-234	Amended	10	sb0347	1	3-7-2013	1
4-29-234	Amended	11	sb0349	1	3-7-2013	1
4-29-234	Amended	12	sb0350	1	3-7-2013	1
4-29-234	Amended	13	sb0354	1	3-7-2013	1
4-29-234	Amended	14	sb0367	1	3-7-2013	1
4-29-234	Amended	17	hb0752	1	3-14-2013	1
4-29-234	Amended	19	sb0342	1	3-14-2013	1
4-29-234	Amended	20	sb0362	1	3-14-2013	1
4-29-234	Amended	24	sb0315	1	3-20-2013	1
4-29-234	Amended	25	sb0323	1	3-20-2013	1

*Section number(s) not assigned by General Assembly

T.C.A. Sec.	Action	Ch. No.	Bill No.	Sec. No.	Eff. Date	Pamphlet No.
4-29-234	Amended	26	sb0324	1	3-20-2013	1
4-29-234	Amended	27	sb0325	1	3-20-2013	1
4-29-234	Amended	28	sb0344	1	3-20-2013	1
4-29-234	Amended	29	sb0345	1	3-20-2013	1
4-29-234	Amended	30	sb0346	1	3-20-2013	1
4-29-234	Amended	38	hb0753	1	3-22-2013	1
4-29-234	Amended	39	hb0774	1	3-22-2013	1
4-29-234	Amended	40	hb0775	1	3-22-2013	1
4-29-234	Amended	41	hb0776	1	3-22-2013	1
4-29-234	Amended	42	hb0777	1	3-22-2013	1
4-29-234	Amended	43	hb0779	1	3-22-2013	1
4-29-234	Amended	44	hb0782	1	3-22-2013	1
4-29-234	Amended	45	hb0783	1	3-22-2013	1
4-29-234	Amended	53	sb0321	1	3-26-2013	1
4-29-234	Amended	54	sb0322	1	3-26-2013	1
4-29-234	Amended	55	sb0329	1	3-26-2013	1
4-29-234	Amended	66	hb0834	1	4-1-2013	1
4-29-234	Amended	77	hb0748	1	4-1-2013	1
4-29-234	Amended	78	hb0762	1	4-1-2013	1
4-29-234	Amended	79	hb0785	1	4-1-2013	1
4-29-234	Amended	80	hb0787	1	4-1-2013	1
4-29-234	Amended	81	hb0789	1	4-1-2013	1
4-29-234	Amended	83	hb0824	1	4-1-2013	1
4-29-234	Amended	86	hb0829	1	4-8-2013	1
4-29-234	Amended	87	hb0750	1	4-8-2013	1
4-29-234	Amended	127	sb0360	1	4-12-2013	1
4-29-234	Amended	128	sb0355	1	4-12-2013	1
4-29-234	Amended	129	sb0351	1	4-12-2013	1
4-29-234	Amended	130	sb0338	1	4-12-2013	1
4-29-234	Amended	131	sb0336	1	4-12-2013	1
4-29-234	Amended	132	sb0331	1	4-12-2013	1
4-29-234	Amended	133	sb0328	1	4-12-2013	1
4-29-234	Amended	252	hb0809	1	4-19-2013	2
4-29-234	Amended	253	hb0837	1	4-19-2013	2
4-29-234	Amended	288	hb0790	1	4-25-2013	2
4-29-234	Amended	330	hb0755	1	5-13-2013	2
4-29-234	Amended	331	hb0766	1	5-13-2013	2

*Section number(s) not assigned by General Assembly

T.C.A. Sec.	Action	Ch. No.	Bill No.	Sec. No.	Eff. Date	Pamphlet No.
4-29-234	Amended	332	hb0780	1	5-13-2013	2
4-29-234	Amended	333	hb0794	1	5-13-2013	2
4-29-234	Amended	334	hb0810	1	5-13-2013	2
4-29-234	Amended	438	sb0333	1	5-16-2013	2
4-29-234	Amended	454	sb0501	4	7-1-2013	2
4-29-235	Amended	52	sb0305	2	3-26-2013	1
4-29-235	Amended	66	hb0834	2	4-1-2013	1
4-29-235	Amended	81	hb0789	2	4-1-2013	1
4-29-235	Amended	82	hb0793	2	4-1-2013	1
4-29-235	Amended	126	sb0369	2	7-1-2013	1
4-29-235	Amended	143	sb0791	1	4-12-2013	1
4-29-235	Amended	253	hb0837	2	4-19-2013	2
4-29-235	Amended	333	hb0794	2	5-13-2013	2
4-29-235	Amended	438	sb0333	2	5-16-2013	2
4-29-236	Amended	31	sb0375	1	3-20-2013	1
4-29-236	Amended	86	hb0829	2	4-8-2013	1
4-29-236	Amended	127	sb0360	2	4-12-2013	1
4-29-236	Amended	133	sb0328	2	4-12-2013	1
4-29-236	Amended	288	hb0790	2	4-25-2013	2
4-29-236	Amended	289	sb0200	102	7-1-2014	2
4-29-236	Amended	330	hb0755	2	5-13-2013	2
4-29-236	Amended	334	hb0810	2	5-13-2013	2
4-29-236	Amended	348	hb0830	1	5-13-2013	2
4-29-236	Amended	374	sb1246	1	5-6-2013	2
4-29-236	Amended	455	sb1392	1	7-1-2013	2
4-29-237	Amended	76	hb0747	2	4-1-2013	1
4-29-237	Amended	126	sb0369	3	4-12-2013	1
4-29-238	Amended	13	sb0354	2	3-7-2013	1
4-29-238	Amended	20	sb0362	2	3-14-2013	1
4-29-238	Amended	38	hb0753	2	3-22-2013	1
4-29-238	Amended	39	hb0774	2	3-22-2013	1
4-29-238	Amended	40	hb0775	2	3-22-2013	1
4-29-238	Amended	41	hb0776	2	3-22-2013	1
4-29-238	Amended	42	hb0777	2	3-22-2013	1
4-29-238	Amended	43	hb0779	2	3-22-2013	1
4-29-238	Amended	44	hb0782	2	3-22-2013	1
4-29-238	Amended	45	hb0783	2	3-22-2013	1

*Section number(s) not assigned by General Assembly

T.C.A. Sec.	Action	Ch. No.	Bill No.	Sec. No.	Eff. Date	Pamphlet No.
4-29-238	Amended	55	sb0329	2	3-26-2013	1
4-29-238	Amended	79	hb0785	2	4-1-2013	1
4-29-238	Amended	83	hb0824	2	4-1-2013	1
4-29-238	Amended	87	hb0750	2	4-8-2013	1
4-29-238	Amended	128	sb0355	2	4-12-2013	1
4-29-238	Amended	130	sb0338	2	4-12-2013	1
4-29-238	Amended	131	sb0336	2	4-12-2013	1
4-29-238	Amended	134	sb0304	2	4-12-2013	1
4-29-238	Amended	252	hb0809	2	4-19-2013	2
4-29-238	Amended	332	hb0780	2	5-13-2013	2
4-29-239	Added	8	sb0340	2	3-7-2013	1
4-29-239	Amended	9	sb0341	2	3-7-2013	1
4-29-239	Amended	10	sb0347	2	3-7-2013	1
4-29-239	Amended	17	hb0752	2	3-14-2013	1
4-29-239	Amended	19	sb0342	2	3-14-2013	1
4-29-239	Amended	24	sb0315	2	3-20-2013	1
4-29-239	Amended	25	sb0323	2	3-20-2013	1
4-29-239	Amended	26	sb0324	2	3-20-2013	1
4-29-239	Amended	27	sb0325	2	3-20-2013	1
4-29-239	Amended	28	sb0344	2	3-20-2013	1
4-29-239	Amended	29	sb0345	2	3-20-2013	1
4-29-239	Amended	30	sb0346	2	3-20-2013	1
4-29-239	Amended	54	sb0322	2	3-26-2013	1
4-29-239	Amended	78	hb0762	2	4-1-2013	1
4-29-239	Amended	132	sb0331	2	4-12-2013	1
4-29-239	Amended	289	sb0200	105	7-1-2014	2
4-29-240	Added	6	sb0307	2	3-7-2013	1
4-29-240	Amended	7	sb0335	2	3-7-2013	1
4-29-240	Amended	11	sb0349	2	3-7-2013	1
4-29-240	Amended	12	sb0350	2	3-7-2013	1
4-29-240	Amended	14	sb0367	2	3-7-2013	1
4-29-240	Amended	53	sb0321	2	3-26-2013	1
4-29-240	Amended	77	hb0748	2	4-1-2013	1
4-29-240	Amended	80	hb0787	2	4-1-2013	1
4-29-240	Amended	129	sb0351	2	4-12-2013	1
4-29-240	Amended	331	hb0766	2	5-13-2013	2
4-32-101; 4-32-103	Repealed	454	sb0501	3	7-1-2013	2

*Section number(s) not assigned by General Assembly

T.C.A. Sec.	Action	Ch. No.	Bill No.	Sec. No.	Eff. Date	Pamphlet No.
4-35-107	Amended	64	sb0138	1	4-1-2013	1
4-38-103	Amended	236	sb1218	71	4-19-2013	2
4-47-101–4-47-105	Repealed	308	sb0521	22	7-1-2013	2
4-51-109; 4-51-111	Amended	236	sb1218	64	4-19-2013	2
4-51-112; 4-51-116	Amended	236	sb1218	65	4-19-2013	2
4-51-129	Amended	236	sb1218	72	4-19-2013	2
4-56-102	Amended	403	sb0170	1	7-1-2013	2
4-56-103	Amended	403	sb0170	2	7-1-2013	2
4-56-104	Amended	403	sb0170	3	7-1-2013	2
4-56-105	Amended	403	sb0170	4	7-1-2013	2
4-56-106	Amended	403	sb0170	5	7-1-2013	2
4-56-107	Transferred from 4-56-108	403	sb0170	6	7-1-2013	2
4-56-107	Repealed	403	sb0170	6	7-1-2013	2
4-56-108	Added	403	sb0170	7	7-1-2013	2
4-56-108	Transferred to 4-56-107	403	sb0170	6	7-1-2013	2
4-56-109	Repealed	403	sb0170	7	7-1-2013	2
4-56-110	Repealed	403	sb0170	7	7-1-2013	2
4-58-102	Amended	120	sb0597	1	7-1-2013	1
4-58-103	Amended	120	sb0597	2, 3	7-1-2013	1
5-1-104	Amended	231	sb0906	11	7-1-2013	2
5-6-109	Amended	315	sb0135	7	4-29-2013	2
5-12-104	Amended	237	hb0087	1, 2	4-23-2013	2
5-13-103	Amended	315	sb0135	11, 12	4-29-2013	2
5-14-103	Amended	315	sb0135	13, 14	4-29-2013	2
5-14-108	Amended	162	hb0073	1	4-16-2013	2
5-20-101	Amended	145	sb0848	1	4-12-2013	1
5-21-109	Amended	315	sb0135	15, 16	4-29-2013	2
6-51-103	Amended	462	sb1054	3, 4	5-20-2013	2
6-51-108	Amended	462	sb1054	1	5-20-2013	2
6-51-115	Amended	480	sb0182	1	5-20-2013	2
6-51-122	Added	441	sb0279	1	5-16-2013	2
6-54-141	Amended	154	sb0186	27	7-1-2013	1
6-55-202	Amended	353	hb0493	8	5-13-2013	2
6-56-402	Amended	153	sb0136	1-3	7-1-2013	1
6-56-403	Amended	153	sb0136	4	7-1-2013	1
6-56-404	Amended	153	sb0136	5, 6	7-1-2013	1

*Section number(s) not assigned by General Assembly

T.C.A. Sec.	Action	Ch. No.	Bill No.	Sec. No.	Eff. Date	Pamphlet No.
6-56-406	Amended	153	sb0136	7	7-1-2013	1
6-56-407	Amended	153	sb0136	8	7-1-2013	1
6-58-112	Amended	256	hb1288	1	4-24-2013	2
7-3-316	Amended	154	sb0186	28	7-1-2013	1
7-4-202	Amended	340	hb1213	1	7-1-2013	2
7-4-205	Amended	280	sb1209	16, 17	1-1-2014	2
7-4-206	Amended	236	sb1218	66	4-19-2013	2
7-51-1802	Amended	91	hb0501	2	4-11-2013	1
7-52-103	Amended	2	sb0078	1	3-7-2013	1
7-52-408	Repealed	204	sb0776	1	4-23-2013	2
7-52-409	Repealed	204	sb0776	2	4-23-2013	2
7-52-410	Repealed	204	sb0776	3	4-23-2013	2
7-53-305	Amended	302	sb0661	1	4-29-2013	2
7-59-311	Amended	204	sb0776	4	4-23-2013	2
7-59-315	Amended	204	sb0776	5	4-23-2013	2
7-82-102	Amended	141	sb0764	9, 10	4-12-2013	1
7-82-307	Amended	141	sb0764	1, 11	4-12-2013	1
7-82-307	Amended	320	hb0116	1	5-13-2013	2
7-82-401	Amended	141	sb0764	2, 3	4-12-2013	1
7-82-401	Amended	236	sb1218	6	4-19-2013	2
7-82-402	Amended	141	sb0764	12	4-12-2013	1
7-82-702	Amended	141	sb0764	4	4-12-2013	1
7-82-709	Amended	141	sb0764	5	4-12-2013	1
7-83-101–7-83-105; 7-83-201–7-83-206; 7-83-301–7-83-311; 7-83-401–7-83-404	Repealed	211	sb1208	6	7-1-2013	2
7-86-105	Amended	34	hb0076	1	3-22-2013	1
7-86-119	Amended	315	sb0135	21, 22	4-29-2013	2
7-86-302	Amended	438	sb0333	3	5-16-2013	2
7-86-316	Amended	116	sb0033	1-3	7-1-2013	1
7-88-112; 7-88-116	Amended	236	sb1218	66	4-19-2013	2
7-88-117	Added	347	hb1341	1	1-1-2014	2
8-4-103	Amended	236	sb1218	5	4-19-2013	2
8-4-602	Amended	236	sb1218	65	4-19-2013	2
8-4-705	Amended	236	sb1218	12	4-19-2013	2
8-7-231	Amended	68	hb1040	2	7-1-2013	1
8-7-315	Amended	236	sb1218	40	4-19-2013	2

*Section number(s) not assigned by General Assembly

T.C.A. Sec.	Action	Ch. No.	Bill No.	Sec. No.	Eff. Date	Pamphlet No.
8-8-102	Amended	137	sb0175	1	4-12-2013	1
8-8-103	Amended	315	sb0135	8	4-29-2013	2
8-8-201	Amended	154	sb0186	29	7-1-2013	1
8-11-102	Amended	315	sb0135	4	4-29-2013	2
8-11-103	Amended	315	sb0135	5, 6	4-29-2013	2
8-13-102	Amended	315	sb0135	9	4-29-2013	2
8-13-103	Amended	315	sb0135	10	4-29-2013	2
8-14-210	Amended	286	hb0158	1	4-25-2013	2
8-14-408	Amended	236	sb1218	40	4-19-2013	2
8-19-101	Amended	315	sb0135	30	4-29-2013	2
8-19-102	Amended	315	sb0135	1, 2	4-29-2013	2
8-19-115	Amended	315	sb0135	3	4-29-2013	2
8-19-122	Added	315	sb0135	29	4-29-2013	2
8-19-203	Amended	315	sb0135	23	4-29-2013	2
8-19-208	Amended	315	sb0135	24	4-29-2013	2
8-21-401	Amended	412	sb1089	1	5-16-2013	2
8-21-901	Amended	388	sb0736	3	5-6-2013	2
8-23-202	Amended	454	sb0501	28	5-16-2013	2
8-25-104	Amended	296	sb1003	1	4-29-2013	2
8-25-105	Amended	259	sb1005	2	7-1-2014	2
8-25-111	Amended	296	sb1003	2	4-29-2013	2
8-25-113	Added	389	sb0728	1	5-14-2013	2
8-25-301	Amended	259	sb1005	3	7-1-2014	2
8-25-301	Amended	296	sb1003	3	4-29-2013	2
8-25-304	Amended	296	sb1003	4	4-29-2013	2
8-25-309	Added	454	sb0501	19	5-16-2013	2
8-25-501	Amended	454	sb0501	20	5-16-2013	2
8-26-101	Amended	454	sb0501	22	5-16-2013	2
8-26-116	Added	454	sb0501	21	5-16-2013	2
8-27-201	Amended	245	hb0191	1	4-19-2013	2
8-30-104	Amended	454	sb0501	27	5-16-2013	2
8-30-313	Amended	236	sb1218	65	4-19-2013	2
8-33-109	Amended	432	sb0667	1	7-1-2013	2
8-34-101	Amended	296	sb1003	5, 6	4-29-2013	2
8-35-201	Amended	296	sb1003	7, 8	4-29-2013	2
8-35-218	Amended	296	sb1003	9	4-29-2013	2
8-35-226	Amended	296	sb1003	10	4-29-2013	2

*Section number(s) not assigned by General Assembly

T.C.A. Sec.	Action	Ch. No.	Bill No.	Sec. No.	Eff. Date	Pamphlet No.
8-35-227; 8-35-229; 8-35-233	Repealed	296	sb1003	11	4-29-2013	2
8-35-253	Amended	296	sb1003	12	4-29-2013	2
8-35-255	Amended	296	sb1003	13	4-29-2013	2
8-35-256	Amended	296	sb1003	14	4-29-2013	2
8-35-319	Added*	296	sb1003	15	4-29-2013	2
8-36-101	Transferred to 8-36-601	296	sb1003	17	4-29-2013	2
8-36-116	Amended	296	sb1003	18	4-29-2013	2
8-36-128	Added*	296	sb1003	16	4-29-2013	2
8-36-204	Amended	296	sb1003	20	4-29-2013	2
8-36-213	Added*	296	sb1003	19	4-29-2013	2
8-36-601	Transferred from 8-36-101	296	sb1003	17	4-29-2013	2
8-36-801	Amended	296	sb1003	21, 22	4-29-2013	2
8-36-804	Amended	296	sb1003	23	4-29-2013	2
8-36-901–8-36-923	Added	259	sb1005	1	7-1-2014	2
8-37-104	Amended	259	sb1005	4	7-1-2014	2
8-37-108	Amended	296	sb1003	24	4-29-2013	2
8-37-220	Amended	296	sb1003	25, 26	4-29-2013	2
8-38-101	Amended	170	hb1035	1	4-16-2013	2
8-38-103	Amended	170	hb1035	2	4-16-2013	2
8-38-104	Amended	170	hb1035	3	4-16-2013	2
8-38-105	Amended	170	hb1035	4	4-16-2013	2
8-38-107	Repealed	170	hb1035	5	4-16-2013	2
8-38-111	Amended	170	hb1035	6	4-16-2013	2
8-38-112	Amended	170	hb1035	7	4-16-2013	2
8-38-113	Repealed	170	hb1035	8	4-16-2013	2
8-38-114	Repealed	170	hb1035	9	4-16-2013	2
8-38-115	Repealed	170	hb1035	10	4-16-2013	2
8-38-117	Repealed	170	hb1035	11	4-16-2013	2
8-38-118	Repealed	170	hb1035	12	4-16-2013	2
8-38-119	Repealed	170	hb1035	13	4-16-2013	2
8-38-120	Repealed	170	hb1035	14	4-16-2013	2
8-38-123	Amended	170	hb1035	15	4-16-2013	2
8-38-125	Repealed	170	hb1035	16	4-16-2013	2
8-38-127	Added	170	hb1035	17	4-16-2013	2
8-38-128	Added	170	hb1035	18	4-16-2013	2

*Section number(s) not assigned by General Assembly

T.C.A. Sec.	Action	Ch. No.	Bill No.	Sec. No.	Eff. Date	Pamphlet No.
8-42-101	Amended	32	sb0442	3	7-1-2013	1
8-42-103	Amended	212	sb1210	1	4-23-2013	2
8-50-114	Amended	473	sb0643	9	7-1-2013	2
8-50-1204	Amended	140	sb0134	1	4-12-2013	1
9-1-103	Added*	454	sb0501	31	5-16-2013	2
9-3-301	Amended	315	sb0135	20	4-29-2013	2
9-3-406	Amended	64	sb0138	2	4-1-2013	1
9-4-103	Amended	202	sb0773	1	4-23-2013	2
9-4-206	Amended	154	sb0186	30	7-1-2013	1
9-4-211	Amended	175	sb0994	1	7-1-2013	2
9-4-213	Amended	236	sb1218	21	4-19-2013	2
9-4-506	Amended	54	sb0322	3	3-26-2013	1
9-4-601	Amended	454	sb0501	30	5-16-2013	2
9-4-603	Amended	208	sb0920	1-3	4-23-2013	2
9-4-608	Amended	208	sb0920	4-7	4-23-2013	2
9-4-610	Amended	20	sb0362	3	3-14-2013	1
9-4-611	Added	454	sb0501	17	5-16-2013	2
9-4-702	Amended	208	sb0920	8	4-23-2013	2
9-4-704	Amended	208	sb0920	9, 10	4-23-2013	2
9-4-904	Amended	454	sb0501	38	5-16-2013	2
9-4-907	Amended	454	sb0501	39	5-16-2013	2
9-4-5101	Amended	243	hb0155	3	4-19-2013	2
9-4-5102	Amended	243	hb0155	4	4-19-2013	2
9-4-5103	Amended	243	hb0155	5	4-19-2013	2
9-4-5106	Amended	243	hb0155	6, 19, 20	4-19-2013	2
9-4-5106	Amended	454	sb0501	16, 40	5-16-2013	2
9-4-5110	Amended	454	sb0501	33	5-16-2013	2
9-4-5112	Amended	454	sb0501	34	5-16-2013	2
9-4-5113	Amended	454	sb0501	24	5-16-2013	2
9-4-5115	Repealed	454	sb0501	40	5-16-2013	2
9-4-5117	Transferred from 4-3-1011	454	sb0501	13	5-16-2013	2
9-4-5203	Amended	451	sb0504	1	5-16-2013	2
9-4-5404	Amended	236	sb1218	83	4-19-2013	2
9-4-5501	Repealed	454	sb0501	7	5-16-2013	2
9-4-5502	Amended	164	hb0396	1	7-1-2013	2
9-4-5502	Repealed	454	sb0501	7	5-16-2013	2

*Section number(s) not assigned by General Assembly

T.C.A. Sec.	Action	Ch. No.	Bill No.	Sec. No.	Eff. Date	Pamphlet No.
9-4-5503	Amended	164	hb0396	2	7-1-2013	2
9-4-5503	Repealed	454	sb0501	7	5-16-2013	2
9-4-5601	Amended	243	hb0155	7	4-19-2013	2
9-4-5602	Amended	243	hb0155	8	4-19-2013	2
9-4-5603	Amended	243	hb0155	9	4-19-2013	2
9-4-5604	Amended	243	hb0155	10	4-19-2013	2
9-4-5605	Amended	243	hb0155	11	4-19-2013	2
9-4-5606	Amended	243	hb0155	12	4-19-2013	2
9-4-5607	Repealed	243	hb0155	13	4-19-2013	2
9-4-5608	Amended	243	hb0155	14	4-19-2013	2
9-4-5609	Amended	243	hb0155	15	4-19-2013	2
9-4-5612	Amended	243	hb0155	16	4-19-2013	2
9-4-5613	Repealed	243	hb0155	17	4-19-2013	2
9-4-5614	Repealed	200	sb0771	1	4-23-2013	2
9-4-5614	Repealed	243	hb0155	18	4-19-2013	2
9-8-108	Amended	164	hb0396	3	7-1-2013	2
9-8-307	Amended	289	sb0200	94, 95	7-1-2014	2
9-8-309	Amended	380	sb1043	1	5-6-2013	2
9-8-402	Amended	289	sb0200	96-99	7-1-2014	2
9-9-101	Amended	176	sb0999	2	7-1-2013	2
9-9-102	Amended	176	sb0999	3	7-1-2013	2
9-9-103	Amended	176	sb0999	4	7-1-2013	2
9-9-104–9-9-107	Amended	176	sb0999	5	7-1-2013	2
9-9-111, 9-9-112	Amended	176	sb0999	6	7-1-2013	2
9-9-118	Repealed	176	sb0999	7	7-1-2013	2
9-9-119	Repealed	176	sb0999	8	7-1-2013	2
9-9-207	Amended	176	sb0999	9	7-1-2013	2
9-9-301	Transferred from 9-10-101	176	sb0999	10	7-1-2013	2
9-10-101	Transferred to 9-9-301	176	sb0999	10	7-1-2013	2
9-21-105	Amended	467	sb0875	1-4	5-20-2013	2
9-21-127	Amended	467	sb0875	5	5-20-2013	2
10-7-301	Amended	207	sb0902	1	4-23-2013	2
10-7-302	Amended	207	sb0902	2	4-23-2013	2
10-7-303	Amended	207	sb0902	3, 4	4-23-2013	2
10-7-304	Amended	207	sb0902	5	4-23-2013	2
10-7-401	Amended	135	sb0284	1, 2	4-12-2013	1

*Section number(s) not assigned by General Assembly

T.C.A. Sec.	Action	Ch. No.	Bill No.	Sec. No.	Eff. Date	Pamphlet No.
10-7-404	Amended	207	sb0902	6	4-23-2013	2
10-7-501	Amended	207	sb0902	7	4-23-2013	2
10-7-504	Amended	15	sb0083	1	3-14-2013	1
10-7-504	Amended	229	sb0834	1-5	4-19-2013	2
10-7-504	Amended	284	hb0009	1	4-25-2013	2
10-7-504	Amended	314	sb0154	1	4-29-2013	2
10-7-508	Amended	207	sb0902	8, 9	4-23-2013	2
11-1-104	Amended	93	hb0338	1	4-8-2013	1
11-1-116	Amended	236	sb1218	7	4-19-2013	2
11-3-120	Amended	236	sb1218	6	4-19-2013	2
11-3-121	Amended	236	sb1218	8	4-19-2013	2
11-4-201	Amended	112	sb0144	1-4	4-10-2013	1
11-4-201; 11-4-308	Amended	236	sb1218	6	4-19-2013	2
11-7-104	Amended	236	sb1218	9	4-19-2013	2
11-11-203	Amended	226	sb0395	1	7-1-2013	2
11-11-203	Amended	378	sb1127	1	5-14-2013	2
11-11-204	Amended	378	sb1127	4	5-14-2013	2
11-11-205	Amended	378	sb1127	3	5-14-2013	2
11-14-104	Amended	93	hb0338	2	4-8-2013	1
11-14-108	Amended	111	sb0160	1, 2	4-10-2013	1
11-14-116	Amended	93	hb0338	3	4-8-2013	1
11-21-104	Amended	93	hb0338	4	4-8-2013	1
12-2-102	Amended	454	sb0501	35	5-16-2013	2
12-2-103–12-2-106; 12-2-108, 12-2-109; 12-2-111, 12-2-112	Amended	454	sb0501	36	5-16-2013	2
12-2-112	Amended	454	sb0501	37	5-16-2013	2
12-2-114; 12-2-116	Amended	454	sb0501	36	5-16-2013	2
12-2-117	Amended	454	sb0501	5	5-16-2013	2
12-2-119–12-2-121	Added	454	sb0501	9	5-16-2013	2
12-2-418	Repealed	118	sb0627	1	4-12-2013	1
12-2-501	Added	115	sb0074	1	4-12-2013	1
12-3-101	Amended	403	sb0170	8	7-1-2013	2
12-3-102	Repealed and reenacted	403	sb0170	9	7-1-2013	2
12-3-103	Repealed and reenacted	403	sb0170	10	7-1-2013	2
12-3-104	Repealed and reenacted	403	sb0170	11	7-1-2013	2

*Section number(s) not assigned by General Assembly

T.C.A. Sec.	Action	Ch. No.	Bill No.	Sec. No.	Eff. Date	Pamphlet No.
12-3-105–12-3-133	Repealed	403	sb0170	12	7-1-2013	2
12-3-134	Added*	217	sb1328	1	4-23-2013	2
12-3-201	Repealed and reenacted	403	sb0170	13	7-1-2013	2
12-3-202	Repealed and reenacted	403	sb0170	14	7-1-2013	2
12-3-203–12-3-262	Repealed	403	sb0170	15	7-1-2013	2
12-3-301	Repealed and reenacted	403	sb0170	16	7-1-2013	2
12-3-302	Repealed and reenacted	403	sb0170	17	7-1-2013	2
12-3-303–12-3-310	Repealed and reenacted	403	sb0170	18	7-1-2013	2
12-3-311–12-3-314	Repealed	403	sb0170	18	7-1-2013	2
12-3-401	Added	403	sb0170	19	7-1-2013	2
12-3-501	Repealed and reenacted	403	sb0170	20	7-1-2013	2
12-3-502	Repealed and reenacted	403	sb0170	21	7-1-2013	2
12-3-503	Repealed and reenacted	403	sb0170	22	7-1-2013	2
12-3-504	Repealed and reenacted	403	sb0170	23	7-1-2013	2
12-3-505	Repealed and reenacted	403	sb0170	24	7-1-2013	2
12-3-506	Repealed and reenacted	403	sb0170	25	7-1-2013	2
12-3-507	Repealed and reenacted	403	sb0170	26	7-1-2013	2
12-3-508	Repealed and reenacted	403	sb0170	27	7-1-2013	2
12-3-509	Repealed and reenacted	403	sb0170	28	7-1-2013	2
12-3-510	Repealed and reenacted	403	sb0170	29	7-1-2013	2
12-3-511	Repealed and reenacted	403	sb0170	30	7-1-2013	2
12-3-512	Repealed and reenacted	403	sb0170	31	7-1-2013	2
12-3-513	Repealed and reenacted	403	sb0170	32	7-1-2013	2
12-3-514	Repealed and reenacted	403	sb0170	33	7-1-2013	2

*Section number(s) not assigned by General Assembly

T.C.A. Sec.	Action	Ch. No.	Bill No.	Sec. No.	Eff. Date	Pamphlet No.
12-3-515–12-3-531	Repealed	403	sb0170	34	7-1-2013	2
12-3-601	Added	403	sb0170	35	7-1-2013	2
12-3-601	Transferred to 12-3-901	403	sb0170	50	7-1-2013	2
12-3-602	Added	403	sb0170	36	7-1-2013	2
12-3-602	Transferred to 12-3-902	403	sb0170	51	7-1-2013	2
12-3-603	Added	403	sb0170	37	7-1-2013	2
12-3-603	Transferred to 12-3-903	403	sb0170	52	7-1-2013	2
12-3-604	Transferred to 12-3-904	403	sb0170	53	7-1-2013	2
12-3-605	Transferred to 12-3-905	403	sb0170	54	7-1-2013	2
12-3-606	Transferred to 12-3-906	403	sb0170	55	7-1-2013	2
12-3-607	Transferred to 12-3-907	403	sb0170	56	7-1-2013	2
12-3-608	Transferred to 12-3-908	403	sb0170	57	7-1-2013	2
12-3-609	Transferred to 12-3-909	403	sb0170	58	7-1-2013	2
12-3-610	Transferred to 12-3-910	403	sb0170	58	7-1-2013	2
12-3-611	Transferred to 12-3-911	403	sb0170	58	7-1-2013	2
12-3-612	Transferred to 12-3-912	403	sb0170	58	7-1-2013	2
12-3-701	Repealed and reenacted	403	sb0170	39	7-1-2013	2
12-3-702–12-3-704	Repealed	403	sb0170	40	7-1-2013	2
12-3-801	Added	403	sb0170	41	7-1-2013	2
12-3-801	Transferred to 12-3-1101	403	sb0170	64	7-1-2013	2
12-3-802	Added	403	sb0170	42	7-1-2013	2
12-3-802	Transferred to 12-3-1102	403	sb0170	65	7-1-2013	2
12-3-803	Added	403	sb0170	43	7-1-2013	2
12-3-803	Transferred to 12-3-1103	403	sb0170	66	7-1-2013	2
12-3-804	Added	403	sb0170	44	7-1-2013	2
12-3-804	Transferred to 12-3-1104	403	sb0170	67	7-1-2013	2

*Section number(s) not assigned by General Assembly

T.C.A. Sec.	Action	Ch. No.	Bill No.	Sec. No.	Eff. Date	Pamphlet No.
12-3-805	Added	403	sb0170	45	7-1-2013	2
12-3-805	Transferred to 12-3-1105	403	sb0170	67	7-1-2013	2
12-3-806	Added	403	sb0170	46	7-1-2013	2
12-3-806	Transferred to 12-3-1106	403	sb0170	67	7-1-2013	2
12-3-807	Added	403	sb0170	47	7-1-2013	2
12-3-807	Transferred to 12-3-1107	403	sb0170	67	7-1-2013	2
12-3-808	Added	403	sb0170	48	7-1-2013	2
12-3-808	Transferred to 12-3-1108	403	sb0170	67	7-1-2013	2
12-3-809	Transferred to 12-3-1109	403	sb0170	49	7-1-2013	2
12-3-810	Transferred to 12-3-1110	403	sb0170	67	7-1-2013	2
12-3-811	Transferred to 12-3-1111	403	sb0170	67	7-1-2013	2
12-3-812	Transferred to 12-3-1112	403	sb0170	67	7-1-2013	2
12-3-813	Transferred to 12-3-1113	403	sb0170	67	7-1-2013	2
12-3-901	Transferred from 12-3-601	403	sb0170	50	7-1-2013	2
12-3-902	Transferred from 12-3-602	403	sb0170	51	7-1-2013	2
12-3-903	Transferred from 12-3-603	403	sb0170	52	7-1-2013	2
12-3-904	Transferred from 12-3-604	403	sb0170	53	7-1-2013	2
12-3-905	Transferred from 12-3-605	403	sb0170	54	7-1-2013	2
12-3-906	Transferred from 12-3-606	403	sb0170	55	7-1-2013	2
12-3-907	Transferred from 12-3-607	403	sb0170	56	7-1-2013	2
12-3-908	Transferred from 12-3-608	403	sb0170	57	7-1-2013	2
12-3-909–12-3-912	Transferred from 12-3-609–12-3-612	403	sb0170	58	7-1-2013	2
12-3-1001	Repealed and reenacted	403	sb0170	59	7-1-2013	2

*Section number(s) not assigned by General Assembly

T.C.A. Sec.	Action	Ch. No.	Bill No.	Sec. No.	Eff. Date	Pamphlet No.
12-3-1002	Repealed and reenacted	403	sb0170	60	7-1-2013	2
12-3-1003	Repealed and reenacted	403	sb0170	61	7-1-2013	2
12-3-1004	Amended	329	hb0739	1	5-13-2013	2
12-3-1004	Repealed and reenacted	403	sb0170	62	7-1-2013	2
12-3-1007	Repealed	403	sb0170	63	7-1-2013	2
12-3-1008	Repealed	329	hb0739	2	5-13-2013	2
12-3-1008	Repealed	403	sb0170	63	7-1-2013	2
12-3-1009	Amended	329	hb0739	3	5-13-2013	2
12-3-1009–12-3-1011	Repealed	403	sb0170	63	7-1-2013	2
12-3-1012	Amended	329	hb0739	6	5-13-2013	2
12-3-1012	Repealed	403	sb0170	63	7-1-2013	2
12-3-1101	Transferred from 12-3-801	403	sb0170	64	7-1-2013	2
12-3-1101	Repealed	272	sb0774	1	4-25-2013	2
12-3-1102	Transferred from 12-3-802	403	sb0170	65	7-1-2013	2
12-3-1102	Repealed	272	sb0774	1	4-25-2013	2
12-3-1103	Transferred from 12-3-803	403	sb0170	66	7-1-2013	2
12-3-1103	Repealed	272	sb0774	1	4-25-2013	2
12-3-1104–12-3-1113	Transferred from 12-3-804–12-3-813	403	sb0170	67	7-1-2013	2
12-3-1201	Repealed and reenacted	403	sb0170	68	7-1-2013	2
12-3-1202	Repealed and reenacted	403	sb0170	69	7-1-2013	2
12-3-1203–12-3-1205	Repealed and reenacted	403	sb0170	70	7-1-2013	2
12-3-1206	Amended	403	sb0170	70	7-1-2013	2
12-3-1207–12-3-1211	Repealed and reenacted	403	sb0170	70	7-1-2013	2
12-4-101	Repealed and reenacted	403	sb0170	71	7-1-2013	2
12-4-103	Repealed and reenacted	403	sb0170	73	7-1-2013	2
12-4-104	Repealed and reenacted	403	sb0170	74	7-1-2013	2

*Section number(s) not assigned by General Assembly

T.C.A. Sec.	Action	Ch. No.	Bill No.	Sec. No.	Eff. Date	Pamphlet No.
12-4-106	Repealed and reenacted	403	sb0170	75	7-1-2013	2
12-4-107	Repealed and reenacted	403	sb0170	76	7-1-2013	2
12-4-109	Repealed and reenacted	403	sb0170	77	7-1-2013	2
12-4-110	Repealed and reenacted	403	sb0170	78	7-1-2013	2
12-4-111	Repealed and reenacted	403	sb0170	79	7-1-2013	2
12-4-112	Repealed and reenacted	403	sb0170	80	7-1-2013	2
12-4-113	Repealed and reenacted	403	sb0170	72	7-1-2013	2
12-4-114–12-4-125	Repealed	403	sb0170	81	7-1-2013	2
12-4-126	Amended	329	hb0739	4, 5	5-13-2013	2
12-4-126	Transferred to 12-4-113	403	sb0170	81	7-1-2013	2
12-4-201	Amended	195	sb0647	1	4-23-2013	2
12-4-320	Repealed	454	sb0501	2	7-1-2013	2
12-4-401	Amended	280	sb1209	1	1-1-2014	2
12-4-402	Amended	280	sb1209	2	1-1-2014	2
12-4-403	Amended	280	sb1209	3, 4	1-1-2014	2
12-4-404	Amended	280	sb1209	5	1-1-2014	2
12-4-405	Amended	280	sb1209	4, 6, 8, 9, 10	1-1-2014	2
12-4-406	Amended	280	sb1209	6	1-1-2014	2
12-4-407	Amended	280	sb1209	7	1-1-2014	2
12-4-408	Amended	280	sb1209	4	1-1-2014	2
12-4-409	Amended	280	sb1209	7, 11	1-1-2014	2
12-4-410	Amended	280	sb1209	13	1-1-2014	2
12-4-411	Amended	280	sb1209	4, 7	1-1-2014	2
12-4-412	Amended	280	sb1209	11	1-1-2014	2
12-4-903	Amended	335	hb0841	1	5-13-2013	2
12-4-903	Amended	91	hb0501	3	4-11-2013	1
12-4-903	Amended	280	sb1209	12	1-1-2014	2
12-4-906, 12-4-907	Added	280	sb1209	14	1-1-2014	2
12-4-1001–12-4-1007	Added	403	sb0170	82	7-1-2013	2
13-3-101	Amended	456	sb1380	4	5-20-2013	2
13-14-111	Amended	456	sb1380	1-3	5-20-2013	2

*Section number(s) not assigned by General Assembly

T.C.A. Sec.	Action	Ch. No.	Bill No.	Sec. No.	Eff. Date	Pamphlet No.
13-14-114	Amended	315	sb0135	25, 26	4-29-2013	2
13-16-301–13-16-306	Repealed	202	sb0773	2	4-23-2013	2
13-23-107	Amended	414	sb1042	1, 3	5-16-2013	2
13-23-110	Amended	414	sb1042	4	5-16-2013	2
13-23-112	Amended	414	sb1042	2	5-16-2013	2
13-23-128	Amended	405	sb0122	1, 2	5-14-2013	2
13-23-403	Amended	198	sb0769	1	4-23-2013	2
13-26-110	Amended	315	sb0135	27, 28	4-29-2013	2
13-30-119	Amended	236	sb1218	67	4-19-2013	2
15-2-123	Added	22	sb0256	1	3-20-2013	1
16-1-117	Amended	236	sb1218	37	4-19-2013	2
16-1-117	Amended	300	sb0789	1	7-1-2013	2
16-1-118	Added*	279	sb1057	1	7-1-2013	2
16-2-508	Amended	21	sb0080	2	3-20-2013	1
16-2-508	Amended	68	hb1040	3	7-1-2013	1
16-2-521	Added*	68	hb1040	1	7-1-2013	1
16-3-803	Amended	236	sb1218	45	4-19-2013	2
16-3-811	Amended	236	sb1218	32	4-19-2013	2
16-3-812	Amended	300	sb0789	2	7-1-2013	2
16-3-815	Amended	97	hb0232	1	4-8-2013	1
16-10-213	Amended	300	sb0789	3	7-1-2013	2
16-11-206	Amended	300	sb0789	4	7-1-2013	2
16-15-303	Amended	300	sb0789	5	7-1-2013	2
16-16-120	Amended	300	sb0789	6	7-1-2013	2
16-18-311; 16-21-101	Amended	236	sb1218	32	4-19-2013	2
16-21-102	Amended	236	sb1218	48	4-19-2013	2
16-21-107; 16-21-111	Amended	236	sb1218	32	4-19-2013	2
17-1-107	Amended	236	sb1218	37	4-19-2013	2
17-2-309	Amended	236	sb1218	46	4-19-2013	2
17-5-311	Amended	236	sb1218	41	4-19-2013	2
18-2-201	Amended	315	sb0135	17	4-29-2013	2
18-2-205	Amended	315	sb0135	18	4-29-2013	2
23-1-101	Amended	236	sb1218	47	4-19-2013	2
24-7-120	Amended	251	hb0742	1	7-1-2013	2
26-2-225	Added	187	sb0243	1	7-1-2013	2
26-4-101	Amended	390	sb0713	25	7-1-2013	2
29-3-101	Amended	247	hb0225	1	7-1-2013	2

*Section number(s) not assigned by General Assembly

T.C.A. Sec.	Action	Ch. No.	Bill No.	Sec. No.	Eff. Date	Pamphlet No.
29-3-110	Amended	463	sb1040	1	5-20-2013	2
29-11-107	Added	317	sb0056	1	7-1-2013	2
29-13-111	Amended	324	hb0234	2	5-13-2013	2
29-13-308	Amended	324	hb0234	1	5-13-2013	2
29-20-107	Amended	96	hb0282	1	4-11-2013	1
29-20-401	Amended	289	sb0200	100	7-1-2014	2
29-20-408	Amended	236	sb1218	84	4-19-2013	2
29-26-121	Amended	23	sb0273	1	7-1-2013	1
29-34-501	Added*	246	hb0197	2	7-1-2013	2
29-34-502	Added*	246	hb0197	3	7-1-2013	2
29-34-503	Added*	246	hb0197	4	7-1-2013	2
29-34-504	Added*	246	hb0197	5	7-1-2013	2
29-34-505	Added*	246	hb0197	6	7-1-2013	2
29-34-506	Added*	246	hb0197	7	7-1-2013	2
29-34-507	Added*	246	hb0197	8	7-1-2013	2
29-39-103	Amended	379	sb1053	1	5-14-2013	2
29-39-104	Amended	224	sb0222	1	7-1-2013	2
30-4-103	Amended	360	hb0987	1	7-1-2013	2
33-2-106	Amended	236	sb1218	50	4-19-2013	2
33-3-104	Amended	238	hb1073	4	7-1-2013	2
33-3-115	Amended	300	sb0789	7	7-1-2013	2
33-3-117	Added	300	sb0789	8	7-1-2013	2
33-3-209	Amended	300	sb0789	10	7-1-2013	2
33-3-210	Added	300	sb0789	9	7-1-2013	2
33-6-109	Amended	236	sb1218	51	4-19-2013	2
33-6-201	Amended	238	hb1073	1	7-1-2013	2
33-6-206	Amended	238	hb1073	2	7-1-2013	2
33-6-407	Amended	32	sb0442	1	7-1-2013	1
33-6-901	Amended	32	sb0442	2	7-1-2013	1
33-7-301	Amended	100	hb0174	1, 2	4-10-2013	1
33-10-104	Amended	398	sb0459	2	5-14-2013	2
34-1-101	Amended	435	sb0555	2-6	7-1-2013	2
34-1-104	Amended	435	sb0555	7, 46	7-1-2013	2
34-1-105	Amended	435	sb0555	38, 46	7-1-2013	2
34-1-106	Amended	435	sb0555	8	7-1-2013	2
34-1-107	Amended	435	sb0555	9-13, 46	7-1-2013	2
34-1-108	Amended	435	sb0555	14, 15, 46	7-1-2013	2

*Section number(s) not assigned by General Assembly

T.C.A. Sec.	Action	Ch. No.	Bill No.	Sec. No.	Eff. Date	Pamphlet No.
34-1-109	Amended	435	sb0555	34	7-1-2013	2
34-1-109, 34-1-110	Amended	435	sb0555	46	7-1-2013	2
34-1-111	Amended	435	sb0555	16-20	7-1-2013	2
34-1-111, 34-1-112	Amended	435	sb0555	46	7-1-2013	2
34-1-113	Amended	435	sb0555	35, 46	7-1-2013	2
34-1-114	Amended	435	sb0555	21	7-1-2013	2
34-1-115, 34-1-116	Amended	435	sb0555	46	7-1-2013	2
34-1-117	Amended	435	sb0555	39	7-1-2013	2
34-1-117, 34-1-118	Amended	435	sb0555	46	7-1-2013	2
34-1-119	Amended	435	sb0555	22	7-1-2013	2
34-1-119, 34-1-120	Amended	435	sb0555	46	7-1-2013	2
34-1-121	Amended	435	sb0555	40, 46	7-1-2013	2
34-1-122	Amended	435	sb0555	41, 46	7-1-2013	2
34-1-127	Amended	435	sb0555	42, 46	7-1-2013	2
34-1-129	Amended	435	sb0555	23	7-1-2013	2
34-1-132	Added	435	sb0555	24	7-1-2013	2
34-1-133	Added	435	sb0555	47	7-1-2013	2
34-3-101	Amended	435	sb0555	1, 46	7-1-2013	2
34-3-103	Amended	435	sb0555	36	7-1-2013	2
34-3-104	Amended	435	sb0555	25, 26	7-1-2013	2
34-3-105	Amended	435	sb0555	27, 46	7-1-2013	2
34-3-106	Amended	435	sb0555	28	7-1-2013	2
34-3-107	Amended	435	sb0555	29, 30, 37, 43, 46	7-1-2013	2
34-3-108	Amended	435	sb0555	31, 32, 44, 46	7-1-2013	2
34-3-109	Amended	435	sb0555	45, 46	7-1-2013	2
34-6-203	Amended	215	sb1294	1	7-1-2013	2
35-6-601	Amended	390	sb0713	1	7-1-2013	2
35-9-108	Added	193	sb0527	1	4-23-2013	2
35-14-102	Amended	390	sb0713	2	7-1-2013	2
35-15-103	Amended	390	sb0713	3, 49	7-1-2013	2
35-15-105	Amended	390	sb0713	4-6	7-1-2013	2
35-15-106	Amended	390	sb0713	7	7-1-2013	2
35-15-107	Amended	390	sb0713	8	7-1-2013	2
35-15-108	Amended	390	sb0713	9, 10	7-1-2013	2
35-15-404	Amended	390	sb0713	50	7-1-2013	2

*Section number(s) not assigned by General Assembly

T.C.A. Sec.	Action	Ch. No.	Bill No.	Sec. No.	Eff. Date	Pamphlet No.
35-15-408	Amended	390	sb0713	11	7-1-2013	2
35-15-409	Amended	390	sb0713	12	7-1-2013	2
35-15-410	Amended	390	sb0713	51	7-1-2013	2
35-15-413	Amended	390	sb0713	13, 14	7-1-2013	2
35-15-501	Amended	390	sb0713	15	7-1-2013	2
35-15-502	Amended	390	sb0713	16	7-1-2013	2
35-15-504	Amended	390	sb0713	17	7-1-2013	2
35-15-505	Amended	390	sb0713	18-21	7-1-2013	2
35-15-506	Amended	390	sb0713	22	7-1-2013	2
35-15-508	Added	390	sb0713	23	7-1-2013	2
35-15-509	Added	390	sb0713	24	7-1-2013	2
35-15-703	Amended	390	sb0713	26	7-1-2013	2
35-15-708	Amended	390	sb0713	27	7-1-2013	2
35-15-709	Amended	390	sb0713	28	7-1-2013	2
35-15-710–35-15-715	Added	390	sb0713	29	7-1-2013	2
35-15-802	Amended	390	sb0713	30	7-1-2013	2
35-15-808	Amended	390	sb0713	31	7-1-2013	2
35-15-813	Amended	390	sb0713	32-35	7-1-2013	2
35-15-814	Amended	390	sb0713	36	7-1-2013	2
35-15-816	Amended	390	sb0713	37, 38	7-1-2013	2
35-15-901	Amended	390	sb0713	39	7-1-2013	2
35-15-1005	Amended	390	sb0713	40	7-1-2013	2
35-15-1014	Added	390	sb0713	41	7-1-2013	2
35-15-1101	Amended	390	sb0713	42	7-1-2013	2
35-15-1104, 35-15-1105	Added	390	sb0713	52	7-1-2013	2
35-15-1201–35-15-1206	Added	390	sb0713	43	7-1-2013	2
35-16-102	Amended	390	sb0713	44	7-1-2013	2
35-16-104	Amended	390	sb0713	45-47	7-1-2013	2
35-16-111	Amended	390	sb0713	53	7-1-2013	2
36-1-113	Amended	298	sb0923	1	4-29-2013	2
36-1-113	Amended	365	hb0710	1	7-1-2013	2
36-1-126	Amended	207	sb0902	11	4-23-2013	2
36-2-401–36-2-403	Added	309	sb0473	1	7-1-2013	2
36-5-101	Amended	236	sb1218	22	4-19-2013	2
36-5-112; 36-5-114	Amended	236	sb1218	21	4-19-2013	2
36-6-106	Amended	220	sb0028	1	7-1-2013	2
36-6-106	Amended	385	sb0749	1	5-14-2013	2

*Section number(s) not assigned by General Assembly

T.C.A. Sec.	Action	Ch. No.	Bill No.	Sec. No.	Eff. Date	Pamphlet No.
36-6-108	Amended	352	hb0597	1	7-1-2013	2
37-1-114	Amended	255	hb1050	1	4-19-2013	2
37-1-128	Amended	255	hb1050	2	4-19-2013	2
37-1-130	Amended	397	sb0496	1	7-1-2013	2
37-1-131	Amended	343	hb0453	1	7-1-2013	2
37-1-166	Amended	354	hb0488	1	5-13-2013	2
37-1-182	Amended	236	sb1218	21	4-19-2013	2
37-1-403	Amended	154	sb0186	31	7-1-2013	1
37-1-406	Amended	236	sb1218	21	4-19-2013	2
37-1-607	Amended	236	sb1218	81	4-19-2013	2
37-2-205	Amended	236	sb1218	21	4-19-2013	2
37-2-403	Amended	354	hb0488	2	5-13-2013	2
37-2-601	Amended	236	sb1218	78	4-19-2013	2
37-3-115, 37-3-116	Amended	236	sb1218	79	4-19-2013	2
37-3-501	Amended	236	sb1218	21	4-19-2013	2
37-3-604	Amended	236	sb1218	25	4-19-2013	2
37-3-703	Amended	236	sb1218	52	4-19-2013	2
37-3-803	Amended	236	sb1218	80	4-19-2013	2
37-5-105	Amended	236	sb1218	82	4-19-2013	2
37-5-115	Amended	236	sb1218	53	4-19-2013	2
37-5-117	Amended	137	sb0175	2	4-12-2013	1
37-5-125; 37-5-128, 37-5-129	Amended	236	sb1218	21	4-19-2013	2
37-5-603	Amended	236	sb1218	28	4-19-2013	2
37-5-605	Amended	236	sb1218	27	4-19-2013	2
37-10-401	Amended	236	sb1218	54	4-19-2013	2
38-5-118	Amended	287	hb0715	5	4-25-2013	2
38-6-103	Amended	154	sb0186	32	7-1-2013	1
38-6-207	Amended	236	sb1218	39	4-19-2013	2
38-7-105	Amended	67	hb0901	1	4-1-2013	1
38-8-104	Amended	137	sb0175	3	4-12-2013	1
38-8-106	Amended	137	sb0175	4	4-12-2013	1
38-11-206	Amended	236	sb1218	67	4-19-2013	2
38-12-110	Amended	349	hb0489	1	5-13-2013	2
38-13-101	Repealed	201	sb0772	1	4-23-2013	2
38-13-102	Amended	236	sb1218	35	4-19-2013	2
38-13-102–38-13-104	Repealed	201	sb0772	1	4-23-2013	2

*Section number(s) not assigned by General Assembly

T.C.A. Sec.	Action	Ch. No.	Bill No.	Sec. No.	Eff. Date	Pamphlet No.
39-11-118	Amended	242	hb0128	1	7-1-2013	2
39-11-502	Amended	337	hb0920	1	7-1-2013	2
39-12-203	Amended	278	sb1038	1	7-1-2013	2
39-13-101	Amended	325	hb0306	1, 3	7-1-2013	2
39-13-102	Amended	325	hb0306	2	7-1-2013	2
39-13-102	Amended	407	sb0066	1	7-1-2013	2
39-13-102	Amended	461	sb1064	2, 3	7-1-2013	2
39-13-103	Amended	154	sb0186	53, 54	7-1-2013	1
39-13-106	Amended	154	sb0186	49	7-1-2013	1
39-13-114	Amended	473	sb0643	10	7-1-2013	2
39-13-213	Amended	154	sb0186	50	7-1-2013	1
39-13-301	Amended	465	sb1033	3	7-1-2013	2
39-13-309	Amended	465	sb1033	2	7-1-2013	2
39-13-501	Amended	172	hb1093	1	7-1-2013	2
39-13-515	Amended	485	sb1032	1	7-1-2013	2
39-13-528	Amended	436	sb0446	1	7-1-2013	2
39-13-529	Amended	337	hb0920	2	7-1-2013	2
39-13-529	Amended	350	hb0521	1	7-1-2013	2
39-13-529	Amended	416	sb1028	2	7-1-2013	2
39-13-530	Amended	236	sb1218	23	4-19-2013	2
39-13-533	Added	465	sb1033	1	7-1-2013	2
39-13-609	Added*	470	sb0796	1	7-1-2013	2
39-14-150	Amended	151	sb1363	1, 2	7-1-2013	1
39-14-210	Amended	157	sb0581	1	7-1-2013	1
39-15-301	Amended	227	sb0542	1, 2	7-1-2013	2
39-15-413	Amended	319	hb0088	1	5-13-2013	2
39-17-116	Amended	413	sb1052	1	7-1-2013	2
39-17-117	Amended	413	sb1052	2	7-1-2013	2
39-17-431	Amended	236	sb1218	61	4-19-2013	2
39-17-438	Amended	161	hb0012	1	7-1-2013	2
39-17-452	Amended	161	hb0012	5, 6	7-1-2013	2
39-17-453	Amended	433	sb0614	1	7-1-2013	2
39-17-454	Amended	161	hb0012	2-4, 7	7-1-2013	2
39-17-907	Amended	459	sb1140	1	5-20-2013	2
39-17-1003	Amended	350	hb0521	2	7-1-2013	2
39-17-1004	Amended	350	hb0521	3	7-1-2013	2
39-17-1005	Amended	350	hb0521	4	7-1-2013	2

*Section number(s) not assigned by General Assembly

T.C.A. Sec.	Action	Ch. No.	Bill No.	Sec. No.	Eff. Date	Pamphlet No.
39-17-1313	Added	16	sb0142	1	7-1-2013	1
39-17-1314	Amended	418	sb1015	1	7-1-2013	2
39-17-1316	Amended	236	sb1218	36	4-19-2013	2
39-17-1351	Amended	236	sb1218	35	4-19-2013	2
39-17-1351	Amended	270	sb0714	1	7-1-2013	2
39-17-1359	Amended	16	sb0142	2	7-1-2013	1
39-17-1504	Amended	319	hb0088	2	5-13-2013	2
39-17-1511	Added*	194	sb0544	1	7-1-2013	2
40-1-111	Amended	236	sb1218	33	4-19-2013	2
40-2-101	Amended	416	sb1028	1	7-1-2013	2
40-2-104	Amended	205	sb0831	1	7-1-2013	2
40-11-125	Amended	169	hb0947	1	4-16-2013	2
40-11-138	Amended	388	sb0736	2	5-6-2013	2
40-11-139	Amended	388	sb0736	1	5-6-2013	2
40-17-125	Amended	236	sb1218	35	4-19-2013	2
40-18-107	Amended	454	sb0501	23	5-16-2013	2
40-20-115	Amended	435	sb0555	33	7-1-2013	2
40-29-203	Amended	231	sb0906	12, 13	7-1-2013	2
40-30-111	Amended	236	sb1218	38	4-19-2013	2
40-31-107	Amended	236	sb1218	35	4-19-2013	2
40-32-101	Amended	384	sb0860	1, 2	7-1-2013	2
40-32-101	Amended	443	sb0237	1-3	7-1-2013	2
40-33-101	Amended	285	hb0093	1	7-1-2013	2
40-33-201	Amended	154	sb0186	33	7-1-2013	1
40-33-203	Amended	382	sb0891	1	1-1-2014	2
40-33-204	Amended	382	sb0891	2, 3	1-1-2014	2
40-33-210	Amended	154	sb0186	34	7-1-2013	1
40-33-211	Amended	154	sb0186	35	7-1-2013	1
40-33-214	Amended	154	sb0186	36	7-1-2013	1
40-34-107	Amended	236	sb1218	64	4-19-2013	2
40-35-121	Amended	357	hb0196	1-3	7-1-2013	2
40-35-121	Amended	415	sb1029	1	7-1-2013	2
40-35-216	Amended	154	sb0186	37	7-1-2013	1
40-35-303	Amended	33	sb0560	1	7-1-2013	1
40-35-303	Amended	154	sb0186	38	7-1-2013	1
40-35-314	Amended	168	hb0681	1	7-1-2013	2
40-35-501	Amended	425	sb0832	1	7-1-2013	2

*Section number(s) not assigned by General Assembly

T.C.A. Sec.	Action	Ch. No.	Bill No.	Sec. No.	Eff. Date	Pamphlet No.
40-35-501	Amended	426	sb0828	1	7-1-2013	2
40-35-501	Amended	461	sb1064	4	7-1-2013	2
40-36-105	Amended	236	sb1218	44	4-19-2013	2
41-1-116	Amended	137	sb0175	5	4-12-2013	1
41-1-502	Amended	236	sb1218	85	4-19-2013	2
41-1-503; 41-1-507	Amended	236	sb1218	64	4-19-2013	2
41-2-128	Amended	154	sb0186	39, 40	7-1-2013	1
41-4-144	Amended	173	hb1339	2	7-1-2013	2
41-6-204	Amended	280	sb1209	15	1-1-2014	2
41-7-104	Amended	236	sb1218	73	4-19-2013	2
41-7-106	Amended	173	hb1339	1	7-1-2013	2
41-8-105	Amended	236	sb1218	65	4-19-2013	2
41-21-236	Amended	154	sb0186	41	7-1-2013	1
41-21-238; 41-21-243, 41-21-244; 41-22-116; 41-22-405, 41-22-406; 41-22-408; 41-22-411	Amended	236	sb1218	64	4-19-2013	2
41-23-103	Amended	236	sb1218	36	4-19-2013	2
41-24-104	Amended	165	hb0441	1	4-16-2013	2
41-24-104	Amended	236	sb1218	65	4-19-2013	2
41-24-106; 41-24-109	Amended	236	sb1218	64	4-19-2013	2
41-52-101–41-52-104	Repealed	454	sb0501	4	7-1-2013	2
42-1-203	Amended	154	sb0186	46, 47	7-1-2013	1
43-1-607	Amended	236	sb1218	1	4-19-2013	2
43-1-704	Amended	236	sb1218	2	4-19-2013	2
43-6-502	Amended	236	sb1218	75	4-19-2013	2
43-24-102	Amended	3	sb0102	1	3-7-2013	1
45-1-107	Amended	102	hb0163	1	4-11-2013	1
45-2-303	Added	119	sb0615	1	7-1-2013	1
45-2-607	Amended	233	sb1020	1	4-19-2013	2
45-2-1603	Amended	36	hb0161	1, 2	3-22-2013	1
45-4-205	Amended	59	sb0587	1	7-1-2013	1
45-7-211	Amended	103	hb0162	1	7-1-2013	1
45-7-227	Added	103	hb0162	2	7-1-2013	1
45-7-228	Added	103	hb0162	3	7-1-2013	1
45-7-229	Added	103	hb0162	4	7-1-2013	1
45-8-221	Amended	211	sb1208	7	7-1-2013	2
45-13-201	Amended	104	hb0160	1-4	4-11-2013	1

*Section number(s) not assigned by General Assembly

T.C.A. Sec.	Action	Ch. No.	Bill No.	Sec. No.	Eff. Date	Pamphlet No.
45-15-115	Amended	70	hb0086	1	4-1-2013	1
46-6-101	Amended	73	hb0187	1, 2	4-2-2013	1
47-4A-108	Amended	51	sb0219	1	3-26-2013	1
47-18-1310	Amended	236	sb1218	92	4-19-2013	2
47-18-5002	Amended	236	sb1218	15	4-19-2013	2
47-22-301, 47-22-302	Added	186	sb0224	1	7-1-2013	2
47-25-503	Amended	123	sb0476	1	7-1-2013	1
47-25-1902	Amended	226	sb0395	2	7-1-2013	2
48-1-103	Amended	261	sb0151	1	10-31-2013	2
49-1-211	Amended	306	sb0531	1	7-1-2013	2
49-1-221	Amended	274	sb0857	1	4-25-2013	2
49-1-302	Amended	105	hb0150	1	4-11-2013	1
49-1-302	Amended	214	sb1291	2	4-23-2013	2
49-1-308	Added*	351	hb0705	1	7-1-2013	2
49-1-606	Amended	105	hb0150	2	4-11-2013	1
49-1-614	Amended	263	sb0233	1	7-1-2013	2
49-1-907	Amended	236	sb1218	26	4-19-2013	2
49-2-116	Amended	473	sb0643	11	7-1-2013	2
49-2-127	Amended	256	hb1288	2, 3	4-24-2013	2
49-2-128	Added	411	sb1175	1	7-1-2013	2
49-2-202	Amended	301	sb0663	1	7-1-2013	2
49-2-203	Amended	281	sb1270	1	4-25-2013	2
49-2-501	Amended	292	sb1354	1	4-29-2013	2
49-2-701	Added*	393	sb0592	2	5-6-2013	2
49-2-702	Added*	393	sb0592	3	5-6-2013	2
49-2-703	Added*	393	sb0592	4	5-6-2013	2
49-2-704	Added*	393	sb0592	5	5-6-2013	2
49-3-314	Amended	305	sb0612	1	4-29-2013	2
49-3-315	Amended	315	sb0135	19	4-29-2013	2
49-3-318	Amended	473	sb0643	12	7-1-2013	2
49-3-351	Amended	454	sb0501	1	7-1-2013	2
49-3-352	Amended	214	sb1291	5	4-23-2013	2
49-3-1202	Amended	174	sb0978	1	4-23-2013	2
49-4-203	Amended	98	hb0188	1	4-11-2013	1
49-4-708	Added	98	hb0188	2	4-11-2013	1
49-4-902	Amended	473	sb0643	13	7-1-2013	2
49-4-902	Amended	361	hb1055	1	5-13-2013	2

*Section number(s) not assigned by General Assembly

T.C.A. Sec.	Action	Ch. No.	Bill No.	Sec. No.	Eff. Date	Pamphlet No.
49-4-921	Amended	473	sb0643	13	7-1-2013	2
49-4-932	Amended	167	hb0599	1	4-16-2013	2
49-4-937	Amended	473	sb0643	13	7-1-2013	2
49-4-942	Added	428	sb0719	1	5-16-2013	2
49-4-942	Added*	483	sb0036	1	5-20-2013	2
49-5-201	Amended	188	sb0267	1	7-1-2013	2
49-5-203	Amended	256	hb1288	4	4-24-2013	2
49-5-413	Amended	177	sb0016	1	4-23-2013	2
49-5-413	Amended	381	sb0922	2	5-14-2013	2
49-5-415	Amended	294	sb1146	1	4-29-2013	2
49-5-418	Added*	383	sb0867	1	7-1-2013	2
49-5-511	Amended	369	hb1112	1	7-1-2014	2
49-5-512	Amended	214	sb1291	3	4-23-2013	2
49-5-714	Amended	439	sb0302	1	5-16-2013	2
49-5-715	Amended	275	sb0866	1	4-25-2013	2
49-5-5001–49-5-5016; 49-5-5021; 49-5-5023; 49-5-5201–49-5-5213; 49-5-5232; 49-5-5241; 49-5-5301–49-5-5308; 49-5-5401–49-5-5408; 49-5-5501–49-5-5509	Repealed	214	sb1291	1	4-23-2013	2
49-5-5612	Added*	46	sb0059	1	3-26-2013	1
49-6-104	Amended	85	hb0839	1	4-8-2013	1
49-6-703	Amended	236	sb1218	64	4-19-2013	2
49-6-815	Added	358	hb0006	2	7-1-2013	2
49-6-902	Amended	397	sb0496	2	7-1-2013	2
49-6-1018	Amended	375	sb1215	2	7-1-2013	2
49-6-1703	Amended	273	sb0792	1, 2	4-25-2013	2
49-6-2009	Added*	395	sb0547	1	7-1-2013	2
49-6-3001	Amended	85	hb0839	2	4-8-2013	1
49-6-3009	Amended	304	sb0640	2	7-1-2013	2
49-6-3019	Amended	155	sb1161	1	7-1-2013	1
49-6-3020	Amended	262	sb0158	1	4-25-2013	2
49-6-3021	Amended	304	sb0640	1	7-1-2013	2
49-6-3050	Amended	225	sb0240	1	7-1-2013	2
49-6-3102	Amended	397	sb0496	3, 4	7-1-2013	2
49-6-3105	Amended	214	sb1291	6	4-23-2013	2
49-6-3201	Amended	397	sb0496	5, 6	7-1-2013	2

*Section number(s) not assigned by General Assembly

T.C.A. Sec.	Action	Ch. No.	Bill No.	Sec. No.	Eff. Date	Pamphlet No.
49-6-3401	Amended	214	sb1291	4	4-23-2013	2
49-6-3401	Amended	222	sb0113	1, 2	7-1-2013	2
49-6-3401	Amended	442	sb0264	1	7-1-2013	2
49-6-4216	Amended	375	sb1215	1	7-1-2013	2
49-6-6001	Amended	422	sb0886	1	7-1-2013	2
49-6-6006	Amended	18	sb0268	1	3-14-2013	1
49-7-102	Amended	473	sb0643	14	7-1-2013	2
49-7-112	Added*	88	hb0566	1	4-8-2013	1
49-7-116	Amended	473	sb0643	15	7-1-2013	2
49-7-118	Amended	368	hb1331	1	5-13-2013	2
49-7-119	Amended	345	hb0283	1	7-1-2013	2
49-7-124	Amended	114	sb0093	1	7-1-2013	1
49-7-155	Amended	473	sb0643	16	7-1-2013	2
49-7-156	Added*	283	hb0534	1	7-1-2013	2
49-7-202	Amended	473	sb0643	17	7-1-2013	2
49-7-205	Amended	296	sb1003	27	4-29-2013	2
49-7-211	Added	429	sb0687	1	7-1-2013	2
49-7-216	Amended	136	sb0223	1	4-12-2013	1
49-7-805	Amended	389	sb0728	2	5-14-2013	2
49-7-808	Amended	359	hb0982	2	7-1-2013	2
49-7-1201	Added*	338	hb1276	2	1-1-2014	2
49-7-1202	Added*	338	hb1276	3	1-1-2014	2
49-7-1203	Added*	338	hb1276	4	1-1-2014	2
49-7-1204	Added*	338	hb1276	5	1-1-2014	2
49-7-1205	Added*	338	hb1276	6	1-1-2014	2
49-7-1206	Added*	338	hb1276	7	1-1-2014	2
49-7-1207	Added*	338	hb1276	8	1-1-2014	2
49-7-1208	Added*	338	hb1276	9	1-1-2014	2
49-7-1209	Added*	338	hb1276	10	5-13-2013	2
49-7-1210	Added*	338	hb1276	11	1-1-2014	2
49-7-1211	Added*	338	hb1276	12	1-1-2014	2
49-7-1212	Added*	338	hb1276	13	1-1-2014	2
49-7-2004	Amended	158	sb1186	1	4-16-2013	1
49-7-2004	Amended	185	sb0195	1, 2	4-23-2013	2
49-7-2004	Amended	307	sb0525	1	4-29-2013	2
49-7-2004	Amended	473	sb0643	18	7-1-2013	2
49-7-2202	Amended	473	sb0643	19	7-1-2013	2

*Section number(s) not assigned by General Assembly

T.C.A. Sec.	Action	Ch. No.	Bill No.	Sec. No.	Eff. Date	Pamphlet No.
49-7-2205	Amended	236	sb1218	74	4-19-2013	2
49-8-101	Amended	473	sb0643	7	7-1-2013	2
49-8-109	Amended	473	sb0643	20	7-1-2013	2
49-8-201	Amended	473	sb0643	21	7-1-2013	2
49-8-401	Amended	473	sb0643	22	7-1-2013	2
49-10-608	Repealed	381	sb0922	1	5-14-2013	2
49-11-104	Amended	473	sb0643	6	7-1-2013	2
49-11-401	Amended	473	sb0643	1	7-1-2013	2
49-11-401	Amended	473	sb0643	2	7-1-2013	2
49-11-402	Amended	473	sb0643	1, 3-5	7-1-2013	2
49-11-403–49-11-408	Amended	473	sb0643	1	7-1-2013	2
49-13-102	Amended	326	hb0315	8	7-1-2013	2
49-13-104	Amended	326	hb0315	5, 7	7-1-2013	2
49-13-104	Amended	351	hb0705	2, 4	7-1-2013	2
49-13-106	Amended	326	hb0315	2, 3, 13, 14	7-1-2013	2
49-13-108	Amended	326	hb0315	15	7-1-2013	2
49-13-108	Amended	351	hb0705	6	7-1-2013	2
49-13-109	Added*	326	hb0315	6	7-1-2013	2
49-13-111	Amended	326	hb0315	1	7-1-2013	2
49-13-112	Amended	326	hb0315	4, 9	7-1-2013	2
49-13-113	Amended	326	hb0315	11	7-1-2013	2
49-13-121	Amended	326	hb0315	10	7-1-2013	2
49-13-127	Amended	326	hb0315	12	7-1-2013	2
49-13-127	Amended	351	hb0705	5	7-1-2013	2
49-13-143	Added*	351	hb0705	3	7-1-2013	2
49-15-101	Amended	473	sb0643	23	7-1-2013	2
49-15-105	Amended	473	sb0643	24	7-1-2013	2
49-16-211	Amended	404	sb0157	1	5-14-2013	2
49-16-213	Amended	404	sb0157	2	5-14-2013	2
50-1-207	Added	277	sb1017	1	4-25-2013	2
50-1-703	Amended	147	sb0879	1-6	4-12-2013	1
50-2-101	Amended	240	hb1223	1, 2	4-23-2013	2
50-2-112	Added*	91	hb0501	1	4-11-2013	1
50-2-113	Added*	91	hb0501	4	4-11-2013	1
50-3-2001	Added, Repealed	257	sb0179	1	4-23-2013	2
50-3-2002–50-3-2019	Repealed	257	sb0179	2	4-23-2013	2

*Section number(s) not assigned by General Assembly

T.C.A. Sec.	Action	Ch. No.	Bill No.	Sec. No.	Eff. Date	Pamphlet No.
50-6-101	Amended	289	sb0200	3	7-1-2014	2
50-6-102	Amended	282	sb1275	2	7-1-2014	2
50-6-102	Amended	289	sb0200	4-9	7-1-2014	2
50-6-103	Amended	289	sb0200	10, 11	7-1-2014	2
50-6-104	Amended	289	sb0200	12	7-1-2014	2
50-6-106	Amended	282	sb1275	1	7-1-2014	2
50-6-108	Amended	289	sb0200	13	7-1-2014	2
50-6-110	Amended	282	sb1275	1	7-1-2014	2
50-6-111	Repealed	289	sb0200	14	7-1-2014	2
50-6-113	Amended	282	sb1275	1	7-1-2014	2
50-6-115	Amended	367	hb0864	1	5-13-2013	2
50-6-116	Amended	289	sb0200	15	7-1-2014	2
50-6-117	Repealed	289	sb0200	16	7-1-2014	2
50-6-118	Amended	289	sb0200	17, 18	7-1-2014	2
50-6-121	Amended	236	sb1218	29	4-19-2013	2
50-6-121	Amended	282	sb1275	1	7-1-2014	2
50-6-121	Amended	289	sb0200	19	7-1-2014	2
50-6-122	Amended	289	sb0200	20, 21	7-1-2014	2
50-6-123, 50-6-124	Amended	282	sb1275	1	7-1-2014	2
50-6-124	Amended	289	sb0200	22	7-1-2014	2
50-6-125	Amended	282	sb1275	1	7-1-2014	2
50-6-125	Amended	289	sb0200	23	7-1-2014	2
50-6-126–50-6-128	Amended	282	sb1275	1	7-1-2014	2
50-6-131	Amended	289	sb0200	25	7-1-2014	2
50-6-132	Amended	236	sb1218	30	4-19-2013	2
50-6-132	Amended	289	sb0200	26	7-1-2014	2
50-6-133	Repealed	289	sb0200	27	7-1-2014	2
50-6-134	Amended	289	sb0200	28	7-1-2014	2
50-6-135	Added*	289	sb0200	24	7-1-2014	2
50-6-201	Amended	289	sb0200	29	7-1-2014	2
50-6-202	Amended	289	sb0200	30	7-1-2014	2
50-6-203	Amended	282	sb1275	1	7-1-2014	2
50-6-203	Amended	289	sb0200	31-34	7-1-2014	2
50-6-204	Amended	282	sb1275	1, 3	7-1-2014	2
50-6-204	Amended	289	sb0200	35-43	7-1-2014	2
50-6-205	Amended	289	sb0200	44, 45	7-1-2014	2
50-6-206	Amended	282	sb1275	1	7-1-2014	2

*Section number(s) not assigned by General Assembly

T.C.A. Sec.	Action	Ch. No.	Bill No.	Sec. No.	Eff. Date	Pamphlet No.
50-6-206	Repealed	289	sb0200	46	7-1-2014	2
50-6-207	Amended	282	sb1275	4, 5	7-1-2014	2
50-6-207	Amended	289	sb0200	47-53	7-1-2014	2
50-6-208	Amended	282	sb1275	1, 6	7-1-2014	2
50-6-208	Amended	289	sb0200	54, 55	7-1-2014	2
50-6-210	Amended	289	sb0200	56	7-1-2014	2
50-6-212	Amended	289	sb0200	57, 58	7-1-2014	2
50-6-214	Amended	282	sb1275	1, 7	7-1-2014	2
50-6-216	Added*	289	sb0200	77	7-1-2014	2
50-6-217	Added*	289	sb0200	80	7-1-2014	2
50-6-218	Added*	289	sb0200	81	7-1-2014	2
50-6-219	Added*	289	sb0200	83	7-1-2014	2
50-6-224	Amended	282	sb1275	1	7-1-2014	2
50-6-224	Repealed	289	sb0200	59	7-1-2014	2
50-6-225	Amended	282	sb1275	1	7-1-2014	2
50-6-225	Amended	289	sb0200	60	7-1-2014	2
50-6-226	Amended	282	sb1275	1	7-1-2014	2
50-6-226	Amended	289	sb0200	61-64	7-1-2014	2
50-6-227	Amended	282	sb1275	1	7-1-2014	2
50-6-227	Repealed	289	sb0200	65	7-1-2014	2
50-6-228	Repealed	289	sb0200	66	7-1-2014	2
50-6-229	Amended	289	sb0200	67, 68	7-1-2014	2
50-6-230	Repealed	289	sb0200	69	7-1-2014	2
50-6-231	Repealed	289	sb0200	70	7-1-2014	2
50-6-232	Amended	289	sb0200	71, 72	7-1-2014	2
50-6-233	Amended	282	sb1275	1	7-1-2014	2
50-6-233	Amended	289	sb0200	73	7-1-2014	2
50-6-234	Amended	289	sb0200	74	7-1-2014	2
50-6-235	Amended	282	sb1275	1	7-1-2014	2
50-6-235	Amended	289	sb0200	75	7-1-2014	2
50-6-236	Amended	282	sb1275	1	7-1-2014	2
50-6-236	Amended	289	sb0200	76	7-1-2014	2
50-6-237	Amended	282	sb1275	1	7-1-2014	2
50-6-237	Amended	289	sb0200	78	7-1-2014	2
50-6-238	Amended	282	sb1275	1	7-1-2014	2
50-6-238	Amended	289	sb0200	79	7-1-2014	2
50-6-239	Amended	282	sb1275	1	7-1-2014	2

*Section number(s) not assigned by General Assembly

T.C.A. Sec.	Action	Ch. No.	Bill No.	Sec. No.	Eff. Date	Pamphlet No.
50-6-239	Amended	289	sb0200	82	7-1-2014	2
50-6-240	Amended	282	sb1275	1	7-1-2014	2
50-6-240	Amended	289	sb0200	84	7-1-2014	2
50-6-241	Amended	289	sb0200	85-89	7-1-2014	2
50-6-242	Amended	282	sb1275	8	7-1-2014	2
50-6-242	Amended	289	sb0200	90	7-1-2014	2
50-6-243	Repealed	289	sb0200	91	7-1-2014	2
50-6-244	Amended	236	sb1218	31	4-19-2013	2
50-6-244; 50-6-246	Amended	282	sb1275	1	7-1-2014	2
50-6-246	Repealed	289	sb0200	92	7-1-2014	2
50-6-301	Repealed	289	sb0200	93	7-1-2014	2
50-6-401	Amended	210	sb1174	1	4-23-2013	2
50-6-402	Amended	236	sb1218	31	4-19-2013	2
50-6-404–50-6-407	Amended	282	sb1275	1	7-1-2014	2
50-6-411	Added	424	sb0833	1	7-1-2013	2
50-6-415	Amended	236	sb1218	31	4-19-2013	2
50-6-415; 50-6-418, 50-6-419	Amended	282	sb1275	1	7-1-2014	2
50-6-421	Added	50	sb0124	1	3-26-2013	1
50-6-501, 50-6-502	Amended	282	sb1275	1	7-1-2014	2
50-6-609	Amended	282	sb1275	9	7-1-2014	2
50-6-902	Amended	282	sb1275	1	7-1-2014	2
50-6-903	Amended	476	sb0519	1	1-1-2014	2
50-6-904	Amended	476	sb0519	2, 3	1-1-2014	2
50-6-913	Amended	282	sb1275	1	7-1-2014	2
50-6-913	Amended	424	sb0833	2	7-1-2013	2
50-6-919	Amended	236	sb1218	31	4-19-2013	2
50-6-919	Amended	282	sb1275	1	7-1-2014	2
50-7-218	Amended	427	sb0783	1	7-1-2013	2
50-7-301	Amended	427	sb0783	2	7-1-2013	2
50-7-302	Amended	427	sb0783	6, 7	7-1-2013	2
50-7-303	Amended	427	sb0783	3, 9, 10	7-1-2013	2
50-7-304	Amended	427	sb0783	4, 5	7-1-2013	2
50-7-407	Added	166	hb0554	1	4-16-2013	2
50-7-451	Amended	236	sb1218	16	4-19-2013	2
50-7-807	Amended	236	sb1218	12	4-19-2013	2
53-8-111	Amended	182	sb0172	49	7-1-2015	2

*Section number(s) not assigned by General Assembly

T.C.A. Sec.	Action	Ch. No.	Bill No.	Sec. No.	Eff. Date	Pamphlet No.
53-8-201	Repealed and reenacted	182	sb0172	1	7-1-2015	2
53-8-202	Repealed and reenacted	182	sb0172	2	7-1-2015	2
53-8-203	Repealed and reenacted	182	sb0172	3	7-1-2015	2
53-8-204	Repealed and reenacted	182	sb0172	4	7-1-2015	2
53-8-205	Repealed and reenacted	182	sb0172	5	7-1-2015	2
53-8-206	Repealed and reenacted	182	sb0172	6	7-1-2015	2
53-8-207	Repealed and reenacted	182	sb0172	7	7-1-2015	2
53-8-208	Repealed and reenacted	182	sb0172	8	7-1-2015	2
53-8-209	Repealed and reenacted	182	sb0172	9	7-1-2015	2
53-8-210	Repealed and reenacted	182	sb0172	10	7-1-2015	2
53-8-211	Repealed and reenacted	182	sb0172	11	7-1-2015	2
53-8-212	Repealed and reenacted	182	sb0172	12	7-1-2015	2
53-8-213	Repealed and reenacted	182	sb0172	13	7-1-2015	2
53-8-214	Repealed and reenacted	182	sb0172	14	7-1-2015	2
53-8-215	Repealed and reenacted	182	sb0172	15	7-1-2015	2
53-8-216	Repealed and reenacted	182	sb0172	16	7-1-2015	2
53-8-217	Repealed and reenacted	182	sb0172	17	7-1-2015	2
53-8-218	Repealed and reenacted	182	sb0172	18	7-1-2015	2
53-8-219	Repealed and reenacted	182	sb0172	19	7-1-2015	2
53-8-220	Repealed and reenacted	182	sb0172	20	7-1-2015	2
53-8-221	Repealed and reenacted	182	sb0172	21	7-1-2015	2
53-8-222	Repealed	182	sb0172	21	7-1-2015	2
53-10-112	Added	276	sb0962	1	7-1-2013	2

*Section number(s) not assigned by General Assembly

T.C.A. Sec.	Action	Ch. No.	Bill No.	Sec. No.	Eff. Date	Pamphlet No.
53-10-302	Amended	430	sb0676	3, 5	10-1-2013	2
53-10-309	Amended	236	sb1218	50	4-19-2013	2
53-10-310	Amended	430	sb0676	15	5-16-2013	2
53-10-312	Added	430	sb0676	6	10-1-2013	2
53-10-401	Amended	74	hb0319	1	4-1-2013	1
53-11-308	Amended	430	sb0676	4	10-1-2013	2
53-11-416	Added*	151	sb1363	3	7-1-2013	1
54-1-119	Amended	236	sb1218	90	4-19-2013	2
54-1-125	Repealed	308	sb0521	23	7-1-2013	2
54-1-133	Amended	308	sb0521	1	7-1-2013	2
54-1-134	Amended	472	sb0653	1	7-1-2013	2
54-1-205	Amended	308	sb0521	6	7-1-2013	2
54-1-401	Amended	308	sb0521	4	7-1-2013	2
54-1-402	Amended	308	sb0521	5	7-1-2013	2
54-1-501–54-1-508	Added	366	hb0183	1	7-1-2014	2
54-2-201–54-2-209	Repealed	203	sb0775	1	4-23-2013	2
54-2-201–54-2-209	Repealed	308	sb0521	24	7-1-2013	2
54-2-201–54-2-209	Repealed	454	sb0501	8	5-16-2013	2
54-3-113	Amended	236	sb1218	90	4-19-2013	2
54-3-113	Amended	308	sb0521	7, 25	7-1-2013	2
54-5-114	Amended	244	hb0182	1	4-19-2013	2
54-5-133	Amended	308	sb0521	26	7-1-2013	2
54-5-145	Amended	154	sb0186	45	7-1-2013	1
54-5-207	Amended	308	sb0521	8	7-1-2013	2
54-5-701, 54-5-702	Repealed	472	sb0653	2	7-1-2013	2
54-5-708	Amended	473	sb0643	25	7-1-2013	2
54-5-1003	Repealed	308	sb0521	2	7-1-2013	2
54-5-1103	Amended	471	sb0657	1, 5	5-20-2013	2
54-5-1104	Repealed	471	sb0657	2	5-20-2013	2
54-5-1105	Amended	308	sb0521	27	7-1-2013	2
54-5-1106	Amended	471	sb0657	3	5-20-2013	2
54-5-1109	Repealed	308	sb0521	28	7-1-2013	2
54-5-1110	Amended	471	sb0657	4	5-20-2013	2
54-7-201	Amended	472	sb0653	3	7-1-2013	2
54-7-206	Amended	308	sb0521	9	7-1-2013	2
54-7-207	Added*	472	sb0653	4	7-1-2013	2
54-8-101–54-8-107	Repealed	308	sb0521	34	7-1-2013	2

*Section number(s) not assigned by General Assembly

T.C.A. Sec.	Action	Ch. No.	Bill No.	Sec. No.	Eff. Date	Pamphlet No.
54-10-103	Amended	308	sb0521	35, 36	7-1-2013	2
54-10-108–54-10-110	Repealed	308	sb0521	37	7-1-2013	2
54-11-206	Repealed	308	sb0521	10	7-1-2013	2
54-11-308	Amended	308	sb0521	29	7-1-2013	2
54-11-309	Repealed and reenacted	308	sb0521	11	7-1-2013	2
54-13-101	Amended	308	sb0521	12	7-1-2013	2
54-13-104	Repealed	308	sb0521	13	7-1-2013	2
54-13-201–54-13-212	Repealed	308	sb0521	14	7-1-2013	2
54-13-301–54-13-321	Repealed	308	sb0521	15	7-1-2013	2
54-16-112	Amended	308	sb0521	16, 30	7-1-2013	2
54-17-105	Amended	308	sb0521	31	7-1-2013	2
54-17-106	Repealed	308	sb0521	32	7-1-2013	2
54-17-107	Amended	308	sb0521	33	7-1-2013	2
54-17-114	Amended	196	sb0655	1	4-23-2013	2
54-21-110	Amended	308	sb0521	3	7-1-2013	2
54-21-122	Amended	401	sb0399	1	7-1-2014	2
55-4-103	Amended	183	sb0184	1	7-1-2013	2
55-4-105	Amended	376	sb1178	1	5-6-2013	2
55-4-110	Amended	223	sb0131	1, 2	7-1-2013	2
55-4-113	Amended	183	sb0184	2	7-1-2013	2
55-4-132	Amended	236	sb1218	88, 90	4-19-2013	2
55-4-135	Amended	183	sb0184	3	7-1-2013	2
55-4-201	Amended	264	sb0259	1	4-25-2013	2
55-4-202	Amended	183	sb0184	4	7-1-2013	2
55-4-202	Amended	303	sb0652	1	4-29-2013	2
55-4-202	Amended	308	sb0521	18	7-1-2013	2
55-4-202	Amended	318	hb0032	6, 7	6-21-2013	2
55-4-202	Amended	484	sb0023	1, 3, 5, 7, 9, 12, 14, 16, 20, 22, 24	7-1-2013	2
55-4-203	Amended	318	hb0032	8, 9	6-21-2013	2
55-4-209	Amended	117	sb0629	1	4-12-2013	1
55-4-213	Amended	236	sb1218	90	4-19-2013	2
55-4-221	Amended	117	sb0629	2, 3	4-12-2013	1
55-4-221	Amended	183	sb0184	5	7-1-2013	2
55-4-230	Added*	303	sb0652	2	4-29-2013	2

*Section number(s) not assigned by General Assembly

T.C.A. Sec.	Action	Ch. No.	Bill No.	Sec. No.	Eff. Date	Pamphlet No.
55-4-231	Amended	318	hb0032	10-12	6-21-2013	2
55-4-232	Amended	183	sb0184	6	7-1-2013	2
55-4-233	Added*	318	hb0032	2	6-21-2013	2
55-4-236	Amended	318	hb0032	1, 3	6-21-2013	2
55-4-240	Amended	318	hb0032	4	6-21-2013	2
55-4-246	Added*	484	sb0023	2	7-1-2013	2
55-4-248	Amended	484	sb0023	11	7-1-2013	2
55-4-253	Amended	484	sb0023	27	7-1-2013	2
55-4-254	Added*	484	sb0023	4	7-1-2013	2
55-4-278	Amended	318	hb0032	5	6-21-2013	2
55-4-282	Added*	484	sb0023	6	7-1-2013	2
55-4-283	Added*	484	sb0023	8	7-1-2013	2
55-4-284	Added*	484	sb0023	10	7-1-2013	2
55-4-285	Added*	484	sb0023	13	7-1-2013	2
55-4-289	Added*	484	sb0023	15	7-1-2013	2
55-4-297	Added*	484	sb0023	17	7-1-2013	2
55-4-301	Added*	484	sb0023	18	7-1-2013	2
55-4-303	Added*	484	sb0023	21	7-1-2013	2
55-4-304	Added*	484	sb0023	23	7-1-2013	2
55-4-305	Added*	484	sb0023	25	7-1-2013	2
55-4-306	Amended	484	sb0023	26	7-1-2013	2
55-4-313	Amended	484	sb0023	34	5-20-2013	2
55-4-347	Amended	484	sb0023	35	5-20-2013	2
55-4-358	Amended	484	sb0023	32	5-20-2013	2
55-4-360	Amended	484	sb0023	33	5-20-2013	2
55-4-361	Amended	484	sb0023	31	5-20-2013	2
55-4-365	Amended	484	sb0023	29	5-20-2013	2
55-4-368	Amended	484	sb0023	30	5-20-2013	2
55-4-374	Amended	484	sb0023	28	5-20-2013	2
55-5-131	Added*	481	sb0069	1	5-20-2013	2
55-7-203	Amended	47	sb0065	1	7-1-2013	1
55-8-201	Amended	219	sb1337	1-3	4-23-2013	2
55-8-201	Amended	236	sb1218	91	4-19-2013	2
55-9-408	Amended	308	sb0521	39	7-1-2013	2
55-9-409	Amended	308	sb0521	40, 41	7-1-2013	2
55-9-411	Repealed	308	sb0521	42	7-1-2013	2
55-9-412	Repealed	308	sb0521	43	7-1-2013	2

*Section number(s) not assigned by General Assembly

T.C.A. Sec.	Action	Ch. No.	Bill No.	Sec. No.	Eff. Date	Pamphlet No.
55-10-203	Amended	308	sb0521	44	7-1-2013	2
55-10-205	Amended	154	sb0186	55, 56	7-1-2013	1
55-10-308	Amended	90	hb0505	1	7-1-2013	1
55-10-401	Repealed and reenacted	154	sb0186	1	7-1-2013	1
55-10-402	Amended	161	hb0012	8, 9	7-1-2013	2
55-10-402	Repealed and reenacted	154	sb0186	2	7-1-2013	1
55-10-403	Repealed and reenacted	154	sb0186	3	7-1-2013	1
55-10-404	Amended	344	hb0353	1	7-1-2013	2
55-10-404	Repealed and reenacted	154	sb0186	4	7-1-2013	1
55-10-405	Repealed and reenacted	154	sb0186	5	7-1-2013	1
55-10-406	Repealed and reenacted	154	sb0186	6	7-1-2013	1
55-10-407	Amended	344	hb0353	2, 3	7-1-2013	2
55-10-407	Repealed and reenacted	154	sb0186	7	7-1-2013	1
55-10-408	Repealed and reenacted	154	sb0186	8	7-1-2013	1
55-10-409	Amended	344	hb0353	4-9	7-1-2013	2
55-10-409	Repealed and reenacted	154	sb0186	9	7-1-2013	1
55-10-410	Repealed and reenacted	154	sb0186	10	7-1-2013	1
55-10-411	Amended	344	hb0353	10	7-1-2013	2
55-10-411	Repealed and reenacted	154	sb0186	11	7-1-2013	1
55-10-412	Repealed and reenacted	154	sb0186	12	7-1-2013	1
55-10-413	Repealed and reenacted	154	sb0186	13	7-1-2013	1
55-10-414	Repealed and reenacted	154	sb0186	14	7-1-2013	1
55-10-415	Repealed and reenacted	154	sb0186	15	7-1-2013	1
55-10-417	Amended	344	hb0353	11	7-1-2013	2
55-10-417	Repealed	344	hb0353	12	7-1-2013	2
55-10-417	Repealed and reenacted	154	sb0186	16	7-1-2013	1

*Section number(s) not assigned by General Assembly

T.C.A. Sec.	Action	Ch. No.	Bill No.	Sec. No.	Eff. Date	Pamphlet No.
55-10-418	Repealed and reenacted	154	sb0186	17	7-1-2013	1
55-10-419	Amended	344	hb0353	13	7-1-2013	2
55-10-419	Repealed and reenacted	154	sb0186	18	7-1-2013	1
55-10-420	Repealed and reenacted	154	sb0186	19	7-1-2013	1
55-10-421	Repealed and reenacted	154	sb0186	20	7-1-2013	1
55-10-422	Added	344	hb0353	20	5-13-2013	2
55-10-422	Amended	236	sb1218	36	4-19-2013	2
55-10-422	Repealed	154	sb0186	21	7-1-2013	1
55-10-423	Repealed	154	sb0186	22	7-1-2013	1
55-10-451	Repealed	154	sb0186	23	7-1-2013	1
55-10-452	Repealed	154	sb0186	24	7-1-2013	1
55-10-453	Repealed	154	sb0186	25	7-1-2013	1
55-10-454	Repealed	154	sb0186	26	7-1-2013	1
55-10-503	Amended	154	sb0186	42	7-1-2013	1
55-10-603	Amended	154	sb0186	51	7-1-2013	1
55-12-102	Amended	308	sb0521	38	7-1-2013	2
55-12-114	Amended	154	sb0186	43	7-1-2013	1
55-12-139	Amended	327	hb0478	1, 2	5-13-2013	2
55-12-139	Amended	479	sb0251	1	7-1-2013	2
55-17-111	Amended	192	sb0440	1	7-1-2013	2
55-17-114	Amended	192	sb0440	2	7-1-2013	2
55-17-123	Amended	258	sb0249	1-5	4-23-2013	2
55-25-107	Amended	183	sb0184	7	7-1-2013	2
55-50-322	Amended	62	sb0010	1	7-1-2013	1
55-50-405	Amended	154	sb0186	44	7-1-2013	1
55-50-502	Amended	154	sb0186	48, 52	7-1-2013	1
55-50-502	Amended	344	hb0353	14-19	7-1-2013	2
56-1-302	Amended	138	sb0149	1	4-12-2013	1
56-1-308	Amended	138	sb0149	2	4-12-2013	1
56-1-402, 56-1-403	Repealed	260	sb0145	1	7-1-2013	2
56-1-415	Amended	260	sb0145	2	7-1-2013	2
56-1-901–56-1-919	Added	260	sb0145	3	7-1-2013	2
56-2-104	Amended	5	sb0146	1, 2	3-7-2013	1
56-2-201	Amended	409	sb1292	2	5-16-2013	2

*Section number(s) not assigned by General Assembly

T.C.A. Sec.	Action	Ch. No.	Bill No.	Sec. No.	Eff. Date	Pamphlet No.
56-6-104	Amended	293	sb1147	10	7-1-2013	2
56-6-110	Amended	293	sb1147	9	7-1-2013	2
56-6-1201	Added	377	sb1145	1	7-1-2013	2
56-6-1201	Added*	293	sb1147	2	7-1-2013	2
56-6-1202	Added	377	sb1145	1	7-1-2013	2
56-6-1202	Added*	293	sb1147	3	7-1-2013	2
56-6-1203	Added	377	sb1145	1	7-1-2013	2
56-6-1203	Added*	293	sb1147	4	7-1-2013	2
56-6-1204	Added	377	sb1145	1	7-1-2013	2
56-6-1204	Added*	293	sb1147	5	7-1-2013	2
56-6-1205	Added	377	sb1145	1	7-1-2013	2
56-6-1205	Added*	293	sb1147	6	7-1-2013	2
56-6-1206	Added*	293	sb1147	7	7-1-2013	2
56-6-1207	Added*	293	sb1147	8	7-1-2013	2
56-7-401	Amended	260	sb0145	4-7	7-1-2013	2
56-7-2914	Amended	236	sb1218	17	4-19-2013	2
56-7-2915	Repealed	211	sb1208	1	7-1-2013	2
56-7-3024	Amended	236	sb1218	18	4-19-2013	2
56-7-3025	Amended	236	sb1218	17	4-19-2013	2
56-7-3026	Repealed	211	sb1208	2	7-1-2013	2
56-13-105	Amended	139	sb0141	1	4-12-2013	1
56-13-114	Amended	139	sb0141	2	4-12-2013	1
56-13-122	Amended	236	sb1218	19	4-19-2013	2
56-13-201	Amended	139	sb0141	3	4-12-2013	1
56-13-202	Amended	139	sb0141	4-8	4-12-2013	1
56-13-204	Amended	139	sb0141	9-12	4-12-2013	1
56-13-205	Amended	139	sb0141	13, 14	4-12-2013	1
56-14-113	Amended	444	sb0150	1	1-1-2014	2
56-32-104	Amended	409	sb1292	1	5-16-2013	2
56-32-128	Amended	92	hb0400	1	4-8-2013	1
56-37-102	Amended	121	sb0596	1	4-12-2013	1
56-37-112	Amended	121	sb0596	2	4-12-2013	1
56-61-116	Amended	106	hb0141	2-4	4-11-2013	1
56-61-116	Amended	106	hb0141	1	4-11-2013	1
57-1-209	Amended	236	sb1218	68	4-19-2013	2
57-1-214	Added*	316	sb0091	1	4-29-2013	2
57-2-103	Amended	445	sb0129	1, 2	7-1-2013	2

*Section number(s) not assigned by General Assembly

T.C.A. Sec.	Action	Ch. No.	Bill No.	Sec. No.	Eff. Date	Pamphlet No.
57-2-104	Amended	341	hb1084	2	7-1-2013	2
57-2-106	Added*	341	hb1084	1	7-1-2013	2
57-2-110	Added*	341	hb1084	3	7-1-2013	2
57-3-202	Amended	445	sb0129	3	7-1-2013	2
57-3-203	Amended	394	sb0590	1	5-14-2013	2
57-3-301	Amended	171	hb1044	1, 2	4-16-2013	2
57-4-102	Amended	37	hb0211	1	3-22-2013	1
57-4-102	Amended	160	sb0924	1	4-12-2013	2
57-4-102	Amended	218	sb1333	1	4-23-2013	2
57-4-102	Amended	230	sb0841	1	4-19-2013	2
57-4-102	Amended	295	sb1129	1, 2	4-29-2013	2
57-4-102	Amended	371	sb1327	1	5-6-2013	2
57-4-102	Amended	458	sb1345	1, 2	5-20-2013	2
57-4-202	Amended	236	sb1218	68	4-19-2013	2
57-4-203	Amended	386	sb0747	2	5-14-2013	2
57-4-301	Amended	371	sb1327	2	5-6-2013	2
57-5-101	Amended	386	sb0747	1, 3	5-14-2013	2
57-5-605	Amended	236	sb1218	68	4-19-2013	2
57-6-103	Amended	189	sb0422	1-7	7-1-2013	2
58-1-106	Amended	364	hb0848	2-4	5-13-2013	2
58-1-412	Added	364	hb0848	1	5-13-2013	2
58-1-601	Amended	308	sb0521	17	7-1-2013	2
60-1-401	Amended	181	sb0159	1	7-1-2013	2
60-1-404	Amended	94	hb0337	1	4-8-2013	1
62-2-401	Amended	180	sb0148	1	4-23-2013	2
62-2-402	Amended	180	sb0148	2	4-23-2013	2
62-2-404	Amended	180	sb0148	3	4-23-2013	2
62-2-405	Amended	180	sb0148	4	4-23-2013	2
62-4-120	Amended	447	sb0109	1	7-1-2013	2
62-4-125	Amended	477	sb0491	1	5-20-2013	2
62-5-101	Amended	437	sb0416	1	1-1-2014	2
62-5-318	Added*	437	sb0416	2	1-1-2014	2
62-6-102	Amended	355	hb0480	1-3	1-1-2014	2
62-6-103	Amended	355	hb0480	4	1-1-2014	2
62-6-103	Amended	469	sb0835	1, 2	7-1-2013	2
62-6-120	Amended	180	sb0148	5	4-23-2013	2
62-6-127	Repealed	211	sb1208	3	7-1-2013	2

*Section number(s) not assigned by General Assembly

T.C.A. Sec.	Action	Ch. No.	Bill No.	Sec. No.	Eff. Date	Pamphlet No.
62-6-605	Amended	355	hb0480	5	1-1-2014	2
62-7-112	Amended	69	hb0085	1	7-1-2013	1
62-9-102	Amended	271	sb0733	1	7-1-2013	2
62-9-113	Amended	211	sb1208	4	7-1-2013	2
62-11-104	Amended	269	sb0693	1, 2	7-1-2013	2
62-11-111	Amended	269	sb0693	3	7-1-2013	2
62-11-112	Amended	269	sb0693	4	7-1-2013	2
62-13-112	Amended	84	sb0646	1	7-1-2013	1
62-13-303	Amended	420	sb0942	1	1-1-2014	2
62-16-101–62-16-103	Repealed	211	sb1208	8	7-1-2013	2
62-20-102	Amended	180	sb0148	6	4-23-2013	2
62-20-108	Amended	180	sb0148	7	4-23-2013	2
62-20-112	Amended	180	sb0148	8	4-23-2013	2
62-20-116	Amended	180	sb0148	9	4-23-2013	2
62-20-125	Repealed	180	sb0148	10	4-23-2013	2
62-20-126	Repealed	180	sb0148	11	4-23-2013	2
62-32-313	Amended	142	sb0781	1	4-12-2013	1
62-32-321	Amended	191	sb0436	1	4-23-2013	2
62-39-322	Amended	180	sb0148	14	4-23-2013	2
62-39-414–62-39-416	Amended	180	sb0148	12	4-23-2013	2
62-39-416	Amended	180	sb0148	13	4-23-2013	2
62-39-417	Amended	180	sb0148	12	4-23-2013	2
63-1-151	Added*	232	sb0955	1	7-1-2013	2
63-1-301	Amended	336	hb0868	2	7-1-2013	2
63-1-301	Amended	430	sb0676	7	10-1-2013	2
63-1-303	Amended	430	sb0676	8	10-1-2013	2
63-1-309	Amended	336	hb0868	3	7-1-2013	2
63-1-309	Amended	336	hb0868	4	7-1-2016	2
63-1-309	Amended	430	sb0676	9	10-1-2013	2
63-1-310	Amended	430	sb0676	10	10-1-2013	2
63-1-311	Amended	430	sb0676	12, 13	10-1-2013	2
63-1-313	Added	336	hb0868	1	7-1-2013	2
63-1-314	Added	430	sb0676	14	10-1-2013	2
63-1-401, 63-1-402	Added	430	sb0676	2	10-1-2013	2
63-2-103	Added	113	sb0103	2	4-12-2013	1
63-3-127	Amended	74	hb0319	2	4-1-2013	1
63-5-109	Amended	110	sb0171	1-3	7-1-2013	1

*Section number(s) not assigned by General Assembly

T.C.A. Sec.	Action	Ch. No.	Bill No.	Sec. No.	Eff. Date	Pamphlet No.
63-5-122	Amended	74	hb0319	3	4-1-2013	1
63-6-236	Amended	74	hb0319	4	4-1-2013	1
63-6-245	Added	387	sb0745	1	1-1-2014	2
63-6-703	Amended	235	sb1201	1	7-1-2013	2
63-7-123	Amended	74	hb0319	5	4-1-2013	1
63-7-123	Amended	396	sb0529	1	7-1-2013	2
63-8-126	Amended	74	hb0319	6	4-1-2013	1
63-9-116	Amended	74	hb0319	7	4-1-2013	1
63-10-204	Amended	266	sb0582	1, 2	4-25-2013	2
63-10-216	Added	266	sb0582	3	4-25-2013	2
63-12-108	Amended	440	sb0265	1	7-1-2013	2
63-12-135	Amended	440	sb0265	2	7-1-2013	2
63-12-139	Amended	440	sb0265	3, 4	7-1-2013	2
63-19-107	Amended	74	hb0319	8	4-1-2013	1
63-19-107	Amended	396	sb0529	2	7-1-2013	2
63-31-107	Amended	236	sb1218	55	4-19-2013	2
64-1-102	Amended	149	sb1007	1	4-12-2013	1
64-5-213	Amended	236	sb1218	69	4-19-2013	2
64-6-105	Amended	265	sb0568	1	4-25-2013	2
64-6-110	Amended	265	sb0568	2	4-25-2013	2
64-10-201–64-10-222	Added	474	sb0608	1	5-20-2013	2
65-1-102	Amended	245	hb0191	2	4-19-2013	2
65-2-122	Added*	245	hb0191	3	4-19-2013	2
65-4-303	Amended	245	hb0191	4	4-19-2013	2
65-5-103	Amended	245	hb0191	5	4-19-2013	2
65-5-107	Amended	61	sb1180	1	3-26-2013	1
65-5-109	Amended	61	sb1180	2-4	3-26-2013	1
65-5-113	Amended	359	hb0982	1	7-1-2013	2
65-23-101–65-23-123	Repealed	211	sb1208	5	7-1-2013	2
65-31-114	Added*	65	sb0851	1, 2	4-1-2013	1
65-32-104	Amended	373	sb1319	1	7-1-2013	2
66-11-101	Amended	469	sb0835	4	7-1-2013	2
66-11-102	Amended	469	sb0835	3	7-1-2013	2
66-11-104	Amended	469	sb0835	5	7-1-2013	2
66-28-201	Amended	206	sb0844	1	4-23-2013	2
66-28-503	Amended	107	hb0106	1, 2	7-1-2013	1
67-1-401	Amended	209	sb1002	1, 2	4-23-2013	2

*Section number(s) not assigned by General Assembly

T.C.A. Sec.	Action	Ch. No.	Bill No.	Sec. No.	Eff. Date	Pamphlet No.
67-1-402	Amended	209	sb1002	3	4-23-2013	2
67-1-507	Amended	209	sb1002	4	4-23-2013	2
67-1-1441	Amended	434	sb0599	1	5-16-2013	2
67-1-1702	Amended	400	sb0405	1	5-6-2013	2
67-1-1709	Amended	400	sb0405	2	5-6-2013	2
67-2-104	Amended	322	hb0192	1	5-13-2013	2
67-2-110	Amended	480	sb0182	2	5-20-2013	2
67-3-206	Amended	164	hb0396	4	7-1-2013	2
67-4-409	Amended	236	sb1218	76	4-19-2013	2
67-4-504	Added*	108	hb0023	1	4-8-2013	1
67-4-601	Amended	450	sb0024	1	5-16-2013	2
67-4-703	Amended	313	sb0183	2	1-1-2014	2
67-4-704	Amended	313	sb0183	3	1-1-2014	2
67-4-705	Amended	313	sb0183	4	1-1-2014	2
67-4-706	Amended	313	sb0183	5	1-1-2014	2
67-4-707	Amended	313	sb0183	6	1-1-2014	2
67-4-708	Amended	313	sb0183	7	1-1-2014	2
67-4-709	Amended	313	sb0183	8, 9	1-1-2014	2
67-4-710	Amended	313	sb0183	10, 11	1-1-2014	2
67-4-711	Amended	313	sb0183	12	1-1-2014	2
67-4-712	Amended	313	sb0183	13	1-1-2014	2
67-4-713	Amended	313	sb0183	14, 15	1-1-2014	2
67-4-714	Amended	313	sb0183	16	1-1-2014	2
67-4-715	Amended	313	sb0183	17	1-1-2014	2
67-4-717	Added	313	sb0183	18	1-1-2014	2
67-4-719	Amended	313	sb0183	19	1-1-2014	2
67-4-723	Amended	313	sb0183	20	1-1-2014	2
67-4-724	Amended	313	sb0183	21	1-1-2014	2
67-4-725	Repealed	313	sb0183	22	1-1-2014	2
67-4-1610	Amended	457	sb1349	1, 2	7-1-2014	2
67-4-1709	Amended	454	sb0501	18	5-16-2013	2
67-4-2004	Amended	321	hb0175	1	5-13-2013	2
67-4-2004	Amended	423	sb0852	5	5-16-2013	2
67-4-2006	Amended	321	hb0175	8	5-13-2013	2
67-4-2008	Amended	164	hb0396	5	7-1-2013	2
67-4-2015	Amended	321	hb0175	2	5-13-2013	2
67-4-2105	Amended	321	hb0175	3	5-13-2013	2

*Section number(s) not assigned by General Assembly

T.C.A. Sec.	Action	Ch. No.	Bill No.	Sec. No.	Eff. Date	Pamphlet No.
67-4-2107	Amended	321	hb0175	4, 5	5-13-2013	2
67-4-2109	Amended	378	sb1127	2	5-14-2013	2
67-4-2111	Amended	321	hb0175	6	5-13-2013	2
67-4-2115	Amended	321	hb0175	7	5-13-2013	2
67-4-2301–67-4-2308; 67-4-2401–67-4-2410; 67-4-2501–67-4-2508; 67-4-2701–67-4-2712	Amended	480	sb0182	1	5-20-2013	2
67-5-105	Amended	353	hb0493	1	5-13-2013	2
67-5-209	Amended	417	sb1024	1	5-16-2013	2
67-5-212	Amended	209	sb1002	5	4-23-2013	2
67-5-303	Amended	209	sb1002	6, 7	4-23-2013	2
67-5-504	Amended	462	sb1054	2	5-20-2013	2
67-5-508	Amended	209	sb1002	8	4-23-2013	2
67-5-509	Amended	209	sb1002	9	4-23-2013	2
67-5-513	Amended	353	hb0493	32	5-13-2013	2
67-5-601	Amended	297	sb1000	1	4-29-2013	2
67-5-601	Amended	423	sb0852	4	5-16-2013	2
67-5-604	Amended	297	sb1000	2	4-29-2013	2
67-5-701	Amended	63	sb0137	1	4-1-2013	1
67-5-703	Amended	63	sb0137	2	4-1-2013	1
67-5-704	Amended	63	sb0137	3	4-1-2013	1
67-5-705	Amended	63	sb0137	4	4-1-2013	1
67-5-806	Amended	209	sb1002	10	4-23-2013	2
67-5-903	Amended	353	hb0493	33	5-13-2013	2
67-5-1203	Amended	328	hb0574	1, 2	5-13-2013	2
67-5-1302	Amended	209	sb1002	11	4-23-2013	2
67-5-1407	Amended	209	sb1002	12	4-23-2013	2
67-5-1501	Amended	209	sb1002	13	4-23-2013	2
67-5-1509	Amended	209	sb1002	14	4-23-2013	2
67-5-1601	Amended	209	sb1002	15, 16	4-23-2013	2
67-5-1806	Amended	353	hb0493	6	5-13-2013	2
67-5-2003	Amended	353	hb0493	9-11	5-13-2013	2
67-5-2010	Amended	370	sb1346	1	5-14-2013	2
67-5-2103	Amended	353	hb0493	13	5-13-2013	2
67-5-2401	Amended	353	hb0493	2	5-13-2013	2
67-5-2402	Amended	353	hb0493	3	5-13-2013	2
67-5-2403	Amended	353	hb0493	4	5-13-2013	2

*Section number(s) not assigned by General Assembly

T.C.A. Sec.	Action	Ch. No.	Bill No.	Sec. No.	Eff. Date	Pamphlet No.
67-5-2404	Amended	353	hb0493	12	5-13-2013	2
67-5-2405	Amended	353	hb0493	7	5-13-2013	2
67-5-2409	Amended	353	hb0493	14	5-13-2013	2
67-5-2415	Amended	353	hb0493	15	5-13-2013	2
67-5-2422	Added	353	hb0493	5	5-13-2013	2
67-5-2423	Added	353	hb0493	16	5-13-2013	2
67-5-2501	Amended	353	hb0493	19	5-13-2013	2
67-5-2502	Amended	353	hb0493	17	5-13-2013	2
67-5-2504	Amended	353	hb0493	20	5-13-2013	2
67-5-2507	Amended	353	hb0493	21-24	5-13-2013	2
67-5-2508	Amended	353	hb0493	25, 26	5-13-2013	2
67-5-2509	Amended	353	hb0493	27, 28	5-13-2013	2
67-5-2702	Amended	353	hb0493	29	5-13-2013	2
67-5-2704	Amended	353	hb0493	30	5-13-2013	2
67-5-2707	Added	353	hb0493	31	5-13-2013	2
67-5-2801	Amended	353	hb0493	18	5-13-2013	2
67-6-102, 67-6-103; 67-6-201–67-6-203; 67-6-205, 67-6-206; 67-6-209; 67-6-217; 67-6-219; 67-6-221	Amended	480	sb0182	1	5-20-2013	2
67-6-222	Amended	61	sb1180	5	3-26-2013	1
67-6-226, 67-6-227	Amended	480	sb0182	1	5-20-2013	2
67-6-228	Amended	323	hb0193	1	7-1-2013	2
67-6-313; 67-6-322; 67-6-329	Amended	480	sb0182	1	5-20-2013	2
67-6-329	Amended	473	sb0643	26	7-1-2013	2
67-6-349; 67-6-385, 67-6-386; 67-6-407, 67-6-408; 67-6-504; 67-6-528; 67-6-536; 67-6-539; 67-6-601; 67-6-702; 67-6-704; 67-6-706; 67-6-710; 67-6-712; 67-6-714–67-6-716; 67-6-901, 67-6-902; 67-6-904–67-6-907	Amended	480	sb0182	1	5-20-2013	2
68-1-101	Amended	122	sb0493	1, 3, 5	7-1-2013	1
68-1-108	Amended	236	sb1218	49	4-19-2013	2
68-1-110	Amended	236	sb1218	87	4-19-2013	2
68-1-123	Amended	236	sb1218	63	4-19-2013	2
68-1-125	Amended	236	sb1218	24	4-19-2013	2

*Section number(s) not assigned by General Assembly

T.C.A. Sec.	Action	Ch. No.	Bill No.	Sec. No.	Eff. Date	Pamphlet No.
68-1-128	Added*	396	sb0529	3	7-1-2013	2
68-4-103	Amended	287	hb0715	2-4	4-25-2013	2
68-4-113	Added	287	hb0715	1	4-25-2013	2
68-5-111	Added	60	sb0979	1	7-1-2013	1
68-5-112	Added*	197	sb0665	1	7-1-2013	2
68-8-108	Amended	58	sb0561	1	3-26-2013	1
68-11-201	Amended	89	hb0518	1	7-1-2013	1
68-11-203	Amended	89	hb0518	2	7-1-2013	1
68-11-209	Amended	236	sb1218	55	4-19-2013	2
68-11-216	Amended	356	hb0342	1	7-1-2013	2
68-11-216	Amended	410	sb1245	1, 2	5-16-2013	2
68-11-224	Amended	238	hb1073	3	7-1-2013	2
68-11-224	Amended	254	hb1019	1	7-1-2013	2
68-11-251	Amended	236	sb1218	56	4-19-2013	2
68-11-305	Amended	113	sb0103	1	4-12-2013	1
68-11-310	Amended	4	sb0104	1	3-7-2013	1
68-11-830	Amended	163	hb0157	1, 2	7-1-2013	2
68-11-1604	Amended	131	sb0336	3, 4	4-12-2013	1
68-11-1609	Amended	311	sb0431	1	7-1-2013	2
68-11-1622	Amended	311	sb0431	2	7-1-2013	2
68-11-1628	Amended	234	sb1048	1	7-1-2013	2
68-14-301	Amended	182	sb0172	22	7-1-2015	2
68-14-302	Amended	182	sb0172	23	7-1-2015	2
68-14-303	Amended	182	sb0172	24	7-1-2015	2
68-14-305	Amended	182	sb0172	25	7-1-2015	2
68-14-306	Amended	182	sb0172	26	7-1-2015	2
68-14-307	Amended	182	sb0172	27	7-1-2015	2
68-14-311	Amended	182	sb0172	28	7-1-2015	2
68-14-313	Repealed	182	sb0172	29	7-1-2015	2
68-14-314	Transferred to 68-14-313	182	sb0172	29	7-1-2015	2
68-14-315	Transferred to 68-14-314	182	sb0172	30	7-1-2015	2
68-14-316	Transferred to 68-14-315	182	sb0172	31	7-1-2015	2
68-14-317	Transferred to 68-14-316	182	sb0172	32	7-1-2015	2
68-14-318	Transferred to 68-14-317	182	sb0172	33	7-1-2015	2

*Section number(s) not assigned by General Assembly

T.C.A. Sec.	Action	Ch. No.	Bill No.	Sec. No.	Eff. Date	Pamphlet No.
68-14-318	Transferred from 68-14-320	182	sb0172	34	7-1-2015	2
68-14-319	Repealed	182	sb0172	35	7-1-2015	2
68-14-319	Transferred from 68-14-321	182	sb0172	35	7-1-2015	2
68-14-320	Transferred from 68-14-322	182	sb0172	34, 36	7-1-2015	2
68-14-321	Transferred from 68-14-323	182	sb0172	35, 37	7-1-2015	2
68-14-322	Transferred from 68-14-325	182	sb0172	36, 38	7-1-2015	2
68-14-323	Transferred from 68-14-326	182	sb0172	37, 39	7-1-2015	2
68-14-324	Repealed	182	sb0172	40	7-1-2015	2
68-14-325	Transferred to 68-14-322	182	sb0172	38	7-1-2015	2
68-14-326	Transferred to 68-14-323	182	sb0172	39	7-1-2015	2
68-14-701	Added	182	sb0172	43	7-1-2015	2
68-14-701	Repealed	182	sb0172	43	7-1-2015	2
68-14-702	Added	182	sb0172	44	7-1-2015	2
68-14-702	Repealed	182	sb0172	44	7-1-2015	2
68-14-703	Added	182	sb0172	45	7-1-2015	2
68-14-703	Repealed	182	sb0172	45	7-1-2015	2
68-14-704	Added	182	sb0172	46	7-1-2015	2
68-14-704	Repealed	182	sb0172	46	7-1-2015	2
68-14-705	Added	182	sb0172	47	7-1-2015	2
68-14-705	Repealed	182	sb0172	47	7-1-2015	2
68-14-706–68-14-726	Added	182	sb0172	48	7-1-2015	2
68-24-606	Amended	190	sb0424	1	7-1-2013	2
68-29-138	Amended	213	sb1269	1	7-1-2013	2
68-55-205	Amended	236	sb1218	55	4-19-2013	2
68-55-501–68-55-503	Added	148	sb0882	1	1-1-2014	1
68-57-101	Amended	391	sb0623	1, 2, 3, 5	7-1-2013	2
68-57-102	Amended	391	sb0623	4	7-1-2013	2
68-59-103	Amended	236	sb1218	55	4-19-2013	2
68-101-104	Amended	56	sb0492	1, 2	1-1-2014	1
68-101-108	Amended	93	hb0338	5	4-8-2013	1
68-102-143	Amended	150	sb1176	1	1-1-2014	1

*Section number(s) not assigned by General Assembly

T.C.A. Sec.	Action	Ch. No.	Bill No.	Sec. No.	Eff. Date	Pamphlet No.
68-102-147	Amended	150	sb1176	2-4	1-1-2014	1
68-105-103	Amended	236	sb1218	20	4-19-2013	2
68-106-101, 68-106-102	Added	249	hb0348	1	7-1-2013	2
68-115-211	Amended	468	sb0856	1	5-20-2013	2
68-140-321	Amended	236	sb1218	56	4-19-2013	2
68-142-103	Amended	89	hb0518	3	7-1-2013	1
68-142-103	Amended	236	sb1218	57	4-19-2013	2
68-201-107	Amended	181	sb0159	2	7-1-2013	2
68-201-108	Amended	181	sb0159	3	7-1-2013	2
68-201-115	Amended	156	sb0943	1	4-16-2013	1
68-203-104	Amended	454	sb0501	14, 15	5-16-2013	2
68-211-113	Amended	181	sb0159	4-6	7-1-2013	2
68-211-117	Amended	181	sb0159	7	7-1-2013	2
68-211-701	Amended	342	hb0952	1	5-13-2013	2
68-211-707	Amended	342	hb0952	2	5-13-2013	2
68-211-861	Amended	421	sb0941	1	5-16-2013	2
68-211-874	Amended	49	sb0082	1, 2	3-26-2013	1
68-212-113	Amended	181	sb0159	8	7-1-2013	2
68-212-117	Amended	181	sb0159	9	7-1-2013	2
68-215-115	Amended	181	sb0159	10	7-1-2013	2
68-215-119	Amended	181	sb0159	11	7-1-2013	2
68-215-123	Amended	181	sb0159	12	7-1-2013	2
68-221-901	Amended	362	hb1066	1	7-1-2013	2
68-221-904	Amended	362	hb1066	2	7-1-2013	2
68-221-905	Amended	362	hb1066	3, 4, 9	7-1-2013	2
68-221-906	Amended	362	hb1066	5	7-1-2013	2
68-221-911	Amended	362	hb1066	6, 7	7-1-2013	2
68-221-914	Amended	362	hb1066	8	7-1-2013	2
68-221-1009	Amended	141	sb0764	6	4-12-2013	1
68-221-1010	Amended	141	sb0764	7, 13	4-12-2013	1
68-221-1012	Amended	141	sb0764	8	4-12-2013	1
69-3-105	Amended	181	sb0159	13, 14	7-1-2013	2
69-3-110	Amended	181	sb0159	15, 16	7-1-2013	2
69-3-111	Amended	181	sb0159	17	7-1-2013	2
69-3-142	Amended	236	sb1218	10	4-19-2013	2
69-3-302	Amended	181	sb0159	18	7-1-2013	2
70-1-201	Amended	236	sb1218	6	4-19-2013	2
70-1-206	Amended	236	sb1218	7	4-19-2013	2

*Section number(s) not assigned by General Assembly

T.C.A. Sec.	Action	Ch. No.	Bill No.	Sec. No.	Eff. Date	Pamphlet No.
70-2-226	Amended	95	hb0336	1	4-8-2013	1
70-5-101	Amended	236	sb1218	11	4-19-2013	2
71-1-105	Amended	402	sb0176	1	5-14-2013	2
71-1-126	Amended	236	sb1218	62	4-19-2013	2
71-1-135	Amended	236	sb1218	33	4-19-2013	2
71-2-105	Amended	236	sb1218	58	4-19-2013	2
71-2-403	Amended	101	hb0171	1	4-8-2013	1
71-2-412	Amended	236	sb1218	59	4-19-2013	2
71-3-106	Repealed	454	sb0501	6	5-16-2013	2
71-3-110	Amended	402	sb0176	3	5-14-2013	2
71-3-126	Added	312	sb0244	1	7-1-2014	2
71-3-503	Amended	72	hb0172	1, 2	4-1-2013	1
71-3-507	Amended	101	hb0171	2	4-8-2013	1
71-3-515	Amended	101	hb0171	3	4-8-2013	1
71-3-517	Added	216	sb1302	1	7-1-2013	2
71-3-518	Added*	291	sb1370	1	7-1-2013	2
71-3-1111	Amended	236	sb1218	17	4-19-2013	2
71-3-1202, 71-3-1203	Amended	236	sb1218	60	4-19-2013	2
71-4-2101–71-4-2109	Amended	455	sb1392	1	7-1-2013	2
71-5-105	Amended	239	hb1097	1	7-1-2013	2
71-5-106	Amended	236	sb1218	86	4-19-2013	2
71-5-107	Amended	236	sb1218	77	4-19-2013	2
71-5-118	Amended	236	sb1218	43	4-19-2013	2
71-5-137	Amended	89	hb0518	4	7-1-2013	1
71-5-160	Amended	250	hb0544	2	7-1-2013	2
71-5-182	Amended	99	hb0184	1	4-11-2013	1
71-5-183	Amended	99	hb0184	2	4-11-2013	1
71-5-190	Amended	236	sb1218	53	4-19-2013	2
71-5-314	Amended	402	sb0176	2	5-14-2013	2
71-5-701–71-5-705	Added*	250	hb0544	1	7-1-2013	2
71-5-706	Added*	250	hb0544	2	7-1-2013	2
71-5-1422	Amended	236	sb1218	50	4-19-2013	2
71-5-2508	Amended	236	sb1218	42	4-19-2013	2
71-5-2512	Amended	236	sb1218	19	4-19-2013	2
71-5-2601	Amended	159	sb0500	1, 2	4-16-2013	1
71-5-2705	Amended	236	sb1218	49	4-19-2013	2
71-6-102	Amended	431	sb0675	1, 2	7-1-2013	2

*Section number(s) not assigned by General Assembly

Ch. No.	Date	Ch. No.	Date
1	3-7-2013	34	3-22-2013
2	3-7-2013	35	3-22-2013
3	3-7-2013	36	3-22-2013
4	3-7-2013	37	3-22-2013
5	3-7-2013	38	3-22-2013
6	3-7-2013	39	3-22-2013
7	3-7-2013	40	3-22-2013
8	3-7-2013	41	3-22-2013
9	3-7-2013	42	3-22-2013
10	3-7-2013	43	3-22-2013
11	3-7-2013	44	3-22-2013
12	3-7-2013	45	3-22-2013
13	3-7-2013	46	3-26-2013
14	3-7-2013	47	7-1-2013
15	3-14-2013	48	3-26-2013
16	7-1-2013	49	3-26-2013
17	3-14-2013	50	3-26-2013
18	3-14-2013	51	3-26-2013
19	3-14-2013	52	3-26-2013
20	3-14-2013	53	3-26-2013
21	3-20-2013	54	3-26-2013
22	3-20-2013	55	3-26-2013
23	7-1-2013	56	1-1-2014
24	3-20-2013	57	3-26-2013
25	3-20-2013	58	3-26-2013
26	3-20-2013	59	7-1-2013
27	3-20-2013	60	7-1-2013
28	3-20-2013	61	3-26-2013
29	3-20-2013	62	7-1-2013
30	3-20-2013	63	4-1-2013
31	3-20-2013	64	4-1-2013
32	7-1-2013	65	4-1-2013
33	7-1-2013	66	4-1-2013

Ch. No.	Date	Ch. No.	Date
67	4-1-2013	100	4-10-2013
68	7-1-2013	101	4-8-2013
69	7-1-2013	102	4-11-2013
70	4-1-2013	103	7-1-2013
71	4-2-2013	104	4-11-2013
72	4-1-2013	105	4-11-2013
73	4-2-2013	106	4-11-2013
74	4-1-2013	107	7-1-2013
75	4-1-2013	108	4-8-2013
76	4-1-2013	109	4-8-2013
77	4-1-2013	110	7-1-2013
78	4-1-2013	111	4-10-2013
79	4-1-2013	112	4-10-2013
80	4-1-2013	113	4-12-2013
81	4-1-2013	114	7-1-2013
82	4-1-2013	115	4-12-2013
83	4-1-2013	116	7-1-2013
84	7-1-2013	117	4-12-2013
85	4-8-2013	118	4-12-2013
86	4-8-2013	119	7-1-2013
87	4-8-2013	120	7-1-2013
88	4-8-2013	121	4-12-2013
89	7-1-2013	122	7-1-2013
90	7-1-2013	123	7-1-2013
91	4-11-2013	124	4-12-2013
92	4-8-2013	125	4-12-2013
93	4-8-2013	126	4-12-2013; 7-1-2013
94	4-8-2013	127	4-12-2013
95	4-8-2013	128	4-12-2013
96	4-11-2013	129	4-12-2013
97	4-8-2013	130	4-12-2013
98	4-11-2013	131	4-12-2013
99	4-11-2013		

Ch. No.	Date	Ch. No.	Date
132	4-12-2013	165	4-16-2013
133	4-12-2013	166	4-16-2013
134	4-12-2013	167	4-16-2013
135	4-12-2013	168	7-1-2013
136	4-12-2013	169	4-16-2013
137	4-12-2013	170	4-16-2013
138	4-12-2013	171	4-16-2013
139	4-12-2013	172	7-1-2013
140	4-12-2013	173	7-1-2013
141	4-12-2013	174	4-23-2013
142	4-12-2013	175	7-1-2013
143	4-12-2013	176	7-1-2013
144	4-12-2013	177	4-23-2013
145	4-12-2013	178	4-23-2013
146	4-12-2013	179	7-1-2013
147	4-12-2013	180	4-23-2013
148	1-1-2014	181	7-1-2013
149	4-12-2013	182	7-1-2015
150	1-1-2014	183	7-1-2013
151	7-1-2013	184	4-23-2013
152	4-16-2013	185	4-23-2013
153	7-1-2013	186	7-1-2013
154	7-1-2013	187	7-1-2013
155	7-1-2013	188	7-1-2013
156	4-16-2013	189	7-1-2013
157	7-1-2013	190	7-1-2013
158	4-16-2013	191	4-23-2013
159	4-16-2013	192	7-1-2013
160	4-12-2013	193	4-23-2013
161	7-1-2013	194	7-1-2013
162	4-16-2013	195	4-23-2013
163	7-1-2013	196	4-23-2013
164	7-1-2013	197	7-1-2013

Ch. No.	Date
198	4-23-2013
199	4-23-2013
200	4-23-2013
201	4-23-2013
202	4-23-2013
203	4-23-2013
204	4-23-2013
205	7-1-2013
206	4-23-2013
207	4-23-2013
208	4-23-2013
209	4-23-2013
210	4-23-2013
211	7-1-2013
212	4-23-2013
213	7-1-2013
214	4-23-2013
215	7-1-2013
216	7-1-2013
217	4-23-2013
218	4-23-2013
219	4-23-2013
220	7-1-2013
221	4-19-2013
222	7-1-2013
223	7-1-2013
224	7-1-2013
225	7-1-2013
226	7-1-2013
227	7-1-2013
228	4-19-2013
229	4-19-2013
230	4-19-2013
231	7-1-2013
232	7-1-2013
233	4-19-2013
234	7-1-2013
235	7-1-2013
236	4-19-2013
237	4-23-2013
238	7-1-2013
239	7-1-2013
240	4-23-2013
241	11-4-2014
242	7-1-2013
243	4-19-2013
244	4-19-2013
245	4-19-2013
246	7-1-2013
247	7-1-2013
248	4-19-2013
249	7-1-2013
250	7-1-2013
251	7-1-2013
252	4-19-2013
253	4-19-2013
254	7-1-2013
255	4-19-2013
256	4-24-2013
257	4-23-2013
258	4-23-2013
259	7-1-2014
260	7-1-2013
261	10-31-2013
262	4-25-2013
263	7-1-2013

Ch. No.	Date	Ch. No.	Date
264	4-25-2013	297	4-29-2013
265	4-25-2013	298	4-29-2013
266	4-25-2013	299	4-29-2013
267	7-1-2013	300	7-1-2013
268	4-25-2013	301	7-1-2013
269	7-1-2013	302	4-29-2013
270	7-1-2013	303	4-29-2013
271	7-1-2013	304	7-1-2013
272	4-25-2013	305	4-29-2013
273	4-25-2013	306	7-1-2013
274	4-25-2013	307	4-29-2013
275	4-25-2013	308	7-1-2013
276	7-1-2013	309	7-1-2013
277	4-25-2013	310	4-29-2013
278	7-1-2013	311	7-1-2013
279	7-1-2013	312	7-1-2014
280	1-1-2014	313	1-1-2014
281	4-25-2013	314	4-29-2013
282	7-1-2014	315	4-29-2013
283	7-1-2013	316	4-29-2013
284	4-25-2013	317	7-1-2013
285	7-1-2013	318	6-21-2013
286	4-25-2013	319	5-13-2013
287	4-25-2013	320	5-13-2013
288	4-25-2013	321	5-13-2013
289	7-1-2014	322	5-13-2013
290	6-28-2014	323	7-1-2013
291	7-1-2013	324	5-13-2013
292	4-29-2013	325	7-1-2013
293	7-1-2013	326	7-1-2013
294	4-29-2013	327	5-13-2013
295	4-29-2013	328	5-13-2013
296	4-29-2013	329	5-13-2013

Ch. No.	Date
330	5-13-2013
331	5-13-2013
332	5-13-2013
333	5-13-2013
334	5-13-2013
335	5-13-2013
336	7-1-2013
337	7-1-2013
338	1-1-2014
339	5-13-2013
340	7-1-2013
341	7-1-2013
342	5-13-2013
343	7-1-2013
344	5-13-2013; 7-1-2013
345	7-1-2013
346	5-13-2013
347	1-1-2014
348	5-13-2013
349	5-13-2013
350	7-1-2013
351	7-1-2013
352	7-1-2013
353	5-13-2013
354	5-13-2013
355	1-1-2014
356	7-1-2013
357	7-1-2013
358	7-1-2013
359	7-1-2013
360	7-1-2013
361	5-13-2013
362	7-1-2013
363	5-13-2013
364	5-13-2013
365	7-1-2013
366	7-1-2014
367	5-13-2013
368	5-13-2013
369	7-1-2014
370	5-14-2013
371	5-6-2013
373	7-1-2013
374	5-6-2013
375	7-1-2013
376	5-6-2013
377	7-1-2013
378	5-14-2013
379	5-14-2013
380	5-6-2013
381	5-14-2013
382	1-1-2014
383	7-1-2013
384	7-1-2013
385	5-14-2013
386	5-14-2013
387	1-1-2014
388	5-6-2013
389	5-14-2013
390	7-1-2013
391	7-1-2013
392	5-14-2013
393	5-6-2013
394	5-14-2013
395	7-1-2013

Ch. No.	Date	Ch. No.	Date
396	7-1-2013	429	7-1-2013
397	7-1-2013	430	10-1-2013
398	5-14-2013	431	7-1-2013
399	1-1-2014	432	7-1-2013
400	5-6-2013	433	7-1-2013
401	7-1-2014	434	5-16-2013
402	5-14-2013	435	7-1-2013
403	7-1-2013	436	7-1-2013
404	5-14-2013	437	1-1-2014
405	5-14-2013	438	5-16-2013
406	5-14-2013	439	5-16-2013
407	7-1-2013	440	7-1-2013
408	5-14-2013	441	5-16-2013
409	5-16-2013	442	7-1-2013
410	5-16-2013	443	7-1-2013
411	7-1-2013	444	1-1-2014
412	5-16-2013	445	7-1-2013
413	7-1-2013	446	5-16-2013
414	5-16-2013	447	7-1-2013
415	7-1-2013	448	5-16-2013
416	7-1-2013	449	7-1-2013
417	5-16-2013	450	5-16-2013
418	7-1-2013	451	5-16-2013
419	5-16-2013	452	5-16-2013
420	1-1-2014	453	7-1-2013
421	5-16-2013	454	5-16-2013; 7-1-2013
422	7-1-2013	455	7-1-2013
423	5-16-2013	456	5-20-2013
424	7-1-2013	457	7-1-2014
425	7-1-2013	458	5-20-2013
426	7-1-2013	459	5-20-2013
427	7-1-2013	460	5-20-2013
428	5-16-2013		

Ch. No.	Date	Ch. No.	Date
461	7-1-2013	474	5-20-2013
462	5-20-2013	475	7-1-2013
463	5-20-2013	476	1-1-2014
464	7-1-2013	477	5-20-2013
465	7-1-2013	478	5-20-2013
466	5-20-2013	479	7-1-2013
467	5-20-2013	480	5-20-2013
468	5-20-2013	481	5-20-2013
469	7-1-2013	482	5-20-2013
470	7-1-2013	483	5-20-2013
471	5-20-2013	484	5-20-2013; 7-1-2013
472	7-1-2013	485	7-1-2013
473	7-1-2013		

PUBLIC CHAPTER NO. 160

PUBLIC CHAPTER NO. 160

SENATE BILL NO. 924

By Johnson

Substituted for: House Bill No. 1088

By Sanderson, Casada, Sargent, Durham

AN ACT to amend Tennessee Code Annotated, Section 57-4-102, relative to premier type tourist resorts.

BE IT ENACTED BY THE GENERAL ASSEMBLY OF THE STATE OF TENNESSEE:

57-4-102 SECTION 1. Tennessee Code Annotated, Section 57-4-102(26), is amended by adding the following as a new subdivision thereto:

(OOO)

(i) A commercially operated recreational facility possessing all of the following characteristics:

(*a*) A golf course of at least eighteen (18) holes;

(*b*) Wooded trails for horseback riding;

(*c*) A fully stocked fishing pond;

(*d*) At least three (3) tennis courts;

(*e*) Located in any county having a population of not less than one hundred eighty-three thousand one hundred (183,100) nor more than one hundred eighty-three thousand two hundred (183,200) according to the 2010 federal census or any subsequent federal census; and

(*f*) Is located no more than two thousand feet (2,000') from the right-of-way of Interstate 840 and must be directly adjacent to Arno Road.

(ii) The premises of any facility licensed under this subdivision (26)(OOO) means any or all of the property that constitutes the facility, including swimming pools, tennis courts, golf courses, paths, and road crossings. A license shall designate the premises to be licensed by the commission by filing a drawing of the premises, which may be amended by the licensee filing a new drawing;

Effective date 4/12/2013 SECTION 2. This act shall take effect upon becoming law, the public welfare requiring it.

PUBLIC CHAPTER NO. 161

PUBLIC CHAPTER NO. 161

HOUSE BILL NO. 12

By Representatives Shipley, Kent Williams, Rogers, Hardaway

Substituted for: Senate Bill No. 48

By Senator Beavers

AN ACT to amend Tennessee Code Annotated, Title 39, Chapter 17, Part 4 and Title 55, Chapter 10, Part 4, relative to illegal drugs and analogues of drugs.

BE IT ENACTED BY THE GENERAL ASSEMBLY OF THE STATE OF TENNESSEE:

39-17-438 SECTION 1. Tennessee Code Annotated, Section 39-17-438, is amended by deleting subsection (a) and substituting instead the following:

(a)

(1) It is an offense to knowingly produce, manufacture, distribute, possess or possess with intent to produce, manufacture or distribute the active chemical ingredient in the hallucinogenic plant salvia divinorum or the following synthetic cannabinoids:

(A) (6a,10a)-9-(hydroxymethyl)-6, 6-dimethyl-3-(2methyloctan-2-yl)-6a, 7,10,10a-tetrahydrobenzo[c]chromen-1-ol; including, but not limited to HU 210 or HU 211;

(B) Naphthoylindoles being any compound structurally derived from 3-(1-naphthoyl) indole with substitution at the nitrogen atom of the indole ring whether or not further substituted in the indole ring to any extent, whether or not substituted in the naphthyl ring to any extent; including, but not limited to JWH-015, JWH-018, JWH-019, JWH-073, JWH-081, JWH-122, JWH-200, JWH-210, AM-1220, MAM-2201 or AM-2201;

(C) Naphthylmethylindoles being any compound structurally derived from a 1 H-indole-3-yl-(1-naphthyl)methane structure with substitution at the nitrogen atom of the indole ring whether or not further substituted in the indole ring to any extent, whether or not substituted in the naphthyl ring to any extent; including, but not limited to JWH-175, JWH-184 or JWH-199;

(D) Naphthoylpyrroles, being any compound structurally derived from 3-(1-naphthoyl) pyrrole with substitution at the nitrogen atom of the pyrrole ring whether or not further substituted in the pyrrole ring to any extent, whether or not substituted in the naphthyl ring to any extent; including, but not limited to JWH-307;

(E) Naphthylmethylindenes, being any compound structurally derived from 1-(1-naphthylmethyl) indene with substitution at the 3-position of the indene ring whether or not further substituted in the indene ring to any extent, whether or not substituted in the naphthyl ring to any extent; including, but not limited to JWH-176;

(F) Phenylacetylindoles, being any compound structurally derived from 3-phenylacetylindole with substitution at the nitrogen atom of the indole ring whether or not further substituted in the indole ring to any extent, whether or not substituted in the phenyl ring to any extent; including but not limited to JWH-167, JWH-201, JWH-203, JWH-250, JWH-251, JWH-302 or RCS-8;

(G) Cyclohexylphenols, being any compound structurally derived from 2-(3-hydroxycyclohexyl) phenol with substitution at the 5-position of the phenolic ring whether or not further substituted in the whether or not substituted in the cyclohexyl ring to any extent; including, but not limited to CP 47,497 or the dimethylhexyl, dimethyloctyl or dimethylnonyl homologues of CP 47,497;

(H) Tetrahydro derivatives of cannabinol and 3-alkyl homologues of cannabiniol or of its tetrahydro derivatives, except where contained in cannabis or cannabis resin;

(I) Benzoylindoles, being any compound containing a 3-(benzoyl) indole structure with substitution at the nitrogen atom of the indole ring whether or not further substituted in the indole ring to any extent and whether or not substituted in the phenyl ring to any extent; including, but not limited to AM-694, Pravadoline (WIN 48, 098), RCS-4, AM-1241 or AM-2233;

(J) WIN-55, 212-2 or 2, 3-Dihydro-5-methyl-3-(4 Morpholinylmethyl) pyrrolo [1,2,3-de]-1, 4—benzoxazin-6-yl]-1-napthalenylmethanone;

(K) Cyclopropanoylindoles, being any compound structurally derived from a 3-(cyclopropylmethanoyl)indole structure with substitution at the nitrogen atom of the indole ring, whether or not further substituted in the indole ring to any extent and whether or not substituted in the cyclopropyl ring to any extent; including, but not limited to UR-144, XLR-11 or A-796,260;

(L) Adamantoylindoles, being any compound structurally derived from a 3-(1-adamantoyl)indole structure with substitution at the nitrogen atom of the indole ring, whether or not further substituted in the indole ring to any extent and whether or not substituted in the adamantly ring to any extent; including, but not limited to AM-1248 or AB-001;

(M) Adamantoylindolecarboxamides, being any compound structurally derived from a N-adamantyl-1-indole-3-carboxamide with substitution at the nitrogen atom of the indole ring, whether or not further substituted in the indole ring to any extent and whether or not substituted in the adamantyl ring to any extent; including but not limited to STS-135, 2NE1;

(N) Adamantylindazolecarboxamides, being any compound structurally derived from a N-adamantyl-1-indazole-3-carboxamide with substitution at the nitrogen atom of the indazole ring, whether or not further substituted in the indazole ring to any extent and whether or not substituted in the adamantly ring to any extent; including, but not limited to AKB-48; and

(O) Naphthoylnaphthalene, being any compound structurally derived from naphthalene-1-yl-(naphthalene-1-yl) methanone with substitutions on either of the naphthalene rings to any extent; including, but not limited to CB-13.

(2) Subdivision (a)(1) concerning synthetic cannabinoids shall not apply to drugs or substances lawfully prescribed or to drugs or substances which have been approved or approved for study by the federal food and drug administration.

39-17-454 SECTION 2. Tennessee Code Annotated, Section 39-17-454, is amended by deleting subdivision (a)(1) and substituting instead the following:

(1) As used in this section, "controlled substance analogue" means a capsule, pill, powder, product or other substance, however constituted, that has the stimulant, depressant or hallucinogenic effect on the central nervous system of a controlled substance; and

(A) Has a chemical structure which is a derivative or structural analogue of the chemical structure of a controlled substance; provided, that as used in this subdivision, "analogue" means the structure of the tested item differs in no more than two (2) atoms, one (1) functional group, or one (1) double bond, from the structure of a controlled substance; or

(B) Is prohibited by § 39-17-452.

39-17-454 SECTION 3. Tennessee Code Annotated, Section 39-17-454, is amended by deleting subdivision (f)(1) and substituting instead the following:

(1) It is an offense for a person to represent, orally or in writing, advertise, infer or intend that a controlled substance analogue has the stimulant, depressant or hallucinogenic effect on the central nervous system of a controlled substance; and

(A) Has a chemical structure which is a derivative or structural analogue of the chemical structure of a controlled substance; provided, that as used in this subdivision, "analogue" means the structure of the tested item differs in no more than two (2) atoms, one (1) functional group, or one (1) double bond, from the structure of a controlled substance; or

(B) Is prohibited by § 39-17-452.

39-17-454 SECTION 4. Tennessee Code Annotated, Section 39-17-454, is amended by deleting subdivision (f)(2)(B) and substituting instead the following:

(B) Does not have a chemical structure which is a derivative or analogue, as defined in subdivision (f)(1)(A), of the chemical structure of a controlled substance;

39-17-452 SECTION 5. Tennessee Code Annotated, Section 39-17-452, is amended by deleting subdivision (a)(2)(F) in its entirety.

39-17-452 SECTION 6. Tennessee Code Annotated, Section 39-17-452(a)(2), is amended by adding the following language as new, appropriately designated subdivisions:

( ) Mitragynine and hydroxymitragynine;

( ) Desoxypipradol;

( ) URB 754;

( ) URB602;

39-17-454 SECTION 7. Tennessee Code Annotated, Section 39-17-454(h), is amended by adding the following language as a new, appropriately designated subdivision:

(3) If the chemical analysis of a controlled substance analogue determines that it also contains a hazardous substance as defined by § 68-131-102, nothing in this section shall preclude a violation of this section from also being prosecuted and punished under title 68, chapter 131, part 1.

55-10-402 SECTION 8. Tennessee Code Annotated, Section 55-10-402, is amended by deleting the language "controlled substance" and substituting instead the language "controlled substance, controlled substance analogue,".

55-10-402 SECTION 9. Tennessee Code Annotated, Section 55-10-402, is amended by deleting the language "controlled substances" and substituting instead the language "controlled substances, controlled substance analogues,".

Effective date 4/12/2013 SECTION 10. This act shall take effect July 1, 2013, the public welfare requiring it.

PUBLIC CHAPTER NO. 162

PUBLIC CHAPTER NO. 162

HOUSE BILL NO. 73

By Representative Sargent

Substituted for: Senate Bill No. 588

By Senators Johnson, Ketron

AN ACT to amend Tennessee Code Annotated, Title 5, Chapter 14, relative to disposing of surplus property.

BE IT ENACTED BY THE GENERAL ASSEMBLY OF THE STATE OF TENNESSEE:

5-14-108 SECTION 1. Tennessee Code Annotated, Section 5-14-108(o), is amended by adding the following language as a new subdivision:

(4) Notwithstanding any other provision of law, a procedure may be established upon approval by resolution or ordinance, by a two-thirds (2/3) majority vote of the county legislative body, to provide the purchasing agent, upon request of the county mayor, the authority to declare county owned personal property with an accumulative estimated value of one thousand dollars ($1,000) or less surplus, obsolete, or unusable personal property and to dispose of the personal property, at the purchasing agent's discretion, by selling the personal property on the open market or by gift, trade, or barter to a nonprofit or charitable organization properly incorporated under the laws of this state and in which no part of the net earnings of the organization inures or may lawfully inure to the benefit of any private shareholder or individual and that it provides services benefiting the general welfare of the residents of the county. Items having an accumulative estimated value that exceeds one thousand dollars ($1,000) shall not be subdivided in order to circumvent the requirement for public notice or receipt of sealed bids or selling the property through public or internet auction. The purchasing agent shall keep all records of transactions of the disposal of personal property under this subdivision for a minimum of five (5) years.

Effective date 4/16/2013 SECTION 2. This act shall take effect upon becoming a law, the public welfare requiring it.

PUBLIC CHAPTER NO. 163

PUBLIC CHAPTER NO. 163

HOUSE BILL NO. 157

By Representatives McCormick, Harrison

Substituted for: Senate Bill No. 163

By Senators Norris, Watson, Massey

AN ACT to amend Tennessee Code Annotated, Section 68-11-830, relative to the taxation of licensed facilities.

BE IT ENACTED BY THE GENERAL ASSEMBLY OF THE STATE OF TENNESSEE:

68-11-830 SECTION 1. Tennessee Code Annotated, Section 68-11-830(d)(2), is amended by deleting the language "July 15, 2013" and substituting instead the language "July 15, 2015".

68-11-830 SECTION 2. Tennessee Code Annotated, Section 68-11-830(d)(10), is amended by deleting the language "July 15, 2013" and substituting instead the language "July 15, 2015".

Effective date 7/1/2013 SECTION 3. This act shall take effect on July 1, 2013, the public welfare requiring it.

PUBLIC CHAPTER NO. 164

PUBLIC CHAPTER NO. 164

HOUSE BILL NO. 396

By Madam Speaker Harwell and Representatives Butt, Alexander

Substituted for: Senate Bill No. 511

By Senator Hensley

AN ACT to amend Tennessee Code Annotated, Title 9, Chapter 4, Part 55; Title 9, Chapter 8 and Title 67, relative to deleting obsolete and antiquated statutory text and references concerning finance.

BE IT ENACTED BY THE GENERAL ASSEMBLY OF THE STATE OF TENNESSEE:

9-4-5502 SECTION 1. Tennessee Code Annotated, Section 9-4-5502, is amended by deleting the following language:

> Such committee shall make recommendations to the general assembly, no later than January 15, 2001, regarding uses and expenditure of funds in the agricultural reserve account and future payments, if any, received pursuant to the master settlement agreement entered into by Tennessee and other states, United States territories and possessions, and participating tobacco manufacturers, dated November 23, 1998.

9-4-5503 SECTION 2. Tennessee Code Annotated, Section 9-4-5503, is amended by deleting the following language:

> Such committee shall make recommendations, no later than January 15, 2001, to the general assembly regarding uses and expenditure of funds in the health reserve account and future payments, if any, received pursuant to the master settlement agreement entered into by Tennessee and other states, United States territories and possessions, and participating tobacco manufacturers, dated November 23, 1998.

9-8-108 SECTION 3. Tennessee Code Annotated, Section 9-8-108(a)(9), is amended by deleting the language:

> (F) No award shall be made for damages occurring prior to February 4, 1987; provided, that claims made pursuant to this subdivision (a)(9) for damages that occurred between January 1, 1987 and February 29, 1988 must be filed with the board of claims within sixty (60) days of February 29, 1988;

67-3-206 SECTION 4. Tennessee Code Annotated, Section 67-3-206, is amended by deleting the following language:

> (b) This section shall cease to be effective until July 1, 2009, at which time this section shall have full effect of law.

67-4-2008 SECTION 5. Tennessee Code Annotated, Section 67-4-2008(e), is amended by deleting the following language:

> (2) No later than January 20, 2009, the commissioner shall submit to the finance, ways and means committees of the senate and the house of representatives a summary report of the information so compiled. The report shall include analyses of the utilization, costs and benefits of the exemption, as well as findings and recommendations pertaining to continuation of the exemption.

Effective date 7/1/2013 SECTION 6. This act shall take effect July 1, 2013, the public welfare requiring it.

PUBLIC CHAPTER NO. 165

PUBLIC CHAPTER NO. 165

HOUSE BILL NO. 441

By Representatives Kane, Haynes

Substituted for: Senate Bill No. 610

By Senator Yager

AN ACT to amend Tennessee Code Annotated, Section 41-24-104, relative to state and local government.

BE IT ENACTED BY THE GENERAL ASSEMBLY OF THE STATE OF TENNESSEE:

41-24-104 SECTION 1. Tennessee Code Annotated, Section 41-24-104(a)(2)(A) and (B), are amended by deleting the last sentence in each subdivision and by substituting instead the following language:

> The authorities listed in subdivision (a)(1) shall withhold their final action until such thirty-day period has ended or until they have received the committee's comments, whichever first occurs;

Effective date 4/16/2013 SECTION 2. This act shall take effect upon becoming a law, the public welfare requiring it.

PUBLIC CHAPTER NO. 166

PUBLIC CHAPTER NO. 166

HOUSE BILL NO. 554

By Representative McDaniel

Substituted for: Senate Bill No. 628

By Senators Gresham, Yager

AN ACT to amend Tennessee Code Annotated, Title 50, Chapter 7, relative to the "Tennessee Employment Security Law".

BE IT ENACTED BY THE GENERAL ASSEMBLY OF THE STATE OF TENNESSEE:

50-7-407 SECTION 1. Tennessee Code Annotated, Title 50, Chapter 7, Part 4, is amended by adding the following language as a new section:

50-7-407.

(a) Notwithstanding any other provision of this chapter to the contrary, if a claimant employed by a reimbursing employer on a continuous part-time basis continues to be employed by the reimbursing employer while separated from other employment and is eligible for benefits, any benefits paid will not be considered attributable to the service with the reimbursing employer.

(b) For the purposes of this section, "reimbursing employer" means an eligible employer who elects to reimburse the state for benefits paid in lieu of premiums, as provided by the Federal Unemployment Tax Act, compiled in 26 U.S.C. 3301 et. seq., or this chapter.

SECTION 2. This act shall take effect upon becoming law, the public welfare requiring it, and shall apply to unemployment benefits accruing on or after the effective date of this act.

PUBLIC CHAPTER NO. 167

PUBLIC CHAPTER NO. 167

HOUSE BILL NO. 599

By Representative Forgety

Substituted for: Senate Bill No. 545

By Senator Bell

AN ACT to amend Tennessee Code Annotated, Title 49, Chapter 4, Part 9, relative to state lottery proceeds.

BE IT ENACTED BY THE GENERAL ASSEMBLY OF THE STATE OF TENNESSEE:

49-4-932 SECTION 1. Tennessee Code Annotated, Section 49-4-932, is amended by adding the following language as new subsection (k):

(k) The Tennessee higher education commission, the University of Tennessee system, and the state university and community college system may also provide information on financial assistance available from net lottery proceeds for attendance at eligible postsecondary institutions in the normal course of their business of development and recruitment of Tennessee students.

Effective date 4/16/2013 SECTION 2. This act shall take effect upon becoming law, the public welfare requiring it.

PUBLIC CHAPTER NO. 168

PUBLIC CHAPTER NO. 168

HOUSE BILL NO. 681

By Representatives Swann, Harry Brooks, Mark White, Dale Carr, Dean, Butt, Kane

Substituted for: Senate Bill No. 524

By Senators Bowling, Ford

AN ACT to amend Tennessee Code Annotated, Title 40, Chapter 35, relative to persons serving felony sentences in local jails or workhouses.

BE IT ENACTED BY THE GENERAL ASSEMBLY OF THE STATE OF TENNESSEE:

40-35-314 SECTION 1. Tennessee Code Annotated, Section 40-35-314, is amended by adding the following new subsection:

(g)

(1) Any defendant convicted of a felony and sentenced to serve such sentence in a local jail or workhouse pursuant to this section, § 40-35-104(b), § 40-35-306, or § 40-35-307 shall be ordered, as a part of the sentence, to participate in any work program operated by the jail or workhouse in which the defendant is incarcerated.

(2) The sheriff may opt the county out of the requirements of this subsection (g) if the sheriff's local jail or workhouse does not operate a work program or, if it does operate such a program, the increased number of inmates participating would exceed the sheriff's ability to provide security, transportation, or requested work projects.

(3) The sheriff may excuse any one (1) or more individual inmates sentenced to the work program if, in the judgment of the sheriff:

(A) The inmate would pose a security or escape risk to the public or other inmates if allowed to participate in a work program outside the facility;

(B) The inmate has physical or mental health conditions that would preclude the inmate from successfully participating in a work program or would endanger others if allowed to participate; or

(C) The county cannot afford to provide the security or transportation for one (1) or more inmates sentenced to the work program pursuant to this section.

(4) Any inmate who knowingly refuses to participate in a work program after being sentenced to do so pursuant to this section shall be considered to have violated a rule of the local jail or workhouse and the court may act upon such violation as provided in subsection (d).

(5) The liability of any county whose local jail or workhouse operates a work program, shall not be increased or changed solely because the work program uses inmates sentenced to the program pursuant to this subsection (g).

Effective date 7/1/2013 SECTION 2. This act shall take effect July 1, 2013, the public welfare requiring it and shall apply to any person sentenced to a local jail or workhouse pursuant to this section, § 40-35-104(b), § 40-35-306 or § 40-35-307 on or after such date.

PUBLIC CHAPTER NO. 169

PUBLIC CHAPTER NO. 169

HOUSE BILL NO. 947

By Representative Lynn

Substituted for: Senate Bill No. 1339

By Senator Bell

AN ACT to amend Tennessee Code Annotated, Section 40-11-125, relative to bondsmen.

WHEREAS, it is desirable that persons who are applicants for approval as a professional bondsman be law abiding citizens; now, therefore,

BE IT ENACTED BY THE GENERAL ASSEMBLY OF THE STATE OF TENNESSEE:

40-11-125

SECTION 1. Tennessee Code Annotated, Section 40-11-125(a), is amended by deleting the language and punctuation "; or" at the end of subsection (a)(2), by deleting the period at the end of subsection (a)(3), and by substituting instead the language and punctuation "; or"; and by adding the following new subdivision (4):

(4) If applying for approval as a professional bondsman, has been convicted in any state of the United States of two (2) or more misdemeanors which are equivalent to Tennessee Class A or Class B misdemeanors; provided, however, that the misdemeanor convictions shall have occurred within five (5) years of the date the application for approval is filed.

Effective date 4/16/2013

SECTION 2. This act shall take effect upon becoming a law, the public welfare requiring it.

PUBLIC CHAPTER NO. 170

PUBLIC CHAPTER NO. 170

HOUSE BILL NO. 1035

By Representative Littleton

Substituted for: Senate Bill No. 742

By Senator Dickerson

AN ACT to amend Tennessee Code Annotated, Section 4-3-2403 and Title 8, Chapter 38, relative to social security for public officers and employees.

BE IT ENACTED BY THE GENERAL ASSEMBLY OF THE STATE OF TENNESSEE:

8-38-101 SECTION 1. Tennessee Code Annotated, Section 8-38-101, is amended by adding the appropriately designated subsections:

( ) "Agreement" means the federal-state agreement between the federal agency and the State of Tennessee entered into on August 16, 1951 as authorized by the Social Security Enabling Act for the purpose of extending coverage under Title II of the Social Security Act.

( ) "Employer" means the state, a political subdivision, or a local instrumentality of either.

( ) "Modification" means an amendment to the original federal-state agreement to modify coverage for coverage groups or to extend coverage to additional coverage groups consistent with the provisions of Section 218 of the Social Security Act and this chapter.

( ) "Plan of agreement" means an agreement between the state social security administrator and an employer for the purpose of extending the benefits of the Social Security Act to coverage groups within its employ.

8-38-103 SECTION 2. Tennessee Code Annotated, Section 8-38-103(b)(2), is amended by deleting the language "state" and by substituting instead the language "employer" and by deleting the language "secretary of the treasury" and by substituting instead the language "Internal Revenue Service".

8-38-104 SECTION 3. Tennessee Code Annotated, Section 8-38-104(a)(3), is amended by deleting the language "secretary of the treasury" and by substituting instead the language "Internal Revenue Service".

8-38-105 SECTION 4. Tennessee Code Annotated, Section 8-38-105, is amended by deleting the language "into the contribution fund established by § 8-38-115" and by deleting the language "§ 3101 of the Federal Insurance Contributions Act, codified in 26 U.S.C. § 3101" and substituting instead "the "Rate of Tax" sections of the Federal Insurance Contributions Act".

8-38-107 SECTION 5. Tennessee Code Annotated, Section 8-38-107, is amended by deleting it in its entirety.

8-38-111 SECTION 6. Tennessee Code Annotated, Section 8-38-111, is amended by deleting the section language in its entirety and substituting instead the language "Each political subdivision that has an approved plan under §§ 8-38-108 – 8-38-110 shall pay to the Internal Revenue Service, at such time or times as may be required by applicable federal law, contributions with respect to wages, equal to the applicable taxes which would be imposed by the "Rate of Tax" sections of the Federal Insurance Contributions Act if the services covered by the agreement constituted employment within the meaning of that Act."

8-38-112 SECTION 7. Tennessee Code Annotated, Section 8-38-112, is amended by deleting the section language in its entirety and substituting instead the language "Each political subdivision required to make payments under § 8-38-111 is authorized to impose upon each of its employees, as to services which are covered by an approved plan of agreement, a contribution with respect to the employee's wages, not exceeding the amount of the employee's tax which would be imposed by the "Rate of Tax" sections of the Federal Insurance Contributions Act, if such services constituted employment within the meaning of that act. Each political subdivision is authorized to deduct the amount of such contribution from the employee's wages. Failure to deduct such contributions shall not relieve the employee or employer of liability for such contributions".

8-38-113 SECTION 8. Tennessee Code Annotated, Section 8-38-113, is amended by deleting it in its entirety.

8-38-114 SECTION 9. Tennessee Code Annotated, Section 8-38-114, is amended by deleting it in its entirety.

8-38-115 SECTION 10. Tennessee Code Annotated, Section 8-38-115, is amended by deleting it in its entirety.

8-38-117 SECTION 11. Tennessee Code Annotated, Section 8-38-117, is amended by deleting it in its entirety.

8-38-118 SECTION 12. Tennessee Code Annotated, Section 8-38-118, is amended by deleting it in its entirety.

8-38-119 SECTION 13. Tennessee Code Annotated, Section 8-38-119, is amended by deleting it in its entirety.

8-38-120 SECTION 14. Tennessee Code Annotated, Section 8-38-120, is amended by deleting it in its entirety.

8-38-123 SECTION 15. Tennessee Code Annotated, Section 8-38-123, is amended by adding a new subsection as follows:

(e) The governor shall delegate signature authority to the state treasurer, who is the administrator for the state of Tennessee. The governor shall also delegate the authority to designate an agency or individual to supervise the state old age and survivors insurance agency, and shall delegate the authority to supervise referenda to the state treasurer. The state treasurer may designate an individual to administer the state old age and survivors insurance agency and to supervise referenda as needed.

8-38-125 SECTION 16. Tennessee Code Annotated, Section 8-38-125, is amended by deleting it in its entirety.

8-38-127 SECTION 17. Tennessee Code Annotated, Title 8, Chapter 38, Part 1, is amended by adding the following language as a new, appropriately designated section:

8-38-127.

(a) The old age and survivors' insurance agency shall be attached to the Department of the Treasury in a division as designated by the state treasurer.

8-38-128 SECTION 18. Tennessee Code Annotated, Title 8, Chapter 38, Part 1, is amended by adding the following language as a new, appropriately designated section:

8-38-128.

(a) The state social security administrator may implement procedures for the filing and retention of social security documents by electronic means and may authorize electronic signatures in the signing of such documents.

(b) If a document is filed by electronic means pursuant to this section, the electronic record and the electronic signature of the person who executes the same shall be binding on all persons. The use of an electronic signature shall have the same validity and effect as the use of a signature affixed by hand.

(c) For the purposes of this section, the following definitions shall apply:

(1) "Electronic" means relating to technology having electrical, digital, magnetic, wireless, optical, electromagnetic, or similar capabilities;

(2) "Electronic record" means information which is created, generated, sent, communicated, received, or stored by electronic means;

(3) "Electronic signature" means an electronic sound, symbol, or process, attached to or logically associated with an electronic record and executed or adopted by a person with the intent to sign the electronic record.

4-3-2403 SECTION 19. Tennessee Code Annotated, Section 4-3-2403(b) (4), is amended by deleting this subsection in its entirety.

Effective date 4/16/2013 SECTION 20. This act shall take effect upon becoming a law, the public welfare requiring it.

PUBLIC CHAPTER NO. 171

PUBLIC CHAPTER NO. 171

HOUSE BILL NO. 1044

By Representative Todd

Substituted for: Senate Bill No. 1347

By Senator Yager

AN ACT to amend Tennessee Code Annotated, Section 57-3-301, relative to brand and contract registrations.

BE IT ENACTED BY THE GENERAL ASSEMBLY OF THE STATE OF TENNESSEE:

57-3-301 SECTION 1. Tennessee Code Annotated, Section 57-3-301(a), is amended by adding the following language as a new subdivision:

(3) The name, trademark, or trade name of the product, as indicated on the certificate of label approval as registered with the alcohol and tobacco tax and trade bureau of the United States department of the treasury, or, if no certificate of label approval is required, then the name, trademark, or trade name of the product.

57-3-301 SECTION 2. Tennessee Code Annotated, Section 57-3-301, is amended by adding the following language as a new subsection (g) and by redesignating the subsequent subsection accordingly:

(g) The department of revenue is authorized to accept the brand registrations required under this section and the contracts described in subdivision (e)(1) by electronic means. The department of revenue is authorized to approve one (1) or more third parties to facilitate electronic submissions on behalf of importers, manufacturers, suppliers, or wholesalers; provided, that such third parties shall:

(1) Be permitted to assess a reasonable cost against the importer, supplier, manufacturer, or wholesaler that elects to use the electronic service;

(2) Not assess any fees or costs against the state for providing such service;

(3) Adhere to the records requirements, privacy requirements, and technical requirements imposed by the department of revenue;

(4) Agree to provide documentation and support for all brand registrations and contract registrations as required by the department of revenue as part of the electronic process; and

(5) Agree to facilitate communication between the department of revenue and the affected importers, manufacturers, suppliers, and wholesalers to relate the status of any filing, transfer, or tax liability.

Effective date 4/16/2013 SECTION 3. This act shall take effect upon becoming a law, the public welfare requiring it.

PUBLIC CHAPTER NO. 172

PUBLIC CHAPTER NO. 172

HOUSE BILL NO. 1093

By Representatives Lynn, Durham

Substituted for: Senate Bill No. 1237

By Senators Bowling, Ford

AN ACT to amend Tennessee Code Annotated, Section 39-13-501, relative to the definition of intimate parts.

BE IT ENACTED BY THE GENERAL ASSEMBLY OF THE STATE OF TENNESSEE:

39-13-501 SECTION 1. Tennessee Code Annotated, Section 39-13-501(2), is amended by inserting the language "semen, vaginal fluid," between the language "includes" and "the primary genital area".

Effective date 7/1/2013 SECTION 2. This act shall take effect July 1, 2013, the public welfare requiring it.

PUBLIC CHAPTER NO. 173

PUBLIC CHAPTER NO. 173

HOUSE BILL NO. 1339

By Representative Dawn White

Substituted for: Senate Bill No. 1376

By Senators Johnson, Yager

AN ACT to amend Tennessee Code Annotated, Title 41, relative to waivers of minimum qualifications of county correctional officers.

BE IT ENACTED BY THE GENERAL ASSEMBLY OF THE STATE OF TENNESSEE:

41-7-106 SECTION 1. Tennessee Code Annotated, Section 41-7-106, is amended by deleting subsection (g) in its entirety and by substituting instead the following language:

(g) The board shall not grant waivers for any person hired as a jail administrator, workhouse administrator, jailer, corrections officer, or guard in any county jail or workhouse who has been dishonorably discharged from the military, has any mental impairment which affects the person's ability to perform any essential function of the job with or without a reasonable accommodation, has a conviction for domestic assault or a felony conviction.

41-4-144 SECTION 2. Tennessee Code Annotated, Section 41-4-144(9), is amended by deleting the subdivision in its entirety and by substituting instead the following language:

(9) Have been certified by a Tennessee licensed health care provider qualified in the psychiatric or psychological field as being free from any impairment, as set forth in the current edition of the Diagnostic and Statistical Manual of Mental Disorders (DSM) of the American Psychiatric Association at the time of the examination, that would, in the professional judgment of the examiner, affect the person's ability to perform an essential function of the job, with or without a reasonable accommodation.

Effective date 7/1/2013 SECTION 3. This act shall take effect July 1, 2013, the public welfare requiring it.

PUBLIC CHAPTER NO. 174

PUBLIC CHAPTER NO. 174

SENATE BILL NO. 978

By McNally, Ketron, Crowe, Niceley, Green

Substituted for: House Bill No. 445

By Sargent, Curtis Johnson, Kent Williams, Pitts, Marsh

AN ACT to amend Tennessee Code Annotated, Title 49, Chapter 3, Part 12, relative to the Tennessee State School Bond Authority.

BE IT ENACTED BY THE GENERAL ASSEMBLY OF THE STATE OF TENNESSEE:

49-3-1202 SECTION 1. Tennessee Code Annotated, Section 49-3-1202(4), is amended by deleting the subdivision in its entirety and by substituting instead the following:

(4) "Institution" means:

(A) The University of Tennessee system, including all of its branches and divisions wherever located, and the services, programs and activities provided therein, and the board of trustees of the University of Tennessee, in the aggregate; and

(B) The state university and community college system, including all of its constituent institutions wherever located (whether or not conferring degrees), and the services, programs and activities provided therein, and the Board of Regents of the state university and community college system, in the aggregate;

Effective date 4/23/2013 SECTION 2. This act shall take effect upon becoming a law, the public welfare requiring it.

PUBLIC CHAPTER NO. 175

PUBLIC CHAPTER NO. 175

SENATE BILL NO. 994

By McNally, Henry, Bowling, Crowe

Substituted for: House Bill No. 330

By Matlock, Rogers, Evans

AN ACT to amend Tennessee Code Annotated, Title 9, relative to budget procedures pertaining to reserves.

BE IT ENACTED BY THE GENERAL ASSEMBLY OF THE STATE OF TENNESSEE:

9-4-211 SECTION 1. Tennessee Code Annotated, Section 9-4-211(a)(2), is amended by deleting the language "five percent (5%)" wherever it appears and substituting instead the language "eight percent (8%)".

Effective date 7/1/2013 SECTION 2. This act shall take effect July 1, 2013, the public welfare requiring it.

PUBLIC CHAPTER NO. 176

PUBLIC CHAPTER NO. 176

SENATE BILL NO. 999

By McNally

Substituted for: House Bill No. 58

By Roach, Sargent

AN ACT to amend Tennessee Code Annotated, Title 9, relative to public finances.

BE IT ENACTED BY THE GENERAL ASSEMBLY OF THE STATE OF TENNESSEE:

SECTION 1. This act shall be known and may be cited as the "Hawkins-Wilson Act".

9-9-101 SECTION 2. Tennessee Code Annotated, Section 9-9-101, is amended by deleting subsection (b).

9-9-102 SECTION 3. Tennessee Code Annotated, Section 9-9-102, is amended by deleting the existing language and substituting the following:

> The commissioner of finance and administration shall maintain, or cause to be maintained, records on the condition of all debt obligations described in § 9-9-105(a) and of the payment of the principal of and premium, if any, and interest on such obligations.

9-9-103 SECTION 4. Tennessee Code Annotated, Section 9-9-103, is amended by deleting subsection (a).

9-9-104
9-9-105
9-9-106
9-9-107 SECTION 5. Tennessee Code Annotated, Sections 9-9-104 through 107, are amended by deleting the existing language and substituting the following:

> 9-9-104.
>
> (a) For the payment of the principal of and interest on the bonds of the state of Tennessee issued under this chapter outstanding as of the effective date of this act, there is hereby pledged the annual proceeds of a tax of not less than five cents (5¢) per gallon upon gasoline, the annual proceeds of the special tax on petroleum products provided for by § 67-3-203, one half (1/2) of the annual proceeds of motor vehicle registration fees now or hereafter required to be paid to the state, and the entire annual proceeds of franchise taxes imposed by the franchise tax law, compiled in title 67, chapter 4, part 21. This pledge shall not extend to any bonds issued under this chapter after the effective date of this act.
>
> (b) As long as any bonds issued under this chapter that were outstanding as of the effective date of this act remain outstanding, the state of Tennessee hereby covenants with the persons who now or may hereafter hold such bonds that it will not decrease by legislative action any of the fees or taxes that constitute the special revenues pledged by this section, or eliminate from the requirement to pay such fees or taxes any substance, motor vehicle or corporation on account of which the payment of such fees or taxes is now required, and that it will levy a tax of not less than five cents (5¢) per gallon upon gasoline or other motor vehicle fuel, unless the state funding board shall certify that all payments due the state funding board under the provisions of this chapter have been made in full, that the state is not in default in the payment of any outstanding debt or in the payment of interest thereon, and that such fees and taxes at lower rates to be specified by the state funding board, in such year or years (not exceeding two (2) years), will be sufficient to provide funds adequate to meet all payments required to be made by the state funding board in such year or years, as well as to provide for the other obligations and expenses of the state for such year or years, to be defrayed therefrom, in which event the state of Tennessee shall be under no obligation to charge or levy in such year or years fees or taxes in excess of the rates so certified by the state funding board.
>
> (c) In no event shall the pledge and covenants set forth in this section extend past or be effective after June 30, 2033.
>
> 9-9-105.

(a) All bonds issued (and to be issued) under this chapter, all notes issued (and to be issued) in anticipation of such bonds, and all tax revenue anticipation notes issued (and to be issued) under this chapter shall constitute direct general obligations of the state of Tennessee for the payment of the principal of and premium, if any, and interest on which there is also pledged the full faith and credit of the state of Tennessee. Subject only to § 9-9-104(a), all such debt obligations shall constitute a charge and lien upon the entire fees, taxes and other revenues and funds allocated to the general fund, the debt service fund, and the highway fund; and, if necessary, upon the first such fees, taxes, revenues and funds thereafter received and allocated to such funds, except only such fees, taxes, revenues and funds as may be otherwise legally restricted.

(b) The state of Tennessee hereby covenants with the persons who now or may hereafter hold any debt obligations described in § 9-9-105(a) that it will raise fees, taxes and other revenues sufficient, together with funds on hand derived from all sources, to pay the principal of and premium, if any, and interest on such obligations as and when due and payable.

(c) The state of Tennessee hereby covenants with the persons who now or may hereafter hold any bonds issued under this chapter that no bonds shall be issued under this chapter after the effective date of this act unless the following debt service coverage test is satisfied: the amount necessary to pay the maximum annual debt service payable in the then current or any future fiscal year, is not greater than ten percent (10%) of the amount of total state tax revenue allocated to the general fund, to the debt service fund, and to the highway fund for the immediately preceding fiscal year. For purposes of satisfying this test, "state tax revenues" are defined as those taxes, licenses, fees, fines, and permits collected by the Department of Revenue and allocated to the general fund, the debt service fund, and the highway fund excluding the portion of those taxes shared with local governments. "Debt service", for this purpose, means and includes principal of and interest on all outstanding bonds issued under this chapter and the bonds then proposed to be issued under this chapter, in the aggregate; provided, that in determining the outstanding bonds, there shall be excluded any outstanding bonds the payment of which has been fully provided for by funds or securities (including expected income therefrom), or both, set aside for that purpose.

9-9-106.

The state funding board shall certify to the commissioner of finance and administration from time to time, but not less than annually, the amount necessary, together with funds on hand derived from all sources, to enable the board to provide for the payment of the principal of and premium, if any, and interest on all debt obligations described in § 9-9-105(a) as and when the same shall become due and payable.

9-9-107.

The state funding board shall provide for the payment of the principal of and premium, if any, and interest on all bonds issued under this chapter, all notes issued in anticipation of such bonds and all tax revenue anticipation notes issued under this chapter, amounts due on contracts or agreements described in § 9-9-202(g) and (h) or other contracts or agreements relating to such debt obligations, and necessary related expenses incurred under this chapter as the same shall become due, out of the fees, taxes and other revenues and funds available for such purposes.

9-9-111 SECTION 6. Tennessee Code Annotated, Sections 9-9-111 and 112, are amended by
9-9-112 deleting the existing language and substituting the following:

9-9-111.

The holders of all debt obligations of the state of Tennessee described in § 9-9-105(a) and all persons who may hereafter purchase such obligations shall have, and are hereby declared to have, a vested right in the performance of the covenants and pledges contained in this chapter, and the performance of the duties imposed upon any officer or agency of the state of Tennessee by or pursuant to the provisions of this chapter may be enforced by the holder of any such obligation by appropriate proceedings; provided, no such holders or purchasers of debt obligations issued after the effective date of this act shall have any such rights with respect to § 9-9-104.

9-9-112.

Principal of and interest on debt obligations issued under this chapter shall be exempt from taxation by the state, or by any county, municipality or taxing district of the state, except inheritance, transfer and estate taxes.

9-9-118 SECTION 7. Tennessee Code Annotated, Section 9-9-118, is amended by deleting the section.

9-9-119 SECTION 8. Tennessee Code Annotated, Section 9-9-119, is amended by deleting the section.

9-9-207 SECTION 9. Tennessee Code Annotated, Section 9-9-207(a), is amended by deleting subsection (a) in its entirety and by substituting instead the following language:

(a) The funding board may issue general obligation refunding bonds to refund outstanding obligations previously issued under the authority of this chapter, upon the determination by the board that such bonds are necessary:

(1) To accomplish cost savings to the public; or

(2) For the administrative convenience of the board; or

(3) To pay or discharge all or any part of an issue or series of bonds, including any interest thereon, in arrears or to become due and for the payment of which sufficient funds are not available; or

(4) To eliminate bond covenants that have been determined to be burdensome to the state due to a change in circumstances if such elimination is not otherwise prohibited by law. Such determination shall be clearly stated in any resolution authorizing such refunding bonds and shall be conclusive.

9-9-301 SECTION 10. Tennessee Code Annotated, Section 9-10-101, is amended by deleting subsections (d) and (e) and by moving the section to part 3 of title 9, chapter 9.

SECTION 11. Nothing in this act shall be construed so as to impair the obligation of any contract made by the state of Tennessee upon any bond of the state issued under title 9, chapter 9 outstanding as of the effective date of this act.

Effective date 7/1/2013 SECTION 12. This act shall take effect July 1, 2013, the public welfare requiring it.

PUBLIC CHAPTER NO. 177

PUBLIC CHAPTER NO. 177

SENATE BILL NO. 16

By Gresham, Burks

Substituted for: House Bill No. 237

By Harry Brooks, Rogers, Moody, Powers

AN ACT to amend Tennessee Code Annotated, Section 49-5-413, relative to background checks.

BE IT ENACTED BY THE GENERAL ASSEMBLY OF THE STATE OF TENNESSEE:

49-5-413 SECTION 1. Tennessee Code Annotated, Section 49-5-413(d)(3)(B), is amended by deleting the subdivision in its entirety and by substituting instead the following:

(B) No employer, or employee of the employer, to whom this subsection (d) applies shall come in direct contact with school children or to children in a child care program or enter the grounds of a school or child care center when children are present if the criminal history records check indicates that the employer or employee has been convicted of an offense that, if committed on or after July 1, 2007, is classified as a sexual offense or a violent sexual offense as defined in § 40-39-202 or, if committed on or after July 1, 2013, is listed in § 39-17-417 or § 40-35-501(i)(2).

Effective date 4/23/2013 SECTION 2. This act shall take effect upon becoming a law, the public welfare requiring it.

PUBLIC CHAPTER NO. 178

PUBLIC CHAPTER NO. 178

SENATE BILL NO. 125

By Ketron

Substituted for: House Bill No. 229

By Lynn, Powers, Rich

AN ACT to amend Tennessee Code Annotated, Title 2, Chapter 7, Part 1, relative to identification for voting purposes.

BE IT ENACTED BY THE GENERAL ASSEMBLY OF THE STATE OF TENNESSEE:

2-7-112 SECTION 1. Tennessee Code Annotated, Section 2-7-112(c), is amended by deleting subdivision (2)(A) and by substituting instead the following:

(2)(A) Except as provided in subdivision (c)(2)(B), a valid identification card issued by the state of Tennessee, or the United States where authorized by law to issue personal identification; provided, that such identification card contains a photograph of the voter;

2-7-112 SECTION 2. Tennessee Code Annotated, Section 2-7-112(c), is further amended by deleting subdivision (5) and by substituting instead the following:

(5) A valid employee identification card issued by the state of Tennessee, or the United States where authorized by law to issue employee identification; provided, that such identification card contains a photograph of the voter;

2-7-112 SECTION 3. Tennessee Code Annotated, Section 2-7-112, is amended by adding the following as a new subsection thereto:

(g) An identification card issued by a county or municipality or entity thereof, including a public library, containing a photograph shall not be evidence of identification for purposes of verifying the person's identification on the application for ballot.

Effective date 4/23/2013 SECTION 4. This act shall take effect upon becoming a law, the public welfare requiring it.

PUBLIC CHAPTER NO. 179

PUBLIC CHAPTER NO. 179

SENATE BILL NO. 127

By Ketron

Substituted for: House Bill No. 889

By Lynn

AN ACT to amend Tennessee Code Annotated, Title 2, relative to elections.

BE IT ENACTED BY THE GENERAL ASSEMBLY OF THE STATE OF TENNESSEE:

2-8-101 SECTION 1. Tennessee Code Annotated, Section 2-8-101, is amended by adding the following language as a new subsection (e):

(e) Upon certifying the results of a referendum held by a municipality or county pursuant to title 57, the county election commission shall send certification of the results to the alcoholic beverage commission.

2-2-109 SECTION 2. Tennessee Code Annotated, Section 2-2-109, is amended by deleting the first sentence of subsection (b) and by substituting instead the following language:

When the thirtieth day before an election falls on a Saturday, Sunday, or legal holiday, applications for registration shall be accepted and processed the next business day following such Saturday, Sunday, or legal holiday.

2-5-211 SECTION 3. Tennessee Code Annotated, Section 2-5-211(b), is amended by deleting the subsection in its entirety and by substituting instead the following:

(b) At least five (5) days before the beginning of an early voting period and at least five (5) days before an election, the county election commission shall:

(1) Publish a sample ballot in a newspaper of general circulation. Where voting machines are used, the sample ballot shall be the machine sample ballot. The sample ballot shall contain the names of all candidates and all offices and a statement of all questions on which voters may vote. A sample ballot does not have to be published in a newspaper of general circulation if a sample ballot that complies with this section has been mailed at least five (5) days prior to the beginning of the early voting period to every active registered voter. If more than one (1) registered voter is at the same address, then only one (1) sample ballot may be sent to that address; and

(2) Post a sample ballot on a website maintained by the county election commission or, if the county election commission does not have or maintain a website, on the website maintained by the secretary of state. The sample ballot shall contain the names of all candidates and all offices and a statement of all questions on which voters may vote.

Effective date 7/1/2013 SECTION 4. This act shall take effect July 1, 2013, the public welfare requiring it.

PUBLIC CHAPTER NO. 180

PUBLIC CHAPTER NO. 180

SENATE BILL NO. 148

By Norris

Substituted for: House Bill No. 142

By McCormick, Roach, Carter

AN ACT to amend Tennessee Code Annotated, Title 62, Chapters 2, 6, 20 and 39, relative to regulatory boards and commissions.

BE IT ENACTED BY THE GENERAL ASSEMBLY OF THE STATE OF TENNESSEE:

62-2-401 SECTION 1. Tennessee Code Annotated, Section 62-2-401, is amended by deleting the language "a minimum eight-hour written" wherever it appears and substituting instead the word "an".

62-2-402 SECTION 2. Tennessee Code Annotated, Section 62-2-402, is amended by deleting the language "a minimum eight-hour written" and substituting instead the word "an", and further amend by deleting the language ", conducted by the board".

62-2-404 SECTION 3. Tennessee Code Annotated, Section 62-2-404(b)(3), is amended by deleting the subdivision and renumbering the remaining subdivisions accordingly.

62-2-405 SECTION 4. Tennessee Code Annotated, Section 62-2-405, is amended by deleting the language "a minimum eight-hour" wherever it appears and substituting instead the word "an".

62-6-120 SECTION 5. Tennessee Code Annotated, Section 62-6-120(a)(2), is amended by deleting the first sentence and substituting instead the following:

> Any person, firm or corporation that engages or offers to engage in contracting without a license as required by § 62-6-103 may, in the discretion of the board, be deemed ineligible to receive a license until six (6) months after the date the person, firm or corporation engaged or offered to engage in contracting.

62-20-102 SECTION 6. Tennessee Code Annotated, Section 62-20-102(6) and (7), is amended by deleting the subdivisions and renumbering the remaining subdivisions accordingly.

62-20-108 SECTION 7. Tennessee Code Annotated, Section 62-20-108, is amended by deleting the section and substituting instead the following:

> The board shall be promptly notified in writing of any change in address, management or ownership of a collection service business.

62-20-112 SECTION 8. Tennessee Code Annotated, Section 62-20-112(d), is amended by deleting the subsection.

62-20-116 SECTION 9. Tennessee Code Annotated, Section 62-20-116(b)(3), is amended by deleting the subdivision.

62-20-125 SECTION 10. Tennessee Code Annotated, Section 62-20-125, is amended by deleting the section.

62-20-126 SECTION 11. Tennessee Code Annotated, Section 62-20-126, is amended by deleting the section.

62-39-414– 62-39-417 SECTION 12. Tennessee Code Annotated, Sections 62-39-414, 62-39-415, 62-39-416 and 62-39-417, are amended by deleting the word "biannual" wherever it appears and substituting instead the word "biennial", and are further amended by deleting the word "biannually" wherever it appears and substituting instead the word "biennially".

62-39-416 SECTION 13. Tennessee Code Annotated, Section 62-39-416, is further amended by deleting the language "USPAP or state/federal laws" and substituting instead the language "USPAP, state laws or federal laws".

62-39-322 SECTION 14. Tennessee Code Annotated, Section 62-39-322(a), is amended by deleting the language "and if that state grants reciprocity to Tennessee licensees and certificate holders".

Effective date 4/23/2013 SECTION 15. This act shall take effect upon becoming a law, the public welfare requiring it.

PUBLIC CHAPTER NO. 181

PUBLIC CHAPTER NO. 181

SENATE BILL NO. 159

By Norris, Southerland

Substituted for: House Bill No. 153

By McCormick, Rogers

AN ACT to amend Tennessee Code Annotated, Title 60; Title 68 and Title 69, relative to the contested case hearing process.

BE IT ENACTED BY THE GENERAL ASSEMBLY OF THE STATE OF TENNESSEE:

60-1-401 SECTION 1. Tennessee Code Annotated, Section 60-1-401, is amended by deleting subsection (h) in its entirety and by substituting instead the following language:

(h) If the operator files an appeal of such citation or assessment of a penalty as provided by subsection (g), the proceedings on such appeal shall be conducted as a contested case and shall be heard before an administrative judge sitting alone pursuant to §§ 4-5-301(a)(2) and 4-5-314(b), unless settled by the parties. The administrative judge to whom the case has been assigned shall convene the parties for a scheduling conference within thirty (30) days of the date the appeal is filed. The scheduling order for the contested case issued by the administrative judge shall establish a schedule that results in a hearing being completed within one hundred eighty (180) days of the scheduling conference, unless the parties agree to a longer time or the administrative judge allows otherwise for good cause shown, and an initial order being issued within sixty (60) days of completion of the record of the hearing. The administrative judge's initial order, together with any earlier orders issued by the administrative judge, shall become final unless appealed to the board by the commissioner or other party within thirty (30) days of entry of the initial order or, unless the board passes a motion to review the initial order pursuant to § 4-5-315, within the longer of thirty (30) days or seven (7) days after the first board meeting to occur after entry of the initial order. Upon appeal to the board by a party, or upon passage of a motion of the board to review the administrative judge's initial order, the board shall afford each party an opportunity to present briefs, shall review the record and allow each party an opportunity to present oral argument. If appealed to the board, the review of the administrative judge's initial order shall be limited to the record, but shall be de novo with no presumption of correctness. In such appeals, the board shall thereafter render a final order, in accordance with the provisions of § 4-5-314, affirming, modifying, remanding, or vacating the supervisor's citation or assessment of a penalty. A final order rendered pursuant to this section is effective upon its entry, except as provided in § 4-5-320(b) unless a later effective date shall be stated therein. A petition to stay the effective date of a final order may be filed under the provisions of § 4-5-316. A petition for reconsideration of a final order may be filed pursuant to § 4-5-317. Judicial review of a final order may be sought by filing a petition for review in accordance with § 4-5-322. An order of an administrative judge that becomes final in the absence of an appeal or review by the board shall be deemed to be a decision of the board in that case for purposes of the standard of review by a court, however, in other matters before the board, it may be considered but shall not be binding on the board.

68-201-107 SECTION 2. Tennessee Code Annotated, Section 68-201-107, is amended by deleting subsection (b) in its entirety.

68-201-108 SECTION 3. Tennessee Code Annotated, Section 68-201-108, is amended by deleting subsection (a) in its entirety and by substituting instead the following language:

(a)(1) A person aggrieved by a final action of the technical secretary on a permit, order, or assessment may request a hearing before the board pursuant to this section by filing a petition with the technical secretary within thirty (30) days of issuance of the permit or service of the order or assessment. The hearing shall be conducted as a contested case and shall be heard before an administrative judge sitting alone pursuant to §§ 4-5-301(a)(2) and 4-5-314(b), unless settled by the parties. The administrative judge to whom the case has been assigned shall convene the parties for a scheduling conference within thirty (30) days of the date the petition is filed. The scheduling order for the contested case issued by the administrative judge shall establish a schedule that results in a hearing being completed within one hundred eighty (180) days of the scheduling conference, unless the parties agree to a longer time or the administrative judge allows otherwise for good cause shown, and an initial order being issued within sixty (60) days of completion of the record of the hearing. The administrative judge's initial order, together with any earlier orders issued by the administrative judge, shall become final unless appealed to the board by the commissioner or other party within thirty (30) days of entry of the initial order or, unless the board passes a motion to review the initial order pursuant to § 4-5-315, within the longer of thirty (30) days or seven (7) days after the first board meeting to occur after entry of the initial order. Upon appeal to the board by a party, or upon passage of a motion of the board to review the administrative judge's initial order, the board shall afford each party an opportunity to present briefs, shall review the record and allow each party an opportunity to present oral argument. If appealed to the board, the review of the administrative judge's initial order shall be limited to the record, but shall be de novo with no presumption of correctness. In such appeals, the board shall thereafter render a final order, in accordance with the provisions of § 4-5-314, affirming, modifying, remanding, or vacating the administrative judge's order. A final order rendered pursuant to this section is effective upon its entry, except as provided in § 4-5-320(b) unless a later effective date shall be stated therein. A petition to stay the effective date of a final order may be filed under the provisions of § 4-5-316. A petition for reconsideration of a final order may be filed pursuant to § 4-5-317. Judicial review of a final order may be sought by filing a petition for review in accordance with § 4-5-322. An order of an administrative judge that becomes final in the absence of an appeal or review by the board shall be deemed to be a decision of the board in that case for purposes of the standard of review by a court; however, in other matters before the board, it may be considered but shall not be binding on the board.

(2) Hearings before the board on requests for variances and certificates of exemption may be conducted as contested case hearings in accordance with the Uniform Administrative Procedures Act, compiled in chapter 4, part 5.

68-211-113 SECTION 4. Tennessee Code Annotated, Section 68-211-113, is amended by deleting subsections (a) and (b) in their entirety and by substituting instead the following language:

(a)(1) Any person whose plans for the construction of, or change in, any solid waste processing facility or disposal facility are disapproved by the commissioner may secure a review of the commissioner's disapproval by filing with the commissioner a written petition setting forth the grounds and reasons for such person's objections to the commissioner's disapproval, and asking for a hearing before the board. Any disapproval of such plans shall become final and not subject to review unless such petition for a hearing before the board is filed no later than thirty (30) days after the notice of disapproval is served.

(2) Any person against whom an order for correction is issued may secure a review of such order by filing with the commissioner a written petition setting forth the grounds and reasons for any objection to the order and asking for a hearing before the board. The order shall become final and not subject to review unless the person named in the order files a petition under this section no later than thirty (30) days after the date the order is served.

(b) The hearing before the board on any petition filed under subsection (a) shall be conducted as a contested case and shall be heard before an administrative judge sitting alone pursuant to §§ 4-5-301(a)(2) and 4-5-314(b), unless settled by the parties. The administrative judge to whom the case has been assigned shall convene the parties for a scheduling conference within thirty (30) days of the date the petition is filed. The scheduling order for the contested case issued by the administrative judge shall establish a schedule that results in a hearing being completed within one hundred eighty (180) days of the scheduling conference, unless the parties agree to a longer time or the administrative judge allows otherwise for good cause shown, and an initial order being issued within sixty (60) days of completion of the record of the hearing. The administrative judge's initial order, together with any earlier orders issued by the administrative judge, shall become final unless appealed to the board by the commissioner or other party within thirty (30) days of entry of the initial order or, unless the board passes a motion to review the initial order pursuant to § 4-5-315, within the longer of thirty (30) days or seven (7) days after the first board meeting to occur after entry of the initial order. Upon appeal to the board by a party, or upon passage of a motion of the board to review the administrative judge's initial order, the board shall afford each party an opportunity to present briefs, shall review the record and allow each party an opportunity to present oral argument. If appealed to the board, the review of the administrative judge's initial order shall be limited to the record, but shall be de novo with no presumption of correctness. In such appeals, the board shall thereafter render a final order, in accordance with the provisions of § 4-5-314, affirming, modifying, remanding, or vacating the administrative judge's order. A final order rendered pursuant to this section is effective upon its entry, except as provided in § 4-5-320(b) unless a later effective date is stated therein. A petition to stay the effective date of a final order may be filed under the provisions of § 4-5-316. A petition for reconsideration of a final order may be filed pursuant to § 4-5-317. Judicial review of a final order may be sought by filing a petition for review in accordance with § 4-5-322. An order of an administrative judge that becomes final in the absence of an appeal or review by the board shall be deemed to be a decision of the board in that case for purposes of the standard of review by a court; however, in other matters before the board, it may be considered but shall not be binding on the board.

68-211-113 SECTION 5. Tennessee Code Annotated, Section 68-211-113, is further amended by deleting subsections (e) and (f) in their entirety.

68-211-113 SECTION 6. Tennessee Code Annotated, Section 68-211-113, is further amended by adding the following sentence at the end of subsection (h):

When such an appeal is timely filed, the procedure for conducting the contested case shall be in accordance with the provisions of § 68-211-113(b).

68-211-117 SECTION 7. Tennessee Code Annotated, Section 68-211-117, is amended by deleting subdivision (b)(2) in its entirety and by substituting instead the following language:

(2) Any person against whom an assessment has been issued may secure a review of the assessment by filing with the commissioner a written petition setting forth the grounds and reasons for such person's objections and asking for a hearing in the matter involved before the board. When such a petition is timely filed, the procedure for conducting the contested case shall be in accordance with the provisions of § 68-211-113(b).

68-212-113 SECTION 8. Tennessee Code Annotated, Section 68-212-113, is amended by deleting subsection (b) in its entirety and by substituting instead the following language:

(b) The hearing before the board on any petition filed under subsection (a) shall be conducted as a contested case and shall be heard before an administrative judge sitting alone pursuant to §§ 4-5-301(a)(2) and 4-5-314(b), unless settled by the parties; provided that in a petition filed under subdivision (a)(2)(B) the judge shall hold the hearing in the county where the facility or site is proposed to be located. The administrative judge to whom the case has been assigned shall convene the parties for a scheduling conference within thirty (30) days of the date the petition is filed. The scheduling order for the contested case, issued by the administrative judge, shall establish a schedule that results in a hearing being completed within one hundred eighty (180) days of the scheduling conference, unless the parties agree to a longer time or the administrative judge allows otherwise for good cause shown, and an initial order being issued within sixty (60) days of completion of the record of the hearing. The administrative judge's initial order, together with any earlier orders issued by the administrative judge, shall become final unless appealed to the board by the commissioner or other party within thirty (30) days of entry of the initial order or, unless the board passes a motion to review the initial order pursuant to § 4-5-315, within the longer of thirty (30) days or seven (7) days after the first board meeting to occur after entry of the initial order. Upon appeal to the board by a party, or upon passage of a motion of the board to review the administrative judge's initial order, the board shall afford each party an opportunity to present briefs, shall review the record and allow each party an opportunity to present oral argument. If appealed to the board, the review of the administrative judge's initial order shall be limited to the record, but shall be de novo with no presumption of correctness. In such appeals, the board shall thereafter render a final order, in accordance with the provisions of § 4-5-314, affirming, modifying, remanding, or vacating the administrative judge's order. A final order rendered pursuant to this section is effective upon its entry, except as provided in § 4-5-320(b) unless a later effective date is stated therein. A petition to stay the effective date of a final order may be filed under the provisions of § 4-5-316. A petition for reconsideration of a final order may be filed under the provisions of § 4-5-317. Judicial review of a final order may be sought by filing a petition for review in accordance with § 4-5-322. An order of an administrative judge that becomes final in the absence of an appeal or review by the board shall be deemed to be a decision of the board in that case for purposes of the standard of review by a court; however, in other matters before the board, it may be considered but shall not be binding on the board.

68-212-117 SECTION 9. Tennessee Code Annotated, Section 68-212-117(a), is amended by deleting the last sentence in its entirety and by substituting instead the following new language:

When such an appeal is timely filed, the procedure for conducting the contested case shall be in accordance with the provisions of § 68-212-113(b). The department shall not be obligated to assist a complainant in gathering information or making investigations or to provide counsel for the purpose of drawing the complaint.

68-215-115 SECTION 10. Tennessee Code Annotated, Section 68-215-115, is amended by deleting subdivision (b)(2) in its entirety and by substituting instead the following language:

Any person against whom an assessment is issued may secure a review of the propriety or amount of the assessment by filing with the commissioner a written petition setting forth the grounds and reasons for the objection and asking for a hearing before the board. Any such assessment shall become final and not subject to review unless the person named therein files the petition within thirty (30) days after the assessment is received. When the petition is timely filed, the procedure for conducting the contested case shall be in accordance with the provisions of § 68-215-119(b).

68-215-119 SECTION 11. Tennessee Code Annotated, Section 68-215-119, is amended by deleting subsection (b) in its entirety and by substituting instead the following language:

(b) Hearings before the board shall be conducted as contested cases and shall be heard before an administrative judge sitting alone pursuant to §§ 4-5-301(a)(2) and 4-5-314(b), unless settled by the parties. The administrative judge to whom the case has been assigned shall convene the parties for a scheduling conference within thirty (30) days of the date the petition is filed. The scheduling order for the contested case issued by the administrative judge shall establish a schedule that results in a hearing being completed within one hundred eighty (180) days of the scheduling conference, unless the parties agree to a longer time or the administrative judge allows otherwise for good cause shown, and an initial order being issued within sixty (60) days of completion of the record of the hearing. The administrative judge's initial order, together with any earlier orders issued by the administrative judge, shall become final unless appealed to the board by the commissioner or other party within thirty (30) days of entry of the initial order or, unless the board passes a motion to review the initial order pursuant to § 4-5-315, within the longer of thirty (30) days or seven (7) days after the first board meeting to occur after entry of the initial order. Upon appeal to the board by a party, or upon passage of a motion of the board to review the administrative judge's initial order, the board shall afford each party an opportunity to present briefs, shall review the record and allow each party an opportunity to present oral argument. If appealed to the board, the review of the administrative judge's initial order shall be limited to the record, but shall be de novo with no presumption of correctness. In such appeals, the board shall thereafter render a final order, in accordance with the provisions of § 4-5-314, affirming, modifying, remanding, or vacating the administrative judge's order. A final order rendered pursuant to this section is effective upon its entry, except as provided in § 4-5-320(b) unless a later effective date is stated therein. A petition to stay the effective date of a final order may be filed under the provisions of § 4-5-316. A petition for reconsideration of a final order may be filed pursuant to § 4-5-317. Judicial review of a final order may be sought by filing a petition for review in accordance with § 4-5-322. An order of an administrative judge that becomes final in the absence of an appeal or review by the board shall be deemed to be a decision of the board in that case for purposes of the standard of review by a court; however, in other matters before the board, it may be considered but shall not be binding on the board.

68-215-123 SECTION 12. Tennessee Code Annotated, Section 68-215-123, is amended by deleting subdivision (a)(2) in its entirety and by substituting instead the following language:

(2) If either the complainant or the alleged violator believes the commissioner's or board's action or determination is or will be inadequate or too severe, such complainant or alleged violator may appeal to the board for a hearing by filing a petition for review. Such appeal must be made within thirty (30) days after receipt of the notification sent by the commissioner or board. When such a petition is timely filed, the procedure for conducting the contested case shall be in accordance with the provisions of § 68-215-119(b).

69-3-105 SECTION 13. Tennessee Code Annotated, Section 69-3-105, is amended by deleting subsection (f) in its entirety and by substituting instead the following language:

(f)(1) The board has and shall exercise the power, duty, and responsibility to:

(A) Hear appeals as specified in subsection (i) from administrative judges' orders assessing penalties or damages, or issuing, denying, revoking or modifying a permit; and

(B) Affirm, modify, or revoke such orders, as specified in subsection (i).

69-3-105 SECTION 14. Tennessee Code Annotated, Section 69-3-105, is amended by deleting subdivision (i) in its entirety and by substituting instead the following language:

(i) A petition for permit appeal may be filed by the permit applicant or by any aggrieved person who participated in the public comment period or gave testimony at a formal public hearing whose appeal is based upon any of the issues that were provided to the commissioner in writing during the public comment period or in testimony at a formal public hearing on the permit application. Additionally, for those permits for which the department gives public notice of a draft permit, any permit applicant or aggrieved person may base a permit appeal on any material change to conditions in the final permit from those in the draft, unless the material change has been subject to additional opportunity for public comment. Any petition for permit appeal under this subsection (i) shall be filed with the board within thirty (30) days after public notice of the commissioner's decision to issue or deny the permit. Notwithstanding the provisions of § 4-5-223 or § 69-3-118(a), or any other provision of law to the contrary, this subsection (i) and the established procedures of Tennessee's antidegradation statement, found in the rules promulgated by the department, shall be the exclusive means for obtaining administrative review of the commissioner's issuance or denial of a permit. When such a petition is timely filed, the procedure for conducting the contested case shall be in accordance with § 69-3-110(a).

69-3-110 SECTION 15. Tennessee Code Annotated, Section 69-3-110, is amended by deleting subsection (a) in its entirety and by substituting instead the following language:

(a) Any hearing brought before the board pursuant to § 69-3-105(i), § 69-3-109, or § 69-3-118 shall be conducted as a contested case. The hearing shall be heard before an administrative judge sitting alone pursuant to §§ 4-5-301(a)(2) and 4-5-314(b), unless settled by the parties. The administrative judge to whom the case has been assigned shall convene the parties for a scheduling conference within thirty (30) days of the date the petition is filed. The scheduling order for the contested case issued by the administrative judge shall establish a schedule that results in a hearing being completed within one hundred eighty (180) days of the scheduling conference, unless the parties agree to a longer time or the administrative judge allows otherwise for good cause shown, and an initial order being issued within sixty (60) days of completion of the record of the hearing. The administrative judge's initial order, together with any earlier orders issued by the administrative judge, shall become final unless appealed to the board by the commissioner or other party within thirty (30) days of entry of the initial order or, unless the board passes a motion to review the initial order pursuant to § 4-5-315, within the longer of thirty (30) days or seven (7) days after the first board meeting to occur after entry of the initial order. Upon appeal to the board by a party, or upon passage of a motion of the board to review the administrative judge's initial order, the board shall afford each party an opportunity to present briefs, shall review the record and allow each party an opportunity to present oral argument. If appealed to the board, the review of the administrative judge's initial order shall be limited to the record, but shall be de novo with no presumption of correctness. In such appeals, the board shall thereafter render a final order, in accordance with the provisions of § 4-5-314, affirming, modifying, remanding, or vacating the administrative judge's order. A final order rendered pursuant to this section is effective upon its entry, except as provided in § 4-5-320(b) unless a later effective date is stated therein. A petition to stay the effective date of a final order may be filed under the provisions of § 4-5-316. A petition for reconsideration of a final order may be filed pursuant to § 4-5-317. Judicial review of a final order may be sought by filing a petition for review in accordance with § 4-5-322. An order of an administrative judge that becomes final in the absence of an appeal or review by the board shall be deemed to be a decision of the board in that case for purposes of the standard of review by a court; however, in other matters before the board, it may be considered but shall not be binding on the board.

69-3-110 SECTION 16. Tennessee Code Annotated, Section 69-3-110, is amended by deleting subsection (c) in its entirety.

69-3-111 SECTION 17. Tennessee Code Annotated, Section 69-3-111, is amended by deleting the following language:

Any appeals from any final order or other final determination of the board by any party shall be conducted in accordance with the Uniform Administrative Procedures Act, compiled in title 4, chapter 5.

69-3-302 SECTION 18. Tennessee Code Annotated, Section 69-3-302, is amended by deleting the section in its entirety and substituting instead the following language:

PUBLIC CHAPTER NO. 181 (cont'd)

69-3-302. Final orders by the board or an administrative judge shall be published on the department website within five (5) business days, in addition to other publication required by law.

SECTION 19. For the purpose of construing this act in relation to the Uniform Administrative Procedures Act, compiled in title 4, chapter 5, this act shall be deemed to be procedural in nature. It is the intent of the general assembly that this act and the Uniform Administrative Procedures Act shall be complied with, however when in conflict, the provisions of this act shall govern.

Effective date 7/1/2013

SECTION 20. This act shall take effect July 1, 2013, the public welfare requiring it and shall apply to all cases filed on or after such date.

PUBLIC CHAPTER NO. 182

PUBLIC CHAPTER NO. 182

SENATE BILL NO. 172

By Norris, Watson, Ketron

Substituted for: House Bill No. 166

By McCormick, Alexander

AN ACT to amend Tennessee Code Annotated, Title 53, Chapter 8 and Title 68, Chapter 14, relative to food safety.

BE IT ENACTED BY THE GENERAL ASSEMBLY OF THE STATE OF TENNESSEE:

53-8-201 SECTION 1. Tennessee Code Annotated, Section 53-8-201, is amended by deleting the section in its entirety and substituting instead the following language:

53-8-201. This part shall be known as the Tennessee Retail Food Safety Act.

53-8-202 SECTION 2. Tennessee Code Annotated, Section 53-8-202, is amended by deleting the section in its entirety and substituting instead the following language:

53-8-202. It is the purpose of this part to ensure that foods offered for public consumption in Tennessee are safe as prepared, processed, served, packaged, and delivered. Food service establishments that are located within retail food stores are subject to this part and exempt from regulation in accordance with title 68, chapter 14, part 7.

53-8-203 SECTION 3. Tennessee Code Annotated, Section 53-8-203, is amended by deleting the section in its entirety and substituting instead the following language:

53-8-203. As used in this part:

(1) "Alteration" shall be defined by rule, but shall not mean function replacement that equals or makes better the existing operation of the facility;

(2) "Commissioner" means the commissioner of agriculture, the commissioner's duly authorized representative, and in the event of the commissioner's absence or vacancy in the office of commissioner, the deputy commissioner;

(3) "Department" means the department of agriculture;

(4) "Demonstration of knowledge" means the ability to demonstrate knowledge of food safety principles as applicable to establishments regulated in accordance with this part. For the purposes of this part, "demonstration of knowledge" may be accomplished by one (1) or more of the following means:

(A) Completing an inspection that reflects no priority item violation;

(B) Employing at least one (1) person certified as a food protection manager who has shown proficiency of food protection information through passing a test that is part of a certification program that is evaluated and listed by an accrediting agency recognized by the Conference for Food Protection as conforming to the Conference for Food Protection Standards for Accreditation of Food Protection Manager Certification Programs; or

(C) Responding correctly to food protection questions related to the specific food operation. A person responding to the questions may be aided by the utilization of food safety procedures posted prominently for employees who may use the procedures as reference guides. The commissioner shall assist establishments that request information relative to risks associated with the establishments' specific food operation, which may be posed as questions during the inspection;

(5) "Employee" means a person:

(A) In charge of a food establishment;

(B) Engaged in the preparation of food or drink;

(C) Engaged in service of food to the establishment's clientele; or

(D) Engaged in ware washing;

(6) "Extensive remodeling" means the repair, construction, alteration or installation of new equipment, modification of existing equipment or fixtures, changes in floor plan layout, addition of new processes, expansion to new space, or significant changes to use of space or equipment;

(7) "Food Code" means the 2009 Food Code as published by the U.S. Department of Health and Human Services, Public Health Service, Food and Drug Administration;

(8) "Food establishments" means retail food stores, and food service establishments located within retail food stores. The term "food establishments" is to be used throughout this part when a provision is applicable to both retail food stores and food service establishments located within retail food stores;

(9)(A) "Food service establishment" means any establishment, place or location, whether permanent, temporary, seasonal, or itinerant, where food is prepared and the public is offered to be served or is served food, including, but not limited to, foods, vegetables, or beverages not in an original package or container, food and beverages dispensed at soda fountains and delicatessens, sliced watermelon, ice balls, or water mixtures;

(B) "Food service establishment" includes places identified in subdivision (A), regardless of whether there is a charge for the food;

(C) "Food service establishment" does not include private homes where food is prepared or served and not offered for sale, retail food store operations other than delicatessens, the location of vending machines or supply vehicles;

(D) "Food service establishment" does not include churches, temples, synagogues or other religious institutions, civic, fraternal, or veteran's organizations where food is prepared, served, transported, or stored by volunteer personnel only on non-consecutive days; however, the storage of unopened, commercially canned food, packaged bulk food that is not potentially hazardous as defined by department rules and regulations, and dry goods shall not apply for these purposes;

(E) "Food service establishment" does not include grocery stores that may, incidentally, make infrequent casual sales of uncooked foods for consumption on the premises, or any establishment whose primary business is other than food service, that may, incidentally, make infrequent casual sales of coffee or prepackaged foods, or both, for consumption on the premises. For the purposes of this subdivision, "infrequent casual sales" means sales not in excess of one hundred fifty dollars ($150) per day on any particular day;

(F) "Food service establishment" does not include a location from which casual, occasional food sales are conducted solely in connection with youth-related amateur athletic or recreational activities or primary or secondary school-related clubs by volunteer personnel and that are in operation for twenty-four (24) consecutive hours or less;

(G) "Food service establishment" does not include a catering business that employs no regular, full-time employees, the food preparation for such business is solely performed within the confines of the principal residence of the proprietor, and the catering business makes only "occasional sales" during any thirty-day period; and

(H) "Food service establishment" does not include a house or other residential structure where seriously ill or injured children and their families are provided temporary accommodations in proximity to their treatment hospitals and where food is prepared, served, transported or stored by volunteer personnel; provided, that the house or structure is supported by a § 501(c)(3) organization, as defined in 26 U.S.C. § 501(c)(3), that has as a component of its mission the support of programs that directly improve the health and well-being of children;

(10) "Imminent health hazard" means any condition, deficiency, or practice that, if not corrected, is very likely to result in illness, injury, or loss of life to any person;

(11) "Person" means any individual, partnership, firm, corporation, agency, municipality, state or political subdivision, or the federal government and its agencies and departments;

(12) "Person in charge" means an individual present at a food establishment who is responsible for the operation at the time of inspection. A "person in charge" shall be present at the establishment during food preparation and handling, and may put instructions in place for cleaning and preparing the establishment prior to the preparation of any food or beverage; and

(13) "Retail food store" means any establishment or a section of an establishment where food and food products are offered to the consumer and intended for off-premise consumption. "Retail food store" does not include establishments that handle only prepackaged, non-potentially hazardous foods, as defined by department rules and regulations; roadside markets that offer only fresh fruits and fresh vegetables; food and beverage vending machines; food service establishments not located within a retail food store; or a person who makes infrequent casual sales of honey or who packs or sells less than one hundred fifty (150) gallons of honey per year.

53-8-204 SECTION 4. Tennessee Code Annotated, Section 53-8-204, is amended by deleting the section in its entirety and substituting instead the following language:

53-8-204. The commissioner is authorized to:

(1) Carry out or cause to be carried out all provisions of this part;

(2) Collect all fees established pursuant to this part and apply the fees in accordance with the procedures of the department of finance and administration to the necessary and incidental costs of the administration of this part. Nothing in this subdivision (2) shall be construed to prohibit the department from receiving, by way of general appropriation, such sums as may be required to fund adequately the implementation of this part, as recommended in the annual budget by the governor to the general assembly;

(3) Prescribe rules and regulations, including emergency rules, governing the alteration, construction, sanitation, safety of food, and operation of food establishments as may be necessary to protect the health and safety of the public, and require food establishments to comply with these rules and regulations. A non-elected body of any municipality, county, or metropolitan government shall not enact any ordinance or issue any rule or regulation pertaining to food safety or the provision of nutritional information related to food or drink, or otherwise regulate menus at food establishments. If, upon the effective date of this act, the federal government takes action regarding the provision of food nutritional information at food establishments, and the federal action specifically authorizes state agencies to enforce such action, then the department of agriculture shall be the department that is primarily responsible for the implementation and supervision of any new requirements and shall have the authority to promulgate rules and regulations in accordance with the Uniform Administrative Procedures Act, compiled in title 4, chapter 5, as necessary to effectuate the purposes of such requirements. The commissioner shall not prescribe any such rules and regulations that are in conflict with the minimum statewide building construction standards established by the state fire marshal pursuant to § 68-120-101. The rules with respect to food temperature shall be specific with respect to the types of food prepared and the risks presented by those foods. Except as specifically provided herein, the commissioner may, by the promulgation of rules and regulations, adopt all or part of the Food Code;

(4) Inspect or cause to be inspected as often as the commissioner, in the commissioner's discretion may deem necessary, every food establishment in the state as authorized by this part, to determine compliance with this part and with rules and regulations;

PUBLIC CHAPTER NO. 182 (cont'd)

(5) Issue or cause to be issued, suspend, and revoke permits to operate food establishments as provided in this part;

(6) Notify the owner, proprietor, or agent of any food establishment of such changes or alterations as may be necessary, to effect complete compliance with this part and with rules and regulations governing the construction, alteration, and operation of the facilities, and close the facilities for failure to comply within specified times as provided in this part and in rules and regulations;

(7) Enter into agreements or contracts with the Shelby, Davidson, and Knox county health departments for the health departments to implement this part in their areas of jurisdiction, if the commissioner deems it appropriate; provided, that the following conditions shall apply:

(A) State reporting requirements shall be met by the county health department or departments;

(B) The county health department program standards shall be identical to those of the state law, and to rules and regulations;

(C) The commissioner shall retain the right to exercise oversight and evaluation of performance of the county health department or departments and terminate the agreement or contract for cause immediately, or otherwise upon reasonable notice;

(D) The commissioner may set such other fiscal, administrative, or program requirements as the commissioner deems necessary to maintain consistency and integrity of the statewide program;

(E) Staffing and resources shall be adequate to implement and enforce the program in the local jurisdiction;

(F) Contract county health departments that collect the applicable permit fees from food establishments located within the county shall retain one hundred percent (100%) of the permit fees and penalty fees. Contract counties that utilize the services of the department for the collection of permit fees shall receive ninety-five percent (95%) of permit fees collected within a contract county pursuant to §§ 53-8-204 – 53-8-206. This amount shall be calculated based upon fees collected in the contract county during the state's fiscal year multiplied by ninety-five percent (95%).

(8)(A) Upon the application of a food establishment for a variance based on a showing of good cause and an affirmative demonstration that the risks to the public attendant to the limited activities have been mitigated, the commissioner shall grant the establishment a variance from the limitations in the Food Code regarding restrictions pertaining to bare hand contact. A request for a variance shall be granted or denied within sixty (60) days of the commissioner's receipt of the application for variance. A request for a variance shall include the following:

(i) A listing of the specific ready-to-eat foods that are touched by bare hands;

(ii) Diagrams and other information showing that hand washing facilities are located and equipped as prescribed by the applicable provisions of the Food Code;

(iii) An employee health policy documenting that the food service establishment complies with:

(a) The person in charge requirements; and

(b) Requirements for monitoring the health of food service employees;

(iv) Documentation that food service employees have received training on the:

(a) Risks of contacting ready-to-eat foods with bare hands;

(b) Practice of proper hand washing;

(c) Proper fingernail maintenance;

(d) Prohibition on jewelry; and

(e) Good hygienic practices;

(v) Documentation that food employees contacting ready-to-eat foods with bare hands used two (2) or more of the following control measures:

(a) Double hand washing;

(b) Nail brushes;

(c) A hand antiseptic after hand washing;

(d) Incentive programs that assist or encourage food service employees not to work when they are ill; or

(e) Other control measures approved by the commissioner.

(B) Notwithstanding any provisions of the Food Code to the contrary, the commissioner shall not require any further documentation for the granting of a variance other than those contained in this section.

53-8-205 SECTION 5. Tennessee Code Annotated, Section 53-8-205, is amended by deleting the section in its entirety and substituting instead the following language:

53-8-205. All monies coming into the state treasury pursuant to this part from fees, fines, and penalties shall be appropriated to the department for the payment of necessary expenses incident to the administration of this part, as determined by the commissioner. Any unexpended balance of the fund in any fiscal year shall be retained by the department to be used to provide or expand training for food service operators and the department's food safety staff.

53-8-206 SECTION 6. Tennessee Code Annotated, Section 53-8-206, is amended by deleting the section in its entirety and substituting instead the following language:

53-8-206.

(a) No person shall operate a food establishment who does not hold a valid permit issued to the person by the commissioner on or before July 1 of each year, or as the commissioner may otherwise provide by rule and regulation.

(b) Every person now engaged in the business of operating a food establishment, and every person who, upon the effective date of this act, engages in such a business, shall procure a permit from the commissioner for each food establishment so operated or proposed to be operated.

(c) Each permit for food establishments shall expire on June 30 following its issuance or as the commissioner may otherwise provide by rule and regulation.

(d) No permit shall be transferred from one location or person to another.

(e) The permit shall be kept and displayed in a conspicuous manner, and visible to the public in the food establishment for which it is issued.

53-8-207 SECTION 7. Tennessee Code Annotated, Section 53-8-207, is amended by deleting the section in its entirety and substituting instead the following language:

53-8-207.

(a) Any person planning to operate a food establishment shall first submit an application for a permit on forms provided by the commissioner. The application shall be completed and submitted to the commissioner with the proper permit fee.

(b) Prior to the approval of the application for a permit, the commissioner shall inspect the proposed facility to determine if the person applying for the permit is in compliance with the requirements of this part and with applicable rules and regulations. The commissioner shall issue a permit to the applicant if the inspection reveals that the facility is in compliance with such requirements.

(c) Applications for renewal of permits for existing food establishments will be issued to the operators prior to the expiration date of the permit. When completed applications and the proper permit fees are returned to the commissioner, the commissioner shall issue new permits to applicants.

53-8-208 SECTION 8. Tennessee Code Annotated, Section 53-8-208, is amended by deleting the section in its entirety and substituting instead the following language:

53-8-208.

(a) The commissioner has the authority to suspend any permit to operate a food establishment issued pursuant to this part if the commissioner has reasonable cause to believe that the permittee is not in compliance with this part; provided, that the permittee shall be given the opportunity to correct violations as provided in § 53-8-215.

(b) Suspension of permits, other than those for temporary food service establishments, shall be of the following two (2) types:

(1) A Class 1 suspension, which provides an opportunity for a hearing prior to the effective date of the suspension; and

(2) A Class 2 suspension, which provides an opportunity for a hearing after the effective date of the suspension and is effective immediately.

(c) Notice of either type of suspension may be given by the inspector on the inspector's regular inspection form or by written notification from the commissioner. When a permit suspension is effective, all food establishment operations shall cease. Class 2 suspensions shall only be issued if an imminent health hazard exists.

(d) A written request for a hearing on either type of suspension shall be filed by the permittee within ten (10) days of the receipt of notice. This ten-day period may run concurrently with the ten-day period set forth in § 53-8-215. If a hearing is requested, it shall be commenced within a reasonable time of the request. If no request for a hearing is made within ten (10) days of receipt of notice, the suspension becomes final and is not subject to review.

(e) The commissioner may end the suspension at any time if the reasons for the suspension no longer exist.

53-8-209 SECTION 9. Tennessee Code Annotated, Section 53-8-209, is amended by deleting the section in its entirety and substituting instead the following language:

53-8-209.

(a) The commissioner may, after providing opportunity for a hearing, revoke a permit for serious or repeated violations of the requirements of this part or for interference with the commissioner in the performance of the commissioner's duty.

(b) Prior to revocation, the commissioner shall notify the permittee, in writing, of the specific reason or reasons for which the permit is being revoked at the end of ten (10) days following service of the notice, unless a written request for a hearing is filed with the commissioner within the ten-day period. If no request for a hearing is filed within the ten-day period, the revocation of the permit becomes final.

53-8-210 SECTION 10. Tennessee Code Annotated, Section 53-8-210, is amended by deleting the section in its entirety and substituting instead the following language:

53-8-210. A notice provided for in this part is properly served when it is delivered to the permittee or person in charge, or when it is sent by certified mail, return receipt requested, to the last known address of the permittee. A copy of the notice shall be filed in the records of the commissioner.

53-8-211 SECTION 11. Tennessee Code Annotated, Section 53-8-211, is amended by deleting the section in its entirety and substituting instead the following:

53-8-211.

(a) The hearings provided for in this part shall be conducted by the commissioner in accordance with the Uniform Administrative Procedures Act, compiled in title 4, chapter 5.

(b) Appeals from any final decision after a hearing shall be pursued in accordance with the Uniform Administrative Procedures Act, compiled in title 4, chapter 5.

(c) Subsections (a) and (b) shall not apply in a county where the health department is operating a program pursuant to § 53-8-204(7) that meets the minimum requirements of due process; provided, that appeals from final decisions made under such programs may be made to the commissioner, for the limited purpose of determining whether a material error of law was made at the county level. The appeal to the commissioner shall not be de novo, but shall be limited to a review of the record of the hearing at the county level.

53-8-212 SECTION 12. Tennessee Code Annotated, Section 53-8-212, is amended by deleting the section in its entirety and substituting instead the following language:

53-8-212. Whenever revocation of a permit becomes final, upon demonstration that the conditions which led to the revocation have been cured, the holder of the revoked permit may make written application for a new permit.

53-8-213 SECTION 13. Tennessee Code Annotated, Section 53-8-213, is amended by deleting the section in its entirety and substituting instead the following language:

53-8-213.

(a) The permit fee to operate a food establishment shall be in accordance with the following schedule:

(1) Retail food stores that contain within the premises a food service establishment that prepares potentially hazardous food, as defined by department rules and regulations, shall pay a permit fee as follows:

No. of Seats	Fee Amount
0-50	$210
51 or more seats	$360

(2) Retail food stores that contain within the premises a food service establishment that offers self-service foods and does not prepare potentially hazardous foods, as defined by department rules and regulations, shall pay a permit fee of thirty-five dollars ($35.00); and

(3) In addition to the fees in subdivision (a)(1) or (a)(2), all retail food stores shall pay an annual permit fee of fifty dollars ($50.00).

(b) If the permit fee is delinquent for more than thirty (30) calendar days, a penalty fee of one half (1/2) the permit fee shall be assessed, in addition to the permit fee. If a check is returned for any reason, a penalty fee of one half (1/2) the permit fee shall be assessed, in addition to the permit fee. The permit fee, plus any penalty fee, must be paid before the permit is issued.

(c) When application is made for a permit to operate any food establishment after January 1 of any year, or such other date as the commissioner may establish by regulation, the fee charged for the permit shall be one half (1/2) the annual rate; however, where the establishment was subject to permit requirements prior to January 1 or such other date as the commissioner may establish by rule and regulation, of any year, no such fractional rate shall be allowed.

53-8-214 SECTION 14. Tennessee Code Annotated, Section 53-8-214, is amended by deleting the section in its entirety and substituting instead the following language:

53-8-214.

(a) Inspection results for food establishments shall be recorded on standard departmental forms that summarize the requirements of the law and rules and regulations.

(b) A copy of the completed inspection report shall be furnished to the person in charge of the facility at the conclusion of the inspection.

(c) The most current inspection report furnished to the operator or person in charge of the establishment shall be made available at the facility for public disclosure to any person who requests to review it.

53-8-215 SECTION 15. Tennessee Code Annotated, Section 53-8-215, is amended by deleting the section in its entirety and substituting instead the following language:

53-8-215.

(a) The completed inspection report shall specify a reasonable period of time for correction of violations found.

(b) Corrections of violations shall be accomplished within the period specified in accordance with the following:

(1) If an imminent health hazard exists, the facility shall immediately cease operations until authorized to reopen by the commissioner;

(2) All violations of priority items shall be corrected as soon as possible and in any event within ten (10) days following inspection. Within fifteen (15) days after inspection, the permittee shall notify the commissioner stating that priority item violations have been corrected. A follow-up inspection may be made for confirmation;

(3) All other items shall be corrected as soon as possible, but no later than the time of the next routine inspection.

(c) The inspection report shall state that failure to comply with any time limits specified by the commissioner for correction may result in cessation of operations. An opportunity for a hearing on the ordered corrective action shall be provided, if a written request is filed with the commissioner within ten (10) days following cessation of operations. If a request for a hearing is received, a hearing shall be held within a reasonable time after receipt of the request.

(d) Whenever a facility is required under this section to cease operations, it shall not resume operations until it has shown on reinspection that the conditions that led to the order to cease operations no longer exist. Opportunity for reinspection shall be offered within a reasonable time.

53-8-216 SECTION 16. Tennessee Code Annotated, Section 53-8-216, is amended by deleting the section in its entirety and substituting instead the following language:

53-8-216. Food may be examined or sampled by the commissioner as deemed necessary for the enforcement of this part. The commissioner may place a hold order on any food that the commissioner believes is in violation of this part or rules and regulations, upon written notice to the operator specifying particular reasons for the hold order. The commissioner shall tag, label, or otherwise identify any food subject to a hold order. No food subject to a hold order shall be used, served, sold, or moved from the establishment. The hold order may state that the food be held while confirmation is obtained that the condition violates this part or rules and regulations. The hold order may also order the operator to destroy food that violates this part or rules and regulations. The commissioner shall permit storage of the food under the conditions specified in the hold order, unless storage is not possible without risk to the health of the public, in which case immediate destruction shall be ordered and accomplished. The hold order shall state that a request for a hearing may be filed within ten (10) days. If a request for a hearing is received, the hearing shall be held within a reasonable time after receipt of the request. On the basis of evidence produced at the hearing, the hold order may be rescinded, or the owner or person in charge may be directed by written order to denature or destroy such food or to bring it into compliance with this part.

53-8-217 SECTION 17. Tennessee Code Annotated, Section 53-8-217, is amended by deleting the section in its entirety and substituting instead the following language:

53-8-217. Whenever a food establishment is constructed or extensively remodeled, and whenever an existing structure is converted to use as a food establishment, plans and specifications shall be submitted to the commissioner for review and approval before construction, remodeling, or conversion begins. The plans and specifications shall indicate the proposed layout, arrangement, mechanical plans, construction materials and work areas, and the type and model of proposed fixed equipment and facilities. The commissioner shall approve the plans and specifications, if they meet the requirements of this part and rules and regulations. No food establishment shall be constructed, extensively remodeled or converted, except in accordance with plans and specifications approved by the commissioner. Any deviation from the submitted plans and specifications previously approved by the commissioner discovered during an inspection that would not compromise the safety of food products shall not delay the issuance of a permit to operate a food establishment.

53-8-218 SECTION 18. Tennessee Code Annotated, Section 53-8-218, is amended by deleting the section in its entirety and substituting instead the following language:

53-8-218.

(a) When the commissioner has reasonable cause to suspect possible disease transmission by an employee of the facility, the commissioner may secure information about any recent illness of the employee or make other investigations as may be indicated. The commissioner may require any of the following:

(1) The immediate exclusion of the employee from employment in the food establishment;

(2) The immediate closing of the facility until, in the commissioner's opinion, no further danger of disease outbreak exists;

(3) Restricting the employee's service to some area of the facility where there would be little likelihood of transmitting disease; or

(4) Adequate medical and laboratory examinations of the employee and of other employees.

(b) A person in charge, having been provided by the employee with written documentation from a person who practices in a medical profession in accordance with title 63 that the employee has been diagnosed with a condition set forth in Chapter 2, § 2-201.11(B)(2) of the Food Code shall have an affirmative duty to notify the commissioner or the commissioner's designee. A person in charge shall not be required to obtain medical records from a prospective employee prior to hiring such individual as an employee.

53-8-219 SECTION 19. Tennessee Code Annotated, Section 53-8-219, is amended by deleting the section in its entirety and substituting instead the following language:

53-8-219. Any person operating a food establishment who fails or refuses to comply with any provision of this part or of rules and regulations, or obstructs or hinders the regulatory authority in the discharge of the regulatory authority's duties, or otherwise operates a food establishment in violation of this part or of rules and regulations commits a Class C misdemeanor. Each day of operation after notice of non-compliance of violation has been given and such violation has not been corrected constitutes a separate offense.

53-8-220 SECTION 20. Tennessee Code Annotated, Section 53-8-220, is amended by deleting the section in its entirety and substituting instead the following language:

53-8-220. When the commissioner has reason to believe that a person is causing, is about to cause, or has caused a violation of this part or of the rules and regulations promulgated under this part, the commissioner may initiate proceedings in either the chancery court of Davidson County or the chancery court of the county where the violation is occurring, for injunctive relief to prevent the continuance of the violation or to correct the conditions resulting in, or about to result in, the violation.

53-8-221 SECTION 21. Tennessee Code Annotated, Section 53-8-221, is amended by deleting the
53-8-222 section in its entirety and substituting instead the following language:

53-8-221. Notwithstanding this part to the contrary, children eighteen (18) years of age or less do not need a license or permit to sell bakery goods, homemade or otherwise, soft drinks, or other similar food commodities at public events.

PUBLIC CHAPTER NO. 182 (cont'd)

68-14-301 SECTION 22. Tennessee Code Annotated, Section 68-14-301, is amended by deleting the section in its entirety and substituting instead the following language:

68-14-301. This part shall be known and cited as the "Hotel and Public Swimming Pool Inspection Act".

68-14-302 SECTION 23. Tennessee Code Annotated, Section 68-14-302, is amended by deleting the section in its entirety and by substituting instead the following new language:

68-14-302. As used in this part, unless the context otherwise requires:

(1) "Alteration" shall be defined by rule, but shall not mean function replacement that equals or makes better the existing operation of the facility;

(2) "Commissioner" means the commissioner of health, the commissioner's duly authorized representative, and in the event of the commissioner's absence or vacancy in the office of commissioner, the deputy commissioner;

(3) "Critical items" means those aspects of operation or conditions of facilities or equipment that, if in violation, constitute the greatest hazards to health and safety, including imminent health hazards. Critical items shall include, but are not limited to, the following:

(A) Restriction of employees with infection - (hotels, pools);

(B) Proper cleanliness and good hygiene practices of employees - (hotels);

(C) Proper sanitizing of utensils and equipment - (hotels);

(D) Approved water supply, hot and cold running water under pressure - (hotels, pools);

(E) Sewage, liquid waste disposal - (hotels, pools);

(F) No cross connection, backsiphonage - (hotels, pools);

(G) Toilet and hand washing facilities for employees - (hotels);

(H) Insects and rodents - (hotels);

(I) Toxic items properly stored and labeled - (hotels);

(J) Fire safety - (hotels);

(K) Safety - (pools);

(L) Excessive turbidity - (pools);

(M) Total absence of approved sanitizing residuals - (pools);

(N) Failure or lack of filtration, sanitizing and cleaning equipment and chemicals - (pools); and

(O) Absence or lack of required supervisory personnel - (pools).

(4) "Department" means the department of health;

(5) "Homeowners' association" means a nonprofit corporation that manages or contracts for the management of the common areas of a residential multi-family housing development. A homeowners' association is governed by a board of directors elected by a majority vote of the individual homeowners;

(6) "Hotel" means any building or establishment kept, used, or maintained as, or advertised as, or offered to the public to be, a place where sleeping accommodations are furnished for pay to transients or travelers, whether or not meals are served to transients or travelers;

(7) "Imminent health hazard" means any condition, deficiency, or practice that, if not corrected, is very likely to result in illness, injury, or loss of life to any person;

(8) "Multi-family residential housing" means condominiums, subdivisions, and individual residential housing developments that share common grounds, parking facilities, tennis courts, swimming pools and similar recreational facilities that are operated by a homeowners' association;

(9) "Multi-family residential housing swimming pool" means a private swimming pool maintained by a homeowners' association solely for the use and benefit of the members of the homeowners' association and their guests;

(10) "Person" means any individual, partnership, firm, corporation, agency, municipality, state or political subdivision, or the federal government and its agencies and departments; and

(11) "Public swimming pools" means a structure of man-made materials, located either indoors or outdoors, used for bathing or swimming, or for instructional purposes in swimming, diving, or other aquatic activities by humans, together with buildings, appurtenances, and equipment used in connection with the structure. "Public swimming pools" also includes spa-type, wading, special purpose pools or water recreation attractions including, but not limited to, those operated at or in camps, child care facilities, cities, clubs, subdivisions, apartment buildings, counties, institutions, schools, motels, hotels, and mobile home parks to which admission may be gained with or without payment of a fee.

68-14-303 SECTION 24. Tennessee Code Annotated, Section 68-14-303, is amended by deleting the section in its entirety and substituting instead the following language:

68-14-303. The commissioner is authorized to:

(1) Carry out or cause to be carried out this part;

(2) Collect all fees established in this part and apply the fees in accordance with the procedures of the department of finance and administration to the necessary and incidental costs of administration of this part. Nothing in this subdivision (2) shall be construed to prohibit the department from receiving by way of general appropriation such sums as may be required to fund adequately the implementation of this part, as recommended in the annual budget by the governor to the general assembly;

(3) Prescribe rules and regulations governing the alteration, construction, sanitation, safety and operation of hotels, and public swimming pools, as may be necessary to protect the health and safety of the public, and enforce compliance with these rules and regulations by every hotel and public swimming pool, and grant variances and waivers for public swimming pools from the requirements of this part or applicable rules and regulations; provided, that such variance or waiver shall not constitute a health or safety hazard as determined by the commissioner. The commissioner shall not prescribe any such rules and regulations that are in conflict with the minimum statewide building construction standards established by the state fire marshal pursuant to § 68-120-101;

(4) Inspect or cause to be inspected at least once every six (6) months, and as often as the commissioner may deem necessary, every hotel in the state, and inspect or cause to be inspected at least once per month, and as often as the commissioner deems necessary, every public swimming pool in the state to determine compliance with this part and with rules and regulations;

(5) Issue or cause to be issued, suspend and revoke permits to operate hotels, and public swimming pools as provided in this part;

(6) Notify the owner, proprietor, or agent in charge of any hotel, or public swimming pool of such changes or alterations as may be necessary to effect compliance with this part and with rules and regulations governing the construction, alteration, and operation of the facilities, and close the facilities for failure to comply within specified times as provided in this part and in rules and regulations;

(7) Enter into an agreement or contract with county health departments whereby the departments would implement this part or its equivalent in their respective areas of jurisdiction, if the commissioner deems it to be appropriate; provided, that the following conditions shall apply:

(A) State reporting requirements shall be met by the county health department or departments;

(B) The county health department program standards shall be at least as stringent as those of state law and of rules and regulations;

(C) The commissioner shall retain the right to exercise oversight and evaluation of performance of the county health department or departments and terminate the agreement or contract for cause immediately or otherwise upon reasonable notice;

(D) The commissioner may set such other fiscal, administrative, or program requirements as the commissioner deems necessary to maintain consistency and integrity of the statewide program;

(E) Staffing and resources shall be adequate to implement and enforce the program in the local jurisdiction;

(F) All permit fees, fines, and penalties shall be deposited directly into the state treasury;

(G) Beginning with fiscal year 2004-2005, all fees under this chapter shall be reviewed biennially to determine the appropriateness and amount relative to the overall cost of the program; and

(H)(i) Ninety-five percent (95%) of permit fees collected within a contract county pursuant to §§ 68-14-312 – 68-14-314 shall be conveyed by contract to the respective county health department to assist the county health department in implementing the program in the local jurisdiction. This amount shall be calculated based upon fees collected in the contract county during the state's fiscal year multiplied by ninety-five percent (95%);

(ii) No contract county shall charge a local permit fee. By July 30 of each year, each contract county shall provide a report to the commissioner for the preceding fiscal year documenting the total cost relative to carrying out the provisions of the contract and the amount of state and local permit fees collected. The report shall be on a form provided by the commissioner.

68-14-305 SECTION 25. Tennessee Code Annotated, Section 68-14-305, is amended by deleting the section in its entirety and substituting instead the following language:

68-14-305.

(a) No person shall operate a hotel who does not hold a valid permit issued to the person by the commissioner on or before July 1 of each year.

(b) No person shall operate a public swimming pool who does not hold a valid permit issued to the person by the commissioner on or before April 1 of each year.

(c) Every person now engaged in the business of operating a hotel, or public swimming pool, and every person who, upon the effective date of this act, shall engage in such a business, shall procure a permit from the commissioner for each hotel, or public swimming pool so operated or proposed to be operated.

(d) Each permit for hotels shall expire on June 30 next following its issuance.

(e) Each permit for public swimming pools shall expire on March 31 next following its issuance.

(f) No permit shall be transferred from one (1) location or person to another.

(g) Permits shall be posted in a conspicuous manner.

68-14-306 SECTION 26. Tennessee Code Annotated, Section 68-14-306, is amended by deleting the section in its entirety and substituting instead the following language:

68-14-306.

(a)(1) Any person planning to operate a hotel or public swimming pool shall first make written application for a permit on forms provided by the commissioner. The application shall be completed and returned to the commissioner with the proper permit fee.

(2) Prior to the approval of the application for a permit, the commissioner shall inspect the proposed facility to determine if the person applying for the permit is in compliance with the requirements of this part, and with applicable rules and regulations. The commissioner shall issue a permit to the applicant if the inspection reveals that the facility is in compliance with such requirements.

(b) Applications for renewal of permits for existing hotels will be issued to operators prior to July 1 of each year. Applications for renewal of permits for existing public swimming pools shall be issued to operators prior to April 1 of each year. When completed applications and the proper permit fees are returned to the commission, the commissioner shall issue new permits to applicants.

68-14-307 SECTION 27. Tennessee Code Annotated, Section 68-14-307, is amended by deleting the section in its entirety and substituting instead the following language:

68-14-307.

(a) The commissioner has the authority to suspend any permit to operate a hotel or public swimming pool issued pursuant to this part, if the commissioner has reasonable cause to believe that the permittee is not in compliance with this part; provided, that the permittee shall be given the opportunity to correct violations as provided in § 68-14-317.

(b) There shall be two (2) types of suspensions as follows:

(1) A Class 1 suspension with an opportunity for a hearing prior to the effective date of the suspension; and

(2) A Class 2 suspension to be effective immediately with an opportunity for a hearing after the effective date of the suspension.

(c) Notice of either type of suspension may be given by the inspector on the inspector's regular inspection form or by written notification from the commissioner. When a permit suspension is effective, all operations shall cease. Such suspensions may only be made if an imminent health hazard exists.

(d) A written request for a hearing on either type of suspension shall be filed by the permittee within ten (10) days of the receipt of notice. This ten-day period may run concurrently with the ten-day period set forth in § 68-14-317(b). If a hearing is requested, it shall commence within a reasonable time of the request. If no request for a hearing is made within ten (10) days of the receipt of notice, the suspension becomes final and is not subject to review.

(e) The commissioner may end the suspension at any time if reasons for the suspension no longer exist.

68-14-311 SECTION 28. Tennessee Code Annotated, Section 68-14-311, is amended by deleting the section in its entirety and substituting instead the following language:

68-14-311. Whenever revocation of a permit becomes final, upon demonstration that the conditions which led to the revocation have been cured, the holder of the revoked permit may make written application for a new permit.

68-14-313 SECTION 29. Tennessee Code Annotated, Section 68-14-313, is amended by deleting the section in its entirety and substituting instead the following language:

68-14-313.

(a)(1) The permit fee to operate a public swimming pool shall be three hundred forty dollars ($340).

(2) If the permit fee is delinquent for more than thirty (30) calendar days, a penalty of one half (1/2) the permit fee shall be assessed in addition to

the permit fee. If a check is returned for any reason, a penalty of one half (1/2) the permit fee shall be assessed in addition to the permit fee. The permit fee, plus any penalty, shall be paid to the commissioner before the permit is issued.

(b) The permit shall be kept and displayed in a conspicuous manner, properly framed, at the pool for which it was issued. The permit fee shall not be collected by the commissioner if the permit is not issued in the calendar year in which the swimming pool is operated.

68-14-314 SECTION 30. Tennessee Code Annotated, Section 68-14-314, is amended by deleting the section in its entirety and substituting instead the following language:

68-14-314. Institutions and organizations that have received a determination of exemption from the internal revenue service under 26 U.S.C. § 501(c)(19), of the Internal Revenue Code, and that are currently operating under such exemption shall be exempt from the payment of the permit fees required for a public swimming pool. The exemption is expressly limited to the payment of fees and does not exempt these organizations from any other provisions of this part.

68-14-315 SECTION 31. Tennessee Code Annotated, Section 68-14-315, is amended by deleting the section in its entirety and substituting instead the following language:

68-14-315.

(a) When application is made for a permit to operate any hotel after January 1 of any year, the fee charged for the permit shall be one half (1/2) the annual rate.

(b) When application is made for a permit to operate any public swimming pool after October 1 of any year, the fee charged for the permit shall be one half (1/2) the annual rate.

(c) When the hotel was subject to permit requirements prior to January 1 of any year, or where the public swimming pool was subject to permit requirements prior to April 1 of any year, no such fractional rate shall be allowed.

68-14-316 SECTION 32. Tennessee Code Annotated, Section 68-14-316, is amended by deleting the section in its entirety and substituting instead the following language:

68-14-316.

(a) Inspection results for hotels and swimming pools shall be recorded on standard departmental forms that summarize the requirements of the law and of rules and regulations.

(b)(1) The scoring system for inspections shall include a weighted point value for each requirement in which critical requirements are assigned values of four (4) and five (5) points, with less critical items having assigned values of one (1) and two (2) points.

(2) The rating score of the facilities shall be the total of the weighted point values for all violations subtracted from one hundred (100).

(c) A copy of the completed inspection report shall be furnished to the person in charge of the facility at the conclusion of the inspection.

68-14-317 SECTION 33. Tennessee Code Annotated, Section 68-14-317, is amended by deleting the section in its entirety and substituting instead the following language:

68-14-317.

(a)(1) The completed inspection report shall specify a reasonable period of time for correction of violations found.

(2) If, after the first reinspection, the item or items noted in violation remain in violation, according to the inspection report, the department shall provide for the supervisor of the employee making the prior inspections to accompany the employee for the second and any subsequent reinspections required for the same continuing item or items in violation.

(3) The correction of violations shall be accomplished within the time periods specified below:

(A) If an imminent health hazard exists, sewage back-up into the facility, or contaminated water supply, the facility shall immediately cease operations until authorized to reopen by the commissioner;

(B) All violations of critical items shall be corrected as soon as possible and in any event within ten (10) days following inspection. A follow-up inspection may be made for confirmation;

(C) All other items shall be corrected as soon as possible, but no later than the time of the next routine inspection;

(D) When the overall rating score of any facility is less than seventy (70) on forms prepared pursuant to § 68-14-316, the facility shall initiate corrective action on all identified violations within forty-eight (48) hours. One (1) or more inspections shall be conducted at reasonable intervals to assure correction.

(b) The inspection report shall state that failure to comply with any time limits specified by the commissioner for correction may result in cessation of operations. An opportunity for a hearing on the ordered corrective action shall be provided if a written request is filed with the commissioner within ten (10) days following cessation of operations. If a request for a hearing is received, a hearing shall be held within a reasonable time after receipt of the request.

(c) Whenever a facility is required under this section to cease operations, it shall not resume operations until it is shown on reinspection that conditions responsible for the order to cease operations no longer exist. Opportunity for reinspection shall be offered within a reasonable time.

68-14-318 SECTION 34. Tennessee Code Annotated, Section 68-14-318, is amended by deleting the section in its entirety and substituting instead the following language:

68-14-318. Whenever a hotel or swimming pool is constructed or extensively remodeled, or whenever an existing structure is converted to use as a hotel, plans and specifications shall be submitted to the commissioner for review and approval before construction, remodeling, or conversion is begun. The plans and specifications shall indicate the proposed layout, arrangement, mechanical plans, construction materials and work areas, and the type and model of proposed fixed equipment and facilities. The commissioner shall approve the plans and specifications, if they meet the requirements of this part and rules and regulations. No hotel or swimming pool shall be constructed, extensively remodeled, or converted except in accordance with plans and specifications approved by the commissioner.

68-14-319 SECTION 35. Tennessee Code Annotated, Section 68-14-319, is amended by deleting the section in its entirety and substituting instead the following language:

08-14-319. When the commissioner has reasonable cause to suspect possible disease transmission by an employee of the facility, the commissioner may obtain information about any recent illness of the employee or make other investigations as may be indicated. The commissioner may require any of the following:

(1) The immediate exclusion of the employee from employment in the hotel or public pool;

(2) The immediate closing of the facility until, in the commissioner's opinion, no further danger of disease outbreak exists;

(3) Restricting the employee's service to some area of the facility where there would be little likelihood of transmitting disease; or

(4) Adequate medical and laboratory examinations of the employee and of other employees.

68-14-320 SECTION 36. Tennessee Code Annotated, Section 68-14-320, is amended by deleting the section in its entirety and substituting instead the following language:

68-14-320. Any person operating a hotel or public swimming pool who fails or refuses to comply with any provision of this part or with rules and regulations, obstructs or hinders the regulatory authority in the discharge of the regulatory authority's duties, or otherwise operates a hotel or swimming pool in violation of this part or of rules and regulations commits a Class C misdemeanor. Each day of operation after notice of non-compliance of violation has been given and such violation has not been corrected constitutes a separate offense.

68-14-321 SECTION 37. Tennessee Code Annotated, Section 68-14-321, is amended by deleting the section in its entirety and substituting instead the following language:

68-14-321. When the commissioner has reason to believe that a person is causing, is about to cause, or has caused a violation of this part or of the rules and regulations promulgated under this part, the commissioner may initiate proceedings in either the chancery court of Davidson County or the chancery court of the county where the violation is occurring for injunctive relief to prevent the continuance of the violation or to correct the conditions resulting in, or about to result in, the violation.

68-14-322 SECTION 38. Tennessee Code Annotated, Section 68-14-322, is amended by deleting the section in its entirety and substituting instead the following language:

68-14-322. This part shall not apply to privately owned swimming facilities that are constructed upon private property by a group of not more than twenty (20) households.

68-14-323 SECTION 39. Tennessee Code Annotated, Section 68-14-323, is amended by deleting the section in its entirety and substituting instead the following language:

68-14-323. The commissioner may grant waivers from rules and regulations governing public swimming pools in excess of fifty thousand square feet (50,000 sq. ft.), or may promulgate additional rules and regulations governing such pools. Waivers or regulations shall be designed to protect the health, safety, and welfare of patrons when adequate standards do not exist to provide sufficient guidance regarding preventive maintenance, pool structure, operating systems, water turnover, circulatory systems, or innovative designs due to the size of the public swimming pools or due to the source of water supply for such pools.

68-14-324 SECTION 40. Tennessee Code Annotated, Section 68-14-324, is amended by deleting the section in its entirety.

68-14-325 SECTION 41. Tennessee Code Annotated, Section 68-14-325, is amended by deleting the section in its entirety.

68-14-326 SECTION 42. Tennessee Code Annotated, Section 68-14-326, is amended by deleting the section in its entirety.

68-14-701 SECTION 43. Tennessee Code Annotated, Section 68-14-701, is amended by deleting the section in its entirety and by substituting instead the following new language:

68-14-701. This part shall be known and may be cited as the Tennessee Food Safety Act.

68-14-702 SECTION 44. Tennessee Code Annotated, Section 68-14-702, is amended by deleting the section in its entirety and substituting instead the following:

68-14-702. It is the purpose of this part to ensure that foods served for public consumption in Tennessee are safe as prepared, served and delivered.

68-14-703 SECTION 45. Tennessee Code Annotated, Section 68-14-703, is amended by deleting the section in its entirety and substituting instead the following:

68-14-703. As used in this part:

(1) "Alteration" shall be defined by rule, but shall not mean function replacement that equals or makes better the existing operation of the facility;

(2) "Auxiliary food service operation" means a designated area located within or adjacent to a food service establishment sharing common ownership or management, and whose primary purpose is serving beverages. For determining the amount of the permit fee for the food service establishment associated with the auxiliary food service operation, all seating in the auxiliary food service operation shall be included in the seating count of the primary food service establishment;

(3) "Commissioner" means the commissioner of health, the commissioner's duly authorized representative, and in the event of the commissioner's absence or vacancy in the office of commissioner, the deputy commissioner;

(4) "Department" means the department of health;

(5) "Demonstration of knowledge" means the ability to demonstrate knowledge of food safety principles as applicable to establishments regulated in accordance with this part. For the purposes of this part, "demonstration of knowledge" may be accomplished by one (1) or more of the following means:

(A) Completing an inspection that reflects no priority item violation;

(B) Employing at least one (1) person certified as a food protection manager who has shown proficiency of food protection information through passing a test that is part of a certification program evaluated and listed by an accrediting agency recognized by the Conference for Food Protection as conforming to the Conference for Food Protection Standards for Accreditation of Food Protection Manager Certification Programs; or

(C) Responding correctly to food protection questions related to the specific food operation. A person responding to the questions may be aided by the utilization of food safety procedures posted prominently for employees who may use the procedures as reference guides. The commissioner shall assist establishments that request information relative to risks associated to their specific food operation, which may be posed as questions during the inspection.

(6) "Employee" means a person:

(A) In charge of a food establishment;

(B) Engaged in the preparation of food or drink;

(C) Engaged in service of food to the establishment's guests or clientele; or

(D) Engaged in ware washing;

(7) "Extensive remodeling" means the repair, construction, alteration or installation of new equipment, modification of existing equipment or fixtures, changes in floor plan layout, addition of new processes, expansion to new space, or significant changes to use of space or equipment.

(8) "Food Code" means the 2009 Food Code as published by the U.S. Department of Health and Human Services, Public Health Service, Food and Drug Administration.

(9)(A) "Food service establishment" means any establishment, place or location, whether permanent, temporary, seasonal or itinerant, other than retail food stores, where food is prepared and the public is offered to be served or is served food, including, but not limited to, foods, vegetables, or beverages not in an original package or container, food and beverages dispensed at soda fountains and delicatessens, sliced watermelon, ice balls, or water mixtures;

(B) "Food service establishment" includes places identified above in (A) regardless of whether there is a charge for the food;

(C) "Food service establishment" does not include private homes where food is prepared or served and not offered for sale, retail food store operations, food service establishments located within a retail food store, the location of vending machines, and supply vehicles;

(D) "Food service establishment" does not include churches, temples, synagogues or other religious institutions, civic, fraternal, or veteran's organizations where food is prepared, served, transported, or stored by volunteer personnel only on non-consecutive days. However, the storage of unopened, commercially canned food, packaged bulk food that is not potentially hazardous, and dry goods shall not apply for these purposes;

(E) "Food service establishment" does not include grocery stores that may, incidentally, make infrequent casual sales of uncooked foods for consumption on the premises, or any establishment whose primary business is other than food service, that may, incidentally, make infrequent casual sales of coffee or prepackaged foods, or both, for consumption on the premises. For the purposes of this subdivision, "infrequent casual sales" means sales not in excess of one hundred fifty dollars ($150) per day on any particular day;

(F) "Food service establishment" does not include a location from which casual, occasional food sales are conducted solely in connection with youth-related amateur athletic or recreational activities or primary or secondary school-related clubs by volunteer personnel and that are in operation for twenty-four (24) consecutive hours or less;

(G) "Food service establishment" does not include a catering business that employs no regular, full-time employees, the food preparation for such business is solely performed within the confines of the principal residence of the proprietor, and the catering business makes only "occasional sales" during any thirty-day period; and

(H) "Food service establishment" does not include a house or other residential structure where seriously ill or injured children and their families are provided temporary accommodations in proximity to their treatment hospitals and where food is prepared, served, transported or stored by volunteer personnel; provided, that the house or structure is supported by a § 501(c)(3) organization, as defined in 26 U.S.C. § 501(c)(3), that has as a component of its mission the support of programs that directly improve the health and well-being of children;

(10) "Imminent health hazard" means any condition, deficiency, or practice that, if not corrected, is very likely to result in illness, injury, or loss of life to any person;

(11) "Person" means any individual, partnership, firm, corporation, agency, municipality, state or political subdivision, or the federal government and its agencies and departments;

(12) "Person in charge" means an individual present at a food service establishment who is responsible for the operation at the time of inspection. A person in charge shall be present at the establishment during food preparation and handling, and may put instructions in place for cleaning or preparing the establishment prior to the preparation of any food or beverage;

(13) "Quick fast food establishment" means those food establishments that only prepare food to be eaten off premises and that provide delivery services for such food but provide no set up, serving, or clean-up services; and

(14) "Temporary food service establishment" means a food service establishment that operates at a fixed location for a period of time of not more than fourteen (14) consecutive days.

68-14-704 SECTION 46. Tennessee Code Annotated, Section 68-14-704, is amended by deleting the section in its entirety and by substituting instead the following new language:

68-14-704. The commissioner is authorized to:

(1) Carry out or cause to be carried out all provisions of this part;

(2) Collect all fees established pursuant to this part and apply the fees in accordance with the procedures of the department of finance and administration to the necessary and incidental costs of the administration of this part. Nothing in this subdivision (2) shall be construed to prohibit the department from receiving by way of general appropriation such sums as may be required to fund adequately the implementation of this part, as recommended in the annual budget by the governor to the general assembly;

(3) Prescribe rules and regulations, including emergency rules, governing the alteration, construction, sanitation, safety of food and operation of food service establishments as may be necessary to protect the health and safety of the public, and require food service establishments to comply with these rules and regulations. A

non-elected body of any municipality, county, or metropolitan government shall not enact any ordinance or issue any rule or regulation pertaining to food safety or the provision of nutritional information related to food or drink, or otherwise regulate menus at food service establishments. If, upon the effective date of this act, the federal government takes action regarding the provision of food nutritional information at food service establishments, and the federal action specifically authorizes state agencies to enforce such action, then the department of health shall be the department that is primarily responsible for the implementation and supervision of any new requirements and shall have the authority to promulgate rules and regulations, pursuant to the Uniform Administrative Procedures Act, compiled in title 4, chapter 5, as are necessary to effectuate the purposes of such requirements. The rules and regulations prohibiting live animals in the presence of dining facilities shall be waived if an adequately engineered forced air exhaust system is installed for the permitted facility. The rules and regulations requiring that food be obtained from sources that comply with all laws relating to food and food labeling shall be waived for churches, temples, synagogues and other religious institutions, civic, fraternal or veterans' organizations, if the food is served only to the homeless and the food is prepared in a church, temple, synagogue or other religious institution, civic, fraternal, or veterans' organization or in a private home or homes by persons who have successfully completed a training course of at least two (2) hours, conducted by the department, and the consumer is informed by a clearly visible placard, readily understandable to the average person, stating that the food may have been prepared in a facility that is not subject to regulation or inspection by the department. The commissioner shall not prescribe any such rules and regulations in conflict with the minimum statewide building construction standards established by the state fire marshal pursuant to § 68-120-101. The rules with respect to food temperature shall be specific with respect to the types of food prepared and the risks presented by those foods. Except as specifically provided herein, the commissioner may adopt, by rule and regulation, all or part of the Food Code;

(4) Inspect or cause to be inspected as often as the commissioner, in the commissioner's discretion, may deem necessary, every food service establishment in the state as authorized by this part, with the exception of those food service establishments licensed by the department of mental health, to determine compliance with this part and with rules and regulations;

(5) Issue or cause to be issued, suspend, and revoke permits to operate food service establishments as provided in this part;

(6) Notify the owner, proprietor, or agent of any food service establishment of such changes or alterations as may be necessary to effect complete compliance with this part and with rules and regulations governing the construction, alteration, and operation of the facilities, and close the facilities for failure to comply within specified times as provided in this part and rules and regulations;

(7) Enter into agreements or contracts with county health departments for the departments to implement this part or its equivalent in their areas of jurisdiction, if the commissioner deems it to be appropriate; provided, that the following conditions shall apply:

(A) State reporting requirements shall be met by the county health department or departments;

(B) The county health department program standards shall be identical to those of the state law and to rules and regulations;

(C) The commissioner shall retain the right to exercise oversight and evaluation of performance of the county health department or departments and terminate the agreement or contract for cause immediately or otherwise upon reasonable notice;

(D) The commissioner may set such other fiscal, administrative, or program requirements as the commissioner deems necessary to maintain consistency and integrity of the statewide program;

(E) Staffing and resources shall be adequate to implement and enforce the program in the local jurisdiction; and

(F) Contract county health departments that collect the applicable permit fees from food establishments located within the county shall retain one hundred percent (100%) of the permit fees and penalty fees. Contract counties that utilize the services of the department for the collection of permit fees shall receive ninety-five percent (95%) of permit fees collected within a contract county pursuant to §§ 68-14-705 through 68-14-707. This amount shall be calculated based upon fees collected in the contract county during the state's fiscal year multiplied by ninety-five percent (95%).

(8)(A) Upon the application of a food service establishment for a variance based on a showing of good cause and an affirmative demonstration that the risks to the public attendant to the limited activities have been mitigated, the commissioner shall grant the establishment a variance from the limitations in the Food Code regarding restrictions pertaining to bare hand contact. A request for a variance shall be granted or denied within sixty (60) days of the commissioner's receipt of the application for variance. A request for a variance shall include the following information:

(i) A listing of the specific ready-to-eat foods that are touched by bare hands;

(ii) Diagrams and other information showing that hand washing facilities are located and equipped as prescribed by the applicable provisions of the Food Code;

(iii) An employee health policy documenting that the food service establishment complies with:

(a) The person in charge requirements; and

(b) Requirements for monitoring the health of food service employees;

(iv) Documentation that food service employees have received training on the:

(a) Risks of contacting ready-to-eat foods with bare hands;

(b) Proper hand washing;

(c) Proper fingernail maintenance;

(d) Prohibition on jewelry;

(e) Good hygienic practices; and

(B) Documentation that food employees contacting ready-to-eat foods with bare hands used two (2) or more of the following control measures:

(i) Double hand washing;

(ii) Nail brushes;

(iii) A hand antiseptic after hand washing;

(iv) Incentive programs that assist or encourage food service employees not to work when they are ill; or

(v) Other control measures approved by the commissioner; and

(C) Notwithstanding any provision of the Food Code to the contrary, the commissioner shall not require any further documentation for the granting of a variance other than those contained in this section.

68-14-705 SECTION 47. Tennessee Code Annotated, Section 68-14-705, is amended by deleting the section in its entirety and by substituting instead the following new language:

68-14-705. All monies coming into the state treasury pursuant to this part from fees, fines, and penalties shall be appropriated to the department of health for the payment of necessary expenses incident to the administration of this part, as determined by the commissioner. Any unexpended balance of the fund in any fiscal year shall be retained by the department to be used to provide or expand training for food service operators and the department's environmentalists.

68-14-706– 68-14-726 SECTION 48. Tennessee Code Annotated, is amended by adding the following language as new sections:

68-14-706.

(a) No person shall operate a food service establishment who does not hold a valid permit issued to the person by the commissioner on or before July 1 of each year or as the commissioner may otherwise provide by rule and regulation.

(b) Every person now engaged in the business of operating a food service establishment, and every person who, upon the effective date of this act engages in such a business, shall procure a permit from the commissioner for each food service establishment so operated or proposed to be operated.

(c) Each permit for food service establishments shall expire on June 30 next following its issuance or as the commissioner may otherwise provide by rule.

(d) No permit shall be transferred from one location or person to another.

(e) The permit shall be kept and displayed in a conspicuous manner and visible to the public in the food service establishment for which it is issued.

68-14-707.

(a)(1) Any person planning to operate a food service establishment shall first submit an application for a permit on forms provided by the commissioner. The application shall be completed and submitted to the commissioner with the proper permit fee.

(2) Prior to the approval of the application for a permit, the commissioner shall inspect the proposed facility to determine if the person applying for the permit is in compliance with the requirements of this part and with applicable rules and regulations. The commissioner shall issue a permit to the applicant if the inspection reveals that the facility is in compliance with such requirements.

(b) Applications for renewal of permits for existing food service establishments will be issued to the operators prior to July 1 of each year or as the commissioner may provide by rule. When completed applications and the proper permit fees are returned to the commissioner, the commissioner shall issue new permits to applicants.

68-14-708.

(a) The commissioner has the authority to suspend any permit to operate a food service establishment issued pursuant to this part if the commissioner has reasonable cause to believe that the permittee is not in compliance with this part; provided, that the permittee shall be given the opportunity to correct violations as provided in § 68-14-709.

(b) Suspension of permits, other than those for temporary food service establishments shall be of two (2) types:

(1) A Class 1 suspension, which provides an opportunity for a hearing prior to the effective date of the suspension; and

(2) A Class 2 suspension, which provides an opportunity for a hearing after the effective date of the suspension, and is effective immediately.

(c) Notice of either type of suspension may be given by the inspector on the inspector's regular inspection form or by written notification from the commissioner. When a permit suspension is effective, all operations shall cease. Class 2 suspensions shall only be issued if an imminent health hazard exists.

(d) A written request for a hearing on either type of suspension shall be filed by the permittee within ten (10) days of the receipt of notice. This ten-day period may run concurrently with the ten-day period set forth in § 68-14-709. If a hearing is requested, it shall be commenced within a reasonable time of the request. If no request for a hearing is made within ten (10) days of the receipt of notice, the suspension becomes final and is not subject to review.

(e) The commissioner may end the suspension at any time if reasons for suspension no longer exist.

68-14-709.

(a) The commissioner may, after providing opportunity for a hearing, revoke a permit for serious or repeated violations of requirements of this part or for interference with the commissioner in the performance of the commissioner's duty.

(b) Prior to revocation, the commissioner shall notify, in writing, the permittee of the specific reason or reasons for which the permit is to be revoked, and that the permit shall be revoked at the end of ten (10) days following service of such notice, unless a written request for a hearing is filed with the commissioner within the ten-day period. If no request for hearing is filed within the ten-day period, the revocation of the permit becomes final.

68-14-710. A notice provided for in this part is properly served when it is delivered to the permittee or person in charge, or when it is sent by certified mail, return receipt requested, to the last known address of the permittee. A copy of the notice shall be filed in the records of the commissioner.

68-14-711.

(a) The hearings provided for in this part shall be conducted by the commissioner in accordance with the Uniform Administrative Procedures Act, compiled in title 4, chapter 5.

(b) Appeals from any final decision after a hearing shall be pursued in accordance with the Uniform Administrative Procedures Act, compiled in title 4, chapter 5, part 3.

(c) Subsections (a) and (b) shall not apply in a county in which the health department is operating a program pursuant to § 68-14-704(7) that meets the minimum requirements of due process; provided, that appeals from final decisions made under such programs may be made to the commissioner, for the limited purpose of determining whether a material error of law was made at the county level. Such appeal to the commissioner shall not be de novo, but shall be limited to a review of the record of the hearing at the county level.

68-14-712. Whenever the revocation of a permit becomes final, upon demonstration that the conditions that led to the revocation have been cured, the holder of the revoked permit may make written application for a new permit.

68-14-713.

(a)(1) The permit fee to operate a food service establishment shall be in accordance with the following schedule:

No. of Seats	Fee Amount
0-50	$210
51 or more seats	$360

(2) Auxiliary food service operations shall pay a permit fee of one hundred dollars ($100);

(3) Temporary food service establishments shall pay a permit fee of thirty dollars ($30.00);

(4) Child care center food service establishments and congregate meal sites funded through the commission on aging and disability that are food service establishments shall pay according to the following schedule:

No. of Seats	Fee Amount

0-50	$50.00
51 or more seats	$80.00

(5) School food services establishments shall pay a permit fee of eighty dollars ($80.00).

(b) This section shall not apply to family child care homes, as defined in § 71-3-501.

(c) If the permit fee is delinquent for more than thirty (30) calendar days, a penalty fee of one half (1/2) the permit fee shall be assessed, in addition to the permit fee. If a check is returned for any reason, a penalty fee of one half (1/2) the permit fee shall be assessed in addition to the permit fee. The permit fee, plus any penalty, shall be paid before the permit is issued.

(d) When an institution operates several group homes within close proximity to each other, the permit fee established in this section shall be assessed only against the institution and not against each individual group home.

(e) This section shall not apply to a blind vendor subject to § 71-4-501.

68-14-714.

(a) Churches, schools, civic, fraternal or veterans' organizations serving food are exempt from the payment of food service establishment permit fees; provided, that food is served on no more than fifty-two (52) separate days in one (1) fiscal year. The exemption is expressly limited to the payment of fees and shall not exempt these organizations from any other provisions of this part.

(b) In addition to the exemption established in subsection (a), churches involved in the sale of food at a four-day, multi-regional event sponsored by a local chamber of commerce, whose primary purpose is to generate economic interest in the regions, shall further be exempt from the payment of food service establishment permit fees for the event.

(c) A bona fide charitable or nonprofit organization that operates a food bank and an on-site feeding program for the free distribution of food to combat poverty and hunger shall be exempt from the payment of food service establishment permit fees.

(d) When application is made for a permit to operate any food service establishment after January 1 of any year, or such other date as the commissioner may establish by rule and regulation, the fee charged for the permit shall be one half (1/2) the annual rate; however, where the establishment was subject to permit requirements prior to January 1 or such other date as the commissioner may establish by rule and regulation, of any year, no such fractional rate shall be allowed.

68-14-715.

(a) Inspection results for food service establishments shall be recorded on standard departmental forms that summarize the requirements of the law and rules and regulations.

(b) A copy of the completed inspection report shall be furnished in a manner prescribed by the commissioner to the person in charge of the facility at the conclusion of the inspection.

(c) The most current inspection report furnished to the operator or person in charge of the establishment shall be posted in a conspicuous manner. If any violation noted on the report is required to be corrected within ten (10) days of the issuance of the report and the department determines that the violation has been corrected within the period of time, then a final report without notation of the violation shall be furnished to the operator or person in charge of the food service establishment and the report shall be posted in lieu of the original report.

68-14-716.

(a) The completed inspection report shall specify a reasonable period of time for correction of violations found.

(b) Corrections of violations shall be accomplished within the following periods:

(1) If an imminent health hazard exists, the facility shall immediately cease operations until authorized to reopen by the commissioner;

(2) All violations of priority items shall be corrected as soon as possible and in any event within ten (10) days following inspection. A follow-up inspection may be made for confirmation;

(3) All other items should be corrected as soon as possible, but in any event by the time of the next routine inspection; and

(4) In the case of temporary food service establishments, all violations shall be corrected within twenty-four (24) hours. If violations are not corrected within twenty-four (24) hours, the establishment shall immediately cease food service operations until authorized to resume by the commissioner.

(c) The inspection report shall state that failure to comply with any time limits specified by the commissioner for correction may result in cessation of operations. An opportunity for a hearing on the ordered corrective action shall be provided if a written request is filed with the commissioner within ten (10) days following cessation of operations. If a request for a hearing is received, a hearing shall be held within a reasonable time after receipt of the request.

(d) Whenever a facility is required under this section to cease operations, it shall not resume operations until it is shown on reinspection that conditions responsible for the order to cease operations no longer exist. Opportunity for reinspection shall be offered within a reasonable time.

68-14-717. Food may be examined or sampled by the commissioner as deemed necessary for the enforcement of this part. The commissioner may place a hold order on any food that the commissioner believes is in violation of this part or of rules and regulations, upon written notice to the operator specifying particular reasons for the hold order. The commissioner shall tag, label, or otherwise identify any food subject to a hold order. No food subject to a hold order shall be used, served, sold, or moved from the establishment. The hold order may state that the food be held while confirmation is obtained that the condition violates this part or rules or regulations. The hold order may also order the operator to destroy food that violates this part or rules or regulations. The commissioner shall permit storage of the food under the conditions specified in the hold order, unless storage is not possible without risk to the health of the public, in which case immediate destruction shall be ordered and accomplished. The hold order shall state that a request for a hearing may be filed within ten (10) days. If a request for a hearing is received, the hearing shall be held within a reasonable time after receipt of the request. On the basis of evidence produced at the hearing, the hold order may be rescinded, or the owner or person in charge may be directed by written order to denature or destroy such food or to bring it into compliance with this part.

68-14-718. Whenever a food service establishment is constructed or extensively remodeled, and whenever an existing structure is converted to use as a food service establishment, plans and specifications shall be submitted to the commissioner for review and approval before construction, remodeling, or conversion is begun. The plans and specifications shall indicate the proposed layout, arrangement, mechanical plans, and construction materials and work areas, and the type and model of proposed fixed equipment and facilities. The commissioner shall approve the plans and specifications if they meet the requirements of this part and of rules and regulations. No food service establishment shall be constructed, extensively remodeled, or converted, except in accordance with plans and specifications approved by the commissioner. Any deviation from the submitted plans and specifications previously approved by the commissioner discovered during an inspection that would not compromise the safety of food products shall not delay the issuance of a permit to operate a food service establishment.

68-14-719.

(a) When the commissioner has reasonable cause to suspect possible disease transmission by an employee of the facility, the commissioner may obtain information about any recent illness of the employee or make other investigations as may be indicated. The commissioner may require any of the following:

(1) The immediate exclusion of the employee from employment in the food service establishment;

(2) The immediate closing of the facility until, in the commissioner's opinion, no further danger of disease outbreak exists;

(3) Restricting the employee's service to some area of the facility where there would be little likelihood of transmitting disease; or

(4) Adequate medical and laboratory examinations of the employee and of other employees.

(b) A person in charge, having been provided by the employee with written documentation from a person who practices in a medical profession in accordance with title 63 that the employee has been diagnosed with a condition set forth in Chapter 2, § 2-201.11(B)(2) of the Food Code shall have an affirmative duty to notify the commissioner or the commissioner's designee. A person in charge shall not be required to obtain medical records from a prospective employee prior to hiring such individual as an employee.

68-14-720. Any person operating a food service establishment who fails or refuses to comply with any of this part or with rules and regulations, obstructs or hinders the regulatory authority in the discharge of the regulatory authority's duties, or otherwise operates a food service establishment in violation of this part or rules and regulations commits a Class C misdemeanor. Each day of operation after notice of non-compliance of violation has been given and such violation has not been corrected constitutes a separate offense.

68-14-721. When the commissioner has reason to believe that a person is causing, is about to cause, or has caused a violation of this part or of the rules and regulations promulgated under this part, the commissioner may initiate proceedings in either the chancery court of Davidson County or the chancery court of the county where the violation is occurring, for injunctive relief to prevent the continuance of the violation or to correct the conditions resulting in, or about to result in, the violation.

68-14-722. Notwithstanding provisions of this part to the contrary, children eighteen (18) years of age or less do not need a license or permit to sell bakery goods, homemade or otherwise, soft drinks, or other similar food commodities at public events.

68-14-723.

(a) Every quick fast food establishment delivery vehicle, whether owned by the establishment or not, that is used in the delivery of prepared food shall be clearly marked with the name and logo of the quick fast food establishment.

(b) If the quick fast food establishment or one (1) of its delivery employees reasonably believes that providing delivery services to an address would expose delivery personnel to a risk of harm, the name or logo may be temporarily removed.

68-14-724. All vehicles owned by a quick fast food establishment used in the delivery of its products shall meet the requirements for proof of financial responsibility in accordance with § 55-12-102(12)(C).

68-14-725.

(a) Every quick fast food establishment shall maintain accurate and current files on each employee hired to provide delivery services that verify the employee has met the requirements of this part. Such files shall be open for inspection by the commissioner of health or the commissioner's authorized agent.

(b) A fine not to exceed two hundred fifty dollars ($250) for each violation as defined in subsection (a) shall be assessed by the commissioner or the commissioner's authorized agent after providing an opportunity for a hearing; provided, that in addition to assessing such fines, the commissioner or the commissioner's authorized agent may revoke a permit for repeated violations of the requirements of this part or for interference with the commissioner or the commissioner's agent in the performance of the official's duty.

68-14-726. The files required to be maintained in accordance with this part shall be kept by all quick fast food establishments that employ drivers or that contract with drivers or contract with companies that provide drivers for the delivery of food. If a quick fast food service establishment contracts with a company that provides drivers for the delivery of food, the company shall provide to the food service establishment proof of financial responsibility for each of the company's employees providing the driving services under the contract.

53-8-111 SECTION 49. Tennessee Code Annotated, Section 53-8-111, is amended by deleting subsections (b)-(f).

Effective date 7/1/2015 SECTION 50. For rulemaking purposes, this act shall become effective upon becoming law, the public welfare requiring it. For all other purposes, this act shall take effect July 1, 2015, the public welfare requiring it.

PUBLIC CHAPTER NO. 183

PUBLIC CHAPTER NO. 183

SENATE BILL NO. 184

By Norris, Yager

Substituted for: House Bill No. 178

By McCormick

AN ACT to amend Tennessee Code Annotated, Title 55, relative to the taxation, titling, registration, and regulation of motor vehicles.

BE IT ENACTED BY THE GENERAL ASSEMBLY OF THE STATE OF TENNESSEE:

55-4-103 SECTION 1. Tennessee Code Annotated, Section 55-4-103(b)(1), is amended by deleting the language "six (6)" in the second sentence and substituting instead the language "seven (7)".

55-4-113 SECTION 2. Tennessee Code Annotated, Section 55-4-113, is amended by deleting the language "; and" at the end of subdivision (a)(5)(B), placing a period at the end of the word "trailers" when it last appears in subdivision (a)(5)(B), and adding the following language as new subdivisions (a)(5)(B)(i), (ii), (iii), and (iv):

(i) The commissioner may, in his discretion, require an owner of a freight trailer, semi-trailer, or pole trailer registered in this state pursuant to subdivision (5)(A) above to provide written confirmation to the department as to whether or not the trailer has been destroyed, abandoned, sold, or otherwise transferred to another owner and still bears the permanent registration plate originally issued to the trailer.

(ii) If such owner provides written confirmation to the department that the trailer has been destroyed, abandoned, sold, or otherwise transferred to another owner and the trailer has not been properly registered to the new owner, the commissioner shall immediately terminate the registration and plate originally assigned to the trailer under the name of the owner of record.

(iii) If such owner fails to provide written confirmation within ninety (90) days of the date of the commissioner's request, the commissioner may, in his discretion, terminate the registration and plate originally assigned to the trailer under the name of the owner of record.

(iv) Whenever the title to a freight trailer, semi-trailer, or pole trailer registered in this state pursuant to subdivision (5)(A) above is destroyed, abandoned, sold, or otherwise transferred to another owner, the registration of the trailer shall expire. If the trailer is sold or otherwise transferred to a new owner, the new owner shall obtain a new registration of the trailer. Notwithstanding any law to the contrary, the department may issue to such new owner a new or existing registration plate bearing the same alpha-numerical characters as was affixed to such trailer at the time of transfer to the new owner.

55-4-135 SECTION 3. Tennessee Code Annotated, Section 55-4-135, is amended by deleting the language "fourteen (14)" appearing therein and substituting instead the language "thirty (30)".

55-4-202 SECTION 4. Tennessee Code Annotated, Section 55-4-202, is amended in subdivision (b)(1) by deleting the language " "national guard", and "OEM headquarters company" " and by substituting instead the language "and "national guard" ".

55-4-221 SECTION 5. Tennessee Code Annotated, Section 55-4-221, is amended by deleting the language "twenty-four (24)" from subdivision (b)(1) and by substituting instead the language "seventy-two (72)"; and is further amended by adding the following language as a new sentence at the end of subdivision (b)(1):

The dealer may further authorize the operation of the vehicle bearing such plates by any customer who is using the vehicle, without charge, while the customer's vehicle is being serviced or repaired by the dealer or by any person who is participating in a driver's education program and is operating a vehicle that was provided by the dealer to a school for use in the driver's education program.

55-4-232 SECTION 6. Tennessee Code Annotated, Section 55-4-232(b), is amended by deleting the language "shall contain an appropriate logo, legend or other design, and" in the first sentence.

PUBLIC CHAPTER NO. 183 (cont'd)

55-25-107 SECTION 7. Tennessee Code Annotated, Section 55-25-107(a), is amended by deleting from subdivision (1) the language "about any individual" and by substituting instead the language "about any person"; and is further amended by deleting from subdivision (2) the language "about any individual" and by substituting instead the language "about any person".

Effective date 7/1/2013 SECTION 8. This act shall take effect on July 1, 2013, the public welfare requiring it.

PUBLIC CHAPTER NO. 184

PUBLIC CHAPTER NO. 184

SENATE BILL NO. 187

By Norris

Substituted for: House Bill No. 181

By McCormick, Dean

AN ACT to amend Tennessee Code Annotated, Title 4, Chapter 3, Part 20, relative to the Department of Safety and Homeland Security and its statewide wireless communications system.

BE IT ENACTED BY THE GENERAL ASSEMBLY OF THE STATE OF TENNESSEE:

4-3-2018 SECTION 1. Tennessee Code Annotated, Title 4, Chapter 3, Part 20, is amended by adding the following language as a new, appropriately designated section:

(a) The department has the authority to promulgate rules and regulations regarding access to its statewide P25 Interoperable Communications System, including the authority to collect, by rules or regulations, assessments for the use and/or maintenance of the system.

(b) Any assessments collected by the department pursuant to the rules and regulations established in subsection (a) shall be expendable receipts of the department for use in maintaining the statewide P25 Interoperable Communications System.

Effective date 4/23/2013 SECTION 2. This act shall take effect upon becoming law, the public welfare requiring it.

PUBLIC CHAPTER NO. 185

PUBLIC CHAPTER NO. 185

SENATE BILL NO. 195

By Norris

Substituted for: House Bill No. 189

By McCormick, Lynn

AN ACT to amend Tennessee Code Annotated, Title 49, Chapter 7, Part 20, relative to post-secondary education authorization.

BE IT ENACTED BY THE GENERAL ASSEMBLY OF THE STATE OF TENNESSEE:

49-7-2004 SECTION 1. Tennessee Code Annotated, Section 49-7-2004(a), is amended by adding the following language as a new, appropriately designated subdivision:

(10) A nonprofit, regionally accredited educational institution:

(A) Offering online, competency-based education to adult students;

(B) Led by a chief executive or chancellor domiciled in Tennessee; and

(C) With activities and operations limited to the scope of a memorandum of understanding executed with the state of Tennessee in 2013.

49-7-2004 SECTION 2. Tennessee Code Annotated, Section 49-7-2004(b), is amended by inserting the language "or (a)(10)" between the language "(a)(6)" and "shall" in the first sentence of the subsection.

Effective date 4/23/2013 SECTION 3. This act shall take effect upon becoming a law, the public welfare requiring it.

PUBLIC CHAPTER NO. 186

PUBLIC CHAPTER NO. 186

SENATE BILL NO. 224

By Massey

Substituted for: House Bill No. 443

By Kane, Haynes, Sexton, Dunn

AN ACT to amend Tennessee Code Annotated, Title 47, Chapter 22, relative to credit cards.

BE IT ENACTED BY THE GENERAL ASSEMBLY OF THE STATE OF TENNESSEE:

47-22-301 47-22-302 SECTION 1. Tennessee Code Annotated, Title 47, Chapter 22, is amended by adding the following language as a new part:

47-22-301. As used in this part:

(1) "Account purchase transaction" means an agreement under which a commercial entity sells accounts, instruments, documents, or chattel paper to another commercial entity subject to a discount or fee, regardless of whether the commercial entity has a repurchase obligation related to the transaction;

(2) "Acquired" means the obtaining of business records, a credit card account, or an instrument evidencing an outstanding debt through an ownership transfer, including a contractual agreement, an account purchase transaction or assignment in a creditor's regularly conducted business;

(3) "Cardholder" means any person who has agreed with a card issuer to pay debts arising from card transactions, whether the card used in such transactions has been issued to the cardholder or to another person;

(4) "Credit card account" means any account that can be accessed by a credit card, including a debit card with a credit feature, whereby the cardholder may obtain loans from time to time either by credit card cash advance or by the purchase or satisfactions by the bank of obligations of the cardholder incurred pursuant to a credit card;

(5) "Creditor" means the person, business, financial institution or commercial entity that currently owns a credit card account or an instrument evidencing outstanding debt;

(6) "Custodian" means and includes an individual, agent, employee, representative, or officer of a creditor, or an individual, agent, employee, representative, or officer of a management company charged with keeping a creditor's records, or any individual familiar with the books and records of a creditor or an appropriately designated person who is an official custodian of records;

(7) "Electronic records" means that information evidenced by a record or records consisting of information stored electronically which may be produced tangibly;

(8) "Financial institution" means:

(A) A banking institution that is authorized to issue credit cards pursuant to federal or state law;

(B) A banking subsidiary owned by a bank holding company as defined in 12 U.S.C. § 1841, or by a savings and loan holding company as defined in 12 U.S.C. § 1467a(a)(1)(D); or

(C) Any other federally regulated banking institution;

PUBLIC CHAPTER NO. 186 (cont'd)

(9) "Incorporated" means to integrate into records, to make a part of records, to place within records, or to treat as records;

(10) "Issuer" means a person, business, financial institution, commercial entity or authorized agent of a financial institution that currently issues a credit card account or an instrument evidencing outstanding debt;

(11) "Original creditor" means the person, business, financial institution or commercial entity that had the original contractual agreement with a cardholder on a credit card account or an instrument evidencing outstanding debt;

(12) "Person" means an individual, corporation, business trust, estate, trust, partnership, limited liability company, association, joint venture, or any other legal entity; and

(13) "Succeeding creditor" means any creditor, not the originating creditor, succeeding to an ownership interest in a credit card account or an instrument evidencing outstanding debt by bill of sale or assignment.

47-22-302.

(a) A creditor's records shall include, but are not limited to, written or electronic records of an original creditor, issuer, or succeeding creditor that have been acquired by the creditor through a contractual agreement, an account purchase transaction or assignment in the creditor's regularly conducted business and such records are:

(1) Incorporated as a business duty into the records of the creditor's regularly maintained records; and

(2) Relied upon in the creditor's regularly conducted business activity.

(b)(1) Except as provided in subdivision (b)(2), records described in subsection (a) shall be considered records of the creditor and the creditor's records custodian may testify with respect to such records as if they are records of the creditor.

(2) The provisions of subdivision (b)(1) shall not apply if the source of information or the method or circumstances of preparation indicate the records described in subsection (a) lack trustworthiness.

(c) The records described in this section may be submitted as records of regularly conducted activity pursuant to Rule 803(6) of the Tennessee Rules of Evidence.

Effective date 7/1/2013

SECTION 2. This act shall take effect July 1, 2013, the public welfare requiring it.

PUBLIC CHAPTER NO. 187

PUBLIC CHAPTER NO. 187

SENATE BILL NO. 243

By Campfield

Substituted for: House Bill No. 548

By Curtiss

AN ACT to amend Tennessee Code Annotated, relative to garnishment.

BE IT ENACTED BY THE GENERAL ASSEMBLY OF THE STATE OF TENNESSEE:

26-2-225 SECTION 1. Tennessee Code Annotated, Title 26, Chapter 2, Part 2, is amended by adding a new section thereto, as follows:

26-2-225.

(a) A judgment debtor whose salaries, wages or other compensation are subject to a garnishment shall notify the judgment creditor who filed the writ of garnishment within ten (10) days, as computed in § 1-3-102, of obtaining any new employment. Notice to the judgment creditor shall be by certified mail and shall include the name, address and telephone number of the new employer. A judgment debtor who fails to provide notice of new employment in compliance with this section is in contempt of court and, upon the court making a determination of contempt, may be punished the same as contempt of court in a judicial proceeding. For purposes of a determination of contempt the debtor's notification of new employment to the judgment creditor shall be considered timely sent if mailed less than ten (10) days from the date of obtaining new employment.

(b) Any fees imposed by the clerk or any other party on the transfer of garnishment to the debtor's new employment shall be imposed on the debtor by adding the amount to the debt to be collected.

Effective date 7/1/2013 SECTION 2. This act shall take effect July 1, 2013, the public welfare requiring it and shall apply to all garnishments filed after such date.

PUBLIC CHAPTER NO. 188

PUBLIC CHAPTER NO. 188

SENATE BILL NO. 267

By Massey

Substituted for: House Bill No. 137

By Hall

AN ACT to amend Tennessee Code Annotated, Title 49, relative to education.

BE IT ENACTED BY THE GENERAL ASSEMBLY OF THE STATE OF TENNESSEE:

49-5-201 SECTION 1. Tennessee Code Annotated, Section 49-5-201(a)(6), is amended by deleting the following language:

(6) Give one (1) fire drill requiring full evacuation every month during the school year, with an additional fire drill to be conducted within the first thirty (30) days of operation, and three (3) additional safety drills during the school year, which may include inclement weather, earthquake, intruder or other emergency drills not requiring full evacuation;

and by substituting instead the following language:

(6) Give the following:

(A) One (1) fire drill requiring full evacuation every month during the school year, with an additional fire drill to be conducted within the first fifteen (15) days of operation;

(B) One (1) intruder drill to be conducted within the first thirty (30) days of operation; and

(C) Three (3) additional safety drills during the school year, which may include inclement weather, earthquake, intruder or other emergency drills not requiring full evacuation;

Effective date 7/1/2013 SECTION 2. This act shall take effect July 1, 2013, the public welfare requiring it.

PUBLIC CHAPTER NO. 189

PUBLIC CHAPTER NO. 189

SENATE BILL NO. 422

By Kelsey, Green, Ketron, Tate, Bowling, Harper, Yager, Ford

Substituted for: House Bill No. 999

By Sexton, Durham, McCormick, Miller, Parkinson, Todd, Fitzhugh, Casada, Odom, Ryan Williams, Haynes, Littleton, Kane, Mitchell, Curtis Johnson, Sparks, Eldridge, Dawn White, Lundberg, McManus, Farmer, Forgety, Travis, Carter

AN ACT to amend Tennessee Code Annotated, Title 57, Chapter 6, relative to the taxation of sales of beer at wholesale.

BE IT ENACTED BY THE GENERAL ASSEMBLY OF THE STATE OF TENNESSEE:

57-6-103 SECTION 1. Tennessee Code Annotated, Section 57-6-103(a), is amended by deleting the first sentence of that subsection in its entirety and substituting instead the following:

> There is hereby imposed on the sale of beer at wholesale a tax equal to thirty-five dollars and sixty cents ($35.60) per barrel of thirty-one liquid gallons (31 gals.) of beer sold. The tax upon barrels containing more or less than thirty-one gallons (31 gals.) shall be taxed at a proportionate rate.

57-6-103 SECTION 2. Tennessee Code Annotated, Section 57-6-103, is amended by deleting subsection (b) in its entirety.

57-6-103 SECTION 3. Tennessee Code Annotated, Section 57-6-103(c), is amended by inserting the language "as well as any sale or transfer contemplated by § 57-5-101(c)(2) by a manufacturer operating as a retailer to a location owned or operated by such manufacturer-retailer," between the language "business" and the language "shall".

57-6-103 SECTION 4. Tennessee Code Annotated, Section 57-6-103, is amended by deleting subsection (e) in its entirety.

57-6-103 SECTION 5. Tennessee Code Annotated, Section 57-6-103(f), is amended by deleting the subsection in its entirety and substituting instead the following:

> (f) Seventeen cents (17¢) of the gross tax owed per barrel shall be remitted at the same time to the department, to be kept in a special fund and to be used only for expenses of the department in the administration of this chapter.

57-6-103 SECTION 6. Tennessee Code Annotated, Section 57-6-103(g), is amended by deleting the subsection in its entirety and substituting instead the following:

> (g) Ninety-two cents (92¢) of the gross tax owed per barrel shall be retained by the wholesaler or manufacturer operating as a retailer to defray the cost of collecting and remitting the tax.

57-6-103 SECTION 7. Tennessee Code Annotated, Section 57-6-103(i)(1), is amended by deleting the last sentence of the subdivision and substituting instead the following:

> The tax imposed by this section shall be due to the municipality beginning with the first full calendar month after receipt of the notice required by this subsection (i) and thereafter.

Effective date 7/1/2013 SECTION 8. This act shall take effect July 1, 2013, the public welfare requiring it.

PUBLIC CHAPTER NO. 190

PUBLIC CHAPTER NO. 190

SENATE BILL NO. 424

By Crowe

Substituted for: House Bill No. 355

By Ramsey

AN ACT to amend Tennessee Code Annotated, Title 68, Chapter 24, Part 6, relative to functions that may be performed by alcohol and drug abuse counselors.

BE IT ENACTED BY THE GENERAL ASSEMBLY OF THE STATE OF TENNESSEE:

68-24-606 SECTION 1. Tennessee Code Annotated, Section 68-24-606, is amended by deleting the existing language in its entirety and substituting instead the following:

(a) The purpose of this section is to adopt nationally recognized and accepted professional practice domains for licensed alcohol and drug abuse counselors.

(b) The professional practice domains and transdisciplinary competencies in which licensed alcohol and drug abuse counselors may engage are as follows:

(1) Clinical evaluation;

(2) Treatment planning;

(3) Referral;

(4) Service coordination;

(5) Counseling;

(6) Client, family, and community education;

(7) Documentation; and

(8) Professional and ethical responsibilities.

Effective date 7/1/2013 SECTION 2. This act shall take effect on July 1, 2013, the public welfare requiring it.

PUBLIC CHAPTER NO. 191

PUBLIC CHAPTER NO. 191

SENATE BILL NO. 436

By Overbey

Substituted for: House Bill No. 263

By Roach

AN ACT to amend Tennessee Code Annotated, Title 62, relative to professions, businesses and trades.

BE IT ENACTED BY THE GENERAL ASSEMBLY OF THE STATE OF TENNESSEE:

62-32-321 SECTION 1. Tennessee Code Annotated, Section 62-32-321(e), is amended by deleting the language "twenty-five dollars ($25.00)" and substituting the language "fifty dollars ($50.00)".

Effective date 4/23/2013 SECTION 2. This act shall take effect upon becoming a law, the public welfare requiring it.

PUBLIC CHAPTER NO. 192

PUBLIC CHAPTER NO. 192

SENATE BILL NO. 440

By Overbey

Substituted for: House Bill No. 13

By Curtis Johnson

AN ACT to amend Tennessee Code Annotated, Title 55, relative to motor vehicles.

BE IT ENACTED BY THE GENERAL ASSEMBLY OF THE STATE OF TENNESSEE:

55-17-111 SECTION 1. Tennessee Code Annotated, Section 55-17-111, is amended by adding the following as a new subsection:

(h)(1) All applications for issuance or renewal of a motor vehicle dealer license shall contain an attestation that the applicant will comply with each of the following requirements:

(A) The applicant shall maintain the surety bond required by subsections (d) and (g), as applicable, in full force and effect during all times that the license is active; and

(B) The applicant shall notify the commission upon a change in ownership or location of the dealership as required by § 55-17-113.

(2) Additionally, all applications for issuance or renewal of a motor vehicle dealer license shall contain the following statement, immediately following the attestation required by subdivision (h)(1):

FAILURE TO MAINTAIN A SURETY BOND AS REQUIRED BY T.C.A. § 55-17-111, OR NOTIFY THE MOTOR VEHICLE COMMISSION OF A CHANGE IN THE OWNERSHIP OR LOCATION OF THE DEALERSHIP AS REQUIRED BY T.C.A. § 55-17-113, MAY RESULT IN THE ASSESSMENT OF A CIVIL PENALTY AND/OR SUSPENSION OR REVOCATION OF THE MOTOR VEHICLE DEALER LICENSE.

55-17-114 SECTION 2. Tennessee Code Annotated, Section 55-17-114, is amended by adding the following as a new subsection:

(e) The commission may revoke or suspend any license that the commission has issued upon finding that the licensee has not maintained any of the requirements for issuance of such license.

Effective date 7/1/2013 SECTION 3. This act shall take effect July 1, 2013, the public welfare requiring it.

PUBLIC CHAPTER NO. 193

PUBLIC CHAPTER NO. 193

SENATE BILL NO. 527

By Dickerson, Henry

Substituted for: House Bill No. 423

By Pitts, Sargent

AN ACT to amend Tennessee Code Annotated, Title 35, Chapter 9, Part 1 and Title 48, relative to administration of private foundations.

BE IT ENACTED BY THE GENERAL ASSEMBLY OF THE STATE OF TENNESSEE:

35-9-108 SECTION 1. Tennessee Code Annotated, Title 35, Chapter 9, Part 1, is amended by adding the following language as a new section:

35-9-108.

(a) For the purposes of this section, "private foundation" has the same meaning ascribed to "private foundation" in § 509(a) of the Internal Revenue Code of 1986, as amended.

(b) No private foundation shall be required by a department, agency, board, or other entity of state or local government to:

(1) Disclose the race, religion, gender, national origin, socioeconomic status, age, ethnicity, disability, marital status, or sexual orientation of:

(A) The foundation's employees, officers, directors, trustees, or contributors, without the prior written consent of the individual or individuals in question; or

(B) Any individual, or of the employees, officers, directors, trustees, members, or owners of any entity, that has received monetary or in-kind contributions or grants from, or contracted with, the foundation, without the prior written consent of the individual or individuals in question;

(2) Hire, appoint, or elect an individual of any particular race, religion, gender, national origin, socioeconomic status, age, ethnicity, disability, marital status, or sexual orientation as an employee, officer, director, or trustee of the foundation;

(3) Disqualify, remove, or prohibit service of an individual as an officer, director, or trustee of the foundation based upon such individual's familial relationship to other officers, directors, or trustees of the foundation or a contributor to the foundation;

(4) Hire, appoint, or elect an individual as an officer, director, or trustee of the foundation who does not share a familial relationship with the other officers, directors, or trustees of the foundation or with a contributor to the foundation; or

(5) Except as a lawful condition or requirement on the expenditure of particular funds imposed by the contributor or grantor of such funds, distribute the foundation's funds to, or contract with, any individual or entity based upon the:

(A) Race, religion, gender, national origin, socioeconomic status, age, ethnicity, disability, marital status, or sexual orientation of the individual or of the employees, officers, directors, trustees, members, or owners of the entity; or

(B) Populations, locales, or communities served by the individual or entity.

Effective date 4/23/2013 SECTION 2. This act shall take effect upon becoming a law, the public welfare requiring it.

PUBLIC CHAPTER NO. 194

PUBLIC CHAPTER NO. 194

SENATE BILL NO. 544

By Bell

Substituted for: House Bill No. 216

By Forgety, Hardaway

AN ACT to amend Tennessee Code Annotated, Title 39, Chapter 15 and Title 39, Chapter 17, relative to smoking.

BE IT ENACTED BY THE GENERAL ASSEMBLY OF THE STATE OF TENNESSEE:

39-17-1511 SECTION 1. Tennessee Code Annotated, Title 39, Chapter 17, Part 15, is amended by adding the following language as a new, appropriately designated section:

39-17-15__.

(a) For the purpose of this section:

(1) "Counter" means the point of purchase at a retail establishment;

(2) "Retail establishment" means a place of business open to the general public for the sale of goods or services; and

(3) "Smoking paraphernalia" means:

(i) A cigarette holder;

(ii) A smoking pipe made of metal, wood, acrylic, glass, stone, or plastic with or without screens, permanent screens, hashish heads or punctured metal bowls;

(iii) A water pipe; or

(iv) Rose and pen combinations.

(4) "Smoking paraphernalia" does not include a smoking pipe or smoking device when sold at retail, if the smoking pipe or smoking device is primarily made of briar, meerschaum, clay or corn cob.

(b) All smoking paraphernalia shall be maintained behind the counter of a retail establishment in an area inaccessible to a customer or in a locked display case that makes the products unavailable to a customer without the assistance of an employee.

(c)(1) A violation of this section is punishable as provided in § 39-17-1509.

(2) If smoking paraphernalia is sold in violation of this section by an employee, the owner or operator of the retail establishment where the employee sold the products shall be in violation of this section.

Effective date 7/1/2013 SECTION 2. This act shall take effect July 1, 2013, the public welfare requiring it.

PUBLIC CHAPTER NO. 195

PUBLIC CHAPTER NO. 195

SENATE BILL NO. 647

By Tracy, Ketron

Substituted for: House Bill No. 219

By Keisling, Mark White

AN ACT to amend Tennessee Code Annotated, Title 12, Chapter 4, Part 2, relative to bonding requirements on public works.

WHEREAS, it is within the public interest of the citizens of Tennessee to ensure that good and solvent bonds are provided by contractors entering into contracts with any city, county or state authority for public works within this state; and

WHEREAS, while Tennessee Code Annotated, § 12-4-201, requires a good and solvent bond to be provided by a contractor entering into a contract for public work with any city, county or state authority within this state, such section currently does not define "good and solvent bond"; and

WHEREAS, it is within the public interest of the citizens of Tennessee to specifically define "good and solvent bonds", and to further provide assurances of compliance with the statutory bonding requirements of this state; now, therefore,

BE IT ENACTED BY THE GENERAL ASSEMBLY OF THE STATE OF TENNESSEE:

12-4-201 SECTION 1. Tennessee Code Annotated, Section 12-4-201(a), is amended by designating the existing language as subdivision (1) and by adding the following language as new, appropriately designated subdivisions:

(2) A good and solvent bond means a bond written by a surety or insurance company listed on the United States department of the treasury financial management service list of approved bonding companies which is published annually in the federal register at the time the bond is provided in accordance with this part.

(3) No bond shall be deemed to be a good and solvent bond if it is written for an amount which is in excess of the amount indicated as approved for sureties or insurance companies by the United States department of the treasury financial management service list published at the time the bond is provided.

(4) Any surety bond written for a public work project shall be written by a surety or insurance company that is licensed and authorized to do business as a surety or insurer in this state.

(5) Any bond which is not in accordance with this section shall be null and void as against the public policy of this state and shall be rejected by the building or bidding authority.

Effective date 4/23/2013 SECTION 2. This act shall take effect upon becoming a law, the public welfare requiring it.

PUBLIC CHAPTER NO. 196

PUBLIC CHAPTER NO. 196

SENATE BILL NO. 655

By Campfield, Massey

Substituted for: House Bill No. 513

By Hall

AN ACT to amend Tennessee Code Annotated, Title 4 and Title 54, relative to transportation.

BE IT ENACTED BY THE GENERAL ASSEMBLY OF THE STATE OF TENNESSEE:

54-17-114 SECTION 1. Tennessee Code Annotated, Section 54-17-114(a)(1), is amended by deleting subdivision (I) in its entirety and by substituting instead the following language:

(I) That segment of State Route 169 (Middlebrook Road which is commonly referred to as Middlebrook Pike) in Knox County from the western boundary of the right-of-way of Whitehall Road in the City of Knoxville westward to its terminus at that route's intersection with Hardin Valley Road, but excluding any part of that segment of State Route 169 that has property fronting on the route that was zoned on April 16, 1996, with the commercial designation of CA, CB or C3, or the industrial designation of I or I-3 under the Knox County or City of Knoxville zoning ordinances;

Effective date 4/23/2013 SECTION 2. This act shall take effect upon becoming a law, the public welfare requiring it.

PUBLIC CHAPTER NO. 197

PUBLIC CHAPTER NO. 197

SENATE BILL NO. 665

By Gresham

Substituted for: House Bill No. 611

By Faison, Shipley, Towns

AN ACT to amend Tennessee Code Annotated, Title 63 and Title 68, relative to cardiopulmonary resuscitation for infants.

BE IT ENACTED BY THE GENERAL ASSEMBLY OF THE STATE OF TENNESSEE:

68-5-112 SECTION 1. Tennessee Code Annotated, Title 68, Chapter 5, Part 1, is amended by adding the following language as a new, appropriately designated section:

68-5-___.

(a) Hospitals, birthing centers, health care facilities, physicians, nurse practitioners, physician assistants or other health care practitioners who provide medical care to newborns as well as obstetricians who provide routine care for prenatal patients shall make available information and instruction concerning the appropriate use and techniques of infant cardiopulmonary resuscitation (CPR) to at least one (1) parent or caregiver of a newborn infant. Nothing in this section shall require classes in certification of infant CPR. This section shall also not constitute a requirement to be assessed during any inspection under chapter 11, part 2 of this title.

(b) Any facility or practitioner acting within the scope of their licensure or practice shall be immune from any civil liability under this section and shall have an affirmative defense to any criminal liability arising from making such information available.

Effective date 7/1/2013 SECTION 2. This act shall take effect July 1, 2013, the public welfare requiring it.

PUBLIC CHAPTER NO. 198

PUBLIC CHAPTER NO. 198

SENATE BILL NO. 769

By Bowling

Substituted for: House Bill No. 658

By Faison

AN ACT to amend Tennessee Code Annotated, Title 4, Chapter 17 and Section 13-23-403, relative to the industrial finance corporation.

BE IT ENACTED BY THE GENERAL ASSEMBLY OF THE STATE OF TENNESSEE:

13-23-403 SECTION 1. Tennessee Code Annotated, Section 13-23-403(a), is amended by deleting subdivision (5) in its entirety.

4-17-401– 4-17-415 SECTION 2. Tennessee Code Annotated, Title 4, Chapter 17, is amended by deleting Part 4 in its entirety.

Effective date 4/23/2013 SECTION 3. This act shall take effect upon becoming a law, the public welfare requiring it.

PUBLIC CHAPTER NO. 199

PUBLIC CHAPTER NO. 199

SENATE BILL NO. 770

By Hensley

Substituted for: House Bill No. 659

By Carter

AN ACT to amend Tennessee Code Annotated, Title 4, Chapter 3, relative to the state government quality improvement task force.

BE IT ENACTED BY THE GENERAL ASSEMBLY OF THE STATE OF TENNESSEE:

4-3-5301– 4-3-5305 SECTION 1. Tennessee Code Annotated, Title 4, Chapter 3, is amended by deleting Part 53 in its entirety.

Effective date 4/23/2013 SECTION 2. This act shall take effect upon becoming a law, the public welfare requiring it.

PUBLIC CHAPTER NO. 200

PUBLIC CHAPTER NO. 200

SENATE BILL NO. 771

By Massey

Substituted for: House Bill No. 660

By Travis, Sexton

AN ACT to amend Tennessee Code Annotated, Section 9-4-5614, relative to the Tennessee governmental accountability commission.

BE IT ENACTED BY THE GENERAL ASSEMBLY OF THE STATE OF TENNESSEE:

9-4-5614 SECTION 1. Tennessee Code Annotated, Section 9-4-5614, is amended by deleting such section in its entirety.

Effective date 4/23/2013 SECTION 2. This act shall take effect upon becoming a law, the public welfare requiring it.

PUBLIC CHAPTER NO. 201

PUBLIC CHAPTER NO. 201

SENATE BILL NO. 772

By Green

Substituted for: House Bill No. 661

By Van Huss, Sexton

AN ACT to amend Tennessee Code Annotated, Title 38, Chapter 13, relative to the Tennessee law enforcement advisory council.

BE IT ENACTED BY THE GENERAL ASSEMBLY OF THE STATE OF TENNESSEE:

38-13-101 – 38-13-104

SECTION 1. Tennessee Code Annotated, Title 38, is amended by deleting Chapter 13 in its entirety.

Effective date 4/23/2013

SECTION 2. This act shall take effect upon becoming a law, the public welfare requiring it.

PUBLIC CHAPTER NO. 202

PUBLIC CHAPTER NO. 202

SENATE BILL NO. 773

By Hensley

Substituted for: House Bill No. 662

By Rogers, Sexton

AN ACT to amend Tennessee Code Annotated, Section 9-4-103 and Title 13, Chapter 16, relative to the Tennessee industrial development authority.

BE IT ENACTED BY THE GENERAL ASSEMBLY OF THE STATE OF TENNESSEE:

9-4-103 SECTION 1. Tennessee Code Annotated, Section 9-4-103, is amended by deleting subdivision (3) in its entirety and by renumbering all subsequent subdivisions accordingly.

13-16-301– 13-16-306 SECTION 2. Tennessee Code Annotated, Title 13, Chapter 16, is amended by deleting Part 3 in its entirety.

Effective date 4/23/2013 SECTION 3. This act shall take effect upon becoming a law, the public welfare requiring it.

PUBLIC CHAPTER NO. 203

PUBLIC CHAPTER NO. 203

SENATE BILL NO. 775

By Haile

Substituted for: House Bill No. 664

By Littleton

AN ACT to amend Tennessee Code Annotated, Title 54, Chapter 2, relative to access improvement projects.

BE IT ENACTED BY THE GENERAL ASSEMBLY OF THE STATE OF TENNESSEE:

54-2-201–54-2-209 SECTION 1. Tennessee Code Annotated, Title 54, Chapter 2, is amended by deleting Part 2 in its entirety.

Effective date 4/23/2013 SECTION 2. This act shall take effect upon becoming a law, the public welfare requiring it.

PUBLIC CHAPTER NO. 204

PUBLIC CHAPTER NO. 204

SENATE BILL NO. 776

By Massey

Substituted for: House Bill No. 665

By Dawn White, Sexton

AN ACT to amend Tennessee Code Annotated, Title 7, Chapter 52, Part 4 and Title 7, Chapter 59, Part 3, relative to the Tennessee broadband task force.

BE IT ENACTED BY THE GENERAL ASSEMBLY OF THE STATE OF TENNESSEE:

7-52-408 SECTION 1. Tennessee Code Annotated, Section 7-52-408, is amended by deleting the section in its entirety.

7-52-409 SECTION 2. Tennessee Code Annotated, Section 7-52-409, is amended by deleting the section in its entirety.

7-52-410 SECTION 3. Tennessee Code Annotated, Section 7-52-410, is amended by deleting the section in its entirety.

7-59-311 SECTION 4. Tennessee Code Annotated, Section 7-59-311(d), is amended by deleting subdivision (2) in its entirety and by substituting instead the following new language:

> (2) It is the legislative intent that in measuring compliance with this section, the department may rely upon verification provided by Connected Tennessee, as to the expansion of access to broadband Internet service to households by a holder of a state-issued certificate of franchise authority.

7-59-315 SECTION 5. Tennessee Code Annotated, Section 7-59-315(b), is amended by deleting subdivision (1) in its entirety and by substituting instead the following new language:

> (1) Monies shall be deposited into the fund as provided by law or provisions of the General Appropriations Act. Monies in the fund shall be used by the department to promote the deployment of broadband Internet service to unserved areas of the state pursuant to guidelines developed by the department in consultation with Connected Tennessee. The guidelines shall provide for the making of grants to political subdivisions or entities of political subdivisions, cable service providers, video service providers, telecommunications companies, and similar entities as the department may determine.

Effective date 4/23/2013 SECTION 6. This act shall take effect upon becoming a law, the public welfare requiring it.

PUBLIC CHAPTER NO. 205

PUBLIC CHAPTER NO. 205

SENATE BILL NO. 831

By Green, Ketron, Finney, Bowling, Burks, Campfield, Haile, McNally, Norris, Stevens, Beavers, Tracy

Substituted for: House Bill No. 1037

By Haynes, Lamberth, Rogers, Weaver, Shipley, Hardaway, Rich, Watson, Parkinson, Faison, Lundberg, Curtis Johnson, Travis, Fitzhugh, Camper, Mark White, Shepard, Eldridge, Kane, Marsh, Doss

AN ACT to amend Tennessee Code Annotated, Title 40, Chapter 2, Part 1, relative to the commencement of prosecutions.

BE IT ENACTED BY THE GENERAL ASSEMBLY OF THE STATE OF TENNESSEE:

40-2-104 SECTION 1. Tennessee Code Annotated, Section 40-2-104, is amended by adding the following at the end of the section:

> A prosecution is also commenced, within the meaning of this chapter, by finding an indictment or presentment or the issuing of a warrant identifying the offender by a deoxyribonucleic acid (DNA) profile.

Effective date 7/1/2013 SECTION 2. This act shall take effect on July 1, 2013, the public welfare requiring it and shall apply to commencement of prosecution for any offense, regardless of when committed, except those offenses for which prosecution is barred on July 1, 2013, because the applicable time limitation set out in § 40-2-101 has expired.

PUBLIC CHAPTER NO. 206

PUBLIC CHAPTER NO. 206

SENATE BILL NO. 844

By Ketron

Substituted for: House Bill No. 706

By Carter, Todd, Dean, McCormick

AN ACT to amend Tennessee Code Annotated, Section 66-28-201, relative to fees charged by public housing projects.

BE IT ENACTED BY THE GENERAL ASSEMBLY OF THE STATE OF TENNESSEE:

66-28-201 SECTION 1. Tennessee Code Annotated, Section 66-28-201, is amended by deleting subsection (e) in its entirety.

Effective date 4/23/2013 SECTION 2. This act shall take effect upon becoming law, the public welfare requiring it, and shall apply to any rental agreement in which title 66, chapter 28 applies that does not incorporate § 66-28-201(e), as it existed prior to the effective date of this act, as a term of the rental agreement, or to any rental agreement in which title 66, chapter 28 applies that does incorporate § 66-28-201(e), as it existed prior to the effective date of this act, as a term of the rental agreement if the rental agreement was entered into on or after the effective date of this act.

PUBLIC CHAPTER NO. 207

PUBLIC CHAPTER NO. 207

SENATE BILL NO. 902

By Yager

Substituted for: House Bill No. 496

By Sanderson

AN ACT to amend Tennessee Code Annotated, Section 4-3-1104; Title 10, Chapter 7 and Section 36-1-126, relative to public records.

BE IT ENACTED BY THE GENERAL ASSEMBLY OF THE STATE OF TENNESSEE:

10-7-301 SECTION 1. Tennessee Code Annotated, Section 10-7-301(12), is amended by deleting the subdivision in its entirety and by substituting instead the following language:

(12) "Section" and "division" means the division of records management of the department of state;

10-7-302 SECTION 2. Tennessee Code Annotated, Section 10-7-302, is amended by deleting the language "general services to initiate, through the records management division" and by substituting instead the language "state to initiate, through the division of records management".

10-7-303 SECTION 3. Tennessee Code Annotated, Section 10-7-303(a), is amended by deleting the language "records management division of the department of general services" and by substituting instead the language "division of records management of the department of state".

10-7-303 SECTION 4. Tennessee Code Annotated, Section 10-7-303, is amended by inserting the following language as a new, appropriately designated subsection:

(_)(1)(A) The division is authorized to develop a protocol manual or to adopt a published protocol manual to be adopted by the executive, judicial and legislative branches of state government.

(B) The division is authorized to develop a style manual or guide or to adopt a published style manual or guide to be adopted by the executive, judicial and legislative branches of state government.

(2) A branch of state government may modify an adopted protocol manual or style guide.

10-7-304 SECTION 5. Tennessee Code Annotated, Section 10-7-304, is amended by deleting the language "records management division" and by substituting instead the language "division of records management of the department of state".

10-7-404 SECTION 6. Tennessee Code Annotated, Section 10-7-404(b), is amended by deleting the language "general services" and by substituting instead the language "state".

10-7-501 SECTION 7. Tennessee Code Annotated, Section 10-7-501, is amended by deleting the language "records management division of the department of general services" and by substituting instead the language "division of records management of the department of state".

10-7-508 SECTION 8. Tennessee Code Annotated, Section 10-7-508(a), is amended by deleting the language "director of the records management division" and by substituting instead the language "secretary of state or his designated representative".

10-7-508 SECTION 9. Tennessee Code Annotated, Section 10-7-508(b), is amended by deleting the language "director of records management" and by substituting instead the language "secretary of state" everywhere it appears.

4-3-1104 SECTION 10. Tennessee Code Annotated, Section 4-3-1104(a)(8), is amended by deleting the subdivision in its entirety.

36-1-126 SECTION 11. Tennessee Code Annotated, Section 36-1-126(c)(2), is amended by deleting the language "with the state records management unit of the department of general services, or its successor" and substituting instead the language "with the division of records management of the department of state".

PUBLIC CHAPTER NO. 207 (cont'd)

Effective date 4/23/2013

SECTION 12. This act shall take effect upon becoming a law, the public welfare requiring it.

PUBLIC CHAPTER NO. 208

PUBLIC CHAPTER NO. 208

SENATE BILL NO. 920

By Haile

Substituted for: House Bill No. 956

By Shipley, Sexton

AN ACT to amend Tennessee Code Annotated, Title 9, Chapter 4, Part 6 and Title 9, Chapter 4, Part 7, relative to investment funds.

BE IT ENACTED BY THE GENERAL ASSEMBLY OF THE STATE OF TENNESSEE:

9-4-603 SECTION 1. Tennessee Code Annotated, Section 9-4-603(c), is amended by deleting subsection (c) in its entirety and substituting it instead with the following:

(c) The state treasurer shall administer the pooled investment fund on behalf of the participants in accordance with § 9-4-602 and shall have the authority to establish accounts and different classes of shares within the fund.

9-4-603 SECTION 2. Tennessee Code Annotated, Section 9-4-603(g), is amended by deleting the second sentence in subsection (g) and substituting it instead with the following:

The state treasurer may deduct from each participant's pro rata earnings through the fund a reasonable charge for administering the fund. In the event that the state treasurer does deduct an administrative fee, it shall be deposited and expended through the revolving account.

9-4-603 SECTION 3. Tennessee Code Annotated, Section 9-4-603(h), is amended by deleting the language contained in subsection (h) in its entirety and substituting it instead with the following, and adding the following language as a new subsection (i):

(h) As the administrator of the pooled investment fund, the state treasurer is authorized to receive, invest and distribute a participant's funds by means of an electronic transfer or other reasonable methods. The state funding board may establish limits, restrictions or conditions on the acceptance of monies into the fund and the withdrawal of monies from the fund.

(i) At any time, a participant in the fund may request the return of its principal investment or investment income or both; however, a redemption of shares does not guarantee that a participant will receive the entire amount of the principal investment or investment income or both.

9-4-608 SECTION 4. Tennessee Code Annotated, Section 9-4-608(b), is amended by deleting the language contained in subsection (b) in its entirety and substituting it instead with the following:

(b) The authorized instruments for investment in the intermediate-term investment fund shall be those instruments contained in § 9-4-602, as well as the pooled investment fund set forth in § 9-4-603.

9-4-608 SECTION 5. Tennessee Code Annotated, Section 9-4-608(g), is amended by deleting the second sentence in subsection (g) and substituting it instead with the following:

(g) The state treasurer may deduct from each participant's pro rata earnings through the fund, a reasonable charge for administering the fund. In the event that the state treasurer does deduct an administrative fee, it shall be deposited and expended through the revolving account.

9-4-608 SECTION 6. Tennessee Code Annotated, Section 9-4-608, is amended by adding a new subsection as follows:

(j) Local governments may invest in the intermediate-term investment fund by having the local government's legislative body, council, commission or other authorizing individual or authorizing governing body submit a duly adopted resolution to the state treasurer demonstrating its authority to participate, along with any other documents required by the state treasurer. The resolution shall contain a disclosure statement as the state treasurer shall periodically require.

9-4-608 SECTION 7. Tennessee Code Annotated, Section 9-4-608, is amended by adding a new subsection as follows:

(k) As the administrator of the intermediate-term investment fund, the state treasurer is authorized to receive, invest and distribute a participant's funds by means of an electronic transfer or other reasonable methods. The state funding board may establish limits, conditions or restrictions on the acceptance of monies into the fund and the withdrawal of monies from the fund.

9-4-702 SECTION 8. Tennessee Code Annotated, Section 9-4-702, is amended by deleting this section in its entirety and substituting it instead with the following:

A local government investment pool is hereby created consisting of the aggregate of all funds from local governments that are placed in the custody of the state treasurer or the agents of the state treasurer for investment, reinvestment and the administration of the fund.

9-4-704 SECTION 9. Tennessee Code Annotated, Section 9-4-704(a), is amended by deleting subsection (a) in its entirety and substituting it instead with the following:

(a) Funds in the local government investment pool established by this part may be commingled, for investment purposes, with state funds held in the pooled investment fund created under § 9-4-603 or may be maintained in a separate pool that is subject to the provisions set forth in §§ 9-4-602 and 9-4-603. The state funding board shall determine whether the funds shall be commingled with the pooled investment fund or maintained in a separate pool. The local government investment pool funds shall be commingled with the pooled investment fund unless the state funding board decides otherwise. The commingling of the local government investment pool with the pooled investment fund for investment purposes shall not prohibit the funds from being established as two (2) separate funds and accounted for separately with accurate and detailed accounting records. As the administrator of the local government investment pool, the state treasurer is authorized to receive, invest and distribute a participant's funds by means of an electronic transfer or other reasonable methods. The state funding board may establish limits, conditions or restrictions on the acceptance of monies into the fund and the withdrawal of monies from the fund.

9-4-704 SECTION 10. Tennessee Code Annotated, Section 9-4-704(b), is amended by deleting subsection (b) in its entirety and substituting it instead with the following:

(b) The state treasurer may deduct from each participant's pro rata earnings through the fund a reasonable charge for administering the fund. In the event that the state treasurer does deduct an administrative fee, it shall be deposited and expended through the revolving account established in § 9-4-603(g).

Effective date 4/23/2013 SECTION 11. This act shall take effect immediately upon becoming a law, the public welfare requiring it.

PUBLIC CHAPTER NO. 209

PUBLIC CHAPTER NO. 209

SENATE BILL NO. 1002

By McNally

Substituted for: House Bill No. 656

By Sparks

AN ACT to amend Tennessee Code Annotated, Title 67, relative to taxation.

BE IT ENACTED BY THE GENERAL ASSEMBLY OF THE STATE OF TENNESSEE:

67-1-401 SECTION 1. Tennessee Code Annotated, Section 67-1-401, is amended by deleting subdivision (a)(2) and substituting instead the following:

> (a)(2) In counties having one or more cities with population exceeding sixty thousand (60,000) according to the federal census of 1970 or any subsequent federal census, two (2) of the members of the board shall be appointed by the governing body of the largest city.

67-1-401 SECTION 2. Tennessee Code Annotated, Section 67-1-401, is further amended by adding the following new, appropriately designated subsection:

> ( ) In addition to its regular appointments under this section, an appointing authority may designate one or more alternates, and the board of equalization chair may call upon an alternate to sit for a regular member who becomes unavailable for a particular hearing due to disqualification or other reason. A duly appointed alternate shall be sworn in the same manner as regular members, and any action taken by a duly appointed alternate shall be as effective as if taken by the unavailable individual.

67-1-402 SECTION 3. Tennessee Code Annotated, Section 67-1-402, is amended by deleting the words "county mayor" in subsection (a) and by substituting instead the words "county mayor or other official authorized by law to administer oaths".

67-1-507 SECTION 4. Tennessee Code Annotated, Section 67-1-507, is amended by deleting the words "county mayor" in subsection (a) and by substituting instead the words "county mayor or other official authorized by law to administer oaths".

67-5-212 SECTION 5. Tennessee Code Annotated, Section 67-5-212, is amended by adding the following sentence after the first sentence of subdivision (b)(2):

> Written notice includes notification by electronic means and notice may be preserved in digital or electronic format.

67-5-303 SECTION 6. Tennessee Code Annotated, Section 67-5-303, is amended by adding the following language at the end of the sentence in subdivision (a)(2):

> and the power to inspect or require the production of books and papers

67-5-303 SECTION 7. Tennessee Code Annotated, Section 67-5-303, is further amended by deleting subsection (d) in its entirety and substituting instead the following:

> (d)(1) The assessor or deputy assessor shall reduce to writing all statements made by the owner of any property interest or witness under the provisions of this section, and such statement shall be filed and maintained in the office of the assessor for a period of not less than three (3) years or the end of the then current reappraisal cycle, whichever is greater.
>
> (2) Information obtained pursuant to this section shall be confidential and shall not be disclosed by state or local officials, agents or employees, except as authorized by this part. Violations of confidentiality as provided herein shall be punishable in the

same manner as violations of § 67-5-401 regarding taxpayer records of the department of revenue.

(3) Pursuant to rules of the state board of equalization, information otherwise confidential may be disclosed to:

(A) The taxpayer or the taxpayer's authorized designee, upon written request;

(B) Individuals designated by a judge presiding in court or administrative proceedings, subject to protective orders issued in the proceedings;

(C) Officials, and their agents or employees, responsible for the administration or collection of taxes due from the taxpayer, but only to the extent necessary for this purpose and subject otherwise to the confidentiality required by this section.

67-5-508 SECTION 8. Tennessee Code Annotated, Section 67-5-508, is amended by adding the following new, appropriately designated subsection:

( ) As an alternative to notice by mail as provided in this section, notice may be sent by email using the email address provided to the assessor by the taxpayer.

67-5-509 SECTION 9. Tennessee Code Annotated, Section 67-5-509, is amended by adding the following sentence at the end of subsection (b):

As used in this subsection, "assessment" includes a back assessment, reassessment, or correction of assessment error.

67-5-806 SECTION 10. Tennessee Code Annotated, Section 67-5-806, is amended by adding the following sentence at the end of subsection (a):

Property maps prepared for property tax and assessment purposes shall not be conclusive evidence of property ownership in any court of law.

67-5-1302 SECTION 11. Tennessee Code Annotated, Section 67-5-1302, is amended by adding the following language at the end of subdivision (b)(1):

; provided, that no equalization factor for purposes of this section may exceed a factor of one (1.000).

67-5-1407 SECTION 12. Tennessee Code Annotated, Section 67-5-1407, is amended by adding the following new, appropriately designated subsection:

( ) Wherever in this section personal appearance at a hearing is required, in the discretion of the board all or part of the hearing may be conducted by telephone, television, software or other electronic means, if each participant in the hearing has an opportunity to participate in, to hear, and, if technically feasible, to see the entire proceedings while taking place.

67-5-1501 SECTION 13. Tennessee Code Annotated, Section 67-5-1501, is amended by deleting in its entirety subdivision (d)(2) and renumbering existing subdivisions accordingly.

67-5-1509 SECTION 14. Tennessee Code Annotated, Section 67-5-1509, is amended by adding the following language at the end of the second sentence of subsection (a):

; provided, that no equalization factor for purposes of this section may exceed a factor of one (1.000).

67-5-1601 SECTION 15. Tennessee Code Annotated, Section 67-5-1601, is amended by deleting the words "the review cycle" in the first sentence of subdivision (a)(2) and substituting instead the words "a six year reappraisal cycle".

67-5-1601 SECTION 16. Tennessee Code Annotated, Section 67-5-1601, is further amended by deleting the first sentence of subdivision (a)(3) and substituting instead the following:

The board may approve a reappraisal plan specifying a schedule for on-site review that is different than the standard schedule provided in subdivision (a)(1), but is no longer than five (5) years, whether the frequency of revaluation is four, five, or six years.

Effective date 4/23/2013

SECTION 17. This act shall take effect upon becoming a law, the public welfare requiring it.

PUBLIC CHAPTER NO. 210

PUBLIC CHAPTER NO. 210

SENATE BILL NO. 1174

By Bowling, Ketron, Summerville, Yager, Bell, Burks, Tracy, Mr. Speaker Ramsey

Substituted for: House Bill No. 626

By Evans

AN ACT to amend Tennessee Code Annotated, Title 50, Chapter 6, relative to workers' compensation.

BE IT ENACTED BY THE GENERAL ASSEMBLY OF THE STATE OF TENNESSEE:

50-6-401 SECTION 1. Tennessee Code Annotated, Section 50-6-401(a)(1), is amended by adding the following language to the end of the subdivision:

For purposes of this subdivision (a)(1), "volunteer firefighter" means any member or personnel of a fire department, volunteer fire department, rescue squad or volunteer rescue squad, including, but not limited to, a junior member, a board member or an auxiliary member of the department or squad.

Effective date 4/23/2013 SECTION 2. This act shall take effect upon becoming a law, the public welfare requiring it.

PUBLIC CHAPTER NO. 211

PUBLIC CHAPTER NO. 211

SENATE BILL NO. 1208

By Johnson

Substituted for: House Bill No. 890

By Madam Speaker Harwell, Lynn

AN ACT to amend Tennessee Code Annotated, Title 7; Title 45; Title 46; Title 47; Title 55; Title 56; Title 62; Title 65 and Title 68, relative to deleting obsolete and antiquated statutory text and references concerning business, insurance and utilities.

BE IT ENACTED BY THE GENERAL ASSEMBLY OF THE STATE OF TENNESSEE:

56-7-2915 SECTION 1. Tennessee Code Annotated, Section 56-7-2915, is amended by deleting the section in its entirety.

56-7-3026 SECTION 2. Tennessee Code Annotated, Section 56-7-3026, is amended by deleting the section in its entirety.

62-6-127 SECTION 3. Tennessee Code Annotated, Section 62-6-127, is amended by deleting the section in its entirety.

62-9-113 SECTION 4. Tennessee Code Annotated, Section 62-9-113(c), is amended by deleting the subsection in its entirety.

65-23-101 – 65-23-123 SECTION 5. Tennessee Code Annotated, Title 65, Chapter 23, is amended by deleting the chapter in its entirety.

3-101 – 7-83-105; 3-201 – 7-83-206; 3-301 – 7-83-311; 3-401 – 7-83-404 SECTION 6. Tennessee Code Annotated, Title 7, Chapter 83, is amended by deleting the chapter in its entirety.

45-8-221 SECTION 7. Tennessee Code Annotated, Section 45-8-221(a)(8), is amended by deleting the subdivision in its entirety.

-101 – 62-16-103 SECTION 8. Tennessee Code Annotated, Title 62, Chapter 16, is amended by deleting the chapter in its entirety.

Effective date 7/1/2013 SECTION 9. This act shall take effect July 1, 2013, the public welfare requiring it.

PUBLIC CHAPTER NO. 212

PUBLIC CHAPTER NO. 212

SENATE BILL NO. 1210

By Dickerson

Substituted for: House Bill No. 1060

By Shepard

AN ACT to amend Tennessee Code Annotated, Title 8, Chapter 42, relative to defense of state employees.

BE IT ENACTED BY THE GENERAL ASSEMBLY OF THE STATE OF TENNESSEE:

8-42-103 SECTION 1. Tennessee Code Annotated, Section 8-42-103, is amended by adding the following language as a new subsection (d):

(d) For the exclusive purpose of this section, "state employee" also includes any expert witness appearing and testifying on behalf of the department of health at any administrative hearing or other similar proceeding held with respect to a disciplinary or other action against any person or entity required to be licensed, permitted, certified, or authorized by any board, council, committee, or agency created pursuant to title 63 and title 68, when a civil action for damages is commenced against such expert witness for any act or omission in the course of appearing and testifying. Notwithstanding any provision of law to the contrary, such witness shall not be considered a state employee for any other purpose including, but not limited to, §§ 9-8-112 and 9-8-307.

Effective date 4/23/2013 SECTION 2. This act shall take effect upon becoming a law, the public welfare requiring it.

PUBLIC CHAPTER NO. 213

PUBLIC CHAPTER NO. 213

SENATE BILL NO. 1269

By Watson, Harper, Crowe, Dickerson, Southerland, Bowling, Campfield, Norris

Substituted for: House Bill No. 1164

By McCormick, Ramsey, Rich, Mark White, Love, Ryan Williams, Durham

AN ACT to amend Tennessee Code Annotated, Title 68, Chapter 29, relative to medical laboratories.

BE IT ENACTED BY THE GENERAL ASSEMBLY OF THE STATE OF TENNESSEE:

68-29-138 SECTION 1. Tennessee Code Annotated, Section 68-29-138, is amended by deleting the current section in its entirety and replacing it with the following:

68-29-138.

(a) Notwithstanding any provisions of official compilation Rules and Regulations of the State of Tennessee, Rule 1200-6-1, or any other rule promulgated by the medical laboratory board to the contrary, a Tennessee medical laboratory shall be licensed in accordance with the rules promulgated under authority of this chapter and as provided in this section if the laboratory:

(1) Is engaged in advanced esoteric applied toxicological, forensic, or biochemical laboratory analysis utilizing emerging technologies, such as chromatographic and non-chromatographic techniques coupled with mass spectrometer based detector systems and molecular diagnostic techniques; and

(2) Is licensed, certified, or accredited by the United States department of health and human resources substance abuse and mental health service administrations (SAMHSA), the American Society of Crime Laboratory Directors Laboratory Accreditation Board (ASCLD/LAB), the American Board of Forensic Toxicology (ABFT), the College of American Pathologists Laboratory Accreditation Program (CAP LAP), or a state that has been determined to be exempt in accordance with Section 353(p) of the Public Health Services Act, 42 U.S.C. § 263a, as having enacted laboratory requirements that are equal to or more stringent than the statutory and regulatory requirements of the Clinical Laboratory Improvement Amendments of 1988 (CLIA).

(b) A laboratory licensed under subsection (a) shall be exempt from the provisions of this chapter, including any rules promulgated under this chapter, that require persons who accept specimens for laboratory examination and perform analytical testing or report the results of a laboratory examination, be licensed as a technologist, technician, laboratory trainee, or special analyst.

(c) In such medical laboratories, laboratory personnel who analyze or report laboratory results shall possess a baccalaureate or advanced degree in the appropriate sciences with at least sixteen (16) semester hours of chemistry and/or biological science courses. Nothing in this section shall be construed to prohibit licensed personnel from performing the tasks for which they are appropriately licensed and trained in such medical laboratories.

(d) Except as provided in subsection (b), such laboratories shall be subject to all other provisions of this chapter, including any rules promulgated under this chapter.

Effective date 7/1/2013 SECTION 2. This act shall take effect July 1, 2013, the public welfare requiring it.

PUBLIC CHAPTER NO. 214

PUBLIC CHAPTER NO. 214

SENATE BILL NO. 1291

By Dickerson, Tracy

Substituted for: House Bill No. 1270

By Forgety

AN ACT to amend Tennessee Code Annotated, Section 49-1-302; Section 49-3-352; Title 49, Chapter 5; Section 49-5-512; Section 49-6-3105 and Section 49-6-3401, relative to education.

BE IT ENACTED BY THE GENERAL ASSEMBLY OF THE STATE OF TENNESSEE:

49-5-5001 – 49-5-5023; 49-5-5201 – 49-5-5241; 49-5-5301– 49-5-5308; 49-5-5401 – 49-5-5408; 49-5-5501 – 49-5-5509

SECTION 1. Tennessee Code Annotated, Title 49, Chapter 5, is amended by deleting Parts 50, 52, 53, 54 and 55 in their entireties.

49-1-302

SECTION 2. Tennessee Code Annotated, Section 49-1-302, is amended by adding the following language as new subdivision (n):

(n) The board shall develop guidelines, criteria and administrative rules as necessary to assure the payment of career ladder supplements to eligible recipients so long as they remain in positions in the public schools that qualify for such supplements. The board shall notify the commissioner of finance and administration at such time as the last eligible recipient separates from service to a local board of education. At the time of the notice to the commissioner of finance and administration, all rules, regulations and policies pertaining to the career ladder program shall become void and of no effect.

49-5-512

SECTION 3. Tennessee Code Annotated, Section 49-5-512(d), is amended by deleting the language ", (b)" in the first sentence of the subdivision, so that the remaining language reads as follows:

(d) Subsections (a) and (c) shall not apply to a disciplinary suspension by the director of schools that is for a period of three (3) days or less and that is not made in anticipation of dismissal.

49-6-3401

SECTION 4. Tennessee Code Annotated, Section 49-6-3401(a)(1), is amended by deleting the words "or truancy" so that the remaining language reads as follows:

(1) Willful and persistent violation of the rules of the school;

49-3-352

SECTION 5. Tennessee Code Annotated, Section 49-3-352(b), is amended by deleting the first sentence of the subsection and by substituting instead the following new language:

All appropriations from all sources intended to fund any function or expense of the LEA shall be appropriated to this account and an affirmative vote by a majority of the membership of the board shall be required to disburse funds from the account.

49-6-3105

SECTION 6. Tennessee Code Annotated, Section 49-6-3105, is amended by adding the following language at the end of the section:

Any transfer student who is admitted to the school system consistent with a policy deadline established according to this section shall be enrolled for one (1) complete school year. School board policies adopted consistent with this section shall establish a date upon which the parent, guardian, or student, as appropriate, shall receive notice of eligibility for re-enrollment.

Effective date 4/23/2013

SECTION 7. This act shall take effect upon becoming a law, the public welfare requiring it.

PUBLIC CHAPTER NO. 215

PUBLIC CHAPTER NO. 215

SENATE BILL NO. 1294

By Watson, Beavers

Substituted for: House Bill No. 1092

By Lynn

AN ACT to amend Tennessee Code Annotated, Title 34, Chapter 6, relative to power of attorney.

BE IT ENACTED BY THE GENERAL ASSEMBLY OF THE STATE OF TENNESSEE:

34-6-203 SECTION 1. Tennessee Code Annotated, Section 34-6-203(b)(1) and (d), are amended by adding the word "treating" immediately before the language "health care institution".

Effective date 7/1/2013 SECTION 2. This act shall take effect July 1, 2013, the public welfare requiring it.

PUBLIC CHAPTER NO. 216

PUBLIC CHAPTER NO. 216

SENATE BILL NO. 1302

By Kyle, Ford

Substituted for: House Bill No. 1163

By Mitchell, Hardaway

AN ACT to amend Tennessee Code Annotated, Title 4 and Title 71, Chapter 3, Part 5, relative to child care agencies.

BE IT ENACTED BY THE GENERAL ASSEMBLY OF THE STATE OF TENNESSEE:

71-3-517 SECTION 1. Tennessee Code Annotated, Title 71, Chapter 3, Part 5, is amended by adding the following language as a new section:

71-3-517.

(a) All persons or entities operating a child care agency as defined in this part, excluding drop-in child care centers and those programs and facilities exempt from licensing as provided in § 71-3-503, shall, in consultation with appropriate local authorities and local emergency management, develop a written multi-hazard plan to protect children in the event of emergencies, including, but not limited to, fires, tornados, earthquakes, chemical spills, and floods. Such persons or entities shall also inform parents and guardians of children attending the child care agency of the plan.

(b) The written plan required pursuant to this section shall include:

(1) Procedures for child care agency staff to notify parents in an emergency;

(2) The development of designated relocation sites and evacuation routes to those sites;

(3) Reunification plans for children and families; and

(4) Written individualized plans for accommodating a child's special needs in an emergency situation.

(c) The child care agency shall maintain documentation that the emergency plan is reviewed monthly.

(d) All child care agency staff persons shall be trained on the plan annually.

(e) The child care agency shall implement these emergency procedures through timely practice drills to meet local regulations and local emergency services plans and shall maintain documentation of drills for one (1) year. Such drills shall involve the following:

(1) At least one (1) fire drill shall be conducted monthly;

(2) Child care agencies shall alternate drills each month to cover each shift while children are present, including extended care hours;

(3) At least one (1) drill other than fire shall be conducted every six (6) months; and

(4) All drills shall be conducted in such a way as to simulate, as closely as is practical, conditions of a real emergency, with alarms to be utilized and evacuation plans to be practiced.

(f)(1) Emergency telephone numbers for the following entities shall be posted next to all child care agency telephones and shall be readily available to all child care agency staff members:

(A) Fire department;

(B) Police department and sheriff's office;

(C) Nearest hospital emergency room;

(D) Department of children's services child abuse hotline;

(E) Local emergency management agency;

(F) Ambulance or rescue squad;

(G) Poison control center; and

(H) Department of human services child care complaint hotline.

(2) If a generic emergency number, including, but not limited to, 911 service, is operable in the community, it shall also be posted in the manner prescribed in this subsection.

(g) All contact information for parents, guardians, and emergency personnel shall be readily available to all child care agency staff, including work, home and cell phone numbers.

Effective date 7/1/2013

SECTION 2. This act shall take effect July 1, 2013, the public welfare requiring it.

PUBLIC CHAPTER NO. 217

PUBLIC CHAPTER NO. 217

SENATE BILL NO. 1328

By Ketron

Substituted for: House Bill No. 1299

By Todd

AN ACT to amend Tennessee Code Annotated, Title 4; Title 12 and Title 54, relative to procurement by the department of transportation.

BE IT ENACTED BY THE GENERAL ASSEMBLY OF THE STATE OF TENNESSEE:

12-3-134 SECTION 1. Tennessee Code Annotated, Title 12, Chapter 3, is amended by adding the following as a new, appropriately designated section:

(_) All noncompetitive purchases and contracts entered into by the department of transportation for non-construction and non-engineering projects or services with a term of more than one (1) year or which are renewable by either party that would extend the contract beyond twelve (12) months and which have a cumulative value of not less than two hundred fifty thousand dollars ($250,000), including all possible renewals, shall be subject to the approval of the comptroller of the treasury. A list of all such purchases and contracts shall be filed with and subject to review by the fiscal review committee.

Effective date 4/23/2013 SECTION 2. This act shall take effect upon becoming law, the public welfare requiring it.

PUBLIC CHAPTER NO. 218

PUBLIC CHAPTER NO. 218

SENATE BILL NO. 1333

By Massey, Tracy, Ford

Substituted for: House Bill No. 1266

By Marsh

AN ACT to amend Tennessee Code Annotated, Title 57, Chapter 4, relative to consumption of alcoholic beverages on premises.

BE IT ENACTED BY THE GENERAL ASSEMBLY OF THE STATE OF TENNESSEE:

57-4-102 SECTION 1. Tennessee Code Annotated, Section 57-4-102(38), is amended by adding the following as a new subdivision thereto:

(E) "Urban park center" also means a facility that possesses each of the following characteristics:

(i) Is owned and maintained by a bona fide charitable or nonprofit organization;

(ii) Is used for the periodic showing or exhibition of animals;

(iii) Has a seating capacity of not less than twenty-five thousand (25,000) persons;

(iv) Includes an arena and a permanently constructed clubhouse or meeting room located on the grounds; and

(v) Is located in any county having a population of not less than forty-five thousand (45,000) nor more than forty-five thousand one hundred (45,100) according to the 2010 federal census or any subsequent federal census.

Effective date 4/23/2013 SECTION 2. This act shall take effect upon becoming a law, the public welfare requiring it.

PUBLIC CHAPTER NO. 219

PUBLIC CHAPTER NO. 219

SENATE BILL NO. 1337

By Bell

Substituted for: House Bill No. 1271

By Forgety, Towns

AN ACT to amend Tennessee Code Annotated, Title 55, Chapter 8, Part 2, relative to the use of golf carts on certain highways.

BE IT ENACTED BY THE GENERAL ASSEMBLY OF THE STATE OF TENNESSEE:

55-8-201 SECTION 1. Tennessee Code Annotated, Section 55-8-201, is amended by deleting subsection (b) in its entirety and by substituting instead the following:

(b)(1) This section shall only apply in municipalities having the following populations, according to the 2010 federal census or any subsequent federal census:

not less than:	nor more than:
719	730
955	965
1,955	1,965
4,050	4,060
29,130	29,140

(2) Until January 1, 2014, the governing body of any municipality to which this section applies may authorize and regulate the operation of a golf cart on any public roadway within such municipality that is not a part of the county highway system or the state system of highways or the interstate and national defense highway system upon the governing body of such municipality adopting an ordinance by a two-thirds (2/3) vote specifying each roadway that is open for golf cart use.

55-8-201 SECTION 2. Tennessee Code Annotated, Section 55-8-201(h), is amended by deleting the first and second sentences in their entirety and by substituting instead the following:

Each municipality participating in such pilot program shall submit a report to the department of safety, the transportation and safety committee of the senate, and the transportation committee of the house of representatives no later than the fifth of each month after the governing body enacts the ordinance authorizing golf carts on certain roadways detailing the program in such municipality. In addition to such monthly report, each municipality participating in the pilot program shall submit a cumulative report to the transportation and safety committee of the senate and the transportation committee of the house of representatives no later than February 1 of each year, detailing the program in such municipality.

55-8-201 SECTION 3. Tennessee Code Annotated, Section 55-8-201, is amended by deleting subsection (i) in its entirety and by substituting instead the following new subsections (i) and (j):

(i)(1) Notwithstanding the provisions of any ordinance or any other law to the contrary, if any municipality fails to submit a total of three (3) monthly reports or a cumulative report as required by subsection (h), the department of safety shall revoke the municipality's authority under this section to allow golf cart use on public roadways designated in subsection (b). Revocation of authorization shall be made in writing and sent by certified mail, return receipt requested, to the chief law enforcement officer and the mayor of the municipality no less than twenty (20) days prior to the effective date of the revocation of authority.

(2) No municipality participating in the pilot program shall issue any permit, registration or sticker for the operation of any low speed vehicle or medium speed vehicle, as defined in § 55-8-101.

(j) This section shall terminate on July 1, 2015, unless reenacted or extended by the general assembly prior to such date.

Effective date 4/23/2013 SECTION 4. This act shall take effect upon becoming a law, the public welfare requiring it.

PUBLIC CHAPTER NO. 220

PUBLIC CHAPTER NO. 220

SENATE BILL NO. 28

By Beavers

Substituted for: House Bill No. 68

By Weaver

AN ACT to amend Tennessee Code Annotated, Title 10; Title 33; Title 36 and Title 63, relative to consideration of health care records of a parent in a child custody case.

BE IT ENACTED BY THE GENERAL ASSEMBLY OF THE STATE OF TENNESSEE:

36-6-106 SECTION 1. Tennessee Code Annotated, Section 36-6-106(a)(5), is amended by deleting the semicolon (;) and adding a period (.) at the end of the subdivision, and is further amended by adding the following language after the language "caregivers;":

> The court may, when it deems appropriate, order an examination of a party pursuant to Rule 35 of the Tennessee Rules of Civil Procedure and, if necessary for the conduct of the proceedings, order the disclosure of confidential mental health information of a party pursuant to § 33-3-105(3). The court order required by § 33-3-105(3) shall contain a qualified protective order that, at a minimum, expressly limits the dissemination of confidential protected mental health information for the purpose of the litigation pending before the court and provides for the return or destruction of the confidential protected mental health information at the conclusion of the proceedings.

Effective date 7/1/2013 SECTION 2. This act shall take effect July 1, 2013, the public welfare requiring it.

PUBLIC CHAPTER NO. 221

PUBLIC CHAPTER NO. 221

SENATE BILL NO. 2

By Yager

Substituted for: House Bill No. 17

By Calfee

AN ACT to name bridges at the Midtown interchange on Interstate 40 in Roane County.

BE IT ENACTED BY THE GENERAL ASSEMBLY OF THE STATE OF TENNESSEE:

SECTION 1. Notwithstanding any provision of law to the contrary, the eastbound bridge spanning Interstate 40 on State Route 29 (Pine Ridge Road) at the Midtown interchange (Exit 350) on Interstate 40 in Roane County is hereby designated the "Paul E. Easter Bridge".

SECTION 2. Notwithstanding any provision of law to the contrary, the westbound bridge spanning Interstate 40 on State Route 29 (Pine Ridge Road) at the Midtown interchange (Exit 350) on Interstate 40 in Roane County is hereby designated the "James W. Harmon Bridge".

SECTION 3. The department of transportation is directed to erect suitable signs or to affix suitable markers designating the bridge described in Section 1 as the "Paul E. Easter Bridge" and the bridge described in Section 2 as the "James W. Harmon Bridge".

SECTION 4. The erection of such signs shall be within the guidelines prescribed by the Manual on Uniform Traffic Control Devices.

SECTION 5. This act shall become operative only if the federal highway administrator advises the commissioner of transportation in writing that the provisions of this act shall not render Tennessee in violation of federal laws and regulations and subject to penalties prescribed therein.

SECTION 6. This act shall become operative only if the cost of the manufacture and installation of each sign is paid to the department of transportation from non-state funds within one (1) year of the effective date of this act; provided, however, lack of funding for one sign shall not negate the erection of the other sign if adequate funding has been provided therefor. Such payment shall be made prior to any expenditure by the state for the manufacture or installation of any such sign. The department shall return any unused portion of the estimated cost to the person or entity paying for any such sign within thirty (30) days of the erection of such sign. If the actual cost exceeds the estimated cost, an amount equal to the difference in such costs shall be remitted to the department in non-state funds within thirty (30) days of the sponsoring person or entity receiving an itemized invoice of the actual cost from the department.

Effective date 4/19/2013

SECTION 7. This act shall take effect upon becoming a law, the public welfare requiring it.

PUBLIC CHAPTER NO. 222

PUBLIC CHAPTER NO. 222

SENATE BILL NO. 113

By Tate, Ketron, Ford, Gresham

Substituted for: House Bill No. 860

By Weaver, Butt, Joe Carr, John Deberry, Dunn, Lamberth, Rogers, Dean, Love, Moody, Womick, Sargent, Sparks

AN ACT to amend Tennessee Code Annotated, Title 49, relative to student discipline.

BE IT ENACTED BY THE GENERAL ASSEMBLY OF THE STATE OF TENNESSEE:

49-6-3401 SECTION 1. Tennessee Code Annotated, Section 49-6-3401, is amended by adding the following language as a new subsection:

(i) Notwithstanding subsection (a) or (b) or any other law to the contrary, if a pupil is determined, via a fair and thorough investigation made by the principal or the principal's appointed representative, to have acted in self-defense under a reasonable belief that the student, or another to whom the student was coming to the defense of, may have been facing the threat of imminent danger of death or serious bodily injury, which the student honestly believed to be real at that time, then, at the principal's recommendation, the student may not face any disciplinary action.

49-6-3401 SECTION 2. Tennessee Code Annotated, Section 49-6-3401, is further amended by deleting subdivision (a)(11) in its entirety and substituting instead the following:

(11) One (1) or more students initiating a physical attack on an individual student on school property or at a school activity, including travel to and from school or a school activity;

Effective date 7/1/2013 SECTION 3. This act shall take effect July 1, 2013, the public welfare requiring it.

PUBLIC CHAPTER NO. 223

PUBLIC CHAPTER NO. 223

SENATE BILL NO. 131

By Hensley

Substituted for: House Bill No. 266

By Hawk, Roach

AN ACT to amend Tennessee Code Annotated, Title 55, Chapter 4, Part 1 and Title 55, Chapter 9, Part 4, relative to display of registration plates.

BE IT ENACTED BY THE GENERAL ASSEMBLY OF THE STATE OF TENNESSEE:

55-4-110 SECTION 1. Tennessee Code Annotated, Section 55-4-110, is amended by adding the following language as subsection (c) and by redesignating the subsequent subsection accordingly:

(c)(1) Except as provided in subdivision (c)(2), for all motor vehicles that are factory-equipped to illuminate the registration plate, the registration plate shall be illuminated at all times that headlights are illuminated.

(2) Subdivision (c)(1) shall not apply to any antique motor vehicle as defined in § 55-4-111(b).

55-4-110 SECTION 2. Tennessee Code Annotated, Section 55-4-110, is amended by adding the following new subdivision (c)(3):

(3) If the violation of this section results solely from the failure to illuminate the registration plate at all times headlights are required to be displayed, the fine set out in this subsection shall be the only amount the person is assessed. No litigation tax levied pursuant to title 67, chapter 4, part 6, shall be imposed or assessed against anyone convicted of a violation of this section nor shall any clerk's fee or court costs, including but not limited to any statutory fees of officers, be imposed or assessed against anyone convicted of a violation of this section. Further, the lighting violation described in this subdivision shall be considered a nonmoving traffic violation and no points shall be added to a driver's record for such violation.

Effective date 7/1/2013 SECTION 3. This act shall take effect July 1, 2013, the public welfare requiring it, and shall apply to any violations occurring on or after such date.

PUBLIC CHAPTER NO. 224

PUBLIC CHAPTER NO. 224

SENATE BILL NO. 222

By Kelsey, Green

Substituted for: House Bill No. 126

By Womick, Dennis, Durham, Mark White, Joe Carr

AN ACT to amend Tennessee Code Annotated, Section 29-39-104, relative to punitive damage awards based on vicarious liability.

BE IT ENACTED BY THE GENERAL ASSEMBLY OF THE STATE OF TENNESSEE:

29-39-104 SECTION 1. Tennessee Code Annotated, Section 29-39-104, is amended by adding the following as a new subsection (g):

(g)(1) Notwithstanding subdivision (a)(9), punitive damages may be awarded against a defendant based on vicarious liability for the acts or omissions of an agent or employee only if the finder of fact determines by special verdict based on clear and convincing evidence that one or more of the following has occurred:

(A) The act or omission was committed by a person employed in a management capacity while that person was acting within the scope of employment;

(B) The defendant was reckless in hiring, retaining, supervising or training the agent or employee and that recklessness was the proximate cause of the act or omission that caused the loss or injury; or

(C) The defendant authorized, ratified or approved the act or omission with knowledge or conscious or reckless disregard that the act or omission may result in the loss or injury.

(2) Nothing in this subsection shall be construed to expand or increase the scope of vicarious liability or punitive damages liability under Tennessee law.

(3) For purposes of this subsection, "a person employed in a management capacity" means an employee with authority to set policy and exercise control, discretion, and independent judgment over a significant scope of the employer's business.

Effective date 7/1/2013 SECTION 2. This act shall take effect July 1, 2013, and shall apply to all actions accruing on or after that date, the public welfare requiring it.

PUBLIC CHAPTER NO. 225

PUBLIC CHAPTER NO. 225

SENATE BILL NO. 240

By Campfield, Burks

Substituted for: House Bill No. 222

By Kane, Sargent, Durham, Hall, Moody, Timothy Hill, Dunn, Womick, Matthew Hill, Dean, Van Huss, Holt, Joe Carr, Sparks, Spivey, Lundberg, Butt, Todd, Weaver, Carter, Kevin Brooks

AN ACT to amend Tennessee Code Annotated, Section 49-50-801 and Title 49, Chapter 6, relative to participation in athletics by home school students.

BE IT ENACTED BY THE GENERAL ASSEMBLY OF THE STATE OF TENNESSEE:

49-6-3050 SECTION 1. Tennessee Code Annotated, Section 49-6-3050, is amended by adding the following language as new subsection (e):

(e)(1) If any of the public schools established under the jurisdiction of an LEA are members of an organization or an association that regulates interscholastic athletic competition, and if such organization or association establishes or maintains eligibility requirements for home school students desiring to participate in interscholastic athletics at a member school, then the LEA shall permit participation in interscholastic athletics at those schools by home school students who satisfy the eligibility requirements established by the organization or association.

(2) This subsection (e) does not guarantee that a home school student trying out for an interscholastic athletics team will make the team or supplant the authority of coaches or other school officials in deciding who makes the team. This subsection (e) is intended to guarantee only that the home school student shall not be prohibited from trying out for an interscholastic athletics team, if the student is eligible under the rules of the organization or association, solely by reason of the student's status as a home school student.

(3) This subsection (e) shall not be construed to limit or supplant the authority of the organization or association to determine eligibility and to establish, modify and enforce its rules and eligibility requirements, including those applicable to home school students.

Effective date 7/1/2013 SECTION 2. This act shall take effect July 1, 2013, the public welfare requiring it, and shall apply to participation in extracurricular athletics beginning with the 2013-2014 academic year.

PUBLIC CHAPTER NO. 226

PUBLIC CHAPTER NO. 226

SENATE BILL NO. 395

By Southerland, Ford

Substituted for: House Bill No. 134

By Keisling

AN ACT to amend Tennessee Code Annotated, Title 11 and Title 47, relative to adventure tourism.

BE IT ENACTED BY THE GENERAL ASSEMBLY OF THE STATE OF TENNESSEE:

11-11-203 SECTION 1. Tennessee Code Annotated, Section 11-11-203, is amended by deleting subdivision (3) in its entirety and by substituting instead the following new language:

(3) "All-terrain vehicle" means either:

(A) A motorized vehicle with no less than four (4) non-highway tires, but no more than six (6) non-highway tires, that is limited in engine displacement to one thousand cubic centimeters (1,000 cc) or less, in total dry weight to less than one thousand five hundred pounds (1,500 lbs.), and is fifty inches (50") or less in width;

(B) A motorized vehicle with not less than four (4) non-highway tires, nor more than six (6) non-highway tires, that is limited in engine displacement to one thousand cubic centimeters (1,000 cc) or less and in total dry weight up to two thousand pounds (2,000 lbs.), and is sixty-five inches (65") or less in width;

(C) A motor vehicle as defined in § 55-1-103, which possesses a four-wheel drive capability and that is designed and suitable for operation off the highway on natural terrain; or

(D) A motorized vehicle designed for or capable of cross-country travel on or immediately over land, water, snow, or other natural terrain and not intended for use on public roads traveling on two (2) wheels and having a seat or saddle designed to be straddled by the operator and handlebars for steering control;

47-25-1902 SECTION 2. Tennessee Code Annotated, Section 47-25-1902, is amended by deleting subdivision (1) in its entirety and by substituting instead the following new language:

(1) "All terrain vehicle" means a motorized vehicle with no less than four (4) non-highway tires, but no more than six (6) non-highway tires, that is limited in engine displacement to one thousand cubic centimeters (1,000 cc) or less and in total dry weight to less than one thousand five hundred pounds (1,500 lbs.), and is fifty inches (50") or less in width;

SECTION 3. If any provision of this act or the application thereof to any person or circumstance is held invalid, such invalidity shall not affect other provisions or applications of the act which can be given effect without the invalid provision or application, and to that end the provisions of this act are declared to be severable.

Effective date 7/1/2013 SECTION 4. This act shall take effect July 1, 2013, the public welfare requiring it.

PUBLIC CHAPTER NO. 227

PUBLIC CHAPTER NO. 227

SENATE BILL NO. 542

By Bell, Ford

Substituted for: House Bill No. 218

By Forgety

AN ACT to amend Tennessee Code Annotated, Title 39, Chapter 15, Part 3; Title 40, Chapter 2 and Title 40, Chapter 35, relative to bigamy.

BE IT ENACTED BY THE GENERAL ASSEMBLY OF THE STATE OF TENNESSEE:

39-15-301 SECTION 1. Tennessee Code Annotated, Section 39-15-301(a), is amended by deleting the subsection in its entirety and by substituting instead the following:

(a) A person commits bigamy who:

(1) Is married and purports to marry or be married to a person other than the person's spouse in this state under circumstances that would, but for the person's existing marriage, constitute a marriage; or

(2) Knows that a person other than the person's spouse is married and purports to marry or be married to the person in this state under circumstances that would, but for the person's existing marriage, constitute a marriage.

39-15-301 SECTION 2. Tennessee Code Annotated, Section 39-15-301, is amended by adding a new subsection thereto, as follows:

(c) For purposes of determining when prosecution for this offense must begin under § 40-2-101:

(1) A violation of this section is a continuing offense; and

(2) Nothing in this section shall be construed as limiting the applicability of § 40-2-103.

(d) Bigamy is a Class A misdemeanor and, in addition to the authorized term of imprisonment, shall be punishable by a fine not to exceed five thousand dollars ($5,000).

Effective date 7/1/2013 SECTION 3. This act shall take effect July 1, 2013, the public welfare requiring it.

PUBLIC CHAPTER NO. 228

PUBLIC CHAPTER NO. 228

SENATE BILL NO. 578

By Haile

Substituted for: House Bill No. 375

By Womick

AN ACT to amend Tennessee Code Annotated, Title 4, Chapter 22, Part 1 and Section 4-3-1109, relative to state owned motor vehicle fleets.

BE IT ENACTED BY THE GENERAL ASSEMBLY OF THE STATE OF TENNESSEE:

4-22-101 SECTION 1. Tennessee Code Annotated, Section 4-22-101(a), is amended by deleting the subsection in its entirety and by substituting instead the following language:

(a) All state agencies, universities, and community colleges that have state owned motor vehicle fleets consisting of more than ten (10) motor vehicles shall develop and implement plans to increase the state's use of alternative fuels, synthetic lubricants, and fuel-efficient or low-emission vehicles. Each entity's plan shall have a goal of reducing or displacing at least twenty percent (20%) of the current petroleum products consumed by each entity's motor vehicle fleet by January 1, 2015. All entities shall initiate plan implementation by January 1, 2014.

4-22-101 SECTION 2. Tennessee Code Annotated, Section 4-22-101, is amended by adding the following at the end of subsection (c):

Technological exceptions may include, but not be limited to, that the entity's vehicles will be operating primarily in an area in which there is no refueling station established for alternative fuels.

Effective date 4/19/2013 SECTION 3. This act shall take effect upon becoming a law, the public welfare requiring it.

PUBLIC CHAPTER NO. 229

PUBLIC CHAPTER NO. 229

SENATE BILL NO. 834

By Ketron

Substituted for: House Bill No. 942

By Ramsey, Hardaway, Towns

AN ACT to amend Tennessee Code Annotated, Title 10, Chapter 7, Part 5, relative to public records.

BE IT ENACTED BY THE GENERAL ASSEMBLY OF THE STATE OF TENNESSEE:

10-7-504 SECTION 1. Tennessee Code Annotated, Section 10-7-504(f)(1), is amended by adding the following language as a new subdivision thereto:

(H) Personal, non-government issued, email address;

10-7-504 SECTION 2. Tennessee Code Annotated, Section 10-7-504(f)(1), is amended by adding the following language between the language "former employee," and the language "or of any law enforcement officer":

or applicant to such position,

10-7-504 SECTION 3. Tennessee Code Annotated, Section 10-7-504(f)(1)(F), is amended by adding the following language between the language "immediate family members" and "or household members":

, whether or not the immediate family member resides with the employee,

10-7-504 SECTION 4. Tennessee Code Annotated, Section 10-7-504(a)(18), is amended by adding the following language between the language, "agencies," and "or higher education institutions":

political subdivisions,

10-7-504 SECTION 5. Tennessee Code Annotated, Section 10-7-504(a), is amended by deleting subdivision (17) and substituting the following:

(17) The telephone number, address and any other information which could be used to locate the whereabouts of a domestic violence shelter, family safety center or rape crisis center may be treated as confidential by a governmental entity, and shall be treated as confidential by a utility service provider as defined in subdivision (a)(15) upon the director of the shelter, family safety center or crisis center giving written notice to the records custodian of the appropriate entity or utility that such shelter, family safety center or crisis center desires that such identifying information be maintained as confidential. The records of family safety centers shall be treated as confidential in the same manner as the records of domestic violence shelters pursuant to § 36-3-623.

Effective date 4/19/2013 SECTION 6. This act shall take effect upon becoming a law, the public welfare requiring it.

PUBLIC CHAPTER NO. 230

PUBLIC CHAPTER NO. 230

SENATE BILL NO. 841

By Ketron

Substituted for: House Bill No. 349

By Todd, Gilmore, Odom

AN ACT to amend Tennessee Code Annotated, Title 57, Chapter 4, relative to authorizing the issuance of licenses to sell alcoholic beverages for consumption on the premises of certain facilities.

BE IT ENACTED BY THE GENERAL ASSEMBLY OF THE STATE OF TENNESSEE:

57-4-102 SECTION 1. Tennessee Code Annotated, Section 57-4-102(38), is amended by adding the following language as a new subdivision thereto:

(E)(i) "Urban park center" also means a facility possessing each of the following characteristics:

(a) Is located on a tract or tracts of land having at least five (5) contiguous acres;

(b) Is located directly adjacent to property owned or leased by an airport authority created under state law;

(c) Has an enclosed facility of at least twenty thousand square feet (20,000 sq. ft.) and one (1) room with more than fourteen thousand square feet (14,000 sq. ft.);

(d) Has an exterior garden or gardens with sculpture;

(e) Is leased or owned by a not-for-profit corporation that qualifies under § 501(c)(3) of the Internal Revenue Code; and

(f) Is located within a county having a metropolitan form of government with a population of not less than six hundred thousand (600,000) according to the 2010 federal census or any subsequent federal census.

(ii) An urban park center licensed under this subdivision (38)(E) shall have the privilege of granting a franchise for the provision of food or beverage, including alcoholic beverages, on its premises, and the holder of such franchise shall also be considered an urban park center under this subdivision (38)(E). The premises of an urban park center under this subdivision (38)(E) shall include all enclosed and outdoor areas of the property described in this subdivision (38)(E).

Effective date 4/19/2013 SECTION 2. This act shall take effect upon becoming a law, the public welfare requiring it.

PUBLIC CHAPTER NO. 231

PUBLIC CHAPTER NO. 231

SENATE BILL NO. 906

By Yager, Beavers

Substituted for: House Bill No. 704

By Sanderson

AN ACT to amend Tennessee Code Annotated, Section 2-10-101(b); Section 2-2-111(b); Section 2-3-107(b)(1); Section 2-4-102(a)(2); Section 2-5-151(f)(2); Section 2-5-208(f)(1); Section 2-6-102(a)(1); Section 2-6-201(9); Section 2-6-401(a)(3); Section 2-7-112(a)(2)(B); Section 2-7-112(a)(3)(A); Section 2-2-109(a); Section 2-2-109(b); Section 5-1-104(b)(1) and Section 40-29-203(b), relative to elections.

BE IT ENACTED BY THE GENERAL ASSEMBLY OF THE STATE OF TENNESSEE:

2-2-109 SECTION 1. Tennessee Code Annotated, Section 2-2-109(a), is amended by adding the language "except as provided in subsection (b)" after the language "twenty-nine (29) days before an election" in the first sentence.

2-2-111 SECTION 2. Tennessee Code Annotated, Section 2-2-111(b), is amended by deleting the language "for a period of at least four (4) hours".

2-3-107 SECTION 3. Tennessee Code Annotated, Section 2-3-107(b)(1), is amended by adding the language "on election day and during the early voting period" after the language "for polling places".

2-4-102 SECTION 4. Tennessee Code Annotated, Section 2-4-102(a)(2), is amended by deleting the subdivision in its entirety.

2-5-151 SECTION 5. Tennessee Code Annotated, Section 2-5-151(f)(2), is amended by deleting the language "sixty (60)" and by substituting instead the language "ninety (90)" in the first and second sentences of the subdivision.

2-5-208 SECTION 6. Tennessee Code Annotated, Section 2-5-208(f)(1), is amended by deleting the subdivision in its entirety and by substituting instead the following language:

(1) Whenever a question is submitted to the vote of the people, it shall be placed at the end of the ballot, followed by the words "Yes" and "No", so that the voter can vote a preference by making a cross mark (X) opposite the proper word. If a retention judicial question is on the ballot as provided for in subdivision (c)(3), this question shall be placed after the retention judicial question, provided, that whenever the question of a state constitutional amendment is submitted to the vote of the people pursuant to Tenn. Const., art. XI, § 3, para. 1, it shall be printed upon the ballot directly after the list of candidates for governor followed by the words "Yes" and "No", so that the voter can vote a preference by making a cross mark (X) opposite the proper word. Any question submitted to the people shall be worded in such a manner that a "yes" vote would indicate support for the measure and a "no" vote would indicate opposition.

2-6-201 SECTION 7. Tennessee Code Annotated, Section 2-6-201(9), is amended by deleting the subsection in its entirety and substituting instead the following language:

(9) A voter who possesses a valid commercial driver license or a valid transportation worker identification credential and who certifies that the voter:

(A) Will be working outside of the county or state where the voter is registered during the early voting period and on election day during all the hours the polls are open; and

(B) Has no specific out-of-county or out-of-state location to which mail may be sent or received during such time;

may complete an application to vote absentee by mail at the voter's county election commission office or complete an absentee by-mail application pursuant to § 2-6-202(a)(3); provided, that if applicable, such voter satisfies the requirements of § 2-2-115(b)(7). In order for the absentee application to be processed, the voter must provide a photocopy of the commercial driver license or transportation worker identification credential, the commercial driver license number on the voter's current commercial driver license, if applicable, and provide a current residential address and a mailing address to which the ballot shall be mailed. This subsection (9) also applies to the spouse of the person who possesses the commercial driver license.

2-6-401 SECTION 8. Tennessee Code Annotated, 2-6-401(a)(3), is amended by deleting the language "and by a notary public".

2-7-112 SECTION 9. Tennessee Code Annotated, Section 2-7-112(a)(2)(B), is amended by deleting the subdivision in its entirety and substituting instead the following language:

(B) For those counties using the electronic poll book, the following procedure shall be followed: After completing the application for ballot which shall include the voter's signature, if, upon comparison of the information, the registrar determines that the voter is entitled to vote, the registrar shall initial the application for ballot and shall give the voter the ballot application, which is the voter's authorization to vote.

2-10-101 SECTION 10. Tennessee Code Annotated, Section 2-10-101(b), is amended by deleting the language "five hundred dollars ($500)" and substituting instead the language "one thousand dollars ($1,000)".

5-1-104 SECTION 11. Tennessee Code Annotated, Section 5-1-104(b)(1), is amended by deleting the language "; provided, that the candidates have sufficient time to qualify for the office, as provided for in § 2-14-106" in the first sentence of the subdivision.

40-29-203 SECTION 12. Tennessee Code Annotated, Section 40-29-203(b)(1), is amended by deleting the subdivision in its entirety.

40-29-203 SECTION 13. Tennessee Code Annotated, Section 40-29-203(b)(2), is amended by deleting the language "also" after the language "issuing authority shall".

Effective date 7/1/2013 SECTION 14. This act shall take effect July 1, 2013, the public welfare requiring it.

PUBLIC CHAPTER NO. 232

PUBLIC CHAPTER NO. 232

SENATE BILL NO. 955

By McNally, Overbey, Burks

Substituted for: House Bill No. 541

By Shepard

AN ACT to amend Tennessee Code Annotated, Title 63, relative to review of certain conduct of health care practitioners by licensing boards.

BE IT ENACTED BY THE GENERAL ASSEMBLY OF THE STATE OF TENNESSEE:

63-1-151 SECTION 1. Tennessee Code Annotated, Title 63, Chapter 1, Part 1, is amended by adding the following as a new, appropriately designated section:

(a)(1) Notwithstanding any other provision of this chapter or of chapters 3, 5, 6, 7, 8, 9 or 19 of this title, when a practitioner licensed under any of such chapters is under state or federal indictment in this state for an offense involving the sale or dispensing of controlled substances under state or federal law, the practitioner shall report the indictment to the practitioner's licensing board in writing within seven (7) calendar days of acquiring actual knowledge of the indictment. Such report shall include the jurisdiction in which the indictment is pending, if known, and shall also be accompanied by a copy of the indictment, if the practitioner has one.

(2) A district attorney general and appropriate attorneys for the federal government are strongly encouraged, when appropriate, to promptly notify a practitioner's licensing board when a practitioner covered under subdivision (a)(1) is indicted in this state for an offense involving the sale or dispensing of controlled substances under state or federal law.

(b) The knowing failure of a practitioner to submit the report required in subdivision (a)(1) above to the licensing board shall be considered unprofessional, dishonorable or unethical conduct and may be grounds for such licensing board to take disciplinary action against the practitioner's license. The fact an indictment was sealed and the practitioner could not have actual knowledge of its existence excuses the practitioner from discipline based on the failure of the practitioner to submit a report. However, the claim that the practitioner was not aware of the obligation required in subdivision (a)(1) may not excuse the practitioner from discipline based on the failure of the practitioner to submit a report.

(c) Upon receiving a report of an indictment pursuant to subdivision (a)(1), (a)(2) or from any other source, the practitioner's licensing board, through the board's consultant or other person designated by the board, shall within fifteen (15) calendar days, conduct an expedited review of the practitioner's conduct alleged in the indictment. The purpose of such expedited review shall be to determine if the matter merits an expedited investigation by the board. If so, such a directive shall be given to the department of health's office of investigations. All review activity under this subsection (c) shall be confidential pursuant to § 63-1-117(f).

(d) For the purposes of this section, "controlled substances" means substances regulated as controlled substances under title 39, chapter 17, part 4, or title 53, chapters 10 and 11, or the federal Controlled Substances Act, compiled at 21 U.S.C. § 801, et seq.

Effective date 7/1/2013 SECTION 2. This act shall take effect July 1, 2013, the public welfare requiring it.

PUBLIC CHAPTER NO. 233

PUBLIC CHAPTER NO. 233

SENATE BILL NO. 1020

By Bell

Substituted for: House Bill No. 870

By Sexton, Marsh, Fitzhugh

AN ACT to amend Tennessee Code Annotated, Title 45, relative to banks.

BE IT ENACTED BY THE GENERAL ASSEMBLY OF THE STATE OF TENNESSEE:

45-2-607 SECTION 1. Tennessee Code Annotated, Section 45-2-607(b)(2), is amended by deleting the subdivision in its entirety and by substituting instead the following:

(2)(A) Except as provided in subdivision (b)(2)(B), real property shall be sold within ten (10) years;

(B) If the bank holds the real property for a period longer than five (5) years, then after an initial five-year period, the bank, in reporting its financial status to the department, shall write off twenty percent (20%) of the appraised value of the real property each subsequent year it is held until the real property is either sold or the ten-year period has elapsed. Upon application of the bank, the commissioner may, in extraordinary circumstances, adjust or waive the percentage a bank shall write off the real property each year, may extend the period in which the real property may be held beyond ten (10) years, or any combination of the foregoing. If the commissioner reduces, waives, or adjusts the amount of write-off, the real property may not be carried at more than the appraised value of the property;

(C) Real property which has been written off but not disposed of shall be maintained on the bank's books at some nominal value;

(D) If the bank's board of directors deem the real property owned to be a prudent investment for income or appreciation for the bank, the board may take action to maintain the real property on the bank's books as an investment, pursuant to subdivision (a)(9);

(E) Not more than one hundred twenty (120) days before or thirty (30) days after the date the parcel is acquired by the bank as real property owned, or from the date on which the bank legally acquires the real property for investment purposes, the bank shall obtain from an independent, qualified appraiser an appraisal of the parcel; provided, however, that:

(i) For parcels whose book value is two hundred fifty thousand dollars ($250,000) or less, the bank may obtain an evaluation in lieu of an appraisal; and

(ii) For parcels whose book value is one hundred thousand dollars ($100,000) or less, no appraisal or evaluation shall be required; and

(F) Within twelve (12) months from the date the bank acquires the real property, and every twelve (12) months thereafter for as long as the bank owns the real property, the bank shall obtain another appraisal or evaluation, whichever is appropriate as provided for in subdivision (b)(2)(E).

SECTION 2. The department of financial institutions is authorized to promulgate such rules and regulations in accordance with the Uniform Administrative Procedures Act, compiled in title 4, chapter 5, or issue departmental bulletins in lieu of such regulations, to implement the provisions of this act.

Effective date 4/19/2013 SECTION 3. This act shall take effect upon becoming a law, the public welfare requiring it.

PUBLIC CHAPTER NO. 234

PUBLIC CHAPTER NO. 234

SENATE BILL NO. 1048

By Kelsey

Substituted for: House Bill No. 575

By Todd

AN ACT to amend Tennessee Code Annotated, Section 68-11-1628, relative to relocation of certain nursing home beds.

BE IT ENACTED BY THE GENERAL ASSEMBLY OF THE STATE OF TENNESSEE:

68-11-1628 SECTION 1. Tennessee Code Annotated, Section 68-11-1628, is amended by adding the following language as a new subsection:

(d) Any existing licensed and operating nursing home which has been operated as part of a continuing care retirement community that offers long term care, including services that included skilled nursing facility (SNF) services, assisted living, and independent living for at least twenty (20) years may relocate thirty (30) or fewer of its licensed beds to a new, separately licensed nursing home which will also operate as part of a continuing care retirement community if all the following conditions are satisfied:

(1) The proposed location for the relocation of beds is within the same county as the original facility;

(2) Both the original licensed facility and the new separately licensed facility will be licensed to not-for-profit corporations, and are affiliated through common management;

(3) The original facility is certified for participation in the medicare program, but is not and was not certified for the medicaid program within the ten (10) years preceding the filing of a certificate of need application for the relocation of beds, and any beds relocated to a new location shall initially have the same medicare and medicaid certification status that the original, existing nursing home relocating its beds maintains when the certificate of need is granted allowing the relocation of beds;

(4) The original facility is licensed for at least one hundred twenty (120) nursing home beds by the department of health; and

(5) An application for the relocation of the beds is filed with and approved by the health services development agency pursuant to this part.

Effective date 7/1/2013 SECTION 2. This act shall take effect July 1, 2013, the public welfare requiring it.

PUBLIC CHAPTER NO. 235

PUBLIC CHAPTER NO. 235

SENATE BILL NO. 1201

By Dickerson

Substituted for: House Bill No. 938

By Kane, Haynes, Hardaway

AN ACT to amend Tennessee Code Annotated, Title 63, Chapter 6, Part 7, relative to voluntary provision of health care services.

BE IT ENACTED BY THE GENERAL ASSEMBLY OF THE STATE OF TENNESSEE:

63-6-703 SECTION 1. Tennessee Code Annotated, Section 63-6-703, is amended by deleting subdivisions (4) and (5) in their entireties and by substituting instead the following:

(4) "Sponsoring organization" means any organization that organizes or arranges for the voluntary provision of health care services and that registers with the department of health as a sponsoring organization in accordance with § 63-6-706 and charges recipients based on one (1) of the following criteria:

(A) On a sliding scale according to income;

(B) A fee at the time of service of no more than the state regulatory fee paid biennially as provided for in § 4-3-1011; or

(C) No fee to the recipient; and

(5) "Voluntary provision of health care services" means the providing of professional health services by the health care provider without charge to the recipient of the services or to a third party. Nothing shall preclude a health care provider from collecting the charges described in § 63-6-703(4)(A) or (B) on behalf of the sponsoring organization as long as the health care provider retains none of the payment and forwards all collections to the sponsoring organization.

Effective date 7/1/2013 SECTION 2. This act shall take effect July 1, 2013, the public welfare requiring it.

PUBLIC CHAPTER NO. 236

PUBLIC CHAPTER NO. 236

SENATE BILL NO. 1218

By Mr. Speaker Ramsey

Substituted for: House Bill No. 976

By Madam Speaker Harwell; McDaniel, McCormick, Fitzhugh

AN ACT to amend Tennessee Code Annotated, to revise committee names in accordance with the Rules of Order of the Tennessee House of Representatives and the Tennessee Senate.

BE IT ENACTED BY THE GENERAL ASSEMBLY OF THE STATE OF TENNESSEE:

43-1-607

SECTION 1. Tennessee Code Annotated, Section 43-1-607, is amended by deleting the language "the chair of the house agriculture committee and the chair of the senate labor, commerce and agriculture committee" and substituting instead "the chair of the agriculture and natural resources committee of the house of representatives and the chair of the senate energy, agriculture and natural resources committee".

43-1-704

SECTION 2. Tennessee Code Annotated, Section 43-1-704(c), is amended by deleting the language "the chair of the agriculture committee of the house of representatives and the chair of the commerce, labor and agriculture committee of the senate" wherever it appears and substituting instead "the chair of the agriculture and natural resources committee of the house of representatives and the chair of the energy, agriculture and natural resources committee of the senate".

4-3-1012, 4-3-1018, 4-3-1105

SECTION 3. Tennessee Code Annotated, Sections 4-3-1012(b)(5), 4-3-1018(d)(4), and 4-3-1105(20), are amended by deleting the language "the energy and environment committee of the senate and the conservation and environment committee of the house of representatives" and substituting instead "the energy, agriculture and natural resources committee of the senate and the agriculture and natural resources committee of the house of representatives".

4-3-1109

SECTION 4. Tennessee Code Annotated, Section 4-3-1109(b)(3), is amended by deleting the language "the chair of the energy and environment committee of the senate, the chair of the conservation and environment committee of the house of representatives" and substituting instead "the chair of the energy, agriculture and natural resources committee of the senate, the chair of the agriculture and natural resources committee of the house of representatives".

4-22-103, 8-4-103

SECTION 5. Tennessee Code Annotated, Sections 4-22-103 and 8-4-103(a), are amended by deleting the language "the energy and environment committee of the senate, the conservation and environment committee of the house of representatives" and substituting instead "the energy, agriculture and natural resources committee of the senate, the agriculture and natural resources committee of the house of representatives".

7-82-401
11-3-120, 11-4-201,
11-4-308, 70-1-201

SECTION 6. Tennessee Code Annotated, Sections 7-82-401(i), 11-3-120(b), 11-4-201(i)(3), 11-14-308(b) and 70-1-201(b)(1), are amended by deleting the language "the conservation and environment committee of the house of representatives and the energy and environment committee of the senate" and substituting instead "the agriculture and natural resources committee of the house of representatives and the energy, agriculture and natural resources committee of the senate".

11-1-116, 70-1-206

SECTION 7. Tennessee Code Annotated, Sections 11-1-116 and 70-1-206(a)(7), are amended by deleting the language "the energy and environment committee of the senate and to the conservation and environment committee of the house of representatives" and substituting instead "the energy, agriculture and natural resources committee of the senate and to the agriculture and natural resources committee of the house of representatives".

11-3-121

SECTION 8. Tennessee Code Annotated, Section 11-3-121(c), is amended by deleting the language "the parks and tourism subcommittee of the conservation and environment committee of the house of representatives, and approved by such standing committee of the house of representatives, as well as approved by the energy and environment committee of the senate" and substituting instead "the agriculture and natural resources subcommittee of the house of representatives, and approved by such standing committee of the house of representatives, as well as approved by the energy, agriculture and natural resources committee of the senate".

11-7-104

SECTION 9. Tennessee Code Annotated, Section 11-7-104(h), is amended by deleting the language "chair of the energy and environment committee of the senate, chair of the conservation and environment committee of the house of representatives" and substituting instead "chair of the

PUBLIC CHAPTER NO. 236 (cont'd)

energy, agriculture and natural resources committee of the senate, chair of the agriculture and natural resources committee of the house of representatives".

69-3-142 SECTION 10. Tennessee Code Annotated, Section 69-3-142(a), (b) and (d), is amended by deleting the language "the chair of the energy and environment committee of the senate and the chair of the conservation and environment committee of the house of representatives" and substituting instead "the chair of the energy, agriculture and natural resources committee of the senate and the chair of the agriculture and natural resources committee of the house of representatives".

70-5-101 SECTION 11. Tennessee Code Annotated, Section 70-5-101(f)(6), is amended by deleting the language "the chair of the conservation and environment committee of the house of representatives and the chair of the energy and environment committee of the senate" and substituting instead "the chair of the agriculture and natural resources committee of the house of representatives and the chair of the energy, agriculture and natural resources committee of the senate".

4-3-737, 8-4-705, 50-7-807 SECTION 12. Tennessee Code Annotated, Sections 4-3-737(d), 8-4-705 and 50-7-807, are amended by deleting the language "the commerce, labor and agriculture committee of the senate and the commerce committee of the house of representatives" and substituting instead "the commerce and labor committee of the senate and the business and utilities committee of the house of representatives".

4-10-112 SECTION 13. Tennessee Code Annotated, Section 4-10-112, is amended by deleting the language "the commerce, labor and agriculture committee of the senate, the commerce committee of the house of representatives" and substituting instead "the commerce and labor committee of the senate, the business and utilities committee of the house of representatives".

4-26-105 SECTION 14. Tennessee Code Annotated, Section 4-26-105(a), is amended by deleting the language "the chair of the senate commerce, labor and agriculture committee, the chair of the house of representatives commerce committee" and substituting instead "the chair of the senate commerce and labor committee, the chair of the house of representatives business and utilities committee".

47-18-5002 SECTION 15. Tennessee Code Annotated, Section 47-18-5002(3), is amended by deleting the language "the commerce, labor and agricultural committee of the senate and to the commerce committee of the house" and substituting instead "the commerce and labor committee of the senate and to the consumer and human resources committee of the house of representatives".

50-7-451 SECTION 16. Tennessee Code Annotated, Section 50-7-451(d)(2), is amended by deleting the language "the commerce committee of the house of representatives, the commerce, labor and agriculture committee of the senate" and substituting instead "the consumer and human resources committee of the house of representatives, the commerce and labor committee of the senate".

56-7-2914, 56-7-3025, 71-3-1111 SECTION 17. Tennessee Code Annotated, Sections 56-7-2914, 56-7-3025 and 71-3-1111, are amended by deleting the language "the commerce, labor and agriculture committee of the senate, the commerce committee of the house of representatives" and substituting instead "the commerce and labor committee of the senate, the insurance and banking committee of the house of representatives".

56-7-3024 SECTION 18. Tennessee Code Annotated, Section 56-7-3024, is amended by deleting the language "the commerce committee of the house of representatives, the commerce, labor and agriculture committee of the senate" and substituting instead "the insurance and banking committee of the house of representatives, the commerce and labor committee of the senate".

56-13-122 71-5-2512 SECTION 19. Tennessee Code Annotated, Sections 56-13-122(b) and 71-5-2512(d), are amended by deleting the language "the commerce, labor and agriculture committee of the senate, and the commerce committee of the house of representatives" and substituting instead "the commerce and labor committee of the senate, and the insurance and banking committee of the house of representatives".

68-105-103 SECTION 20. Tennessee Code Annotated, Section 68-105-103(k)(4), is amended by deleting the language "the commerce committee of the house of representatives and the commerce, labor and agriculture committee of the senate" and substituting instead "the business and utilities committee of the house of representatives and the commerce and labor committee of the senate".

9-4-213, 36-5-112, 36-5-114, 37-1-182, 37-1-406, 37-2-205, 37-3-501, 37-5-125, 37-5-128, 37-5-129 SECTION 21. Tennessee Code Annotated, Sections 9-4-213(a)(8), 36-5-112(d), 36-5-114(a)(2)(B), 37-1-182(a)(2)(F), 37-1-406(m)(2), 37-2-205(f)(3), 37-3-501(e), 37-5-125(c), 37-5-128, and 37-5-129, are amended by deleting the language "children and family affairs" and substituting instead "civil justice".

36-5-101 SECTION 22. Tennessee Code Annotated, Section 36-5-101(e)(3), is amended by deleting the language "the children and family affairs committee of the house of representatives and the general welfare, health and human services committee of the senate" and substituting instead "the civil justice committee of the house of representatives and the health and welfare committee of the senate".

39-13-530 SECTION 23. Tennessee Code Annotated, Section 39-13-530(j), is amended by deleting the language "the general welfare committee of the senate, the children and family affairs committee of the house of representatives" and substituting instead "the health and welfare committee of the senate and the civil justice committee of the house of representatives".

68-1-125 SECTION 24. Tennessee Code Annotated, Section 68-1-125(d), is amended by deleting the language "the general welfare, health and human resources committee of the senate, the children and family affairs committee of the house of representatives" and substituting instead "the health and welfare committee of the senate, the civil justice committee of the house of representatives".

37-3-604 SECTION 25. Tennessee Code Annotated, Section 37-3-604, is amended by deleting the language "the chair of the general welfare, health and human resources committee of the senate, the chair of the committee on child and family affairs of the house of representatives" and substituting instead "the chair of the health and welfare committee of the senate, the chair of the civil justice committee of the house of representatives".

49-1-907 SECTION 26. Tennessee Code Annotated, Section 49-1-907(b)(9), is amended by deleting the language "or the committee on children and family affairs of the house of representatives".

37-5-605 SECTION 27. Tennessee Code Annotated, Section 37-5-605(a), is amended by deleting the language "the senate general welfare, health and human resources committee, the committee on children and family affairs of the house of representatives" and substituting instead "the senate health and welfare committee, the civil justice committee of the house of representatives".

37-5-603 SECTION 28. Tennessee Code Annotated, Section 37-5-603(b), is amended by deleting the language "the children and family affairs committee of the house of representatives, the senate general welfare, health and human resources committee, and the children and family affairs committee of the house of representatives" and substituting instead "the civil justice committee of the house of representatives and the health and welfare committee of the senate".

50-6-121 SECTION 29. Tennessee Code Annotated, Section 50-6-121, is amended by deleting in subdivision (a)(1)(F) the language "The chair of the commerce, labor and agriculture committee of the senate, the chair of the consumer and employee affairs committee of the house of representatives" and substituting instead "The chair of the commerce and labor committee of the senate, the chair of the consumer and human resources committee of the house of representatives"; by deleting in subsection (i) the language "the chair of the consumer and employee affairs committee of the house of representatives, the chair of the commerce, labor and agriculture committee of the senate" and substituting instead "the chair of the consumer and human resources committee of the house of representatives, the chair of the commerce and labor committee of the senate"; and by deleting in subsection (j) the language "the consumer and employee affairs committee of the house of representatives and commerce, labor and agriculture committee of the senate" and substituting instead "the consumer and human resources committee of the house of representatives and the commerce and labor committee of the senate".

50-6-132 SECTION 30. Tennessee Code Annotated, Section 50-6-132, is amended by deleting the language "the chairs of the senate commerce, labor and agriculture committee and the consumer and employee affairs committee of the house of representatives" and substituting instead "the chairs of the senate commerce and labor committee and the consumer and human resources committee of the house of representatives".

50-6-244, 50-6-402, 50-6-415, 50-6-919 SECTION 31. Tennessee Code Annotated, Sections 50-6-244(a), 50-6-402(b), 50-6-415(a)(2), and 50-6-919(g), are amended by deleting the language "the commerce, labor and agriculture committee of the senate, and the consumer and employee affairs committee of the house of representatives" and substituting instead, "the commerce and labor committee of the senate, and the consumer and human resources committee of the house of representatives".

16-3-811, 16-18-311, 16-21-101, 16-21-107, 16-21-111 SECTION 32. Tennessee Code Annotated, Sections 16-3-811(a)(1)(D)(iv) and (e), 16-18-311(a)(8)(A) and (b), 16-21-101, 16-21-107(a)(3)(B), and 16-21-111(c), are amended by deleting the language "judiciary committee of the house of representatives" and substituting instead "civil justice committee of the house of representatives".

40-1-111 71-1-135 SECTION 33. Tennessee Code Annotated, Sections 40-1-111(a)(1)(D)(iii) and 71-1-135(d), are amended by deleting the language "judiciary committee of the house of representatives" and substituting instead "criminal justice committee of the house of representatives".

PUBLIC CHAPTER NO. 236 (cont'd)

1-1-108 SECTION 34. Tennessee Code Annotated, Section 1-1-108(a), is amended by deleting the language "judiciary committees of the senate and house of representatives" and substituting instead "judiciary committee of the senate and the civil justice committee of the house of representatives".

38-13-102, 39-17-1351, 40-17-125, 40-31-107 SECTION 35. Tennessee Code Annotated, Sections 38-13-102, 39-17-1351(p)(1), 40-17-125(h), and 40-31-107(b), are amended by deleting the language "judiciary committees of the senate and house of representatives" and substituting instead "senate judiciary committee and the criminal justice committee of the house of representatives".

39-17-1316, 41-23-103, 55-10-422 SECTION 36. Tennessee Code Annotated, Sections 39-17-1316(e)(2), 41-23-103(b), and 55-10-422(a) and (b), are amended by deleting the language "judiciary committees of the senate and the house of representatives" and substituting instead "senate judiciary committee and the criminal justice committee of the house of representatives".

16-1-117, 17-1-107 SECTION 37. Tennessee Code Annotated, Sections 16-1-117(a)(5) and 17-1-107, are amended by deleting the language "the judiciary committees of the house of representatives and the senate" and by substituting instead "the civil justice committee of the house of representatives and the senate judiciary committee".

40-30-111 SECTION 38. Tennessee Code Annotated, Section 40-30-111(e)(1), is amended by deleting the language "the judiciary committee of the house of representatives and the senate" and substituting instead "the criminal justice committee of the house of representatives and the senate judiciary committee".

38-6-207 SECTION 39. Tennessee Code Annotated, Section 38-6-207, is amended by deleting the language "the house of representatives and senate judiciary committees" and substituting instead "the criminal justice committee of the house of representatives and the senate judiciary committee".

8-7-315, 8-14-408 SECTION 40. Tennessee Code Annotated, Sections 8-7-315 and 8-14-408, are amended by deleting the language "the judiciary committees of the respective houses of the general assembly" and substituting instead "the criminal justice committee of the house of representatives and the senate judiciary committee".

17-5-311 SECTION 41. Tennessee Code Annotated, Section 17-5-311(c), is amended by deleting the language "five (5) members of the judiciary committees of the respective houses" and substituting instead "five (5) members each from the senate judiciary committee and the civil justice committee of the house of representatives".

71-5-2508 SECTION 42. Tennessee Code Annotated, Section 71-5-2508, is amended by deleting the language "governor and the judiciary committees of the general assembly" and substituting instead "governor, senate judiciary committee, and criminal justice committee of the house of representatives".

71-5-118 SECTION 43. Tennessee Code Annotated, Section 71-5-118(c), is amended by deleting the language "judiciary committees of the general assembly" and substituting instead "criminal justice committee of the house of representatives and the senate judiciary committee".

40-36-105 SECTION 44. Tennessee Code Annotated, Section 40-36-105(2), is amended by deleting the language "the judiciary and fiscal review committees of the general assembly" and substituting instead "the criminal justice committee of the house of representatives, senate judiciary committee, and fiscal review committee".

16-3-803 SECTION 45. Tennessee Code Annotated, Section 16-3-803, is amended by deleting in subdivision (l)(1) the language "judiciary committees and" and substituting instead "civil justice committee of the house of representatives, the senate judiciary committee, and"; and by deleting in subsection (m) the language "judiciary committees of the senate and the house of representatives" and substituting instead "senate judiciary committee and civil justice committee of the house of representatives".

17-2-309 SECTION 46. Tennessee Code Annotated, Section 17-2-309, is amended by deleting in subsections (a), (b) and (c) the language "the judiciary and finance, ways and means committees of the senate and the house of representatives" and substituting instead "the civil justice and finance, ways and means committees of the house of representatives and the judiciary and finance, ways and means committees of the senate".

23-1-101 SECTION 47. Tennessee Code Annotated, Section 23-1-101(b)(1), is amended by deleting the language "the judiciary committees and the finance, ways and means committees of the senate and the house of representatives" and substituting instead "the civil justice and finance, ways and means committees of the house of representatives and the judiciary and finance, ways and means committees of the senate".

16-21-102 SECTION 48. Tennessee Code Annotated, Section 16-21-102, is amended by deleting from the first sentence the language "judiciary committee of the house of representatives" and substituting instead "civil justice committee of the house of representatives"; and by deleting from the second sentence the language "the judiciary committees of the senate and house of representatives" and substituting instead "the civil justice committee of the house of representatives and judiciary committee of the senate".

4-3-1013, 68-1-108, 71-5-2705 SECTION 49. Tennessee Code Annotated, Sections 4-3-1013(f), 68-1-108(f), and 71-5-2705(h), are amended by deleting the language "health and human resources" and substituting instead "health".

33-2-106, 53-10-309, 71-5-1422 SECTION 50. Tennessee Code Annotated, Sections 33-2-106(b)(1), 53-10-309, and 71-5-1422(a), are amended by deleting the language "the general welfare, health and human resources committee of the senate and the health and human resources committee of the house of representatives" and substituting instead "the health and welfare committee of the senate and the health committee of the house of representatives".

33-6-109 SECTION 51. Tennessee Code Annotated, Section 33-6-109, is amended by deleting the language "the health and human resources committee of the house of representatives, the general welfare, health and human resources committee of the senate" and substituting instead "the health committee of the house of representatives, the health and welfare committee of the senate".

37-3-703 SECTION 52. Tennessee Code Annotated, Section 37-3-703(d), is amended by deleting the language "the governor, the chair of the general welfare, health and human resources committee of the senate, and the chair of the health and human resources committee of the house of representatives" and substituting instead "the governor and the chairs of the health and welfare committee of the senate and health committee of the house of representatives".

37-5-115 71-5-190 SECTION 53. Tennessee Code Annotated, Sections 37-5-115 and 71-5-190(a), are amended by deleting the language "the general welfare, health and human resources committee of the senate, the health and human resources committee of the house of representatives" and substituting instead "the health and welfare committee of the senate, the health committee of the house of representatives".

37-10-401 SECTION 54. Tennessee Code Annotated, Section 37-10-401(d), is amended by deleting the language "the health and human resources committee of the house of representatives, and the senate general welfare, health and human resources committee" and substituting instead "the health committee of the house of representatives, and the senate health and welfare committee".

63-31-107 68-11-209 68-55-205 68-59-103 SECTION 55. Tennessee Code Annotated, Sections 63-31-107(a)(5), 68-11-209(a)(2), 68-55-205, and 68-59-103(a), are amended by deleting the language "the health and human resources committee of the house of representatives and the general welfare, health and human resources committee of the senate" and substituting instead "the health committee of the house of representatives and the health and welfare committee of the senate".

68-11-251 68-140-321 SECTION 56. Tennessee Code Annotated, Sections 68-11-251(f) and 68-140-321(e), are amended by deleting the language "the general welfare, health and human resources committee of the senate, to the health and human resources committee of the house of representatives" and substituting instead "the health and welfare committee of the senate, to the health committee of the house of representatives".

68-142-103 SECTION 57. Tennessee Code Annotated, Section 68-142-103, is amended in subdivision (13) by deleting the language "health and human resources" and substituting instead "health" and by deleting in subdivision (14) the language "the general welfare, health and human resources" and substituting instead "the health and welfare".

71-2-105 SECTION 58. Tennessee Code Annotated, Section 71-2-105(c)(7), is amended by deleting the language "senate commerce, labor and agriculture committee and the house health and human resources committee" and substituting instead "senate commerce and labor committee and the health committee of the house of representatives".

71-2-412 SECTION 59. Tennessee Code Annotated, Section 71-2-412(b), is amended by deleting the language "the senate general welfare, health and human resources committee and the house health and human resources committee" and substituting instead "the senate health and welfare committee and the health committee of the house of representatives".

71-3-1202 71-3-1203 SECTION 60. Tennessee Code Annotated, Sections 71-3-1202(c) and 71-3-1203, are amended by deleting the language "the general health and welfare committee of the senate and the health and human resources committee of the house of representatives" and substituting instead "the health and welfare committee of the senate and the health committee of the house of representatives".

39-17-431 SECTION 61. Tennessee Code Annotated, Section 39-17-431(o)(2), is amended by deleting the language "the house of representatives health and human resources committee and the senate general welfare, health and human resources committee" and substituting instead "the house of representatives health committee and the senate health and welfare committee".

71-1-126 SECTION 62. Tennessee Code Annotated, Section 71-1-126, is amended by deleting the language "the chair of the senate general welfare, health and human resources committee, the chair of the house finance, ways and means committee, the chair of the house health and human resources committee" and substituting instead "the chair of the senate health and welfare committee, the chair of the house of representatives finance, ways and means committee, the chair of the house of representatives health committee".

68-1-123 SECTION 63. Tennessee Code Annotated, Section 68-1-123, is amended by deleting the language "the general welfare, health and human resources committee of the senate and the health and human services committee of the house of representatives" and substituting instead "the health and welfare committee of the senate and the health committee of the house of representatives".

3-17-108, 4-51-109
4-51-111, 40-34-107
41-1-503, 41-1-507
41-21-238, 41-21-243
41-21-244, 41-22-116
41-22-405, 41-22-406
41-22-408, 41-22-411
41-24-106, 41-24-109
49-6-703

SECTION 64. Tennessee Code Annotated, Sections 3-17-108(b), 4-51-109(a)(7), 4-51-111(c)(2)(A)(i), 40-34-107(a), 41-1-503(b), 41-1-507(a), (a)(6) and (c), 41-21-238(d), 41-21-243(g), 41-21-244, 41-22-116(f), 41-22-405(a)(1), 41-22-406(a)(1)(E), 41-22-408(e) and (f)(3)(B), 41-22-411, 41-24-106(1) and (2), 41-24-109, and 49-6-703, are amended by deleting the language "the state and local government committee of the house of representatives" and substituting instead "the state government committee of the house of representatives".

2-2-140, 2-3-308
4-51-112, 4-51-116,
8-4-602, 8-30-313,
41-8-105, 41-24-104

SECTION 65. Tennessee Code Annotated, Sections 2-2-140(b), 2-3-308, 4-51-112(b)(2), 4-51-116(c), 8-4-602(b)(2), 8-30-313(f), 41-8-105(b), and 41-24-104(a)(2)(B), are amended by deleting the language "the state and local government committees of the senate and the house of representatives" and substituting instead "the state and local government committee of the senate and the state government committee of the house of representatives".

7-4-206
7-88-112
7-88-116

SECTION 66. Tennessee Code Annotated, Sections 7-4-206(b)(5), 7-88-112(c)(3), and 7-88-116(c)(3), are amended by deleting the language "the state and local government committees of the senate and the house of representatives" and substituting instead "the state and local government committee of the senate and the local government committee of the house of representatives".

13-30-119
38-11-206

SECTION 67. Tennessee Code Annotated, Sections 13-30-119(b) and 38-11-206, are amended by deleting the language "the state and local government committees of each house" and substituting instead "the state and local government committee of the senate and the local government committee of the house of representatives".

57-1-209
57-4-202
57-5-605

SECTION 68. Tennessee Code Annotated, Sections 57-1-209(b), 57-4-202(e), and 57-5-605(e)(3), are amended by deleting the language "the state and local government committees of each house" and substituting instead "the state and local government committee of the senate and the state government committee of the house of representatives".

64-5-213 SECTION 69. Tennessee Code Annotated, Section 64-5-213(b), is amended by deleting the language "house state and local government" and substituting instead "state government of the house of representatives".

4-25-107 SECTION 70. Tennessee Code Annotated, Section 4-25-107(a), is amended by deleting the language "the chairs of the senate and house of representatives state and local government committees" and substituting instead "the chairs of the state and local government committee of the senate and the state government committee of the house of representatives".

4-38-103 SECTION 71. Tennessee Code Annotated, Section 4-38-103(4), is amended by deleting the language "the chairman of the house of representatives and senate committees on state and local government respectively" and substituting instead "the chairs of the house of representatives state government committee and senate state and local government committee".

4-51-129 SECTION 72. Tennessee Code Annotated, Section 4-51-129, is amended by deleting in subdivision (1) the language "the state and local government committee of the house of representatives" and substituting instead "the state government committee of the house of representatives" and by deleting in subdivision (4)(C) the language "the chairs of the state and local government committees of the senate and house of representatives" and substituting instead the language "the chairs of the state and local government committee of the senate and the state government committee of the house of representatives".

PUBLIC CHAPTER NO. 236 (cont'd)

41-7-104 SECTION 73. Tennessee Code Annotated, Section 41-7-104(c), is amended by deleting the language "chairs of the state and local government committees and finance, ways and means committees of the senate and the house of representatives" and substituting instead "chairs of the state and local government and finance, ways and means committees of the senate and the local government and finance, ways and means committees of the house of representatives".

49-7-2205 SECTION 74. Tennessee Code Annotated, Section 49-7-2205(a), is amended by deleting the language "the state and local government committees and education committees of the house of representatives and the senate" and substituting instead the language "the state and local government and education committees of the senate and the state government and education committees of the house of representatives".

43-6-502 SECTION 75. Tennessee Code Annotated, Section 43-6-502(a), is amended by deleting the language "the commerce, labor, and agriculture committee of the senate, the energy and environment committee of the senate, the agriculture committee of the house of representatives, and the conservation and environment committee of the house of representatives" and substituting instead "the energy, agriculture and natural resources committee of the senate and the agriculture and natural resources committee of the house of representatives".

67-4-409 SECTION 76. Tennessee Code Annotated, Section 67-4-409, is amended in subdivisions (m)(1)(A) and (B) and (m)(2)(A), by deleting the language "the energy and environment committee of the senate and the conservation and environment committee of the house of representatives" and substituting instead "the energy, agriculture and natural resources committee of the senate and the agriculture and natural resources committee of the house of representatives"; and is amended in subdivisions (m)(1)(C) and (m)(2)(B), by deleting the language "the energy and environment and commerce, labor and agriculture committees of the senate and the agriculture and conservation and environment committees of the house of representatives" and substituting instead "the energy, agriculture and natural resources committee of the senate and the agriculture and natural resources committee of the house of representatives".

71-5-107 SECTION 77. Tennessee Code Annotated, Section 71-5-107(f)(2)(H), is amended by deleting the language "the general welfare, health and human resources committee of the senate, the health and human resources committee of the house of representatives, and the commerce committees of the general assembly" and substituting instead "the health and welfare committee and commerce and labor committee of the senate and the health committee and insurance and banking committee of the house of representatives".

37-2-601 SECTION 78. Tennessee Code Annotated, Section 37-2-601(a)(2), is amended by deleting the language "the children and family affairs committee of the house of representatives, the health and human resources committee of the house of representatives and the general welfare, health and human resources committee of the senate" and substituting instead "the civil justice committee and health committee of the house of representatives and the health and welfare committee of the senate".

37-3-115
37-3-116 SECTION 79. Tennessee Code Annotated, Sections 37-3-115(c) and 37-3-116(d), are amended by deleting the language "the judiciary committees of the senate and the house of representatives, the general welfare, health and human resources committee of the senate, the education committees of the senate and the house of representatives, the health and human resources committee of the house of representatives, the children and family affairs committee of the house of representatives" and substituting instead "the judiciary, education, and health and welfare committees of the senate and the civil justice, education and health committees of the house of representatives".

37-3-803 SECTION 80. Tennessee Code Annotated, Section 37-3-803(d)(2), is amended by deleting the language "the judiciary committees of the senate and the house of representatives, the general welfare, health and human resources committee of the senate, and the children and family affairs committee of the house of representatives" and substituting instead "the judiciary and health and welfare committees of the senate and the civil justice committee of the house of representatives".

37-1-607 SECTION 81. Tennessee Code Annotated, Section 37-1-607, is amended in subdivision (a)(1)(A) by deleting the language "the judiciary committees of the senate and house of representatives" and substituting instead the language "the judiciary committee of the senate and the civil justice committee of the house of representatives" and by deleting the language "The procedure and format, including an implementation plan with timelines, shall be cooperatively developed and presented to the judiciary committees of the senate and house of representatives and the children and family affairs committee of the house of representatives on or before January 15, 2000."; and is amended in subdivision (a)(1)(B) by deleting the language "the judiciary committees of the senate and house of representatives and the children and family affairs committee of the house of representatives" and substituting instead the language "the judiciary committee of the senate and the civil justice committee of the house of representatives".

37-5-105 SECTION 82. Tennessee Code Annotated, Section 37-5-105, is amended in subdivision (4)(A) by deleting the language "including the children and family affairs committee of the house of representatives,"; and is amended in subdivision (15) by deleting the language "the judiciary committees of the senate and house of representatives, and the children and family affairs committee of the house of representatives" and substituting instead "the judiciary committee of the senate and the civil justice committee of the house of representatives".

9-4-5404 SECTION 83. Tennessee Code Annotated, Section 9-4-5404, is amended by deleting the language "the general welfare, health and human resources committee of the senate; the health and human resources committee of the house of representatives; the energy and environment committee of the senate; the conservation and environment committee of the house of representatives" and by substituting instead "the health and welfare committee of the senate; the health committee of the house of representatives; the energy, agriculture and natural resources committee of the senate; the agriculture and natural resources committee of the house of representatives".

29-20-408 SECTION 84. Tennessee Code Annotated, Section 29-20-408(a)(6), is amended by deleting the language "chair of the senate and house of representatives state and local government committees, judiciary committees and finance ways and means committees, or such chair's designees" and substituting instead "chairs of the judiciary, state and local government and finance, ways and means committees of the senate and the civil justice, state government, and finance, ways and means committees of the house of representatives, or such chairs' designees".

41-1-502 SECTION 85. Tennessee Code Annotated, Section 41-1-502(a), is amended by deleting the language "the chairs of the judiciary committees of the senate and house of representatives, and the chairs of the state and local government committees of the senate and house of representatives" and substituting instead "the chairs of the judiciary and state and local government committees of the senate and the criminal justice and state government committees of the house of representatives".

71-5-106 SECTION 86. Tennessee Code Annotated, Section 71-5-106(a)(1), is amended by deleting the language "the general welfare, health and human resources committee of the senate and the general welfare committee of the house of representatives" and substituting instead "the health and welfare committee of the senate and the health committee of the house of representatives".

68-1-110 SECTION 87. Tennessee Code Annotated, Section 68-1-110, is amended by deleting the language "general welfare committee of each house, the senate and the house of representatives" and substituting instead "health and welfare committee of the senate and the health committee of the house of representatives".

4-3-2305
4-3-2311
55-4-132 SECTION 88. Tennessee Code Annotated, Sections 4-3-2305(c)(4), 4-3-2311(b)(2)(A), and 55-4-132(e), are amended by deleting the language "the senate transportation committee" and substituting "the senate transportation and safety committee".

4-3-2303 SECTION 89. Tennessee Code Annotated, Section 4-3-2303(6), is amended by deleting the language "house of representatives and senate transportation committees" and substituting instead "the transportation committee of the house of representatives and the transportation and safety committee of the senate".

4-3-2311
54-1-119
54-3-113
55-4-132
55-4-213 SECTION 90. Tennessee Code Annotated, Sections 4-3-2311(f), 54-1-119(e), 54-3-113(d)(1), 55-4-132(d), and 55-4-213(b)(1)(C), are amended by deleting the language "the transportation committees of the senate and house of representatives" and substituting instead "the transportation and safety committee of the senate and transportation committee of the house of representatives".

55-8-201 SECTION 91. Tennessee Code Annotated, Section 55-8-201(h), is amended by deleting the language "the transportation committees of the house of representatives and the senate" and substituting instead "the transportation committee of the house of representatives and the transportation and safety committee of the senate".

47-18-1310 SECTION 92. Tennessee Code Annotated, Section 47-18-1310, is amended by deleting the language "chairs of the house and senate transportation committees of the general assembly" and substituting instead "chairs of the transportation committee of the house of representatives and the transportation and safety committee of the senate".

3-9-101 SECTION 93. Tennessee Code Annotated, Section 3-9-101, is amended in subdivision (a)(3) by deleting the language "The chair, vice chair and secretary of the senate committee on finance, ways and means" and substituting instead the language "The chair, chairman emeritus and first vice chair of the senate committee on finance, ways and means; provided, that if the office of the chairman emeritus is vacant, the second vice chair"; and is amended in subdivision (a)(4) by deleting the language "The chair, vice chair and secretary of the house committee on finance, ways and means" and substituting instead "The chair, vice chair and subcommittee chair of the house of representatives committee on finance, ways and means".

Effective date 4/19/2013

SECTION 94. This act shall take effect upon becoming a law, the public welfare requiring it.

PUBLIC CHAPTER NO. 237

PUBLIC CHAPTER NO. 237

HOUSE BILL NO. 87

By Representatives Lundberg, Shipley, Timothy Hill

Substituted for: Senate Bill No. 1156

By Senator Crowe

AN ACT to amend Tennessee Code Annotated, Title 5, relative to the county budget committee under the county budgeting law of 1957.

BE IT ENACTED BY THE GENERAL ASSEMBLY OF THE STATE OF TENNESSEE:

5-12-104 SECTION 1. Tennessee Code Annotated, Section 5-12-104(b)(1), is amended by deleting the language "The committee shall" and by substituting instead the language "Except as provided in subsection (e), the committee shall".

5-12-104 SECTION 2. Tennessee Code Annotated, Section 5-12-104, is amended by adding the following language as a new subsection (e):

> (e) In any county having a population of not less than one hundred fifty-six thousand eight hundred (156,800) nor more than one hundred fifty-six thousand nine hundred (156,900) according to the 2010 federal census or any subsequent federal census, the committee shall consist of not more than nine (9) nor less than five (5) members, one (1) of whom shall be the county mayor. The other members shall be appointed by the county mayor with the approval of the county governing body at its regular January session of each year or at any subsequent session. The number of members shall be determined annually by the legislative body of the county.

Effective date 4/23/2013 SECTION 3. This act shall take effect upon becoming a law, the public welfare requiring it.

PUBLIC CHAPTER NO. 238

PUBLIC CHAPTER NO. 238

HOUSE BILL NO. 1073

By Representatives Rich, Sexton, Michael Turner, Ramsey, Rogers

Substituted for: Senate Bill No. 884

By Senator Hensley

AN ACT to amend Tennessee Code Annotated, Title 33 and Title 68, relative to voluntary admission to inpatient treatment.

BE IT ENACTED BY THE GENERAL ASSEMBLY OF THE STATE OF TENNESSEE:

33-6-201 SECTION 1. Tennessee Code Annotated, Section 33-6-201, is amended designating the present language as subsection (a) and further amended by adding the following new subdivision to subsection (a):

( ) An individual acting as an agent under the Tennessee Health Care Decisions Act, Title 68, Chapter 11, Part 18 or an individual designated as a surrogate under TCA § 68-11-1806(a).

And further amend Tennessee Code Annotated, Section 33-6-201, by adding the following as a new subsection:

(b) An individual's surrogate as designated under § 68-11-1806(c) may also apply for such admission provided no person may be admitted by a surrogate under this subsection for more than twenty-one (21) consecutive days unless a petition has been filed pursuant to Title 33, Chapter 6, Part 5, or unless an individual who meets any of the criteria set out in subdivisions (a)(1)-(7) of this section applies for voluntary admission subsequent to an application by a surrogate for voluntary admission under this section.

33-6-206 SECTION 2. Tennessee Code Annotated, Section 33-6-206(a), is amended by adding the following new subdivision:

( ) An individual acting as an agent under the Tennessee Health Care Decisions Act, Title 68, Chapter 11, Part 18 or a person's surrogate as designated under Title 68, Chapter 11, Part 18.

68-11-224 SECTION 3. Tennessee Code Annotated, Section 68-11-224, is amended by deleting the last sentence of subdivision (j)(4).

33-3-104 SECTION 4. Tennessee Code Annotated, Section 33-3-104, is amended by adding the following new subdivision:

( ) An individual acting as an agent under the Tennessee Health Care Decisions Act, Title 68, Chapter 11, Part 18 or a person's surrogate as designated under Title 68, Chapter 11, Part 18.

Effective date 7/1/2013 SECTION 5. This act shall take effect July 1, 2013, the public welfare requiring it.

PUBLIC CHAPTER NO. 239

PUBLIC CHAPTER NO. 239

HOUSE BILL NO. 1097

By Representatives Floyd, Favors, McCormick, Dean, Carter

Substituted for: Senate Bill No. 1223

By Senator Watson

AN ACT to amend Tennessee Code Annotated, Section 71-5-105, relative to ICF/MR beds.

BE IT ENACTED BY THE GENERAL ASSEMBLY OF THE STATE OF TENNESSEE:

71-5-105 SECTION 1. Tennessee Code Annotated, Section 71-5-105(b)(2), is amended by deleting the following language:

These new beds shall be filled by persons exiting the developmental centers.

and by substituting instead the following language:

These new beds shall be initially filled by persons exiting the developmental centers and upon the death of the person who exited the developmental center, the bed may be filled by individuals from the home and community based services (HCBS) waiver waiting list for individuals with intellectual disabilities, subject to the individual's freedom of choice and pursuant to a process established and administered by the department of intellectual and developmental disabilities (DIDD) in order to ensure that such placement is the most integrated and cost-effective setting appropriate.

Effective date 7/1/2013 SECTION 2. This act shall take effect July 1, 2013, the public welfare requiring it.

PUBLIC CHAPTER NO. 240

PUBLIC CHAPTER NO. 240

HOUSE BILL NO. 1223

By Representatives Hall, Haynes

Substituted for: Senate Bill No. 1295

By Senator Massey

AN ACT to amend Tennessee Code Annotated, Title 50, Chapter 2, Part 1 and Title 50, Chapter 4, Part 1, relative to wages.

BE IT ENACTED BY THE GENERAL ASSEMBLY OF THE STATE OF TENNESSEE:

50-2-101 SECTION 1. Tennessee Code Annotated, Section 50-2-101, is amended by deleting subsection (b) in its entirety and by substituting instead the following language:

(b) It is unlawful for any proprietor, foreman, owner or other person to employ, permit or suffer to work for hire, in, about, or in connection with any workshop or factory any person whatsoever without first informing the employee of the amount of wages to be paid for the labor. This shall not apply to farm labor. Nothing in this section shall apply to railroad companies engaged in interstate commerce and subject to the federal Railway Labor Act, compiled in 45 U.S.C. § 151 et seq.

50-2-101 SECTION 2. Tennessee Code Annotated, Section 50-2-101, is amended by adding the following language as a new subsection (d):

(d) The department of labor and workforce development shall enforce this section.

Effective date 4/23/2013 SECTION 3. This act shall take effect upon becoming a law, the public welfare requiring it.

PUBLIC CHAPTER NO. 241

PUBLIC CHAPTER NO. 241

HOUSE BILL NO. 80

By Representatives Womick, Madam Speaker Harwell, Evans, Rogers, Durham, Lamberth, Sargent, Dawn White, Littleton

Substituted for: Senate Bill No. 107

By Senators Haile, Dickerson, Johnson, Green, Ketron

AN ACT to amend Tennessee Code Annotated, Section 3-1-106, relative to allowances for expenses.

BE IT ENACTED BY THE GENERAL ASSEMBLY OF THE STATE OF TENNESSEE:

3-1-106 SECTION 1. Tennessee Code Annotated, Section 3-1-106(a), is amended by deleting the language "Each member of the general assembly" and by substituting instead the language "Except as otherwise provided in this section, each member of the general assembly".

3-1-106 SECTION 2. Tennessee Code Annotated, Section 3-1-106(b), is amended by adding the following language as a new subdivision:

> (3) A member whose principal residence is fifty (50) miles from the capitol or less shall only be paid an expense allowance for meals and incidentals equal to the allowance granted federal employees for such expenses in the Nashville area for each legislative day in Nashville or any day the member participates in any other meeting or endeavor as described in subsection (a) held in Nashville; provided however, if such member is unable to return home at the conclusion of any such day, with the express approval of the speaker of such member's house, the member shall be reimbursed an expense allowance for lodging equal to the allowance granted federal employees for lodging expense in the Nashville area.

3-1-106 SECTION 3. Tennessee Code Annotated, Section 3-1-106(c), is amended by deleting the first sentence in its entirety and by substituting instead the following:
Each member shall be paid a mileage allowance per mile, equal to the mileage allowance authorized for state employees who have been authorized to use personally owned vehicles in the daily performance of their duties, for each mile traveled from the member's home to the seat of government and back, limited to one (1) round trip each week of any legislative session, and one (1) round trip from the member's home to the site of any such other meeting as described in subsection (a); provided, that a member whose principal residence is fifty (50) miles from the capitol or less shall be paid a mileage allowance per mile traveled for each legislative day in Nashville or any Monday, Tuesday, Wednesday or Thursday that the member participates in any other meeting or endeavor as described in subsection (a) held in Nashville, limited to one (1) round trip per day.

3-1-106 SECTION 4. Tennessee Code Annotated, Section 3-1-106, is amended by adding the following language as a new subsection:

> (h) For the purpose of this section, "fifty (50) miles from the capitol" means the most commonly traveled route between the member's principal residence and the state capitol building.

Effective date 11/4/2014 SECTION 5. This act shall take effect November 4, 2014, the public welfare requiring it.

PUBLIC CHAPTER NO. 242

PUBLIC CHAPTER NO. 242

HOUSE BILL NO. 128

By Representatives Coley, Hardaway, Rogers, Littleton, Moody, Weaver, Camper, Parkinson, Jones, Lollar, Goins, Todd, Lundberg, Evans, Eldridge, Haynes, Ryan Williams, Windle

Substituted for: Senate Bill No. 1035

By Senators Kelsey, Ford, Crowe, Beavers

AN ACT to amend Tennessee Code Annotated, Section 39-11-118, relative to restitution to crime victims.

BE IT ENACTED BY THE GENERAL ASSEMBLY OF THE STATE OF TENNESSEE:

39-11-118 SECTION 1. Tennessee Code Annotated, Section 39-11-118, is amended by designating the existing language as subsection (a) and by adding the following language as a new subsection (b):

(b) In addition to the punishment authorized by the specific statute prohibiting the conduct, it is a part of the punishment for the offenses named in this subsection that the defendant be sentenced by the court to pay restitution to the victim or victims of §§ 39-13-309, 39-13-514, 39-17-1005(a), 39-13-528(a), and 39-13-529(a) in accordance with the provisions of §§ 40-35-104(c)(2) and 40-35-304.

Effective date 7/1/2013 SECTION 2. This act shall take effect July 1, 2013, the public welfare requiring it and shall apply to all applicable offenses committed on or after such date.

PUBLIC CHAPTER NO. 243

PUBLIC CHAPTER NO. 243

HOUSE BILL NO. 155

By Representatives McCormick, Kevin Brooks, Fitzhugh

Substituted for: Senate Bill No. 161

By Senators Norris, Watson

AN ACT to amend Tennessee Code Annotated, Section 4-4-119; Section 9-4-5101; Section 9-4-5102; Section 9-4-5103; Section 9-4-5106 and Title 9, Chapter 4, Part 56, relative to budgeting process and performance-based budgeting.

BE IT ENACTED BY THE GENERAL ASSEMBLY OF THE STATE OF TENNESSEE:

SECTION 1. This act shall be known and cited as the "Tennessee Governmental Accountability Act of 2013."

4-4-119 SECTION 2. Tennessee Code Annotated, Section 4-4-119, is amended by deleting the section in its entirety.

9-4-5101 SECTION 3. Tennessee Code Annotated, Section 9-4-5101(d), is amended by deleting the subsection in its entirety.

9-4-5102 SECTION 4. Tennessee Code Annotated, Section 9-4-5102, is amended by deleting the phrase "using performance-based program budgeting principles." and replacing it with "using performance data and other relevant program measures."

9-4-5103 SECTION 5. Tennessee Code Annotated, Section 9-4-5103(b), is amended by deleting the subsection in its entirety and substituting instead the following:

(b) Any state agency subject to part 56 of this chapter shall include with its budget request the performance measures and standards required by 9-4-5606.

9-4-5106 SECTION 6. Tennessee Code Annotated, Section 9-4-5106(a)(3), is amended by deleting the phrase "it also shall include a performance-based program budget for all state agencies subject to performance-based budgeting, including program statements and performance measures" and replacing it with the phrase "it also shall include performance measures and standards required by 9-4-5606".

9-4-5601 Part 56 SECTION 7. Tennessee Code Annotated, Section 9-4-5601, is amended by deleting this section in its entirety and substituting instead the following.

This part shall be known and may be cited as the "Tennessee Governmental Accountability Act of 2013."

9-4-5602 SECTION 8. Tennessee Code Annotated, Section 9-4-5602, is amended by deleting this section in its entirety and substituting instead the following.

The general assembly finds and declares that accountability in program performance is vital to effective and efficient delivery of governmental services, and to maintain public confidence and trust in government. To maximize accountability, a system of strategic planning, program performance measures, and performance audits should be implemented to measure the effectiveness and efficiency of governmental services. It is of paramount public importance that this system encourages full and candid participation by all agencies of state government. This system will generate information necessary to inform the public fully and for the general assembly to make meaningful decisions about the allocation of scarce resources in meeting vital needs.

9-4-5603 SECTION 9. Tennessee Code Annotated, Section 9-4-5603, is amended by deleting this section in its entirety and substituting instead the following.

The strategic planning, program performance measures, and performance review requirements of this part shall apply to all agencies unless exempted in this part or exempted by the Commissioner of Finance and Administration.

9-4-5604 SECTION 10. Tennessee Code Annotated, Section 9-4-5604, is amended by deleting this section in its entirety and substituting instead the following.
As used in this part, unless the context otherwise requires:

(1) "Agency" or "state agency" means any unit organization of the executive department, including any official, department, board, commission, division, bureau, section, district, office, authority, committee, or council or any other unit of state government, however designated, including, without limitation, higher education. For purposes of this part, "agency" or "state agency" shall not include the governor's office, the judicial department, the comptroller of the treasurer, state treasurer, secretary of state, attorney general and reporter or the legislative department. For purposes of this part, "judicial department" means the court system, district attorneys general conference, district public defenders conference, and the office of post-conviction defender;

(2) "Baseline data" means indicators of a state agency's current performance level, pursuant to guidelines established by the commissioner of finance and administration;

(3) "Commissioner" means the commissioner of finance and administration;

(4) "Outcome" means an indicator of the actual impact or public benefit of a program;

(5) "Output" means the actual service or product delivered by a state agency;

(6) "Performance measure" means a quantitative or qualitative indicator used to assess state agency performance, including outcome and output indicators;

(7) "Program" means a set of activities undertaken in accordance with a plan of action organized to realize identifiable goals and objectives. These activities are chosen by department of finance and administration in consultation with the agency or state agency to be measured in order to support the overall goals and objectives of the department.

(8) "Standard" means the desired level of performance of a program, measured by outcome or output.

9-4-5605 SECTION 11. Tennessee Code Annotated, Section 9-4-5605, is amended by deleting this section in its entirety and substituting instead the following.

(a) It is the legislative intent that the requirements of this part constitute a new approach to measuring the strategic functions and operations of each department in order for the state government to operate more efficiently and effectively.

(b) The comptroller of the treasury shall have authority to employ outside consultants and entities with expertise in governmental finance and performance review for the purpose of conducting performance reviews or otherwise fulfilling the comptroller's duties under this part. The performance reviews required under this part may be conducted by a private entity selected by the comptroller, subject to the competitive bidding requirements of title 12, chapter 4.

9-4-5606 SECTION 12. Tennessee Code Annotated, Section 9-4-5606, is amended by deleting this section in its entirety and substituting instead the following.

(a) The commissioner of finance and administration shall annually issue instructions for the strategic plans and for the development of performance measures and standards for each program.

(b) By August 15 of each year, each state agency subject to this part is required to submit to the commissioner of finance and administration, in a form to be specified by the commissioner, a draft strategic plan and proposed performance measures and standards for each program. Such state agencies shall also identify the outputs or outcomes produced by each program, baseline data associated with each performance measure, and performance standards. Performance measures and standards shall be reviewed by the commissioner of finance and administration and revised as deemed necessary by the commissioner of finance and administration.

(c) Each state agency subject to this part shall submit to the commissioner of finance and administration any documentation required by the commissioner regarding the validity, reliability, and appropriateness of each performance measure and standard and regarding how the strategic plan and the performance measures are used in management decision-making and other agency processes.

(d)

(1) Annually, at a time to be determined by the commissioner of finance and administration after the general appropriations act becomes law, state agencies may submit to the commissioner any adjustments to their performance measures and standards based on the amounts appropriated for each program by the general assembly. The chairs of the finance, ways and means committees of the senate and the house may request updated performance measures based on the increase or decrease of appropriations in the given year.

(2) At any time during the fiscal year in which a state agency, by restraining order, injunction, consent decree, settlement, or any final judgment of a court of competent jurisdiction, or by law or executive order, is required to modify its operations, or the state agency receives additional federal or other funding, the state agency may submit to the commissioner of finance and administration any necessary adjustments to its performance measures and standards.

(3) When an adjustment is made pursuant to subdivisions (d)(1) and (2), all performance measures and standards, including any adjustments made, shall be submitted to and reviewed and revised as necessary by the commissioner of finance and administration. The commissioner shall maintain the official record of adjustments to the performance measures and standards and shall update the reports accordingly. Programs that have been eliminated or added from the report in a given year shall be indicated in the annual report or when the report is updated.

9-4-5607 SECTION 13. Tennessee Code Annotated, Section 9-4-5607, is amended by deleting the section in its entirety.

9-4-5608 SECTION 14. Tennessee Code Annotated, Section 9-4-5608, is amended by deleting this section in its entirety and substituting instead the following.

(a) The commissioner of finance and administration shall evaluate at least annually each state agency's strategic plan and program performance measures. When necessary the commissioner of finance and administration shall update each state agency's strategic plan and program performance measures. Such updates shall include comments from the state agency when necessary to explain how the program is performing.

(b) The commissioner of finance and administration may make recommendations to the governor and the finance, ways, and means committees of the senate and the house of representatives concerning the following non-exhaustive performance measure incentives or disincentives for potential inclusion in the appropriations bill:

(1) Incentives may include, but are not limited to:

(A) Additional flexibility in budget management;

(B) Additional flexibility in salary rate and position management, notwithstanding title 8, chapter 23, or any other law to the contrary;

(C) Retention of up to fifty percent (50%) of unexpended and unencumbered balances of appropriations, excluding special categories and grants in aid, that may be used for non-recurring purposes including, but not limited to, lump-sum bonuses, employee training, or productivity enhancements, including technology and other improvements; and

(D) Additional funds to be used for, but not limited to, lump-sum bonuses, employee training, or productivity enhancements, including technology and other improvements;

(2) Disincentives may include, but are not limited to:

(A) Mandatory quarterly reports to the governor on the agency's progress in meeting performance standards;

(B) Mandatory quarterly appearances before the governor to report on the agency's progress in meeting performance standards;

(C) Elimination or restructuring of the program, which may include, but not be limited to, transfer of the program or outsourcing all or a portion of the program;

(D) Reduction of total positions for a program;

(E) Restriction on or reduction of the appropriation for the program; and

(F) Reduction of managerial salaries, notwithstanding the requirements of title 8, chapter 23, or any other law to the contrary.

9-4-5609 SECTION 15. Tennessee Code Annotated, Section 9-4-5609, is amended by deleting this section in its entirety and substituting instead the following.

(a) Beginning August 15, 2013, and each year thereafter, each state agency subject to this part, shall submit a draft strategic plan and the agency's programs chosen for the program performance measures to the department of finance and administration for review, modification, and approval. Each strategic plan and program performance plan shall be submitted to the general assembly and the governor not later than September 30 of each year and shall cover the fiscal year in effect as of the date of the report.

The programs report shall include, but not be limited to, the following matters:

1. A clear statement of the purpose for each program.

2. A description of the program, when such information is needed to explain the program.

3. The funding amount of each program, when such information is identifiable by agency.

4. The outcomes or outputs produced by each program.

5. The historical trends of outputs or outcomes of the program, when such information is available.

(b)

(1)

(A) The Tennessee higher education commission shall submit to the commissioner of finance and administration a single strategic plan, with the advice of the University of Tennessee, the state university and community college system, and the Tennessee student assistance corporation.

(B) The comptroller of the treasury, state treasurer, secretary of state, and attorney general and reporter shall prepare their strategic plans separately.

(C) The administrative office of the courts shall prepare a strategic plan separately on behalf of the court system. Such plan shall include the court system, the district attorneys general conference, the district public defenders conference, and the office of post-conviction defender.

(D) The joint legislative services committee shall prepare a strategic plan separately on behalf of the legislative department.

(2) Each strategic plan shall be submitted to the general assembly and the governor not later than September 30 of each year and shall cover the fiscal year in effect as of the date of the report.

9-4-5612 SECTION 16. Tennessee Code Annotated, Section 9-4-5612, is amended by deleting this section in its entirety and substituting instead the following.

The director of the office of legislative administration shall develop and submit to the joint legislative services committee proposed instructions for the development of performance measures for the legislative department. The joint legislative services committee shall review such proposed instructions, may revise or amend the proposed instructions, and shall adopt final instructions for the development of such performance measures.

9-4-5613 SECTION 17. Tennessee Code Annotated, Section 9-4-5613, is amended by deleting this section in its entirety.

9-4-5614 SECTION 18. Tennessee Code Annotated, Section 9-4-5614, is amended by deleting this section in its entirety.

9-4-5106 SECTION 19. Tennessee Code Annotated, Section 9-4-5106(a), is amended by:

(1) Deleting subdivision (2) in its entirety and by renumbering the remaining subdivisions accordingly;

(2) Deleting from the introductory sentence the language "four (4) parts" and by substituting instead the language "three (3) parts";

(3) Deleting the language "Part 3" in subdivision (2), as amended, and by substituting instead the language "Part 2"; and

(4) Deleting the language "Part 4" in subdivision (3), as amended, and by substituting instead the language "Part 3".

9-4-5106 SECTION 20. Tennessee Code Annotated, Section 9-4-5106(b), is amended by deleting the language "part 3" and by substituting instead the language "part 2".

Effective date 4/19/2013 SECTION 21. This act shall take effect upon becoming law, the public welfare requiring it.

PUBLIC CHAPTER NO. 244

PUBLIC CHAPTER NO. 244

HOUSE BILL NO. 182

By Representatives McCormick, Casada

Substituted for: Senate Bill No. 188

By Senators Norris, Ketron

AN ACT to amend Tennessee Code Annotated, Section 54-5-114, relative to advertising for bids.

BE IT ENACTED BY THE GENERAL ASSEMBLY OF THE STATE OF TENNESSEE:

54-5-114 SECTION 1. Tennessee Code Annotated, Title 54, Chapter 5, Section 114, is amended by deleting the section in its entirety and substituting instead the following language:

(a) The department, before making contracts on its own behalf, or when acting as an agent, shall advertise for bids at least two (2) weeks prior to the date set for receiving bids by publishing a written notice on the department's internet website. The department may advertise for bids by publishing notice in a newspaper located in the county where the money is to be expended, in one of the widely circulated daily newspapers in the grand division of the state where the work is to be done, or in other internet or print media as the department may deem appropriate or necessary. Funding allocated by the department for purchasing advertising in a county having a population greater than two hundred fifty thousand (250,000), according to the 1990 federal census or any subsequent federal census, and in counties located in rural west Tennessee, may be expended to purchase advertisements in one or more newspapers published primarily for distribution within the county's African-American community.

(b) The notice shall describe the work to be performed and shall enable the bidders to prepare their bids. All bids must be sealed and filed with the commissioner or the authorized agent of the department at the place designated in the notice on or before the time fixed in the notice.

(c) The requirements of this section may be modified by the department in order to conform to any federal requirements that may accompany federal funds.

(d) The requirements of this section may be waived as provided in § 54-1-135.

Effective date 4/19/2013 SECTION 2. This act shall take effect upon becoming a law, the public welfare requiring it.

PUBLIC CHAPTER NO. 245

PUBLIC CHAPTER NO. 245

HOUSE BILL NO. 191

By Representative McCormick

Substituted for: Senate Bill No. 197

By Senator Norris

AN ACT to amend Tennessee Code Annotated, Section 8-27-201; Title 65, Chapter 2; Section 65-4-303; Section 65-5-101; Section 65-5-103 and Section 65-1-102, relative to the Tennessee Regulatory Authority and the regulation of public utilities and carriers.

BE IT ENACTED BY THE GENERAL ASSEMBLY OF THE STATE OF TENNESSEE:

8-27-201 SECTION 1. Tennessee Code Annotated, Section 8-27-201(g), is amended by deleting the subsection and substituting instead the following:

(g)

(1) "State employee":

(A) Means

(i) Any person who is a state official, including members of the general assembly and legislative officials elected by the general assembly;

(ii) Any person who is employed in the service of, and whose compensation is payable by, the state;

(iii) Any person who is employed by the state whose compensation is paid, in whole or in part, from federal or other funds; or

(iv) Any director of the Tennessee regulatory authority; and

(B) Does not include any person performing services on a contractual or percentage basis.

(2) The committee shall, subject to the availability of funds as certified by the commissioner of finance and administration, have the authority to establish additional criteria that must be met by a state employee to be eligible for participation in any insurance plan offered by the committee; provided, that persons currently participating in any plan offered by the committee who are not state employees as defined in this subsection (g) shall remain eligible to participate until such time as coverage is provided by an alternative state administered plan offered by the committee.

65-1-102 SECTION 2. Tennessee Code Annotated, Section 65-1-102(b), is amended by deleting the subsection and substituting instead the following:

(b) No person who owns, in an individual capacity or jointly with another person, any bonds, stocks, equity interest or other property in any business or entity regulated by the Tennessee regulatory authority, or who is an agent or employee in any way of any such business or entity, shall be eligible to serve as a director of the Tennessee regulatory authority.

65-2-122 SECTION 3. Tennessee Code Annotated, Section Title 65, Chapter 2, is amended by adding the following language as a new section:

65-2-122

(a) The authority may establish optional services that may be purchased by regulated entities or other unregulated service providers, which are related to the exercise, administration or enforcement of jurisdiction delegated to the authority by state or federal law.

(b) The establishment of charges for services described in subsection (a) shall be cost-based.

(c) No charge for services as established in this section shall be applied to any party that does not expressly elect to use such services, and no party shall be required to elect to use such optional services as a condition of initiating any case before the authority.

65-4-303 SECTION 4. Tennessee Code Annotated, Section 65-4-303, is amended by deleting the section and substituting instead the following:

(a) The amount of the fee provided for in this section shall be measured by the amount of the gross receipts from intrastate operations of each public utility in excess of five thousand dollars ($5,000).

(b)

(1) Except as provided in subdivision (b)(2), "gross receipts from intrastate operations":

(A) Means total revenues, before any deductions, which are recognized by the authority as utility revenue for the purpose of setting intrastate rates under chapter 5 of this title; and

(B) Does not include any revenues from directory operations; provided, the exclusion of these revenues from directory operations shall not affect the power of the authority to include or exclude these revenues in setting intrastate rates.

(2) For companies that elect market regulation pursuant to § 65-5-109(m), "gross receipts from intrastate operations" means the total revenue derived from the provision of intrastate services to non-affiliated telecommunications carriers, including specifically revenue from interconnection, collocation, billing and collection, inter-carrier compensation, services sold for resale and carrier access; provided, revenue derived from the provision of retail services and products to consumers that are not telecommunications carriers is excluded.

(c)

(1) The fee fixed and assessed against and to be paid by each public utility shall be due and payable on or before April 1, 2014, and each April 1 thereafter, and shall be based on the previous calendar year's gross receipts from intrastate operations. The fee shall be four dollars and twenty-five cents ($4.25) per one thousand dollars ($1,000) of such gross receipts over five thousand dollars ($5,000), except as set forth in subdivision (c)(2) for companies that provide telecommunications services.

(2)

(i) Notwithstanding the calculations in subdivision (c)(1), the minimum inspection fee for companies that elect market regulation pursuant to § 65-5-109(m) shall be forty-nine percent (49%) of the inspection fee that was due by such company on April 1, 2012. Such companies shall file with their fee payments a calculation of both the fee as calculated under subdivision (c)(1) and the alternative minimum calculation established in this subdivision (c)(2)(i).

(ii) Notwithstanding the calculation in subdivision (c)(1), the maximum inspection fee for a company providing telecommunications services that does not elect to enter market regulation shall be the inspection fee that was due by such company on April 1, 2012.

(iii) In no event, however, shall the minimum inspection fee for any telecommunications service company be less than one hundred dollars ($100).

(d) The fee shall be due and payable on or before April 1, 2014, and each April 1 thereafter.

(e) The fee provided for in this section may be recovered by a public utility operating under rate of return regulation through either a rate case proceeding pursuant to § 65-5-103 or through a separate recovery mechanism to be determined by the authority. Nothing in this section shall alter the manner in which public utilities that operate under price regulation or market regulation, pursuant to § 65-5-109, may set rates. Nothing in this section shall alter the limitations on the jurisdiction of the authority over market-regulated companies in § 65-5-109. A public utility may recoup its inspection fees by including a line item on its subscribers' bills.

65-5-103 SECTION 5. Tennessee Code Annotated, Section 65-5-103, is amended by adding the following language as a new subsection:

(d) The authority is authorized to implement alternative regulatory methods to allow for public utility rate reviews and cost recovery in lieu of a general rate case proceeding before the authority.

(1)

(A) For all alternative regulatory methods, the authority is authorized to develop minimum filing requirements and procedural schedules; provided, however, a final determination of the authority pursuant to any alternative regulatory method be made by the authority no later than one hundred twenty (120) days from the initial filing by the public utility.

(B) If the authority denies an alternative regulatory method filed by a public utility, the authority shall set forth with specificity the reasons for its denial and the public utility shall have the right to re-file, without prejudice, an amended plan or amendment within sixty (60) days of the issuance of a final order. The authority shall thereafter have sixty (60) days to approve or deny the amended plan or amendment.

(2)

(A) A public utility may request and the authority may authorize a mechanism to recover the operational expenses, capital costs or both, if such expenses or costs are found by the authority to be in the public interest, related to any one (1) of the following:

(i) Safety requirements imposed by the state or federal government;

(ii) Insuring the reliability of the public utility plant in service; or

(iii) Weather-related natural disasters.

(B) The authority shall grant recovery and shall authorize a separate recovery mechanism or adjust rates to recover operational expenses, capital costs or both associated with the investment in such safety and reliability facilities, including the return on safety and reliability investments at the rate of return approved by the authority at the public utility's most recent general rate case pursuant to §§ 65-5-101 and 65-5-

103(a), upon a finding that such mechanism or adjustment is in the public interest.

(3)

(A) A public utility may request and the authority may authorize a mechanism to recover the operational expenses, capital costs or both related to the expansion of infrastructure for the purpose of economic development, if such expenses or costs are found by the authority to be in the public interest. Expansion of economic development infrastructure may include, but is not limited to, the following:

(i) Infrastructure and equipment associated with alternative motor vehicle transportation fuel;

(ii) Infrastructure and equipment associated with combined heat and power installations in industrial or commercial sites; and

(iii) Infrastructure that will provide opportunities for economic development benefits in the area to be directly served by the infrastructure.

(B) The authority shall grant recovery and shall authorize a separate recovery mechanism or adjust rates to recover operational expenses, capital costs or both associated with the investment in such economic development facilities, including the return on such economic development investments at the rate of return approved by the authority at the public utility's most recent general rate case pursuant to §§ 65-5-101 and 65-5-103(a), upon a finding that such mechanism or adjustment is in the public interest.

(4)

(A) A public utility may request and the authority may authorize a mechanism to recover expenses associated with efforts to promote economic development in its service territory, if such expenses are found by the authority to be in the public interest.

(i) Efforts to promote economic development may include, but are not limited to, foregone revenues associated with economic development riders and rates.

(ii) Expenses described in subdivision (d)(4)(A)(i) may be reflected in cost of service and be subject to recovery through the annual review process in subdivision (d)(6).

(B) Upon a finding that expenses to promote economic development have been incurred, the authority shall authorize a separate recovery mechanism or adjust rates to recover such expenses or grant recovery through the annual review process set forth in subdivision (d)(6), upon a finding that such mechanism or adjustment is in the public interest.

(5)

(A) A public utility may request and the authority may authorize a mechanism to recover the operational expenses, capital costs or both related to other programs that are in the public interest.

(B) A utility may request and the authority may authorize a mechanism to allow for and permit a more timely adjustment of rates resulting from changes in essential, non-discretionary expenses, such as fuel and power and chemical expenses.

(C) Upon a finding that such programs are in the public interest, the authority shall grant recovery and shall authorize a separate recovery mechanism or adjust rates to recover operational expenses, capital costs or both associated with the investment in other programs, including the rate of return approved by the authority at the public utility's most recent general rate case pursuant to §§ 65-5-101 and 65-5-103(a).

(6)

(A) A public utility may opt to file for an annual review of its rates based upon the methodology adopted in its most recent rate case pursuant to §§ 65-5-101 and 65-5-103(a), if applicable.

(B) In order for a public utility to be eligible to make an election to opt into an annual rate review, the public utility must have engaged in a general rate case pursuant to §§ 65-5-101 and 65-5-103(a) within the last five (5) years; provided, however, the authority may waive such requirement or increase the eligibility period upon a finding that doing such would be in the public interest.

(C) Pursuant to the procedures set forth in subdivision (d)(1), the authority shall review the annual filing by the public utility within one hundred twenty (120) days of receipt and order the public utility to make the adjustments to its tariff rates to provide that the public utility earns the authorized return on equity established in the public utility's most recent general rate case pursuant to §§ 65-5-101 and 65-5-103(a).

(D)

(i) A public utility may terminate an approved annual review plan only by filing a general rate case pursuant to §§ 65-5-101 and 65-5-103(a).

(ii) The authority may terminate an approved annual review plan only after citing the public utility to appear and show cause why the authority should not take such action pursuant to the procedures in § 65-2-106.

(iii) The authority or the public utility may propose a modification to the approved annual review plan for consideration by the authority. The authority shall determine whether any proposed modification is in the public interest and should be approved within the time frame set forth in subdivision (d)(6)(C). If the authority denies a modification to the approved annual review plan, the authority shall set forth with specificity the reasons for its denial.

(7) In addition to the alternative regulatory methods described in this subsection (d), a public utility may opt to file for other alternative regulatory methods. Upon a filing by a public utility for an alternative method not prescribed, the authority is empowered to adopt policies or procedures, that would permit a more timely review and revisions of the rates, tolls, fares, charges, schedules, classifications or rate structures of public utilities, and that would further streamline the regulatory process and reduce the cost and time associated with the ratemaking processes in §§ 65-5-101 and 65-5-103(a).

(e) For purposes of this section, the term "public utility" does not include a telecommunications carrier that elects market regulation pursuant to § 65-5-109.

Effective date 4/19/2013

SECTION 6. This act shall take effect upon becoming law, the public welfare requiring it.

PUBLIC CHAPTER NO. 246

PUBLIC CHAPTER NO. 246

HOUSE BILL NO. 197

By Representative Farmer

Substituted for: Senate Bill No. 622

By Senator Stevens

AN ACT to amend Tennessee Code Annotated, Title 29, Chapter 34, relative to successor corporation asbestos-related liabilities.

BE IT ENACTED BY THE GENERAL ASSEMBLY OF THE STATE OF TENNESSEE:

SECTION 1. Tennessee Code Annotated, Title 29, Chapter 34, is amended by adding Sections 2 through 8 of this act as a new part.

29-34-501 — 29-34-507 SECTION 2. This part shall be known and may be cited as the "Successor Corporation Asbestos-Related Liability Fairness Act".

SECTION 3. For purposes of this part:

(1) "Asbestos claim" means any claim, wherever or whenever made, for damages, losses, indemnification, contribution, or other relief arising out of, based on, or in any way related to asbestos, including:

(A) The health effects of exposure to asbestos, including a claim for personal injury or death, mental or emotional injury, risk of disease or other injury, or the costs of medical monitoring or surveillance;

(B) Any claim made by or on behalf of any person exposed to asbestos, or a representative, spouse, parent, child or other relative of the person; and

(C) Any claim for damage or loss caused by the installation, presence, or removal of asbestos;

(2) "Corporation" means a corporation for profit, including a domestic corporation organized under the laws of this state or a foreign corporation organized under laws other than the laws of this state;

(3) "Successor" means a corporation that assumes or incurs or has assumed or incurred successor asbestos-related liabilities that is a successor and became a successor before January 1, 1972, or is any of such successor corporation's successors;

(4) "Successor asbestos-related liabilities" means any liabilities, whether known or unknown, asserted or unasserted, absolute or contingent, accrued or unaccrued, liquidated or unliquidated, or due or to become due, that are related in any way to asbestos claims and were assumed or incurred by a corporation as a result of or in connection with a merger or consolidation, or the plan of merger or consolidation related to the merger or consolidation with or into another corporation, or that are related in any way to asbestos claims based on the exercise of control or the ownership of stock of the corporation before the merger or consolidation. "Successor asbestos-related liabilities" includes liabilities that, after the time of the merger or consolidation for which the fair market value of total gross assets is determined under section 6, were or are paid or otherwise discharged, or committed to be paid or otherwise discharged, by or on behalf of the corporation, or a successor of the corporation, or by or on behalf of a transferor, in connection with settlements, judgments, or other discharges in this state or another jurisdiction; and

(5) "Transferor" means a corporation from which successor asbestos-related liabilities are or were assumed or incurred.

PUBLIC CHAPTER NO. 246 (cont'd)

SECTION 4.

(a) The limitations in Section 5 shall apply to any successor corporation.

(b) The limitations of Section 5 shall not apply to:

(1) Workers' compensation benefits paid by or on behalf of an employer to an employee under the provisions of title 50, chapter 6, or a comparable workers' compensation law of another jurisdiction;

(2) Any claim against a corporation that does not constitute a successor asbestos-related liability;

(3) Any obligation under the National Labor Relations Act, 29 U.S.C. Section 151 et seq., as amended or under any collective bargaining agreement; or

(4) A successor that, after a merger or consolidation, continued in the business of mining asbestos or in the business of selling or distributing asbestos fibers or in the business of manufacturing, distributing, removing, or installing asbestos-containing products which were the same or substantially the same as those products previously manufactured, distributed, removed, or installed by the transferor.

SECTION 5.

(a) Except as otherwise provided in subsection (b), the cumulative successor asbestos-related liabilities of a successor corporation are limited to the fair market value of the total gross assets of the transferor determined as of the time of the merger or consolidation. The successor corporation does not have responsibility for successor asbestos-related liabilities in excess of this limitation.

(b) If the transferor had assumed or incurred successor asbestos-related liabilities in connection with a prior merger or consolidation with a prior transferor, then the fair market value of the total assets of the prior transferor determined as of the time of the earlier merger or consolidation shall be substituted for the limitation set forth in subsection (a) for purposes of determining the limitation of liability of a successor corporation.

SECTION 6.

(a) A successor corporation may establish the fair market value of total gross assets for the purpose of the limitations under Section 5 through generally accepted accounting principles, including:

(1) By reference to the going concern value of the assets or to the purchase price attributable to or paid for the assets in an arms-length transaction; or

(2) In the absence of other readily available information from which the fair market value can be determined, by reference to the value of the assets recorded on a balance sheet.

(b) For purposes of this section, total gross assets may include any intangible assets.

(c) To the extent total gross assets include any liability insurance that was issued to the transferor whose assets are being valued for purposes of this section, the applicability, terms, conditions and limits of such insurance shall not be affected by this statute, nor shall this statute otherwise affect the rights and obligations of an insurer, transferor or successor under any insurance contract or any related agreements, including, without limitation, preenactment settlements resolving coverage-related disputes, and the rights of an insurer to seek payment for applicable deductibles, retrospective premiums or self-insured retentions or to seek contribution from a successor for uninsured or self-insured periods or periods where insurance is uncollectible or otherwise unavailable. Without limiting the foregoing, to the extent total gross assets include any such liability insurance, a settlement of a dispute concerning any such liability insurance coverage entered into by a transferor or successor with the insurers of the transferor before July 1, 2013, shall be determinative of the total coverage of such liability insurance to be included in the calculation of the transferor's total gross assets.

SECTION 7.

(a) Except as otherwise provided in this section, the fair market value of total gross assets at the time of the merger or consolidation shall increase annually at a rate equal to the sum of:

(1) The prime rate as listed in the first edition of the Wall Street Journal published for each calendar year since the merger or consolidation, unless the prime rate is not published in that edition of the Wall Street Journal, in which case any reasonable determination of the prime rate on the first day of the year may be used; and

(2) One percent (1%).

(b) The rate determined pursuant to subsection (a) shall not be compounded.

(c) The adjustment of the fair market value of total gross assets shall continue as provided in subsection (a) until the date the adjusted value is first exceeded by the cumulative amounts of successor asbestos-related liabilities paid or committed to be paid by or on behalf of the successor corporation or a predecessor or by or on behalf of a transferor after the time of the merger or consolidation for which the fair market value of total gross assets is determined.

(d) No adjustment of the fair market value of total gross assets shall be applied to any liability insurance that may be included in total gross assets pursuant to Section 6 (c).

SECTION 8.

(a) The courts of this state shall construe this act liberally with regard to successors.

(b) This act shall apply to all asbestos claims filed against a successor on or after July 1, 2013.

(c) This act shall also apply to any pending asbestos claims against a successor in which trial has not commenced as of July 1, 2013, except that any provisions of these sections which would be unconstitutional if applied retroactively shall be applied prospectively.

Effective date 7/1/2013

SECTION 9. This act shall take effect July 1, 2013, the public welfare requiring it.

PUBLIC CHAPTER NO. 247

PUBLIC CHAPTER NO. 247

House Bill No. 225

By Representative Sparks

Substituted for: Senate Bill No. 633

By Senators Tracy, Finney

AN ACT to amend Tennessee Code Annotated, Title 29, Chapter 3 and Title 39, relative to drug paraphernalia.

BE IT ENACTED BY THE GENERAL ASSEMBLY OF THE STATE OF TENNESSEE:

29-3-101 **SECTION 1. Tennessee Code Annotated, Section 29-3-101(a)(2)(A), is amended by deleting the language "other controlled substance or controlled substance analogue" and by substituting instead the language "other controlled substance or controlled substance analogue, any sale or possession with intent to sell of drug paraphernalia, as defined by § 39-17-402".**

Effective date 7/1/2013 **SECTION 2. This act shall take effect July 1, 2013, the public welfare requiring it.**

PUBLIC CHAPTER NO. 248

PUBLIC CHAPTER NO. 248

HOUSE BILL NO. 301

By Representatives McDaniel, Kent Williams, Goins

Substituted for: Senate Bill No. 642

By Senators Tracy, Ketron, Burks, Gardenhire

AN ACT to amend Tennessee Code Annotated, Title 4, Chapter 11, Part 1, relative to historical preservation.

BE IT ENACTED BY THE GENERAL ASSEMBLY OF THE STATE OF TENNESSEE:

SECTION 1. This act shall be known and may be cited as the "Tennessee Civil War or War Between the States Site Preservation Act of 2013".

4-11-112 SECTION 2. Tennessee Code Annotated, Title 4, Chapter 11, Part 1, is amended by adding the following language as a new section:

4-11-112.

(a) There is created a special account in the state treasury to be known as the Tennessee Civil War or War Between the States site preservation fund, hereinafter referred to as the "preservation fund".

(b)

(1) Moneys in the preservation fund shall be used exclusively by the Tennessee historical commission to provide grants to private nonprofit organizations to match federal and other matching funds. All such grants shall be made solely for the fee simple purchase of, or purchase of protective interests in, any Tennessee Civil War or War Between the States historic site listed in the Report on the Nation's Civil War Battlefields, issued in 1993, or as amended or reissued pursuant to the Civil War Battlefield Preservation Act of 2002 (P.L. 107-359) as amended or supplemented by new information by the National Park Service's American Battlefield Protection Program, hereinafter referred to as "the report" or any historic site associated with the Underground Railroad that is eligible for National Historic Landmark designation or for listing in the National Register of Historic Places".

(2) The commission shall establish, administer, manage and make expenditures and allocations from the preservation fund.

(3)

(A) Private nonprofit organizations seeking grant funding from the preservation fund shall be required to provide matching funds from any non-state sources on a dollar-for-dollar basis.

(B) For the purposes of this section, "matching funds" means both cash and the value of any non-cash contribution due to a bargain sale or the donation of land or interest therein made by the landowner as part of the proposed project.

(C) No state funds may be included in determining the amount of the match.

(4) Eligible costs for which moneys from the preservation fund may be allocated include acquisition of land and any improvements thereon or permanent protective interests, including, but not limited to, conservation easements, and costs associated with such acquisitions, including, but

not limited to, the cost of appraisals, environmental reports, surveys, title searches and title insurance, and other closing costs.

(5) Grants from the preservation fund shall not exceed fifty percent (50%) of the appraised value of the land or permanent protective interest therein.

(6) Grants from the preservation fund may be awarded for prospective purchases or for acquisitions which the applicant has closed; provided, that for closed acquisitions, the applicant shall demonstrate that:

(A) The closing occurred no more than twelve (12) months prior to the date of application for the grant; and

(B) An identifiable threat to the resource or compelling need for preservation existed at the time of the purchase.

(7) Any eligible organization making an acquisition of land or interest therein pursuant to this section shall grant to the state or other qualified holder a perpetual easement placing restrictions on the use or development of the land. In cases where the easement is granted to a holder other than the state, all terms and conditions of the easement shall be reviewed by and found by the commission to be consistent with the intent and purpose of the Conservation Easement Act, compiled in title 66, chapter 9, part 3, and to accomplish the perpetual preservation of Civil War or War Between the States historic site or historic site associated with the Underground Railroad. Such other holder shall demonstrate to the commission that it has the capacity and expertise to manage and enforce the terms of the easement.

(8) Nothing in this section shall be construed to prevent the subsequent transfer of property acquired pursuant to this section to the United States of America, its agencies or instrumentalities.

(9) The commission shall establish, administer, manage and make expenditures and allocations from the preservation fund and shall establish guidelines for applications, prioritization and award of grants from the preservation fund in consultation with appropriate "site" preservation interests. Consideration shall be given, but not limited to, the following:

(A) Significance of the battlefield and the location of the proposed project in relation to core and study areas as identified in the report as well as proximity to other protected lands;

(B) Threat to and integrity of the features associated with the battle which occurred there; and

(C) The financial and administrative capacity of the applicant to complete the project and to maintain and manage the property consistent with the public investment and public interests, such as education, recreation, research, heritage tourism promotion or orderly community development.

(10) All grant recipients are subject to audit by the comptroller of the treasury as to the funds received pursuant to this section.

(c)

(1) In addition to appropriations made to the preservation fund, the commission may accept other funds, public or private, by way of gift or grant to the fund. Any such gift or grant shall be deposited into the preservation fund to be distributed in accordance with this section.

(2) Moneys in the preservation fund may be invested by the state treasurer in accordance with § 9-4-602.

(3) Notwithstanding any law to the contrary, interest accruing on investments and deposits of the preservation fund shall be credited to such fund, shall not revert to the general fund, and shall be carried forward into the subsequent fiscal year.

(4) Any balance remaining unexpended at the end of a fiscal year in the preservation fund shall not revert to the general fund but shall be carried forward into the subsequent fiscal year.

Effective date 4/19/2013

SECTION 3. This act shall take effect upon becoming a law, the public welfare requiring it.

PUBLIC CHAPTER NO. 249

PUBLIC CHAPTER NO. 249

HOUSE BILL NO. 348

By Representative Todd

Substituted for: Senate Bill No. 62

By Senators Tate, Ford, Harper

AN ACT to amend Tennessee Code Annotated, Title 5; Title 6; Title 7; Title 39, Chapter 17; Title 54; Title 55, Chapter 20; Title 55, Chapter 52 and Title 68, relative to safety of children.

BE IT ENACTED BY THE GENERAL ASSEMBLY OF THE STATE OF TENNESSEE:

68-106-101, 68-106-102

SECTION 1. Tennessee Code Annotated, Title 68, is amended by adding the following language as a new, appropriately designated chapter:

68-106-101. For purposes of this part, unless the context otherwise requires:

(1) "Child" means any person under eighteen (18) years of age;

(2) "Highway" means the entire width between the boundary lines of every way when any part thereto is open to the use of the public for the purpose of vehicular travel;

(3) "Intersection" means the area embraced within the prolongation or connection of the lateral curb lines, or, if none, then the lateral boundary lines of the roadways of two (2) highways that join one another at, or approximately at, right angles, or the areas within which vehicles traveling upon different highways joining at any other angle may come in conflict;

(4) "Roadway" means that portion of a highway improved, designed or ordinarily used for vehicular travel, exclusive of the berm or shoulder. In the event a highway includes two (2) or more separate roadways, "roadway" refers to any such roadway separately but not to all such roadways collectively; and

(5) "Sidewalk" means the portion of a street between the curb lines, or the lateral lines of a roadway, and the adjacent property lines, intended for use by pedestrians.

68-106-102.

(a) A county may by resolution, and a municipality may by ordinance, prohibit or restrict a child from being present in the roadway of a highway or an intersection for the purpose of the child's participation in soliciting or collecting money.

(b) This section shall not apply to private roads or driveways, nor shall this section prevent children from using sidewalks.

Effective date 7/1/2013

SECTION 2. This act shall take effect July 1, 2013, the public welfare requiring it.

PUBLIC CHAPTER NO. 250

PUBLIC CHAPTER NO. 250

HOUSE BILL NO. 544

By Representatives Harrison, Casada, Sargent, Hardaway, Miller, Roach

Substituted for: Senate Bill No. 441

By Senators Overbey, Massey, Bowling, Burks, Ford, Gardenhire

AN ACT to amend Tennessee Code Annotated, Title 71, Chapter 5, and Chapter 645 of the Public Acts of 2012, relative to the Annual Coverage Assessment.

BE IT ENACTED BY THE GENERAL ASSEMBLY OF THE STATE OF TENNESSEE:

71-5-701 — 71-5-705 SECTION 1. Tennessee Code Annotated, Title 71, Chapter 5, is amended by adding the following as a new part to be appropriately designated:

71-5-__01. This part shall be known and may be cited as the "Annual Coverage Assessment Act of 2013".

71-5-__02. As used in this part, unless the context otherwise requires:

(1) "Annual coverage assessment" means the annual assessment imposed on covered hospitals as set forth in this part;

(2) "Annual coverage assessment base" is a covered hospital's net patient revenue as shown in its medicare cost report for its fiscal year that ended during calendar year 2008 on file with the centers for medicare and medicaid services ("CMS") as of September 30, 2009, subject to the following qualifications:

(A) If a covered hospital does not have a full twelve-month medicare cost report for 2008 on file with CMS as of September 30, 2009, but does have a full twelve-month medicare cost report for 2008 on file as of September 30, 2010, the twelve-month medicare cost report for 2008 on file with CMS as of September 30, 2010, will be the annual coverage assessment base;

(B) If a covered hospital does not have a full twelve-month medicare cost report on file with CMS for 2008, but does have a medicare cost report on file with CMS for 2009, that medicare cost report will be the annual coverage assessment base. If the covered hospital's 2009 medicare cost report is for a partial year only, the net patient revenue in such medicare cost report shall be annualized to determine the hospital's annual coverage assessment base;

(C) If a covered hospital was first licensed in 2010 or later and did not replace an existing hospital, the annual coverage assessment base is the covered hospital's projected net patient revenue for its first full year of operation as shown in its certificate of need application filed with the health services and development agency;

(D) If a covered hospital was first licensed in 2010 or later and replaced an existing hospital, the annual coverage assessment base shall be the predecessor hospital's net patient revenue as shown in its medicare cost report for its fiscal year that ended during calendar year 2008 on file with CMS as of September 30, 2009, subject to the qualifications of subdivisions (2)(A) and (2)(B);

(E) If a covered hospital is not required to file an annual medicare cost report with CMS, then its annual coverage assessment base shall be its net patient revenue for the fiscal year ending during calendar year 2008 or the first fiscal year that the hospital was in operation if after 2008 as shown in the covered hospital's joint annual report filed with the department of health;

(F) If a covered hospital's fiscal year 2008 medicare cost report is not contained in the centers for medicare and medicaid services' healthcare cost report information system file dated September 30, 2009, and does not meet any of the other qualifications listed in subdivisions (2)(A)-(E), then the hospital shall submit a copy of the hospital's 2008 medicare cost report to the bureau of TennCare in order to allow for the determination of the hospital's net patient revenue for the state fiscal year 2013-2014 annual coverage assessment;

(3) "Bureau" means the bureau of TennCare;

(4) "CMS" means the federal centers for medicare and medicaid services;

(5) "Controlling person" means a person who, by ownership, contract or otherwise, has the authority to control the business operations of a covered hospital. Indirect or direct ownership of ten percent (10%) or more of a covered hospital shall constitute control;

(6) "Covered hospital" means a hospital licensed under title 33 or title 68, as of the effective date of this part, except an excluded hospital;

(7) "Excluded hospital" means:

(A) A hospital that has been designated by CMS as a critical access hospital;

(B) A mental health hospital owned by the state of Tennessee;

(C) A hospital providing primarily rehabilitative or long-term acute care services;

(D) A children's research hospital that does not charge patients for services beyond that reimbursed by third party payors; and

(E) A hospital that is determined by the bureau of TennCare as eligible to certify public expenditures for the purpose of securing federal medical assistance percentage payments;

(8) "Medicare cost report" means CMS-2552-96, the cost report for electronic filing of hospitals, for the period applicable as set forth in this section; and

(9) "Net patient revenue" means the amount calculated in accordance with generally accepted accounting principles for hospitals that is reported on Worksheet G-3, Column 1, Line 3, of the medicare cost report, excluding long-term care inpatient ancillary revenues.

71-5-__03.

(a) There is imposed on each covered hospital licensed as of the effective date, an annual coverage assessment for fiscal year (FY) 2013-2014 as set forth in this part.

(b) The annual coverage assessment imposed by this part shall not be effective and validly imposed until the bureau has provided the Tennessee Hospital Association with written notice that includes:

(1) A determination from CMS that the annual coverage assessment is a permissible source of revenue that shall not adversely affect the amount of federal financial participation in the TennCare program;

(2) Approval from CMS for the distribution of additional payments to hospitals to offset unreimbursed TennCare costs as set forth in § 71-5-_05(d)(2); and

(3) Evidence that the TennCare Bureau will implement the remaining rate changes effective July 1, 2013, that establish a floor and ceiling for hospital reimbursement that reduce the amount of variation in reimbursement rates to hospitals for the same or similar services.

(c) The general assembly intends that the proceeds of the annual coverage assessment not be used as a justification to reduce or eliminate the state funding to the TennCare program. To this end, the annual coverage assessment shall not be effective and validly imposed if the coverage or the amount of revenue available for expenditure by the TennCare program in FY 2013-2014 is less than:

(1) The governor's FY 2013-2014 recommended budget level; plus

(2) All annual appropriations made by the general assembly to the TennCare program for FY 2013-2014, except to the extent new federal funding is available to replace funds that are appropriated as described in subdivision (c)(1) and that are above the amount that the state receives from CMS under the regular federal matching assistance percentage.

(d)

(1)

(A) The general assembly intends that the proceeds of the annual coverage assessment not be used as justification for any TennCare managed care organization to implement across the board rate reductions to negotiated rates with covered or excluded hospitals or physicians in existence on July 1, 2013. To this end, for those rates in effect on July 1, 2013, the bureau shall include provisions in the managed care organizations' contractor risk agreements that prohibit the managed care organizations from implementing across the board rate reductions to covered or excluded network hospitals or physicians either by category or type of provider. The requirements of the preceding sentence shall also apply to services or settings of care that are ancillary to a covered or excluded hospital or physician's primary license, but shall not apply to reductions in benefits or reimbursement for such ancillary services if:

(i) Such reductions are different from those items being restored in § 71-5-__05(d); and

(ii) Such reductions have been communicated in advance of implementation to the general assembly and the Tennessee Hospital Association.

(B) For purposes of this subsection (d), services or settings of care that are ancillary to a covered or excluded hospital or physician's primary license shall include all services where the physician or covered or excluded hospital, including a wholly owned subsidiary or controlled affiliate of a covered or excluded hospital or hospital system, holds more than a fifty percent (50%) controlling interest in such ancillary services or settings of care, but shall not include any other ancillary services or settings of care. For across the board rate reductions to ancillary services or settings of care, the bureau shall include appropriate requirements for notice to providers in the managed care organizations' contractor risk agreements. For purposes of this subsection (d), services or settings of care that are "ancillary" mean, but is not limited to, ambulatory surgical facilities, outpatient treatment clinics or imaging centers, dialysis centers, home health and related services, home infusion therapy services, outpatient rehabilitation or skilled nursing services. For purposes of this subsection (d), "physician" includes a physician licensed under title 63, chapter 6 or chapter 9 and a group practice of physicians that hold a contract with a managed care organization.

(2) This subsection (d) does not preclude good faith negotiations between managed care organizations and covered or excluded hospitals, hospital systems and physicians on an individualized, case-by-case basis, nor is this subsection (d) intended by the general assembly to serve as justification for Tennessee managed care organizations, covered or excluded hospitals, hospital

systems or physicians to unreasonably deny any party the ability to enter into such individualized, case-by-case "good faith" negotiations. Such "good faith" negotiation necessarily implies mutual cooperation between the negotiating parties and may include, but is not limited to, the right to terminate contractual agreements, the ability to modify negotiated rates, pricing or units of service, the ability to alter payment methodologies, and the ability to enforce existing managed care techniques or implement new managed care techniques.

(3) Notwithstanding the other provisions of this subsection (d), if CMS mandates a TennCare program change or a change is required by federal law that impacts rates and that is required to be implemented by the MCOs in accordance with their contracts, or the annual coverage assessment becomes invalid, then nothing in this part shall prohibit the managed care organizations from implementing any rate changes as may be mandated by TennCare or federal law.

71-5-__04.

(a) The annual coverage assessment established for this part shall be four and fifty-two hundredths percent (4.52%) of a covered hospital's annual coverage assessment base.

(b) The annual coverage assessment shall be paid in equal quarterly installments, with the first quarterly payment due on the fifteenth day of the first month of the first quarter of the state fiscal year after the bureau has obtained the determination and approval from CMS described in § 71-5-__03(b). Subsequent installments shall be due on the fifteenth day of the first month of the three (3) successive calendar quarters following the calendar quarter in which the first installment is due.

(c) To facilitate collection of the annual coverage assessment, the bureau shall send to each covered hospital, at least thirty (30) days in advance of each quarterly payment due date, a notice of payment along with a return form developed by the bureau. Failure of a covered hospital to receive a notice and return form, however, shall not relieve a covered hospital from the obligation of timely payment. The bureau shall also post the return form on its web site.

(d) Failure of a covered hospital to pay a quarterly installment of the annual coverage assessment when due shall result in an imposition of a penalty of five hundred dollars ($500) per day until such installment is paid in full.

(e) If a covered hospital ceases to operate after July 1, 2013, and before July 1, 2014, its total annual coverage assessment shall be equal to its annual coverage assessment base multiplied by a fraction, the denominator of which is the number of calendar days from July 1, 2013, until July 1, 2014, and the numerator of which is the number of days from July 1, 2013, until the date the Tennessee division of health care facilities has recorded as the date that the hospital ceased operation.

(f) If a covered hospital ceases operation prior to payment of its full annual coverage assessment, then the person or persons controlling the hospital as of the date the hospital ceased operation shall be jointly and severally responsible for any remaining annual coverage assessment installments and unpaid penalties associated with previous late payments.

(g) If a covered hospital fails to pay a quarterly installment of the annual coverage assessment within thirty (30) days of its due date, the bureau shall report such failure to the department which licenses the covered hospital. Notwithstanding any other law, failure of a covered hospital to pay a quarterly installment of the annual coverage assessment or any refund required by this part shall be considered a license deficiency and grounds for disciplinary action as set forth in the statutes and rules under which the covered hospital is licensed.

(h) In addition to the action required by subsection (g), the bureau is authorized to file a civil action against a covered hospital and its controlling person or persons to collect delinquent annual coverage assessment installments, late penalties and refund obligations established by this part. Exclusive jurisdiction and venue for a civil action authorized by this subsection (h) shall be in the chancery court for Davidson County.

(i)

(1) If any federal agency with jurisdiction over this annual coverage assessment determines that the annual coverage assessment is not a valid source of revenue or that the methodology for distribution of the additional payments to hospitals from the annual coverage assessment is not valid after an installment has been collected, or if there is a reduction of the coverage and funding of the TennCare program contrary to § 71-5-__03(c), or if one (1) or more managed care organizations impose rate reductions contrary to § 71-5- __03(d), then:

(A) The bureau shall refund to covered hospitals all installment payments previously collected within forty-five (45) days of such event;

(B) No subsequent installments of the annual coverage assessment shall be due and payable; and

(C) Covered hospitals that received payments pursuant to § 71-5-__05(d)(2) shall refund to the bureau all such payments within forty-five (45) days of such event, or shall establish a payment plan that has been approved by the bureau within forty-five (45) days of such event.

(2) The bureau will then have authority to make necessary changes to the TennCare budget to account for the loss of the annual coverage assessment revenue.

(j) A covered hospital or an association, the membership of which includes thirty (30) or more covered hospitals, shall have the right to file a petition for declaratory order pursuant to § 4-5-223 to determine if there has been a failure to satisfy one (1) of the conditions precedent to the valid imposition of the annual coverage assessment.

(k) A covered hospital may not increase charges or add a surcharge based on or as a result of the annual coverage assessment.

(l) Notwithstanding any other provision of this part, if the bureau receives from CMS notification of the determination and approval set forth in § 71-5-__ 03(b), and if such determination and approval have retroactive effective dates, then:

(1) Quarterly annual coverage assessment payments that become due by application of the retroactive determination date from CMS shall be paid to the bureau within thirty (30) days of the bureau notifying the Tennessee Hospital Association that CMS has issued such determination; and

(2) Quarterly payments to covered hospitals required by § 71-5- __05(d) (2) that become due by application of the retroactive approval date from CMS shall be paid within fifteen (15) days of the bureau notifying the Tennessee Hospital Association that CMS has issued such approval.

71-5-__05.

(a) The funds generated as a result of this part shall be deposited in the maintenance of coverage trust fund created by the section formerly codified as § 71-5-1005, extended by §§ 71-5-1006, 71-5-2006, and 71-5-2706, and by § 71-5-160, the existence of which is continued by subsection (b). The fund shall not be used to replace any monies otherwise appropriated to the TennCare program by the general assembly or to replace any monies appropriated outside of the TennCare program.

(b) Notwithstanding the section formerly codified as § 71-5-1006, the maintenance of coverage trust fund created by the section formerly codified as § 71-5-1005, extended by §§ 71-5-1006, 71-5-2006, and 71-5-2706, and by § 71-5-160, shall continue without interruption and shall be operated in accordance with this section.

(c) The maintenance of coverage trust fund shall consist of:

(1) All annual coverage assessments received by the bureau; and

(2) Investment earnings credited to the assets of the maintenance of coverage trust fund.

(d) Monies credited or deposited to the maintenance of coverage trust fund together with all federal matching funds shall be available to and used by the bureau only for expenditures in the TennCare program and shall include the following purposes:

(1) Expenditure for benefits and services under the TennCare program that would have been subject to reduction or elimination from TennCare funding for FY 2012-2013, except for the availability of one-time funding for that year only, as follows:

(A) Replacement of seven percent (7%) reduction in covered and excluded hospital and professional reimbursement rates described in the governor's FY 2013-2014 recommended budget;

(B) Maintenance of essential access hospital payments of at least one hundred million dollars ($100,000,000);

(C) Maintenance of payments to critical access hospitals to achieve reimbursement of full cost of benefits provided to TennCare enrollees up to sixteen million dollars ($16,000,000);

(D) Maintenance of payments for the graduate medical education of at least fifty million dollars ($50,000,000);

(E) Maintenance of reimbursement for medicare part A crossover claims at the lesser of one hundred percent (100%) of medicare allowable or the billed amount;

(F) Funding to increase the rates for the lowest paid hospitals to reduce the amount of variation in TennCare hospital rates for the same or similar services;

(G) Avoidance of any coverage limitations relative to the number of hospital inpatient days per year or annual cost of inpatient services for a TennCare enrollee;

(H) Avoidance of any coverage limitations relative to the number of non-emergency outpatient visits per year for a TennCare enrollee;

(I) Avoidance of any coverage limitations relative to the number of physician office visits per year for a TennCare enrollee;

(J) Avoidance of coverage limitations relative to the number of laboratory and diagnostic imaging encounters per year for a TennCare

(K) Maintenance of coverage for occupational therapy, physical therapy and speech therapy services; and

(L) Making medicaid disproportionate share hospital payments at the maximum amount authorized by the federal Social Security Act for FY 2013-2014;

(2)

PUBLIC CHAPTER NO. 250 (cont'd)

(A) Solely from the annual coverage assessment payments received by the bureau, payments to covered hospitals to offset losses incurred in providing services to TennCare enrollees as set forth in this subdivision (d)(2);

(B) Each covered hospital shall be entitled to payments for FY 2013-2014 of a portion of its unreimbursed cost of providing services to TennCare enrollees. Unreimbursed TennCare costs are defined as the excess of cost over TennCare net revenue as reported on the hospital's 2011 joint annual report filed with the department of health. TennCare costs are defined as the product of a facility's cost-to-charge ratio times TennCare charges. The amount of the payment to covered hospitals shall be no less than fifty-four and two tenths percent (54.20%) of unreimbursed TennCare cost for all hospitals licensed by the state of Tennessee excluding state owned hospitals;

(C) The payments required by this subdivision (d)(2) shall be made in four (4) equal installments. Each installment payment shall be made by the third business day of four (4) successive calendar quarters, with the first calendar quarter to be the calendar quarter in which the annual coverage assessment is first levied in accordance with § 71-5-__04. The bureau shall provide to the Tennessee Hospital Association a schedule showing the quarterly payments to each hospital at least seven (7) days in advance of such payments;

(D) The payments required by this subdivision (d)(2) may be made by the bureau directly to the hospitals or the bureau may transfer the funds to one (1) or more managed care organizations with the direction to make payments to hospitals as required by this subsection. The payments to a hospital pursuant to this subdivision (d)(2) shall not be considered as part of the reimbursement to which a hospital is entitled under its contract with a TennCare managed care organization; and

(3) Refunds to covered hospitals on the basis of payment of annual coverage assessments or penalties to the bureau through error, mistake, or a determination that the annual coverage assessment was invalidly imposed.

(e) If a hospital closes or changes status from a covered hospital to an excluded hospital and consequently reduces the amount of the annual coverage assessment such that the amount is no longer sufficient to cover the total cost of the items included in subsection (d), the payments for these items may be adjusted by an amount equal to the shortfall including the federal financial participation. The items to be adjusted and the amounts of the adjustments shall be determined by the bureau in consultation with hospitals.

(f) The bureau shall modify the contracts with TennCare managed care organizations and otherwise take action necessary to assure the use and application of the assets of the maintenance of coverage trust fund, as described in subsection (d).

(g) The bureau shall submit requests to CMS to modify the medicaid state plan, the contractor risk agreements or the TennCare II Section 1115 demonstration project as necessary to implement the requirements of this part.

(h) At quarterly intervals beginning September 1, 2013, the bureau shall submit a report to the finance, ways and means committees of the senate and house of representatives, to the health and welfare committee of the senate and to the health committee of the house of representatives, which report shall include:

(1) The status if applicable of the determination and approval by CMS set forth in § 71-5-03(b) of the annual coverage assessment;

(2) The balance of funds in the maintenance of coverage trust fund; and

(3) The extent of which the maintenance of coverage trust fund has been used to carry out this part.

(i) No part of the maintenance of coverage trust fund shall be diverted to the general fund or used for any purpose other than set forth in this part.

71-5-160
71-5-706

SECTION 2. Tennessee Code Annotated, Section 71-5-160, is amended by adding the following as a new subsection:

(e) The Annual Coverage Assessment Act of 2013, enacted by this act, shall expire on June 30, 2014; provided, however, the following rights and obligations shall survive such expiration:

(1) The authority of the bureau to impose late payment penalties and to collect unpaid annual coverage assessments and required refunds;

(2) The rights of a covered hospital or an association of covered hospitals to file a petition for declaratory order to determine whether the annual coverage assessment has been validly imposed; and

(3) The existence of the maintenance of coverage trust fund and the obligation of the bureau to use and apply the assets of the maintenance of coverage trust fund.

Effective date 7/1/2013

SECTION 3. This act shall take effect July 1, 2013, the public welfare requiring it.

PUBLIC CHAPTER NO. 251

PUBLIC CHAPTER NO. 251

HOUSE BILL NO. 742

By Representatives Coley, Rogers, Littleton, Moody, Weaver, Camper, Parkinson, Jones, Favors, Lollar, Goins, Todd, Dean, Lundberg, Sexton, Ryan Williams, Mark White, Hardaway, Eldridge

Substituted for: Senate Bill No. 1027

By Senators Ketron, Ford, Crowe, Beavers, Burks, Overbey

AN ACT to amend Tennessee Code Annotated, Title 24, Chapter 7, Part 1, relative to the admissibility of evidence in certain cases.

BE IT ENACTED BY THE GENERAL ASSEMBLY OF THE STATE OF TENNESSEE:

24-7-120 SECTION 1. Tennessee Code Annotated, Section 24-7-120, is amended by adding the following new subdivisions to subsection (e):

( ) Trafficking for commercial sex act as defined in § 39-13-309;

( ) Patronizing prostitution as defined in § 39-13-514

Effective date 7/1/2013 SECTION 2. This act shall take effect July 1, 2013, the public welfare requiring it.

PUBLIC CHAPTER NO. 252

PUBLIC CHAPTER NO. 252

HOUSE BILL NO. 809

By Representatives Matheny, Ragan, Hardaway

Substituted for: Senate Bill No. 327

By Senator Bell

AN ACT to amend Tennessee Code Annotated, Title 4, relative to the department of economic and community development.

BE IT ENACTED BY THE GENERAL ASSEMBLY OF THE STATE OF TENNESSEE:

4-29-234 SECTION 1. Tennessee Code Annotated, Section 4-29-234(a), is amended by deleting subdivision (21) in its entirety.

4-29-238 SECTION 2. Tennessee Code Annotated, Section 4-29-238(a), is amended by adding a new subdivision thereto, as follows:

( ) Department of economic and community development, created by §§ 4-3-101 and 4-3-701;

4-14-303 SECTION 3. Tennessee Code Annotated, Section 4-14-303, is amended by adding a new subsection thereto, as follows:
(j) The board of directors shall adopt and implement a conflict of interest policy for board members. The policy shall mandate annual written disclosures of financial interests, other possible conflicts of interest, and an acknowledgement by board members that they have read and understand all aspects of the policy. The policy shall also require persons who are to be appointed to the board of directors to acknowledge, as a condition of appointment, that they are not in conflict with the conditions of the policy.

4-14-109 SECTION 4. Tennessee Code Annotated, Section 4-14-109, is amended by adding a new subsection thereto, as follows:
(m) The committee shall adopt and implement a conflict of interest policy for committee members. The policy shall mandate annual written disclosures of financial interests, other possible conflicts of interest, and an acknowledgement by committee members that they have read and understand all aspects of the policy. The policy shall also require persons who are to be appointed to the committee to acknowledge, as a condition of appointment, that they are not in conflict with the conditions of the policy.

4-3-727 SECTION 5. Tennessee Code Annotated, Section 4-3-727, is amended by adding a new subsection thereto, as follows:
(g) The committee shall adopt and implement a conflict of interest policy for committee members. The policy shall mandate annual written disclosures of financial interests, other possible conflicts of interest, and an acknowledgement by committee members that they have read and understand all aspects of the policy. The policy shall also require persons who are to be appointed to the committee to acknowledge, as a condition of appointment, that they are not in conflict with the conditions of the policy.

SECTION 6. The department of economic and community development shall appear back before the Government Operations Joint Subcommittee on Commerce, Labor, Transportation and Agriculture in November, 2013 to update the subcommittee on its progress in addressing the first four findings of the October, 2012 performance audit report.

Effective date 4/19/2013 SECTION 7. This act shall take effect upon becoming a law, the public welfare requiring it.

PUBLIC CHAPTER NO. 253

PUBLIC CHAPTER NO. 253

HOUSE BILL NO. 837

By Representatives Matheny, Ragan

Substituted for: Senate Bill No. 361

By Senators Bell, Ford

AN ACT to amend Tennessee Code Annotated, Title 4, Chapter 29 and Title 4, Chapter 3, relative to the Tennessee film, entertainment and music commission.

BE IT ENACTED BY THE GENERAL ASSEMBLY OF THE STATE OF TENNESSEE:

4-29-234 SECTION 1. Tennessee Code Annotated, Section 4-29-234(a), is amended by deleting subdivision (57) in its entirety.

4-29-235 SECTION 2. Tennessee Code Annotated, Section 4-29-235(a), is amended by adding a new subdivision thereto, as follows:

( ) Tennessee film, entertainment and music commission, created by § 4-3-5003;

Effective date 4/19/2013 SECTION 3. This act shall take effect upon becoming a law, the public welfare requiring it.

PUBLIC CHAPTER NO. 254

PUBLIC CHAPTER NO. 254

HOUSE BILL NO. 1019

By Representative Sexton

Substituted for: Senate Bill No. 257

By Senators Crowe, Overby

AN ACT to amend Tennessee Code Annotated, Title 32, Chapter 11; Title 34, Chapter 6 and Title 68, Chapter 11, relative to health care decisions.

BE IT ENACTED BY THE GENERAL ASSEMBLY OF THE STATE OF TENNESSEE:

68-11-224 SECTION 1. Tennessee Code Annotated, Section 68-11-224, is amended by deleting the section in its entirety and by substituting instead the following:

(a) For the purposes of this section:

(1) "Clinical nurse specialist" means a nurse duly licensed under title 63, chapter 7 who has a master's degree or higher in a nursing specialty, has national specialty certification as a clinical nurse specialist, and is recognized by the board of nursing as an advanced practice nurse under § 63-7-126; and

(2) "Do-not-resuscitate order' means a written order, other than a "POST" as defined by this section, not to resuscitate a patient in the event of cardiac or respiratory arrest in accordance with accepted medical practices; and

(3) "Emergency responder" means a paid or volunteer firefighter, law enforcement officer, or other public safety official or volunteer operating within the scope of the person's proper function under the law or rendering emergency care at the scene of an emergency; and

(4) "Health care provider" shall have the same meaning as ascribed to that term in § 68-11-1802(a), and shall include, but shall not be limited to, qualified emergency medical services personnel; and

(5) "Nurse practitioner" means a nurse duly licensed under title 63, chapter 7 who has a master's degree or higher in a nursing specialty, has national specialty certification as a nurse practitioner, and is recognized by the board of nursing as an advanced practice nurse under § 63-7-126;

(6) "Person authorized to consent on the patient's behalf" means any person authorized by law to consent on behalf of the patient incapable of making any informed decision or, in the case of a minor child, the parent or parents having custody of the child or the child's legal guardian or as otherwise provided by law;

(7) "Physician assistant" means a person who has graduated from a physician assistant educational program accredited by the Accreditation Review Commission on Education for the Physician Assistant, has passed the Physician Assistant National Certifying Examination, and is currently licensed in Tennessee as a physician assistant under title 63, chapter 19;

(8) "Physician orders for scope of treatment" or "POST" means written orders that:

(A) Are on a form approved by the board for licensing health care facilities;

(B) Apply regardless of the treatment setting that are signed as required herein by the patient's physician, physician assistant, nurse practitioner, or clinical nurse specialist; and

(C)

(i) Specify whether, in the event the patient suffers cardiac or respiratory arrest, cardiopulmonary resuscitation should or should not be attempted;

(ii) Specify other medical interventions that are to be provided or withheld; or

(iii) Specify both (i) and (ii); and

(9) "Qualified emergency medical service personnel" includes, but is not limited to, emergency medical technicians, paramedics, or other emergency services personnel, providers, or entities acting within the course of their professions, and other emergency responders; and

(10) "Unlicensed individuals who provide direct care and support to persons supported" means the unlicensed individuals, including their unlicensed direct care and support supervisors, who are employed to provide direct care and support to persons supported within the department of intellectual and developmental disabilities ICF/ID homes and facilities or by agencies that are licensed under title 33 and under contract with this department.

(b) Physician orders for scope of treatment (POST) may be issued by a physician for a patient with whom the physician has a bona fide physician-patient relationship, but only:

(1) With the informed consent of the patient;

(2) If the patient is a minor or is otherwise incapable of making an informed decision regarding consent for such an order, upon the request of and with the consent of the agent, surrogate, or other person authorized to consent on the patient's behalf under the Tennessee Health Care Decisions Act, compiled in part 18 of this chapter; or

(3) Where the patient is a minor or is otherwise incapable of making an informed decision regarding consent for such an order and the agent, surrogate, or other person authorized to consent on the patient's behalf under the Tennessee Health Care Decisions Act, is not reasonably available, if the physician determines that the provision of cardio pulmonary resuscitation would be contrary to accepted medical standards.

(c) A POST may be issued by a physician assistant, nurse practitioner or clinical nurse specialist for a patient with whom such physician assistant, nurse practitioner or clinical nurse specialist has a bona fide physician assistant-patient or nurse-patient relationship, but only if:

(1) No physician who has a bona fide physician-patient relationship with the patient is present and available for discussion with the patient (or if the patient is a minor or is otherwise incapable of making an informed decision, with the agent, surrogate, or other person authorized to consent on the patient's behalf under the Tennessee Health Care Decisions Act;

(2) Such authority to issue is contained in the physician assistant's, nurse practitioner's or clinical nurse specialist's protocols;

(3) Either:

(A) The patient is a resident of a nursing home licensed under this title or an ICF/MR facility licensed under title 33 and is in the process of being discharged from the nursing home or transferred to another facility at the time the POST is being issued; or

(B) The patient is a hospital patient and is in the process of being discharged from the hospital or transferred to another facility at the time the POST is being issued; and

(4) Either:

(A) With the informed consent of the patient;

(B) If the patient is a minor or is otherwise incapable of making an informed decision regarding consent for such an order, upon the request of and with the consent of the agent, surrogate, or other person authorized to consent on the patient's behalf under the Tennessee Health Care Decisions Act; or

(C) If the patient is a minor or is otherwise incapable of making an informed decision regarding consent for such an order and the agent, surrogate, or other person authorized to consent on the patient's behalf under the Tennessee Health Care Decisions Act, is not reasonably available and such authority to issue is contained in the physician assistant, nurse practitioner or clinical nurse specialist's protocols and the physician assistant or nurse determines that the provision of cardio pulmonary resuscitation would be contrary to accepted medical standards.

(d) If the patient is an adult who is capable of making an informed decision, the patient's expression of the desire to be resuscitated in the event of cardiac or respiratory arrest shall revoke any contrary order in the POST. If the patient is a minor or is otherwise incapable of making an informed decision, the expression of the desire that the patient be resuscitated by the person authorized to consent on the patient's behalf shall revoke any contrary order in the POST. Nothing in this section shall be construed to require cardiopulmonary resuscitation of a patient for whom the physician or physician assistant or nurse practitioner or clinical nurse specialist determines cardiopulmonary resuscitation is not medically appropriate.

(e)

(1) A POST issued in accordance with this section shall remain valid and in effect until revoked. In accordance with this section and applicable regulations, qualified emergency medical services personnel; and licensed health care practitioners in any facility, program, or organization operated or licensed by the board for licensing health care facilities, the department of mental health and substance abuse services, or the department of intellectual and developmental disabilities, or operated, licensed, or owned by another state agency, shall follow a POST that is available to such persons in a form approved by the board for licensing health care facilities.

(2) The department of intellectual and developmental disabilities shall allow unlicensed individuals who provide direct support and care to persons supported and who are employed by agencies that are licensed under title 33 and under contract to provide residential or adult day programs and personal assistance

or who provide direct support and care to persons supported within the ICE/ID homes and department facilities, to follow universal do not resuscitate orders that are made available to them in a form approved by the board.

(f) Nothing in this section shall authorize the withholding of other medical interventions, such as medications, positioning, wound care, oxygen, suction, treatment of airway obstruction or other therapies deemed necessary to provide comfort care or to alleviate pain.

(g) If a person has a do-not-resuscitate order in effect at the time of such person's discharge from a health care facility, the facility shall complete a POST prior to discharge. If a person with a POST is transferred from one health care facility to another health care facility, the health care facility initiating the transfer shall communicate the existence of the POST to qualified emergency medical service personnel and to the receiving facility prior to the transfer. The transferring facility shall provide a copy of the POST that accompanies the patient in transport to the receiving health care facility. Upon admission, the receiving facility shall make the POST a part of the patient's record.

(h) This section shall not prevent, prohibit, or limit a physician from using a written order, other than a POST, not to resuscitate a patient in the event of cardiac or respiratory arrest in accordance with accepted medical practices. This action shall have no application to any do not resuscitate order that is not a POST, as defined in this section.

(i) Valid do not resuscitate orders or emergency medical services do not resuscitate orders issued before July 1, 2004, pursuant to the then-current law, shall remain valid and shall be given effect as provided, in this section.

(j)

(1) The board for licensing health care facilities shall promulgate rules and create forms regarding procedures for the withholding of resuscitative services from patients in accordance with the Tennessee Health Care Decisions Act, and this section.

(2) The rules shall address:

(A) The mechanism or mechanisms for reaching decisions about the withholding of resuscitative services from individual patients;

(B) The mechanism or mechanisms for resolving conflicts in decision making, should they arise; and

(C) The roles of physicians, physician assistant, nurse practitioner or clinical nurse specialists and, when applicable, other nursing personnel, other appropriate staff, and family members in the decision to withhold resuscitative services.

(3) The rules shall include provisions designed to assure that patients' rights are respected when decisions are made to withhold resuscitative services and shall include the requirement that appropriate orders be written by the physician, physician assistant, nurse practitioner or clinical nurse specialist, primarily responsible for the patient, and that documentation be made in the patient's current clinical record if resuscitative services are to be withheld.

(4) This section shall not be construed or implemented in any manner which restricts or impairs the decision-making

authority of the agent, surrogate, or other person designated in the Tennessee Health Care Decisions Act. This section does not authorize a surrogate to give consent for or take any action on behalf of a patient on any matter governed by title 33.

(k) A health care provider or institution acting in good faith and in accordance with generally accepted health care standards applicable to the health care provider or institution is not subject to civil or criminal liability for:

(1) Complying with a POST;

(2) Declining to comply with a POST based on reasonable belief that the order then lacked validity; or

(3) Complying with a POST and assuming that the order was valid when made and has not been revoked or terminated.

Effective date 7/1/2013

SECTION 2. For purposes of rulemaking this act shall take effect on becoming a law, for all other purposes this act shall take effect July 1, 2013, the public welfare requiring it.

PUBLIC CHAPTER NO. 255

PUBLIC CHAPTER NO. 255

HOUSE BILL NO. 1050

By Representatives Coley, Hardaway, Ryan Williams, Miller, Mark White, Sparks, Lollar, Goins, Todd, Lundberg, Dean, Butt, Eldridge

Substituted for: Senate Bill No. 1390

By Senators Kelsey, Summerville, Ford, Crowe

AN ACT to amend Tennessee Code Annotated, Title 37, relative to protective custody of children.

BE IT ENACTED BY THE GENERAL ASSEMBLY OF THE STATE OF TENNESSEE:

37-1-114 SECTION 1. Tennessee Code Annotated, Section 37-1-114(a)(2), is amended by deleting the language "parent, guardian or legal custodian" and by substituting instead the language "parent, guardian, legal custodian or the person who physically possesses or controls the child".

37-1-128 SECTION 2. Tennessee Code Annotated, Section 37-1-128(b)(2), is amended by deleting the language "the court may order that the child be removed from the custody of the child's parent, guardian or legal custodian" and by substituting instead the language "the court may order that the child be removed from the custody of the child's parent, guardian, legal custodian or the person who physically possesses or controls the child".

Effective date 4/19/2013 SECTION 3. This act shall take effect upon becoming a law, the public welfare requiring it.

PUBLIC CHAPTER NO. 256

PUBLIC CHAPTER NO. 256

HOUSE BILL NO. 1288

By Representatives Todd, Coley, Mark White, Lollar, McManus, Harry Brooks, Madam Speaker Harwell and Representatives McCormick, Rich, Sexton, Ryan Williams, Carter, Travis, Curtis Johnson, Forgety, Hawk, Swann, Lynn, Matheny, Halford, Matlock, Sanderson, Moody, Ragan, Goins, Watson, Weaver, Kevin Brooks, Faison, Pody, Lundberg, Marsh, Rogers, Floyd, Sparks, Wirgau, Joe Carr, Shipley, Powers, Dennis, Calfee, Holt, Kent Williams, McDaniel, Harrison, Roach, Eldridge, Keisling, Casada, Ramsey, Sargent, Durham, Butt, Dawn White, Littleton, Kane, Womick, Dean, Farmer, Doss

Substituted for: Senate Bill No. 1353

By Senators Norris, Gresham, Tate

AN ACT to amend Tennessee Code Annotated, Section 6-58-112 and Title 49, relative to local education agencies.

WHEREAS, the General Assembly enacted Chapter 115 of the Public Acts of 1925, giving birth to large school systems through the consolidation movement in public education; and

WHEREAS, Tennessee encouraged consolidation through laws governing student body size, prohibiting establishment of new school systems, and establishing funding policies to encourage consolidation within each county; and

WHEREAS, the premise that bigger schools and larger school systems necessarily produce cost efficiencies and successful student outcomes has come into question as research now demonstrates that, as school systems grow, classroom performance may actually decrease and per-pupil costs increase; and

WHEREAS, notwithstanding the earlier prohibition against establishing new school systems, since 2002 Tennessee has nevertheless created new types of schools - charter schools, achievement schools, and even virtual schools - thereby avoiding artificial barriers to innovation; and

WHEREAS, education reform and innovation will be further enhanced if the statewide prohibition against establishment of municipal school systems is abolished and local communities are, once again, granted the flexibility to assess and determine, on a case-by-case basis, the best path to greater cost efficiencies and more effective student outcomes; and

WHEREAS, the provisions of this act will in no way diminish the obligation of any newly created city school system to comply with all state requirements pertaining to K-12 public education, including requirements to ensure maintenance of effort; now, therefore,

BE IT ENACTED BY THE GENERAL ASSEMBLY OF THE STATE OF TENNESSEE:

6-58-112 SECTION 1. Tennessee Code Annotated, Section 6-58-112(b), is amended by deleting the subsection in its entirety.

49-2-127 SECTION 2. Tennessee Code Annotated, Section 49-2-127(a), is amended by deleting the language "If a municipality is located within any county in which a transition planning commission has been created pursuant to § 49-2-502(b);" and by substituting instead the following:

If a municipality seeks to create a city school system;

PUBLIC CHAPTER NO. 256 (cont'd)

49-2-127 SECTION 3. Tennessee Code Annotated, Section 49-2-127(d), is amended by deleting the subsection in its entirety and by substituting instead the following:

(d) The new city school system shall commence student instruction no earlier than August 1 following the commissioner's determination that:

(1) Rights and privileges protected by § 49-5-203 will not be impaired, interrupted or diminished;

(2) There is, or will be, timely compliance with state law pertaining to creation of city school systems, including § 49-2-106 and state board of education rules promulgated pursuant thereto; and

(3) The system has demonstrated, to the commissioner's satisfaction, its general readiness to commence student instruction.

49-5-203 SECTION 4. Tennessee Code Annotated, Section 49-5-203(a), is amended by deleting the subsection in its entirety and by substituting instead the following:

(a) The change in the governmental structure of a school system or institution through the process of annexation, unification, consolidation, abolition, reorganization, transfer of the control and operation of a school system or institution to a different type governmental structure, organization or administration, or creation of a city school system shall not impair, interrupt or diminish the rights and privileges of a then existing teacher; and such rights and privileges shall continue without impairment, interruption or diminution.

Effective date 4/24/2013 SECTION 5. This act shall take effect upon becoming a law, the public welfare requiring it.

PUBLIC CHAPTER NO. 257

PUBLIC CHAPTER NO. 257

SENATE BILL NO. 179

By Norris, Tracy

Substituted for: House Bill No. 173

By McCormick, Ragan, Towns

AN ACT to amend Tennessee Code Annotated, Section 50-3-2001 et seq., relative to the Hazardous Chemical Right to Know Law.

BE IT ENACTED BY THE GENERAL ASSEMBLY OF THE STATE OF TENNESSEE:

50-3-2001 SECTION 1. The language of Tennessee Code Annotated, Section 50-3-2001, is deleted in its entirety and replaced with the following language:

§ 50-3-2001.

(a) Each employer shall comply with all of the requirements of the federal Hazard Communication Standard codified in 29 CFR 1910.1200. In addition to the requirements set forth in 29 CFR 1910.1200 each employer must also comply with the following:

(1)(A) Employers shall keep a record of the dates of training sessions given to their employees.

(B) The hazard communication program and employee information and training required of employers pursuant to 29 CFR 1910.1200 and the education and training program pursuant to subsection (a)(1) shall require annual refresher training after the initial training pursuant to 29 CFR 1910.1200 is conducted, unless the commissioner grants an exemption from annual refresher training. The exemption may be granted if the commissioner determines that the nature of the work assignment, the level of exposure or the nature of the hazardous chemical involved would not reasonably require annual refresher training.

(2)(A) For the purposes of this section only, "workplace" means any workplace as defined in 29 CFR 1910.1200(c) that is located within the fire chief's actual jurisdiction or that is located in a jurisdiction to which the fire chief responds pursuant to a mutual aid pact.

(B) Employers and distributors who normally store a hazardous chemical in excess of fifty-five gallons (55 gal.) or five hundred pounds (500 lbs.) shall provide the fire chief, in writing, the names and telephone numbers of knowledgeable representatives of the manufacturing employer, non-manufacturing employer or distributor who can be contacted for further information or in the event of an emergency.

(C) Each employer and distributor shall provide a copy of the workplace chemical list to the fire chief and shall thereafter notify the fire chief of any significant changes that occur in the workplace chemical list.

(D) The fire chief or the fire chief's representative, upon request, shall be permitted on-site inspections of the hazardous chemicals on the workplace chemical list during normal business hours for the sole purpose of preplanning emergency fire department activities.

(E) Employers and distributors, upon written request, shall provide the fire chief a copy of the safety data sheet (SDS) for any chemical on their workplace chemical list.

(F) The fire chief shall, upon request, make the workplace chemical list and SDSs available to members of the fire chief's fire company having jurisdiction over the workplace, or their designated representatives, but shall not otherwise distribute the information without written approval of the manufacturing employer, non-manufacturing employer or distributor who provided the workplace chemical list or SDSs; except that approval shall not be required in an emergency situation in which human life is at stake. In the event the workplace chemical list or SDSs are released under an emergency situation, the fire chief shall promptly notify the supplier of the workplace chemical list or SDSs, in writing, as to whom the information was released and the circumstances of the emergency. Persons receiving workplace chemical lists or SDSs from the fire chief shall hold the information contained in the workplace chemical lists or SDSs in confidence.

(G)(i) Employers and distributors shall place one (1) sign in accordance with the NFPA704M series on the outside of any building that contains a class A explosive, class B explosive, poison gas (poison A), water-reactive flammable solid (flammable solid W), or radioactive material as listed in Table 1 of the federal department of transportation (DOT) regulations at 49 CFR, Part 172, and further defined in federal DOT regulations at 49 CFR, Part 173, or any other hazardous chemical in excess of the amounts listed in subsection (a).

(ii) The commissioner shall promulgate rules in accordance with § 50-3-102(b)(3) to establish specifications on the size, color, lettering and posting requirements pursuant to the series. The regulations shall provide that the number used shall be determined by the hazardous chemical that presents the greatest danger.

(iii) The commissioner shall exempt an employer from this subdivision (G) who can satisfactorily demonstrate that:

(a) The employer maintains a trained fire or emergency preparedness team considered capable of handling workplace chemical or fire emergencies without external assistance; or

(b) The employer maintains twenty-four (24) hour security personnel who maintain accurate records of the location of chemicals and who can readily direct emergency personnel from outside sources to affected company facilities.

(H) The department of labor and workforce development shall assist employers and fire personnel to effectuate the purposes of this section.

(3)(A)*(1)* Manufacturing employers shall compile and maintain a workplace chemical list, which shall contain the following information for each hazardous chemical known to be present in the workplace:

(a) The chemical name or common name used on the SDS or the container label, or both;

(b) The chemical abstract service (CAS) number for the hazardous chemical, if the number is included on the SDS; and

(c) The work area or workplace in which the hazardous chemical is normally used or stored.

(2) The manufacturing employer shall maintain the workplace chemical list for no less than thirty (30) years. The manufacturing employer shall send complete records pertinent to the workplace chemical list to the commissioner if the

manufacturing employer generating the list ceases to operate a business within the state.

(3) The workplace chemical list shall be filed with the commissioner within ninety-six (96) hours of a request by an authorized representative of the commissioner.

(B)*(1)* Non-manufacturing employers shall compile and maintain a workplace chemical list, which shall contain the following information for each hazardous chemical normally used or stored in the workplace in excess of fifty-five gallons (55 gal.) or five hundred pounds (500 lbs.):

(a) The chemical name or the common name used on the SDS or container label, or both;

(b) The CAS number, if the number is included on the SDS; and

(c) The work area or workplace in which the hazardous chemical is normally stored or used.

(2) The non-manufacturing employer shall maintain the workplace chemical list for no less than thirty (30) years. The non-manufacturing employer shall send complete records pertinent to the workplace chemical list to the commissioner if the non-manufacturing employer generating the list ceases to operate a business within the state.

(3) The non-manufacturing employer shall notify new or newly assigned employees about the workplace chemical list and its contents before working in a work area containing hazardous chemicals.

(4) The non-manufacturing employer shall file the workplace chemical list with the commissioner within ninety-six (96) hours of a request by an authorized representative of the commissioner.

(C) The workplace chemical list may consist of either a single listing prepared for the workplace as a whole or a collection of lists prepared for each work area individually.

(D) The department of labor and workforce development shall provide the following information and services:

(1) The CAS number for any hazardous chemical on the workplace chemical list that is not included by the manufacturing or non-manufacturing employer pursuant to subsection (a) or (b) *if:*

(a) The chemical is not a mixture; and

(b) A CAS number exists for the chemical.

(2) The employer shall make available a copy of the workplace chemical list for inspection by the public during regular office hours at the division's central office or any division field office. The copy must be requested by the public and received by the division as specified by this section.

(3) Copies of any workplace chemical list may be obtained from the division of occupational safety and health upon written request and payment of a reasonable copying and mailing fee. The division shall provide the list within ten (10) business days of receipt of the written request.

(E) It is the intention of the general assembly, pursuant to this section, to provide access to information concerning hazardous chemicals used and stored in this state to the citizens of this state who

PUBLIC CHAPTER NO. 257 (cont'd)

live and work in proximity to the chemicals to enable the citizens to make informed decisions concerning their health, safety and welfare.

50-3-2001 — 50-3-2019

SECTION 2. Tennessee Code Annotated, Sections 50-3-2002 through 50-3-2019, are repealed.

Effective date 4/23/2013

SECTION 3. This act shall take effect upon becoming law, the public welfare requiring it.

PUBLIC CHAPTER NO. 258

PUBLIC CHAPTER NO. 258

SENATE BILL NO. 249

By Ketron, Bowling, Tracy, Johnson

Substituted for: House Bill No. 863

By Alexander, Durham, Sparks, Joe Carr, Casada, Womick, Sargent, Dawn White, Sexton

AN ACT to amend Tennessee Code Annotated, Section 55-17-123, relative to motor vehicles.

BE IT ENACTED BY THE GENERAL ASSEMBLY OF THE STATE OF TENNESSEE:

55-17-123 SECTION 1. Tennessee Code Annotated, Section 55-17-123, is amended by:

(1) Deleting subsections (b), (c), and (e) in their entirety;

(2) Redesignating present subsection (d) as subsection (b); and

(3) Adding the following as a new subsection (c):

(c)(1) A producer of motor vehicles may lease no more than four (4) motor vehicles, and provide any maintenance ancillary to the motor vehicles, of the same line-make as the producer or any related business entity produces, to each eligible employee of the producer, under no less than a twelve-month closed-end lease; provided, that the total number of vehicles so leased to such eligible employees in this state shall not exceed the producer's total number of eligible employees in this state. For purposes of this section, an "eligible employee" shall include:

(A) Each full-time employee, as defined in § 67-6-394(c), on producer's payroll; and

(B) Each leased employee, as defined under Section 414(n) of the Internal Revenue Code as such section exists as of the effective date of this act, of the producer who works onsite at one of the producer's facilities in this state.

(2) Any motor vehicle that is subject to a lease permitted under this subsection (c) shall be purchased by the producer from any dealer of the same line-make as the leased motor vehicle.

55-17-123 SECTION 2. Tennessee Code Annotated, Section 55-17-123(f), is amended by redesignating the subsection as a new subsection (d).

55-17-123 SECTION 3. Tennessee Code Annotated, Section 55-17-123(d)(1), is amended by deleting the language "subsection (e)" and by substituting instead the language "subsection (c)".

55-17-123 SECTION 4. Tennessee Code Annotated, Section 55-17-123(d)(1), is further amended by deleting the language "a regular full-time working employee" and by substituting instead the language "an eligible employee".

55-17-123 SECTION 5. Tennessee Code Annotated, Section 55-17-123(d)(1), is further amended by deleting the language "full-time working employee" and by substituting instead the language "eligible employee".

Effective date 4/23/2013 SECTION 6. This act shall take effect upon becoming a law, the public welfare requiring it.

PUBLIC CHAPTER NO. 259

PUBLIC CHAPTER NO. 259

SENATE BILL NO. 1005

By McNally, Kelsey, Mr. Speaker Ramsey

Substituted for: House Bill No. 948

By McManus; Madam Speaker Harwell; Sargent, Durham, Pody, Lundberg

AN ACT to amend Tennessee Code Annotated, Title 8, Chapter 25; Title 8, Chapter 34; Title 8, Chapter 35; Title 8, Chapter 36 and Title 8, Chapter 37, relative to retirement.

BE IT ENACTED BY THE GENERAL ASSEMBLY OF THE STATE OF TENNESSEE:

8-36-901 — 8-36-923 SECTION 1. Tennessee Code Annotated, Title 8, Chapter 36, is amended by adding a new part thereto as follows:

8-36-901. This part shall be known and may be cited as the "Hybrid Retirement Plan for State Employees and Teachers".

8-36-902.

(a) As used in this part, unless the context otherwise requires:

(1) "Hybrid plan" means a plan that provides a combination of a defined benefit plan and a defined contribution plan which, together, are intended to comply with the provisions of the Internal Revenue Code that are applicable to governmental plans;

(2) "Defined benefit component" means the portion of the hybrid plan that provides a defined benefit plan within the provisions of the retirement system, but which has its own vesting, benefit structure, and contribution requirements as set forth in this part;

(3) "Defined contribution component" means the portion of the hybrid plan that provides a defined contribution plan within the provisions of the profit sharing and/or salary reduction plan established under chapter 25, part 3 of this title;

(4) "Participant" means any state employee, teacher, or political subdivision employee participating in the hybrid plan;

(5) "Political subdivision" means any entity authorized to participate in the retirement system pursuant to chapter 35, part 2 of this title;

(6) "Political subdivision employee" means any person in the employ of a political subdivision, including a county judge, but does not include any person performing services on a contractual or percentage basis;

(7) "County judge" means a judge of a general sessions court, probate judge, or judge of a juvenile and/or domestic relations court;

(8) "State employee" means any person who is a state official, including members of the general assembly, the attorney general and reporter, district attorneys general, and district public defenders, or any person who is employed in the service of and whose compensation is payable by the state, or any person who is employed by the state whose compensation is paid in whole or in part from federal or other funds. "State employee" also means any person who is employed in the service of and whose compensation is payable by a public institution of higher education, or any person who is employed by a public institution of higher education whose compensation is paid in whole or in part from federal or other funds. For purposes of this part, "state employee" does not include the governor or any person employed on a contractual or percentage basis. Any retirement allowances payable in respect of a former governor shall be as prescribed by the provisions of chapter 39, part 2 of this title in lieu of any other benefits to

which the governor may otherwise be entitled under chapters 34 – 37 of this title;

(9) "State judge" has the meaning set forth in § 8-34-101(41); and

(10) "Teacher" has the meaning set forth in § 8-34-101(46)(B), but does not include any person employed by a public institution of higher education.

(b) Terms used in this part that are not otherwise defined shall have the same meaning ascribed to them in chapters 34 – 37 of this title.

8-36-903.

(a) Notwithstanding any other law to the contrary and except as provided in this section, any person otherwise eligible to participate in the retirement system who enters service as a state employee or teacher on or after July 1, 2014, shall participate in the hybrid plan established under this part. Provided, however, any person who enters service with a state-supported institution of higher education on or after July 1, 2014, and who is exempt from the Fair Labor Standards Act, compiled in 29 U.S.C. § 201 et seq., may elect membership in the optional retirement program as provided in § 8-36-923 in lieu of the hybrid plan. In all cases of doubt, the retirement system shall determine whether the person is eligible to participate in the optional retirement program.

(b) Any state employee or teacher who is a member of the retirement system on June 30, 2014, shall continue membership in the retirement system pursuant to the terms of chapters 34 – 37 of this title that were in effect on June 30, 2014. Any person who reenters service as a state employee or teacher on or after July 1, 2014, having previously served as a state employee or teacher prior to July 1, 2014, and who has not been refunded such previous service pursuant to § 8-37-210, shall continue membership in the retirement system pursuant to the terms of chapters 34 – 37 of this title that were in effect on June 30, 2014.

(c) Membership in the hybrid plan or the optional retirement program, as applicable, shall not be required for any part-time state employee or part-time teacher who would otherwise be covered under the provisions of this part, or for any state employee who has optional membership in the retirement system pursuant to chapters 34 – 37 of this title. Any election made by a state employee or teacher to become a participant shall be irrevocable and such employee or teacher shall thereafter be subject to the terms and conditions of the hybrid plan or the optional retirement program, as applicable, which are in effect at the time of the election.

(d) All provisions of chapters 34 – 37 of this title that are not inconsistent with the provisions of this part shall continue to apply, as applicable, to participants in the hybrid plan or the optional retirement program.

8-36-904.

(a) Participants in the hybrid plan shall be excluded from the noncontributory provisions of § 8-34-206 and shall be required to make employee contributions to the defined benefit component of the plan equal to five percent (5%) of the participant's earnable compensation.

(b) Each employer shall pick up the employee contributions required under this section. The contributions so picked up shall be treated as employer contributions pursuant to § 414(h) of the Internal Revenue Code in determining tax treatment under said Code. The employee shall not have the option of choosing to receive the contributions in the form of cash or cash equivalents instead of having them paid by the employer into the hybrid plan benefits trust account created pursuant to § 8-36-920.

8-36-905. Any participant who desires to establish service credit pursuant to the provisions of chapters 34 – 37 of this title shall pay employee contributions to the defined benefit component of the plan equal to the amount of the employee contributions required under the terms of the hybrid plan as they existed at the time the service was established, plus interest at the rate provided in § 8-37-214. In the case of refunded service, the amount shall be equal to the total amount that was previously withdrawn, plus interest at the rate provided in § 8-37-124. Any service established or reestablished pursuant to this section shall be credited under the terms of the hybrid plan as they existed at the time the service was established and not at the time the service was rendered.

8-36-906.

(a)(1) Except as otherwise provided in this section and in § 8-36-921, any participant shall be eligible for a service retirement allowance from the defined benefit component of the plan upon attainment of sixty-five (65) years of age and completion of five (5) years of creditable service, or upon attainment of a combination of age and years of creditable service as to equal ninety (90).

(2) Any participant serving in a position covered by the mandatory retirement provisions of § 8-36-205 shall be eligible for a service retirement allowance from the defined benefit component of the plan upon attainment of sixty (60) years of age and upon completion of five (5) years of creditable service, or at any age upon completion of thirty (30) years of creditable service. Further, any participant who has creditable service in a position covered by the mandatory retirement provisions of § 8-36-205 and who is entitled to the supplemental bridge benefit pursuant to § 8-36-211 shall be eligible for a service retirement allowance from the defined benefit component of the plan upon attainment of fifty-five (55) years of age and upon completion of twenty-five (25) years of creditable service; provided that the service rendered while the participant was in a position covered by the mandatory retirement provisions shall be independent of all other creditable service for the purpose of calculating the participant's retirement allowance under § 8-36-907.

(b) Any participant serving as the attorney general and reporter, a district attorney general, district public defender, or state judge shall be eligible for a service retirement allowance from the defined benefit component of the plan upon attainment of sixty (60) years of age and upon completion of eight (8) years of creditable service, or upon the attainment of fifty-five (55) years of age and upon completion of twenty-four (24) years of creditable service.

(c) Any participant serving as a member of the general assembly shall be eligible for a service retirement allowance from the defined benefit component of the plan upon attainment of sixty (60) years of age and upon completion of four (4) years of creditable service.

8-36-907.

(a) Except as provided in §§ 8-36-908 and 8-36-909, the service retirement allowance payable to a participant under § 8-36-906 shall consist of a member annuity which shall be the actuarial equivalent of the participant's accumulated contributions in the defined benefit component of the plan at retirement, plus a state annuity which, when added to the member annuity, shall be equal to:

(1) In the case of a participant, other than those participants described in subdivision (a)(2) below, one percent (1.0%) of the participant's average final compensation, multiplied by the number of years of creditable service, unless reduced in accordance with § 8-36-921 or § 8-36-922; and

(2) In the case of a participant who is the attorney general and reporter, a district attorney general, district public defender, or state judge, one and six-tenths percent (1.6%) of the participant's average final compensation, multiplied by the number of years of creditable service, unless reduced in accordance with § 8-36-921 or § 8-36-922.

(b) Section 8-36-124 shall not apply in determining the retirement allowance payable under this section.

8-36-908.

(a) Notwithstanding any provision of the law to the contrary, the base annual service retirement allowance payable to a participant under the defined benefit component of the plan shall not exceed the amount determined and in effect on July 1, 2014, pursuant to § 8-35-256(h). Provided, however, commencing on July 1, 2015, and on each July 1 thereafter, this amount shall be increased or decreased in accordance with the consumer price index as defined in § 8-36-701(c), and the amount of increase or decrease shall be based on the prior calendar year. Such participant's annual pension benefit shall be limited to the base benefit in effect at the time of the participant's retirement, but shall be subject to increase in accordance with the cost-of-living provisions of § 8-36-701(b)(1) and (b)(2).

(b) Notwithstanding subsection (a), the service retirement allowance payable under the provisions of this part shall not exceed ninety percent (90%) of the participant's average final compensation as may be adjusted by the cost-of-living provisions of § 8-36-701(b)(1) and (b)(2).

8-36-909.

(a) Notwithstanding § 8-36-209 or any other law to the contrary, there shall be no minimum service retirement allowance payable under the defined benefit component of the plan except as otherwise provided in subsections (b) and (c) below. Instead, the retirement allowance shall be determined in accordance with § 8-36-907.

(b)(1) The minimum service retirement allowance payable under the defined benefit component of the plan with respect to creditable service established pursuant to § 8-35-226 shall not be less than seven dollars ($7.00) per month for each year of such creditable service, except as provided in subsection (e) below.

(2) Notwithstanding subdivision (b)(1), the chief legislative body of any city, special school district or county may set the minimum service retirement allowance payable with respect to creditable service established pursuant to § 8-35-226 in the amount as determined and in effect pursuant to § 8-36-209(a)(2)(A)(i) or § 8-36-209(a)(2)(A)(ii). Such amount shall be adjusted on each July 1 thereafter pursuant to the cost-of-living provisions in § 8-36-701(b)(1) and (2).

(3) To set the minimum service retirement allowance under either § 8-36-209(a)(2)(A)(i) or § 8-36-209(a)(2)(A)(ii), the chief legislative body of the respective city, special school district or county must pass a resolution authorizing the provisions of either § 8-36-209(a)(2)(A)(i) or § 8-36-209(a)(2)(A)(ii) and accepting the liability therefore. Any such resolution shall apply to current and future retirees of the hybrid plan and shall become effective on the first day of any quarter following the filing of the resolution with the retirement system. No retroactive benefits shall be paid under the provisions of subdivision (b)(2).

(c)(1) The minimum retirement allowance payable under the defined benefit component with respect to creditable service rendered as a member of the general assembly shall not be less than fifty-five dollars ($55.00) per month for each year of creditable service adjusted effective July 1, 2015, and on each July 1 thereafter pursuant to the cost-of-living provisions in § 8-36-701(b)(1) and (2) except as provided in subsection (e).

(2) Any recipient eligible for a benefit pursuant to subdivision (c)(1) may elect to receive an amount less than the amount that the recipient is otherwise eligible to receive; provided that the election is in writing and irrevocable.

(d) Section 8-36-124 shall not apply in determining the retirement allowance payable under this section.

(e) In no event shall the minimum retirement allowance payable hereunder exceed ninety percent (90%) of the participant's average final compensation as may be adjusted by the cost-of-living provisions of § 8-36-701(b)(1) and (b)(2).

For purposes of determining the limitations on the amount of the retirement allowance as provided in this subsection (e), the average final compensation for service granted under § 8-35-226 shall be independent of the average final compensation calculation on any other creditable service in the retirement system, and the average final compensation for service granted as a member of the general assembly shall be independent of the average final compensation calculation on any other creditable service in the retirement system.

8-36-910.

(a) Except as otherwise provided in this section and in § 8-36-921, any participant shall be eligible for an early service retirement allowance from the defined benefit component of the plan upon attainment of sixty (60) years of age and completion of five (5) years of creditable service, or upon attainment of a combination of age and years of creditable service as to equal eighty (80).

(b) Any participant serving in a position covered by the mandatory retirement provisions of § 8-36-205 shall be eligible for an early service retirement allowance from the defined benefit component of the plan upon attainment of fifty-five (55) years of age and upon completion of five (5) years of creditable service, or at any age upon completion of twenty-five (25) years of creditable service.

(c) Any participant serving as the attorney general and reporter, a district attorney general, district public defender, state judge, or as a member of the general assembly shall not be eligible for an early service retirement allowance under the defined benefit component of the plan. Instead, such participants shall be eligible for a retirement allowance from the defined benefit component of the plan upon meeting the applicable conditions set forth in § 8-36-906.

8-36-911.

(a) Except as provided in § 8-36-912, the early service retirement allowance payable to a participant under § 8-36-910 shall be computed as a service retirement allowance in accordance with § 8-36-907, but reduced by an actuarially determined factor as set by the board from time to time.

(b) Section 8-36-124 shall not apply in determining the retirement allowance payable under this section. Further, Section 8-36-211(a)(2) shall not apply in calculating the supplemental bridge benefit for participants covered by the mandatory retirement provisions of § 8-36-205(a)(1) who retire on an early service retirement allowance pursuant to this section, nor shall § 8-36-211(b)(2) apply in calculating the supplemental bridge benefit for participants covered by the mandatory retirement provisions of § 8-36-205(a)(2) who retire on an early service retirement allowance pursuant to this section and whose employer adopted the provisions of this part. Instead, the supplemental bridge benefit shall be equal to three-fourths of one percent (0.75%) of the participant's average final compensation, multiplied by the participant's years of creditable service when the participant was in a position covered by the mandatory retirement provisions of § 8-36-205, but reduced by an actuarially determined factor as set by the board from time to time.

8-36-912. The minimum early service retirement allowance payable under the defined benefit component of the plan pursuant to § 8-36-911 shall be the minimum service retirement allowance computed in accordance with § 8-36-909 on the basis of the participant's creditable service at the time of early retirement, reduced by an actuarially determined factor as set by the board from time to time. Section 8-36-124 shall not apply in determining the retirement allowance payable under this section.

8-36-913. Any participant may apply for a disability retirement benefit pursuant to the provisions and criteria set forth in part 5 of this chapter. All provisions of part 5 of this chapter shall be applicable, except that the disability retirement allowance shall be equal to nine-tenths (9/10) of a service retirement allowance as computed in § 8-36-907 and as may be further reduced in accordance with part 5 of this chapter. Sections 8-36-124 and 8-36-209 shall not apply in determining any disability retirement benefit allowance payable under this section. The minimum disability retirement allowance, if applicable, shall be computed in accordance with § 8-36-909.

8-36-914. Sections 8-36-109(b)(1)(C) and 8-36-123(a)(2) shall not apply in determining the retirement allowance payable under § 8-36-109(b) or under § 8-36-123(a) to a deceased participant's surviving spouse, if any. Instead, the retirement allowance payable under such sections shall be reduced by an actuarially determined factor as set by the board from time to time.

8-36-915. Except as otherwise provided in this part, administration of the defined benefit component of the hybrid plan and the optional retirement program shall be governed by the provisions of chapters 34 – 37 of this title. Provided, however, any reference in chapters 34 – 37 of this title to the eligibility requirements for an early or service retirement allowance under the hybrid plan shall for purposes of this part mean the eligibility requirements set forth in §§ 8-36-906 and 8-36-910. Any reference in chapters 34 – 37 of this title to the formula for computing an early or service retirement allowance, or for computing a disability retirement allowance under the hybrid plan shall for purposes of this part mean the applicable formula as set out in §§ 8-36-907 – 8-36-909 and §§ 8-36-911 – 8-36-913.

8-36-916.

(a) There is established the defined contribution component of the hybrid plan that provides a defined contribution plan within the provisions of the profit sharing and/or salary reduction plan established under chapter 25, part 3 of this title and as supplemented pursuant to this part.

(b)(1) Any person who becomes a participant in the hybrid plan shall have an initial two percent (2%) of that participant's compensation automatically deferred into the defined contribution component of the plan during the initial year of participation, unless such participant files with that participant's employer a notice of that participant's election not to contribute. Any notice of non-election shall be made in such format and through such medium as prescribed by the retirement system and must be filed with that participant's employer by no later than thirty (30) calendar days from the date of the notice of automatic deferral letter.

(2) All contributions made by or on behalf of a participant to the defined contribution component of the plan who does not file a notice of non-election within the prescribed period shall be directed to the default option established by the trustees of the profit sharing and/or salary reduction plan established under chapter 25, part 3 of this title until such time as the participant selects a different investment option or options. Notwithstanding any provision of this section or any other law to the contrary, future deferrals may be cancelled or adjusted at any time by a participant provided the participant notifies that participant's employer in such format and through such medium as may be prescribed by the retirement system at least one month before the payday on which the cancellation or change is to be effective. Provided, however, any adjustment in the deferrals, other than a cancellation, cannot cause the amount of the deferrals to be less than twenty dollars ($20.00) per month, or if the employee is paid twice a month, ten dollars ($10.00) semimonthly, or such other lower amount as may be established under chapter 25, part 3 of this title. In addition, any adjustment in the deferrals cannot cause the amount of the deferrals to exceed the maximum allowed under the Internal Revenue Code.

(3) Any participant who affirmatively declines to make employee deferrals after the first automatic enrollment contribution was made, may make an election to withdraw that participant's entire automatic enrollment contribution. This election must be submitted no later than ninety (90) calendar days after the payroll date in which the first automatic enrollment contribution is made on behalf of the participant. The amount of the distribution shall be the value of the automatic enrollment contributions plus or minus investment gains or losses as of the date the distribution is processed. Automatic enrollment contributions made after such date shall remain in the defined contribution component of the plan and shall be subject to the plan's regular distribution rules. Further, a participant who has made an election to withdraw and who thereafter leaves employment and is then rehired by the same employer as defined below or, by the same political subdivision in the case of a political subdivision employee, before a twelve (12) continuous month absence shall not be permitted to make another election to withdraw that participant's automatic enrollment contribution. For purposes of this subdivision, "same employer" means the employer for which the person last worked prior to separation from covered employment. All departments, agencies and instrumentalities in the executive, legislative and judicial branches of state government, including public institutions of higher education, shall be deemed one and the same employer. All public schools within the Tennessee public school system, except for public institutions of higher education, shall be deemed one and the same employer. Notwithstanding subsection (d) below, the employer matching contributions described in subsection (c) that are attributable to the distribution of the automatic enrollment contributions shall be forfeited and placed in a forfeiture account. Amounts in the forfeiture account shall be used in the manner provided in the plan document established for the profit sharing and/or salary reduction plan established under chapter 25, part 3 of this title. The employer matching contributions described in subsection (c) shall not be made if a permissible

withdrawal is taken pursuant to this subsection before the date the matching contribution is allocated.

(4) The initial two percent (2%) automatic enrollment contribution described in this subsection shall be subject to a percentage annual increase thereafter if provided for in the plan document established for the profit sharing and/or salary reduction plan established under chapter 25, part 3 of this title.

(5) The automatic deferrals shall be contributed on a pre-tax basis and shall continue until the participant affirmatively elects otherwise.

(c)(1) Notwithstanding § 8-35-111, each employer shall make a mandatory contribution to the defined contribution component of the plan on behalf of each of its employees participating in the hybrid plan, regardless of whether the employees make any employee contributions pursuant to subsection (b). Employer contributions for kindergarten through twelfth grade teachers shall be paid by the respective local education agency for which the teachers are employed. The amount of the contribution shall be five percent (5%) of the respective employee's salary. The mandatory contributions required in this subdivision (c)(1) shall be in addition to any match provided for in § 8-25-303 to participants who otherwise participate in the profit sharing and/or salary reduction plan under chapter 25, part 3 of this title; provided that the total combined employer contributions to all defined contribution plans on behalf of a single employee shall not exceed the maximum allowed under the Internal Revenue Code, and shall conform to all applicable laws, rules and regulations of the internal revenue service governing profit sharing and/or salary reduction plans for governmental employees. If the employer contributions to all such plans combined exceed such amount, the employer shall reduce its contributions to any other defined contribution plans such that the contributions to the defined contribution component of the plan and to the other plans do not exceed the limit.

(2) Each participant who affirmatively elects to make employee deferrals shall select the investment option or options in which the contributions made by or on behalf of such participant are to be directed. Should a participant fail to select an investment option, the contributions attributable to the participant shall be directed to the default option established for the defined contribution component of the plan until such time as the person selects a different investment option or options.

(d) The total amount contributed by the employee and employer under this section shall vest to the participant's benefit immediately.

(e) The state treasurer may offer financial educational services for participants in the defined contribution component of the hybrid plan. The services may include, but are not limited to, offering financial planning guidance on matters such as investment diversification, investment risks, investment costs, asset allocation, and other topics regarding investing, generally.

8-36-917. Except as otherwise provided in part 8 of this chapter, any retired participant who returns to service in a position covered by the retirement system shall have such participant's retirement allowance under the defined benefit component of the plan suspended while so employed. The participant shall be subject to the provisions of §§ 8-36-801 – 8-36-804. Provided, however, reemployment in a covered position shall have no effect on a payment under the defined contribution component of the plan.

8-36-918.

(a) Notwithstanding § 8-35-124 or any other law to the contrary, an employee or elected or appointed official of this state, an employee or elected or appointed official of any political subdivision thereof, or a teacher employed with a local education agency who is convicted in any state or federal court of a felony arising out of that employee's or official's employment or official capacity constituting malfeasance in office shall forfeit that person's retirement benefits under the defined benefit component of the plan.

(b) Upon initial conviction, or upon a plea of guilty or nolo contendere, any person subject to the provisions of this section shall:

(1) Have the employee's or official's benefit stopped immediately, if the employee or official is receiving a benefit under the defined benefit component of the plan; and

(2) Receive a refund of the employee contributions and interest credited to the employee's or official's account, less any benefits received, unless the person elected to have a monthly retirement allowance paid upon such person's death in accordance with subsection (e).

(c) The employing agency is responsible for immediately notifying the administrator of the retirement system of the conviction of any person subject to the provisions of this section.

(d) In the event the conviction of such person is later overturned in any court and such person is acquitted, or is granted a full pardon, the person shall be restored to all rights, privileges and benefits as if the conviction had never occurred.

(e) Any person convicted of a felony as provided in this section may elect, within six (6) months of the person's conviction, to have a monthly retirement allowance paid to whomever that person had designated as beneficiary on file with the retirement system at the time of that person's conviction; provided, that, such beneficiary must have been that person's spouse or child at the time of that person's conviction. The amount of any allowance payable hereunder shall be equal to the retirement allowance which would have been payable under the defined benefit component of the plan had the person retired under an effective election of Option 1 as provided in part 6 of this chapter. The benefits shall be paid to such beneficiary following the person's death and upon meeting all other eligibility requirements applicable to a beneficiary.

8-36-919.

(a) A political subdivision that is not otherwise participating under any of the plans afforded under chapters 34 – 37 of this title may, by resolution legally adopted and approved by its chief governing body and in accordance with the procedure set out in § 8-35-201, authorize its employees in all of its departments or instrumentalities to become eligible to participate in the hybrid plan. Membership in the hybrid plan for employees of political subdivisions that are admitted into the hybrid plan pursuant to this subsection shall be:

(1) Optional for all employees in the service of the political subdivision on the date the approval is given; and

(2) Mandatory for all eligible employees entering the service of the political subdivision thereafter. Provided, however, membership shall not be required for any part-time employee who would otherwise be covered under the provisions of this part, or for any employee who has optional membership in the retirement system pursuant to chapters 34 – 37 of this title. Any election made by an employee to become a participant shall be irrevocable and such employee shall thereafter be subject to the terms and conditions of the hybrid plan.

(b) Any political subdivision electing to participate in the hybrid plan pursuant to this section shall participate in the provisions of the plan as they exist for state employees on the date of participation or at any other given time pursuant to any changes made pursuant to §§ 8-36-921 and 8-36-922. Provided, however, any subsequent changes that increase the liability of a participating political subdivision within the meaning of Article II, Section 24 of the Tennessee Constitution shall not apply to the political subdivision unless the chief governing body of the political subdivision agrees to such changes and accepts the liability therefore. Notwithstanding this subsection, the following provisions shall remain optional to political subdivisions:

(1) Part-time, seasonal, or temporary employee service credit in accordance with § 8-34-621; and

(2) Mandatory retirement in accordance with § 8-36-205.

(c) A political subdivision already participating in the retirement system under one of the additional plans afforded under chapters 34 – 37 of this title may change from that plan to the hybrid plan on a prospective basis by passage of a resolution pursuant to subsection (a) above. Any such resolution shall set forth the effective date of the change; provided that the date shall be on the first day of any quarter following a minimum of six (6) months' notice to the retirement system. The actuarial value of accrued benefits earned by employees of the political subdivision prior to the effective date of the change shall remain an enforceable right and may not be reduced or otherwise forfeited except by the consent of the employee or in accordance with § 8-35-124.

(d) Any political subdivision that participates in the hybrid plan shall have the right to change from the hybrid plan to any of the additional plans afforded to the political subdivision under chapters 34 – 37. Any such change shall be in accordance with and subject to the terms and conditions of §§ 8-35-253 – 8-35-256. In addition, any political subdivision that participates in the hybrid plan shall be subject to the withdrawal provisions of §§ 8-35-211 and 8-35-218. Benefits accrued under the hybrid plan or under any of the plans adopted pursuant to §§ 8-35-253 – 8-35-256 shall be in accordance with 26 U.S.C. § 411. Notwithstanding this section or any other law to the contrary, the cost-of-living provisions of § 8-36-701 shall not be deemed an accrued benefit and may be subject to change pursuant to this section and §§ 8-36-921 and 8-36-922.

(e) Notwithstanding this section or any other law to the contrary, a political subdivision may authorize its county judges to participate in the hybrid plan under the same provisions governing state judges as set forth in this part provided the political subdivision authorizes and pays for the cost of an actuarial study to determine the liability associated with such membership and, following review of the cost of such membership, the chief governing body of the political subdivision passes a resolution authorizing the membership and accepting the liability therefor. In addition, a political subdivision may authorize its county judge to participate in the hybrid plan under the provisions of this subsection (e) without extending retirement coverage to its other employees provided the political subdivision authorizes and pays for the cost of an actuarial study to determine the liability associated with such membership and, following review of the cost of such membership, the chief governing body of the political subdivision passes a resolution authorizing the membership and accepting the liability therefor. The retirement system shall not be liable for the payment of retirement allowances or other payments on account of such membership for which reserves have not been previously created from funds contributed by the political division and/or its county judges. It is the legislative intent that the state shall realize no increased cost as a result of this section. All costs associated with retirement coverage, including administrative costs, shall be the responsibility of the political subdivision.

(f) Notwithstanding this part or any law to the contrary, a political subdivision that extends retirement coverage to its employees under this section may elect to provide its own profit sharing and/or salary reduction plan that is authorized under § 401(k) of the Internal Revenue Code in lieu of participating in the state's profit sharing and/or salary reduction plan established under chapter 25, part 3 of this title; provided that the political subdivision makes mandatory contributions to such plan on behalf of each of its employees participating in the hybrid plan, regardless of whether the employees make any employee contributions to that plan. The amount of the employer contributions shall be five percent (5%) of the respective employee's salary unless suspended or reduced pursuant to § 8-36-922.

8-36-920.

(a) There shall be established in the retirement system trust fund a hybrid plan benefits trust account into which contributions made to the defined benefit component of the plan shall be deposited.

(b) All interest and dividends earned on the funds of the defined benefit component of the hybrid plan shall be credited to the hybrid plan benefits trust account.

(c) Within the hybrid plan benefits trust account created pursuant to this section, there shall be established a reserve trust account, which shall consist of two (2) subaccounts as follows:

(1)(A) An employer reserve trust account into which shall be deposited:

(i) The employer contributions as determined by the actuary pursuant to § 8-36-922(b) and any payments made to establish service credit in the hybrid plan that result from employer contributions rolled over or otherwise transferred from another qualified plan;

(ii) All amounts transferred from the participants' reserve trust account pursuant to subdivision (c)(2)(B) below;

(iii) Transfers from the stabilization reserve trust account pursuant to subdivision (d)(2) below;

(iv) A pro rata share of the interest and dividends earned on the funds of the defined benefit component of the hybrid plan; and

(v) Any penalties assessed against an employer pursuant to § 8-37-504;

(B) All costs of administering the hybrid plan, and all retirement allowances and other benefits payable under the defined benefit component of the hybrid plan other than those payable from the participants' reserve trust account established in subdivision (c)(2) below shall be paid from the employer reserve trust account.

(2)(A) A participants' reserve trust account shall also be established within the reserve trust account into which shall be deposited:

(i) The contributions deducted from the compensation of participants to provide for their member annuities, together with any contributions of participants and interest thereon to establish service credit in the hybrid plan; and

(ii) All amounts transferred from the employer reserve trust account pursuant to subdivision (2)(C) below.

(B) The accumulated contributions of a participant that are withdrawn by the participant, or paid to the participant's designated beneficiary or to the participant's estate pursuant to § 8-36-120, shall be paid from the participants' reserve trust account. Upon the retirement of a participant, or if a retirement allowance becomes payable on account of the participant's death prior to retirement, the participant's accumulated contributions shall be transferred from the participants' reserve trust account to the employer reserve trust account.

(C) The board of trustees shall annually show interest at such rate or rates as it shall determine from time to time on the individual accounts of participants in the participants' reserve trust account and shall transfer such amounts from the employer reserve trust account.

(d)(1) Unless prohibited by an agency of the federal government or contrary to the advice of competent legal counsel or government accounting professionals, there shall be established within the hybrid plan benefits trust account a stabilization reserve trust account into which shall be deposited:

(A) All employer contributions made in excess of the actuarial rate determined pursuant to § 8-36-922(b); and

(B) A pro rata share of the interest and dividends earned on the funds of the defined benefit component of the hybrid plan.

(2) If in any given year the total amount in the employer reserve account is not sufficient to meet the benefit liabilities of the defined benefit component of the plan as determined by the most recent actuarial study, then such amount as may be necessary to fund the benefits shall be transferred from the stabilization reserve trust account to the employer reserve trust account.

(e)(1) For accounting purposes only, the reserve trust account and the stabilization reserve trust account created by this section shall each consist of the following individual separate accounts for the purpose of accounting for:

(A) The benefits payable to state employees other than those described in subdivisions (1)(B) and (1)(C) below;

(B) The benefits payable to the attorney general and reporter, district attorneys general, district public defenders and state judges;

(C) The supplemental bridge benefits payable to state employees pursuant to § 8-36-211; and

(D) The benefits payable to teachers.

(2) In addition and for accounting purposes only, the reserve trust account and the stabilization reserve trust account shall each consist of individual separate accounts established in the name of each political subdivision participating under the provisions of this part. Each political subdivision shall have the following three (3) separate subaccounts for the purpose of accounting for:

(A) The benefits payable to employees of the political subdivision other than those described in subdivisions (2)(B) and (2)(C) below;

(B) The benefits payable to its county judges pursuant to § 8-36-919(e); and

(C) The supplemental bridge benefits payable to its employees pursuant to § 8-36-211.

(f) All monies deposited into the hybrid benefits plan trust account shall be used exclusively for the purposes set forth in this section.

8-36-921. The general assembly shall have the right to freeze, suspend, or modify benefits, employee and employer contributions, plan terms, and design of the hybrid plan on a prospective basis through amendments to or repeals of chapters 34 – 37 of this title. Nothing under state law may confer to participants in the hybrid plan an implied right to future retirement benefit arrangements and such participants may not assert the indefinite continuation of the retirement formulas, contribution rates, eligibility ages, or any other provision of the plan. Provided, however, the actuarial value of accrued benefits earned by participants prior to the effective date of any such amendment or repeal shall remain an enforceable right and may not be reduced or otherwise forfeited except by the consent of the participant or in accordance with § 8-36-918. Notwithstanding this section or any other law to the contrary, the cost-of-living provisions of § 8-36-701 shall not be deemed an accrued benefit and may be subject to change pursuant to this section and § 8-36-922.

8-36-922.

(a) Every employer participating in the hybrid plan shall contribute to the hybrid plan benefits trust account each year a sum equal to the greater of (i) the normal contribution rate and the accrued liability contribution rate as determined pursuant to subsection (b) below, multiplied by the earnable compensation of all its participating employees, or (ii) four percent (4%) of the earnable compensation of all its participating employees. Employer contributions for kindergarten through twelfth grade teachers shall be paid by the respective local education agency for which the teachers are employed.

(b) The actuary of the retirement system shall compute the normal contribution rate and the accrued liability contribution rate payable to the defined benefit component of the plan for each account described in § 8-36-920(e). The computation shall be made by an actuarial valuation in the manner provided by chapter 37, part 3 of this title; provided, that the entry age actuarial cost method, as defined by the Actuarial Standards Board, shall be used in determining normal costs and contributions for unfunded accrued liabilities. Level dollar amortization of unfunded accrued liabilities shall be used over a period of time as set by the board, but not to exceed twenty (20) years. The asset valuation method shall be based on the market value of plan assets and provide for smoothing of investment gains and losses over a period of time established by the board, but not to exceed ten (10) years. In addition, the actuarial demographic assumptions shall include projections of mortality improvement.

(c)(1) Notwithstanding this part or any other law to the contrary, if the actuarial valuation as of any year establishes a normal contribution rate and an accrued liability contribution rate, combined, that exceeds four percent (4%), the following steps in the order provided below shall automatically take effect the next July 1 immediately following the actuarial valuation as determined by the actuarial valuation process:

(A) Transfer such amounts as may be necessary from the stabilization reserve trust account created in § 8-36-920 to the reserve trust account to fund the increase in the employer contribution rate;

(B) Suspend or reduce, as necessary, the three percent (3%) maximum cost-of-living adjustment as provided for in § 8-36-701(b)(1). Any such suspension or reduction shall begin on the July 1 next following the actuarial valuation;

(C) Suspend or reduce, as necessary, the amount of employer contributions required to the defined contribution component of the plan and redirect such amount to the reserve trust account to fund the increase in the employer contribution rate;

(D) Increase the employee contributions required in § 8-36-904 from five percent (5%) to six percent (6%) of the participant's earnable compensation;

(E) Reduce the retirement allowance formulas in § 8-36-907 from one percent (1.0%) and one and six-tenths percent (1.6%) to such lesser amount as is necessary to reduce the employer contribution rate to four percent (4%). The reduction in formulas shall only apply to future service accruals; and

(F) If the employer contribution rate still exceeds four percent (4%) after taking the above steps, then the hybrid plan shall be suspended for future service accruals until such time as the employer rate equals four percent (4%) or lower.

(2) If the actuarial valuation as of any year establishes a normal contribution rate and an accrued liability contribution rate, combined, that equals four percent (4%) or lower, the above steps in the reversed order as provided above shall automatically take effect the next July 1 immediately following the actuarial valuation as determined by the actuarial valuation process.

(d)(1) The actuary of the retirement system shall determine the amount of the unfunded accrued liability for the defined benefit component of the hybrid plan. If the unfunded liability exceeds the maximum unfunded liability, the following steps in the order provided below shall automatically apply on the effective date that the maximum unfunded liability has been reached. The unfunded liability shall be determined by the calculation of the net pension liability in accordance with the standards and other pronouncements issued by the governmental accounting standards board. For purposes of this section, "maximum unfunded liability" means with respect to state employees an unfunded liability of no greater than twelve and one-half percent (12½%) of a five-year moving market average of the general obligation debt of the state of Tennessee, including its commercial paper. With respect to teachers, "maximum unfunded liability" means an unfunded liability of no greater than twelve and one-half percent (12½%) of a five-year moving market average of the general obligation debt of the state of Tennessee, including its commercial paper. With respect to political subdivision employees, "maximum unfunded liability" means an unfunded liability of no greater than the amount as determined by the employees' respective employer and as shall be set forth in the political subdivision's participation resolution.

(A) Transfer such amounts as may be necessary from the stabilization reserve trust account created in § 8-36-920 to the reserve trust account to fund the increase in the maximum unfunded liability;

(B) Suspend or reduce, as necessary, the three percent (3%) maximum cost-of-living adjustment as provided for in § 8-36-701(b)(1). Any such suspension or reduction shall begin on the July 1 next following the actuarial valuation;

(C) Suspend or reduce, as necessary, the amount of employer contributions required to the defined contribution component of the plan and redirect such amount to the reserve trust account to fund the increase in the maximum unfunded liability;

(D) Increase the employee contributions required in § 8-36-904 from five percent (5%) to six percent (6%) of the participant's earnable compensation;

(E) Reduce the retirement allowance formulas in § 8-36-907 from one percent (1.0%) and one and six-tenths percent (1.6%) to such lesser amount as is necessary to reduce the unfunded liability to the maximum unfunded liability. The reduction in formulas shall only apply to future service accruals; and

(F) If the maximum unfunded liability is still exceeded, then the hybrid plan shall be suspended for future service accruals until such time as the unfunded liability equals or is less than the maximum unfunded liability.

(2) If the unfunded liability equals or is less than the maximum unfunded liability, the above steps in the reversed order as provided above shall automatically apply on the effective date that the unfunded liability equals or is less than maximum unfunded liability.

8-36-923.

(a) Notwithstanding any other law to the contrary and except as otherwise provided in § 8-36-903(c), any person who enters service with a state-supported institution of higher education on or after July 1, 2014, and who is exempt from the Fair Labor Standards Act, compiled in 29 U.S.C. § 201 et seq., may elect membership in the optional retirement program established in part 4 of this chapter in lieu of the hybrid plan. The election shall be made on election forms as shall be prescribed by the retirement system and shall be filed with the retirement system and with the institution of higher education where the employee is employed. The election shall be made within the time frame described in § 8-36-403. In all cases of doubt, the retirement system shall determine whether the person is eligible to participate in the optional retirement program.

(b) Any employee participating in the optional retirement program as provided in this part who attains either five (5) or more but less than six (6) years of creditable service in the optional retirement program, or five (5) or more but less than six (6) years of creditable service in the retirement system and the optional retirement program combined, shall have the option of transferring membership from the optional retirement program to the hybrid plan under the terms and conditions prescribed in § 8-35-403. The amount paid by the employee pursuant to § 8-35-403 shall be credited to the individual account of the employee in an amount equal to the employee contributions, if any, that were in the employee's optional retirement accounts immediately before the transfer, plus any difference between the amount paid and the employee's account balance in the optional retirement program immediately before the transfer. All other sums shall be credited to the employer reserve trust account established in § 8-36-920.

(c) Any person who elects to participate in the optional retirement program as provided in subsection (a) shall participate in the program under the provisions of part 4 of this chapter except as otherwise provided in subsection (d) below.

(d) The employer and employee contribution provisions of § 8-35-404(b)(1) shall not apply. Instead, the employer shall make employer contributions on behalf of each such eligible employee at the rate of nine percent (9%) of the employee's earnable compensation, or such alternate amount as may be prescribed in the general appropriations act each year. In addition, each such eligible employee shall contribute five percent (5%) of the employee's earnable compensation to the optional retirement program. The contributions made by such employees shall be treated as employer contributions pursuant to § 8-36-904(b).

(e) The general assembly shall have the right to freeze, suspend, or modify benefits, employee and employer contributions, plan terms, and design of the optional retirement program on a prospective basis through amendments to or repeals of chapters 34 – 37 of this title. Nothing under state law may confer to participants in the optional retirement program an implied right to future retirement benefit arrangements and such participants may not assert the indefinite continuation of the retirement formulas, contribution rates and eligibility ages in effect at the time of employment. Provided, however, the actuarial value of accrued benefits earned by participants prior to the effective date of any such amendment or repeal shall remain an enforceable right and may not be reduced or otherwise forfeited except by the consent of the employee.

8-25-105 SECTION 2. Tennessee Code Annotated, Section 8-25-105, is amended by adding the following language as a new second sentence:

It is the intent of the general assembly that a variety of investment options be offered to participants in the plan, which may include one or more comingled funds whereby assets in the custody of the state treasurer are pooled.

8-25-301 SECTION 3. Tennessee Code Annotated, Section 8-25-301, is amended by adding the following new sentence at the end thereof:

It is the intent of the general assembly that a variety of investment options be offered to participants in the plan, which may include one or more comingled funds whereby assets in the custody of the state treasurer are pooled.

8-37-104 SECTION 4. Tennessee Code Annotated, Section 8-37-104, is amended by adding the following as a new, appropriately designated subsection:

(_) The board may authorize assets of the funds of the retirement system to be pooled for investment purposes with any assets under the custody of the state treasurer.

SECTION 5. If any provision of this act or the application thereof to any person or circumstance is held invalid, such invalidity shall not affect other provisions or applications of the act which can be given effect without the invalid provision or application, and to that end, the provisions of this act are declared to be severable.

SECTION 6. The board may promulgate rules, including emergency rules, in accordance with the Uniform Administrative Procedures Act, compiled in Title 4, Chapter 5, that the board deems necessary to effectuate this part.

Effective date 7/1/2014 SECTION 7. This act shall take effect immediately for purposes of rulemaking and for all other purposes on July 1, 2014, the public welfare requiring it.

PUBLIC CHAPTER NO. 260

PUBLIC CHAPTER NO. 260

SENATE BILL NO. 145

By Norris, Johnson, Ketron

Substituted for: House Bill No. 139

By McCormick

AN ACT to amend Tennessee Code Annotated, Title 56, Chapter 1 and Title 56, Chapter 7, relative to requirements for Principle-Based Valuation.

BE IT ENACTED BY THE GENERAL ASSEMBLY OF THE STATE OF TENNESSEE:

56-1-402 56-1-403 SECTION 1. Tennessee Code Annotated, Sections 56-1-402 and 56-1-403, are amended by deleting the sections in their entirety.

56-1-415 SECTION 2. Tennessee Code Annotated, Section 56-1-415, is amended by deleting the language "§§ 56-1-402 -- 56-1-405" and substituting instead the language "part 9 of this chapter".

56-1-901 — 56-1-919 SECTION 3. Tennessee Code Annotated, Title 56, Chapter 1, is amended by adding the following language as a new part:

56-1-901. Title and Definitions.

(a) This part shall be known and may be cited as the "Standard Valuation Law".

(b) For purposes of this part, the following definitions shall apply on or after the operative date of the valuation manual:

(1) "Accident and health insurance contracts" means contracts that incorporate morbidity risk and provide protection against economic loss resulting from accident, sickness or medical conditions and as may be specified in the valuation manual;

(2) "Appointed actuary" means a qualified actuary who is appointed in accordance with the valuation manual to prepare the actuarial opinion required in § 56-1-903;

(3) "Company" means an entity that:

(A) Has written, issued, or reinsured life insurance contracts, accident and health insurance contracts, or deposit-type contracts in this state and has at least one (1) such policy in force or on claim; or

(B) Has written, issued, or reinsured life insurance contracts, accident and health insurance contracts, or deposit-type contracts in any state and is required to hold a certificate of authority to write life insurance, accident and health insurance or deposit-type contracts in this state;

(4) "Deposit-type contract" means contracts that do not incorporate mortality or morbidity risks, and as may be specified in the valuation manual;

(5) "Life insurance" means contracts that incorporate mortality risk, including annuity and pure endowment contracts, and as may be specified in the valuation manual;

(6) "NAIC" means the National Association of Insurance Commissioners;

(7) "Policyholder behavior" means any action a policyholder, contract holder or any other person with the right to elect options, such as a certificate holder, may take under a policy or contract subject to this part including, but not limited to, lapse, withdrawal, transfer, deposit, premium payment, loan, annuitization or benefit elections prescribed by the policy or contract but

excluding events of mortality or morbidity that result in benefits prescribed in their essential aspects by the terms of the policy or contract;

(8) "Principle-based valuation" means a reserve valuation that uses one (1) or more methods or one (1) or more assumptions determined by the insurer and is required to comply with § 56-1-915 as specified in the valuation manual;

(9) "Qualified actuary" means an individual who is qualified to sign the applicable statement of actuarial opinion in accordance with the American Academy of Actuaries' qualification standards for actuaries signing such statements and who meets the requirements specified in the valuation manual;

(10) The term "tail risk" means a risk that occurs either where the frequency of low probability events is higher than expected under a normal probability distribution or where there are observed events of very significant size or magnitude; and

(11) The term "valuation manual" means the manual of valuation instructions adopted by the NAIC as specified in this part or as subsequently amended.

56-1-902. Reserve Valuation.

(a) For policies and contracts issued prior to the operative date of the valuation manual:

(1) The commissioner shall annually value, or cause to be valued, the reserve liabilities ("reserves") for all outstanding life insurance policies and annuity and pure endowment contracts of every life insurance company doing business in this state issued on or after January 1, 1962, and prior to the operative date of the valuation manual. In calculating reserves, the commissioner may use group methods and approximate averages for fractions of a year or otherwise. In lieu of the valuation of the reserves required of a foreign or alien company, the commissioner may accept a valuation made, or caused to be made, by the insurance supervisory official of any state or other jurisdiction when the valuation complies with the minimum standard provided in this part.

(2) Sections 56-1-904 through 56-1-913 of this part shall apply to all policies and contracts, as appropriate, subject to this part issued on or after January 1, 1962, and prior to the operative date of the valuation manual and the provisions set forth in 56-1-914 through 56-1-915 of this part shall not apply to any such policies and contracts.

(3) The minimum standard for the valuation of policies and contracts issued prior to January 1, 1962, shall be that provided by the laws in effect immediately prior to that date.

(b) For policies and contracts issued on or after the operative date of the valuation manual:

(1) The commissioner shall annually value, or cause to be valued, the reserves for all outstanding life insurance contracts, annuity and pure endowment contracts, accident and health contracts, and deposit-type contracts of every company issued on or after the operative date of the valuation manual. In lieu of the valuation of the reserves required of a foreign or alien company, the commissioner may accept a valuation made, or caused to be made, by the insurance supervisory official of any state or other jurisdiction when the valuation complies with the minimum standard provided in this part; and

(2) Sections 56-1-914 through 56-1-915 shall apply to all policies and contracts issued on or after the operative date of the valuation manual.

56-1-903. Actuarial Opinion of Reserves.

(a) For an actuarial opinion prior to the operative date of the valuation manual:

(1) Every life insurance company doing business in this state shall annually submit the opinion of a qualified actuary as to whether the reserves and related actuarial items held in support of the policies and contracts specified by the commissioner by regulation are computed appropriately, are based on assumptions that satisfy contractual provisions, are consistent with prior reported amounts and comply with applicable laws of this state. The commissioner shall define by regulation the specifics of this opinion and add any other items deemed to be necessary to its scope.

(2) For actuarial analysis of reserves and assets supporting reserves:

(A) Every life insurance company, except as exempted by regulation, shall also annually include in the opinion required by subdivision (a)(1), an opinion of the same qualified actuary as to whether the reserves and related actuarial items held in support of the policies and contracts specified by the commissioner by regulation, when considered in light of the assets held by the company with respect to the reserves and related actuarial items, including, but not limited to, the investment earnings on the assets and the considerations anticipated to be received and retained under the policies and contracts, make adequate provision for the company's obligations under the policies and contracts, including, but not limited to, the benefits under, and expenses associated with, the policies and contracts.

(B) The commissioner may provide by regulation for a transition period for establishing any higher reserves that the qualified actuary may deem necessary in order to render the opinion required by this section.

(3) Each opinion required by subdivision (a)(2) shall be governed by the following provisions:

(A) A memorandum, in form and substance acceptable to the commissioner as specified by regulation, shall be prepared to support each actuarial opinion.

(B) If the insurance company fails to provide a supporting memorandum at the request of the commissioner within a period specified by regulation or the commissioner determines that the supporting memorandum provided by the insurance company fails to meet the standards prescribed by regulations promulgated by the commissioner or is otherwise unacceptable to the commissioner, the commissioner may engage a qualified actuary at the expense of the company to review the opinion and the basis for the opinion and prepare the supporting memorandum required by the commissioner.

(4) Every opinion required by this subsection (a) shall be governed by the following provisions:

(A) The opinion shall be submitted with the annual statement reflecting the valuation of such reserve liabilities for each year ending on or after December 31, 1995;

(B) The opinion shall apply to all business in force including individual and group health insurance plans, in form and substance acceptable to the commissioner as specified by regulation;

(C) The opinion shall be based on standards adopted from time to time by the Actuarial Standards Board and on such additional standards as the commissioner prescribes by regulation;

(D) In the case of an opinion required to be submitted by a foreign or alien company, the commissioner may accept the opinion filed by that company with the insurance supervisory official of another state if the commissioner determines that the opinion reasonably meets the requirements applicable to a company domiciled in this state;

(E) For purposes of this section, "qualified actuary" means a member in good standing of the American Academy of Actuaries who meets the requirements set forth in the regulation;

(F) Except in cases of fraud or willful misconduct, the qualified actuary shall not be liable for damages to any person, other than the insurance company and the commissioner, for any act, error, omission, decision or conduct with respect to the actuary's opinion;

(G) Disciplinary action by the commissioner against the company or the qualified actuary shall be defined in regulations promulgated by the commissioner;

(H) Except as provided in subdivisions (a)(4)(L)-(N), documents, materials or other information in the possession or control of the department that are a memorandum in support of the opinion, and any other material provided by the company to the commissioner in connection with the memorandum, shall be confidential by law and privileged, shall not be subject to § 10-7-501 or § 56-1-602, shall not be subject to subpoena, and shall not be subject to discovery or admissible in evidence in any private civil action. However, the commissioner is authorized to use the documents, materials or other information in the furtherance of any regulatory or legal action brought as a part of the commissioner's official duties;

(I) Neither the commissioner nor any person who received documents, materials or other information while acting under the authority of the commissioner shall be permitted or required to testify in any private civil action concerning any confidential documents, materials or information subject to subdivision (a)(4)(H);

(J) In order to assist in the performance of the commissioner's duties, the commissioner may:

(i) Share documents, materials or other information, including the confidential and privileged documents, materials or information subject to subdivision (a)(4)(H) with other state, federal and international regulatory agencies, with the NAIC and its affiliates and subsidiaries, and with state, federal and international law enforcement authorities; provided, the recipient agrees to maintain the confidentiality and privileged status of the document, material or other information;

(ii) Receive documents, materials or information, including otherwise confidential and privileged documents, materials or information, from the NAIC and its affiliates and subsidiaries, and from regulatory and law enforcement officials of other foreign or domestic jurisdictions, and shall maintain as confidential or privileged any document, material or information received with notice or the understanding that it is confidential or privileged under the laws of the jurisdiction that is the source of the document, material or information; and

(iii) Enter into agreements governing sharing and use of information consistent with subdivisions (a)(4)(H)-(J);

(K) No waiver of any applicable privilege or claim of confidentiality in the documents, materials or information shall occur as a result of disclosure to the commissioner under § 56-1-903 or as a result of sharing as authorized in subdivision (a)(4)(J);

(L) A memorandum in support of the opinion, and any other material provided by the company to the commissioner in connection with the memorandum, may be subject to subpoena for the purpose of defending an action seeking damages from the actuary submitting the memorandum by reason of an action required by this section or by regulation;

(M) The memorandum or other material may otherwise be released by the commissioner with the written consent of the company or to the American Academy of Actuaries upon request stating that the memorandum or other material is required for the purpose of professional disciplinary proceedings and setting forth procedures satisfactory to the commissioner for preserving the confidentiality of the memorandum or other material; and

(N) Once any portion of the confidential memorandum is cited by the company in its marketing or is cited before a governmental agency other than a state insurance department or is released by the company to the news media, all portions of the confidential memorandum shall be no longer confidential.

(b) For an actuarial opinion of reserves after the operative date of the valuation manual:

(1) Every company with outstanding life insurance contracts, accident and health insurance contracts or deposit-type contracts in this state and subject to regulation by the commissioner shall annually submit the opinion of the appointed actuary as to whether the reserves and related actuarial items held in support of the policies and contracts are computed appropriately, are based on assumptions that satisfy contractual provisions, are consistent with prior reported amounts and comply with applicable laws of this state. The valuation manual will prescribe the specifics of this opinion including any items deemed to be necessary to its scope;

(2) For actuarial analysis of reserves and assets supporting reserves, every company with outstanding life insurance contracts, accident and health insurance contracts or deposit-type contracts in this state and subject to regulation by the commissioner, except as exempted in the valuation manual, shall also annually include in the opinion required by subdivision (b)(1), an opinion of the same appointed actuary as to whether the reserves and related actuarial items held in support of the policies and contracts specified in the valuation manual, when considered in light of the assets held by the company with respect to the reserves and related actuarial items, including, but not limited to, the investment earnings on the assets and the considerations anticipated to be received and retained under the policies and contracts, make adequate provision for the company's obligations under the policies and contracts, including, but not limited to, the benefits under, and expenses associated with, the policies and contracts.

(3) Each opinion required by subdivision (b)(2) shall be governed by the following provisions:

(A) A memorandum, in form and substance as specified in the valuation manual, and acceptable to the commissioner, shall be prepared to support each actuarial opinion; and

(B) If the insurance company fails to provide a supporting memorandum at the request of the commissioner within a period specified in the valuation manual or the commissioner determines that the supporting memorandum provided by the insurance company fails to meet the standards prescribed by the valuation manual or is otherwise unacceptable to the commissioner, the commissioner may engage a qualified actuary at the expense of the company to review the opinion and the basis for the opinion and prepare the supporting memorandum required by the commissioner.

(4) Every opinion shall be governed by the following provisions:

(A) The opinion shall be in form and substance as specified in the valuation manual and acceptable to the commissioner;

(B) The opinion shall be submitted with the annual statement reflecting the valuation of such reserve liabilities for each year ending on or after the operative date of the valuation manual;

(C) The opinion shall apply to all policies and contracts subject to this subsection (b), plus other actuarial liabilities as may be specified in the valuation manual;

(D) The opinion shall be based on standards adopted from time to time by the Actuarial Standards Board or its successor, and on such additional standards as may be prescribed in the valuation manual;

(E) In the case of an opinion required to be submitted by a foreign or alien company, the commissioner may accept the opinion filed by that company with the insurance supervisory official of another state if the commissioner determines that the opinion reasonably meets the requirements applicable to a company domiciled in this state;

(F) Except in cases of fraud or willful misconduct, the appointed actuary shall not be liable for damages to any person, other than the insurance company and the commissioner for any act, error, omission, decision or conduct with respect to the appointed actuary's opinion; and

(G) Disciplinary action by the commissioner against the company or the appointed actuary shall be defined in regulations promulgated by the commissioner.

56-1-904. Computation of Minimum Standard.

Except as provided in §§ 56-1-905, 56-1-906 and 56-1-913, the minimum standard for the valuation of policies and contracts issued prior to January 1, 1962, shall be that provided by the laws in effect immediately prior to that date. Except as otherwise provided in §§ 56-1-905, 56-1-906 and 56-1-913, the minimum standard for the valuation of all policies and contracts issued on or after January 1, 1962, shall be the commissioner's reserve valuation methods defined in §§ 56-1-907, 56-1-908, 56-1-911 and 56-1-913, three and one half percent (3.5%) interest, or in the case of life insurance policies and contracts, other than annuity and pure endowment contracts, issued on or after May 6, 1973, four percent (4%) interest for policies issued prior to March 13, 1978, five and one half percent (5.5%) interest for single premium life insurance policies and four and one half percent (4.5%) interest for all other policies issued on or after March 13, 1978, and the following tables:

(1) For ordinary policies of life insurance issued on the standard basis, excluding any disability and accidental death benefits in the policies: the Commissioners 1941 Standard Ordinary Mortality Table for policies issued prior to the operative date of § 56-7-401(f), the Commissioners 1958 Standard Ordinary Mortality Table for policies issued on or after the operative date of § 56-7-401(f) and prior to the operative date of § 56-7-401(h), provided that for any category of policies issued on female risks, all modified net premiums and present values referred to in this part may be calculated according to an age not more than six (6) years younger than the actual age of the insured; and for policies issued on or after the operative date of § 56-7-401(h):

(A) The Commissioners 1980 Standard Ordinary Mortality Table;

(B) At the election of the company for any one (1) or more specified plans of life insurance, the Commissioners 1980 Standard Ordinary Mortality Table with Ten-Year Select Mortality Factors; or

(C) Any ordinary mortality table, adopted after 1980 by the NAIC, which is approved by regulation promulgated by the commissioner for use in determining the minimum standard of valuation for such policies;

(2) For industrial life insurance policies issued on the standard basis, excluding any disability and accidental death benefits in the policies: the 1941 Standard Industrial Mortality Table for policies issued prior to the operative date of § 56-7-401(g), and for policies issued on or after the operative date of § 56-7-401(g), the Commissioners 1961 Standard Industrial Mortality Table or any industrial mortality table adopted after 1980 by the NAIC that is approved by regulation promulgated by the commissioner for use in determining the minimum standard of valuation for the policies;

(3) For individual annuity and pure endowment contracts, excluding any disability and accidental death benefits in the policies: the 1937 Standard Annuity Mortality Table, or at the option of the company, the Annuity Mortality Table for 1949, Ultimate or any modification of either of these tables approved by the commissioner;

(4) For group annuity and pure endowment contracts, excluding any disability and accidental death benefits in the policies: the Group Annuity Mortality Table for 1951, a modification of the table approved by the commissioner, or at the option of the company, any of the tables or modifications of tables specified for individual annuity and pure endowment contracts;

(5) For total and permanent disability benefits in or supplementary to ordinary policies or contracts: for policies or contracts issued on or after January 1, 1966, the tables of Period 2 disablement rates and the 1930 to 1950 termination rates of the 1952 Disability Study of the Society of Actuaries, with due regard to the type of benefit or any tables of disablement rates and termination rates adopted after 1980 by the NAIC, that are approved by regulation promulgated by the commissioner for use in determining the minimum standard of valuation for those policies; for policies or contracts issued on or after January 1, 1961, and prior to January 1, 1966, either those tables or, at the option of the company, the Class (3) Disability Table (1926); and for policies issued prior to January 1, 1961, the Class (3) Disability Table (1926). Any such table shall, for active lives, be combined with a mortality table permitted for calculating the reserves for life insurance policies;

(6) For accidental death benefits in or supplementary to policies issued on or after January 1, 1966: the 1959 Accidental Death Benefits Table or any accidental death benefits table adopted after 1980 by the NAIC that is approved by regulation promulgated by the commissioner for use in determining the minimum standard of valuation for those policies, for policies issued on or after January 1, 1961, and prior to January 1, 1966, either that table or, at the option of the company, the Inter-Company Double Indemnity Mortality Table; and for policies issued prior to January 1, 1961, the Inter-Company Double Indemnity Mortality Table. Either table shall be combined with a mortality table for calculating the reserves for life insurance policies; and

(7) For group life insurance, life insurance issued on the substandard basis and other special benefits: tables approved by the commissioner.

56-1-905. Computation of Minimum Standard for Annuities.

(a) Except as provided in § 56-1-906, the minimum standard of valuation for individual annuity and pure endowment contracts issued on or after the operative date of this section and for annuities and pure endowments purchased on or after the operative date under group annuity and pure endowment contracts, shall be the commissioner's reserve valuation methods defined in §§ 56-1-907 and 56-1-908 and the following tables and interest rates:

(1) For individual annuity and pure endowment contracts issued prior to March 13, 1978, excluding any disability and accidental death benefits in those contracts: the 1971 Individual Annuity Mortality Table, or any modification of this table approved by the commissioner, and six percent (6%) interest for single premium immediate annuity contracts and four percent (4%) interest for all other individual annuity and pure endowment contracts;

(2) For individual single premium immediate annuity contracts issued on or after March 13, 1978, excluding any disability and accidental death benefits in those contracts: the 1971 Individual Annuity Mortality Table or any individual annuity mortality table adopted after 1980 by the NAIC that is approved by regulation promulgated by the commissioner for use in determining the minimum standard of valuation for these contracts, or any modification of these tables approved by the commissioner, and seven and one half percent (7.5%) interest;

(3) For individual annuity and pure endowment contracts issued on or after March 13, 1978, other than single premium immediate annuity contracts, excluding any disability and accidental death benefits in those contracts: the 1971 Individual Annuity Mortality Table or any individual annuity mortality table adopted after 1980 by the NAIC, that is approved by regulation promulgated by the commissioner for use in determining the minimum standard of valuation for those contracts, or any modification of these tables approved by the commissioner, and five and one half percent (5.5%) interest for single premium deferred annuity and pure endowment contracts and four and one half percent (4.5%) interest for all other individual annuity and pure endowment contracts;

(4) For annuities and pure endowments purchased prior to March 13, 1978, under group annuity and pure endowment contracts, excluding any disability and accidental death benefits purchased under those contracts: the 1971 Group Annuity Mortality Table or any modification of this table approved by the commissioner, and six percent (6%) interest; and

(5) For annuities and pure endowments purchased on or after March 13, 1978, under group annuity and pure endowment contracts, excluding any disability and accidental death benefits purchased under those contracts: the 1971 Group Annuity Mortality Table, or any group annuity mortality table adopted after 1980 by the NAIC that is approved by regulation promulgated by the commissioner for use in determining the minimum standard of valuation for annuities and pure endowments, or any modification of these tables approved by the commissioner, and seven and one half percent (7.5%) interest.

(b) After May 6, 1973, any company may file with the commissioner a written notice of its election to comply with this section after a specified date before January 1, 1979, which shall be the operative date of this section for that company. If a company makes no election, the operative date of this section for that company shall be January 1, 1979.

56-1-906. Computation of Minimum Standard by Calendar Year of Issue.

(a) The interest rates used in determining the minimum standard for the valuation of the following shall be the calendar year statutory valuation interest rates as defined in this section:

(1) Life insurance policies issued in a particular calendar year, on or after the operative date of § 56-7-401(h);

(2) Individual annuity and pure endowment contracts issued in a particular calendar year, on or after January 1, 1983;

(3) Annuities and pure endowments purchased in a particular calendar year, on or after January 1, 1983, under group annuity and pure endowment contracts; and

(4) The net increase, if any, in a particular calendar year after January 1, 1983, in amounts held under guaranteed interest contracts.

(b) For calendar year statutory valuation interest rates:

(1) The calendar year statutory valuation interest rates, I, shall be determined as follows and the results rounded to the nearer one-quarter of one percent (0.25%), where R_1 is the lesser of R and .09, R_2 is the greater of R and .09, R is the reference interest rate defined in this section, and W is the weighting factor defined in this section:

(A) For life insurance:

$$I = .03 + W \cdot (R_1 - .03) + \frac{W}{2} \cdot (R_2 - .09)$$

(B) For single premium immediate annuities and for annuity benefits involving life contingencies arising from other annuities with cash settlement options and from guaranteed interest contracts with cash settlement options:

$$I = .03 + W \cdot (R - .03)$$

(C) For other annuities with cash settlement options and guaranteed interest contracts with cash settlement options, valued on an issue year basis, except as stated in subdivision (b)(1)(B), the formula for life insurance in subdivision (b)(1)(A) shall apply to annuities and guaranteed interest contracts with guarantee durations in excess of ten (10) years and the formula for single premium immediate annuities in subdivision (b)(1)(B) shall apply to annuities and guaranteed interest contracts with guarantee duration of ten (10) years or less.

(D) For other annuities with no cash settlement options and for guaranteed interest contracts with no cash settlement options, the formula for single premium immediate annuities in subdivision (b)(1)(B) shall apply.

(E) For other annuities with cash settlement options and guaranteed interest contracts with cash settlement options, valued on a change in fund basis, the formula for single premium immediate annuities in subdivision (b)(1)(B) shall apply.

(2)(A) However, if the calendar year statutory valuation interest rate for a life insurance policy issued in any calendar year determined without reference to this subdivision (b)(2)(A) differs from the corresponding actual rate for similar policies issued in the immediately preceding calendar year by less than one half of one percent (0.5%), the calendar year statutory valuation interest rate for the life insurance policies shall be equal to the corresponding actual rate for the immediately preceding calendar year.

(B) For purposes of applying subdivision (b)(2)(A), the calendar year statutory valuation interest rate for life insurance policies issued in a calendar year shall be determined for 1980, using the reference interest rate defined in 1979, and shall be determined for each subsequent calendar year regardless of when § 56-7-401(h) becomes operative.

(c) The weighting factors referred to in the formulas described in subsection (b) are given in the following tables:

(1)(A) Weighting factors for life insurance:

Guarantee Duration (Years)	Weighting Factors
10 or less	.50
More than 10, but not more than 20	.45
More than 20	.35

(B) For life insurance, the guarantee duration is the maximum number of years the life insurance can remain in force on a basis guaranteed in the policy or under options to convert to plans of life insurance with premium rates or nonforfeiture values or both which are guaranteed in the original policy;

(2) Weighting factor for single premium immediate annuities and for annuity benefits involving life contingencies arising from other annuities with cash settlement options and guaranteed interest contracts with cash settlement options: .80

(3) Weighting factors for other annuities and for guaranteed interest contracts, except as provided in subdivision (c)(2), shall be as specified in subdivisions (c)(3)(A), (B) and (C), according to the rules and definitions in subdivisions (c)(3)(D), (E) and (F):

(A) For annuities and guaranteed interest contracts valued on an issue year basis:

Guarantee Duration	Weighting Factor for Plan Type		
(Years)	A	B	C
5 or less:	.80	.60	.50
More than 5, but not more than 10:	.75	.60	.50

More than 10, but not more than 20:	.65	.50	.45
More than 20:	.45	.35	.35

(B) For annuities and guaranteed interest contracts valued on a change in fund basis, the factors in subdivision (c)(3)(A) increased by:

Plan Type		
A	B	C
.15	.25	.05

(C) For annuities and guaranteed interest contracts valued on an issue year basis, other than those with no cash settlement options, that do not guarantee interest on considerations received more than one (1) year after issue or purchase and for annuities and guaranteed interest contracts valued on a change in fund basis that do not guarantee interest rates on considerations received more than twelve (12) months beyond the valuation date, the factors in subdivision (c)(3)(A) or derived in subdivision (c)(3)(B) increased by:

Plan Type		
A	B	C
.05	.05	.05

(D) For other annuities with cash settlement options and guaranteed interest contracts with cash settlement options, the guarantee duration is the number of years for which the contract guarantees interest rates in excess of the calendar year statutory valuation interest rate for life insurance policies with guarantee duration in excess of twenty (20) years. For other annuities with no cash settlement options and for guaranteed interest contracts with no cash settlement options, the guaranteed duration is the number of years from the date of issue or date of purchase to the date annuity benefits are scheduled to commence.

(E) Plan type as used in subdivisions (c)(3)(A)-(C) is defined as follows:

(i) Plan Type A: At any time policyholder may withdraw funds only:

(a) With an adjustment to reflect changes in interest rates or asset values since receipt of the funds by the insurance company;

(b) Without an adjustment but installments over five (5) years or more;

(c) As an immediate life annuity; or

(d) No withdrawal permitted.

(ii) Plan Type B: Before expiration of the interest rate guarantee, policyholder may withdraw funds only:

(a) With an adjustment to reflect changes in interest rates or asset values since receipt of the funds by the insurance company;

(b) Without an adjustment but in installments over five (5) years or more;

(c) No withdrawal permitted; or

(d) At the end of interest rate guarantee, funds may be withdrawn without an adjustment in a single sum or installments over less than five (5) years.

(iii) Plan Type C: Policyholder may withdraw funds before expiration of interest rate guarantee in a single sum or installments over less than five (5) years either:

(a) Without adjustment to reflect changes in interest rates or asset values since receipt of the funds by the insurance company; or

(b) Subject only to a fixed surrender charge stipulated in the contract as a percentage of the fund.

(F) A company may elect to value guaranteed interest contracts with cash settlement options and annuities with cash settlement options on either an issue year basis or on a change in fund basis. Guaranteed interest contracts with no cash settlement options and other annuities with no cash settlement options must be valued on an issue year basis. As used in this section, an issue year basis of valuation refers to a valuation basis under which the interest rate used to determine the minimum valuation standard for the entire duration of the annuity or guaranteed interest contract is the calendar year valuation interest rate for the year of issue or year of purchase of the annuity or guaranteed interest contract, and the change in fund basis of valuation refers to a valuation basis under which the interest rate used to determine the minimum valuation standard applicable to each change in the fund held under the annuity or guaranteed interest contract is the calendar year valuation interest rate for the year of the change in the fund.

(d) The reference interest rate referred to in subsection (b) means:

(1) For life insurance, the lesser of the average over a period of thirty-six (36) months and the average over a period of twelve (12) months, ending on June 30 of the calendar year preceding the year of issue, of the monthly average of the composite yield on seasoned corporate bonds, as published by Moody's Investors Service, Inc.;

(2) For single premium immediate annuities and for annuity benefits involving life contingencies arising from other annuities with cash settlement options and guaranteed interest contracts with cash settlement options, the average over a period of twelve (12) months, ending on June 30 of the calendar year of issue or year of purchase, of the monthly average of the composite yield on seasoned corporate bonds, as published by Moody's Investors Service, Inc.;

(3) For other annuities with cash settlement options and guaranteed interest contracts with cash settlement options, valued on a year of issue basis, except as stated in subdivision (d)(2), with guarantee duration in excess of ten (10) years, the lesser of the average over a period of thirty-six (36) months and the average over a period of twelve (12) months, ending on June 30 of the calendar year of issue or purchase, of the monthly average of the composite yield on seasoned corporate bonds, as published by Moody's Investors Service, Inc.;

(4) For other annuities with cash settlement options and guaranteed interest contracts with cash settlement options, valued on a year of issue basis, except as stated in subdivision (d)(2), with guarantee duration of ten (10) years or less, the average over a period of twelve (12) months, ending on June 30 of the calendar year of issue or purchase, of the monthly average of the composite yield on seasoned corporate bonds, as published by Moody's Investors Service, Inc.;

(5) For other annuities with no cash settlement options and for guaranteed interest contracts with no cash settlement options, the average over a period of twelve (12) months, ending on June 30 of the calendar year of issue or purchase, of the monthly average of the composite yield on seasoned corporate bonds, as published by Moody's Investors Service, Inc.; or

(6) For other annuities with cash settlement options and guaranteed interest contracts with cash settlement options, valued on a change in fund

basis, except as stated in subdivision (d)(2), the average over a period of twelve (12) months, ending on June 30 of the calendar year of the change in the fund, of the monthly average of the composite yield on seasoned corporate bonds, as published by Moody's Investors Service, Inc.

(e) For alternative method for determining reference interest rates, in the event that the monthly average of the composite yield on seasoned corporate bonds is no longer published by Moody's Investors Service, Inc., or in the event that the NAIC determines that the monthly average of the composite yield on seasoned corporate bonds as published by Moody's Investors Service, Inc., is no longer appropriate for the determination of the reference interest rate, then an alternative method for determination of the reference interest rate adopted by the NAIC and approved by regulations promulgated by the commissioner may be substituted.

56-1-907. Reserve Valuation Method—Life Insurance and Endowment Benefits.

(a) Except as otherwise provided in §§ 56-1-908, 56-1-911 and 56-1-913, reserves according to the commissioner's reserve valuation method, for the life insurance and endowment benefits of policies providing for a uniform amount of insurance and requiring the payment of uniform premiums, shall be the excess, if any, of the present value, at the date of valuation, of the future guaranteed benefits provided for by those policies, over the then present value of any future modified net premiums therefore. The modified net premiums for a policy shall be the uniform percentage of the respective contract premiums for the benefits such that the present value, at the date of issue of the policy, of all modified net premiums shall be equal to the sum of the then present value of the benefits provided for by the policy and the excess of subdivision (a)(1) over subdivision (a)(2), as follows:

(1) A net level annual premium equal to the present value, at the date of issue, of the benefits provided for after the first policy year, divided by the present value, at the date of issue, of an annuity of one (1) per annum payable on the first and each subsequent anniversary of the policy on which a premium falls due. However, the net level annual premium shall not exceed the net level annual premium on the nineteen (19) year premium whole life plan for insurance of the same amount at an age one (1) year higher than the age at issue of the policy;

(2) A net one (1) year term premium for the benefits provided for in the first policy year.

(b) For a life insurance policy issued on or after January 1, 1986, for which the contract premium in the first policy year exceeds that of the second year and for which no comparable additional benefit is provided in the first year for the excess and which provides an endowment benefit or a cash surrender value or a combination in an amount greater than the excess premium, the reserve according to the commissioner's reserve valuation method as of any policy anniversary occurring on or before the assumed ending date defined in this part as the first policy anniversary on which the sum of any endowment benefit and any cash surrender value then available is greater than the excess premium shall, except as otherwise provided in § 56-1-911, be the greater of the reserve as of the policy anniversary calculated as described in subsection (a) and the reserve as of the policy anniversary calculated as described in subsection (a), but with:

(1) The value defined in subdivision (a)(1) being reduced by fifteen percent (15%) of the amount of such excess first year premium;

(2) All present values of benefits and premiums being determined without reference to premiums or benefits provided for by the policy after the assumed ending date;

(3) The policy being assumed to mature on that date as an endowment; and

(4) The cash surrender value provided on that date being considered as an endowment benefit.

(c) In making the comparison the mortality and interest bases in §§ 56-1-904 and 56-1-906 shall be used.

(d) Reserves according to the commissioner's reserve valuation method shall be calculated by a method consistent with subsections (a) and (b) for:

(1) Life insurance policies providing for a varying amount of insurance or requiring the payment of varying premiums;

(2) Group annuity and pure endowment contracts purchased under a retirement plan or plan of deferred compensation, established or maintained by an employer, including a partnership or sole proprietorship, or by an employee organization, or by both, other than a plan providing individual retirement accounts or individual retirement annuities under § 408 of the Internal Revenue Code, codified in 26 U.S.C. § 408, as amended;

(3) Disability and accidental death benefits in all policies and contracts; and

(4) All other benefits, except life insurance and endowment benefits in life insurance policies and benefits provided by all other annuity and pure endowment contracts.

56-1-908. Reserve Valuation Method—Annuity and Pure Endowment Benefits.

(a) This section shall apply to all annuity and pure endowment contracts other than group annuity and pure endowment contracts purchased under a retirement plan or plan of deferred compensation, established or maintained by an employer, including a partnership or sole proprietorship, or by an employee organization, or by both, other than a plan providing individual retirement accounts or individual retirement annuities under § 408 of the Internal Revenue Code, codified in 26 U.S.C. § 408, as amended.

(b) Reserves according to the commissioners annuity reserve method for benefits under annuity or pure endowment contracts, excluding any disability and accidental death benefits in the contracts, shall be the greatest of the respective excesses of the present values, at the date of valuation, of the future guaranteed benefits, including guaranteed nonforfeiture benefits, provided for by the contracts at the end of each respective contract year, over the present value, at the date of valuation, of any future valuation considerations derived from future gross considerations, required by the terms of the contract, that become payable prior to the end of the respective contract year. The future guaranteed benefits shall be determined by using the mortality table, if any, and the interest rate, or rates, specified in the contracts for determining guaranteed benefits. The valuation considerations are the portions of the respective gross considerations applied under the terms of the contracts to determine nonforfeiture values.

56-1-909. Minimum Reserves.

(a) In no event shall a company's aggregate reserves for all life insurance policies, excluding disability and accidental death benefits, issued on or after March 13, 1978, be less than the aggregate reserves calculated in accordance with the methods set forth in §§ 56-1-907, 56-1-908, 56-1-911 and 56-1-912 and the mortality table or tables and rate or rates of interest used in calculating nonforfeiture benefits for the policies.

(b) In no event shall the aggregate reserves for all policies, contracts and benefits be less than the aggregate reserves determined by the appointed actuary to be necessary to render the opinion required by § 56-1-903.

56-1-910. Optional Reserve Calculation.

(a) Reserves for policies and contracts issued prior to March 13, 1978, may be calculated, at the option of the company, according to any standards that produce greater aggregate reserves for all such policies and contracts than the minimum reserves required by the laws in effect immediately prior to March 13, 1978.

(b) Reserves for any category of policies, contracts or benefits established by the commissioner, issued on or after March 13, 1978, may be calculated, at the option of the company, according to any standards that produce greater aggregate reserves for the category than those calculated according to the minimum standard provided in this part, but the rate or rates of interest used for policies and contracts, other than annuity and pure endowment contracts, shall not be greater than the corresponding rate or rates of interest used in calculating any nonforfeiture benefits provided in the policies or contracts.

(c) A company, which adopts at any time a standard of valuation producing greater aggregate reserves than those calculated according to the minimum standard provided under this part may adopt a lower standard of valuation with the approval of the commissioner, but not lower than the minimum provided herein; provided that, for the purposes of this section, the holding of additional reserves previously determined by the appointed actuary to be necessary to render the opinion required by § 56-1-903 shall not be deemed to be the adoption of a higher standard of valuation.

56-1-911. Reserve Calculation—Valuation Net Premium Exceeding the Gross Premium Charged.

(a) If in any contract year the gross premium charged by a company on a policy or contract is less than the valuation net premium for the policy or contract calculated by the method used in calculating the reserve but using the minimum valuation standards of mortality and rate of interest, the minimum reserve required for the policy or contract shall be the greater of either the reserve calculated according to the mortality table, rate of interest and method actually used for the policy or contract; or the reserve calculated by the method actually used for the policy or contract but using the minimum valuation standards of mortality and rate of interest and replacing the valuation net premium by the actual gross premium in each contract year for which the valuation net premium exceeds the actual gross premium. The minimum valuation standards of mortality and rate of interest referred to in this section are those standards stated in §§ 56-1-904 and 56-1-906.

(b) For a life insurance policy issued on or after January 1, 1986, for which the gross premium in the first policy year exceeds that of the second year and for which no comparable additional benefit is provided in the first year for the excess and which provides an endowment benefit or a cash surrender value, or a combination, in an amount greater than the excess premium, § 56-1-911(a) shall be applied as if the method actually used in calculating the reserve for the policy were the method described in § 56-1-907, without consideration of § 56-1-907(b). The minimum reserve at each policy anniversary of such a policy shall be the greater of the minimum reserve calculated in accordance with § 56-1-907, including 56-1-907(b), and the minimum reserve calculated in accordance with this section.

56-1-912. Reserve Calculation—Indeterminate Premium Plans.

In the case of a plan of life insurance that provides for future premium determination, the amounts of which are to be determined by the insurance company based on then estimates of future experience, or in the case of a plan of life insurance or annuity that is of such a nature that the minimum reserves cannot be determined by the methods described in §§ 56-1-907, 56-1-908 and 56-1-911, the reserves that are held under the plan shall, as determined by regulations promulgated by the commissioner:

(1) Be appropriate in relation to the benefits and the pattern of premiums for that plan; and

(2) Be computed by a method that is consistent with the principles of this part.

56-1-913. Minimum Standard for Accident and Health Insurance Contracts.

(a) For accident and health insurance contracts issued on or after the operative date of the valuation manual, the standard prescribed in the valuation manual is the minimum standard of valuation required under § 56-1-902(b).

(b) For disability, accident and sickness, accident and health insurance contracts issued on or after January 1, 1962, and prior to the operative date of the valuation manual, the minimum standard of valuation is the standard adopted by the commissioner by regulation.

56-1-914. Valuation Manual for Policies Issued On or After the Operative Date of the Valuation Manual.

(a) For policies issued on or after the operative date of the valuation manual, the standard prescribed in the valuation manual is the minimum standard of valuation required under § 56-1-902(b), except as provided under subsections (e) or (g).

(b) The operative date of the valuation manual is January 1 of the first calendar year following the first July 1 as of which all of the following have occurred:

(1) The valuation manual has been adopted by the NAIC by an affirmative vote of at least forty-two (42) members, or three-fourths (¾) of the members voting, whichever is greater.

(2) The Standard Valuation Law, as amended by the NAIC in 2009, or legislation including substantially similar terms and provisions, has been enacted by states representing greater than seventy-five percent (75%) of the direct premiums written as reported in the following annual statements submitted for 2008: life, accident and health annual statements; health annual statements; or fraternal annual statements.

(3) The Standard Valuation Law, as amended by the NAIC in 2009, or legislation including substantially similar terms and provisions, has been enacted by at least forty-two (42) of the following fifty-five (55) jurisdictions: The fifty (50) states of the United States, American Samoa, the American Virgin Islands, the District of Columbia, Guam and Puerto Rico.

(c) Unless a change in the valuation manual specifies a later effective date, changes to the valuation manual shall be effective on January 1 following the date when the change to the valuation manual has been adopted by the NAIC by an affirmative vote representing:

(1) At least three-fourths (¾) of the members of the NAIC voting, but not less than a majority of the total membership; and

(2) Members of the NAIC representing jurisdictions totaling greater than seventy-five percent (75%) of the direct premiums written as reported in the following annual statements most recently available prior to the vote in subdivision (c)(1): life, accident and health annual statements, health annual statements or fraternal annual statements.

(d) The valuation manual shall specify all of the following:

(1) Minimum valuation standards for and definitions of the policies or contracts subject to § 56-1-902(b). Such minimum valuation standards shall be:

(A) The commissioner's reserve valuation method for life insurance contracts, other than annuity contracts, subject to § 56-1-902(b);

(B) The commissioner's annuity reserve valuation method for annuity contracts subject to § 56-1-902(b); and

(C) Minimum reserves for all other policies or contracts subject to § 56-1-902(b).

(2) Which policies or contracts or types of policies or contracts that are subject to the requirements of a principle-based valuation in § 56-1-915(a) and the minimum valuation standards consistent with those requirements;

(3) For policies and contracts subject to a principle-based valuation under § 56-1-915:

(A) Requirements for the format of reports to the commissioner under § 56-1-915(b)(2) and which shall include information necessary to determine if the valuation is appropriate and in compliance with this part;

(B) Assumptions shall be prescribed for risks over which the company does not have significant control or influence; and

(C) Procedures for corporate governance and oversight of the actuarial function, and a process for appropriate waiver or modification of such procedures.

(4) For policies not subject to a principle-based valuation under § 56-1-915, the minimum valuation standard shall either:

(A) Be consistent with the minimum standard of valuation prior to the operative date of the valuation manual; or

(B) Develop reserves that quantify the benefits and guarantees, and the funding, associated with the contracts and their risks at a level of conservatism that reflects conditions that include unfavorable events that have a reasonable probability of occurring;

(5) Other requirements, including, but not limited to, those relating to reserve methods, models for measuring risk, generation of economic scenarios, assumptions, margins, use of company experience, risk measurement, disclosure, certifications, reports, actuarial opinions and memorandums, transition rules and internal controls; and

(6) The data and form of the data required under § 56-1-916, with whom the data must be submitted, and may specify other requirements including data analyses and reporting of analyses.

(e) In the absence of a specific valuation requirement or if a specific valuation requirement in the valuation manual is not, in the opinion of the commissioner, in compliance with this part, then the company shall, with respect to such requirements, comply with minimum valuation standards prescribed by the commissioner by regulation.

(f) The commissioner may engage a qualified actuary, at the expense of the company, to perform an actuarial examination of the company and opine on the appropriateness of any reserve assumption or method used by the company, or to review and opine on a company's compliance with any requirement set forth in this part. The commissioner may rely upon the opinion, regarding provisions contained within this part, of a qualified actuary engaged by the commissioner of another state, district or territory of the United States. As used in this subsection (f), "engage" includes employment and contracting.

(g) The commissioner may require a company to change any assumption or method that in the opinion of the commissioner is necessary in order to comply with the requirements of the valuation manual or this part; and the company shall adjust the reserves as required by the commissioner. The commissioner may take other disciplinary action as permitted pursuant to § 56-2-305 and the Uniform Administrative Procedures Act, compiled in title 4, chapter 5.

56-1-915. Requirements of a Principle-Based Valuation.

(a) A company shall establish reserves using a principle-based valuation that meets the following conditions for policies or contracts as specified in the valuation manual:

(1) Quantify the benefits and guarantees, and the funding, associated with the contracts and their risks at a level of conservatism that reflects conditions that include unfavorable events that have a reasonable probability of occurring during the lifetime of the contracts. For policies or contracts with significant tail risk, reflects conditions appropriately adverse to quantify the tail risk.

(2) Incorporate assumptions, risk analysis methods and financial models and management techniques that are consistent with, but not necessarily identical to, those utilized within the company's overall risk assessment process, while recognizing potential differences in financial reporting structures and any prescribed assumptions or methods.

(3) Incorporate assumptions that are derived in one (1) of the following manners:

(A) The assumption is prescribed in the valuation manual.

(B) For assumptions that are not prescribed, the assumptions shall:

(i) Be established utilizing the company's available experience to the extent it is relevant and statistically credible; or

(ii) To the extent that company data is not available, relevant, or statistically credible, be established utilizing other relevant, statistically credible experience.

(4) Provide margins for uncertainty including adverse deviation and estimation error, such that the greater the uncertainty the larger the margin and resulting reserve.

(b) A company using a principle-based valuation for one (1) or more policies or contracts subject to this section as specified in the valuation manual shall:

(1) Establish procedures for corporate governance and oversight of the actuarial valuation function consistent with those described in the valuation manual.

(2) Provide to the commissioner and the board of directors an annual certification of the effectiveness of the internal controls with respect to the principle-based valuation. Such controls shall be designed to assure that all material risks inherent in the liabilities and associated assets subject to such valuation are included in the valuation, and that valuations are made in accordance with the valuation manual. The certification shall be based on the controls in place as of the end of the preceding calendar year.

(3) Develop, and file with the commissioner upon request, a principle-based valuation report that complies with standards prescribed in the valuation manual.

(c) A principle-based valuation may include a prescribed formulaic reserve component.

56-1-916. Experience Reporting for Policies In Force On or After the Operative Date of the Valuation Manual.

A company shall submit mortality, morbidity, policyholder behavior, or expense experience and other data as prescribed in the valuation manual.

56-1-917. Confidentiality.

(a) For purposes of this section, "Confidential Information" shall mean:

(1) A memorandum in support of an opinion submitted under § 56-1-903 and any other documents, materials and other information, including, but not limited to, all working papers, and copies thereof, created, produced or obtained by or disclosed to the commissioner or any other person in connection with such memorandum;

(2) All documents, materials and other information, including, but not limited to, all working papers and copies thereof, created, produced or obtained by or disclosed to the commissioner or any other person in the course of an examination made under § 56-1-914(f); provided, however, that if an examination report or other material prepared in connection with an examination made under § 56-1-411 is not held as private and confidential information under § 56-1-411, an examination report or other material prepared in connection with an examination made under § 56-1-914(f) shall not be "confidential information" to the same extent as if such examination report or other material had been prepared under § 56-1-411;

(3) Any reports, documents, materials and other information developed by a company in support of, or in connection with, an annual certification by the company under § 56-1-915(b)(2) evaluating the effectiveness of the company's internal controls with respect to a principle-based valuation and any other documents, materials and other information, including, but not limited to, all working papers and copies thereof, created, produced or obtained by or disclosed to the commissioner or any other person in connection with such reports, documents, materials and other information;

(4) Any principle-based valuation report developed under § 56-1-915(b)(3) and any other documents, materials and other information, including, but not limited to, all working papers and copies thereof, created, produced or obtained by or disclosed to the commissioner or any other person in connection with such report; and

(5) Any documents, materials, data and other information submitted by a company under § 56-1-916, collectively, "experience data," and any other documents, materials, data and other information, including, but not limited to, all working papers, and copies thereof, created or produced in connection with such experience data, in each case that include any potentially company-identifying or personally identifiable information, that is provided to or obtained by the commissioner (together with any "experience data", the "experience materials") and any other documents, materials, data and other information, including, but not limited to, all working papers, and copies thereof, created, produced or obtained by or disclosed to the commissioner or any other person in connection with such experience materials.

(b) For privilege for, and confidentiality of, confidential information:

(1) Except as provided in this section, a company's confidential information is confidential by law and privileged, and shall not be subject to § 10-7-503 or § 56-1-602, shall not be subject to subpoena and shall not be subject to discovery or admissible in evidence in any private civil action; provided, however, that the commissioner is authorized to use the confidential information in the furtherance of any regulatory or legal action brought against the company as a part of the commissioner's official duties.

(2) Neither the commissioner nor any person who received confidential information while acting under the authority of the commissioner shall be permitted or required to testify in any private civil action concerning any confidential information.

(3) In order to assist in the performance of the commissioner's duties, the commissioner may share confidential information:

(A) With other state, federal and international regulatory agencies and with the NAIC and its affiliates and subsidiaries;

(B) In the case of confidential information specified in subdivisions (a)(1) and (a)(4) only, with the Actuarial Board for Counseling and Discipline or its successor upon request stating that the confidential information is required for the purpose of professional disciplinary proceedings and with state, federal and international law enforcement officials; and

(C) Provided that such recipient agrees, and has the legal authority to agree, to maintain the confidentiality and privileged status of such documents, materials, data and other information in the same manner and to the same extent as required for the commissioner.

(4) The commissioner may receive documents, materials, data and other information, including otherwise confidential and privileged documents, materials, data or information, from the NAIC and its affiliates and subsidiaries, from regulatory or law enforcement officials of other foreign or domestic jurisdictions and from the Actuarial Board for Counseling and Discipline or its successor and shall maintain as confidential or privileged any document, material, data or other information received with notice or the understanding that it is confidential or privileged under the laws of the jurisdiction that is the source of the document, material or other information.

(5) The commissioner may enter into agreements governing sharing and use of information consistent with this subsection (b).

(6) No waiver of any applicable privilege or claim of confidentiality in the confidential information shall occur as a result of disclosure to the commissioner under this section or as a result of sharing as authorized in subdivision (b)(3).

(7) A privilege established under the law of any state or jurisdiction that is substantially similar to the privilege established under subsection (b) shall be available and enforced in any proceeding in, and in any court of, this state.

(8) In this section, "regulatory agency," "law enforcement agency" and "NAIC" include, but are not limited to, their employees, agents, consultants and contractors.

(c) Notwithstanding subsection (b), any confidential information specified in subdivisions (a)(1) and (a)(4):

(1) May be subject to subpoena for the purpose of defending an action seeking damages from the appointed actuary submitting the related memorandum in support of an opinion submitted under § 56-1-903 or principle-based valuation report developed under § 56-1-915(b)(3) by reason of an action required pursuant to this part or by regulations promulgated by the commissioner;

(2) May otherwise be released by the commissioner with the written consent of the company; and

(3) Once any portion of a memorandum in support of an opinion submitted under § 56-1-903 or a principle-based valuation report developed under § 56-1-915(b)(3) is cited by the company in its marketing or is publicly volunteered to or before a governmental agency other than a state insurance department or is released by the company to the news media, all portions of such memorandum or report shall no longer be confidential.

56-1-918. Single State Exemption.

(a) The commissioner may exempt specific product forms or product lines of a domestic company that is licensed and doing business only in this state from § 56-1-914 provided:

(1) The commissioner has issued an exemption in writing to the company and has not subsequently revoked the exemption in writing; and

(2) The company computes reserves using assumptions and methods used prior to the operative date of the valuation manual in addition to any requirements established by the commissioner and promulgated by regulation.

(b) For any company granted an exemption under this section, §§ 56-1-903 through 913 shall be applicable. With respect to any company applying this exemption, any reference to § 56-1-914 found in §§ 56-1-903 through 913 shall not be applicable.

56-1-919. Effective Date.

To the extent that this part conflicts with or is inconsistent with any law, the provisions of this part shall control. This part shall apply to policies and contracts issued on or after January 1, 1962.

56-7-401 SECTION 4. Tennessee Code Annotated, Section 56-7-401(h)(8)(B)(vi), is amended by deleting the subdivision and substituting instead the following:

(vi) For policies issued prior to the operative date of the valuation manual, any Commissioners' Standard ordinary mortality tables, adopted after 1980 by the National Association of Insurance Commissioners, that are approved by regulation promulgated by the commissioner for use in determining the minimum nonforfeiture standard may be substituted for the Commissioners 1980 Standard Ordinary Mortality Table with or without Ten-Year Select Mortality Factors or for the Commissioners 1980 Extended Term Insurance Table. For policies issued on or after the operative date of the valuation manual the valuation manual shall provide the Commissioners' Standard mortality table for use in determining the minimum nonforfeiture standard that may be substituted for the Commissioners 1980 Standard Ordinary Mortality Table with or without Ten-Year Select Mortality Factors or for the Commissioners 1980 Extended Term Insurance Table. If the commissioner approves by regulation any Commissioners' Standard ordinary mortality table adopted by the National Association of Insurance Commissioners for use in determining the minimum nonforfeiture standard for policies issued on or after the operative date of the valuation manual then that minimum nonforfeiture standard supersedes the minimum nonforfeiture standard provided by the valuation manual.

56-7-401 SECTION 5. Tennessee Code Annotated, Section 56-7-401(h)(8)(B)(vii), is amended by deleting the subdivision and substituting instead the following:

(vii) For policies issued prior to the operative date of the valuation manual, any Commissioners' Standard industrial mortality tables, adopted after 1980 by the National Association of Insurance Commissioners, that are approved by regulation promulgated by the commissioner for use in determining the minimum nonforfeiture standard may be substituted for the Commissioners 1961 Standard Industrial Mortality Table or the Commissioners 1961 Industrial Extended Term Insurance Table. For policies issued on or after the operative date of the valuation manual the valuation manual shall provide the Commissioners' Standard mortality table for use in determining the minimum nonforfeiture standard that may be substituted for the Commissioners 1961 Standard Industrial Mortality Table or the Commissioners 1961 Industrial Extended Term Insurance Table. If the commissioner approves by regulation any Commissioners' Standard industrial mortality table adopted by the National Association of Insurance Commissioners for use in determining the minimum nonforfeiture standard for policies issued on or after the operative date of the valuation manual then that minimum nonforfeiture standard supersedes the minimum nonforfeiture standard provided by the valuation manual.

56-7-401 SECTION 6. Tennessee Code Annotated, Section 56-7-401(h)(9), is amended by deleting the subdivision and substituting instead the following:

(9)(A) For policies issued prior to the operative date of the valuation manual, the nonforfeiture interest rate per annum for any policy issued in a particular calendar year shall be equal to one hundred and twenty-five percent (125%) of the calendar year statutory valuation interest rate for such policy as defined in the Standard Valuation Law, rounded to the nearer one quarter of one percent (0.25%).

(B) For policies issued on or after the operative date of the valuation manual the nonforfeiture interest rate per annum for any policy issued in a particular calendar year shall be provided by the valuation manual.

56-7-401 SECTION 7. Tennessee Code Annotated, Section 56-7-401, is further amended by adding the following language as a new subsection:

(o) "Operative date of the valuation manual" means the January 1 of the first calendar year that the valuation manual is effective as defined in § 56-1-914;

Effective date 7/1/2013 SECTION 8. This act shall become effective July 1, 2013, the public welfare requiring it.

PUBLIC CHAPTER NO. 261

PUBLIC CHAPTER NO. 261

SENATE BILL NO. 151

By Norris, Stevens

Substituted for: House Bill No. 145

By McCormick, Matthew Hill

AN ACT to amend Tennessee Code Annotated, Title 48, Chapter 1, Part 1, relative to regulation of securities.

BE IT ENACTED BY THE GENERAL ASSEMBLY OF THE STATE OF TENNESSEE:

48-1-103 SECTION 1. Tennessee Code Annotated, Section 48-1-103(b), is amended by adding the following language as a new, appropriately designated subdivision:

( ) Any non-issuer transaction by or through a broker-dealer, registered or exempt from registration under this chapter, effecting an unsolicited order or offer to purchase, provided that the broker-dealer acts solely as an agent for the purchaser, has no direct or indirect interest in the sale or distribution of the security ordered, and receives no commission, profit, or other compensation from any source other than the purchaser; and further provided, that the commissioner may by rule require that the customer acknowledge upon a specified form that the sale was unsolicited, and that a signed copy of each such form be preserved by the broker-dealer for a specified period;

Effective date 10/31/2013 SECTION 2. For purposes of promulgating rules and regulations, this act shall take effect upon becoming law, the public welfare requiring it. For all other purposes, this act shall take effect October 31, 2013, the public welfare requiring it.

PUBLIC CHAPTER NO. 262

PUBLIC CHAPTER NO. 262

SENATE BILL NO. 158

By Norris, Gardenhire

Substituted for: House Bill No. 152

By McCormick, Moody

AN ACT to amend Tennessee Code Annotated, Section 49-6-3020, relative to student withdrawal and transfer.

BE IT ENACTED BY THE GENERAL ASSEMBLY OF THE STATE OF TENNESSEE:

49-6-3020 SECTION 1. Tennessee Code Annotated, Section 49-6-3020(b), is amended by deleting the subsection in its entirety and replacing it with the following:

(b) The department of education shall require an LEA to obtain formal written proof that a child who has moved out-of-state has enrolled in a school or program leading to the award of a regular high school diploma in order to not count such student as a dropout.

Effective date 4/25/2013 SECTION 2. This act shall take effect upon becoming law, the public welfare requiring it.

PUBLIC CHAPTER NO. 263

PUBLIC CHAPTER NO. 263

SENATE BILL NO. 233

By Kelsey, Crowe

Substituted for: House Bill No. 221

By Mark White

AN ACT to amend Tennessee Code Annotated, Section 49-1-614, relative to employment of teachers.

BE IT ENACTED BY THE GENERAL ASSEMBLY OF THE STATE OF TENNESSEE:

49-1-614 SECTION 1. Tennessee Code Annotated, Section 49-1-614(g)(2), is amended by deleting the second sentence of the subdivision and substituting instead:

> Any tenured teacher not given that option shall remain an employee of the LEA, subject to § 49-5-511. The LEA, if it so chooses, may continue the employment of a nontenured teacher not given that option.

Effective date 7/1/2013 SECTION 2. This act shall take effect July 1, 2013, the public welfare requiring it.

PUBLIC CHAPTER NO. 264

PUBLIC CHAPTER NO. 264

SENATE BILL NO. 259

By Crowe, Overbey, Yager

Substituted for: House Bill No. 687

By Matthew Hill, Dunn, Dean

AN ACT to amend Tennessee Code Annotated, Title 55, Chapter 4, relative to motor vehicle license plates.

BE IT ENACTED BY THE GENERAL ASSEMBLY OF THE STATE OF TENNESSEE:

55-4-201 SECTION 1. Tennessee Code Annotated, Section 55-4-201, is amended by adding a new subsection thereto, as follows:

(l)(1) Notwithstanding any provision of this part to the contrary, any cultural or new specialty earmarked license plate authorized by statute on or after July 1, 2013, shall be subject to a minimum order of at least one thousand (1,000) plates prior to initial issuance. Any cultural or new specialty earmarked license plate authorized by statute shall be subject to a minimum order of at least eight hundred (800) plates for the renewal of such cultural or new specialty earmarked plates. Any such plate that does not meet the minimum order requirements of this subdivision (l)(1) within one (1) year of the effective date of the act authorizing that plate, or does not meet the renewal requirements for any two (2) successive renewal periods thereafter, shall not be issued, reissued, or renewed and shall be deemed obsolete and invalid. The commissioner shall annually notify the executive secretary of the Tennessee code commission of the sections of the code authorizing the issuance of plates deemed obsolete and invalid pursuant to this subdivision (l)(1).

(2) Subdivision (l)(1) shall not apply to collegiate plates otherwise administered pursuant to this part; provided, that on and after July 1, 2013, collegiate plates for four-year colleges or universities located outside Tennessee shall be subject to a minimum order of at least one thousand (1,000) plates prior to initial issuance by the department. The renewal of any collegiate plates for four-year colleges or universities located outside Tennessee issued by the department on or after July 1, 2013, shall be subject to a minimum order of at least eight hundred (800) plates. Any such plate that does not meet the minimum order requirements of this subdivision (l)(2) or does not meet the renewal requirements for any two (2) successive renewal periods, shall not be administratively issued, reissued, or renewed by the department and shall be deemed obsolete and invalid.

Effective date 4/25/2013 SECTION 2. This act shall take effect upon becoming a law, the public welfare requiring it.

PUBLIC CHAPTER NO. 265

PUBLIC CHAPTER NO. 265

SENATE BILL NO. 568

By Bell

Substituted for: House Bill No. 838

By Matheny, Ragan

AN ACT to amend Tennessee Code Annotated, Title 4 and Title 64, Chapter 6, relative to regional megasite authorities.

BE IT ENACTED BY THE GENERAL ASSEMBLY OF THE STATE OF TENNESSEE:

64-6-105 SECTION 1. Tennessee Code Annotated, Section 64-6-105, is amended by deleting subsection (a) in its entirety and by substituting instead the following new language:

(a)(1) The authority shall be governed by a board of directors in which all powers of the corporation shall be vested. The membership of the board shall include the following:

(A) For each county that chooses to be a participating municipality in accordance with § 64-6-104(a), the county mayor or a designee of the county mayor of that county;

(B) The mayor or the designee of the mayor in an incorporated municipality that chooses to be a participating municipality in accordance with § 64-6-104(a);

(C) The two (2) speakers of the respective houses acting jointly after consultation with the members whose districts lie within the participating counties shall appoint one (1) member;

(D) The governor, after consultation with the mayors of the participating municipalities, shall appoint one (1) member; and

(E) The chancellor of the board of regents shall appoint one (1) member from the presidents of the community colleges that have a campus within the participating counties.

(2) For the purposes of calculating terms, members serving on a board as of January 1, 2013, shall serve until December 31, 2014. At the conclusion of such terms:

(A) Each regular term of the board member appointed jointly by the speakers beginning January 1, 2015, shall be two (2) years, to be coterminous with the terms of office of the speakers;

(B) Each regular term of the board member appointed by the governor beginning January 1, 2015, shall be four (4) years, to be coterminous with the term of office of the governor; and

(C) Each regular term of all other board members appointed in accordance with this subsection (a) beginning January 1, 2015, shall be for three (3) years.

(3) Board members shall serve until their successors are appointed. If a vacancy occurs on the board, the remainder of the term shall be filled by the respective appointing authorities in accordance with this subsection (a).

(4) Any board created pursuant to this subsection (a) shall cease to exist upon the completion of the sale of a megasite governed by such board.

64-6-110 SECTION 2. Tennessee Code Annotated, Section 64-6-110, is amended by deleting subsection (c) in its entirety and by substituting instead the following new language:

PUBLIC CHAPTER NO. 265 (cont'd)

(c)(1) The authority formed pursuant to this section shall be governed by a board of directors in which all powers of the corporation shall be vested. The membership of the board shall include the following:

(A) The county mayor or a designee of the county mayor of the county in which the megasite is located or, if it is located in more than one (1) county, the county in which the megasite is predominately located;

(B) The mayor or the designee of the mayor in the incorporated municipality with the largest population in a county in which the megasite is located or, if it is located in more than one (1) county, the county in which the megasite is predominately located;

(C) The two (2) speakers of the respective houses acting jointly after consultation with the members whose districts lie within the participating counties shall appoint two (2) members;

(D) The governor shall appoint two (2) at-large members and three (3) additional members representing and residing in counties contiguous to the county in which the megasite is located. At the time of initial appointment, the three (3) additional members shall be selected from counties not otherwise represented on the board. Notwithstanding any provision of this part to the contrary, the three (3) additional members shall serve without reimbursement for their actual travel expenses;

(E) The chancellor of the board of regents shall appoint one (1) member from the presidents of the community colleges that have a campus within a county in which the megasite is wholly or partially located or within a county contiguous thereto; and

(F) The executive director of the development district in which the megasite is located.

(2) For the purposes of calculating terms, members serving on a board as of January 1, 2013, shall serve until December 31, 2014, at which time their terms shall expire. At the conclusion of such terms:

(A) Each regular term of the board members appointed jointly by the speakers beginning January 1, 2015, shall be two (2) years, to be coterminous with the terms of office of the speakers;

(B) Each regular term of the board members appointed by the governor beginning January 1, 2015, shall be four (4) years, to be coterminous with the term of office of the governor; and

(C) Each regular term of all other board members appointed in accordance with this subsection (c) beginning January 1, 2015, shall be for three (3) years.

(3) Board members shall serve until their successors are appointed. If a vacancy occurs on the board, the remainder of the term shall be filled by the respective appointing authorities in accordance with this subsection (c).

(4) Any board created pursuant to this subsection (c) shall cease to exist upon the completion of the sale of a megasite governed by such board.

Effective date 4/25/2013

SECTION 3. This act shall take effect upon becoming a law, the public welfare requiring it.

PUBLIC CHAPTER NO. 266

PUBLIC CHAPTER NO. 266

SENATE BILL NO. 582

By Haile

Substituted for: House Bill No. 317

By Shepard, Sexton

AN ACT to amend Tennessee Code Annotated, Title 63, Chapter 10, relative to compounding, compounding pharmacies, and the dispensing and transfer of compounded products.

BE IT ENACTED BY THE GENERAL ASSEMBLY OF THE STATE OF TENNESSEE:

63-10-204 SECTION 1. Tennessee Code Annotated, Section 63-10-204(4), is amended by adding the following new language as new subdivisions:

(D) For use in a licensed prescribing practitioner's office for administration to the prescribing practitioner's patient or patients when the product is not commercially available upon receipt of an order from the prescriber;

(E) For use in a health care facility for administration to a patient or patients receiving treatment or services provided by that facility when the product is not commercially available upon receipt of an order from an authorized licensed medical practitioner of the facility;

(F) For use by emergency medical services for administration to a patient or patients receiving services from them under authorized medical control when the product is not commercially available upon receipt of an order from a licensed prescriber authorized to provide medical control; or

(G) For use by a licensed veterinarian for administration to their non-human patient or patients or for dispensing to non-human patients in the course of the practice of veterinary medicine upon receipt of an order from a veterinarian when the product is not commercially available.

63-10-204 SECTION 2. Tennessee Code Annotated, Section 63-10-204(12), is amended by inserting the following new language following the words "to a patient or the patient's agent" and before "by or pursuant to the lawful order of a prescriber":

, to include a licensed health care practitioner or a health care facility providing services or treatment to the patient or patients,

63-10-216 SECTION 3. Tennessee Code Annotated, Title 63, Chapter 10, Part 2, is amended by adding the following as a new section:

63-10-216.

(a) Prior to initial licensure in this state as a compounding pharmacy, a pharmacy located outside of this state must have an inspection by the regulatory or licensing agency of the state in which the pharmacy practice site is physically located. Out-of-state pharmacy practice sites must provide a copy of the most recent inspection by the regulatory or licensing agency of the state in which the pharmacy practice site is physically located, which must have been within the previous twelve (12) months. Prior to renewal of its license in this state, an out-of-state pharmacy practice site must provide the most recent inspection by the regulatory or licensing agency of the state in which the pharmacy practice site is physically located or equivalent regulatory entity, and which must have been within the previous twelve (12) months. The board of pharmacy shall have the right to require additional information before issuing or renewing a pharmacy license to insure compliance with applicable laws of this state and any rules and policies of the board.

(b) Any compounding pharmacy having an active Tennessee license shall notify the board within fourteen (14) business days of receipt of any order or decision by a regulatory agency, other than the Tennessee board of pharmacy, imposing any disciplinary action, including any warning, on the pharmacy.

(c) Any pharmacies engaged in sterile compounding must comply with relevant United States Pharmacopeia (USP) guidelines as adopted by the board by rule or policy.

(d) Any pharmacies engaging in sterile compounding, except hospital pharmacies compounding for inpatients of a hospital, shall report on a quarterly basis to the board the quantity of sterile compounded products dispensed in a defined time period in accordance with policies adopted by the board; provided, however, the executive director of the board may request this information from a hospital pharmacy for cause and the hospital pharmacy shall be required to respond in a timely manner as defined by the executive director of the board.

Effective date 4/25/2013

SECTION 4. This act shall take effect upon becoming a law, the public welfare requiring it.

PUBLIC CHAPTER NO. 267

PUBLIC CHAPTER NO. 267

SENATE BILL NO. 605

By Finney, Yager, McNally, Burks, Bell, Bowling, Campfield, Gardenhire

Substituted for: House Bill No. 378

By Fitzhugh, Sexton, Rogers, Evans, Camper, Ryan Williams, Dennis, Dunn, Holt, Hardaway, Kane, Littleton, Hall, Keisling, Mark White, Roach, Wirgau, Haynes, Marsh, Durham, Lollar, McManus, Eldridge, Ragan, Lundberg, Harry Brooks, Carter

AN ACT to amend Tennessee Code Annotated, Title 4, Chapter 3, Part 7 and Title 64, Chapter 6, relative to economic and community development.

BE IT ENACTED BY THE GENERAL ASSEMBLY OF THE STATE OF TENNESSEE:

4-3-731 SECTION 1. Tennessee Code Annotated, Title 4, Chapter 3, Part 7, is amended by adding the following language as a new, appropriately designated section:

> Notwithstanding any law to the contrary, the department of economic and community development shall execute a separate agreement in conjunction with any grant or loan contract awarded pursuant to § 4-3-717(d)(1) that reserves the right of the department to recover the amount of money, grants, funds, or other incentives disbursed by the department, in whole or in part, if the person or entity benefitting from such money, grants, funds, or other incentives fails to fulfill the commitments made by such person or entity to the department.

Effective date 7/1/2013 SECTION 2. This act shall take effect July 1, 2013, the public welfare requiring it, and shall apply to all contracts entered into or renewed on or after such date.

PUBLIC CHAPTER NO. 268

PUBLIC CHAPTER NO. 268

SENATE BILL NO. 626

By Norris, Kelsey

Substituted for: House Bill No. 1033

By Mark White, Lollar

AN ACT to amend Tennessee Code Annotated, Title 2, Chapter 12, relative to county election commissions.

BE IT ENACTED BY THE GENERAL ASSEMBLY OF THE STATE OF TENNESSEE:

2-12-116 SECTION 1. Tennessee Code Annotated, Section 2-12-116, is amended by deleting subsection (b) in its entirety.

2-12-201 SECTION 2. Tennessee Code Annotated, Section 2-12-201, is amended by deleting subsection (b) in its entirety.

2-12-201 SECTION 3. Tennessee Code Annotated, Section 2-12-201(a), is amended by deleting the language "Except as provided in subsection (b), the" and substituting instead the language "The".

2-12-202 SECTION 4. Tennessee Code Annotated, Section 2-12-202, is amended by deleting subdivision (a)(2) in its entirety.

2-12-202 SECTION 5. Tennessee Code Annotated, Section 2-12-202(a)(1), is amended by deleting the language "Except as provided in subdivision (a)(2), the" and substituting instead the language "The".

2-12-116 SECTION 6. Tennessee Code Annotated, Section 2-12-116(a), is amended by deleting the language "Except as provided in subsection (b), the" and by substituting instead the language "The".

Effective date 4/25/2013 SECTION 7. This act shall take effect upon becoming a law, the public welfare requiring it.

PUBLIC CHAPTER NO. 269

PUBLIC CHAPTER NO. 269

SENATE BILL NO. 693

By Tate

Substituted for: House Bill No. 1065

By Powell

AN ACT to amend Tennessee Code Annotated, Title 62, relative to locksmiths.

BE IT ENACTED BY THE GENERAL ASSEMBLY OF THE STATE OF TENNESSEE:

62-11-104 SECTION 1. Tennessee Code Annotated, Section 62-11-104(a)(2), is amended by deleting the language "in Tennessee".

62-11-104 SECTION 2. Tennessee Code Annotated, Section 62-11-104, is further amended by adding the following language as a new subsection:

( ) On or after July 1, 2013, any partnership, association, company or corporation seeking initial licensure pursuant to this chapter shall be placed on a probationary licensure status pursuant to a probation period, the requirements of which shall be determined by the commissioner.

62-11-111 SECTION 3. Tennessee Code Annotated, Section 62-11-111(a), is amended by adding the following language as a new subdivision:

( ) Proof of a permanent, fixed business address as determined appropriate by the department;

62-11-112 SECTION 4. Tennessee Code Annotated, Section 62-11-112, is amended by adding the following language as a new subsection:

(i)(1) An individual holding a valid certificate of registration as an apprentice pursuant to this section for at least two (2) years shall be eligible to take any examination required by the commissioner for initial licensure.

(2) An individual holding a valid certificate of registration as an apprentice pursuant to this section for at least four (4) years shall be exempt from taking any qualifying education as required by the commissioner prior to initial licensure.

Effective date 7/1/2013 SECTION 5. This act shall take effect July 1, 2013, the public welfare requiring it.

PUBLIC CHAPTER NO. 270

PUBLIC CHAPTER NO. 270

SENATE BILL NO. 714

By Campfield

Substituted for: House Bill No. 1282

By Goins, Lamberth, Faison, Matheny, Dunn, Powers, Casada, Rich, Carter, Durham, Halford, Keisling, Sparks, Holt, Kane, Moody, Shipley, Forgety, Hall, Hawk, Dale Carr, Ragan, Rogers, Tidwell, Harry Brooks, Eldridge, Evans, Weaver, Ryan Williams, Todd, Lollar, Spivey

AN ACT to amend Tennessee Code Annotated, Section 39-17-1351, relative to handgun carry permits.

BE IT ENACTED BY THE GENERAL ASSEMBLY OF THE STATE OF TENNESSEE:

39-17-1351 SECTION 1. Tennessee Code Annotated, Section 39-17-1351(c), is amended by deleting subdivision (10) and substituting the following:

(10) That the applicant is not an unlawful user of or addicted to alcohol, any controlled substance or controlled substance analogue, and the applicant has not been either:

(A) A patient in a rehabilitation program pursuant to a court order or hospitalized for alcohol, controlled substance or controlled substance analogue abuse or addiction pursuant to a court order within ten (10) years from the date of application; or

(B) A voluntary patient in a rehabilitation program or voluntarily hospitalized for alcohol, controlled substance or controlled substance analogue abuse or addiction within three (3) years from the date of application;

Effective date 7/1/2013 SECTION 2. This act shall take effect July 1, 2013, the public welfare requiring it.

PUBLIC CHAPTER NO. 271

PUBLIC CHAPTER NO. 271

SENATE BILL NO. 733

By Watson

Substituted for: House Bill No. 474

By Carter

AN ACT to amend Tennessee Code Annotated, Title 4; Title 5; Title 6; Title 7; Title 38; Title 43; Title 44; Title 45; Title 48; Title 53; Title 55; Title 56; Title 57; Title 59; Title 60; Title 62; Title 67; Title 68 and Title 71, relative to licenses and registrations.

BE IT ENACTED BY THE GENERAL ASSEMBLY OF THE STATE OF TENNESSEE:

62-9-102 SECTION 1. Tennessee Code Annotated, Section 62-9-102, is amended by adding the following language as new, appropriately designated subsections:

(d) Notwithstanding any law to the contrary, a registration issued pursuant to this part shall not expire immediately upon the death of the registrant. Such registration shall continue to be effective for the locations designated in such registration for a period of at least sixty (60) days; provided, such 60-day period may be extended by the commissioner for good cause.

(e) Notwithstanding any law to the contrary, a registration issued pursuant to this part shall expire upon notification to the department by the location registered with the department that the registrant is no longer an employee or agent of the location.

Effective date 7/1/2013 SECTION 2. This act shall take effect July 1, 2013, the public welfare requiring it.

PUBLIC CHAPTER NO. 272

PUBLIC CHAPTER NO. 272

SENATE BILL NO. 774

By Haile

Substituted for: House Bill No. 663

By Farmer

AN ACT to amend Tennessee Code Annotated, Title 12, Chapter 3, relative to the state and local government advisory committee.

BE IT ENACTED BY THE GENERAL ASSEMBLY OF THE STATE OF TENNESSEE:

12-3-1101 — 12-3-1103 SECTION 1. Tennessee Code Annotated, Title 12, Chapter 3, is amended by deleting Part 11 in its entirety.

Effective date 4/25/2013 SECTION 2. This act shall take effect upon becoming a law, the public welfare requiring it.

PUBLIC CHAPTER NO. 273

PUBLIC CHAPTER NO. 273

SENATE BILL NO. 792

By Bowling

Substituted for: House Bill No. 1042

By Moody

AN ACT to amend Tennessee Code Annotated, Title 49, Chapter 6, Part 17, relative to the Financial Literacy Program Act of 2010.

BE IT ENACTED BY THE GENERAL ASSEMBLY OF THE STATE OF TENNESSEE:

49-6-1703 SECTION 1. Tennessee Code Annotated, Section 49-6-1703(b), is amended by deleting the second sentence in the subsection and substituting it instead with the following:

In making appointments to the board, the speaker of the house of representatives and the speaker of the senate shall appoint individuals who are actively involved in financial literacy; provided, however, one (1) such individual appointed by the speaker of the house of representatives shall be a teacher or administrator of a Tennessee public elementary school.

49-6-1703 SECTION 2. Tennessee Code Annotated, Section 49-6-1703(e), is amended by deleting the subsection in its entirety and substituting it instead with the following:

The state treasurer shall serve as the chair of the commission. The board shall annually elect a vice-chair, a secretary and such other officers as it deems necessary from its membership to perform the business of the commission. Such officers and the ex-officio members, or the ex-officios' designees, shall comprise the executive committee. The board may also appoint advisory boards or committees to report to the executive committee as deemed necessary.

Effective date 4/25/2013 SECTION 3. This act shall take effect upon becoming a law, the public welfare requiring it.

PUBLIC CHAPTER NO. 274

PUBLIC CHAPTER NO. 274

SENATE BILL NO. 857

By Tate, Harper

Substituted for: House Bill No. 1047

By Parkinson

AN ACT to amend Tennessee Code Annotated, Title 49, relative to education.

BE IT ENACTED BY THE GENERAL ASSEMBLY OF THE STATE OF TENNESSEE:

49-1-221 SECTION 1. Tennessee Code Annotated, Section 49-1-221(c), is amended by adding the following language at the end of the subsection:

> In lieu of submitting the biennial report to the chairs of the education committees of the senate and the house of representatives, the commissioner is authorized to post the report on the department's website and give notice of the posting via email to the chairs.

Effective date 4/25/2013 SECTION 2. This act shall take effect upon becoming a law, the public welfare requiring it.

PUBLIC CHAPTER NO. 275

PUBLIC CHAPTER NO. 275

SENATE BILL NO. 866

By Gresham, Hensley

Substituted for: House Bill No. 408

By Casada, Butt, Joe Carr

AN ACT to amend Tennessee Code Annotated, Title 49, relative to granting of special privileges to professional employees' organizations.

BE IT ENACTED BY THE GENERAL ASSEMBLY OF THE STATE OF TENNESSEE:

49-5-715 SECTION 1. Tennessee Code Annotated, Section 49-5-715, is amended by deleting the section in its entirety and by substituting instead the following:

49-5-715.

(a) Leave to hold statewide office as an officer, director, trustee or agent of a professional employees' association may be granted if the local board approves the leave after the person requesting the leave provides the director of schools with proof of election and proof of the term of office. Acceptable proof of election shall include, but not be limited to, certification by the professional employees' association of the date of the election and the results of the election. Leave shall be granted from a date certain to a date certain pursuant to § 49-5-704.

(b) For purposes of this section only, "professional employees' association" or "association" means any organization or association granting membership to professional employees of LEAs and professionals employed by the state department of education; provided, however, that membership in the organization or association statewide exceeds one thousand (1,000) dues-paying members.

(c) Any person on leave under this section shall retain all rights enumerated in § 49-5-708.

(d) Association service leave shall be leave without pay. The person on leave is entitled to maintain benefits only if the full cost of the benefits is paid by either the person on leave or the association for which the person is serving as an officer, director, trustee or agent. During the leave period, the person's position with the LEA shall be maintained without advancement on the salary scale and with no accrual of sick leave or personal and professional leave. At the end of leave taken pursuant to this section, the person taking the leave shall be returned to the person's former position or a comparable position. Leave shall only be granted with the understanding that the recipient, immediately following the leave of absence, will return to the LEA for a period at least equal to the period of the leave. Prior to the person being allowed to return to a position in the LEA, the person or the association shall reimburse the LEA for any additional expenses incurred in staffing the position while the person was on leave.

(e) Any president of a professional employees' association who was granted leave from an LEA to hold the office prior to the effective date of this act may continue to hold the office of president with leave from the LEA until the end of the leave and termination of the agreement that covers the leave; provided, however, that the agreement shall not be modified or extended after the effective date of this act. If a person who was president of an association before the effective date of this act is re-elected after the effective date of this act, then any new agreement between an LEA and a person who is re-elected shall be entered in accordance with subsections (a) through (d).

Effective date 4/25/2013 SECTION 2. This act shall take effect upon becoming law, the public welfare requiring it.

PUBLIC CHAPTER NO. 276

PUBLIC CHAPTER NO. 276

SENATE BILL NO. 962

By McNally, Campfield, Crowe, Bowling, Burks, Haile, Johnson, Niceley, Stevens, Yager

Substituted for: House Bill No. 542

By Shepard, Sexton, Stewart, Dunn, Hardaway, Ryan Williams

AN ACT to amend Tennessee Code Annotated, Title 39, Chapter 17, Part 4; Title 53, Chapter 10; Title 56; Title 63, Chapter 1; Title 63, Chapter 10; Title 67 and Title 68, relative to certain duties of pharmacists.

BE IT ENACTED BY THE GENERAL ASSEMBLY OF THE STATE OF TENNESSEE:

53-10-112 SECTION 1. Tennessee Code Annotated, Title 53, Chapter 10, Part 1, is amended by adding the following language as a new section:

53-10-112.

(a) For purposes of this section:

(1) "Pharmacist" has the same meaning as defined in § 63-10-204; and

(2) "Pharmacy" has the same meaning as defined in § 63-10-204.

(b) A pharmacy owner, manager or operator shall respect the professional judgment of the pharmacist in holding the health and safety of a patient to be their first consideration.

(c) A pharmacist shall, by utilizing education, skill, experience and professional judgment, make every reasonable effort to prevent the abuse of drugs which the pharmacist dispenses. In doing so, a pharmacist may decline to dispense to a patient a legend drug which in that pharmacist's professional judgment, lacks a therapeutic value for the patient or which is not for a legitimate medical purpose.

(d) A pharmacist shall not be subject to any penalty or fine when fulfilling their obligation to uphold the health and safety of a patient which results in their decline to dispense any legend drug.

(e) It shall be a Class A misdemeanor, punishable by fine only, for the owner, manager or operator of a pharmacy to knowingly restrict or interfere with, or knowingly require a protocol or procedure that restricts or interferes with, a pharmacist's professional duty to counsel with patients and to evaluate the patients' appropriate pharmaceutical needs and the exercise of the pharmacist's professional judgment as to whether it is appropriate to dispense a legend drug to a patient.

Effective date 7/1/2013 SECTION 2. This act shall take effect July 1, 2013, the public welfare requiring it.

PUBLIC CHAPTER NO. 277

PUBLIC CHAPTER NO. 277

SENATE BILL NO. 1017

By Bell, Kelsey

Substituted for: House Bill No. 915

By Holt

AN ACT to amend Tennessee Code Annotated, Title 50, Chapter 1, Part 2, relative to right to work.

WHEREAS, Tennessee is a right to work state; and

WHEREAS, Tennessee's right to work laws are premised on the belief in free choice whereby employees have a right to freely decide whether to join, be represented by, or financially support a union or employee organization; and

WHEREAS, the labor neutrality agreement is used as a tool to pressure company ownership and management to agree to union demands before ever approaching employees; and

WHEREAS, labor neutrality agreements have become increasingly common in recent years and need to be regulated as to their use to ensure both the employer and employee are treated in the fairest way possible; now, therefore,

BE IT ENACTED BY THE GENERAL ASSEMBLY OF THE STATE OF TENNESSEE:

50-1-207 SECTION 1. Tennessee Code Annotated, Title 50, Chapter 1, Part 2, is amended to add the following as a new section:

50-1-207.

(a) For purposes of this section:

(1) "Employee" means a natural person who performs services for an employer for valuable consideration, and does not include a self-employed independent contractor;

(2) "Employer" means a person, association, or legal or commercial entity receiving services from an employee and, in return, giving compensation of any kind to such employee;

(3) "Federal labor laws" means the National Labor Relations Act, compiled in 29 U.S.C. § 151 et seq., and the Labor Management Relations Act, compiled in 29 U.S.C. § 141 et seq., as amended, presidential executive orders, and federal administrative regulations relating to labor and management or employee and employer issues, and the United States Constitution as amended;

(4) "Multi-employer association" means a bargaining unit composed of independent employers who associate together to negotiate jointly with one or more labor organizations representing the employees of the independent employers within the bargaining unit;

(5) "Political subdivision" means any local governmental entity, including but not limited to, any municipality, metropolitan government, county, utility district, school district, public building authority, and development district created and existing pursuant to the laws of this state, or any instrumentality of government created by any one (1) or more of the named local governmental entities; and

(6) "State" means the state of Tennessee and its political subdivisions, agencies and instrumentalities.

(b) No law, ordinance, or regulation shall impose any contractual, zoning, permitting, licensing, or other condition that requires any employer or employee to waive their rights under the National Labor Relations Act, compiled in 29 U.S.C. § 151 et seq.

PUBLIC CHAPTER NO. 277 (cont'd)

(c) No law, regulation, or ordinance shall require, in whole or in part, an employer or multi-employer association to accept or otherwise agree to any provisions that are mandatory or non-mandatory subjects of collective bargaining under federal labor laws, including but not limited to, any limitations on an employer or multi-employer association's rights to engage in collective bargaining with a labor organization, to lock out employees, or to operate during a work stoppage; provided, this subsection shall not invalidate or otherwise restrict the state from requiring the use of project labor agreements to the extent permissible under federal labor laws.

(d) This section shall be interpreted and enforced consistent with the National Labor Relations Act, compiled in 29 U.S.C. § 151 et seq.

(e)(1) Any agreement, contract, understanding, or practice, written or oral, implied or expressed, between any employer and any labor organization required in violation of this section is declared to be unlawful, null, and void, and of no legal effect.

(2) An employer or employee may seek injunctive relief in the chancery court of Davidson County to prevent the state from violating this section.

Effective date 4/25/2013

SECTION 2. This act shall take effect upon becoming a law, the public welfare requiring it.

PUBLIC CHAPTER NO. 278

PUBLIC CHAPTER NO. 278

SENATE BILL NO. 1038

By Kelsey, Ford, Crowe, Burks, Stevens, Overbey, Yager

Substituted for: House Bill No. 358

By Coley, Rogers, Littleton, Moody, Weaver, Camper, Parkinson, Jones, Lollar

AN ACT to amend Tennessee Code Annotated, Title 39 and Title 40, relative to organized crime.

BE IT ENACTED BY THE GENERAL ASSEMBLY OF THE STATE OF TENNESSEE:

39-12-203 SECTION 1. Tennessee Code Annotated, Section 39-12-203, is amended by deleting subdivision (13) in its entirety and substituting the following:

(13) "Unlawful debt" means any money or other thing of value constituting principal or interest of a debt that is legally unenforceable in this state in whole or in part, because the debt was incurred or contracted in violation of:

(A) Chapter 17, part 4 of this title, and the amount of controlled substances involved in the violation is included under § 39-17-417(i) or (j);

(B) Sections 39-17-1004(b)(1)(A) and 39-17-1005(a)(1), involving especially aggravated sexual exploitation of a minor;

(C) Section 39-13-309, involving trafficking for commercial sex acts;

(D) Section 39-13-515, involving promoting prostitution;

(E) Section 39-13-514(b)(4)(A), involving patronizing prostitution;

(F) Section 39-13-528(a), involving solicitation of a minor; or

(G) Section 39-13-529, involving soliciting sexual exploitation of a minor, exploitation of a minor by electronic means.

Effective date 7/1/2013 SECTION 2. This act shall take effect July 1, 2013, the public welfare requiring it.

PUBLIC CHAPTER NO. 279

PUBLIC CHAPTER NO. 279

SENATE BILL NO. 1057

By Kelsey

Substituted for: House Bill No. 1226

By Dennis

AN ACT to amend Tennessee Code Annotated, Title 16 and Title 17, relative to the judiciary.

BE IT ENACTED BY THE GENERAL ASSEMBLY OF THE STATE OF TENNESSEE:

16-1-118 SECTION 1. Tennessee Code Annotated, Title 16, Chapter 1, Part 1, is amended by adding the following language as a new, appropriately designated section:

> Unless otherwise provided by law, all courts in this state that implement an electronic court filing system pursuant to Tennessee Supreme Court Rule 46 and Tennessee Rule of Civil Procedure 5B shall utilize only a system provider authorized by the administrative office of the courts. The administrative office of the courts shall establish technical standards with the goals of ensuring integrity of filings, assuring an environment that promotes uniformity and ease of filing, and providing the framework for future compatibility among e-filing solutions implemented by local and state courts. Nothing in this section shall require the administrative office of the courts to begin implementing a statewide e-filing system.

Effective date 7/1/2013 SECTION 2. This act shall take effect on July 1, 2013, the public welfare requiring it.

PUBLIC CHAPTER NO. 280

PUBLIC CHAPTER NO. 280

SENATE BILL NO. 1209

By Johnson; Mr. Speaker Ramsey; Kelsey

Substituted for: House Bill No. 850

By Marsh, McCormick, Hawk, Doss, Casada, Durham, Ryan Williams, Carter, Hall, Holt

AN ACT to amend Tennessee Code Annotated, Title 4; Title 7; Title 12; Title 41; Title 50; Title 58 and Title 62, relative to certain wage requirements.

BE IT ENACTED BY THE GENERAL ASSEMBLY OF THE STATE OF TENNESSEE:

12-4-401 SECTION 1. Tennessee Code Annotated, Section 12-4-401, is amended by deleting the section and substituting instead the following:

This part shall be known and may be cited as the "Prevailing Wage Act for State Highway Construction Projects".

12-4-402 SECTION 2. Tennessee Code Annotated, Section 12-4-402, is amended by deleting the section and substituting instead the following:

As used in this part, unless the context otherwise requires:

(1) "Commission" means the prevailing wage commission;

(2) "Highway contractor" means any contractor, subcontractor, person, firm or corporation engaged in a state construction project for the purpose of building, rebuilding, locating, relocating or repairing any streets, highways or bridges;

(3) "Prevailing wage" means the rate of pay as determined according to this part;

(4) "State contract" means any contractual agreement, written or oral, entered into by any person, firm or corporation with this state for the performance of work on a state highway construction project; and

(5) "State highway construction project" means any construction project for the purpose of building, rebuilding, locating, relocating or repairing any streets, highways or bridges.

12-4-403 SECTION 3. Tennessee Code Annotated, Section 12-4-403, is amended by deleting the language "state construction projects" wherever it may appear and substituting instead "state highway construction projects".

12-4-403
12-4-405 SECTION 4. Tennessee Code Annotated, Sections 12-4-403, 12-4-405(1), 12-4-408 and 12-
12-4-408 4-411(a), are amended by deleting the language "contractor" wherever it may appear and
12-4-411 substituting instead "highway contractor".

12-4-404 SECTION 5. Tennessee Code Annotated, Section 12-4-404(b), is amended by deleting the language "state construction" and substituting instead the language "state highway construction".

12-4-405 SECTION 6. Tennessee Code Annotated, Sections 12-4-405(5) and 12-4-406(a), are
12-4-406 amended by deleting the language "contractors" wherever it may appear and substituting instead "highway contractors".

12-4-407 SECTION 7. Tennessee Code Annotated, Sections 12-4-407, 12-4-409 and 12-4-411(b) are
12-4-409 amended by deleting the language "state construction project" wherever it may appear and
12-4-411 substituting instead "state highway construction project".

12-4-405 SECTION 8. Tennessee Code Annotated, Section 12-4-405(2)(A), is amended by deleting the subdivision and redesignating existing subdivisions accordingly.

12-4-405 SECTION 9. Tennessee Code Annotated, Section 12-4-405(3)(A), is amended by deleting the subdivision and redesignating existing subdivisions accordingly.

PUBLIC CHAPTER NO. 280 (cont'd)

12-4-405 SECTION 10. Tennessee Code Annotated, Section 12-4-405(4), is amended by deleting the language "and biennially for building construction", and further amended by adding the word "highway" immediately before the language "contractor or contractors".

12-4-409
12-4-412 SECTION 11. Tennessee Code Annotated, Sections 12-4-409 and 12-4-412, are amended by deleting the language "contractor or subcontractor" wherever it may appear and substituting instead the language "highway contractor or subcontractor".

12-4-903 SECTION 12. Tennessee Code Annotated, Section 12-4-903(3)(C)(i), is amended by deleting the subdivision and substituting instead the following:

(i) Wages that exceed:

(*a*) The state's most current prevailing wage scale established pursuant to part 4 of this chapter if the agreement involves a state highway construction project, as defined by § 12-4-402; or

(*b*) The Tennessee Occupational Wages Report, as defined by § 12-4-907, if the agreement involves a construction project other than a project described in subdivision (3)(C)(i)(*a*); or

12-4-410 SECTION 13. Tennessee Code Annotated, Section 12-4-410, is amended by deleting the language "contractor and subcontractor" wherever it may appear and substituting instead the language "highway contractor and subcontractor".

12-4-906
12-4-907 SECTION 14. Tennessee Code Annotated, Title 12, Chapter 4, Part 9, is amended by adding the following new sections thereto:

12-4-906.

If compliance with this part by the state and its political subdivisions, agencies and instrumentalities, relative to a specific contract, project, or program would result in the denial of federal funds that would otherwise be available to the state and its political subdivisions, agencies and instrumentalities, then the state or its political subdivisions, agencies or instrumentalities may require a private employer to pay its employees a wage necessary to meet the federal requirements to obtain the federal funds, but only relative to such contract, project or program.

12-4-907.

For purposes of this part, Tennessee Occupational Wages Report means the applicable report that is published by the department of labor and workforce development, employment security division.

41-6-204 SECTION 15. Tennessee Code Annotated, Section 41-6-204, is amended by deleting the language "prescribed by the Prevailing Wage Act of 1975, compiled in title 12, chapter 4, part 4" and substituting instead the language "the mean wage for the applicable occupation under the "construction and extraction occupations" published in the Tennessee Occupational Wages Report, as defined in § 12-4-907".

7-4-205 SECTION 16. Tennessee Code Annotated, Section 7-4-205(a), is amended by deleting the language:

the prevailing wage rate for all types and classifications of work for contractors entering into a state contract pursuant to the Prevailing Wage Act of 1975, compiled in title 12, chapter 4, part 4

and substituting instead the language:

the mean wage for the applicable occupation under the "construction and extraction occupations" published in the Tennessee Occupational Wages Report, as defined in § 12-4-907

7-4-205 SECTION 17. Tennessee Code Annotated, Section 7-4-205(b), is amended by deleting the language:

an average of the prevailing wage rate for all types and classifications of work for contractors entering into a state contract pursuant to the Prevailing Wage Act of 1975, compiled in title 12, chapter 4, part 4

PUBLIC CHAPTER NO. 280 (cont'd)

and substituting instead the language:

> the mean wage for the applicable occupation under the "construction and extraction occupations" published in the Tennessee Occupational Wages Report, as defined in § 12-4-907

Effective date 1/1/2014

SECTION 18. This act shall take effect January 1, 2014, the public welfare requiring it, and shall apply to contracts entered into or renewed on or after that date.

PUBLIC CHAPTER NO. 281

PUBLIC CHAPTER NO. 281

SENATE BILL NO. 1270

By Hensley

Substituted for: House Bill No. 1193

By Butt, Sexton

AN ACT to amend Tennessee Code Annotated, Title 49, relative to finances.

BE IT ENACTED BY THE GENERAL ASSEMBLY OF THE STATE OF TENNESSEE:

49-2-203 SECTION 1. Tennessee Code Annotated, Section 49-2-203(a)(3), is amended by adding the following language as new subdivision (F):

> (F)(i) Notwithstanding any law to the contrary, contracts for energy-related services that include both engineering services and equipment, and have as their purpose the reduction of energy costs in public schools or school facilities shall be awarded on the basis of recognized competence and integrity and shall not be competitively bid.
>
> (ii) In the procurement of engineering services under this subdivision (F), the local board may seek qualifications and experience data from any firm or firms licensed in Tennessee and interview such firm or firms. The local board shall evaluate statements of qualifications and experience data regarding the procurement of engineering services, and shall conduct discussions with such firm or firms regarding the furnishing of required services and equipment and then shall select the firm deemed to be qualified to provide the services and equipment required.
>
> (iii) The local board shall negotiate a contract with the qualified firm for engineering services and equipment at compensation which the local board determines to be fair and reasonable to the LEA. In making such determination, the local board shall take into account the estimated value of the services to be rendered, the scope of work, complexity and professional nature thereof and the value of the equipment.
>
> (iv) Should the local board be unable to negotiate a satisfactory contract with the firm considered to be qualified, at a price determined to be fair and reasonable, negotiations shall continue with other qualified firms until an agreement is reached.
>
> (V) A local board having a satisfactory existing working relationship for engineering services and equipment under this subdivision (F) may expand the scope of the services; provided, that they are within the technical competency of the existing firm, without exercising the provisions of this subdivision.
>
> (vi) The provisions of this subdivision (a)(3)(F) shall not prohibit or prevent the energy efficient schools council from establishing required design criteria in accordance with industry standards.

Effective date 4/25/2013 SECTION 2. This act shall take effect upon becoming a law, the public welfare requiring it.

PUBLIC CHAPTER NO. 282

PUBLIC CHAPTER NO. 282

SENATE BILL NO. 1275

By Norris

50-6-106, 110, 113, 121, 123, 124, 125, 126, 127, 128, 203, 204, 206, 208, 214, 224, 225, 226, 227, 233, 235, 236, 237, 238, 239, 240, 244, 246, 404, 405, 406, 407, 415, 418, 419, 501, 502, 902, 913, 919

Substituted for: House Bill No. 1159

By McCormick, Kevin Brooks, Eldridge

AN ACT to amend Tennessee Code Annotated, Title 50, Chapter 6, relative to the workers' compensation system.

BE IT ENACTED BY THE GENERAL ASSEMBLY OF THE STATE OF TENNESSEE:

SECTION 1. The Tennessee Code Commission is requested to change appropriate references in Title 50, Chapter 6 from "commissioner" to "administrator" whenever the reference is to the commissioner of labor and workforce development in the code as supplements are issued and volumes are replaced, except in Sections 50-6-102, 50-6-118 and 50-6-412.

50-6-102 SECTION 2. Tennessee Code Annotated, Section 50-6-102(4), is amended by deleting the subdivision in its entirety and by renumbering the remaining subdivisions accordingly.

50-6-204 SECTION 3. Tennessee Code Annotated, Section 50-6-204(j)(4)(E)(i), is amended by deleting the language "may either file a:" and by substituting, instead, "may file a petition for benefit determination.", and is further amended by deleting subsections (a) and (b).

50-6-207 SECTION 4. Tennessee Code Annotated, Section 50-6-207(4)(C)(v), is amended by deleting the subdivision in its entirety and substituting, instead, the following language:

> Prior to filing any request for reconsideration, the employer, insurer or department shall file a petition for benefit determination and participate in alternative dispute resolution pursuant to § 50-6-236. In the event the parties are unable to reach an agreement through alternative dispute resolution, the workers' compensation mediator shall issue a dispute certification notice and the employer, insurer or department may file a request for a hearing, as provided in § 50-6-239, to determine the issue of reconsideration.

50-6-207 SECTION 5. Tennessee Code Annotated, Section 50-6-207(5), is amended by adding the word "primarily" between the words "arising" and "out" and by adding the phrase "and scope" between the words "course" and "of".

50-6-208 SECTION 6. Tennessee Code Annotated, Section 50-6-208(h), is amended by deleting the language "benefit review conference" and substituting, instead, "alternative dispute resolution".

50-6-214 SECTION 7. Tennessee Code Annotated, Section 50-6-214(a)(2)(B), is amended by deleting the language "specialist" and substituting, instead, "judge".

50-6-242 SECTION 8. Tennessee Code Annotated, Section 50-6-242, is amended by deleting the reference to "§ 50-6-241(d)(1)(B) or (d)(2)" and by substituting instead a reference to "§ 50-6-207(3)(B)" and further amend by deleting the language "court or workers' compensation specialist" and replacing it, instead, with "workers' compensation judge".

50-6-609 SECTION 9. Tennessee Code Annotated, Section 50-6-609, is amended by adding the word "primarily" between the words "arising" and "out" and by adding the phrase "and scope" between the words "course" and "of".

Effective date 7/1/2014 SECTION 10. This act shall take effect July 1, 2014, the public welfare requiring it.

PUBLIC CHAPTER NO. 283

PUBLIC CHAPTER NO. 283

HOUSE BILL NO. 534

By Representatives Pody, Rogers, Powers, Evans

Substituted for: Senate Bill No. 802

By Senatosr Beavers, Bowling

AN ACT to amend Tennessee Code Annotated, Title 49, Chapter 7, Part 1; Title 49, Chapter 8, Part 1 and Title 49, Chapter 9, Part 1, relative to public higher education institutions.

BE IT ENACTED BY THE GENERAL ASSEMBLY OF THE STATE OF TENNESSEE:

49-7-156 SECTION 1. Tennessee Code Annotated, Title 49, Chapter 7, Part 1, is amended by adding the following language as a new section:
49-7-150.

(a) No state higher education institution that grants recognition to any student organization shall discriminate against or deny recognition to a student organization, or deny to a student organization access to programs, funding, or facilities otherwise available to another student organization, on the basis of:

(1) The religious content of the organization's speech including, but not limited to, worship; or

(2) The organization's exercise of its rights pursuant to subsection (b).

(b) A religious student organization may determine that the organization's religious mission requires that only persons professing the faith of the group and comporting themselves in conformity with it qualify to serve as members or leaders.

(c) As used in this section, "state higher education institution" means any higher education institution governed by chapter 8 or 9 of this title.

Effective date 7/1/2013 SECTION 2. This act shall take effect July 1, 2013, the public welfare requiring it.

PUBLIC CHAPTER NO. 284

PUBLIC CHAPTER NO. 284

HOUSE BILL NO. 9

By Representatives Lamberth, Watson, Lundberg, Durham, Evans, Weaver, Curtis Johnson, Rogers, Womick, Eldridge, Tidwell, Spivey, Joe Carr, Goins, Doss, Micah Van Huss, Shipley, Kane, Carter, Travis, Lollar, Todd, Forgety, McDaniel, Moody, Timothy Hill, Towns, Matheny, Casada, Sexton, Ryan Williams, Powers, Farmer, Dale Carr, Hall, Butt, Alexander, Littleton, Hawk, Coley, Sparks, Floyd, Marsh, Wirgau, Harry Brooks, Rich, McManus, Holt, Windle, Matthew Hill, Powell

Substituted for: Senate Bill No. 108

By Senators Haile, Green, Beavers, Bell, Bowling, Campfield, Gardenhire, Gresham, Johnson, Niceley, Norris, Tracy

AN ACT to amend Tennessee Code Annotated, Section 10-7-504 and Title 39, Chapter 17, Part 13, relative to confidential records.

BE IT ENACTED BY THE GENERAL ASSEMBLY OF THE STATE OF TENNESSEE:

10-7-504 SECTION 1. Tennessee Code Annotated, Section 10-7-504, is amended by adding the following new subsection:

(o)

(1) Except as provided in subdivisions (2)-(4), the following information and records are confidential, not open or available for public inspection and shall not be released in any manner:

(A) All information contained in any application for a handgun carry permit issued pursuant to § 39-17-1351, a permit renewal application, or contained in any materials required to be submitted in order to obtain such a permit;

(B) All information provided to any state or federal agency, to any county, municipality, or other political subdivision, to any official, agent, or employee of any state or federal agency, or obtained by any state or federal agency in the course of its investigation of an applicant for a handgun carry permit; and

(C) Any and all records maintained relative to an application for a handgun carry permit issued pursuant to § 39-17-1351, a permit renewal application, the issuance, renewal, expiration, suspension, or revocation of a handgun carry permit, or the result of any criminal history record check conducted under this part.

(2) Any information or other records regarding an applicant or permit holder may be released to a law enforcement agency for the purpose of conducting an investigation or prosecution, or for determining the validity of a handgun carry permit, or to a child support enforcement agency for purposes of child support enforcement, but shall not be publicly disclosed except as evidence in a criminal or child support enforcement proceeding.

(3) Any person or entity may request the department of safety to search its handgun permit holder database to determine if a named person has a Tennessee handgun carry permit, as of the date of the request, if the person or entity presents with the request a judgment of conviction, criminal history report, order of protection, or other official government document or record that indicates the named person is not eligible to possess a handgun carry permit under the requirements of § 39-17-1351.

(4) Nothing in this subsection (o) shall prohibit release of the handgun carry permit statistical reports authorized by § 39-17-1351(s).

Effective date 4/25/2013

SECTION 2. This act shall take effect upon becoming a law, the public welfare requiring it.

PUBLIC CHAPTER NO. 285

PUBLIC CHAPTER NO. 285

HOUSE BILL NO. 93

By Representatives Eldridge, Lamberth, Hardaway, Sargent, Hawk, Durham, Lollar, Matlock, Calfee, Alexander, Floyd, Carter, Joe Carr, Fitzhugh, Miller, Casada, Towns, Dunn, Curtis Johnson, Matheny, McCormick, Shaw, Wirgau, Halford, McDaniel

Substituted for: Senate Bill No. 823

By Senators Stevens, Burks, Ford

AN ACT to amend Tennessee Code Annotated, Title 39, Chapter 11, Part 7 and Title 40, Chapter 33, Part 1, relative to forfeiture.

BE IT ENACTED BY THE GENERAL ASSEMBLY OF THE STATE OF TENNESSEE:

40-33-101 SECTION 1. Tennessee Code Annotated, Section 40-33-101, is amended by deleting the section in its entirety and by substituting instead the following:

(a) Except as provided in subsection (b), where there is a final judgment of conviction, in the discretion of the court, conveyances, including vehicles, aircraft or vessels, are subject to forfeiture if used in the commission of:

(1) Any offense under title 39, chapter 13, part 5;

(2) Any robbery offense under title 39, chapter 13, part 4;

(3) A burglary, aggravated burglary, or especially aggravated burglary offense under title 39, chapter 14, part 4; or

(4) A felony theft offense under title 39, chapter 14, part 1.

(b)

(1) No conveyance used by any person as a common carrier in the transaction of business as a common carrier is subject to forfeiture under this part, unless it appears that the owner or other person in charge of the conveyance is a consenting party or privy to any of the offenses listed in subdivisions (a)(2)-(4).

(2) No conveyance is subject to forfeiture under this part by reason of any act or omission established by the owner thereof to have been committed or omitted without the owner's knowledge or consent; provided, that if the conveyance belongs to an automobile or truck rental company, the burden of proof shall be on the state to prove that the automobile or truck rental company knew, or had reason to know, that the conveyance was or would be used in the commission of an offense for which this part provides for forfeiture of the conveyance.

(3) A forfeiture of a conveyance encumbered by a bona fide security interest is subject to the interest of the secured party if the secured party neither had knowledge of nor consented to the act or omission.

Effective date 7/1/2013 SECTION 2. This act shall take effect July 1, 2013, the public welfare requiring it.

PUBLIC CHAPTER NO. 286

PUBLIC CHAPTER NO. 286

HOUSE BILL NO. 158

By Representatives McCormick, Camper

Substituted for: Senate Bill No. 164

By Senator Norris

AN ACT to amend Tennessee Code Annotated, Title 8, Chapter 14, relating to funding for public defenders in the twentieth and thirtieth judicial districts.

BE IT ENACTED BY THE GENERAL ASSEMBLY OF THE STATE OF TENNESSEE:

8-14-210 SECTION 1. Tennessee Code Annotated, Section 8-14-210, is amended by deleting the present section in its entirety and substituting the following:

> For the twentieth and thirtieth judicial districts, the state shall pay, in equal quarterly installments, to the county or metropolitan government which has a local public defender, an amount annually appropriated for that purpose. Such amount shall not be less than the amount appropriated in fiscal year 1992-1993. In addition to the amount appropriated in 1992-1993 the base level of state support on July 1, 2013 shall be adjusted to reflect the percent of change in the average consumer price index (all items-city average) as published by the United States department of labor, bureau of labor statistics, between that figure for the calendar year 2011 and the calendar year 2012. Each succeeding July 1, a similar adjustment shall be made, based on the percent of change in the average consumer price index between the two (2) calendar years preceding July 1 of the year in which the adjustment is made. No adjustment provided for herein shall exceed five percent (5%) per annum. The base level of state support may be adjusted accordingly each year to meet state budget requirements or to reflect changes to programs, workloads or other operational costs.

Effective date 4/25/2013

SECTION 2. This act shall take effect upon becoming law, the public welfare requiring it.

PUBLIC CHAPTER NO. 287

PUBLIC CHAPTER NO. 287

HOUSE BILL NO. 715

By Representatives Carter, Dean

Substituted for: Senate Bill No. 727

By Senators Watson, Ketron

AN ACT to amend Tennessee Code Annotated, Title 38; Title 46; Title 62 and Title 68, relative to human remains.

BE IT ENACTED BY THE GENERAL ASSEMBLY OF THE STATE OF TENNESSEE:

68-4-113 SECTION 1. Tennessee Code Annotated, Title 68, Chapter 4, Part 1, is amended by adding the following language as a new section:

68-4-113. Notwithstanding any law to the contrary, the coroner, medical investigator or county medical examiner may direct the cremation of an unclaimed dead body; provided:

(1) Proper notice is given in accordance with § 68-4-103; and

(2) The body is held for the time period provided in § 68-4-103.

68-4-103 SECTION 2. Tennessee Code Annotated, Section 68-4-103(a), is amended by deleting the subsection and by substituting instead the following:

(a) Whenever a person dies in any hospital, infirmary, mental health institute, poorhouse, penitentiary, house of correction, workhouse, jail, or other charitable or penal institution that is supported in whole or in part at public expense, or whenever a body is delivered to a public official for the purpose of determining the cause of death or for the purpose of burial of the body or the cremated remains at public expense, it is the duty of the public official or of the custodian, superintendent or active head of such institution to immediately notify the nearest relative of the person, if any relative be known, of the person's death.

68-4-103 SECTION 3. Tennessee Code Annotated, Section 68-4-103(b)(1), is amended by deleting the language "made for its interment" and substituting instead "made for its interment by burial of the body or the cremated remains".

68-4-103 SECTION 4. Tennessee Code Annotated, Section 68-4-103(c), is amended by deleting the subsection and by substituting instead the following:

(c) If the chief medical examiner or the chief medical examiner's representative, upon receipt of the notification, does not, within seventy two (72) hours, make a demand for the body, then the body or the cremated remains shall be buried as provided by law or cremated in accordance with § 68-4-113. The public official or the custodian, superintendent or active head of such institution as referred to in subsection (a) may, in such person's discretion, choose to have the body cremated prior to burial.

38-5-118 SECTION 5. Tennessee Code Annotated, Section 38-5-118, is amended by deleting the section in its entirety and substituting instead the following language:

After the inquisition, the coroner or medical investigator may deliver the body of the deceased to the deceased's relatives, if there are any; but if not, the coroner or the medical investigator shall cause the deceased to be decently buried or cremated in accordance with § 68-4-113, and the expense to be paid from the property found with the body, or, if there is none, from the county treasury, by certifying an account of the expenses to the county mayor, who shall allow and pay the expenses, if deemed reasonable, as other claims on the county.

PUBLIC CHAPTER NO. 287 (cont'd)

Effective date 4/25/2013

SECTION 6. This act shall take effect upon becoming a law, the public welfare requiring it.

PUBLIC CHAPTER NO. 288

PUBLIC CHAPTER NO. 288

HOUSE BILL NO. 790

By Representatives Matheny, Ragan

Substituted for: Senate Bill No. 364

By Senators Bell, Crowe

AN ACT to amend Tennessee Code Annotated, Title 4, Chapter 29 and Title 58, Chapter 7, relative to the Tennessee state veterans' home board.

BE IT ENACTED BY THE GENERAL ASSEMBLY OF THE STATE OF TENNESSEE:

4-29-234 SECTION 1. Tennessee Code Annotated, Section 4-29-234(a), is amended by deleting subdivision (60) in its entirety.

4-29-236 SECTION 2. Tennessee Code Annotated, Section 4-29-236(a), is amended by adding a new subdivision thereto, as follows:

( ) Tennessee state veterans' home board, created by § 58-7-102;

SECTION 3. The division of state audit shall return to the Tennessee state veterans' home board in 2014 for the purpose of conducting a limited audit to review actions taken to address the issues raised in the findings of the September, 2012 audit report for the board. The division of state audit shall complete the limited audit within a period sufficient to allow for its review by the Government Operations Joint Subcommittee on Education, Health and General Welfare no later than December 1, 2014.

Effective date 4/25/2013 SECTION 4. This act shall take effect upon becoming a law, the public welfare requiring it.

PUBLIC CHAPTER NO. 289

PUBLIC CHAPTER NO. 289

SENATE BILL NO. 200

By Norris, Johnson, Kelsey

Substituted for: House Bill No. 194

By McCormick, Kevin Brooks, Eldridge, Dennis, Todd, Kane, Hall

AN ACT to amend Tennessee Code Annotated, Title 4, Chapter 3, Part 14; Title 9, Chapter 8, Part 3; Title 9, Chapter 8, Part 4; Title 29, Chapter 20, Part 4; Title 50, Chapter 6, Part 1; Title 50, Chapter 6, Part 2 and Title 50, Chapter 6, Part 3, relative to the improvement of workers' compensation system.

BE IT ENACTED BY THE GENERAL ASSEMBLY OF THE STATE OF TENNESSEE:

4-3-1408 SECTION 1. Tennessee Code Annotated, Section 4-3-1408, is amended by deleting the section in its entirety and substituting instead the following:

(a) In addition to the creation of the division of the Tennessee state employment service within the department of labor and workforce development as provided in § 50-7-601, there are created within the department, the following divisions:

(1) The division of employment security;

(2) The division of workers' compensation; and

(3) The division of occupational safety and health.

(b) The division of employment security and the division of occupational health and safety shall be under the supervision and charge of the commissioner of labor and workforce development, and shall be separate administrative entities for programs, personnel, and budgets. The division of workers' compensation shall also be a separate administrative entity for programs, personnel, and budgets; the supervision and charge of the division shall be in accordance with § 4-3-1409.

(c)(1) The office of administrator is hereby created for each division created pursuant to subdivisions (a)(1)-(3). The administrator shall have the general administrative authority of the division.

(A) Except as otherwise provided in this chapter, the administrator of the division of employment security is responsible, to the greatest extent possible, for administering, implementing, and enforcing title 50, chapter 7, and any rules or regulations promulgated in accordance with such chapter that are within the purview of employment security, but not including WOTC alien certification, veterans' programs and the Tennessee state employment service. The administrator shall have a minimum of five (5) years' credible experience in the field of employment security and shall have a comprehensive knowledge of and experience in the operation and programs of the division. The administrator shall be recognized by the representatives of the business and labor communities as a person of good standing and reputation in matters concerning employment security.

(B) The administrator of the division of workers' compensation is responsible for administering, implementing, and enforcing all of the provisions enacted into law and compiled in title 50, chapter 6, and any rules or regulations promulgated in accordance with such chapter.

(C) The administrator of the division of occupational safety and health shall be responsible for administering, implementing, and enforcing all of the provisions enacted into law and compiled in title 50, chapter 3, and any rules or regulations promulgated in accordance with such chapter. The administrator shall have a minimum of five (5) years' credible experience in the field of occupational safety and health and shall have a comprehensive knowledge of and experience in the operation and programs of the division. The administrator shall be recognized by the representatives of the business and labor communities as a person of good standing and reputation in matters concerning occupational safety and health.

(2) In addition to other duties, each administrator is responsible for preparing and submitting to the commissioner of labor and workforce development an annual budget for the division the administrator heads.

(3) The administrators of the division of employment security and the division of occupational safety and health shall be appointed by the commissioner of labor and workforce development for a term of four (4) years. The first appointment shall be made July 1, 1999, or as soon as practical thereafter. The four-year terms shall begin on July 1 and end on June 30 of appropriate years. The commissioner of labor and workforce development has the authority to remove an administrator only for non-performance of duties and responsibilities. If removed, a vacancy shall exist in the office of the administrator. A vacancy in the office shall be filled for the unexpired term with a person meeting the requirements applicable to the original appointee.

(4) The administrator of the division of workers' compensation shall be appointed in the manner provided in § 4-3-1409.

(d) The transfer of the functions and activities of the various departments and programs to the department of labor and workforce development shall not, because of the transfer, result in any preferred service employee suffering loss of employment, compensation, benefits, or state service status. Such rights, benefits, and compensation shall continue without any impairment, interruption, or diminution; provided, that the department may engage in disciplinary actions or reductions in force as provided for by law. The commissioner of human resources is authorized to enforce this section and shall determine whenever the rights, benefits, and compensation are impaired, interrupted, or diminished. Any employee aggrieved by any impairment in violation of this section shall have the right to seek redress through the grievance procedure established in § 8-30-318.

4-3-1409 SECTION 2. Tennessee Code Annotated, Title 4, Chapter 3, Part 14, is amended by adding the following as a new section to be designated as the formerly obsolete Section 4-3-1409:

(a) In recognition of Tennessee's endeavor to reform the workers' compensation law in a manner designed to ensure the health and safety of Tennessee workers and to promote Tennessee as an attractive destination for business, the General Assembly has determined that the independence of the workers' compensation division is paramount. The workers' compensation division shall be an autonomous unit that shall be attached to the department of labor and workforce development for administrative matters only.

(b)(1) The division of workers' compensation shall be under the charge and general supervision of the administrator.

(2) The administrator or the administrator's designee has the following powers and duties, in addition to other powers and duties specifically provided by law:

(A) Development and maintenance of an organizational structure to ensure fair, equitable, expeditious, and efficient administration of the workers' compensation law; and

(B) Responsibility for the administration of a workers' compensation system that protects the life, health, and safety of Tennessee's workforce and ensures the continued viability of Tennessee's business environment.

(c)(1) The administrator of the division of workers' compensation shall be appointed by the governor for a term of six (6) years. No administrator shall serve more than two (2) full terms, and service of more than half of a six (6) year term shall constitute service of one (1) full term; provided, that any administrator appointed to serve less than a full term to fill a vacancy created by the removal or resignation of the previous administrator shall be eligible to serve an additional two (2) full terms. The first appointment shall be made July 1, 2013, or as soon as practical thereafter. The first six-year term shall begin on July 1, 2013, and end on June 30, 2019. Thereafter, all terms shall begin on July 1 and end, six (6) years later, on June 30 of the following years. The governor has the authority to remove the administrator for nonperformance of duties and responsibilities or for cause. If the administrator is removed or resigns, a vacancy shall exist in the office, which shall be filled for the unexpired term by a person meeting the requirements of subdivision (c)(2) of this section.

(2) The administrator shall have a minimum of seven (7) years' credible experience in the field of workers' compensation and shall have a comprehensive knowledge of and experience in the operation and programs of the workers' compensation industry. The administrator shall be recognized by the representatives of the business and labor communities as a person of good standing and reputation in matters concerning workers' compensation.

50-6-101 SECTION 3. Tennessee Code Annotated, Section 50-6-101, is amended by deleting the section in its entirety and substituting instead the following:

This chapter shall be cited to as the "Workers' Compensation Law" and shall be controlling for any claim for workers' compensation benefits for an injury, as defined in this chapter, when the date of injury is on or after July 1, 2014. All claims having a date of injury prior to July 1, 2014, shall be governed by prior law.

50-6-102 SECTION 4. Tennessee Code Annotated, Section 50-6-102(2), is amended by deleting the language "§ 50-6-204(d)(3)(C)" and replacing it with the language "§ 50-6-204( )(1)(A)".

50-6-102 SECTION 5. Tennessee Code Annotated, Section 50-6-102(12), is amended by deleting the subdivision in its entirety and substituting instead the following:

(12) "Injury" and "personal injury" mean an injury by accident, a mental injury, occupational disease including diseases of the heart, lung and hypertension, or cumulative trauma conditions including hearing loss, carpal tunnel syndrome or any other repetitive motion conditions, arising primarily out of and in the course and scope of employment, that causes death, disablement or the need for medical treatment of the employee; provided, that:

(A) An injury is "accidental" only if the injury is caused by a specific incident, or set of incidents, arising primarily out of and in the course and scope of employment, and is identifiable by time and place of occurrence, and shall not include the aggravation of a preexisting disease, condition or ailment unless it can be shown to a reasonable degree of medical certainty that the aggravation arose primarily out of and in the course and scope of employment;

(B) An injury "arises primarily out of and in the course and scope of employment" only if it has been shown by a preponderance of the evidence that the employment contributed more than fifty percent (50%) in causing the injury, considering all causes;

(C) An injury causes death, disablement or the need for medical treatment only if it has been shown to a reasonable degree of medical certainty that it contributed more than fifty percent (50%) in causing the death, disablement or need for medical treatment, considering all causes;

(D) "Shown to a reasonable degree of medical certainty" shall mean that, in the opinion of the physician, it is more likely than not considering all causes, as opposed to speculation or possibility;

(E) The opinion of the treating physician, selected by the employee from the employer's designated panel of physicians pursuant to § 50-6-204(a)(3), shall be presumed correct on the issue of causation but this presumption shall be rebuttable by a preponderance of the evidence;

50-6-102 SECTION 6. Tennessee Code Annotated, Section 50-6-102(13), is amended by deleting the subdivision in its entirety and substituting instead the following:

(13) "Maximum total benefit" means the sum of all weekly benefits to which a worker may be entitled;

(A) For injuries occurring on or after July 1, 1992, but before July 1, 2009, the maximum total benefit shall be four hundred (400) weeks times the maximum weekly benefit, except in instances of permanent total disability;

(B) For injuries occurring on or after July 1, 2009, but before July 1, 2014, the maximum total benefit shall be four hundred (400) weeks times one hundred percent (100%) of the state's average weekly wage, as determined pursuant to subdivision (14)(B), except in instances of permanent total disability. Temporary total disability benefits paid to the injured worker shall not be included in calculating the maximum total benefit;

(C) For injuries occurring on or after July 1, 2014, the maximum total benefit shall be four hundred fifty (450) weeks times one hundred percent (100%) of the state's average weekly wage, as determined pursuant to subdivision (14)(B), except in instances of permanent total disability. Temporary total disability benefits paid to the injured worker before the employee attains maximum medical improvement shall not be included in calculating the maximum total benefit;

50-6-102 SECTION 7. Tennessee Code Annotated, Section 50-6-102(16), is amended by deleting the subdivision in its entirety and substituting instead the following:

(16) "Minimum weekly benefit" means the minimum compensation per week payable to the worker, which shall be fifteen percent (15%) of the state's average weekly wage, as determined by the department.

50-6-102 SECTION 8. Tennessee Code Annotated, Section 50-6-102(15) and (18), is amended by deleting the subdivisions in their entirety and renumbering subsequent subdivisions accordingly.

50-6-102 SECTION 9. Tennessee Code Annotated, Section 50-6-102, is amended by adding the following as new, appropriately designated subdivisions and renumbering the remaining subdivisions accordingly:

( ) "Court of workers' compensation claims" means the adjudicative function within the division of workers' compensation;

( ) "Mental injury" means a loss of mental faculties or a mental or behavioral disorder, arising primarily out of a compensable physical injury or an identifiable work related event resulting in a sudden or unusual stimulus, and shall not include a psychological or psychiatric response due to the loss of employment or employment opportunities;

50-6-103 SECTION 10. Tennessee Code Annotated, Section 50-6-103(a), is amended by adding the word "primarily" between the words "arising" and "out" and by adding the phrase "and scope" between the words "course" and "of".

50-6-103 SECTION 11. Tennessee Code Annotated, Section 50-6-103(b), is amended by deleting the subsection in its entirety.

50-6-104 SECTION 12. Tennessee Code Annotated, Section 50-6-104, is amended by adding the phrase "or member of a limited liability company" to subsection (a) between the words "corporation" and "may", and by deleting subsection (d), and by adding the following language as new, appropriately designated subsections:

( ) The election by any employee, who is a corporate officer of the employer or member of a limited liability company, to be exempted from this chapter, shall not reduce the number of employees of the employer for the purposes of determining the requirements of coverage of the employer under this chapter.

( ) Every employee who is a corporate officer or member of a limited liability company and who elects not to operate under this chapter, in any action to recover damages for personal injury or death by accident brought against an employer who has elected to operate under this chapter, shall proceed as at common law, and the employer may make use of all common law defenses. This section shall not apply to any officer of a corporation, member of a limited liability company, partner, or sole proprietor who is engaged in the construction industry, as defined by § 50-6-901; instead, part 9 of this chapter shall apply to such officer, member, partner or sole proprietor.

50-6-108 SECTION 13. Tennessee Code Annotated, Section 50-6-108, is amended by adding the following language as a new, appropriately designated subsection:

( ) No employer who fails to secure payment of compensation as required by this chapter, shall be permitted to defend the suit upon any of the following grounds, in any suit brought against the employer by an employee covered by this chapter or by the dependent or dependents of the employee, to recover damages for personal injury or death arising from an accident:

(1) The employee was negligent;

(2) The injury was caused by the negligence of a fellow servant or fellow employee; or

(3) The employee had assumed the risk of the injury.

50-6-111 SECTION 14. Tennessee Code Annotated, Section 50-6-111, is amended by deleting the section in its entirety.

50-6-116 SECTION 15. Tennessee Code Annotated, Section 50-6-116, is amended by deleting the section in its entirety and substituting instead the following:

For any claim for workers' compensation benefits for an injury, as defined in this chapter, when the date of injury is on or after July 1, 2014, this chapter shall not be remedially or liberally construed but shall be construed fairly, impartially, and in accordance with basic principles of statutory construction and this chapter shall not be construed in a manner favoring either the employee or the employer.

50-6-117 SECTION 16. Tennessee Code Annotated, Section 50-6-117, is amended by deleting the section in its entirety.

50-6-118 SECTION 17. Tennessee Code Annotated, Section 50-6-118, is amended by deleting subdivisions (a)(5), (a)(6) and (a)(7) in their entirety and by adding the following as new, appropriately numbered subdivisions:

( ) Failure of any party to appear or to mediate in good faith at any alternative dispute resolution proceeding;

( ) Failure of any party to comply, within the designated timeframe, with any order or judgment issued by a workers' compensation judge;

( ) Performance of any enumerated action provided in § 29-9-102 in relation to any proceedings in the court of workers' compensation claims;

( ) Failure of any employer to timely provide medical treatment made reasonably necessary by the accident and recommended by the authorized treating physician or operating physician;

( ) Failure of an employer to timely provide a panel of physicians that meets the statutory requirements of this chapter;

( ) Wrongful failure of an employer to pay an employee's claim for temporary total disability payments;

( ) Wrongful failure to satisfy the terms of an approved settlement; and

( ) Refusal to cooperate with the services provided by an ombudsman;

50-6-118 SECTION 18. Tennessee Code Annotated, Section 50-6-118, is amended by deleting subsection (c) in its entirety and substituting instead the following new subsections (c) and (d):

(c) The division of workers' compensation may assess the penalties authorized by this chapter, upon providing notice and an opportunity for a hearing to an employer, an employee, an insurer, or a self-insured pool or trust. If a hearing is requested, the commissioner, commissioner's designee, or an agency member appointed by the commissioner shall have the authority to hear the matter as a contested case, and the authority to hear the administrative appeal of an agency decision, relating to the assessment of the penalties authorized by this chapter. When a hearing or review of an agency decision is requested, the requesting party shall have the burden of proving, by a preponderance of the evidence, that the penalized party was either not subject to this chapter, or that the penalties assessed pursuant to this chapter should not have been assessed. Any party assessed a penalty pursuant to this section shall have the right to appeal the penalty assessed by the division and affirmed by the commissioner, the commissioner's designee or an agency member in the manner provided in this subsection, pursuant to the Uniform Administrative Procedures Act, compiled in title 4, chapter 5.

(d) If an employee receives a settlement, judgment or decree under this chapter that includes the payment of medical expenses and the employer or workers' compensation carrier wrongfully fails to reimburse an employee for any medical expenses actually paid by the employee within sixty (60) days of the settlement, judgment or decree, or fails to provide reasonable and necessary medical expenses and treatment, including failure to reimburse for reasonable and necessary medical expenses, in bad faith after receiving reasonable notice of their obligation to provide the medical treatment, the employer or workers' compensation carrier shall be liable, in the discretion of the court, to pay the employee, in addition to the amount due for medical expenses paid, a sum not exceeding twenty-five percent (25%) of the expenses; provided, that it is made to appear to the court that the

PUBLIC CHAPTER NO. 289 (cont'd)

refusal to pay the claim was not in good faith and that the failure to pay inflicted additional expense, loss or injury upon the employee.

50-6-121 SECTION 19. Tennessee Code Annotated, Section 50-6-121(a)(1)(C), is amended by deleting the final two sentences of the subdivision and substituting instead the following language:

All four-year terms shall begin on July 1 and terminate on June 30, four (4) years thereafter.

50-6-122 SECTION 20. Tennessee Code Annotated, Section 50-6-122(a)(3), is amended by deleting the language "50-6-204(a)(4)" wherever it may appear in the subdivision and replacing it with the language "50-6-204(a)(3)".

50-6-122 SECTION 21. Tennessee Code Annotated, Section 50-6-122(c), is amended by deleting the subsection in its entirety.

50-6-124 SECTION 22. Tennessee Code Annotated, Section 50-6-124, is amended by adding the following language as appropriately numbered subsections:

( ) In consultation with the administrator's medical advisory committee, the administrator shall, by rules to become effective on January 1, 2016, adopt guidelines for the diagnosis and treatment of commonly occurring workers' compensation injuries.

( ) Any treatment that explicitly follows the treatment guidelines adopted by the administrator or is reasonably derived therefrom, including allowances for specific adjustments to treatment, shall have a presumption of medical necessity for utilization review purposes. This presumption shall be rebuttable only by clear and convincing evidence that the treatment erroneously applies the guidelines or that the treatment presents an unwarranted risk to the injured worker.

( ) The administrator may assess a reasonable fee, not to exceed two hundred fifty dollars ($250), for an appeal of any utilization review decision.

50-6-125 SECTION 23. Tennessee Code Annotated, Section 50-6-125, is amended by deleting the section in its entirety and substituting instead the following language:

(a)(1) The administrator shall appoint a medical payment committee. The committee shall hear disputes on medical bill payments between providers and insurers and advise the administrator on issues relating to the medical fee schedule and medical care cost containment in the workers' compensation system. Upon hearing disputes on medical bill payments between providers and insurers, the medical payment committee shall have authority to render a decision on the merits of a dispute. If the medical payment committee determines that a provider or insurer has acted in bad faith in refusing to provide payment for a medical bill or refusing to provide reimbursement for overpayment, the medical payment committee, upon a majority vote, shall refer the malfeasant provider or insurer to the division for consideration of assessment of a civil penalty of no more than one thousand dollars ($1,000) per occurrence. Any provider or insurer aggrieved by the assessment of a penalty under this subsection shall have the right to seek review of the penalty assessment in the manner provided by § 50-6-118(c).

(2) The committee shall be comprised of seven (7) voting members appointed by the administrator as follows:

(A) Three (3) members shall be representative of the medical provider industry;

(B) Three (3) members shall be representative of the workers' compensation insurance industry; and

(C) The medical director shall serve as the final member of the committee but shall not cast a vote unless a vote taken by members results in a tie. In that case, the medical director shall cast the deciding vote.

(b) In making appointments, the administrator shall strive to achieve a geographic balance and, in the case of the physician members of the committee, shall assure, to the extent possible, that the membership of the committee reflects the diversity of specialties involved in the medical treatment and management of workers' compensation claimants.

(c) Members of the committee shall serve without compensation but, when engaged in the conduct of their official duties as members of the committee, shall be entitled to reimbursement for travel expenses in accordance with uniform regulations promulgated by the department of finance and administration and approved by the attorney general and reporter.

(d) Each member appointed shall serve a term of four (4) years and may be reappointed by the administrator. If a member leaves the position prior to the expiration of the term, the administrator shall appoint an individual meeting the qualifications of this section to serve the unexpired portion of the term, and the individual may be reappointed by the administrator upon expiration of the term.

50-6-135 SECTION 24. Tennessee Code Annotated, Title 50, Chapter 6, Part 1, is amended by adding the following as a new section:

(a)(1) The administrator shall appoint a medical advisory committee comprised of practitioners in the medical community having experience in the treatment of workers' compensation injuries, representatives of the insurance industry, employer representatives, and employee representatives to assist the administrator in the development of treatment guidelines and advise the administrator on issues relating to medical care in the workers' compensation system.

(2) The medical director shall serve as a non-voting ex-officio member of the committee.

(b) In making appointments, the administrator shall strive to achieve a geographic balance and, in the case of the physician members of the committee, shall assure, to the extent possible, that the membership of the committee reflects the diversity of specialties involved in the medical treatment and management of workers' compensation claimants.

(c) Members of the committee shall serve without compensation but, when engaged in the conduct of their official duties as members of the committee, shall be entitled to reimbursement for travel expenses in accordance with uniform regulations promulgated by the department of finance and administration and approved by the attorney general and reporter.

(d) Each member appointed shall serve a term of four (4) years and may be reappointed by the administrator. If a member leaves the position prior to the expiration of the term, the administrator shall appoint an individual meeting the qualifications of this section to serve the unexpired portion of the term. The individual may be reappointed by the administrator upon expiration of the term.

50-6-131 SECTION 25. Tennessee Code Annotated, Section 50-6-131, is amended by deleting the language "relative to benefit review conferences".

50-6-132 SECTION 26. Tennessee Code Annotated, Section 50-6-132, is amended by deleting the language "senate commerce, labor and agriculture committee and the consumer and employee affairs committee of the house of representatives" and substituting instead the language "senate commerce and labor committee and the consumer and human resources committee of the house of representatives".

50-6-133 SECTION 27. Tennessee Code Annotated, Section 50-6-133, is amended by deleting the section in its entirety.

50-6-134 SECTION 28. Tennessee Code Annotated, Section 50-6-134, is amended by deleting the section in its entirety and substituting instead the following:

The division shall, on or before July 1, 2015, and annually thereafter, review the impact of the Workers' Compensation Reform Act of 2013 on the workers' compensation system in this state and deliver a report of its findings to each member of the General Assembly.

50-6-201 SECTION 29. Tennessee Code Annotated, Section 50-6-201, is amended by deleting subsection (c) in its entirety and by adding the following language as new subdivisions under subsection (a):

(1) The notice of the occurrence of an accident by the employee required to be given to the employer shall state in plain and simple language the name and address of the employee and the time, place, nature, and cause of the accident resulting in injury or death. The notice shall be signed by the claimant or by some person authorized to sign on the claimant's behalf, or by any one (1) or more of the claimant's dependents if the accident resulted in death to the employee.

(2) No defect or inaccuracy in the notice shall be a bar to compensation, unless the employer can show, to the satisfaction of the workers' compensation judge before which the matter is pending, that the employer was prejudiced by the failure to give the proper notice, and then only to the extent of the prejudice.

(3) The notice shall be given personally to the employer or to the employer's agent or agents having charge of the business at which the injury was sustained by the employee.

50-6-202 SECTION 30. Tennessee Code Annotated, Section 50-6-202, is amended by deleting the section in its entirety and substituting instead the following language:

(a) On or after July 1, 2014, the administrator, in cooperation with the commissioner of commerce and insurance, shall adopt rules regarding the electronic submission and processing of medical bills by health care providers to insurance carriers.

(b) Insurance carriers shall accept medical bills submitted electronically by health care providers in accordance with the administrator's rules.

(c) The administrator shall establish by rule the criteria for granting exceptions to insurance carriers and health care providers who are unable to submit or accept medical bills electronically.

50-6-203 SECTION 31. Tennessee Code Annotated, Section 50-6-203, is amended by deleting subsections (a) and (b) in their entirety and substituting instead the following language:

(a) No request for a hearing by a workers' compensation judge under this chapter shall be filed with the court of workers' compensation claims, other than a request for settlement approval, until a workers' compensation mediator has issued a dispute certification notice certifying issues in dispute for hearing before a workers' compensation judge.

(b)(1) In instances when the employer has not paid workers' compensation benefits to or on behalf of the employee, the right to compensation under this chapter shall be forever barred, unless the notice required by § 50-6-201 is given to the employer and a petition for benefit determination is filed with the division on a form prescribed by the administrator within one (1) year after the accident resulting in injury.

(2) In instances when the employer has voluntarily paid workers' compensation benefits, within one (1) year following the accident resulting in injury, the right to compensation is forever barred, unless a petition for benefit determination is filed with the division on a form prescribed by the administrator within one (1) year from the latter of the date of the last authorized treatment or the time the employer ceased to make payments of compensation to or on behalf of the employee.

50-6-203 SECTION 32. Tennessee Code Annotated, Section 50-6-203(e)(1), is amended by deleting the subdivision in its entirety and substituting instead the following language:

Unless a claim for death benefits is settled or voluntarily paid, the dependent or dependents of a deceased employee shall file a petition for benefit determination on a form prescribed by the administrator within one (1) year after the date of the employee's death.

50-6-203 SECTION 33. Tennessee Code Annotated, Section 50-6-203(f), is amended by deleting the subsection in its entirety and substituting instead the following language:

(f) If the employee fails to appear and participate in alternative dispute resolution as scheduled by the division, a workers' compensation judge shall have the authority to dismiss the employee's claim by sending a copy of the order of dismissal by certified mail with return receipt requested to the employee's last known address. The order of dismissal for failure to participate in alternative dispute resolution shall become final and the claim shall be forever barred, unless the employee contacts the division to schedule mediation and attends mediation within sixty (60) days after the date on which the workers' compensation judge enters the order of dismissal. If the employee complies with the requirements of this subsection within the timeframe provided, the workers' compensation judge shall rescind the order dismissing the employee's claim for failure to participate in alternative dispute resolution.

50-6-203 SECTION 34. Tennessee Code Annotated, Section 50-6-203, is amended by deleting subsections (g) and (h) in their entirety and renumbering the remaining subsections accordingly.

50-6-204 SECTION 35. Tennessee Code Annotated, Section 50-6-204(a)(2), is amended by deleting the current language of subdivisions (A) and (B) in their entirety and substituting instead the following language:

(A) It is the intent of the general assembly that the administration of the workers' compensation system proceed in a timely manner and that the parties and the division have reasonable access to the employee's medical records and medical providers that are pertinent to and necessary for the efficient resolution of the employee's workers' compensation claim in a timely manner. To that end, employers or case managers may communicate with the employee's authorized treating physician, orally or in writing, and each medical provider shall be required to release the records of any employee treated for a work-related injury to both the employer and the employee within thirty (30) days after admission or treatment. There shall be no implied covenant of confidentiality with respect to those records, which will include all written memoranda or visual or recorded materials, e-mails and any written materials provided to the employee's authorized treating physician, by case managers, employers, insurance companies, or their attorneys or received from the employee's authorized treating physician.

(B) For purposes of subdivision (a)(2), "employer" means the employer, the employer's attorney, the employer's insurance carrier or third party administrator, a case manager as authorized by § 50-6-123, or any utilization review agent as authorized by § 50-6-124 during the employee's treatment for the claimed workers' compensation injury.

50-6-204 SECTION 36. Tennessee Code Annotated, Section 50-6-204(a)(2)(C), is amended by deleting the subdivision in its entirety and substituting instead the following:

(C) If the division becomes involved in the appeal of a utilization review issue, then the division is authorized to communicate with the medical provider involved in the dispute, either orally or in writing, to permit the timely resolution of the issue and shall notify the employee, employer, and any attorney representing the employee or employer that they may review or copy the documents and responses. Each party requesting copies of records shall pay a fee authorized by subdivision (a)(1)(B) prior to the division providing the requested copies.

50-6-204 SECTION 37. Tennessee Code Annotated, Section 50-6-204(a)(3), is amended by deleting the subdivision in its entirety and substituting instead the following language:

(3)(A) The injured employee shall accept the medical benefits afforded under this section; provided that in any case when the employee has suffered an injury and expressed a need for medical care, the employer shall designate a group of three (3) or more independent reputable physicians, surgeons, chiropractors or specialty practice groups if available in the injured employee's community or, if not so available, in accordance with subdivision (B), from which the injured employee shall select one (1) to be the treating physician.

(i) When necessary, the treating physician selected in accordance with subdivision (a)(3)(A) shall make referrals to a specialist physician, surgeon, or chiropractor and immediately notify the employer. The employer shall be deemed to have accepted the referral, unless the employer, within three (3) business days, provides the employee a panel of three (3) or more independent reputable physicians, surgeons, chiropractors or specialty practice groups. In this case, the employee may choose a specialist physician, surgeon, chiropractor or specialty practice group to provide treatment only from the panel provided by the employer.

(ii) The liability of the employer for the services provided to the employee shall be limited to the maximum allowable fees that are established in the applicable medical fee schedule adopted pursuant to this section.

(iii) The division shall have authority to waive subdivision (ii) when necessary to provide treatment for an injured employee.

(B) If three (3) or more independent reputable physicians, surgeons, chiropractors or specialty practice groups are not available in the employee's community, the employer shall provide a list of three (3) independent reputable physicians, surgeons, chiropractors or specialty practice groups, within a one hundred (100) mile radius of the employee's community.

(C) When the treating physician or chiropractor refers the injured employee, the employee shall be entitled to have a second opinion on the issue of surgery and diagnosis from a physician or chiropractor specified in the initial panel of physicians provided by the employer pursuant to subdivision (a)(3)(A). The employee's decision to obtain a second opinion shall not alter the previous selection of the treating physician or chiropractor.

(D) The employer shall provide the applicable panel of physicians or chiropractors to the employee in writing on a form prescribed by the division, and the employee shall select a physician or chiropractor from the panel, sign and date the completed form, and return the form to the employer. The employer shall provide a copy of the completed form to the employee and shall maintain a copy of the completed form in the records of the employer and shall produce a copy of the completed form upon request by the division.

In any case when the employee has been presented the physician selection form but has failed to sign the completed form and return it to the employer, the employee's receipt of treatment from any physician provided in the panel after the date the panel was provided shall constitute acceptance of the panel and selection of the physician from whom the employee received treatment as the treating physician, specialist physician, chiropractor or surgeon.

(E) In all cases where the treating physician has referred the employee to a specialist physician, surgeon, chiropractor or specialty practice group, the specialist physician, surgeon, or chiropractor to which the employee has been referred, or selected by the employee from a panel provided by the employer, shall become the treating physician until treatment by the specialist physician, surgeon, or chiropractor concludes and the employee has been referred back to the treating physician selected by the employee from the initial panel provided by the employer under subdivision (a)(3)(A).

(F) In all cases when an employee changes his or her community of residence after selection of a physician under this subdivision (a)(3), the employer shall provide the employee, upon written request, a new panel of reputable physicians, surgeons, chiropractors or specialty practice groups, as provided in subdivision (a)(3)(A), from which the injured employee shall select one (1) to be the treating physician.

(G) If any physician, surgeon, chiropractor or specialty practice group included on a panel provided to an employee under this subsection declines to accept the employee as a patient for the purpose of providing treatment to the employee for his workers' compensation injury, the employee may either select a physician from the remaining physicians, surgeons or chiropractors included on the initial panel provided to the employee pursuant to subdivision (a)(3)(A) or request that the employer provide an additional choice of a physician, surgeon, chiropractor or specialty practice group to replace the physician, surgeon or chiropractor who refused to accept the injured employee as a patient for the purpose of treating his or her workers' compensation injury.

(H) Any treatment recommended by a physician or chiropractor selected pursuant to this subdivision (a)(3) or by referral, if applicable, shall be presumed to be medically necessary for treatment of the injured employee.

(I) Following the adoption of treatment guidelines pursuant to § 50-6-124, the presumption of medical necessity for treatment recommended by a physician or chiropractor selected pursuant to this subsection or by referral, if applicable, shall be rebuttable only by clear and convincing evidence demonstrating that the recommended treatment substantially deviates from, or presents an unreasonable interpretation of, the treatment guidelines.

50-6-204 SECTION 38. Tennessee Code Annotated, Section 50-6-204(a)(4), is amended by deleting the subdivision in its entirety and renumbering the remaining subdivisions accordingly.

50-6-204 SECTION 39. Tennessee Code Annotated, Section 50-6-204(a)(5), is amended by deleting the subdivision in its entirety and renumbering the remaining subdivisions accordingly.

50-6-204 SECTION 40. Tennessee Code Annotated, Section 50-6-204(b)(2), is amended by deleting the subdivision in its entirety and renumbering the remaining subdivisions accordingly.

50-6-204 SECTION 41. Tennessee Code Annotated, Section 50-6-204(d)(3), is amended by deleting the subdivision in its entirety and renumbering the remaining subdivisions accordingly.

50-6-204 SECTION 42. Tennessee Code Annotated, Section 50-6-204, is amended by adding the following language as an appropriately numbered subsection:

( ) All permanent impairment ratings shall be assigned by the treating physician or chiropractor.

(1) The treating physician or chiropractor shall utilize the applicable edition of the AMA guides as established by this chapter.

(A) The medical advisory committee shall, within six (6) months of the release of a new edition, conduct an evaluation of the new edition, report the committee's findings to the administrator and recommend to the administrator whether the new edition should be designated for application to the provisions of this chapter. The administrator shall report the committee's findings and recommendation to the general assembly. The AMA guides, as defined in § 50-6-102, shall remain in effect until a new edition is designated by the general assembly.

(B) No impairment rating, whether contained in a medical record, medical report, including a medical report pursuant to § 50-6-235(c), deposition, or oral expert opinion testimony shall be accepted during alternative dispute resolution proceedings or be admissible into evidence at the trial of a workers' compensation claim unless the impairment rating is based on the applicable edition of the AMA guides or, in cases not covered by the AMA guides, an impairment rating by any appropriate method used and accepted by the medical community.

(2) The treating physician or chiropractor shall assign impairment ratings as a percentage of the body as a whole and shall not consider complaints of pain in calculating the degree of impairment, notwithstanding allowances for pain provided by the applicable edition of the AMA guides as established by this chapter.

(3) The treating physician or chiropractor shall evaluate the employee for purposes of assigning an impairment rating and the employee shall attend the evaluation. An employee who fails to attend a scheduled evaluation without justifiable cause shall be subject to sanctions up to and including dismissal of the employee's claim for workers' compensation benefits.

(4) Scheduling of the evaluation shall occur within time limits and according to procedures promulgated by the administrator by rule.

(5) The treating physician or chiropractor shall complete the evaluation and submit an impairment rating report, on a form prescribed by the administrator, within time limits imposed by the administrator through the promulgation of rules.

(6) The treating physician's or chiropractor's written opinion of the injured employee's permanent impairment rating shall be presumed to be the accurate impairment rating. This presumption shall be rebuttable by the presentation of contrary evidence that satisfies a preponderance of the evidence standard.

50-6-204 SECTION 43. Tennessee Code Annotated, Section 50-6-204(g)(2), is amended by deleting the subdivision in its entirety and substituting instead the following:

(2)(A) If an employer does not provide medical care and treatment, medical services or medical benefits, or both, that an employee contends should be provided as a result of a judgment or decree entered by a workers' compensation judge following a workers' compensation trial or as a result of a workers' compensation settlement agreement, either the employee or the employer, or the attorney for the employee or employer, shall request the assistance of a workers' compensation mediator to determine whether such medical care and treatment, medical services or medical benefits, or both, are appropriate by filing a petition for benefit determination and participating in alternative dispute resolution as provided in § 50-6-236. If the parties do not resolve the dispute by agreement, either party may file a request for a hearing and submit the dispute to a workers' compensation judge for resolution after the workers' compensation mediator has issued a dispute certification notice in accordance with § 50-6-236.

(B) A workers' compensation judge shall have the authority to determine whether it is appropriate to order the employer or the employer's insurer to provide specific medical care and treatment, medical services or medical benefits, or both, to the employee pursuant to a judgment or decree entered by a judge following a workers' compensation trial or pursuant to a workers' compensation settlement agreement approved by a workers' compensation judge pursuant to § 50-6-240. The workers' compensation judge's authority shall include, but is not limited to, the authority to order specific medical care and treatment, medical services or medical benefits, or both. The authority of a workers' compensation judge to order the provision of benefits under this section shall include authority to order specific medical care and treatment, medical services or medical benefits, or both for all settlements approved by the department, the division, the commissioner, the commissioner's designee or a workers' compensation specialist even if the settlement was approved under prior law.

50-6-205 SECTION 44. Tennessee Code Annotated, Section 50-6-205(b)(3), is amended by deleting the term "specialist" in the subdivision and substituting instead the term "judge".

50-6-205 SECTION 45. Tennessee Code Annotated, Section 50-6-205(c)(2), is amended by deleting the subdivision in its entirety and renumbering the remaining subdivision accordingly.

50-6-206 SECTION 46. Tennessee Code Annotated, Section 50-6-206, is amended by deleting the section in its entirety.

50-6-207 SECTION 47. Tennessee Code Annotated, Section 50-6-207(1)(D)(ii), is amended by deleting the subdivision in its entirety.

50-6-207 SECTION 48. Tennessee Code Annotated, Section 50-6-207(1)(E), is amended by deleting the subdivision in its entirety and substituting instead the following:

(E) An employee claiming an injury as defined in § 50-6-102, other than a mental injury, when the date of injury is on or after July 1, 2014, shall be conclusively presumed to be at maximum medical improvement when the treating physician ends all active medical treatment and the only care provided is for the treatment of pain. The employer shall be given credit against an award of permanent disability for any amount of temporary total disability benefits paid to the employee after the date that the employee attains maximum medical improvement as determined by a workers' compensation judge.

50-6-207 SECTION 49. Tennessee Code Annotated, Section 50-6-207(2), is amended by designating the existing language as subdivision (A), and by deleting the phrase "four hundred (400)" and replacing it instead with the phrase "four hundred fifty (450)" and is further amended by adding the following as new subdivisions (B) and (C):

(B) In all cases of temporary partial disability for claims with a date of injury on or after July 1, 2014, the compensation shall be sixty-six and two-thirds percent (66 2/3%) of the difference between the average weekly wage of the worker at the time of the injury and the wage the worker is able to earn in the worker's partially disabled condition. This compensation shall be paid during the period of the disability, but payment shall not extend beyond four hundred fifty (450) weeks. Payment shall be made at the intervals when the wage was payable, as nearly as may be, and subject to the same maximum, as stated in subdivision (1). In no event shall the compensation be less than the minimum weekly benefit;

(C) In any case when a dispute exists over the date of the employee's attainment of maximum medical improvement, the employer shall be given credit against an award of permanent disability for any amount of temporary partial disability paid to the employee after the date on which the workers' compensation judge determines maximum medical improvement;

50-6-207 SECTION 50. Tennessee Code Annotated, Section 50-6-207(3), is amended by deleting the subsection in its entirety and substituting instead the following:

(3) Permanent Partial Disability.

(A) In case of disability partial in character but adjudged to be permanent, at the time the injured employee reaches maximum medical improvement the injured employee shall be paid sixty-six and two-thirds percent (66 2/3%) of the employee's average weekly wages for the period of compensation, which shall be determined by multiplying the employee's impairment rating by four hundred fifty (450) weeks. The injured employee shall receive these benefits, in addition to the benefits provided in subdivisions (1) and (2) and those provided by § 50-6-204, whether the employee has returned to work or not; and

PUBLIC CHAPTER NO. 289 (cont'd)

(B) If at the time the period of compensation provided by subdivision (3)(A) ends, the employee has not returned to work with any employer or has returned to work and is receiving wages or a salary that is less than one hundred percent (100%) of the wages or salary the employee received from his pre-injury employer on the date of injury, the injured employee may file a claim for increased benefits. If appropriate, the injured employee's award as determined under subdivision (3)(A) shall be increased by multiplying the award by a factor of one and thirty-five one hundredths (1.35); in addition, the injured employee's award shall be further increased by multiplying the award by the product of the following factors, if applicable:

(1) Education: One and forty-five one hundredths (1.45), if the employee lacks a high school diploma or general equivalency diploma;

(2) Age: One and two tenths (1.2), if the employee was more than forty (40) years of age at the time the period of compensation ends; and

(3) Unemployment rate: One and three tenths (1.3), if the unemployment rate, in the Tennessee county where the employee was employed by the employer on the date of the workers' compensation injury, was at least two percentage (2%) points greater than the yearly average unemployment rate in Tennessee according to the yearly average unemployment rate compiled by the department for the year immediately prior to the expiration of the period of compensation.

(C) In determining the employee's increased award pursuant to subdivision (3)(B), the employer shall be given credit for payment of the original award of benefits as determined under subdivision (3)(A) against the increased award.

(D) Any employee may file a claim for increased benefits under subdivision (3)(B) by filing a new petition for benefit determination, on a form prescribed by the administrator, with the division no more than one (1) year after the period of compensation provided in section (3)(A) ends. Any claim for increased benefits under this subdivision (3)(D) shall be forever barred, unless the employee files a new petition for benefit determination with the division within one (1) year after the period of compensation for the subject injury ends. Under no circumstances shall an employee be entitled to additional benefits when:

(1) The employee's loss of employment is due to the employee's voluntary resignation or retirement; provided, however, that the resignation or retirement does not result from the work-related disability;

(2) The employee's loss of employment is due to the employee's misconduct connected with the employee's employment; or

(3) The employee remains employed but received a reduction in salary, wages, or hours that is concurrent with a reduction in salary, wages or reduction in hours that affected at least fifty percent (50%) of all hourly employees operating at or out of the same location.

(E) Nothing in this subsection shall prohibit the employer and employee from settling the issue of additional benefits at any time after the employee reaches maximum medical improvement. Any settlement or award of additional permanent partial disability benefits pursuant to this subdivision shall give the employer credit for prior permanent partial disability benefits paid to the employee.

(F) Subdivision (3)(B) shall not apply to injuries sustained by an employee who is not eligible or authorized to work in the United States under federal immigration laws.

(G) The total amount of compensation payable in this subdivision 50-6-207(3) shall not exceed the maximum total benefit. The payment of temporary total disability benefits or temporary partial disability benefits shall not be included in calculating the maximum total benefit.

(H) All cases of permanent partial disability shall be apportioned to the body as a whole, which shall have a value of four hundred fifty (450) weeks, and there shall be paid compensation to the injured employee for the proportionate loss of use of the body as a whole resulting from the injury. If an employee has previously sustained an injury compensable under this section and has been awarded benefits for that injury, the injured employee shall be paid compensation for the period of temporary total disability or temporary partial disability and only for the degree of permanent disability that results from the subsequent injury.

50-6-207 SECTION 51. Tennessee Code Annotated, Section 50-6-207(4)(A)(i), is amended by deleting the phrase "after sixty (60) years of age, regardless of the age of the employee" and substituting instead the phrase "less than five (5) years before the date when the employee is eligible for full benefits in the Old Age Insurance Benefit Program as referenced previously in this subdivision or after the employee is eligible for such benefits".

50-6-207 SECTION 52. Tennessee Code Annotated, Section 50-6-207(4)(A)(iii), is amended by deleting the subdivision in its entirety and substituting instead the following:

(iii) For injuries occurring before July 1, 2014, attorneys' fees in contested cases of permanent total disability shall be calculated upon the first four hundred (400) weeks of disability only; for injuries occurring on or after July 1, 2014, attorneys' fees in contested cases of permanent disability shall be calculated upon the first four hundred fifty (450) weeks of disability only;

50-6-207 SECTION 53. Tennessee Code Annotated, Section 50-6-207(6), is amended by deleting the phrase "from this code" and substituting instead the phrase "maintained by the United States Centers for Disease Control and Prevention".

50-6-208 SECTION 54. Tennessee Code Annotated, Section 50-6-208(a), is amended by adding the following as subdivisions (5) and (6):

(5) Claims against the fund shall be made by either the injured employee or the employer in the manner prescribed in § 50-6-239. In all cases when a party is making a claim against the fund, the party advancing the claim shall give notice to the fund of any alternative dispute resolution proceedings scheduled pursuant to § 50-6-236.

(6) Nothing in this section shall relieve the employer or its insurance company of liability for other benefits that may be due the injured employee, including temporary benefits, medical expenses and permanent benefits for injuries.

50-6-208 SECTION 55. Tennessee Code Annotated, Section 50-6-208(b), is amended by deleting the subsection in its entirety and renumbering the remaining subsections accordingly.

50-6-210 SECTION 56. Tennessee Code Annotated, Section 50-6-210, is amended by adding the following as a new subsection (f):

(f)(1)(A) If compensation is payable due to the death of an employee under this chapter, and the decedent leaves an alien dependent or dependents residing outside of the United States, a workers' compensation mediator is authorized to conduct alternative dispute resolution proceedings to attempt to resolve the issues; provided, that a representative or representatives of the employer and a duly authorized representative or representatives of the consul or other representative of the foreign country in which the dependent or dependents reside are present. If the parties reach a settlement agreement, the administrator or administrator's designee is authorized to approve the settlement, and the order of the administrator or the administrator's designee shall be entitled to the same standing as a judgment of a court of record for all purposes. If the parties are unable to reach an agreement, the employer or employee's representative may seek relief pursuant to § 50-6-239 following the issuance of a dispute certification notice.

(B) The administrator, or administrator's designee, or the court shall order payment of any compensation due from the employer to be made to the duly accredited consular officer of the country where the beneficiaries are citizens. The consular officer or the consular officer's representative shall be fully authorized and empowered by this law to settle all claims for compensation and to receive the compensation for distribution to the persons entitled to the compensation.

(2) The distribution of funds in cases described in subdivision (1)(A) shall be made only upon the order of the administrator, the administrator's designee, or the court that heard the matter. If required to do so by the administrator, the administrator's designee, or the court, the consular officer or the consular officer's representative shall execute a good and sufficient bond to be approved by the administrator, the administrator's designee, or the court, conditioned upon the faithful accounting of the monies so received by the consular officer or the consular officer's

representative. Before the bond is discharged, a verified statement of receipts and disbursements of the monies shall be made and filed with the administrator or the court, as appropriate.

(3) The consular officer or the consular officer's representative shall, before receiving the first payment of the compensation, and at reasonable times thereafter, upon the request of the employer, furnish to the employer a sworn statement containing a list of the dependents with the name, age, residence, extent of dependency and relation to the deceased of each dependent.

50-6-212 SECTION 57. Tennessee Code Annotated, Section 50-6-212(a), is amended by adding the term "primarily" between the terms "arising" and "out" and by adding the phrase "and scope" between the terms "course" and "of".

50-6-212 SECTION 58. Tennessee Code Annotated, Section 50-6-212(b), is amended by adding the term "primarily" between the terms "arising" and "out" and by adding the phrase "and scope" between the terms "course" and "of" in the first sentence of the subsection.

50-6-224 SECTION 59. Tennessee Code Annotated, Section 50-6-224, is amended by deleting the section in its entirety.

50-6-225 SECTION 60. Tennessee Code Annotated, Section 50-6-225, is amended by deleting the section in its entirety and substituting instead the following:

(a)(1) Any party to the proceedings in the court of workers' compensation claims may, if dissatisfied or aggrieved by the judgment of that court, appeal to the supreme court, where the cause shall be heard and determined as provided in the Tennessee Rules of Appellate Procedure.

(2) Review of the workers' compensation court's findings of fact shall be de novo upon the record of the workers' compensation court, accompanied by a presumption of the correctness of the finding, unless the preponderance of the evidence is otherwise.

(3) The supreme court may, by order, refer workers' compensation cases to a panel known as the special workers' compensation appeals panel. This panel shall consist of three (3) judges designated by the chief justice, at least one (1) of whom shall be a member of the supreme court.

(4) Any case that the supreme court by order or rule refers to the special workers' compensation appeals panel shall be briefed, and oral argument shall be heard pursuant to the Tennessee Rules of Appellate Procedure as if the appeal were being heard by the entire supreme court.

(5)(A) The special workers' compensation appeals panel shall reduce to writing its findings and conclusions in all cases. The decision of the panel shall become the judgment of the supreme court thirty (30) days after it is issued unless:

(i) Any member of the supreme court files with the clerk a written request within the thirty-day period that the case be heard by the entire supreme court, in which event a final judgment will not be entered until the supreme court, after due consideration of the case, enters final judgment; or

(ii) Any party to the appeal files a motion requesting review by the entire supreme court within fifteen (15) days after issuance of the decision by the panel, in which event a final judgment will not be entered:

(a) Until the motion is denied; or

(b) If the motion is granted, until the supreme court enters final judgment after its consideration of the case.

(B) For purposes of this subsection (a), a decision of the panel shall be deemed to be issued on the day it is mailed to the parties, which date shall be noted on the decision by the clerk. Section 27-1-122 applies to all motions made pursuant to this subsection (e).

(b) Appeal of all cases under this chapter shall be expedited by:

(1) Giving the cases priority over all cases on the appellate dockets; and

(2) Allowing any case on appeal in the supreme court to be on motion of either party transferred to the division where the supreme court is then or will next be in session.

(c)(1) If the judgment or decree is appealed pursuant to subsection (a), interest on the judgment or decree shall be computed from the date that the judgment is entered by the court of workers' compensation claims at an annual rate as defined in § 47-14-121. For purposes of calculating the accrual of interest pursuant to this subdivision (c)(1), the average prime loan rate on the day the judgment or decree is entered by the trial court shall be used.

(2) Total judgment awarded is computed by the total number of weeks multiplied by the benefit rate without any reduction.

(d) When a reviewing court determines pursuant to motion or sua sponte that the appeal of an employer or insurer is frivolous, or taken for purposes of delay, a penalty may be assessed by the court, without remand, against the appellant for a liquidated amount.

(e) When a reviewing court determines pursuant to motion or sua sponte that the appeal of an employee is frivolous, a penalty may be assessed by the court, without remand, against the appellant for a liquidated amount.

50-6-226 SECTION 61. Tennessee Code Annotated, Section 50-6-226(a)(1), is amended by deleting the subdivision in its entirety, and substituting instead the following language:

(a)(1) The fees of attorneys for services to employees under this chapter, shall be subject to the approval of the workers' compensation judge before which the matter is pending, as appropriate; provided, that no attorney's fees to be charged employees shall be in excess of twenty percent (20%) of the amount of the recovery or award to be paid by the party employing the attorney. The department shall deem the attorney's fee to be reasonable if the fee does not exceed twenty percent (20%) of the award to the injured worker, or, in cases governed by § 50-6-207(4), twenty percent (20%) of the first four hundred fifty (450) weeks of the award. All attorney's fees for attorneys representing employers shall be subject to review for reasonableness of the fee and shall be subject to approval by a workers' compensation judge when the fee exceeds ten thousand dollars ($10,000).

50-6-226 SECTION 62. Tennessee Code Annotated, Section 50-6-226(a)(2)(B), is amended by deleting the subdivision in its entirety and renumbering the remaining subdivisions accordingly.

50-6-226 SECTION 63. Tennessee Code Annotated, Section 50-6-226(c)(2), is amended by deleting the phrase "trial judge" in the subdivision and replacing it, instead, with the phrase "workers' compensation judge".

50-6-226 SECTION 64. Tennessee Code Annotated, Section 50-6-226, is amended by adding the following as appropriately numbered subsections:

( ) In addition to any attorneys' fees provided for in this section, the court of workers' compensation claims may award attorneys' fees and reasonable costs, including reasonable and necessary court reporter expenses and expert witness fees for depositions and trials incurred when the employer fails to furnish appropriate medical, surgical and dental treatment or care, medicine, medical and surgical supplies, crutches, artificial members and other apparatus to an employee provided for in a settlement or judgment under this chapter.

( ) A health care provider shall not employ a collection agency or make a report to a credit bureau concerning a private claim against an employer for all or part of the costs of medical care provided to an employee that are not paid by the employer's workers' compensation insurer without having first given notice of the dispute to the medical payment committee. The medical director may include the insurer in the administrative process.

50-6-227 SECTION 65. Tennessee Code Annotated, Section 50-6-227, is amended by deleting the section in its entirety.

50-6-228 SECTION 66. Tennessee Code Annotated, Section 50-6-228, is amended by deleting the section in its entirety.

50-6-229 SECTION 67. Tennessee Code Annotated, Section 50-6-229(b), is amended by deleting the subsection in its entirety and substituting instead the following:

(b) All settlements of compensation by agreement of the parties and all awards of compensation made by the court of workers' compensation claims, when the amount paid or to be paid in settlement or by award does not exceed the compensation for twenty-six (26) weeks of disability, shall be final and not subject to readjustment.

50-6-229 SECTION 68. Tennessee Code Annotated, Section 50-6-229, is amended by adding the following as a new subsection (c):

(c) All amounts paid by the employer and received by the employee or the employee's dependents, by lump sum payments, shall be final, but the amount of any award payable periodically for more than twenty-six (26) weeks may be modified as follows:

(1) At any time by agreement of the parties and approval by the court; or

(2) If the parties do not agree, then at any time after twenty-six (26) weeks from the date of the award, either party may file an application to the court of workers' compensation claims, on the ground of increase or decrease of incapacity due solely to the injury.

50-6-230 SECTION 69. Tennessee Code Annotated, Section 50-6-230, is amended by deleting the section in its entirety.

50-6-231 SECTION 70. Tennessee Code Annotated, Section 50-6-231, is amended by deleting the section in its entirety.

50-6-232 SECTION 71. Tennessee Code Annotated, Section 50-6-232(b), is amended by deleting the subsection in its entirety and substituting instead the following:

(b) The payment of the sum by the employer evidenced by the receipts of the trustee, which shall be filed with the division, shall constitute satisfaction of the award by the employer.

50-6-232 SECTION 72. Tennessee Code Annotated, Section 50-6-232(d), is amended by deleting the term "court" from the subsection and substituting instead the phrase "court of workers' compensation claims".

50-6-233 SECTION 73. Tennessee Code Annotated, Section 50-6-233, is amended by deleting the language of the section in its entirety and substituting instead the following language:

(a)(1) There is conferred upon the administrator the power to enforce this chapter that relate to the assurance of payments of the awards under this chapter.

(2) In no event shall the division of workers' compensation charge a fee or impose a cost for any necessary or required forms needed to process a workers' compensation claim.

(b) The administrator shall cause the division of workers' compensation to refer all feasible cases for vocational rehabilitation to the department of education.

(c) In addition to the rulemaking authority granted in § 50-6-118, and subsection (a) of this section, the administrator or the commissioner of commerce and insurance, as appropriate, may promulgate rules and regulations implementing this chapter. The rules and regulations shall be promulgated pursuant to the Uniform Administrative Procedures Act, compiled in title 4, chapter 5.

50-6-234 SECTION 74. Tennessee Code Annotated, Section 50-6-234, is amended by deleting the section in its entirety and substituting instead the following language:

(a) In any case when the employer has commenced paying temporary disability benefits to the employee and has then stopped or changed the benefits for any cause other than failure of an employee to submit to employer requests for reasonable medical examinations by the treating physician or final settlement, the employee may request the assistance of a workers' compensation mediator who shall mediate the dispute, in accordance with § 50-6-236. If the dispute is not resolved by agreement, the parties may submit the dispute to a workers' compensation judge for resolution after the workers' compensation mediator has issued a dispute certification notice in accordance with § 50-6-236.

PUBLIC CHAPTER NO. 289 (cont'd)

(b) After temporary disability payments have commenced, when the injured employee reaches maximum medical improvement and the compensability of the injury has not been contested by the employer, then payments shall continue until the injured employee accepts or rejects a job offered by any employer at a wage equal to or greater than the employee's pre-injury wage, if the employee is able to perform the duties of the position within any restrictions placed on the employee by the physician selected pursuant to § 50-6-204. In no case may temporary payments pursuant to this subsection (b) exceed the lesser of sixty (60) days or the value of the employee's permanent partial disability award calculated solely upon the medical impairment; provided, that these limits may be exceeded if agreed to by all parties. The amount of the payment shall be credited against any permanent award. For purposes of this subsection (b), the determination of attainment of maximum medical improvement and the employee's medical impairment shall be made by the physician selected in accordance with § 50-6-204. Nothing in this subsection (b) shall require an employer to return any employee to work.

50-6-235 SECTION 75. Tennessee Code Annotated, Section 50-6-235, is amended by deleting every mention of the term "commissioner" or any derivation thereof in the section and replacing it, instead, with the term "administrator" or an appropriate derivation, and is further amended by deleting the phrase "medical care and cost containment committee" in subsection (d) and replacing it, instead, with the phrase "medical payment committee".

50-6-236 SECTION 76. Tennessee Code Annotated, Section 50-6-236, is amended by deleting the section in its entirety and substituting instead the following:

(a) The administrator shall establish a workers' compensation mediators program to assist injured or disabled employees, persons claiming death benefits, employers and other persons in protecting their rights, resolving disputes, and obtaining information pertinent to workers' compensation laws and practices.

(b) In accordance with rules adopted by the administrator, the mediator shall conduct alternative dispute resolution and the mediator shall:

(1) Mediate all disputes between the parties related to the resolution of a claim for workers' compensation benefits and assist in the adjustment of claims consistent with this chapter and the policies of the administrator;

(2) Thoroughly inform all parties of their rights and responsibilities under this chapter, including the right of any party to be represented by an attorney of the party's choice;

(3) Accept all documents and information presented to the division relating to the employee's wages, medical condition, and any other information pertinent to the resolution of disputed issues and include them in the claim file; and

(4) If the parties reach a full and final settlement, the mediator shall reduce the settlement to writing and each party, or their representative, shall sign. Any settlement reached during alternative dispute resolution proceedings shall not become effective, until it has been approved by a workers' compensation judge in accordance with the procedure provided in this chapter.

(c)(1) When mediation is held, a person representing the employee and the employer, or the employer's insurer, with the authority to settle, shall attend. It shall not be required that the state or its representative who attends mediation have final settlement authority. Parties entering into mediation shall be prepared to mediate all disputed issues at the beginning of mediation and shall mediate all issues in good faith.

(2) When a mediator determines that a party is not prepared to mediate as required or believes a party is not mediating in good faith, the mediator shall include comments to that effect in the dispute certification notice.

(3) The administrator is authorized to promulgate rules to effectuate the purposes of this subsection in accordance with the Uniform Administrative Procedures Act, compiled in title 4, chapter 5. The violation of those rules or the provisions of this subsection may subject the party or their representative to a civil penalty of not less than fifty dollars ($50.00) or more than five thousand dollars ($5,000).

(d) If the parties are unable to reach settlement of any disputed issues, the mediator shall issue a written dispute certification notice setting forth all unresolved issues for hearing before a workers' compensation judge.

(1) The dispute certification shall be issued on a form prescribed by the administrator and signed by the assigned workers' compensation mediator who shall distribute a copy of the signed dispute certification notice to all parties in accordance with rules adopted by the administrator.

(2) No party is entitled to a hearing before a workers' compensation judge to determine temporary or permanent benefits or to resolve a dispute over the terms of an agreed settlement of a workers' compensation claim, unless a workers' compensation mediator has issued a dispute certification notice setting forth the issues for adjudication by a workers' compensation judge.

(A) Within five (5) business days after a copy of the dispute certification notice signed by the mediator has been distributed to the parties, any party may, on no more than one (1) occasion for each notice, present a written request that the contents of the dispute certification notice be amended to the mediator who presided over the alternative dispute resolution proceeding.

(B) If a written request to amend the dispute certification notice is presented to the mediator before the expiration of the five (5) business day period provided in subdivision (d)(2)(A), the mediator shall, within three (3) business days after the initial five (5) business day period ends, issue an amended dispute certification notice. If no amended dispute certification notice is signed by the mediator and distributed to the parties, the initial dispute certification notice distributed to the parties pursuant to subdivision (d)(2) of this section shall remain in effect.

(e) A workers' compensation mediator shall not be an advocate for either party and shall mediate all issues without favor or presumption for or against either party. A mediator shall have no authority to order the provision of workers' compensation benefits.

(f) Any person employed as a workers' compensation mediator shall not engage in mediation, litigation, or determination of workers' compensation claims outside of the workers' compensation mediator's duties as a workers' compensation mediator.

(g) If, following a request by the mediator, a party fails to produce documents, to cooperate in scheduling mediation, or to provide a representative authorized to settle a matter in attendance at mediation, then the mediator may issue a dispute certification notice and include a statement detailing the party's failure to cooperate, produce documents or to ensure attendance of a representative authorized to settle the claim. On the motion of either party or on the workers' compensation judge's motion, a workers' compensation judge is authorized, but not required, to hold a hearing on the failure to produce documents requested by the mediator, to cooperate in scheduling and to provide a representative who possessed settlement authority. If the workers' compensation judge determines that the failure lacked good cause or resulted from bad faith, then the workers' compensation judge may assess the offending party who failed to take the requested action with attorney's fees and costs related only to the mediation and the hearing. The administrator is authorized to promulgate rules to effectuate the purposes of this subsection (g) in accordance with the Uniform Administrative Procedures Act, compiled in title 4, chapter 5.

50-6-216 SECTION 77. Tennessee Code Annotated, Title 50, Chapter 6, Part 2, is amended by adding the following as a new section:

(a) The administrator shall establish a workers' compensation ombudsman program to assist injured or disabled employees, persons claiming death benefits, employers, and other persons in protecting their rights, resolving disputes, and obtaining information available under workers' compensation laws. The ombudsman program shall be available only to those individuals or organizations that are not represented by an attorney in the claim for workers' compensation benefits.

(b) No statement, discussion, evidence, allegation or other matter of legal significance that occurs in the presence of an ombudsman shall be admissible as evidence in any other proceeding.

(c) The administrator may adopt rules and regulations consistent with this chapter in order to fulfill the purposes of this section in an orderly and efficient manner.

(d) The division shall have authority to assess a civil penalty against any person or organization, with the exception of the state or a representative of the state, that refuses to cooperate with the services provided by an ombudsman as provided in § 50-6-118.

50-6-237 SECTION 78. Tennessee Code Annotated, Section 50-6-237, is amended by deleting the section in its entirety and substituting instead the following:

There is created the court of workers' compensation claims in the division of workers' compensation, which shall have original and exclusive jurisdiction over all contested claims for workers' compensation benefits when the date of the alleged injury is on or after July 1, 2014. The administrator shall have sole administrative authority over the court including authority to appoint, and to remove, workers' compensation judges. The administrator shall promulgate rules and regulations consistent with this chapter in order to fulfill the purposes of this chapter in an orderly and efficient manner.

50-6-238 SECTION 79. Tennessee Code Annotated, Section 50-6-238, is amended by deleting the section in its entirety and substituting instead the following:

(a)(1) On or after July 1, 2013, the administrator shall appoint qualified individuals to serve as workers' compensation judges. Workers' compensation judges shall be Tennessee licensed attorneys in good standing with at least five (5) years experience in workers' compensation matters and shall be at least thirty (30) years of age. Workers' compensation judges shall be executive service employees of the state as defined in § 8-30-103(7).

(2)(A) In making the initial appointments, the administrator shall have authority to shorten and stagger the terms of workers' compensation judges to ensure that the terms of no more than seven (7) workers' compensation judges shall terminate at the same time.

(B) Except for the initial appointment of candidates to fill the position of workers' compensation judge, upon appointment, each workers' compensation judge shall serve a term of six (6) years. Terms shall begin on July 1 and expire six (6) years later, on June 30. No workers' compensation judge shall serve more than three (3) full terms, and service of more than half of a six (6) year term shall constitute service of one (1) full term. If a sitting workers' compensation judge is removed or resigns, a vacancy shall exist in the office, which shall be filled for the unexpired term by a person meeting the requirements of subdivision (a)(1) of this section.

(C) Any workers' compensation judge may be reappointed by the administrator upon expiration of the term.

(D) If a workers' compensation judge leaves the position prior to the expiration of the term, the administrator shall appoint an individual meeting the qualifications of this section to serve the unexpired portion of the term. The individual may be reappointed by the administrator upon expiration of the term. Any workers' compensation judge appointed to serve less than a full term to fill a vacancy created by the removal or resignation of a sitting workers' compensation judge shall be eligible to serve an additional three (3) full terms.

(3) It shall be the duty of a workers' compensation judge to hear and determine claims for compensation, to approve settlements of claims for compensation, to conduct hearings, and to make orders, decisions, and determinations. Workers' compensation judges shall conduct hearings in accordance with the Tennessee Rules of Civil Procedure, the Tennessee Rules of Evidence and the rules adopted by the division and shall have authority to issue subpoenas and to compel obedience to their judgments, orders, and process through the assessment of a penalty as provided in § 50-6-118.

(b)(1) On or after July 1, 2013, the administrator shall appoint a qualified individual to serve as chief judge of the court of workers' compensation claims. The individual shall be a Tennessee licensed attorney in good standing with at least seven (7) years experience in workers' compensation matters. The chief judge shall be an executive service employee of the state as defined in § 8-30-103(7).

(2) In addition to performing the duties required of a workers' compensation judge by subdivision (a)(3) of this section, it shall be the duty of the chief judge, under the rules adopted by the division, to administer the day to day operations of the court

of workers' compensation claims and supervise the activities of workers' compensation judges.

(3) Upon appointment, the chief judge shall serve a term of six (6) years and may be reappointed by the administrator upon expiration of the term. No chief judge of the court of workers' compensation claims shall serve more than two (2) full terms, and service of more than half of a six (6) year term shall constitute service of one (1) full term. Any chief judge of the court of workers' compensation claims appointed to serve less than a full term to fill a vacancy created by the removal or resignation of the previous chief judge shall be eligible to serve an additional two (2) full terms.

(c) Unless otherwise provided by law or clearly inapplicable in context, the Tennessee Code of Judicial Conduct, Rule 10, Canons 1 through 4, of the Rules of the Tennessee Supreme Court, and any subsequent amendments thereto, shall apply to all workers' compensation judges. However, any complaints regarding the conduct of a workers' compensation judge under the code shall be made to the chief workers' compensation judge. Any complaints about the chief judge shall be made to the administrator.

(d) The administrator shall have authority to remove a workers' compensation judge or the chief judge during an unexpired term for the commission of any of the judicial offenses provided in § 17-5-302.

(e) Any person appointed to serve as a workers' compensation judge or as the chief judge shall be required to take an oath or affirmation to support the constitutions of the United States and of this state, and to administer justice without respect of persons, and impartially to discharge all the duties incumbent upon a judge to the best of the judge's skill and ability. The oath may be taken before another workers' compensation judge, any inferior court judge, a retired judge, a retired chancellor or an active or retired judge of the court of general sessions.

(f) No workers' compensation judge or chief judge shall practice law, or perform any of the functions of attorney or counsel, in any of the courts of this state, except in cases in which the judge may have been employed as counsel previous to the appointment as a workers' compensation judge or chief judge. A newly appointed workers' compensation judge or chief judge can practice law only in an effort to wind up the judge's practice and must end the practice of law as soon as reasonably possible and in no event longer than one hundred eighty (180) days after assuming the position of workers' compensation judge or chief judge.

(g) When considering the appointment of an individual to serve as a workers' compensation judge or as the chief judge, the administrator shall consider comment from the members of the business, labor and legal communities concerning the suitability of the individual for appointment as a workers' compensation judge or the chief judge.

(h) On or after July 1, 2013, the administrator shall appoint a qualified individual to serve as the clerk of the court of workers' compensation claims whose duty it shall be to perform all the clerical functions of the court. The clerk of the court of workers' compensation claims shall be an executive service employee of the state as defined in § 8-30-103(7).

50-6-217 SECTION 80. Tennessee Code Annotated, Title 50, Chapter 6, Part 2, is amended by adding the following as a new section:

(a)(1) The governor shall appoint three (3) qualified individuals to serve as judges on the workers' compensation appeals board. Each individual selected shall be a Tennessee licensed attorney, with at least seven (7) years' experience in workers' compensation matters, shall be at least thirty (30) years of age, and shall be required to attend annual training on workers' compensation laws.

(2) Upon appointment, each judge of the workers' compensation appeals board shall serve a term of six (6) years and may be reappointed for an additional term by the governor upon expiration of the initial term. No judge appointed to the workers' compensation appeals board shall serve more than two (2) full terms, and service of more than half of a six (6) year term shall constitute service of one (1) full term. Any judge appointed to the workers' compensation appeals board to serve less than a full term to fill a vacancy created by the removal or resignation of a judge sitting on the workers' compensation appeals board shall be eligible to serve an additional two (2) full terms. In the initial appointment of judges to the workers' compensation appeals board, one judge appointed shall serve a term of two (2) years, one judge appointed shall serve a term of four (4) years, and one judge appointed shall serve a term of six (6) years.

(3) The governor shall have authority to remove a judge sitting on the workers' compensation appeals board during an unexpired term for the commission of any of the judicial offenses provided in § 17-5-302.

(4) Any person appointed to serve as a judge on the workers' compensation appeals board shall be required to take an oath or affirmation to support the constitutions of the United States and of this state, and to administer justice without respect of persons, and impartially to discharge all the duties incumbent upon a judge to the best of the judge's skill and ability. The oath may be taken before another workers' compensation judge, any inferior court judge, a retired judge, a retired chancellor or an active or retired judge of the court of general sessions.

(5) No person appointed to serve as a judge on the workers' compensation appeals board shall practice law, or perform any of the functions of attorney or counsel, in any of the courts of this state, except in cases in which the judge may have been employed as counsel previous to the appointment as a judge on the workers' compensation appeals board. A newly appointed judge on the workers' compensation appeals board can practice law only in an effort to wind up the judge's practice and must end the practice of law as soon as reasonably possible and in no event longer than one hundred eighty (180) days after assuming the position of judge on the board of administrative review.

50-6-218 SECTION 81. Tennessee Code Annotated, Title 50, Chapter 6, Part 2, is amended by adding the following as a new section:

The administrator shall institute and maintain an education and training program for workers' compensation mediators, workers' compensation judges, the chief judge, ombudsmen, and the judges of the workers' compensation appeals board in order to assure that these persons maintain current and appropriate skills and knowledge in performing their duties. Before assuming their duties, all persons selected to serve or appointed as workers' compensation mediators, workers' compensation judges, the chief judge, ombudsmen, or as judge of the workers' compensation appeals board shall be provided formal training and education, which shall include training on the department's workers' compensation system, the Tennessee workers' compensation statutes and case law, and the rules and regulations of the division of workers' compensation. In addition, such persons shall attend at least seven (7) hours of training each year that is focused on workers' compensation statutes and case law, and the rules and regulations of the division of workers' compensation.

50-6-239 SECTION 82. Tennessee Code Annotated, Section 50-6-239, is amended by deleting the section in its entirety and substituting instead the following:

(a) Within sixty (60) days after issuance of a dispute certification notice by a workers' compensation mediator, a party seeking further resolution of disputed issues shall file a request for a hearing with the division, and the clerk of the court of workers' compensation claims shall issue notice to all parties identifying the judge to whom the claim has been assigned and the procedure for scheduling and preparing for a hearing.

(b) Unless permission has been granted by the assigned workers' compensation judge, only issues that have been certified by a workers' compensation mediator within a dispute certification notice may be presented to the workers' compensation judge for adjudication.

(1) Following the issuance of a dispute certification notice and assignment of the claim to a workers' compensation judge, the workers' compensation judge may grant permission for parties to present issues that have not been certified by a workers' compensation mediator only upon finding that:

(A) The parties did not have knowledge of the issue prior to issuance of the dispute certification and could not have known of the issue despite reasonable investigation; and

(B) Prohibiting presentation of the issue would result in substantial injustice to the petitioning party.

(c) Hearings of disputes shall be conducted in the following manner:

(1) All hearings shall be conducted within the timeframes adopted by the administrator through the promulgation of rules. The Tennessee Rules of Evidence and the Tennessee Rules of Civil Procedure shall govern proceedings at all hearings before a workers' compensation judge unless an alternate procedural or evidentiary

rule has been adopted by the administrator. Whenever the administrator has adopted an alternate procedural or evidentiary rule that conflicts with the Tennessee Rules of Civil Procedure or the Tennessee Rules of Evidence, the rule adopted by the administrator shall apply.

(2) Following the hearing, the workers' compensation judge shall issue a compensation order that sets forth findings of fact and conclusions of law, and, if appropriate, an order for the payment of benefits under the workers' compensation law. The workers' compensation judge shall note the date of entry on the order and a copy of the order shall be distributed to the parties in accordance with procedures adopted by the administrator.

(3) If a party who has filed a request for hearing files a notice of nonsuit of the action, either party shall have ninety (90) days from the date of the order of dismissal to institute an action for recovery of benefits under this chapter.

(4) All hearings before the workers' compensation judge shall be open to the public. The parties may provide a court reporter for the preparation of a record.

(5) The testimony of any witness may be taken by deposition according to the Tennessee Rules of Civil Procedure or may be taken before the workers' compensation judge. No costs shall be charged, taxed or collected by the workers' compensation judge for the appearance of witnesses except fees for witnesses who testify under subpoena. The witnesses shall be allowed the same fee for attendance and mileage as is fixed by law in civil actions.

(6) Unless the statute provides for a different standard of proof, at a hearing the employee shall bear the burden of proving each and every element of the claim by a preponderance of the evidence.

(7) There shall be a presumption that the findings and conclusions of the workers' compensation judge are correct, unless the preponderance of the evidence is otherwise. The decision of the workers' compensation judge shall become final thirty (30) days after the workers' compensation judge enters a compensation order, unless a party in interest seeks an appeal of the decision from the workers' compensation appeals board pursuant to this chapter. If a party in interest does not file a timely request for appeal to the workers' compensation appeals board, the order of the workers' compensation judge shall become final and may be appealed to the state supreme court in the manner provided by § 50-6-225.

(8) The workers' compensation judge may, in his discretion, assess discretionary costs including reasonable fees for depositions of medical experts against the employer upon adjudication of the employee's claim as compensable.

(9) After an order entered by a workers' compensation judge has become final, the parties subject to the order shall have five (5) business days after all appeals are exhausted to comply with the order or the noncompliant parties shall be subject to penalization as provided by § 50-6-118.

(10) In any claim where the employee has suffered a catastrophic injury, the workers' compensation judge assigned to the claim shall have discretion to order that the claim be heard on an expedited basis. If the assigned workers' compensation judge orders an expedited hearing of the claim, the claim shall be given priority over all cases on the workers' compensation judge's trial docket with the exception of any other claims that the workers' compensation judge has previously ordered to be heard on an expedited basis under this subdivision.

(d) Hearings of disputes on an expedited basis shall be conducted in the following manner:

(1) Upon motion of either party made at any time after a dispute certification notice has been issued by a workers' compensation mediator, a workers' compensation judge may, at the judge's discretion, hear disputes over issues provided in the dispute certification notice concerning the provision of temporary disability or medical benefits on an expedited basis and enter an interlocutory order upon determining that the injured employee would likely prevail at a hearing on the merits. A copy of the motion shall be served by the moving party on all other parties to the claim in accordance with procedures adopted by the administrator.

(2) A workers' compensation judge is not required to hold a full evidentiary hearing before issuing an interlocutory order for temporary disability or medical benefits.

(3) If temporary disability or medical benefits are ordered, the employer shall have seven (7) business days to comply with the order or to request an appeal from the workers' compensation appeals board. Unless modified by the workers' compensation appeals board following an appeal or unless a subsequent order to modify an interlocutory order for temporary disability or medical benefits is issued by the workers' compensation judge presiding over the claim, the interlocutory order shall remain in effect pending conclusion of the matter by hearing according to the procedure provided in subsection (c).

(4) If a motion for temporary disability or medical benefits is denied on the basis that the claim is not compensable, the proceeding shall continue according to the procedure provided in subsection (c) unless the employee files a request for an appeal to the workers' compensation appeals board. At any time after the employee has exhausted the procedures for seeking an appeal from the workers' compensation appeals board, as provided in this chapter, the workers' compensation judge may entertain an appropriate motion from the employer for dismissal of the claim.

(e) All discovery disputes, including motions to compel and for protective order, shall be adjudicated upon the review of written motions and affidavits. A workers' compensation judge may, in his or her discretion, convene a hearing on a discovery dispute only upon a finding that good cause to convene a hearing exists.

(f) The failure of any party to comply in a timely manner with an interlocutory or final order issued by a workers' compensation judge may result in the assessment of a penalty as provided in § 50-6-118.

(g) The administrator shall have authority to assess a filing fee sufficient to offset the cost of administering this chapter.

(h) Except as otherwise provided in § 50-6-118, no order issued by a workers' compensation judge shall be subject to judicial review pursuant to the Uniform Administrative Procedures Act, compiled in title 4, chapter 5.

50-6-219 SECTION 83. Tennessee Code Annotated, Title 50, Chapter 6, Part 2, is amended by adding a new section:

(a) The administrator shall establish a workers' compensation appeals board, which shall be wholly separate from the court of workers' compensation claims, to review interlocutory and final orders entered by workers' compensation judges upon application of any party to a workers' compensation claim.

(1) Any party aggrieved by an order for temporary disability or medical benefits or an order either awarding permanent disability or medical benefits or denying a claim for permanent disability or medical benefits issued by a workers' compensation judge may request review of the order by the workers' compensation appeals board by filing a request for appeal, on a form prescribed by the administrator. Review shall be accomplished in the following manner:

(A) Within seven (7) business days after issuance of an interlocutory order for temporary disability or medical benefits by a workers' compensation judge, either party may request an appeal of the decision. Within seven (7) business days of receiving an appeal of an interlocutory order, the workers' compensation appeals board shall enter an order affirming, reversing, remanding, or modifying the decision of the workers' compensation judge. The workers' compensation appeals board's decision on an appeal of an interlocutory order shall not be subject to further review.

(B) Within thirty (30) calendar days after issuance of a compensation order pursuant to § 50-6-239(c)(2), either party may request an appeal of the decision by filing a notice of appeal with the workers' compensation appeals board. Parties shall have fifteen (15) calendar days after an appeal is filed to file briefs with the workers' compensation appeals board. Within forty-five (45) calendar days after receiving an appeal of a compensation order, the workers' compensation appeals board shall issue a decision either affirming the judgment and certifying the workers' compensation judge's order as final or remanding the case. If judgment is affirmed, the final order of the workers' compensation judge shall be immediately appealable to the state supreme court. If a request for administrative review is timely filed, the order issued by the workers' compensation judge shall not become final, as provided in § 50-6-239(c)(7), until the workers' compensation appeals board issues a written decision certifying the order as a final order.

(2) The workers' compensation appeals board may remand the decision of the workers' compensation judge, if the rights of the party seeking review have been prejudiced because findings, inferences, conclusions, or decisions of a workers' compensation judge:

(A) Violate constitutional or statutory provisions;

(B) Exceed the statutory authority of the workers' compensation judge;

(C) Do not comply with lawful procedure;

(D) Are arbitrary, capricious, characterized by abuse of discretion, or clearly unwarranted exercise of discretion; or

(E) Are not supported by evidence that is both substantial and material in the light of the entire record.

(b) This section shall have no effect on the procedures established for filing a claim for workers' compensation benefits in the division of claims administration, pursuant to § 9-8-402, or in the claims commission, pursuant to section 9-8-307. The workers' compensation appeals board shall have no jurisdiction over an appeal of a decision of a commissioner of the claims commission.

(c) The decisions of the workers' compensation appeals board shall not be subject to judicial review pursuant to the Uniform Administrative Procedures Act, compiled in title 4, chapter 5.

50-6-240 SECTION 84. Tennessee Code Annotated, Section 50-6-240, is amended by deleting the section in its entirety and substituting instead the following:

(a) A workers' compensation judge may approve a proposed settlement among the parties if:

(1) The settlement agreement has been signed by the parties; and

(2) The workers' compensation judge has determined that the employee is receiving, substantially, the benefits provided by this chapter, or, in cases subject to subsection (d), if the workers' compensation judge has determined that the settlement is in the best interest of the employee.

(b) A workers' compensation judge shall approve or reject settlements submitted to the division within three (3) business days after the settlement has been received by the division and assigned to a workers' compensation judge for consideration.

(c) In approving settlements, a workers' compensation judge shall consider all pertinent factors and if the injured employee is not represented by counsel, then the workers' compensation judge shall thoroughly inform the employee of the scope of benefits available under this chapter and the employee's rights and the procedures necessary to protect those rights.

(d) Notwithstanding any other provision of this chapter, an employee who is determined to be permanently and totally disabled shall not be allowed to compromise and settle the employee's rights to future medical benefits.

(e) Notwithstanding any other provision of this section, if there is a dispute between the parties as to whether a claim is compensable, or as to the amount of compensation due, the parties may settle the matter without regard to whether the employee is receiving substantially the benefits provided by this chapter; provided that the settlement is determined by a workers' compensation judge to be in the best interest of the employee.

50-6-241 SECTION 85. Tennessee Code Annotated, Section 50-6-241(d)(1)(A), is amended by adding the language "but before July 1, 2014," between the language "July 1, 2004," and the term "in" to the first line of the subdivision.

50-6-241 SECTION 86. Tennessee Code Annotated, Section 50-6-241(d)(1)(C)(i), is amended by adding the language "but before July 1, 2014," between the language "July 1, 2009," and the word "if" to the first line of the subdivision.

50-6-241 SECTION 87. Tennessee Code Annotated, Section 50-6-241(d)(2)(A), is amended by deleting the subdivision in its entirety and substituting instead the following as an appropriately numbered subdivision:

For injuries arising on or after July 1, 2004, but before July 1, 2014, in cases in which the pre-injury employer did not return the injured employee to employment at a wage equal to or greater than the wage the employee was receiving at the time of the injury, the maximum permanent partial disability benefits that the employee may receive for body as a whole and schedule member injuries may not exceed six (6) times the medical impairment rating determined pursuant to the provisions of § 50-6-204(d)(3). The maximum permanent partial disability benefits to which the employee is entitled shall be computed utilizing the appropriate maximum number of weeks as set forth in § 50-6-207 for the type of injury sustained by the employee. In making such determinations, the court shall consider all pertinent factors, including lay and expert testimony, the employee's age, education, skills and training, local job opportunities, and capacity to work at the types of employment available in claimant's disabled condition.

50-6-241 SECTION 88. Tennessee Code Annotated, Section 50-6-241(e)(2)(A), is amended by adding the language "but before July 1, 2014," between the language "July 1, 2009," and the word "in" to the first line of the subdivision.

50-6-241 SECTION 89. Tennessee Code Annotated, Section 50-6-241, is amended by deleting subsections (a), (b), and (c) in their entirety, renumbering the remaining subsections accordingly, deleting any reference to subsection (d) and substituting instead subsection (a), and deleting any reference to subsection (e) and substituting instead subsection (b).

50-6-242 SECTION 90. Tennessee Code Annotated, Section 50-6-242(a), is amended by deleting the subsection in its entirety and substituting instead the following:

For those injuries that occur on or after July 1, 2014, in appropriate cases where the employee has not returned to work and is entitled to additional benefits under § 50-6-207(3)(B), the employee may receive additional disability benefits not to exceed the maximum number of weeks as set forth in § 50-6-207(2)(B). In such cases, the court or the workers' compensation judge shall make specific documented findings, supported by clear and convincing evidence, that as of the date of the award or settlement, at least three (3) of the following facts concerning the employee are true:

(1) The employee lacks a high school diploma or general equivalency diploma, or the employee cannot read or write on a grade eight (8) level;

(2) The employee is fifty-five (55) years of age or older;

(3) The employee has no reasonably transferable job skills from prior vocational background and training; and

(4) The employee has no reasonable employment opportunities available locally considering the employee's permanent medical condition.

50-6-243 SECTION 91. Tennessee Code Annotated, Section 50-6-243, is amended by deleting the section in its entirety.

50-6-246 SECTION 92. Tennessee Code Annotated, Section 50-6-246, is amended by deleting the section in its entirety.

50-6-301 SECTION 93. Tennessee Code Annotated, Section 50-6-301, is amended by deleting the section in its entirety.

9-8-307 SECTION 94. Tennessee Code Annotated, Section 9-8-307(a)(1)(K)(ii), is amended by deleting the references to Sections 50-6-117, 50-6-203(a)-(e) and (g)-(h), 50-6-206(a)(1), 50-6-224(a)(2), 50-6-225(a)-(d), (g) and (k), 50-6-227, 50-6-228, 50-6-236(a), (b), (e) and (h), and 50-6-237(c), and replacing them, instead, with references to Sections 50-6-203(a)-(e) and (g), 50-6-210(f), 50-6-225(d), 50-6-236(c)(2)-(3) and (g), 50-6-239, and 50-6-237.

9-8-307 SECTION 95. Tennessee Code Annotated, Section 9-8-307(a)(1)(K)(iv), is amended by deleting the phrase "or by the commissioner of labor and workforce development or the commissioner's designee pursuant to § 50-6-206(c)" and replacing it, instead, with the following "or to a workers' compensation judge pursuant to § 50-6-240".

9-8-402 SECTION 96. Tennessee Code Annotated, Section 9-8-402(d)(2), is amended by deleting the phrase "request for a benefits review conference" and replacing it, instead, with the phrase "petition for benefit determination".

9-8-402 SECTION 97. Tennessee Code Annotated, Section 9-8-402(d)(4), is amended by deleting the subdivision in its entirety and substituting instead the following language:

> In the event an agreement cannot be reached through alternative dispute resolution as to all issues related to the claim, the claimant shall have ninety (90) days, after the issuance of a dispute certification notice as provided in § 50-6-236, to file a claim with the claims commission. A claim for workers' compensation benefits must be instituted in the claims commission within that ninety (90) days.

9-8-402 SECTION 98. Tennessee Code Annotated, Section 9-8-402(d)(5), is amended by deleting the phrase "or to the commissioner of labor and workforce development or the commissioner's designee, pursuant to § 50-6-206(c)" and replacing it, instead, with the following "or to a workers' compensation judge pursuant to § 50-6-240".

9-8-402 SECTION 99. Tennessee Code Annotated, Section 9-8-402, is amended by deleting all references to Section 50-6-239 and replacing them, instead, with references to Section 50-6-236; and is further amended by deleting every mention of the phrase "benefit review conference" in the section and replacing it, instead, with the phrase "alternative dispute resolution".

29-20-401 SECTION 100. Tennessee Code Annotated, Section 29-20-401(f)(1), is amended by deleting the reference to Section "50-6-208(c) and (d)" and replacing it, instead, with a reference to Section "50-6-208(b) and (c)".

SECTION 101. Any guidelines issued by the medical care and cost containment committee issued at the time this act becomes law shall remain in effect and not be added to, altered, or amended until or unless the medical advisory committee, created pursuant to Section 24 of this act, or the medical payment committee, created pursuant to Section 23 of this act, issue new guidelines pursuant to this act.

4-29-236 SECTION 102. The medical payment committee and the medical advisory committee, created pursuant to Sections 23 and 24 of this act, shall each terminate on the termination date established for the medical care and cost containment committee pursuant to § 4-29-236.

SECTION 103. This act shall be known and may be cited as "The Workers' Compensation Reform Act of 2013".

SECTION 104. If any provision of this act or the application thereof to any person or circumstance is held invalid, such invalidity shall not affect other provisions or applications of the act which can be given effect without the invalid provision or application, and to that end the provisions of this act are declared to be severable.

4-29-239 SECTION 105. The division of workers' compensation created pursuant to this act shall terminate pursuant to title 4, chapter 29 on June 30, 2018.

Effective date 7/1/2014 SECTION 106. For purposes of promulgating rules and regulations, making appointments and making necessary provisions for the implementation of this act, this act shall take effect upon becoming a law, the public welfare requiring it. Additionally, Sections 1 and 2 of this act shall take effect upon becoming a law, the public welfare requiring it. For all other purposes, this act shall take effect on July 1, 2014, the public welfare requiring it.

PUBLIC CHAPTER NO. 290

PUBLIC CHAPTER NO. 290

SENATE BILL NO. 9

By Summerville, Henry

Substituted for: House Bill No. 1296

By Tidwell, Hardaway

AN ACT to amend Tennessee Code Annotated, Title 4, Chapter 11; Title 4, Chapter 29 and Title 58, relative to the Great War Commission.

BE IT ENACTED BY THE GENERAL ASSEMBLY OF THE STATE OF TENNESSEE:

SECTION 1. Tennessee Code Annotated, Title 4, Chapter 11, is amended by adding Sections 2 through 5 of this act as a new part.

4-11-401 – 4-11-405 SECTION 2. There is created the Great War Commission, hereinafter "the commission", to facilitate the appropriate recognition by Tennessee, along with other states and nations, of the centenary of the cataclysm of 1914 through 1919, later called World War I.

SECTION 3. (a) The commission shall be composed of nine (9) members: three (3) members to be appointed by the governor, three (3) members to be appointed by the speaker of the house of representatives, and three (3) members to be appointed by the speaker of the senate. Each appointing authority shall select persons who reside in each of the three (3) grand divisions of the state to serve on the commission. Vacancies shall be filled by the original appointing authority. All appointees to the commission shall be persons who have demonstrated an interest in Tennessee history, twentieth century world history, modern European world history, or the continuing significance of World War I.

(b) Any survivor of a World War I veteran may serve as an honorary, nonvoting member of the commission.

(c) From its membership, the commission shall elect a chairman and such other officers as the commission deems necessary to effectuate the purposes for which the commission was created.

(d) Members of the commission shall not receive travel expenses or compensation for their service.

(e) For administrative purposes only, the commission shall be attached to the office of the secretary of state.

SECTION 4. (a) The Great War Commission has the power and duty to formulate, develop and execute plans for projects and activities that facilitate the appropriate recognition by Tennessee, along with other states and nations, of the centenary of World War I, with particular emphasis on those Tennesseans who made the supreme sacrifice and those who returned home gravely wounded.

(b) The commission is authorized to:

(1) Cooperate with national and international activities that commemorate World War I with appropriate solemnity and accurate scholarship;

(2) Elevate young Tennesseans' knowledge and understanding of World War I, in connection with the teaching of Tennessee, American or World History in public schools and public institutions of higher education; and

(3) Receive and accept loans, gifts, grants, donations or contributions of property, facilities, or services, with or without consideration from any person, firm or corporation or from the state of Tennessee or any agency or instrumentality thereof or from any county, municipal corporation or local government or governing body.

SECTION 5. Beginning July 15, 2015, the commission shall file an annual report with the chair of the government operations committee of the senate and the chair of the government operations committee of the house of representatives that details the commission's activities for the prior fiscal year. The report shall also include, but not be limited to, all commission plans and projects, in addition to an accounting of commission revenues by source and expenditures by item.

SECTION 6. The commission shall cease to exist on November 11, 2018, at which time all of the commission's minutes, files, papers, recordings, publications, and any other items of historical value shall be delivered to the state library and archives to ensure the preservation of such items.

Effective date 6/28/2014

SECTION 7. For purposes of making initial appointments to the commission, this act shall take effect upon becoming a law, for all other purposes this act shall take effect June 28, 2014, the public welfare requiring it.

PUBLIC CHAPTER NO. 291

PUBLIC CHAPTER NO. 291

SENATE BILL NO. 1370

By Tate, Ford

Substituted for: House Bill No. 1106

By Camper

AN ACT to amend Tennessee Code Annotated, Title 37; Title 49; Title 58 and Title 71, relative to services for the care of children.

BE IT ENACTED BY THE GENERAL ASSEMBLY OF THE STATE OF TENNESSEE:

71-3-518 SECTION 1. Tennessee Code Annotated, Title 71, Chapter 3, Part 5, is amended by adding the following language as a new, appropriately designated section:

On or after July 1, 2013, unless otherwise prohibited by federal or state law, no child care agency licensed pursuant to this part shall place a child with at least one (1) parent or legal guardian that serves on active duty in the armed forces of the United States on a wait list behind a child with no parent or legal guardian serving on active duty in the armed forces of the United States.

Effective date 7/1/2013 SECTION 2. This act shall take effect July 1, 2013, the public welfare requiring it.

PUBLIC CHAPTER NO. 292

PUBLIC CHAPTER NO. 292

SENATE BILL NO. 1354

By Norris

Substituted for: House Bill No. 1291

By Lollar, Mark White, Coley, Todd, McManus, Harry Brooks

AN ACT to amend Tennessee Code Annotated, Title 6 and Title 49, relative to K-12 education.

BE IT ENACTED BY THE GENERAL ASSEMBLY OF THE STATE OF TENNESSEE:

49-2-501 SECTION 1. Tennessee Code Annotated, Section 49-2-501(b), is amended by deleting subdivision (1) in its entirety.

Effective date 4/29/2013 SECTION 2. This act shall take effect upon becoming a law, the public welfare requiring it.

PUBLIC CHAPTER NO. 293

PUBLIC CHAPTER NO. 293

SENATE BILL NO. 1147

By Tracy

Substituted for: House Bill No. 980

By Sargent, Pitts, Haynes, Watson, Eldridge, Keisling, Powers, Kevin Brooks

AN ACT to amend Tennessee Code Annotated, Title 56, Chapter 6 and Title 66, Chapter 31, relative to the sale of insurance for self storage unit possessions in a storage facility.

BE IT ENACTED BY THE GENERAL ASSEMBLY OF THE STATE OF TENNESSEE:

SECTION 1. Tennessee Code Annotated, Title 56, Chapter 6, is amended by adding Sections 2 through 8 as a new, appropriately designated part:

56-6-1201 SECTION 2. For purposes of this part:

(1) "Commissioner" means the commissioner of commerce and insurance or the commissioner's designee;

(2) "Covered personal property" means personal property covered under an occupant's self-service storage insurance policy;

(3) "Department" means the department of commerce and insurance;

(4) "Enrolled occupant" means an occupant who elects coverage under a self-service storage insurance policy issued to an owner;

(5) "Leased space" means the storage space or spaces at the self-service storage facility that is leased or rented to an occupant pursuant to a rental agreement;

(6) "Location" means any physical location in this state or any website, or similar location directed to residents of this state;

(7) "Occupant" means a person, or a sublessee, successor or assign of such person, entitled to the use of leased or rented storage space at a self-service storage facility under a rental agreement, to the exclusion of others;

(8) "Owner" means:

(A) The owner, operator, lessor or sublessor of a self-service storage facility, the agent of such person; or

(B) Any person authorized by such person to manage the facility or to receive rent from an occupant under a rental agreement;

(9) "Personal property" means movable property not affixed to land and includes, but is not limited to, goods, wares, merchandise, household items and vehicles;

(10) "Rental agreement" means any agreement or lease, written or oral, that establishes or modifies the terms, conditions, rules or any other provisions concerning the use and occupancy of leased or rented storage space at a self-service storage facility;

(11) "Self-service storage facility":

(A) Means any real property designed and used for the purpose of renting or leasing storage space to occupants who are to have access to such space for the purpose of storing and removing personal property; and

(B) Does not include any part of the real property used for residential purposes;

(12) "Self-service storage insurance":

PUBLIC CHAPTER NO. 293 (cont'd)

(A) Means insurance which may provide coverage for the repair or replacement of covered personal property against any one (1) or more of the following causes:

(i) Loss;

(ii) Theft;

(iii) Damage; or

(iv) Other similar causes of loss; and

(B) Does not include a homeowner's, renter's, private passenger automobile, commercial multi-peril or similar policy;

(13) "Self-service storage transaction" means the lease of self-service storage space by an owner to an occupant pursuant to a rental agreement;

(14) "Supervising entity" means a business entity that is a licensed insurance producer or insurer; and

(15) "Vehicle" means a motor vehicle, a trailer or a semitrailer as defined in §§ 55-1-103 and 55-1-105 and a vessel as defined in § 69-9-204.

56-6-1202 SECTION 3. (a) An owner shall hold a limited lines business entity producer's license to sell or offer coverage under a policy of self-service storage insurance. An owner who complies with this part shall be entitled to a limited lines license, without examination, authorizing the owner to sell or offer coverage under a policy of self-service storage insurance.

(b) A limited lines license issued to an owner under this section shall authorize any employee or authorized representative of the owner to sell or offer coverage under a policy of self-service storage insurance to an occupant at each location at which the owner engages in self-service storage transactions.

(c) In connection with an owner's initial application for licensure and at renewal, the owner shall provide a list to the commissioner of all locations in this state at which the owner offers coverage.

(d) Notwithstanding any law to the contrary, a license issued pursuant to this section shall authorize the licensee and its employees or authorized representatives to engage in activities permitted in this part.

56-6-1203 SECTION 4. (a) At every location where self-service storage insurance is offered to occupants, brochures or other written materials shall be made available that:

(1) Disclose that self-service storage insurance may provide a duplication of coverage already provided by an occupant's homeowner's insurance policy, renter's insurance policy or other source of coverage;

(2) State that the enrollment by the occupant in a self-service storage insurance program is not required in order to lease self-service storage space;

(3) Summarize the material terms of the insurance coverage, including:

(A) The identity of the insurer;

(B) The identity of the supervising entity;

(C) The amount of any applicable deductible and how it is to be paid;

(D) Benefits of the coverage; and

(E) Key terms and conditions of coverage such as whether covered personal property may be repaired or replaced;

(4) Summarize the process for filing a claim; and

(5) State that the enrolled occupant may cancel enrollment for coverage under a self-service storage insurance policy at any time and the person paying the premium shall receive a refund of any applicable unearned premium.

(b) Self-service storage insurance may only be offered or sold on a periodic basis in connection with the rental of leased space at the self-service storage facility on a master, corporate, commercial, group, or individual policy basis and only with respect to personal property insurance that provides coverage to an occupant at the self-service storage facility where the insurance is transacted for the loss of or damage to stored personal property that occurs at such facility.

(c) Eligibility and underwriting standards for occupants electing to enroll in coverage shall be established for each self-service storage insurance program.

56-6-1204 SECTION 5. (a) Notwithstanding any law to the contrary, the employees and authorized representatives of an owner may sell or offer self-service storage insurance to occupants and shall not be subject to licensure as an insurance producer under this part; provided, that:

(1) The owner obtains a limited lines license to authorize its employees or authorized representatives to sell or offer self-service storage insurance pursuant to Section 3 of this act;

(2) The insurer issuing the self-service storage insurance either directly supervises or appoints a supervising entity to supervise the administration of the program, including development of a training program for employees and authorized representatives of the owner. The training required by this subdivision (a)(2) shall comply with the following:

(A) The training shall be delivered to employees and authorized representatives of an owner who are directly engaged in the activity of selling or offering self-service storage insurance;

(B) The training may be provided in electronic form. If the training is conducted in an electronic form, the supervising entity shall implement a supplemental education program regarding self-service storage insurance that is conducted and overseen by the supervising entity; and

(C) Each employee and authorized representative shall receive basic instruction concerning the self-service storage insurance offered to customers and the disclosures required under Section 4;

(3) No employee or authorized representative of an owner of self-service storage space shall advertise, represent or otherwise hold themselves out as a non-limited lines licensed insurance producer; and

(4) No employee or authorized representative of an owner shall be compensated based primarily on the number of occupants enrolled for self-service storage coverage; provided, however, the employee or authorized representative may receive compensation for activities under the limited lines license which is incidental to overall compensation.

(b)(1) The charge for self-service storage insurance coverage may be assessed and collected by the owner; provided, however, such charge shall be a separate item within or an addendum to a rental agreement.

(2) Owners assessing and collecting such charges shall not be required to maintain such funds in a segregated account; provided, the owner is authorized by the insurer to hold such funds in a non-segregated account and remits such amounts to the supervising entity within sixty (60) days of receipt.

(3) All funds received by an owner from an enrolled occupant for the sale of self-service storage insurance shall be considered funds held in trust by the owner in a fiduciary capacity for the benefit of the insurer.

(4) Owners may receive compensation for assessing and collection services.

56-6-1205 SECTION 6. If an owner or its employee or authorized representative violates this part, the commissioner is authorized to:

(1) After notice and hearing, impose on a person licensed pursuant to this act civil penalties not to exceed five hundred dollars ($500) per violation and five thousand dollars ($5,000) in the aggregate for such conduct; and

(2) After notice and hearing, impose on a person licensed pursuant to this act other penalties that the commissioner deems necessary and reasonable to carry out the purpose of this act, including:

(A) Suspending the privilege of transacting self-service storage insurance pursuant to this act at specific business locations where violations have occurred; and

(B) Suspending or revoking the authority of individual employees or authorized representatives to act under a license issued pursuant to Section 3.

56-6-1206 SECTION 7. Notwithstanding any other law to the contrary:

(1) An insurer may terminate or otherwise change the terms and conditions of a policy of self-service storage insurance only upon providing the policyholder and enrolled occupants with at least thirty (30) days written notice;

(2) If the insurer changes the terms and conditions, then the insurer shall provide the owner with a revised policy or endorsement and each enrolled occupant with a revised certificate, endorsement, updated brochure or other evidence indicating a change in the terms and conditions has occurred and a summary of material changes;

(3) Notwithstanding subdivision (1):

(A) An insurer may terminate an enrolled occupant's enrollment under a self-service storage insurance policy upon fifteen (15) days written notice for discovery of fraud or material misrepresentation in obtaining coverage or in the presentation of a claim thereunder; and

(B) An insurer may immediately terminate an enrolled occupant's enrollment under a self-service storage insurance policy:

(i) For nonpayment of premium;

(ii) If the enrolled occupant ceases to have active business with the owner; or

(iii) If an enrolled occupant exhausts the aggregate limit of liability, if any, under the terms of the self-service storage insurance policy and the insurer sends written notice of termination to the enrolled occupant within thirty (30) calendar days after exhaustion of the limit. Provided, however, if notice is not timely sent, enrollment shall continue notwithstanding the aggregate limit of liability until the insurer sends written notice of termination to the enrolled occupant;

(4) If a self-service storage insurance policy is terminated by a policyholder, then the policyholder shall mail or deliver written notice to each enrolled occupant advising the enrolled occupant of the termination of the policy and the effective date of termination. The written notice shall be mailed or delivered to the enrolled occupant at least thirty (30) days prior to the termination; and

(5)(A) Whenever notice by an insurer is required pursuant to this section, the notice shall be in writing and may be mailed or delivered to the owner at the owner's mailing address and to its affected enrolled occupants' last known mailing addresses on file with the insurer;

(B) If notice is mailed pursuant to this section, then the insurer or owner, as the case may be, shall maintain proof of mailing in a form authorized or accepted by the United States Postal Service or other commercial mail delivery service;

(C) An insurer or owner may comply with any notice required by this section by providing electronic notice to an owner or its affected enrolled occupants, as the case may be, by electronic means. If notice is accomplished through electronic means, the insurer or owner, as the case may be, shall maintain proof that the notice was sent.

56-6-1207 SECTION 8. (a) A sworn application for a license under this part shall be made to and filed with the commissioner on forms prescribed and furnished by the department.

(b) The application shall:

(1) Provide the name, residence address and other information required by the department for an individual that is designated by the applicant as the individual responsible for the owner's compliance with this part and the name of the principal, officer, employee, or representative who holds a current producer license in this state; and

(2) Provide the location of the applicant's home office.

(c) Initial licenses issued pursuant to this part shall be valid for a period of twenty-four (24) months and expire biennially on March 1 of the renewal year assigned by the commissioner.

(d)(1) Except as provided in subdivision (d)(2), each owner licensed under this part shall pay to the commissioner a fee as prescribed by the commissioner, but in no event shall the fee exceed one thousand dollars ($1,000) for an initial self-service storage limited lines license and five hundred dollars ($500) for each renewal.

(2) The fee prescribed for an owner that is engaged in self-service storage transactions at ten (10) or fewer locations in this state shall not exceed one hundred dollars ($100) for an initial license and for each renewal.

56-6-110 SECTION 9. Tennessee Code Annotated, Section 56-6-110, is amended by adding the following new, appropriately designated subdivision thereto:

( ) Self-service storage insurance;

56-6-104 SECTION 10. Tennessee Code Annotated, Section 56-6-104(b), is amended by adding the following new, appropriately designated subdivision thereto:

( ) An officer, director, employee or authorized representative of a business entity engaged in the sale, solicitation or negotiation of self-service storage insurance licensed pursuant to and acting in compliance with Sections 2-8 of this act;

SECTION 11. The commissioner is authorized to promulgate rules and regulations to effectuate the purposes of this act. All such rules and regulations shall be promulgated in accordance with Tennessee Code Annotated, Title 4, Chapter 5.

Effective date 7/1/2013 SECTION 12. For the purpose of promulgating rules and regulations, this act shall take effect upon becoming law, the public welfare requiring it. For all other purposes, this act shall take effect July 1, 2013, the public welfare requiring it.

PUBLIC CHAPTER NO. 294

PUBLIC CHAPTER NO. 294

SENATE BILL NO. 1146

By Green, Haile

Substituted for: House Bill No. 866

By Sexton, Goins, Ryan Williams

AN ACT to amend Tennessee Code Annotated, Title 49, relative to education.

BE IT ENACTED BY THE GENERAL ASSEMBLY OF THE STATE OF TENNESSEE:

49-5-415 SECTION 1. Tennessee Code Annotated, Section 49-5-415(f), is amended by adding the following language as a new subdivision (3):

(3)(A) It is the intent of the general assembly that schools, both public and nonpublic, be prepared to treat allergic reaction in the event a student's personal epinephrine auto-injector is not available or the student is having a reaction for the first time.

(B) Each school in an LEA and each nonpublic school is authorized to maintain at the school in at least two (2) unlocked, secure locations, including, but not limited to, the school office and the school cafeteria, epinephrine auto-injectors so that epinephrine may be administered to any student believed to be having a life-threatening allergic or anaphylactic reaction.

(C) Notwithstanding any provision of title 63 to the contrary, a physician may prescribe epinephrine auto-injectors in the name of an LEA or nonpublic school to be maintained for use in schools when necessary.

(D) When a student does not have an epinephrine auto-injector or a prescription for an epinephrine auto-injector on file, the school nurse or other trained school personnel may utilize the LEA or nonpublic school supply of epinephrine auto-injectors to respond to an anaphylactic reaction, under a standing protocol from a physician licensed to practice medicine in all its branches.

(E) If a student is injured or harmed due to the administration of epinephrine that a physician has prescribed to an LEA or nonpublic school under this subdivision (f)(3), the physician shall not be held responsible for the injury unless the physician issued the prescription or standing protocol with intentional disregard for safety.

(F) Similarly, if a student is injured or harmed due to administration of epinephrine to the student by a school nurse or other trained school personnel under this subdivision (f)(3), the school nurse or school employee shall not be held responsible for the injury unless the school nurse or school employee administered the epinephrine injection with an intentional disregard for safety.

Effective date 4/29/2013 SECTION 2. This act shall take effect upon becoming a law, the public welfare requiring it.

PUBLIC CHAPTER NO. 295

PUBLIC CHAPTER NO. 295

SENATE BILL NO. 1129

By Niceley

Substituted for: House Bill No. 971

By Matheny

AN ACT to amend Tennessee Code Annotated, Title 57, Chapter 4, Part 1, relative to premier type tourist resort licenses.

BE IT ENACTED BY THE GENERAL ASSEMBLY OF THE STATE OF TENNESSEE:

57-4-102 SECTION 1. Tennessee Code Annotated, Section 57-4-102(26), is amended by adding the following language as a new, appropriately designated subdivision:

( ) A commercially owned marina containing all of the following characteristics:

(i) Operates as a marina on approximately forty-six (46) acres of land;

(ii) Has a restaurant with at least one hundred ten (110) seats;

(iii) Has approximately two hundred (200) boat slips;

(iv) Has seven (7) cabins; and

(v) Is located in a county having a population of not less than forty-four thousand five hundred (44,500) nor more than forty-four thousand six hundred (44,600) according to the 2010 federal census or any subsequent federal census.

57-4-102 SECTION 2. Tennessee Code Annotated, Section 57-4-102(26), is amended by adding the following language as new, appropriately designated subdivisions:

( ) A commercially operated facility containing all of the following characteristics:

(i) Operates as a hunting lodge on approximately four hundred (400) acres of land;

(ii) Has adequate kitchen facilities and a dining area within the hunting lodge with seating of at least fifty (50) at tables;

(iii) Has capacity to sleep at least thirty (30) guests within the main hunting lodge and at least twenty (20) guests in a cabin located on the property; and

(iv) Is located off I-40 at Exit 311 in any county having a population of not less than fifty-six thousand (56,000) nor more than fifty-six thousand one hundred (56,100) according to the 2010 federal census or any subsequent federal census.

( )(i) A commercially operated facility, including any location within the property designated by the licensee, containing all of the following characteristics:

(*a*) Is located four (4) miles off Exit 144 on Interstate 75;

(*b*) Contains at least one hundred (100) acres on multiple parcels divided by a creek;

(*c*) Contains at least thirty (30) cabins which are fully plumbed with septic systems;

(*d*) Contains at least thirty (30) recreational vehicle sites with full hookups;

(*e*) Contains at least three (3) miles of all terrain vehicle trailheads, which connect and border the North Cumberland Wildlife Area which is governed by the Tennessee wildlife resources agency;

PUBLIC CHAPTER NO. 295 (cont'd)

(*f*) Contains a convenience store which sells gasoline, snacks, drinks, and all terrain vehicle recreational permits which total at least three hundred thousand dollars ($300,000) in annual sales;

(*g*) Contains a restaurant which seats at least seventy-five (75) persons at tables both indoors and outdoors which serve at least six (6) meals on a weekly basis, with the exception of closures for private groups or events, and seasonal closures, vacations, general maintenance, and remodeling by the owners;

(*h*) Does not discriminate against any patron on the basis of age, gender, race, religion, or national origin; and

(*i*) Is located in a county having a population of not less than forty thousand seven hundred (40,700) nor more than forty thousand eight hundred (40,800) according to the 2010 federal census or any subsequent federal census.

(ii) A licensee licensed under this subdivision ( ) shall designate the premises to be licensed by the commission by filing a drawing of the premises, which may be amended by the licensee filing a new drawing.

Effective date 4/29/2013

SECTION 3. This act shall take effect upon becoming a law, the public welfare requiring it.

PUBLIC CHAPTER NO. 296

PUBLIC CHAPTER NO. 296

SENATE BILL NO. 1003

By McNally

Substituted for: House Bill No. 950

By McManus

AN ACT to amend Tennessee Code Annotated, Title 8, Chapter 25; Title 8, Chapter 34; Title 8, Chapter 35; Title 8, Chapter 36; Title 8, Chapter 37 and Title 49, Chapter 7, Part 2, relative to retirement.

BE IT ENACTED BY THE GENERAL ASSEMBLY OF THE STATE OF TENNESSEE:

8-25-104 SECTION 1. Tennessee Code Annotated, Section 8-25-104, is amended by adding the following language as new, appropriately designated subsections:

(_) Notwithstanding any provision of the law to the contrary, the chair of the consolidated retirement board, with the concurrence of the commissioner of finance and administration, has the authority to implement an automatic deferred or tax-sheltered compensation plan. Such plan shall provide that any person who becomes a full-time state employee on or after the implementation date of the plan, including a full-time employee of an institution of higher education, who is eligible to participate in one of the deferred or tax-sheltered compensation plans established pursuant to parts 1 or 3 of this chapter shall participate in at least one of the plans as a condition of employment, unless such employee files with that person's employer a notice of that person's election not to participate.

(_) Any notice of non-election shall be made in such format and through such medium as prescribed by the chair of the Tennessee consolidated retirement system and must be filed with that employee's employer by no later than thirty (30) calendar days from the date of the notice of automatic deferral letter. Any employee who does not file a notice of non-election within the prescribed period shall be automatically enrolled in the state's salary reduction plan established in part 3 of this chapter with a salary deferral of two percent (2%) of that employee's compensation. All contributions made by or on behalf of the employee shall be directed to such default option as shall be established by the chair of the consolidated retirement board until such time as the employee selects a different investment option or options. Notwithstanding any provision of this section or any other law to the contrary, future deferrals may be cancelled or adjusted at any time by the employee provided the employee notifies that employee's employer in such format and through such medium as may be prescribed by the chair of the Tennessee consolidated retirement system at least one month before the payday on which the cancellation or change is to be effective. Provided, however, any adjustment in the deferrals, other than a cancellation, cannot cause the amount of the deferrals to be less than twenty dollars ($20.00) per month, or if the employee is paid twice a month, ten dollars ($10.00) semimonthly, or such other lower amount as may be established under chapter 25, part 3 of this title. In addition, any adjustment in the deferrals cannot cause the amount of the deferrals to exceed the maximum allowed under the Internal Revenue Code.

(_) Any employee who affirmatively declines to make employee deferrals after the first automatic enrollment contribution was made, may make an election to withdraw that employee's entire automatic enrollment contribution. This election must be submitted no later than ninety (90) calendar days after the payroll date in which the first automatic enrollment contribution is made on behalf of the employee. The amount of the distribution shall be the value of the automatic enrollment contributions plus or minus investment gains or losses as of the date the distribution is processed. Automatic enrollment contributions made after such date shall remain in the plan and shall be subject to the plan's regular distribution rules. Further, an employee who has made an election to withdraw and who thereafter leaves employment and is then rehired by the same employer as defined below or, by the same political subdivision in the case of a political subdivision employee, before a twelve (12) continuous month absence shall not be permitted to make another election to withdraw that participant's automatic enrollment contribution. For purposes of this subdivision, "same employer" means the employer for which the person last worked prior to separation from covered employment. All departments, agencies and instrumentalities in the executive, legislative and judicial branches of state government, including public institutions of higher education, shall be deemed one and the same employer. All public schools within the Tennessee public school system, except for public institutions of higher education, shall be deemed one and the same employer. Notwithstanding the vesting provisions of the plan's document, the employer matching contributions described in § 8-25-303 that are attributable to the distribution of the automatic enrollment contributions shall be forfeited and placed in a forfeiture account. Amounts in the forfeiture account shall be used in the manner provided in the plan document established for the profit sharing and/or salary reduction plan established under chapter 25, part 3 of this title. The employer matching contributions described in § 8-25-303 shall not be made if a permissible withdrawal is taken pursuant to this subsection before the date the matching contribution is allocated.

(_) The initial two percent (2%) automatic enrollment contribution described in this section shall be subject to a percentage annual increase thereafter if provided for in the plan document established for the profit sharing and/or salary reduction plan established under chapter 25, part 3 of this title.

(_) The automatic deferrals shall be contributed on a pre-tax basis and shall continue until the employee affirmatively elects otherwise.

8-25-111 SECTION 2. Tennessee Code Annotated, Section 8-25-111, is amended by adding the following language as a new, appropriately designated subsection:

(_) A local board of education may elect to participate in the plan separately from the political subdivision with which it is associated. A political subdivision may elect to participate in the plan without extending coverage to the employees of the local board of education that is associated with the participating political subdivision. In the event that a political subdivision withdraws its participation in the deferred compensation plan, the local board of education, which is a part of the political subdivision, may continue its participation in the plan separately.

8-25-301 SECTION 3. Tennessee Code Annotated, Section 8-25-301, is amended by deleting the first sentence in this section in its entirety and by substituting instead with the following:

The state treasurer is directed to develop and obtain internal revenue service approval of a profit sharing or salary reduction plan for state employees as permitted by the internal revenue service.

8-25-304 SECTION 4. Tennessee Code Annotated, Section 8-25-304(a), is amended by deleting the subsection in its entirety and by substituting instead with the following:

(a) Any political subdivision or instrumentality of the state, by resolution or ordinance of its governing body, is authorized to make available to its employees a profit sharing or salary reduction plan approved by the internal revenue service.

8-34-101 SECTION 5. Tennessee Code Annotated, Section 8-34-101(34), is amended by deleting from the third sentence thereof the language "fifty dollars ($50.00)" and by substituting instead the language "seventy-five dollars ($75.00)".

8-34-101 SECTION 6. Tennessee Code Annotated, Section 8-34-101(34), is further amended by adding the following new sentence at the end thereof:

Notwithstanding this subdivision (34) to the contrary, any retirement allowance that equals ten dollars ($10.00) or more per month but less than seventy-five dollars ($75.00) per month shall be paid in a lump sum of equivalent actuarial value if such allowance is payable on account of a person who became a member of the retirement system on or after July 1, 2013;

8-35-201 SECTION 7. Tennessee Code Annotated, Section 8-35-201, is amended by adding a new, appropriately designated subsection as follows:

(_) A local board of education may elect to participate in the retirement system separately from the political subdivision with which it is associated. If a local board of education elects to participate in the retirement system separately, the local board of education shall designate, by resolution, which city or the county shall accept financial responsibility for the liabilities associated with participation. The city or county that accepts the financial responsibility for the local board of education's participation in the retirement system, through its chief legislative body, governing body or authorizing body shall, by resolution, authorize and approve the local board of education's participation and shall demonstrate the city or county's acceptance of the liability associated with that participation. A political subdivision may elect to participate in the retirement system without extending coverage to the employees of the local board of education that is associated with the participating political subdivision. In the event that a political subdivision withdraws its participation from the retirement system, the political subdivision may allow the local board of education, which is a part of the political subdivision, to continue its participation in the retirement system separately.

8-35-201 SECTION 8. Tennessee Code Annotated, Section 8-35-201, is amended by adding a new, appropriately designated subsection as follows:

(_) All political subdivisions that participate in or desire to participate in the retirement system shall have a governing body and shall meet all applicable state and federal law requirements that are necessary for the retirement system to maintain its status as a qualified plan under the Internal Revenue Code

8-35-218 SECTION 9. Tennessee Code Annotated, Section 8-35-218(a), is amended by adding the following language as a new, appropriately designated subdivision:

(_) A political subdivision that withdraws its participation from the retirement system and elects to participate in the state's deferred compensation plan pursuant to § 8-25-111, shall not be subject to the one (1) year's advance notice requirement in this section; instead, the political subdivision shall give the board of trustees at least six (6) months advance written notice of the effective date of the withdrawal. The political subdivision shall submit a withdrawal resolution, legally adopted by two-thirds (2/3) of the membership of the chief legislative body of the political subdivision, at least six (6) months in advance of the political subdivision's effective date of the withdrawal, which shall be submitted on the first day of any quarter following the six (6) months' minimum notice requirement. Such resolution to withdraw may be rescinded and withdrawn by a resolution legally adopted and approved by the chief legislative body of the political subdivision at any time prior to the expiration of the six (6) month notice period.

8-35-226 SECTION 10. Tennessee Code Annotated, Section 8-35-226(c), is amended by deleting the second sentence in the subsection in its entirety and by substituting instead with the following:

In no event shall the benefit payable on such service be less than that provided under § 8-36-209(a)(1)(A), (a)(1)(B), (a)(2)(A)(i) or (a)(2)(A)(ii), depending upon which option is exercised by the chief legislative body.

8-35-227
8-35-229
8-35-233 SECTION 11. Tennessee Code Annotated, Sections 8-35-227, 8-35-229 and 8-35-233, are amended by deleting them in their entirety.

8-35-253 SECTION 12. Tennessee Code Annotated, Section 8-35-253(f), is amended by adding the language "for employees hired on or after the effective date of this act", after the word "prospectively" in the second sentence in this subsection.

8-35-255 SECTION 13. Tennessee Code Annotated, Section 8-35-255(d), is amended by deleting the language "twenty (20) years" and substituting instead the language "five (5) years".

8-35-256 SECTION 14. Tennessee Code Annotated, Section 8-35-256(d), is amended by deleting the language "twenty (20) years" and substituting instead the language "five (5) years".

8-35-319 SECTION 15. Tennessee Code Annotated, Title 8, Chapter 35, Part 3, is amended by adding the following language as a new, appropriately designated section:

8-35-3___.

Notwithstanding any provision of this chapter to the contrary, no entity shall be eligible to participate in the retirement system if the chair of the Tennessee consolidated retirement system determines, in the chair's sole discretion, that the entity's participation could have a potentially adverse effect on the retirement system's status as a qualified plan under the Internal Revenue Code, codified in U.S.C. title 26, and regulations. In making such determination, the chair may rely on the advice of a nationally recognized counsel in the area of government employee benefit plans.

8-36-128 SECTION 16. Tennessee Code Annotated, Title 8, Chapter 36, Part 1, is amended by adding a new, appropriately designated section as follows:

8-36-1___.

The retirement system shall honor claims under a qualified domestic relations order at a time designated by the state treasurer. For purposes of this section, "qualified domestic relations order" has the same meaning as provided in §414(p) of the Internal Revenue Code of 1986, codified in 26 U.S.C. §414(p); provided, that such order may only relate to the provision of marital property rights relating to the retirement system for the benefit of the retirement system member's former spouse.

8-36-601 SECTION 17. Tennessee Code Annotated, Section 8-36-101, is amended by deleting the language contained in this section and inserting it in Section 8-36-601 as new subsections (c) and (d).

8-36-116 SECTION 18. Tennessee Code Annotated, Section 8-36-116, is amended by adding a new subsection (6) as follows:

(6) In the event that a retired member receives an overpayment in retirement benefits from the retirement system and that member returns to service, the retirement system may initiate an automatic payroll deduction to recoup the overpaid amount. The employer shall comply with the retirement system's request for an automatic payroll deduction.

8-36-213 SECTION 19. Tennessee Code Annotated, Title 8, Chapter 36, Part 2, is amended by adding the following language as a new, appropriately designated section:

8-36-2___.

(a) Notwithstanding any provision of the law to the contrary, no benefit shall be paid to a member from the retirement system in excess of benefit limitations established in 26 U.S.C. §415 and applicable federal rules and regulations.

(b) The board may establish a separate qualified excess benefit arrangement ("QEBA") pursuant to 26 U.S.C. §415(m) solely for the purpose of providing eligible members with retirement system benefits that are in excess of the benefit limits established in 26 U.S.C. §415. For purposes of this section, "eligible member" means any person included in the membership of the retirement system as provided in chapter 35, part 1 of this title who is entitled to receive a retirement benefit in excess of the limits imposed by 26 U.S.C. §415.

(c) The board shall have the authority to adopt a plan document and a trust agreement as well as administer, maintain, modify, terminate or reestablish the QEBA, and may, in its discretion, delegate its authority to the state treasurer.

(d) On or after the date that the QEBA is established, the retirement system shall pay from the QEBA to each eligible member or beneficiary a supplemental retirement allowance equal to the difference between the eligible member's monthly benefit otherwise payable from the applicable retirement system prior to any reduction or limitation because of 26 U.S.C. §415 and the actual monthly benefit payable from the retirement system as limited by 26 U.S.C. §415. The retirement system shall compute and pay the supplemental retirement allowance in the same form, at the same time, and to the same persons as such benefits would have otherwise been paid as a monthly pension under the retirement system except for 26 U.S.C. §415 limitations.

(e) The retirement system shall determine the amount of an eligible member's benefits that cannot be provided to the member or beneficiary because of limitations established by 26 U.S.C. §415, and the amount of employer contributions that must be made to the QEBA as a separate fund, separate and apart from the retirement system, for each eligible member whose retirement allowance would exceed federal law limitations. The retirement system shall engage actuarial services required to make these determinations.

(f) The eligible member's employer shall pay the excess benefits for an eligible member to the separate QEBA fund when the retirement system makes the assessment that the member's retirement allowance would exceed federal law limitations established by 26 U.S.C. §415. An employer's contribution to the QEBA shall be a separate contribution from the employer contributions made pursuant to chapter 35 of this title.

(g) Payments under a QEBA are exempt from garnishment, assignment, alienation, judgments, and other legal processes to the same extent as the retirement allowance under the retirement system.

(h) An eligible member shall not elect to defer the receipt of all or any part of the payments due under a QEBA.

(i) The board shall have the authority to promulgate rules as may be necessary to implement a QEBA plan as provided in this section.

8-36-204 SECTION 20. Tennessee Code Annotated, Section 8-36-204(b)(2), is amended by adding the following language after the first sentence in the subdivision:

Subsequent to an employer's election to decrease the required years of service from ten (10) to five (5) years, the employer, through a resolution passed by the employer's chief governing body, may then increase the required years of service from five (5) to ten (10) for employees hired on or after the increase in the years of service, without any limit to the number of increases or decreases that an employer may make by resolution from its chief governing body; provided that, any increases in the number of required years of service shall be applied prospectively for employees hired on or after the increase in the years of service.

8-36-801 SECTION 21. Tennessee Code Annotated, Section 8-36-801(a), is amended by deleting the language in the subsection in its entirety and substituting instead the following:

(a) Except as provided in this part, any retired member of the Tennessee consolidated retirement system, or of any superseded system, or of any local retirement fund established pursuant to chapter 35, part 3 of this title who accepts employment in a position covered by the Tennessee consolidated retirement system shall, as a condition of such employment, cease to draw the member's retirement allowance during the period of the employment; however, the member shall keep his or her retirement benefit in the month that he or she returns to work.

8-36-801 SECTION 22. Tennessee Code Annotated, Section 8-36-801(b), is amended by deleting the third sentence thereof in its entirety and by substituting it instead with the following:

Any retiree restored to employment who reenrolls as an active member of the retirement system shall be treated as voiding any optional benefit previously elected under § 8-36-601 for purposes of in-service death benefits.

8-36-804 SECTION 23. Tennessee Code Annotated, Section 8-36-804, is amended by deleting this section in its entirety and by substituting instead the following:

No member shall be entitled to establish retirement credit for any period during which the member received a retirement allowance; however, should a member return to a position covered by the retirement system, the member shall be able to obtain retirement credit for the month in which he or she returns to work even though the member shall keep his or her retirement benefit in the month that the member returns to work as provided in § 8-36-801(a).

8-37-108 SECTION 24. Tennessee Code Annotated, Section 8-37-108, is amended by adding a new subsection (d) and renumbering the subsequent subsections accordingly:

(d) The council shall annually elect a chair and vice chair from its membership.

8-37-220 SECTION 25. Tennessee Code Annotated, Section 8-37-220(a), is amended by deleting this subsection in its entirety and by substituting instead the following:

(a) Subject to the conditions set forth in this section, the board of trustees may promulgate substantive and procedural rules to permit members, including retired members, to establish the retirement credit authorized in chapters 34-37 of this title through equal monthly installments over a period not to exceed five (5) years from the date the first monthly installment payment is due and payable. Any rules promulgated under this section shall set forth the date on which the retirement system may begin accepting monthly installment payments pursuant hereto. Nothing in this section shall be construed to allow a member or retired member to establish retirement credit unless such member otherwise meets all the eligibility requirements to establish the credit.

8-37-220 SECTION 26. Tennessee Code Annotated, Section 8-37-220(c), is amended by deleting the second sentence in the subsection and by substituting instead the following:

Each installment shall be due and payable on the first business day of each calendar month during the payment period or on a date designated by the member. If a member does not designate a date, then the date that each installment shall be due and payable will default to the first business day of each calendar month during the payment period.

49-7-205 SECTION 27. Tennessee Code Annotated, Section 49-7-205(d), is amended by deleting subdivisions (d)(1) and (d)(2) in their entirety.

Effective date 4/29/2013

SECTION 28. This act shall take effect immediately upon becoming a law, the public welfare requiring it.

PUBLIC CHAPTER NO. 297

PUBLIC CHAPTER NO. 297

SENATE BILL NO. 1000

By McNally, Finney, Ford

Substituted for: House Bill No. 62

By Hawk

AN ACT to amend Tennessee Code Annotated, Title 67, to assure equitable taxation of green energy production facilities.

BE IT ENACTED BY THE GENERAL ASSEMBLY OF THE STATE OF TENNESSEE:

67-5-601 SECTION 1. Tennessee Code Annotated, Section 67-5-601, is amended by deleting subsection (e) and substituting instead the following:

(e)(1) The general assembly finds that any property that generates electricity using green sources such as geothermal, hydrogen, solar or wind, is generally capable of producing less electricity than conventional sources due to uncertain or intermittent energy sources or other factors, that net operating income will be affected by unusual cost and market conditions, and that the commercially competitive disadvantage of these green energy source properties evidences that their sound, intrinsic and immediate value is significantly less than their total installed costs. The general assembly further finds that unless these circumstances are considered in the determination of value for tax purposes under this chapter, investment in property to generate electricity from green sources will be unreasonably discouraged, denying the citizens of Tennessee the environmental benefits associated with the greater use of these domestic renewable energy sources for power generation.

(2) Based on the foregoing findings, the sound, intrinsic and immediate value of green energy source property should not initially exceed a percentage of total installed costs equal to the ratio of projected electricity output over a period of one (1) year to the maximum capacity of the property, as follows:

(i) The sound, intrinsic and immediate value of wind source property should not initially exceed one-third (1/3) of total installed costs;

(ii) The sound, intrinsic and immediate value of solar source property should not initially exceed twelve and one-half percent (12.5%) of total installed costs; and

(iii) The sound, intrinsic and immediate value of other green source property should not initially exceed its appropriate capacity factor as determined by the state board of equalization in consultation with the department of environment and conservation.

(3) The assessor of property, or the comptroller of the treasury, in the case of public utility property, shall take the foregoing findings into account in determining the sound, intrinsic and immediate value of green source property when the property is initially appraised and each time the property is reappraised. A copy of the green energy production facility certification issued by the department of environment and conservation, or filing of a schedule or statement pursuant to § 67-5-1303, effective as of January 1 of the year for which valuation under this subsection is claimed, shall be required and shall be provided by the property owner to the comptroller's office by March 1 of the first year for which valuation under this subsection is claimed. The department of environment and conservation shall report each month to the comptroller a listing of certifications approved in the preceding month, and shall provide copies of certification records to the comptroller on request. On or before the scheduled reappraisal in each county, the comptroller shall advise the assessor of known locations of certified or other green energy property and whether the property is assessable locally or centrally.

67-5-604 SECTION 2. Tennessee Code Annotated, Section 67-5-604, is amended by deleting subsection (d) in its entirety.

Effective date 4/29/2013 SECTION 3. This act shall take effect upon becoming law, the public welfare requiring it, and shall apply retroactively for tax year 2013.

PUBLIC CHAPTER NO. 298

PUBLIC CHAPTER NO. 298

SENATE BILL NO. 923

By Johnson, Burks

Substituted for: House Bill No. 1303

By Littleton, Durham, Moody, Casada, Farmer, Hardaway, Evans, Holt

AN ACT to amend Tennessee Code Annotated, Title 36 and Title 39, relative to termination of parental rights.

BE IT ENACTED BY THE GENERAL ASSEMBLY OF THE STATE OF TENNESSEE:

36-1-113 SECTION 1. Tennessee Code Annotated, Section 36-1-113(g), is amended by deleting subdivision (10) in its entirety and substituting instead the following:

(10)(A) The parent has been convicted of aggravated rape pursuant to § 39-13-502, rape pursuant to § 39-13-503, or rape of a child pursuant to § 39-13-522, from which crime the child was conceived. A certified copy of the conviction suffices to prove this ground.

(B) When one (1) of the child's parents has been convicted of one (1) of the offenses specified in subdivision (g)(10)(A), the child's other parent shall have standing to file a petition to terminate the parental rights of the convicted parent. Nothing in this section shall give a parent standing to file a petition to terminate parental rights based on grounds other than those listed in this subdivision (g)(10).

Effective date 4/29/2013 SECTION 2. This act shall take effect upon becoming a law, the public welfare requiring it.

PUBLIC CHAPTER NO. 299

PUBLIC CHAPTER NO. 299

SENATE BILL NO. 806

By Finney, Henry, Beavers, Bowling, Burks, Campfield, Johnson, Kyle, Massey

Substituted for: House Bill No. 718

By Powell, Mitchell, Curtiss, Love, Swann, Eldridge, Moody, Hardaway, Stewart, Evans, Armstrong, Harry Brooks, Kane, Haynes, Camper, Halford

AN ACT to amend Tennessee Code Annotated, Title 4, Chapter 3, Part 7, relative to promoting certain goods and products.

BE IT ENACTED BY THE GENERAL ASSEMBLY OF THE STATE OF TENNESSEE:

4-3-738 SECTION 1. Tennessee Code Annotated, Title 4, Chapter 3, Part 7, is amended by adding the following language as a new section:

(a) This section shall be known and may be cited as the "Made in Tennessee Act".

(b) The purpose of this section is to create a pilot project that will terminate January 1, 2016, unless extended by the general assembly, to encourage producers and promotion of non-agricultural products made in this state.

(c) The University of Tennessee Center for Industrial Services may:

(1) Use a logo or seal for "Made in Tennessee" products and goods, except for food and agricultural products, that have been substantially processed, fabricated, manufactured or otherwise transformed in this state; and

(2) Take appropriate steps to protect the logo or seal from misuse or infringement as deemed necessary by the center.

(d) Prior to use of the logo or seal, a producer or retailer shall register with the center and comply with all terms, conditions and requirements for use of the logo or seal as determined by the center. A list of all producers and retailers registered with the center may be made available on the center's website.

(e) The center may deny, suspend or revoke a producer or retailer's registration and the ability to use the logo or seal if the producer or retailer fails to comply with the terms, conditions and requirements promulgated by the center.

(f) The department may provide technical assistance to the center upon request.

(g) The center may seek any available grants and other sources of funding to implement and administer the pilot program described in this section.

(h) The center shall report on the pilot project to the commerce and labor committee of the senate and the business and utilities committee of the house of representatives no later than February 1, 2015, and annually thereafter if the pilot project is extended by the general assembly.

(i) As used in this section, unless the context requires otherwise:

(1) "Agricultural products" means horticultural, poultry, dairy and farm products, livestock and livestock products, harvested trees, nursery stock and nursery products;

(2) "Center" means the University of Tennessee Center for Industrial Services;

(3) "Department" means the department of economic and community development;

(4) "Producer" means any individual or legal entity engaged in the processing, fabrication, manufacture or other transformation of goods or products, other than food and agricultural products, in this state; and

PUBLIC CHAPTER NO. 299 (cont'd)

(5) "Retailer" means any individual or legal entity engaged in the business of making sales of a producer's goods or products to the public.

Effective date 4/29/2013

SECTION 2. This act shall take effect upon becoming a law, the public welfare requiring it.

PUBLIC CHAPTER NO. 300

PUBLIC CHAPTER NO. 300

SENATE BILL NO. 789

By Haile; Mr. Speaker Ramsey; Bowling, Burks, Crowe

Substituted for: House Bill No. 645

By Lamberth, Dean, Hardaway

AN ACT to amend Tennessee Code Annotated, Title 4; Title 8; Title 16; Title 29; Title 33; Title 38; Title 39; Title 40; Title 49; Title 54; Title 55 and Title 65, relative to firearm ownership by mental health patients.

BE IT ENACTED BY THE GENERAL ASSEMBLY OF THE STATE OF TENNESSEE:

16-1-117 SECTION 1. Tennessee Code Annotated, Section 16-1-117(a), is amended by adding the following new subdivision:

(6)(A) The clerks of those courts wherein commitments to a mental institution, as defined in § 16-10-213, are ordered or persons are adjudicated as a mental defective, as defined in § 16-10-213, shall report information described in § 16-10-213(c) regarding individuals who have been adjudicated as a mental defective or judicially committed to a mental institution. Included in the report pursuant to this subdivision (a)(6)(A) shall be the date in which such information was also reported to the federal bureau of investigation-NICS Index.

(B) The clerks of those courts unable to make direct reports to the federal bureau of investigation-NICS Index, pursuant to the reporting requirements of §§ 16-10-213, 16-11-206, 16-15-303 and 16-16-120, shall provide sufficient information to the administrative office of the courts who shall make such reports on behalf of those clerks as soon as practicable, but no later than the third business day following the date of receipt of signed order.

(C) The information reported pursuant to subdivision (a)(6)(A) shall be maintained as confidential and not subject to public inspection, except for such use as may be necessary in the conduct of any proceedings pursuant to §§ 39-17-1316, 39-17-1353 and 39-17-1354.

(D) The administrative office of the courts shall provide written notification to any responsible party found not to be in compliance with the reporting requirements of this subdivision (a)(6) or with the reporting requirements of §§ 16-10-213, 16-11-206, 16-15-303 and 16-16-120. If compliance is not achieved during the subsequent reporting period following notification, the administrative office of the courts will no longer accept data from the office not in compliance. Notification of this action will be sent to all judges, district attorneys general, district public defenders and court clerks within the district where the noncomplying office is located. Notification will also be sent to the district attorneys general conference, the district public defenders conference, the administrative office of the courts and the county officials association of Tennessee. Any periods of noncompliance will also be reported in the annual report to the chair of the senate judiciary committee and the chair of the house of representatives civil justice committee.

16-3-812 SECTION 2. Tennessee Code Annotated, Section 16-3-812, is amended by deleting it in its entirety and substituting instead the following:

(a) The administrative office of the courts (AOC) shall be responsible for making available to the Tennessee bureau of investigation in a mutually agreeable form all information the AOC receives from the various courts regarding disposition of cases.

(b) The administrative office of the courts (AOC) shall be responsible for making available, upon request, to the Tennessee bureau of investigation in a mutually agreeable form all information the AOC receives from the various courts regarding compliance with the reporting requirements of §§ 16-10-213, 16-11-206, 16-15-303, 16-16-120 and reports made by the AOC pursuant to § 16-1-117(a)(6)(B) for purposes of auditing compliance and accuracy of the required reports.

16-10-213 SECTION 3. Tennessee Code Annotated, Section 16-10-213(b), is amended by deleting the following language:

January 1, April 1, July 1, and October 1 of every year beginning January 1, 2010

and by substituting instead the following language:

as soon as practicable, but no later than the third business day following the date of such an order or adjudication

16-11-206 SECTION 4. Tennessee Code Annotated, Section 16-11-206(b), is amended by deleting the following language:

January 1, April 1, July 1, and October 1 of every year beginning January 1, 2010

and by substituting instead the following language:

as soon as practicable, but no later than the third business day following the date of such an order or adjudication

16-15-303 SECTION 5. Tennessee Code Annotated, Section 16-15-303(g)(2), is amended by deleting the following language:

January 1, April 1, July 1, and October 1 of every year beginning January 1, 2010

and by substituting instead the following language:

as soon as practicable, but no later than the third business day following the date of such an order or adjudication

16-16-120 SECTION 6. Tennessee Code Annotated, Section 16-16-120(b), is amended by deleting the following language:

January 1, April 1, July 1, and October 1 of every year beginning January 1, 2010

and by substituting instead the following language:

as soon as practicable, but no later than the third business day following the date of such an order or adjudication

33-3-115 SECTION 7. Tennessee Code Annotated, Section 33-3-115(a), is amended by deleting the language "39-17-1352 and" and by substituting instead the language "39-17-1352, 16-1-117(a)(6) and".

33-3-117 SECTION 8. Tennessee Code Annotated, Title 33, Chapter 3, Part 1, is amended by adding the following new section thereto:

33-3-117.

(a) If a service recipient is involuntarily committed to an inpatient treatment facility under this title, the inpatient treatment facility shall report the service recipient to local law enforcement as soon as practicable, but no later than the third business day following the date of such commitment, who shall report the service recipient to the federal bureau of investigation-NICS Index and the department of safety as soon as practicable, but no later than the third business day following the date of receiving such notification, for the purposes of complying with the NICS Improvement Amendments Act of 2007, Public Law 110-180, as enacted and as may be amended in the future.

(b) If an inpatient treatment facility is required to report pursuant to subsection (a), the facility shall report the following information:

(1) Complete name of the person involuntarily committed;

(2) Date involuntary commitment was ordered;

(3) Private or state hospital or treatment resource to which the individual was involuntarily committed; and

(4) Date of birth of the person involuntarily committed.

(c) The information in subdivisions (b)(1)-(4), the confidentiality of which is protected by other statutes or regulations, shall be maintained as confidential and not subject to public inspection pursuant to such statutes or regulations, except for such use as may be necessary in the conduct of any proceedings pursuant to §§ 39-17-1316, 39-17-1353 and 39-17-1354.

33-3-210 SECTION 9. Tennessee Code Annotated, Title 33, Chapter 3, Part 2, is amended by adding the following new section thereto:

33-3-210.

(a) If a service recipient has communicated to a qualified mental health professional or behavior analyst an actual threat of serious bodily harm or death against a reasonably identifiable victim or victims, the qualified mental health professional or behavior analyst, using the reasonable skill, knowledge, and care ordinarily possessed and exercised by the professional's specialty under similar circumstances, who has determined or reasonably should have determined that the service recipient has the apparent ability to commit such an act and is likely to carry out the threat unless prevented from doing so, shall immediately report the service recipient to local law enforcement, who shall take appropriate action based upon the information reported.

(b) If a mental health professional or behavior analyst is required to report pursuant to subsection (a), the professional or analyst shall report the following information:

(1) Complete name and all aliases of the service recipient;

(2) Name of the mental health professional or behavior analyst and name of private or state hospital or treatment resource from which the individual may be receiving services; and

(3) Date of birth of the service recipient.

(c) The information in subdivisions (b)(1)-(3), the confidentiality of which is protected by other statutes or regulations, shall be maintained as confidential and not subject to public inspection pursuant to such statutes or regulations, except for such use as may be necessary in the conduct of any proceedings pursuant to §§ 39-17-1316, 39-17-1353 and 39-17-1354.

33-3-209 SECTION 10. Tennessee Code Annotated, Section 33-3-209, is amended by deleting the language "§ 33-3-206 or § 33-3-208" and substituting instead the language "§§ 33-3-206, 33-3-208, or 33-3-210".

Effective date 7/1/2013 SECTION 11. This act shall take effect July 1, 2013, the public welfare requiring it.

PUBLIC CHAPTER NO. 301

PUBLIC CHAPTER NO. 301

SENATE BILL NO. 663

By Gresham

Substituted for: House Bill No. 449

By Dunn, Wirgau, Hardaway, Holt, Eldridge, Powers

AN ACT to amend Tennessee Code Annotated, Title 49, Chapter 2, Part 2 and Title 49, Chapter 5, Part 4, relative to employment of school personnel.

BE IT ENACTED BY THE GENERAL ASSEMBLY OF THE STATE OF TENNESSEE:

49-2-202 SECTION 1. Tennessee Code Annotated, Section 49-2-202(a), is amended by adding the following language as a new subdivision (3) and by renumbering the subsequent subdivisions accordingly:

(3)(i) Each member of the board of education who has a relative employed by the board shall declare such relationship prior to voting on any matter of business that shall have an effect upon the employment of the relative. In making the declaration, such board member shall certify that the vote that is about to be cast on the pending matter is in the best interest of the school system. Such matters shall include, but shall not be limited to, the school system annual budget, tenure considerations and personnel policies. The director of schools shall give notice to the board each time there is intent to employ a relative of a school board member. The director of schools of a county school system shall also give notice to the county school board each time there is intent to employ a relative of an elected county official. The director of schools of a city school system shall also give notice to the city school board each time there is intent to employ a relative of an elected city official. In giving such notice, the director of schools shall certify that the prospective employee is duly qualified by training and licensure to occupy the position.

(ii) As used in this subdivision (3), unless the context otherwise requires, "relative" means a spouse, parent, parent-in-law, child, son-in-law, daughter-in-law, grandparent, grandchild, brother, sister, uncle, aunt, nephew, niece, or any person who resides in the same household as any of the officials referenced in subdivision (3)(i).

(iii) The provisions of this subdivision (3) shall not be construed to prohibit two (2) or more relatives from working for the LEA. If two (2) or more employees who are relatives are within the same direct line of supervision, or become within the same direct line of supervision by marriage or promotion, then the director of schools shall attempt to resolve this issue by transfer of one (1) of the employees. If the director finds that transfer is not feasible or is not in the best interest of students, then an alternate evaluation plan shall be devised for one (1) of the employees.

Effective date 7/1/2013 SECTION 2. This act shall take effect July 1, 2013, the public welfare requiring it.

PUBLIC CHAPTER NO. 302

PUBLIC CHAPTER NO. 302

SENATE BILL NO. 661

By Massey

Substituted for: House Bill No. 558

By Harrison

AN ACT to amend Tennessee Code Annotated, Title 7, Chapter 53, Part 3, relative to industrial development corporations.

BE IT ENACTED BY THE GENERAL ASSEMBLY OF THE STATE OF TENNESSEE:

7-53-305 SECTION 1. Tennessee Code Annotated, Section 7-53-305, is amended by adding the following language as a new subsection:

( ) Notwithstanding this section or any other law to the contrary, an industrial development corporation organized solely by a municipality that does not impose a real property tax may only enter into a payment in lieu of ad valorem tax agreement or lease if:

(1) The county in which the municipality is located has approved the entering into a payment in lieu of ad valorem tax agreement or lease with respect to the property at issue; or

(2) Either the industrial development corporation or the municipality which organized the industrial development corporation agrees to pay to the county in which the municipality is located an amount equal to the amount of real property tax that would have been assessed to the property at issue for each year in which the payment in lieu of ad valorem tax agreement or lease is effective were the property not owned by the industrial development corporation during such time period.

Effective date 4/29/2013 SECTION 2. This act shall take effect upon becoming a law, the public welfare requiring it.

PUBLIC CHAPTER NO. 303

PUBLIC CHAPTER NO. 303

SENATE BILL NO. 652

By Niceley, Ford, Crowe

Substituted for: House Bill No. 1238

By Tidwell, Hardaway

AN ACT to amend Tennessee Code Annotated, Title 55, Chapter 4, relative to special license plates.

BE IT ENACTED BY THE GENERAL ASSEMBLY OF THE STATE OF TENNESSEE:

55-4-202 SECTION 1. Tennessee Code Annotated, Section 55-4-202(c)(7), is amended by adding the following as a new, appropriately designated subdivision:

( ) Native American Indian Association;

55-4-230 SECTION 2. Tennessee Code Annotated, Title 55, Chapter 4, is amended by adding the following as a new, appropriately designated section:

55-4-___.

(a) An owner or lessee of a motor vehicle who is a resident of this state upon complying with state motor vehicle laws relating to registration and licensing of motor vehicles and paying the regular fee applicable to the motor vehicle and the fee provided in § 55-4-203, shall be issued a Native American Indian Association new specialty earmarked license plate for a motor vehicle authorized by § 55-4-210(c).

(b) The new specialty earmarked license plates shall be of an appropriate design representative of the Native American Indian Association of Tennessee, Inc. The plates shall be designed in consultation with the Native American Indian Association of Tennessee, Inc.

(c) The funds produced from the sale of the Native American Indian Association new specialty earmarked license plates shall be allocated to the Native American Indian Association of Tennessee, Inc., in accordance with § 55-4-215. The funds shall be used exclusively for the association's emergency assistance and education program, which provides services to American Indians in Tennessee, including emergency assistance, educational services, job training, and health services in times of crisis.

Effective date 4/29/2013 SECTION 3. This act shall take effect upon becoming a law, the public welfare requiring it.

PUBLIC CHAPTER NO. 304

PUBLIC CHAPTER NO. 304

SENATE BILL NO. 640

By Tracy

Substituted for: House Bill No. 285

By Forgety, Hardaway

AN ACT to amend Tennessee Code Annotated, Title 49, Chapter 6, Part 30, relative to remediation and truancy.

BE IT ENACTED BY THE GENERAL ASSEMBLY OF THE STATE OF TENNESSEE:

49-6-3021 SECTION 1. Tennessee Code Annotated, Section 49-6-3021, is amended by adding the following language as new subsection (c):

(c)(1) The principal of a school shall report promptly to the director of schools, or the director's designated representative, the name of any student required to attend a remedial program who has been absent from the remedial program five (5) times without adequate excuse. The principal shall make the report after the fifth unexcused absence whether the absences have been consecutive or not. The principal shall also report each successive accumulation of five (5) unexcused absences by the student.

(2) If a student's unexcused absences from remedial instruction are reported to the director of schools, or the director's representative, then the director, or the director's representative, shall proceed, pursuant to § 49-6-3007, in the same manner as required for unexcused absences from the regular school day. The appropriate judge having juvenile jurisdiction in the county shall deal with the case in such manner as the judge may determine to be in the best interest of the child, consistent with §§ 37-1-132, 37-1-168 and 37-1-169 and in the event the child is adjudicated to be unruly, the judge may assess a fine of up to fifty dollars ($50.00) or five (5) hours of community service, in the discretion of the judge, against the parents or legal guardians of such student.

(3) This subsection (c) shall only apply to remedial programs that are offered at no cost to the parent; provided, that prior to the LEA requiring the student to attend the remedial program, the LEA commits to provide transportation to those students in the remedial program who qualify for transportation to and from school.

49-6-3009 SECTION 2. Tennessee Code Annotated, Section 49-6-3009, is amended by adding the following language as new subsection (d):

(d) Parents, guardians or other persons having control of a child who is required to attend remedial instruction under § 49-6-3021 commit educational neglect as defined in subsection (a), if the child is truant from the instruction.

Effective date 7/1/2013 SECTION 3. This act shall take effect July 1, 2013, the public welfare requiring it.

PUBLIC CHAPTER NO. 305

PUBLIC CHAPTER NO. 305

SENATE BILL NO. 612

By Yager

Substituted for: House Bill No. 1156

By Dawn White, Hardaway

AN ACT to amend Tennessee Code Annotated, Title 5; Title 6; Title 7 and Title 49, relative to K-12 education funding.

BE IT ENACTED BY THE GENERAL ASSEMBLY OF THE STATE OF TENNESSEE:

49-3-314 SECTION 1. Tennessee Code Annotated, Section 49-3-314(c), is amended by adding the following language as a new subdivision (3):

(3) Notwithstanding any other law to the contrary, if in any fiscal year a local government appropriates funds for education for non-recurring expenditures evidenced by a written agreement with the LEA establishing the non-recurring use of the funds, such funds shall be excluded from this maintenance of local funding requirement and from any apportionment requirement under § 49-3-315(a). Before any such agreement takes effect, it shall be subject to review by the department to ensure the non-recurring nature of the expenditures.

Effective date 4/29/2013 SECTION 2. This act shall take effect upon becoming a law, the public welfare requiring it.

PUBLIC CHAPTER NO. 306

PUBLIC CHAPTER NO. 306

SENATE BILL NO. 531

By Dickerson, McNally, Yager

Substituted for: House Bill No. 647

By Powell, Love, Coley, Jernigan, Casada, Dunn

AN ACT to amend Tennessee Code Annotated, Title 49, Chapter 1, Part 2, relative to the department of education.

BE IT ENACTED BY THE GENERAL ASSEMBLY OF THE STATE OF TENNESSEE:

49-1-211 SECTION 1. Tennessee Code Annotated, Section 49-1-211(a), is amended by adding the following language as new subdivisions:

(14) ACT academic achievement data including the number and percentage of students with a 21 composite score or higher and the number and percentage of students meeting the college readiness benchmark in English, mathematics, reading, and science for each LEA and high school with at least ten (10) students taking the exam. This data shall not contain private or individual student information. The ACT data shall be included on the department's website; provided it is received by the department from ACT.

(15) SAT college-bound seniors district profile for each LEA with at least twenty-five (25) students taking the SAT. This data shall not contain private or individual student information. This data shall be included on the department's website; provided it is received by the department from the college board.

Effective date 7/1/2013 SECTION 2. This act shall take effect July 1, 2013, the public welfare requiring it.

PUBLIC CHAPTER NO. 307

PUBLIC CHAPTER NO. 307

SENATE BILL NO. 525

By Dickerson, Massey

Substituted for: House Bill No. 447

By Matheny, Hardaway

AN ACT to amend Tennessee Code Annotated, Title 49, relative to education.

BE IT ENACTED BY THE GENERAL ASSEMBLY OF THE STATE OF TENNESSEE:

49-7-2004 SECTION 1. Tennessee Code Annotated, Section 49-7-2004(a)(7), is amended by adding the language "auction schools," between the word "as" and the words "barber schools".

Effective date 4/29/2013 SECTION 2. This act shall take effect upon becoming a law, the public welfare requiring it.

PUBLIC CHAPTER NO. 308

PUBLIC CHAPTER NO. 308

SENATE BILL NO. 521

By Bowling, Tracy

Substituted for: House Bill No. 325

By Madam Speaker Harwell, Joe Carr

AN ACT to amend Tennessee Code Annotated, Title 4; Title 54; Title 55 and Section 58-1-601, relative to transportation.

BE IT ENACTED BY THE GENERAL ASSEMBLY OF THE STATE OF TENNESSEE:

54-1-133 SECTION 1. Tennessee Code Annotated, Section 54-1-133, is amended by deleting the language "The department" and by substituting instead the language "The department, subject to appropriation by the general assembly,".

54-5-1003 SECTION 2. Tennessee Code Annotated, Section 54-5-1003, is amended by deleting the section in its entirety.

54-21-110 SECTION 3. Tennessee Code Annotated, Section 54-21-110, is amended by deleting the section in its entirety and by substituting instead the following:

54-21-110. No person shall affix any outdoor advertising on any sign erected under the authority of the department, or on any right-of-way of any state highway.

54-1-401 SECTION 4. Tennessee Code Annotated, Section 54-1-401, is amended by deleting the language "to be known as "Don't Trash Tennessee"".

54-1-402 SECTION 5. Tennessee Code Annotated, Section 54-1-402, is amended by deleting the language ""Don't Trash Tennessee"" and by substituting instead the language "litter prevention and control".

54-1-205 SECTION 6. Tennessee Code Annotated, Section 54-1-205, is amended by deleting the language "the state of Tennessee" and by substituting instead the language "this state when such employee is directly interested as defined in § 12-4-101 in such material or product".

54-3-113 SECTION 7. Tennessee Code Annotated, Section 54-3-113(e), is amended by deleting the subsection in its entirety and by substituting instead the following:

(e) The department shall not develop any tollway project or toll facility project that is not within the pilot program created in this section until after the general assembly has expressly authorized the department to proceed with additional tollway projects and toll facility projects.

54-5-207 SECTION 8. Tennessee Code Annotated, Section 54-5-207, is amended in the first sentence by deleting the word "retarded" and by substituting instead the word "delayed".

54-7-206 SECTION 9. Tennessee Code Annotated, Section 54-7-206, is amended by deleting the section in its entirety and by substituting instead the following:

54-7-206.

(a) Any theft by a chief administrative officer, either directly or indirectly, of county highway or road money shall be punished under § 39-14-105.

(b) If any chief administrative officer charged with the collection, safekeeping, transfer, or disbursement of money or property belonging to the county highway department uses or diverts any part of the money or property by loan, investment, or otherwise, without authority of law, or converts any part of the money or property to the chief administrative officer's own use in any way whatsoever, the chief administrative officer commits embezzlement, and for every act, upon conviction, shall be punished as in the case of larceny, and in addition shall be required to pay to the court an amount equal to the amount embezzled. The amount shall be forwarded by the clerk to the county highway department.

54-11-206 SECTION 10. Tennessee Code Annotated, Section 54-11-206, is amended by deleting the section in its entirety.

54-11-309 SECTION 11. Tennessee Code Annotated, Section 54-11-309, is amended by deleting the section in its entirety and by substituting instead the following:

54-11-309.

(a) Except as otherwise provided in subsection (b), no person shall charge as ferriage on any stream on any highway included in the state highway system or maintained in whole or part by the department of transportation more than the rate fixed as follows:

Automobile and passengers	$2.00
Person, each, on foot	.50
Truck or bus (one (1) ton capacity and under) and driver	2.00
Truck or bus (one (1) ton capacity and over) and driver	4.00
Automobile trailer	1.50
Truck trailer or bus trailer	3.00
Motorcycle and driver	2.00

(b) Upon application submitted to the department requesting a waiver of the maximum rate fixed within subsection (a), the commissioner may fix a maximum rate in excess of that fixed within subsection (a). Any maximum rate fixed by the commissioner pursuant to this subsection (b) shall be promulgated as a rule in accordance with the Uniform Administrative Procedures Act, compiled in title 4, chapter 5. In promulgating any such rule, the commissioner shall give due consideration to:

(1) The public's need for adequate and efficient ferriage service at a reasonable and prudent cost; and

(2) The ferry operator's need of revenues sufficient to enable the operator, using honest, economical, and efficient management, to provide the ferriage services and to earn a reasonable profit.

54-13-101 SECTION 12. Tennessee Code Annotated, Section 54-13-101, is amended by deleting the language "toll bridges, causeways across bottoms, fish traps, milldams, ferries, public roads," and by substituting instead the language "public roads".

54-13-104 SECTION 13. Tennessee Code Annotated, Section 54-13-104, is amended by deleting such section in its entirety.

54-13-201 — 54-13-212 SECTION 14. Tennessee Code Annotated, Title 54, Chapter 13, is amended by deleting Part 2 in its entirety.

54-13-301 — 54-13-321 SECTION 15. Tennessee Code Annotated, Title 54, Chapter 13, is amended by deleting Part 3 in its entirety.

54-16-112 SECTION 16. Tennessee Code Annotated, Section 54-16-112(h), is amended by deleting the subsection in its entirety and by redesignating the remaining subsections accordingly.

58-1-601 SECTION 17. Tennessee Code Annotated, Section 58-1-601(b), is amended by deleting the subsection in its entirety.

4-7-119 55-4-202 SECTION 18.

(1) The Code Commission is directed to delete § 4-7-119 as obsolete.

(2) At each time when the applicable volume of Tennessee Code Annotated is replaced, the Code Commission is requested to delete the language "[Obsolete.]" with reference to sections in parts 2 and 3 of title 55, chapter 4, which have been deemed obsolete by the commission, to delete from the subdivisions of § 55-4-202 the names of license plates deemed obsolete, to delete the language "[Obsolete]" appearing immediately after such names, and to redesignate, alphabetically or numerically, the subdivisions.

4-3-2010 SECTION 19. Tennessee Code Annotated, Section 4-3-2010(c), is amended by deleting the subsection in its entirety and by redesignating the remaining subsection (d) accordingly.

4-3-2305 SECTION 20. Tennessee Code Annotated, Section 4-3-2305(c)(4), is amended by deleting the first sentence in its entirety and by substituting instead the following:

The commissioner shall report in writing the progress of this program to any member of the general assembly upon request.

4-3-2308 SECTION 21. Tennessee Code Annotated, Section 4-3-2308, is amended by deleting the section in its entirety.

4-47-101 — 4-47-105 SECTION 22. Tennessee Code Annotated, Title 4, Chapter 47, is amended by deleting the chapter in its entirety.

54-1-125 SECTION 23. Tennessee Code Annotated, Section 54-1-125, is amended by deleting the section in its entirety.

54-2-201 — 54-2-209 SECTION 24. Tennessee Code Annotated, Title 54, Chapter 2, Part 2, is amended by deleting the part in its entirety.

54-3-113 SECTION 25. Tennessee Code Annotated, Section 54-3-113(c), is amended by deleting the second sentence in its entirety.

54-5-133 SECTION 26. Tennessee Code Annotated, Section 54-5-133, is amended by deleting the section in its entirety and by substituting instead the following:

54-5-133. The commissioner shall adequately eradicate or control, or both, by chemical or other means, noxious weeds growing on state highway rights-of-way whenever areas adjacent to the rights-of-way are determined by the commissioner of agriculture, in accordance with § 43-1-106, to be row crop areas or grassland areas.

54-5-1105 SECTION 27. Tennessee Code Annotated, Section 54-5-1105, is amended by deleting subsection (b) in its entirety.

54-5-1109 SECTION 28. Tennessee Code Annotated, Section 54-5-1109, is amended by deleting the section in its entirety.

54-11-308 SECTION 29. Tennessee Code Annotated, Section 54-11-308(e), is amended by deleting the subsection in its entirety.

54-16-112 SECTION 30. Tennessee Code Annotated, Section 54-16-112, is amended by deleting subsections (i) and (j) in their entirety.

54-17-105 SECTION 31. Tennessee Code Annotated, Section 54-17-105(c), is amended by deleting the first two sentences in their entirety and by substituting instead the following:

The commissioner of transportation shall, in accordance with the rules, regulations, policies and procedures of the state publications committee, prepare a comprehensive statewide scenic highway plan. In the preparation of this plan, the commissioner may consult as necessary with the department of environment and conservation, the department of agriculture, the department of economic and community development, the respective development districts across the state, and the Tennessee historical commission.

54-17-106 SECTION 32. Tennessee Code Annotated, Section 54-17-106, is amended by deleting the section in its entirety.

54-17-107 SECTION 33. Tennessee Code Annotated, Section 54-17-107(d), is amended by deleting the subsection in its entirety.

54-8-101 — 54-8-107 SECTION 34. Tennessee Code Annotated, Title 54, Chapter 8, is amended by deleting the chapter in its entirety.

54-10-103 SECTION 35. Tennessee Code Annotated, Section 54-10-103(a), is amended by deleting the language "at a January session".

54-10-103 SECTION 36. Tennessee Code Annotated, Section 54-10-103(b), is amended by deleting the language "the previous year" and by substituting instead the language "previously".

54-10-108 — 54-10-110 SECTION 37. Tennessee Code Annotated, Title 54, Chapter 10, Part 1, is amended by deleting Sections 54-10-108, 54-10-109 and 54-10-110 in their entirety.

55-12-102 SECTION 38. Tennessee Code Annotated, Section 55-12-102, is amended by deleting subdivision (12) in its entirety and by substituting instead the following:

(12) "Proof of financial responsibility" or "proof of financial security" means:

(A)(i) If proof is required after December 31, 1989, but prior to January 1, 2009, such proof means:

(*a*) A written proof of liability insurance coverage provided by a single limit policy with a limit of not less than sixty thousand dollars ($60,000) applicable to one (1) accident;

(*b*) A split-limit policy with a limit of not less than twenty-five thousand dollars ($25,000) for bodily injury to or death of one (1) person, not less than fifty thousand dollars ($50,000) for bodily injury to or death of two (2) or more persons in any one (1) accident, and not less than ten thousand dollars ($10,000) for damage to property in any one (1) accident;

(*c*) A deposit of cash with the commissioner in the amount of sixty thousand dollars ($60,000); or

(*d*) The execution and filing of a bond with the commissioner in the amount of sixty thousand dollars ($60,000).

(ii) An insured holding a policy that complies with the insurance requirements of the financial responsibility law on December 31, 1989, will not be deemed to be in violation of the law if the policy meets the limits specified in subdivisions (12)(A)(i)(*a*)-(*d*) as of the first renewal after that date;

(B)(i) If proof is required after December 31, 2008, proof means:

(*a*) A written proof of liability insurance coverage provided by a single limit policy with a limit of not less than sixty thousand dollars ($60,000) applicable to one (1) accident;

(*b*) A split-limit policy with a limit of not less than twenty-five thousand dollars ($25,000) for bodily injury to or death of one (1) person, not less than fifty thousand dollars ($50,000) for bodily injury to or death of two (2) or more persons in any one (1) accident, and not less than fifteen thousand dollars ($15,000) for damage to property in any one (1) accident;

(*c*) A deposit of cash with the commissioner in the amount of sixty thousand dollars ($60,000); or

(*d*) The execution and filing of a bond with the commissioner in the amount of sixty thousand dollars ($60,000).

(ii) An insured holding a policy that complies with the insurance requirements of the financial responsibility law on December 31, 2008, will not be deemed to be in violation of the law if the policy meets the limits specified in subdivision (12)(B)(i)(*a*)-(*d*) as of the first renewal after December 31, 2008;

55-9-408 SECTION 39. Tennessee Code Annotated, Section 55-9-408, is amended by deleting the section in its entirety and by substituting instead the following:

55-9-408. Headlights shall be deemed to comply with the provisions of § 55-9-406, prohibiting glaring and dazzling lights, if the headlights are of a type customarily employed by manufacturers of automobiles and in addition are equipped with some anti-glare device; provided, that the anti-glare device, or any combination thereof, when properly adjusted, shall prevent any of the bright portions of the headlight beams from rising above a horizontal plane passing through the lamp centers parallel to a level road upon which the loaded vehicle stands and in no case higher than forty-two inches (42"), seventy-five feet (75') ahead of the vehicle.

55-9-409 SECTION 40. Tennessee Code Annotated, Section 55-9-409(a), is amended by deleting the subsection in its entirety and by substituting instead the following:

PUBLIC CHAPTER NO. 308 (cont'd)

(a) Any member of the highway patrol having reasonable ground to believe that any headlamp or auxiliary driving or fog lamp or any device upon a vehicle emits a glaring light as defined in §§ 55-9-406 and 55-9-408, or otherwise fails to comply with the requirements of this part, may require the driver of the vehicle to stop and submit the lamp to an inspection or test. The officer making the inspection shall require the driver of the vehicle to remove the illegal lamp within twenty-four (24) hours, and may arrest the driver and give the driver a notice to appear, and may further require the driver or the owner of the vehicle to produce in court satisfactory evidence of the removal of the illegal lamp.

55-9-409 SECTION 41. Tennessee Code Annotated, Section 55-9-409(b), is amended by deleting the language "of a type that has been approved by the department".

55-9-411 SECTION 42. Tennessee Code Annotated, Section 55-9-411, is amended by deleting the section in its entirety.

55-9-412 SECTION 43. Tennessee Code Annotated, Section 55-9-412, is amended by deleting the section in its entirety.

55-10-203 SECTION 44. Tennessee Code Annotated, Section 55-10-203(a)(2), is amended by deleting the language "involuntary manslaughter" and by substituting instead the language "criminally negligent homicide".

SECTION 45. If any provision of this act or the application thereof to any person or circumstance is held invalid, such invalidity shall not affect other provisions or applications of the act which can be given effect without the invalid provision or application, and to that end the provisions of this act are declared to be severable.

Effective date 7/1/2013 SECTION 46. This act shall take effect July 1, 2013, the public welfare requiring it.

PUBLIC CHAPTER NO. 309

PUBLIC CHAPTER NO. 309

SENATE BILL NO. 473

By Massey, Finney, Ford, Burks, Campfield

Substituted for: House Bill No. 401

By Haynes, Lundberg

AN ACT to amend Tennessee Code Annotated, Title 34; Title 36 and Title 37, relative to relinquishment of rights involving an embryo.

BE IT ENACTED BY THE GENERAL ASSEMBLY OF THE STATE OF TENNESSEE:

36-2-401 — 36-2-403 SECTION 1. Tennessee Code Annotated, Title 36, Chapter 2, is amended by adding the following as a new part:

36-2-401. This chapter provides a single means to establish parentage of children born of donated embryo transfer to recipient intended parent. It is intended to promote the interests of children who may be born as a result of donated embryo transfer. It is the intent that no adoption pursuant to chapter 1 of this title or no parentage pursuant to chapter 3 of this title shall be required to create parentage in recipient intended parent pursuant to this part.

36-2-402. As used in this part:

(1) "Embryo" or "human embryo" means an individual fertilized ovum of the human species from the single-cell stage to eight-week development;

(2) "Embryo parentage" means the acceptance of rights and responsibilities for an embryo by a recipient intended parent;

(3) "Embryo relinquishment" or "legal transfer of rights to an embryo" means the relinquishment of rights and responsibilities by the person or persons who hold the legal rights and responsibilities for an embryo;

(4) "Embryo transfer" means the medical procedure of physically placing an embryo into the uterus of a female recipient intended parent;

(5) "Legal embryo custodian" means the person or entity, including an embryo transfer clinic, who hold the legal rights and responsibilities for a human embryo and who relinquishes said embryo to another person; and

(6) "Recipient intended parent" means a person or persons who receive a relinquished embryo and who accepts full legal rights and responsibilities for such embryo and any child that may be born as a result of embryo transfer.

36-2-403.

(a)(1) A legal embryo custodian may relinquish all rights and responsibilities for an embryo prior to embryo transfer. A written contract shall be entered into as appropriate when establishing embryo parentage prior to embryo transfer for the legal transfer of rights to an embryo and to any child that may result from the embryo transfer:

(A) Between legal embryo custodians and the embryo transfer clinic; or

(B) Between a legal embryo custodian and each recipient intended parent.

(2) The contract shall be signed, as appropriate, by each legal embryo custodian for such embryo, by the embryo transfer clinic or by each recipient intended parent in the presence of a notary public. Initials or other designations may be used if the individuals desire anonymity.

(b) If the embryo was created using donor gametes, the sperm or oocyte donors who irrevocably relinquished their rights in connection with in vitro fertilization shall not be entitled to any notice of the embryo relinquishment, nor shall their consent to the embryo relinquishment be required.

(c) Upon embryo relinquishment by each legal embryo custodian pursuant to subsection (a), the legal transfer of rights to an embryo shall be considered complete at the time of thawing or to such other time as the parties may agree, and the embryo transfer shall be authorized.

(d) A child born to a recipient intended parent as the result of embryo relinquishment pursuant to subsection (a) shall be presumed to be the legal child of the recipient intended parent; provided, that each legal embryo custodian and each recipient intended parent has entered into a written contract pursuant to this part.

(e) Any and all prior legal embryo custodians whose donation of an embryo has resulted in the birth of a child to a recipient intended parent pursuant to subsection (a) shall have no rights or responsibilities with such child and of the child to them.

Effective date 7/1/2013

SECTION 2. This act shall take effect July 1, 2013, the public welfare requiring it.

PUBLIC CHAPTER NO. 310

PUBLIC CHAPTER NO. 310

SENATE BILL NO. 453

By Summerville, Johnson

Substituted for: House Bill No. 711

By Littleton, Shepard

AN ACT to amend Tennessee Code Annotated, Section 4-24-112, relative to minimum training requirements for firefighters.

BE IT ENACTED BY THE GENERAL ASSEMBLY OF THE STATE OF TENNESSEE:

4-24-112 SECTION 1. Tennessee Code Annotated, Section 4-24-112(g)(1), is amended by deleting the language "43,100" and "43,200".

Effective date 4/29/2013 SECTION 2. This act shall take effect upon becoming a law, the public welfare requiring it.

PUBLIC CHAPTER NO. 311

PUBLIC CHAPTER NO. 311

SENATE BILL NO. 431

By Overbey, Bowling, Ford

Substituted for: House Bill No. 345

By Harrison

AN ACT to amend Tennessee Code Annotated, Title 68 and Title 71, relative to nursing homes.

BE IT ENACTED BY THE GENERAL ASSEMBLY OF THE STATE OF TENNESSEE:

68-11-1609 SECTION 1. Tennessee Code Annotated, Section 68-11-1609(b), is amended by deleting the language "years of July 1, 2011, to June 30, 2012, and July 1, 2012, to June 30, 2013," and by substituting instead the language "year of July 1, 2013, to June 30, 2014,".

68-11-1622 SECTION 2. Tennessee Code Annotated, Section 68-11-1622(a), is amended by deleting the words "years of July 1, 2011, to June 30, 2012, and July 1, 2012, to June 30, 2013," and by substituting instead the language "year of July 1, 2013, to June 30, 2014,".

Effective date 7/1/2013 SECTION 3. This act shall take effect on July 1, 2013, the public welfare requiring it.

PUBLIC CHAPTER NO. 312

PUBLIC CHAPTER NO. 312

SENATE BILL NO. 244

By Tracy, Crowe, Ketron, Bell, Bowling, Campfield, Gresham, Kelsey, Norris, Overbey, Watson

Substituted for: House Bill No. 119

By Weaver, Evans, Womick, Joe Carr, Lamberth, Todd, Kent Williams, Sparks, Lollar, Forgety, Harrison, Mark White, Matlock, Dale Carr, Shipley, Littleton, Lynn, Moody, Timothy Hill, Curtiss, Kevin Brooks, Eldridge, Sexton, Ragan, Durham, Butt, Sanderson, Powers, Travis, Goins, Hall, Carter, Lundberg, Haynes, Dean

AN ACT to amend Tennessee Code Annotated, Title 71, relative to electronic benefit card transactions involving persons receiving certain assistance.

BE IT ENACTED BY THE GENERAL ASSEMBLY OF THE STATE OF TENNESSEE:

71-3-126 SECTION 1. Tennessee Code Annotated, Title 71, Chapter 3, Part 1, is amended by adding the following as a new section:

71-3-126.

(a) For the purposes of this section, the term "public assistance benefits" means money or property provided directly or indirectly to eligible persons through the temporary assistance to needy families program.

(b)(1) A recipient of public assistance benefits shall not knowingly use an electronic benefits transfer card in:

(A) A liquor store as defined in 42 U.S.C. § 608(a)(12)(B)(i);

(B) A casino, gambling casino, or gaming establishment as defined in 42 U.S.C. § 608(a)(12)(B)(ii); or

(C) An adult cabaret as defined in § 7-51-1102.

(2) To the extent permitted by federal law, any person who violates this subsection shall reimburse the department for the purchase;

(c)(1) A person or business entity, or any agent or employee of the person or business entity shall not knowingly accept public assistance benefits from an electronic benefits transfer card for the purchase of any goods or services in:

(A) A liquor store as defined in 42 U.S.C. § 608(a)(12)(B)(i);

(B) A casino, gambling casino, or gaming establishment as defined in 42 U.S.C. § 608(a)(12)(B)(ii); or

(C) An adult cabaret as defined in § 7-51-1102.

(2) Any person or business entity who knowingly violates this subsection shall be subject to the following civil penalties:

(1) One thousand dollars ($1,000) for the first violation.

(2) Twenty-five hundred dollars ($2,500) for the second violation within five (5) years.

(3) Five thousand dollars ($5,000) for a third or a subsequent violation within five (5) years. The district attorney general may bring an action to suspend the business licenses and permits of the person or business entity for one (1) year for any violation under this subsection. The department is authorized to bring an action to enforce any civil penalty under this subsection in a complaint filed in the chancery court of the county where the merchant is located.

(d)(1) A recipient of public assistance benefits shall not knowingly use an electronic benefit transfer card in an automated teller machine or point-of-sale device located in:

(A) A liquor store as defined in 42 U.S.C. § 608(a)(12)(B)(i);

(B) A casino, gambling casino, or gaming establishment as defined in 42 U.S.C. § 608(a)(12)(B)(ii); or

(C) An adult cabaret as defined in § 7-51-1102.

(2) Any person who knowingly violates this subsection shall reimburse the department for the amount withdrawn and used subject to any prohibition in federal law. Upon a third or subsequent violation, if permitted by federal law, the person shall be permanently disqualified from receiving public assistance benefits by means of direct cash payment or an electronic benefits transfer access card.

(e) The department of human services shall establish a system for reviewing electronic benefit transactions of recipients pursuant to this section on such basis as the commissioner may determine, but not less than on a quarterly basis.

(f) A person or entity subject to a penalty or sanction under this section shall have the right to a hearing pursuant to the Uniform Administrative Procedures Act, compiled in title 4, chapter 5.

(g)(1) The commissioner of human services is authorized to promulgate rules and regulations, including emergency rules, to effectuate the purposes of this section. All such rules and regulations shall be promulgated in accordance with the Uniform Administrative Procedures Act, compiled in title 4, chapter 5.

(2) The department shall add by rule to the prohibited use of an electronic benefits transfer card other purchases to the fullest extent later permitted by federal law.

(h) Any revenues deposited or civil fines collected pursuant to subsection (c) shall be deposited into the general fund.

Effective date 7/1/2014

SECTION 2. For rulemaking purposes this act shall take effect on becoming law and for all other purposes this act shall take effect July 1, 2014, the public welfare requiring it.

PUBLIC CHAPTER NO. 313

PUBLIC CHAPTER NO. 313

SENATE BILL NO. 183

By Norris

Substituted for: House Bill No. 177

By McCormick

AN ACT to amend Tennessee Code Annotated, Title 67, Chapter 4, Part 7, relative to business tax.

BE IT ENACTED BY THE GENERAL ASSEMBLY OF THE STATE OF TENNESSEE:

SECTION 1. This act shall be known and may be cited as the "Uniformity and Small Business Relief Act of 2013."

67-4-703 SECTION 2. Tennessee Code Annotated, Section 67-4-703(a), is amended by deleting the first two sentences and by substituting instead the following language:

The commissioner is authorized to collect and administer the taxes levied by this part.

and is further amended by deleting from subsection (c) the language "July 1, 2009, through October 1, 2010," and by substituting instead the language "July 1, 2013, through December 31, 2014,".

67-4-704 SECTION 3. Tennessee Code Annotated, Title 67, Chapter 4, Part 7, is amended by deleting Section 67-4-704 in its entirety and by substituting instead the following:

67-4-704.

(a) Except as otherwise provided in § 67-4-710, the making of sales by engaging in any vocation, occupation, business, or business activity enumerated, described, or referred to in § 67-4-708(1)-(5) is declared to be a privilege upon which a state tax is levied at the rates fixed and provided in § 67-4-709.

(b) Notwithstanding subsection (a) or any other provision to the contrary, the tax provided for in this section shall not be imposed on receipts from sales of any services or tangible personal property made by a provider of direct-to-home satellite television programming services.

67-4-705 SECTION 4. Tennessee Code Annotated, Title 67, Chapter 4, Part 7, is amended by deleting Section 67-4-705 in its entirety and by substituting instead the following:

67-4-705.

(a) The making of sales by engaging in any vocation, occupation, business, or business activity enumerated, described, or referred to in § 67-4-708(1)-(4) is declared to be a privilege upon which each incorporated municipality in which the vocation, occupation, business, or business activity is carried on, by ordinance of its governing body, may levy a privilege tax at the rates fixed and provided in § 67-4-709. The tax imposed by this subsection shall be collected by the commissioner in the same manner as the tax imposed by § 67-4-704.

(b) Notwithstanding subsection (a) or any other provision to the contrary, every incorporated municipality levying such tax as of the effective date of this act, shall be deemed to have made an effective election to continue the imposition of such tax at the same rate that was in effect on such date and shall not be required to pass any additional ordinance. Any incorporated municipality that elects after the effective date of this act, to levy the tax authorized by this section, or elects to change the rate of tax imposed by the municipality, must levy such tax at the rates fixed and provided in § 67-4-709. Every municipality that levies the tax described in subsection (a) is authorized to repeal such tax by ordinance of its governing body.

(c) The making of sales by engaging in any vocation, occupation, business, or business activity enumerated, described, or referred to in § 67-4-710 is declared to be a privilege upon which each county or incorporated municipality, or both, in which the business, business activity, vocation, or occupation is carried on, by ordinance of its governing body, may levy a privilege tax at the rates fixed and provided in § 67-4-710.

(d) Notwithstanding subsection (a) or any other provision to the contrary, no incorporated municipality shall impose the tax provided for in this section on receipts from sales of any services or tangible personal property made by a provider of direct-to-home satellite television programming services.

67-4-706 SECTION 5. Tennessee Code Annotated, Section 67-4-706, is amended by deleting subsection (a) in its entirety and by substituting instead the following:

(a) For purposes of filing the returns required by § 67-4-715 and paying the taxes levied by §§ 67-4-704 and 67-4-705, every person taxable under §§ 67-4-704 and 67-4-705 shall, prior to engaging in business as defined in § 67-4-702, register with the commissioner or the county clerk, in the case of businesses located within the county, and with the commissioner or the appropriate city official, in the case of businesses located within the incorporated municipality. Any person that is subject to the tax levied by § 67-4-704 but has no established physical location, outlet, or other place of business in the state shall register with the commissioner for purposes of this section.

and is further amended by deleting from subsection (c) the language "taxable under §§ 67-4-705 and 67-4-709(5)" and by substituting instead the language "described in § 67-4-708(5) and taxable under § 67-4-709(5)".

67-4-707 SECTION 6. Tennessee Code Annotated, Section 67-4-707, is amended by designating the current language as subsection (a) and by adding the following language as subsection (b):

(b) Notwithstanding subsection (a), any county or municipality may, but shall not be required to, enter an agreement with the commissioner pursuant to which the bond or escrow account required by subsection (a) will be filed with the commissioner rather than the county or municipality.

67-4-708 SECTION 7. Tennessee Code Annotated, Section 67-4-708(1), is amended by deleting from subdivision (B) the language "gasoline and diesel fuel sold at wholesale;" and by adding the following language as a new subdivision (E):

(E) Gasoline and diesel fuel sold at wholesale;

67-4-709 SECTION 8. Tennessee Code Annotated, Section 67-4-709, is amended by deleting the following language:

For the exercise of the privileges described or enumerated in § 67-4-708, persons shall pay a tax, according to the dominant business activity of the persons as follows:

and by substituting instead the following language:

For the exercise of the privileges described, enumerated, or referred to in § 67-4-708, every person shall pay the taxes imposed by §§ 67-4-704 and 67-4-705 according to the dominant business activity of the person as follows:

67-4-709 SECTION 9. Tennessee Code Annotated, Section 67-4-709(1), is amended by adding the following language as a new subdivision (E):

(E) One thirty-second of one percent (1/32 of 1%) of all sales by a wholesaler classified under § 67-4-708(1)(E);

67-4-710 SECTION 10. Tennessee Code Annotated, Section 67-4-710(a), is amended by deleting the following language:

For the exercise of the privileges described or enumerated in this section, persons shall pay a fee directly to the county clerk, in the case of activities carried on within the county, and to the city official designated as the collector of tax by city charter or ordinance, in the case of activities carried on within the municipality:

and by substituting instead the following language:

Any county, by resolution of its county legislative body, or any incorporated municipality, by ordinance of its governing body, is authorized to impose a fee on the exercise of the privileges described or enumerated in this section. Notwithstanding any provision to the contrary, every county and incorporated municipality imposing the fee provided by this section as of the effective date of this act, shall be deemed to have made an effective election to continue the imposition of such fee and shall not be required to pass any additional resolution or ordinance. Persons exercising such privileges shall pay the applicable fee directly to the county clerk, in the case of activities carried on within the county, and to the city official designated as the collector of tax by city charter or ordinance, in the case of activities carried on within the municipality:

67-4-710 SECTION 11. Tennessee Code Annotated, Section 67-4-710, is amended by deleting subsection (b) in its entirety.

67-4-711 SECTION 12. Tennessee Code Annotated, Section 67-4-711(a), is amended by deleting subdivision (6) in its entirety and by substituting instead the following:

(6) Sales of services that are received by customers located outside the state;

67-4-712 SECTION 13. Tennessee Code Annotated, Section 67-4-712, is amended by deleting subsection (d) in its entirety and by substituting instead the following:

(d)(1) Any person having sales of less than ten thousand dollars ($10,000) within a county shall be exempt from the tax and licensing provisions in §§ 67-4-704 and 67-4-723(a) with respect to the sales sourced to that county as provided in § 67-4-717(b).

(2) Any person having sales of less than ten thousand dollars ($10,000) within an incorporated municipality shall be exempt from the tax and licensing provisions in §§ 67-4-705 and 67-4-723(a) with respect to the sales sourced to that municipality as provided in § 67-4-717(c).

(3) Any person subject to the tax imposed by this chapter due to the operation of § 67-4-717(a) and having sales of less than ten thousand dollars ($10,000) within a county shall be exempt from the taxing provision in § 67-4-704 with respect to the sales occurring in that county.

67-4-713 SECTION 14. Tennessee Code Annotated, Section 67-4-713(a)(2)(A), is amended by deleting the language "levied the tax under this part" and by substituting instead the language "receives the allocation of tax under § 67-4-724".

67-4-713 SECTION 15. Tennessee Code Annotated, Section 67-4-713(a)(2), is amended by adding the following as a new subdivision (D):

(D) Notwithstanding subdivision (a)(2)(A), providers of video programming services, as defined in § 67-6-102, shall be allowed the credit provided by this subdivision (a)(2) to the extent that the property is located in a jurisdiction to which the taxpayer's receipts are sourced in accordance with § 67-4-717 and the property is taxed by that jurisdiction;

67-4-714 SECTION 16. Tennessee Code Annotated, Section 67-4-714(a), is amended by inserting the language "per location" between the word "annum" and the word "after" in subdivision (1) and is further amended by inserting the following language between the first and second sentences of subdivision (1):

Any person subject to tax under this part that has no established physical location, outlet, or other place of business in the state shall be subject to a single minimum tax as provided in this subdivision for all activity within the state.

67-4-715 SECTION 17. Tennessee Code Annotated, Section 67-4-715, is amended by deleting from subsection (b) the language "taxes levied by the county" and by substituting instead the language "taxes levied by the state", and is further amended by deleting subsection (g) in its entirety and by substituting instead the following as a new subsection (g):

(g) Notwithstanding any provision of this section to the contrary, the commissioner is authorized to change the tax period established by this part to correspond to the taxpayer's fiscal year and change the due date of the associated tax return to a date that is not less than two (2) calendar months following the end of such tax period. Such change is authorized to occur no sooner than ninety (90) days after the commissioner has certified that a system is in place for the electronic submission of such returns. Such certification shall be accomplished by the commissioner prominently posting a notice on the department's website. The commissioner shall allow the submission of a single, electronic filing that includes all of the information required by the commissioner to determine the amount of tax, if any, that is properly due under this part and allocated to each jurisdiction. Nothing in this subsection (g) shall be construed to either increase or decrease the amount of tax otherwise due under the provisions of this part.

PUBLIC CHAPTER NO. 313 (cont'd)

67-4-717 SECTION 18. Tennessee Code Annotated, Title 67, Chapter 4, Part 7, is amended by adding the following as a new section designated as Section 67-4-717:

67-4-717.

(a) Any person engaged in this state in any vocation, occupation, business, or business activity enumerated, described, or referred to in § 67-4-708(1)-(4) without establishing a physical location, outlet, or other place of business in the state shall be subject to the tax levied by § 67-4-704 and shall be exempt from the tax levied by § 67-4-705. For purposes of this section, the term "engaged in this state" shall be limited to the following activities:

(1) Performing any service in this state, to the extent such service is received by a customer located in the state;

(2) Leasing tangible personal property that is located in this state;

(3) Delivering tangible personal property to a buyer in this state, when delivered by the seller in the seller's own vehicle; and

(4) Purchasing and subsequently selling tangible personal property in this state in a wholly in-state transaction, where the purchase and subsequent sale are accomplished through the presence in this state of the seller's employees, agents, or independent contractors acting on behalf of the seller.

(b)(1) For purposes of distributing the state business tax as provided in § 67-4-724(a), receipts from sales made by a person subject to the tax levied by § 67-4-704 shall be sourced to the county in which the person's established physical location, outlet, or other place of business is located. Receipts from sales made by persons operating from an established physical location, outlet, or other place of business in one county who extend their operations into other counties without establishing a physical location, outlet, or other place of business therein shall be sourced to the county in which the person's established physical location, outlet, or other place of business is located. If the person has no established physical location, outlet, or other place of business in the state, then such receipts shall be sourced to the state and the taxes shall be earmarked and allocated to the state's general fund in accordance with § 67-4-724(a)(5).

(2) Notwithstanding subdivision (b)(1), receipts from all taxable sales of any services or tangible personal property by a provider of video programming services, as defined in § 67-6-102, shall be sourced to the county where the property or service is received by the customer, regardless of whether the provider has a physical location, outlet, or other place of business in that county.

(3) Notwithstanding subdivision (b)(1), compensation of more than fifty thousand dollars ($50,000) from contracts performed in one county by a person described in § 67-4-708(4)(A) shall be sourced to that county as provided in § 67-4-709(4)(A)(i) and the tax on such compensation shall be distributed to that county pursuant to § 67-4-724(a). Compensation of fifty thousand dollars ($50,000) or less from contracts performed in one county by a person described in § 67-4-708(4)(A) shall be sourced to the county of such person's domicile or location. If such person does not have a domicile or location in the state, such compensation shall be earmarked and allocated to the state's general fund in accordance with § 67-4-724(a)(5).

(c)(1) For purposes of levying the tax set forth in § 67-4-705, receipts from sales made by a person subject to the tax levied by § 67-4-705 shall be sourced to the incorporated municipality in which the person's established physical location, outlet, or other place of business is located and shall be subject to the tax, if any, that is levied by such incorporated municipality. Receipts from sales made by persons operating from an established physical location, outlet, or other place of business in one incorporated municipality who extend their operations outside the boundaries of the incorporated municipality that levied the tax without establishing a physical location, outlet, or other place of business outside such incorporated municipality shall be sourced to the incorporated municipality in which the person's established physical location, outlet, or other place of business is located and shall be subject to the tax, if any, that is levied by such incorporated municipality. If the person has no established physical location, outlet, or other place of business in the state, then such receipts shall not be subject to tax under § 67-4-705.

(2) Notwithstanding subdivision (c)(1), receipts from all taxable sales of any services or tangible personal property by a provider of video programming services, as defined in § 67-6-102, shall be sourced to the incorporated municipality where the property or service is received by the customer, regardless of whether the provider has a physical location, outlet, or other place of business in that incorporated municipality.

(3) Notwithstanding subdivision (c)(1), compensation of more than fifty thousand dollars ($50,000) from contracts performed in one incorporated municipality by a person described in § 67-4-708(4)(A) shall be sourced to that incorporated municipality as provided in § 67-4-709(4)(A)(i) and such compensation shall be subject to the tax, if any, that is levied by such incorporated municipality. Compensation of fifty thousand dollars ($50,000) or less from contracts performed in one incorporated municipality by a person described in § 67-4-708(4)(A) shall be sourced to the incorporated municipality of such person's domicile or location; provided, if such person does not have a domicile or location in the state, such compensation shall not be subject to tax under § 67-4-705.

67-4-719 SECTION 19. Tennessee Code Annotated, Section 67-4-719, is amended by deleting the language "levied by a county" from the first sentence of the section and by substituting instead the language "levied by the state".

67-4-723 SECTION 20. Tennessee Code Annotated, Title 67, Chapter 4, Part 7, is amended by deleting Section 67-4-723 in its entirety and by substituting instead the following:

67-4-723.

(a)(1) Upon receipt of the prescribed application and payment of fifteen dollars ($15.00), together with any other information reasonably required, it shall be the duty of the county clerk, in the case of taxpayers located within the county, and the appropriate city official, in the case of taxpayers located within the incorporated municipality, to issue a license to the taxpayer. If a taxpayer has more than one location within the county or incorporated municipality, a separate license, including payment of the fifteen dollar ($15.00) fee required by this subsection, shall be required for each location.

(2) In addition to the initial license issued under subdivision (a)(1), the issuing official shall renew the license upon notification from the department that the taxpayer has filed the return required under § 67-4-715 and remitted the amount shown to be due on the return. There shall be no fee charged for the renewal of a license issued under this subsection.

(3) Each license issued under this subsection shall expire thirty (30) days after the date that the taxpayer's return is due under § 67-4-715.

(4) No person shall conduct business in this state without first acquiring the license required by this subsection.

(5) Notwithstanding subdivisions (a)(1) and (2), any county or municipality may, but shall not be required to, enter an agreement with the commissioner pursuant to which the department will issue or renew, or both, the license required by this subsection on behalf of the county or municipality.

(b)(1) Notwithstanding any provision to the contrary, any incorporated municipality that imposes the tax authorized by § 67-4-705(a) and every county shall issue a minimal activity license to any person that is exempt from taxation and licensing pursuant to § 67-4-712(d), provided that such person has sales of more than three thousand dollars ($3,000) but less than ten thousand dollars ($10,000) per year within the jurisdiction. Such license shall be issued upon receipt of an application, to be prescribed by the department, and payment of fifteen dollars ($15.00). The application shall require the applicant to attest that the applicant is engaged in business within such county or incorporated municipality but has sales of less than ten thousand dollars ($10,000) per year within such county or incorporated municipality. No person with sales of more than three thousand dollars ($3,000) but less than ten thousand dollars ($10,000) per year within such county or incorporated municipality shall conduct business in such county or incorporated municipality without first acquiring the license required by this subsection. If a person has more than one location within the county or incorporated municipality, a separate minimal activity license, including payment of the fifteen dollar ($15.00) fee required by this subsection, shall be required for each location. Every county or incorporated municipality that issues minimal activity licenses pursuant to this subsection shall provide the department, if requested, with the identity of each licensee and any other information reasonably required by the department to verify the licensee's compliance with this part.

(2) Persons with sales of three thousand dollars ($3,000) or less per year in any incorporated municipality or county may, but do not have to, apply for a minimal activity license, as provided for in this subsection (b).

(3) Each minimal activity license issued under this subsection shall expire thirty (30) days after the dates set forth in § 67-4-715 as if the person were filing a return.

(4) This subsection shall not operate to exempt any person from filing a tax return pursuant to § 67-4-715 in the event that the person's sales exceed ten thousand dollars ($10,000) during their tax year as otherwise provided in § 67-4-715.

(5) Notwithstanding subdivision (b)(1), any county or municipality may, but shall not be required to, enter an agreement with the commissioner pursuant to which the department will issue or renew, or both, the license required by this subsection on behalf of the county or municipality.

(c) It shall be the duty of each taxpayer that receives a license under this section to exhibit such license.

(d) An amount equal to three dollars ($3.00) per minimal activity license shall be retained by the county clerk or city official that issues such license. In the case of a county clerk, such amount shall be earmarked for computer hardware purchases or replacement but may be used for other usual and necessary computer-related expenses at the discretion of the county clerk. The amount shall be preserved for these purposes and shall not revert to the general fund at the end of a budget year if unexpended. Notwithstanding § 8-21-701, no additional fee shall be charged to any person for the filing of the application or issuance of the license provided for in this section.

(e) Licenses already in effect as of the effective date of this act continue to be valid until their original renewal date.

67-4-724 SECTION 21. Tennessee Code Annotated, Title 67, Chapter 4, Part 7, is amended by deleting Section 67-4-724 in its entirety and by substituting instead the following:

67-4-724.

(a) The tax levied by the state under § 67-4-704, including any associated interest and penalties, shall be distributed as follows:

(1) An amount equal to seven dollars ($7.00) per return shall be paid to the county clerk with respect to each tax return filed under § 67-4-715 by a taxpayer that is either located within the county or otherwise obtains a license under § 67-4-723(a). Of that amount, three dollars ($3.00) shall be earmarked for computer hardware purchases or replacement, but may be used for other usual and necessary computer-related expenses at the discretion of the county clerk. The amount shall be preserved for these purposes and shall not revert to the general fund at the end of a budget year if unexpended.

(2) After the distribution provided in subdivision (a)(1), an amount equal to five percent (5%) of the remaining proceeds of the tax shall be paid to the county clerk in the case of returns filed under § 67-4-715 by taxpayers located or otherwise licensed under § 67-4-723(a) within the county.

PUBLIC CHAPTER NO. 313 (cont'd)

(3) After the distributions provided in subdivisions (a)(1) and (2), forty-three percent (43%) of the remaining proceeds of the tax shall be earmarked and allocated specifically and exclusively to the state's general fund.

(4) After the distributions provided in subdivisions (a)(1)-(3), an administration fee of one and one hundred twenty-five thousandths percent (1.125%) of the remaining proceeds of the tax shall be allocated to the department to cover the expenses of administration and collection.

(5) After the distributions provided in subdivisions (a)(1)-(4), the remaining proceeds of the tax collected under § 67-4-704 shall be distributed to the county in which the taxpayer has established a physical location, outlet, or other place of business from which the sales are made.

(b) The tax levied by an incorporated municipality under § 67-4-705, including any associated interest and penalties, shall be distributed as follows:

(1) An amount equal to seven dollars ($7.00) per return shall be paid to the appropriate city official with respect to each tax return filed under § 67-4-715 by a taxpayer that is either located within the municipality or otherwise obtains a license under § 67-4-723(a).

(2) After the distribution provided in subdivision (b)(1), an amount equal to five percent (5%) of the remaining proceeds of the tax shall be paid to the appropriate city official in the case of returns filed under § 67-4-715 by taxpayers located or otherwise licensed under § 67-4-723(a) within the municipality.

(3) After the distributions provided in subdivisions (b)(1) and (2), forty-three percent (43%) of the remaining proceeds of the tax shall be earmarked and allocated specifically to a fund held by the state to be used for purposes of the municipality that levied the tax. The fund shall be preserved for these purposes and shall not revert to the general fund at the end of a budget year if unexpended.

(4) After the distributions provided in subdivisions (b)(1)-(3), an administration fee of one and one hundred twenty-five thousandths percent (1.125%) of the remaining proceeds of the tax shall be allocated to the department to cover the expenses of administration and collection.

(5) After the distributions provided in subdivisions (b)(1)-(4), the remaining proceeds of the tax collected by the commissioner under § 67-4-705 shall be distributed to the municipality that levied the tax.

(c) Notwithstanding subsections (a) and (b), one hundred percent (100%) of the tax, interest, and penalty collected from a taxpayer that does not have either a license under § 67-4-723(a) or an established physical location, outlet, or other place of business in any county or incorporated municipality in the state shall be earmarked and allocated specifically and exclusively to the state's general fund. In addition, one hundred percent (100%) of the amount of any tax, interest, and penalty assessed by the commissioner pursuant to § 67-4-704 as a result of an audit of the taxpayer's books and records shall be earmarked and allocated specifically and exclusively to the state's general fund.

(d) The fee levied by a county or incorporated municipality under § 67-4-710, including any associated interest and penalties, shall be retained by the county or incorporated municipality that levied the fee. Notwithstanding the preceding sentence, an amount equal to five percent (5%) of the proceeds of the fee shall be paid to the county clerk, in the case of fees collected under § 67-4-710 by a county, and to the appropriate city official, in the case of fees collected under § 67-4-710 by a municipality.

67-4-725 SECTION 22. Tennessee Code Annotated, Title 67, Chapter 4, Part 7, is amended by deleting Section 67-4-725 in its entirety.

Effective date 1/1/2014 SECTION 23. This act shall take effect on January 1, 2014, the public welfare requiring it, and shall apply to tax periods that begin on or after such date.

PUBLIC CHAPTER NO. 314

PUBLIC CHAPTER NO. 314

SENATE BILL NO. 154

By Norris, Yager, Ketron

Substituted for: House Bill No. 148

By McCormick, Carter, Lamberth, Shipley, Calfee, Butt, Hawk, Faison, Curtiss, Travis, Sexton, Curtis Johnson, Kane, Moody, Hall, Lynn, Durham, Ragan, Goins, Sanderson

AN ACT to amend Tennessee Code Annotated, Title 10 and Title 40, relative to the department of correction.

BE IT ENACTED BY THE GENERAL ASSEMBLY OF THE STATE OF TENNESSEE:

10-7-504 SECTION 1. Tennessee Code Annotated, Section 10-7-504, is amended by deleting the language in subdivision (h)(1) and substituting instead the following:

> (h)(1) Notwithstanding any other law to the contrary, those parts of the record identifying an individual or entity as a person or entity who or that has been or may in the future be directly involved in the process of executing a sentence of death shall be treated as confidential and shall not be open to public inspection. For the purposes of this section "person or entity" includes, but is not limited to, an employee of the state who has training related to direct involvement in the process of executing a sentence of death, a contractor or employee of a contractor, a volunteer who has direct involvement in the process of executing a sentence of death, or a person or entity involved in the procurement or provision of chemicals, equipment, supplies and other items for use in carrying out a sentence of death. Records made confidential by this section include, but are not limited to, records related to remuneration to a person or entity in connection with such person's or entity's participation in or preparation for the execution of a sentence of death. Such payments shall be made in accordance with a memorandum of understanding between the commissioner of correction and the commissioner of finance and administration in a manner that will protect the public identity of the recipients; provided, that, if a contractor is employed to participate in or prepare for the execution of a sentence of death, the amount of the special payment made to such contractor pursuant to the contract shall be reported by the commissioner of correction to the comptroller of the treasury and such amount shall be a public record.

Effective date 4/29/2013 SECTION 2. This act shall take effect upon becoming a law, the public welfare requiring it.

PUBLIC CHAPTER NO. 315

PUBLIC CHAPTER NO. 315

SENATE BILL NO. 135

By Ketron, Bowling

Substituted for: House Bill No. 100

By Matlock

AN ACT to amend Tennessee Code Annotated, Title 5; Title 6; Title 7; Title 8; Title 9; Title 13; Title 18; Title 49; Title 54 and Title 67, relative to official bonds required of certain public officials and public employees.

BE IT ENACTED BY THE GENERAL ASSEMBLY OF THE STATE OF TENNESSEE:

8-19-102 SECTION 1. Tennessee Code Annotated, Section 8-19-102(a), is amended by deleting the subsection in its entirety and substituting instead the following language:

(a) The official bonds of county officials required by law to execute such bonds shall be transmitted to the office of county clerk for safekeeping immediately upon their execution, approval and recordation in the office of the county register of deeds.

8-19-102 SECTION 2. Tennessee Code Annotated, Section 8-19-102(b), is amended by deleting the language "the comptroller of the treasury or" wherever it appears.

8-19-115 SECTION 3. Tennessee Code Annotated, Section 8-19-115, is amended by deleting the language "office of the comptroller of the treasury" wherever it appears and by substituting instead the language "office of the county clerk".

8-11-102 SECTION 4. Tennessee Code Annotated, Section 8-11-102, is amended by deleting the language "comptroller of the treasury" and by substituting instead the language "office of the county clerk".

8-11-103 SECTION 5. Tennessee Code Annotated, Section 8-11-103(b), is amended by deleting the subsection in its entirety and by substituting instead the following:

(b) If the official bond of the county trustee is executed by a surety company authorized to transact business in this state, the minimum amount of the bond shall be based on the revenues as follows:

(1) Four percent (4%) up to three million dollars ($3,000,000) of the funds collected by the office;

(2) Two percent (2%) of the excess over three million dollars ($3,000,000) shall be added; and

(3) The amounts indicated in subdivisions (b)(1)-(2) shall be cumulative.

8-11-103 SECTION 6. Tennessee Code Annotated, Section 8-11-103(c), is amended by deleting the subsection in its entirety and by substituting instead the following:

(c) If the official bond of the county trustee is executed by personal sureties, the minimum amount of the bond shall be based on revenues as follows:

(1) Six percent (6%) up to three million dollars ($3,000,000) of the funds collected by the office;

(2) Four percent (4%) of the excess over three million dollars ($3,000,000) shall be added; and

(3) The amounts indicated in subdivisions (c)(1)-(2) shall be cumulative.

5-6-109 SECTION 7. Tennessee Code Annotated, Section 5-6-109, is amended by deleting the section in its entirety and by substituting instead the following:

Section 5-6-109. All county mayors shall, before entering upon the discharge of their duties, enter into an official bond prepared in accordance with title 8, chapter 19, to be approved by the county legislative bodies, in the sum of one hundred thousand dollars

($100,000), or in a greater sum as the county legislative body may determine, payable to the state of Tennessee, for the use of their respective counties, conditioned for the faithful discharge of their duties as accounting officers and general agents of their counties, during their official terms, as set forth in § 5-6-108. The bond shall be recorded in the office of the county register of deeds and transmitted to the office of the county clerk for safekeeping.

8-8-103 SECTION 8. Tennessee Code Annotated, Section 8-8-103, is amended by deleting the language "twenty-five thousand dollars ($25,000)" and by substituting instead the language "one hundred thousand dollars ($100,000)" and further amended by deleting the language "comptroller of the treasury" and by substituting instead the language "office of the county clerk".

8-13-102 SECTION 9. Tennessee Code Annotated, Section 8-13-102(a), is amended by deleting the language "comptroller of the treasury" and by substituting instead the language "office of the county clerk".

8-13-103 SECTION 10. Tennessee Code Annotated, Section 8-13-103, is amended by deleting the language "fifteen thousand dollars ($15,000) in counties with population of less than fifteen thousand (15,000), and twenty-five thousand dollars ($25,000) in counties with population of fifteen thousand (15,000) or more, according to the 1970 federal census or any subsequent federal census" and by substituting instead the following: "fifty thousand dollars ($50,000) in counties with a population of less than fifteen thousand (15,000), and one hundred thousand dollars ($100,000) in counties with a population of fifteen thousand (15,000) or more, according to the 2010 federal census or any subsequent federal census".

5-13-103 SECTION 11. Tennessee Code Annotated, Section 5-13-103(c)(1), is amended by deleting the subdivision in its entirety and by substituting instead the following:

(1) Before assuming the director's duties the director shall execute a corporate surety bond, the amount of which shall be established by the county mayor at not less than one hundred thousand dollars ($100,000).

5-13-103 SECTION 12. Tennessee Code Annotated, Section 5-13-103(c)(2), is amended by deleting the language "comptroller of the treasury" and by substituting instead the language "office of the county clerk".

5-14-103 SECTION 13. Tennessee Code Annotated, Section 5-14-103(c)(1), is amended by deleting the language "not less than ten thousand dollars ($10,000) nor more than twenty-five thousand dollars ($25,000)" and by substituting instead the language "not less than one hundred thousand dollars ($100,000)".

5-14-103 SECTION 14. Tennessee Code Annotated, Section 5-14-103(c)(2), is amended by deleting the language "comptroller of the treasury" and by substituting instead the language "office of the county clerk".

5-21-109 SECTION 15. Tennessee Code Annotated, Section 5-21-109(a), is amended by deleting the language "fifty thousand dollars ($50,000)" and by substituting instead the language "one hundred thousand dollars ($100,000)".

5-21-109 SECTION 16. Tennessee Code Annotated, Section 5-21-109(d), is amended by deleting the language "comptroller of the treasury" and by substituting instead the language "office of the county clerk".

18-2-201 SECTION 17. Tennessee Code Annotated, Section 18-2-201(a), is amended by deleting the language "twenty-five thousand dollars ($25,000) in counties with population of less than fifteen thousand (15,000) and fifty thousand dollars ($50,000) in counties with population of fifteen thousand (15,000) or more, according to the 1970 federal census or any subsequent federal census" and by substituting instead the following: "fifty thousand dollars ($50,000) in counties with a population of less than fifteen thousand (15,000) and one hundred thousand dollars ($100,000) in counties with a population of fifteen thousand (15,000) or more, according to the 2010 federal census or any subsequent federal census".

18-2-205 SECTION 18. Tennessee Code Annotated, Section 18-2-205, is amended by deleting the language "comptroller of the treasury" and by substituting instead the language "office of the county clerk".

49-3-315 SECTION 19. Tennessee Code Annotated, Section 49-3-315(b)(3), is amended by deleting the language "comptroller of the treasury" and by substituting instead the language "office of the county clerk".

PUBLIC CHAPTER NO. 315 (cont'd)

9-3-301 SECTION 20. Tennessee Code Annotated, Section 9-3-301(c), is amended by deleting the language "fifty thousand dollars ($50,000)" and by substituting instead the language "one hundred thousand dollars ($100,000)" and further amended by deleting the language "comptroller of the treasury" and by substituting instead the language "office of the county clerk".

7-86-119 SECTION 21. Tennessee Code Annotated, Section 7-86-119(c)(2), is amended by deleting the subdivision in its entirety and by substituting instead the following:

(2) Effective July 1, 2013, the minimum amount of such required bond shall be determined from the amount of revenues handled by the respective emergency communications district as reported in the last audit approved by the comptroller of the treasury. The minimum amount of the bond shall be based on revenues as follows:

(A) Four percent (4%) of the revenues up to three million dollars ($3,000,000);

(B) Two percent (2%) of the excess over three million dollars ($3,000,000) shall be added; and

(C) The amounts indicated in subdivisions (2)(A)-(B) shall be cumulative.

7-86-119 SECTION 22. Tennessee Code Annotated, Section 7-86-119(e), is amended by deleting the subsection in its entirety and by substituting instead the following:

(e) The official bonds required under this section are hereby required to be recorded in the office of the register of deeds where the office of the emergency communications district is located and transmitted to the office of the county clerk in the same county for safekeeping.

8-19-203 SECTION 23. Tennessee Code Annotated, Section 8-19-203, is amended by deleting the language "comptroller of the treasury" wherever it appears and by substituting instead the language "office of the county clerk".

8-19-208 SECTION 24. Tennessee Code Annotated, Section 8-19-208, is amended by deleting the section in its entirety and substituting instead the following:

8-19-208. The bonds of the revenue officers, shall within ten (10) days after the same have been examined or taken, and after they shall have been attested, recorded and certified, according to law, be filed in the office of the county clerk for safekeeping.

13-14-114 SECTION 25. Tennessee Code Annotated, Section 13-14-114(c), is amended by deleting the subsection in its entirety and by substituting instead the following:

(c) Effective July 1, 2013, the minimum amount of such required bond shall be determined from the amount of revenues handled by the respective development district as reported in the last audit approved by the comptroller of the treasury. The minimum amount of the bond shall be based on revenues as follows:

(1) Four percent (4%) of the revenues up to three million dollars ($3,000,000);

(2) Two percent (2%) of the excess over three million dollars ($3,000,000) shall be added; and

(3) The amounts indicated in subdivisions (c)(1)-(2) shall be cumulative.

13-14-114 SECTION 26. Tennessee Code Annotated, Section 13-14-114(e), is amended by deleting the subsection in its entirety and by substituting instead the following:

(e) The official bonds required under this section are hereby required to be recorded in the office of the register of deeds where the office of the development district is located and transmitted to the office of the county clerk in the same county for safekeeping.

13-26-110 SECTION 27. Tennessee Code Annotated, Section 13-26-110(c), is amended by deleting the subsection in its entirety and by substituting instead the following:

(c) Effective July 1, 2013, the minimum amount of such required bond shall be determined from the amount of revenues handled by the respective human resource agency as reported in the last audit approved by the comptroller of the treasury. The minimum amount of the bond shall be based on revenues as follows:

(1) Four percent (4%) of the revenues up to three million dollars ($3,000,000);

PUBLIC CHAPTER NO. 315 (cont'd)

(2) Two percent (2%) of the excess over three million dollars ($3,000,000) shall be added; and

(3) The amounts indicated in subdivisions (c)(1)-(2) shall be cumulative.

13-26-110 SECTION 28. Tennessee Code Annotated, Section 13-26-110(e), is amended by deleting the subsection in its entirety and by substituting instead the following:

(e) The official bonds required under this section are hereby required to be recorded in the office of the register of deeds where the office of the human resource agency is located and transmitted to the office of the county clerk in the same county for safekeeping.

8-19-122 SECTION 29. Tennessee Code Annotated, Title 8, Chapter 19, Part 1, is amended by adding a new section thereto, as follows:

8-19-122. No bond required by this chapter shall be renewed upon its expiration or in the event of the reappointment or re-election of any officer or employee to a position for which a bond is required, but a new bond shall be furnished.

8-19-101 SECTION 30. Tennessee Code Annotated, Section 8-19-101, is amended by adding the following as a new subsection:

(e) County governments are required to obtain and maintain blanket surety bond coverage for all county employees not covered by individual bonds referenced elsewhere in statute. The minimum amount of such blanket bonds shall be one hundred fifty thousand dollars ($150,000).

Effective date 4/29/2013 SECTION 31. This act shall take effect upon becoming a law, the public welfare requiring it, and shall apply to the renewal or obtaining an official bond for any bonding after the effective date.

PUBLIC CHAPTER NO. 316

PUBLIC CHAPTER NO. 316

SENATE BILL NO. 91

By Finney, Burks

Substituted for: House Bill No. 294

By Fitzhugh

AN ACT to amend Tennessee Code Annotated, Title 4; Title 5; Title 6; Title 7 and Title 57, relative to suspension and revocation of licenses to sell alcoholic beverages and beer.

BE IT ENACTED BY THE GENERAL ASSEMBLY OF THE STATE OF TENNESSEE:

57-1-214 SECTION 1. Tennessee Code Annotated, Title 57, Chapter 1, Part 2, is amended by adding the following language as a new, appropriately designated section:

(a)(1) In any county other than those included in §§ 57-4-202(d) and 57-5-108(p), if the alcoholic beverage commission suspends or revokes a license to sell alcoholic beverages on the premises at any establishment for any violation or violations as provided in title 57, chapter 4, then the commission shall notify the local beer board responsible for controlling the sale of beer or malt beverages within such county by certified mail, return receipt requested, of the action taken by the commission. Such notice shall include the record of evidence and the determination made by the commission in suspending or revoking the license of the establishment.

(2) Upon receipt of such notice, the local beer board may temporarily suspend the beer permit of the establishment and shall:

(A) Schedule a hearing for the next regularly scheduled meeting of the local beer board to be held at least fourteen (14) days following the date the local beer board receives the certified letter to provide an opportunity for the permit holder to appear and show cause why the permit to sell beer on the premises should not be suspended or revoked for a violation or violations as provided in title 57, chapter 4, based on actions taken by the commission; and

(B) Notify the individual or business entity, which is listed as the permit holder at the same location where the alcoholic beverage license had been suspended or revoked, of the date and time of the hearing.

(3) If the local beer board finds at a hearing that a sufficient violation or violations have occurred as provided in title 57, chapter 4, at such location, then the local beer board may suspend or revoke the permit to the same extent and at least for the same period of time as the commission has suspended or revoked the license of the establishment.

(4) If the permit holder fails to appear or decides to surrender the permit to the local beer board in lieu of appearing at the hearing, the permit may be suspended or revoked by the local beer board; provided, that if the permit is suspended or revoked, no permit to sell beer or malt beverages on the premises shall be issued by the local beer board to any person for the location where the commission had suspended or revoked the license for the period of time included in the decision of the commission.

(5) The decision of the local beer board is final, and any party aggrieved thereby may appeal the decision of the local beer board in accordance with § 57-5-108.

(b)(1) In any county other than those included in §§ 57-4-202(d) and 57-5-108(p), if a local beer board responsible for controlling the sale of beer or malt beverages finds a violation or violations, as provided in title 57, chapter 4, in the sale of beer or malt beverages consumed on-premises of an establishment located within the local beer board's jurisdiction that result in the local beer board suspending the operation of or revoking the permit of the establishment where the violation or violations occurred, then the local beer board shall notify the executive director of the commission by certified mail, return receipt requested, of the action taken by the local beer board. Such notice shall include the record of evidence and the determination made by the local beer board in suspending or revoking the permit.

(2) Upon receipt of such notice, the executive director of the commission may take the action with respect to a violation or violations as provided in title 57, chapter 4, related to the license for the sale of alcoholic beverages for consumption on the premises at the location where the violation or violations of the chapter occurred.

(3) The suspension or revocation decision of the local beer board made pursuant to subsection (b) is final, and any party aggrieved thereby may appeal the decision of the local beer board in accordance with § 57-5-108.

Effective date 4/29/2013

SECTION 2. This act shall take effect upon becoming a law, the public welfare requiring it.

PUBLIC CHAPTER NO. 317

PUBLIC CHAPTER NO. 317

SENATE BILL NO. 56

By Kelsey, Gardenhire, Overbey

Substituted for: House Bill No. 1099

By Durham, Womick, Lamberth, Casada, Rich, Littleton, Holt, Dawn White, Ragan, Carter, Eldridge

AN ACT to amend Tennessee Code Annotated, Title 29, Chapter 11, Part 1, relative to the doctrine of joint and several liability.

BE IT ENACTED BY THE GENERAL ASSEMBLY OF THE STATE OF TENNESSEE:

29-11-107 SECTION 1. Tennessee Code Annotated, Title 29, Chapter 11, Part 1, is amended by adding the following new section:

29-11-107.

(a) If multiple defendants are found liable in a civil action governed by comparative fault, a defendant shall only be severally liable for the percentage of damages for which fault is attributed to such defendant by the trier of fact, and no defendant shall be held jointly liable for any damages.

(b) Notwithstanding subsection (a), the doctrine of joint and several liability remains in effect:

(1) To apportion financial responsibility in a civil conspiracy among two (2) or more at-fault defendants who, each having the intent and knowledge of the other's intent, accomplish by concert an unlawful purpose, or accomplish by concert a lawful purpose by unlawful means, which results in damage to the plaintiff; and

(2) Among manufacturers only in a product liability action as defined in § 29-28-102, but only if such action is based upon a theory of strict liability or breach of warranty. Nothing in this subsection (b) eliminates or affects the limitations on product liability actions found in § 29-28-106.

(c) Nothing in this section eliminates or affects the doctrines of vicarious liability or respondeat superior.

(d) Nothing in this section limits the ability of the trier of fact to allocate fault to a nonparty to the suit, including, but not limited to, an immune third party or a settling party, person, or entity. Allocations of fault to nonparties shall be used only to determine the liability of named parties and shall not subject nonparties to liability in the action in which the allocation occurred or in any other action.

(e) Nothing in this section eliminates or diminishes:

(1) The filing of cross-claims or counterclaims against any party or third party under Tennessee Rules of Civil Procedure 13 and 14;

(2) The assertion by a party of rights to contribution or indemnity;

(3) The assertion by a party of comparative fault under Tennessee Rule of Civil Procedure 8.03;

(4) The doctrine of superseding and independent intervening cause; or

(5) Any defenses or immunities that exist as of the effective date of this act.

(f) This section shall not prevent parties from entering into a legally enforceable contract that allocates fault in a civil action among the parties to the contract.

PUBLIC CHAPTER NO. 317 (cont'd)

Effective date 7/1/2013

SECTION 2. This act shall take effect July 1, 2013, the public welfare requiring it, and shall apply to all actions accruing on or after that date.

PUBLIC CHAPTER NO. 318

PUBLIC CHAPTER NO. 318

HOUSE BILL NO. 32

By Representatives Sexton, Goins, Powell, Van Huss, Eldridge, Ryan Williams, Joe Carr, Shipley

Substituted for: Senate Bill No. 1152

By Senators Burks, Crowe

AN ACT to amend Tennessee Code Annotated, Title 55, Chapter 4, Part 2, relative to memorial plates.

BE IT ENACTED BY THE GENERAL ASSEMBLY OF THE STATE OF TENNESSEE

55-4-236 SECTION 1. Tennessee Code Annotated, Section 55-4-236(a), is amended by deleting the language "the Congressional Medal of Honor," and "the Air Medal,".

55-4-233 SECTION 2. Tennessee Code Annotated, Title 55, Chapter 4, is amended by adding the following as a new, appropriately designated section:

55-4-___.

(a) Notwithstanding any other law to the contrary, the department shall provide and issue, free of charge, to each resident of this state who is a recipient of the Congressional Medal of Honor, upon presentation of proper application, Medal of Honor memorial registration plates for no more than two (2) motor vehicles or motor homes which are registered or leased for private use in the name of any one (1) recipient. For the purposes of this section, "private use" vehicle means any motor vehicle authorized by § 55-4-210(c) or motor home that is not used for rehire or for any other commercial purpose.

(b) The Medal of Honor memorial plates provided for in this section shall be the same as regular registration plates, but shall be of a distinctive design which denotes the importance of these distinguished veterans and the high regard in which this state holds the heroic recipients of the highest military decoration. The legend shall read "Medal of Honor." The registration number of the plate shall include the letters "CM" and a unique identifying number.

(c)

(1) Notwithstanding any other law to the contrary, eligibility for the Medal of Honor memorial plate shall be determined by the department by consulting the appropriate information on the:

(A) DD214 form and a copy of the orders that awarded the medal or copy of the certificate or citation granting the medal, in the case of an applicant who has been discharged from the armed forces;

(B) Copy of the orders that awarded the medal or copy of the certificate or citation granting the medal, in the case of an applicant who has not been discharged from the armed forces; or

(C) A written communication from the department of veterans affairs, in the case of an applicant who does not possess the documentation required by subdivision (A) or (B).

(2) The form, documentation or communication required by subdivision (c)(1) shall certify that the application for the plate is submitted by a recipient of the Congressional Medal of Honor.

(3) Any person issued a Medal of Honor plate under this chapter prior to the effective date of this act, shall submit to the department of revenue the

appropriate information required by this subsection within thirty (30) days after the effective date of this act. If any such person to whom a Medal of Honor plate has been issued does not comply with this subdivision (c)(3) or the department of revenue determines that the person is not eligible for the plate, the person shall surrender the plate to the county clerk of the county of the person's residence within thirty (30) days of noncompliance or determination of ineligibility, whichever is sooner.

55-4-236 SECTION 3. Tennessee Code Annotated, Section 55-4-236, is amended by adding the following as a new, appropriately designated subsection:

( )

(1) Notwithstanding any provision of this section or any other law to the contrary, eligibility for the memorial plates provided for in this section shall be determined by the department by consulting the appropriate information on the:

(A) DD214 form and a copy of the orders that awarded the medal or copy of the certificate or citation granting the medal, in the case of an applicant who has been discharged from the armed forces;

(B) Copy of the orders that awarded the medal or copy of the certificate or citation granting the medal, in the case of an applicant who has not been discharged from the armed forces; or

(C) A written communication from the department of veterans affairs, in the case of an applicant who does not possess the documentation required by subdivision (A) or (B).

(2) The form, documentation, or communication required by subdivision ( )(1) shall certify that the application for the plate is submitted by a recipient of the military decorations described in this section, as appropriate.

55-4-240 SECTION 4. Tennessee Code Annotated, Section 55-4-240, is amended by:

(1) Deleting the language "Air Medal," and "Medal of Honor," and

(2) Inserting the language "§ 55-4-___ pertaining to recipients of the Congressional Medal of Honor," between the language "former prisoners of war," and the language "§ 55-4-236".

55-4-278 SECTION 5. Tennessee Code Annotated, Section 55-4-278, is amended by:

(1) Deleting the language "the Air Medal," and "the Medal of Honor," wherever it appears;

(2) Inserting the language "by § 55-4-___ pertaining to recipients of the Congressional Medal of Honor," between the language "former prisoners of war," and the language "by § 55-4-236" wherever such language appears; and

(3) Deleting the language "Silver Star" and by substituting instead the language "Air Medal, Silver Star,".

55-4-202 SECTION 6. Tennessee Code Annotated, Section 55-4-202(c)(4)(B), is amended by deleting the subdivision and redesignating the remaining subdivisions accordingly.

55-4-202 SECTION 7. Tennessee Code Annotated, Section 55-4-202(c)(5)(E), is amended by adding the following as a new, appropriately designated subdivision:

( ) Air Medal recipients;

55-4-203 SECTION 8. Tennessee Code Annotated, Section 55-4-203(b), is amended by deleting subdivision (2) in its entirety and by renumbering the remaining subdivisions accordingly.

55-4-203 SECTION 9. Tennessee Code Annotated, Section 55-4-203(c)(1), is amended by adding the following as a new, appropriately designated subdivision:

( ) Air Medal recipients;

55-4-231 SECTION 10. Tennessee Code Annotated, Section 55-4-231(a), is amended by:

(1) Deleting the language "A recipient of the Silver Star or a recipient of the Bronze Star" and by substituting instead the language "A recipient of the Silver Star, the Bronze Star, or the Air Medal"; and

(2) Deleting the language "Silver Star or Bronze Star" and by substituting instead the language "Air Medal, Silver Star, or Bronze Star".

55-4-231 SECTION 11. Tennessee Code Annotated, Section 55-4-231(b), is amended by adding the following as a new subdivision (3):

(3) The Air Medal plates provided for in this section shall include an identification legend distinctive to recipients of the Air Medal. The legend shall read "Air Medal." The registration number of the plate shall include the letters "RE" and a unique identifying number.

55-4-231 SECTION 12. Tennessee Code Annotated, Section 55-4-231(c), is amended by:

(1) Deleting the language "Silver Star plates and Bronze Star plates" and by substituting instead the language "Air Medal plates, Silver Star plates, and Bronze Star plates"; and

(2) Deleting the language "by a recipient of the Silver Star or a recipient of the Bronze Star" and by substituting instead the language "by a recipient of the Silver Star, the Bronze Star, or the Air Medal".

SECTION 13. Notwithstanding any law to the contrary, any person issued an Air Medal memorial license plate prior to the effective date of this act, shall be entitled to retain the plate for vehicular use upon compliance with all motor vehicle laws relating to registration and licensing of motor vehicles. Such Air Medal memorial license plates issued prior to the effective date of this act, shall be considered military cultural plates upon their first renewal on or after July 1, 2014; provided, that upon such renewal, the plates shall be subject to the annual regular registration fee. Any Air Medal military cultural plates initially issued on or after the effective date of this act, shall be subject to the annual regular registration fee and the fee applicable to that category of plates pursuant to § 55-4-203(c)(1).

Effective date 6/21/2013 SECTION 14. This act shall take effect upon becoming a law, the public welfare requiring it.

PUBLIC CHAPTER NO. 319

PUBLIC CHAPTER NO. 319

HOUSE BILL NO. 88

By Representative Lundberg

Substituted for: Senate Bill No. 1250

By Senator Stevens

AN ACT to amend Tennessee Code Annotated, Title 39, Chapter 15, Part 4 and Title 39, Chapter 17, Part 15, relative to law enforcement efforts involving the use of minors.

BE IT ENACTED BY THE GENERAL ASSEMBLY OF THE STATE OF TENNESSEE:

39-15-413 SECTION 1. Tennessee Code Annotated, Section 39-15-413, is amended by deleting the language "and the juvenile court" wherever it appears in the Section.

39-17-1504 SECTION 2. Tennessee Code Annotated, Section 39-17-1504(b), is amended by deleting the language "a parent of the individual" and by substituting instead the language "the minor's parent or legal guardian".

Effective date 5/13/2013 SECTION 3. This act shall take effect upon becoming a law, the public welfare requiring it.

PUBLIC CHAPTER NO. 320

PUBLIC CHAPTER NO. 320

HOUSE BILL NO. 116

By Representative Dunn

Substituted for: Senate Bill No. 73

By Senator Massey

AN ACT to amend Tennessee Code Annotated, Section 7-82-307, relative to vacancies on the board of commissioners of utility districts.

BE IT ENACTED BY THE GENERAL ASSEMBLY OF THE STATE OF TENNESSEE:

7-82-307 SECTION 1 Tennessee Code Annotated, Section 7-82-307, is amended by deleting the last sentence in subdivision (a)(4) and substituting instead the following:
If the county mayor enters an order rejecting the third list of nominees within twenty-one (21) days after the submission of the third list of nominees, then the county legislative body shall appoint a commissioner from the third list of nominees to fill the vacancy at the meeting of the county legislative body in which the mayor's order rejecting the third list of nominees is entered of record on the minutes of the county legislative body.

Effective date 5/13/2013 SECTION 2. This act shall take effect upon becoming a law, the public welfare requiring it.

PUBLIC CHAPTER NO. 321

PUBLIC CHAPTER NO. 321

HOUSE BILL NO. 175

By Representatives McCormick, Goins

Substituted for: Senate Bill No. 181

By Senator Norris

AN ACT to amend Tennessee Code Annotated, Title 67, Chapter 4, Part 20, relative to excise tax, and Title 67, Chapter 4, Part 21, relative to franchise tax.

BE IT ENACTED BY THE GENERAL ASSEMBLY OF THE STATE OF TENNESSEE:

67-4-2004 SECTION 1. Tennessee Code Annotated, Section 67-4-2004, is amended by adding the following as a new, appropriately designated subdivision:

( ) "Final return status" means the status of any person or taxpayer that has commenced the process of effecting a surrender of charter, withdrawal of qualification to do business in this state, merger, consolidation, liquidation, complete sale, transfer or distribution of assets, conversion, dissolution, or any similar event that results in, or is intended to result in, the taxpayer ceasing to exist, or no longer being subject to the tax imposed by this part, or no longer having any substantial remaining business or financial activity.

67-4-2015 SECTION 2. Tennessee Code Annotated, Section 67-4-2015, is amended by adding the following as a new, appropriately designated subsection:

(h) Final return status shall apply to the first return that reflects any activity or event giving rise to such status, and shall apply to all subsequent returns filed by the taxpayer. The taxpayer shall file a return for each tax period during which the taxpayer is in final return status. This requirement shall include returns of taxpayers with any remaining assets, activity, equity, or proceeds; or with installment sales attributable to any Tennessee assets regardless of whether the entity has any remaining in-state activity.

67-4-2105 SECTION 3. Tennessee Code Annotated, Section 67-4-2105(a), is amended by deleting the following language:

or under subsection (b)

67-4-2107 SECTION 4. Tennessee Code Annotated, Section 67-4-2107(b)(1), is amended by deleting the following language at the end of the last sentence:

the methods of allocation set forth in subdivision (b)(2) shall be used.

.and by substituting instead the following language:

the methods of allocation set forth in this part shall be used.

67-4-2107 SECTION 5. Tennessee Code Annotated, Section 67-4-2107(b)(2), is amended by deleting the subdivision in its entirety and renumbering the remaining subdivisions accordingly.

67-4-2111 SECTION 6. Tennessee Code Annotated, Section 67-4-2111(e)(3)(C), is amended by deleting the following language at the end of the last sentence:

the classification groupings enumerated in § 67-4-2013(a)(1)-(6) shall be used.
and by substituting instead the following language:

the classification groupings enumerated in § 67-4-2013(a)(1)-(7) shall be used.

67-4-2115 SECTION 7. Tennessee Code Annotated, Section 67-4-2115, is amended by deleting the section in its entirety and by substituting instead the following:

§ 67-4-2115

(a) The franchise tax return shall be filed as provided in § 67-4-2015. On any return covering less than a twelve (12) month period, including the return of a taxpayer in final return status, but excluding any return based on a 52-53 week year, the franchise tax shall be prorated to cover the proportionate part of the year covered by the return. In the event the taxpayer's taxable year is closed within less than twelve (12) months of incorporation, formation, domestication, or commencing of business, the franchise tax of a domestic entity shall be prorated to cover the proportionate part of the year since the date of incorporation or formation, or the date of commencing business, whichever occurred first. The franchise tax of a taxpayer formed outside of Tennessee shall be prorated to cover the proportionate part of the year since beginning business in this state. On any return where the franchise tax is prorated, annualization of rent paid shall be required when determining the minimum franchise tax measure under § 67-4-2108. Proration of the franchise tax and annualization of rent paid shall be computed by a fraction based on a days method.

(b) If a person or taxpayer in final return status effects a complete liquidation that is initiated and completed on the same date, then the franchise tax shall be computed utilizing net worth, or the minimum franchise tax base under § 67-4-2108, on the date immediately preceding the liquidating event; otherwise, on any return of a taxpayer in final return status, the franchise tax shall be computed by using the average monthly value of net worth or the average monthly value of the real and tangible property owned in Tennessee. Such average monthly value shall be determined by totaling the value of net worth as of the final day of each month of the tax period, or the book value of the real and tangible property owned in Tennessee as of the final day of each month of the tax period, and then dividing that total by the number of months in the tax period. In the event the taxpayer is part of an affiliated group that has elected to compute its net worth on a consolidated basis, such election shall not apply to the taxpayer while it is in final return status unless the entire affiliated group is in final return status during the same tax period, in which case the election shall continue to apply to the taxpayer.

67-4-2006 SECTION 8. Tennessee Code Annotated, Section 67-4-2006(c), is amended by deleting the following language from the first paragraph of the subsection:

The taxpayer shall then deduct any loss carryovers, computed in accordance with subdivisions (c)(1)-(5), from its net earnings so determined.

and substituting instead the following language:

The taxpayer shall then deduct any loss carryovers, computed in accordance with this subsection (c), from its net earnings so determined.

and is further amended by adding the following language as a new subdivision (8):

(8)

(A)

(i) There shall be added to the net loss as determined for excise tax purposes the amount excluded from federal gross income under 26 U.S.C. § 108(a)(1)(A), (B), or (C) for the taxable year of the discharge.

(ii) There shall be added to any qualified net operating loss as determined for excise tax purposes and carried forward to the year of the discharge the amount excluded from federal gross income under 26 U.S.C. § 108(a)(1)(A), (B), or (C) allocable or apportionable to this state for the taxable year of the discharge.

(B) The adjustments described in subdivision (A) shall be made first in the loss for the taxable year of the discharge and then in the carryforwards to such taxable year in the order of the taxable years from which each such carryforward arose.

Effective date 5/13/2013 SECTION 9. Sections 1 - 7 of this act shall take effect upon becoming a law, the public welfare requiring it. Section 8 of this act shall take effect upon becoming a law and shall apply to any tax year in which a discharge of indebtedness occurred on or after October 1, 2013, the public welfare requiring it.

PUBLIC CHAPTER NO. 322

PUBLIC CHAPTER NO. 322

HOUSE BILL NO. 192

By Representatives McCormick, Sexton, Evans, Kevin Brooks, Lundberg, McManus, Ryan Williams, Rogers, Durham, Dawn White, Moody, Timothy Hill, Hall, Kane, Haynes, Butt, Matthew Hill, Sanderson, Eldridge, Rich, Pody, Coley, Powers, Wirgau, Harry Brooks, Travis, Carter, Mark White, Marsh, Van Huss, Swann, Halford, Sparks, Goins

Substituted for: Senate Bill No. 198

By Senators Norris, Ketron, Kelsey, Crowe, Beavers, Bowling, Campfield, Johnson, Massey

AN ACT to amend Tennessee Code Annotated, Title 67, Chapter 2, Part 1, relative to income tax.

BE IT ENACTED BY THE GENERAL ASSEMBLY OF THE STATE OF TENNESSEE:

67-2-104 SECTION 1. Tennessee Code Annotated, Section 67-2-104, is amended by deleting subsection (b) in its entirety and by substituting instead the following:

(b) For tax years beginning January 1, 2000, and thereafter, any person sixty-five (65) years of age or older having a total annual income derived from any and all sources of sixteen thousand two hundred dollars ($16,200) or less, or any persons who file a joint return and either spouse is sixty-five (65) years of age or older having a total annual joint income derived from any and all sources of not more than twenty seven thousand dollars ($27,000), are exempt from the income tax imposed by this chapter upon submission of evidence deemed acceptable by the commissioner to establish the age and income limitations stated in this subsection (b). For tax years beginning January 1, 2012, and thereafter, the income levels specified in the previous sentence in this subsection (b) shall change to twenty-six thousand two hundred dollars ($26,200) for single filers and to thirty-seven thousand dollars ($37,000) for persons filing jointly. For tax years beginning January 1, 2013, and thereafter, the income levels specified in the previous sentence in this subsection (b) shall change to thirty-three thousand dollars ($33,000) for single filers and to fifty-nine thousand dollars ($59,000) for persons filing jointly.

Effective date 5/13/2013

SECTION 2. This act shall take effect upon becoming a law, the public welfare requiring it.

PUBLIC CHAPTER NO. 323

PUBLIC CHAPTER NO. 323

HOUSE BILL NO. 193

By Representatives McCormick, Haynes, Evans, Kevin Brooks, Dunn, Goins, Ragan, Coley, Ryan Williams, Powers, Kane, Sparks, Matthew Hill, Van Huss, Timothy Hill, Moody, Littleton, Shipley, Butt, Lynn, Womick, Watson, Gilmore, Favors, Hardaway, Durham, Sargent, Miller, Hall, Curtis Johnson, Pitts, Travis, Lamberth

Substituted for: Senate Bill No. 199

By Senators Norris, Kelsey, Yager, Crowe, Beavers, Bowling, Campfield, Gresham, Harper, Johnson, Ketron, Massey

AN ACT to amend Tennessee Code Annotated, Title 67, Chapter 6, relative to the sales and use tax on food.

BE IT ENACTED BY THE GENERAL ASSEMBLY OF THE STATE OF TENNESSEE:

67-6-228 SECTION 1. Tennessee Code Annotated, Section 67-6-228(a), is amended by deleting the subsection in its entirety and substituting instead the following language:

(a) Notwithstanding any provision of this part to the contrary, except as otherwise provided in subsection (b), the retail sale of food and food ingredients for human consumption shall be taxed at the rate of five percent (5%) of the sales price.

Effective date 7/1/2013 SECTION 2. This act shall take effect on July 1, 2013, the public welfare requiring it.

PUBLIC CHAPTER NO. 324

PUBLIC CHAPTER NO. 324

HOUSE BILL NO. 234

By Representatives Carter, Moody, Timothy Hill, Lollar

Substituted for: Senate Bill No. 294

By Senators Watson, Gardenhire

AN ACT to amend Tennessee Code Annotated, Title 29, Chapter 13, relative to criminal injuries compensation.

BE IT ENACTED BY THE GENERAL ASSEMBLY OF THE STATE OF TENNESSEE:

29-13-308 SECTION 1. Tennessee Code Annotated, Section 29-13-308, is amended by deleting the section in its entirety and by substituting instead the following language:

> Upon attaining eighteen (18) years of age, the minor may terminate the trust by submitting a written request therefor with the court clerk. The court clerk shall deliver to the minor all funds and interest income remaining in the trust less any outstanding fees, court costs, fines, or restitutions resulting from the minor beneficiary's actions pending in juvenile court within sixty (60) calendar days from the date of the request.

29-13-111 SECTION 2. Tennessee Code Annotated, Section 29-13-111(e)(1), is amended by deleting the language "Except as provided in subdivision (e)(2)" and by substituting instead the language "Except as provided in subdivisions (e)(2) and (e)(3)".

29-13-111 SECTION 2. Tennessee Code Annotated, Section 29-13-111(e), is amended by adding the following language as a new subdivision:

> (e)(3) If any minor claimant is entitled to direct compensation pursuant to this chapter and a trust fund has been established for the minor claimant in accordance with part 3 of this chapter, the juvenile court clerk may, without further order of the court, withhold any funds within the trust for the purpose of paying court costs, fines, fees, or restitutions resulting from the minor beneficiary's actions pending in juvenile court.

Effective date 5-13-2013 SECTION 4. This act shall take effect upon becoming a law, the public welfare requiring it.

PUBLIC CHAPTER NO. 325

PUBLIC CHAPTER NO. 325

HOUSE BILL NO. 306

By Representatives Favors, Shipley, Jernigan, Hardaway, Evans, Powell, Parkinson, Miller

Substituted for: Senate Bill No. 412

By Senators Green, Massey, Kelsey

AN ACT to amend Tennessee Code Annotated, Title 39, Chapter 13, relative to assaultive offenses.

BE IT ENACTED BY THE GENERAL ASSEMBLY OF THE STATE OF TENNESSEE:

39-13-101 SECTION 1. Tennessee Code Annotated, Section 39-13-101(b)(1), is amended by deleting the language "under this section" and by substituting instead the language "or a health care provider acting in the discharge of the provider's duty".

39-13-102 SECTION 2. Tennessee Code Annotated, Section 39-13-102(e)(1), is amended by adding the language "or a health care provider acting in the discharge of the provider's duty" after the language "law enforcement officer".

39-13-101 SECTION 3. Tennessee Code Annotated, Section 39-13-101, is amended by adding the following as a new subsection:

( ) For purposes of this section and § 39-13-102, "health care provider" means a person who is licensed, certified or otherwise authorized or permitted by the laws of this state to administer health care in the ordinary course of business in the practicing of a profession.

Effective date 7/1/2013 SECTION 4. This act shall take effect July 1, 2013, the public welfare requiring it.

PUBLIC CHAPTER NO. 326

PUBLIC CHAPTER NO. 326

HOUSE BILL NO. 315

By Representative Harry Brooks

Substituted for: Senate Bill No. 205

By Senator Gresham

AN ACT to amend Tennessee Code Annotated, Title 8; Title 9; Title 12 and Title 49, relative to charter schools.

BE IT ENACTED BY THE GENERAL ASSEMBLY OF THE STATE OF TENNESSEE:

49-13-111 SECTION 1. Tennessee Code Annotated, Section 49-13-111(e), is amended by deleting the subsection in its entirety and by substituting instead the following:

(e) All contracts for goods in excess of ten thousand dollars ($10,000) shall be bid and must be approved by the governing body of each public charter school.

49-13-106 SECTION 2. Tennessee Code Annotated, Section 49-13-106(b)(2)(B), is amended by designating the existing language as subdivision (i) and by adding the following language as a new subdivision (ii)

(ii) Conversion of a public school to a public charter school at the request of the local board of education:

(*a*) Upon a local board's review of a charter school application, the local board may request that the sponsor amend the application to provide for the conversion of an existing public school.

(*b*) If the sponsor declines the request of the local board, then the local board shall proceed with the review of the application under § 49-13-108.

49-13-106 SECTION 3. Tennessee Code Annotated, Section 49-13-106(b), is amended by adding the following language as a new subdivision (3).

(3) Conversion of a school to a charter school by a charter school sponsor:

(A) A charter school sponsor may apply to an LEA to convert an existing public school to a charter school to serve the students zoned to the school. A charter school sponsor shall submit its application to the LEA and the LEA shall act on the application within the time frames set under §§ 49-13-107 and 49-13-108.

(B) Students living in other school zones may enroll after those living in the school zone, but only if there is program, class, grade level and building capacity to serve the out-of-zone students. If applications by out-of-zone students exceed the charter school's capacity, then enrollment of out-of-zone students shall be determined on the basis of a lottery. Out-of-zone students who attended the school the previous school year and such students' siblings may be given preference in enrollment. Parents whose children are enrolled in the existing public school to be converted shall have the option to enroll their children in another public school operated by the LEA without penalty.

(C) The conversion shall occur at the beginning of an academic school year and shall be subject to compliance with this chapter.

(D) If the application to convert an existing public school to a charter school is approved, then the charter school shall occupy the existing public school's facility.

PUBLIC CHAPTER NO. 326 (cont'd)

(E) If the application to convert an existing public school to a charter school is approved, then any teacher or administrator in the school converted to a charter school may be allowed to transfer into vacant positions for which they are certified in other schools in the LEA. Personnel who transfer into vacant positions in other schools in the LEA shall suffer no impairment, interruption or diminution of the rights and privileges of a then existing teacher or administrator, and the rights and privileges shall continue without impairment, interruption or diminution with the local board of education. "Rights and privileges," as used in this subdivision (E), include, but are not limited to, salary, pension or retirement benefits, sick leave accumulation and tenure with the local board of education. The director of schools shall have the option to specifically assign these teachers or administrators to those vacant positions.

(F) If the LEA denies the application, the LEA's decision is final and no appeal of the denial may be made.

49-13-112 SECTION 4. Tennessee Code Annotated, Section 49-13-112(b)(3)(C), is amended by adding the following language at the end of the subdivision:

Notwithstanding subdivision (b)(3)(B), if the charter agreement includes an agreement with the LEA for administrative or other services, then the LEA may withhold funds to cover the costs of those services.

49-13-104 SECTION 5. Tennessee Code Annotated, Section 49-13-104(6), is amended by deleting the subdivision in its entirety and by substituting instead the following:

(6) "Governing body" means the organized group of persons who will operate a public charter school or schools by deciding matters, including, but not limited to, budgeting, curriculum and other operating procedures for the public charter school and by overseeing management and administration of a public charter school.

49-13-109 SECTION 6. Tennessee Code Annotated, Title 49, Chapter 13, is amended by adding the following language as a new, appropriately designated section:

49-13-1__.

(a) The membership of a governing body shall include at least one (1) parent representative whose child is currently enrolled in a charter school operated by the governing body. The parent representative shall be appointed by the governing body within six (6) months of the school's opening date. A charter management organization may satisfy this requirement by establishing an advisory school council at each school that it operates. An advisory school council shall consist of no fewer than five (5) members and shall include the principal, at least one (1) parent and at least one (1) teacher representative.

(b) A local board of education shall not serve as the governing body of a public charter school;

49-13-104 SECTION 7. Tennessee Code Annotated, Section 49-13-104, is amended by adding the following language as new subdivision (4) and by renumbering subsequent subdivisions accordingly:

(4) "Charter management organization" or "CMO" means a nonprofit entity that operates multiple charter schools at least one (1) of which is in Tennessee.

49-13-102 SECTION 8. Tennessee Code Annotated, Section 49-13-102(a)(2), is amended by deleting the words "in high priority schools".

49-13-112 SECTION 9. Tennessee Code Annotated, Section 49-13-112(b)(3), is amended by adding the following language as new subdivision (D):

(D) Any fee for service that is agreed to by a charter school and the chartering authority shall be set forth in an addendum to the charter school agreement or in a separate document.

49-13-121 SECTION 10. Tennessee Code Annotated, Section 49-13-121, is amended by adding the following language as new subsection (e):

(e) One (1) year prior to the date on which a charter school is required to submit a renew application, the chartering authority shall submit to the charter school a performance report that directly reflects the renewal evaluation.

49-13-113 SECTION 11. Tennessee Code Annotated, Section 49-13-113(b)(2)(A), is amended by deleting subdivision (ii) in its entirety and substituting instead the following:

(ii) Pupils attending during the previous school year:

(*a*) Another charter school that has an articulation agreement with the enrolling public charter school; provided, that the articulation agreement has been approved by the chartering authority; or

(*b*) A pre-K program operated by the charter school sponsor;

49-13-127 SECTION 12. Tennessee Code Annotated, Section 49-13-127(b), is amended by adding the following language as a new subdivision (3):

(3) A CMO may comply with subdivision (b)(1) by submitting one (1) audit for all the charter schools operated in Tennessee by the CMO; provided, that such audit includes all information required under this section for each school.

49-13-106 SECTION 13. Tennessee Code Annotated, Section 49-13-106(b), is amended by deleting the words "an eligible public school" wherever they appear and substituting instead the words "a school".

49-13-106 SECTION 14. Tennessee Code Annotated, Section 49-13-106(b)(2), is amended by deleting the language "Conversion of eligible schools" and substituting instead the language "Conversion of schools".

49-13-108 SECTION 15. Tennessee Code Annotated, Section 49-13-108(b), is amended by deleting the subsection in its entirety and by substituting instead the following:

(b) The local board of education may consider whether the establishment of the charter school will have a substantial negative fiscal impact on the LEA such that authorization of the charter school would be contrary to the best interest of the pupils, school district or community.

Effective date 7/1/2013 SECTION 16. This act shall take effect July 1, 2013, the public welfare requiring it.

PUBLIC CHAPTER NO. 327

PUBLIC CHAPTER NO. 327

HOUSE BILL NO. 478

By Representatives Travis, Moody, Hardaway

Substituted for: Senate Bill No. 512

By Senators Hensley, Norris

AN ACT to amend Tennessee Code Annotated, Title 55 and Title 56, relative to insurance.

BE IT ENACTED BY THE GENERAL ASSEMBLY OF THE STATE OF TENNESSEE:

55-12-139 SECTION 1. Tennessee Code Annotated, Section 55-12-139(b)(1), is amended by adding the language "whether in paper or electronic format," immediately after the language "Tennessee,".

55-12-139 SECTION 2. Tennessee Code Annotated, Section 55-12-139, is amended by adding the following new subsections:

(g) For purposes of this section, acceptable electronic formats include display of electronic images on a cellular phone or any other type of portable electronic device.

(h) If a person displays the evidence in an electronic format pursuant to this section, the person is not consenting for law enforcement to access any other contents of the electronic device.

Effective date 5/13/2013 SECTION 3. This act shall take effect upon becoming a law, the public welfare requiring it.

PUBLIC CHAPTER NO. 328

PUBLIC CHAPTER NO. 328

HOUSE BILL NO. 574

By Representatives Dunn, Eldridge, Sargent

Substituted for: Senate Bill No. 885

By Senator Hensley

AN ACT to amend Tennessee Code Annotated, Title 67, relative to taxes.

BE IT ENACTED BY THE GENERAL ASSEMBLY OF THE STATE OF TENNESSEE:

67-5-1203 SECTION 1. Tennessee Code Annotated, Section 67-5-1203(b), is amended by deleting the language "by such company" from the introductory clause of the subsection and substituting instead "by an insurance company with stockholders".

67-5-1203 SECTION 2. Tennessee Code Annotated, Section 67-5-1203, is amended by redesignating subsection (c) as a new subsection (d), and is further amended by adding the following language as new subsection (c):

(c) In the case of an insurance company without stockholders, the value of the corporate property of such company for purposes of this section, excluding real property and tangible personal property, shall be equal to the total dividends paid to policyholders in the preceding calendar year. For purposes of this subsection (c), "dividends" do not include returns or reductions of premiums or credits applied to premiums.

SECTION 3.

(a) This act shall apply to all assessments issued under this part regardless of the year in which the assessment applies.

(b) This act shall not apply to an insurance company which, after the effective date of this act, is either:

(1) Converted from a stock insurance company; or

(2) Organized to receive the assets of a stock insurance company.

Effective date 5/13/2013 SECTION 4. This act shall take effect upon becoming a law, the public welfare requiring it.

PUBLIC CHAPTER NO. 329

PUBLIC CHAPTER NO. 329

HOUSE BILL NO. 739

By Representative Sanderson

Substituted for: Senate Bill No. 458

By Senator Yager

AN ACT to amend Tennessee Code Annotated, Title 12, Chapter 3, Part 10 and Section 12-4-126, relative to local government purchasing.

BE IT ENACTED BY THE GENERAL ASSEMBLY OF THE STATE OF TENNESSEE:

12-3-1004 SECTION 1. Tennessee Code Annotated, Section 12-3-1004, is amended by deleting subsection (c) and substituting instead the following:

(c)

(1) Any municipality, county, utility district, or other local governmental unit of this state may purchase supplies, goods, equipment, and services under contracts or price agreements entered into by any other local governmental unit of this state. Such purchases shall be made on the same terms and under the same rules and regulations as regular purchases of the purchasing entity. Any local governmental unit that purchases supplies, goods, equipment, or services under this section shall directly handle payment, refunds, returns, and any other communication or requirements involved in the purchase without involving the local governmental unit that originated the contract. The originating local governmental unit shall have no liability or responsibility for any purchases made by another local governmental unit under a contract that the originating local governmental unit negotiated and consummated. Where any local or private act, charter, or general law requires that a local governmental unit purchase by competitive bidding, the local governmental unit may, notwithstanding the local or private act, charter, or general law, purchase without public advertisement or competitive bidding in accordance with this section.

(2) This subsection (c) shall not apply to:

(A) Purchases of new or unused motor vehicles, unless the motor vehicles are manufactured for a special purpose as defined in § 12-3-1012; and

(B) Purchases related to any transportation infrastructure project, including, but not limited to, projects for the construction or improvement of streets, highways, bridges, tunnels, or any roadway related facility.

12-3-1008 SECTION 2. Tennessee Code Annotated, Section 12-3-1008, is amended by deleting the section.

12-3-1009 SECTION 3. Tennessee Code Annotated, Section 12-3-1009, is amended by deleting subsection (b) and substituting instead the following:

(b)

(1) Notwithstanding any other law to the contrary, any municipality county, utility district, or other local government of the state may participate in, sponsor, conduct, or administer a cooperative purchasing agreement for the procurement of any goods, supplies, services, or equipment with one (1) or more other governmental entities outside this state, to the extent the laws of the other state permit the joint exercise of purchasing authority, in accordance with an agreement entered into between or among the participants; provided, such goods, supplies, services, or equipment were procured in a manner that

constitutes competitive bidding and were advertised, evaluated, and awarded by a governmental entity and made available for use by other governmental entities.

(2) A municipality, county, utility district, or other local government of the state may participate in a master agreement by adopting a resolution accepting the terms of the master agreement. If a participant in a joint or multi-party agreement is required to advertise and receive bids, then it will be deemed sufficient for those purposes that the purchasing entity or the entity that procured the bid complied with its own purchasing requirements. The participant shall acquire and maintain documentation that the purchasing entity or entities that procured the bid complied with its own purchasing requirements.

(3) The powers conferred by this section are in addition and supplemental to the powers conferred by any other law, and any limitations imposed by this section shall not affect powers conferred by any other law.

(4) This subsection (b) shall not apply to:

(A) Purchases of new or unused motor vehicles, unless the motor vehicles are manufactured for a special purpose as defined in § 12-3-1012; or

(B) Purchases of construction, engineering or architectural services, or construction materials.

(c) The chief procurement officer may collect information from municipalities, counties, utility districts, or any other local government unit concerning the type, cost, quality, and quantity of commonly used goods, supplies, services, or equipment being procured under cooperative purchasing agreements. The chief procurement officer may make available all such information to any municipality, county, utility district, or other local government unit upon request.

12-4-126 SECTION 4. Tennessee Code Annotated, Section 12-4-126, is amended by deleting the language "within less than forty-eight (48) hours of the bid opening date" and substituting instead the language "within less than forty-eight (48) hours of the bid opening date, excluding weekends and legal holidays designated in § 15-1-101,".

12-4-126 SECTION 5. Tennessee Code Annotated, Section 12-4-126, is further amended by adding the following language immediately before the period (.) at the end of subsection (a):

unless the bid deadline is extended for a reasonable time as determined by the purchasing agent, which shall not be less than forty-eight (48) hours excluding weekends and legal holidays designated in § 15-1-101, to allow for any necessary changes to the bid documents and to allow bidders to resubmit their bids accordingly

12-3-1012 SECTION 6. Tennessee Code Annotated, Section 12-3-1012(a), is amended by inserting the following language in subdivision (3)(C) between "school buses," and "garbage trucks": buses with capacity exceeding twenty-two (22) passengers used to provide public transportation,

Effective date 5/13/2013 SECTION 7. This act shall take effect upon becoming a law, the public welfare requiring it.

PUBLIC CHAPTER NO. 330

PUBLIC CHAPTER NO. 330

HOUSE BILL NO. 755

By Representatives Matheny, Ragan

Substituted for: Senate Bill No. 353

By Senator Bell

AN ACT to amend Tennessee Code Annotated, Title 4, Chapter 29 and Title 49, Chapter 1, relative to the state board of education.

BE IT ENACTED BY THE GENERAL ASSEMBLY OF THE STATE OF TENNESSEE:

4-29-234 SECTION 1. Tennessee Code Annotated, Section 4-29-234(a), is amended by deleting subdivision (49) in its entirety.

4-29-236 SECTION 2. Tennessee Code Annotated, Section 4-29-236(a), is amended by adding a new subdivision thereto, as follows:

( ) State board of education, created by § 49-1-301;

Effective date 5/13/2013 SECTION 3. This act shall take effect upon becoming a law, the public welfare requiring it.

PUBLIC CHAPTER NO. 331

PUBLIC CHAPTER NO. 331

HOUSE BILL NO. 766

By Representatives Matheny, Ragan

Substituted for: Senate Bill No. 337

By Senator Bell

AN ACT to amend Tennessee Code Annotated, Title 4, Chapter 11 and Title 4, Chapter 29, relative to the historical commission.

BE IT ENACTED BY THE GENERAL ASSEMBLY OF THE STATE OF TENNESSEE:

4-29-234 SECTION 1. Tennessee Code Annotated, Section 4-29-234(a), is amended by deleting subdivision (31) in its entirety.

4-29-240 SECTION 2. Tennessee Code Annotated, Title 4, Chapter 29, Part 2, is amended by adding a new section thereto, as follows:

4-29-240.

(a) The following governmental entities shall terminate on June 30, 2019:

( ) Historical commission, created by § 4-11-102;

(b) Each department, commission, board, agency or council of state government created during calendar year 2017 terminates on June 30, 2019.

(c) Any governmental entity that has been terminated under this section may be continued, reestablished, or restructured in accordance with this chapter.

Effective date 5/13/2013 SECTION 3. This act shall take effect upon becoming a law, the public welfare requiring it.

PUBLIC CHAPTER NO. 332

PUBLIC CHAPTER NO. 332

HOUSE BILL NO. 780

By Representatives Matheny, Ragan

Substituted for: Senate Bill No. 313

By Senator Bell

AN ACT to amend Tennessee Code Annotated, Title 4, Chapter 29 and Title 63, Chapter 5, relative to the board of dentistry.

BE IT ENACTED BY THE GENERAL ASSEMBLY OF THE STATE OF TENNESSEE:

4-29-234 SECTION 1. Tennessee Code Annotated, Section 4-29-234(a), is amended by deleting subdivision (7) in its entirety.

4-29-238 SECTION 2. Tennessee Code Annotated, Section 4-29-238(a), is amended by adding a new subdivision thereto, as follows:

( ) Board of dentistry, created by § 63-5-101;

Effective date 5/13/2013 SECTION 3. This act shall take effect upon becoming a law, the public welfare requiring it.

PUBLIC CHAPTER NO. 333

PUBLIC CHAPTER NO. 333

HOUSE BILL NO. 794

By Representatives Matheny, Ragan

Substituted for: Senate Bill No. 334

By Senator Bell

AN ACT to amend Tennessee Code Annotated, Title 4, Chapter 29 and Title 49, Chapter 17, relative to the energy efficient schools council.

BE IT ENACTED BY THE GENERAL ASSEMBLY OF THE STATE OF TENNESSEE:

4-29-234 SECTION 1. Tennessee Code Annotated, Section 4-29-234(a), is amended by deleting subdivision (28) in its entirety.

4-29-235 SECTION 2. Tennessee Code Annotated, Section 4-29-235(a), is amended by adding a new subdivision thereto, as follows:

( ) Energy efficient schools council, created by § 49-17-103;

Effective date 5/13/2013 SECTION 3. This act shall take effect upon becoming a law, the public welfare requiring it.

PUBLIC CHAPTER NO. 334

PUBLIC CHAPTER NO. 334

HOUSE BILL NO. 810

By Representatives Matheny, Ragan,

Substituted for: Senate Bill No. 326

By Senator Bell

AN ACT to amend Tennessee Code Annotated, Title 4, Chapter 29 and Title 4, Chapter 3, relative to the department of correction.

BE IT ENACTED BY THE GENERAL ASSEMBLY OF THE STATE OF TENNESSEE:

4-29-234 SECTION 1. Tennessee Code Annotated, Section 4-29-234(a), is amended by deleting subdivision (20) in its entirety.

4-29-236 SECTION 2. Tennessee Code Annotated, Section 4-29-236(a), is amended by adding a new subdivision thereto, as follows:

( ) Department of correction, created by §§ 4-3-101 and 4-3-601;

SECTION 3. The division of state audit shall return to the department of correction in 2014 for the purpose of conducting a limited audit to review actions taken by the department to address the issues raised in the findings of the September, 2012 performance audit report. The division of state audit shall complete the limited audit within a period sufficient to allow for its review by the Government Operations Joint Subcommittee on Judiciary and Government no later than December 1, 2014.

Effective date 5/13/2013 SECTION 4. This act shall take effect upon becoming a law, the public welfare requiring it.

PUBLIC CHAPTER NO. 335

PUBLIC CHAPTER NO. 335

HOUSE BILL NO. 841

By Representatives Durham, Holt

Substituted for: Senate Bill No. 591

By Senator Johnson

AN ACT to amend Tennessee Code Annotated, Title 12, Chapter 4, Part 1, relative to public contracts.

BE IT ENACTED BY THE GENERAL ASSEMBLY OF THE STATE OF TENNESSEE:

12-4-903 SECTION 1. Tennessee Code Annotated, Title 12, Chapter 4, is amended by deleting the language "for manufacture of public works, or overseeing such procurement, construction or manufacture".

Effective date 5/13/2013 SECTION 2. This act shall take effect upon becoming a law and shall apply to any action filed on or after that date, the public welfare requiring it.

PUBLIC CHAPTER NO. 336

PUBLIC CHAPTER NO. 336

HOUSE BILL NO. 868

By Representatives Sexton, Dale Carr, Doss, McCormick, Haynes, Ryan Williams

Substituted for: Senate Bill No. 705

By Senators McNally, Overbey, Burks, Campfield, Yager

AN ACT to amend Tennessee Code Annotated, Title 39, Chapter 17, Part 4; Title 53; Title 63 and Chapter 880 of the Private Acts of 2012, relative to dispensing prescription medicines.

BE IT ENACTED BY THE GENERAL ASSEMBLY OF THE STATE OF TENNESSEE:

63-1-313 SECTION 1. Tennessee Code Annotated, Title 63, Chapter 1, Part 3, is amended by adding the following as a new section:

63-1-313.

(a) Notwithstanding any provision of this title or title 53, chapters 10 and 11 to the contrary, no pain management clinic or medical doctor, osteopathic physician, advanced practice nurse with certificates of fitness to prescribe, or physician assistant working at a pain management clinic shall be permitted to dispense controlled substances; provided, however, this subsection shall not prohibit a medical doctor, osteopathic physician, advanced practice nurse with certificates of fitness to prescribe, or physician assistant working at a pain management clinic from providing to that practitioner's patient, without charge, a sample of a schedule IV or schedule V controlled substance in a quantity limited to an amount that is adequate to treat the patient for a maximum of seventy-two (72) hours.

(b) For the purposes of this section, "controlled substance" has the meaning given in § 39-17-402.

63-1-301 SECTION 2. Tennessee Code Annotated, Title 63-1-301(5), is amended by deleting the language "or dispensed," in its entirety.

63-1-309 SECTION 3. Tennessee Code Annotated, Section 63-1-309(c), is amended by deleting the language "dispenses or" and "or dispensing" in their entireties.

63-1-309 SECTION 4. Tennessee Code Annotated, Section 63-1-309(c), is amended by deleting the language "dispenses or" and "or dispensing" in their entireties.

Effective date 7/1/2013 SECTION 5. Section 4 of this act shall take effect 12:01 a.m. July 1, 2016, the public welfare requiring it. The remainder of this act shall take effect July 1, 2013, the public welfare requiring it.

PUBLIC CHAPTER NO. 337

PUBLIC CHAPTER NO. 337

HOUSE BILL NO. 920

By Representatives Moody, Coley, Rogers, Littleton, Weaver, Camper, Parkinson, Gilmore, Hardaway, Miller, Lollar, Towns, Mark White

Substituted for: Senate Bill No. 1031

By Senators Kelsey, Yager, Beavers, Haile, Overbey, Stevens

AN ACT to amend Tennessee Code Annotated, Title 39 and Title 40, relative to criminal defenses.

BE IT ENACTED BY THE GENERAL ASSEMBLY OF THE STATE OF TENNESSEE:

39-11-502 SECTION 1. Tennessee Code Annotated, Section 39-11-502, is amended by adding the following as a new, appropriately designated subsection:

( ) It shall not be a defense to prosecution for a violation of § 39-13-514 or § 39-13-529(a), (b)(1) or (b)(2) that the person charged was ignorant or mistaken as to the age of a minor.

39-13-529 SECTION 2. Tennessee Code Annotated, Section 39-13-529, is amended by adding the following new subdivision (4) to subsection (b):

(4)

(A) Except as provided in subdivision (B), it is an exception to the application of this subsection that the victim is at least fifteen (15) but less than eighteen (18) years of age and the defendant is no more than four (4) years older than the victim.

(B) Subdivision (A) shall not apply or be an exception to the application of subdivision (A), if the defendant intentionally commanded, hired, induced or caused the victim to violate this subsection (b).

Effective date 7/1/2013 SECTION 3. This act shall take effect July 1, 2013, the public welfare requiring it.

PUBLIC CHAPTER NO. 338

PUBLIC CHAPTER NO. 338

HOUSE BILL NO. 1276

By Representatives McCormick, Mark White, Camper, Favors, Hardaway, Parkinson, Powers, Johnnie Turner, Roach, Harry Brooks, Halford, Kane, Weaver

Substituted for: Senate Bill No. 1330

By Senators Norris, Burks, Tate

AN ACT to amend Tennessee Code Annotated, Title 4; Title 9; Title 49; Title 50 and Title 67, relative to creating the Labor Education Alignment Program ("LEAP").

BE IT ENACTED BY THE GENERAL ASSEMBLY OF THE STATE OF TENNESSEE:

SECTION 1. Tennessee Code Annotated, Title 49, Chapter 7, is amended by adding Sections 2 through 13 of this act as a new, appropriately designated part.

49-7-1201 – 49-7-1212

SECTION 2. The purposes of this part are to establish a statewide, comprehensive labor education alignment program, also referred to as the "program" or "LEAP," to enable students in technology centers and community colleges to participate in employment training and to attain industry-recognized post-secondary credentials for sustaining gainful and quality employment in this state; and to enable students to more adequately meet the advanced technical training needs required by current and future employers of existing and prospective industries and businesses in this state.

SECTION 3. The purpose of the labor education alignment program is to provide students at technology centers and community colleges the opportunity to combine occupational training in a high-skill or high-technology industry with academic credit and to apply that combined work and academic experience towards acquiring a post-secondary credential. Any technology center or community college may establish a labor education alignment program under this part, subject to the approval of the board of regents. The labor education alignment program shall enable employers to employ a participating student on such basis as the employer determines appropriate, and to provide occupational training to the student during the period of employment; provided, that any cooperative education earnings, wages, salary, or other compensation received by the student shall not be included in any determination of the student's eligibility for any state financial assistance or grants. The labor education alignment program shall also allow the transferability of the student's completed occupational training and academic hours at other technology centers, community colleges, and post-secondary institutions in this state in accordance with established transfer pathways, and institution and program accreditation requirements. Notwithstanding any provision of this part to the contrary, the labor education alignment program shall not in any way adversely affect the accreditation of an institution.

SECTION 4. The higher education commission shall coordinate efforts with the department of labor and workforce development and the department of economic and community development in developing, administering, and implementing a labor education alignment program pursuant to this part. The higher education commission shall make specific efforts to encourage technology centers and community colleges in this state to offer a labor education alignment program under this part, in an effort to train students in needed high-skill and high-technology industries in this state. The higher education commission shall coordinate the following priorities to the extent possible:

(1) Creating a labor education alignment program at community colleges and technology centers in this state with students having the opportunity to participate;

(2) Planning and partnership with business, labor, education, government, community-based organizations, employers, and students;

(3) Providing training in regions identified in the report submitted by the department of economic and community development as workforce needs pursuant to Section 10;

(4) Career preparation and guidance incorporated in the curriculum and materials;

(5) Job placement and job retention support services;

(6) Applied learning experiences, including prior learning assessments;

(7) Integration of basic skills and work-readiness training with occupational skills training;

(8) Performance assessment of the programs created under this initiative;

(9) Actual or simulated learning at the worksite;

(10) Curriculum and employment training for industries that promote high-skill jobs in high-technology areas, emerging occupations, or skilled manufacturing jobs; including, but not limited to, the following:

(A) Advanced manufacturing;

(B) Electronics;

(C) Information technology;

(D) Infrastructure engineering; and

(E) Transportation and logistics.

SECTION 5. The department of labor and workforce development shall utilize existing staff to assist individuals interested in seeking post-secondary degrees. Efforts shall be made to encourage individuals to enroll in labor education alignment programs offered at technology centers and community colleges, and to seek employment in high-skill or high-technology industries.

SECTION 6. The board of regents, with input from the higher education commission, shall coordinate curriculum development by the faculty and related resource materials to assist educators, employers, and students with workplace training and placement. The curriculum and materials shall, at a minimum, meet the necessary skill standards of high-skill and high-technology industries in this state. The curriculum and materials shall define courses that are necessary for each technical career field that may lead to a post-secondary credential. The curriculum shall be developed by faculty who teach within the field and shall outline the academic and technical courses that are necessary for each post-secondary award, credential or degree to be awarded under this part.

SECTION 7. Subject to appropriation by the general assembly in the annual appropriations act, the department of economic and community development, in consultation with the board of regents and higher education commission, may award a grant to any technology center or community college in this state that is located in a region where advanced training opportunities or a highly-skilled workforce is lacking. The funds from such grant shall be used to establish and implement a labor education alignment program under this part. The department shall establish procedures for grant applications, eligibility and reporting requirements, and the maximum amount of the grant authorized by this section.

SECTION 8. Each community college and technology center in this state is authorized to establish a labor education alignment program under this part, with the appropriate approvals as required by the higher education commission and the board of regents; provided, that the labor education alignment program shall enable students to obtain a post-secondary credential; and to achieve one (1) or more of the following outcomes:

(1) Acquire and demonstrate competency in basic skills, including English and math;

(2) Acquire and demonstrate competency in a specified technical field; and

(3) Any other goals identified by the departments and the higher education commission, made in consultation and agreement with the board of regents.

SECTION 9. There is created in the state treasury a "workforce advanced training fund," referred to in this part as the "fund." The fund shall consist of monies appropriated to the fund by the general assembly. Interest accruing on investments and deposits of the fund shall be carried forward into the subsequent fiscal year. Any fund balance remaining unexpended at the end of a fiscal year shall remain in the fund and shall not be transferred or revert to the general fund of the state at the end of any fiscal year. Monies in the fund shall be invested by the state treasurer in accordance with § 9-4-603. The fund shall be administered by the department of economic and community development. Monies in the fund shall be subject to annual appropriation by the general assembly to the department of economic and community development to cover the costs associated with the establishment of the labor education alignment program and any grants authorized pursuant to this part.

SECTION 10. On or before November 1, 2013, and on or before November 1 of each subsequent year, the department of economic and community development shall submit a report to the higher education commission and the department of labor and workforce development on any workforce needs within existing and prospective businesses or industries in this state, including any areas of specialization within a vocation, identified by the department to be necessary to attract, develop, and retain high-skill or high-technology businesses and industries in this state.

SECTION 11. On or before January 1, 2016, the higher education commission shall submit a report to the education committees of the senate and the house of representatives detailing degree completion of participants in each labor education alignment program established in the state and the program goals for the upcoming year, in addition to any recommendations for legislation. On or before January 1, 2016, and on or before January 1 of each subsequent year, the higher education commission shall submit a report to the commerce and labor committee of the senate, and the consumer and human resources committee of the house of representatives, which shall include findings regarding job placement and any recommendations for legislation.

SECTION 12. The higher education commission, in consultation with the department of labor and workforce development and the department of economic and community development, is authorized to establish any policies and guidelines, and to promulgate rules and regulations, to effectuate the purposes of this part. Such rules and regulations shall be promulgated in accordance with the Uniform Administrative Procedures Act, compiled in title 4, chapter 5.

SECTION 13. The higher education commission shall monitor the operation of the labor education alignment program, and require periodic reporting by the technology centers and community colleges conducting the programs as the executive director deems appropriate, reasonable and necessary to evaluate the performance and effectiveness of the programs throughout the state.

SECTION 14. Nothing in this act shall be construed to be an appropriation of funds and no funds shall be obligated or expended pursuant to the act unless such funds are specifically appropriated by the general appropriations act.

Effective date 1-1-2014

SECTION 15. For the purposes of promulgating rules and regulations, this act shall take effect upon becoming a law, the public welfare requiring it. Section 10 of this act shall take effect upon becoming a law, the public welfare requiring it. The remaining sections of this act shall take effect January 1, 2014, the public welfare requiring it.

PUBLIC CHAPTER NO. 339

PUBLIC CHAPTER NO. 339

HOUSE BILL NO. 1246

By Representative Curtis Johnson

Substituted for: Senate Bill No. 1303

By Senator McNally

AN ACT to amend Tennessee Code Annotated, Title 8; Title 38; Title 39; Title 40; Title 48 and Title 67, relative to criminal law.

WHEREAS, combating sales tax fraud must be vigorously and consistently pursued to assure that law abiding citizens and taxpayers of Tennessee do not bear undue burdens because of those who cheat and break the sales tax law; and

WHEREAS, when sales tax receipts fall below estimates due to fraud the reduction in resources may negatively impact the health, education and safety of our citizens; and

WHEREAS, district attorneys general recognize the need to work closely with the Tennessee Department of Revenue to combat sales tax fraud; and

WHEREAS, the commissioner of revenue was invited to attend and did attend the September 2012 meeting of the Tennessee district attorneys conference; and

WHEREAS, at that meeting the commissioner and the district attorneys discussed ways to better investigate, prepare for and prosecute sales tax fraud cases; and

WHEREAS, discussion continues as they collaborate on this subject and a report to the general assembly will be helpful to ensure the elected senators and representatives of this state are kept apprised of these discussions and of any legislative recommendations which may come from those discussions; now, therefore

BE IT ENACTED BY THE GENERAL ASSEMBLY OF THE STATE OF TENNESSEE:

SECTION 1. The general assembly hereby directs the executive director of the Tennessee district attorneys general conference, in consultation with the commissioner of revenue shall prepare a report to the general assembly on steps which should be taken with respect to improvement of sales tax fraud investigations and prosecutions. The report shall include, but not be limited to, the following:

(1) Recommendations on hiring additional investigators, accountants, auditors or staff by the department of revenue including computer specialists and clerical staff and any specialized training needed for investigators and staff members to enhance their knowledge and skills for combating sales tax fraud;

(2) Any recommendations by the Tennessee district attorneys general conference on hiring prosecutors or district attorneys general pro tem, accountants or auditors, expert witnesses, including computer specialists and clerical staff and any specialized training needed for prosecutors and staff members to enhance their knowledge and skills for combating sales tax fraud.

SECTION 2. The executive director of the Tennessee district attorneys general conference, in consultation with the commissioner of revenue, may take any steps under current authority to better combat sales tax fraud as may be found during the course of the reporting period.

SECTION 3. The report to the general assembly shall be completed and transmitted to the chief clerk of the Senate and the chief clerk of the House of Representatives no later than March 15, 2014.

Effective date 5/13/2013

SECTION 4. This act shall take effect upon becoming a law, the public welfare requiring it.

PUBLIC CHAPTER NO. 340

PUBLIC CHAPTER NO. 340

HOUSE BILL NO. 1213

By Representative Michael Turner

Substituted for: Senate Bill No. 707

By Senator Harper

AN ACT to amend Tennessee Code Annotated, Title 7, Chapter 4, Part 2, relative to an additional tourist accommodation tax upon the occupancy of each hotel room located within the territory of certain metropolitan governments.

BE IT ENACTED BY THE GENERAL ASSEMBLY OF THE STATE OF TENNESSEE:

7-4-202 SECTION 1. Tennessee Code Annotated, Section 7-4-202(d), is amended by deleting subdivision (2) in its entirety and by substituting instead the following new language:

> (2) The authority to charge the amount of the privilege tax imposed on hotel room occupancy by subsection (a) in excess of two dollars ($2.00) and the terms of the committee members shall expire six (6) years from May 21, 2014.

Effective date 7/1/2013 SECTION 2. This act shall take effect July 1, 2013, the public welfare requiring it.

PUBLIC CHAPTER NO. 341

PUBLIC CHAPTER NO. 341

HOUSE BILL NO. 1084

By Representatives Alexander, Sexton, Ryan Williams

Substituted for: Senate Bill No. 1195

By Senators Tracy, Bowling

AN ACT to amend Tennessee Code Annotated, Title 57, Chapter 2, relative to the manufacturing of intoxicating liquors.

BE IT ENACTED BY THE GENERAL ASSEMBLY OF THE STATE OF TENNESSEE:

57-2-106 SECTION 1. Tennessee Code Annotated, Title 57, Chapter 2 is amended by adding the following language as a new section:

(a) An intoxicating liquor may not be advertised, described, labeled, named, sold or referred to for marketing or sales purposes as "Tennessee Whiskey", "Tennessee Whisky", "Tennessee Sour Mash Whiskey" or "Tennessee Sour Mash Whisky" unless the intoxicating liquor is:

(1) Manufactured in Tennessee;

(2) Made of a grain mixture that is at least fifty-one percent (51%) corn;

(3) Distilled to no more than 160 proof or eighty percent (80%) alcohol by volume;

(4) Aged in new, charred oak barrels in Tennessee;

(5) Filtered through maple charcoal prior to aging;

(6) Placed in the barrel at no more than 125 proof or sixty-two and one-half percent (62.5 %) alcohol by volume; and

(7) Bottled at not less than 80 proof or forty percent (40%) alcohol by volume.

(b) Any manufacturer who violates this section shall be subject to suspension or revocation of its license for a period of not less than one (1) year.

(c) Subdivision (a)(5) of this section shall not apply to intoxicating liquor manufactured at a distillery located in a county that authorized the manufacturing process by referendum after January 1, 1979, and prior to January 1, 1980; provided, however, that any such distillery was first licensed by the state alcoholic beverage commission after January 1, 2000, and before January 1, 2001.

(d)

(1) Any Tennessee corporation, limited liability company or proprietorship that holds a federal distiller basic permit pursuant to 27 U.S.C. § 204 and had a licensed manufacturing operation in this state as of January 1, 2013, may label, market and sell any product owned or contracted to purchase by such permit holder on or after the effective date of this act for a period of thirty-six (36) months; provided, however, any product manufactured at such distillery after the effective date of this act shall meet all the requirements of subsection (a) to be advertised, described, labeled, named, sold or referred to for marketing or sales purposes as "Tennessee Whiskey", "Tennessee Whisky", "Tennessee Sour Mash Whiskey", or "Tennessee Sour Mash Whisky".

(2) This subsection (d) shall apply to any product that is referred to as "Tennessee Whiskey", "Tennessee Whisky", "Tennessee Sour Mash Whiskey",

or "Tennessee Sour Mash Whisky" under 27 CFR Part 5 on the effective date of this act.

57-2-104 SECTION 2. Tennessee Code Annotated, Section 57-2-104, is amended by deleting the comma after the language “only within the county authorizing the operation,” and adding the language “or in a county adjacent to the county authorizing the manufacturing operation,”.

57-2-110 SECTION 3. Tennessee Code Annotated, Title 57, chapter 2, part 1, is amended by adding the following as a new section thereto:

57-2-1__.

The hours of sale for a manufacturer licensed to sell products at retail under § 57-3-204(f) shall be the same as for a manufacturer licensed to sell products at retail under § 57-3-202.

Effective date 7/1/2013 SECTION 4. This act shall take effect July 1, 2013, the public welfare requiring it.

PUBLIC CHAPTER NO. 342

PUBLIC CHAPTER NO. 342

HOUSE BILL NO. 952

By Representative Wirgau

Substituted for: Senate Bill No. 1160

By Senator Stevens

AN ACT to amend Tennessee Code Annotated, Title 68, Chapter 211, Part 7, relative to landfills.

BE IT ENACTED BY THE GENERAL ASSEMBLY OF THE STATE OF TENNESSEE:

68-211-701 SECTION 1. Tennessee Code Annotated, Section 68-211-701, is amended by designating the existing language as subsection (a) and adding the following language:

(b) Prior to accepting any waste that would require a change in the classification of a landfill under rules promulgated pursuant to this chapter to a classification with higher standards including, but not limited to, changing the classification from a Class III or IV to a Class I or II or from a Class II to a Class I, the plans for which were approved pursuant to subsection (a), the landfill operator shall first submit the proposal to accept the waste to:

(1) The county legislative body in which the landfill that is the subject of the proposed change in classification is located, if such landfill is located in an unincorporated area;

(2) Both the county legislative body and the governing body of the municipality in which the landfill that is the subject of the proposed change in classification is located, if such landfill is located in an incorporated area; or

(3) Both the county legislative body of the county in which the landfill that is the subject of the proposed change in classification is located and the governing body of any municipality which is located within one (1) mile of such landfill.

(c) After submission to the county legislative body or municipality under subsection (b), the county legislative body or the municipality or both shall give public notice and an opportunity for public hearing on the proposal and then approve or disapprove it in accordance with § 68-211-704(a) and (b). Judicial review of the decision shall be available in accordance with § 68-211-704(c).

68-211-707 SECTION 2. Tennessee Code Annotated, Section 68-211-707, is amended by adding the following as a new subsection (b) and redesignating the existing subsection (b) as subsection (c):

(b) In any county or municipality in which §§ 68-211-701 — 68-211-704 and this section have been approved by a two-thirds (2/3) vote of the appropriate legislative body prior to the effective date of this act, § 68-211-701(b) shall only apply if it is approved by a two-thirds (2/3) vote of the appropriate legislative body.

Effective date 5/13/2013 SECTION 3. This act shall take effect upon becoming a law, the public welfare requiring it.

PUBLIC CHAPTER NO. 343

PUBLIC CHAPTER NO. 343

HOUSE BILL NO. 453

By Representatives Hardaway, Towns, Parkinson, Camper

Substituted for: Senate Bill No. 934

By Senator Ford

AN ACT to amend Tennessee Code Annotated, Title 37, relative to juveniles.

BE IT ENACTED BY THE GENERAL ASSEMBLY OF THE STATE OF TENNESSEE:

37-1-131 SECTION 1. Tennessee Code Annotated, Section 37-1-131(a), is amended by adding the following language as a new subdivision:

(8)

(A) In lieu of committing a child to the custody of the department of children's services and subject to the requirements of subdivision (a)(8)(B), the court may order any of the following if the child is found to be a delinquent child:

(i) Assign a long-term mentor to such child; or

(ii) Require that the delinquent child or any of the child's family members receive counseling services from any counseling service provided through or approved by the juvenile court.

(B) An order may be issued under subdivision (a)(8)(A) only if the funding necessary to implement such order is appropriated by the legislative body of the county in which the court is located or is provided by grants from public or private sources.

Effective date 7/1/2013 SECTION 2. This act shall take effect July 1, 2013, the public welfare requiring it.

PUBLIC CHAPTER NO. 344

PUBLIC CHAPTER NO. 344

HOUSE BILL NO. 353

By Representatives Shipley, Lamberth, Weaver, Faison, Casada, Evans, Watson, Sexton, Rogers, Jernigan, Kevin Brooks, John DeBerry, Sargent, Littleton, Moody, Durham, Farmer, Butt, Camper, Stewart, Calfee, Eldridge, Ryan Williams, Shepard, Shaw, Roach, Hardaway, Dale Carr, Dean, McDaniel, Harry Brooks, Lollar, Travis, Coley, Alexander, Powell, McManus, Powers, Dunn, Mark White, Kane, Ragan, Hall

Substituted for: Senate Bill No. 670

By Senators Beavers, Haile, Bell, Campfield, Gardenhire, Dickerson, Bowling, Green, Johnson, Yager, Harper, Burks

AN ACT to amend Tennessee Code Annotated, Title 55, relative to ignition interlock.

BE IT ENACTED BY THE GENERAL ASSEMBLY OF THE STATE OF TENNESSEE:

55-10-404 SECTION 1. Tennessee Code Annotated, Section 55-10-404(a), as created by Chapter __ of the Public Acts of 2013 (HB 180/SB 186), is amended by deleting the subsection and substituting instead the following:

(a)

(1) The court shall prohibit any person convicted of a violation of § 55-10-401 from driving a vehicle in this state for a period of:

(A) One (1) year, if the conviction is a first offense;

(B) Two (2) years for a second offense;

(C) Six (6) years for a third offense; and,

(D) Eight (8) years for a fourth or subsequent offense.

(2) In the interest of public safety, a driver who has been prohibited from driving a vehicle in this state pursuant to this subsection (a) may apply for a restricted license subject to § 55-10-409.

55-10-407 SECTION 2. Tennessee Code Annotated, Section 55-10-407(c)(1), as created by Chapter __ of the Public Acts of 2013 (HB 180/SB 186), is amended by adding the language "person's driver license is currently suspended for an" between the language "the" and "implied consent" and by deleting the language "result" and by substituting instead "resulted".

55-10-407 SECTION 3. Tennessee Code Annotated, Section 55-10-407(d)(2) and (3), as created by Chapter __ of the Public Acts of 2013 (HB 180/SB 186), are amended by deleting the subdivisions in their entireties and redesignating the remaining subdivision appropriately.

55-10-409 SECTION 4. Tennessee Code Annotated, Section 55-10-409(a)(2) and (3), as created by Chapter __ of the Public Acts of 2013 (HB 180/SB 186), are amended by deleting the subdivisions and substituting instead the following:

(2) Seriously injured or killed another person in the course of the conduct that resulted in the driver's conviction under § 55-10-401 or a similar offense in another state. A driver who has committed such an offense shall not be eligible for and the court shall not have the authority to grant the issuance of a restricted motor vehicle operator's license until such time as the period of suspension mandated by § 55-10-404 has expired, notwithstanding the fact that it may be the driver's first conviction.

55-10-409 SECTION 5. Tennessee Code Annotated, Section 55-10-409(b)(1), as created by Chapter __ of the Public Acts of 2013 (HB 180/SB 186), is amended by deleting the subdivision in its entirety and substituting instead the following:

PUBLIC CHAPTER NO. 344 (cont'd)

(1)

(A) Except as provided in subsection (a), if a person's motor vehicle operator's license has been revoked pursuant to § 55-10-404 or § 55-10-406, the person may apply to the trial judge or a judge of any court in the person's county of residence having jurisdiction to try charges for driving under the influence for a restricted driver license.

(i) If the person's present conviction for driving under the influence of an intoxicant is an offense for which subdivision (b)(2)(B) requires the court to order the person to operate only a motor vehicle that is equipped with a functioning ignition interlock device, the court may order the issuance of a restricted motor vehicle operator's license subject to such limitations. The court shall have discretion to order additional limitations, including but not limited to geographic restrictions as provided in subsection (c), on the restricted motor vehicle license.

(ii) If the person's violation of § 55-10-406 or present conviction for driving under the influence of an intoxicant is not an offense for which subdivision (b)(2)(B) requires the court to order the person to operate only a motor vehicle that is equipped with a functioning ignition interlock device, the court may order the issuance of a restricted motor vehicle operator's license. The court shall have discretion to order the person to operate only a motor vehicle that is equipped with a functioning ignition interlock device or place additional limitations on the person's restricted license; provided, however, that a restricted license issued pursuant to this subdivision (b)(1)(A)(ii) without an ignition interlock requirement shall be subject to geographic restrictions as provided in subsection (c).

(B)

(i) A Tennessee resident, whose operator's license has been revoked because of a conviction in another jurisdiction for operating a motor vehicle while under the influence of an intoxicant, may apply for a restricted license to a judge of any court in the person's county of residence having jurisdiction to try charges for driving under the influence. The court may order the issuance of a restricted motor vehicle operator's license. The court shall have discretion to order the person to operate only a motor vehicle that is equipped with a functioning ignition interlock device or place additional limitations on the person's restricted license; provided, however, that a restricted license issued pursuant to this subdivision (b)(1)(B)(i) without an ignition interlock requirement shall be subject to geographic restrictions as provided in subsection (c). If the person has a prior conviction within the past ten (10) years for a violation of § 55-10-401 or § 55-10-421, in this state or a similar offense in any other jurisdiction, the court shall be required to order the person to operate only a motor vehicle that is equipped with a functioning ignition interlock device.

(ii) If a copy of the judgment of conviction certified by the court that tried the case in the other jurisdiction accompanies the restricted license application, the court may issue such order allowing the person so convicted to operate a motor vehicle including such restrictions ordered by the court that tried the case in the other jurisdiction provided such restrictions do not conflict with Tennessee statutes or regulations.

(C) A person ordered to operate only a motor vehicle that is equipped with a functioning ignition interlock device pursuant to this subsection (b) may apply for assistance to meet the requirement pursuant to § 55-10-419, except as provided in subdivision (b)(2)(C).

55-10-409 SECTION 6. Tennessee Code Annotated, Section 55-10-409(b)(2)(B)(i), as created by Chapter __ of the Public Acts of 2013 (HB 180/SB 186), is amended by deleting the subdivision and substituting instead the following:

(i) The person was convicted of a violation of § 55-10-401 and had a blood or breath alcohol concentration of eight hundredths of one percent (.08%) or higher or a combination of alcohol in any amount and marijuana, a controlled substance, controlled substance analogue, drug, or any substance affecting the central nervous system;

55-10-409 SECTION 7. Tennessee Code Annotated, Section 55-10-409(b)(2), as created by Chapter __ of the Public Acts of 2013 (HB 180/SB 186), is amended by deleting subdivisions (b)(2)(C) – (E) in their entireties and substituting instead the following:

(C) A person convicted of § 55-10-401, who is eligible for a restricted license under subsection (a) and who is not required to have an interlock device pursuant to subdivision (b)(2) or other statute, may request the court order the installation and use of an ignition interlock in lieu of geographic restrictions or additional limitations on the restricted license. The person shall pay all costs associated with the device and is not eligible for ignition interlock fund assistance under § 55-10-419.

(D) A court may also order a person whose license has been suspended pursuant to § 55-10-407 to operate only a motor vehicle that is equipped with a functioning ignition interlock with or without geographic restrictions which shall remain on the vehicle during the entire period of the restricted license. A person ordered to operate only a motor vehicle that is equipped with a functioning ignition interlock device pursuant to this subdivision (b)(2)(D) may apply for assistance to meet the requirement pursuant to § 55-10-419.

55-10-409 SECTION 8. Tennessee Code Annotated, Section 55-10-409(c), as created by Chapter __ of the Public Acts of 2013 (HB 180/SB 186), is amended by deleting the subsection in its entirety and substituting instead the following:

(c)

(1) If a court issues an order allowing a person to operate a motor vehicle with geographic restrictions, the court shall specify the necessary time and places of permissible operation of a motor vehicle, for the limited purposes of going to and from:

(A) And working at the person's regular place of employment;

(B) The office of the person's probation officer or other similar location for the sole purpose of attending a regularly scheduled meeting or other function with the probation officer by a route to be designated by the probation officer;

(C) A court-ordered alcohol safety program;

(D) A college or university in the case of a student enrolled full time in the college or university;

(E) A scheduled interlock monitoring appointment;

(F) A court ordered outpatient alcohol and drug treatment program; and

(G) The person's regular place of worship for regularly scheduled religious services conducted by a bona fide religious institution as defined in § 48-101-502(c).

(2) A court order issued under subsection (b) may be presented within ten (10) days after the date of issuance to the department, accompanied by a fee of sixty-five dollars ($65.00) and proof to the satisfaction of the department that a functioning ignition interlock device has been installed and will be maintained on one (1) or more vehicles to be operated by the person for the duration of the restricted license, if such installation and maintenance is required by subdivision (b)(2)(B) or the court's order. If the person has first successfully completed a driver license examination, the department shall forthwith issue a restricted license specifying that such restricted license authorizes the person, except as

provided in § 55-10-415(m)(1), to operate only noncommercial vehicles equipped with a functioning ignition interlock device, if required, and embodying additional limitations imposed by the court upon the person.

(3) If the violation resulting in the person's conviction for driving under the influence or the person's violation of § 55-10-406 occurred prior to July 1, 2013, the law in effect when the violation occurred shall govern the person's eligibility for a restricted motor vehicle operator license unless the person petitions the court to consider the person's eligibility under the law in effect when the petition is filed.

55-10-409 SECTION 9. Tennessee Code Annotated, Section 55-10-409(d), as created by Chapter __ of the Public Acts of 2013 (HB 180/SB 186), is amended by deleting the subsection in its entirety and substituting instead the following:

(d)

(1) Unless otherwise prohibited by subsection (a), the trial judge or a judge of any court in the person's county of residence having jurisdiction to try charges for driving under the influence may order the issuance of a restricted motor vehicle operator's license in accordance with § 55-50-502 to any person whose motor vehicle operator's license has been revoked pursuant to § 55-10-404 and who has a prior conviction within the past ten (10) years for a violation of § 55-10-401 or § 55-10-421, in this state or a similar offense in any other jurisdiction.

(2)

(i) If the court orders the issuance of a restricted motor vehicle operator's license pursuant to this subsection (d), the court shall also order the person, except as provided in § 55-10-417(m)(1), to operate only a motor vehicle that is equipped with a functioning ignition interlock device. The restriction shall be for the entire period of the restricted license and for a period of six (6) months after the license revocation period has expired if required by § 55-10-417(l).

(ii) Sections 55-10-417, 55-10-418 and 55-10-419 shall apply when a person is ordered to operate only a motor vehicle that is equipped with a functioning ignition interlock device pursuant to this subsection (d).

55-10-411 SECTION 10. Tennessee Code Annotated, Section 55-10-411(h)(3), as created by Chapter __ of the Public Acts of 2013 (HB 180/SB 186), is amended by deleting the subdivision in its entirety and substituting instead the following:

(3) "Functioning ignition interlock device" means a device that connects a motor vehicle ignition system to a breath-alcohol analyzer and prevents a motor vehicle ignition from starting if a driver's blood alcohol level exceeds the calibrated setting on the device and which devices, on all new installations after the effective date of this act, must employ technology capable of taking a photo identifying the person providing the breath sample, recording the date, the time and the test result along with the photo of the person providing the test and storing such information on the device for transfer to remote storage and reporting; provided, however, that the department of safety shall permit the continued installation by an ignition interlock provider of an ignition interlock device that is not capable taking photos or recording and storing the information required by this subdivision for up to six (6) months from the earliest effective date of this act; and

55-10-417 SECTION 11. Tennessee Code Annotated, Section 55-10-417(a)(2), as created by Chapter __ of the Public Acts of 2013 (HB 180/SB 186), is amended by deleting the subdivision and substituting the following:

(2) If a person is convicted of a first offense of § 55-10-401, and the person is not required to operate only a motor vehicle with an ignition interlock device pursuant to § 55-10-409(b)(2)(B), and the person is otherwise eligible for a restricted license pursuant to § 55-10-409(b)(1)(A), such person may request and the court may order the installation and use of an ignition interlock device in lieu of geographic restrictions or additional limitations on the restricted license. A person so requesting shall pay all costs associated with the ignition interlock

device and no funds from the interlock assistance fund shall be used to pay any cost associated with the device, regardless of whether or not the person is indigent.

55-10-417 SECTION 12. Tennessee Code Annotated, Section 55-10-417(b), as created by Chapter __ of the Public Acts of 2013 (HB 180/SB 186), is amended by deleting the subsection in its entirety.

55-10-419 SECTION 13. Tennessee Code Annotated, Section 55-10-419(g)(3)(B) and (C), as created by Chapter __ of the Public Acts of 2013 (HB 180/SB 186), are amended by deleting the subdivisions and substituting instead the following:

(B) Beginning on July 1, 2013, and annually thereafter, the treasurer shall conduct an analysis to determine the solvency of the interlock assistance fund. The treasurer may declare a surplus if the analysis determines that there is a balance in excess of the amount necessary to maintain the solvency of the fund, and shall report the amount of any surplus to the commissioner of finance and administration for inclusion in the annual budget document prepared pursuant to title 9, chapter 4, part 51.

55-50-502 SECTION 14. Tennessee Code Annotated, Section 55-50-502(c)(3)(A), is amended by deleting the language:

to operate a motor vehicle for the purpose of going to and from and working at the person's regular place of employment.

and substituting instead the language:

to operate a motor vehicle for the purpose of going to and from and working at the person's regular place of employment or to operate only a motor vehicle that is equipped with a functioning ignition interlock device. The trial judge may order the issuance of a restricted license allowing a person whose license has been suspended due to a conviction for violating § 39-14-151 or title 55, chapter 10, part 5 to operate a motor vehicle for the purpose of going to and from and working at the person's regular place of employment.

55-50-502 SECTION 15. Tennessee Code Annotated, Section 55-50-502(c)(3)(B), is amended by deleting the subdivision in its entirety and substituting instead the following:

(B) The judge may order the issuance of a restricted license, if

(i) Based upon the records of the department of safety the person does not have a prior conviction for a violation of § 39-13-106, § 39-13-213(a)(2), or § 39-13-218 in this state, or a similar offense in another state; and

(ii) No person was seriously injured or killed in the course of the conduct that resulted in the driver's conviction under § 55-10-401.

55-50-502 SECTION 16. Tennessee Code Annotated, Section 55-50-502(c)(3)(C), is amended by deleting the language "The trial judge", substituting instead the language "If the trial judge imposes geographic restrictions, the trial judge", adding the following subdivision, and redesignating the current subdivision (vi):

(vi) A court ordered outpatient alcohol and drug treatment program; and

55-50-502 SECTION 17. Tennessee Code Annotated, Section 55-50-502, is amended by deleting subdivision (c)(3)(D) and by substituting instead the following:

(D) If the violation resulting in the person's conviction for driving under the influence occurred prior to July 1, 2013, the law in effect when the violation occurred shall govern the person's eligibility for a restricted motor vehicle operator license unless the person petitions the court to consider the person's eligibility under the law in effect when the petition is filed.

55-50-502 SECTION 18. Tennessee Code Annotated, Section 55-50-502(c)(3)(E), is amended by deleting the subdivision in its entirety and substituting instead the following:

(E) The person so arrested may obtain a certified copy of the order and within ten (10) days after it is issued present it, together with an application fee of sixty-five dollars ($65.00), to the department, which shall forthwith issue a restricted license embodying the limitations imposed in the order.

55-50-502 SECTION 19. Tennessee Code Annotated, Section 55-50-502(c)(4), is amended by deleting the subdivision in its entirety and substituting instead the following:

(4) Where a nonresident whose license has been suspended or revoked by any other state subsequently becomes a bona fide resident of this state, and where the person has been granted a restricted license by the other state if the triggering offense would under the laws of this state provide for the issuance of a restricted driver license upon petition to a judge of the court of general sessions, or its equivalent, for the county wherein the person resides, the court may order the issuance of a restricted motor vehicle operator's license. The court shall have discretion to order the person to operate only a motor vehicle that is equipped with a functioning ignition interlock device or place additional limitations on the person's restricted license; provided, however, that a restricted license issued pursuant to this subdivision (c)(4) without an ignition interlock requirement shall be subject to geographic restrictions, as provided in subdivision (c)(3), during the mandatory revocation/suspension period. If the person has a prior conviction within the past ten (10) years for a violation of § 55-10-401 or § 55-10-421, in this state or a similar offense in any other jurisdiction, the court shall be required to order the person to operate only a motor vehicle that is equipped with a functioning ignition interlock device. The person may obtain a certified copy of the order and within thirty (30) days after it is issued present it, together with an application fee of sixty-five dollars ($65.00), to the department, which shall then issue a restricted license embodying the limitations imposed in the order.

55-10-422 SECTION 20. Tennessee Code Annotated, Title 55, Chapter 10, Part 4, is amended by adding the following as a new section:

55-10-422.

A person whose license has been suspended pursuant to this part and who applies for a restricted license to operate only a motor vehicle that is equipped with a functioning ignition interlock device shall be required to pay a program development fee of eight dollars ($8.00). The fee required by this section shall terminate on June 30, 2014.

SECTION 21. All documents, records, identifying information, monitoring data or results and other information recorded, collected, maintained, transmitted or stored by an Ignition Interlock Provider about or concerning an Interlock Program Participant is confidential and not available for public inspection. All such information shall retain its confidentiality when it is transmitted, electronically or otherwise, maintained and stored, examined or used by a Monitoring Authority. Only authorized employees of an Ignition Interlock Provider or Monitoring Authority may view any document made confidential by this section.

Effective date 7/1/2013 SECTION 22. Section 20 of this act shall take effect upon becoming law, the public welfare requiring it. All other sections of this act shall take effect July 1, 2013, the public welfare requiring it, and shall apply to offenses committed on or after such date.

PUBLIC CHAPTER NO. 345

PUBLIC CHAPTER NO. 345

HOUSE BILL NO. 283

By Representatives Forgety, Lynn, Shepard, Kevin Brooks, Powers, Keisling, Sexton, Travis, Harry Brooks, Fitzhugh

Substituted for: Senate Bill No. 543

By Senators Bell, Crowe, Burks

AN ACT to amend Tennessee Code Annotated, Title 49, Chapter 7, relative to tuition discounts.

BE IT ENACTED BY THE GENERAL ASSEMBLY OF THE STATE OF TENNESSEE:

49-7-119 SECTION 1. Tennessee Code Annotated, Section 49-7-119(a), is amended by adding the following sentence after the first sentence of the subsection:

> Every child in Tennessee under twenty-four (24) years of age whose parent is a retired teacher who retired after a minimum of thirty (30) years of full-time creditable service in Tennessee public schools of this state or who received disability retirement after a minimum of twenty-five (25) years of full-time creditable service in Tennessee public schools shall receive a twenty-five percent (25%) reduction on tuition to any state-operated institution of higher learning.

Effective date 7/1/2013 SECTION 2. This act shall take effect July 1, 2013, the public welfare requiring it.

PUBLIC CHAPTER NO. 346

PUBLIC CHAPTER NO. 346

HOUSE BILL NO. 1154

By Representatives Rogers, Joe Carr, Womick, Butt, Dunn, Evans, Weaver, Dale Carr, Alexander, Forgety, Dennis, Powers, Floyd, Eldridge, Ragan, Marsh, Doss, Casada, Lundberg, Carter, McCormick, Dean, Lollar, Hall, Haynes, Pody

Substituted for: Senate Bill No. 1235

By Senators Henry, Bell, Bowling, Gardenshire, Tracy

AN ACT to amend Tennessee Code Annotated, Title 4; Title 9 and Title 67, relative to limitations on appropriations.

BE IT ENACTED BY THE GENERAL ASSEMBLY OF THE STATE OF TENNESSEE:

SECTION 1.

(a) The state funding board shall:

(1) Study the current constitutional provision commonly known as the "Copeland Cap" provided for in article II, § 24 of the Constitution of Tennessee;

(2) Study the current statutory method of estimating the rate of growth of the state's economy pursuant to title 9, chapter 4, part 52;

(3) Identify alternative methods of estimating the rate of growth of the state's economy;

(4) Identify practices as adopted through statutory or constitutional provisions in other states designed to limit or establish boundaries for state spending or to hold elected officials accountable for spending above defined limits or boundaries; and

(5) Recommend statutory revisions, constitutional revisions, combination of statutory and constitutional revisions, if any, to clarify, modify, reform or replace Tennessee's current spending limitations or boundaries and the accountability of its elected officials for actions that may exceed the limitations or boundaries.

(b) The attorney general and reporter shall furnish such assistance to the state funding board as shall be requested by the state funding board.

(c) The state funding board shall complete the duties described in subsection (a) and make its final report, including its findings and recommendations, to the speakers of the senate and house of representatives by February 1, 2014.

Effective date 5/13/2013

SECTION 2. This act shall take effect upon becoming a law, the public welfare requiring it.

PUBLIC CHAPTER NO. 347

PUBLIC CHAPTER NO. 347

HOUSE BILL NO. 1341

By Representatives Powell, Michael Turner, Odom, Gilmore, Jones, Stewart, Mitchell, Love, Jernigan

Substituted for: Senate Bill No. 1212

By Senators Harper, Henry

AN ACT to amend Tennessee Code Annotated, Title 7, Chapter 88 and Title 67, relative to activity in central business improvement districts which lie within a tourism development zone.

BE IT ENACTED BY THE GENERAL ASSEMBLY OF THE STATE OF TENNESSEE:

7-88-117 SECTION 1. Tennessee Code Annotated, Title 7, Chapter 88, Part 1, is amended by adding the following language as a new section:

7-88-117.

(a)

(1) Notwithstanding any provision of law to the contrary, any metropolitan government which has created a tourism development zone pursuant to this chapter and which tourism development zone completely includes one (1) or more central business improvement districts, may, by resolution of its governing body, impose an additional fee on the sales price of services and tangible personal property sold at retail within one (1) central business improvement district located within the tourism development zone; provided that there shall be exempt from the fee imposed by this chapter any sales of the following:

(A) Professional services;

(B) Lodging provided to transients;

(C) Tickets to sporting events or other live ticketed events;

(D) Alcoholic beverages which are subject to the liquor by the drink tax in addition to sales tax;

(E) Newspapers and other publications; and

(F) Overnight and long term parking.

(2) The fee authorized by this section shall not exceed the rate of twenty-five hundredths percent (.25%).

(b)

(1) The metropolitan government shall furnish a certified copy of the adopting resolution to the department of revenue in accordance with regulations prescribed by the department. Such resolution shall clearly designate the one (1) central business improvement district within which the additional fee applies and shall include a description of the boundaries of such district.

(2) The department of revenue shall collect such fee concurrently with the collection of the state sales tax in the same manner as the state sales tax is collected.

(3) Except as provided in subdivision (4), the proceeds of the fee provided for in this section shall be distributed to the metropolitan government from which the fee was collected to be deposited into the event and marketing fund of such government. The funds derived from the collection of this fee shall

be used to assist in the recruitment of major conventions and group meetings, the improvement of promotion, and to provide additional focused security in the central business improvement districts located within a tourism development zone. The funds derived from the collection of this fee shall not be used to assist in the recruitment of, directly or indirectly, conventions or group meetings which are considering, or would otherwise consider absent the use of this fee, other meeting and convention venues located in a county in which such fee is imposed.

(4)

(A) For fiscal year 2013-2014, the first one hundred sixty-five thousand dollars ($165,000) of the fee collected shall be deposited into the state general fund prior to any distribution to metropolitan government.

(B) For fiscal year 2014-2015 and subsequent fiscal years, the first fifty thousand dollars ($50,000) of the fee collected shall be deposited into the state general fund prior to any distribution to metropolitan government.

Effective date 1/1/2014

SECTION 2. This act shall take effect January 1, 2014, the public welfare requiring it.

PUBLIC CHAPTER NO. 348

PUBLIC CHAPTER NO. 348

HOUSE BILL NO. 830

By Representatives Matheny, Ragan

Substituted for: Senate Bill No. 376

By Senator Bell

AN ACT to amend Tennessee Code Annotated, Title 4, Chapter 29 and Title 65, Chapter 4, Part 1, relative to the consumer advocate division in the office of the attorney general and reporter.

BE IT ENACTED BY THE GENERAL ASSEMBLY OF THE STATE OF TENNESSEE:

4-29-236 SECTION 1. Tennessee Code Annotated, Section 4-29-236(a), is amended by adding a new subdivision thereto, as follows:

( ) Consumer advocate division in the office of the attorney general and reporter, created by § 65-4-118;

Effective date 5/13/2013 SECTION 2. This act shall take effect upon becoming a law, the public welfare requiring it.

PUBLIC CHAPTER NO. 349

PUBLIC CHAPTER NO. 349

HOUSE BILL NO. 489

By Representative Jones

Substituted for: Senate Bill No. 425

By Senator Burks

AN ACT to amend Tennessee Code Annotated, Title 38, Chapter 12, Part 1, relative to the certification of batterers' intervention programs.

BE IT ENACTED BY THE GENERAL ASSEMBLY OF THE STATE OF TENNESSEE:

38-12-110 SECTION 1. Tennessee Code Annotated, Section 38-12-110, is amended by adding the following new subsection (c):

(c) The council may prescribe fees, not to exceed three hundred dollars ($300), for the certification of such programs.

Effective date 5/13/2013 SECTION 2. This act shall take effect upon becoming a law, the public welfare requiring it.

PUBLIC CHAPTER NO. 350

PUBLIC CHAPTER NO. 350

HOUSE BILL NO. 521

By Representatives Watson, Coley, Hardaway, Parkinson, Rogers, Littleton, Moody, Weaver, Camper, Jones, Lamberth, Johnnie Turner, Lollar, Butt, Haynes, Dean, Floyd, Sexton, Todd, Hall, Ragan

Substituted for: Senate Bill No. 1030

By Senators Kelsey, Ford, Crowe, Bowling, Burks, Campfield, Massey, Stevens, Overbey

AN ACT to amend Tennessee Code Annotated, Title 39 and Title 40, relative to defenses to sex crimes.

BE IT ENACTED BY THE GENERAL ASSEMBLY OF THE STATE OF TENNESSEE:

39-13-529 SECTION 1. Tennessee Code Annotated, Section 39-13-529, is amended by adding the following as a new subsection:

( ) It shall not be a defense to a violation of this section that a minor victim of the offense consented to the conduct that constituted the offense.

39-17-1003 SECTION 2. Tennessee Code Annotated, Section 39-17-1003, is amended by adding the following as a new subsection:

( ) It shall not be a defense to a violation of this section that a minor victim of the offense consented to the conduct that constituted the offense.

39-17-1004 SECTION 3. Tennessee Code Annotated, Section 39-17-1004, is amended by adding the following as a new subsection:

( ) It shall not be a defense to a violation of subsection (a) that the minor victim of the offense consented to the conduct that constituted the offense.

39-17-1005 SECTION 4. Tennessee Code Annotated, Section 39-17-1005, is amended by adding the following as a new subsection:

( ) It shall not be a defense to a violation of subsection (a) that the minor victim of the offense consented to the conduct that constituted the offense.

Effective date 7/1/2013 SECTION 5. This act shall take effect July 1, 2013, the public welfare requiring it.

PUBLIC CHAPTER NO. 351

PUBLIC CHAPTER NO. 351

HOUSE BILL NO. 705

By Representatives Harry Brooks, John DeBerry, Lollar

Substituted for: Senate Bill No. 634

By Senator Tracy

AN ACT to amend Tennessee Code Annotated, Title 49, relative to education.

WHEREAS, the general assembly finds that high school students should be encouraged to enroll in and successfully complete more rigorous coursework, such as Advanced Placement (AP) courses, to enable success in postsecondary students; and

WHEREAS, the general assembly wishes to enhance the accessibility of AP courses for all students; and

WHEREAS, the general assembly finds that high school students interested in career and technical training also should be encouraged to pursue completion of rigorous coursework and successful passage of career and technical certification examinations; and

WHEREAS, the cost of taking AP examinations and career and technical certification examinations may discourage students from attempting these exams; now, therefore,

BE IT ENACTED BY THE GENERAL ASSEMBLY OF THE STATE OF TENNESSEE:

49-1-308 SECTION 1. Tennessee Code Annotated, Title 49, Chapter 1, Part 3, is amended by adding the following language as a new, appropriately designated section:

49-1-3__.

(a)

(1) There is established a two-year pilot project to be operated by the department of education. The purpose of the project shall be to determine whether enhanced accessibility of AP courses and examinations and career and technical certification examinations encourages students to pursue completion of rigorous course work and successfully pass AP examinations and career and technical certification examinations.

(2) Pilot project participants enrolled In Advanced Placement courses shall not be required to pay any fee to take the AP examination.

(3) Pilot project participants enrolled in career and technical courses leading to certification or licensure in the field of study shall not be required to pay any fee to take the certification or licensure examination.

(4) The cost of the examination shall be the responsibility of the state, regardless of the score achieved on the examination by the student.

(b) The pilot project shall be conducted in high schools to be selected by the commissioner of education. The high schools shall be selected so that the cost of the pilot project is no more than one hundred thousand dollars ($100,000) per year.

(c)

(1) The office of research and education accountability (OREA) in the office of the comptroller of the treasury, with the assistance of the department of education, shall study the pilot project and shall report on the effectiveness of the project after the initial year of the project and at the conclusion of the project. In its report at the conclusion of pilot

project, OREA shall make findings as to whether the project encouraged students to pursue completion of rigorous course work and successfully pass AP examinations and career and technical certification examinations. OREA shall make recommendations as to the potential of the project for expansion statewide. OREA shall submit its initial report to the education committees of the senate and the house of representatives by November 1, 2014, and its final report to the committees by November 1, 2015.

(2) If OREA, in consultation with the department, finds that the results of the two-year pilot project are promising, but that more study needs to be done before a final recommendation is issued, then department is authorized to continue the pilot program for an additional two (2) years, if funded.

49-13-104 SECTION 2. Tennessee Code Annotated, Section 49-13-104(6), is amended by deleting the subdivision in its entirety and by substituting instead the following:

(6) "Governing body" means the organized group of persons who will operate a public charter school or schools by deciding matters, including, but not limited to, budgeting, curriculum and other operating procedures for the public charter school and by overseeing management and administration of a public charter school.

49-13-143 SECTION 3. Tennessee Code Annotated, Title 49, Chapter 13, is amended by adding the following language as a new, appropriately designated section:

49-13-1__.

(a) The membership of a governing body shall include at least one (1) parent representative whose child is currently enrolled in a charter school operated by the governing body. The parent representative shall be appointed by the governing body within six (6) months of the school's opening date. A charter management organization may satisfy this requirement by establishing an advisory school council at each school that it operates. An advisory school council shall consist of no fewer than five (5) members and shall include the principal, at least one (1) parent and at least one (1) teacher representative.

(b) A local board of education shall not serve as the governing body of a public charter school;

49-13-104 SECTION 4. Tennessee Code Annotated, Section 49-13-104, is amended by adding the following language as new subdivision (4) and by renumbering subsequent subdivisions accordingly:

(4) "Charter management organization" or "CMO" means a nonprofit entity that operates multiple charter schools at least one (1) of which is in Tennessee.

49-13-127 SECTION 5. Tennessee Code Annotated, Section 49-13-127(b), is amended by adding the following language as a new subdivision (3):

(3) A CMO may comply with subdivision (b)(1) by submitting one (1) audit for all the charter schools operated in Tennessee by the CMO; provided, that such audit includes all information required under this section for each school.

49-13-108 SECTION 6. Tennessee Code Annotated, Section 49-13-108(b), is amended by deleting the subsection in its entirety and by substituting instead the following:

(b) The local board of education may consider whether the establishment of the charter school will have a substantial negative fiscal impact on the LEA such that authorization of the charter school would be contrary to the best interest of the pupils, school district or community.

Effective date 7/1/2013 SECTION 7. This act shall take effect July 1, 2013, the public welfare requiring it.

PUBLIC CHAPTER NO. 352

PUBLIC CHAPTER NO. 352

HOUSE BILL NO. 597

By Representatives Ryan Williams, Hardaway

Substituted for: Senate Bill No. 1068

By Senator Burks

AN ACT to amend Tennessee Code Annotated, Section 36-6-108, relative to parental relocation.

BE IT ENACTED BY THE GENERAL ASSEMBLY OF THE STATE OF TENNESSEE:

36-6-108 SECTION 1. Tennessee Code Annotated, Section 36-6-108, is amended by deleting the language "one hundred (100) miles" and by substituting instead the language "fifty (50) miles".

Effective date 7/1/2013 SECTION 2. This act shall take effect July 1, 2013, the public welfare requiring it and shall only apply to relocations occurring on or after such date.

PUBLIC CHAPTER NO. 353

PUBLIC CHAPTER NO. 353

HOUSE BILL NO. 493

By Representative Sargent

Substituted for: Senate Bill No. 601

By Senator Johnson

AN ACT to amend Tennessee Code Annotated, Section 6-55-202 and Title 67, relative to taxes.

BE IT ENACTED BY THE GENERAL ASSEMBLY OF THE STATE OF TENNESSEE:

67-5-105 SECTION 1. Tennessee Code Annotated, Title 67, Chapter 5, Part 1, is amended by adding the following language as a new Section 67-5-105:

67-5-105. As used in this chapter:

(1) "Collector" means in the case of any tax entity, other than a county, that collects its own taxes, assessments, or other charges secured by property, the officer of such tax entity responsible for collecting such taxes, assessments, or charges;

(2) "Tax entity" includes counties, cities, metropolitan governments, municipal corporations, quasi-municipal corporations, and political subdivisions having authority to levy a property tax; and

(3) "Taxpayer" means any owner of property subject to taxation or any party liable for property taxes.

67-5-2401 SECTION 2. Tennessee Code Annotated, Section 67-5-2401, is amended by deleting the section in its entirety and by substituting instead the following language:

(a) As a preliminary step toward enforcing the lien for uncollected property taxes, the trustee or collector shall cause to be inserted, once a week for two (2) consecutive weeks in the month of January, in a newspaper of general circulation as defined in § 2-1-104 or one (1) or more newspapers published or widely distributed in the county, a notice as follows:

You are advised that after February 1, additional penalties and costs will be imposed in consequence of suits to be filed for enforcement of the lien for property taxes for prior tax years; until the filing of such suits, taxes may be paid in my office.

____
County Trustee (or other Collector)

(b) The cost of publication shall be paid by the tax entity, and, if no newspaper is published in the county, notice shall be posted on the courthouse door.

67-5-2402 SECTION 3. Tennessee Code Annotated, Section 67-5-2402, is amended by deleting subsection (a) in its entirety and by substituting instead the following language:

(a) The trustee or collector shall likewise prepare from the rolls held by the trustee's or the collector's office, a list of taxpayers and identification of property for which property taxes are delinquent, as of June 1 of the current calendar year, and include the following notice or equivalent language in the current tax bills sent to property owners appearing on either the trustee's or the collector's list or the list received from the clerk of court pursuant to § 67-5-2403:

IN ADDITION TO THIS AMOUNT, YOU OWE BACK TAXES. CONTACT THIS OFFICE IMMEDIATELY OR YOUR PROPERTY MAY BE SOLD.

____
County Trustee (or other Collector)

67-5-2403 SECTION 4. Tennessee Code Annotated, Section 67-5-2403, is amended by deleting the section in its entirety and by substituting instead the following language:

Additionally, it is the duty of the clerk of any court in which suits for the enforcement of property tax liens have been filed, if requested by the trustee, collector or by the attorney prosecuting the suit, to annually provide to such requesting party or parties, no earlier than June 1 nor later than July 1, a complete list of unpaid delinquent taxes pending in the court as of June 1 of the current calendar year, with identification of the property involved in such suits, and the years for which taxes are delinquent.

67-5-2422 SECTION 5. Tennessee Code Annotated, Title 67, Chapter 5, Part 24, is amended by adding the following language as a new Section 67-5-2422:

67-5-2422. The legislative body of every county having a charter form of government or metropolitan form of government and every municipality which has adopted home rule in accordance with Article XI, Section 9 of the Tennessee Constitution, is authorized to establish any percentage to be applied as interest, penalties, court costs, attorney fees, and fees to provide compensation for the prosecution of the delinquent taxes, and is authorized to apply such percentages on its own accord, §§ 67-5-2010, 67-5-2404, 67-5-2410, and 67-5-2501 notwithstanding. If such a county or municipal government has not elected to establish and to specifically identify its own percentages, §§ 67-5-2010, 67-5-2404, 67-5-2410, and 67-5-2501 shall remain in effect until the legislative body of the county or municipal government so acts.

67-5-1806 SECTION 6. Tennessee Code Annotated, Section 67-5-1806, is amended by deleting the section in its entirety and by substituting instead the following language:

(a) All taxes assessed against real and personal property in this state shall be barred, discharged and uncollectible after the lapse of ten (10) years from April 1 of the year following the year in which such taxes become delinquent, whether suit be brought within that time or not to collect the taxes, and whether this § 67-5-1806 be pleaded in bar of such collection or not, unless the property in question be struck off and sold within such period of ten (10) years.

(b) The bar against collection provided in subsection (a) shall be tolled:

(1) As to taxes at issue in an administrative appeal before the state board of equalization, from the date of filing the appeal through issuance of the final assessment certificate and during the pendency of any judicial review thereof;

(2) During the pendency of any appeal of an action to collect or enforce a lien for unpaid taxes;

(3) During the pendency of any recovery action under title 67, chapter 1, part 9;

(4) During the pendency of any suit to invalidate a tax sale; or

(5) During the pendency of any bankruptcy or receivership proceedings affecting the taxing entity's collection rights or the term of any payment plan ordered in such proceedings.

67-5-2405 SECTION 7. Tennessee Code Annotated, Section 67-5-2405, is amended by deleting the section in its entirety and by substituting instead the following language:

(a) The attorney shall after February 1, and not later than April 1, file suits in the circuit or chancery court of the county for the collection of delinquent land taxes due the state, county and municipality, as well as the interest, penalties, and costs attached to and a part of such taxes, which taxes, interest, penalties, and costs are declared a lien upon the land; and, for the enforcement of this lien, suits shall be brought in the name of the county, in its own behalf and for the use and benefit of the state, municipality or other tax entity that has certified a delinquent tax list, or in the name of any such tax entity that has certified a delinquent tax list, in its own behalf and for its own use and benefit.

(b)

(1) The complaint shall be in substance and form as other complaints for the enforcement of liens and may be filed against and contain the names of all the delinquent taxpayers in the county, and the fact that the complaint contains the names of more than one (1) defendant shall not be considered by the court multifarious, or a misjoinder of parties.

(2) Additional defendants and delinquent taxes may be added to the suit as a matter of right upon the filing of a notice on behalf of the complainant to add additional defendants and without the necessity of amending the complaint. Upon the filing of such notice, the additional defendants shall be served with process pursuant to the Rules of Civil Procedure and § 67-5-2415.

(c) Suits for the collection of delinquent taxes are to be prosecuted to a conclusion as soon as practicable, and for this purpose proceedings in respect thereto are to be accorded priority by the court.

(d) At any time after suit has been filed pursuant to subsection (a), whether delinquent tax defendants have or have not been served with a copy of such suit, the court may amend this suit by adding delinquent taxes that became delinquent more recently than the taxes being enforced pursuant to subsection (a) of this section.

6-55-202 SECTION 8. Tennessee Code Annotated, Section 6-55-202, is amended by deleting the section in its entirety and by substituting instead the following language:

6-55-202. It is lawful for any incorporated municipality to sue in the chancery court of the county in which it is located for taxes due the municipality upon real estate, whenever the taxes are past due and unpaid. The fact that the complaint contains the names of more than one (1) defendant shall not subject the complaint to an objection for misjoinder by reason of the distinct interests the several defendants have in the properties proceeded against.

67-5-2003 SECTION 9. Tennessee Code Annotated, Section 67-5-2003, is amended by deleting subsection (a) in its entirety and by substituting instead the following language;

(a) All delinquent personal property taxes, including but not limited to, public utility personal property taxes, may be immediately collected by the county trustee or collector, with the assistance of the delinquent tax attorney selected pursuant to § 67-5-2404 or § 67-5-2001, if such delinquent tax attorney's assistance is requested by the trustee or collector. The tax books in the hands of the trustee or collector and the delinquent lists furnished to deputy trustees or the collector's deputies, or the sheriff or constables in any county where the taxpayer or any property liable for the taxes may be found, or the delinquent tax attorney, shall have the force and effect of a judgment and execution from a court of record, and shall be ample authority for the officers or delinquent tax attorney having such taxes for collection to distrain and sell a sufficient amount of the personal property to satisfy the delinquent taxes, interest, penalties, costs and attorneys' fees. However, leased personal property assessed to a lessee shall not be distrained and sold pursuant to this section.

67-5-2003 SECTION 10. Tennessee Code Annotated, Section 67-5-2003, is amended by deleting subsection (g) and substituting instead the following language:

(g)

(1) The trustee or collector may turn over the delinquent list thirty (30) days after such taxes become delinquent to the delinquent tax attorney, selected pursuant to § 67-5-2404 or § 67-5-2001, to file suit to collect delinquent personal property taxes, as part of any pending suit to collect real property taxes, as part of a separate mass lawsuit pursuant to the procedures set forth in this chapter, or as a separate lawsuit. Such can be done without having first issued a distress warrant.

(2) In the event the trustee or collector turns over the delinquent list prior to the mailing of the notice pursuant to § 67-5-2402, the trustee or collector shall

be required to forward written notice by first class mail to the last known property owner at least ten (10) days before the delinquent list is turned over to the delinquent tax attorney.

(3) If the procedure in this subsection (g) is used, the trustee or collector is also authorized, as with real property tax records, to turn over records to the clerk of court.

(4) A judgment obtained against a delinquent taxpayer may be enforced as a lien on the property, or as any other judgment, including garnishment or sale of property by the sheriff.

(5) Following entry of a personal judgment for delinquent personal property taxes, a tax entity may enter into a written agreement for the payment of such judgment in installments, pursuant to § 26-2-218, on such terms as the tax entity may deem appropriate, provided that such agreement must provide for payment of all taxes, interest, penalties, fees, and costs in full, including any interest and penalties that accrue during the term of the installment payments.

(6) Any tax entity may file suit to collect any other taxes it is authorized by law to collect thirty (30) days after such taxes become delinquent, as part of any pending suit to collect property taxes, or as a separate mass lawsuit pursuant to the procedures set forth in this chapter.

67-5-2003 SECTION 11. Tennessee Code Annotated, Section 67-5-2003, is amended by adding the following language as a new subsection (i):

(i) Delinquent public utility taxes may not be immediately collected under this section if the local assessment includes any real property. The trustee or collector shall confirm with the comptroller of the treasury whether the public utility company's local assessment includes any real property.

67-5-2404 SECTION 12. Tennessee Code Annotated, Section 67-5-2404, is amended by adding the following language as a new subsection (d):

(d) If a taxpayer or other adverse party to the tax entity appeals a judgment or other order in an action to collect or enforce a lien for unpaid taxes, or files suit for recovery pursuant to title 67, chapter 1, part 9, or to set aside a tax sale pursuant to § 67-5-2504, the court may, in its discretion, and upon the tax entity prevailing in such action, award reasonable attorneys' fees in addition to the compensation set forth in this section. Any request for such fees shall be supported by affidavit and such fees shall become additional expenses of the tax suit for the purposes of § 67-5-2410(d), and shall be secured by the lien in favor of the tax entity as costs accruing on the taxes pursuant to § 67-5-2101(a). Nothing in this subsection shall be construed as authorizing an award of attorney's fees in favor of a taxpayer or other adverse party to the tax entity.

67-5-2103 SECTION 13. Tennessee Code Annotated, Section 67-5-2103, is amended by deleting the section in its entirety and by substituting instead the following language:

The whole proceeding for the enforcement of property tax liens, from the assessment to sale for delinquency, shall be a proceeding in rem, and shall not be invalid on account of such land having been listed or assessed for taxation to anyone as owner or owners or to any person or persons not the owner or owners or to unknown owner or owners.

67-5-2409 SECTION 14. Tennessee Code Annotated, Section 67-5-2409, is amended by designating the existing language as subsection (a), and by adding the following language as a new subsection (b):

(b) At any time after suit has been filed, whether delinquent tax defendants have or have not been served with a copy of such suit, the court may amend the suit by adding delinquent taxes that became delinquent more recently than the taxes being enforced pursuant to subsection (a). Once amended, all delinquent taxes, both delinquent prior to filing the complaint and added later by amendment, shall be included in the first bid submitted to purchase the property at the tax sale. Amendment of the suit to include more recent delinquent taxes owed shall not require the issuance of leading process and formal service upon the defendant or defendants, as all property owners are already on notice pursuant to this title that taxes are due every year and become delinquent, if not paid by March 1 of the following year.

67-5-2415 SECTION 15. Tennessee Code Annotated, Section 67-5-2415(e), is amended by deleting subdivision (1) in its entirety and by substituting instead the following language:

(1) The return of the receipt signed by the defendant, spouse, or other person deemed appropriate to receive summons or notice as provided for in the Rules of Civil Procedure, or its return marked "refused," "unclaimed", or other similar notation, as evidenced by appropriate notation of such fact by the postal authorities, and filed as a part of the record by the clerk, with notation on the docket of the true facts, shall be evidence of personal notice.

67-5-2423 SECTION 16. Tennessee Code Annotated, Title 67, Chapter 5, Part 24, is amended by adding the following language as a new Section 67-5-2423:

67-5-2423. A delinquent tax roll, certified by the appropriate collecting official, shall constitute prima facie evidence that the underlying tax assessment has become conclusively established pursuant to § 67-5-1329 or § 67-5-1401, that each person charged with a duty relating to the imposition of the tax has complied with all requirements of law, and that the tax, including all applicable penalties, interest, costs, and fees, remains due and owing, and constitutes a good and valid lien on the subject property, as well as a personal liability of the taxpayer.

67-5-2502 SECTION 17. Tennessee Code Annotated, Section 67-5-2502, is amended by adding the following language as a new subsection (d) and by designating the current subsection (d) as subsection (e):

(d) A tax sale notice, which shall be the same or substantially the same as the advertised notice, may be recorded in the register of deeds' office for the county in which the property is located upon the setting of the tax sale date. The recording cost shall be divided between the parcels of land listed in the tax sale notice and added as an additional court cost to each such parcel of land. This tax sale notice shall be recorded for informational purposes only and no release shall be required.

67-5-2801 SECTION 18. Tennessee Code Annotated, Section 67-5-2801, is amended by deleting the section in its entirety and by substituting instead the following language:

(a) The trustee or collector may request the delinquent tax attorney to seek court approval in order to waive the enforcement and collection of all, but not a portion of, industrial and commercial personal property taxes, penalties, interest, attorney fees and costs. All of the following must be determined and attested to by the trustee or collector before a court may approve a waiver:

(1) The taxpayer has ceased all business operations;

(2) No personal property subject to the tax can be found; and

(3) Neither fraud nor an intention to avoid payment of the taxes on the part of the taxpayer caused the circumstances giving rise to such waiver.

(b) In order to waive the enforcement and collection of public utility personal property taxes, including penalties, interest, attorney fees and costs, the trustee or collector must first confirm with the comptroller of the treasury that the public utility's local assessment only includes personal property and does not include any real property. If the public utility is still operating, then no waiver may be requested or approved even if the local assessment only includes personal property and no personal property can be found in the trustee's or the collector's jurisdiction. If the public utility has ceased all operations and the local assessment does not include any real property, then the trustee or the collector may request a waiver in accordance with subdivisions (a)(1)-(3)

(c) The trustee or collector is required to submit a report to the chief executive officer of the local government and the county assessor of all waivers approved by the court when no delinquent tax lawsuit has been filed. The report shall contain the taxpayer's name and amount of taxes, penalties, interest, attorney fees, and costs waived. The waivers approved by the court under this subsection are to be included and written as a credit in the monthly settlement and annual statement in accordance with §§ 67-5-1903 and 67-5-1904.

(d) With respect to delinquent personal property taxes being waived under this section, for which the delinquent lawsuit has been filed, the court having jurisdiction of the delinquent tax lawsuit may, upon motion by the delinquent tax attorney and a finding that the factors outlined in subdivisions (a)(1)-(3) or subsection (b) exist, order the waiver of enforcement and collection of all, but not a portion of, such personal property taxes, penalties, interest, attorney fees and costs.

67-5-2501 SECTION 19. Tennessee Code Annotated, Section 67-5-2501, is amended by deleting subdivision (a)(2) and subdivision (b)(2) in their entirety and by substituting instead the following language in each such subdivision:

(2) At all sales, the clerk of the court, acting for a tax entity or entities prosecuting the suit, shall bid the debt ascertained to be due for taxes, interest, penalties, and the costs and fees incident to the collection thereof, where no other bidder offers the same or larger bid; provided, that, when the legislative body of a tax entity determines that the environmental risks are such that it is not in the best interests of the tax entity for a minimum bid to be offered at the tax sale, the clerk shall not offer a bid on the property at the tax sale.

67-5-2504 SECTION 20. Tennessee Code Annotated, Section 67-5-2504, is amended by deleting subsection (d) in its entirety and by substituting instead the following language:

(d)

(1) A suit to invalidate any tax title to land shall be commenced within one (1) year from the date the cause of action accrued, which is the date of the entry of the order confirming the tax sale.

(2) The statute of limitations to invalidate the sale of any tax title shall be one (1) year as set forth is subdivision (1) of this subsection, except that it may be extended to one (1) year after the plaintiff discovered or with the exercise of reasonable due diligence should have discovered the existence of such cause of action.

(3) In no event shall any action to invalidate any tax sale title be brought more than three (3) years after the entry of the order confirming the tax sale.

(4) This subsection (d) shall not be construed to prevent or delay issuance of an order quieting title to land at the suit of a delinquent tax sale purchaser. After expiration of the period of redemption provided in § 67-5-2702, the delinquent tax sale purchaser may file suit to quiet title, notwithstanding the deadline for tax sale challenges provided in this subsection (d).

(5) Nothing in this subsection (d) shall limit the time in which a motion for excess proceeds may be filed pursuant to § 67-5-2707.

67-5-2507 SECTION 21. Tennessee Code Annotated, Section 67-5-2507(a), is amended by deleting the language "to sell" and by substituting instead the language "for the disposition of".

67-5-2507 SECTION 22. Tennessee Code Annotated, Section 67-5-2507(b), is amended by deleting subdivision (3) in its entirety and by substituting instead the following language:

(3) No tract of land shall be sold for an amount less than the total amount of the taxes, penalty, cost and interest, unless the legislative body, upon application, determines that it is impossible to sell the tract of land for this amount, and grants permission to offer the land for sale at some amount to be fixed by such legislative body.

67-5-2507 SECTION 23. Tennessee Code Annotated, Section 67-5-2507(b), is further amended by deleting subdivision (5) in its entirety.

67-5-2507 SECTION 24. Tennessee Code Annotated, Section 67-5-2507(b), is further amended by adding the following language as new, appropriately designated subdivisions:

( ) The county may, upon a majority vote of its legislative body determining it in the best interests of the county to use the property for a public purpose, decide to retain ownership and possession of such property.

( ) This section shall not apply in any county having a metropolitan form of government and a population in excess of five hundred thousand (500,000) according to the 2010 federal census or any subsequent federal census.

67-5-2508 SECTION 25. Tennessee Code Annotated, Section 67-5-2508(c), is amended by adding the following language as a new subdivision (3):

(3) The municipality may, upon a majority vote of its legislative body determining it in the best interests of the municipality to use the property for a public purpose, decide to retain ownership and possession of such property.

67-5-2508 SECTION 26. Tennessee Code Annotated, Section 67-5-2508(d), is amended by adding the following language as a new subdivision (4):

(4) The county or municipality may, upon a majority vote of its legislative body determining it in the best interests of such county or municipality to use the property for a public purpose, decide to retain ownership and possession of such property. The county or municipality wishing to retain the property shall pay to the other governmental entity its pro rata share of the joint bid amount at the tax sale, upon receipt of which the other governmental entity shall execute a quitclaim deed conveying its interest in the property.

67-5-2509 SECTION 27. Tennessee Code Annotated, Section 67-5-2509(a), is amended by deleting the language "two-year period of redemption," and by substituting instead the language "period of redemption provided in § 67-5-2702,".

67-5-2509 SECTION 28. Tennessee Code Annotated, Section 67-5-2509, is amended by deleting subsection (b) in its entirety and by deleting the language "subsection (b)," wherever it appears in subdivision (d) and by substituting instead the language "§§ 67-5-2505, 67-5-2507 and 67-5-2508,".

67-5-2702 SECTION 29. Tennessee Code Annotated, Section 67-5-2702, is amended by deleting the section in its entirety and by substituting instead the following language:

(a) Persons entitled to redeem property may do so by paying the moneys to the clerk as required by § 67-5-2703 within one (1) year from the date of entry of the order of confirmation of sale, as evidenced by the records in the office of the clerk of the court responsible for the sale.

(b) A taxpayer may redeem property that has been previously redeemed by paying to the clerk the moneys as required by § 67-5-2703 within one (1) year from the date the property was sold, as evidenced by entry of the order of confirmation of sale. Upon the entry of the order of redemption using the procedure outlined in § 67-5-2704, the clerk shall disburse the moneys paid to redeem, plus interest at a rate of ten percent (10%) per annum computed from the date of the order of the previous redemption to the person previously redeeming as ordered by the court.

67-5-2704 SECTION 30. Tennessee Code Annotated, Section 67-5-2704(a), is amended by inserting the following language after the fourth sentence:

In addition, the court shall direct the person entitled to redeem to pay a reasonable fee to the clerk and master or delinquent tax attorney for the preparation of the notices, motions, and orders required to give effect to the request to redeem the property.

67-5-2707 SECTION 31. Tennessee Code Annotated, Title 67, Chapter 5, Part 27, is amended by adding the following language as a new section 67-5-2707:

67-5-2707.

(a) Following entry of the order of confirmation of sale, any "person entitled to redeem property," as defined in § 67-5-2701(a), may file a motion with the court setting forth a claim to any excess sale proceeds.

(b) A copy of such motion shall be served, in the manner prescribed by the Rules of Civil Procedure, on all parties to the underlying action, no later than thirty (30) days prior to the hearing date of the motion.

(c) At the hearing, the court shall order that any remaining redemption period shall be terminated as to the movant and as to any other person entitled to redeem property who consents to such termination as evidenced by their signature on such order, and any excess proceeds be paid according to the following priorities to each party that establishes its claim to the proceeds:

(1) To the tax entity or entities prosecuting the delinquent tax sale, for any remaining or subsequent outstanding taxes that are a lien against the property;

(2) To any lienholder, private or public, holding a claim against the property at the time of the tax sale, for the amount proven to be due under such lien, in accordance with priorities established by applicable law;

(3) To any lienholder, private or public, holding a claim against the property arising after the tax sale, for the amount proven to be due under such lien, in accordance with priorities established by applicable law;

(4) To any taxpayer, according to such taxpayer's interest at the time of the tax sale, provided that such taxpayer was a defendant in the underlying action, or acquired by will or intestate succession the interest in the property of a former taxpayer who was a defendant in the underlying action; and

(5) If no such motion is filed within the period set forth in § 67-5-2504(d), any such excess proceeds shall escheat to the state of Tennessee pursuant to the Uniform Disposition of Unclaimed Property Act, compiled in title 66, chapter 29.

67-5-513 SECTION 32. Tennessee Code Annotated, Section 67-5-513(a), is amended by inserting the language "limited liability company," after the language "corporation,"

67-5-903 SECTION 33. Tennessee Code Annotated, Section 67-5-903(b), is amended by adding the following language at the end of the subsection:

The taxpayer shall designate on the schedule one (1) or more individuals as owner or owners of the business, or responsible person or persons in the event of dissolution of a corporate or limited liability entity, for the purposes of § 67-5-513(a).

Effective date 5/13/2013 SECTION 34. This act shall take effect upon becoming a law, the public welfare requiring it.

PUBLIC CHAPTER NO. 354

PUBLIC CHAPTER NO. 354

HOUSE BILL NO. 488

By Representatives Jones, Hardaway

Substituted for: Senate Bill No. 575

By Senator Burks

AN ACT to amend Tennessee Code Annotated, Title 37, relative to foster care.

BE IT ENACTED BY THE GENERAL ASSEMBLY OF THE STATE OF TENNESSEE:

37-1-166 SECTION 1. Tennessee Code Annotated, Section 37-1-166, is amended by adding the following as a new subsection:

(h) In determining whether to continue or restore custody to a parent is in the best interest of a child, the department shall not require a parent to:

(1) Obtain employment if such parent has sufficient resources from other means to care for the child; or

(2) Provide the child with the child's own bedroom, unless there are specific safety or medical reasons that would make placement of the child with another child unsafe.

37-2-403 SECTION 2. Tennessee Code Annotated, Section 37-2-403(a)(2)(C), is amended by adding the following language to the end of the subdivision:

The permanency plan shall not require the parent to obtain employment if such parent has sufficient resources from other means to care for the child, and shall not require the parent to provide the child with the child's own bedroom unless specific safety or medical reasons exist that would make bedroom placement of the child with another child unsafe.

Effective date 5/13/2013 SECTION 3. This act shall take effect upon becoming a law, the public welfare requiring it.

PUBLIC CHAPTER NO. 355

PUBLIC CHAPTER NO. 355

HOUSE BILL NO. 480

By Representative Powers

Substituted for: Senate Bill No. 631

By Senators Johnson, Bowling

AN ACT to amend Tennessee Code Annotated, Title 62, Chapter 6, relative to roofing contractors.

BE IT ENACTED BY THE GENERAL ASSEMBLY OF THE STATE OF TENNESSEE:

62-6-102 SECTION 1. Tennessee Code Annotated, Section 62-6-102, is amended by adding the following language as a new, appropriately designated subdivision:

( ) "Roofing work" means the act of removing, installing, repairing or otherwise maintaining any covering to any at- or above-grade structure for the purpose of providing weather proof protection or ornamental enhancement to such structure;

62-6-102 SECTION 2. Tennessee Code Annotated, Section 62-6-102(4)(A)(ii), is amended by deleting the language "and licensed masonry contractor" and by substituting instead the language "masonry contractor, and roofing subcontractor where the total cost of the roofing portion of the construction project is twenty-five thousand dollars ($25,000) or more".

62-6-102 SECTION 3. Tennessee Code Annotated, Section 62-6-102(4)(D)(ii), is amended by deleting the language "licensed masonry contractors" and by substituting instead the language "licensed masonry contractors, and roofing subcontractors where the total cost of the roofing portion of the construction project is twenty-five thousand dollars ($25,000) or more".

62-6-103 SECTION 4. Tennessee Code Annotated, Section 62-6-103, is amended by adding the following language as a new, appropriately designated subsection:

( ) No contractor shall be authorized to perform roofing work on a construction project where the roofing portion of the construction project is twenty-five thousand dollars ($25,000) or more unless the contractor is licensed; provided:

(1) Any person who holds a license issued by the department as either a manufactured home installer or a manufactured home retailer, pursuant to title 68, chapter 126, shall not be required to be a licensed contractor in order to perform roofing work on a manufactured home as defined in § 68-126-202; provided, such work is related to the construction of a manufactured home or performed in connection with a manufacturer's warranty covering a manufactured home, or the repair of such home; and

(2) Any person who holds a license issued by the department as to the manufacture or installation of modular building units, pursuant to title 68, chapter 126, shall not be required to be a licensed contractor in order to perform roofing work on a modular building unit as defined in § 68-126-303; provided, such work is related to the construction or installation of a modular building unit, or performed in connection with a manufacturer's warranty covering a modular building unit, or the repair of such unit.

62-6-605 SECTION 5. Tennessee Code Annotated, Section 62-6-605, is amended by deleting the section and substituting instead the following:

No residential roofing services provider shall act or hold out as being a public adjuster, as defined in § 56-6-902, unless licensed as a public adjuster in accordance with title 56, chapter 6, part 9.

Effective date 1/1/2014 SECTION 6. For the purpose of promulgating rules and regulations, this act shall take effect upon becoming a law, the public welfare requiring it. For all other purposes, this act shall take effect January 1, 2014, the public welfare requiring it.

PUBLIC CHAPTER NO. 356

PUBLIC CHAPTER NO. 356

HOUSE BILL NO. 342

By Representative Harrison

Substituted for: Senate Bill No. 430

By Senators Overbey, Massey, Bowling, Burks, Yager

AN ACT to amend Tennessee Code Annotated, Title 68 and Title 71, relative to nursing homes.

BE IT ENACTED BY THE GENERAL ASSEMBLY OF THE STATE OF TENNESSEE:

68-11-216 SECTION 1. Tennessee Code Annotated, Section 68-11-216, is amended by deleting subsection (c) in its entirety and substituting the following:

(c)

(1) It is declared to be the legislative intent that every person is exercising a taxable privilege who engages in the business of providing nursing home care. The assessment fee imposed by this subsection (c) shall be in addition to all other privilege taxes.

(2) Effective for one (1) year beginning July 1, 2013, in addition to the fees set forth in subsection (a), each nursing home shall pay a nursing home annual assessment fee as set forth in this subsection (c). Such assessment fee shall be paid in equal monthly installments of one-twelfth (1/12) of the annual amount established by this subsection (c). The installments are due on the fifteenth day of each following month beginning August 15, 2013, for the July 2013 installment and ending with a final payment on July 15, 2014.

(3) The nursing home annual assessment fee shall be based on the number of nursing home beds licensed by this state on July 1, 2013, for the fiscal year following such date, excluding beds in nursing homes specifically certified as intermediate care beds for the mentally retarded. The assessment fee shall be uniformly applied to all licensed beds at the rate of two thousand two hundred twenty-five dollars ($2,225) per licensed bed per year. Licensed facilities that are owned or operated by an agency of this state are not excluded from paying the assessment fee. There shall be no exclusions, deductions or adjustments applied to the assessment fee of any licensed facility different from any other such facility. Beds licensed after July 1, 2013, shall pay a prorated amount of the annual assessment fee for the fiscal year following such date; provided, that no such assessment fee shall be due to the extent that the beds licensed after July 1, 2013, were the result of the transfer of such beds from one (1) licensed facility to another licensed facility, where the transferor facility had already paid the full amount of the assessment fee on such beds, or where the transferor facility agrees to continue to pay the monthly installments due with respect to such beds.

(4) The commissioner shall adopt rules and regulations governing the collection of such assessment fees. Notwithstanding any other provision of law, the commissioner is authorized to promulgate such rules as emergency rules pursuant to the Uniform Administrative Procedures Act, compiled in title 4, chapter 5.

(5) Any challenge to the assessment fee imposed by this subsection (c) shall be brought pursuant to title 67, chapter 1, part 9 and § 9-8-307(a)(1)(O).

(6)

(A) All revenue collected pursuant to this subsection (c) shall be deposited in the general fund.

(B) All nursing home annual assessment fee payments made by nursing homes under this section and received by this state; all investment earnings credited to the nursing home annual assessment fee payments; any interest and penalties paid under this section by any nursing home; and all funds generated by federal matching payments made relative to the nursing home annual assessment fee shall be available to and used by the bureau of TennCare for the sole purpose of providing payment to nursing homes.

(C) No part of the nursing home annual assessment fee payments made by nursing homes under this section and received by this state; the investment earnings credited to the nursing home annual assessment fee payments; the interest and penalties paid under this section by any nursing home; or the funds generated by federal matching payments made relative to the nursing home annual assessment fee shall be used for any purpose other than providing payment to nursing homes.

(7)

(A) If any part of any assessment fee imposed under this subsection (c) is not paid on or before the due date, a penalty of five percent (5%) of the amount due shall at once accrue and be added to such assessment fee. Thereafter, on the first day of each month during which any part of any assessment fee or any prior accrued penalty remains unpaid, an additional penalty of five percent (5%) of the then unpaid balance shall accrue and be added to such assessment fee or prior accrued penalty. In addition, assessment fees under this subsection (c) not paid on the due date shall bear interest at the maximum lawful rate from the due date to the date paid. Payment shall be deemed to have been made upon date of deposit in the United States mail. The commissioner may for good cause approve an alternative payment plan, as long as full payment of the assessment fee plus penalty and interest is made.

(B) If a nursing home is more than sixty (60) days delinquent in paying an installment of its nursing home annual assessment fee, the commissioner shall be authorized to initiate proceedings before the board in accordance with the Uniform Administrative Procedures Act, compiled in title 4, chapter 5, so that the board may suspend admissions to the facility or otherwise direct the facility to pay the assessment fee and any accrued penalties and interest in full within a prescribed period of time. If the facility does not pay the assessment fee and any accrued penalties and interest in full within the prescribed period of time as directed by the board, the board shall suspend admissions to the facility. Any suspension of admissions imposed according to this section shall immediately be lifted following the full payment of the assessment fee and any accrued penalties and interest by the facility. If full payment of the assessment fee and any accrued penalties and interest is not paid within sixty (60) days from the first day of the suspension of admissions, the commissioner shall be authorized to initiate proceedings before the board in accordance with the Uniform Administrative Procedures Act, compiled in title 4, chapter 5, so that the board may consider the revocation of the facility's license.

(8) The assessment fee imposed by this subsection (c) may not be billed by the nursing home as a separately stated charge, but this shall not prevent the nursing home from adjusting its rates to defray the cost associated with the assessment fee.

(9) The fiscal review committee shall review and have oversight of the implementation of this subsection (c).

(10) Enactment of this subsection (c) and any amendments to this subsection (c) shall not operate to excuse the monthly installment payment of the nursing home assessment fee due on July 15, 2013.

(11) Any assessment fee obligation imposed by this subsection (c) shall be suspended to the extent that, and for the period that receipt of the assessment fee by the state results in, a corresponding reduction in federal financial participation under Title XIX of the federal Social Security Act, compiled in 42 U.S.C. § 1396 et seq.

(12) The nursing home annual assessment fee established by this subsection (c) shall terminate on June 30, 2014.

Effective date 7/1/2013

SECTION 2. This act shall take effect July 1, 2013, the public welfare requiring it.

PUBLIC CHAPTER NO. 357

PUBLIC CHAPTER NO. 357

HOUSE BILL NO. 196

By Representatives McCormick, Rich, Hardaway, Dean, Sexton, Evans, Eldridge, Watson, McManus, Hall, Kane, Harry Brooks, Shipley, Kevin Brooks, Haynes, Ryan Williams, Todd

Substituted for: Senate Bill No. 202

By Senators Norris, Tate, Finney, Burks

AN ACT to amend Tennessee Code Annotated, Section 40-35-121, relative to criminal gang offenses.

BE IT ENACTED BY THE GENERAL ASSEMBLY OF THE STATE OF TENNESSEE:

40-35-121 SECTION 1. Tennessee Code Annotated, Section 40-35-121(a)(3), is amended by deleting the subdivision in its entirety and substituting the following:

(3) "Criminal gang offense" means:

(A) A criminal offense committed prior to July 1, 2013 that:

(i) During the perpetration of which the defendant knowingly causes, or threatens to cause, death or bodily injury to another person or persons and specifically includes rape of a child, aggravated rape and rape; or

(ii) Results, or was intended to result, in the defendant's receiving income, benefit, property, money or anything of value from the commission of any aggravated burglary, or from the illegal sale, delivery, or manufacture of a controlled substance, controlled substance analogue, or firearm; or

(B) The commission or attempted commission, facilitation of, solicitation of, or conspiracy to commit any of the following offenses on or after July 1, 2013:

(i) First degree murder, as defined in § 39-13-202;

(ii) Second degree murder, as defined in § 39-13-210;

(iii) Voluntary manslaughter, as defined in § 39-13-211;

(iv) Assault, as defined in § 39-13-101;

(v) Aggravated assault, as defined in § 39-13-102;

(vi) Kidnapping, as defined in § 39-13-303;

(vii) Aggravated kidnapping, as defined in § 39-13-304;

(viii) Especially aggravated kidnapping, as defined in § 39-13-305;

(ix) Robbery, as defined in § 39-13-401;

(x) Aggravated robbery, as defined in § 39-13-402;

(xi) Especially aggravated robbery, as defined in § 39-13-403;

(xii) Carjacking, as defined in § 39-13-404;

(xiii) Rape, as defined in § 39-13-503;

(xiv) Aggravated rape, as defined in § 39-13-502;

(xv) Rape of a child, as defined in § 39-13-522;

(xvi) Aggravated burglary, as defined in § 39-14-403;

(xvii) Especially aggravated burglary, as defined in § 39-14-404;

(xviii) Aggravated criminal trespass, as defined in § 39-14-406;

(xix) Coercion of witness, as defined in § 39-16-507;

(xx) Retaliation for past action, as defined in § 39-16-510;

(xxi) Riot, as defined in § 39-17-302;

(xxii) Aggravated riot, as defined in § 39-17-303;

(xxiii) Inciting to riot, as defined in §39-17-304;

(xxiv) The illegal sale, delivery or manufacture of a controlled substance or controlled substance analogue, as defined in §§ 39-17-417 and 39-17-454;

(xxv) Possession of a controlled substance or controlled substance analogue with intent to sell, deliver, or manufacture, as defined in § 39-17-417(a)(4) and § 39 17-454;

(xxvi) Unlawful carrying or possession of a weapon, as defined in § 39-17-1307;

40-35-121 SECTION 2. Tennessee Code Annotated Section, 40-35-121(a)(4)(A), is amended by deleting the language "or solicitation or conspiracy to commit" and substituting instead the language "facilitation of, solicitation of, or conspiracy to commit".

40-35-121 SECTION 3. Tennessee Code Annotated, Section 40-35-121, is amended by adding the following language as a new subsection (i):

(i) For purposes of establishing a "pattern of criminal gang activity" the following offenses may be considered:

(1) Criminal gang offenses, as defined by subdivision (a)(3)(A), committed prior to July 1, 2013; and,

(2) Criminal gang offenses, as defined by subdivision (a)(3)(B), committed on or after July 1, 2013.

Effective date 7/1/2013 SECTION 4. This act shall take effect July 1, 2013, the public welfare requiring it.

PUBLIC CHAPTER NO. 358

PUBLIC CHAPTER NO. 358

HOUSE BILL NO. 6

By Representatives Watson, Joe Carr, Evans, Weaver, Alexander, Carter, Hardaway, Sparks, Matthew Hill, Kane, Dean, Hall, McCormick, Mark White, Todd, Littleton, Powers, Moody, Van Huss, Womick, Shipley, Butt, Ryan Williams, Lollar, Forgety, Sanderson, Rogers, Keisling, Curtis Johnson

Substituted for: Senate Bill No. 570

By Senators Niceley, Crowe, Bowling

AN ACT to amend Tennessee Code Annotated, Title 39, Chapter 17, Part 13 and Title 49, Chapter 6, relative to carrying weapons on school property by certain employees.

BE IT ENACTED BY THE GENERAL ASSEMBLY OF THE STATE OF TENNESSEE:

SECTION 1. This act shall be known and may be cited as the "School Security Act of 2013".

49-6-815 SECTION 2. Tennessee Code Annotated, Title 49, Chapter 6, Part 8, is amended by adding the following new section:

49-6-815.

(a) Notwithstanding § 39-17-1309 or any other provision of title 39, chapter 17, part 13 to the contrary, the following people are permitted to possess and carry a firearm on the grounds of the school at which they are assigned:

(1) A person employed by an LEA as a faculty or staff member at a school within the LEA; or

(2) A person assigned to a school in accordance with a memorandum of understanding between the chief of the appropriate law enforcement agency and the LEA.

(b) In order to possess and carry a firearm on the grounds of the school pursuant to subsection (a), the person must:

(1) Be authorized to possess and carry a firearm pursuant to § 39-17-1351;

(2) Have the joint written authorization of the director of schools in conjunction with the principal of the school to carry or possess a firearm on school property; and

(3) Be a law enforcement officer, or have prior service as a law enforcement officer, as defined in § 39-11-106, and be in compliance with all laws, rules and regulations of the peace officer standards and training (POST) commission, and have successfully completed forty (40) hours in basic training in school policing as required by § 49-6-4217. Any such training shall be approved by the LEA and the cost of the training, firearm and ammunition shall be at the expense of the person seeking authorization and not the LEA.

(c)

(1) Within ten (10) days after the director of schools has authorized a person to carry or possess a firearm on school property pursuant to subdivision (a)(1) or (a)(2), the director shall notify the chief of the appropriate law enforcement agency of each such authorization.

(2) The notification pursuant to this subsection shall contain basic information about each such person including name, address, contact

information and whether the person is authorized under subdivision (a)(1) or (a)(2).

(d) The joint written authorization of the director of schools and the principal of the school given pursuant to subdivision (b)(2), the notification transmitted to the chief of the appropriate law enforcement agency pursuant to subdivision (c)(1), the names and contact information of any person authorized to carry or possess a firearm on school property pursuant to subdivision (c)(2), any listing or compilation of names or individual names of persons who are authorized to carry or possess a firearm on school property, whether the director of schools and the principal of the school have or have not issued joint written authorization to carry or possess a firearm on school property, or any other document, file, record, information or material relating to the carrying or possessing of a firearm on school property pursuant to this section that is received by, transmitted to, maintained, stored or compiled by the director of schools, the principal of the school, any LEA, or city, county or municipal law enforcement agency, shall be confidential and not open for public inspection.

(e) Nothing in § 49-3-315 shall be construed to require an LEA or a law enforcement agency of the county to assign or provide funding for a school resource officer as defined in § 49-6-4202 to any city school system within that county on the basis of the WFTEADA as defined by § 49-3-302. The providing of security or school resource officers by a sheriff shall be considered a law enforcement function and not a school operation or maintenance purpose that requires the apportionment of funds pursuant to § 49-3-315.

Effective date 7/1/2013

SECTION 3. This act shall take effect July 1, 2013 the public welfare requiring it and shall apply to the 2013-2014 academic year and each academic year thereafter.

PUBLIC CHAPTER NO. 359

PUBLIC CHAPTER NO. 359

HOUSE BILL NO. 982

By Representatives Sanderson, Hardaway

Substituted for: Senate Bill No. 1133

By Senator Norris

AN ACT to amend Tennessee Code Annotated, Title 49, Chapter 7, Part 8 and Title 65, Chapter 5, Part 1, relative to the transfer of the small and minority-owned business assistance program.

BE IT ENACTED BY THE GENERAL ASSEMBLY OF THE STATE OF TENNESSEE:

65-5-113 SECTION 1. Tennessee Code Annotated, Section 65-5-113, is amended by adding the following as a new subsection (c):

(c) It is within the state treasurer's discretion to accept new applications to participate in the small and minority-owned business assistance program after July 1, 2013. After July 1, 2013, the program shall administer all loans that are outstanding as of July 1, 2013, until the loans are matured or written-off. After July 1, 2013, and notwithstanding subsection (b) of this section, a portion of the small and minority-owned business program funds shall be transferred to the board of trustees of the baccalaureate education system trust fund program to be utilized in an incentive plan or plans authorized in §49-7-805(4), reserving such amounts that the state treasurer deems necessary for the administration of the small and minority-owned business program, as well as the administration and marketing of the incentive plan or plans. At least annually, the state treasurer shall evaluate the loan payments received by the small and minority-owned business assistance program and shall have the authority to transfer the funds from loan payments to the baccalaureate education system trust fund program while reserving amounts for continued administration of the small and minority-owned business assistance program.

49-7-808 SECTION 2. Tennessee Code Annotated, Section 49-7-808, is amended by adding a new, appropriately designated subsection as follows:

(d) The funds from the small and minority-owned business assistance program that are transferred to the board pursuant to §65-5-113(c) shall be used for the establishment of an incentive plan or plans as authorized in §49-7-805(4) for the benefit of low-income individuals. The board shall have the authority to promulgate rules relative to the implementation and administration of the incentive plan or plans. The state treasurer shall be responsible for the day-to-day administration and implementation of the plan or plans as established by the board.

Effective date 7/1/2013 SECTION 3. This act shall take effect on July 1, 2013, the public welfare requiring it.

PUBLIC CHAPTER NO. 360

PUBLIC CHAPTER NO. 360

HOUSE BILL NO. 987

By Representative Goins

Substituted for: Senate Bill No. 937

By Senator Southerland

AN ACT to amend Tennessee Code Annotated, Title 30, Chapter 4, relative to administration of estates.

BE IT ENACTED BY THE GENERAL ASSEMBLY OF THE STATE OF TENNESSEE:

30-4-103 SECTION 1. Tennessee Code Annotated, Section 30-4-103, is amended by deleting the section in its entirety and substituting instead the following:

Whenever a decedent leaves a small estate, it may be administered in the following manner:

(1)

(A) After the expiration of forty-five (45) days from the date of decedent's death, provided no petition for the appointment of a personal representative of the decedent has been filed in that period of time and decedent's estate is a small estate within the meaning of this chapter, one (1) or more of decedent's competent, adult legatees or devisees or personal representatives named in the decedent's will, if a will was left, or heirs or next of kin, if no will was left, or in either a testate or intestate estate, any creditor proving that creditor's debt on oath before the court, shall file with the clerk of the court an affidavit which shall set forth the following facts:

(i) Whether or not decedent left a will, and if so, the original shall be presented to the court for examination by the clerk. The original will has not been proven and therefore shall not be recorded. A copy of the original will shall be filed to support the affidavit. The original will shall be deposited with the court for safekeeping;

(ii) A list of unpaid debts left by decedent and the name and address of each creditor and the amount due that creditor;

(iii) An itemized description and the value of all of decedent's property, the names and addresses of all persons known to have possession of any of decedent's property, and a schedule of all insurance on decedent's life payable to the decedent's estate;

(iv) The name, age, address and relationship, if any, of each devisee, legatee or heir entitled to receive any of decedent's property; and

(B) The form of the affidavit required by this section shall disclose that the affiant evidences by signature that, subject to the penalty for perjury, the affidavit is not false or misleading and that the affiant is mindful of all duties imposed upon the affiant by this chapter. No clerk or assistant shall be liable as a result of services rendered to the affiant in good faith in completing the affidavit based upon information furnished by the affiant.

(C) Upon the motion of one (1) or more of the decedent's competent, adult legatees or devisees if a will was left, or the decedent's heirs or next of kin if no will was left, or upon its own motion, the court may, in its discretion for good cause shown, reduce the forty-five day period required by subdivision (1)(A).

(D) A competent adult who is not a legatee or devisee or personal representative named in the decedent's will, or an heir or next of kin of the deceased, may be appointed as the affiant for a small estate by the court, if all competent adult legatees or devisees or personal representatives named in the decedent's will, if a will was left, or heirs or next of kin, if no will was left, consent in writing to the appointment of the competent adult as the affiant; provided, that any person who is appointed as an affiant pursuant to these provisions shall comply with all other provisions of this section, including the bond provisions contained in subdivision (5). The consent shall not be required of any personal representative who is named in the decedent's will and who has renounced the appointment, in order for the court to appoint an affiant for a small estate.

(2) The court shall receive and file the original affidavit as a part of the court's permanent records, shall assign it a number and shall index it as other estates are indexed. The clerk shall deliver to the affiant as many certified copies of the affidavit as are requested, onto which are affixed a clerk's stamp and seal certifying that the affidavit has been filed in the office of the probate court. An affidavit may be amended to the extent that the aggregate amount does not exceed the statutory limitation.

(3) The clerk shall charge and receive such fees for processing a small estate as authorized and provided in §§ 8-21-401 and 32-1-112

(4) The affiant shall make bond payable to the state for the benefit of those entitled with two (2) or more sufficient sureties or one (1) corporate surety. The amount of the bond shall equal the value of the decedent's estate to be administered under this chapter. However, bond shall not be required of the affiant if § 30-1-201 would not require such from a personal representative.

(5) The affiant and the sureties on the affiant's bond may obtain discharge from liability under the bond in either of two (2) ways:

(A) The court may enter an order discharging the affiant and the sureties on the affiant's bond after the affiant files:

(i) Either the tax receipt issued pursuant to § 67-8-420, or the certificate issued pursuant to § 67-8-409; and

(ii) An affidavit that each debt of the decedent is paid.

(B) Instead of filing as provided in subdivision (A), the affiant and the sureties on the affiant's bond may wait until the first anniversary of the filing of the affidavit when the court shall automatically discharge them from liability.

Effective date 7/1/2013

SECTION 2. This act shall take effect July 1, 2013, the public welfare requiring it, and shall apply to small estate affidavits filed on or after such date.

PUBLIC CHAPTER NO. 361

PUBLIC CHAPTER NO. 361

HOUSE BILL NO. 1055

By Representatives Durham, Matthew Hill, Casada, Evans, Weaver, Kevin Brooks, Pitts, Timothy Hill, Moody, Littleton, Lynn, Shipley, Butt, Dunn, Kane, Ryan Williams

Substituted for: Senate Bill No. 538

By Senators Bell, Johnson, Kelsey, Beavers, Burks, Gardenshire, Yager

AN ACT to amend Tennessee Code Annotated, Section 49-4-902, relative to the definition of "home school student" for purposes of the Tennessee HOPE scholarship.

BE IT ENACTED BY THE GENERAL ASSEMBLY OF THE STATE OF TENNESSEE:

49-4-902 SECTION 1. Tennessee Code Annotated, Section 49-4-902(23), is amended by deleting the words "two (2) years" and by substituting instead the words "one (1) year" in the second sentence of the subdivision.

Effective date 5/13/2013 SECTION 2. This act shall take effect upon becoming a law, the public welfare requiring it, and shall apply to students applying for postsecondary financial assistance from net lottery proceeds for the 2013-2014 academic year and academic years thereafter.

PUBLIC CHAPTER NO. 362

PUBLIC CHAPTER NO. 362

HOUSE BILL NO. 1066

By Representative Keisling

Substituted for: Senate Bill No. 1232

By Senators Tracy, Bell

AN ACT to amend Tennessee Code Annotated, Title 62 and Title 68, Chapter 221, Part 9, relative to water.

BE IT ENACTED BY THE GENERAL ASSEMBLY OF THE STATE OF TENNESSEE:

68-221-901 SECTION 1. Tennessee Code Annotated, Section 68-221-901, is amended by deleting the language "Water Environmental Health Act" and by substituting instead the language "Water and Wastewater Operator Certification Act."

68-221-904 SECTION 2. Tennessee Code Annotated, Section 68-221-904(c), is amended by deleting subdivision (2) in its entirety and by substituting instead the following:

(2) The commissioner has the duty and authority to levy civil penalties authorized in subdivision (1), the duty and authority to issue orders requiring compliance with this part, and to hold show cause meetings with the persons or entities to whom the orders are proposed to be issued.

68-221-905 SECTION 3. Tennessee Code Annotated, Section 68-221-905, is amended by deleting subsection (b) in its entirety and by substituting instead the following:

(b)

(1) Such board shall be composed of the following members, appointed by the governor:

(A) One (1) member shall be a certified operator of a water or wastewater system who holds a certificate of the highest class issued by the board, who may be appointed from lists of qualified persons submitted by interested water and wastewater groups including, but not limited to, the Tennessee Water and Wastewater Association;

(B) One (1) member shall be a certified operator of a water or wastewater utility district, who may be appointed from lists of qualified persons submitted by interested utility district groups including, but not limited to, the Tennessee Association of Utility Districts;

(C) One (1) member shall be a person knowledgeable about water or wastewater systems with experience working for such systems, who may be appointed from lists of qualified persons submitted by interested municipal groups including, but not limited to, the Tennessee Municipal League;

(D) One member shall be a faculty member of a college, university or state technical institute whose major field is related to water or wastewater systems, who may be appointed from lists of qualified persons submitted by interested engineering groups including, but not limited to, the Tennessee Society of Professional Engineers; and

(E) The commissioner or such qualified member of the commissioner's staff as the commissioner may designate.

(2) The governor shall consult with interested groups including, but not limited to, the organizations listed in subdivision (b)(1) to determine qualified persons to fill positions on the board.

PUBLIC CHAPTER NO. 362 (cont'd)

68-221-905 SECTION 4. Tennessee Code Annotated, Section 68-221-905, is amended by deleting the language "water management" wherever it appears and by substituting instead the language "water resources".

68-221-906 SECTION 5. Tennessee Code Annotated, Section 68-221-906 is amended by deleting the language "revocations,".

68-221-911 SECTION 6. Tennessee Code Annotated, Section 68-221-911(a), is amended by deleting the language "commissioner, in accordance with the rules and regulations of the".

68-221-911 SECTION 7. Tennessee Code Annotated, Section 68-221-911 is amended by deleting subsections (b) and (c) in their entirety and by substituting instead the following:

(b) When the commissioner believes an operator has engaged in any of the activities set forth in subsection (a), the commissioner may issue an order suspending the operator's certificate until the board conducts a hearing on the revocation of the operator's certificate for such activities. When the commissioner has issued a suspension order, the board shall conduct its revocation hearing and render its decision within ninety (90) days of the operator's suspension. In the event the board does not render its decision within ninety (90) days of the operator's suspension, the suspension order shall expire and no longer be in force or effect. However, the commissioner may reissue an order of suspension for a period not to exceed ninety (90) days.

(c) When the board determines an operator's certificate should be revoked under subsection (a), the board shall establish the timing, terms and conditions for any reinstatement of the operator's certificate.

68-221-914 SECTION 8. Tennessee Code Annotated, Section 68-221-914, is amended by deleting subsection (a) in its entirety and by substituting instead the following:

(a) Any party to a hearing before the board regarding a revocation or an appeal of an order or assessment of a civil penalty by the commissioner may appeal the final order of the board to the chancery court of Davidson County.

68-221-905 SECTION 9. Tennessee Code Annotated, Section 68-221-905(e), is amended by deleting the language "water management" and by substituting instead the language "water resources".

Effective date 7/1/2013 SECTION 10. This act shall take effect on July 1, 2013, the public welfare requiring it, and the provisions of Section 3 shall apply to all appointments to the board made on or after that date.

PUBLIC CHAPTER NO. 363

PUBLIC CHAPTER NO. 363

HOUSE BILL NO. 1268

By Representatives Farmer, Hardaway, Stewart

Substituted for: Senate Bill No. 1307

By Senators Southerland, Bowling

AN ACT to amend Tennessee Code Annotated, Title 4; Title 11; Title 12; Title 13; Title 43 and Title 49, Chapter 17, relative to building materials used for public projects.

BE IT ENACTED BY THE GENERAL ASSEMBLY OF THE STATE OF TENNESSEE:

4-15-104 SECTION 1. Tennessee Code Annotated, Section 4-15-104 is amended by deleting subsection (b) in its entirety and substituting the following:

(b) The commission is encouraged to prescribe high performance building requirements and other standards, and promulgate rules and regulations, which meet or exceed the 2005 Sustainable Design Guidelines that the commission implemented, that are necessary to ensure all state buildings perform in an energy efficient manner.

(c) Notwithstanding subsection (b), the commission shall not prescribe any high performance building requirement or any other standard, nor promulgate any rules and regulations, which require or permit any wood products harvested or manufactured in this state, or any wood products designed or manufactured by a forest products company that is headquartered in this state, to be in any way less preferred in the design and construction of state buildings than any wood products harvested or manufactured outside this state, or to be in any way less preferred than any other wood products grown or harvested in this state, that have been certified or graded by any certifying or grading association or agency, including but not limited to the Sustainable Forestry Initiative, the American Tree Farm System, or the Forest Stewardship Council.

Effective date 5/13/2013 SECTION 2. This act shall take effect upon becoming law, the public welfare requiring it.

PUBLIC CHAPTER NO. 364

PUBLIC CHAPTER NO. 364

HOUSE BILL NO. 848

By Representative Ragan

Substituted for: Senate Bill No. 1006

By Senators Gresham, Crowe

AN ACT to amend Tennessee Code Annotated, Title 58, Chapter 1, relative to the Tennessee state guard.

BE IT ENACTED BY THE GENERAL ASSEMBLY OF THE STATE OF TENNESSEE:

58-1-412 SECTION 1. Tennessee Code Annotated, Title 58, Chapter 1, Part 4, is amended by adding the following language as a new section:

58-1-412.

The governor is authorized and empowered to call members of the state guard to active state duty with the member's consent, for the performance of any official duty in connection with state guard activities. Inactive reserve status may include voluntary unpaid state service for assistance to local authorities during times of disaster, or other times of crisis, when requested from and approved by the adjutant general by city, county or metropolitan local authorities.

58-1-106 SECTION 2. Tennessee Code Annotated, Section 58-1-106(b), is amended by deleting the language "prescribed by § 58-1-109." and by substituting instead the language "prescribed by § 58-1-109 for the national guard and § 58-1-411 for the Tennessee state guard."

58-1-106 SECTION 3. Tennessee Code Annotated, Section 58-1-106(c), is amended by deleting the language "in § 58-1-109," and by substituting instead the language "in § 58-1-109 for the national guard and § 58-1-411 for the Tennessee state guard,".

58-1-106 SECTION 4. Tennessee Code Annotated, Section 58-1-106(c), is amended by adding the following language as the fourth and final sentence of the subsection:

Assistance authorized by, and requested from, competent authority provided only by the Tennessee state guard at the request of a city, county, or other local authority pursuant to this section by volunteers without compensation, shall not require the county or city to reimburse the military department; provided, however, that any travel expenses resulting from the authorized assistance of Tennessee state guard members from outside the requesting city or county shall require reimbursement from the city, county or local authority to the military department, when the department incurs an expense as a result of the travel for costs directly paid by the department or for travel claims filed by Tennessee state guard members.

Effective date 5/13/2013 SECTION 5. This act shall take effect upon becoming law, the public welfare requiring it.

PUBLIC CHAPTER NO. 365

PUBLIC CHAPTER NO. 365

HOUSE BILL NO. 710

By Representatives Littleton, Mark White, Hardaway, Jones, Coley, Rogers, Moody, Weaver, Camper, Parkinson, Holt, Wirgau, Dunn, Harry Brooks, Ryan Williams, Kane, Kevin Brooks, Sexton, McManus, Lollar

Substituted for: Senate Bill No. 1034

By Senators Kelsey, Bowling, Crowe, Gresham, Yager

AN ACT to amend Tennessee Code Annotated, Title 36, Chapter 1, Part 1, relative to the termination of parental rights.

BE IT ENACTED BY THE GENERAL ASSEMBLY OF THE STATE OF TENNESSEE:

36-1-113 SECTION 1. Tennessee Code Annotated, Section 36-1-113, is amended by adding the following new subdivision to subsection (g):

( ) The parent or guardian has been convicted of trafficking for commercial sex act under § 39-13-309;

Effective date 7/1/2013 SECTION 2. This act shall take effect July 1, 2013, the public welfare requiring it.

PUBLIC CHAPTER NO. 366

PUBLIC CHAPTER NO. 366

HOUSE BILL NO. 183

By Representatives McCormick, Kevin Brooks

Substituted for: Senate Bill No. 189

By Senator Norris

AN ACT to amend Tennessee Code Annotated, Title 54, Chapter 1, relative to construction manager/general contractor services for the delivery of transportation projects.

BE IT ENACTED BY THE GENERAL ASSEMBLY OF THE STATE OF TENNESSEE:

54-1-501—54-1-508

SECTION 1. Tennessee Code Annotated, Title 54, Chapter 1, is amended by adding the following language as a new Part 5:

54-1-501.

(a) This part shall be known and may be cited as the "Tennessee Department of Transportation Contracts for Construction Manager/General Contractor Services Pilot Program".

(b) This part provides a pilot program that allows the department to engage in an alternative procurement procedure for certain transportation projects performed by the department of transportation.

(c) It is the intent of the general assembly in enacting this part to provide a pilot program to test the utilization of a construction manager/general contractor ("CM/GC") method as a cost-effective and efficient option for constructing transportation projects.

(d) The construction manager/general contractor method allows the department to engage a construction manager during the design process to provide input on the design. During the design phase, the construction manager provides advice including, but not limited to, constructability review, scheduling, pricing, and phasing to assist the department to design a more efficient and well-designed project. The construction manager/general contractor may subsequently construct the project if the department and the CM/GC reach agreement on a guaranteed maximum price for construction.

54-1-502. As used in this part:

(1) "Authorized contingency" means the contingency prepared and submitted by the CM/GC as part of the GMP, which is designed to cover costs that may result from incomplete design, unforeseen and unpredictable conditions, or uncertainties within the defined project scope which a prudent CM/GC would not have reasonably detected or anticipated during the discharge of CM/GC's pre-construction duties;

(2) "Commissioner" means the commissioner of transportation;

(3) "Construction manager/general contractor" or "CM/GC" means a business firm, separate from the project designer, that is able to provide pre-construction services during the design and development phase of a project;

(4) "Construction manager/general contractor method" or "CM/GC method" means a project delivery method in which a construction manager is procured to provide pre-construction services and the CM/GC may subsequently construct the project, or any part of the project, if the department and the firm reach agreement on a guaranteed maximum price;

(5) "Department" means the department of transportation;

(6) "Guaranteed maximum price" or "GMP" means the total dollar amount within which the CM/GC commits to complete construction of the project, including the CM/GC's direct costs, overhead, and profit, plus any authorized contingency. The GMP may be supplemented at a later date to cover additional costs arising from changes in the scope of work as the department may subsequently direct in writing; and

(7) "Pre-construction services" may include, but not be limited to, cost estimates, schedule analysis, sequencing of work, risk identification and mitigation, constructability reviews, evaluation of alternative construction options, assistance with various permits, coordination with public or private utility service providers, communication with third-party stakeholders and/or the public, development of a GMP, and any directly related or similar services as may be necessary or useful to assist the department with the design and development of a project to the construction phase.

54-1-503.

(a) Notwithstanding any other provision of law to the contrary, during the term of this pilot program, the commissioner may select up to a total of three (3) projects for the use of the CM/GC method of project delivery. The aggregate total construction costs of the pilot program projects shall not exceed two hundred million dollars ($200,000,000). The first CM/GC project shall not exceed seventy million dollars ($70,000,000) in construction costs, and no CM/GC project shall exceed one hundred million dollars ($100,000,000) in construction costs.

(b) After the first project subject to the construction manager/general contractor method has begun, the department shall not initiate any other project using the CM/GC method until after a contract for construction of the first CM/GC project has been awarded.

(c) Before using the CM/GC method of project delivery, the commissioner shall send written notice to the chair of the transportation and safety committee of the senate and the chair of the transportation committee of the house of representatives. The written notice shall identify the project and the reasons for deciding to use the CM/GC method.

54-1-504. If the commissioner determines that the CM/GC method of procurement is appropriate for a project, the commissioner shall establish a multi-phase process as described in subdivisions (1) - (4) to select the CM/GC that is the most responsive and responsible proposer.

(1) Phase 1 of the process is the appointment of the selection committee, as follows:

(A) For each request for proposal ("RFP") for CM/GC services, the commissioner shall appoint a selection committee to evaluate and score all responsive proposals in accordance with the procedures established in the RFP.

(i) The selection committee shall have a total of eight (8) members. The commissioner shall appoint five (5) department employees to the selection committee based on their qualifications and experience, including at least one (1) employee who is a licensed professional engineer in this state.

(ii) In addition, the commissioner shall appoint three (3) members who are not employees of the department, all of whom shall be residents of this state. At least one (1) member shall be appointed from and reside in each of the grand divisions of this state. At least one (1) of these three (3) members shall have a degree in banking, finance or accounting and a minimum of five (5) years of employment experience in a banking, finance or accounting position. Each of the other two (2) members shall have a minimum of ten (10) years of construction or highway engineering design experience, and at least one (1) of these two (2) members shall have a valid professional engineering license.

(2) Phase 2 of the process is the development and issuance of the request for proposals ("RFP"), as follows:

(A) The RFP used to solicit a CM/GC proposal shall be reviewed by the selection committee established under subdivision (1). Prior to the issuance of the RFP, the selection committee shall approve the proposed RFP indicating that the RFP complies with the requirements in this part, in a closed meeting that is not open to the public and by a majority vote.

(B) For the purposes of the pilot program, the RFP shall not require prior experience with any particular project delivery method as a condition for submitting a responsive proposal. Further, the RFP shall not solicit information concerning prior experience with any particular contract delivery method, and the RFP shall not give any credit or preference for any particular contract delivery method experience in the scoring of any proposal. The RFP shall include, but not be limited to, the following:

(i) The procedures for submitting proposals and the criteria for evaluating qualifications and the relative weight for each criteria as indicated in the technical score matrix, which shall be attached to the RFP;

(ii) The form of the contract to be awarded for pre-construction services;

(iii) A listing of the types and scope of pre-construction services that will be required;

(iv) The scope of the intended construction work, with a requirement that the CM/GC, if awarded the construction contract, shall complete at least thirty percent (30%) of the negotiated construction cost of the entire project internally. The cost for pre-construction services shall not be considered part of the thirty percent (30%) but may be considered a specialty item;

(v) Any budget limits for the construction project and the pre-construction services;

(vi) The method of payment and structure of fees for the pre-construction services;

(vii) A requirement that the proposer submit relevant information regarding any licenses, registration and credentials that may be required to construct the project, including information on the revocation or suspension of any license, registration or credential. A Tennessee contractor's license shall not be required to submit a proposal or to be considered for award of a contract for pre-construction services; provided, however, that a Tennessee contractor's license shall be required prior to the execution of any contract for pre-construction services or to construct the project;

(viii) A requirement that the proposer submit evidence that establishes the entity has the capacity to obtain the required bonding and insurance for the project;

(ix) A requirement that the proposer submit information concerning any debarment or default from a federal, state or local government project within the past five (5) years;

(x) A requirement that the proposer provide information concerning the bankruptcy or receivership of any member of the entity including information concerning any work completed by a surety;

(xi) A requirement that the proposing firm provide evidence that the proposing firm has actual experience in the successful construction of other highway transportation projects, as well as the competency, capability and capacity to complete a project of similar size, scope or complexity; and further, the proposing firm may not rely on the construction experience of a subcontractor or other team member for the purpose of meeting this requirement;

(xii) An affidavit that shall be signed by each proposer competing for a CM/GC contract affirming that the company, its agents, subcontractors and employees have not violated the prohibitions described in subdivisions (3)(F) and(3)(G); and

(xiii) A prohibition that excludes any person or firm that has received compensation for assisting the department in preparing the RFP from submitting a proposal in response to the RFP, or participating as a CM/GC team member.

(C) Once the selection committee has approved the RFP and determined that it complies with the requirements of this part, the RFP shall be published on the department's Internet web site, and may be advertised in a newspaper of general circulation in the region of the state where the work is to be performed and/or published in such other internet or print media of general circulation so as to afford an opportunity for qualified firms to be considered for award of the contract.

(3) Phase 3 of the process, which may be known as the "CM/GC Selection-Design Phase," is as follows:

(A) The department's RFP shall establish a procedure for the evaluation and selection of a CM/GC to perform pre-construction services and potentially construct the project. Members of the selection committee are to be instructed as to their responsibilities and duties, as established in this part, prior to their review or evaluation of the proposals.

(B) All proposals received by the department in response to the RFP, and any documents used by the selection committee to evaluate and score the proposals, shall remain confidential and not subject to disclosure to any proposer or to the public until after the department issues a written notice of award as provided in subdivision (3)(E).

(C) The RFP may provide for the selection committee to make an initial review and evaluation of interested proposers through a request for qualifications (RFQ), with a more detailed proposal to be submitted by a selected list of proposers, and it may provide for interviews or presentations. The RFP may also provide for a process by which members of the selection committee, through a department employee identified in the RFP as a point of contact, may request and obtain information on technical matters to assist them in the evaluation of proposals.

(D) Upon completion of the evaluation process, each member of the selection committee shall independently review and score the proposals. Each member shall score the proposals pursuant to the scoring matrix that the department provides in the RFP and based on the RFP's evaluation criteria. The scores will be tallied and averaged according to the procedure established in the RFP; provided, however, that the scores of the two (2) selection committee members giving the highest and lowest scores on a proposal shall be excluded when computing the average score for each proposal. Upon completion of the scoring, the proposals will be ranked in order of the highest aggregate score to the lowest aggregate score. The proposer whose proposal receives the highest aggregate score will be considered the best-evaluated proposer.

(E) The proposals shall be submitted in rank order to the commissioner. The commissioner may either accept the selection committee's recommendation of the best-evaluated proposer, or the commissioner may reject all proposals and proceed with construction of the project through any lawful method for procuring a construction services contract. The department shall send all proposers a written notice of award to the best-evaluated proposer, or a written notice that all proposals have been rejected. If the department issues a written notice of award, the notice shall include a copy of the scores from each member of the selection committee for each RFP proposal.

(F) Throughout the selection process:

(i) The members of the selection committee shall not communicate with each other concerning their review or evaluation of the proposals.

(ii) Any entity that submits a proposal in response to the RFP, as well as their employees, agents and subcontractors, shall not communicate with any member of the selection committee, or with any employee or official of the department, concerning the review or evaluation of any proposal, except that a proposer may communicate with those department employees who are specifically listed in the RFP as appropriate points of contact. Any proposer's failure to comply with this restriction shall render said proposer's RFP response ineligible for selection.

(iii) To confirm that no member of the selection committee has been improperly influenced, prior to reviewing the RFP responses, each committee member must affirmatively complete an affidavit indicating that such member has not discussed the proposals or such member's review of the same with any other selection committee member, with any department employee other than those listed in the RFP as an appropriate point of contact, or with any of the proposers, their agents, employees or subcontractors.

(iv) Each member of the selection committee shall also be required to complete an affidavit stating that such member is not aware of having any conflict of interest, financial or otherwise, regarding the member's ability to fairly evaluate all proposals.

(G) Entities competing for a CM/GC contract are also prohibited from offering or paying a contingency fee of any type that is directly tied to specific actions or work designed to help the proposer obtain a contract through the CM/GC RFP process. The selected CM/GC firm shall complete an affidavit affirming this information before being awarded a contract. Falsely affirming that a contingency fee, associated with the CM/GC RFP process, was neither offered nor paid shall be grounds for debarment of the proposer under official compilation Rules and Regulations of the State of Tennessee, Chapter 1680-5-1, governing suspension and debarment for department contractors.

(4) Phase IV of the process, which may be known as the "CM/GC Selection-Construction Phase," is as follows:

(A) Once the design has been completed, or has been sufficiently developed to allow the CM/GC to prepare a proposed guaranteed maximum price for construction of the project, or a part of the project, the department shall conduct the steps described in subdivision (4)(B) before proceeding with any construction of the project.

(B) The department shall:

(i) Prepare and compile the contract plans, specifications, special provisions, and other requirements which will comprise the contract for construction of the project;

(ii) Prepare a detailed construction cost estimate to evaluate the appropriate price for construction of the project as designed; and

PUBLIC CHAPTER NO. 366 (cont'd)

(iii) If directed by the commissioner, have an independent third-party estimator prepare a detailed construction cost estimate to confirm the appropriate price for construction of the project as designed.

(C) The department's detailed construction cost estimate, and any construction cost estimate prepared by an independent third-party estimator, shall not be disclosed to the CM/GC, and shall remain confidential and not subject to public disclosure until after award of the contract for construction of the project.

(D) The contract shall require the CM/GC to self-perform a portion of the construction work comprising at least thirty percent (30%) of the total cost for construction, excluding specialty items. The cost for pre-construction services shall not be considered part of the thirty percent (30%) but may be considered a specialty item.

(E) Based on the contract plans, specifications, special provisions, and other contract terms and conditions compiled by the department, the CM/GC shall prepare a guaranteed maximum price, including any authorized contingency, for construction of the project. When completed, the CM/GC's proposed GMP shall be submitted to the department for review. The CM/GC's proposed GMP shall otherwise remain confidential and not subject to public disclosure until after award of the contract for construction of the project.

(F) The department shall compare the CM/GC's proposed GMP with its own confidential construction estimate, and with any construction estimate prepared by an independent third-party estimator. If the GMP does not exceed the department's estimate, or the independent third-party estimate, by more than ten percent (10%), the commissioner may, but is not required to, award the contract for construction of the project to the CM/GC.

(G) If the commissioner rejects the proposed GMP, the department may continue to conduct contract discussions with the CM/GC to develop an acceptable GMP for the project as designed. Alternatively, the department may direct the CM/GC to provide additional pre-construction services as needed to assist in the further development of contract plans, terms, or specifications for the purpose of repeating the Phase IV process steps established in this subdivision (4).

(H) If the CM/GC and the commissioner are unable to reach agreement on the GMP, the commissioner may proceed with construction of the project through the low bid procurement process.

54-1-505.

(a) A proposer who participated in the CM/GC RFP process may protest the award of a CM/GC contract to the commissioner. The protest shall be submitted in writing within seven (7) calendar days after the proposer knows or should have known of the facts giving rise to the protest. In the case of a pending award, a stay of award may be requested. The commissioner or the commissioner's designee has the authority to settle and resolve a protest.

(b) Upon receipt of the "notice of award" letter which will be sent to all proposers by email, facsimile or mail prior to awarding the contract to the recommended proposer, the proposers shall have seven (7) calendar days to review the procurement file and to file a protest. In no event shall any protest be allowed, however, more than seven (7) calendar days after the proposer knew or should have known of the facts giving rise to the protest. If no protest letter with a protest bond is received in accordance with the requirements described in this subsection, then the department shall proceed with the award. The protest procedures and protest bond requirements are as follows:

(1) The protester shall deliver by mail or hand delivery an original protest letter, manually signed in ink, with a protest bond to the commissioner within seven (7) calendar days after the proposer knew or should have known of the

facts giving rise to the protest. The protest letter shall include the solicitation number, the reason or reasons for the protest, and the signature of an attorney or protesting party indicating that the signer has read the document, and that to the best of the signer's knowledge, information, and belief formed after reasonable inquiry, it is well grounded in fact and is warranted by existing law or a good faith argument for the extension, modification, or reversal of existing law, and that it is not interposed for any improper purpose, such as to harass, limit competition, or to cause unnecessary delay or needless increase in the cost of the procurement or of the litigation.

(2) The protest, and any review or appeal thereof, shall be based exclusively on the written record of the CM/GC procurement process described in § 54-1-504(2) and (3), unless there are specific factual allegations that, in the course of evaluating or scoring the proposals, the selection committee or a member thereof has engaged in unlawful conduct or conduct so arbitrary and capricious as to amount to an illegality, in which case evidence outside the written record may be submitted.

(3) The protest bond shall be in the amount of five percent (5%) of the department's estimate of the total project cost.

(4) If the protest is not resolved by mutual agreement, the protester may request that the matter be considered at a meeting with the state protest committee created in § 4-56-103. The protester shall be required to submit a letter of appeal to the commissioner of general services and the commissioner of transportation requesting a meeting with the state protest committee within seven (7) calendar days from the date of the final determination letter provided by the commissioner or the commissioner's designee. In the event that a letter of appeal is not received within the seven (7) calendar days, the department shall proceed with an award.

(5) If the protester submits a letter of appeal to the state protest committee within the seven (7) calendar days, the state protest committee shall hold a protest meeting and make a final determination in writing to the protester and the commissioner.

(6) The department shall hold the protest bond for at least eleven (11) calendar days after the date of the final determination by the commissioner or the commissioner's designee. If the protester appeals the commissioner's final determination to the state protest committee, the protest bond shall be held until the commissioner is instructed by the state protest committee to either keep the bond or return it to the protester. The protester shall be notified in writing of the decision to keep the protest bond or shall be sent the protest bond by certified mail; provided, however, the bond may only be retained if the commissioner determines that there is substantial evidence in the record to establish that the protest was brought or pursued in bad faith, or that the protest does not state on its face a valid basis for protest.

(7) A decision rendered by the state protest committee may be appealed by filing a petition for a writ of certiorari with the chancery court of Davidson County within sixty (60) days of the state protest committee's final decision.

54-1-506. After the protest period has expired, and the contract for pre-construction services has been awarded, the department's procurement files shall be subject to public inspection pursuant to § 10-7-504(a)(7), and the department shall within five (5) business days after the protest period has expired, provide any unsuccessful proposer with a debriefing on the selection process. The debriefing shall be provided within the earliest mutually convenient time after award of the contract. The debriefing shall be limited to discussion of the strengths and weaknesses of the proposal submitted by the unsuccessful proposer and shall not include specific discussion of any other firm's competing proposal.

54-1-507. The department may establish agency policies and/or promulgate rules and regulations in accordance with the Uniform Administrative Procedures Act, compiled in title 4, chapter 5, in furtherance of the provisions of this part.

54-1-508. This part shall terminate on July 1, 2019, unless re-enacted or extended by the general assembly prior to such date. It is the legislative intent that any such legislative proposals to re-enact or extend this part be referred to the transportation and safety committee of the senate and the transportation committee of the house of representatives. No later than February 1, 2019, the department shall submit a detailed report to the transportation and safety committee of the senate and the transportation committee of the house of representatives containing relevant data that shall include, but not be limited to, the estimated actual cost of each project upon completion, the estimated and actual time of completion, and the number and value of any change orders for the project.

Effective date 7/1/2014

SECTION 2. For the purpose of promulgating rules and regulations, this act shall take effect upon becoming a law, the public welfare requiring it. For all other purposes this act shall take effect July 1, 2014, the public welfare requiring it.

PUBLIC CHAPTER NO. 367

PUBLIC CHAPTER NO. 367

HOUSE BILL NO. 864

By Representatives Lollar, Dennis

Substituted for: Senate Bill No. 432

By Senator Overbey

AN ACT to amend Tennessee Code Annotated, Title 50, relative to workers' compensation.

BE IT ENACTED BY THE GENERAL ASSEMBLY OF THE STATE OF TENNESSEE:

50-6-115 SECTION 1. Tennessee Code Annotated, Section 50-6-115, is amended by deleting the section in its entirety and substituting the following:

50-6-115.

(a) For purposes of this section, an employee is considered to be temporarily in a state working for an employer if the employee is working for such employee's employer in a state other than the state where such employee is primarily employed for no more than fourteen (14) consecutive days, or no more than twenty-five (25) days total, during a calendar year.

(b)

(1) If an employee in this state who is subject to this chapter temporarily leaves this state incidental to the employee's employment and receives an accidental injury arising out of and in the course and scope of the employee's employment, the employee, or the employee's beneficiaries in the case of an injury that results in the employee's death, shall be entitled to the benefits of this chapter as if the employee was injured in this state.

(2) If an employee, while working outside the territorial limits of this state other than temporarily, suffers an injury on account of which the employee, or, in the event of the employee's death, the employee's dependents, would have been entitled to the benefits provided by this chapter had the injury occurred within this state, the employee, or in the event of the employee's death resulting from the injury, the employee's dependents, shall be entitled to the benefits provided by this chapter; provided, that at the time of the injury:

(1) The employment was principally localized within this state;

(2) The contract of hire was made in this state; or

(3) If at the time of the injury the injured worker was a Tennessee resident and there existed a substantial connection between this state and the particular employer and employee relationship.

(c)

(1) An employee from another state and the employee's employer are exempt from this chapter while the employee is temporarily in this state performing work for the employer if:

(A) The employer has furnished workers' compensation insurance coverage under the workers' compensation insurance or similar laws of the other state to cover the employee's employment while in this state;

(B) The extraterritorial provisions of this chapter are recognized in the other state; and

(C) Employees and employers who are covered in this state are likewise exempted from the application of the workers' compensation insurance or similar laws of the other state.

(2) The benefits under the workers' compensation insurance or similar laws of the other state, or other remedies under similar law, are the exclusive remedy against the employer for any injury, whether resulting in death or not, received by the employee while temporarily working for that employer in this state.

(3) A certificate from the duly authorized officer of the appropriate department of another state certifying that the employer of such other state is insured in that state and has provided extraterritorial coverage insuring employees while working in this state is prima facie evidence that the employer carries such workers' compensation insurance.

(4) Whenever in any appeal or other litigation the construction of the laws of another jurisdiction is required, the courts shall take judicial notice of such construction of the laws of the other jurisdiction.

(5) When an employee has a claim under the workers' compensation insurance laws of another state, territory, province, or foreign nation for the same injury or occupational disease as the claim filed in this state, the total amount of compensation paid or awarded under such other workers' compensation law shall be credited against the compensation due under this chapter.

(d)

(1) Any employer who is insured in this state for workers' compensation under title 50, chapter 6, and who has extraterritorial coverage under title 50, chapter 6, for their employees while such employees are temporarily working outside this state within the meaning of subsection (a) may obtain a certificate evidencing such coverage at the time that the application for certification is made from the commissioner of commerce and insurance.

(2) In order to obtain a certificate under subdivision (d)(1), an employer shall:

(A) File an application with the commissioner of commerce and insurance, on a form that is approved by the commissioner of commerce and insurance;

(B) Pay a filing fee to the department of commerce and insurance in the amount of one hundred dollars ($100). The commissioner of commerce and insurance may change the amount of the filing fee required by this subdivision (B) by promulgating a rule pursuant to the Uniform Administrative Procedures Act, compiled in title 4, chapter 5, as necessary to ensure that the proceeds of such filing fees are sufficient to offset the cost of processing applications and issuing the certificates authorized by this subsection (d); and

(C) Submit to the commissioner of commerce and insurance a copy of the declaration page from the employer's workers' compensation insurance policy, or such proof as the commissioner of commerce and insurance may require to demonstrate that the employer is self insured for workers' compensation and the territorial limits of such coverage.

(3) The commissioner of commerce and insurance is authorized to issue a certificate that certifies that, at the time that the application for certification is made, the applicant employer in this state is insured for workers' compensation under title 50, chapter 6, and that such employers have extraterritorial coverage under title 50, chapter 6, for their employees while such employees are temporarily working outside this state within the meaning of subsection (a).

Effective date 5/13/2013

SECTION 2. This act shall take effect upon becoming a law, and shall apply to any claim filed on or after such date regardless of the date of the injury, the public welfare requiring it.

PUBLIC CHAPTER NO. 368

PUBLIC CHAPTER NO. 368

HOUSE BILL NO. 1331

By Representatives John DeBerry, McDaniel

Substituted for: Senate Bill No. 1382

By Senator Gresham

AN ACT to amend Tennessee Code Annotated, Section 49-7-118, relative to university and college police and security departments.

BE IT ENACTED BY THE GENERAL ASSEMBLY OF THE STATE OF TENNESSEE:

49-7-118 SECTION 1. Tennessee Code Annotated, Section 49-7-118, is amended by adding the following language as new subsection (h) and by relettering subsequent subsections accordingly:

(h)

(1) Private universities or colleges that are accredited by the Southern Association of Colleges and Schools and that have an enrollment which is thirty percent (30%) or more of the population of the municipality in which the main campus is located may employ and commission campus police officers for the main campus under the conditions of this section; provided, that the chief law enforcement officer of the municipality has appointed the police officer as a special deputy in accordance with § 8-8-212 or has appointed the police officer as a special police officer.

(2) The chief law enforcement officer of the municipality in which the main campus is located shall define any geographical limitation on the exercise of police power of the special deputy or special police officer.

(3) Notwithstanding any law to the contrary, the law enforcement agency having jurisdiction where the private university or campus is located shall be immune from any suit by anyone incurring any wrong, injury, loss, damage, or expense resulting from any act or failure to act on the part of any special deputy or special police officer commissioned as a campus police officer by a private university or college.

(4) No person shall be appointed as a special deputy or a special police officer or be commissioned as a campus police officer by a private university or college under this subsection (h), unless the person proves to the chief law enforcement officer in which the main campus is located that the person's financial responsibility is in accordance with § 8-8-303(c) and the person has successfully completed the certification requirements of the peace officers standards and training commission (POST), or at least the equivalent thereof.

(5) This subsection (h) shall not entitle the campus police officers to any public funding, for training or otherwise.

Effective date 5/13/2013 SECTION 2. This act shall take effect upon becoming a law, the public welfare requiring it.

PUBLIC CHAPTER NO. 369

PUBLIC CHAPTER NO. 369

HOUSE BILL NO. 1112

By Representative Haynes

Substituted for: Senate Bill No. 1149

By Senator Gresham

AN ACT to amend Tennessee Code Annotated, Section 49-5-511, relative to dismissal or suspension of teachers.

BE IT ENACTED BY THE GENERAL ASSEMBLY OF THE STATE OF TENNESSEE:

49-5-511 SECTION 1. Tennessee Code Annotated, Section Section 49-5-511, is amended by deleting the section in its entirety and substituting instead the following:

49-5-511.

(a)

(1) No teacher shall be dismissed or suspended except as provided in this part.

(2) The causes for which a teacher may be dismissed or suspended are as follows: incompetence, inefficiency, neglect of duty, unprofessional conduct, and insubordination, as defined in § 49-5-501.

(3) A director of schools may suspend a teacher at any time that may seem necessary, pending investigation or final disposition of a case before the board or an appeal. If vindicated or reinstated, the teacher shall be paid the full salary for the period during which the teacher was suspended.

(4) When charges are made to the board of education against a teacher, charging the teacher with offenses that would justify dismissal of the teacher under the terms of this part, the charges shall be made in writing, specifically stating the offenses that are charged, and shall be signed by the party or parties making the charges.

(5) If, in the opinion of the board, charges are of such a nature as to warrant the dismissal of the teacher, the director of schools shall give the teacher a written notice of this decision, together with a copy of the charges and a copy of a form, which shall be provided by the commissioner of education, advising the teacher as to the teacher's legal duties, rights, and recourse under the terms of this part.

(b)

(1) When it becomes necessary to reduce the number of teaching positions or nonlicensed positions in the system because of a decrease in enrollment or for other good reasons, the board shall be empowered to dismiss such teachers or nonlicensed employees based on their level of effectiveness determined by the evaluation pursuant to § 49-1-302 for licensed employees and an evaluation of work performance for nonlicensed employees.

(2) The board shall give the teacher or nonlicensed employee written notice of dismissal explaining fully the circumstances or conditions making the dismissal necessary.

(3) A teacher rated in the three (3) highest categories based on evaluations pursuant to 49-1-302 who has been dismissed because of abolition of a position shall be placed on a list for reemployment. Nothing in this

PUBLIC CHAPTER NO. 369 (cont'd)

subsection (b) shall be construed to deprive the director of schools of the power to determine the filling of such vacancy on the basis of the director's of schools evaluation of the teacher's competence, compatibility, and suitability to properly discharge the duties required for the vacant position considered in the light of the best interest of the students in the school where the vacancy exists. A principal may refuse to accept the placement or transfer of a teacher by the director of schools to the principal's school. The teacher's most recent evaluations shall be a factor in such determination.

(4) The right to remain on the preferred list for employment shall remain in effect until:

(A) The teacher accepts a bona fide offer of reemployment for a comparable position within the LEA; or

(B) The teacher rejects four (4) bona fide offers of reemployment for comparable positions within the LEA.

(c)

(1) Notwithstanding subsection (a), but subject to the appeal and review provisions of §§ 49-5-512 and 49-5-513, any teacher convicted of a felony listed in § 40-35-501(i)(2) or convicted of an offense listed in § 39-17-417 shall be immediately suspended, and dismissed subject to subdivision (c)(2).

(2) If the dismissal of the teacher is upheld in the board and court reviews provided for in §§ 49-5-512 and 49-5-513, the director shall notify in writing the commissioner of education who shall begin licensure revocation proceedings under applicable rules of the state board of education.

Effective date 7/1/2014

SECTION 2. This act shall take effect July 1, 2014, the public welfare requiring it.

PUBLIC CHAPTER NO. 370

PUBLIC CHAPTER NO. 370

SENATE BILL NO. 1346

By Yager

Substituted for: House Bill No. 1313

By Calfee

AN ACT to amend Tennessee Code Annotated, Title 67, Chapter 5, relative to tax relief for certain disaster claimants.

BE IT ENACTED BY THE GENERAL ASSEMBLY OF THE STATE OF TENNESSEE:

67-5-2010 SECTION 1. Tennessee Code Annotated, Section 67-5-2010, is amended by adding the following as a new subsection:

(c)(1) Delinquent taxes on property that was demolished, impaired, or substantially damaged as a result of a coal ash spill occurring in this state after December 1, 2008, and before January 1, 2009, shall not be subject to the penalty and interest provided in subsection (a) but shall only accrue interest from the delinquency date of the respective tax year at the composite prime rate published by the federal reserve board as of the delinquency date, minus two (2) points. Property shall be deemed substantially damaged when, as a consequence of such coal ash spill, it has been rendered unfit for use or occupancy, or the owner has filed legal action against TVA in the appropriate court of law and the court has issued an order finding TVA responsible for the damage.

(2) The owner must apply for this relief to the appropriate collecting official by September 1, 2013, using a form approved by the director of the state division of property assessments and shall file a copy with the assessor of property. The owner shall provide the address and description of any destroyed, impaired, demolished or substantially damaged real property for which such relief under this subsection (c) is sought and a copy of the legal action filed against TVA. The collecting official shall adjust the penalty and interest in accordance with this subsection (c) and collection of such tax, penalty and interest shall be in full satisfaction of the property tax assessment for those tax years.

(3) This subsection (c) shall be effective retroactively to January 1, 2009, and shall only apply to penalties and interest imposed for the 2009 and 2010 tax years.

SECTION 2. If any provision of this act or the application thereof to any person or circumstance is held invalid, then all provisions and applications of this act are declared to be invalid and void.

Effective date 5/14/2013 SECTION 3. This act shall take effect on becoming law, the public welfare requiring it and shall cease to be effective on January 1, 2014.

PUBLIC CHAPTER NO. 371

PUBLIC CHAPTER NO. 371

SENATE BILL NO. 1327

By Ketron, Harper

Substituted for: House Bill No. 1254

By Todd

AN ACT to amend Tennessee Code Annotated, Title 57, Chapter 4, relative to the consumption of alcoholic beverages on premises.

BE IT ENACTED BY THE GENERAL ASSEMBLY OF THE STATE OF TENNESSEE:

57-4-102 SECTION 1. Tennessee Code Annotated, Section 57-4-102(38), is amended by adding the following as new subdivisions thereto:

(E) "Urban park center" also includes a facility possessing each of the following characteristics:

(i) Is located in a building constructed in 1883 that was originally used as a flour mill and eventually became a cannery;

(ii) Is an entertainment complex open to the public with three (3) facilities used for live music performances;

(iii) Serves or sells food to patrons;

(iv) Is approximately fifty-two thousand square feet (52,000 sq. ft.); and

(v) Is located within a county having a metropolitan form of government and a population in excess of five hundred thousand (500,000), according to the 2010 federal census or any subsequent federal census;

(F) "Urban park center" also includes a facility possessing each of the following characteristics:

(i) Is located approximately two (2) blocks from Interstate 40;

(ii) Is located in a building constructed in the 1920s as an automobile factory;

(iii) Is located in a building remodeled in 2011 as a live music venue open to the public;

(iv) Serves or sells food to patrons;

(v) Is approximately fourteen thousand square feet (14,000 sq. ft.); and

(vi) Is located within a county having a metropolitan form of government and a population in excess of five hundred thousand (500,000), according to the 2010 federal census or any subsequent federal census;

(G) "Urban park center" also includes a facility possessing each of the following characteristics:

(i) Is located in the historic Elliston Place neighborhood;

(ii) Is located approximately three (3) blocks from a private university and approximately one (1) block from a non-profit hospital;

(iii) Serves or sells food to patrons;

(iv) Was opened to the public in 1971 as a live music venue;

(v) Has a stage that is four feet (4 ft.) high and has an indoor balcony; and

(vi) Is located within a county having a metropolitan form of government and a population in excess of five hundred thousand (500,000), according to the 2010 federal census or any subsequent federal census;

(H) "Urban park center" also includes a facility possessing each of the following characteristics:

(i) Is located on 8th Avenue approximately one (1) block from Interstate 65;

(ii) Is a live music venue that opened to the public in 2001;

(iii) Is located beneath an independent and nationally acclaimed record store;

(iv) Serves or sells food to patrons;

(v) Is approximately one thousand eight hundred square feet (1,800 sq. ft.); and

(vi) Is located within a county having a metropolitan form of government and a population in excess of five hundred thousand (500,000), according to the 2010 federal census or any subsequent federal census;

(I) "Urban park center" also includes a facility possessing each of the following characteristics:

(i) Is located on Forrest Avenue across from a branch of a public library;

(ii) Is a live music venue that promotes local artists that opened to the public in 2003;

(iii) Serves or sells food to patrons;

(iv) Is approximately two thousand seven hundred square feet (2,700 sq. ft.) and has an enclosed exterior patio; and

(v) Is located within a county having a metropolitan form of government and a population in excess of five hundred thousand (500,000), according to the 2010 federal census or any subsequent federal census;

57-4-301 SECTION 2. Tennessee Code Annotated, Section 57-4-301(b), is amended by adding the following as a new subdivision thereto:

(3) Notwithstanding subdivision (b)(1)(E) to the contrary, "urban park centers" under § 57-4-102(38)(E) through (I) shall pay an annual privilege tax of four thousand dollars ($4,000) to be earmarked for and allocated to the commission for the purpose of administration and enforcement of the duties, powers, and functions of the commission.

Effective date 5/6/2013 SECTION 3. This act shall take effect upon becoming a law, the public welfare requiring it.

PUBLIC CHAPTER NO. 373

PUBLIC CHAPTER NO. 373

SENATE BILL NO. 1319

By Dickerson

Substituted for: House Bill No. 1207

By Odom, Cooper

AN ACT to amend Tennessee Code Annotated, Title 65, Chapter 32, relative to utility procedures in certain counties.

BE IT ENACTED BY THE GENERAL ASSEMBLY OF THE STATE OF TENNESSEE:

65-32-104

SECTION 1. Tennessee Code Annotated, Section 65-32-104(2), is amended by deleting the second sentence in its entirety and substituting instead the following:

Placing a telephone call or sending electronic mail by the utility representative constitutes a reasonable good faith effort; provided, however, the utility representative need not place a telephone call or send electronic mail to any residence where service has been discontinued within the previous four (4) years.

Effective date 7/1/2013

SECTION 2. This act shall take effect July 1, 2013, the public welfare requiring it.

PUBLIC CHAPTER NO. 374

PUBLIC CHAPTER NO. 374

SENATE BILL NO. 1246

By Hensley, Bowling, Campfield

Substituted for: House Bill No. 1114

By Joe Carr, Armstrong

AN ACT to amend Tennessee Code Annotated, Title 3; Title 4 and Title 71, relative to oversight of the TennCare program.

BE IT ENACTED BY THE GENERAL ASSEMBLY OF THE STATE OF TENNESSEE:

4-29-236 SECTION 1. Tennessee Code Annotated, Section 4-29-236(a), is amended by adding a new subdivision thereto, as follows:

( ) Bureau of TennCare within the department of finance and administration, pursuant to Executive Order No. 23 on October 19, 1999;

Effective date 5/6/2013 SECTION 2. This act shall take effect upon becoming a law, the public welfare requiring it.

PUBLIC CHAPTER NO. 375

PUBLIC CHAPTER NO. 375

SENATE BILL NO. 1215

By Green, Bowling, Campfield

Substituted for: House Bill No. 1158

By Curtis Johnson

AN ACT to amend Tennessee Code Annotated, Title 39 and Title 49, relative to certain criminal offenses.

BE IT ENACTED BY THE GENERAL ASSEMBLY OF THE STATE OF TENNESSEE:

49-6-4216 SECTION 1. Tennessee Code Annotated, Section 49-6-4216(a)(2), is amended by adding the following language as a new, appropriately designated subdivision:

(C) Who transmits by an electronic device any communication containing a credible threat to cause bodily injury or death to another student or school employee and the transmission of such threat creates actual disruptive activity at the school that requires administrative intervention.

49-6-1018 SECTION 2. Tennessee Code Annotated, Section 49-6-1018, is amended by adding the following language as a new, appropriately designated subsection:

(d) Notwithstanding subsections (b) and (c), a school employee, student or volunteer who witnesses or possesses reliable information that a student has transmitted by an electronic device any communication containing a credible threat to cause bodily injury or death to another student or school employee, as prohibited by § 49-6-4216, shall report such information to the appropriate school official designated by the policy of the school district. Such school official shall make a determination regarding the administration of the report.

Effective date 7/1/2013 SECTION 3. This act shall take effect July 1, 2013, the public welfare requiring it, and shall apply to any communication transmitted on or after the effective date of this act.

PUBLIC CHAPTER NO. 376

PUBLIC CHAPTER NO. 376

SENATE BILL NO. 1178

By Gardenhire

Substituted for: House Bill No. 849

By Carter

AN ACT to amend Tennessee Code Annotated, Title 4; Title 5; Title 6; Title 7; Title 55 and Title 67, relative to registration and licensing of motor vehicles.

BE IT ENACTED BY THE GENERAL ASSEMBLY OF THE STATE OF TENNESSEE:

55-4-105 SECTION 1. Tennessee Code Annotated, Section 55-4-105, is amended by adding the following language as a new subsection:

( )(1) If a person makes an application for a renewal certificate of registration or registration plate pursuant to this section and at the time of application, owes any motor vehicle registration fee to the office of the county clerk, then the clerk may deny the application until the person makes full payment on such fee amount.

(2) In addition to the fee amount described in subdivision ( )(1), the clerk may charge the person a clerk's fee, which shall be equal to ten percent (10%) of the fee amount described in subdivision ( )(1); provided, eighty percent (80%) of such clerk's fee may be retained by the county and the remaining twenty percent (20%) of such clerk's fee shall be forwarded by the clerk to the department.

Effective date 5/6/2013 SECTION 2. This act shall take effect upon becoming a law, the public welfare requiring it.

PUBLIC CHAPTER NO. 377

PUBLIC CHAPTER NO. 377

SENATE BILL NO. 1145

By Green, Bowling, Gardenhire, Yager

Substituted for: House Bill No. 881

By Pitts, Sargent, Favors, Camper

AN ACT to amend Tennessee Code Annotated, Title 56, Chapter 6, relative to the regulation of navigators in the implementation of the Patient Protection and Affordable Care Act regarding health insurance exchanges.

WHEREAS, HR. 3590, the Patient Protection and Affordable Care Act (PPACA) became law on March 23, 2010; and

WHEREAS, PPACA established health care exchanges to facilitate the purchase of health insurance; and

WHEREAS, currently health insurance agents must be licensed under the Tennessee Insurance Producer Licensing Act of 2002, Tenn. Code Ann. § 56-6-101; and

WHEREAS, the act requires insurance agents to complete both prelicensing and continuing education, undergo background checks, fingerprinting, and other consumer protections; and

WHEREAS, the United States Congress has declared in the McCarran-Ferguson Act and the Gramm-Leach-Bliley Act that states should regulate the business of insurance; and

WHEREAS, PPACA has created a new, federally mandated program which requires that exchanges must establish a navigator program to assist in the enrollment of exchanges; and

WHEREAS, navigators assisting consumers will obtain disclosure of private personal information such as social security numbers, tax returns, income, and personal health information; and

WHEREAS, it is in the best interest of the people of the State of Tennessee that navigators be licensed and regulated insofar as is consistent with PPACA; now, therefore,

BE IT ENACTED BY THE GENERAL ASSEMBLY OF THE STATE OF TENNESSEE:

56-6-1201 — 56-6-1205 SECTION 1. Tennessee Code Annotated, Title 56, Chapter 6, is amended by adding the following language as a new part:

56-6-1201. For purposes of this part:

(1) "Commissioner" means the commissioner of commerce and insurance;

(2) "Exchange" means any health benefit exchange established or operating in this state, including any exchange established or operated by the United States department of health and human services; and

(3) "Navigator" means any person, other than an insurance producer, who:

(A) Receives any funding, directly or indirectly, from an exchange, this state or the federal government to perform any of the activities and duties identified in 42 U.S.C. § 18031(i);

(B) Facilitates enrollment of individuals or employers in health plans or public insurance programs offered through an exchange;

(C) Conducts public education or consumer assistance activities for, or on behalf of, an exchange; or

(D) Is described or designated by an exchange, this state or the United States department of health and human services, or could reasonably be described or designated as, a navigator, an in-person assister, enrollment assister, application assister or application counselor.

56-6-1202. No navigator shall sell, solicit or negotiate any policy of insurance, either within or outside of an exchange.

56-6-1203. The commissioner may:

(1) Issue a cease and desist order to a navigator for violating state or federal law pertaining to an exchange; and

(2) Seek injunctive relief against a navigator acting in violation of state or federal law pertaining to an exchange.

56-6-1204. The commissioner may promulgate such rules and regulations as may be necessary or appropriate to regulate the activities of navigators as may be consistent with the Patient Protection and Affordable Care Act.

56-6-1205. If any provision of this act or the application thereof to any person or circumstance is held invalid, such invalidity shall not affect other provisions or applications of the act which can be given effect without the invalid provision or application, and to that end the provisions of this act are declared to be severable.

Effective date 7/1/2013

SECTION 2. This act shall take effect July 1, 2013, the public welfare requiring it.

PUBLIC CHAPTER NO. 378

PUBLIC CHAPTER NO. 378

SENATE BILL NO. 1127

By Yager, Finney, Ford

Substituted for: House Bill No. 855

By Keisling

AN ACT to amend Tennessee Code Annotated, Title 11, Chapter 11 and Title 67, Chapter 4, relative to adventure tourism districts.

BE IT ENACTED BY THE GENERAL ASSEMBLY OF THE STATE OF TENNESSEE:

11-11-203 SECTION 1. Tennessee Code Annotated, Section 11-11-203(4), is amended by deleting the subdivision in its entirety and substituting instead the following:

(4) "Best interests of the state" means a determination by the commissioner of revenue, with approval by the commissioner of economic and community development, that:

(A) The qualified business enterprise or enterprises made within an adventure tourism district are a result of the special allocation and tax credits provided for in § 67-4-2109(b)(2)(C);

(B) The adventure tourism district is a result of such qualified business enterprise or enterprises; and

(C) The zone is not structured to create a competitive advantage for one business.

67-4-2109 SECTION 2. Tennessee Code Annotated, Section 67-4-2109(b)(2)(C), is amended by deleting the subdivision in its entirety and substituting instead the following:

(C) If the qualified business enterprise is located in an area designated as an adventure tourism zone pursuant to § 11-11-204(c), an annual credit shall be allowed as follows:

(i) If the qualified business enterprise is located in a tier 1 enhancement county, the additional annual credit shall be allowed if the qualified business enterprise meets one hundred percent (100%) of the job creation requirement in subdivision (b)(1)(C);

(ii) If the qualified business enterprise is located in a tier 2 enhancement county, the additional annual credit shall be allowed if the qualified business enterprise meets at least seventy-five percent (75%) of the job creation requirement in subdivision (b)(1)(C);

(iii) If the qualified business enterprise is located in a tier 3 enhancement county, the additional annual credit shall be allowed if the qualified business enterprise meets at least fifty percent (50%) of the job creation requirement in subdivision (b)(1)(C);

(iv) The additional annual credit shall be allowed for a period of three (3) years for a qualified business enterprise located in a tier 1 or tier 2 enhancement county, beginning with the first tax year in which the qualified business enterprise applies the credit in accordance with subdivision (b)(2)(D);

(v) The additional annual credit shall be allowed for a period of five (5) years for a qualified business enterprise located in a tier 3 enhancement county, beginning with the first tax year in which the qualified business enterprise applies the credit in accordance with subdivision (b)(2)(D); and

(vi) The additional annual credit shall equal four thousand five hundred dollars ($4,500) for each qualified job; provided, that the job remains filled by employees during the year in which the credit is being taken. This annual credit may be used to offset up to one hundred percent (100%) of the taxpayer's franchise and excise tax liability for that year. Any unused annual credit, however, shall not be carried forward beyond the year in which the credit originated.

11-11-205 SECTION 3. Tennessee Code Annotated, Section 11-11-205(d), is amended by deleting the subsection in its entirety and substituting instead the following:

(d) The signs and contracts described in subsection (c) shall contain the following warning notice:

Under Tennessee Law, an adventure tourism professional is not liable for an injury to or the death of a participant in adventure tourism activities resulting from the inherent risks of such activities, pursuant to Tennessee Code Annotated, title 11, chapter 11.

The State of Tennessee is held harmless for any act of approval of an adventure tourism business. State approval is limited to determining eligibility for tax credits only.

11-11-204 SECTION 4. Tennessee Code Annotated, Section 11-11-204(c), is amended by deleting the language "best interest of the state" and by substituting instead the language "best interests of the state".

Effective date 5/14/2013 SECTION 5. This act shall take effect upon becoming a law, the public welfare requiring it.

PUBLIC CHAPTER NO. 379

PUBLIC CHAPTER NO. 379

SENATE BILL NO. 1053

By Kelsey

Substituted for: House Bill No. 1244

By Doss, Dennis

AN ACT to amend Tennessee Code Annotated, Section 29-39-103, relative to determination of future damages by the trier of fact.

BE IT ENACTED BY THE GENERAL ASSEMBLY OF THE STATE OF TENNESSEE:

29-39-103 SECTION 1. Tennessee Code Annotated, Section 29-39-103(a)(2), is amended by deleting the language ", on an annual basis,".

Effective date 5/14/2013 SECTION 2. This act shall take effect upon becoming law, the public welfare requiring it.

PUBLIC CHAPTER NO. 380

PUBLIC CHAPTER NO. 380

SENATE BILL NO. 1043

By Kelsey

Substituted for: House Bill No. 1232

By Dennis

AN ACT to amend Tennessee Code Annotated, Title 9, Chapter 8, Part 3, relative to the Tennessee claims commission.

BE IT ENACTED BY THE GENERAL ASSEMBLY OF THE STATE OF TENNESSEE:

9-8-309 SECTION 1. Tennessee Code Annotated, Section 9-8-309, is amended by deleting the first sentence in this section and substituting instead the following:

> Upon the request of the governor, or of an individual claims commissioner as to claims within that commissioner's grand division, or of a majority of the claims commissioners as to claims within any grand division, the secretary of state may assign administrative law judges from the administrative procedures division of the secretary of state's office to assist in the removal of unacceptable congestion, delay on the claims commission docket or in the event of a claims commissioner's recusal or disability.

Effective date 5/6/2013 SECTION 2. This act shall take effect upon becoming a law, the public welfare requiring it.

PUBLIC CHAPTER NO. 381

PUBLIC CHAPTER NO. 381

SENATE BILL NO. 922

By Haile

Substituted for: House Bill No. 1064

By Odom, Gilmore, Love, Powell, Mitchell, Jernigan, Jones, Stewart

AN ACT to amend Tennessee Code Annotated, Title 37 and Title 49, relative to education.

BE IT ENACTED BY THE GENERAL ASSEMBLY OF THE STATE OF TENNESSEE:

49-10-608 SECTION 1. Tennessee Code Annotated, Section 49-10-608, is deleted in its entirety.

49-5-413 SECTION 2. Tennessee Code Annotated, Section 49-5-413, is amended by adding the following subsection (e):

(e)(1) The department of education, the state board of education, local boards of education, and LEAs are prohibited from hiring or retaining any individual whom the department of children's services has found to have committed child abuse, severe child abuse, child sexual abuse, or child neglect pursuant to title 37, except that no individual or employee shall be reported as a perpetrator by the department of children's services unless the department of children's services has determined that the due process rights of the individual or employee were either offered but not accepted, or were fully concluded, pursuant to the department of children's services rules and regulations and state and federal law.

(2) Any individual who is currently employed with, or has been conditionally offered employment with, the department of education, any local board of education, or any LEA, and has ever been found by the department of children's services to have committed child abuse, severe child abuse, child sexual abuse, or child neglect, shall be offered due process rights. Once the due process rights of the individual or employee have either been offered but not accepted, or have been fully concluded and the finding upheld, the department of children's services shall disclose such finding to the department of education, local board of education, or LEA.

(3) If an individual is currently employed with, or has been conditionally offered employment with, the department of education, any local board of education, or any LEA, and the department of children's services has ever found the individual to have committed child abuse, severe child abuse, child sexual abuse, or child neglect, but the due process rights of the individual or employee have not yet been offered or are still pending, the department of children's services shall conduct an emergency file review to determine if the individual poses an immediate threat to the health, safety, or welfare of children. If the emergency file review results in a finding that the individual poses an immediate threat to the health, safety or welfare of children, the department of children's services shall disclose the threat to the department of education, local board of education, or LEA.

(4) If an individual is currently employed with, or has been conditionally offered employment with, the department of education, any local board of education, or any LEA, and the department of children's services has commenced an investigation of the individual that has not yet been concluded, the department of children's services shall conduct an emergency file review to determine if the individual poses an immediate threat to the health, safety, or welfare of children. If the emergency file review results in a finding that the individual poses an immediate threat to the health, safety or welfare of children, the department of children's services shall disclose the threat to the department of education, local board of education, or LEA.

(5) If due process proceedings have been stayed due to a pending criminal charge against an individual who is currently employed or has been conditionally offered employment by the department of education, any local board of education, or any LEA, the department of children's services shall notify the department of education, local board of education, or LEA of the pending criminal charge.

(6) The department of education, the state board of education and the department of children's services, in consultation, shall develop a procedure whereby

local boards of education or LEAs may submit to the department of children's services the names of current employees and individuals who have been conditionally offered employment with the local board of education or LEA, to determine if the employee or individual has been found by the department of children's services to have committed child abuse, severe child abuse, child sexual abuse, or child neglect, or to pose an immediate threat to the health, safety, or welfare of children. Upon submission by the local board of education or LEA of the names of current employees and individuals who have been conditionally offered employment, the department of children's services shall timely provide the local board of education or LEA with the information in (2)-(5).

(7) The department of education, local board of education, and LEAs shall not hire or retain any individual whose name has been placed on the state's vulnerable person's registry or the state's sex offender registry.

(8) The department of children's services shall have authority to promulgate as emergency rules the procedures described in (2)-(5) and shall promulgate such rules within 60 days of this becoming law.

Effective date 5/14/2013

SECTION 3. This act shall take effect upon becoming a law, the public welfare requiring it.

PUBLIC CHAPTER NO. 382

PUBLIC CHAPTER NO. 382

SENATE BILL NO. 891

By Hensley, Gresham, Gardenhire

Substituted for: House Bill No. 1078

By Rich, Lollar, Dennis, Holt, Shipley, Faison, Casada, Farmer, Halford, Rogers, Spivey, Hardaway, Sparks

AN ACT to amend Tennessee Code Annotated, Title 40, Chapter 6 and Title 40, Chapter 33, Part 2, relative to asset forfeitures.

BE IT ENACTED BY THE GENERAL ASSEMBLY OF THE STATE OF TENNESSEE:

40-33-203 SECTION 1. Tennessee Code Annotated, Section 40-33-203, is amended by adding the following language as a new subsection (d):

(d) Upon the seizure of any personal property subject to forfeiture pursuant to § 40-33-201 where the person in possession is not being arrested, the seizing officer shall provide the person found in possession of the property, if known, a notice entitled "Notice of Forfeiture Warrant Hearing". This notice shall contain the following:

(1) the date, time, and court in which the seizing officer will be seeking a forfeiture warrant against the property pursuant to § 40-33-204;

(2) a statement that the person in possession is entitled to appear in court at the stated date and time to contest the issuance of a forfeiture warrant against the seized property and that this hearing shall be civil in nature pursuant to § 40-33-204(b); and,

(3) a statement that if the person in possession does not appear in court, a forfeiture warrant may be issued and the property subject to the forfeiture process set forth in title 40, chapter 33, part 2 and as stated in the Notice of Seizure.

40-33-204 SECTION 2. Tennessee Code Annotated, Section 40-33-204(b), is amended by deleting the section in its entirety and substituting the following language:

(b)(1) Any affidavit in support of a forfeiture warrant shall be sworn to and state the following:

(A) The legal and factual basis making the property subject to forfeiture;

(B) If the owner or co-owner of the property was not the person in possession of the property at the time of seizure and can be determined from public records of titles, registrations or other recorded documents, the affidavit shall state with particular specificity the officer's probable cause for believing that the owner or co-owner of the property knew that the property was of a nature making its possession illegal or was being used in a manner making it subject to forfeiture as well as the legal, and factual basis for forfeiture of the interest; and

(C) If the interest of a secured party with a duly perfected security interest as reflected in the public records of titles, registrations or other recorded documents, is sought to be forfeited, the affidavit shall state with particular specificity the officer's probable cause that the secured party's interest in the property is nevertheless subject to forfeiture as well as the legal and factual basis for forfeiture of the interest.

(2) If an arrest was made at the time of the seizure, the officer making the seizure shall apply for a forfeiture warrant by filing a sworn affidavit within five (5) working days following the property seizure. The forfeiture warrant shall be based upon proof by affidavit and shall have attached to it a copy of the notice of seizure. The hearing on the application for a forfeiture warrant shall be ex parte and based upon the application, the affidavit, and any testimony as may be required in this section.

(3) If no arrest was made at the time of the seizure, the officer making the seizure shall present to the court, at the date and time specified on the notice of forfeiture warrant hearing, the application for a forfeiture warrant, the affidavit in support, the notice of seizure, and the notice of forfeiture warrant hearing. At the hearing on the forfeiture warrant application, the court shall:

(A) Review the application for a forfeiture warrant and the affidavit in support and take testimony from the seizing officer regarding the probable cause to issue a forfeiture warrant, including any testimony as may be required in this section; and

(B) Review any evidence presented by and take testimony from the person in possession at the time of the seizure regarding why no probable cause exists to issue a forfeiture warrant.

(C) If the person in possession at the time of the seizure does not appear at the hearing and has received notice of the hearing, then the court shall review the application for a forfeiture warrant ex parte as under subsection (b)(2).

(D) The taking of testimony shall consist solely of the judge putting the seizing officer and person in possession under oath and asking questions to determine if probable cause exists for a forfeiture warrant to be issued under this section. Any examination by the judge of the seizing officer shall in no form or manner extend to whether the seizure is part of an ongoing investigation, nor shall the judge's examination extend in any form or manner to the source of any confidential information used in making a stop leading to seizure of the property.

(4) All hearings on applications for forfeiture warrants under this section shall be recorded. It is the duty of the court to maintain the recording. Certified copies of the proceeding shall be made available to any party requesting them, and the same shall be admissible as evidence.

40-33-204

SECTION 3. Tennessee Code Annotated, Section 40-33-204(c)(2), is amended by inserting the language "In a proceeding under subsection (b)(2)," at the beginning of the first paragraph so that, as amended, the subsection shall read:

(c)(2) In a proceeding under subsection (b)(2), if the seizing officer asserts to the judge that the officer was unable to determine the owner of the seized property or whether the owner's interest is subject to forfeiture within the required five-day period, the judge may grant up to ten (10) additional days to seek a forfeiture warrant if the judge finds that the seizing officer has:

Effective date 1/1/2014

SECTION 4. This act shall take effect January 1, 2014, the public welfare requiring it.

PUBLIC CHAPTER NO. 383

PUBLIC CHAPTER NO. 383

SENATE BILL NO. 867

By Gresham, Hensley

Substituted for: House Bill No. 847

By Ragan

AN ACT to amend Tennessee Code Annotated, Title 49, Chapter 5, Part 4, relative to teachers acting as representatives of a professional employees' organization.

BE IT ENACTED BY THE GENERAL ASSEMBLY OF THE STATE OF TENNESSEE:

49-5-418 SECTION 1. Tennessee Code Annotated, Title 49, Chapter 5, Part 4, is amended by adding the following language as a new, appropriately designated section:

49-5-4__.

(a) An LEA may grant release-time to a professional employee to hold office as a representative of a local professional employees' organization as defined in § 49-5-602. Release-time may be granted if the local board approves the request or if release-time is agreed to as part of a memorandum of understanding under the Professional Educators Collaborative Conferencing Act of 2011. Release-time may be granted for a portion of the year or for an entire year. If the release is granted for an entire year, the release-time shall be granted from a date certain to a date certain.

(b) If an LEA grants release-time, the professional employees' organization shall:

(1) Reimburse the LEA the full per diem salary of the professional employees' organization representative for each day of service the employee is released from duty, or the LEA shall deduct the day from the employee's accumulated personal leave, if the release is granted for less than the entire school year; or

(2) Reimburse the LEA the full cost of the employee's salary and benefits, if the release is granted for an entire school year.

(c) If release-time is granted to a professional employee for more than ninety (90) days, the LEA shall maintain the employee's position without advancement on the salary scale.

(d) An LEA may allow a teacher representative of a professional employees' organization whose presence has been requested by another teacher participating in a grievance procedural meeting or a disciplinary or employment rights meeting to attend the meeting. The teacher representative's attendance shall be considered as engaging in school duties.

(e) This section does not apply if an agreement is made between a professional employees' organization and the LEA granting release-time of less than one (1) full day per week to perform organizational duties.

(f) This section does not apply to an LEA, in which a collective bargaining agreement between the LEA and its professional employees is in effect on July 1, 2013, until the collective bargaining agreement's scheduled expiration.

Effective date 7/1/2013 SECTION 2. This act shall take effect July 1, 2013, the public welfare requiring it.

PUBLIC CHAPTER NO. 384

PUBLIC CHAPTER NO. 384

SENATE BILL NO. 860

By Tate, Harper

Substituted for: House Bill No. 1275

By Faison, Dennis, Gilmore, Hardaway, Camper, Favors, Johnnie Turner, Miller

AN ACT to amend Tennessee Code Annotated, Title 40, Chapter 32, relative to criminal records.

BE IT ENACTED BY THE GENERAL ASSEMBLY OF THE STATE OF TENNESSEE:

40-32-101 SECTION 1. Tennessee Code Annotated, Section 40-32-101, is amended by adding the following language as a new subsection:

(h)(1) For purposes of this subsection (h), "eligible petitioner" means a person who was convicted of a non-violent crime after January 1, 1980, if the person:

(A) Petitioned the court in which the petitioner was convicted of the offense and the judge finds that the offense was a non-violent crime;

(B) Petitioned for and received a positive vote from the board of parole to receive a pardon; and

(C) Received a pardon by the governor.

(2) Notwithstanding the provisions of this section, effective July 1, 2013, an eligible petitioner under subdivision (h)(1) may file a petition for expunction of that person's public records involving the crime. The procedures in subdivisions (g)(3)-(6), (8), (10), (14) and (15) will apply to a petitioner under this subsection (h).

40-32-101 SECTION 2. Tennessee Code Annotated, Section 40-32-101, is amended in subdivisions (g)(10) and (11) by deleting the language "this subsection" and substituting instead the language "this subsection (g) or subsection (h)" and is amended in subdivisions (g)(14) and (15) by deleting the language "this subsection (g)" and substituting instead the language "this subsection (g) or subsection (h)" wherever it appears.

Effective date 7/1/2013 SECTION 3. This act shall take effect July 1, 2013, the public welfare requiring it.

PUBLIC CHAPTER NO. 385

PUBLIC CHAPTER NO. 385

SENATE BILL NO. 749

By Massey, Ford, Campfield

Substituted for: House Bill No. 693

By Farmer, Hawk, Harry Brooks

AN ACT to amend Tennessee Code Annotated, Title 33; Title 36 and Title 37, relative to custody determinations involving disabled parents.

WHEREAS, the Tennessee General Assembly finds that thousands of Tennesseans are disabled as the result of disease, accident, injuries sustained in the service of our country, genetic causes, or congenital defects; and

WHEREAS, the General Assembly further finds that Tennesseans with disabilities have contributed in no small manner to the prosperity and welfare of the State of Tennessee in the practice of various professions, in the arts, in business, in the sciences, as teachers and instructors, and as parents and caregivers to countless children in this State; and

WHEREAS, the General Assembly further finds and concludes that strong and healthy families are the foundation of an orderly and prosperous society; and

WHEREAS, it is the policy of the State of Tennessee to foster the growth and preservation of strong and healthy families in Tennessee; and

WHEREAS, the General Assembly finds that Tennesseans with disabilities have suffered invidious discrimination in child welfare and custody proceedings throughout this State on account of such disability; and

WHEREAS, it is the policy of the State of Tennessee that no citizen of this State shall suffer discrimination from any child welfare agency or in any custody proceeding solely because of such person's disability; now, therefore,

BE IT ENACTED BY THE GENERAL ASSEMBLY OF THE STATE OF TENNESSEE:

36-6-106 SECTION 1. Tennessee Code Annotated, Section 36-6-106, is amended by adding the following as a new subsection:

(e) The disability of a parent seeking custody shall not create a presumption for or against awarding custody to such a party but may be a factor to be considered by the court.

Effective date 5/14/2013 SECTION 2. This act shall take effect upon becoming law, the public welfare requiring it.

PUBLIC CHAPTER NO. 386

PUBLIC CHAPTER NO. 386

SENATE BILL NO. 747

By Massey

Substituted for: House Bill No. 903

By Kane, Haynes, Fitzhugh

AN ACT to amend Tennessee Code Annotated, Title 57, Chapter 4 and Title 57, Chapter 5, relative to sales of beer at certain licensed establishments.

BE IT ENACTED BY THE GENERAL ASSEMBLY OF THE STATE OF TENNESSEE:

57-5-101 SECTION 1. Tennessee Code Annotated, Section 57-5-101(c)(1)(B), is amended by deleting subdivision (B) in its entirety and by substituting instead the following language:

(B) May qualify for and hold a license:

(i) Under the provisions of chapter 4 of this title as a "restaurant" or "limited service restaurant"; provided, that notwithstanding title 57, chapter 4 related to restrictions or prohibitions on licensees under chapter 4, a restaurant or limited service restaurant may sell for off premises consumption beer manufactured pursuant to this section at such location or at any other restaurant or limited service restaurant licensed under chapter 4 that is owned by the same person; or

(ii) As a hotel as defined under § 57-4-102(20)(F)(iii); provided, that the hotel licensee shall only sell beer manufactured pursuant to this section on the premises of the hotel.

57-4-203 SECTION 2. Tennessee Code Annotated, Section 57-4-203(e), is amended by adding the following as a new subdivision (4):

(4) A restaurant or limited service restaurant may sell beer for consumption off premises upon meeting the requirements of § 57-5-101(c)(1)(B).

57-5-101 SECTION 3. Tennessee Code Annotated, Section 57-5-101(c)(1), is amended by deleting the language "or" at the end of subdivision (A) and by substituting instead the language "and".

Effective date 5/14/2013 SECTION 4. This act shall take effect upon becoming a law, the public welfare requiring it.

PUBLIC CHAPTER NO. 387

PUBLIC CHAPTER NO. 387

SENATE BILL NO. 745

By Massey, Beavers, Bowling, Campfield, Ford, Harper, Gresham, Yager

Substituted for: House Bill No. 532

By Powers, Cooper, Gilmore

AN ACT to amend Tennessee Code Annotated, Title 63, relative to communication of mammographic breast density information to patients.

BE IT ENACTED BY THE GENERAL ASSEMBLY OF THE STATE OF TENNESSEE:

63-6-245 SECTION 1. Tennessee Code Annotated, Title 63, Chapter 6, Part 2, is amended by adding the following as a new section:

63-6-245.

(a) As used in this section, "physician" means an individual authorized by this chapter to practice medicine and surgery or osteopathic medicine and surgery pursuant to chapter 9.

(b) If a physician has determined, after a mammogram is performed, that a patient has dense breasts or extremely dense breasts, based on the breast imaging reporting and data system established by the American college of radiology, the facility where the mammogram was performed shall provide the following notice to the patient:

> Your mammogram shows that your breast tissue is dense. Dense breast tissue is common and is not abnormal. However, dense breast tissue can make it harder to evaluate the results of your mammogram and may also be associated with an increased risk of breast cancer. This information about the results of your mammogram is given to you to raise your awareness and to inform your conversations with your doctor. Together, you can decide which screening options are right for you. A report of your results was sent to your physician.

(c) This section shall become operative on January 1, 2014. Nothing in this section shall be construed to create or impose liability for failing to comply with the requirements of this section. Nothing in this section shall be deemed to create a duty of care or other legal obligation beyond the duty to provide notice as set forth in this section. Nothing in this section shall be deemed to require a notice that is inconsistent with the provisions of the federal mammography quality standards act, as compiled in 42 U.S.C. § 263b or any regulations promulgated pursuant to that act.

SECTION 2. This act may be known and cited as "The Breast Cancer Prevention Act."

Effective date 1/1/2014 SECTION 3. This act shall take effect January 1, 2014, the public welfare requiring it.

PUBLIC CHAPTER NO. 388

PUBLIC CHAPTER NO. 388

SENATE BILL NO. 736

By Gardenhire, Yager

Substituted for: House Bill No. 1023

By Dean

AN ACT to amend Tennessee Code Annotated, Section 8-21-901 and Title 40, Chapter 11, Part 1, relative to bonds.

BE IT ENACTED BY THE GENERAL ASSEMBLY OF THE STATE OF TENNESSEE:

40-11-139 SECTION 1. Tennessee Code Annotated, Section 40-11-139, is amended by adding the following new subsection (c):

(c) No execution shall issue upon a final forfeit, nor shall proceedings be taken for its enforcement until the expiration of thirty (30) days after its entry.

40-11-138 SECTION 2. Tennessee Code Annotated, Section 40-11-138, is amended by deleting the following language and punctuation at the end of subsection (b):

; provided, that where the disposition is a conviction or plea of guilty, the surety, unless relieved by the court, shall remain liable on the criminal appearance bond until the court renders the defendant's sentence

8-21-901 SECTION 3. Tennessee Code Annotated, Section 8-21-901(a)(3), is amended by deleting subdivision (C) in its entirety and by substituting the following:

(C) For every bail bond to be paid as cost at the time there is a disposition of the case: $10.00

Effective date 5/6/2013 SECTION 4. This act shall take effect upon becoming a law, the public welfare requiring it.

PUBLIC CHAPTER NO. 389

PUBLIC CHAPTER NO. 389

SENATE BILL NO. 728

By Watson

Substituted for: House Bill No. 954

By Curtis Johnson

AN ACT to amend Tennessee Code Annotated, Title 8, Chapter 25, Part 1 and Title 49, Chapter 7, Part 8, relative to procurement.

BE IT ENACTED BY THE GENERAL ASSEMBLY OF THE STATE OF TENNESSEE:

8-25-113 SECTION 1. Tennessee Code Annotated, Title 8, Chapter 25, Part 1, is amended by adding a new, appropriately designated section as follows:

8-25-113.

The trustees of any deferred or tax sheltered compensation plans established pursuant to this part are expressly authorized to contract for investment management services, personal services, professional services and consultant services for the deferred compensation programs. The trustees shall provide for the powers, duties, functions and compensation of any investment managers, professionals or consultants so engaged. Any contract for investment management services, personal services, professional services and consultant services may be procured in the manner prescribed by the trustees without regard to the requirements of § 12-4-109, if it is determined that the services are necessary or desirable for the efficient administration of the deferred compensation programs. All expenses and fees incidental to the procurement of services shall be charged to and paid from participant accounts.

49-7-805 SECTION 2. Tennessee Code Annotated, Section 49-7-805(5), is amended by deleting this subsection in its entirety and substituting it instead with the following language:

(5) Contract with financial consultants, actuaries, auditors, investment managers and other consultants and professionals as necessary to carry out its responsibilities under this part. These services may be procured in the manner prescribed by the board without regard to the requirements of § 12-4-109, if the board determines that the services are necessary or desirable for the efficient administration of the board programs. All expenses and fees incidental to securing these services shall be charged to and paid from earnings.

Effective date 5/14/2013 SECTION 3. This act shall take effect upon becoming a law, the public welfare requiring it.

PUBLIC CHAPTER NO. 390

PUBLIC CHAPTER NO. 390

SENATE BILL NO. 713

By Stevens, Bowling, Henry

Substituted for: House Bill No. 873

By Rich, Dennis, Shepard, Keisling, Fitzhugh, Doss, Ryan Williams, Marsh

AN ACT to amend Tennessee Code Annotated, Title 35, relative to fiduciaries and trust estates.

BE IT ENACTED BY THE GENERAL ASSEMBLY OF THE STATE OF TENNESSEE:

35-6-601 SECTION 1. Tennessee Code Annotated, Section 35-6-601, is amended by deleting the section in its entirety and by substituting instead the following:

Section 35-15-1101 controls all application and construction of chapter 6.

35-14-102 SECTION 2. Tennessee Code Annotated, Section 35-14-102, is amended by deleting subdivisions (1) and (3) and by substituting instead the following:

(1) "Governing instrument" means:

(A) A will, deed, trust instrument or agency agreement;

(B) For purposes of subdivision (1)(A), an agency agreement includes but is not limited, to any agreement under which any delegation is made, either pursuant to § 35-15-807 or by anyone holding a power or duty pursuant to chapter 15, part 12;

(3) "Trustee" means any fiduciary as defined in § 35-15-103.

35-15-103 SECTION 3. Tennessee Code Annotated, Section 35-15-103, is amended by deleting subdivision (3)(B) and by adding the following new subdivisions:

( ) "Another state" or "other state" means any state other than this state;

( ) "Beneficial interest" means a distribution interest or a remainder interest; provided however, a beneficial interest specifically excludes a power of appointment or a power reserved by a settlor;

( ) "Distribution beneficiary" means a beneficiary who is an eligible distributee or permissible distributee of the income or principal of a trust;

( ) "Distribution interest" means:

(A) An interest, other than a remainder interest, held by a distribution beneficiary under a trust and may be a current distribution interest or a future distribution interest;

(B) Relative to a distribution interest:

(i) Neither the existence of a distribution interest or the provision of services by a spouse in that spouse's capacity as a fiduciary of the trust creating the distribution interest is relevant in the equitable division of marital property;

(ii) None of the factors in subdivision (B)(i) or the exercise or non-exercise of any power or discretion by a spouse in that spouse's capacity as a fiduciary of the trust creating the distribution interest (even if that spouse is also a beneficiary of the trust creating the distribution interest) are relevant to, indicative of or effect the transmutation or other conversion of separate property to community property;

(iii) The expending of any community funds by a spouse in that spouse's capacity as a fiduciary of the trust creating the distribution interest relative to the operation or maintenance of property related to a distribution interest is not relevant to or indicative of, and does not effect a transmutation or other conversion of separate property to community property;

(iv) Any funds expended pursuant to subdivision (B)(iii) shall be valid debts of the trust and shall be repaid to the community with appropriate interest;

(C) A distribution interest is classified as either a mandatory interest, a support interest or a discretionary interest; and although not the exclusive means to create each such respective distribution interest, absent clear and convincing evidence to the contrary, use of the example language accompanying the following definitions of each such respective distribution interest results in the indicated classification of distribution interest:

(i) A mandatory interest means a distribution interest in which the timing of any distribution must occur within one (1) year from the date the right to the distribution arises and the trustee has no discretion in determining whether a distribution shall be made or the amount of such distribution; example distribution language indicating a mandatory interest includes, but is not limited to:

(a) All income shall be distributed to a named beneficiary; or

(b) One hundred thousand dollars ($100,000) a year shall be distributed to a named beneficiary;

(ii) A support interest means a distribution interest that is not a mandatory interest but still contains mandatory language such as "shall make distributions" and is coupled with a standard capable of judicial interpretation; example distribution language indicating a support interest includes, but is not limited to:

(a) The trustee shall make distributions for health, education, maintenance, and support;

(b) Notwithstanding the distribution language used, if a trust instrument containing such distribution language specifically provides that the trustee exercise discretion in a reasonable manner with regard to a discretionary interest, then notwithstanding any other provision of this subdivision defining distribution interests, the distribution interest shall be classified as a support interest;

(iii) A discretionary interest means any interest that is not a mandatory or a support interest and is any distribution interest where a trustee has any discretion to make or withhold a distribution; example distribution language indicating a discretionary interest includes, but is not limited to:

(a) The trustee may, in the trustee's sole and absolute discretion, make distributions for health, education, maintenance, and support;

(b) The trustee, in the trustee's sole and absolute discretion, shall make distributions for health, education, maintenance, and support;

(c) The trustee may make distributions for health, education, maintenance, and support;

(d) The trustee shall make distributions for health, education, maintenance, and support; however, the trustee may exclude any of the beneficiaries or may make unequal distributions among them; or

(e) The trustee may make distributions for health, education, maintenance, support, comfort, and general welfare;

(f) A discretionary interest may also be evidenced by:

(1) Permissive distribution language such as "may make distributions";

(2) Mandatory distribution language that is negated by the discretionary distribution language contained in the trust

such as "the trustee shall make distributions in the trustee's sole and absolute discretion";

(g) An interest that includes mandatory distribution language such as "shall" but is subsequently qualified by discretionary distribution language shall be classified as a discretionary interest and not as a support or a mandatory interest;

(D)(i) To the extent a trust contains distribution language indicating the existence of any combination of a mandatory, support and discretionary interest, that combined interest of the trust shall be divided and treated separately as follows:

(*a*) The trust shall be a mandatory interest only to the extent of the mandatory distribution language;

(*b*) The trust shall be a support interest only to the extent of such support distribution language; and

(*c*) The remaining trust property shall be held as a discretionary interest;

(ii) For purposes of this subdivision (D), a support interest that includes mandatory distribution language such as "shall" but is subsequently qualified by discretionary distribution language, shall be classified as a discretionary interest and not as a support interest;

( ) "Directed trust" means a trust where either through the terms of the trust, an agreement of the qualified beneficiaries or a court order, one or more persons are given the authority to direct or consent to a fiduciary's actual or proposed investment decision, distribution decision, or any other decision of the fiduciary;

( ) "Excluded fiduciary" means any trustee, trust advisor, or trust protector to the extent that, under the terms of a trust, an agreement of the qualified beneficiaries, or court order:

(A) The trustee, trust advisor, or trust protector is excluded from exercising a power, or is relieved of a duty; and

(B) The power or duty is granted or reserved to another person.

( ) "Fiduciary" means:

(A) A trustee, conservator, guardian, agent under any agency agreement or other instrument, an executor, personal representative or administrator of a decedent's estate, or any other party, including a trust advisor or a trust protector, who is acting in a fiduciary capacity for any person, trust, or estate;

(B) Fiduciary also means a trustee as defined in § 35-14-102;

(C) For purposes of subdivision ( )(A), an agency agreement includes but is not limited to, any agreement under which any delegation is made, either pursuant to § 35-15-807 or by anyone holding a power or duty pursuant to part 12;

(D) For purposes of the definition of fiduciary in § 35-15-103, fiduciary does not mean any person who is an excluded fiduciary as such is defined in § 35-15-103;

( ) "Foreign" or "foreign country" means any jurisdiction, subdivision, territory or possession thereof, other than that of the United States of America or of a state;

( ) "Foreign jurisdiction" means any jurisdiction, subdivision, territory or possession thereof, other than this state;

( ) "Internal Revenue Code" means the Internal Revenue Code of 1986, as in effect on July 1, 2004, or as later amended;

( ) "Power of appointment" means:

PUBLIC CHAPTER NO. 390 (cont'd)

(A) An inter vivos or testamentary power to direct the disposition of trust property, other than a distribution decision made by a trustee or other fiduciary to a beneficiary;

(B) Powers of appointment are held by the person to whom such power has been given, and not by a settlor in that person's capacity as settlor;

( ) "Reach" means, with respect to a distribution interest or any power held by anyone relative to a trust, to subject such distribution interest or such power to a judgment, decree, garnishment, attachment, execution, levy, creditor's bill or other legal, equitable, or administrative process, relief, or control of any court, tribunal, agency, or other entity that, by power of law, is provided with powers or jurisdiction similar to those described in this subdivision;

( ) "Remainder interest" means an interest under which a trust beneficiary will receive property held by a trust outright at some time during the future; relative to a remainder interest:

(A) Neither the existence of a remainder interest or the provision of services by a spouse in that spouse's capacity as a fiduciary of the trust creating the remainder interest is relevant in the equitable division of marital property;

(B) None of the factors in subdivision ( )(A) or the exercise or non-exercise of any power or discretion by a spouse in that spouse's capacity as a fiduciary of the trust creating the remainder interest (even if that spouse is also a beneficiary of the trust creating the remainder interest) are relevant to, indicative of or effect the transmutation or other conversion of separate property to community property;

(C) The expending of any community funds by a spouse in that spouse's capacity as a fiduciary of the trust creating the remainder interest relative to the operation or maintenance of property related to a remainder interest is not relevant to or indicative of, and does not effect a transmutation or other conversion of separate property to community property;

(D) Any funds expended pursuant to subdivision ( )(C) shall be valid debts of the trust and shall be repaid to the community with appropriate interest;

( ) "Reserved power" means a power held by a settlor;

( ) "This state" means the State of Tennessee;

( ) "Trust advisor" means any person described in § 35-15-1201(a); and

( ) "Trust protector" means any person described in § 35-15-1201(a).

35-15-105 SECTION 4. Tennessee Code Annotated, Section 35-15-105, is amended by deleting subsection (a) and by substituting instead the following:

(a) Except as otherwise provided in the terms of the trust, this chapter governs the duties and powers of a trustee or any other fiduciary under this chapter, relations among trustees and such other fiduciaries, and the rights and interests of a beneficiary. The terms of a trust may expand, restrict, eliminate, or otherwise vary the duties and powers of a trustee, any such other fiduciary, relations among any of them, and the rights and interests of a beneficiary; provided, however, that nothing contained in this subsection shall be construed to override or nullify the provisions of subsection (b). The rule of statutory construction that states that statutes in derogation of the common law are to be strictly construed shall have no application to this section. Except as restricted by subsection (b), pursuant to this section, courts shall give maximum effect to the principle of freedom of disposition and to the enforceability of trust instruments.

35-15-105 SECTION 5. Tennessee Code Annotated, Section 35-15-105, is further amended by deleting subdivision (b)(3) and by substituting instead the following:

(b)(3) The requirement that a trust and its terms be for the benefit of its beneficiaries as the interests of such beneficiaries are defined under the terms of the trust, and that the trust has a purpose that is lawful and possible to achieve;

35-15-105 SECTION 6. Tennessee Code Annotated, Section 35-15-105, is further amended by adding the following new subsection (c):

(c) Any purpose enunciated as a material purpose of a trust in that trust's trust instrument shall be treated as a material purpose of that trust for all purposes of this chapter and chapter 16.

35-15-106 SECTION 7. Tennessee Code Annotated, Section 35-15-106, is amended by deleting the section in its entirety and by substituting instead the following:

35-15-106. Common law of trusts – Principles of equity.

(a) The common law of trusts and principles of equity supplement this chapter, except to the extent modified by this chapter or another statute of this state.

(b) Notwithstanding the provisions of subsection (a):

(1) No provision in a trust directing or authorizing accumulation of trust income shall be invalid; and

(2) The traditional common law distinction between a discretionary trust and a support trust and the dual judicial review standards related to this distinction shall be maintained. Unless specifically provided otherwise in this chapter, courts shall not consult, rely on or give any persuasive value to the Restatement (Third) of Trusts §§ 50, 56, 58, 59 or 60, nor any of the comments under such sections or related thereto, none of which have any force or effect relative to trusts governed by the laws of this state.

35-15-107 SECTION 8. Tennessee Code Annotated, Section 35-15-107, is amended by deleting the section in its entirety and by substituting instead the following:

35-15-107. Governing Law.

(a) The validity, construction and administration of a trust are determined by the law of the jurisdiction designated in the terms of the trust instrument, which is called a state jurisdiction provision.

(b) When a state jurisdiction provision designates that the law of this state controls:

(1) This state and its courts have jurisdiction over a trust created in a foreign jurisdiction;

(2) The validity, construction, and administration of a trust are determined by the laws of this state, including but not limited to:

(A) The capacity of the settlor;

(B) The powers, obligations, liabilities, and rights of the trustees and other fiduciaries;

(C) The appointment and removal of the trustees and other fiduciaries;

(D) The existence and extent of all powers conferred on a trustee or other fiduciary, including but not limited to, any trustee's or other fiduciary's discretionary powers, as well as the existence and extent of all powers retained by a settlor and the validity of the exercise of any such power, whether conferred on a trustee or other fiduciary or retained by a settlor;

(3)(A) Neither a trust nor any disposition made subject to the terms of such trust is subject to the laws of any foreign country, nor is any such trust or such disposition void, voidable, liable to be set aside or defective in any manner for any reason including but not limited to:

(i) The law of any foreign country prohibits or does not recognize the concept of a trust; or

(ii) The trust or disposition avoids or defeats any right, claim, or interest conferred by the law of a foreign country upon any person by reason of a personal relationship to the settlor or by way of heirship rights or contravenes any rule or law of a

PUBLIC CHAPTER NO. 390 (cont'd)

foreign country or any foreign country's judicial or administrative order or action intended to recognize, protect, enforce, or give effect to such right, claim, or interest;

(B) Relative to any foreign country or any interest in property arising or originating under the laws of any foreign country:

(i) No form of forced heirship, legitime, forced share or any similar heirship rights or form of transmission or transfer of property from a decedent or from a living person, or any restrictions on transmission or transfer of property from a decedent or a living person is recognized by this state; or

(ii) No heirship rights described in subdivision (C)(i) conferred under the law of a foreign country shall constitute an obligation or liability, the transfer, conveyance or devise of which, would violate title 66, chapter 3; and

(C) Subdivision (b)(3) shall apply to all realty or other forms of immovable property physically in this state, as well as to all personal or movable property wherever situated if owned by a trust containing a state jurisdiction provision designating that the law of this state controls such trust;

(4) No judgment or other holding of any judicial body of any foreign country, including but not limited to, any court, administrative body or other entity or organization purportedly having the power to make judicial or administrative decisions of any foreign country, shall be recognized or enforced or give rise to any equitable forms of relief, including but not limited to, estoppel, to the extent such judgment or other holding concerns a trust containing a state jurisdiction provision designating that the law of this state controls such trust or to the extent such judgment or other holding concerns property held by such trust;

(5) If, in any action brought against a trustee or other fiduciary of a trust, any judicial body of any foreign country, including but not limited to, any court, administrative body or other entity or organization purportedly having the power to make judicial or administrative decisions of any foreign country, takes any action whereby such judicial body declines to apply the law of this state in determining the validity, construction, or administration of a trust, or the effect of a spendthrift provision or discretionary interest of a trust, the trustee or other fiduciary, as applicable, shall immediately upon the action of the judicial body of the foreign country and without the further order of any court of this state, cease in all respects to be trustee or other fiduciary, as applicable, of the trust and a vacancy in the office of trustee or other fiduciary, as applicable, shall immediately exist:

(A) Upon the existence of such vacancy, the trustee or other fiduciary, as applicable, has no power or authority other than to convey the trust property to the successor trustee or other fiduciary who fills such vacancy as provided in subdivision (5)(B);

(B) Such vacancy shall be filled in the same manner as would a vacancy in trusteeship that is required to be filled, either as provided by § 35-15-704(c) if the trust is a noncharitable trust, or as provided by § 35-15-704(d) if the trust is a charitable trust; and

(C) Section 35-15-704(e) shall also apply relative to such trustee or other fiduciary, as applicable, in the same manner as that subsection does to trustees and vacancies in trusteeship in general; however, when exercising its power provided by § 35-15-704(e), the court shall consider the purposes of this subsection (b) and make any such appointments pursuant to § 35-15-704(e) in a manner designed to give full force and effect to this subsection (b) to the maximum extent allowed by the laws of this state or of the United States.

(c) In the absence of the existence of a state jurisdiction provision, the laws of the jurisdiction where the trust was executed determine the validity of the trust and the laws of descent, while the laws of the principal place of administration determine the administration of the trust.

35-15-108 SECTION 9. Tennessee Code Annotated, Section 35-15-108, is amended by deleting subsection (a) and by substituting instead the following:

(a) Without limiting or precluding other means for establishing a sufficient connection with a jurisdiction, the terms of a trust designating that jurisdiction's laws in a state jurisdiction provision are valid and controlling if:

(1) A trustee's principal place of business is located in or a trustee is a resident of the designated jurisdiction; or

(2) All or part of the administration occurs in the designated jurisdiction; which such administration, includes but is not limited to:

(A) Maintenance of some trust records physically in the designated jurisdiction; and

(B) Wholly or partly preparing or arranging for the preparation, either on an exclusive or a nonexclusive basis, in the designated jurisdiction of an income tax return that must be filed by the trust; or

(3) Some or all of the trust assets are deposited in the designated jurisdiction or physical evidence of such assets is held in the designated jurisdiction and the trust is being administered by a person defined in subdivision (a)(1). For purposes of this subdivision (a)(3), "deposited in the designated jurisdiction," includes assets being held in any of a checking account, time deposit, certificate of deposit, brokerage account, trust company fiduciary account, or other similar account or deposit that is located in the designated jurisdiction.

35-15-108 SECTION 10. Tennessee Code Annotated, Section 35-15-108, is further amended by adding the following new subsection (b) and redesignating existing subsections accordingly:

(b) Except as otherwise expressly provided by the terms of a governing instrument specifically addressing the governing law for trust administration or by court order, the laws of this state shall govern the administration of a trust while the trust is administered in this state. Without precluding other means for establishing that a trust is administered in this state, if any of the activities described in subsection (a) occur in this state, the trust is administered in this state.

35-15-408 SECTION 11. Tennessee Code Annotated, Section 35-15-408, is amended by deleting subsection (b) and by substituting instead:

(b) A trust authorized by this section may be enforced by any of the following who are appointed under the terms of a trust: a trustee, trust advisor, trust protector or other person or, if no person is so appointed, by a person appointed by the court. In addition, a person having an interest in the welfare of the animal may request the court to appoint a person to enforce the trust or to remove a person appointed.

35-15-409 SECTION 12. Tennessee Code Annotated, Section 35-15-409, is amended by deleting subdivision (2) and by substituting instead:

(2) A trust authorized by this section may be enforced by any of the following who are appointed under the terms of a trust: a trustee, trust advisor, trust protector or other person; or if no person is so appointed, by a person appointed by the court.

35-15-413 SECTION 13. Tennessee Code Annotated, Section 35-15-413(a), is amended by deleting the language "or wasteful" before the colon in subsection (a) and by instead substituting the language "obsolete or ineffective".

35-15-413 SECTION 14. Tennessee Code Annotated, Section 35-15-413, is further amended by deleting the remainder of the language following the last comma in subdivision (a)(3) and by instead substituting the words "in a manner that fulfills as nearly as possible the settlor's charitable intent and purposes."

35-15-501 SECTION 15. Tennessee Code Annotated, Section 35-15-501, is amended by deleting the section in its entirety and by substituting instead the following:

35-15-501. Application of part 5; rights of beneficiary's creditor or assignee.

This part applies to a creditor's or assignee's claims and ability to reach mandatory, support and discretionary interests regardless of whether such interests are subject to a spendthrift provision. To the extent not otherwise prohibited by this part, the court may authorize a creditor or assignee of the beneficiary to reach the beneficiary's distribution interest by attachment of present or future distributions to or for the benefit of the beneficiary or other means. The court may limit the award to such relief as is appropriate under the circumstances.

35-15-502 SECTION 16. Tennessee Code Annotated, Section 35-15-502, is amended by deleting the current subsection (c) and by substituting instead the following subsection (c) and by adding the following new subsections:

(c) A spendthrift provision applies to all beneficial interests, including distribution interests and remainder interests.

(d) A beneficiary may not transfer an interest in a trust in violation of a valid spendthrift provision and a creditor or assignee of the beneficiary may not reach any of, the interest, or a present, future or prospective distribution at the trust level. Similarly, no creditor or assignee of the beneficiary may force any distribution from the trust. This subsection remains applicable regardless of the beneficiary's potential right to force a distribution under § 35-15-814.

(e) Notwithstanding any other provision of this section to the contrary, regardless of whether a beneficiary has any outstanding creditor, a trustee, cotrustee or other fiduciary of a trust subject to a spendthrift provision may directly pay any expense on behalf of such beneficiary and may exhaust the income and principal of the trust for the benefit of such beneficiary. No trustee, cotrustee or other fiduciary is liable to any creditor for paying the expenses of a beneficiary under a trust subject to a spendthrift provision. This subsection remains applicable regardless of whether the beneficiary for whom such direct payment was made held a mandatory, support, discretionary or remainder interest.

35-15-504 SECTION 17. Tennessee Code Annotated, Section 35-15-504, is amended by deleting the entire section and by substituting instead the following:

35-15-504. Discretionary interests – Effect thereof.

(a) A discretionary interest is neither a property interest nor an enforceable right; it is a mere expectancy.

(b) Relative to a discretionary interest, whether or not a trust contains a spendthrift provision:

(1) No creditor or assignee shall force or otherwise reach a distribution with regard to a discretionary interest;

(2) No creditor or assignee shall require a trustee, cotrustee or other fiduciary to exercise the trustee's, cotrustee's or other fiduciary's discretion to make a distribution with regard to a discretionary interest;

(3) Regardless of whether a beneficiary has any outstanding creditors or assignees, a trustee, cotrustee or other fiduciary of a discretionary interest may directly pay any expense on behalf of such beneficiary and may exhaust the income and principal of the trust for the benefit of such beneficiary;

(4) No trustee, cotrustee or other fiduciary is liable to any creditor or assignee for paying the expenses of a beneficiary of a discretionary interest;

(5)(A) Regardless of whether a beneficiary holding a discretionary interest is also a trustee, cotrustee or other fiduciary, subdivisions (b)(1) through (b)(4) remain applicable if:

(i) The beneficiary-fiduciary does not have the discretion to make or participate in making distributions to himself or herself;

(ii) The beneficiary-fiduciary's discretion to make or participate in making distributions to himself or herself is limited by an ascertainable standard; or

(iii) The beneficiary-fiduciary's discretion to make or participate in making distributions to himself or herself is exercisable only with the consent of a cotrustee or another person holding an adverse interest.

(B) A creditor or assignee may compel or otherwise reach a distribution only to the extent the creditor or assignee may compel or otherwise reach a distribution if the beneficiary was not acting as a trustee, cotrustee or other fiduciary.

35-15-505 SECTION 18. Tennessee Code Annotated, Section 35-15-505, is amended by renumbering subdivision (a)(5) as subdivision (a)(6).

35-15-505 SECTION 19. Tennessee Code Annotated, Section 35-15-505, is further amended by adding a new subdivision (a)(5) as follows:

(a)(5) Notwithstanding any law to the contrary, neither a creditor nor any other person shall have any claim or cause of action against the trustee or other fiduciary, or an advisor of an irrevocable special needs trust. For purposes of this subdivision (a)(5), an advisor of an irrevocable special needs trust includes any person involved in the counseling, drafting, preparation, execution or funding of an irrevocable special needs trust.

35-15-505 SECTION 20. Tennessee Code Annotated, Section 35-15-505, is further amended by deleting from subdivision (a)(2) the introductory phrase: "Except as provided in chapter 16 of this title regarding investment services trusts and subdivision (a)(3) regarding an irrevocable special needs trust," and replacing it with the introductory phrase: "Except as provided in chapter 16 of this title regarding investment services trusts and subdivisions (a)(3) through (a)(5) regarding an irrevocable special needs trust,".

35-15-505 SECTION 21. Tennessee Code Annotated, Section 35-15-505, is further amended by adding the following new subsections (e), (f) and (g):

(e) For purposes of subdivision (a)(2) and subsection (g), a person who is the holder of a power of withdrawal is not considered a settlor of the trust by failing to exercise that power of withdrawal or letting that power of withdrawal lapse.

(f) For purposes of subdivision (a)(2) and subsection (g), a person who becomes a beneficiary of a trust due to the exercise of a power of appointment by someone other than such person shall not be considered a settlor of the trust.

(g)(1) Notwithstanding § 66-3-310, no person shall bring an action with respect to a transfer of property to a spendthrift trust:

(A) If the person is a creditor when the transfer is made, unless the action is commenced within the later of two (2) years after the transfer is made or six (6) months after the person discovers or reasonably should have discovered the transfer; or

(B) If the person becomes a creditor after the transfer is made, unless the action is commenced within two (2) years after the transfer is made; and

(2) If subdivision (g)(1) applies:

(A) A person shall be deemed to have discovered the existence of a transfer at the time any public record is made of the transfer, including but not limited to, a conveyance of real property that is recorded in the office of the county register of deeds of the county in which the property is located or the filing of a financing statement under title 47, chapter 9, or the equivalent recording or filing of either with the appropriate person or official under the laws of a jurisdiction other than this state;

(B) No creditor shall bring an action with respect to a transfer of property to a spendthrift trust unless that creditor proves by clear and convincing evidence that the settlor's transfer to the trust was made with the intent to defraud that specific creditor; and

(i) Notwithstanding any law to the contrary, neither a creditor nor any other person shall have any claim or cause of action against the trustee or other fiduciary or an advisor of a spendthrift trust if that claim or cause of action is based in any way on any person availing themselves of the benefits of this subsection;

(ii) For purposes of subdivision (g)(2)(C), an advisor of a spendthrift trust includes, but is not limited to, any person involved in the counseling, drafting, preparation, execution or funding of a spendthrift trust;

(iii) For purposes of subdivision (g)(2)(C)(i), counseling, drafting, preparation, execution or funding of a spendthrift trust includes the counseling, drafting, preparation, execution and funding of a limited partnership, a limited liability company or any other type of entity if interests in the limited partnership, limited liability company or other entity are subsequently transferred to a spendthrift trust;

(3) Notwithstanding subdivision (g)(2)(C), in the same manner as provided other than by this section to trusts in general, a beneficiary, settlor, cotrustee, trust advisor or trust protector retains the right to bring a claim against a trustee or against another cotrustee, trust advisor, trust protector or any of their predecessors; however, no such claim shall arise solely because a person availed themselves, or attempted to avail themselves, of the benefits of this subsection;

(4) If more than one transfer of property is made to a spendthrift trust, the subsequent transfer of property to the spendthrift trust shall be disregarded for the purpose of determining whether a person may bring an action pursuant to this subsection with respect to a prior transfer of property to the spendthrift trust; and any distribution to a beneficiary from the spendthrift trust shall be deemed to have been made from the most recent transfer made to the spendthrift trust;

(5) With the exception of any claim brought pursuant to subdivision (g)(3), notwithstanding any other provision of law, no action of any kind, including, without limitation, an action to enforce a judgment entered by a court or other body having adjudicative authority, shall be brought at law or in equity against the trustee, other fiduciary or advisor of a spendthrift trust if, as of the date such action is brought, an action by a creditor with respect to a transfer of property to the spendthrift trust would be barred pursuant to this subsection; and

(6) This subsection shall not abridge the rights of a creditor, to the extent otherwise provided by this section, to reach the maximum amount that can be distributed to or for the settlor's benefit under a spendthrift trust.

35-15-506 SECTION 22. Tennessee Code Annotated, Section 35-15-506, is amended by deleting the section in its entirety and by substituting instead the following:

35-15-506. Distributions relative to support, mandatory and certain remainder interests.

(a) Relative to a support interest, whether or not a trust contains a spendthrift provision:

(1) Although a beneficiary of a support interest has enforceable rights under § 35-15-814, those rights do not raise the beneficiary's support interest to the level of a property interest;

(2) No creditor or assignee shall reach that support interest until a distribution from the support interest is actually made to the beneficiary;

(3) After all or a portion of a support interest is distributed to the beneficiary, no portion of the distribution made from the support interest shall be reached by a creditor or assignee of the beneficiary except to the extent that the distribution made from the support interest exceeds the amount necessary for the health, education, maintenance and support of the beneficiary who received the distribution made from the support interest;

(4) In the case of a beneficiary who holds a support interest, the use or enjoyment of property belonging to the trust by that beneficiary shall not be transferred and shall not be reached by creditors or assignees of that beneficiary;

(5) Regardless of whether a beneficiary has any outstanding creditors or assignees, a trustee or other fiduciary of a support interest may directly pay any expense on behalf of such beneficiary and may exhaust the income and principal of the trust for the benefit of such beneficiary; and

(6) No trustee or other fiduciary is liable to any creditor or assignee for paying the expenses of a beneficiary of a support interest.

(b) Relative to a mandatory interest, whether or not a trust contains a spendthrift provision:

(1) While a court may order a trustee or other fiduciary to distribute a past due mandatory distribution to its beneficiary, no court shall order a trustee or other fiduciary to distribute such past due mandatory distribution directly to a creditor or assignee;

(2) Regardless of whether a beneficiary has any outstanding creditors or assignees, a trustee or other fiduciary of a mandatory interest may directly pay any expense on behalf of such beneficiary and may exhaust the income and principal of the trust for the benefit of such beneficiary;

(3) No trustee or other fiduciary is liable to any creditor or assignee for paying the expenses of a beneficiary of a mandatory interest.

(c) Although a remainder interest may be an enforceable right, where it is not absolutely certain based on the language of the trust that the remainder interest will be distributed within one (1) year, it shall not be classified as a property interest. This subsection does not affect eligibility for any public assistance program administered by the department of human services.

35-15-508 SECTION 23. Tennessee Code Annotated, Title 35, Chapter 15, Part 5, is amended by adding the following new section:

35-15-508. Removal or replacement power over trustee or other fiduciary not reachable by holder's creditors -- Interests of beneficiary who is also a trustee or other fiduciary not reachable.

(a) No creditor or assignee of a beneficiary shall have the power to reach an interest of a beneficiary or any other person who holds an unconditional or conditional removal or replacement power over a trustee or other fiduciary. Such power over a trustee or other fiduciary is personal to the holder and shall not be exercised by the holder's creditors. No court shall direct a holder to exercise the power.

(b) Subject to § 35-15-504(b)(3):

(1) No creditor or assignee of a beneficiary may reach an interest of a beneficiary who is also a trustee, cotrustee or other fiduciary, or otherwise compel a distribution because the beneficiary is then serving as a trustee, cotrustee or other fiduciary; and

(2) No court may foreclose against a beneficiary's interest described in subdivision (b)(1).

35-15-509 SECTION 24. Tennessee Code Annotated, Title 35, Chapter 15, Part 5, is further amended by adding the following new section:

35-15-509. Judicial foreclosure of beneficial interests, powers of appointment, and reserved powers prohibited -- Certain reaches prohibited.

Regardless of whether or not a trust contains a spendthrift provision:

(1) No beneficial interest, power of appointment, or reserved power in a trust shall be judicially foreclosed;

(2) No creditor or assignee shall reach a power of appointment or a remainder interest at the trust level and such creditor or assignee shall wait until any funds are distributed relative to such power of appointment or remainder interest before such creditor or assignee may reach such funds; and

(3) No power of appointment is a property interest.

26-4-101 SECTION 25. Tennessee Code Annotated, Section 26-4-101, is amended by deleting the language "§§ 35-15-501 – 35-15-507" and substituting instead the language "§§ 35-15-501 – 35-15-509".

35-15-703 SECTION 26. Tennessee Code Annotated, Section 35-15-703, is amended by adding a new subsection (i) as follows:

(i) A trustee shall keep each cotrustee and any other fiduciary reasonably informed about the administration of the trust, to the extent the trustee has knowledge that each such cotrustee or other fiduciary does not have such knowledge of the trustee's actions, or regarding other material information or the availability of such information, related to the administration of the trust that would be reasonably necessary for each such cotrustee or other fiduciary to perform his or her duties as a trustee or other fiduciary of the trust.

35-15-708 SECTION 27. Tennessee Code Annotated, Section 35-15-708, is amended by deleting the section in its entirety and by substituting instead the following:

35-15-708. Compensation of trustees, trust advisors and trust protectors.

(a) If the terms of a trust do not specify a trustee's, trust advisor's or trust protector's compensation, and if the settlor, if living, or otherwise a majority of the qualified beneficiaries as defined in § 35-15-103(13)(A), have not otherwise agreed, a trustee, trust advisor or trust protector is entitled to compensation that is reasonable under the circumstances.

(b) If the terms of a trust specify a trustee's, trust advisor's or trust protector's compensation, the trustee, trust advisor or trust protector is entitled to be compensated as specified in the trust, but the court may allow more or less compensation if:

(1) The duties of the trustee, trust advisor or trust protector are substantially different from those contemplated when the trust was created; or

(2) The compensation specified by the terms of the trust would be unreasonably low or high.

(c) Factors for the court to consider in deciding upon a trustee's, trust advisor's or trust protector's compensation shall include the size of the trust, the nature and number of the assets, the income produced, the time and responsibility required, the expertise required, any management or sale of real property or closely held business interests, any involvement in litigation to protect trust property, and other relevant factors.

(d) Subject to the court's authority as provided in subsection (b), regardless of its form of entity, the fees set forth in the published fee schedule of a trustee, trust advisor or trust protector that is regulated by the department of financial institutions, the equivalent regulatory agency of another state, the office of the comptroller of the currency or the office of thrift supervision shall be presumed to be reasonable, unless otherwise provided by the terms of the trust.

35-15-709 SECTION 28. Tennessee Code Annotated, Section 35-15-709, is amended by deleting the section in its entirety and by substituting instead the following:

(a) A trustee, trust advisor or trust protector is entitled to be reimbursed out of the trust property, with interest as appropriate, for:

(1) Expenses that were properly incurred in the administration of the trust; and

(2) To the extent necessary to prevent unjust enrichment of the trust, expenses that were not properly incurred in the administration of the trust.

(b) An advance, either by the trustee, trust advisor or trust protector or by a person named in § 35-15-701(c)(1), of money for the protection of the trust gives rise to a lien against trust property to secure reimbursement with reasonable interest.

35-15-710 — 35-15-715 SECTION 29. Tennessee Code Annotated, Title 35, Chapter 15, Part 7, is amended by adding the following new sections:

35-15-710. Directed trusts.

If the terms of the trust, an agreement of the qualified beneficiaries, or a court order requires a trustee, trust advisor, or trust protector to follow the direction of a trust advisor or trust protector, and the trustee, trust advisor, or trust protector acts in accordance with such direction, then the trustee, trust advisor, or trust protector so directed shall be treated as an excluded fiduciary.

35-15-711. Directed Trusts; Accepting or declining fiduciary appointment.

(a) A trust advisor, trust protector or other fiduciary other than a cotrustee, such cotrustee already being provided for in § 35-15-701(a), may accept its appointment as such respective fiduciary in a like manner as provided for a trustee under § 35-15-701(a).

(b) A trust advisor, trust protector or other fiduciary other than a cotrustee, such cotrustee already being provided for in § 35-15-701(b), may reject its appointment as such respective fiduciary in a like manner as provided for a trustee under § 35-15-701(b).

(c) A trust advisor, trust protector or other fiduciary other than a cotrustee, such cotrustee already being provided for in § 35-15-701(c), may, without accepting its appointment as such respective fiduciary, carry out the appropriate activities relative to such respective fiduciary as are provided for a trustee under § 35-15-701(c).

35-15-712. Directed Trusts; Fiduciary's bond.

(a) Section 35-15-702 applies to trust advisors, trust protectors or other fiduciaries other than cotrustees, such cotrustees already being provided for in § 35-15-702.

(b) When exercising its powers under this section, the court shall consider the powers, duties and liabilities relative to such respective fiduciaries other than a cotrustee and whether any of such respective fiduciaries are excluded fiduciaries.

35-15-713. Vacancy; Directed Trusts.

(a) Except as otherwise provided by the terms of the trust upon obtaining knowledge of a vacancy in the office of trust advisor or trust protector, the trustee shall be vested with any fiduciary power or duty that otherwise would be vested in the trustee but that by the terms of the trust was vested in the trust advisor or trust protector, until such time that the vacancy in the office of trust advisor or trust protector, as applicable is filled.

(b) Such vacancy shall be filled in the same manner as would a vacancy in trusteeship that is required to be filled, either as provided by § 35-15-704(c) if the trust is a noncharitable trust, or as provided by § 35-15-704(d) if the trust is a charitable trust. Section 35-15-704(e) shall also apply relative to trust advisors and trust protectors in the same manner as that subsection does to trustees and vacancies in trusteeship.

(c) Notwithstanding subsection (a), a trustee shall not be liable for failing to exercise or assume any power or duty held by a trust advisor or trust protector and conferred upon the trustee by subsection (a) for the sixty-day period immediately following the date the trustee obtains knowledge of such vacancy.

35-15-714. Directed Trusts; Resignation of fiduciary.

(a) A trust advisor, trust protector or other fiduciary other than a cotrustee, such cotrustee's resignation already being provided for in § 35-15-705, may resign its appointment as such respective fiduciary in a like manner as provided for a trustee under § 35-15-705.

(b) When exercising its powers under this section relative to resignation, the court shall consider the powers, duties and liabilities relative to such respective fiduciaries other than a cotrustee and whether any of such respective fiduciaries are excluded fiduciaries.

35-15-715. Directed Trusts; Removal of fiduciary.

(a) A trust advisor, trust protector or other fiduciary other than a cotrustee, such cotrustee's removal already being provided for in § 35-15-706, may be removed as such respective fiduciary in a like manner as provided for a trustee under § 35-15-706.

(b) When exercising its powers under this section relative to removal of such respective fiduciary, the court shall consider the powers, duties and liabilities relative to such respective fiduciaries other than a cotrustee and whether any of such respective fiduciaries are excluded fiduciaries.

35-15-802 SECTION 30. Tennessee Code Annotated, Section 35-15-802(g)(5), is amended by deleting that subdivision and by substituting instead the following:

(g)(5) For purposes of this section, "fiduciary" means any fiduciary as defined in § 35-15-103, as well as any other fiduciary; and

35-15-808 SECTION 31. Tennessee Code Annotated, Section 35-15-808, is amended by deleting subsections (b), (d) and (e) and by substituting instead new subsections (b), (d), (e) and (f) as follows:

(b) If the terms of a trust, an agreement of the qualified beneficiaries, or a court order, confer upon a person other than the settlor of a revocable trust power to direct certain actions of the trustee, the trustee shall act in accordance with an exercise of the power.

(d) Unless the terms of a trust provide otherwise, if a person holds a power to perform any act in reliance on §§ 35-3-122 and 35-3-123, and that power holder is other than a beneficiary, that person is a fiduciary who, as such, is required to act in good faith with regard to the purposes of the trust and the interests of the beneficiaries. The holder of a power to perform any act under this subsection is liable for any loss that results from breach of a fiduciary duty. In so following the directions of such person the trustee is protected from liability as provided in §§ 35-3-122 and 35-3-123.

(e) If a person holds a power to direct pursuant to part 12 of this chapter, that person is a trust advisor, trust protector or both. Such power holder is subject to all the provisions of part 12, including any duties prescribed by part 12 and any provisions that make the power holder a fiduciary. Any trustee or other person that under part 12 is relieved of any duty or any liability, or is otherwise protected under part 12, shall be so relieved and otherwise protected.

(f) Transitional provisions applicable to this section shall be as follows:

(1) Powers to direct or perform any act held in reliance on or that are subject to §§ 35-3-122 and 35-3-123 that are in existence prior to July 1, 2013, remain effective thereafter and remain subject to the provisions of those sections and their protections;

(2) Notwithstanding subdivision (f)(1), should any power that is described in part 12 of this chapter be held under a trust instrument that was in existence or became irrevocable before July 1, 2013, and that power is not held in reliance on nor is it subject to §§ 35-3-122 and 35-3-123, then from July 1, 2013, all law relative to such power shall be controlled by and subject to part 12 of this chapter, along with any amendments made to this chapter in furtherance of the implementation and effectiveness of such part 12; and

(3) For all trust instruments entered into, that become irrevocable or that are amended relative to any power that is described in part 12 of this chapter on or after July 1, 2013, part 12 of this chapter, along with any amendments made to this chapter in furtherance of the implementation and effectiveness of such part 12, shall be the exclusive method to create a directed trust or a provision regarding such and shall control such. Relative to trusts described in this subdivision and subdivision (f)(2), §§ 35-3-122 and 35-3-123 shall be of no further force and effect.

35-15-813 SECTION 32. Tennessee Code Annotated, Section 35-15-813, is amended by adding the following new subdivision (a)(3):

(a)(3) The requirements of subdivisions (a)(1) and (a)(2) shall also apply to the benefit of anyone who, in a capacity other than that of a fiduciary, as defined by § 35-15-103, holds a power of appointment.

35-15-813 SECTION 33. Tennessee Code Annotated, Section 35-15-813, is further amended by deleting subsection (b) and substituting instead the following:

(b) The trustee of an irrevocable or non-grantor trust within sixty (60) days after the acceptance and funding of a trust, excluding nominal funding for the trust to have corpus or the depositing of insurance policies on the life of a living person, shall notify each current income beneficiary, each vested ultimate beneficiary of a remainder interest and anyone who, in a capacity other than that of a fiduciary, as defined by § 35-15-103, holds a power of appointment, that the trust has been established.

35-15-813 SECTION 34. Tennessee Code Annotated, Section 35-15-813, is further amended by adding a new subdivision (b)(2)(D) as follows:

(b)(2)(D) If for anyone who, in a capacity other than that of a fiduciary, as defined by § 35-15-103, holds a power of appointment, all of the information required by subdivisions (b)(2)(A) through (C) necessary or beneficial for that person to effectively determine whether or not to exercise that power of appointment.

35-15-813 SECTION 35. Tennessee Code Annotated, Section 35-15-813, is further amended by deleting subsections (c) through (e) and substituting new subsections (c) through (e) and adding a new subsection (h) as follows:

(c) Upon the termination of an interest of any one (1) or more of the current income beneficiaries:

(1) The trustee shall similarly notify the income beneficiaries who are takers of the terminated interest of their interest by sending or delivering them the notice required in subsection (b); and

(2) If at that time the period described in subsection (b) has lapsed, the trustee shall similarly notify anyone who, in a capacity other than that of a fiduciary, as defined by § 35-15-103, holds a power of appointment by sending or delivering to such person the notice required in subsection (b).

(d) A beneficiary may waive the right to a trustee's report or other information otherwise required to be furnished under this section. A beneficiary, with respect to future reports and other information, may withdraw a waiver previously given. Anyone who, in a capacity other than that of a fiduciary, as defined by § 35-15-103, holds a power of appointment has the same power as provided a beneficiary in this subsection to waive reports and other information and to withdraw a waiver previously given.

(e) Subsections (a) and (b) shall not apply to the extent that the terms of the trust provide otherwise or the settlor of the trust, or a trust protector or trust advisor under part 12 that holds the power to so direct, directs otherwise in a writing delivered to the trustee.

(h) A trust advisor, trust protector, or other fiduciary designated by the terms of the trust shall keep each excluded fiduciary designated by the terms of the trust reasonably informed about:

(1) The administration of the trust with respect to any specific duty or function being performed by the trust advisor, trust protector, or other fiduciary to the extent that the duty or function would normally be performed by the excluded fiduciary or to the extent that providing such information to the excluded fiduciary is reasonably necessary for the excluded fiduciary to perform its duties; and

(2) Any other material information that the excluded fiduciary would be required to disclose to the specified beneficiaries under subsection (a) regardless of whether the terms of the trust relieve the excluded fiduciary from providing such information to qualified beneficiaries. Neither the performance nor the failure to perform of a trust advisor, trust protector, or other fiduciary designated by the terms of the trust as provided in this subsection shall affect the limitation on the liability of any excluded fiduciary provided by part 12 of this chapter.

35-15-814 SECTION 36. Tennessee Code Annotated, Section 35-15-814, is amended by deleting the section in its entirety and substituting instead the following:

35-15-814. Exercise of Powers Over Discretionary and Other Interests; Tax Savings.

(a) Relative to exercise of powers over discretionary and other interests:

PUBLIC CHAPTER NO. 390 (cont'd)

(1) "Improper motive" means to demonstrate action such as the following:

(A) A trustee refusing to make or limiting distributions to beneficiaries other than the trustee due to the trustee's self interest when the trustee also holds a beneficial interest subject to a discretionary interest; or

(B) A trustee making a distribution in excess of an ascertainable standard to himself or herself as beneficiary when the trustee is restricted by an ascertainable standard in the trust.

(2) Unless otherwise provided in the trust:

(A) If the settlor's spouse is named as a beneficiary, the settlor's spouse is still living and the trust is classified as a support trust, then the trustee shall consider the resources of the settlor's spouse, including the settlor's obligation of support, prior to making a distribution; and

(B) In all other cases, unless otherwise provided in the trust, the trustee need not consider the beneficiary's resources in determining whether a distribution should be made.

(b) The following provisions apply only to discretionary interests:

(1) A discretionary interest is neither a property interest nor an enforceable right; it is a mere expectancy;

(2) A court may review a trustee's distribution discretion only if the trustee acts dishonestly, acts with an improper motive, or fails to act if under a duty to do so;

(3) A reasonableness standard shall not be applied to the exercise of discretion by the trustee with regard to a discretionary interest;

(4) Other than for the three circumstances listed in subdivision (b)(2), a court has no jurisdiction to review the trustee's discretion or to force a distribution; and

(5) Absent express language in the trust instrument to the contrary, in the event that the distribution language in a discretionary interest permits unequal distributions between beneficiaries or distributions to the exclusion of other beneficiaries, the trustee may distribute all of the accumulated, accrued, or undistributed income and principal to one beneficiary in the trustee's discretion.

(c) The following provisions apply only to mandatory or support interests:

(1) A beneficiary of a mandatory or a support interest has an enforceable right to a distribution pursuant to a court's review;

(2) A trustee's distribution decision may be reviewed for unreasonableness, dishonesty, improper motivation, or failure to act if under a duty to do so; and

(3) In the case of a support interest, nothing in this section shall raise a beneficiary's support interest to the level of a property interest.

(d) Unless otherwise provided in subsection (f), and unless the terms of the trust expressly indicate that a rule in this subsection does not apply:

(1) A person other than a settlor who is a beneficiary and trustee of a trust that confers on the trustee a power to make discretionary distributions to or for the trustee's personal benefit may exercise the power only in accordance with an ascertainable standard; and

(2) A trustee may not exercise a power to make discretionary distributions to satisfy a legal obligation of support that the trustee personally owes another person.

(e) A power that is limited or prohibited by subsection (d) may be exercised by a majority of the remaining trustees whose exercise of the power is not so limited or prohibited. If the power of all trustees is so limited or prohibited, the court may appoint a special fiduciary with authority to exercise the power.

(f) Subsection (d) shall not apply to:

(1) A power held by the settlor's spouse who is the trustee of a trust for which a marital deduction, as defined in section 2056(b)(5) or 2523(e) of the Internal Revenue Code was previously allowed;

(2) Any trust during any period that the trust may be revoked or amended by its settlor; or

(3) A trust if contributions to the trust qualify for the annual exclusion under section 2503(c) of the Internal Revenue Code.

35-15-816 SECTION 37. Tennessee Code Annotated, Section 35-15-816(b)(19), is amended by deleting the phrase "provided, however, that this power shall not apply to any beneficiary's interest that is subject to a spendthrift provision;".

35-15-816 SECTION 38. Tennessee Code Annotated, Section 35-15-816(b)(27), is amended by adding the following new subdivisions:

(E) The exercise of the power to appoint principal under subdivision (b)(27)(A) shall be considered an exercise of a power of appointment, other than a power to appoint to the trustee, the trustee's creditors, the trustee's estate, or the creditors of the trustee's estate;

(F) The second trust:

(i) May confer a power of appointment upon a beneficiary of the original trust to whom or for the benefit of whom the trustee has the power to distribute principal of the original trust;

(ii) The permissible appointees of the power of appointment conferred upon a beneficiary may include persons who are not beneficiaries of the original or second trust; and

(iii) The power of appointment conferred upon a beneficiary must preclude any exercise that would extend the permissible period of the rule against perpetuities that applies to the trust;

(G) If any contribution to the original trust qualified for the annual exclusion under § 2503(b) of the Internal Revenue Code, the marital deduction under §§ 2056(a) or 2523(a) of the Internal Revenue Code, or the charitable deduction under §§ 170(a), 642(c), 2055(a) or 2522(a) of the Internal Revenue Code, is a direct skip qualifying for treatment under § 2642(c) of the Internal Revenue Code, or qualified for any other specific tax benefit that would be lost by the existence of the authorized trustee's authority under subdivision (b)(27)(A) for income, gift, estate, or generation-skipping transfer tax purposes under the Internal Revenue Code, then the authorized trustee shall not have the power to distribute the principal of a trust pursuant to subdivision (b)(27)(A) in a manner that would prevent the contribution to the original trust from qualifying for or would reduce the exclusion, deduction, or other tax benefit that was originally claimed with respect to that contribution;

(H) During any period when the original trust owns stock in a subchapter S corporation as defined in § 1361(a)(1) of the Internal Revenue Code, an authorized trustee shall not exercise a power authorized by subdivision (b)(27)(A) to distribute part or all of the stock of the S corporation to a second trust that is not a permitted shareholder under § 1361(c)(2) of the Internal Revenue Code;

(I) This section applies to any trust that is administered in this state; and

(J) For purposes of this section, the term "original trust" refers to the trust from which principal is being distributed and the phrase "second trust" refers to the trust to which assets are being distributed from the original trust.

35-15-901 SECTION 39. Tennessee Code Annotated, Section 35-15-901, is amended by deleting the section in its entirety and by substituting instead the following:

35-15-901. Uniform Principal and Income Act and Tennessee Uniform Prudent Investor Act of 2002 incorporated by reference.

Title 35, chapter 6 and chapter 14 are incorporated in this chapter by reference.

35-15-1005 SECTION 40. Tennessee Code Annotated, Section 35-15-1005, is amended by adding the following new sections:

(d) A trustee may not commence a proceeding against a cotrustee or a former trustee for breach of trust more than one (1) year after the date the trustee or a representative of the trustee was sent a report that adequately disclosed facts indicating the existence of a potential claim for breach of trust.

(e) A report adequately discloses facts indicating the existence of a potential claim for breach of trust if it provides sufficient information so that the trustee or the trustee's representative knows of the potential claim or has sufficient information to be presumed to know of it, or to be put on notice to inquire into its existence.

(f) If subsection (d) does not apply, a judicial proceeding by a trustee against a cotrustee or former trustee for breach of trust must be commenced within three (3) years after the first to occur of:

(1) The removal, resignation, or death of the cotrustee or a former trustee;

(2) The termination of the beneficiary's interest in the trust; or

(3) The termination of the trust.

(g) A trust advisor or trust protector may not commence a proceeding against a trustee or a former trustee for breach of trust more than one (1) year after the date the trust advisor or trust protector or the respective representative of each was sent a report that adequately disclosed facts indicating the existence of a potential claim for breach of trust.

(h) A report adequately discloses facts indicating the existence of a potential claim for breach of trust if it provides sufficient information so that the trust advisor or trust protector or the respective representative of each knows of the potential claim or has sufficient information to be presumed to know of it, or to be put on notice to inquire into its existence.

(i) If subsection (g) does not apply, a judicial proceeding by a trust advisor or trust protector against a trustee or former trustee for breach of trust must be commenced within three (3) years after the first to occur of:

(1) The removal, resignation, or death of the trustee or a former trustee;

(2) The termination of the beneficiary's interest in the trust; or

(3) The termination of the trust.

(j) Notwithstanding subsections (d)–(i), no trustee, trust advisor or trust protector, may commence a proceeding against a trustee or a former trustee if, under § 35-15-1005(a)–(c), none of the beneficiaries may commence a proceeding against the cotrustee or former trustee for such breach of trust.

35-15-1014 SECTION 41. Tennessee Code Annotated, Title 35, Chapter 15, Part 10, is amended by adding the following as a new, appropriately numbered section:

35-15-1014. Enforcement of No-contest, In Terrorem or Forfeiture Provisions.

(a) For the purposes of this section, "no-contest provision" includes a "no-contest provision," "in terrorem provision" or "forfeiture provision" of a trust instrument. A "no-contest provision" means a provision that, if given effect, would reduce or eliminate the interest of any beneficiary of such trust who, directly or indirectly, initiates or otherwise pursues:

(1) Any action to contest the validity of the trust or the terms of the trust;

(2) Any action to set aside or vary the terms of the trust;

(3) Any action to challenge the acts of the trustee or other fiduciary of the trust in the performance of the trustee's or other fiduciary's duties as described in the terms of the trust; or

(4) Any other act or proceedings to frustrate or defeat the settlor's intent as expressed in the terms of the trust.

(b) Regardless of whether or not the beneficiary sought, received or relied upon legal counsel, a no-contest provision shall be enforceable according to the express terms of the no-contest provision without regard to the beneficiary's good or bad faith in taking the action that would justify the complete or partial forfeiture of the beneficiary's interest in the trust under the terms of the no-contest provision unless probable cause exists for the beneficiary taking such action on the grounds of:

(1) Fraud;

(2) Duress;

(3) Revocation;

(4) Lack of testamentary capacity;

(5) Undue influence;

(6) Mistake;

(7) Forgery; or

(8) Irregularity in the execution of the trust instrument.

(c) Subsection (b) shall not apply to:

(1) Any action brought solely to challenge the acts of the trustee or other fiduciary of the trust to the extent that the trustee or other fiduciary has committed a breach of fiduciary duties or breach of trust;

(2) Any action brought by the trustee or any other fiduciary serving under the terms of the trust, unless the trustee or other fiduciary is a beneficiary against whom the no-contest provision is otherwise enforceable;

(3) Any agreement among the beneficiaries and any other interested persons in settlement of a dispute or resolution of any other matter relating to the trust, including without limitation any nonjudicial settlement agreement;

(4) Any action to determine whether a proposed or pending motion, petition, or other proceeding constitutes a contest within the meaning of a no-contest provision;

(5) Any action brought by a beneficiary or on behalf of any such beneficiary for a construction or interpretation of the terms of the trust; or

(6) Any action brought by the attorney general for a construction or interpretation of a charitable trust or a trust containing a charitable interest if a provision exists in a trust purporting to penalize a charity or charitable interest for contesting the trust if probable cause exists for instituting proceedings.

(d) Pursuant to this section, courts shall enforce the settlor's intent as reflected in a no-contest provision to the greatest extent possible.

35-15-1101 SECTION 42. Tennessee Code Annotated, Section 35-15-1101, is amended by deleting the section in its entirety and by substituting instead the following:

35-15-1101.

(a) Numerous provisions of each of the following have been modified extensively relative to their respective uniform acts as such uniform acts were drafted and have been amended by the Uniform Law Commission, also known as the National Conference of Commissioners of Uniform State Laws:

(1) Chapter 6, the Uniform Principal and Income Act;

(2) Chapter 14, the Tennessee Uniform Prudent Investor Act of 2002; and

(3) Chapter 15, the Tennessee Uniform Trust Code.

(b) These modifications were undertaken deliberately and after significant consideration:

(1) Therefore, in applying and construing title 35, no consideration shall be given to the need to promote uniformity of the law with respect to its subject matter among states, including any other state that has enacted laws covering the same general subject matter as chapters 9, 14 or 15, either by enacting such respective uniform acts as such uniform acts were originally drafted or as such were originally drafted and subsequently have been amended, or by enacting laws based on or similar to such uniform acts as originally drafted or as such have been amended; and

(2) Unless specifically provided otherwise in this chapter, chapter 6 or chapter 14, courts shall not consult, rely on or give any persuasive value to such uniform acts or any respective other state's acts based on or similar to such uniform acts, or any comments accompanying any such uniform acts or any respective other state's acts based on or similar to such uniform acts; none of which have any force or effect relative to trusts governed by the laws of this state.

35-15-1201 — 35-15-1206 SECTION 43. Tennessee Code Annotated, Title 35, Chapter 15, is amended by adding the following as a new part 12:

35-15-1201. Powers of Trust Advisors and Trust Protectors.

(a) A trust protector or trust advisor is any person, and may be a committee of more than one person, other than a trustee, who under the terms of the trust, an agreement of the qualified beneficiaries, or a court order has a power or duty with respect to a trust, including but not limited to, one or more of the following powers:

(1) The power to modify or amend the trust instrument to achieve favorable tax status or respond to changes in any applicable federal, state, or other tax law affecting the trust, including but not limited to, any rulings, regulations, or other guidance implementing or interpreting such laws;

(2) The power to amend or modify the trust instrument to take advantage of changes in the rule against perpetuities, laws governing restraints on alienation, or other state laws restricting the terms of the trust, the distribution of trust property, or the administration of the trust;

(3) The power to appoint a successor trust protector or trust advisor;

(4) The power to review and approve a trustee's trust reports or accountings;

(5) The power to change the governing law or principal place of administration of the trust;

(6) The power to remove and replace any trust advisor or trust protector for the reasons stated in the trust instrument;

(7) The power to remove a trustee, cotrustee, or successor trustee, for the reasons stated in the trust instrument, and appoint a successor;

(8) The power to consent to a trustee's or cotrustee's action or inaction in making distributions to beneficiaries;

(9) The power to increase or decrease any interest of the beneficiaries in the trust, to grant a power of appointment to one (1) or more trust beneficiaries, or to terminate or amend any power of appointment granted in the trust;

(10) The power to perform a specific duty or function that would normally be required of a trustee or cotrustee;

(11) The power to advise the trustee or cotrustee concerning any beneficiary;

(12) The power to consent to a trustee's or cotrustee's action or inaction relating to investments of trust assets;

(13) The power to direct the acquisition, disposition, or retention of any trust investment;

(14) The power to appoint under § 35-15-816(b)(27);

(15) The power to terminate all or part of a trust;

(16) The power to veto or direct all or part of any trust distribution;

(17) The power to borrow money with or without security, and mortgage or pledge trust property for a period within or extending beyond the duration of the trust;

(18) The power to make loans out of trust property, including but not limited to, loans to a beneficiary on terms and conditions, including without interest, considered to be fair and reasonable under the circumstances;

(19) The power to vote proxies and exercise all other rights of ownership relative to securities and business entities held by the trust;

(20) The power to select one (1) or more investment advisors, managers or counselors, including but not limited to, a trustee and delegate to them any of its powers; and

(21) The power to direct the trustee with respect to any additional powers and discretions over investment and management of trust assets provided in the trust instrument.

(b) The exercise of a power by a trust advisor or a trust protector shall be exercised in the sole and absolute discretion of the trust advisor or trust protector and shall be binding on all other persons.

(c) Any power of a trust advisor or trust protector to directly or indirectly modify a trust may be granted notwithstanding the provisions of §§ 35-15-410 through 35-15-412 and 35-15-414.

(d) An excluded fiduciary may continue to follow the direction of a trust protector or trust advisor upon the incapacity or death of the grantor of a trust to the extent provided in the trust instrument.

(e) Notwithstanding anything in this section to the contrary, no modification, amendment or grant of a power of appointment with respect to a trust all of whose beneficiaries are charitable organizations may authorize a trust protector or trust advisor to grant a beneficial interest in such trust to any non-charitable interest or purpose.

35-15-1202. Trust Advisors and Trust Protectors as Fiduciaries.

(a) A trust advisor or trust protector, other than a beneficiary, is a fiduciary with respect to each power granted to such trust advisor or trust protector. In exercising any power or refraining from exercising any power, a trust advisor or trust protector shall act in good faith and in accordance with the terms and purposes of the trust and the interests of the beneficiaries.

(b) A trust advisor or trust protector is an excluded fiduciary with respect to each power granted or reserved exclusively to any one or more other trustees, trust advisors, or trust protectors.

35-15-1203. Trust Advisor and Trust Protector Subject to Court Jurisdiction.

By accepting appointment to serve as a trust advisor or trust protector, the trust advisor or the trust protector submits personally to the jurisdiction of the courts of this state even if investment advisory agreements or other related agreements provide otherwise, and the trust advisor or trust protector may be made a party to any action or proceeding relating to a decision, action, or inaction of the trust advisor or trust protector.

35-15-1204. No Duty to Review Actions of Trustee, Trust Advisor, or Trust Protector.

(a) Whenever, pursuant to the terms of a trust, an agreement of the qualified beneficiaries, or a court order, an excluded fiduciary is to follow the direction of a trustee, trust advisor, or trust protector with respect to investment decisions, distribution decisions, or other decisions of the non-excluded fiduciary, then, except to the extent that the terms of the trust, the agreement of the qualified beneficiaries, or the court order provide otherwise, the excluded fiduciary shall have no duty to:

(1) Review, evaluate, perform investment reviews, suitability reviews, inquiries, or investigations, or in any other way monitor the conduct of the trustee, trust advisor, or trust protector;

(2) Make recommendations or evaluations or in any way provide advice to the trustee, trust advisor, or trust protector or consult with the trustee, trust advisor, or trust protector; or

(3) Communicate with or warn or apprise any beneficiary or third party concerning instances in which the excluded fiduciary would or might have exercised the excluded fiduciary's own discretion in a manner different from the manner directed by the trustee, trust advisor, or trust protector.

(b) Absent provisions in the trust instrument to the contrary, the actions of the excluded fiduciary pertaining to matters within the scope of the trustee, trust advisor, or trust protector's authority, including but not limited to, confirming that the trustee, trust advisor, or trust protector's directions have been carried out and recording and reporting actions taken at the trustee, trust advisor, or trust protector's direction or other information pursuant to § 35-15-813, shall be deemed to be administrative actions taken by the excluded fiduciary solely to allow the excluded fiduciary to perform those duties assigned to the excluded fiduciary under the terms of the trust, the agreement of the qualified beneficiaries, or the court order; such administrative actions, as well as any communications made by the excluded fiduciary to the trust advisor, trust protector or any of their agents or persons they have selected to provide services to the trust, shall not be deemed to constitute an undertaking by the excluded fiduciary to monitor the trustee, trust advisor, or trust protector or otherwise participate in actions within the scope of the trustee, trust advisor, or trust protector's authority.

35-15-1205. Fiduciary's Liability for Action or Inaction of Trustee, Trust Advisor, and Trust Protector.

An excluded fiduciary is not liable, either individually or as a fiduciary, for:

(1) Any loss resulting from compliance with a direction of a trustee, trust advisor or trust protector, including but not limited to, any loss from the trustee, trust advisor or trust protector breaching fiduciary responsibilities or acting beyond the trustee's, trust advisor's or trust protector's scope of authority;

(2) Any loss resulting from any action or inaction of a trustee, trust advisor, or trust protector; or

(3) Any loss that results from the failure of a trustee, trust advisor, or trust protector to take any action proposed by the excluded fiduciary where such action requires the authorization of the trustee, trust advisor, or trust protector, provided that an excluded fiduciary who had a duty to propose such action timely sought but failed to obtain the authorization.

35-15-1206. Limitation of Action Against a Trust Advisor or Trust Protector.

(a) A beneficiary may not commence a proceeding against a trust advisor or trust protector for breach of trust more than one (1) year after the date the beneficiary or a representative of the beneficiary was sent a report that adequately disclosed facts indicating the existence of a potential claim for breach of trust.

(b) A report adequately discloses facts indicating the existence of a potential claim for breach of trust if it provides sufficient information so that the beneficiary or the beneficiary's representative knows of the potential claim or has sufficient information to be presumed to know of it, or to be put on notice to inquire into its existence.

(c) If subsection (a) does not apply, a judicial proceeding by a beneficiary against a trust advisor or trust protector for breach of trust must be commenced within three (3) years after the first to occur of:

(1) The removal, resignation, or death of the trust advisor or trust protector;

(2) The termination of the beneficiary's interest in the trust; or

(3) The termination of the trust.

(d) A trustee may not commence a proceeding against a trust advisor or trust protector for breach of trust more than one (1) year after the date the trustee or a representative of the trustee was sent a report that adequately disclosed facts indicating the existence of a potential claim for breach of trust.

(e) A report adequately discloses facts indicating the existence of a potential claim for breach of trust if it provides sufficient information so that the trustee or the trustee's representative knows of the potential claim or has sufficient information to be presumed to know of it, or to be put on notice to inquire into its existence.

(f) If subsection (d) does not apply, a judicial proceeding by a trustee against a trust advisor or trust protector for breach of trust must be commenced within three (3) years after the first to occur of:

(1) The removal, resignation, or death of the trust advisor or trust protector;

(2) The termination of the beneficiary's interest in the trust; or

(3) The termination of the trust.

(g) A trust advisor or trust protector may not commence a proceeding against another trust advisor or another trust protector for breach of trust more than one (1) year after the date the trust advisor or trust protector or the respective representative of each was sent a report that adequately disclosed facts indicating the existence of a potential claim for breach of trust.

(h) A report adequately discloses facts indicating the existence of a potential claim for breach of trust if it provides sufficient information so that the trust advisor or trust protector or the respective representative of each knows of the potential claim or has sufficient information to be presumed to know of it, or to be put on notice to inquire into its existence.

(i) If subsection (g) does not apply, a judicial proceeding by a trust advisor or trust protector against another trust advisor or another trust protector for breach of trust must be commenced within three (3) years after the first to occur of:

(1) The removal, resignation, or death of the other trust advisor or other trust protector;

(2) The termination of the beneficiary's interest in the trust; or

(3) The termination of the trust.

(j) Notwithstanding subsections (d)–(i), no trustee, trust advisor or trust protector, may commence a proceeding against a trust advisor or trust protector or another trust advisor or another trust protector if, under either subsections (a)–(c) or § 35-15-1005(a)–(c), none of the beneficiaries may commence a proceeding against the trust advisor or trust protector for such breach of trust.

35-16-102 SECTION 44. Tennessee Code Annotated, Section 35-16-102, is amended by adding a new subdivision (14) as follows:

(14) Unless the context or a provision contained in this chapter provides otherwise, throughout this chapter, any form of the word "trustee," whether singular or plural means

"trustee, cotrustee or any other fiduciary" as fiduciary is defined at § 35-15-103 relative to any power or duty held by such fiduciary that could otherwise be held by a trustee, to the extent that such fiduciary is holding such a power or duty and is not an excluded fiduciary as defined at § 35-15-103 relative to that power or duty.

35-16-104 SECTION 45. Tennessee Code Annotated, Section 35-16-104, is amended by deleting the language "foreign court" in subdivision (i)(2)(A)(i) and replacing it with "court of another state as defined by § 35-15-103".

35-16-104 SECTION 46. Tennessee Code Annotated, Section 35-16-104, is further amended by deleting subsection (b) in its entirety and by substituting instead the following:

(b)(1) Notwithstanding § 66-3-310, a creditor's claim under subsection (a) shall be extinguished:

(A) If the person is a creditor when the qualified disposition to an investment services trust is made, unless the action is commenced within the later of two (2) years after the qualified disposition is made or six (6) months after the person discovers or reasonably should have discovered the qualified disposition; or

(B) If the person becomes a creditor after the qualified disposition to an investment services trust is made, unless the action is commenced within two (2) years after the qualified disposition is made;

(2) If subdivision (b)(1) applies:

(A) A person shall be deemed to have discovered the existence of a qualified disposition to an investment services trust at the time any public record is made of any transfer of property relative to such qualified disposition, including but not limited to, the conveyance of real property that is recorded in the office of the county register of deeds of the county in which the property is located or the filing of a financing statement under title 47, chapter 9, or the equivalent recording or filing of either with the appropriate person or official under the laws of a jurisdiction other than this state; and

(B) No creditor shall bring an action with respect to property that is the subject of a qualified disposition unless that creditor proves by clear and convincing evidence that the settlor's transfer of such property was made with the intent to defraud that specific creditor.

35-16-104 SECTION 47. Tennessee Code Annotated, Section 35-16-104, is further amended by adding a new subsection (k) as follows:

(k) In addition to the provisions of subsection (j) to the extent subsection (j) applies to the laws of any foreign country:

(1) For all purposes under this chapter, the effect of the laws of any foreign country shall be the same as provided in § 35-15-107(b)(3) and (b)(4); and

(2) Subsection (a) applies in addition to all other provisions of this chapter.

SECTION 48. The topic headings and tag-lines in this act are for reference purposes only and do not constitute a part of the law enacted hereby. However, the Tennessee Code Commission is requested to include such descriptive headings in any compilation or publication containing the provisions of this act, and to make any conforming adjustments in other provisions of Title 35 which are amended or revised. Furthermore, the Tennessee Code Commission is requested to change the following topic headings and tag-lines as follows:

(1) **35-15-108. Place of administration – Sufficient nexus for a state jurisdiction provision - Place of administration.**

(2) Tennessee Code Annotated, Title 35, Chapter 15, Part 5; replace the current heading - tag line of the part with the following:

Part 5—Creditor's Claims — Mandatory, Support and Discretionary Interests – Effect of Spendthrift Provision

(3) Tennessee Code Annotated, Title 35, Chapter 15, Part 9; replace the current heading - tag line of the part with the following:

Part 9—"Uniform Principal and Income Act" and "Tennessee Uniform Prudent Investor Act of 2002" Incorporated

(4) § 35-15-1005; replace the current heading - tag line of the section with the following:

§ 35-15-1005. Limitation of action against trustee by a beneficiary; Limitation of action against trustee by a trustee, trust advisor or trust protector.

(5) Tennessee Code Annotated, Title 35, Chapter 15, Part 12; make the heading - tag line of the part the following:

Part 12—Trust Protectors and Trust Advisors

35-15-103 SECTION 49. Tennessee Code Annotated, Section 35-15-103(13), is amended by adding the following new subdivision (D):

(D) Notwithstanding any other provisions of this subdivision (13), no ultimate beneficiary or potential ultimate beneficiary shall be a qualified beneficiary.

(i) In determining who is or may be an ultimate beneficiary, all of the following shall be taken into consideration:

(*a*) The terms of the trust naming any ultimate beneficiary or potential ultimate beneficiary and the intention of the settlor relative to any such beneficiary as expressed in such terms; and

(*b*) Any terms or provisions related to the exercise of any power by any person naming any ultimate beneficiary or potential ultimate beneficiary and the intention of the person exercising such power relative to any such beneficiary as expressed in such terms or provisions;

(ii) Determined as provided in subdivision (13)(D)(i), an ultimate beneficiary or potential ultimate beneficiary is any beneficiary who the settlor or power holder did not reasonably anticipate would take any interest upon termination of all or any part of a trust absent all other beneficiaries or members of classes of beneficiaries named in the trust instrument or in the exercise of the power, respectively, predeceasing or otherwise not being in existence at the time at which such trust or part thereof terminates.

(iii) By way of example and not in limitation of this subdivision (13)(D), an ultimate beneficiary is a person or persons often included in a trust instrument or under the exercise of a power to take an interest in a trust at the time all or any part of such trust terminates only in a case where all other named beneficiaries or classes of beneficiaries that have or had an affinity through either familial connection or friendship with any of:

(*a*) The settlor;

(*b*) The person holding any power; or

(*c*) Any prior beneficiary or potential beneficiary of the trust;

are predeceased or are otherwise not in existence at the time all or any part of the trust terminates.

35-15-404 SECTION 50. Tennessee Code Annotated, Section 35-15-404, is amended by deleting the section and by substituting instead the following:

35-15-404. Trust Purposes.

A trust may be created only to the extent its purposes are lawful and possible to achieve. A trust and its terms must be for the benefit of its beneficiaries as the interests of such beneficiaries are defined under the terms of the trust.

35-15-410 SECTION 51. Tennessee Code Annotated, Section 35-15-410, is amended by deleting subsection (a) and by substituting instead the following:

(a) In addition to the methods of termination prescribed by §§ 35-15-411 – 35-15-414, a trust terminates to the extent the trust is revoked or expires pursuant to its terms, no purpose of the trust remains to be achieved, or the purposes of the trust have become unlawful or impossible to achieve.

35-15-1104, 35-15-1105 SECTION 52. Tennessee Code Annotated, Title 35, Chapter 15, Part 11, is amended by adding the following new, appropriately designated sections thereto:

35-15-1104. Alter Ego.

(a) Absent clear and convincing evidence, no settlor of an irrevocable trust may be deemed to be the alter ego of a trustee of such trust.

(b) None of the following factors, by themselves or in combination, may be considered sufficient evidence for a court to conclude that the settlor controls a trustee, or is the alter ego of a trustee of such trust:

(1) Any combination of the factors listed in § 35-15-1105 regarding dominion and control over a trust;

(2) Isolated occurrences where the settlor has signed checks, made disbursements, or executed other documents related to such trust as a trustee, a trust advisor or a trust protector, when in fact the settlor was not such a trustee, trust advisor or trust protector;

(3) Making any requests for distributions on behalf of beneficiaries; or

(4) Making any requests to the trustee to hold, purchase, or sell any trust property.

35-15-1105. Dominion and Control over a Trust.

In the event a person challenges a settlor's or a beneficiary's influence over a trust, none of the following factors, alone or in combination, shall enter into a determination that dominion and control over a trust exists:

(1) The settlor or a beneficiary is serving as a trustee, a trust advisor, a trust protector or other fiduciary as described in § 35-15-508;

(2) The settlor or a beneficiary holds an unrestricted power to remove or replace a trustee, a trust advisor, a trust protector or other fiduciary;

(3) The settlor or a beneficiary is a trust administrator, a general partner of a partnership, a manager of a limited liability company, an officer of a corporation, or holds any other managerial function relative to any type of entity specified in this subdivision, or relative to any other type of entity not so specified, and part or all of the trust property consists of an interest in such entity;

(4) A person related by blood or adoption to the settlor or a beneficiary is appointed as a trustee, a trust advisor, a trust protector or other fiduciary;

(5) The settlor's or a beneficiary's agent, accountant, attorney, financial advisor, or friend is appointed as a trustee, a trust advisor, a trust protector or other fiduciary;

(6) A business associate is appointed as a trustee, a trust advisor, a trust protector or other fiduciary;

(7) A beneficiary holds any power of appointment over any or all of the trust property;

(8) The settlor holds a power to substitute property of equivalent value for property held by the trust, regardless of whether such power is:

(A) Held in a fiduciary or nonfiduciary capacity;

(B) Exercisable with or without the approval of any person in a fiduciary capacity; or

(C) Exercisable with or without the approval of any person having an interest adverse to such settlor;

(9) A trustee, a trust advisor, a trust protector or other fiduciary has the power to loan trust property to the settlor for less than a full and adequate rate of interest or without adequate security;

(10) Any language relative to the power to make any distribution provides for any discretion relative to such distribution;

(11) The trust has only one beneficiary eligible for current distributions; or

(12) The beneficiary is serving as a cotrustee, or as a trust advisor or trust protector under part 12, or as any other fiduciary.

35-16-111 SECTION 53. Tennessee Code Annotated, Section 35-16-111(2), is amended by deleting the language "exercisable by will or other written instrument of the transferor effective only upon the transferor's death" and by substituting instead the language "either exercisable by written instrument of the transferor during the transferor's life or exercisable by will or other written instrument of the transferor effective upon the transferor's death".

SECTION 54. The Tennessee Code Commission is requested to publish in the Tennessee Code Annotated the revisions required to conform to the current state of the law official comments for Chapters 6, 14, 15 and 16 of Title 35 that are filed with the executive secretary of the Tennessee Code Commission by June 15, 2013, unless a later date is provided by said secretary, by duly authorized representatives of the Estate and Probate Section of the Tennessee Bar Association, the Probate Study Committee of the Tennessee Bar Association and the Trust Committee of the Tennessee Bankers Association.

Effective date 7/1/2013 SECTION 55. (a) This act shall take effect July 1, 2013, the public welfare requiring it.

(b) Except as otherwise provided in this act, on such effective date:

(1) This act applies to all trusts created before, on, or after such effective date;

(2) This act applies to all judicial proceedings concerning trusts commenced on or after such effective date;

(3) This act applies to judicial proceedings concerning trusts commenced before such effective date unless the court finds that application of a particular provision of this act would substantially interfere with the effective conduct of the judicial proceedings or prejudice the rights of the parties, in which case the particular provision of this act does not apply and the superseded law applies;

(4) Any rule of construction or presumption provided in this act applies to trust instruments executed before such effective date unless there is a clear and express indication of a contrary intent in the terms of the trust; and

(5) An act done before such effective date is not affected by this act.

(c) If a right is acquired, extinguished, or barred upon the expiration of a prescribed period that has commenced to run under any other statute before such effective date, that statute continues to apply to the right even if it has been repealed or superseded.

PUBLIC CHAPTER NO. 391

PUBLIC CHAPTER NO. 391

SENATE BILL NO. 623

By Norris

Substituted for: House Bill No. 615

By Shipley

AN ACT to amend Tennessee Code Annotated, Title 68, Chapter 57, Part 1, relative to surgical technologists.

BE IT ENACTED BY THE GENERAL ASSEMBLY OF THE STATE OF TENNESSEE:

68-57-101 SECTION 1. Tennessee Code Annotated, Section 68-57-101(a), is amended by deleting subdivision 1 in its entirety and by substituting instead the following new language:

(1) Hold current national certification established by the National Board of Surgical Technology and Surgical Assisting (NBSTSA);

68-57-101 SECTION 2. Tennessee Code Annotated, Section 68-57-101(a), is further amended by deleting subdivision (4) in its entirety and by substituting instead the following new language:

(4) Successfully complete the surgical technologists NBSTSA certifying exam.

68-57-101 SECTION 3. Tennessee Code Annotated, Section 68-57-101, is amended by adding the following language as a new subsection:

(c) Persons qualified to be employed as a surgical technologist pursuant to subsection (a) shall complete fifteen (15) hours of continuing education or contact hours annually to remain qualified for employment and shall submit verification of having completed such continuing education or contact hours requirements to their employers. The submission of current certification by the NBSTSA shall satisfy the requirements of this subsection (c).

68-57-102 SECTION 4. Tennessee Code Annotated, Section 68-57-102, is amended by adding the following language at the end of subsection (a):

Persons qualified to be employed as surgical technologists pursuant to this subsection shall complete fifteen (15) hours of continuing education or contact hours annually to remain qualified for employment and shall submit verification of having completed such continuing education or contact hours requirements to their employers. The submission of current certification by the NBSTSA shall satisfy this requirement.

68-57-101 SECTION 5. Tennessee Code Annotated, Section 68-57-101, is amended by adding the following as a new subsection (c):

(c) The provisions in this section and § 68-57-102 shall not constitute a requirement to be assessed during any inspection under chapter 11, part 2 of this title.

Effective date 7/1/2013 SECTION 6. This act shall take effect July 1, 2013, the public welfare requiring it.

PUBLIC CHAPTER NO. 392

PUBLIC CHAPTER NO. 392

SENATE BILL NO. 620

By Norris, Ketron

Substituted for: House Bill No. 1234

By McManus

AN ACT to amend Tennessee Code Annotated, Title 55, Chapter 4, relative to purchases of special license plates.

BE IT ENACTED BY THE GENERAL ASSEMBLY OF THE STATE OF TENNESSEE:

SECTION 1. The department of revenue is directed to study the establishment of a program to authorize the sale of nonrefundable gift vouchers that may be redeemed by any person toward the fee required by § 55-4-203(d) for cultural and new specialty earmarked motor vehicle registration plates. The department of revenue shall file a written report, including any recommendations or proposed legislation, to the transportation and safety committee of the senate and the transportation committee of the house of representatives by December 31, 2013.

Effective date 5/14/2013

SECTION 2. This act shall take effect upon becoming a law, the public welfare requiring it.

PUBLIC CHAPTER NO. 393

PUBLIC CHAPTER NO. 393

SENATE BILL NO. 592

By Johnson, Gardenhire, Overbey

Substituted for: House Bill No. 210

By Sargent, Swann, Casada, Mark White

AN ACT to amend Tennessee Code Annotated, Title 49, to enact the "High Performing School Districts Flexibility Act".

BE IT ENACTED BY THE GENERAL ASSEMBLY OF THE STATE OF TENNESSEE:

SECTION 1. Tennessee Code Annotated, Title 49, Chapter 2, is amended by adding Sections 2 through 5 as a new, appropriately designated part.

49-2-701 SECTION 2. This part shall be known and may be cited as the "High Performing School Districts Flexibility Act".

49-2-702 SECTION 3. As used in this part, unless the context otherwise requires:

(1) "Department" means the department of education; and

(2)(A) "High performing school district" means any LEA in the state that satisfies a majority of the following criteria, if applicable to that LEA, according to the state report card:

(i) Reaches a graduation rate of ninety percent (90%) or higher;

(ii) Exhibits an average student ACT score of 21 or higher;

(iii) Exhibits a TCAP three-year average composite normal curve equivalent (NCE) score of 55 or higher;

(iv) Exhibits a TVAAS three-year average composite normal curve equivalent (NCE) gain of 1.75 or higher; or

(v) Meets or exceeds achievement and gap closure annual measurable objectives and receives an "exemplary" or similar status from the department.

(B) Only those criteria in the list in subdivision (2)(A) that apply to a particular LEA and are reported on the state report card shall be considered when calculating whether an LEA is eligible to be declared a high performing school district under this part. If a criterion does not apply to a particular LEA, it shall be removed from consideration for that LEA and a majority of the remaining criteria must be met. Should any of the above criteria cease being reported on the state report card, the department shall designate a replacement measure for purposes of this part. An LEA scoring in the top fifteen percent (15%) of all LEAs in the state under the replacement measure shall meet that criterion.

49-2-703 SECTION 4. Any LEA meeting a majority of the applicable criteria in Section 3 may, by action of its local board of education, declare itself to be a high performing school district. Such designation shall be in effect beginning July 1 following the local board action. The designation shall last for three (3) years, at which time the LEA shall be eligible to declare itself a high performing school district under this part again if a majority of the criteria are met.

49-2-704 SECTION 5. (a) A high performing school district may, during any year in which the designation is in effect, without first seeking or obtaining approval from any other state or local governmental agency or unit:

(1) Appropriate additional funds as needed from the fund balance of self-sustaining or self-sufficient funds, including, but not limited to, the central cafeteria fund and the extended school program fund;

(2) Utilize a teacher evaluation system which varies from the evaluation system established by the department as though a flexibility waiver had been applied for and granted to the district. Notwithstanding the foregoing, the alternative teacher evaluation system used shall comply with all rules of the state board. The high performing school district shall submit the evaluation system it plans to use to the department; and

(3) Add educational days to that district's school calendar, so long as the minimum number of school days required by law is met.

(b) A high performing school district, during any year in which the designation is in effect, may apply to the commissioner of education for a waiver of any state board rule, regulation or statute that inhibits or hinders the district's ability to meet its goals or comply with its mission statement. At the discretion of the commissioner the waiver may be granted, but the commissioner shall not grant a waiver where waivers are otherwise prohibited in this title 49, and shall not waive regulatory or statutory requirements related to:

(1) Federal and state civil rights;

(2) Federal, state, and local health and safety;

(3) Federal and state public records;

(4) Immunizations;

(5) Possession of weapons on school grounds;

(6) Background checks and fingerprinting of personnel;

(7) Federal and state special education services;

(8) Student due process;

(9) Parental rights;

(10) Federal and state student assessment and accountability;

(11) Open meetings; and

(12) At least the same equivalent time of instruction as required in regular public schools.

SECTION 6. If any provision of this act or the application thereof to any person or circumstance is held invalid, such invalidity shall not affect other provisions or applications of the act which can be given effect without the invalid provision or application, and to that end the provisions of this act are declared to be severable.

Effective date 5/6/2013

SECTION 7. This act shall take effect upon becoming law, the public welfare requiring it.

PUBLIC CHAPTER NO. 394

PUBLIC CHAPTER NO. 394

SENATE BILL NO. 590

By Johnson

Substituted for: House Bill No. 70

By Sargent

AN ACT to amend Tennessee Code Annotated, Section 57-3-203, relative to certain requirements for a wholesaler's license for the sale of alcoholic beverages.

BE IT ENACTED BY THE GENERAL ASSEMBLY OF THE STATE OF TENNESSEE:

57-3-203 SECTION 1. Tennessee Code Annotated, Section 57-3-203(i), is amended by designating the existing language as subdivision (i)(1) and by adding the following language as subdivision (i)(2):

(i)(2) Notwithstanding the requirement imposed in subdivision (i)(1), a wholesale liquor license, limited to the sale and distribution of wine only, not to exceed six thousand (6,000) cases of wine per year, may be issued to an entity that is located in any municipality which:

(A) Has authorized the sale of alcoholic beverages for consumption on the premises pursuant to § 57-4-103;

(B) Has a bond rating of AAA issued by a nationally recognized bond rating agency; and

(C) Is located within a county which has a bond rating of AAA issued by a nationally recognized bond rating agency.

Effective date 5/14/2013 SECTION 2. This act shall take effect upon becoming a law, the public welfare requiring it.

PUBLIC CHAPTER NO. 395

PUBLIC CHAPTER NO. 395

SENATE BILL NO. 547

By Bell

Substituted for: House Bill No. 334

By Matlock

AN ACT to amend Tennessee Code Annotated, Title 2 and Title 49, relative to use of school property.

BE IT ENACTED BY THE GENERAL ASSEMBLY OF THE STATE OF TENNESSEE:

49-6-2009 SECTION 1. Tennessee Code Annotated, Title 49, Chapter 6, Part 20, is amended by adding the following language as a new, appropriately designated section:

49-6-20__. No sign or message in support of or opposition to a referendum or initiative placed before the voters shall be displayed on a sign owned by an LEA or its schools or attached to LEA-owned buildings. No audio or video messages in support of or opposition to a referendum or initiative shall be dispersed using LEA or school telephonic or electronic equipment or accounts.

Effective date 7/1/2013 SECTION 2. This act shall take effect July 1, 2013, the public welfare requiring it.

PUBLIC CHAPTER NO. 396

PUBLIC CHAPTER NO. 396

SENATE BILL NO. 529

By McNally, Burks, Yager

Substituted for: House Bill No. 49

By Ramsey, Shepard, Sexton, Ryan Williams

AN ACT to amend Tennessee Code Annotated, Title 63, relative to the healing arts.

BE IT ENACTED BY THE GENERAL ASSEMBLY OF THE STATE OF TENNESSEE:

63-7-123 SECTION 1. Tennessee Code Annotated, Section 63-7-123(b)(2), is amended by deleting the subdivision and substituting instead the following:

(2)(A) The nurse practitioner who holds a certificate of fitness shall be authorized to prescribe and/or issue controlled substances listed in Schedules II, III, IV and V of title 39, chapter 17, part 4 upon joint adoption of physician supervisory rules concerning controlled substances pursuant to subsection (d).

(B) Notwithstanding subdivision (b)(2)(A), a nurse practitioner shall not prescribe Schedules II, III and IV controlled substances unless such prescription is specifically authorized by the formulary or expressly approved after consultation with the supervising physician before the initial issuance of the prescription or dispensing of the medication.

(C) A nurse practitioner who had been issued a certificate of fitness may only prescribe or issue a Schedule II or III opioid listed on the formulary for a maximum of a non-refillable, thirty-day course of treatment unless specifically approved after consultation with the supervising physician before the initial issuance of the prescription or dispensing of the medication. This subdivision (C) shall not apply to prescriptions issued in a hospital, a nursing home licensed under title 68, or inpatient facilities licensed under title 33.

63-19-107 SECTION 2. Tennessee Code Annotated, Section 63-19-107(2)(B), is amended by deleting the subdivision and by substituting instead the following:

(B)(i) A physician assistant to whom the authority to prescribe legend drugs and controlled substances has been delegated by the supervising physician shall file a notice with the committee containing the name of the physician assistant, the name of the licensed physician having supervision, control and responsibility for prescriptive services rendered by the physician assistant and a copy of the formulary describing the categories of legend drugs and controlled substances to be prescribed and/or issued, by the physician assistant. The physician assistant shall be responsible for updating this information;

(ii) Notwithstanding any other rule or law, a physician assistant shall not prescribe Schedules II, III and IV controlled substances unless such prescription is specifically authorized by the formulary or expressly approved after consultation with the supervising physician before the initial issuance of the prescription or dispensing of the medication;

(iii) Any physician assistant to whom the authority to prescribe controlled drugs has been delegated by the supervising physician may only prescribe or issue a Schedule II or III opioid listed on the formulary for a maximum of a non-refillable, thirty-day course of treatment, unless specifically approved after consultation with the supervising physician before the initial issuance of the prescription or dispensing of the medication. This subdivision (iii) shall not apply to prescriptions issued in a hospital, a nursing home licensed under title 68, or inpatient facilities licensed under title 33.

68-1-128 SECTION 3. Tennessee Code Annotated, Title 63, is amended by adding the following as a new section to be appropriately designated:

(a) No later than July 31, 2013, and at least annually thereafter but more often at the discretion of the commissioner, the department of health shall:

(1) Identify the top fifty (50) prescribers who have unique DEA numbers of controlled substances in the previous calendar year, or if implemented more frequently for the relevant time period as determined by the department, from the data available in the controlled substances database established pursuant to title 53, chapter 10, part 3; and

(2) Send a letter through registered mail to each prescriber identified in subdivision (1), and to the physician supervisor as found on the provider's profile established in title 63, chapter 51 of each advanced practice nurse and each physician assistant identified in subdivision (1) that notifies the prescribers and, where appropriate, the supervising physician that the prescriber has been identified pursuant to subdivision (1) and includes the following information:

(A) The significant controlled substances prescribed by the prescriber;

(B) The number of patients prescribed these controlled substances by the prescriber;

(C) The total milligrams in morphine equivalents of controlled substances prescribed during the relevant period of time; and

(D) Any other relevant information sought by the department.

(3) If there is an active investigation against the prescriber or, where appropriate the supervising physician, on the list of prescribers identified in (a)(1) above, the department is authorized to withhold any communication required under this act until such time as charges are brought or the investigation is closed.

(b)(1)(A) At the discretion of the department, each prescriber and each supervising physician of an advanced practice nurse and physician assistant who appear on the top fifty (50) prescribers of controlled substances in the relevant period of time shall submit to the department within fifteen (15) business days through registered mail or electronic mail an explanation justifying the amounts of controlled substances prescribed in the relevant period of time by the prescriber demonstrating that these amounts were medically necessary for the patients treated and that, for advanced practice nurses and physician assistants, the supervising physician had reviewed and approved the prescribing amounts. The department shall consider the prescriber's specialty and the patients' ages to make a determination as to whether the explanation of the prescriber and, where appropriate the supervising physician, for the prescribing habits of the prescriber of controlled substances is justifiable.

(B) The department is authorized to develop a model form to assist the prescriber and where appropriate the supervising physician in completing the explanation required by this subsection (b).

(C) The department is authorized to contract with an expert reviewer to determine if the explanation is acceptable. Should charges ultimately be filed against the prescriber or, where appropriate the supervising physician, any report of the expert reviewer shall be discoverable by the licensee.

(2) If the department is not satisfied with any explanation by the prescriber or where appropriate a supervising physician, it shall communicate via registered mail such concerns to the prescriber and, if appropriate, the supervising physician. The prescriber and, if appropriate, the supervising physician shall have fifteen (15) business days to attempt to rectify the department's stated concerns.

(3) If the department remains unsatisfied after receiving a justification pursuant to subdivision (2), the department may submit its concerns to the member of the controlled substance database committee who represents the board which has licensed the individual. This member shall have access to all of the documents pertaining to the concerns of the department and the expert reviewer. If that member also believes that the explanations which have been provided are not sufficient to justify the prescribing pattern of the prescriber, the concerns may be forwarded to the department's office of investigations. Investigations are conducted by the entity responsible for licensure of that prescriber.

(c) All data, reports and correspondence under this section shall be confidential and shall not be considered to be a public record for purposes of title 10, chapter 7.

PUBLIC CHAPTER NO. 396 (cont'd)

(d) All correspondence and reports can be used by the department's office of investigations and/or the respective entity responsible for licensure to develop a disciplinary case against the prescriber and, where appropriate, the supervising physician of an advanced practice nurse or physician assistant.

(e) The failure of a prescriber or, where appropriate, a supervising physician to respond to the department's request for information in a timely fashion may be a cause for disciplinary action by the prescriber's, or where appropriate the supervising physician's, licensing board and may include a penalty of up to one thousand dollars ($1,000) per day for failure to respond or failure to respond in a timely manner.

(f) All correspondence shall be maintained for five (5) years and kept organized by prescriber so that information on a prescriber who appears on multiple lists compiled pursuant to subsection (a) may be aggregated.

SECTION 4. If any provision of this act or the application thereof to any person or circumstance is held invalid, such invalidity shall not affect other provisions or applications of the act which can be given effect without the invalid provision or application, and to that end the provisions of this act are declared to be severable.

Effective date 7/1/2013

SECTION 5. This act shall take effect July 1, 2013, the public welfare requiring it.

PUBLIC CHAPTER NO. 397

PUBLIC CHAPTER NO. 397

SENATE BILL NO. 496

By Gresham, Ford

Substituted for: House Bill No. 243

By John Deberry, Pitts, Hardaway

AN ACT to amend Tennessee Code Annotated, Title 37, Chapter 1 and Title 49, Chapter 6, relative to the education of children in foster care.

BE IT ENACTED BY THE GENERAL ASSEMBLY OF THE STATE OF TENNESSEE:

37-1-130 SECTION 1. Tennessee Code Annotated, Section 37-1-130(a)(2)(B)(i), is amended by deleting the existing subsection and by substituting instead the following:

(i) Any child placed in the custody of the department of children's services shall become a resident of the county in which such child is placed by the department. The board of education of each local school system shall assign the student to a public school pursuant to § 49-6-3102.

49-6-902 SECTION 2. Tennessee Code Annotated, Section 49-6-902, is amended by adding the following language as subsection (c):

(c) Upon written request from the department of children's services, LEAs shall provide the department of children's services all school records for a child in custody of the department of children's services or receiving foster care services. These records may include, but are not limited to, a copy of the child's report card, notice of school attendance, names of teachers, class schedules, standardized test scores, and any other records customarily available to parents. LEAs shall not charge the department of children's services any cost for the records, even in instances where a debt or restitution is owed to the school by the student. The release of the records to the department of children's services shall not waive or reduce any debt or restitution owed to the school. The student's records shall be made available to the department of children's services no later than five (5) business days from the date the LEA received the records request from the department.

49-6-3102 SECTION 3. Tennessee Code Annotated, Section 49-6-3102(a)(1) and (2), are amended by deleting the word "child", wherever it appears, and by substituting instead the word "student".

49-6-3102 SECTION 4. Tennessee Code Annotated, Section 49-6-3102, is amended by adding the following as a new, appropriately designated subsection (c) and by numbering subsequent subsections accordingly:

(c) Pursuant to 42 U.S.C. § 675, any student placed in the custody of the department of children's services shall remain enrolled in the same public school the student attended prior to entering custody. The department of children's services shall decide if the student's school is in the student's best interest. If the department of children's services determines that enrollment in the public school, which the student attended prior to entering care, is not in the student's best interest, the student shall be enrolled in the local school system where the student is placed or where the parent resides.

49-6-3201 SECTION 5. Tennessee Code Annotated, Section 49-6-3201(a), is amended by deleting the existing subsection in its entirety and by substituting instead the following:

(a) Both parents, if living, or the parent, guardian, legal custodian, guardian ad litem or attorney of any student assigned pursuant to part 31 of this chapter who is dissatisfied with the assignment of the student may, within ten (10) days of the order making the assignment, make written application to the board for a hearing before the board as to the reasonableness of the assignment and asking for a transfer to another school.

49-6-3201 SECTION 6. Tennessee Code Annotated, Section 49-6-3201(b) and (d), are amended by deleting the word "child", wherever it appears, and by substituting instead the word "student".

Effective date 7/1/2013 SECTION 7. This act shall take effect on July 1, 2013, the public welfare requiring it.

PUBLIC CHAPTER NO. 398

PUBLIC CHAPTER NO. 398

SENATE BILL NO. 459

By Yager, Massey, Henry, Burks, Kelsey, Overbey

Substituted for: House Bill No. 277

By Dunn, Lois DeBerry, Ryan Williams, McDaniel, Weaver, Jones, Calfee, Sexton, Moody, Kane, McCormick, Hardaway, Holt, Mark White, Powers, Butt

AN ACT to amend Tennessee Code Annotated, Title 33; Title 36 and Title 37, relative to Neonatal Abstinence Syndrome.

BE IT ENACTED BY THE GENERAL ASSEMBLY OF THE STATE OF TENNESSEE:

WHEREAS, the Tennessee General Assembly declares that the growing misuse of prescription drugs by pregnant women leads too often to drug-affected infants with neonatal abstinence syndrome, that adversely affects the health and welfare of the newborn and places a heavy financial burden on Tennessee's taxpayers and those who pay for health care, so it is the policy of this state to take effective action that will minimize these costs; and

WHEREAS, special attention must be focused on preventive programs and services directed at pregnant women at risk of becoming prescription drug abusers and misusers as well as on pregnant women who use these substances or who are at risk of substance use or abuse; now, therefore,

BE IT ENACTED BY THE GENERAL ASSEMBLY OF THE STATE OF TENNESSEE:

SECTION 1. This act shall be known as the "Safe Harbor Act of 2013".

33-10-104 SECTION 2. Tennessee Code Annotated, Section 33-10-104, is amended by adding the following new subsection:

(f)(1) Notwithstanding subsection (e), a pregnant woman referred for drug abuse or drug dependence treatment at any treatment resource that receives public funding shall be a priority user of available treatment. All records and reports regarding such pregnant woman shall be kept confidential. The department of mental health and substance abuse services shall ensure that family-oriented drug abuse or drug dependence treatment is available, as appropriations allow. A treatment resource that receives public funds shall not refuse to treat a person solely because the person is pregnant as long as appropriate services are offered by the treatment resource.

(2) If during prenatal care, the attending obstetrical provider determines no later than the end of the twentieth week of pregnancy that the patient has used prescription drugs which may place the fetus in jeopardy, and drug abuse or drug dependence treatment is indicated, the provider shall encourage counseling, drug abuse or drug dependence treatment and other assistance to the patient.

(A) If the patient initiates drug abuse or drug dependence treatment based upon a clinical assessment prior to her next regularly scheduled prenatal visit and maintains compliance with both drug abuse or drug dependence treatment based on a clinical assessment as well as prenatal care throughout the remaining term of the pregnancy, then the department of children's services shall not file any petition to terminate the mother's parental rights or otherwise seek protection of the newborn solely because of the patient's use of prescription drugs for non-medical purposes during the term of her pregnancy.

(B) Notwithstanding subdivision (f)(2)(A), nothing shall prevent the department of children's services from filing any petition to terminate the mother's parental rights or seek protection of the newborn should the department determine that the newborn's mother, or any other adult caring for the newborn, is unfit to properly care for such child.

(3) Any physician or other health care provider who does not recognize that the pregnant woman has used prescription drugs that place the fetus in jeopardy after a reasonable inquiry, or who complies with the provisions of this subsection, or any physician or facility that initiates substance abuse treatment consistent with

community standards of care pursuant to this subsection, shall be presumed to be acting in good faith and shall have immunity from any civil liability that might otherwise result by reason of such actions.

(4) The commissioner of mental health and substance abuse services is authorized to promulgate emergency rules and regulations to effectuate the purposes of this act. All such rules and regulations shall be promulgated in accordance with Tennessee Code Annotated, title 4, chapter 5.

Effective date 5/14/2013

SECTION 3. This act shall take effect on becoming law, the public welfare requiring it.

PUBLIC CHAPTER NO. 399

PUBLIC CHAPTER NO. 399

SENATE BILL NO. 408

By Beavers

Substituted for: House Bill No. 251

By Jernigan, Lynn, Pody

AN ACT relative to the boundary line between the counties of Davidson and Wilson.

BE IT ENACTED BY THE GENERAL ASSEMBLY OF THE STATE OF TENNESSEE:

SECTION 1. The boundary line between Davidson County and Wilson County shall be revised so as to include within Wilson County all of the territory described as follows:

> Beginning at a point on the current Davidson County and Wilson County line, as appears on the recorded subdivision plat of Hickory Hills, Phase 3, Section C, said point also being on the northerly line of Lot 244; thence (clockwise) with the county line, as appears on said subdivision plat, S 23°00' E, more or less, a distance of 935', more or less, to a point on the southern boundary of said subdivision, said point being on the northerly line of property now or formerly owned by Eva Richardson, Book 7213, Page 133, R.O.D.C.; thence with said line N 81°02'51" W a distance of 180', more or less, to a point; thence N 82°25'23" W along the line of property now or formerly owned by H.H. Richardson, et al., Book 4159, Page 427, R.O.D.C., a distance of 296.53' to a point; thence N 5°28'09" E a distance of 87.25' to a point; thence N 6°04'33" E a distance of 206.31' to a point; thence N 6°38'38" E a distance of 379.95' to a point; thence N 5°40'05" E a distance of 130.14' to a point, said point also being the northwest corner of aforementioned Lot 244; thence, with the north line of said lot, N 87°23'58" E a distance of 28', more or less, to the point of beginning. Such area consisting of approximately 4.65 acres.

SECTION 2. The boundary line between Davidson County and Wilson County shall be further revised so as to include within Wilson County all of the territory described as follows:

> Beginning at a point on the current Davidson County and Wilson County line north of Stewarts Ferry Pike being marked by United States Army Corps of Engineers monument number 518-1; thence (counterclockwise) in a northwesterly direction 655.98' to a point being marked by United States Army Corps of Engineers monument number 518-2; thence in a southeasterly direction 471.94' to a point being marked by United States Army Corps of Engineers monument number 518-3; thence in a southwesterly direction 1132.13' to a point being marked by United States Army Corps of Engineers monument number 518-4; thence in a northwesterly direction 457.47' to a point being marked by United States Army Corps of Engineers monument number 518-5; thence in a southeasterly direction 1,338.13' to a point being marked by United States Army Corps of Engineers monument number 518-6; thence in a southwesterly direction 856.26' to a point being marked by United States Army Corps of Engineers monument number 518-7; thence continuing in a southwesterly direction 612.14' to a point being marked by United States Army Corps of Engineers monument number 518-8; thence in a southeasterly direction 1046.24' to a point being marked by United States Army Corps of Engineers monument number 611-1; thence continuing in a southeasterly direction 299.99' to a point being marked by United States Army Corps of Engineers monument number 611-2; thence in a northeasterly direction 730.33' to a point being marked by United States Army Corps of Engineers monument number 612-A and further being the current Davidson County and Wilson County line; thence following the current county line to the point of beginning.

Effective date 1/1/2014

SECTION 3. This act shall take effect January 1, 2014, the public welfare requiring it.

PUBLIC CHAPTER NO. 400

PUBLIC CHAPTER NO. 400

SENATE BILL NO. 405

By Beavers

Substituted for: House Bill No. 278

By Womick

AN ACT to amend Tennessee Code Annotated, Title 67, Chapter 1, Part 17, relative to the confidentiality of tax returns and tax information.

BE IT ENACTED BY THE GENERAL ASSEMBLY OF THE STATE OF TENNESSEE:

67-1-1702 SECTION 1. Tennessee Code Annotated, Section 67-1-1702(a), is amended by deleting the following language:

> no officer or employee of the department and no other person, or officer or employee of the state

and by substituting instead the following language:

> no officer or employee of the department or of any office of a district attorney general or any state or local law enforcement agency, and no other person, or officer or employee of the state

67-1-1709 SECTION 2. Tennessee Code Annotated, Section 67-1-1709(a), is amended by inserting the language "or any other officer or employee described in § 67-1-1702(a)" between the language "any officer or employee of the state" and the language ", the officer or employee".

Effective date 5/6/2013 SECTION 3. This act shall take effect upon becoming a law, the public welfare requiring it.

PUBLIC CHAPTER NO. 401

PUBLIC CHAPTER NO. 401

SENATE BILL NO. 399

By Southerland, Ford

Substituted for: House Bill No. 1027

By Dean, Sexton

AN ACT to amend Tennessee Code Annotated, Title 13; Title 29 and Title 54, relative to outdoor advertising.

BE IT ENACTED BY THE GENERAL ASSEMBLY OF THE STATE OF TENNESSEE:

54-21-122 SECTION 1. Tennessee Code Annotated, Section 54-21-122, is amended by adding the following language as a new subsection:

(h)(1) All changeable message signs installed on or after July 1, 2014, shall come equipped with a light sensing device that automatically adjusts the brightness in direct correlation with ambient light conditions.

(2) The brightness of light emitted from a changeable message sign shall not exceed 0.3 foot candles over ambient light levels measured at a distance of one hundred fifty feet (150') for those sign faces less than or equal to three hundred square feet (300 sq. ft.), measured at a distance of two hundred feet (200') for those sign faces greater than three hundred square feet (300 sq. ft.) but less than or equal to three hundred eighty-five square feet (385 sq. ft.), measured at a distance of two hundred fifty feet (250') for those sign faces greater than three hundred eighty-five square feet (385 sq. ft.) and less than or equal to six hundred eighty square feet (680 sq. ft.), measured at a distance of three hundred fifty feet (350') for those sign faces greater than six hundred eighty square feet (680 sq. ft.), or subject to the measuring criteria in the applicable table set forth in subdivision (h)(4).

(3) Any measurements required pursuant to this subsection shall be taken from a point within the highway right-of-way at a safe distance from the lane of the main traveled way and as close to perpendicular to the face of the changeable message sign as practical. If perpendicular measurement is not practical, valid measurements may be taken at an angle up to forty-five degrees (45 degrees) from the center point of the sign face.

(4) In the event it is found not to be practical to measure a changeable message sign at the distances prescribed in subdivision (h)(2) a measurer may opt to measure the sign at any of the alternative measuring distances described in the applicable table set forth in this subdivision (h)(4). In the event the sign measurer chooses to measure the sign using an alternative measuring distance, the prescribed foot candle level above ambient light shall not exceed the prescribed level, to be determined based on the alternative measuring distances set forth in the following tables (A), (B), (C), and (D), as applicable:

(A) For changeable message signs less than or equal to 300 square feet:

Alternative Measuring Distance:	Prescribed Foot Candle Level:
100	0.68
125	0.43
150	0.3
200	0.17
250	0.11
275	0.09
300	0.08
325	0.06
350	0.06
400	0.04

(B) For changeable message signs greater than 300 square feet but less than or equal to 385 square feet:

Alternative Measuring Distance:	Prescribed Foot Candle Level:
100	1.2
125	0.77
150	0.53
200	0.3
250	0.19
275	0.16
300	0.13
325	0.11
350	0.1
400	0.08

(C) For changeable message signs greater than 385 square feet but less than or equal to 680 square feet:

Alternative Measuring Distance:	Prescribed Foot Candle Level:
100	1.88
125	1.2
150	0.83
200	0.47
250	0.3
275	0.25
300	0.21
325	0.18
350	0.15
400	0.12

(D) For changeable Message Sign greater than 680 square feet:

Alternative Measuring Distance:	Prescribed Foot Candle Level:
100	3.675
125	2.35
150	1.63
200	0.92
250	0.59
275	0.49
300	0.41
325	0.35
350	0.3
400	0.23
425	0.2
450	0.18
500	0.15

(5) This subsection shall apply to all changeable message signs located in this state operated pursuant to a permit issued by the commissioner.

Effective date 7/1/2014

SECTION 2. This act shall take effect July 1, 2014, the public welfare requiring it.

PUBLIC CHAPTER NO. 402

PUBLIC CHAPTER NO. 402

SENATE BILL NO. 176

By Norris, Tracy, Bowling, Haile, Stevens

Substituted for: House Bill No. 170

By McCormick, Butt, Littleton

AN ACT to amend Tennessee Code Annotated, Title 71, Chapters 1, 3 and 5, relative to the department of human services.

BE IT ENACTED BY THE GENERAL ASSEMBLY OF THE STATE OF TENNESSEE:

71-1-105 SECTION 1. Tennessee Code Annotated, Section 71-1-105(a), is amended by adding the following language as a new, appropriately designated subdivision:

(16) Conduct investigations, which shall include, but not be limited to, investigation into the existence of:

(A) Trafficking in, or fraud involving, the food assistance program administered by the department pursuant to title 71, chapter 5, part 3;

(B) Fraud, abuse, theft, misappropriation, or misuse of property, funds, or services by any person or entity in any program administered by the department; and

(C) Misconduct by any employee, contractor, or agent of the department concerning or related to the operation of any department program or any laws, regulations or policies governing the department's operations.

71-5-314 SECTION 2. Tennessee Code Annotated, Section 71-5-314, is amended by adding the following language as a new, appropriately designated subsection:

(i)(1) In addition to any criminal provisions provided by this section, the department is authorized to address intentional program violations or overpayments in the food assistance program through any administrative means, including, but not limited to, settlement of such violations or overpayments by a written agreement with recipients or by the provision of administrative hearings pursuant to the Uniform Administrative Procedures Act in title 4, chapter 5, part 3 and federal regulations.

(2) The department is authorized to initiate legal action to collect all overpayments and all payments made due to intentional program violations or fraud in the food assistance program.

71-3-110 SECTION 3. Tennessee Code Annotated, Section 71-3-110, is amended by deleting the section in its entirety and substituting instead the following language:

The commissioner of human services has the authority to establish a system for distribution of any benefits provided by this part, or under the continued provisions of federal law and regulations as provided under § 71-3-108, by means of electronic benefits transfer system and to contract with public or private entities to provide any services necessary to carry out such provision as the commissioner shall determine is appropriate.

SECTION 4. If any provision of this act or the application thereof to any person or circumstance is held invalid, such invalidity shall not affect other provisions or applications of the act which can be given effect without the invalid provision or application, and to that end the provisions of this act are declared to be severable.

Effective date 5/14/2013 SECTION 5. This act shall take effect upon becoming a law, the public welfare requiring it.

PUBLIC CHAPTER NO. 403

PUBLIC CHAPTER NO. 403

SENATE BILL NO. 170

By Norris, Ketron

Substituted for: House Bill No. 164

By McCormick, McDaniel, Hardaway

AN ACT to amend Tennessee Code Annotated, Title 4, Chapter 56; Title 12, Chapter 3 and Title 12, Chapter 4, relative to state procurement.

BE IT ENACTED BY THE GENERAL ASSEMBLY OF THE STATE OF TENNESSEE:

4-56-102 SECTION 1. Tennessee Code Annotated, Section 4-56-102, is amended by deleting the section in its entirety and by substituting instead the following:

4-56-102.

(a)(1) There is created a procurement commission, which shall consist of the commissioners of general services and finance and administration, and the comptroller of the treasury. The chief procurement officer shall serve as a non-voting member.

(2) The commission shall adopt a procedure governing its proceedings, and the chief procurement officer shall keep a permanent and accurate record of all of its proceedings.

(3) All departments and agencies shall submit existing rules related to procurement to the commission for the commission's review, comment, and recommendations for any changes to such rules. Prior to forwarding draft rules related to procurement to the secretary of state, all departments shall submit such draft rules to the commission for the commission's review and comment together with any recommendations for changes to such draft rules.

(4) The attorney general and reporter shall serve as legal counsel to the commission in accordance with the requirements of § 8-6-301.

(b)(1) The commission has the power and authority, except as otherwise provided in this chapter, to review, comment, and approve draft rules and regulations, policies, standards, and procedures to be followed consistent with this chapter and title 12, chapters 3 and 4, and to make recommendations for changes thereto, governing the procurement of goods and services, contracting, agency contract and grant management, training and professional development, and the disposal of goods and services by the state.

(2) The commission is authorized to promulgate necessary rules and regulations in accordance with the Uniform Administrative Procedures Act, compiled in chapter 5 of this title, as well as policies and procedures to implement this chapter.

(3) The commission shall not exercise authority over the award or administration of any particular contract or grant.

4-56-103 SECTION 2. Tennessee Code Annotated, Section 4-56-103, is amended by deleting the section in its entirety and by substituting instead the following:

4-56-103.

(a) Creation of Committee.

(1) There is created a state protest committee, which shall consist of the commissioners of general services and finance and administration, and the treasurer.

(2) The committee shall adopt procedures governing its operations, and the chief procurement officer shall keep a permanent and accurate record of all of its proceedings.

(3) If a member is not available to hear a scheduled protest, the member is authorized to appoint a designee to hear the scheduled protest on the member's behalf.

(b) Appeals to Committee.

(1) The committee is authorized to act on any appeal of the chief procurement officer's decision of a protest.

(2) Any committee member whose department is the requestor of a procurement or the resulting contract may not hear the protest.

(3) The chief procurement officer shall provide the minutes of the protest proceedings to each committee member and to the comptroller of the treasury and shall post the final determination within fifteen (15) business days to the single public procurement website.

4-56-104 SECTION 3. Tennessee Code Annotated, Section 4-56-104, is amended by deleting the section in its entirety and by substituting instead the following:

4-56-104.

(a) There is created a procurement office headed by the chief procurement officer in such department as the governor shall designate, after consulting with the comptroller of the treasury, which shall take effect as provided in § 4-56-104(b).

(b) Effective July 1, 2011, the governor shall appoint the chief procurement officer, who shall be a person:

(1) Qualified by training and relevant and recent experience in large scale public procurement of goods and services, establishment of contracts, contract oversight, providing training and contract administration, and demonstrated executive and organizational ability to perform the duties of this office; and

(2) Qualified by training or relevant and recent experience in administering programs to encourage and enhance economic opportunities for small businesses and minority-owned businesses.

(c) The chief procurement officer shall be a full-time public official of the state as an executive service employee appointed by the governor to serve at the pleasure of the governor.

(d)(1) Necessary personnel in the department of general services involved in the procurement of goods and necessary personnel in the department of finance and administration involved in the procurement of services, as required by the procurement officer, shall be transferred to the procurement office together with the funding for the compensation and benefits for such personnel.

(2) The chief procurement officer is authorized to employ such additional personnel as are necessary to carry out the purposes of this chapter, upon the approval of the governor.

(3) The compensation of employees of the procurement office shall be fixed by the governor.

(e)(1) All contracts and contract rights and responsibilities, and renewals for such contracts, in existence with the department of general services and the department of finance and administration with respect to the duties transferred by this section shall be preserved and transferred to the procurement office.

(2) Any bidding procedure or negotiations concerning any such procedure which is in the process but not complete shall continue under the purview of the procurement officer.

(3) All documents, books, records, papers or other writings in the possession of the department of general services and the department of finance and administration with respect to the duties transferred by this

section shall be transferred to and remain in the custody of the procurement office.

(4) Any rules, regulations, orders, decisions and policies formerly issued or promulgated by the departments of finance and administration or general services whose functions have been transferred under this section to the procurement office shall remain in full force and effect and shall hereafter be administered and enforced by the procurement officer. The commission shall have the authority, consistent with the statutes and regulations pertaining to the programs and functions transferred herein, to modify or rescind orders, rules and regulations, decisions or policies formerly issued and to adopt, issue or promulgate new orders, rules and regulations, decisions or policies as may be necessary for the administration of the programs or functions herein transferred.

(f) Subject to this chapter and other procurement laws under the jurisdiction of the chief procurement office, the chief procurement officer may adopt operational procedures governing the internal functions of the procurement office.

4-56-105 SECTION 4. Tennessee Code Annotated, Section 4-56-105, is amended by deleting the section in its entirety and by substituting instead the following:

4-56-105.

The chief procurement officer has the power and duty to:

(1) Effective January 1, 2012, establish a single, public procurement website that includes how to do business with the state; registration for bidders; posting of all procurements in process and related status to award; and a database of established contracts by state agencies, departments and institutions;

(2) Effective April 1, 2012, develop a transition plan that provides for the implementation by date and action to consolidate the procurement and contracting for goods, services and grants; to include employee job classifications for the state procurement office and agency procurement functions that include development and training plans and other plans as prescribed and approved by the commission;

(3) Develop and propose to the general assembly any changes required to consolidate statutes;

(4) Develop proposed rules and regulations, policies, standards and procedures consistent with this chapter and title 12, chapters 3 and 4 and approved by the commission that establish:

(A) A central procurement process with opportunities for strategic sourcing;

(B) A central contract management process;

(C) A central grant management process that will assist agencies in identifying grant opportunities and provide for a central database of information regarding grant recipients and sub-recipients for monitoring purposes;

(D) A central performance and quality assurance process that assists agencies in identifying risk areas and recommending contract performance and management best practices; and

(E) A central bidder relations management process to include a central bidder registration database and program for conducting business with the state, which provides bidders and vendors with training and assistance with technical matters, procurement notification, and contract and grant awards.

(5) Develop and conduct training to foster professional development and certification for the state procurement office and agency procurement staff to promote procurement excellence, either independently or in cooperation with other state governments, municipalities or other units of local government, or other persons. In conducting this training, the chief procurement officer shall:

(A) Prescribe professional and accountability standards and guidelines for procurement, contract, grant, performance and quality assurance management personnel;

(B) Conduct or participate in procurement education and training programs;

(C) Conduct research into existing and new methods of procurement; and

(D) Establish and maintain an electronic library of education and training courses and technical reference resources;

(6) Delegate authority to designees or to any department, agency, or official, subject to additional approvals including approval by the comptroller of the treasury and such other requirements as prescribed in rules, regulations, standards, policies and procedures approved by the commission;

(7) Establish and maintain agenda and minutes of the commission and the council and all actions of both, which shall be open to public inspection during regular office hours and on the single public procurement website in accordance with bylaws established by the council and commission. The chief procurement officer shall chair the council. Except as otherwise indicated, all requirements of this section shall be ready for implementation by the chief procurement officer by April 1, 2012;

(8) Prescribe the manner in which goods and services shall be purchased, delivered, stored and distributed;

(9) Require periodic reports by departments, institutions and agencies of state government of stocks of supplies, materials, and equipment on hand and prescribe the form of such reports;

(10) Prescribe the dates for making requisitions and estimates, the periods for which they are to be made and the manner of authentication;

(11) Prescribe the manner of inspecting all deliveries of supplies, materials, and equipment and of making chemical and physical tests of samples submitted with solicitation responses, and sample deliveries to determine whether deliveries have been made to departments, institutions, and agencies in compliance with specifications;

(12) Prescribe the manner for the handling and processing of specifications, estimates, requisitions, solicitations, responses to solicitations, and all reports made and required to be made to the department;

(13) Prescribe the manner in which respondents may qualify and show responsibility in compliance;

(14) Prescribe the manner for responding to solicitations on lease-purchase contracts and multi-year contracts for the rental of personal property;

(15) Prescribe the manner that provides for and regulates the advertisement, soliciting, and letting of state contracts that include escalator clauses;

(16) Resolve controversies concerning protests of qualification of respondents, suspension from competing, solicitations, and stay of award prior to actual award;

(17) Prescribe the manner for conducting discussions and negotiations, particularly with respect to participants and safeguarding of information, for all solicitation types;

(18) Prescribe the process to be followed in making data available to respondents of solicitations;

(19) Prescribe the process to be followed by agencies in requisitioning goods or services through the central procurement office; and

(20) Provide for any other matters that may be necessary to give effect to the powers and duties of the chief procurement officer under this section by rules and regulations, standards, policies and procedures approved by the commission.

4-56-106 SECTION 5. Tennessee Code Annotated, Section 4-56-106, is amended by deleting the section in its entirety and by substituting instead the following:

4-56-106.

(a)(1) Effective November 1, 2011, there is created an advisory council on state procurement. There shall be five (5) voting members of the council. There shall be seven (7) non-voting members of the council representing the proposer and vendor community and other procurement professionals. All members shall have a demonstrable working knowledge of the state procurement process. In making the appointments to the advisory council, the appointing authorities shall give due consideration to the need for geographic, age, racial, gender, and ethnic diversity on the council.

(2) The five (5) voting members of the council shall consist of one (1) representative of state agencies appointed by the commissioner of general services, one (1) representative from the department of general services to be appointed by the commissioner of general services, one (1) representative from the department of finance and administration to be appointed by the commissioner of finance and administration, one (1) representative from the office of the comptroller of the treasury to be appointed by the comptroller of the treasury, and the chief procurement officer who shall serve as chair. The initial appointments by the commissioners shall be made prior to November 1, 2011. The initial appointment by the comptroller of the treasury shall be made prior to November 1, 2011. Any vacancy shall be filled for the unexpired term by the appointing authority making the initial appointment. The pattern established for initial appointments shall be followed for appointments by the appropriate officials when appointments are to fill expired terms.

(b)(1) Voting members appointed by the commissioner of general services shall serve a staggered four-year term, beginning November 1, 2011. These voting members of the council shall, upon expiration of the member's term, be eligible for reappointment and shall serve until a successor is appointed.

(2) The terms shall be staggered so that the terms of only two (2) voting members shall terminate at the same time.

(A) The term of one (1) voting member initially appointed by the commissioner of general services and the voting member appointed by the commissioner of finance and administration shall be for a two-year term to begin on November 1, 2011, to expire on October 31, 2013, and the successors shall serve a four-year term to begin on November 1, and expire October 31 of the appropriate year.

(B) The term of the other voting member initially appointed by the commissioner of general services shall be for a three-year term to begin on November 1, 2011, to expire on October 31, 2014, and the successor shall serve a four-year term to begin on November 1, and expire October 31 of the appropriate year.

(C) The chief procurement officer shall be an ex officio member whose term shall begin November 1, 2011.

(D) The one (1) voting member appointed by the comptroller of the treasury shall be appointed for a four-year term to begin on November 1, 2011, to expire on October 31, 2015. The successor shall serve a four-year term to begin on November 1, and expire October 31 of the appropriate year.

(3) Proxy voting is prohibited by voting members of the council; provided, however, that, in instances where a voting member will be absent from a vote of the council, the member's appointing authority is authorized to appoint an alternate or designee for the vote.

(c)(1) Except as provided in subsections (a) and (b), the seven (7) non-voting members shall be selected to serve staggered four-year terms as follows:

(A) The speaker of the house of representatives, the speaker of the senate, and the governor shall each appoint two (2) representatives, with one (1) representative from the bidder or vendor community and one (1) representative recommended by the National Institute of Government Purchasing. The final advisory non-voting member appointment shall be appointed by the chair of the fiscal review committee. The initial appointments to the council shall be made prior to November 1, 2011, by the speaker of the senate and the speaker of the house of representatives. The pattern established for initial appointments shall be followed for appointments by the appropriate officials when appointments are to fill expired terms;

(B) The non-voting member appointed by the chair of the fiscal review committee shall serve a two-year term, beginning November 1, 2011, until the term expires October 31, 2013. The non-voting member appointed by the chair of fiscal review shall be eligible for reappointment to succeeding two-year terms without limitation; the two-year term of office of successor appointees shall begin November 1, and expire October 31 of the appropriate year; and

(C) The initial appointments of the non-voting members shall be staggered. The speaker of the senate and the speaker of the house of representatives shall each initially appoint one (1) member for a two-year term to begin November 1, 2011, and expire October 31, 2013, and one (1) member for a three-year term to begin November 1, 2011, and expire October 31, 2014; and the governor shall initially appoint one (1) member for a two-year term to begin November 1, 2011, and expire October 31, 2013, and one (1) member for a three-year term to begin November 1, 2011, and expire October 31, 2014. All subsequent appointments shall be for a four-year term to begin November 1, and expire October 31 of the appropriate year.

(d) Except as provided in subdivision (c)(1)(B), each non-voting member of the council, upon expiration of the member's term, shall not be eligible for reappointment for two (2) years after the conclusion of that member's term. In no event shall a non-voting member of the council serve more than four (4) consecutive years as a non-voting member of the council. In the event a member resigns or becomes ineligible for service during the member's term, a successor shall be appointed by the appropriate appointing authority to serve the remainder of the term.

(e) No employer shall discriminate in any manner against an employee who serves on the council because of the employee's service on the council. Employees who serve on the council shall not be denied any benefit from their employer because of the employee's service on the council.

(f) Members of the council shall not be paid but may be reimbursed for travel expenses. All reimbursement for travel expenses shall be in accordance with the comprehensive travel regulations promulgated by the department of finance and administration and approved by the attorney general and reporter.

(g) The council shall meet at least twice each year for the discussion of problems and recommendations for improvement of the procurement process or any other matter relevant to procurement as determined by the chief procurement officer.

(h) The council shall review and issue a formal comment approved by the council on procurement policies, standards, guidelines, and procedures established by the chief procurement officer prior to being presented for approval by the commission. All reviews and formal comments shall be issued within sixty (60) days of being presented to the council by the chief procurement officer. The formal comments approved by the council shall be provided to the members of the commission, and the officers of the fiscal review committee.

(i) When requested by the chief procurement officer, the council may conduct studies, research, analyses, and make reports and recommendations with respect to subjects or matters within the authority and duties of the chief procurement officer. The chief procurement officer may appoint advisory groups to assist in specific areas, and with respect to any other matters within the authority of the chief procurement officer.

(j) In performing its responsibilities, the council's role shall be strictly advisory, but it may do any of the following:

(1) Make recommendations to the governor, general assembly, fiscal review committee, commissioner of general services, commissioner of finance and administration, and comptroller of the treasury relating to the enactment or promulgation of laws or rules that affect this title and title 12, chapters 3 and 4;

(2) Make recommendations to the commissioner of general services and commissioner of finance and administration regarding the method and form of statistical data collections; and

(3) Monitor the performance of the chief procurement office in the implementation of legislative directives.

(k) The council may develop evaluations, statistical reports, and other information from which the general assembly may evaluate the impact of legislative changes to procurement laws.

(l) Whenever any bill is introduced in the general assembly proposing to amend this chapter, to make any change in public procurement or contract law, or to make any change in the law that may have a financial or other substantive impact on the administration of public procurement and contract law, the standing committee to which the bill is referred may refer the bill to the council. The council's review of bills relating to procurement and contract law shall include, but not be limited to, bills that propose to amend this chapter and title 12, chapters 3 and 4. All bills referred to the council shall be reported back to the standing committee to which they were assigned in a reasonable time. Notwithstanding the absence of a report from the council, the standing committee may consider the bill at any time. The chair making the referral shall immediately notify the prime sponsors of the bill of the referral and the council shall not review and comment on the proposed legislation until the prime sponsors of the bill have been notified. The comments of the council shall describe the potential effects of the proposed legislation on the procurement and contract process and its operations and any other information or suggestions that the council may determine to be helpful for the sponsors, standing committees, or the general assembly. The comments of the council may include recommendations concerning the proposed legislation. Except for reporting the recommendations for or against passage of proposed bill and responding to any inquiries made by the members of the general assembly, council staff shall not lobby or advocate for or against passage of any proposed legislation.

4-56-107 SECTION 6. Tennessee Code Annotated, Section 4-56-107, is amended by deleting the section in its entirety and by substituting instead the following:

4-56-107.

(a) All requests of the procuring agency to procure goods or services by negotiation with a single service provider, referred to in this section as a noncompetitive contract, shall be contemporaneously filed with the fiscal review committee of the general assembly, comptroller of the treasury and the chief procurement officer. Such requests shall document the following:

(1) Description of the goods or services to be acquired;

(2) Explanation of the need for or requirement to acquire the goods or services;

(3) Name and address of the proposed contractor's principal owner;

(4) Evidence that the proposed contractor has experience in providing the same or similar goods or services and evidence of the length of time the contractor has provided the same or similar goods or services;

(5) Explanation of whether the goods or services were purchased by the procuring agency in the past, and if applicable, the method used to purchase the goods or services and the name and address of the contractor;

(6) Description of the procuring agency's efforts to use existing state employees and resources, or in the alternative, to identify reasonable and

competitive procurement alternatives, rather than to use noncompetitive negotiation;

(7) Justification of why the goods or services should be acquired through noncompetitive negotiation; and

(8) Any additional information that the fiscal review committee may direct the procuring agency to provide that will assist the committee in evaluating the contract.

(b)(1) The following contracts and contract amendments shall be subject to review by the fiscal review committee:

(A) Proposed noncompetitive contracts with a term of more than one (1) year or which contain a provision to allow for extension by either party that would extend the contract beyond twelve (12) months and which have a cumulative value of not less than two hundred fifty thousand dollars ($250,000), including all possible extensions; and

(B) Any amendment to a contract meeting the term and dollar threshold requirements as described in subdivision (b)(1)(A), regardless of whether the original contract was procured through competitive or noncompetitive means, where the amendment:

(i) Increases or decreases the maximum liability;

(ii) Extends or shortens the contract term;

(iii) Changes the entity or name of the entity with which the state is contracting; or

(iv) Otherwise changes an original contract or amended contract in a substantive manner.

(2) If the chief procurement officer or delegated state agency is unable to determine whether a proposed contract or amendment would be subject to review by the fiscal review committee, the chief procurement officer or delegated state agency shall contact the fiscal review committee staff for a determination.

(3) The contracts subject to review shall include all contracts of the executive branch that otherwise meet the requirements of subdivision (b)(1), including, but not limited to, contracts of higher education, including the board of regents, the University of Tennessee, and the Tennessee higher education commission. Highway and road improvement contracts reviewed by the department of transportation, contracts reviewed by the state building commission and debt issuance contracts reviewed by the comptroller of the treasury shall not be subject to this review.

(4) The fiscal review committee, pursuant to its jurisdiction under § 3-7-103(a), is authorized to review any other state contract or contract amendment in accordance with the procedures established in this section without regard to whether the contract or contract amendment meets the requirements of subdivision (b)(1).

(5) The fiscal review committee shall have forty (40) business days from receipt of the request as provided in this section to comment on the proposed contract. After this forty-day period, any such contract authorized by the chief procurement officer may be executed. All other requests to negotiate noncompetitive contracts shall be reviewed by the fiscal review committee after approval by the chief procurement officer. With respect to such requests, the fiscal review committee shall be provided the same information to be submitted in accordance with this subsection (a). The chair or the chair's designee, after consultation with the comptroller of the treasury, shall have authority to waive the forty-day period for comment and authorize the chief procurement officer to execute contracts or amendments that are determined to be in the best interest of the state, and to proceed with reporting and comment by the committee at their next scheduled meeting.

(A) If an exception is granted to any request, approved in accordance with subdivision (a)(1) or rules promulgated pursuant to § 4-56-103, then any such exception shall be filed with the fiscal review committee for its perusal, comment and review.

(B) The procurement office shall file a goods and services contract report quarterly with the fiscal review committee. The report shall list contracts approved in accordance with rules authorized by § 4-56-103 during the prior quarter and detail whether each contract procurement was competitive.

(C) Each procuring agency granted a special delegated authority, pursuant to rules authorized by § 4-56-103, to establish goods and services contracts shall report to the fiscal review committee a list of all contracts awarded under the delegated authority. The list of contracts awarded shall be filed quarterly and shall include the contractor name, contract period, contract amount, method used to select the contractor, and the completion date for a monitoring review, as defined by any applicable policy developed by the chief procurement officer and any other information the procuring agency wishes to include.

(D) The department of transportation shall report to the fiscal review committee on approved highway and road improvement contracts that would otherwise meet the requirements of subdivision (b)(1) within thirty (30) days of approval, including all of the information specified in subsection (a) and any other information the committee deems necessary or helpful. The fiscal review committee shall have the option to conduct a separate hearing on highway and road improvement contracts approved by the department of transportation.

(E) The state building commission shall report to the fiscal review committee on contracts it has approved that would otherwise meet the requirements of subdivision (b)(1) within thirty (30) days of approval, including all of the information specified in subsection (a) and any other information the committee deems necessary or helpful. The committee shall have the option to conduct a separate hearing on contracts approved by the building commission.

4-56-108, 4-56-109, 4-56-110

SECTION 7. Tennessee Code Annotated, Sections 4-56-108 -- 4-56-110, are amended by deleting the sections in their entireties and by substituting instead the following:

4-56-108.

(a) The comptroller of the treasury shall review and approve such procurements, contracts, grants, and other related documents prior to the public posting on the single procurement website of such procurements; after posting any amendments thereto; after recommendation for award; and prior to execution of the contract as applicable for the following:

(1) Delegation of procurement or contract authority by the chief procurement officer. All initial, reduced or revoked delegations as provided under § 12-3-401 shall be reported to the comptroller of the treasury in such format and time interval as reasonable. All periodic reviews of purchasing activities of any state agency granted such delegation shall be provided to the comptroller of the treasury;

(2) Procurement and contracts for goods and services where authority exists under both the state building commission and the central procurement office to procure and contract;

(3) Procurement and contracts for auditing services;

(4) Cooperative agreement to participate, sponsor, conduct or administer as provided in § 12-3-512 with any other entity;

(5) Fee for service procurement or contracts with a maximum liability in excess of five million dollars ($5,000,000), which may be increased or decreased by action of the commission;

(6) Grant contracts with a maximum liability in excess of five million dollars ($5,000,000), which may be increased or decreased by action of the commission;

(7) Fee for service procurement or contracts for new or replacement information systems and technical infrastructure projects for goods and services in excess of five hundred thousand dollars ($500,000), which may be increased or decreased by action of the commission;

(8) Procurement or contracts that would utilize competitive or noncompetitive negotiations with a maximum liability in excess of two hundred fifty thousand dollars ($250,000), which may be increased or decreased by action of the commission. Competitive or noncompetitive negotiation shall not be utilized by a state agency unless such procurement is performed by the central procurement office;

(9) Procurement or contracts for which the state would receive revenue;

(10) Procurement or contracts that would incur no cost;

(11) Procurement or contracts that propose a term that exceeds sixty (60) months;

(12) Procurement or contracts that propose a limitation of liability that is less than two (2) times the maximum liability;

(13) Procurement or contracts that propose to change the records, annual report and audit or monitoring provisions;

(14) Procurement or contracts that would provide for the negotiation of a necessary, mandatory or standard contract clause;

(15) Procurement that would provide that a cost proposal may be evaluated contemporaneously with or prior to evaluation of the technical proposal;

(16) Procurement or contract that provides an automatic price escalator; and

(17) Such other procurements, contracts or other items as may be directed by the commissioner of finance and administration or by the commission.

(b) Without limitation of the audit authority of the comptroller of the treasury, the comptroller is authorized to examine any documents under the authority of the chief procurement officer.

(c) Cancellation of procurements or rejection of all responses to a procurement shall be documented in accordance with rules and regulations, standards, policies and procedures as approved by the commission and the reason for the cancellation or rejection of all bids for a procurement shall be provided to the comptroller of the treasury within three (3) business days after such determination.

(d) Any protest after notice of intent to award by an aggrieved respondent received by the chief procurement officer or the protest committee shall be filed with the comptroller of the treasury within three (3) business days of receipt. All responses to the aggrieved respondent regarding the protest whether allowed or not, shall be filed with the comptroller of the treasury at the same time provided to the aggrieved respondent.

(e) Contracts shall contain on the last page of the secured contract document the signature and approval date of all required approvers to be a fully executed document and for the release of a purchase order against the contract.

(f) The comptroller of the treasury shall be provided view access to any information or data from any system housing procurement and contract related data, information, and processes.

(g) The chief procurement officer shall post on the single procurement website reports or data queries, subject to approval by the comptroller of the treasury as to format and time interval for update. Such reports shall include, but are not limited to, the following:

(1) Noncompetitive, sole source or proprietary contracts;

(2) Cancellation of procurements or contract awards;

(3) Cancellation of contracts before term extension or for cause;

(4) Protests to chief procurement officer and protest committee;

(5) Emergency procurements and contracts;

(6) Contracts with term extensions beyond sixty (60) months;

(7) Rule exceptions approved by the chief procurement officer; and

(8) Persons or entities that are prevented from contracting or submitting a response to a procurement.

12-3-101 SECTION 8. Tennessee Code Annotated, Section 12-3-101, is amended by deleting the section in its entirety and by substituting instead the following:

12-3-101.

Except as provided in §§ 12-3-102 and 12-3-103, all goods and services, and all telephone, telegraph, electric light, gas, power, postal services, and the leasing of any equipment required for the use of state government, shall be purchased and contracted for by the central procurement office consistent with the requirements of this chapter and any rules, regulations or policies and procedures approved by the procurement commission.

12-3-102 SECTION 9. Tennessee Code Annotated, Section 12-3-102, is amended by deleting the section in its entirety and by substituting instead the following:

12-3-102.

(a) Procurements and contracts by and for the following state governmental entities shall be exempt from the operation of this chapter:

(1) The legislative branch;

(2) The judicial branch;

(3) The University of Tennessee system and the Tennessee board of regents system;

(4) Contracts advertised and awarded by the state building commission pursuant to § 4-15-102. If there is a question whether a contract or procurement requires state building commission or central procurement office approval, the chief procurement officer and the state architect shall determine in writing the procurement method or the contract form that is in the best interest of the state. Any such agreement reached by the chief procurement officer and the state architect shall be subject to the approval of the comptroller of the treasury;

(5) Construction and engineering contracts entered into by the department of transportation pursuant to title 54, chapter 5;

(6) Contracts for procurement of services in connection with the issue, sale, purchase, and delivery of bonds, notes and other debt obligations or the administration, safekeeping, and payment after delivery of such debt obligations by the state or any of its agencies;

(7) Contracts for appraisal, relocation or acquisition services related to the acquisition of land that are entered into by the department of transportation pursuant to title 54, chapter 5; and

(8) Administrative contracts for specific service signs pursuant to title 54, chapter 5, part 11, shall be awarded to the vendor who offers the lowest responsible response. The basis of all responses shall be the least cost to the retail user of the signs. All administrative contracts shall be awarded on an objective, competitive basis pursuant to rules and regulations promulgated by the department of transportation.

(b) Notwithstanding subsection (a), any or all state entities exempt from the requirements of this part, as well as any private nonprofit institution of higher education chartered in this state, are authorized to procure goods or services under this chapter through the central procurement office.

12-3-103 SECTION 10. Tennessee Code Annotated, Section 12-3-103, is amended by deleting the section in its entirety and by substituting instead the following:

12-3-103.

(a) Contracts for legal services, fiscal agent, financial advisor or advisory services, educational consultant services, and similar services by professional persons or groups with high ethical standards, shall not be based upon competitive procurement methods, but shall be awarded on the basis of recognized competence and integrity. The prohibition against competitive procurement in this section shall not prohibit any entity enumerated from interviewing eligible persons or entities to determine the capabilities of such persons or entities.

(b) Any person providing fiscal agent, financial advisor or advisory services covered by this part shall perform such services only pursuant to a written contract specifying the services to be rendered, the costs of the services, and the expenses to be covered under such contract.

(c) Any person providing fiscal agent, financial advisor or advisory services covered by this part who desires to respond, directly or indirectly, on any bonds, notes or other obligations of such entity sold pursuant to public, competitive sale shall receive in writing prior to the sale the permission of such entity to respond either directly or indirectly on the obligations.

(d) For the purposes of this section, "providing fiscal agent, financial advisor or advisory services" means a relationship that exists when a person renders, or enters into an agreement to render, financial advisory or consultant services to or on behalf of an issuer with respect to a new issue or issues of municipal securities, including advice with respect to the structure, timing, terms and other similar matters concerning such issue or issues, for a fee or other compensation or in expectation of such compensation for the rendering of such services.

(e) A financial advisory relationship shall not be deemed to exist when, in the course of acting as an underwriter, a municipal securities dealer renders advice to an issuer, including advice with respect to the structure, timing, terms and other similar matters concerning a new issue of municipal securities.

12-3-104 SECTION 11. Tennessee Code Annotated, Section 12-3-104, is amended by deleting the section in its entirety and by substituting instead the following:

12-3-104.

Whenever any state department or agency applies to the department of general services to lease or rent any equipment, the department of general services shall first ascertain whether or not any such equipment is available for use from any other department, institution, or agency. The department of general services shall have the power to request the transfer of any such equipment from one (1) department, institution, or agency to another with the approval of the head of the transferring department, institution, or agency.

12-3-105 — 12-3-133 SECTION 12. Tennessee Code Annotated, Sections 12-3-105 through 12-3-133, are amended by deleting the sections in their entireties.

12-3-201 SECTION 13. Tennessee Code Annotated, Section 12-3-201, is amended by deleting the section in its entirety and by substituting instead the following:

12-3-201.

As used in this chapter, unless the context otherwise requires:

(1) "Central procurement office" means the government agency established in § 4-56-104;

(2) "Chief procurement officer" means the person holding the position established in § 4-56-104, as the head of the central procurement office and with the powers and duties set forth in § 4-56-105;

(3) "Committee" means the state protest committee as established in § 4-56-103;

(4) "Contract" means any duly authorized and legally binding written agreement for the procurement of goods and services;

(5) "Council" means the advisory council on state procurement established in § 4-56-106;

(6) "Data" means any recorded information, regardless of its form or characteristic;

(7) "Energy efficiency standard" means a performance standard that prescribes the relationship of the energy use of a product to its useful output of services;

(8) "Goods" mean all personal property, including, but not limited to, supplies, equipment, materials, printing, and insurance. "Goods" does not include real property;

(9) "Grant" means any grant awarded to the state or awarded by the state to any person to support a program authorized by law. "Grant" does not include an award whose primary purpose is to procure an end product, whether in the form of supplies, services, or construction, or any contract resulting from such an award;

(10) "Invitation to bid" means all documents, whether attached or incorporated by reference, utilized for soliciting bids for the lowest cost, responsive and responsible bidder;

(11) "Major energy-consuming product" means any article so designated by the chief procurement officer in consultation with the central procurement office staff;

(12) "Political subdivision" means any authority, city, town, municipality, county or instrumentality of any authority, city, town, municipality or county within the state;

(13) "Procurement" means buying, purchasing, renting, leasing, or otherwise acquiring of any goods or services. "Procurement" also includes all functions that pertain to the obtaining of goods or services, including the description of requirements, selection and solicitation of sources, preparation and award of a contract, and all phases of contract administration;

(14) "Procurement commission" means the state procurement commission, as established in § 4-56-102;

(15) "Proprietary" means a good or service that is used, produced, or marketed under exclusive legal right of the inventor, maker or service provider that is protected under trade secret, patent, trademark, or copyright law;

(16) "Request for proposal" means a written solicitation for written proposals to provide goods or services to the state or a state governmental entity based upon specified evaluation criteria;

(17) "Respondent" includes a "bidder" or "proposer" that is a natural person or legal entity that has properly registered as required by the state. The terms "bidder" and "proposer" may be used interchangeably as the context requires;

(18) "Response" means a written response to a solicitation for goods and services;

(19) "Responsible" means a person who has the capacity in all respects to perform fully the contract requirements, as well as the integrity and reliability, which will assure good faith performance;

(20) "Responsive" means a person who has submitted a response that conforms in all material respects to the competitive procurement;

(21) "Services" means all services and agreements obligating the state, except services for highway and road improvements governed by title 54 and design and construction services governed by title 4, chapter 15;

(22) "Solicitation" means any type of document that invites responses and may include, by way of example, an "invitation to bid", a "request for proposal" or a "competitive negotiation";

(23) "Specification" means any description of the physical, functional, performance characteristics, or nature of a supply, service, or construction item. "Specification" includes, as appropriate, requirements for inspecting, testing, or preparing a supply, service, or construction item for delivery;

(24) "State agency" means any state governmental entity, other than the central procurement office and those state entities exempted by § 12-3-102, that is authorized to enter into contracts by this title or its implementing regulations, or by way of delegation from the chief procurement officer, or that utilizes any goods or services procured under this title;

(25) "State governmental entity" means any agency, authority, board, commission, department, or office within the executive, legislative or judicial branches of state government or any autonomous state agency, authority, board, commission, council, department, office, or institution of higher education; and

(26) "Vendor" means a natural person or legal entity that has been established by the department of finance and administration's division of accounts as a vendor through proper authority for which payment may be made by the state.

12-3-202 SECTION 14. Tennessee Code Annotated, Section 12-3-202, is amended by deleting the section in its entirety and by substituting instead the following:

12-3-202. Subject to the regulations and requirements of the Tennessee regulatory authority and other state or federal bodies, the central procurement office is authorized to extend the use of the state network long distance telephone service to students at state universities and colleges. If the central procurement office extends such service, it shall charge the institution the amount that it costs the state for such service.

12-3-203 — 12-3-262 SECTION 15. Tennessee Code Annotated, Sections 12-3-203 through 12-3-262, are amended by deleting these sections in their entireties.

12-3-301 — 12-3-314 SECTION 16. Tennessee Code Annotated, Section 12-3-301, is amended by deleting the section in its entirety and by substituting instead the following:

12-3-301.

(a) Before April 1 of each year, each state agency shall compile and submit to the chief procurement officer and the comptroller of the treasury, a written acquisition plan for the upcoming fiscal year forecasting the specific categories and quantities of goods and services anticipated for purchase by the state agency. The chief procurement officer shall develop procedures to ensure uniformity among the various state agencies both in the manner of calculating such forecasts and in the style and format used for submitting such written acquisition plans to the chief procurement officer. The information contained within such forecasts shall be based on good faith estimates and shall not be construed in any way to legally bind or authorize the state agency to make any purchase in conflict with the other requirements of this chapter. This subsection (a) shall not apply to those entities exempt from this chapter pursuant to § 12-3-102.

(b) Before July 1 of each year, the chief procurement officer shall compile and publish the written acquisition plans submitted by the various agencies pursuant to this subsection (a), within an annual report that shall be entitled "The Forecast of Acquisition Plans for State Departments and Agencies for Fiscal Year _____--_____." A copy of the report shall be posted on the central procurement office's website.

(c) It is the duty of all state agencies to furnish to the central procurement office, upon request, data relating to purchases and purchase estimates.

(d) An agency is permitted to amend or supplement its written acquisition plan before the end of a given fiscal year for unforeseen circumstances pursuant to rules, regulations and policies approved by the commission.

SECTION 17. Tennessee Code Annotated, Section 12-3-302, is amended by deleting the section in its entirety and by substituting instead the following:

12-3-302.

(a) Any statement or agreement in which the respondent is asked to indicate a willingness to meet the low price, if such respondent is not the low respondent, is adverse to the competitive procurement standards and shall not be included in any solicitation to be awarded by any state agencies.

(b) This section shall apply to divisible contracts.

(c) This section shall not apply when applicable law permits negotiated contracts.

(d) For the purposes of this section, contracts for the administration of specific service signs pursuant to title 54, chapter 5, part 11, shall not be negotiable.

SECTION 18. Tennessee Code Annotated, Sections 12-3-303 through 12-3-314, are amended by deleting the sections in their entireties and by substituting instead the following:

12-3-303.

(a) Any contract for goods or services entered into by an executive branch state agency shall be executed by the head of such state agency and approved by the chief procurement officer. Notwithstanding any other provision of the law to the contrary, approval of the chief procurement officer and no other officer of the state government is necessary, except as follows:

(1) Contracts for financial management or accounting services shall also be approved by the commissioner of finance and administration;

(2) Contracts for auditing services shall also be approved by the comptroller of the treasury;

(3) Contracts for engineering or architectural services shall also be approved by the office of the state architect;

(4) Contracts of all state colleges and universities operated by the board of trustees of the University of Tennessee or the state board of regents do not need to be approved by the chief procurement officer, provided that those contracts shall be subject to applicable provisions of the rules and policies promulgated by the central procurement office and approved by the procurement commission; or

(5) Those procurements, contracts, grants, and other documents subject to approval by the comptroller of the treasury pursuant to § 4-56-108 or otherwise required by law.

(b) All contracts for rendering public relations, advertising or related services entered into by or on behalf of agencies and departments of the executive branch of state government shall be restricted to provide for only the rendition of media advertising and related design and production services, except as otherwise determined in accordance with policies established by the procurement commission.

(c)(1) This section shall not apply to construction and engineering contracts entered into by the department of transportation pursuant to title 54, chapter 5, or to contracts for projects required by law to be approved by the state building commission.

(2) This section shall not apply to contracts to hire additional counsel for the state or any of its departments, institutions or agencies; provided, that all such contracts shall be made in accordance with § 8-6-106, except for legal counsel employed pursuant to any statute concerning the issuance and sale of bonds, notes, or other obligations.

(3) This section shall not apply to contracts for procurement of services in connection with the issue, sale, purchase, and delivery of bonds, notes and other debt obligations or the administration, safekeeping, and payment after delivery of such debt obligations by the state or any of its agencies.

(d) All contracts for goods and services shall be posted on the state procurement office's website, at a minimum providing the following information, as applicable, regarding each request for goods or services:

(1) Business unit or agency requesting;

(2) Contract number;

(3) Brief description of the contract;

(4) Type of contract;

(5) Commencement date of the contract;

(6) Ending date of the contract;

(7) Maximum liability; and

(8) Status of the contract.

12-3-304.

(a) When any state agency required by this chapter to purchase goods or services through the central procurement office, contracts for the purchase of goods or services contrary to provisions of this chapter or the rules and regulations made hereunder, such contract shall be void and of no effect.

(b) When the central procurement office contracts for the purchase of goods or services contrary to the provisions of this chapter or the rules and regulations made hereunder, such contract shall also be void and of no effect.

(c) If any state agency, including the central procurement office, purchases any goods or services contrary to the provisions of this chapter or the rules and regulations made hereunder, then the chief procurement officer or head of such state agency shall be personally liable for the costs thereof, and if such goods or services are so unlawfully purchased and paid for out of state monies, then the amount thereof may be recovered in the name of the state in an appropriate action instituted by the state.

12-3-305.

(a) The central procurement office or the procuring state governmental entity shall be responsible for the effective management of all contracts procured under its authority and shall adopt regulations or policies that define service contracting fundamentals. Such regulations or policies shall include, but are not limited to, contract management and monitoring of vendors, grants and sub-recipient relationships. The regulations for monitoring shall, at a minimum, require the filing of the monitoring plan with the chief procurement officer before any contracts are approved.

(b) Any state agency, when entering into contracts with any organizations that agree to provide services to third parties, shall, subject to approval by the chief procurement officer and the comptroller of the treasury, establish guidelines for such organizations. These guidelines shall define the responsibility and prescribe procedures to be followed by the contracting agencies including, but not limited to, the use of generally accepted accounting procedures, sound business practices, and compliance with related state and federal regulations regarding the fiscal policies of nonprofit organizations. The guidelines established shall be used as prerequisites for the state's agreement to provide matching or other state funds or federal funds or entering into a third party contract.

(c) Every solicitation issued for the purpose of establishing a contract shall include the maximum liability or total estimated purchase by agencies of state government for the current contract period, if applicable, and for the new contract period. More than one (1) contract may be let for the supply of any given class or type of goods or services and any contract may provide for the cancellation thereof by either party. Contracts executed or proposed to be executed for periods of time of more than twelve (12) months shall be subject to the policies, rules and regulations of the central procurement office, as approved by the procurement commission, and shall meet the following conditions:

(1) Such contracts may contain a provision giving the state the right of cancellation for convenience for periods of time established by the chief procurement officer;

(2) Such contracts shall contain a provision giving the state the right of cancellation at the end of any fiscal year without notice, in the event that funds to support the contract become unavailable; and

(3) No contract may be let for periods of time in excess of sixty (60) months, unless the chief procurement officer determines the contract is in the best interest of the state and approves the contract in accordance with rules and regulations, and policies and procedures approved by the procurement commission, as being in the best interest of the state.

(d) After contracts have been awarded, the chief procurement officer shall certify to state agencies the sources of services and supply and the contract price of the various goods and services covered by the contracts. It is unlawful for any state agency to purchase any goods or services covered thereby from any sources other than those certified by the chief procurement officer, except as otherwise provided in this chapter.

12-3-306.

(a) A state governmental entity shall not contract to acquire goods or services, and no person may contract to supply goods or services to a state governmental entity, unless, prior to, or contemporaneous with, entering into the contract, the person contracting to supply goods or services and its affiliates register with the department of revenue to collect and remit the sales and use tax levied by the Retailers' Sales Tax Act, compiled in title 67, chapter 6. Nothing in this section shall require a person or affiliate to register if the person or affiliate does not make sales to customers in the state of tangible personal property or services, which if the sales occurred wholly within the state, would be taxable under title 67, chapter 6. This provision is specifically applicable to foreign persons, notwithstanding the fact that such foreign persons or their affiliates may not otherwise be legally obligated to collect and remit such tax.

(b) For purposes of this section:

(1) "Affiliates" means each and every affiliate of the person contracting with the state or other state entities, as the term "affiliate" is defined in § 48 103-102;

(2) "Other state entities" has the same meaning as in § 12-4-601; and

(3) "Person" or "persons" has the same meaning as in § 67-6-102.

(c) The commissioner of revenue and the chief procurement officer shall develop procedures for compliance with this section with approval by the procurement commission.

12-3-307.

Contracting state agencies that establish the procedural and administrative accountability requirements shall apply these requirements to all matching funds. The established procedural and administrative requirements shall remain in effect for the entire fiscal year covered by the third party contract, and no contracting agency shall modify or amend these procedures without the state agency's approval.

12-3-308.

(a) Notwithstanding any other provision of law to the contrary, state and local governments shall contract for goods and services provided through, or administered by, the departments of children's services, health, and human services without discrimination against religious organizations or discrimination based on race, age, color, sex, or national origin and shall provide beneficiaries of assistance under the programs established by law with forms of disbursement that are redeemable with these organizations that are awarded a contract. State and local governments may use any state, federal, local or other monies available for these purposes.

(b) State and local governments shall allow contracts with religious organizations to provide goods and services provided through, or administered by, the departments of children's services, health, and human services and to accept forms of disbursement under any program established on the same basis as any other nongovernmental provider without impairing the religious character of these organizations, and without diminishing the religious freedom of beneficiaries of assistance funded under these programs. The programs shall be implemented consistent with the first amendment of the United States Constitution. State and local governments shall not discriminate against an organization that is, or applies to be, a contractor to provide assistance or that accepts forms of disbursement on the basis that the organization has a religious character.

(c) A religious organization with a contract described in this section shall retain its independence from federal, state and local governments, including the religious organization's control over the definition, development, practice and expression of its religious beliefs. State and local governments shall not require a religious organization to alter its form of internal governance or to remove religious art, icons, scripture or other symbols in order to be eligible to contract to provide assistance or to accept grants or other forms of disbursement funded under any program or public contract.

(d) If a person, who applies for or receives goods, services or disbursements, objects to the religious character of the organization or institution from which the person receives, or would receive, assistance funded under any program, the state or local government shall provide the person, within a reasonable period of time after the date of the objection, with assistance from an alternative provider that is accessible to the person if an alternative provider is available and the value of which is not less than the value of assistance that the person would have received from the religious organization. Organizations shall provide notice to people receiving assistance of the right to object pursuant to this subsection (d).

(e) A religious organization's exemption provided under § 702 of the Civil Rights Act of 1964, codified in 42 U.S.C. § 2000e-1(a), regarding employment practices is not affected by its participation in, or receipt of, monies from programs described in this section. Nothing in this section allows religious organizations to discriminate in employment practices on the basis of race, age, color, sex or national origin.

(f) Except as otherwise provided by law, a religious organization shall not discriminate against a person in regard to rendering assistance funded under any program described in this section on the basis of religion, a religious belief or refusal to participate in a religious practice, or on the basis of race, age, color, sex or national origin.

(g) Except as provided in subsection (h), any religious organization that contracts to provide goods, services or assistance funded under any program is subject to audit by the comptroller of the treasury, and is required to comply with the same rules and laws as other contractors to account in accordance with generally accepted auditing principles for the use of the monies provided under the program.

(h) If a religious organization segregates public monies provided under these programs into separate accounts, only the programs funded by financial assistance provided with these monies are subject to audit by the comptroller of the treasury.

(i) Appeals from the decisions of the head of a state agency, board or commission may be made to the commissioner of finance and administration in accordance with the Uniform Administrative Procedures Act, compiled in title 4, chapter 5.

(j) No monies provided directly to institutions or organizations to provide services and administer programs under this section may be spent for sectarian worship, instruction or proselytization. This subsection (j) does not apply to the contracting for the services of chaplains by state and local governments.

(k) For the purposes of this section, "state and local governments" means state agencies, boards and commissions and political subdivisions of this state.

(l) No funds provided by any state or local government for goods and services to religious organizations shall supplant present funding of programs provided by such groups but shall be a supplement to the activities rendered by these groups.

12-3-309.

(a) Prohibited contracts:

(1) No state governmental entity shall contract to acquire goods or services from any person who knowingly utilizes the services of illegal immigrants in the performance of a contract for goods or services entered into with a state governmental entity.

(2) No person may contract to supply goods or services to a state governmental entity if that person knowingly utilizes the services of illegal immigrants in the performance of a contract to supply goods or services entered into with the state or a state entity.

(b) After January 1, 2007, no person may enter into a contract to supply goods or services to a state governmental entity without first attesting in writing that the person will not knowingly utilize the services of illegal immigrants in the performance of the contract, and will not knowingly utilize the services of any subcontractor who will utilize the services of illegal immigrants in the performance of the contract.

(c) If any person who contracts to supply goods or services to a state governmental entity, or who submits a response to contract to supply goods or services to a state governmental entity, is discovered to have knowingly utilized the services of illegal immigrants in the performance of the contract to supply goods or services to a state governmental entity, the chief procurement officer shall declare that person to be prohibited from contracting for or submitting a response for any contract to supply goods or services to a state governmental entity for a period of one (1) year from the date of discovery of the usage of illegal immigrant services in the performance of a contract to supply goods or services to a state governmental entity.

(d) Any person who is prevented from contracting for or submitting a response for a contract to supply goods or services to a state governmental entity for one (1) year pursuant to subsection (c) may appeal the imposition of the one-year prohibition by utilizing an appeals process to be established by the chief procurement officer and approved by the procurement commission.

(e) The chief procurement officer is authorized to promulgate rules and regulations to effectuate the purposes of this section and shall be approved by the procurement commission. All rules and regulations shall be promulgated in accordance with the Uniform Administrative Procedures Act, compiled in title 4, chapter 5.

12-3-310.

(a) As used in this section, "call center" includes a person who performs services, including, but not limited to, data entry services, electronic governmental transfers, or other electronic, telephone and telecommunication services.

(b) The chief procurement officer shall promulgate regulations pursuant to title 4, chapter 56, authorizing a preference in the evaluation of proposals for state contracts requiring vendors of call center services to only employ, use, or contract with citizens of the United States who reside in the United States, or any person authorized to work in the United States pursuant to federal law, including legal resident aliens in the United States to provide call center services.

(c) Any respondent seeking this preference shall supply such supporting documentation as the state may require and shall certify that it will provide services solely by citizens of the United States who reside within the United States, or persons authorized to work in the United States pursuant to federal law, including legal resident aliens in the United States. The certification shall acknowledge and confirm the right of the state to audit and monitor compliance and seek appropriate remedies for noncompliance.

12-3-401 SECTION 19. Tennessee Code Annotated, Title 12, Chapter 3, Part 4, is amended by adding the following language as a new section:

12-3-401.

(a) The chief procurement officer may authorize any or all state agencies to procure all or any specific types and classes of goods or services, without following the procedures relating to the requisitioning of such goods or services through the central procurement office. The comptroller of the treasury shall review and approve such delegations as required by procurement commission policy. The chief procurement officer shall consider the individual state agency's purchasing record in these delegations and shall periodically review purchasing activities of any state agency granted such delegation, and may reduce or revoke such delegated purchasing authority.

(b) It is intended that delegation of purchase authority may be made by state agency, by type of good or service, by dollar amount of procurement, or by any combination thereof, in order to reduce the procurement time required and to increase the amount of purchases made from any minority-owned business, woman-owned business, service-disabled veteran-owned business, or small business, as defined in § 12-3-514.

(c) Upon delegated authority, any procurement not exceeding fifty thousand dollars ($50,000), for which a source of supply has not otherwise been established, shall be made without requisitioning such goods or services through the central procurement office; provided, that procurement requirements shall not be artificially divided so as to constitute a small purchase under this section.

(d) All requisitions and solicitations provided for in this section shall be posted on the state procurement office's website, at a minimum providing the following information, as applicable, regarding each such procurement:

(1) Procuring agency;

(2) Requisition number;

(3) Vendor;

(4) Total amount of requisition;

(5) Line item of description; and

(6) Line item amount.

12-3-501 SECTION 20. Tennessee Code Annotated, Section 12-3-501, is amended by deleting the section in its entirety and by substituting instead the following:

12-3-501.

Unless otherwise authorized by law, state contracts shall be awarded by competitive sealed solicitations by the central procurement office in the manner set forth in § 12-3-502, except as provided in § 12-3-401 and §§ 12-3-503 -- 12-3-508.

12-3-502 SECTION 21. Tennessee Code Annotated, Section 12-3-502, is amended by deleting the section in its entirety and by substituting instead the following:

12-3-502.

(a) The central procurement office shall publicly advertise a copy of the solicitation. All responses received by the central procurement office shall be opened and examined at the time and place specified in the solicitation. Any and all responses may be rejected pursuant to subsection (b).

(b) Whenever the chief procurement officer approves the rejection of all responses for a certain solicitation, the chief procurement officer shall file a notice of such action with the comptroller of the treasury and shall take such action only for one (1) or more of the following reasons:

(1) Unreasonably high prices;

(2) Error in the solicitation;

(3) Cessation of need;

(4) Unavailability of funds; or

(5) Any other reason determined to be in the best interest of the state.

(c) Submission of a response shall not create rights, interests, or claims of entitlement in any respondent, including the lowest apparent respondent in terms of cost.

(d)(1) Correction or withdrawal of inadvertently erroneous responses, before or after award, or cancellation of awards or contracts based on such mistakes, shall be permitted with approval of the chief procurement officer. All cancellation of awards or contracts shall be filed with the comptroller of the treasury.

(2) After response opening, no changes in prices or other provisions of responses prejudicial to the interest of the state or fair competition shall be permitted.

(3) Except as otherwise provided by regulation or policy of the procurement commission, all decisions to permit the correction or withdrawal of responses, or cancel awards or contracts based on response mistakes, shall be supported by a written determination made by the chief procurement officer and such determination shall be filed with the comptroller of the treasury.

(e) Only criteria or factors set forth in the solicitation may be used in evaluating a response.

(f) After response evaluation and prior to award of the contract, the chief procurement officer shall issue a notice of intent to award to all respondents to the solicitation. Notification by the state of intent to award shall not create rights, interests, or claims of entitlement in any respondent.

(g) Upon issuance of the intent to award, all data relating to the procurement shall be made available for inspection to each respondent of the solicitation, upon request. No contract shall be awarded by the chief procurement officer without providing respondents a reasonable opportunity for inspection. The chief procurement officer shall establish procedures for providing inspection by respondents to solicitations. Such procedures shall be approved by the procurement commission. Notification by the state of intent to award shall not create rights, interests, or claims of entitlement in any respondent.

(h) Each contract shall be awarded in the name of the state, with reasonable promptness by written notice to the respondent to whom a contract will be awarded in accordance with the criteria for award as set forth in the solicitation.

(i) Procurement and performance bonds or other security may be required for any contract. Any such requirement shall be set forth in the solicitation. The chief procurement officer shall promulgate rules establishing the requirements for the use and appropriate amount of such bonds or other security with approval by the procurement commission.

12-3-503 SECTION 22. Tennessee Code Annotated, Section 12-3-503, is amended by deleting the section in its entirety and by substituting instead the following:

12-3-503.

(a) The procurement commission may grant the chief procurement officer authority to establish informal solicitation rules, regulations, policies and procedures for procurements. The maximum amount of the procurement shall be determined in accordance with the following:

(1) If all of the members of the procurement commission agree, the amount shall be up to fifty thousand dollars ($50,000) or less; and

(2) Procurement requirements shall not be artificially divided in order to constitute an informal procurement under this section.

(b) The procurement commission may grant the chief procurement officer authority to establish small purchase rules, regulations, policies, and procedures. The maximum amount of the purchases shall be determined in accordance with the following:

(1) If all the members of the procurement commission agree, the amount shall be up to ten thousand dollars ($10,000) or less; and

(2) Purchasing requirements shall not be artificially divided in order to constitute a small purchase under this section.

(c) Notwithstanding subsections (a) and (b), such state agencies shall actively solicit responses from any minority-owned business, woman-owned business, service-disabled veteran-owned business, or small business in accordance with title 12, chapter 3, part 11.

12-3-504 SECTION 23. Tennessee Code Annotated, Section 12-3-504, is amended by deleting the section in its entirety and by substituting instead the following:

12-3-504.

The chief procurement officer shall identify goods or services that may not be procured by competitive means because of the existence of a single source of supply. The chief procurement officer shall submit to the procurement commission, for approval rules, policies, and procedures prescribing the manner in which such procurements may be accomplished, which may include noncompetitive negotiation. Sole source goods and services shall be purchased only in accordance with these rules, policies, and procedures approved by the procurement commission.

12-3-505 SECTION 24. Tennessee Code Annotated, Section 12-3-505, is amended by deleting the section in its entirety and by substituting instead the following:

12-3-505.

The chief procurement officer is authorized to purchase for a state governmental entity in the open market specific goods or services for immediate delivery to meet emergencies arising from any unforeseen cause, including, but not limited to, delays by contractors, delays in transportation, unanticipated volume of work, and acts of God. The chief procurement officer may delegate this authority to any state agency; provided, that a report on the circumstances of any such emergency and the actions taken by such state agency as a result of the emergency shall be transmitted in writing as soon as possible by such state agency to the chief procurement officer. The report shall set forth the prices at which goods and services were purchased and the total amount of the purchase. The chief procurement officer shall keep each report on file in the permanent records of the central procurement office. All emergency purchases shall be posted on the single public Internet website in such form as prescribed by the procurement commission. All emergency purchases shall, if practicable, be made on the basis of competitive procurement.

12-3-506 SECTION 25. Tennessee Code Annotated, Title 12, Chapter 3, Part 5, is amended by adding the following language as a new § 12-3-506:

12-3-506.

In accordance with rules and regulations of the central procurement office approved by the procurement commission and adopted pursuant to title 4, chapter 56, part 1, and title 12, chapters 3 and 4, the chief procurement officer is authorized to negotiate with vendors who maintain a general services administration pricing agreement with the United States or any agency thereof; provided, that no contract executed under this section shall authorize a price higher than is contained in the contract between the general services administration and the affected vendor.

12-3-507 SECTION 26. Tennessee Code Annotated, Title 12, Chapter 3, Part 5, is amended by adding the following language as a new § 12-3-507:

12-3-507.

Except as otherwise provided by law, a contract may be entered into by competitive negotiation when it is determined by the chief procurement officer that it is in the best interest of the state. Each use of competitive negotiation shall be subject to approval by the chief procurement officer and the comptroller of the treasury in accordance with rules, policies, and procedures of the procurement commission. Notice of such approved competitive negotiations shall be posted on the central procurement office's website.

12-3-508 SECTION 27. Tennessee Code Annotated, Title 12, Chapter 3, Part 5, is amended by adding the following language as a new § 12-3-508:

12-3-508.

Subject to rules of the central procurement office approved by the procurement commission, the central procurement office shall purchase or contract for all telephone, telegraph, electric light, gas, power, postal, and other services for which a rate for the use thereof has been established by a public authority, in such manner as the chief procurement officer deems to be in the best interest of the state.

12-3-509 SECTION 28. Tennessee Code Annotated, Section 12-3-509, is amended by deleting the section in its entirety and by substituting instead the following:

12-3-509.

When any goods or services are received by a state agency, the state agency's receiving agent shall certify electronically or in writing that the goods or services received were equal in quality and quantity to those requisitioned or ordered. The certification shall accompany the voucher directing the payment. The state shall not remit funds in payment of any voucher unless the voucher is accompanied by the certification.

12-3-510 SECTION 29. Tennessee Code Annotated, Title 12, Chapter 3, Part 5, is amended by adding the following language as a new § 12-3-510:

12-3-510.

Notwithstanding the provisions of § 12-3-502, all procurement records of the department and all records of the procurement commission shall be open and accessible to the public during the regular office hours of the central procurement office or state agency, when such inspections do not interfere with the orderly operation of the central procurement office or state agency.

12-3-511 SECTION 30. Tennessee Code Annotated, Title 12, Chapter 3, Part 5, is amended by adding the following language as a new § 12-3-511:

12-3-511.

The central procurement office shall not honor or act upon any requisitions from any state agency without first having ascertained from the commissioner of finance and administration, or other responsible official, the availability of funds to cover the proposed expenditure.

12-3-512 SECTION 31. Tennessee Code Annotated, Title 12, Chapter 3, Part 5, is amended by adding the following language as a new § 12-3-512:

12-3-512.

The central procurement office may participate in, sponsor, conduct or administer a cooperative purchasing agreement for the procurement of goods or services with one (1) or more other states or local governments in accordance with an agreement entered into between the participants. All cooperative purchasing conducted under this section shall be awarded through full and open competition and pursuant to policies or rules and regulations approved by the procurement commission.

12-3-513 SECTION 32. Tennessee Code Annotated, Title 12, Chapter 3, Part 5, is amended by adding the following language as a new § 12-3-513:

12-3-513.

(a) For a purchase of goods and services under this chapter, the central procurement office may purchase goods and services through a competitive reverse auction process that allows responses on specified goods or services electronically and adjustments to pricing during a specified time period. An award shall be made to the offeror determined to be the lowest responsible and responsive respondent at the close of the specified solicitation period.

(b) Policies and procedures concerning this procurement methodology, including the criteria, and the evaluation process shall be developed by the central procurement office and approved by the procurement commission.

(c) This section shall not apply to:

(1) Construction services; or

(2) Architectural or engineering services.

12-3-514 SECTION 33. Tennessee Code Annotated, Title 12, Chapter 3, Part 5, is amended by adding the following language as a new § 12-3-514:

12-3-514.

(a) Prior to the commencement of an action in court concerning the controversy, any actual respondent who claims to be aggrieved in connection with a procurement authorized under title 12, chapter 3, may protest to the chief procurement officer. The protest shall be submitted in writing within seven (7) calendar days after such claimant knows or should have known of the facts giving rise to the protest. Any issues raised by the protesting party after the seven-day period shall not be considered as part of the protest. In the case of a pending award, a stay of award in accordance with subsection (e) may be requested.

(b) The signature of an attorney or protesting party on a request for consideration, protest, motion, or other document constitutes a certification by the signer that the signer has read such document, that to the best of the signer's knowledge, information, and belief formed after reasonable inquiry, it is well grounded in fact and is warranted by existing law or a good faith argument for the extension, modification, or reversal of existing law, and that it is not interposed for any improper purpose, such as to harass, limit competition, or to cause unnecessary delay or needless increase in the cost of the procurement or of the litigation. If a request for consideration, protest, pleading, motion, or other document is signed in violation of this subsection (b) before or after appeal to the chief procurement officer and the protest committee, the chief procurement officer or protest committee, upon motion or upon its own initiative, may impose upon the person who signed it, a represented party, or both, an appropriate sanction, which may include an order to pay to the other party or parties, including the affected state agency, the amount of the reasonable expenses, including reasonable attorneys' fees incurred because of the filing of the protest, a petition for a stay of award, pleading, motion, or other paper.

(c) Neither a protest nor a stay of award shall proceed under this section unless the protesting party posts a protest bond. The protesting party shall post with the chief procurement officer, at the time of filing a notice of protest, a bond payable to the state in the amount of five percent (5%) of the lowest cost proposal evaluated or, if a protest is filed prior to the opening of cost proposals, the bond payable shall be five percent (5%) of the estimated maximum liability provided in the procurement document. The protest bond shall be in form and substance acceptable to the state and shall be immediately payable to the state conditioned upon a decision by the protest committee that:

(1) A request for consideration, protest, pleading, motion, or other document is signed, before or after appeal to the chief procurement officer or protest committee, in violation of subsection (b);

(2) The protest has been brought or pursued in bad faith; or

(3) The protest does not state on its face a valid basis for protest.

(d) The bond shall be payable to the state for any other reason approved by the protest committee. The state shall hold the protest bond for at least eleven (11) calendar days after the date of the final determination by the chief procurement officer. If the protesting party appeals the chief procurement officer's determination to the protest committee, the chief procurement officer shall hold the protest bond until instructed by the protest committee to either keep the bond or return it to the protesting party.

(1) At the time of filing notice of a protest of a procurement in which the lowest bid or lowest evaluated cost proposal is less than one million dollars ($1,000,000), a minority-owned business, woman-owned business, service-disabled veteran-owned business, or small business protesting party may submit a written petition for exemption from the protest bond requirement of subsection (c). The petition shall include clear evidence of a minority-owned business, woman-owned business, service-disabled veteran-owned business, or small business status. On the day of receipt, the petition shall be given to the chief procurement officer. The chief procurement officer has seven (7) calendar days in which to make a determination. If an exemption from the protest bond requirement is granted, the protest shall proceed as though the bond were posted. Should the chief procurement officer deny an exemption from the requirement, the protesting party shall post the protest bond with the chief procurement officer as required in subsection (c) within five (5) calendar days of the determination.

(2) For purposes of this subdivision (d)(1):

(A) "Minority" means a person who is a citizen or lawful permanent resident of the United States and who is:

(i) African American: a person having origins in any of the black racial groups of Africa;

(ii) Hispanic: a person of Mexican, Puerto Rican, Cuban, Central or South American, or other Spanish culture or origin, regardless of race;

(iii) Asian American: a person having origins in any of the original peoples of the Far East, Southeast Asia, the Indian subcontinent, or the Pacific Islands; or

(iv) Native American: a person having origins in any of the original peoples of North America;

(B) "Minority-owned business" means a minority-owned business that is a continuing, independent, for-profit business that performs a commercially useful function, and is at least fifty-one percent (51%) owned and controlled by one (1) or more minority individuals who are impeded from normal entry into the economic mainstream because of past practices of discrimination based on race or ethnic background;

(C) "Small business" means a business that is independently owned and operated, has total gross receipts of not more than ten million dollars ($10,000,000) averaged over a three-year period, or employs no more than ninety-nine (99) persons on a full-time basis;

(D) "Tennessee service-disabled veteran-owned business" means a service-disabled veteran-owned business that is a continuing, independent, for-profit business located in this state that performs a commercially useful function, and is at least fifty-one percent (51%) owned and controlled by one (1) or more service-disabled veterans. In the case of a business solely owned by one (1) service-disabled veteran and such person's spouse, is at least fifty percent (50%) owned and controlled by the service-disabled veteran or in the case of any publicly owned business, at least fifty-one percent (51%) of the stock of which is owned and controlled by one (1) or more service-disabled veterans and whose management and daily business operations are under the control of one (1) or more service-disabled veterans; and

(E) "Woman-owned business" means a woman-owned business that is a continuing, independent, for-profit business that performs a commercially useful function, and is at least fifty-one percent (51%) owned and controlled by one (1) or more women; or, in the case of any publicly owned business, at least fifty-one percent (51%) of the stock of which is owned and controlled by one (1) or more women and whose management and daily business operations are under the control of one (1) or more women.

(3) The chief procurement officer, in consultation with the head of the state agency, has the authority to resolve the protest. The chief procurement officer shall have no longer than sixty (60) calendar days from receipt of a protest to resolve the protest. The final determination of the chief procurement officer shall be given in writing and submitted to the protestor and the protest committee, and the comptroller of the treasury. If the chief procurement officer fails to resolve the protest within sixty (60) calendar days, the protesting party may request that the protest committee meet to consider the protest.

(4) If a protest is not resolved by mutual agreement within sixty (60) calendar days, the protesting party may request the matter be considered at a meeting with the protest committee. The request for consideration before the protest committee shall be made in writing within seven (7) calendar days from the date of the chief procurement officer's final determination or within seven (7) calendar days following the chief procurement officer's failure to resolve the protest within sixty (60) calendar days after receipt of the protest.

(e) Prior to the award of a contract, respondents who have protested may submit to the chief procurement officer a written petition for stay of award. Such stay shall become effective upon receipt by the state. The state shall not proceed further with the procurement process or with the award of the contract until the protest has been resolved in accordance with this section, unless the protest committee makes a written determination that continuation of the procurement process or the award of the contract without delay is necessary to protect substantial interests of the state. It shall be the responsibility of the chief procurement officer, with the assistance of the procuring agency, to seek such a determination by the protest committee. The chief procurement officer shall provide the minutes of the protest proceedings to each committee member and to the comptroller of the treasury and shall post the final determination within fifteen (15) business days to the single public procurement website.

(f) Nothing in this section shall be construed to require a contested case hearing as set forth in the Uniform Administrative Procedures Act, compiled in chapter 5 of this title. The protesting party must exhaust all administrative remedies provided in this section prior to the initiation of any judicial review of the protest.

(g) Should a protest be received by the state subsequent to a contract being completely executed pursuant to a procurement process, the Tennessee claims commission has exclusive jurisdiction to determine all monetary claims against the state, including, but not limited to, claims for the negligent deprivation of statutory rights pursuant to § 9-8-307(a)(1)(N).

(h) Protests appealed to the chancery court from the protest committee shall be by common law writ of certiorari. The scope of review in the proceedings shall be limited to the record made before the protest committee and shall involve only an inquiry into whether the protest committee exceeded its jurisdiction, followed an unlawful procedure, or acted illegally, fraudulently, or arbitrarily without material evidence to support its action.

12-3-515 — 12-3-531 SECTION 34. Tennessee Code Annotated, Sections 12-3-515 through 12-3-531, are amended by deleting these sections in their entireties.

12-3-601 SECTION 35. Tennessee Code Annotated, Section 12-3-601, is amended by deleting the section in its entirety and by substituting instead the following:

12-3-601.

(a) A contractor who makes a contract with the state under this chapter shall, except as provided in subsection (c), submit cost or pricing data, and shall certify that, to the best of its knowledge and belief, the cost of pricing data submitted was accurate, complete, and current as of a mutually determined specified date prior to the date of:

(1) The pricing of any contract awarded pursuant to sole source procurement authority pursuant to § 12-3-504, where the total contract price is expected to exceed an amount established by the procurement commission; or

(2) The pricing of any change order or contract modification which is expected to exceed an amount established by the procurement commission.

(b) Any contract, change order, or contract modification under which a certificate is required shall contain a provision that the price to the state, including profit or fee, shall be adjusted to exclude any significant sums by which the state finds that such price was increased because the contractor-furnished cost or pricing data was inaccurate, incomplete, or not current as of the date agreed upon between the parties.

(c) The requirements of this section need not be applied to contracts when:

(1) The contract price is based on adequate price competition;

(2) The contract price is based on established catalogue prices or market prices;

(3) Contract prices are set by law or regulation; or

(4) It is determined in writing in accordance with regulations promulgated by the procurement commission that the requirements of this section may be waived, and the reasons for such waiver are stated in writing.

12-3-602 SECTION 36. Tennessee Code Annotated, Section 12-3-602, is amended by deleting the section in its entirety and by substituting instead the following:

12-3-602.

(a) The state may, at reasonable times, and subject to regulation of the procurement commission, inspect the part of the plant or place of business of a contractor or any subcontractor which is related to the performance of any contract awarded or to be awarded by the state.

(b) The state may, at reasonable times and places, audit the books and records of any person who has submitted cost or pricing data to the extent that such books and records relate to such cost or pricing data. Any person who receives a contract, change order, or contract modification for which cost or pricing data are required, shall maintain such books and records that relate to such cost or pricing data for three (3) years from the date of final payment under the contract, unless a shorter period is otherwise authorized in writing.

(c) The state shall be entitled to audit the books and records of a contractor or any subcontractor under any contract or subcontract other than a firm fixed-price contract, to the extent that such books and records relate to the performance of such contract or subcontract. Such books and records shall be maintained by the contractor for a period of three (3) years from the date of final payment under the prime contract and by the subcontractor for a period of three (3) years from the date of final payment under the subcontract, unless a shorter period is otherwise authorized in writing. All contracts after July 1, 2013, shall include a provision with this statutory requirement and the provision cannot be amended or removed without the written consent of the comptroller of the treasury.

12-3-603 SECTION 37. Tennessee Code Annotated, Section 12-3-603, is amended by deleting the section in its entirety and by substituting instead the following:

12-3-603.

The chief procurement officer shall propose regulations for approval by the procurement commission setting forth cost principles which shall be used to determine the allowability of incurred costs for the purpose of reimbursing costs under contract provisions that provide for the reimbursement of costs; provided, that if a written determination is made by the chief procurement officer to justify such action, such cost principles may be modified by contract and reported to the comptroller of the treasury.

12-3-604 — 12-3-612 SECTION 38. Tennessee Code Annotated, Sections 12-3-604 through 12-3-612, are amended by deleting these sections in their entireties.

12-3-701 SECTION 39. Tennessee Code Annotated, Section 12-3-701, is amended by deleting the section in its entirety and by substituting instead the following:

12-3-701.

(a) The chief procurement officer, pursuant to policies or rules and regulations of the procurement commission, may authorize the procurement of goods and services through a solicitation process in which a limitation of liability is authorized by the chief procurement officer and set forth in the documents initiating the solicitation process. Such procurement may be undertaken only in accordance with rules and regulations describing the circumstances in which such procurement may be permitted and what types of limitations of liability may be allowed.

(b)(1) The rules and regulations, as presented to the procurement commission by the chief procurement officer, may describe the circumstances in which such procurement may be permitted and the types of limitations of liability to be allowed. The chief procurement officer may not authorize limitation of the liability of a contractor to an amount less than two (2) times the value of the contract unless the chief procurement officer determines, and the comptroller of the treasury approves, that:

(A) Allowing the limitation of liability is necessary to prevent harm to the state from failing to obtain the goods or services sought, or from obtaining the goods or services at a higher price, if the state refused to allow a limitation of liability as long as all respondents are offered the same opportunity as provided in the solicitation;

(B) The limitations and any alternative contract language are commercially reasonable in light of the risks to the state created by the type of goods or services purchased and the purposes for which they will be used; and

(C) The state shall not agree to limit the liability of any contractor for intentional torts, criminal acts, or fraudulent conduct.

(2) The rules and regulations shall also allow the chief procurement officer to authorize negotiation of a limitation on a contractor's liability with comptroller of the treasury approval in circumstances when the applicable procurement process has failed to provide a qualified respondent.

(c) Notwithstanding the foregoing or any other law to the contrary, the chief procurement officer and the comptroller of the treasury shall permit a limitation of liability to an amount not less than two (2) times the maximum liability under the contract. The limitation of liability shall not apply to intentional torts, criminal acts, fraudulent conduct or acts or omissions that result in personal injuries or death. If the chief procurement officer determines that it is necessary to protect the interests of the state to increase the limitation of liability to an amount greater than that authorized under this subsection (c), the chief procurement officer, comptroller of the treasury and the commissioner of finance and administration may increase the limitation of liability of the contractor to an amount in excess of two (2) times the value of the contract.

(d) The purpose of this section is to limit the monetary damages recoverable by the state in a claim or legal action against its contractor. This section shall not be construed to authorize any further limitation on the legal rights of the state, and shall not constitute a waiver of sovereign immunity of the state, and shall not authorize a cause of action against the state in any jurisdiction.

12-3-702 — 12-3-704 SECTION 40. Tennessee Code Annotated, Sections 12-3-702 through 12-3-704, are amended by deleting these sections in their entireties.

12-3-801 SECTION 41. Tennessee Code Annotated, Section 12-3-801, is amended by deleting the section in its entirety and by substituting instead the following:

12-3-801.

Whenever possible, all procurement specifications and scopes of work for goods and services to be purchased by the central procurement office or state agencies shall be worded or designed to permit open and competitive soliciting for the supplying of the goods or services to which they apply and all proprietary specifications and scopes of work shall be developed in accordance with rules of the central procurement office approved by the procurement commission.

12-3-802 SECTION 42. Tennessee Code Annotated, Section 12-3-802, is amended by deleting the section in its entirety and by substituting instead the following:

12-3-802.

It is the duty of all state agencies to furnish to the chief procurement officer recommended specifications for all goods and services required and to be required by such state agencies. It is the duty of the chief procurement officer to canvas the recommended specifications and either approve or modify the standard specifications and scopes of work so recommended, subject to the policy and criteria of the procurement commission. All standard specifications and scopes of work shall remain on file in the central procurement office and shall be posted on the central procurement office's website. Each standard specification adopted for any good or service shall fit, insofar as possible, the requirements of the majority of the state agencies that use the same.

12-3-803 SECTION 43. Tennessee Code Annotated, Section 12-3-803, is amended by deleting the section in its entirety and by substituting instead the following:

12-3-803.

After the approval and adoption of standard specifications in the manner provided in § 12-3-802, changes in, alterations to, modifications of, or additions to such standard specifications may be made in accordance with rules or policy of the central procurement office as approved by the procurement commission.

12-3-804 SECTION 44. Tennessee Code Annotated, Section 12-3-804, is amended by deleting the section in its entirety and by substituting instead the following:

12-3-804.

The chief procurement officer shall make use of standard specifications whenever practicable. Goods and services purchased without standard specifications shall be made in accordance with policies and criteria established by the procurement commission.

12-3-805 SECTION 45. Tennessee Code Annotated, Section 12-3-805, is amended by deleting the section in its entirety and by substituting instead the following:

12-3-805.

Whenever any department, institution, or agency of state government requisitions any goods or services for which a standard specification has not been adopted and approved, it shall be accompanied by or contain a recommended specification for such goods or services.

12-3-806 SECTION 46. Tennessee Code Annotated, Section 12-3-806, is amended by deleting the section in its entirety and by substituting instead the following:

12-3-806.

(a) Whenever the chief procurement officer determines it to be advantageous, then specifications for office goods to be purchased by the state agencies shall be worded or designed so as to permit remanufactured office goods to be eligible for purchase. Such specifications may provide that remanufactured office materials, supplies and equipment be comparable in use and quality to new or currently manufactured office materials, supplies and equipment.

(b) The chief procurement officer shall prepare and submit to the governor, the speakers of the senate and the house of representatives, the chairs of the committees on government operations, and the procurement commission, a biennial report concerning the purchase of remanufactured office goods. Such report shall include the amount and frequency of such purchases, the cost savings realized by the state as a result of such purchases, and any remaining issues or areas for improvement.

12-3-807 SECTION 47. Tennessee Code Annotated, Section 12-3-807, is amended by deleting the section in its entirety and by substituting instead the following:

12-3-807.

(a) Standard specifications adopted for lubricating motor oil for competitive solicitations to be let by the central procurement office, or by the appropriate purchasing agencies for any political subdivision of the state, shall be prescribed to include re-refined or recycled lubricating motor oil. Such specifications may exclude re-refined or recycled lubricating motor oil for circumstances or equipment that require specialized treatment, upon submission of documented evidence to the procurement commission or the appropriate purchasing agency of the political subdivision to substantiate each such claim for exclusion.

(b) Standard specifications adopted for lubricating motor oil for competitive solicitations to be let by any state agency or by any political subdivision of the state, shall be prescribed to include re-refined or recycled lubricating motor oil. Such specifications may exclude re-refined or recycled lubricating motor oil for circumstances or equipment that require specialized treatment, upon submission of documented evidence to the appropriate departmental, institutional or agency head to substantiate each such claim for exclusion. The requirements of this section shall not be construed to prohibit such state agency from purchasing and contracting for the purchase of such re-refined or recycled lubricating motor oil through the central procurement office or through the appropriate local purchasing agency.

(c) Any nonprofit corporation receiving funding from the state or contracting with any department, institution, or agency of state government or political subdivision of the state to provide services to the public, shall be authorized to purchase and contract for the purchase of such re-refined or recycled lubricating motor oil as provided in this section through the central procurement office under this chapter or through the appropriate local purchasing agency.

(d)(1) The central procurement office shall compile and publish a list of business entities that commercially distribute re-refined or recycled lubricating motor oil that complies with the standard specifications adopted by the central procurement office pursuant to this section. The central procurement office shall make such list available to the various entities and political subdivisions of state government. The central procurement office shall mail such list to the chief executive of each county and each municipality.

(2) Prior to accepting competitive responses for a contract concerning lubricating motor oil, a county or municipality shall notify each business entity on the central procurement office's list of relevant facts concerning such proposed contract.

12-3-808 SECTION 48. Tennessee Code Annotated, Section 12-3-808, is amended by deleting the section in its entirety and by substituting instead the following:

12-3-808.

(a) Specifications for purchases of chemical products pursuant to this chapter shall require that the manufacturer of the chemical products create and maintain a material safety data sheet (MSDS) for such chemical products on the national MSDSSEARCH repository or the manufacturer's website so that the information can be accessed by means of the Internet. A site operated by or on behalf of the manufacturer or a relevant trade association is acceptable so long as the information is freely accessible to the public. In lieu of posting a MSDS on MSDSSEARCH, a respondent shall include the manufacturer's URL for their MSDS in the response proposal or purchase order.

(b) The chief procurement officer shall post on the chief procurement officer's website the universal resource locator (URL) for MSDSSEARCH.

12-3-809 — 12-3-813 SECTION 49. Tennessee Code Annotated, Sections 12-3-809 through 12-3-813, are amended by deleting these sections in their entirety.

12-3-901 SECTION 50. Tennessee Code Annotated, Section 12-3-901, is amended by deleting the section in its entirety and by substituting instead the following:

12-3-901. This part shall be known as and may be cited as the "Life Cycle Cost and Procurement Act of 1978."

12-3-902 SECTION 51. Tennessee Code Annotated, Section 12-3-902, is amended by deleting the section in its entirety and by substituting instead the following:

12-3-902.

As used in this part, unless the context otherwise requires:

(1) "Energy efficiency standard" means a performance standard which prescribes the relationship of the energy use of a product to its useful output of services;

(2) "Major energy-consuming product" means any article so designated by the chief procurement officer in consultation with the central procurement office staff;

(3) "Political subdivision" means any city, town, municipality or county within the state; and

(4) "State procurement commission" means the commission established as set forth in title 4, chapter 56.

12-3-903 SECTION 52. Tennessee Code Annotated, Section 12-3-903, is amended by deleting the section in its entirety and by substituting instead the following:

12-3-903.

It is hereby declared to be the policy of the state and its political subdivisions to use the life cycle costs of commodities as developed and disseminated by the federal government when purchased by the state or its political subdivisions where feasible as provided in this part.

12-3-904 SECTION 53. Tennessee Code Annotated, Section 12-3-904, is amended by deleting the section in its entirety and by substituting instead the following:

12-3-904.

The chief procurement officer, to the maximum extent feasible, shall determine which commodities and products purchased by the state may be purchased according to energy efficiency standards based on rules and regulations, policies, and procedures approved by the procurement commission.

12-3-905 SECTION 54. Tennessee Code Annotated, Section 12-3-905, is amended by deleting the section in its entirety and by substituting instead the following:

12-3-905.

(a) The chief procurement officer, in consultation with the central procurement office staff, shall adopt rules and regulations approved by the procurement commission relative to energy efficiency standards for major energy-consuming products to be procured by the state.

(b) When federal energy efficiency standards exist, the procurement commission, in consultation with the department of general services, shall, where feasible, adopt standards at least as stringent as the federal standards.

(c) For the purpose of implementing this part only, the central procurement office shall advise and consult with the chief procurement officer as an ex officio member.

(d) All future office equipment, appliances, lighting and heating and cooling products and systems purchased by and for state agencies shall be Energy Star qualified; provided, that such Energy Star qualified products and systems are commercially available.

(e) Existing purchasing contracts for all state agencies that do not provide as options Energy Star qualified office equipment, appliances, lighting and heating and cooling products and systems shall not be renewed upon expiration. All future contracts for state agencies shall provide as options Energy Star qualified office equipment, appliances, lighting and heating and cooling products and systems.

(f) The central procurement office, in consultation with the department of finance and administration, shall establish and publish guidelines providing direction to all state agencies regarding implementation of this section.

12-3-906 SECTION 55. Tennessee Code Annotated, Section 12-3-906, is amended by deleting the section in its entirety and by substituting instead the following:

12-3-906.

When energy efficiency standards are established, the procurement commission shall adopt rules requiring life cycle costs to be used by the chief procurement officer in contracting for major energy-consuming products. In determining life cycle costs, the procurement commission and the chief procurement officer may consider the acquisition cost of the product, the energy consumption and the projected cost of energy over the useful life of the product, and the anticipated resale or salvage value of the product.

12-3-907 SECTION 56. Tennessee Code Annotated, Section 12-3-907, is amended by deleting the section in its entirety and by substituting instead the following:

12-3-907.

Except when private act or state law prohibits, every political subdivision shall adopt and incorporate in its procurement policies energy efficiency standards and life cycle costing employed by the state in its procurement policies.

12-3-908 SECTION 57. Tennessee Code Annotated, Section 12-3-908, is amended by deleting the section in its entirety and by substituting instead the following:

12-3-908.

(a) Executory contracts for the purchase of commodities by a political subdivision included in this part shall be voidable by the circuit courts upon the bringing of an action by an aggrieved party.

(b) The court may void the contract upon the showing by the aggrieved party that:

(1) The party is a seller of the commodity;

(2) The party is doing business in the state;

(3) The commodity to be sold has an energy efficiency rating and life cycle cost lower than the commodity contracted for by the purchaser;

(4) The purchaser is a political subdivision, and the standard for the commodity has been adopted for one (1) year by the procurement commission and has not been incorporated or adopted by the political subdivision; and

(5) The aggrieved party is ready, willing and able, without any other legal constraints, to sell the commodity to the purchaser.

12-3-909, 12-3-910, 12-3-911, 12-3-912 SECTION 58. Tennessee Code Annotated, title 12, chapter 3, part 9, is amended by adding appropriately designated sections as follows:

12-3-909.

The chief procurement officer shall provide technical assistance to aid in the development or implementation of energy efficiency standards for procurement policies to political subdivisions that request assistance.

12-3-910.

The appropriate state agencies shall cooperate and coordinate their efforts in the development and implementation of energy efficiency standards for procurement policies to the fullest extent possible with the Tennessee municipal league, the municipal technical advisory service, the county technical advisory service, the Tennessee county services association, and any other appropriate state or local agency or group.

12-3-911.

Nothing in this part shall be construed to prohibit the adoption of an energy efficiency standard by a political subdivision when that standard has not been adopted by rules of the procurement commission, or where the standard proposed to be adopted by the political subdivision is more stringent than the standard adopted by the rules of the procurement commission.

12-3-912.

The Uniform Administrative Procedures Act, compiled in title 4, chapter 5, shall apply to this part.

12-3-1001 SECTION 59. Tennessee Code Annotated, Section 12-3-1001, is amended by deleting the section in its entirety and by substituting instead the following:

12-3-1001.

No person, firm or corporation shall be considered for contract award by the central procurement office under this chapter or under the rules and regulations established by the central procurement office, unless and until such person, firm, or corporation makes proper application to the central procurement office, as prescribed by rule or policy approved by the procurement commission, to be placed upon the permanent register of respondents. The central procurement office shall establish and maintain the register under and in compliance with the rules and regulations adopted by the procurement commission.

12-3-1002 SECTION 60. Tennessee Code Annotated, Section 12-3-1002, is amended by deleting the section in its entirety and by substituting instead the following:

12-3-1002.

All such applications by prospective respondents shall contain:

(1) A verified statement by the applicant disclosing and setting forth the types or classes of goods or services which the applicant desires to furnish and is able to furnish to the state or any state agency;

(2) A statement disclosing whether such applicant will furnish such goods or services as a manufacturer, dealer, agent, distributor, factor, or otherwise; and

(3) Such other information as may be required by the central procurement office to establish the ability of the applicant to perform any future undertaking for the state.

12-3-1003 SECTION 61. Tennessee Code Annotated, Section 12-3-1003, is amended by deleting the section in its entirety and by substituting instead the following:

12-3-1003.

The central procurement office shall establish and maintain from the permanent register of respondents a permanent mailing list, which shall include the names and mailing addresses of all interested respondents.

12-3-1004 SECTION 62. Tennessee Code Annotated, Section 12-3-1004, is amended by deleting the section in its entirety and by substituting instead the following:

12-3-1004.

Notwithstanding any provision of law, rule or regulation to the contrary, the central procurement office may satisfy any requirement for mailing by distributing solicitations electronically and posting solicitations to the central procurement office Internet website. In addition, the central procurement office may receive responses electronically. In order to assure the fullest possible participation of small businesses and minority-owned businesses, the central procurement office shall not require such small businesses and minority-owned businesses to receive or respond to solicitations electronically.

12-3-1007, 12-3-1008, 12-3-1009, 12-3-1010, 12-3-1011, 12-3-1012 SECTION 63. Tennessee Code Annotated, Sections 12-3-1007 through 12-3-1012, are amended by deleting these sections in their entirety.

12-3-1101 SECTION 64. Tennessee Code Annotated, Section 12-3-1101, is amended by deleting the section in its entirety and by substituting instead the following:

12-3-1101.

Sections 12-3-1101 -- 12-3-1108 shall be known and may be cited as the "Tennessee Minority-Owned, Woman-Owned and Small Business Procurement and Contracting Act."

12-3-1102 SECTION 65. Tennessee Code Annotated, Section 12-3-1102, is amended by deleting the section in its entirety and by substituting instead the following:

12-3-1102.

As used in this part, unless the context otherwise requires:

(1) "Department" means the department of general services;

(2) "Minority" means a person who is a citizen or lawful permanent resident of the United States and who is:

(A) African American, a person having origins in any of the black racial groups of Africa;

(B) Hispanic, a person of Mexican, Puerto Rican, Cuban, Central or South American, or other Spanish culture or origin, regardless of race;

(C) Asian American, a person having origins in any of the original peoples of the Far East, Southeast Asia, the Indian subcontinent, or the Pacific Islands; or

(D) Native American, a person having origins in any of the original peoples of North America;

(3) "Minority-owned business" means a minority-owned business that is a continuing, independent, for profit business that performs a commercially useful function, and is at least fifty-one percent (51%) owned and controlled by one (1) or more minority individuals who are impeded from normal entry into the economic mainstream because of past practices of discrimination based on race or ethnic background;

(4) "Procurement and contracting" means the procurement of equipment, supplies, personal services, professional services, consulting services, construction contracts, and architectural and engineering services;

(5) "Small business" means a business that is a continuing, independent, for profit business which performs a commercially useful function with residence in this state and has total gross receipts of not more than ten million dollars ($10,000,000) averaged over a three-year period or employs no more than ninety-nine (99) persons on a full-time basis;

(6) "State agency" means any department, office, institution of higher education, board, commission, or any other state agency that receives state funds;

(7) "Tennessee service-disabled veteran" means any person who served honorably on active duty in the armed forces of the United States with at least a twenty percent (20%) disability that is service-connected, meaning that such disability was incurred or aggravated in the line of duty in the active military, naval or air service;

(8) "Tennessee service-disabled veteran-owned business" means a service-disabled veteran-owned business that is a continuing, independent, for profit business located in this state that performs a commercially useful function, and:

(A) Is at least fifty-one percent (51%) owned and controlled by one (1) or more service-disabled veterans;

(B) In the case of a business solely owned by one (1) service-disabled veteran and such person's spouse, is at least fifty percent (50%) owned and controlled by the service-disabled veteran; or

(C) In the case of any publicly owned business, at least fifty-one percent (51%) of the stock of which is owned and controlled by one (1) or more service-disabled veterans and whose management and daily business operations are under the control of one (1) or more service-disabled veterans;

(9) "Tennessee small business" means a business that is a continuing, independent, for profit business which performs a commercially useful function with residence in Tennessee and has total gross receipts of no more than ten million dollars ($10,000,000) averaged over a three-year period or employs no more than ninety-nine (99) persons on a full-time basis; and

(10) "Woman-owned business" means a woman-owned business that is a continuing, independent, for profit business that performs a commercially useful function, and is at least fifty-one percent (51%) owned and controlled by one or more women; or, in the case of any publicly owned business, at least fifty-one percent (51%) of the stock of which is owned and controlled by one (1) or more women and whose management and daily business operations are under the control of one (1) or more women.

12-3-1103 SECTION 66. Tennessee Code Annotated, Section 12-3-1103, is amended by deleting the section in its entirety and by substituting instead the following:

12-3-1103.

(a) The procurement commission is authorized to adopt rules and regulations establishing criteria and standards for minority-owned, woman-owned, Tennessee service-disabled veteran-owned and Tennessee small businesses that are eligible to be included under this part. Such rules and regulations shall include methods by which eligibility can be verified and the business deemed certified.

(b) Such criteria and standards for eligibility shall include, but not be limited to, the number of employees, the total gross receipts or annual sales volume, including ownership and control.

(c) The maximum number of employees and the maximum dollar value of a small business under such rules and regulations may vary from industry to industry to the extent necessary to reflect the differing characteristics of any relevant factors of each particular industry.

(d) The governor's office of diversity business enterprises shall implement and administer a certification program and publish a directory of businesses certified as Tennessee small businesses and diversity business enterprises.

(e) Any business desiring to be certified as a Tennessee small business or diversity business enterprise shall make application to the governor's office of diversity business enterprises on an application as prescribed by such office.

12-3-1104 — 12-3-1113 SECTION 67. Tennessee Code Annotated, title 12, chapter 3, part 11, is amended by adding appropriately designated sections as follows:

12-3-1104.

(a)(1) All state agencies are required to actively solicit bids and proposals for equipment, supplies, personal services, professional services, consulting services, construction contracts, and architectural and engineering services from a minority-owned business, woman-owned business, service-disabled veteran-owned business, or small business in order to strive to obtain a fair proportion of procurements from any minority-owned business, woman-owned business, service-disabled veteran-owned business, or small business.

(2) The amount of fair proportion shall be recommended annually by the governor's office of diversity business enterprises to the procurement commission for its review and approval. In annually determining such amount of fair proportion, the procurement commission shall establish, based on the recommendation of the governor's office of diversity business enterprises a separate amount of fair proportion for each of the four (4) subcategories of minority-owned businesses set forth within § 12-3-1102 woman-owned, Tennessee service-disabled veteran-owned businesses and small businesses. Nothing in this part shall be construed as establishing any mandatory goal or quota with respect to minority-owned business, woman-owned business, service-disabled veteran-owned business, or small businesses.

(b) Procurements shall not be deemed to be from either minority-owned business, woman-owned business, service-disabled veteran-owned business, or small business if the business with which such contracting is done is owned by or is under the controlling interest of another business which exceeds the limitations of § 12-3-1103. No minority-owned business, woman-owned business, service-disabled veteran-owned business, or small business to which a contract has been awarded shall subcontract any portion of such contract with any business which exceeds the limitations of § 12-3-1103 and continue to maintain eligibility under this part without express approval of the chief procurement officer.

(c) As used in subsection (a), "actively solicit bids and proposals" may include contacting the governor's office of diversity business enterprises; reviewing compiled directories of a minority-owned business, woman-owned business, service-disabled veteran-owned business, or small business; purchasing publication of notices within newspapers of general circulation or through electronic media; and inviting any minority-owned business, woman-owned business, service-disabled veteran-owned business, or small business to submit bids or to obtain information pertaining to the submission of bids.

12-3-1105.

The departments of general services, finance and administration, transportation and economic and community development, and the state building commission shall cooperate with the governor's office of diversity business enterprises in the design and implementation of procedures for the identification of any minority-owned business, woman-owned business, service-disabled veteran-owned business, or small business, the selection for bid and proposal lists and the monitoring of procurements from minority-owned business, woman-owned business, service-disabled veteran-owned business, or small business.

12-3-1106.

(a) The chief procurement officer, as director of the governor's office of diversity business enterprises, shall appoint a diversity business program director to work in conjunction with the departments of general services, finance and administration, transportation, economic and community development and the state building commission to:

(1) Compile and maintain a comprehensive list of any minority-owned business, woman-owned business, service-disabled veteran-owned business, or small business by cooperating with both governmental and private sector entities in locating potential sources for various products and services;

(2) Assist any minority-owned business, woman-owned business, service-disabled veteran-owned business, or small business in complying with state procurement and contracting procedures and requirements;

(3) Examine requests from state agencies for the purchase of goods or services to help determine which solicitations may offer increased opportunities for any minority-owned business, woman-owned business, service-disabled veteran-owned business, or small business; and

(4) Make recommendations to appropriate state agencies for the simplification of procurement and contract specifications and terms in order to increase the opportunities of participation by any minority-owned business, woman-owned business, service-disabled veteran-owned business, or small business.

(b) All state agencies shall fully cooperate with the governor's office of diversity business enterprises and shall provide staff support and any other assistance upon request of the chief procurement officer. This cooperation specifically includes, but is not limited to, establishing and striving to achieve annual state agency level internal goals for minority-owned business, woman-owned business, service-disabled veteran-owned business, or small business contracting. In establishing and striving to achieve these annual goals, each agency shall work closely with the governor's office of diversity business enterprises. Each agency shall provide as requested to the governor's office of diversity business enterprises periodic reports on upcoming procurement and contract opportunities and on the level of participation by minority-owned business, woman-owned business, service-disabled veteran-owned business, or small business in that agency's procurements and contracts.

12-3-1107.

(a) The chief procurement officer shall annually report, on or before each December 31, to the governor and to each member of the general assembly concerning the awarding of purchases to minority-owned business, woman-owned business, service-disabled veteran-owned business, or small business and the total value of awards made during the preceding fiscal year under this part. The chief procurement officer shall also include in such annual report:

(1) The number of solicitations of minority-owned business, woman-owned business, service-disabled veteran-owned business, or small business by category;

(2) The number of responses received from minority-owned business, woman-owned business, service-disabled veteran-owned business, or small business by category; and

(3) The dollar amount of purchases awarded to such businesses by category.

(b) In annually reporting the information on any minority-owned business, woman-owned business, service-disabled veteran-owned business, or small business, based upon information provided by vendors, the chief procurement officer shall, in a separate section of the report, indicate the number of businesses solicited within each of the four (4) subcategories enumerated within § 12-3-1102, the number of responses received from each of the four (4) subcategories enumerated within § 12-3-1102, and the total number and dollar amount of all purchases awarded within each of the four (4) subcategories enumerated within § 12-3-1102. For purposes of evaluation, the report shall also indicate the total number and dollar amount of all purchases by all state agencies during the reporting period.

12-3-1108.

All departments, agencies and institutions of state government that purchase meat, meat food products or meat by-products, as defined in § 53-7-202, with state funds shall give preference to producers located within the boundaries of this state when awarding contracts or agreements for the purchase of such meat or meat products, so long as the terms, conditions and quality associated with the in-state producers' proposals are equal to those obtainable from producers located elsewhere.

12-3-1109.

All public education institutions using state funds to purchase meat, meat food products, or meat by-products, as defined in § 53-7-202, shall give preference in awarding contracts or agreements for the purchase of such meat or meat products to producers located within the boundaries of this state so long as the terms, conditions and quality associated with the in-state producers' proposals are equal to those obtainable from producers located elsewhere.

12-3-1110.

Notwithstanding any provision of law to the contrary, all state agencies, departments, boards, commissions, institutions, institutions of higher education, schools and all other state entities shall purchase coal mined in this state if such coal is available at a delivered price that is equal to or less than coal mined outside the state.

12-3-1111.

Notwithstanding any provision of law to the contrary, all state agencies, departments, boards, commissions, institutions, institutions of higher education, schools and all other state entities shall purchase natural gas produced from wells located in the state if such gas is available at a price which is equal to or less than natural gas produced from wells located outside the state, transportation costs taken into account.

12-3-1112.

(a) There is created the governor's office of diversity business enterprises to administer this part. All positions, resources and functions of the governor's office of diversity business enterprises existing within the department of general services shall be transferred to the procurement office on October 1, 2011.

(b) The office of diversity business enterprises shall assist small businesses and businesses owned by minorities and women to develop into viable, successful businesses. This work shall include assisting these businesses to compete successfully for the state's expenditures for goods and services.

(c) Each state agency shall designate a staff person as a small business liaison representative to the governor's office of diversity business enterprises to coordinate the agency's efforts to utilize Tennessee small businesses and diversity business enterprises in their procurement and contracting opportunities.

(d) After appointment of the chief procurement officer, such officer, in consultation with the department of general services and the department of economic and community development, shall study opportunities available to Tennessee small businesses and diversity business enterprises in state contracting and the potential effect of enhancing such opportunities through utilization of monetary allowances. It is the legislative intent that such study shall, insofar as possible, assess the impact on Tennessee small businesses and diversity business enterprises that would have occurred if monetary allowances of varying amounts had been available. Further, it is the legislative intent that such study shall estimate the costs to the state that would have resulted from such monetary allowances.

(e) The small business advocate within the office of the comptroller of the treasury shall be qualified by training or relevant and recent experience in administering programs to encourage and enhance economic opportunities for small businesses, woman-owned businesses and minority-owned businesses. At least annually, the advocate shall attend training or other specialized instruction to enhance understanding of the particular obstacles impeding woman-owned and minority-owned businesses from normal entry into the economic mainstream. Such training shall be provided by the governor's office of diversity business enterprises in the normal course of business as part of the regular training program for state agencies. When the advocate position is filled by reassigning a current employee, such employee shall receive the requisite training prior to assuming the advocate duties.

12-3-1113.

(a) Notwithstanding any other provision of law to the contrary, all departments and agencies making purchases of goods, including agricultural products, shall give preference to those produced or grown in this state or offered by Tennessee respondents as follows:

(1) Goods produced in this state or offered by Tennessee respondents shall be given equal preference if the cost to the state and quality are equal; and

(2) Agricultural products grown in this state shall be given first preference and agricultural products offered by Tennessee respondents shall be given second preference, if the cost to the state and quality are equal.

(b) If goods, including agricultural products, produced or grown in this state or offered by Tennessee respondents are not equal in cost and quality to other products, then goods, including agricultural products, produced or grown in other states of the United States shall be given preference over foreign products if the cost to the state and quality are equal.

(c) As used in this section:

(1) "Agricultural products" includes textiles and other similar products; and

(2) "Tennessee respondents" means a business:

(A) Incorporated in this state;

(B) That has its principal place of business in this state; or

(C) That has an established physical presence in this state.

(d) The commission and all state agencies making purchases of vegetation for landscaping purposes, including plants, shall give preference to Tennessee vegetation native to the region if the cost to the state is not greater and the quality is not inferior.

(e) All departments and agencies procuring services shall give preference to services offered by a Tennessee respondent if:

(1) The services meet state requirements regarding the service to be performed and expected quality; and

(2) The cost of the service does not exceed the cost of other similar services of similar expected quality that are not offered by a Tennessee respondent.

12-3-1201 SECTION 68. Tennessee Code Annotated, Section 12-3-1201, is amended by deleting the section in its entirety and by substituting instead the following:

12-3-1201.

(a) The central procurement office may, upon request, purchase goods and services for any county, city, municipality, special district, school district, other local governmental unit of the state, or quasi-governmental entity organized under a city, municipality, or county. The purchases shall be made on the same terms and under the same rules and regulations as now provided for the purchase of goods and services by the central procurement office. The cost of any purchase made pursuant to this section shall be borne by the local governmental unit concerned. The central procurement office has the power to promulgate all rules and regulations necessary for the operation of this section, subject to the approval of the procurement commission.

(b) It is the intent of this section that the central procurement office advise local governments of the benefits to be derived from the use of the purchasing procedures authorized herein. Where any local or private act, charter, or general law requires that a local governmental unit purchase by competitive procurement method, the local unit of government may, notwithstanding the local or private act, charter, or general law, purchase, without public advertisement or competitive soliciting, under the provisions of contracts or price agreements entered into by the central procurement office.

(c) To the extent permitted by federal law or regulations, local governments may make purchases of goods, except motor vehicles, or services included in federal general service administration contracts or other applicable federal open purchase contracts either directly or through the appropriate state agency; provided, that no purchase under this section shall be made at a price higher than that which is contained in the contract between the general services administration and the vendor affected.

(d)(1) Except as provided in subdivision (d)(5), when any local or private act, charter, or general law requires that a local governmental unit purchase by competitive soliciting, the local unit of government may, notwithstanding the local or private act, charter, or general law, purchase, without public advertisement or competitive soliciting, any item from local sources if such item is available for purchase under the provisions of contracts or price agreements entered into by the central procurement office, and such item is available at the same or lower cost from such local sources. This subsection (d) shall apply only in cases where the local governmental entity is not permitted to purchase from an existing contract established by the central procurement office. Any item purchased locally must be of equal or better specifications than the item under the competitive contract.

(2) The legislative body of a county by resolution or a municipality by ordinance may establish and adopt a program to encourage participation in government purchasing programs by minority-owned businesses. Such programs may include set-aside provisions which conform to federal law.

(3) This subsection (d) shall be permissive relative to sellers of motor vehicles.

(4) This subsection (d) shall have no effect unless it is approved by a two-thirds (2/3) vote of the local legislative body and such approval is filed with the comptroller of the treasury.

(5) This subsection (d) does not apply in a county having a metropolitan form of government and a population in excess of five hundred thousand (500,000), or in a county having a population in excess of eight hundred thousand (800,000), according to the 1990 federal census or any subsequent federal census.

12-3-1202 SECTION 69. Tennessee Code Annotated, Section 12-3-1202, is amended by deleting the section in its entirety and by substituting instead the following:

12-3-1202.

(a) Notwithstanding any charter, private act, or general law requirements, any municipality or any county may purchase used or secondhand articles consisting of goods, equipment, materials, supplies, or commodities from any federal, state, or local governmental unit or agency without public advertisement and competitive soliciting.

(b) Notwithstanding any charter, private act, or general law requirements, any municipality or any county may purchase used or secondhand articles consisting of goods, equipment, materials, supplies, or commodities from any private individual or entity without public advertisement and competitive soliciting as long as the purchasing government documents the general range of value of the purchased item through a listing in a nationally recognized publication or through an appraisal by a licensed appraiser, and the price is not more than five percent (5%) higher than the highest value of the documented range.

12-3-1203 — 12-3-1211 SECTION 70. Tennessee Code Annotated, Title 12, Chapter 3, Part 12, is amended by adding appropriately designated sections as follows:

12-3-1203.

(a) Any municipality, county, utility district, or other local governmental unit of the state may, upon request, purchase supplies, equipment, and services for any other municipality, county, utility district, or other local governmental unit.

(1) The purchases shall be made on the same terms and under the same rules and regulations as regular purchases of the purchasing entity.

(2) The cost of the purchase shall be borne by the local government for which the purchase was made.

(3) Where the local government making the request is required to advertise and receive bids, it shall be sufficient for those purposes that the purchasing entity comply only with its own purchasing requirements.

(b)(1) Any local education agency (LEA) may purchase equipment under the same terms of a legal bid initiated by any other LEA in Tennessee.

(2)(A) Any LEA may purchase directly from a vendor the same equipment at the same price and under the same terms as provided in a contract for such equipment entered into by any other LEA.

(B) Any LEA which purchases equipment under this subsection (b) shall directly handle payment, refunds, returns, and any other communications or requirements involved in the purchase of the equipment without involving the LEA which originated the contract. The originating LEA shall have no liability or responsibility for any purchases made by another LEA under a contract which the originating LEA negotiated and consummated.

(c)(1) Any municipality, county, utility district, or other local governmental unit of this state may purchase supplies, goods, equipment, and services under contracts or price agreements entered into by any other local governmental unit of this state. Such purchases shall be made on the same terms and under the same rules and regulations as regular purchases of the purchasing entity. Any local governmental unit that purchases supplies, goods, equipment, or services under this section shall directly handle payment, refunds, returns, and any other communication or requirements involved in the purchase without involving the local governmental unit that originated the contract. The originating local governmental unit shall have no liability or responsibility for any purchases made by another local governmental unit under a contract that the originating local governmental unit negotiated and consummated. Where any local or private act, charter, or general law requires that a local governmental unit purchase by competitive bidding, the local governmental unit may, notwithstanding the local or private act, charter, or general law, purchase without public advertisement or competitive bidding in accordance with this section.

(2) This subsection (c) shall not apply to:

(A) Purchases of new or unused motor vehicles, unless the motor vehicles are manufactured for a special purpose as defined in § 12-3-1208; and

(B) Purchases related to any transportation infrastructure project, including, but not limited to, projects for the construction or improvement of streets, highways, bridges, tunnels, or any roadway related facility.

12-3-1204.

(a) As used in this section, "municipality," "county," and "metropolitan government" apply only to municipalities, counties, and metropolitan governments with a population greater than one hundred fifty thousand (150,000), according to the 1990 federal census or any subsequent federal census.

(b) In any municipality, county, or metropolitan government, notwithstanding any charter provision, private act, or other provision of law, a purchase, lease, or lease-purchase must be preceded by competitive solicitation only if the purchase, lease, or lease-purchase exceeds ten thousand dollars ($10,000).

(c) When the charter of a metropolitan government requires that purchases be made on the basis of competitive bidding, notwithstanding subsection (b), "competitive soliciting" for the metropolitan government means:

Dollar Amount of Purchase	Requirement
$1,000.00 to $3,999.99	Three (3) verbal (including telephone) quotations when possible.
$4,000 to $9,999.99	Three (3) written (including fax) quotations when possible.
$10,000 and above	Competitive sealed bids or proposals for non-emergency and non-proprietary product purchases.

(d) Any municipality, county, or metropolitan government may retain present competitive soliciting requirements and may retain the right to establish, in accordance with charter amendment or private act, whichever is applicable, different dollar amount thresholds and different requirements for competitive bids and competitive proposals from those established in this section.

(e) Nothing in this section shall be deemed to expressly or impliedly repeal § 7-52-117, or any part of that section.

(f) This section shall not supersede or be construed to supersede § 12-3-1201.

12-3-1205.

(a) Any municipality, county, utility district, or other local government of the state may participate in, sponsor, conduct or administer a cooperative purchasing agreement for the procurement of any supplies, services or construction with one (1) or more other local governments in accordance with an agreement entered into between the participants. Such cooperative purchasing may include, but is not limited to, joint or multi-party contracts between local governments. Where the participants in a joint or multi-party contract are required to advertise and receive bids, it shall be sufficient for those purposes that the purchasing entity comply only with its own purchasing requirements.

(b)(1) Notwithstanding any other law to the contrary, any municipality, county, utility district, or other local government of the state may participate in, sponsor, conduct, or administer a cooperative purchasing agreement for the procurement of any goods, supplies, services, or equipment with one (1) or more other governmental entities outside this state, to the extent the laws of the other state permit the joint exercise of purchasing authority, in accordance with an agreement entered into between or among the participants; provided, such goods, supplies, services, or equipment were procured in a manner that constitutes competitive bidding and were advertised, evaluated, and awarded by a governmental entity and made available for use by other governmental entities.

(2) A municipality, county, utility district, or other local government of the state may participate in a master agreement by adopting a resolution accepting the terms of the master agreement. If a participant in a joint or multi-party agreement is required to advertise and receive bids, then it will be deemed sufficient for those purposes that the purchasing entity or the entity that procured the bid complied with its own purchasing requirements. The participant shall acquire and maintain documentation that the purchasing entity or entities that procured the bid complied with its own purchasing requirements.

(3) The powers conferred by this section are in addition and supplemental to the powers conferred by any other law, and any limitations imposed by this section shall not affect powers conferred by any other law.

(4) This subsection (b) shall not apply to:

(A) Purchases of new or unused motor vehicles, unless the motor vehicles are manufactured for a special purpose as defined in § 12-3-1208; or

(B) Purchases of construction, engineering or architectural services, or construction materials.

(c) The chief procurement officer may collect information from municipalities, counties, utility districts, or any other local government unit concerning the type, cost, quality, and quantity of commonly used goods, supplies, services, or equipment being procured under cooperative purchasing agreements. The chief procurement officer may make available all such information to any municipality, county, utility district, or other local government unit upon request.

12-3-1206.

(a) Notwithstanding any other provision of law, a county, municipality and metropolitan government may transfer the ownership of assets for fire protection purchased through or with the proceeds of federal, state or local grants to volunteer fire departments within such county, municipality or metropolitan area; provided, that such volunteer fire departments are registered as non-profit organizations with the office of the secretary of state.

(b) This section shall have no effect in a county, municipality or metropolitan area unless it is approved by the appropriate legislative body.

12-3-1207.

(a) Any municipality may use competitive sealed proposals to purchase goods and services rather than competitive sealed bids when the municipal governing body, acting under the restrictions and requirements of this section and a procurement code adopted by the governing body, determines that the use of competitive sealed bidding is either not practicable or not advantageous to the municipality. In actual emergencies caused by unforeseen circumstances, such as natural or human-made disasters, delays by contractors, delays in transportation, or unanticipated volume of work, purchases through competitive sealed proposals may be made without specific authorizing action of the municipal governing body. A record of any emergency purchase shall be made by the person or body authorizing the emergency purchase, specifying the amount paid, the items and services purchased, from whom the purchase was made, and the nature of the emergency. A report of the emergency purchase through competitive sealed proposals containing all relevant information shall be made as soon as possible by the person or body authorizing the purchase to the municipal governing body.

(b) In the decision to use competitive sealed proposals, the governing body shall follow a procurement code, which shall be adopted by the municipality by ordinance before purchases may be made under this section. The code shall contain criteria for purchasing through competitive sealed proposals and procedures consistent with this section.

(c) The procurement code shall provide that competitive sealed proposals may be used only when qualifications, experience, or competence are more important than price in making the purchase and:

(1) When there is more than one (1) solution to a purchasing issue and the competitive sealed proposals will assist in choosing the best solution; or

(2) When there is no readily identifiable solution to a purchasing issue and the competitive sealed proposals will assist in identifying one (1) or more solutions.

(d) The municipal technical advisory service of the University of Tennessee's institute for public service, in conjunction with the comptroller of the treasury's office, shall develop a model procurement code that may be adopted by any municipality to guide the governing body and purchasing agent in making purchases through requests for competitive sealed proposals. The model procurement code shall contain provisions allowing an aggrieved respondent to protest the intended award to another respondent if the protest is filed within seven (7) calendar days after the intended award is announced. The protest shall be filed with and decided by the municipal governing body.

(e) Adequate public notice of the request for competitive sealed proposals shall be given in the same manner provided for competitive sealed bids.

(f) Competitive sealed proposals shall be opened in a manner that avoids disclosure of contents to competing respondents during the negotiation. The proposals shall be open for public inspection after the intent to award the contract to a particular respondent is announced.

(g) The request for competitive sealed proposals shall state the relative importance of price and other evaluation factors.

(h) As provided in the request for competitive sealed proposals and in the procurement code, discussions may be conducted for clarification to assure full understanding of, and responsiveness to, the solicitation requirements with responsible respondents who submit proposals determined by the purchasing agent to be reasonably susceptible of being selected. These respondents shall be accorded fair and equal treatment with respect to any opportunity for discussion and revision of proposals, and revisions may be permitted after submission and before the intent to award to a particular respondent is announced to obtain the best and final offers. In conducting discussions, the purchasing agent and other municipal personnel may make no disclosure to any respondent of any information derived from proposals submitted by competing respondents.

(i) The award shall be made to the responsible respondent whose proposal the governing body determines is the most advantageous to the municipality, taking into consideration price and the evaluation factors set out in the request for competitive sealed proposals. No other factor may be used in the evaluation. The purchasing agent shall place in the contract file a statement containing the basis on which the award was made.

(j)(1) A governmental utility board shall have the same rights and be subject to the same restrictions and requirements as apply to a municipal governing body under this section. The governmental utility board shall adopt a procurement code by resolution before purchases may be made under this section.

(2) For purposes of subdivision (j)(1), a "governmental utility board" includes a board of public utilities created under title 7, chapter 52, and shall also include any other county, metropolitan government or municipal utility board or supervisory body created by private act, home rule charter or local ordinance or resolution.

(3) Nothing in this subsection (j) shall otherwise modify or impair any limitations on the contracting power of the governmental utility boards as the powers may exist under applicable law.

12-3-1208.

(a)(1) As used in this section, "local governmental unit" means and includes a county, city, municipality, special district, utility district, school district, authority or any other entity created or appointed by a local governmental unit of the state.

(2) For a purchase of goods or services, any local governmental unit may purchase goods or services through a competitive reverse auction process that allows offerors to bid on specified goods or services electronically and adjust bid pricing during a specified time period.

(3) This section shall not apply to:

(A) Construction services, other than those relating to maintenance, repairs and renovations, the cost of which is less than twenty-five thousand dollars ($25,000);

(B) Architectural or engineering services;

(C) New or unused motor vehicles, unless the motor vehicles are manufactured for a special purpose. "Manufactured for a special purpose" includes, but is not limited to, school buses, buses with capacity exceeding twenty-two (22) passengers used to provide public transportation, garbage trucks, fire trucks or ambulances; or

(D) New or unused construction equipment.

(b) The purchasing agent of the local governmental unit shall solicit bids by public notice inserted at least once in a newspaper of countywide circulation five (5) calendar days prior to the first day bids can be submitted. If the county in question has no newspaper with countywide circulation, the purchasing agent shall post notices on a public bulletin board in the county courthouse. The purchasing agent may also solicit bid requests by mail to prospective bidders or by distributing invitations to bid electronically via email or by posting on the entity's website. All invitations to bid shall include a general description of the goods or services to be purchased and information related to the time and place of opening bids.

(c) In order to assure the fullest possible participation of small businesses and minority-owned businesses, a local governmental unit shall provide a mechanism either through the local governmental unit itself or through a third party, if a third party source is utilized to conduct the reverse auction, to facilitate participation of small and minority-owned businesses in a reverse auction.

(d) All bid responses received shall be made available publicly at the time and place identified in the invitation to bid. An award shall be made to the offeror determined to be the lowest responsible and responsive bidder at the close of the specified bid period. Each bid, with the name and address of the bidder, shall be recorded and the names of the bidders, the amounts of their bids and the name of the successful bidder shall, after the award, be open to public inspection. All bids should be preserved for a period of sixty (60) months.

(e)(1) Prior to the initial utilization of a reverse auction, the local governmental unit shall file a plan with the comptroller of the treasury. The plan shall indicate the technology to be utilized, whether a third party source will be utilized to conduct a reverse auction or auctions, a description of policies and procedures related to the implementation of the reverse auction process and documentation of internal controls that will ensure the integrity of the process;

(2) The plan shall also indicate whether such a process will be implemented within the existing operating resources of the local governmental unit or indicate prior approval of the governing body of the local governmental unit if additional operating resources are needed.

12-3-1209.

(a)(1) Contracts by counties, cities, metropolitan governments, towns, utility districts and other municipal and public corporations of the state, for legal services, fiscal agent, financial advisor or advisory services, educational consultant services, and similar services by professional persons or groups of high ethical standards, shall not be based upon competitive solicitations, but shall be awarded on the basis of recognized competence and integrity. The prohibition against competitive soliciting in this section shall not prohibit any entity enumerated from interviewing eligible persons or entities to determine the capabilities of such persons or entities.

(b) Any person providing fiscal agent, financial advisor or advisory services to any county, city, metropolitan government, town, utility district or other municipal or public corporation shall perform such services only pursuant to a written contract, specifying the services to be rendered, the costs therefore, and the expenses to be covered under such contract.

(c) Any person providing fiscal agent, financial advisor or advisory services to any county, city, metropolitan government, town, utility district or other municipal or public corporation of this state who desires to bid, directly or indirectly, on any bonds, notes or other obligations of such entity sold pursuant to public, competitive sale shall receive in writing prior to the sale the permission of such entity to respond either directly or indirectly on the obligations.

(d) For the purposes of this section, "providing fiscal agent, financial advisor or advisory services" means a relationship that exists when a person renders or enters into an agreement to render financial advisory or consultant services to or on behalf of an issuer with respect to a new issue or issues of municipal securities, including advice with respect to the structure, timing, terms and other similar matters concerning such issue or issues, for a fee or other compensation or in expectation of such compensation for the rendering of such services. Notwithstanding the foregoing provisions of this subsection (d), a financial advisory relationship shall not be deemed to exist when, in the course of acting as an underwriter, a municipal securities dealer renders advice to an issuer, including advice with respect to the structure, timing, terms and other similar matters concerning a new issue of municipal securities.

(e)(1) Contracts by counties, cities, metropolitan governments, towns, utility districts and other municipal and public corporations of the state for information management services, including, but not limited to, computer program analyst services shall, upon approval by a two-thirds (2/3) vote of the governing body, be procured through a request for proposals process. The request for proposals process will invite prospective respondents to participate and will indicate the service requirements and the factors used for evaluating the proposals. Such factors shall include cost, the vendor's qualifications and any additional factor or factors deemed relevant by the procuring entity for the procurement of the service. Cost shall not be the sole criterion for evaluation. The contract for such services will be awarded to the best evaluated, responsive respondent.

(2) This subsection (e) shall only apply in counties having a population of not less than four hundred seventy thousand (470,000) nor more than four hundred eighty thousand (480,000), according to the 1980 federal census or any subsequent federal census.

12-3-1210.

Notwithstanding any law to the contrary, the Tennessee Board of Regents system and the University of Tennessee system are authorized to:

(1) Develop procedures to apply the policy of § 12-3-701 to their constituent institutions, including procedures describing the circumstances in which limitations below two (2) times the value of the contract are permitted and procedures for obtaining permission from the appropriate official of the Tennessee board of regents or the University of Tennessee;

(2) Purchase software for use restricted solely to academic teaching or research upon terms that may limit the contractor's liability or warranties; provided that, in no event, shall the liability of the contractor be limited for intentional torts, criminal acts or fraudulent conduct; and

(3) Acquire software or services, materials, supplies and equipment free or at nominal cost upon terms that may limit the contractor's liability or warranties; provided that, in no event, shall the liability of the contractor be limited for intentional torts, criminal acts or fraudulent conduct.

12-3-1211.

The central procurement office may establish contracts for the purchase of personal computers and related devices by public school teachers for use outside the classroom. The computers and related devices shall not be purchased with public funds, but shall be paid for and owned by teachers individually. The contracts shall be established in accordance with this chapter. The central procurement office shall promulgate rules to regulate the purchases authorized in this section. The rules shall be approved by the procurement commission.

12-4-101 SECTION 71. Tennessee Code Annotated, Section 12-4-101, is amended by deleting the section in its entirety and by substituting instead the following:

12-4-101.

(a)(1) It is unlawful for any officer, committee member, director, or other person whose duty it is to vote for, let out, overlook, or in any manner to superintend any work or any contract in which any municipal corporation, county, state, development district, utility district, human resource agency, or other political subdivision created by statute shall or may be interested, to be directly interested in any such contract. "Directly interested" means any contract with the official personally or with any business in which the official is the sole proprietor, a partner, or the person having the controlling interest. "Controlling interest" includes the individual with the ownership or control of the largest number of outstanding shares owned by any single individual or corporation. This subdivision (a)(1) shall not be construed to prohibit any officer, committeeperson, director, or any person, other than a member of a local governing body of a county or municipality, from voting on the budget, appropriation resolution, or tax rate resolution, or amendments thereto, unless the vote is on a specific amendment to the budget or a specific appropriation or resolution in which such person is directly interested.

(2)(A) Subdivision (a)(1) shall also apply to a member of the board of directors of any not-for-profit corporation authorized by the laws of Tennessee to act for the benefit or on behalf of any one (1) or more counties, cities, towns and local governments pursuant to title 7, chapter 54 or 58.

(B) Subdivision (a)(2)(A) shall not apply to any county with a metropolitan form of government and having a population of four hundred thousand (400,000) or more, according to the 1980 federal census or any subsequent federal census.

(b) It is unlawful for any officer, committee member, director, or other person whose duty it is to vote for, let out, overlook, or in any manner to superintend any work or any contract in which any municipal corporation, county, state, development district, utility district, human resource agency, or other political subdivision created by statute shall or may be interested, to be indirectly interested in any such contract unless the officer publicly acknowledges such officer's interest. "Indirectly interested" means any contract in which the officer is interested but not directly so, but includes contracts where the officer is directly interested but is the sole supplier of goods or services in a municipality or county.

(c)(1) Any member of a local governing body of a county or a municipality who is also an employee of such county or municipality and whose employment predates the member's initial election or appointment to the governing body of the county or municipality may vote on matters in which the member has a conflict of interest if the member informs the governing body immediately prior to the vote as follows: "Because I am an employee of (name of governmental unit), I have a conflict of interest in the proposal about to be voted. However, I declare that my argument and my vote answer only to my conscience and to my obligation to my constituents and the citizens this body represents." The vote of any such member having a conflict of interest who does not so inform the governing body of such conflict shall be void if challenged in a timely manner. As used in this subdivision (c)(1), "timely manner" means during the same meeting at which the vote was cast and prior to the transaction of any further business by the body.

(2) Any member of a local governing body of a county or a municipality who is also an employee of such county or municipality and whose employment began on or after the date on which the member was initially elected or appointed to serve on the governing body of the county or municipality shall not vote on matters in which the member has a conflict of interest.

(3)(A) In the event a member of a local governing body of a county or a municipality has a conflict of interest in a matter to be voted upon by the body, such member may abstain for cause by announcing such to the presiding officer.

(B)(i) Any member of a local governing body of a municipality who abstains from voting for cause on any issue coming to a vote before the body shall not be counted for the purpose of determining a majority vote.

(ii) This subdivision (c)(3)(B) shall in no way be construed to apply to any county having a metropolitan form of government and having a population in excess of five hundred thousand (500,000), according to the 1990 federal census or any subsequent federal census.

(d) This section shall apply to a member of the board of directors or officer of any nonprofit corporation required under § 8-44-102 to conduct all meetings of its governing body as open meetings.

12-4-113 SECTION 72. Tennessee Code Annotated, Title 12, Chapter 4, Part 1, is amended by adding the following language as a new, appropriately designated section:

(a)(1) No public officer or employee who is involved in making or administering a contract on behalf of a public agency may derive a direct benefit from the contract except as provided in this section, or as otherwise allowed by law.

(2) No public employee having official responsibility for a procurement transaction shall participate in that transaction on behalf of the public body when the employee knows that:

(A) The employee is contemporaneously employed by a respondent to a solicitation or contractor involved in the procurement transaction;

(B) The employee, the employee's spouse, or any member of the employee's immediate family holds a position with a respondent to a solicitation, a contractor involved in the procurement transaction, such as an officer, director, trustee, partner or the like, or is employed in a capacity involving personal and substantial participation in the procurement transaction, or owns or controls an interest of more than five percent (5%);

(C) The employee, the employee's spouse, or any member of the employee's immediate family has a pecuniary interest arising from the procurement transaction; or

(D) The employee, the employee's spouse, or any member of the employee's immediate family is negotiating, or has an arrangement concerning, prospective employment with a respondent to a solicitation or contractor involved in the procurement transaction.

(3) A public officer or employee who will derive a direct benefit from a contract with the public agency the officer or employee serves, but who is not involved in making or administering the contract, shall not attempt to influence any other person who is involved in making or administering the contract.

(4) No public officer or employee may solicit or receive any gift, reward, or promise of reward in exchange for recommending, influencing, or attempting to influence the award of a contract by the public agency the officer or employee serves.

(b) As used in this section, "immediate family" means spouse, dependent children or stepchildren, or relatives related by blood or marriage.

12-4-103 SECTION 73. Tennessee Code Annotated, Section 12-4-103, is amended by designating the existing language as subsection (a) and adding the following language:

(b) A person violating subsection (a) shall be liable to the state for any and all sums paid out by the state, together with interest at the rate of eight percent (8%) per annum, growing out of any such transaction.

(c) A violation of subsection (a) is a Class E felony.

12-4-104 SECTION 74. Tennessee Code Annotated, Section 12-4-104, is amended by deleting the section in its entirety and by substituting instead the following:

12-4-104.

(a) It is an offense for a public employee or former public employee having official responsibility for procurement transactions to accept employment with any respondent to a solicitation or contractor with whom the employee or former employee dealt in an official capacity concerning procurement transactions for a period of one (1) year from the cessation of employment by the public body unless the employee or former employee provides written notification to the public body, or a public official if designated by the public body, or both, prior to commencement of employment by that respondent to a solicitation or a contractor.

(b) It is an offense for any person who, for compensation, prepares a solicitation for or on behalf of a public body to:

(1) Submit a response to a solicitation for that procurement or any portion thereof; or

(2) Disclose to any respondent to a solicitation information concerning the procurement that is not available to the public. A public body may permit such person to submit response to a solicitation for that procurement or any portion thereof if the public body determines that the exclusion of the person would limit the number of potential qualified respondents to a solicitation in a manner contrary to the best interest of the public body.

(c)(1) It is an offense for a contractor or subcontractor to demand or receive from any of the contractor's or subcontractor's suppliers or for a contractor to demand or receive from the contractor's subcontractors, as an inducement for the award of a subcontract or order, any payment, loan, subscription, advance, deposit of money, services or anything, present or promised, unless consideration of substantially equal or greater value is exchanged.

(2) It is an offense for a subcontractor or supplier to make or offer to make any payment, loan, subscription, advance, deposit of money, services or anything, present or promised, unless consideration of substantially equal or greater value is exchanged.

(3) It is an offense for any person to demand or receive any payment, loan, subscription, advance, deposit of money, services or anything of value in return for an agreement not to compete on a public contract.

(4) If a contractor, subcontractor, supplier or any person violates any provision of this subsection (c), the amount thereof shall be conclusively presumed to have been included in the price of the contract, subcontract or order and ultimately borne by the public body and shall be recoverable from both the maker and recipient. Recovery from one (1) offending party shall not preclude recovery from other offending parties.

(d)(1) A contract entered into in violation of this section on or after October 1, 2011, is void. A contract that is otherwise void under this section may continue in effect until an alternative can be arranged when:

(A) Immediate termination would result in harm to the public health or welfare; and

(B) The continuation is approved by the commission.

(2) Approval of continuation of contracts under this subsection (d) shall be given for the minimum period necessary to protect the public health or welfare. The chief procurement officer and the comptroller of the treasury shall be notified immediately upon a determination that a contract violates this subsection (d).

(e)(1) As used in this section, the term "public officer" means an individual who is elected or appointed to serve or represent a public agency, other than an employee or independent contractor of a public agency.

(2) A public officer or employee is involved in administering a contract if the officer or employee oversees the performance of the contract or has authority to make decisions regarding the contract or to interpret the contract.

(3) A public officer or employee is involved in making a contract if such officer or employee participates in the development of specifications or terms or in the preparation or award of the contract. A public officer is also involved in making a contract if the board, commission, or other body of which such officer is a member takes action on the contract, whether or not the public officer actually participates in that action, unless the contract is approved under an exception to this section under which the public officer is allowed to benefit and is prohibited from voting.

(4) A public officer or employee derives a direct benefit from a contract if the person or the person's spouse:

(A) Has more than a ten-percent ownership or other interest in an entity that is a party to the contract;

(B) Derives any income or commission directly from the contract; or

(C) Acquires property under the contract.

(f) A public officer or employee is not involved in making or administering a contract solely because of the performance of ministerial duties related to the contract.

(g) A violation of this section is a Class A misdemeanor.

12-4-106 SECTION 75. Tennessee Code Annotated, Section 12-4-106, is amended by deleting the section in its entirety and by substituting instead the following:

12-4-106.

(a) No officer or employee of the central procurement office, nor any member of the procurement commission, nor any head of any state department, institution or agency, nor any employee of any state department, institution or agency charged with the responsibility of initiating requisitions, shall accept or receive, directly or indirectly, from any person, firm or corporation to whom any contract for the purchase of goods or services for the state may be awarded, by rebate, gifts, or otherwise, any money or anything of value whatsoever, or any promise, obligation, or contract for future rewards or compensation.

(b)(1) It is a conflict of interest for any person or any company with whom such person is an officer, a director, or an equity owner having an ownership interest greater than one percent (1%) to bid on any public contract for goods or services for a governmental entity if such person or the immediate family member of such person is a member of a board or commission having responsibility for letting or approving such contract.

(2) As used in this subsection (b):

(A) "Governmental entity" means any state agency, authority, board, commission, department, or office within the executive, legislative or judicial branch of state government or any autonomous state agency, authority, board, commission, department, office, or institution of higher education; and

(B) "Immediate family" means spouse, dependent children or stepchildren, or relatives related by blood or marriage.

12-4-107 SECTION 76. Tennessee Code Annotated, Section 12-4-107, is amended by deleting the section in its entirety and by substituting instead the following:

12-4-107.

(a) All contracts for architectural, engineering and construction services procured by any municipal corporation, county, state, development district, utility district, human resource agency, or other political subdivision created by statute shall meet the following requirements:

(1) In the procurement of architectural and engineering services, the selection committee or procurement official may seek qualifications and experience data from any firm or firms licensed in this state and interview such firm or firms. The selection committee or procurement official shall evaluate statements of qualifications and experience data regarding the procurement of architectural and engineering services, and shall conduct discussions with such firm or firms regarding the furnishing of required services and then shall select the firm deemed to be qualified to provide the services required.

(2) The selection committee or procurement official shall negotiate a contract with the qualified firm for architectural and engineering services at compensation which the selection committee or procurement official determines to be fair and reasonable to the government. In making such determination, the selection committee or procurement official shall take into account the estimated value of the services to be rendered, the scope of work, complexity and professional nature thereof.

(3) Should the selection committee or procurement official be unable to negotiate a satisfactory contract with the firm considered to be qualified, at a price determined to be fair and reasonable, negotiations will continue with other qualified firms until an agreement is reached.

(4) A city, county or utility district having a satisfactory existing working relationship for architectural or engineering services may expand the scope of the services; provided, that they are within the technical competency of the existing firm, without exercising this section.

(b) Construction of correctional facility projects of the state, a county, city, metropolitan government or town shall meet the following requirements:

(1) For construction of local correctional facility projects or additions to existing correctional facility buildings, the state, a county, city, metropolitan government or town may contract for construction management agent or advisor services. Construction management services that are provided for a fee and that involve preconstruction and construction administration and management services shall be deemed as professional services and may be performed by a qualified person licensed under the Contractors Licensing Act of 1994, compiled in title 62, chapter 6. Construction management services are to be procured for each project through a written request for proposals process through advertisement. The procurement and advertisement shall be in accordance with laws, regulations, and ordinances of the county, city, metropolitan government or town. The written request for proposals process shall invite prospective proposers to participate and shall indicate the service requirements and the factors used for evaluating the proposals. These factors shall include the construction manager's qualifications and experience on similar projects, qualifications of personnel to be assigned to the project, fees and costs or any additional factors deemed relevant by the procuring entity for procurement of the service. Cost shall not be the sole criterion for evaluation. The contract for such services shall be awarded to the best qualified and responsive responder. A construction manager is prohibited from undertaking actual construction work on a project over which the construction manager coordinates or oversees the planning, bid or construction phases of the project, except in instances when bids have been solicited twice and no bids have been submitted. If the construction manager can document that a good faith effort was made in each bid solicitation to obtain bids and no bids were received, then the construction manager may perform the construction work at

a price agreed upon by the construction manager, the architect and the owner of the project. A governing body, at its own discretion, may perform work on the project with its own employees and may include the coordination and oversight of this work as part of the services of the construction manager. Sealed bids for actual construction work shall be opened at the bid opening and the names of the contractors and their bid amounts shall be announced.

(2) Construction management agent or advisor services for the construction of local correctional facility projects or additions to existing correctional facility buildings in accordance with subdivision (b)(2)(A) may be performed by:

(A) A general contractor licensed in this state pursuant to the Contractors Licensing Act of 1994, compiled in title 62, chapter 6; provided, that none of such services performed by a general contractor involve any of the services exempt from the requirements of title 62, chapter 6 as "normal architectural and engineering services" under § 62-6-102(4)(B) or (C), unless, with regard to the performance of any services defined as normal architectural and engineering services, the general contractor is also licensed as an architect or engineer under title 62, chapter 2; or

(B) An architect or an engineer licensed pursuant to title 62, chapter 2; provided, that none of such services performed by an architect or engineer involve any of the services required to be performed by a contractor within the definition of "contractor" under § 62-6-102, unless with regard to the performance of any services included within the definition of contractor, the architect or engineer is also licensed as a contractor under the Contractors Licensing Act of 1994, compiled in title 62, chapter 6.

(3) Construction work that is under the coordination and oversight of a construction manager shall be procured through competitive bids.

12-4-109 SECTION 77. Tennessee Code Annotated, Section 12-4-109, is amended by deleting the section in its entirety and by substituting instead the following:

12-4-109.

There is hereby established an account to be known as the capital preplanning account, which shall be the funding source for the preplanning of all capital projects undertaken by the departments and agencies of the state. The account shall be reimbursed for the preplanning cost of a capital investment project from the appropriations allocated to that project. Any funds remaining in the account at the end of any fiscal year shall be carried over to the succeeding fiscal year and expended only for the purpose specified in this section.

12-4-110 SECTION 78. Tennessee Code Annotated, Section 12-4-110, is amended by deleting the section in its entirety and by substituting instead the following:

12-4-110.

Contracts by counties, cities, metropolitan governments, towns, utility districts and other municipal and public corporations of this state for energy-related services that include both engineering services and equipment, and have as their purpose the reduction of energy costs in public facilities, shall be awarded on the same basis as contracts for professional services.

12-4-111 SECTION 79. Tennessee Code Annotated, Section 12-4-111, is amended by deleting the section in its entirety and by substituting instead the following:

12-4-111.

(a) For purposes of this part, "state standard prototype," means a design on which a state correctional facility is based so that the design can be used by the state to construct similar buildings at different sites at a future time. The state building commission may designate state standard prototypes from design documents which were originally prepared for the exclusive use of the state. The state architect shall place the appropriate designation on a document which is determined to be a state standard prototype.

(b) Prior to the re-use of documents for a project in which the original architect or engineer is not also involved, the state shall remove and obliterate from all documents the identification of the original architect or engineer, including name, address, professional seal or stamp, and signature. The architect or engineer who is involved in a state standard prototypical re-use project shall affix such architect's or engineer's seal or stamp to such design, and shall be solely responsible for all documents on which such architect's or engineer's seal or stamp is placed, and shall hold the original architect or engineer harmless from suits by third parties.

(c) The original architect or engineer shall not be liable for injury or damage resulting from re-use of plans, designs, details, specifications or construction documents of a state standard prototype by the state or third parties, if the original architect or engineer is not also involved in the re-use project. It is the intent of this section that the architect or engineer who seals or stamps a prototype is legally responsible only for that set of documents on which such architect's or engineer's seal or stamp is placed.

12-4-112 SECTION 80. Tennessee Code Annotated, Section 12-4-112, is amended by deleting the section in its entirety and by substituting instead the following:

12-4-112.

(a) As used in this section, "governmental entity" means any county, municipality, metropolitan government, town, utility district, or other municipal or public corporation of this state.

(b) Notwithstanding any other provision of law or private act to the contrary, a governmental entity may enter into multi-year contracts for painting and other maintenance of water storage tanks and appurtenant facilities procured through a request for proposals process. The request for proposals process shall invite prospective proposers to participate and shall indicate the service requirements and the categories used for evaluating the proposals, together with the relative weight of each category. Such categories shall include such factors as qualifications, experience on similar projects, availability of workers, technical approach, minority participation, cost, and any additional factor or factors deemed relevant by the procuring governmental entity. Cost shall not be the sole criterion for evaluation. Proposers shall be given at least thirty (30) days from public advertisement of the request for proposals to consider the evaluation factors set forth in the solicitation documents before submitting proposals. The contract shall be awarded to the best proposer who meets the minimum required qualifications, using the evaluation criteria set forth in this subsection (b).

(c) Any governmental entity may, at its option, require such multi-year contracts to be competitively bid.

12-4-114 — 12-4-126 SECTION 81. Tennessee Code Annotated, Title 12, Chapter 4, Part 1, is amended by deleting § 12-4-113 through § 12-4-125 in their entireties and by transferring the existing § 12-4-126 to be § 12-4-113.

12-4-1001 — 12-4-1007 SECTION 82. Tennessee Code Annotated, title 12, chapter 4, is amended by adding the following language as a new part:

12-4-1001.

The state treasurer shall investigate alternative methods, including competitive bidding, for purchasing insurance for the use and benefit of the state and its agencies, departments or divisions. The state treasurer shall prepare a plan for purchasing insurance, and shall submit the plan to the board of claims prior to its implementation.

12-4-1002.

The state treasurer shall establish accepted practices and procedures to be followed in purchasing insurance under the plan developed under § 12-4-1001. Such practices and procedures shall be subject to the approval of the board of claims.

12-4-1003.

All officers, officials, agents or employees of the state and its divisions, departments and agencies are prohibited from bidding, selling or contracting to sell any policy of insurance to the state or its divisions, departments and agencies.

12-4-1004.

All buildings and building contents owned by the state shall be insured for not less than their actual cash value subject to an aggregate deductible of not less than one million five hundred thousand dollars ($1,500,000) and to such individual claim deductible as may be commercially reasonable.

12-4-1005.

The repair or replacement of damaged or destroyed buildings and building contents shall include engineering and other services necessary for such an insurance program to be paid from the risk management fund created pursuant to § 9-8-109.

12-4-1006.

The state treasurer shall establish appropriate policies and procedures governing the administration of the insurance program provided herein, including the allocation of premium and other costs and the payment of losses from the risk management fund created pursuant to § 9-8-109. Such policies and procedures shall be subject to the approval of the board of claims.

12-4-1007.

(a)(1) The policy or policies of insurance provided in this part shall be obtained by the state treasurer subject to the approval of the board of claims. Notwithstanding the Surplus Lines Insurance Act, compiled in title 56, chapter 14, part 1, or any other law to the contrary, the state treasurer, with the approval of the board of claims, shall consider proposals from admitted carriers and nonadmitted surplus lines carriers. In order for nonadmitted carriers to be eligible for consideration under this section, at least two (2) admitted carriers must have declined to submit a proposal, and the nonadmitted carriers shall:

(A) Have a minimum A.M. Best financial strength rating of "A-" and an A.M. Best financial size category of no less than "VI", or such other A.M. Best rating as may be established by the board of claims provided that the financial strength rating shall not be less than "A-" and the A.M. Best financial size category shall not be less than "VI"; and

(B) Be a member of an insurance holding company system, as defined in § 56-11-101(b), that has at least one (1) affiliate carrier admitted in this state as a property or casualty insurer.

(2) Should A.M. Best change or amend its rating methodology, then the board of claims shall adopt a minimum rating requirement that is equivalent to the rating as stated in subdivision (a)(1)(A). The state treasurer shall place the insurance directly with the companies without policies being countersigned notwithstanding § 56-2-409.

(b) The state treasurer shall make periodic reports to the fiscal review committee of the general assembly and to the state building commission concerning the operations of the insurance program.

Effective date 7/1/2013

SECTION 83. This act shall take effect upon July 1, 2013, the public welfare requiring it, and shall apply to contracts entered into or renewed on and after such date.

PUBLIC CHAPTER NO. 404

PUBLIC CHAPTER NO. 404

SENATE BILL NO. 157

By Norris

Substituted for: House Bill No. 151

By McCormick, Harry Brooks

AN ACT to amend Tennessee Code Annotated, Title 49, Chapter 16, Part 2, relative to virtual public schools.

BE IT ENACTED BY THE GENERAL ASSEMBLY OF THE STATE OF TENNESSEE:

49-16-211 SECTION 1. Tennessee Code Annotated, Section 49-16-211, is amended by designating the existing language as subsection (a) and adding the following language as a new subsection (b):

(b) Initial enrollment in a public virtual school shall be limited to one thousand five hundred (1,500) students; however, any public virtual school in operation as of January 1, 2013, may continue to serve the number of students enrolled in the school as of the effective date of this act. If a public virtual school demonstrates student achievement growth at a minimum level of "at expectations" as represented by the Tennessee Value-Added Assessment System (TVAAS) developed pursuant to title 49, chapter 1, part 6 and guidelines adopted by the state board of education pursuant to title 49, chapter 1, part 3, the school may exceed the enrollment cap.

49-16-213 SECTION 2. Tennessee Code Annotated, Section 49-16-213, is amended by designating the existing language as subsection (a) and adding the following language as a new subsection (b):

(b) In addition to the intervention options available under § 49-1-602, if a public virtual school is identified as a priority school pursuant to § 49-1-602 or demonstrates student achievement growth at a level of "significantly below expectations" for any three consecutive years of the school's operation, as represented by the Tennessee Value-Added Assessment System (TVAAS) developed pursuant to title 49, chapter 1, part 6 and guidelines adopted by the state board of education pursuant to title 49, chapter 1, part 3, the commissioner shall have the authority to reinstitute the enrollment cap specified in § 49-16-211(b) or direct the LEA to close the school. If the commissioner reinstitutes the enrollment cap pursuant to this subsection, such cap shall not affect students enrolled in the virtual school at the time of the department's action. Notwithstanding § 49-3-351(d), if a public virtual school is closed upon direction of the commissioner or the LEA, the Basic Education Program (BEP) payments for the LEA that established the school shall be exclusive of any student who was enrolled in the school the prior year and did not remain enrolled in the LEA.

SECTION 3. The state board of education is authorized to promulgate rules and regulations to effectuate the purposes of this act. All such rules and regulations shall be promulgated in accordance with Tennessee Code Annotated, title 4, chapter 5.

Effective date 5/14/2013 SECTION 4. This act shall take effect upon becoming law, the public welfare requiring it.

PUBLIC CHAPTER NO. 405

PUBLIC CHAPTER NO. 405

SENATE BILL NO. 122

By Ketron

Substituted for: House Bill No. 1

By Faison

AN ACT to amend Tennessee Code Annotated, Title 13, Chapter 23, relative to conflicts of interest for the Tennessee Housing Development Agency.

BE IT ENACTED BY THE GENERAL ASSEMBLY OF THE STATE OF TENNESSEE:

13-23-128 SECTION 1. Tennessee Code Annotated, Section 13-23-128, is amended by deleting subsection (a) in its entirety and by substituting instead the following:

> (a)(1) No member or employee of the agency, during such member's or employee's tenure or for six (6) months thereafter, shall be employed by, hold any paid official relation to, or have any financial interest in, any housing sponsor or any housing development financed or assisted by the agency.
>
> (2) No real property to which such member or employee holds legal title or in which such person has any financial interest shall be sold, during such member's or employee's tenure or for six (6) months thereafter, to a housing sponsor for a housing development to be financed by the agency.

13-23-128 SECTION 2. Tennessee Code Annotated, Section 13-23-128(b), is amended by deleting the language "prohibited in subsection (a)" wherever it appears and by substituting instead the language "described in subsection (a)".

Effective date 5/14/2013 SECTION 3. This act shall take effect upon becoming a law, the public welfare requiring it.

PUBLIC CHAPTER NO. 406

PUBLIC CHAPTER NO. 406

SENATE BILL NO. 88

By Finney, Kelsey, Ford

Substituted for: House Bill No. 425

By Pitts, Sexton, Ryan Williams

AN ACT to amend Tennessee Code Annotated, Title 49, Chapter 1; Title 49, Chapter 2; Title 49, Chapter 3; Title 49, Chapter 5 and Title 49, Chapter 6, relative to security of standardized tests.

BE IT ENACTED BY THE GENERAL ASSEMBLY OF THE STATE OF TENNESSEE:

SECTION 1. Tennessee Code Annotated, Title 49, Chapter 1, Part 2, is amended by adding the following as a new, appropriately designated section:

49-1-2__. The department shall review all measures that are in place to prevent breaches in the security of standardized tests administered in grades kindergarten through twelve (K-12) in the public schools. The state board of education shall assist the department, as requested, in the review. The department shall consult with the providers of the standardized tests to determine if the providers are aware of issues with security or can recommend changes that need to be made to improve test security. The department shall report its findings and recommendations for improvement of test security to the general assembly before the second Tuesday in January 2014.

Effective date 5/14/2013

SECTION 2. This act shall take effect upon becoming a law, the public welfare requiring it.

PUBLIC CHAPTER NO. 407

PUBLIC CHAPTER NO. 407

SENATE BILL NO. 66

By Green, Bowling, Burks, Yager

Substituted for: House Bill No. 99

By Curtis Johnson, Evans, Jernigan, Timothy Hill, Eldridge, Lamberth, Hardaway, Todd

AN ACT to amend Tennessee Code Annotated, Title 39, relative to criminal offenses.

BE IT ENACTED BY THE GENERAL ASSEMBLY OF THE STATE OF TENNESSEE:

39-13-102

SECTION 1. Tennessee Code Annotated, Section 39-13-102(e)(1), is amended by deleting the last sentence and by substituting instead the following language:

> However, the maximum fine shall be fifteen thousand dollars ($15,000) for an offense under subdivision (a)(1)(A), subdivision (a)(1)(B), subsection (c), or subsection (d) committed against any of the following persons who are discharging or attempting to discharge their official duties:
>
> (A) Law enforcement officer;
>
> (B) Firefighter;
>
> (C) Medical fire responder;
>
> (D) Paramedic;
>
> (E) Emergency medical technician; or
>
> (F) Any other first responder.

Effective date 7/1/2013

SECTION 2. This act shall take effect July 1, 2013, the public welfare requiring it.

PUBLIC CHAPTER NO. 408

PUBLIC CHAPTER NO. 408

SENATE BILL NO. 63

By Yager, Haile

Substituted for: House Bill No. 228

By Sanderson, Sexton, Shepard, Odom, Stewart

AN ACT to amend Tennessee Code Annotated, Title 4 and Title 56, Chapter 7, Part 31, relative to pharmacy benefit contracts.

BE IT ENACTED BY THE GENERAL ASSEMBLY OF THE STATE OF TENNESSEE:

4-3-1021 SECTION 1. Tennessee Code Annotated, Title 4, Chapter 3, Part 10, is amended by adding the following language as a new section:

(a) The department of finance and administration shall monitor, and cause to be audited by its qualified independent auditor, the pharmacy benefits manager's compliance with any state pharmacy benefits management contract. The commissioner of finance and administration, or the commissioner's designee, shall report, by July 1st of each year, on the pharmacy benefits manager's contract compliance to the speaker of the senate, the speaker of the house of representatives and the fiscal review committee.

(b) In order to comply with subsection (a), the department shall, after one (1) year of entering into or renewing any state pharmacy benefits management contract, annually perform a single risk assessment to determine those areas of the contracts that pose the greatest risk of noncompliance, fraud, waste and abuse. Upon completion of the risk assessment, the department shall incorporate the results of the risk assessment into its audit and monitoring plan. The department shall update the risk assessment when contract amendments result in additional risks of noncompliance, fraud, waste, or abuse. The department shall consult with the office of the comptroller of the treasury in determining the scope and extent of the audit and monitoring plan procedures. The department may submit the updated audit and monitoring plan, along with any audit or monitoring findings, to comply with the reporting requirement in subsection (a).

(c) The audit and monitoring plan shall address all state pharmacy benefits management contracts and be designed to examine source documentation whenever such documentation is available. The plan shall include, but not be limited to, a review of:

(1) Repricing of pharmacy claims at the drug level;

(2) Validation of the national drug code (NDC) usage;

(3) Appropriateness of the nationally recognized reference prices, or average wholesale price (AWP), in accordance with § 56-7-3104;

(4) Eligibility of beneficiaries for pharmacy claims paid;

(5) For pharmacy benefits contracts entered into or renewed on or after July 1, 2013, reconciliation of the pharmacy benefits manager's payments to pharmacies with the state's reimbursement to the pharmacy benefits manager;

(6) Confirmation that the pharmacy benefits manager's payments to pharmacies do not reflect disparity among network pharmacies attributable to preferential treatment of one (1) or more pharmacies;

(7) Recalculation of discount and dispensing fee guarantees;

(8) Review of the state's claim utilization to ensure that per claim rebate guarantees were accurately calculated by the pharmacy benefits manager;

(9) Review of rebate contracts between the pharmacy benefits manager and five (5) drug manufacturers, to be selected by the benefits administration division of the department, and the contracted auditor to ensure that eligible rebate utilization was accurately invoiced on behalf of the state;

(10) Comparison of total rebates collected by the PBM (pass-through rebates) to the minimum rebate guarantees (per claim rebates) to ensure that annual reconciliation of rebate payments to the state represented the greater of the two (2) amounts;

(11) Monitor the activities of the pharmacy benefits manager to ensure that the contractor is conducting audits and other reviews of pharmacies as provided in the contractor's scope of services; and

(12) Consideration of other industry related risks to reduce the risk of financial losses due to fraud, waste and abuse.

(d) The department shall seek appropriate remedies for contract noncompliance and occurrences of fraud, waste or abuse that are discovered through monitoring or audits.

(e) The department shall have the authority to contract with a qualified independent auditor experienced in conducting pharmacy audits for auditing the pharmacy benefits manager's compliance with the contract. No contracted qualified independent auditor shall subcontract any part of the plan described in this section without the express written approval by the commissioner, or the commissioner's designee, and notification in writing to the comptroller of the treasury.

(f) This section shall apply to any state or local health insurance plan established under title 8, chapter 27.

Effective date 5/14/2013

SECTION 2. This act shall take effect upon becoming a law, the public welfare requiring it.

PUBLIC CHAPTER NO. 409

PUBLIC CHAPTER NO. 409

SENATE BILL NO. 1292

By Tracy, Yager, Kelsey, Burks, Beavers, Crowe, Haile, Ketron

Substituted for: House Bill No. 1121

By Womick, Jernigan, Durham, Sparks, Forgety

AN ACT to amend Tennessee Code Annotated, Title 4; Title 8; Title 56; Title 68 and Title 71, relative to suppliers of equipment and services to certain healthcare coverage programs.

BE IT ENACTED BY THE GENERAL ASSEMBLY OF THE STATE OF TENNESSEE:

56-32-104 SECTION 1. Tennessee Code Annotated, Section 56-32-104(a)(3)(E), is amended by deleting the subdivision in its entirety and substituting instead the following:

(a)(3)(E) In the event the HMO enters into an agreement with any physician-hospital organization, or any other provider, provider group, or provider network, for the provision of healthcare services on a prepayment basis or other risk sharing basis, the commissioner may not disallow the agreement on the basis that it transfers risk to the physician-hospital organization or other provider, provider group or provider network; or transfers the risk of payment for services to the physician-hospital organization or other provider, provider group or provider network; provided, that the HMO shall:

(i) Remain contractually responsible to its enrollees;

(ii) Enter into contractual arrangements utilizing contract provisions and arrangements that ensure compliance with applicable federal law, rule, regulation or waivers, including federal requirements; and

(iii) Assure the physician-hospital organizations, providers, provider groups, or provider networks that are at substantial financial risk obtain either aggregate or per-patient stop-loss protection insurance coverage for the healthcare services included in the scope of the arrangement; or the HMO remains contractually responsible to the subcontracted providers and provides a system for reserving for its continued liability; and

56-2-201 SECTION 2. Tennessee Code Annotated, Section 56-2-201(1), is amended by deleting the subdivision in its entirety and substituting instead the following:

(1) "Accident and health insurance" means insurance against bodily injury, disablement or death, by accident or accidental means, or the expense of bodily injury, disablement or death, against disablement or expense resulting from sickness, and every insurance pertaining thereto; providing for the mental and emotional welfare of an individual and members of the individual's family by defraying the cost of legal services; or providing aggregate or excess stop-loss coverage in connection with employee welfare benefit plans, managed care organizations participating in commercial plans or the TennCare program, or both, health maintenance organizations, long-term care facilities, physician-hospital organizations as defined in § 56-32-102 and provider aggregate or per-patient stop-loss protection insurance coverage as authorized by § 56-32-104;

SECTION 3. The provisions contained in this act shall terminate on December 31, 2016, and the law in effect prior to this act's effective date shall be restored.

Effective date 5/16/2013 SECTION 4. This act shall take effect upon becoming a law, the public welfare requiring it.

PUBLIC CHAPTER NO. 410

PUBLIC CHAPTER NO. 410

SENATE BILL NO. 1245

By Hensley

Substituted for: House Bill No. 1094

By McDaniel, Shaw

AN ACT to amend Tennessee Code Annotated, Title 67 and Title 68, Chapter 11, relative to nursing homes with delinquent payments of the annual nursing home tax.

BE IT ENACTED BY THE GENERAL ASSEMBLY OF THE STATE OF TENNESSEE:

68-11-216 SECTION 1. Tennessee Code Annotated, Section 68-11-216(c)(7)(B), is amended by deleting the first sentence in its entirety and substituting instead the following:

> If a nursing home is more than ninety (90) days delinquent in paying an installment of its annual nursing home assessment fee, the commissioner shall initiate proceedings before the board in accordance with the Uniform Administrative Procedures Act, compiled in title 4, chapter 5, so that the board may suspend admissions to the facility or otherwise direct the facility to pay the assessment fee and any accrued penalties and interest in full within a prescribed period of time.

68-11-216 SECTION 2. Tennessee Code Annotated, Section 68-11-216(c)(7), is amended by adding the following as a new subdivision (c)(7)(C):

> (C) In cases where a licensed nursing home is delinquent on assessment fees beginning July 1, 2009, and ending June 30, 2012, and is currently participating in a payment plan, the commissioner shall be authorized to reduce the amount of penalties and interest due for that time period to twenty-five percent (25%) of the total assessment fee outstanding balance as of June 30, 2012. For purposes of this subdivision, the total assessment fee outstanding balance is calculated as the total assessment fees owed not including any penalties and interest, less any payments made by the facility, beginning July 1, 2009, and ending June 30, 2012. This subdivision (c)(7)(C) shall terminate on July 1, 2015, unless reenacted or extended by the general assembly prior to such date.

Effective date 5/16/2013 SECTION 3. This act shall take effect upon becoming law, the public welfare requiring it.

PUBLIC CHAPTER NO. 411

PUBLIC CHAPTER NO. 411

SENATE BILL NO. 1175

By Kelsey, Crowe, Gresham, Niceley

Substituted for: House Bill No. 941

By Dunn, Evans

AN ACT to amend Tennessee Code Annotated, Title 49, relative to education.

BE IT ENACTED BY THE GENERAL ASSEMBLY OF THE STATE OF TENNESSEE:

49-2-128 SECTION 1. Tennessee Code Annotated, Title 49, Chapter 2, Part 1, is amended by adding the following language as a new section:

49-2-128. Each LEA shall develop a policy whereby the LEA shall provide for an open enrollment period during which parents or guardians may choose from a list of the LEA schools with available space and request a transfer. The policy shall be developed and implemented to provide an open enrollment period for the 2014-2015 school year and every school year thereafter. If the transfer is granted, the parents or guardians are responsible for transportation to the new school. The student shall maintain satisfactory attendance, behavior and effort to remain in the new school.

Effective date 7/1/2013 SECTION 2. This act shall take effect July 1, 2013, the public welfare requiring it.

PUBLIC CHAPTER NO. 412

PUBLIC CHAPTER NO. 412

SENATE BILL NO. 1089

By Kyle, Ford

Substituted for: House Bill No. 869

By Miller

AN ACT to amend Tennessee Code Annotated, Section 8-21-401, relative to clerks.

BE IT ENACTED BY THE GENERAL ASSEMBLY OF THE STATE OF TENNESSEE:

8-21-401

SECTION 1. Tennessee Code Annotated, Section 8-21-401(i)(6), is amended by deleting the subdivision and substituting instead the following:

> (6) For receiving funds paid into court on confirmation of private sales or other funds paid into the clerk pursuant to court order, and collecting and paying out the proceeds, the fee shall be forty dollars ($40.00). This fee also applies where there is a pre-judgment judicial attachment or similar process to bring property into the court's possession prior to judgment. This fee shall not apply to payments of proceeds made pursuant to court order to any person from funds held by the clerk, except for court orders concerning a redemption of delinquent taxes property sale; in such case, the fee shall only be charged one (1) time against the total amount of proceeds generated from the property.

Effective date 5/16/2013

SECTION 2. This act shall take effect upon becoming a law, the public welfare requiring it.

PUBLIC CHAPTER NO. 413

PUBLIC CHAPTER NO. 413

SENATE BILL NO. 1052

By Kelsey

Substituted for: House Bill No. 354

By Lollar, Hall, Todd

AN ACT to amend Tennessee Code Annotated, Title 39, Chapter 17, Part 1 and Title 66, relative to offenses involving real and personal property.

BE IT ENACTED BY THE GENERAL ASSEMBLY OF THE STATE OF TENNESSEE:

39-17-116 SECTION 1. Tennessee Code Annotated, Section 39-17-116(d), is amended by deleting the language "Class A misdemeanor" and by substituting instead the language "Class E felony".

39-17-117 SECTION 2. Tennessee Code Annotated, Section 39-17-117(d), is amended by deleting the language "Class A misdemeanor" and by substituting instead the language "Class E felony".

Effective date 7/1/2013 SECTION 3. This act shall take effect July 1, 2013, the public welfare requiring it.

PUBLIC CHAPTER NO. 414

PUBLIC CHAPTER NO. 414

SENATE BILL NO. 1042

By Kelsey

Substituted for: House Bill No. 1054

By Faison

AN ACT to amend Tennessee Code Annotated, Title 13, Chapter 23, Part 1, relative to the Tennessee Housing Development Agency Act.

BE IT ENACTED BY THE GENERAL ASSEMBLY OF THE STATE OF TENNESSEE:

13-23-107 SECTION 1. Tennessee Code Annotated, Section 13-23-107(a)(1), is amended by deleting the subdivision in its entirety and substituting instead the following:

> (a)(1) The governor shall appoint the following members to the board of directors for the agency, who shall be citizens of the state and shall not hold public office: a total of six (6) persons representing the following groups, with no more than one (1) person representing each group: retail building material supply; manufactured housing; home building; mortgage banking; licensed real estate brokers; local public housing authority; local government; and a qualifying not-for-profit corporation. After June 30, 2013, the governor shall appoint two (2) persons from the public at large who are knowledgeable about the problems about inadequate housing conditions in the state. Upon the first term expiration for one (1) of the public at large members, that public at large position shall expire, without reappointment, at the end of the member's term. After this term expiration and thereafter, the governor shall appoint one (1) person from the public at large who is knowledgeable about the problems about inadequate housing conditions in the state. When making appointments, the governor shall give due consideration to geographic distribution of the members of the agency to ensure that all parts of the state are adequately represented. In making appointments to the agency board of directors, the governor shall strive to ensure that at least one (1) person appointed to serve on the board is sixty (60) years of age or older and that at least one (1) person appointed to serve on the board is a member of a racial minority.

13-23-112 SECTION 2. Tennessee Code Annotated, Section 13-23-112(h)(1), is amended by deleting the subdivision in its entirety and by substituting instead the following:

> (h)(1) There is hereby created an audit and budget committee of the agency, which shall be composed of the following: the chair of the agency; the vice chair of the agency; the state treasurer; the secretary of state; and two (2) members appointed annually by the chair from among the appointed members of the board. The state treasurer shall serve as the chair of the audit and budget committee in even years and the secretary of state shall serve as the chair of the audit and budget committee in odd years beginning in 2013, and alternating thereafter. The agency's director of internal audit shall serve as the secretary for the committee. The agency's director of internal audit shall serve at the pleasure of the committee. The committee has the authority to employ, terminate and establish the salary of the director of internal audit.

13-23-107 SECTION 3. Tennessee Code Annotated, Section 13-23-107, is further amended by adding the following language as a new, appropriately designated subsection:

> ( ) Other individuals may be directors of the agency as may be required by applicable federal law, regulation or agreement, who shall be eligible to vote on matters before the agency to the extent required by federal law, regulation or agreement.

13-23-110 SECTION 4. Tennessee Code Annotated, Section 13-23-110, is amended by deleting this section in its entirety and substituting it instead with the following:

> A majority of the members of the agency shall constitute a quorum, and the affirmative vote of eight (8) members at a meeting of the members duly called and held shall be necessary for any action taken by the membership of the agency. No vacancy in the membership of the agency shall impair the rights of a quorum to exercise all the rights and to perform all the duties of the agency. For the purposes of determining a quorum and the number of affirmative votes at a meeting, persons who have been delegated the right to vote in accordance with § 13-23-106 shall be considered members of the agency.

SECTION 5. The board members whose terms expire on June 30, 2013, shall continue to serve on the board after the effective date of this act, until the expiration of their terms.

Effective date 5/16/2013

SECTION 6. This act shall take effect upon becoming a law, the public welfare requiring it.

PUBLIC CHAPTER NO. 415

PUBLIC CHAPTER NO. 415

SENATE BILL NO. 1029

By Kelsey, Beavers, Burks, Ford, Haile, Overbey, Stevens, Yager

Substituted for: House Bill No. 416

By McCormick, Coley, Rogers, Littleton, Moody, Weaver, Camper, Parkinson, Jones, Dawn White, Hardaway

AN ACT to amend Tennessee Code Annotated, Title 39 and Title 40, relative to criminal gang offenses.

BE IT ENACTED BY THE GENERAL ASSEMBLY OF THE STATE OF TENNESSEE:

40-35-121 SECTION 1. Tennessee Code Annotated, Section 40-35-121(a)(3)(B), as amended by Senate Bill No. 202/House Bill No. 196, is amended by adding the following new subdivision:

( ) Trafficking for commercial sex acts, as defined in § 39-13-309;

Effective date 7/1/2013 SECTION 2. This act shall take effect July 1, 2013, the public welfare requiring it.

PUBLIC CHAPTER NO. 416

PUBLIC CHAPTER NO. 416

SENATE BILL NO. 1028

By Kelsey, Ketron, Crowe, Bowling, Burks, Campfield, Ford, Haile, Harper, Massey, Overbey, Stevens, Yager

Substituted for: House Bill No. 709

By Littleton, Jones, Coley, Rogers, Moody, Weaver, Camper, Parkinson, Dawn White, Eldridge, Hardaway, Keisling, Evans

AN ACT to amend Tennessee Code Annotated, Title 39 and Title 40, relative to limitation on prosecution of crimes committed against children.

BE IT ENACTED BY THE GENERAL ASSEMBLY OF THE STATE OF TENNESSEE:

40-2-101 SECTION 1. Tennessee Code Annotated, Section 40-2-101, is amended by adding the following as a new subsection:

( )(1) A person may be prosecuted, tried and punished for any offense committed against a child on or after July 1, 2013, that constitutes a criminal offense under § 39-13-309 or § 39-13-529, no later than fifteen (15) years from the date the child becomes eighteen (18) years of age.

(2) A person may be prosecuted, tried and punished for any offense committed against a child on or after July 1, 2013, that constitutes a criminal offense under § 39-13-514 or § 39-13-515 no later than ten (10) years from the date the child becomes eighteen (18) years of age.

39-13-529 SECTION 2. Tennessee Code Annotated, Section 39-13-529(c), is amended by deleting the subsection in its entirety.

Effective date 7/1/2013 SECTION 3. This act shall take effect July 1, 2013, the public welfare requiring it.

PUBLIC CHAPTER NO. 417

PUBLIC CHAPTER NO. 417

SENATE BILL NO. 1024

By Overbey

Substituted for: House Bill No. 737

By Ramsey

AN ACT to amend Tennessee Code Annotated, Section 67-5-209, relative to taxation of private act hospital authorities.

BE IT ENACTED BY THE GENERAL ASSEMBLY OF THE STATE OF TENNESSEE:

67-5-209 SECTION 1. Tennessee Code Annotated, Section 67-5-209, is amended by deleting the section in its entirety and by substituting instead the following language:

In addition to all rights and powers granted to a private act hospital authority under the provisions of title 7, chapter 57, part 6, such a private act hospital authority shall be exempt from the payment of any taxes or fees to the state or any subdivisions thereof, or to any officer or employee of the state or any subdivision thereof, except as hereinafter provided. This exemption does not include fees paid by private act hospital authorities as required by § 68-11-216. All property of an authority residing within the boundaries of its creating or participating governing authorities or entities shall be exempt from all county and municipal taxes; provided, that the authority shall pay all county and municipal fees. An authority may agree to the payment of tax equivalents to the creating or participating governing authority or entity. Authorities shall be required to apply to the state board of equalization for claims for exemption of property residing outside the boundaries of their creating or participating governing authorities or entities. The claims for exemption shall be determined by the state board of equalization, following application in the manner required by § 67-5-212, and exemptions shall be:

(1) Limited to property of the authority which would be exempt if owned and operated by a charitable hospital under § 67-5-212; and

(2) Granted in accordance with the same criteria used by the board of equalization in granting exemptions to property owned and operated by a charitable hospital under § 67-5-212.

Effective date 5/16/2013 SECTION 2. This act shall take effect upon becoming a law, the public welfare requiring it.

PUBLIC CHAPTER NO. 418

PUBLIC CHAPTER NO. 418

SENATE BILL NO. 1015

By Bell

Substituted for: House Bill No. 581

By Dennis

AN ACT to amend Tennessee Code Annotated, Title 39, Chapter 17, Part 13, relative to knives.

BE IT ENACTED BY THE GENERAL ASSEMBLY OF THE STATE OF TENNESSEE:

39-17-1314 SECTION 1. Tennessee Code Annotated, Section 39-17-1314, is amended by adding the following new subsection:

(e) It is the intent of the general assembly that this part is preemptive with respect to the transfer, ownership, possession or transportation of knives and no city, county, or metropolitan government shall occupy any part of the field of regulation of the transfer, ownership, possession or transportation of knives.

Effective date 7/1/2013 SECTION 2. This act shall take effect July 1, 2013, the public welfare requiring it and shall apply to all applicable provisions of law in conflict with this act.

PUBLIC CHAPTER NO. 419

PUBLIC CHAPTER NO. 419

SENATE BILL NO. 982

By McNally, Bowling

Substituted for: House Bill No. 20

By Shepard, Odom, Evans

AN ACT to amend Tennessee Code Annotated, Title 67, Chapter 4, Part 17, relative to the privilege tax imposed on persons engaged in certain occupations.

BE IT ENACTED BY THE GENERAL ASSEMBLY OF THE STATE OF TENNESSEE:

SECTION 1. Tennessee Code Annotated, Title 67, Chapter 4, Part 17, is amended by adding the following as a new section:

67-4-1711.

(a) The commissioner of revenue is urged to study the advisability of using the following criteria in determining the amount of tax to be levied on persons subject to the tax: the profitability ratio for the type of vocation, profession, business, or occupation listed in § 67-4-1702(a) as measured by nationwide averages derived from statistics, classifications, or other information published by the United States office of management and budget or the United States internal revenue service.

(b) If any such study is undertaken, the commissioner is urged to report any findings and recommendations to the chairs of the finance, ways and means committees of the senate and house of representatives by January 15, 2014.

Effective date 5/16/2013

SECTION 2. This act shall take effect upon becoming a law, the public welfare requiring it.

PUBLIC CHAPTER NO. 420

PUBLIC CHAPTER NO. 420

SENATE BILL NO. 942

By Southerland

Substituted for: House Bill No. 944

By Ryan Williams, Sargent

AN ACT to amend Tennessee Code Annotated, Title 62, Chapter 13, Part 3, relative to licensure.

BE IT ENACTED BY THE GENERAL ASSEMBLY OF THE STATE OF TENNESSEE:

62-13-303 SECTION 1. Tennessee Code Annotated, Section 62-13-303, is amended by adding the following as a new, appropriately designated subsection:

(l)(1) The commission shall require all applicants for initial licensure issued under this chapter, including but not limited to a time-share license, on or after January 1, 2014, to submit a complete and legible set of fingerprints, on a form prescribed by the commission or in such electronic format as the commission may require, to the commission or to the Tennessee bureau of investigation for the purpose of obtaining a criminal background check from the Tennessee bureau of investigation and the federal bureau of investigation.

(2) The commission shall refuse to issue a license to an applicant for initial licensure who does not comply with subdivision (l)(1); provided, a licensee who requests to renew an existing license issued under this chapter, or obtain a broker license after being licensed as an affiliate broker, shall not be required to submit a set of fingerprints pursuant to this subsection (l).

(3) The commission shall conduct a criminal background check of each applicant described in subdivision (l)(1) by using information:

(A) Provided by the applicant under this subsection (l); and

(B) Made available to the commission by the Tennessee bureau of investigation, the federal bureau of investigation and any other criminal justice agency.

(4) The commission may:

(A) Enter into an agreement with the Tennessee bureau of investigation to administer a criminal background check required under this subsection (l); and

(B) Authorize the Tennessee bureau of investigation to collect from the applicant the costs incurred by the department in conducting the criminal background check.

SECTION 2. The Tennessee Real Estate Commission is authorized to promulgate rules and regulations to effectuate the purposes of this act. All such rules and regulations shall be promulgated in accordance with Title 4, Chapter 5.

Effective date 1/1/2014 SECTION 3. For purposes of promulgating rules and regulations, this act shall take effect upon becoming a law, the public welfare requiring it. For all other purposes, this act shall take effect January 1, 2014, the public welfare requiring it.

PUBLIC CHAPTER NO. 421

PUBLIC CHAPTER NO. 421

SENATE BILL NO. 941

By Southerland, Overbey

Substituted for: House Bill No. 945

By Swann, Matheny, Gilmore, Powell

AN ACT to amend Tennessee Code Annotated, Title 5; Title 6; Title 7; Title 62, Chapter 9 and Title 68, relative to landfilling of recyclables.

BE IT ENACTED BY THE GENERAL ASSEMBLY OF THE STATE OF TENNESSEE:

68-211-861 SECTION 1. Tennessee Code Annotated, Section 68-211-861, is amended by designating the existing language in subsection (c) as subdivision (c)(1) and adding the following as a new subdivision (c)(2):

(2)(A) As used in this subdivision (c)(2):

(1) "Aluminum cans" means aluminum beverage cans, aluminum food cans, and aluminum bottles; and

(2) "Plastic bottles" means recyclable plastic beverage containers that have a neck smaller than the body of the container.

(B) Any region shall be permitted to multiply by three (3) the gross weight of any aluminum cans and plastic bottles that are diverted from Class I municipal solid waste disposal facilities and incinerators located within the geographic area encompassed by the region for purposes of calculating the total percentage waste reduction and diversion that the region has achieved.

Effective date 5/16/2013 SECTION 2. This act shall take effect upon becoming a law, the public welfare requiring it.

PUBLIC CHAPTER NO. 422

PUBLIC CHAPTER NO. 422

SENATE BILL NO. 886

By Hensley, Burks, Ford

Substituted for: House Bill No. 620

By John Deberry, Kevin Brooks, Womick

AN ACT to amend Tennessee Code Annotated, Title 49, relative to diplomas for students with disabilities.

BE IT ENACTED BY THE GENERAL ASSEMBLY OF THE STATE OF TENNESSEE:

49-6-6001 SECTION 1. Tennessee Code Annotated, Section 49-6-6001, is amended by adding the following as a new subsection:

(g) In addition to a full diploma, a certificate of attendance, or a special education diploma, the board shall adopt an occupational diploma for students with disabilities. The board shall set appropriate standards and benchmarks of attendance, academic achievement, and job readiness skills for the occupational diploma. A student is not required to comply with the testing requirements of subdivision (a)(1) in order to receive an occupational diploma.

Effective date 7/1/2013 SECTION 2. This act shall take effect July 1, 2013, the public welfare requiring it.

PUBLIC CHAPTER NO. 423

PUBLIC CHAPTER NO. 423

SENATE BILL NO. 852

By Ketron, Bell, Tracy

Substituted for: House Bill No. 1272

By Matheny, Sargent, Harrison, Haynes, Swann, Hawk, Dean, Eldridge, Littleton, Jernigan, Shepard, Kevin Brooks, Watson, Forgety, Sparks, Moody, Faison, Weaver, Womick

AN ACT to amend Tennessee Code Annotated, Title 4; Title 67 and Title 68, relative to alternative fuel vehicles and fueling infrastructure.

WHEREAS, the United States consumed nearly eighteen million eight hundred thousand (18,800,000) barrels of oil in 2011; and

WHEREAS, forty-five percent (45%) of the oil consumed was imported from other countries; and

WHEREAS, the petroleum market is a global market, and the price of oil is greatly affected by world events; and

WHEREAS, eighty-five percent (85%) of the natural gas consumed in the United States is produced domestically; and

WHEREAS, U.S. natural gas resources are estimated at one trillion seven hundred billion (1,700,000,000) cubic feet, enough to last one hundred (100) years or more; and

WHEREAS, the newly discovered, domestic natural gas reserves have led to low natural gas prices and price stability. Natural gas prices are unaffected by turmoil in the Middle East; and

WHEREAS, the United States leads the world in natural gas production, but lags in the usage of natural gas vehicles; and

WHEREAS, the price of compressed natural gas is nearly half the price of gasoline or diesel; and

WHEREAS, natural gas powers more than one hundred thousand (100,000) vehicles in the United States and roughly eleven million two hundred thousand (11,200,000) vehicles worldwide and is a good power choice for high-mileage fleets, such as buses and taxis, that are centrally fueled or operate within a limited area; and

WHEREAS, the advantages of natural gas as an alternative fuel include its domestic availability, widespread distribution infrastructure, low cost when compared with gasoline and diesel fuels, and clean-burning qualities; and

WHEREAS, the U.S. Department of Energy found that there are two (2) forms of natural gas which may be used in vehicles and are considered alternative fuels under the Energy Policy Act of 1992: compressed natural gases or liquefied natural gases; and

WHEREAS, the Tennessee general assembly finds that energy independence is a worthy public policy goal; now, therefore,

BE IT ENACTED BY THE GENERAL ASSEMBLY OF THE STATE OF TENNESSEE:

SECTION 1. This act shall be known and may be cited as the "Energy Independence Act of 2013."

4-3-1109 SECTION 2. Tennessee Code Annotated, Section 4-3-1109, is amended by deleting the section in its entirety and substituting the following:

4-3-1109.

(a) The commissioner shall encourage the acquisition of energy-efficient and alternative fuel motor vehicles in the fleet of state vehicles. Each year, every effort should be made to achieve a target goal that one hundred percent (100%) of newly purchased passenger motor vehicles be energy-efficient or alternative fuel motor vehicles. The department shall ensure that at least twenty-five percent (25%) of newly purchased passenger motor vehicles procured for use in areas designated by the United States environmental protection agency (EPA) as nonattainment areas shall be hybrid-electric vehicles or vehicles powered by natural gas; provided, that such vehicles and fueling infrastructure are available at the time of procurement and such vehicles are purchased at competitive prices. In the event that such vehicles or fueling infrastructure is not available at the time of procurement, the department may instead meet this mandate by procuring compact fuel-efficient vehicles. In areas not designated by the EPA as nonattainment areas, the department shall ensure that at least twenty-five percent (25%) of newly purchased passenger motor vehicles are hybrid-electric vehicles, vehicles powered by natural gas, or compact fuel-efficient vehicles; provided, that such vehicles are purchased at competitive prices.

(b)(1) Commencing June 30, 2013, the commissioner shall compile and maintain information on the nature of passenger motor vehicles that are owned and leased by the state, including, but not limited to:

(A) The number of passenger motor vehicles purchased during the fiscal year categorized by energy-efficiency; and

(B) The number of passenger motor vehicles owned as of June 30 of each year categorized by energy-efficiency.

(2) The commissioner shall file an annual report with the governor and the general assembly concerning such passenger motor vehicles. The report shall include at a minimum:

(A) Problems or concerns the state may have experienced in meeting the target goal set pursuant to subsection (a) relative to obtaining such energy-efficient motor vehicles;

(B) Any savings or increased expenditures to the state in the purchase of, as well as the operation and maintenance cost of, such motor vehicles;

(C) Plans for integrating energy-efficient motor vehicles identified in subdivisions (c)(1)(E) and (G) into the state passenger motor vehicle fleet;

(D) The volume of gasoline or diesel displaced by the usage of energy-efficient or alternative fuel vehicles; and

(E) The emissions reduction achieved by the usage of energy-efficient or alternative fuel vehicles.

(3) The information compiled and maintained pursuant to subdivisions (b)(1) and (2) shall be made accessible to the public on the department's website through a prominent link provided on the home page. In addition, the department shall submit an annual report containing the information compiled and maintained pursuant to subdivisions (b)(1) and (2) to the speaker of the senate and the speaker of the house of representatives and to the chairs of the committees concerning government operations and to the chair of the energy, agriculture and natural resources committee of the senate and the chair of the agriculture and natural resources committee of the house of representatives.

(c) For purposes of this section unless the context otherwise requires:

(1) "Energy-efficient motor vehicle" means a passenger motor vehicle that is:

(A) An alternative fuel vehicle as defined by the Energy Policy Act of 1992 (P.L. 102-486);

(B) A flexible fuel vehicle (FFV) utilizing ethanol, biodiesel, or any other commercially available alternative fuel approved by the United States department of energy;

(C) A hybrid-electric vehicle (HEV);

(D) A compact fuel-efficient vehicle, defined as a vehicle powered by unleaded gasoline that has a United States EPA estimated highway gasoline mileage rating of at least twenty-five miles per gallon (25 mpg) or greater for the model year purchased;

(E) An electric vehicle (EV);

(F) A vehicle powered by natural gas; or

(G) A vehicle powered by ultra low sulfur diesel fuel that meets Bin 5, Tier II emission standards mandated by the EPA and that has an EPA-estimated highway mileage rating of at least thirty miles per gallon (30 mpg) or greater for the model year purchased; and

(2) "Passenger motor vehicle" means a motor vehicle designed for carrying six (6) or fewer adult passengers and used for the transportation of persons; provided, that vans, including cargo vans, trucks, sport utility vehicles, and police pursuit vehicles shall not be considered passenger motor vehicles.

(d) For purchases of vehicles that are not passenger motor vehicles, including cargo vans, trucks, and sport utility vehicles, the department is encouraged to make reasonable efforts to achieve a target goal that at least five percent (5%) of newly purchased vehicles are vehicles powered by natural gas, provided that such vehicles and fueling infrastructure are available at the time of procurement and such vehicles are purchased at competitive prices.

(e) In order to facilitate the development of natural gas fueling infrastructure, the department is authorized to participate in such pilot projects as may be necessary to insure the availability of natural gas fueling infrastructure throughout the interstate highway corridors in Tennessee.

4-22-101 SECTION 3. Tennessee Code Annotated, Section 4-22-101(b), is amended by inserting the following language after "hybrid electric vehicles": ", natural gas vehicles".

67-5-601 SECTION 4. Tennessee Code Annotated, Section 67-5-601, is amended by adding the following as a new, appropriately designated subsection:

(f) The general assembly finds that any public utility property or commercial and industrial property that is used to engage in the fueling of natural gas vehicles and that is a certified alternative fueling site as described in the definition of "certified green energy production facility" in § 67-4-2004, is generally capable of fueling fewer types of vehicles due to limited availability from original equipment manufacturers, that use of such alternative, domestically produced transportation fuels should be encouraged to improve air quality and to enhance our nation's energy security, and immediate economic value for all purposes under this chapter should not initially exceed thirty percent (30%) of its total installed costs. The general assembly further finds that, unless the findings are considered in the determination of the sound, intrinsic, and immediate economic value of such property for all purposes under this chapter, investment in property for fueling alternative fuel vehicles will be unreasonably discouraged, denying the citizens of this state the environmental benefits and domestic energy security associated with the use of natural gas as a transportation fuel. The assessor of property, in assessing any such commercial and industrial property, or the comptroller, in assessing any such public utility property, that engages in the fueling of motor vehicles with natural gas, shall take these findings by the general assembly into account in determining the sound, intrinsic, and immediate economic value of such property, when the property is initially appraised and each time the property is reappraised. A copy of the facility certification issued by the department of environment and conservation shall be required in order to qualify for such valuation. The valuation of personal property under this section shall also apply to machinery and equipment utilized in a natural gas vehicle fueling station. Such equipment shall include, but not be limited to: storage vessels, compressors, dryers, dispensers, piping, compressed or liquefied gas appliances, or any other item that is installed by a natural gas provider.

67-4-2004 SECTION 5. Tennessee Code Annotated, Section 67-4-2004(9), is amended by deleting the subsection in its entirety and replacing with the following language:

(9) "Certified green energy production facility" means:

(A) A facility certified by the department of environment and conservation as producing electricity for use and consumption off the premises using clean energy technology. For the purposes of this subdivision (9)(A), clean energy technology means technology used to generate energy from geothermal, hydrogen, solar, and wind sources;

(B) A facility certified by the department of environment and conservation as an alternative motor vehicle fueling station that utilizes natural gas in compressed or liquid form for the purpose of fueling motor vehicles and that is projected to displace more than six thousand (6,000) gallons of petroleum annually; or

(C) A facility which utilizes natural gas in a combined heat and power configuration (CHP) for production of heat and electricity for consumption onsite.

4-22-101 SECTION 6. Tennessee Code Annotated, Section 4-22-101, is amended by deleting the term "fuel-efficient" wherever it appears in the section and substituting the term "energy-efficient motor vehicle", and by deleting subsection (d) and substituting the following:

(d) For purposes of this section:

(1) "Motor vehicle" means a self-propelled vehicle licensed for highway use; and

(2) "Energy-efficient motor vehicle" means a passenger motor vehicle that is:

(A) An alternative fuel vehicle as defined by the Energy Policy Act of 1992 (P.L. 102-486);

(B) A flexible fuel vehicle (FFV) utilizing ethanol, biodiesel, or any other commercially available alternative fuel approved by the United States department of energy;

(C) A hybrid-electric vehicle (HEV);

(D) A compact fuel-efficient vehicle, defined as a vehicle powered by unleaded gasoline that has a United States EPA estimated highway gasoline mileage rating of at least twenty-five miles per gallon (25 mpg) or greater for the model year purchased;

(E) An electric vehicle (EV);

(F) A vehicle powered by natural gas; or

(G) A vehicle powered by ultra low sulfur diesel fuel that meets Bin 5, Tier II emission standards mandated by the EPA and that has an EPA-estimated highway mileage rating of at least thirty miles per gallon (30 mpg) or greater for the model year purchased.

SECTION 7. If any provision of this act or the application thereof to any person or circumstance is held invalid, such invalidity shall not affect other provisions or applications of the act which can be given effect without the invalid provision or application, and to that end the provisions of this act are declared to be severable.

Effective date 5/16/2013 SECTION 8. This act shall take effect upon becoming a law, the public welfare requiring it.

PUBLIC CHAPTER NO. 424

PUBLIC CHAPTER NO. 424

SENATE BILL NO. 833

By Ketron

Substituted for: House Bill No. 551

By Curtiss, Eldridge

AN ACT to amend Tennessee Code Annotated, Title 50 and Title 56, relative to misclassification of employees.

BE IT ENACTED BY THE GENERAL ASSEMBLY OF THE STATE OF TENNESSEE:

50-6-411 SECTION 1. Tennessee Code Annotated, Title 50, Chapter 6, Part 4, is amended by adding the following new section thereto:

50-6-411.

(a)(1) It is a violation of this section if at any time a construction services provider, as defined in § 50-6-901, misclassifies employees to avoid proper classification for premium calculations by concealing any information pertinent to the computation and application of an experience rating modification factor or by materially understating or concealing:

(A) The amount of the construction services provider's payroll;

(B) The number of the construction services provider's employees; or

(C) Any of the construction services provider's employee's duties.

(2) A construction services provider who violates subdivision (a)(1) shall be subject to a penalty issued by the commissioner or commissioner's designee of up to the greater of one thousand dollars ($1,000) or one and one half (1½) times the average yearly workers' compensation premium for such construction services provider based on the appropriate assigned risk plan advisory prospective loss cost and multiplier minus the premium dollars paid on the policy that was the object of the understatement or concealment.

(b) This section shall have no effect upon a construction services provider's or carrier's duty to provide benefits under this chapter or upon any of the construction services provider's or carrier's rights and defenses under this chapter, including, but not limited to, § 50-6-108.

(c) In addition to the penalties provided for in subdivision (a)(2), the department shall refer cases involving business operations that are in violation of this section to the Tennessee bureau of investigation or the appropriate district attorney general for any action deemed necessary under any applicable criminal law.

(d) An individual or entity that is not a successor-in-interest or a principal of a construction services provider who is in violation of this section shall not be liable for the monetary penalties in this section.

(e) The funds collected by the commissioner of labor and workforce development or the commissioner's designee for penalties assessed pursuant to subdivision (a)(2) shall be deposited in the employee misclassification education and enforcement fund established by § 50-6-913 to be administered by the commissioner of labor and workforce development.

50-6-913 SECTION 2. Tennessee Code Annotated, Section 50-6-913(b), is amended by adding the following language to the second sentence of the subsection between the words "development" and "for":

for the purchase of computer software and hardware designed to identify potential employee misclassification activity, for the hiring of additional employees to investigate potential employee misclassification activity,

Effective date 7/1/2013

SECTION 3. This act shall take effect July 1, 2013, the public welfare requiring it, and shall apply to violations occurring on or after the effective date of this act.

PUBLIC CHAPTER NO. 425

PUBLIC CHAPTER NO. 425

SENATE BILL NO. 832

By Overbey, Burks, Haile

Substituted for: House Bill No. 1038

By Rich, Lamberth, Rogers, Weaver, Shipley, Hardaway, Watson, Parkinson, Faison, Lundberg, Curtis Johnson, Travis, Fitzhugh, Camper, Harwell, Mark White, Shepard, Dennis, McCormick, Harrison, McDaniel, Powers, Littleton, Roach, Evans, Eldridge, Butt, Moody

AN ACT to amend Tennessee Code Annotated, Title 39 and Title 40, relative to criminal offenses, sentencing and criminal procedure.

BE IT ENACTED BY THE GENERAL ASSEMBLY OF THE STATE OF TENNESSEE:

40-35-501 SECTION 1. Tennessee Code Annotated, Section 40-35-501, is amended by creating the following new subdivision to subsection (k) to be appropriately designated:

> (k)( ) There shall be no release eligibility for a person committing attempted first degree murder as defined in § 39-13-202 where the victim suffers serious bodily injury as defined in § 39-11-106, on or after July 1, 2013, until the person has served eighty-five percent (85%) of the sentence imposed by the court less sentence credits earned and retained. However, no sentence reduction credits authorized by § 41-21-236, or any other provision of law, shall operate to reduce below seventy-five percent (75%) the percentage of sentence imposed by the court such person must serve before becoming release eligible.

Effective date 7/1/2013 SECTION 2. This act shall take effect July 1, 2013, the public welfare requiring it and shall apply to all offenses committed on or after such date.

PUBLIC CHAPTER NO. 426

PUBLIC CHAPTER NO. 426

SENATE BILL NO. 828

By Gresham, Haile

Substituted for: House Bill No. 1036

By Weaver, Lamberth, Rogers, Rich, Shipley, Hardaway, Watson, Parkinson, Camper, Faison, Lundberg, Curtis Johnson, Dawn White, Evans, Travis, Mark White, Butt, Shepard, Fitzhugh, Womick, Eldridge, Littleton

AN ACT to amend Tennessee Code Annotated, Titles 39 and 40, relative to criminal offenses, sentencing and criminal procedure.

BE IT ENACTED BY THE GENERAL ASSEMBLY OF THE STATE OF TENNESSEE:

40-35-501 SECTION 1. Tennessee Code Annotated, Section 40-35-501(k), is amended by adding the following new, appropriately designated subdivision:

( ) There shall be no release eligibility for a person committing aggravated child neglect or endangerment as defined in § 39-15-402, on or after July 1, 2013, until the person has served seventy percent (70%) of the sentence imposed by the court less sentence credits earned and retained. However, no sentence reduction credits authorized by § 41-21-236, or any other provision of law, shall operate to reduce below fifty-five percent (55%) the percentage of sentence imposed by the court such person must serve before becoming release eligible.

Effective date 7/1/2013 SECTION 2. This act shall take effect July 1, 2013, the public welfare requiring it and shall apply to all offenses committed on or after such date.

PUBLIC CHAPTER NO. 427

PUBLIC CHAPTER NO. 427

SENATE BILL NO. 783

By Johnson, Mr. Speaker Ramsey

Substituted for: House Bill No. 639

By Matlock, Casada, Sexton, Kevin Brooks, Durham, Littleton, Butt, Marsh, Shipley, Spivey, Womick, Kane, Hall, Haynes, Lundberg, Eldridge, Ryan Williams, McManus

AN ACT to amend Tennessee Code Annotated, Title 50, Chapter 7, relative to unemployment insurance.

BE IT ENACTED BY THE GENERAL ASSEMBLY OF THE STATE OF TENNESSEE:

50-7-218 SECTION 1. Tennessee Code Annotated, Section 50-7-218, is amended by deleting the section in its entirety and substituting instead the following:

"Base period" means the first four (4) of the last five (5) completed calendar quarters immediately preceding the first day of an individual's benefit year; provided, that if the first quarter of the last five (5) completed calendar quarters was included in the base period applicable to any individual's previous benefit year, the individual's base period shall be the last four (4) completed calendar quarters. For the purposes of establishing a base period in cases involving persons receiving workers' compensation benefits for temporary total disability, the department shall exclude periods of such disability from the base period and determine the base period from the last four (4) completed quarters of work before any such disability.

50-7-301 SECTION 2. Tennessee Code Annotated, Section 50-7-301, is amended by deleting subsection (e).

50-7-303 SECTION 3. Tennessee Code Annotated, Section 50-7-303(b)(3), is amended by adding the following new subdivision (C) and redesignating existing subdivisions accordingly:

(C) "Misconduct" also includes any conduct constituting a criminal offense for which the claimant has been convicted or charged that:

(i) Involves dishonesty arising out of the claimant's employment; or

(ii) Was committed while the claimant was acting within the scope of employment;

50-7-304 SECTION 4. Tennessee Code Annotated, Section 50-7-304(b)(1)(C), is amended by adding the following language at the end of the subdivision:

There shall be no one (1) year limitation on the agency representative reconsidering a decision if a claimant is subsequently convicted of a misdemeanor or felony that caused the separation from the employer; provided, however, the employer gives notification of the conviction in a reasonable time to the agency. Any overpayment created as a result of a reconsideration because a claimant is subsequently convicted of a misdemeanor or felony that cause the separation from the employer shall be determined to be fraud and the administrator shall not waive repayment of the overpaid amounts.

50-7-304 SECTION 5. Tennessee Code Annotated, Section 50-7-304(d), is amended by adding the following language at the end of the subsection:

The department shall hold annual training for all unemployment hearing officers. Such training shall include updates on any new laws or regulations involving employment security law enacted by the state or federal government.

50-7-302 SECTION 6. Tennessee Code Annotated, Section 50-7-302(a)(4), is amended by deleting subdivision (F) and redesignating existing subdivisions accordingly.

50-7-302 SECTION 7. Tennessee Code Annotated, Section 50-7-302(a)(4), is amended by deleting the language "one thousand (1,000)" and substituting instead the language "one thousand five hundred (1,500)".

PUBLIC CHAPTER NO. 427 (cont'd)

SECTION 8. Notwithstanding any other provision of law to the contrary, any provision of this act shall not apply to the extent that compliance with such provision would violate federal law or cause a loss of federal funding.

50-7-303 SECTION 9. Tennessee Code Annotated, Section 50-7-303(d)(3), is amended by deleting the language "shall" in subdivisions (A) and (B) and substituting instead the language "may".

50-7-303 SECTION 10. Tennessee Code Annotated, Section 50-7-303(d)(3), is amended by adding the following as a new subdivision thereto:

(C) If a waiver is given by the administrator pursuant to subdivision (d)(3)(A) or (d)(3)(B), such waiver shall only be made by the administrator in accordance with § 4-4-120 and procedures established pursuant to such section.

Effective date 7/1/2013 SECTION 11. This act shall take effect July 1, 2013, the public welfare requiring it.

PUBLIC CHAPTER NO. 428

PUBLIC CHAPTER NO. 428

SENATE BILL NO. 719

By Crowe

Substituted for: House Bill No. 862

By Lundberg, Harry Brooks

AN ACT to amend Tennessee Code Annotated, Title 49, Chapter 4, Part 9, relative to postsecondary financial assistance from net lottery proceeds.

BE IT ENACTED BY THE GENERAL ASSEMBLY OF THE STATE OF TENNESSEE:

49-4-942 SECTION 1. Tennessee Code Annotated, Title 49, Chapter 4, Part 9, is amended by adding the following language as a new section:

49-4-942.

(a) As used in this section:

(1) "Dependent child" means a natural or adopted child or stepchild:

(A) Whose parent is a headquarters staff employee;

(B) Whose parent claims the child as a dependent for federal income tax purposes;

(C) Who is under twenty-one (21) years of age; and

(D) Who resides in another nation only while the parent is on full-time work assignment as a headquarters staff employee;

(2) "Qualified headquarters facility" has the same meaning as defined in § 67-6-224(b); and

(3) "Headquarters staff employee" has the same meaning as defined in § 67-6-224(b).

(b) Notwithstanding any provision of this part to the contrary, a student who is a Tennessee citizen and a dependent child of a headquarters staff employee who is on full-time work assignment in a foreign nation shall be eligible for a Tennessee HOPE scholarship as an entering freshman if the student meets all eligibility requirements for the scholarship, except that, while the parent is on full-time work assignment in another nation, the student does not reside in Tennessee immediately preceding the date of application for financial assistance and the student does not meet the requirements of § 49-4-905(b)(2). To be eligible under this section, the student shall:

(1) Graduate from a high school that is accredited by a regional accrediting association as defined in § 49-4-902 in the foreign nation where the student's parent is on work assignment and meet the academic eligibility requirements of § 49-4-907(3); or

(2) Complete high school in a home school in the foreign nation where the student's parent is on work assignment and meet the eligibility requirements of § 49-4-908(2)(A).

(c) This section shall only apply to dependent children of headquarters staff employees who are on full-time work assignment in another nation for more than one (1) year and who were Tennessee residents before leaving the United States and intend to return to Tennessee upon completion of their assignment.

Effective date 5/16/2013 SECTION 2. This act shall take effect upon becoming a law, the public welfare requiring it, and shall apply to students seeking postsecondary financial assistance from net lottery proceeds for the 2013-2014 academic year and academic years thereafter.

PUBLIC CHAPTER NO. 429

PUBLIC CHAPTER NO. 429

SENATE BILL NO. 687

By Tate

Substituted for: House Bill No. 471

By Lois DeBerry, Fitzhugh, Hardaway

AN ACT to amend Tennessee Code Annotated, Title 49, relative to higher education.

BE IT ENACTED BY THE GENERAL ASSEMBLY OF THE STATE OF TENNESSEE:

49-7-211 SECTION 1. Tennessee Code Annotated, Title 49, Chapter 7, Part 2, is amended by adding the following language as a new section:

49-7-211.

(a) Each institution of higher education shall report to the Tennessee higher education commission, on an annual basis, an accounting of student activity fees.

(b) The Tennessee higher education commission shall publish, as part of the Tennessee Postsecondary Education Fact Book, a financial disclosure statement for student activity fees.

(c) The financial disclosure statement shall account for the student activity fees on a campus-by-campus basis. At a minimum the following information shall also be included with the financial disclosure statement:

(1) The number of undergraduate and graduate students enrolled;

(2) Source of any student activity fees according to the number of students enrolled as undergraduate or graduate students;

(3) The expenditure of the student activity fees; and

(4) Funds not expended during the disclosure period.

(d) This section shall only apply to public institutions of higher education operated by the board of regents or the University of Tennessee board of trustees.

Effective date 7/1/2013 SECTION 2. This act shall take effect July 1, 2013, the public welfare requiring it.

PUBLIC CHAPTER NO. 430

PUBLIC CHAPTER NO. 430

SENATE BILL NO. 676

By Yager, Burks, Massey, McNally, Campfield, Gardenhire, Haile, Kelsey, Overbey, Tate

Substituted for: House Bill No. 1264

By Dunn, Haynes, Dean, Sexton, Ramsey, Matlock, Faison, Lamberth, Shipley, Hardaway, Camper, Harry Brooks, Gloria Johnson, Calfee, Powers, Shepard, Kevin Brooks, Kane, Weaver, Evans, Stewart, Rogers, Sparks, Powell, Towns, Ryan Williams, Swann, Travis, Mark White, Johnnie Turner, Hall, Butt

AN ACT to amend Tennessee Code Annotated, Title 39; Title 53 and Title 63, relative to prescription drug abuse.

BE IT ENACTED BY THE GENERAL ASSEMBLY OF THE STATE OF TENNESSEE:

SECTION 1. This act shall be known and may be cited as the "Addison Sharp Prescription Regulatory Act of 2013."

63-1-401, 63-1-402 SECTION 2. Tennessee Code Annotated, Title 63, Chapter 1, is amended by adding a new Part 4 as follows:

63-1-401.

(a) As used in this part:

(1) "Commissioner" means the commissioner of the department of health; and

(2) "Treatment guidelines" means systematically developed statements to assist health care providers in making patient decisions concerning appropriate medical care for specific clinical circumstances.

(b) By January 1, 2014, the commissioner shall develop recommended treatment guidelines for prescribing of opioids, benzodiazepines, barbiturates, and carisoprodol that can be used by prescribers in the state as a guide for caring for patients. This subsection shall not apply to veterinarians.

(c) The commissioner shall review and update the guidelines by September 30th of each year, and shall cause them to be posted on the department's website.

(d) The treatment guidelines shall be submitted to each prescribing board that licenses health professionals who can legally prescribe controlled substances and to the board of pharmacy. Each board shall be charged with review of the treatment guidelines and determining how the guidelines are to be used by its licensees.

(e) Each board shall notify all of its licensees through routine bulletins or newsletters of the existence of the guidelines.

63-1-402.

(a) On or after July 1, 2014, all prescribers who hold a current federal drug enforcement administration (DEA) license and who prescribe controlled substances shall be required to complete a minimum of two (2) hours of continuing education related to controlled substance prescribing biennially to count toward the licensees' mandatory continuing education.

(b) The continuing education must include instruction in the department's treatment guidelines on opioids, benzodiazepines, barbiturates, and carisoprodol, and may include such other topics as medicine addiction, risk management tools, and other topics as approved by the respective licensing boards.

(c) This section shall not apply to veterinarians, providers practicing at a registered pain management clinic as defined in § 63-1-301 or to medical doctors or osteopathic physicians board certified by the American Board of Medical Specialties (ABMS), or American Osteopathic Association (AOA), or the American Board of

Physician Specialties (ABPS) in one or more of the following specialties or subspecialties:

(1) Pain management;

(2) Anesthesiology;

(3) Physical medicine and rehabilitation;

(4) Neurology; or

(5) Rheumatology.

53-10-302 SECTION 3. Tennessee Code Annotated, Section 53-10-302(10), is deleted in its entirety and replaced with the following language:

(10) "Healthcare practitioner extender" means any registered or licensed healthcare professional, and up to two (2) unlicensed persons per prescriber or dispenser designated by the prescriber or dispenser to act as agents of such prescriber or dispenser. A prescriber shall have the ability to authorize a healthcare practitioner extender to check the controlled substance database as stipulated in § 53-10-310(e) for other prescribers in the authorizing prescriber's practice. Notwithstanding the provisions of Section 28 of Chapter 880 of the Public Acts of 2012, any one-time costs required to be made to effectuate the provisions of this act specific to system modifications required by changes in this subdivision shall be shared on a pro-rata basis, excluding the pharmacy board, by the appropriate prescribing boards as enumerated in title 53, chapter 10, part 3. The prescriber or dispenser shall be responsible for actions taken by their agents pursuant to this part;

53-11-308 SECTION 4. Tennessee Code Annotated, Section 53-11-308, is amended by adding the following language as new subsections at the end of the current section:

(e) No prescription for any opioids or benzodiazepines may be dispensed in quantities greater than a thirty (30) day supply.

(f) If a prescriber dispenses any opioids, benzodiazepines, barbiturates, or carisoprodol, then the prescriber shall submit the transaction to the controlled substances monitoring database operated under title 53, chapter 10, part 3.

(g) Any prescribers of opioids, benzodiazepines, barbiturates or carisoprodol, either alone, concurrently, or sequentially with any other opioids, benzodiazepines, barbiturates, or carisoprodol to patients who are chronic, long-term drug therapy for ninety (90) days or longer shall consider mandatory urine drug testing. This subsection shall not supercede any rules promulgated by the commissioner for urine drug testing by registered pain management clinics.

53-10-302 SECTION 5. Tennessee Code Annotated, Section 53-10-302, is hereby amended by adding the following new language as new subsections at the end of the current section:

(_) "Manufacturer" means any person, except a pharmacist compounding in the normal course of professional practice, engaged in the commercial production, preparation, propagation, conversion, or processing of a drug, either directly or indirectly, by extraction from substances of natural origin or independently by means of chemical synthesis, or both, and includes any packaging or repackaging of a drug or the labeling or relabeling of its container and the promotion and marketing of such drugs or devices;

(__) "Wholesaler" means a person whose principal business is buying or otherwise acquiring drugs or devices for resale or distribution to persons other than consumers.

53-10-312 SECTION 6. Tennessee Code Annotated, Title 53, Chapter 10, Part 3, is amended by adding the following language as a new section:

53-10-312.

(a) Wholesalers and manufacturers, as defined in § 63-10-204, that sell controlled substances at wholesale must at least report the following information to the committee in Automation of Reports and Consolidated Orders System (ARCOS) format or other mutually acceptable format:

(1) Wholesaler or manufacturer with a drug enforcement administration registration number; provided that if this number is not applicable, then another mutually acceptable identifier;

(2) Purchaser's drug enforcement administration registration number; provided that if this number is not applicable, then another mutually acceptable identifier;

(3) National drug code number of the actual drug sold;

(4) Quantity of the drug sold;

(5) Date of sale; and

(6) Transaction identifier or invoice number.

(b) The department of health will establish such rules as are necessary to specify which medications shall be reported, the time frames for such reporting, and other reporting requirements as required.

63-1-301 SECTION 7. Tennessee Code Annotated, Section 63-1-301(5), is amended by deleting subdivision (5) in its entirety and by substituting instead the following:

(5) "Pain management clinic" means a privately-owned facility in which a medical doctor, an osteopathic physician, an advanced practice nurse, a physician assistant, or any other health care provider licensed under title 63 provides pain management services to patients, a majority of whom are issued a prescription for, or are dispensed, opioids, benzodiazepines, barbiturates, or carisoprodol and provides prescriptions for more than ninety (90) days in a twelve-month period. For purposes of determining if a clinic should be registered under this part, patients of health care providers who do not prescribe controlled substances shall be excluded from the count. "Pain management clinic" shall also mean any privately owned clinic, facility, or office which advertises in any medium for any type pain management services and in which one (1) or more employees or contractors prescribe controlled substances; and

63-1-303 SECTION 8. Tennessee Code Annotated, Section 63-1-303(c), is amended by deleting subsection (c) in its entirety and by substituting instead the following:

(c) The rules adopted pursuant to subsection (b) shall address the following topics, among others:

(1) The operation of the clinic, including requirements:

(A) That patients have current and valid government issued identification or current health insurance card issued by either a government or private carrier; and

(B) That providers conduct urine drug screening in accordance with a written drug screening and compliance plan, which may include testing on initial assessment or upon new admission;

(2) Personnel requirements for the clinic;

(3) Training requirements for clinic providers who are regulated by that board;

(4) Patient records;

(5) Standards to ensure quality of patient care;

(6) Infection control;

(7) Health and safety requirements;

(8) Certificate application and renewal procedures and requirements;

(9) Data collection and reporting requirements;

(10) Inspections and complaint investigations; and

(11) Patient billing procedures.

63-1-309 SECTION 9. Tennessee Code Annotated, Section 63-1-309(d), is amended by adding the following language at the end of the subsection:

A medical director shall serve as medical director and provide services for no more than four (4) pain management clinics.

63-1-310 SECTION 10. Tennessee Code Annotated, Section 63-1-310(a), is amended by deleting the subsection in its entirety and by substituting instead the following:

(a) A pain management clinic may accept only a check or credit card in payment for services provided at the clinic, except as provided in subsection (b).

SECTION 11. The department of health, the board of pharmacy or any board operating under Tennessee Code Annotated, Title 63, is authorized to use emergency rules under Tennessee Code Annotated, Section 4-5-208(a)(5), in order to promulgate any rules required by this act.

63-1-311 SECTION 12. Tennessee Code Annotated, Section 63-1-311(b), is amended by deleting the language "an administrative penalty of one thousand dollars ($1,000) per day," and by substituting instead the language "an administrative penalty of no less than one thousand dollars ($1,000) per day and which shall not exceed five thousand dollars ($5,000) per day."

63-1-311 SECTION 13. Tennessee Code Annotated, Section 63-1-311, is amended by adding the following as a new subsection (c):

(c) An owner, co-owner, or operator of an uncertified pain management clinic is subject to an administrative penalty of no less than one thousand dollars ($1,000) per day and which shall not exceed five thousand dollars ($5,000) per day, imposed by the department of health, in accordance with the Uniform Administrative Procedures Act, compiled in title 4, chapter 5. Before such a penalty may be assessed by the department, the department shall give at least thirty (30) days notice to the owner, co-owner, or operator of the alleged violation of this part.

63-1-313 SECTION 14. Tennessee Code Annotated, Title 63, Chapter 1, Part 3, is amended by adding the following as a new subsection:

63-1-313. The commissioner of health and each appropriate occupational professional licensing board governing licensees who may legally prescribe or dispense controlled substances shall prepare a comprehensive report on actions relative to prescription drug abuse and pain management clinics to the general assembly no later than January 31st for actions in the prior calendar year. This report shall summarize the number of complaints received, frequent findings, and actions taken.

53-10-310 SECTION 15. Tennessee Code Annotated, Section 53-10-310(e)(5), is amended by adding the following new subdivision:

(E) The controlled substance is prescribed for administration directly to a patient during the course of inpatient or residential treatment in a hospital or nursing home licensed under title 68 or a mental health hospital licensed under title 33.

Effective date 10/1/2013 SECTION 16. For the purpose of promulgating rules and regulations, this act shall take effect upon becoming a law, the public welfare requiring it. The section added to this act by the amendment with draft # 6707 shall take effect upon becoming a law, the public welfare requiring it. All other sections of this act shall take effect October 1, 2013, the public welfare requiring it.

PUBLIC CHAPTER NO. 431

PUBLIC CHAPTER NO. 431

SENATE BILL NO. 675

By Yager, Green, Burks, Ketron

Substituted for: House Bill No. 531

By Powers, Hardaway

AN ACT to amend Tennessee Code Annotated, Title 39, Chapter 15, Part 1 and Title 71, Chapter 6, Part 1, relative to disabled adults.

BE IT ENACTED BY THE GENERAL ASSEMBLY OF THE STATE OF TENNESSEE:

71-6-102 SECTION 1. Tennessee Code Annotated, Section 71-6-102(1), is amended by designating the current language of the subdivision as new subdivision (A) and by adding the following language as a new subdivision (B):

(B) "Abuse or neglect" means transporting an adult and knowingly abandoning, leaving or failing to provide additional planned transportation for the adult if the adult's caretaker knows, or should know, that:

(i) The adult is unable to protect or care for himself or herself without assistance or supervision; and

(ii) The caretaker's conduct causes any of the results listed in subdivision (1)(A) or creates a substantial risk of such results;

71-6-102 SECTION 2. Tennessee Code Annotated, Section 71-6-102(5), is amended by deleting the subdivision and substituting instead the following:

(5) "Caretaker":

(A) Means an individual or institution who has assumed the duty to provide for the care of the adult by contract or agreement;

(B) Includes a parent, spouse, adult child or other relative, both biological or by marriage, who:

(i) Resides with or in the same building with or regularly visits the adult;

(ii) Knows or reasonably should know of the adult's mental or physical dysfunction or advanced age; and

(iii) Knows or reasonably should know that the adult is unable to adequately provide for the adult's own care; and

(C) Does not mean a financial institution as a caretaker of funds or other assets unless such financial institution has entered into an agreement to act as a trustee of such property or has been appointed by a court of competent jurisdiction to act as a trustee with regard to the property of the adult;

SECTION 3. This act shall be known and may be cited as "Lynn's Law".

Effective date 7/1/2013 SECTION 4. This act shall take effect July 1, 2013, the public welfare requiring it.

PUBLIC CHAPTER NO. 432

PUBLIC CHAPTER NO. 432

SENATE BILL NO. 667

By Gresham, Crowe, Green

Substituted for: House Bill No. 1074

By Rich, Evans, Roach, Harrison, Faison, Holt, Halford, Curtiss, Dennis, Moody, Hall, Kane, Kevin Brooks, Goins, Ragan, Hawk, Rogers, Butt, Floyd, Haynes, Mark White, Todd, Carter, Lundberg, Swann, Forgety, Curtis Johnson, Lollar, Lynn, Travis, Watson, Powers, Stewart, Powell, Camper, Shipley, Armstrong, Ryan Williams, Sexton, Eldridge, Harry Brooks, Durham, Van Huss, McDaniel, Towns, Dale Carr, Weaver, Wirgau, McManus, Womick

AN ACT to amend Tennessee Code Annotated, Title 8, Chapter 33, Part 1, relative to leave for employees in the military service.

BE IT ENACTED BY THE GENERAL ASSEMBLY OF THE STATE OF TENNESSEE:

8-33-109 SECTION 1. Tennessee Code Annotated, Section 8-33-109, is amended by adding the following language to the end of the section:

> After the twenty (20) working days of full compensation, members of any reserve component of the armed forces of the United States, including members of the Tennessee army and air national guard, may use up to five (5) days of sick leave in lieu of annual leave for the purposes of not having to take leave without pay.

Effective date 7/1/2013 SECTION 2. This act shall take effect July 1, 2013, the public welfare requiring it.

PUBLIC CHAPTER NO. 433

PUBLIC CHAPTER NO. 433

SENATE BILL NO. 614

By Yager, Burks, Green, Haile

Substituted for: House Bill No. 1043

By Lundberg, Rich, Curtis Johnson, Travis, Mark White, Shepard, Rogers, Shipley, Joe Carr, Butt, Spivey, Matlock, Farmer, Calfee, Faison, Dale Carr, Swann, Keisling, Holt, Doss, Hawk, Carter, Sexton, Towns, Marsh, Wirgau, Eldridge, Powers, Lamberth, Coley, Sparks, Durham, Goins, Womick, Todd, Sanderson, Haynes, McCormick, Hardaway, Matthew Hill, Timothy Hill, Van Huss

AN ACT to amend Tennessee Code Annotated, Title 39, Chapter 17, Part 4, relative to imitation controlled substances.

BE IT ENACTED BY THE GENERAL ASSEMBLY OF THE STATE OF TENNESSEE:

39-17-453 SECTION 1. Tennessee Code Annotated, Section 39-17-453, is amended by deleting subsection (d) and substituting instead the following:

(d) For purposes of this section:

(1) "Imitation controlled substance" means a pill, capsule, tablet, or substance in any form whatsoever if it:

(A) Is not a controlled substance enumerated in this part;

(B) Is subject to abuse;

(C) Purports, by express or implied representations, to act like a controlled substance that is a stimulant or depressant of the central nervous system; and

(D) Is not commonly used or recognized for use in that particular formulation for any purpose other than as a stimulant or depressant of the central nervous system; or

(2)(A) The chemical structure of the substance is a derivative or analogue of the chemical structure of a controlled substance; and

(B) The substance is not commonly used or recognized for use in that particular formulation for any purpose other than as a stimulant or depressant of the central nervous system.

(3) "Imitation controlled substance" does not include a pill, capsule, tablet, or substance in any form whatsoever if it is marketed or promoted, or sold as permitted by the United States food and drug administration.

Effective date 7/1/2013 SECTION 2. This act shall take effect July 1, 2013, the public welfare requiring it.

PUBLIC CHAPTER NO. 434

PUBLIC CHAPTER NO. 434

SENATE BILL NO. 599

By Johnson, Ketron

Substituted for: House Bill No. 1056

By Durham

AN ACT to amend Tennessee Code Annotated, Section 67-1-1441, relative to revenue officers.

BE IT ENACTED BY THE GENERAL ASSEMBLY OF THE STATE OF TENNESSEE:

67-1-1441 SECTION 1. Tennessee Code Annotated, Section 67-1-1441, is amended by adding the following language as a new subsection:

(c)(1) Any duly authorized agent or officer of the department of revenue who retires after twenty-five (25) years of honorable armed service shall be issued a retired commission card by the department, which shall identify the agent or officer and the fact that the agent or officer is retired. Cards issued under this subdivision shall bear the inscription, in print of equal or larger size than the rest of the printing on the card, the words "Not a handgun permit." After twenty-five (25) years of honorable armed service by an authorized agent or officer of the department, the department shall authorize such agent or officer, upon retirement, to retain the agent or officer's service weapon and badge, in recognition of the agent or officer's many years of good and faithful public service.

(2) Any authorized agent or officer of the department, who is issued a retired commission card pursuant to this subsection but who has not completed twenty-five (25) years of honorable armed service, may retain the agent or officer's service weapon and badge in recognition of the agent or officer's years of good and faithful public service; provided, that the agent or officer reimburses the department for the cost of the service weapon and badge.

(3) This subsection shall be retroactive to include officers from the department of safety that were transferred to the department of revenue effective July 1, 2006.

Effective date 5/16/2013 SECTION 2. This act shall take effect upon becoming a law, the public welfare requiring it.

PUBLIC CHAPTER NO. 435

PUBLIC CHAPTER NO. 435

SENATE BILL NO. 555

By Overbey, Kyle, Stevens, Beavers

Substituted for: House Bill No. 692

By Farmer, Harry Brooks, Powell, Eldridge

AN ACT to amend Tennessee Code Annotated, Title 34 and Title 40, relative to a person appointed by a court to exercise duties for another person.

BE IT ENACTED BY THE GENERAL ASSEMBLY OF THE STATE OF TENNESSEE:

34-1-101 SECTION 1. Tennessee Code Annotated, Section 34-3-101, is amended by adding the following as a new subsection:

(c) Nothing in this title shall be construed to supersede the Tennessee Adult Protection Act, § 71-6-101 et seq., or the orders of the court pursuant to such act.

34-1-101 SECTION 2. Tennessee Code Annotated, Section 34-1-101, is amended by deleting subdivision (4) and substituting instead the following:

(4)(A) "Conservator" or "coconservators" means a person or persons or an entity appointed by the court to exercise the decision-making rights and duties of the person with a disability in one or more areas in which the person lacks capacity as determined and required by the orders of the court;

(B) "Conservatorship" is a proceeding in which a court removes the decision-making powers and duties, in whole or in part, in a least restrictive manner, from a person with a disability who lacks capacity to make decisions in one or more important areas and places responsibility for one or more of those decisions in a conservator or coconservators.

34-1-101 SECTION 3. Tennessee Code Annotated, Section 34-1-101, is amended by deleting subdivision (7) and substituting instead the following:

( ) "Person with a disability" means any person eighteen (18) years of age or older determined by the court to be in need of partial or full supervision, protection, and assistance by reason of mental illness, physical illness or injury, developmental disability, or other mental or physical incapacity;

34-1-101 SECTION 4. Tennessee Code Annotated, Section 34-1-101, is amended by deleting subdivision (11) and substituting instead the following:

( ) "Guardian ad litem" means a person meeting the qualifications set forth in § 34-1-107(c) appointed by the court to investigate the allegations in a petition, perform the duties set forth in § 34-1-107(d) and report to the court with recommendations as to the best interests of the respondent;

34-1-101 SECTION 5. Tennessee Code Annotated, Section 34-1-101, is amended by deleting subdivision (15) and substituting instead the following:

( ) "Property management plan" means the plan submitted by the fiduciary for the investment and management of the property of a minor or person with a disability;

34-1-101 SECTION 6. Tennessee Code Annotated, Section 34-1-101, is amended by deleting subdivision (17) and substituting instead the following:

( ) "Respondent" means a person who is a minor or is alleged to be a person with a disability for whom a fiduciary is being sought.

34-1-104 SECTION 7. Tennessee Code Annotated, Section 34-1-104(a), is amended by deleting the subsection in its entirety and substituting instead the following:

(a) Except as provided in subsections (b) and (c), no person shall undertake the administration of the estate of a minor or person with a disability until the person has been issued letters of guardianship or letters of conservatorship; provided, that no guardian or conservator shall be appointed if the property of the minor or person with a disability is deposited with the clerk of the court subject to distribution on order of the court. The letters of conservatorship shall either:

(1) Recite the specific powers to be exercised by the conservator and the specific powers retained by the person with a disability; or

(2) Have attached to them the order or orders of the court specifying the powers to be exercised by the conservator and the powers retained by the person with a disability.

34-1-106 SECTION 8. Tennessee Code Annotated, Section 34-1-106(b), is amended by deleting the language "respondent or with whom the respondent is living" and substituting instead the language "respondent, institution, or residential provider with whom the respondent is living".

34-1-107 SECTION 9. Tennessee Code Annotated, Section 34-1-107(a)(1), is amended by deleting the subdivision in its entirety and substituting instead the following:

The court may appoint a guardian ad litem in any proceeding and, except as provided in this section, shall appoint a guardian ad litem on filing of a petition for appointment of a fiduciary. If the respondent is represented by counsel who has made an appearance for the respondent, the court may appoint or continue the services of a guardian ad litem or may waive appointment or terminate the services of a guardian ad litem in the best interests of the respondent.

34-1-107 SECTION 10. Tennessee Code Annotated, Section 34-1-107(d)(1), is amended by deleting the subdivision in its entirety and substituting instead the following:

(d)(1) The guardian ad litem owes a duty to the court to impartially investigate the facts and make a report and recommendations to the court. The guardian ad litem serves as an agent of the court, and is not an advocate for the respondent or any other party.

34-1-107 SECTION 11. Tennessee Code Annotated, Section 34-1-107(d)(2)(D), is amended by deleting subdivision (D) in its entirety and substituting instead the following:

(D) Make a report and recommendations to the court concerning the issues of:

(i) Whether a fiduciary should be appointed for the respondent;

(ii) If a fiduciary should be appointed, whether the proposed fiduciary is the appropriate person to be appointed; and

(iii) Any other matters as directed by the court.

34-1-107 SECTION 12. Tennessee Code Annotated, Section 34-1-107(d)(3), is amended by deleting subdivision (3) in its entirety and substituting instead the following:

(3) In a proceeding for the appointment of a conservator, the guardian ad litem shall investigate the physical and mental capabilities of the respondent. The guardian ad litem's investigation shall include:

(i) An in-person interview with the respondent; and

(ii) A review of the sworn report required by § 34-3-105 to verify that the sworn statement contains:

(a) A detailed description of the respondent's physical or mental conditions or both that may render the respondent a person with a disability; and

(b) A detailed description of how the respondent's physical or mental conditions or both may impair the respondent's ability to function normally.

34-1-107 SECTION 13. Tennessee Code Annotated, Section 34-1-107(d)(4), is amended by deleting subdivision (4) in its entirety and substituting instead the following:

(4) In a proceeding seeking the appointment of a fiduciary to manage the respondent's property, the guardian ad litem shall investigate the:

(A) Nature and extent of the respondent's property; and

(B) Financial capabilities and integrity of the proposed fiduciary. In evaluating the financial capabilities of the proposed fiduciary, the guardian ad litem may take such actions as directed by the court and as the guardian ad litem deems necessary, which may include but are not limited to:

(i) Obtaining and reviewing the proposed fiduciary's credit report;

(ii) Inquiring into whether and to what extent the proposed fiduciary has previous experience in managing assets of the same or similar type and value as the respondent's assets;

(iii) Inquiring into how the proposed fiduciary plans to manage the respondent's assets;

(iv) Inquiring into whether the proposed fiduciary has previously borrowed funds from the respondent or received any financial assistance or benefits from the respondent; and

(v) Interview any persons with knowledge and review any documents pertinent to the financial capabilities and integrity of the proposed fiduciary.

34-1-108 SECTION 14. Tennessee Code Annotated, Section 34-1-108(c)(1), is amended by deleting the following language:

(c)(1) In a proceeding for the appointment of a conservator, a notice of the hearing shall be served on the respondent. The notice of hearing shall be substantially in the following form:

and substituting instead the following language:

(c)(1) In a proceeding for the appointment of a conservator, a notice of the hearing shall be served on the respondent and any person, institution or residential provider having care or custody of the respondent by the guardian ad litem or as otherwise authorized under the Tennessee Rules of Civil Procedure. The notice of hearing shall be substantially in the following form:

34-1-108 SECTION 15. Tennessee Code Annotated, Section 34-1-108(c), is amended by adding the following new subdivision (3):

(3) The notice shall also be served upon the closest relative or relatives of the respondent, as such persons are described in title 31, chapter 2, but not including the petitioner, and upon the person or institution, if any, having care and custody of the respondent or with whom the respondent is living. Service by mail, sent to the last known address of such persons or institution, shall be sufficient for purposes of this subdivision.

34-1-111 SECTION 16. Tennessee Code Annotated, Section 34-1-111, is amended by deleting subsection (b) and substituting instead the following:

(b) Except as provided in subsection (i), within sixty (60) days after each anniversary of the accounting required in subsection (a) or any other end of an accounting period selected by the fiduciary after the subsection (a) accounting, the fiduciary shall file a sworn accounting with the court. To select an accounting period end other than the end of the month during which the fiduciary was appointed, the fiduciary shall file a statement with the clerk advising of the accounting period selected. The accounting period shall not exceed twelve (12) months.

34-1-111 SECTION 17. Tennessee Code Annotated, Section 34-1-111(h), is amended by deleting the language "Accountings may" and substituting instead the language "Financial accountings may".

34-1-111 SECTION 18. Tennessee Code Annotated, Section 34-1-111(h), is amended by adding the following new subdivision (3):

(3) Subdivision (c)(2) requiring a report regarding the physical or mental condition of the person with a disability may not be waived or excused.

34-1-111 SECTION 19. Tennessee Code Annotated, Section 34-1-111(i), is amended by adding the following language to the end of the subdivision as the last sentence:

The provisions of this section related to financial accountings do not apply to fiduciaries who do not have authority over the property of the person with a disability.

34-1-111 SECTION 20. Tennessee Code Annotated, Section 34-1-111, is amended by adding the following new subsection (a) and redesignating existing subsections accordingly:

(a) Except as provided in subsection (i), within thirty (30) days after the six-month anniversary of the fiduciary's date of appointment, the fiduciary shall file a sworn accounting with the court.

34-1-114 SECTION 21. Tennessee Code Annotated, Section 34-1-114, is amended by deleting the section in its entirety and substituting instead the following:

34-1-114.

(a) The costs of the proceedings, which are the court costs, the guardian ad litem fee and expenses incurred by the guardian ad litem in conducting the required investigations, the required medical examination costs, and the attorney's fee for the petitioner, may, in the court's discretion, be charged against the property of the respondent to the extent the respondent's property exceeds the supplemental security income eligibility limit, or to the petitioner or any other party, or partially to any one or more of them as determined in the court's discretion. In exercising its discretion to charge some or all of the costs against the respondent's property, the fact a conservator is appointed or would have been appointed but for an event beyond the petitioner's control is to be given special consideration. The guardian ad litem fee and the attorney's fee for the petitioner shall be established by the court. If a fiduciary is cited for failure to file an inventory or accounting, the costs incurred in citing the fiduciary, in the discretion of the court, may be charged to and collected from the cited fiduciary.

(b) If the principal purpose for bringing the petition is to benefit the petitioner and there would otherwise be little, if any, need for the appointment of a fiduciary, the costs of the proceedings may be assessed against the petitioner, in the discretion of the court.

34-1-119 SECTION 22. Tennessee Code Annotated, Section 34-1-119(c)(2), is amended by deleting the language "potentially disabled person" and substituting instead the language "person with a potential disability".

34-1-129 SECTION 23. Tennessee Code Annotated, Section 34-1-129, is amended by deleting the section in its entirety and substituting instead the following:

34-1-129. Upon the entry of the order appointing a fiduciary and the submission of a bond consistent with the order, the clerk shall issue letters of conservatorship or letters of guardianship. The letters of conservatorship or guardianship shall either:

(1) Recite the specific powers removed from the minor or person with a disability and transferred to the fiduciary; or

(2) Have attached to them the order or orders of the court specifying the powers removed from the minor or person with a disability and transferred to the fiduciary. If the fiduciary has been granted less than full authority over the person and property of the minor or person with a disability in the order of appointment, the clerk shall mark the letters prominently with the term "LIMITED".

34-1-132 SECTION 24. Tennessee Code Annotated, Title 34, Chapter 1, is amended by adding a new section thereto:

34-1-132.

(a) If the court finds that compliance with the procedures of this title will likely result in substantial harm to the respondent's health, safety, or welfare, and that no other person, including an agent acting under the Health Care Decision Act compiled in title 68, chapter 11, part 18, or a person acting under the Durable Powers of Attorney for Healthcare Act, compiled in chapter 6, part 2 of this title or a living will pursuant to title 32, chapter 11, appears to have authority to act, willingness to act, and is acting in the best interests of the respondent in the circumstances, then the court, on petition by a person interested in the respondent's welfare, may appoint an emergency guardian or conservator whose authority may not exceed sixty (60) days and who may exercise only the powers specified in the order. Immediately upon receipt of the petition for an emergency guardianship or conservatorship, the court shall appoint an attorney ad litem to represent the respondent in the proceeding. Except as otherwise provided in subsection (b), reasonable notice of the time and place of a hearing on the petition shall be given to the respondent and any other person as the court directs.

(b) An emergency guardian or conservator may be appointed without notice to the respondent and the attorney ad litem only if the court finds upon a sworn petition that the respondent will be substantially harmed before a hearing on the appointment can be held. If the court appoints an emergency guardian or conservator without notice to the respondent, the respondent shall be given notice of the appointment within forty-eight (48) hours after the appointment. The court shall hold a hearing on the appropriateness of the appointment within five (5) days after the appointment.

(c) Appointment of an emergency guardian or conservator, with or without notice, is not a determination of the respondent's incapacity.

(d) The court may remove an emergency guardian or conservator at any time. The court may appoint a guardian ad litem to investigate the circumstances. An emergency guardian or conservator shall make any report the court requires. In other respects, the provisions of this title concerning guardians or conservators apply to an emergency guardian or conservator.

(e) The time periods set forth above in this section are mandatory and not directory. Failure to comply with those provisions shall void any emergency appointment and remove the authority previously granted to an emergency fiduciary.

34-3-104 SECTION 25. Tennessee Code Annotated, Section 34-3-104(7)(A) and (B), is amended by deleting the language "medical" wherever it may appear.

34-3-104 SECTION 26. Tennessee Code Annotated, Section 34-3-104, is amended by adding the following new subdivision (10):

(10) A request for a guardian ad litem, conservator or coconservator, or attorney ad litem with specific experience or expertise in matters like those faced by the respondent, if warranted under the circumstances.

34-3-105 SECTION 27. Tennessee Code Annotated, Section 34-3-105, is amended by adding the following new subsections:

(d) The examiner's sworn report shall be prima facie evidence of the respondent's disability and need for the appointment of a fiduciary unless the report is contested and found to be in error.

(e) If upon an additional finding that the person with a disability poses a threat to self or others in accordance with the mental health law, title 33, a court of competent jurisdiction may order a commitment to involuntary care and treatment.

34-3-106 SECTION 28. Tennessee Code Annotated, Section 34-3-106, is amended by deleting subdivisions (3), (4) and (5) and substituting instead the following:

(3) Appeal the final decision on the petition with the assistance of an attorney ad litem or adversary counsel;

(4) Attend any hearing;

(5) Have an attorney ad litem appointed to advocate the interests of the respondent; and

(6) Request a protective order placing under seal the respondent's health and financial information, including reports provided under § 34-3-105(c).

34-3-107 SECTION 29. Tennessee Code Annotated, Section 34-3-107(1), is amended by deleting the language "conservators" and substituting instead the language "coconservators".

34-3-107 SECTION 30. Tennessee Code Annotated, Section 34-3-107, is amended by deleting subdivision (2) and substituting instead the following:

(2) Enumerate the powers removed from the respondent and those to be vested in the conservator. To the extent not specifically removed, the respondent shall retain and shall

exercise all of the powers of a person without a disability. The court may consider removing any rights of the person with a disability and vesting some or all in a conservator. Such rights may include, but are not limited to:

(A) The right to give, withhold, or withdraw consent and make other informed decisions relative to medical and mental examinations and treatment;

(B) The right to make end of life decisions:

(i) To consent, withhold, or withdraw consent for the entry of a "do not resuscitate" order or the application of any heroic measures or medical procedures intended solely to sustain life and other medications; and

(ii) To consent or withhold consent concerning the withholding or withdrawal of artificially provided food, water, or other nourishment or fluids;

(C) The right to consent to admission to hospitalization, and to be discharged or transferred to a residential setting, group home, or other facility for additional care and treatment;

(D) The right to consent to participate in activities and therapies which are reasonable and necessary for the habilitation of the respondent;

(E) The right to consent or withhold consent to any residential or custodial placement;

(F) The power to give, receive, release, or authorize disclosures of confidential information;

(G) The right to apply for benefits, public and private, for which the person with a disability may be eligible;

(H) The right to dispose of personal property and real property subject to statutory and judicial constraints;

(I) The right to determine whether or not the respondent may utilize a Tennessee driver license for the purpose of driving;

(J) The right to make purchases;

(K) The right to enter into contractual relationships;

(L) The right to execute instruments of legal significance;

(M) The right to pay the respondent's bills and protect and invest the respondent's income and assets;

(N) The right to prosecute and defend lawsuits; and

(O) The right to execute, on behalf of the respondent, any and all documents to carry out the authority vested above.

34-3-108 SECTION 31. Tennessee Code Annotated, Section 34-3-108, is amended by deleting subsection (c) and substituting instead the following:

(c) The court, upon receipt of the petition filed under this section, shall conduct a hearing. At the hearing, the person with a disability has all the rights set out in § 34-3-106. Prior to the holding of the hearing, the court may require that the person with a disability submit to an examination as required by § 34-3-105 to support the person with a disability's contention that a conservator is no longer needed.

34-3-108 SECTION 32. Tennessee Code Annotated, Section 34-3-108(e), is amended by deleting the second sentence and substituting instead the following language:

If the conservator has responsibility for the property of the person with a disability, within one hundred twenty (120) days after the date the conservatorship terminates, the conservator shall file a preliminary final accounting with the court, which shall account for all assets, receipts, and disbursements from the date of the last accounting until the date the conservatorship terminates, and shall detail the amount of the final distribution to close the conservatorship.

PUBLIC CHAPTER NO. 435 (cont'd)

40-20-115 SECTION 33. Tennessee Code Annotated, Section 40-20-115, is amended by deleting the language "administrator or guardian" and substituting instead the language "administrator or guardian, fiduciary or conservator".

34-1-109 SECTION 34. Tennessee Code Annotated, Section 34-1-109(b), is amended by deleting the language "disabled person's" between "or" and "property" in the second sentence of the subsection and substituting instead the language "person with a disability's".

34-1-113 SECTION 35. Tennessee Code Annotated, Section 34-1-113(e), is amended by deleting the language "disabled person's" between the words "the" and "funeral" and substituting instead the language "person with a disability's".

34-3-103 SECTION 36. Tennessee Code Annotated, Section 34-3-103, is amended by deleting the section in its entirety and substituting instead the following:

34-3-103.

Subject to the court's determination of what is in the best interests of the person with a disability, the court shall consider the following persons in the order listed for appointment of the conservator:

(1) The person or persons designated in a writing signed by the alleged person with a disability;

(2) The spouse of the person with a disability;

(3) Any child of the person with a disability;

(4) Closest relative or relatives of the person with a disability;

(5) A district public guardian as described by § 34-7-104; and

(6) Other person or persons.

34-3-107 SECTION 37. Tennessee Code Annotated, Section 34-3-107, is amended by adding the following new subdivision (4) and renumbering existing subdivisions accordingly:

(4) Whether a conservator is being appointed from § 34-3-103(6), and if the conservator is being appointed from § 34-3-103(6), the reasons why the court was unable to appoint a conservator from § 34-3-103(1) - (5);

34-1-105 SECTION 38. Tennessee Code Annotated, Section 34-1-105(b)(2), is amended by deleting the language "minor's or disabled person's non-real estate property" and substituting instead the language "minor's non-real estate property or the person with a disability's non-real estate property".

34-1-117 SECTION 39. Tennessee Code Annotated, Section 34-1-117(e)(2)(B), is amended by deleting the language "disabled person's property" and substituting instead the language "person with a disability's property".

34-1-121 SECTION 40. Tennessee Code Annotated, Section 34-1-121(a), is amended by deleting the language "minor's or disabled person's property" and substituting instead the language "property of the minor or the person with a disability".

34-1-122 SECTION 41. Tennessee Code Annotated, Section 34-1-122, is amended by deleting the language "minor's or disabled person's property" and substituting instead the language "property of the minor or person with a disability".

34-1-127 SECTION 42. Tennessee Code Annotated, Section 34-1-127, is amended by deleting the language "disabled person's property" and substituting instead the language "property of the person with a disability".

34-3-107 SECTION 43. Tennessee Code Annotated, Section 34-3-107(3)(C), is amended by deleting the subdivision in its entirety and substituting instead the following:

(C) Set forth the approved management of the property of the disabled person; and

34-3-108 SECTION 44. Tennessee Code Annotated, Section 34-3-108(a), is amended by deleting the subsection in its entirety and substituting instead the following:

PUBLIC CHAPTER NO. 435 (cont'd)

(a) A conservator appointed under this chapter may be discharged or have its duties modified if the court determines that the respondent is no longer a person with a disability, or that it is in the best interests of the person with a disability that the conservatorship be terminated, or that the conservator has failed to perform its duties and obligations in accordance with the law, or that the conservator has failed to act in the best interest of the person with a disability so as to warrant modification or termination. The person with a disability or any interested person on the behalf of the person with a disability may petition the court at any time for a termination or modification order under this section.

34-3-109

SECTION 45. Tennessee Code Annotated, Section 34-3-109, is amended by deleting the language "disabled person's spouse or dependent minor children" and substituting instead the language "spouse or dependent minor children of the person with a disability".

34-1-104, 105, 107, 108, 109, 110, 111, 112, 113, 115, 116, 117, 118, 119, 120, 121, 122, 127; 34-3-101, 105, 107, 108, 109

SECTION 46. Tennessee Code Annotated, Title 34, Chapters 1 and 3, are amended by deleting the language "disabled person" wherever it may appear and substituting instead the language "person with a disability".

34-1-133

SECTION 47. Tennessee Code Annotated, Title 34, Chapter 1, is amended by adding a new section:

34-1-133. Expedited Limited Healthcare Fiduciary.

(a) If the respondent is under hospitalization in a hospital as those terms are defined in TCA title 68, chapter 11, part 2, and no other person, including an agent acting under the Healthcare Decision Act TCA title 68, chapter 11, part 8, a person acting under the Durable Powers of Attorney for Healthcare Act title 34, chapter 6, part 2 or a living will under TCA title 32, chapter 11, Part 1 appears to have the authority and willingness to act and is acting in the best interest of the respondent, the court on petition of a person interested in the respondent's welfare may appoint an expedited limited healthcare fiduciary whose authority is for the limited purpose of consenting to discharge, transfer, and admission and consenting to any financial arrangements or medical care necessary to affect such discharge, transfer or admission to another healthcare facility and whose authority may not exceed sixty (60) days. Immediately upon the receipt of the petition for an expedited limited healthcare fiduciary, the court shall appoint an attorney ad litem to represent the respondent in the proceeding. In expediting the appointment of an expedited limited healthcare fiduciary, the court may vary the time periods for hearings including but not limited to the minimum number of days before a hearing under TCA § 34-1-108 or the number of days before appointment of a guardian ad litem under TCA § 34-1-107 or other time periods, but shall not vary requirements as necessary to determine the respondent is in need of a fiduciary.

(b) The court shall hold a hearing on the appropriateness of the appointment within five (5) days of the appointment.

(c) Appointment of an expedited limited healthcare fiduciary is not a determination of the respondent's incapacity.

(d) The court may remove an expedited limited healthcare fiduciary at any time.

(e) The time periods set forth in this section are mandatory and not directory. Failure to comply with those provisions shall void any expedited appointment and remove the authority previously granted to the expedited limited healthcare fiduciary.

Effective date 7/1/2013

SECTION 48. This act shall take effect July 1, 2013, the public welfare requiring it, and shall apply to actions commenced on or after such date.

PUBLIC CHAPTER NO. 436

PUBLIC CHAPTER NO. 436

SENATE BILL NO. 446

By Overbey, Kelsey, Finney, Ford

Substituted for: House Bill No. 129

By Coley, Hardaway, Rogers, Littleton, Moody, Weaver, Camper, Parkinson, Jones, Miller, Eldridge, Todd, Lollar, Kent Williams, Harry Brooks, Fitzhugh, Haynes

AN ACT to amend Tennessee Code Annotated, Title 39 and Title 40, relative to solicitation of a minor.

BE IT ENACTED BY THE GENERAL ASSEMBLY OF THE STATE OF TENNESSEE:

39-13-528 SECTION 1. Tennessee Code Annotated, Section 39-13-528(a), is amended by adding the following as new, appropriately designated subdivisions:

(10) Trafficking for commercial sex acts, pursuant to § 39-13-309;

(11) Patronizing prostitution, pursuant to § 39-13-514;

(12) Promoting prostitution, pursuant to § 39-13-515;

(13) Aggravated sexual exploitation of a minor, pursuant to § 39-17-1004;

Effective date 7/1/2013 SECTION 2. This act shall take effect July 1, 2013, the public welfare requiring it.

PUBLIC CHAPTER NO. 437

PUBLIC CHAPTER NO. 437

SENATE BILL NO. 416

By Crowe, Ford

Substituted for: House Bill No. 333

By Matlock, Forgety

AN ACT to amend Tennessee Code Annotated, Title 39; Title 47 and Title 62, Chapter 5, relative to human remains.

BE IT ENACTED BY THE GENERAL ASSEMBLY OF THE STATE OF TENNESSEE:

62-5-101 SECTION 1. Tennessee Code Annotated, Section 62-5-101, is amended by adding the following language as a new, appropriately designated subdivision:

( ) "Removal service":

(A) Means any person or entity that engages in arranging, directing, supervising or performing the transportation of deceased human remains for a fee; and

(B) Does not include:

(i) A licensed funeral director, a licensed embalmer, a licensed funeral establishment or person's employees;

(ii) A federal, state or county government agency involved in the transportation of deceased human remains; and

(iii) A private, for-profit ambulance service licensed pursuant to the Emergency Medical Services Act of 1983, compiled in title 68, chapter 140, part 3.

62-5-318 SECTION 2. Tennessee Code Annotated, Title 62, Chapter 5, Part 3, is amended by adding the following language as a new, appropriately designated section:

(a) On or after January 1, 2014, no removal service shall operate in this state unless the removal service is registered with the board of funeral directors and embalmers. All such registrations shall expire two (2) years from the date of the registration or renewal. The board may promulgate and adopt such rules and regulations to establish adequate registration and renewal fees to cover the administrative costs associated with the registration program.

(b) In conjunction with the registration fee, the registrant must provide proof of liability insurance in an amount to be determined by the board by rule.

(c) Included on each registration and renewal form shall be a section whereby the applicant or registrant shall declare, under penalty of perjury pursuant to § 39-16-702(a)(4), whether such registrant or any principal officer, director, or any person owning more than five percent (5%) of the removal service, has ever been convicted of a violation of this chapter or § 39-17-312.

(d) An applicant shall be prohibited from registering under this section for five (5) years from the date of conviction if the applicant or any principal officer, director, or any person owning more than five percent (5%) of the applicant's removal service has been convicted of a violation of this chapter or § 39-17-312.

(e) On or after January 1, 2014, it is an offense for a person to engage in the business of a removal service without registering or after falsely registering with the board.

(f) A violation of this section is a Class C misdemeanor.

(g) The registration of a removal service shall be immediately revoked by operation of law upon the conviction of the removal service or any principal officer, director, or person owning more than five percent (5%) of the removal service of any violation of this chapter or § 39-17-312. A copy of the judgment of conviction shall be transmitted to the board by the law enforcement agency responsible for the conviction.

PUBLIC CHAPTER NO. 437 (cont'd)

Effective date 1/1/2014

SECTION 3. For purposes of rulemaking, this act shall take effect upon becoming a law, the public welfare requiring it; for all other purposes, this act shall take effect January 1, 2014, the public welfare requiring it.

PUBLIC CHAPTER NO. 438

PUBLIC CHAPTER NO. 438

SENATE BILL NO. 333

By Bell, Gardenhire

Substituted for: House Bill No. 807

By Matheny, Ragan

AN ACT to amend Tennessee Code Annotated, Title 4, Chapter 29 and Title 7, Chapter 86, relative to the emergency communications board.

BE IT ENACTED BY THE GENERAL ASSEMBLY OF THE STATE OF TENNESSEE:

4-29-234 SECTION 1. Tennessee Code Annotated, Section 4-29-234(a), is amended by deleting subdivision (27) in its entirety.

4-29-235 SECTION 2. Tennessee Code Annotated, Section 4-29-235(a), is amended by adding a new subdivision thereto, as follows:

( ) Emergency communications board, created by § 7-86-302;

7-86-302 SECTION 3. Tennessee Code Annotated, Section 7-86-302, is amended by deleting subsection (b) in its entirety and by substituting instead the following new language:

(b)(1) The board shall be composed of nine (9) members as follows:

(A) One (1) member, appointed by the governor, who has no connection to emergency communications districts and who does not fulfill any other requirements for appointment to the board;

(B) The comptroller of the treasury or the comptroller's designee. The appointment of the comptroller's designee to the board shall be for the term of office of the comptroller;

(C) One (1) representative of county government, appointed by the governor, who may be appointed from lists of qualified persons submitted by interested county services groups including, but not limited to, the Tennessee County Services Association;

(D) One (1) representative of city government, appointed by the governor, who may be appointed from lists of qualified persons submitted by interested municipal groups including, but not limited to, the Tennessee Municipal League; and

(E)(i) Five (5) members, appointed by the governor, who shall either be current directors of emergency communications districts or current members of emergency communications district boards of directors at the time of their appointment. The governor may appoint such members from lists of qualified persons submitted by interested emergency communications groups including, but not limited to, the Tennessee Emergency Number Association, or from a nominating resolution adopted by an emergency communications district. No more than two (2) members appointed pursuant to this subdivision (b)(5) shall be residents of the same congressional district.

(ii) Nominations shall be made not less than thirty (30) days before the end of a term, and shall be filed with the governor and the board. In appointing members, the governor shall strive to ensure that the composition of the board represents the diversity of persons in Tennessee by considering race, gender, age, and geographical and political interests.

(2) The governor shall consult with interested groups including, but not limited to, the organizations listed in subdivision (b)(1) to determine qualified persons to fill positions on the board.

Effective date 5/16/2013 SECTION 4. This act shall take effect upon becoming a law, the public welfare requiring it.

PUBLIC CHAPTER NO. 439

PUBLIC CHAPTER NO. 439

SENATE BILL NO. 302

By Niceley, Crowe, Ford, Yager

Substituted for: House Bill No. 362

By Farmer, Roach, Harrison, Hardaway, Todd

AN ACT to amend Tennessee Code Annotated, Title 49, Chapter 5, Part 7, relative to leave for teachers.

BE IT ENACTED BY THE GENERAL ASSEMBLY OF THE STATE OF TENNESSEE:

49-5-714 SECTION 1. Tennessee Code Annotated, Section 49-5-714, is amended by designating the current subdivision (b) as subdivision (c) and by adding a new subdivision (b) as follows:

> (b) In the event a teacher is absent from assigned duties as a result of personal injury caused by a physical assault or other violent criminal act committed against the teacher in the course of the teacher's employment activities, the LEA shall continue to pay the teacher's full benefits including, but not limited to, health insurance benefits, until the earlier of the date on which the teacher is released by the teacher's physician to return to work or the date on which the teacher is determined by the teacher's physician to be permanently disabled from returning to work.

Effective date 5/16/2013 SECTION 2. This act shall take effect upon becoming a law, the public welfare requiring it.

PUBLIC CHAPTER NO. 440

PUBLIC CHAPTER NO. 440

SENATE BILL NO. 265

By Massey

Substituted for: House Bill No. 302

By McDaniel

AN ACT to amend Tennessee Code Annotated, Title 63, Chapter 12, relative to veterinary practice.

BE IT ENACTED BY THE GENERAL ASSEMBLY OF THE STATE OF TENNESSEE:

63-12-108 SECTION 1. Tennessee Code Annotated, Section 63-12-108(a), is amended by deleting the language "fifty dollars ($50.00)" and by substituting instead the language "one hundred dollars ($100)".

63-12-135 SECTION 2. Tennessee Code Annotated, Section 63-12-135(b), is amended by deleting the language "direct supervision" and by substituting instead the language "responsible supervision".

63-12-139 SECTION 3. Tennessee Code Annotated, Section 63-12-139(d), is amended by deleting the first four sentences of the subsection and by substituting instead the following language:

Each application for a premises permit submitted by a person not licensed under this chapter shall state the name and address of the licensed veterinarian who will be responsible for the practice of veterinary medicine on the premises. The supervising veterinarian shall be licensed in Tennessee. The applicant shall also include the name or names and address or addresses of the licensee or licensees who will be on-site when the practice of veterinary medicine occurs. The applicant shall affirm that the practice of veterinary medicine shall not be provided on the premises without the physical presence of a veterinarian licensed in Tennessee.

63-12-139 SECTION 4. Tennessee Code Annotated, Section 63-12-139, is amended by adding the following as a new subsection (k):

(k) The board of veterinary examiners is authorized to issue a limited waiver to the requirement for a premises permit under this section to a veterinarian who meets the following requirements:

(1) The waiver is granted for one (1) day, once in a calendar year;

(2) The waiver is applicable to only one (1) county and only one (1) waiver shall be granted in each county in a calendar year;

(3) The waiver is only for livestock testing; and

(4) The waiver is only for one location, which shall be a farm.

Effective date 7/1/2013 SECTION 5. This act shall take effect July 1, 2013, the public welfare requiring it.

PUBLIC CHAPTER NO. 441

PUBLIC CHAPTER NO. 441

SENATE BILL NO. 279

By Watson, Beavers, Bowling, Campfield, Bell, Niceley, Kelsey, Norris

Substituted for: House Bill No. 475

By Carter, Joe Carr, Van Huss, Lollar, McManus, Butt, Lynn, Mark White, Pody, Coley, Todd, Rogers, Rich, Spivey, Travis, Timothy Hill, Rogers, Holt, Hall

AN ACT to amend Tennessee Code Annotated, Title 6, Chapter 51 and Title 6, Chapter 58, relative to annexation.

BE IT ENACTED BY THE GENERAL ASSEMBLY OF THE STATE OF TENNESSEE:

6-51-122 SECTION 1. Tennessee Code Annotated, Title 6, Chapter 51, Part 1, is amended by adding the following language as a new section:

6-51-122.

(a)(1) Notwithstanding the provisions of this part or any other law to the contrary, from April 15, 2013, through May 15, 2014, no municipality shall extend its corporate limits by means of annexation by ordinance upon the municipality's own initiative, pursuant to § 6-51-102, in order to annex territory being used primarily for residential or agricultural purposes; and, except as otherwise permitted pursuant to subdivision (a)(2), no such ordinance to annex such territory shall become operative during such period. As used in this subsection, "municipality" does not include any county having a metropolitan form of government.

(2) If, prior to April 15, 2013, a municipality formally initiated an annexation ordinance delayed by subdivision (a)(1); and if the municipality would suffer substantial and demonstrable financial injury if such ordinance does not become operative prior to May 15, 2014; then, upon petition by the municipality, the county legislative body may, by a majority vote of its membership, waive the restrictions imposed on such ordinance by subdivision (a)(1).

(b) On or before January 14, 2014, the Tennessee advisory commission on intergovernmental relations (TACIR) shall complete a comprehensive review and evaluation of the efficacy of state policies set forth within title 6, chapters 51 and 58, and shall submit a written report of findings and recommendations, including any proposed legislation, to the speaker of the senate and the speaker of the house of representatives.

Effective date 5/16/2013 SECTION 2. This act shall take effect upon becoming a law, the public welfare requiring it.

PUBLIC CHAPTER NO. 442

PUBLIC CHAPTER NO. 442

SENATE BILL NO. 264

By Gresham, Summerville, Tate, Burks, Crowe, Hensley, Ketron, Beavers, Gardenhire, Ford

Substituted for: House Bill No. 966

By Dawn White, Durham, Littleton, Goins, Kane, Kevin Brooks, Hardaway, Watson, Todd

AN ACT to amend Tennessee Code Annotated, Title 49, relative to student discipline.

BE IT ENACTED BY THE GENERAL ASSEMBLY OF THE STATE OF TENNESSEE:

49-6-3401 SECTION 1. Tennessee Code Annotated, Section 49-6-3401(g), is amended by deleting the word "battery" and by substituting instead the language "aggravated assault as defined in § 39-13-102".

Effective date 7/1/2013 SECTION 2. This act shall take effect July 1, 2013, the public welfare requiring it.

PUBLIC CHAPTER NO. 443

PUBLIC CHAPTER NO. 443

SENATE BILL NO. 237

By Campfield, Ford

Substituted for: House Bill No. 457

By Hardaway, Camper, Faison, Parkinson, Towns, Cooper, Miller, Mark White, Eldridge, Johnnie Turner, Shaw, Marsh

AN ACT to amend Tennessee Code Annotated, Title 40, Chapter 32, relative to the expungement of certain criminal records.

BE IT ENACTED BY THE GENERAL ASSEMBLY OF THE STATE OF TENNESSEE:

40-32-101 SECTION 1. Tennessee Code Annotated, Section 40-32-101(g)(10), is amended by deleting the words "The petitioner shall pay" and substituting instead the words "Except as provided in subdivision (g)(16), the petitioner shall pay".

40-32-101 SECTION 2. Tennessee Code Annotated, Section 40-32-101(g), is amended by adding the following new subdivision:

(16) If the petitioner is unable to pay the fee required by subdivision (g)(10), the petitioner may enter into a payment plan with the clerk in order to pay the fee in installment payments; provided, however, that no order of expunction shall be granted pursuant to this subdivision (g)(16) until the total amount of the fee is paid. Once the petitioner has paid to the clerk of the court a total of three hundred fifty dollars ($350.00) the fee shall be allocated by the clerk in the same manner set forth for the disposition of the three hundred fifty dollar ($350.00) fee under subdivision (g)(10).

40-32-101 SECTION 3. Tennessee Code Annotated, Section 40-32-101(g), is amended by adding the following language as a new subdivision (g)(13) and by redesignating the subsequent subdivisions accordingly:

(13) Beginning on July 1, 2013, the department of finance and administration shall review the number of expunction petitions pursuant to this subsection, the cost of processing each petition and the amount of money paid in expunction fees to determine if the amount allotted to the state under subdivision (g)(10)(C) to implement this subsection is adequate and if some portion of such funds could be used for other criminal justice purposes such as the criminal injuries compensation fund or drug court funding. The department shall report its findings to the general assembly in January of 2014.

Effective date 7/1/2013 SECTION 4. This act shall take effect July 1, 2013, the public welfare requiring it.

PUBLIC CHAPTER NO. 444

PUBLIC CHAPTER NO. 444

SENATE BILL NO. 150

By Norris, Ketron

Substituted for: House Bill No. 144

By McCormick

AN ACT to amend Tennessee Code Annotated, Title 56, Chapter 14, relative to Surplus Lines Insurance.

BE IT ENACTED BY THE GENERAL ASSEMBLY OF THE STATE OF TENNESSEE:

56-14-113 SECTION 1. Tennessee Code Annotated, Section 56-14-113, is amended by deleting the section and substituting instead the following:

56-14-113.

(a) The premiums charged for surplus lines insurance are subject to a gross premium tax in an amount to be determined by subsection (b).

(b)(1) In addition to the full amount of gross premiums charged by the insurer for the insurance, every person licensed pursuant to § 56-14-104 shall collect and pay to the commissioner a sum based on the total gross premiums charged, less any return premiums, for surplus lines insurance provided by the surplus lines agent pursuant to the license. Where the insurance covers an insured whose home state is this state, the sum payable shall be computed based on an amount equal to five percent (5%) on the gross premiums, less the amount of gross premiums allocated to this state and returned to the insured.

(2) The tax on any portion of the premium unearned at termination of insurance having been credited by the state to the surplus lines agent shall be returned to the policyholder directly by the surplus lines agent or through the producing broker, if any.

(3) The surplus lines agent is prohibited from rebating, for any reason, any part of the tax.

(4) The commissioner is authorized to contract or compact with other states for the purpose of collecting and disbursing to reciprocal states, defined as those participating in such contract or compact, any funds collected pursuant to subsection (a) that are applicable to other properties, risks, or exposures located or to be performed outside of this state. To the extent that other states where portions of the properties, risks, or exposures reside have failed to enter into compact or reciprocal allocation procedures with this state, the net premium tax collected shall be retained by this state.

(5) On March 1 of each year, at the time of filing the report as set forth in § 56-14-106, each surplus lines licensee shall pay the premium tax due for the policies written during the period covered by the report.

(6) For the purposes of this section, "premium" includes all premiums, membership fees, assessments, dues, or any other consideration for insurance collected under this section.

(7) The tax collected under this section shall be in lieu of all other insurance taxes.

(8) The surplus lines agent shall collect from the insured the amount of the tax at the time of delivery of the cover note, certificate of insurance, policy, or other initial confirmation of insurance, in addition to the full amount of the gross premium charged by the insurer for the insurance. No agent shall absorb the tax nor shall any agent, as an inducement for insurance or for any other reason, rebate all or any part of the tax or the agent's commission.

(c) All surplus lines premium taxes collected by a surplus lines agent under this section are trust funds in the agent's hands and the property of this state. Any surplus lines agent who fails or refuses to pay over to the state the surplus lines premium tax at the time required in this section, or who fraudulently withholds or appropriates or otherwise uses the money or any portions of the money belonging to the state, commits theft and shall be punished as provided by title 39, chapter 14, part 1, regardless of whether the surplus lines agent has or claims to have any interest in the money so received.

(d)(1) Any surplus lines agent or writing agent, holding the premium tax funds in trust, who fails and neglects to make returns and payments promptly and correctly as provided by subdivision (b)(5) shall forfeit and pay to the state, in addition to the amount of these taxes, an amount equal to five percent (5%) for the first month or fractional part of the first month of delinquency; provided, that should the period of delinquency exceed one (1) month, the rate of penalty will be an additional five percent (5%) for the second month or fractional part of the second month and penalty thereafter at the rate of one half of one percent (0.5%) per month of the amount of tax due, the maximum penalty not to exceed ten thousand dollars ($10,000) for any agent not more than three (3) days delinquent. All delinquencies shall bear interest at the rate of ten percent (10%) per annum from the date the amount was due until paid. The penalty and interest shall apply to any part of the tax unpaid by the due date.

(2) The commissioner has the discretion, for good cause shown, upon application made in advance of the delinquency date, to grant an extension of time not to exceed sixty (60) days, to the surplus lines agent or writing agent, holding the premium tax funds in trust, to file the premium tax returns and pay the tax imposed in this part, without penalty attached, but the tax shall bear interest as provided in subdivision (d)(1) from the date the amount was due.

(3) Any surplus lines agent or writing agent, holding the premium tax funds in trust, failing to pay the tax due plus penalty and interest for sixty (60) days beyond the due date may thereafter be debarred from transacting any business of insurance in the state until these taxes and penalties are fully paid, and the commissioner shall revoke the license of the surplus lines agent or writing agent.

(4) The commissioner is authorized to promulgate rules that provide for a convenience fee to cover the cost of accepting electronic monthly affidavits, annual reports and tax payments. Any fee set by rule under the authority of this subdivision (d)(4) may be assessed in addition to any applicable penalty and interest. In no event shall the convenience fee exceed the actual costs incurred by the department in accepting electronic monthly affidavits, annual reports and tax payments. Any convenience fee may be collected from the insured in addition to the premium and tax.

(e) If the property of any surplus lines agent is seized upon any mesne or final process in any court in this state, or when the business of any surplus lines agent is suspended by the action of creditors or put into the hands of any assignee, receiver or trustee, all surplus lines premium tax money and penalties due the state from the surplus lines agent shall be considered preferred claims, and the state shall be a preferred creditor and shall be paid in full.

(f) The attorney general and reporter, upon request of the commissioner, shall proceed in the courts of this or any other state or in any federal court or agency to recover the tax not paid within the time prescribed in this section.

Effective date 1/1/2014

SECTION 2. This act shall take effect January 1, 2014, the public welfare requiring it.

PUBLIC CHAPTER NO. 445

PUBLIC CHAPTER NO. 445

SENATE BILL NO. 129

By Ketron, Tate

Substituted for: House Bill No. 102

By Joe Carr, Durham

AN ACT to amend Tennessee Code Annotated, Title 57, Chapter 3, Part 2 and Title 57, Chapter 2, Part 1, relative to manufacturing of alcoholic beverages.

BE IT ENACTED BY THE GENERAL ASSEMBLY OF THE STATE OF TENNESSEE:

57-2-103 SECTION 1. Tennessee Code Annotated, Section 57-2-103, is amended by deleting subsection (d) and substituting instead the following:

(d)(1) Notwithstanding subsections (a)-(c), it shall be lawful to manufacture intoxicating liquors or intoxicating drinks, or both, within the boundaries of:

(A) A municipality if both retail package sales and consumption of alcoholic beverages on the premises have been approved through referendum of voters within such municipality; or

(B) The unincorporated areas of a county, or a municipality which has a population of less than one thousand (1,000) persons in such county, if any jurisdiction located within such county has approved retail package sales through referendum of voters and any jurisdiction located within such county has approved consumption of alcoholic beverages on the premises through referendum of voters or if the county is included in the Tennessee River resort district as defined in § 57-4-102 and retail package sales have been approved through referendum by the voters in any jurisdiction within such county; or

(C) Any municipality authorized under § 57-4-102(26) to allow facilities or establishments in such municipality to sell alcoholic beverages or wine for on premises consumption.

(D) Any county or municipality where it was lawful to have manufacturing of intoxicating liquors or intoxicating drinks, or both under subsection (d) as it read prior to the effective date of this act.

(2)(A) Notwithstanding subdivision (d)(1), the county legislative body of any such county may adopt a resolution to remove the unincorporated areas of the county from the application of this subsection (d) subject to the restrictions in subdivision (d)(2)(B). The county mayor shall notify the alcoholic beverage commission if such action is taken and approved.

(B) Such action may be taken by the county legislative body pursuant to subdivision (d)(2)(A) until a written notification is filed with the county mayor by any person as an official notice that the person intends to pursue all lawful avenues to manufacture intoxicating liquors or intoxicating drinks, or both, within the unincorporated areas of the county. Once the notice is filed, no action may be taken by the county legislative body unless such interest is withdrawn or the person's application to manufacture such intoxicating liquors or intoxicating drinks, or both, is denied by the state or federal government. A written notification as described pursuant to this subdivision (d)(2)(B) may not be filed with the county mayor until at least forty-five (45) days after the effective date of this act.

(C) If a county adopts a resolution pursuant to subdivision (d)(2)(A), the county may at a later date adopt a resolution reversing such action. The county mayor shall notify the alcoholic beverage commission if such action is taken and approved.

(3)(A) Notwithstanding subdivision (d)(1), the legislative body of any municipality may adopt a resolution to remove the municipality from the application of this subsection (d) subject to the restrictions in subdivision (d)(3)(B). The legislative body of the municipality shall notify the alcoholic beverage commission if such action is taken and approved.

(B) Such action may be taken by the legislative body of the municipality pursuant to subdivision (d)(3)(A) until a written notification is filed with the legislative body of the municipality by any person as an official notice that the person intends to pursue all lawful avenues to manufacture intoxicating liquors or intoxicating drinks, or both, within the boundaries of the municipality. Once the notice is filed, no action may be taken by the legislative body of the municipality unless such interest is withdrawn or the person's application to manufacture such intoxicating liquors or intoxicating drinks, or both, is denied by the state or federal government. A written notification as described pursuant to this subdivision (d)(3)(B) may not be filed with the legislative body of the municipality until at least forty-five (45) days after the effective date of this act.

(C) If a municipality adopts a resolution pursuant to subdivision (d)(3)(A), the municipality may at a later date adopt a resolution reversing such action. The legislative body of the municipality shall notify the alcoholic beverage commission if such action is taken and approved.

(4) If a manufacturer that has been issued a license pursuant to this subsection (d) is also selling the manufacturer's alcoholic beverages or products at retail and the manufacturer is located in a jurisdiction that pursuant to § 57-5-105 has established a distance requirement that restricts the storage, sale or manufacture of beer from places of public gatherings or in a municipality or Class B county that pursuant to § 57-5-106 has adopted proper ordinances governing the storage, sale, manufacture and/or distribution of beer within its jurisdictional boundary, then any distance requirement related to a building used for religious purposes or a building used as an elementary or secondary school in effect in that jurisdiction shall apply to the building used for the retail sale of the manufacturer's alcoholic beverages or products containing alcohol. The measurement shall be a building-to-building measurement.

(5) Notwithstanding subsections (a)-(c) and subdivision (d)(1), it shall be lawful to manufacture intoxicating liquors or intoxicating drinks, or both, on property that is listed on the National Register of Historic Places and where intoxicating liquors or intoxicating drinks, or both, were previously distilled on such property, or approximately on such property.

57-2-103 SECTION 2. Tennessee Code Annotated, Section 57-2-103, is amended by deleting subsection (f) and substituting instead the following:

(f)(1) Notwithstanding subsections (a)-(c), it shall be lawful to manufacture high alcohol content beer as defined in § 57-3-101(a) within the boundaries of:

(A) A municipality if both retail package sales and consumption of alcoholic beverages on the premises have been approved through voter referendum of voters within such municipality; or

(B) The unincorporated areas of a county if any jurisdiction located within such county has approved retail package sales through referendum of voters and any jurisdiction located within such county has approved consumption of alcoholic beverages on the premises through referendum of voters or if the county is included in the Tennessee River resort district as defined in § 57-4-102 and retail package sales have been approved through voter referendum in any jurisdiction within the county.

(2) Any manufacturer authorized pursuant to subdivision (f)(1) must also hold a brewer's notice approved by the United States department of the treasury, alcohol and tobacco tax and trade bureau, or any successor federal beer manufacturing permit granted by a federal bureau having jurisdiction over the manufacture of beer.

(3) In all jurisdictions not meeting the requirements of subdivision (f)(1), it shall be lawful to manufacture high alcohol content beer as defined in § 57-3-101(a) within the boundaries of a municipality or in the unincorporated area of such county upon such jurisdiction meeting the requirements of subsections (a)-(c), and if the manufacturer also holds a brewer's notice approved by the United States department of the treasury, alcohol and tobacco tax and trade bureau, or any successor federal

beer manufacturing permit granted by a federal bureau having jurisdiction over the manufacture of beer.

(4) Notwithstanding any other law to the contrary, it shall be lawful for any manufacturer of high alcohol content beer authorized to manufacture such beverages pursuant to subdivision (f)(1) to also brew beer as this term is defined in § 57-5-101(b) on the same premises of the manufacturer of high alcohol content beer, upon meeting necessary federal, state and local license requirements.

(5) The general assembly hereby ratifies any action which may have been taken by the alcoholic beverage commission in issuing a license to a manufacturer of high alcohol content beer prior to June 10, 2011.

(g) The general assembly hereby ratifies any action which may have been taken by the alcoholic beverage commission in issuing a license to a manufacturer of intoxicating liquors or intoxicating drinks, or both prior to the effective date of this act.

(h)(1) Any person who has received a manufacturing license for intoxicating liquors or intoxicating drinks, or both from the alcoholic beverage commission or who has an application for such manufacturing license pending with the commission on July 1, 2013, may still receive and be able to renew the license if the person was authorized to apply for such license under this section prior to July 1, 2013.

(2) Any person who has received the necessary permit to manufacture intoxicating liquors or intoxicating drinks, or both from the alcohol and tobacco tax and trade bureau (TTB) or who has an application for such permit pending with the TTB on July 1, 2013, may still receive and be able to renew a manufacturing license from the alcoholic beverage commission if the person was authorized to apply for such manufacturing license under this section prior to July 1, 2013.

(3) If any person obtains a manufacturing permit pursuant to this subsection (h), then the jurisdiction such licensee is located in shall be allowed to have other manufacturers located in such jurisdiction, notwithstanding subdivision (d)(1).

57-3-202 SECTION 3. Tennessee Code Annotated, Section 57-3-202, is amended by adding the following as a new subsection thereto:

(i)(1) A manufacturer's license issued or renewed under this section to a manufacturer shall also allow such manufacturer to sell at retail on the licensed premises of the manufacturer products that are manufactured on the manufacturer's premises; provided that no more than five gallons (5 gal.) or one-sixth (1/6) of a barrel of its products may be sold to any one (1) individual per visit to the premises. The manufacturer may serve samples of the product manufactured or distilled at the premises to any person of legal drinking age without cost or may include such samples as part of a tour of the manufacturer's or distiller's premises available to the public with or without cost. Such samples may be made available at any location on the manufacturing premises permitted by federal law. The manufacturer shall disclose to the commission the location where samples are available. The hours of sale for the manufacturer to sell products at retail shall be between the hours of eight o'clock a.m. (8:00 a.m.) and eleven o'clock p.m. (11:00 p.m.) on Monday through Saturday and between the hours of noon (12:00 p.m.) and seven o'clock p.m. (7:00 p.m.) on Sunday.

(2) A manufacturer electing to exercise the rights granted to it under subdivision (i)(1), may only sell at retail or provide samples of product that it has obtained from a wholesaler licensed under § 57-3-203, and such wholesaler shall remit all taxes imposed under §§ 57-3-302, 57-3-501 (which shall be collected from the manufacturer based upon its retail sales), and 57-6-201. For products acquired from a wholesaler by a manufacturer under this section, the wholesaler may permit the manufacturer to deliver its products to the location on its premises where such retail sales and samples will be effected, provided the wholesaler permitting such direct shipment must include the amounts delivered in its inventory and depletions for purposes of tax collections.

(3) Notwithstanding any law to the contrary, any manufacturer selling at retail with the license authorized by this subsection (i) shall pay a municipal inspection fee, described in § 57-3-501, if a municipality the manufacturer is located in imposes such inspection fee which shall then be remitted by the wholesaler as described in subdivision (i)(2).

PUBLIC CHAPTER NO. 445 (cont'd)

SECTION 4. If any provision of this act or the application thereof to any person or circumstance is held invalid, such invalidity shall not affect other provisions or applications of the act which can be given effect without the invalid provision or application, and to that end the provisions of this act are declared to be severable.

Effective date 7/1/2013

SECTION 5. This act shall take effect July 1, 2013, the public welfare requiring it.

PUBLIC CHAPTER NO. 446

PUBLIC CHAPTER NO. 446

SENATE BILL NO. 116

By Ketron, Green, Haile, Beavers, Bowling, Crowe, Watson

Substituted for: House Bill No. 220

By Mark White, Evans, Marsh, Casada, Haynes, Weaver, McManus, Rogers

AN ACT to amend Tennessee Code Annotated, Title 3, Chapter 2, relative to the content of fiscal notes.

BE IT ENACTED BY THE GENERAL ASSEMBLY OF THE STATE OF TENNESSEE:

3-2-107 SECTION 1. Tennessee Code Annotated, Section 3-2-107(a)(2), is amended by designating the existing language as subdivision (A) and adding the following language as a new subdivision (B):

(B)(i) The fiscal note shall also include a statement as to the immediate effect and, if determinable or reasonably foreseeable, the long-range effect on commerce and jobs in this state. Such impact to commerce statement shall also include, if possible, an estimate in dollars of the anticipated change in costs or savings to commerce under the bill or resolution.

(ii) Beginning January 1, 2014, impact to commerce statements shall be required for general bills or resolutions referred to the following standing committees:

(a) House business and utilities committee;

(b) House insurance and banking committee; and

(c) Senate commerce and labor committee.

Effective date 5/16/2013 SECTION 2. This act shall take effect upon becoming a law, the public welfare requiring it.

PUBLIC CHAPTER NO. 447

PUBLIC CHAPTER NO. 447

SENATE BILL NO. 109

By Tate, Ford

Substituted for: House Bill No. 39

By Parkinson, Cooper, Hardaway, Camper, Lois DeBerry, Towns, Love, Miller, Favors, Shaw, Johnnie Turner, John Deberry

AN ACT to amend Tennessee Code Annotated, Section 62-4-120, relative to cosmetology schools.

BE IT ENACTED BY THE GENERAL ASSEMBLY OF THE STATE OF TENNESSEE:

62-4-120 SECTION 1. Tennessee Code Annotated, Section 62-4-120, is amended by adding the following language as new, appropriately designated subsections:

(j) In addition to the schools currently operated pursuant to this section, the board shall establish rules and regulations for separate schools that specialize solely in natural hair styling, manicuring and the practice of aesthetics; provided, at a minimum, such specialized schools remain subject to the requirements of this section.

(k) Notwithstanding any law to the contrary, the board shall establish rules and regulations enabling schools operated pursuant to this section to develop courses of instruction in practice and theory that will satisfy the requirements of § 62-4-110, and that consist of:

(1) Earning fifty percent (50%) of the hours needed for the specific license from classroom training; and

(2) Fifty percent (50%) of the hours needed for the specific license from apprenticing under the supervision of a person licensed pursuant to this chapter, who has at least ten (10) years of experience.

SECTION 2. The state board of cosmetology is authorized to promulgate rules and regulations to effectuate the purposes of this act. All such rules and regulations shall be promulgated in accordance with the Uniform Administrative Procedures Act, compiled in Title 4, Chapter 5.

Effective date 7/1/2013 SECTION 3. For the purpose of promulgating rules and regulations, this act shall take effect upon becoming a law, the public welfare requiring it. For all other purposes, this act shall take effect July 1, 2013, the public welfare requiring it.

PUBLIC CHAPTER NO. 448

PUBLIC CHAPTER NO. 448

SENATE BILL NO. 105

By Massey, Burks, Gresham, Ford, Tracy, Bowling, Harper, Kelsey, Kyle, Overbey, Tate

Substituted for: House Bill No. 387

By Powers, Lois DeBerry, Camper, Pitts, Hardaway, Johnnie Turner, Harry Brooks, Shaw, Parkinson, Favors, Gilmore, Miller, Armstrong, Eldridge, Halford, Roach, Love, Cooper, Lollar, Towns, Windle, Faison, Fitzhugh, Butt, Moody, Pody, Littleton, Shipley, Ryan Williams, Weaver, Rogers

AN ACT to amend Tennessee Code Annotated, relative to creating an educational credential signifying completion of high school and to enact the Tennessee Alternative Diploma Act.

BE IT ENACTED BY THE GENERAL ASSEMBLY OF THE STATE OF TENNESSEE:

4-3-1422 SECTION 1. Tennessee Code Annotated, Section 4-3-1422, is amended by deleting the section in its entirety and by substituting instead the following:

4-3-1422.

(a) This section shall be known and may be cited as the "Lois M. DeBerry Alternative Diploma Act".

(b) The department of labor and workforce development is authorized to make recommendations relative to assessments that lead to the award of a high school equivalency credential. The state board shall review the recommendations of the department. Any recommendation approved by the state board of education shall be considered a high school equivalency assessment and the successful completion of such assessment shall lead to the award of a high school equivalency credential. The department, as needed, may consult with or request assistance from other state agencies in performing its duties under this section.

Effective date 5/16/2013 SECTION 2. This act shall take effect upon becoming a law, the public welfare requiring it.

PUBLIC CHAPTER NO. 449

PUBLIC CHAPTER NO. 449

SENATE BILL NO. 26

By Yager

Substituted for: House Bill No. 16

By Calfee

AN ACT to amend Tennessee Code Annotated, Title 2, Chapter 3 and Title 2, Chapter 8, relative to tie votes in county elections.

BE IT ENACTED BY THE GENERAL ASSEMBLY OF THE STATE OF TENNESSEE:

2-8-111 SECTION 1. Tennessee Code Annotated, Section 2-8-111(1), is amended by deleting the subsection in its entirety and by substituting instead the following:

(1) The county legislative body may cast the deciding vote for offices filled by the votes of a single county or civil district, or, in the alternative, the legislative body may by resolution call for a run-off election between the tied candidates;

Effective date 7/1/2013 SECTION 2. This act shall take effect July 1, 2013, the public welfare requiring it.

PUBLIC CHAPTER NO. 450

PUBLIC CHAPTER NO. 450

SENATE BILL NO. 24

By Southerland

Substituted for: House Bill No. 7

By Faison

AN ACT to amend Tennessee Code Annotated, Section 67-4-601, relative to litigation taxes.

BE IT ENACTED BY THE GENERAL ASSEMBLY OF THE STATE OF TENNESSEE:

67-4-601 SECTION 1. Tennessee Code Annotated, Section 67-4-601, is amended by adding the following language as a new, appropriately designated subsection:

( )(1) In addition to any other tax imposed pursuant to this chapter, there is levied a privilege tax on litigation in all civil and criminal cases instituted in the general sessions court in any county having a population of not less than thirty-five thousand six hundred (35,600) nor more than thirty-five thousand seven hundred (35,700) according to the 2010 federal census or any subsequent federal census, in an amount not to exceed four dollars seventy-five cents ($4.75) and upon the adoption of a resolution by a two-thirds (2/3) majority vote of the county legislative body.

(2) Notwithstanding the apportionment provisions of § 67-4-606, any revenue collected pursuant to this subsection shall be deposited in the county general fund, with the proceeds to be used exclusively for the funding of the general sessions court, and for ensuring compliance with fire codes for the existing courthouse justice center facilities. No proceeds derived from the tax shall be used to increase or decrease the salary of the general sessions judge during such judge's term in office. All expenditures made for courthouse justice center facilities in accordance with this subsection shall be administered by the county sheriff, subject to the appropriation of funds for such purposes by the county legislative body.

(3) No privilege tax shall be levied on litigation in accordance with this subsection on or after July 1, 2020; provided, however, this subdivision (3) shall not be construed to absolve any person of liability for any litigation tax duly imposed by this subsection prior to July 1, 2020.

Effective date 5/16/2013 SECTION 2. This act shall take effect upon becoming a law, the public welfare requiring it.

PUBLIC CHAPTER NO. 451

PUBLIC CHAPTER NO. 451

SENATE BILL NO. 504

By Norris

Substituted for: House Bill No. 509

By Sargent, McCormick

AN ACT pursuant to Article II, Section 24, of the Tennessee Constitution providing for the dollar amount and rate by which the growth of appropriations from State Tax Revenues will exceed the estimated growth in the state's economy and to amend Tennessee Code Annotated, Title 9, Chapter 4, Part 52.

BE IT ENACTED BY THE GENERAL ASSEMBLY OF THE STATE OF TENNESSEE:

9-4-5203 SECTION 1. Tennessee Code Annotated, Section 9-4-5203(e), is amended by adding the following language as a new, appropriately designated subdivision:

( ) The index of appropriations from state tax revenues for the 2012-2013 fiscal year may exceed the index of estimated growth in the state's economy by one hundred thirty-two million five hundred thousand dollars ($132,500,000) or one percent (1.0%).

Effective date 5/16/2013 SECTION 2. This act shall take effect upon becoming law, the public welfare requiring it.

PUBLIC CHAPTER NO. 452

PUBLIC CHAPTER NO. 452

SENATE BILL NO. 503

By Norris

Substituted for: House Bill No. 508

By Sargent, McCormick

AN ACT to authorize the State of Tennessee, acting by resolution of its funding board, to issue and sell its bonds and bond anticipation notes in amounts not to exceed two hundred sixty-six million dollars ($266,000,000) for the purpose of providing funds to the Department of Finance and Administration and the Department of Transportation; to provide for acquisition of equipment and sites, and erection, construction and equipment of sites and buildings, expressly including the acquisition of existing structures for expansion, improvements, betterments, and extraordinary repairs to existing structures, for construction of highways, and repair, replacement or rehabilitation of bridges, and for grants to any county, metropolitan government, incorporated town, city, special district of the state, or any governmental agency or instrumentality of any of them; and to provide for the expenditure of said funds; to issue its debt in excess of the previously stated amount to fund discount and costs of issuance; and to provide for the expenditure of said funds. This act makes appropriations for an indefinite period of time for the purpose of allocating the proceeds of the bonds and notes authorized by this act.

BE IT ENACTED BY THE GENERAL ASSEMBLY OF THE STATE OF TENNESSEE:

SECTION 1. The State of Tennessee, acting by resolutions of its funding board, is hereby authorized and empowered to issue and sell direct general obligation bonds of the State of Tennessee in amounts not to exceed two hundred sixty-six million dollars ($266,000,000) to effectuate the purposes specified in Section 4 of this act. Further, the funding board is authorized to sell bonds in amounts not to exceed 2.5% of the amounts specified above and authorized in Section 4, for the purpose of funding discount and costs of issuance. Such bonds may be issued and sold in one (1) block or in several installments and separately or together with other general obligation bonds of the State of Tennessee as the board may determine, either at public or private sale as provided by law.

SECTION 2. The bonds and the interest coupons attached thereto, if any, shall be in such form, mature at such time or times within twenty (20) years from the date of their issuance (subject to Section 7 of this act), be executed in such manner, be payable at such place or places both as to principal and interest, and be in such denominations and bear such rate or rates of interest, payable in such manner, as the funding board shall by resolution direct; provided, however, that the maximum rate determined by the funding board in no instance shall exceed the legal rate as provided in Section 47-14-103 of the Tennessee Code Annotated. The bonds and interest payable thereon shall be exempt from taxation by the State of Tennessee or by any county, municipality or taxing district of the state except inheritance, transfer and estate taxes.

SECTION 3. When the bonds are so issued and sold, they shall be direct general obligations of the State of Tennessee for the payment of which well and truly to be made according to the tenor, effect and terms thereof the full faith and credit of the state, together with its taxing power, shall irrevocably be pledged; and the bonds as authorized herein shall be issued agreeable to the terms of Title 9, Chapter 9, Tennessee Code Annotated; and they shall be financed, retired, and paid both as to principal and interest as provided in that chapter and shall be subject to the terms and conditions therein and herein contained. When the bonds are sold and proceeds paid over to the state treasurer, the funds shall be paid out by the treasurer and the proper fiscal officers of the state, as provided by general law and this act, but only (except for accrued interest paid as part of the purchase price) on order of the proper administrative authorities of the agency or department herein named for the benefit of which such bonds have been authorized and only to the extent such bonds have in fact been issued for the benefit of such agency or department.

SECTION 4. The proceeds of any and all issues of bonds herein authorized shall be allocated to the following departments:

(1) Department of Finance and Administration in the amount of one hundred eighty-five million dollars ($185,000,000) and expended for the purposes of acquisition of equipment and sites, and erection, construction and equipment of sites and buildings, expressly including the acquisition of existing structures for expansion, improvements, betterments and extraordinary repairs to existing structures, and for the purpose of making

grants to any county, metropolitan government, incorporated town, city, special district of the state, or any governmental agency or instrumentality of any of them, if such project grant is approved by the State Building Commission. Such grants so identified and approved are determined to be for a public purpose.

(2) Department of Transportation in the amount of eighty-one million dollars ($81,000,000) and expended for the construction of highways and for the purpose of acquisition of equipment and sites, and erection, construction and equipment of sites and buildings, expressly including the acquisition of existing structures for expansion, improvements, betterments and extraordinary repairs to existing structures.

In its discretion the funding board is authorized to issue bonds in amounts not to exceed 2.5% of the amounts specified above, the proceeds of which are to be allocated to the funding board and expended for the purpose of funding discount and the costs of issuance.

SECTION 5. The proper authorities heretofore enumerated and charged with the duty of expending the funds shall have authority to proceed with the projects authorized herein and for that purpose may hire an architect or architects, advertise for bids and award contracts, all within the provisions of the general law, expressly including the provisions of Title 4, Chapter 15, Tennessee Code Annotated, and rules of the State Building Commission, and in agreement with the terms of this act. No contract, including a contract for architectural services, involving a project authorized by this act which is subject to the approval of the State Building Commission shall be entered into unless and until that contract shall have been approved by the State Building Commission. The foregoing provisions shall not apply to any grants authorized herein, but the Department of Finance and Administration, charged with the duty of expending funds, shall have the authority to enter into such grant contracts and perform in accordance in their terms only after the projects have been approved by the State Building Commission.

SECTION 6. The appropriation made to each agency or department as provided in Section 4 may be applied as determined by the funding board to bear its appropriate portion of discount and costs of issuance.

SECTION 7. Pending the issuance of the definite bonds authorized by this act, the State of Tennessee, acting by resolutions of its funding board, is hereby authorized and empowered to issue and sell, either at public or private sale, together with accrued interest thereon, its interest-bearing bond anticipation note or notes. Such note or notes shall be authorized by resolution of the funding board. The note or notes shall bear such date or dates, bear interest at such rate or rates, be in such denominations, be in such form, be executed in such manner, be payable in such medium of payment, at such place or places and mature on such date(s), subject to such terms and conditions as such resolution or resolutions may provide. In its discretion, the funding board may provide that a bond anticipation note or any renewal of such note may mature more than five (5) years from the date of issue of the original note; provided, that an amortization schedule of repayment of principal is established for the project funded by the note and provisions are made such that any note or renewal note or bond refunding such note attributed to the financing of such project shall be redeemed or retired no later than either twenty-five (25) years from the date of issue of such original note or twenty (20) years from the date the project is completed and placed in full service, whichever is earlier. Provisions of general law with respect to authentication, execution and registration of general obligation bonds of the State of Tennessee shall also apply to the notes to the extent applicable. The note or notes and the interest payable thereon shall be exempt from taxation by the State of Tennessee or by any county, municipality or taxing district of the state except inheritance, transfer and estate taxes. Any resolution or resolutions of the funding board authorizing the issuance of such bond anticipation note or notes shall provide that the same are issued in anticipation of the bonds authorized hereunder and shall further provide that the full faith and credit and taxing power of the State of Tennessee are pledged to the payment thereof.

In its discretion the funding board is authorized to issue bond anticipation notes, the proceeds of which are to be allocated to the funding board and expended for the purpose of funding discount and the costs of issuance, as part of the 2.5% additional amounts authorized by Section 4 of this act.

SECTION 8. No bonds shall be issued under the authority of this act until such time as the general assembly has appropriated sufficient funds to pay the first year's obligation of principal and interest on the amount of bonds to be issued and the state funding board has determined that such funds are available.

SECTION 9. Notwithstanding any other provision of this act to the contrary, the bonds and bond anticipation notes authorized by this act may be designated "college savings bonds" and be issued pursuant to the provisions of the Baccalaureate Education Savings for Tennessee Act, Chapter 190, Public Acts of 1989.

PUBLIC CHAPTER NO. 452 (cont'd)

SECTION 10. If any provision of this act or the application thereof to any person or circumstance is held invalid, such invalidity shall not affect other provisions or applications of the act which can be given effect without the invalid provision or application, and to that end the provisions of this act are declared to be severable.

SECTION 11. No expenditure of public funds pursuant to this act shall be made in violation of the provisions of Title VI of the Civil Rights Act of 1964, as codified in 42 United States Code 2000(d).

Effective date 5/16/2013

SECTION 12. This act shall take effect upon becoming a law, the public welfare requiring it.

PUBLIC CHAPTER NO. 453

PUBLIC CHAPTER NO. 453

SENATE BILL NO. 502

By Norris

Substituted for: House Bill No. 507

By Sargent, McCormick

AN ACT to make appropriations for the purpose of defraying the expenses of the state government for the fiscal years beginning July 1, 2012, and July 1, 2013, in the administration, operation and maintenance of the legislative, executive and judicial branches of the various departments, institutions, offices and agencies of the state; for certain state aid and obligations; for capital outlay, for the service of the public debt, for emergency and contingency; to repeal certain appropriations and any acts inconsistent herewith; to provide provisional continuing appropriations; and to establish certain provisions, limitations and restrictions under which appropriations may be obligated and expended. This act makes appropriations for the purposes described above for the fiscal years beginning July 1, 2012, and July 1, 2013.

BE IT ENACTED BY THE GENERAL ASSEMBLY OF THE STATE OF TENNESSEE:

SECTION 1. That appropriations hereinafter set out are hereby made for the purpose of defraying the expenses of state government for the fiscal year beginning July 1, 2013, in the administration, operation and maintenance of the legislative, executive and judicial branches of the various departments, institutions, offices and agencies of the state, and for certain state aid and obligations and for capital outlay; for the service of the public debt, and for emergency and contingency, all according to the following schedule:

	I. LEGISLATIVE		2013-2014
1.	Legislature		
	1.1 General Assembly Support Services	$	7,842,500.00
	1.2 House of Representatives		17,666,400.00
	1.3 State Senate		9,821,400.00
	1.4 Legislative Administration Services		4,480,100.00
	1.5 Tennessee Code Commission		68,900.00
	Total Legislature	$	39,879,300.00
2.	Fiscal Review Committee		1,428,100.00
	Total Title I	$	41,307,400.00
	II. JUDICIAL		
1.	Appellate and Trial Courts	$	59,348,100.00
2.	Supreme Court Buildings		2,668,800.00
3.	Child Support Referees		784,300.00
4.	Guardian ad Litem		6,047,500.00
5.	Indigent Defendants' Counsel		30,463,000.00
6.	Civil Legal Representation Fund		3,327,900.00
7.	Court Interpreter Services		3,000,000.00
8.	Verbatim Transcripts		3,930,100.00
9.	Tennessee State Law Libraries		74,500.00
10.	Council of Juvenile and Family Court Judges		60,500.00
11.	Judicial Conference		223,600.00
12.	Judicial Programs and Commissions		430,100.00
13.	State Court Clerks' Conference		260,200.00
14.	Administrative Office of the Courts		8,225,900.00
15.	Appellate Court Clerks		613,500.00
16.	Board of Court Reporting		170,000.00
17.	Board of Law Examiners		730,100.00
18.	Board of Professional Responsibility		3,118,800.00
19.	Tennessee Lawyers Assistance Program		459,400.00
20.	Continuing Legal Education		806,200.00
21.	Client Protection Fund		208,500.00

	Total Title II	$	124,951,000.00
	III. EXECUTIVE		
	1. Constitutional and Quasi-Judicial Offices		
1.	Attorney General and Reporter		
1.1	Attorney General and Reporter	$	24,301,100.00
1.2	Publication of Tennessee Reports		173,700.00
1.3	Special Litigation		289,700.00
	Total Attorney General and Reporter	$	24,764,500.00
2.	District Attorneys General Conference		
2.1	District Attorneys General	$	72,295,700.00
2.2	District Attorneys General Conference		439,000.00
2.3	Executive Director		1,766,200.00
	Total District Attorneys General Conference	$	74,500,900.00
3.	Secretary of State		
3.1	Secretary of State	$	9,489,100.00
3.2	State Election Commission		1,591,900.00
3.3	Public Documents		396,600.00
3.4	State Library and Archives		8,459,000.00
3.5	Regional Library System		6,661,000.00
3.6	Bureau of Ethics and Campaign Finance		634,600.00
3.7	Economic Council on Women		225,200.00
3.8	Charitable Solicitations and Charitable Gaming		90,900.00
	Total Secretary of State.	$	27,548,300.00
4.	District Public Defenders Conference		
4.1	District Public Defenders	$	37,499,700.00
4.2	Executive Director		1,594,600.00
4.3	Shelby County Public Defender		3,917,300.00
4.4	Davidson County Public Defender		2,152,400.00
	Total District Public Defenders Conference	$	45,164,000.00
5.	Comptroller of the Treasury		
5.1	Division of Administration	$	2,113,000.00
5.2	Office of Management Services		10,622,000.00
5.3	Division of State Audit		11,799,000.00
5.4	Division of Local Government Audit		8,461,400.00
5.5	Investigations		2,370,000.00
5.6	Office of State and Local Finance		949,600.00
5.7	Office of Local Government		1,135,400.00
5.8	Division of Property Assessments		7,387,300.00
5.9	Tax Relief		28,402,100.00
5.10	State Board of Equalization		834,600.00
5.11	Offices of Research and Education Accountability		1,419,800.00
5.12	Office of State Assessed Properties		1,003,400.00
5.13	Telecommunications Ad Valorem Tax Equity Payments		7,000,000.00
	Total Comptroller of the Treasury	$	83,497,600.00
6.	Office of the Post-Conviction Defender	$	2,201,500.00
7.	Treasury Department		
7.1	Treasury Department	$	589,600.00
7.2	Certified Public Administrators		407,300.00
7.3	Baccalaureate Education System Trust		1,416,400.00
7.4	Interlock Assistance Fund		463,500.00
	Total Treasury Department	$	2,876,800.00
8.	Claims and Compensation		
8.1	Criminal Injuries Compensation	$	11,170,000.00
8.2	Unclaimed Property		5,250,000.00
	Total Claims and Compensation	$	16,420,000.00
	Total Title III-1	$	276,973,600.00

The appropriation made under Title III-1, Item 8.1, may be increased or decreased as realized receipts of the Criminal Injuries Compensation Fund justify, subject to the provisions of Tennessee Code Annotated, Title 4, Chapter 3, Part 10 and Title 9, Chapter 4, Part 51. To the extent that receipts of the fund are insufficient to meet the fund's expenditure requirements, there is hereby appropriated a sum sufficient to support such expenditures.

2. Executive Offices

1.	Executive Department			
	1.1	Governor's Office	$	4,671,200.00
		Total Executive Department	$	4,671,200.00
2.	Commissions			
	2.1	Commission on Children and Youth	$	2,239,800.00
	2.2	Commission on Aging and Disability		13,694,400.00
	2.3	Alcoholic Beverage Commission		80,700.00
	2.4	Human Rights Commission		1,679,800.00
	2.5	Health Services and Development Agency		1,098,500.00
	2.6	Tennessee Regulatory Authority		6,631,600.00
	2.7	Advisory Commission on Intergovernmental Relations		212,200.00
	2.8	Arts Commission		6,407,600.00
	2.9	State Museum		3,464,600.00
		Total Commissions	$	35,509,200.00
3.	Department of Finance and Administration			
	3.1	Division of Administration	$	2,197,700.00
	3.2	Office for Information Resources		12,150,000.00
	3.3	Division of Accounts		1,800,000.00
	3.4	Division of Budget		5,535,800.00
	3.5	Criminal Justice Programs		3,894,100.00
	3.6	State Architect's Office		1,238,500.00
	3.7	Volunteer Tennessee		246,200.00
	3.8	Business Solutions Delivery		2,636,500.00
		Total Department of Finance and Administration	$	29,698,800.00
4.	Department of General Services			
	4.1	Administration	$	334,900.00
	4.2	Real Estate Asset Management		4,434,600.00
	4.3	Printing and Media Services		309,100.00
	4.4	Procurement Office		2,140,100.00
	4.5	Governor's Books from Birth Fund		3,104,100.00
	4.6	State Facilities Pre-Planning		500,000.00
		Total Department of General Services	$	10,822,800.00
5.	Department of Veterans Affairs		$	5,195,400.00
		Total Title III-2	$	85,897,400.00

3. Department of Agriculture

1.	Administration and Grants	$	5,615,000.00
2.	Regulatory Services		11,912,400.00
3.	Market Development		20,375,900.00
4.	Agricultural Resources Conservation Fund		3,187,500.00
5.	Forestry Operations		21,677,400.00
6.	Forestry Maintenance		157,200.00
7.	Certified Cotton Growers' Organization Fund		607,500.00
8.	Beef Promotion Board		235,000.00
9.	Agricultural Regulatory Fund		3,038,500.00
	Total Title III-3	$	66,806,400.00

4. Department of Tourist Development

1.	Administration and Marketing	$	18,025,200.00
2.	Welcome Centers		1,365,000.00
	Total Title III-4	$	19,390,200.00

5. Department of Environment and Conservation

1.	Administrative Services	$ 6,588,400.00
2.	Recreation Educational Services	807,100.00
3.	Archaeology	785,300.00
4.	Geology	140,400.00
5.	Tennessee State Parks	42,395,300.00
6.	State Parks Maintenance	2,214,100.00
7.	Historical Commission	2,285,200.00
8.	Maintenance of Historic Sites	285,000.00
9.	West Tennessee River Basin Authority	956,400.00
10.	West Tennessee River Basin Authority Maintenance	1,215,500.00
11.	Environment Administration	539,900.00
12.	Used Oil Collection Program	1,104,900.00
13.	Tennessee Dry Cleaners Environmental Response Fund	1,910,400.00
14.	Air Pollution Control	1,104,700.00
15.	Radiological Health	610,400.00
16.	Water Pollution Control	9,324,700.00
17.	Solid Waste Management	1,786,000.00
18.	Abandoned Lands	500,000.00
19.	Hazardous Waste Remedial Action Fund	1,000,000.00
20.	Water Supply	1,002,200.00
21.	Groundwater Protection	2,155,400.00
22.	Underground Storage Tanks	23,099,500.00
23.	Solid Waste Assistance	11,241,000.00
24.	Environmental Protection Fund	52,658,000.00
25.	Clean Water and Drinking Water State Revolving Fund	6,714,000.00
26.	Office of Sustainable Practices	621,200.00
27.	Office of Energy Programs	34,800.00
28.	State Lands Compensation Fund	100,000.00
29.	Conservation Compensation Fund	42,000.00
30.	Local Parks Acquisition Fund	3,718,700.00
31.	State Lands Acquisition Fund	3,087,500.00
	Total Title III-5	$ 180,028,000.00

6. Tennessee Wildlife Resources Agency

1.	Wildlife Resources Agency	$ 41,764,500.00
2.	Boating Safety	6,946,000.00
3.	Wetlands Acquisition Fund	6,506,300.00
4.	Wetlands Compensation Fund	400,000.00
	Total Title III-6	$ 55,616,800.00

The appropriation made under Title III-6 may be increased or decreased as realized receipts of the Wildlife Resources Fund justify, subject to the provisions of Tennessee Code Annotated, Title 4, Chapter 3, Part 10 and Title 9, Chapter 4, Part 51.

7. Department of Correction

1.	Administration	$ 15,983,000.00
2.	Office of Investigations and Compliance	4,408,200.00
3.	Correction Academy	5,089,100.00
4.	Probation and Parole Field Supervision	64,950,500.00
5.	Community Corrections	14,018,100.00
6.	Sex Offender Treatment Program	443,600.00
7.	State Prosecutions	201,252,800.00
8.	Correction Release Centers	1,918,800.00
9.	Tennessee Prison for Women	26,953,200.00
10.	Turney Center Industrial Complex	39,230,700.00
11.	Mark Luttrell Correctional Facility	15,639,900.00
12.	Charles B. Bass Correctional Complex	29,149,500.00
13.	Southeastern Tennessee State Regional Correctional Facility	64,053,200.00
14.	West Tennessee State Penitentiary	57,491,100.00
15.	Riverbend Maximum Security Institution	27,510,500.00
16.	Northeast Correctional Complex	41,676,700.00
17.	Northwest Correctional Complex	52,069,500.00

18.	Morgan County Correctional Complex		67,511,000.00
19.	Lois M. DeBerry Special Needs Facility		48,392,000.00
20.	Hardeman County Incarceration Agreement		39,344,800.00
21.	Hardeman County Agreement – Whiteville		31,746,400.00
22.	South Central Correctional Center		28,261,000.00
23.	Sentencing Act of 1985		17,717,800.00
24.	Major Maintenance		13,910,500.00
	Total Title III-7	$	908,721,900.00

8. Department of Economic and Community Development

1.	Administrative Services	$	5,217,300.00
2.	Business Development		6,170,100.00
3.	Innovation Programs		257,900.00
4.	Headquarters Relocation Assistance		6,000,000.00
5.	TNInvestco Tax Credits		30,000,000.00
6.	Policy and Federal Programs		480,500.00
7.	Economic Development District Grants		1,500,100.00
8.	FastTrack Infrastructure and Job Training Assistance		40,157,400.00
9.	Film and Television Incentive Fund		13,400,000.00
10.	Community and Rural Development		1,996,000.00
	Total Title III-8	$	105,179,300.00

9. Department of Education

1.	Administrative Services		
	1.1 Administration	$	6,672,100.00
	1.2 State Board of Education		864,800.00
2.	Pre-Kindergarten, Kindergarten, Elementary, and Secondary		
	2.1 State Programs		
	a. Curriculum and Instruction		3,623,700.00
	b. Career Ladder		39,000,000.00
	c. Basic Education Program		4,030,319,100.00
	d. Driver Education		1,700,000.00
	e. Training and Professional Development		2,926,100.00
	f. Grants-In-Aid		4,893,900.00
	g. Technology, Infrastructure, and Support Systems		53,382,000.00
	h. Accountability and Assessment		29,602,800.00
	i. Early Childhood Education		91,801,300.00
	j. After-School Programs Special Account (Lottery-Funded)		13,100,000.00
	2.2 Federally Funded and Supported Programs		
	a. Improving Schools Program		20,387,800.00
	b. School Nutrition Program		4,807,200.00
	c. Special Education Services		676,100.00
	d. Tennessee Early Intervention Services		12,083,300.00
	e. ESEA No Child Left Behind		470,000.00
	f. Achievement School District		3,800.00
3.	Career and Technical Education Programs		4,130,800.00
4.	Special Schools		
	4.1 Alvin C. York Institute		5,748,800.00
	4.2 Tennessee School for the Blind		10,910,700.00
	4.3 Tennessee School for the Deaf		15,384,800.00
	4.4 West Tennessee School for the Deaf		2,686,200.00
	4.5 Major Maintenance		239,100.00
	Total Title III-9	$	4,355,414,400.00

10. Higher Education

1.	Administration and Support Services		
	1.1 Tennessee Higher Education Commission	$	2,239,300.00
	1.2 Contract Education		2,178,400.00

PUBLIC CHAPTER NO. 453 (cont'd)

	1.3	Tennessee Student Assistance Awards		57,762,500.00
	1.4	Tennessee Student Assistance Corporation		1,223,100.00
	1.5	Loan/Scholarship Programs		1,191,000.00
	1.6	Foreign Language Institute		378,600.00
	1.7	THEC Grants		7,318,100.00
	1.8	Lottery for Education Account		329,700,000.00
2.		Excellence Initiatives		
	2.1	Academic Scholars Program		401,800.00
	2.2	Centers of Excellence		17,755,200.00
	2.3	Campus Centers of Emphasis		1,281,700.00
		Total Administration and Support Services and Excellence Initiatives	$	421,429,700.00
3.		University of Tennessee System		
	3.1	Administrative and Other Services		
		a. UT University-Wide Administration	$	4,648,000.00
		b. UT Institute for Public Service		4,622,900.00
		c. UT Municipal Technical Advisory Service		2,821,900.00
		d. UT County Technical Assistance Service		1,714,900.00
		e. UT Access and Diversity Initiative		5,550,100.00
		f. UT Space Institute		7,734,700.00
		g. UT Research Initiatives		10,594,300.00
	3.2	Agricultural Services		
		a. UT Agricultural Experiment Station		24,892,600.00
		b. UT Agricultural Extension Service		30,169,500.00
		c. UT Veterinary Medicine		16,476,900.00
	3.3	Medical Education		
		a. UT Health Science Center		74,394,500.00
		b. UT Family Medicine		10,470,400.00
		c. UT College of Medicine		47,273,300.00
	3.4	University Campuses		
		a. UT Chattanooga		36,603,100.00
		b. UT Knoxville		174,723,700.00
		c. UT Martin		25,657,500.00
		Total University of Tennessee System	$	478,348,300.00
4.		Tennessee Board of Regents System		
	4.1	Administration and Other Services		
		a. Tennessee Board of Regents	$	5,124,500.00
		b. Regents Access and Diversity Initiative		9,803,700.00
	4.2	Medical Education		
		a. ETSU College of Medicine		28,987,400.00
		b. ETSU Family Practice		6,124,900.00
	4.3	Regional Universities		
		a. Austin Peay State University		33,041,000.00
		b. East Tennessee State University		48,767,600.00
		c. University of Memphis		94,120,800.00
		d. Middle Tennessee State University		81,158,100.00
		e. Tennessee State University		32,659,300.00
		f. Tennessee Technological University		39,632,100.00
	4.4	Tennessee Community Colleges		211,149,400.00
	4.5	Tennessee Technology Centers		57,445,700.00
	4.6	Equipment for Community Colleges and Technology Centers		16,500,000.00
	4.7	Agricultural Centers		
		a. TSU McMinnville Center		547,100.00

	b. TSU Institute of Agricultural and Environmental Research		2,223,500.00
	c. TSU Cooperative Education		3,031,700.00
	d. TSU McIntire-Stennis Forestry Research		175,000.00
	Total Tennessee Board of Regents System	$	670,491,800.00
	Total Title III-10	$	1,570,269,800.00

11. Department of Commerce and Insurance

1.	Administration	$	1,305,700.00
2.	Consumer Affairs		1,226,200.00
3.	Cemetery Consumer Protection Fund		363,900.00
4.	Pre-Need Funeral Consumer Protection Fund		100,100.00
5.	Fire Service and Codes Enforcement Academy		2,765,400.00
6.	Fire Fighting Personnel Standards and Education		4,109,600.00
7.	Peace Officer Standards and Training (POST) Commission		8,981,900.00
8.	Tennessee Law Enforcement Training Academy		2,377,300.00
9.	911 Emergency Communications Fund		63,140,100.00
10.	Regulatory Boards		18,779,900.00
	10.1 Real Estate Education and Recovery Fund		291,700.00
	10.2 Auctioneer Education and Recovery Fund		81,700.00
11.	Tennessee Athletic Commission		247,000.00
12.	Corrections Institute		1,430,200.00
	Total Title III-11	$	105,200,700.00

12. Department of Financial Institutions	$	9,775,100.00
Total Title III-12	$	9,775,100.00

The appropriation made under Title III-12 may be increased or decreased as realized receipts justify, subject to the provisions of Tennessee Code Annotated, Title 4, Chapter 3, Part 10 and Title 9, Chapter 4, Part 51.

13. Department of Labor and Workforce Development

1.	Administration	$	2,873,100.00
2.	Tennessee Occupational Safety and Health Administration		5,030,600.00
3.	Mines		361,400.00
4.	Boilers and Elevators		4,769,600.00
5.	Labor Standards		1,273,300.00
6.	Workers' Compensation		14,738,700.00
7.	Workers' Compensation Employee Misclassification Education and Enforcement Fund (WCEMEEF)		330,400.00
8.	Second Injury Fund		9,872,400.00
9.	Adult Basic Education		3,889,200.00
10.	Employment Security		4,394,300.00
	Total Title III-13	$	47,533,000.00

14. Department of Mental Health and Substance Abuse Services

1.	Administrative Services Division	$	14,020,000.00
2.	Mental Health Services		
	2.1 Middle Tennessee Mental Health Institute		29,167,400.00
	2.2 Western Mental Health Institute		20,406,100.00
	2.3 Moccasin Bend Mental Health Institute		16,957,800.00
	2.4 Memphis Mental Health Institute		14,512,300.00
	2.5 Community Mental Health Services		77,999,800.00
	2.6 Major Maintenance		450,000.00
3.	Community Substance Abuse Services		22,881,000.00
	Total Title III-14	$	196,394,400.00

PUBLIC CHAPTER NO. 453 (cont'd)

15. Department of Military

1.	Administration	$	2,450,800.00
2.	Army National Guard		1,085,600.00
3.	Air National Guard		2,112,600.00
4.	Tennessee Emergency Management Agency		3,036,500.00
5.	TEMA Disaster Relief Grants		4,000,000.00
6.	Armories Utilities		1,959,100.00
7.	Armories Maintenance		588,200.00
	Total Title III-15	$	15,232,800.00

16. Department of Health

1.	Administration		
	1.1 Executive Administration	$	15,317,000.00
	1.2 Policy Planning and Assessment		4,431,700.00
2.	Manpower Resources and Facilities		
	2.1 Bureau of Health Licensure and Regulation		7,495,000.00
	2.2 Emergency Medical Services		450,700.00
	2.3 Laboratory Services		6,155,100.00
	2.4 Health Related Boards		15,415,900.00
	2.5 Trauma System Fund		8,500,000.00
3.	Community Health Services		
	3.1 General Environmental Health		11,996,300.00
	3.2 Maternal and Child Health		7,332,500.00
	3.3 Communicable and Environmental Disease Services		11,570,700.00
	3.4 Community and Medical Services		25,407,900.00
	3.5 Division of Animal Welfare		670,200.00
4.	Local Health Services		62,547,900.00
	Total Title III-16	$	177,290,900.00

17. Department of Human Services

1.	Administration		
	1.1 Administration	$	21,010,800.00
	1.2 Field Operations		5,542,600.00
	1.3 County Rentals		6,395,600.00
	1.4 Appeals and Hearings		3,319,400.00
	1.5 Organizational Performance Management		2,724,800.00
2.	Family Assistance Services		
	2.1 Child Support		16,157,000.00
	2.2 Family Assistance Services		72,980,400.00
	2.3 Temporary Cash Assistance		19,968,900.00
	2.4 Child Care Benefits		10,667,600.00
3.	Community Services		801,300.00
4.	Rehabilitative Services		
	4.1 Vocational Rehabilitation		9,409,500.00
	Total Title III-17	$	168,977,900.00

18. Department of Revenue

1.	Administration Division	$	6,114,300.00
2.	Tax Enforcement Division		5,583,300.00
3.	Information Technology Resources Division		15,177,500.00
4.	Taxpayer and Vehicle Services Division		24,900,000.00
5.	Processing Division		5,095,200.00
6.	Audit Division		20,927,400.00
7.	Anti-Theft Unit		1,521,500.00
8.	Sales Tax Disaster Relief		250,000.00
9.	Tax Refund Interest Expense		2,500,000.00

PUBLIC CHAPTER NO. 453 (cont'd)

	Total Title III-18	$	82,069,200.00
	19. Tennessee Bureau of Investigation	$	40,717,500.00
	Total Title III-19	$	40,717,500.00
	20. Department of Safety		
1.	Administration	$	8,560,900.00
2.	Driver License Issuance		10,652,900.00
3.	Highway Patrol		92,143,800.00
4.	Office of Homeland Security		1,729,700.00
5.	Motor Vehicle Operations		11,551,100.00
6.	Technical Services		820,900.00
7.	Driver Education		273,000.00
8.	Motorcycle Rider Education		514,100.00
9.	Major Maintenance		10,000.00
	Total Title III-20	$	126,256,400.00
	21. Department of Finance and Administration, Strategic Health-Care Programs		
1.	CoverTN	$	7,982,200.00
2.	AccessTN		19,054,000.00
3.	CoverKids		57,573,700.00
4.	CoverRx		10,689,500.00
5.	Health-Care Planning and Innovation		826,900.00
	Total Title III-21	$	96,126,300.00
	22. Miscellaneous Appropriations		
1.	State Employees' Unemployment Compensation, Sick Leave, Death Benefit Payments and Terminal Leave Payments	$	200,000.00
2.	Consolidated Retirement System		
	2.1 Former Governors and Widows of Former Governors – Pensions		364,700.00
3.	Insurance		
	3.1 Retirees Health Insurance		14,200,000.00
	3.2 Retired Teachers Insurance		20,500,000.00
4.	Attorney's Fees – Civil Rights Cases		500,000.00
5.	Special Election Reimbursement to Counties		400,000.00
6.	Homeland Security Emergency Fund		1,100,000.00
7.	Criminal Justice Programs		700,000.00
8.	Tennessee Association of Rescue Squads		71,300.00
9.	Volunteer Rescue Squad – $25,000 Death Benefit		25,000.00
10.	YMCA Youth Legislature		25,000.00
11.	YMCA Community Action Program		350,000.00
12.	Forensic Center at Quillen College of Medicine		100,000.00
13.	State Employees 1.5% Salary Increase		22,100,000.00
14.	Salary Market Adjustment		
	14.1 Salary Market Adjustment at 7/1/2013		26,668,000.00
	14.2 Salary Market Adjustment at 7/1/2013 – Additional Funds		27,900,000.00
15.	Group Health Insurance Premium – State Employees		9,700,000.00
16.	Deferred Compensation – 401K Match – State Employees		9,197,000.00
17.	Intergovernmental Conference Dues		600,000.00
18.	UT CBER – Research Assistance		159,200.00
19.	UT CBER – State Census Data Center		278,000.00
20.	MVM – Purchase of New Vehicles		3,500,000.00
21.	Statewide Rate Adjustments		
	21.1 Rent Adjustments		1,266,300.00

	21.2 OIR Rate Adjustment for Data Center		3,055,400.00
	21.3 OIR Rate Adjustment		4,900,000.00
	21.4 Edison Rate Adjustment		3,400,000.00
	21.5 Property Insurance Premium		2,000,000.00
	21.6 Central Procurement Office Rate Adjustment		400,000.00
	21.7 Postage Rate Increase - State Agencies		1,000,000.00
22.	Civil Rights Museum		250,000.00
23.	Severance Benefit Plan		2,200,000.00
24.	Swipe and Ride Benefit		500,000.00
25.	American Battle Monuments Commission – Maintenance of Tennessee World War I Monuments in France		3,500.00
26.	Online Innovation Initiative		3,000,000.00
27.	Innovation Fund		750,000.00
28.	General Session Courts Data Repository		1,250,000.00
29.	Contingency Appropriation – Health and Wellness Initiatives (Tobacco MSA Source)		20,000,000.00
30.	Tobacco MSA Diligent Enforcement Systems Development		1,203,100.00
31.	FRF Rent Adjustment - Alternate Lease Space Disposed-Buildings		800,000.00
32.	Weighted Caseload Study, Judges, DAs, and Public Defenders		400,000.00
33.	Pay for Performance Planning		100,000.00
34.	Contingency Appropriation – Grant to Knox County in Lieu of Tax		50,000.00
	Total Title III-22	$	185,166,500.00

23. Department of Children's Services

1.	Administration	$	26,439,600.00
2.	Family Support Services		23,791,300.00
3.	Custody Services		85,257,400.00
4.	Needs Assessment		4,119,400.00
5.	Adoption Services		41,861,400.00
6.	Child and Family Management		81,588,600.00
7.	John S. Wilder Youth Development Center		12,289,000.00
8.	Woodland Hills Youth Development Center		12,051,900.00
9.	Mountain View Youth Development Center		12,044,600.00
10.	New Visions Youth Development Center		3,226,500.00
11.	Major Maintenance		370,100.00
	Total Title III-23	$	303,039,800.00

24.	Board of Parole	$	7,212,300.00
	Total Title III-24	$	7,212,300.00

25. Department of Intellectual and Developmental Disabilities

1.	Intellectual Disabilities Services Administration	$	1,746,900.00
2.	Developmental Disabilities Council		230,600.00
3.	Community Intellectual Disabilities Services		15,034,600.00
4.	Quality Assurance Program		881,500.00
5.	Clover Bottom Developmental Center		95,900.00
6.	Greene Valley Developmental Center		648,900.00
7.	Harold Jordan Center		2,843,800.00
8.	West Tennessee Regional Office		1,284,800.00
9.	Middle Tennessee Regional Office		1,030,900.00
10.	East Tennessee Regional Office		905,900.00
11.	West Tennessee Resource Center		2,268,900.00
12.	Middle Tennessee Resource Center		1,188,700.00
13.	East Tennessee Resource Center		168,700.00
14.	Middle Tennessee Community Homes		241,200.00
15.	East Tennessee Community Homes		56,000.00
16.	Major Maintenance		100,000.00
	Total Title III-25	$	28,727,300.00

26. Department of Finance and Administration, Bureau of TennCare

1.	TennCare Administration	$	108,470,700.00
2.	TennCare Medical Services		2,169,842,800.00

3.	Supplemental Payments		270,403,400.00
4.	Intellectual Disabilities Services		317,951,900.00
5.	Medicare Services		319,274,100.00
	Total Title III-26	$	3,185,942,900.00
27.	Emergency and Contingency Fund	$	819,300.00
	Total Title III-27	$	819,300.00

The Emergency and Contingency Fund may be used for any purpose authorized by law to be allowed on Executive Order of the Governor; provided, however, the Emergency and Contingency Fund shall not be used to fund any law requiring the expenditure of state funds unless an appropriation is made elsewhere for the estimated first year's funding.

28. State Building Commission

1.	Major Maintenance and Equipment	$	250,000.00
	Total Title III-28	$	250,000.00

29. Facilities Revolving Fund

1.	Facilities Operations	$	8,517,200.00
2.	Leases and Space Planning		14,147,600.00
3.	FRF Capital Projects		135,920,000.00
4.	FRF Debt Service		13,000,000.00
	Total Title III-29	$	171,584,800.00

The appropriation to the Facilities Revolving Fund in Section 1, Title III-29, Item 4, in the amount of $13,000,000.00 for FRF Debt Service is intended to provide funds to defease certain outstanding general obligation bonds. The bonds were issued for projects associated with six of eight state office buildings which are recommended for disposition by the state. The six buildings with outstanding general obligation bonds are:

(a) Cordell Hull Building in Nashville;
(b) Chattanooga State Office Building;
(c) James R. Mapp Building in Chattanooga;
(d) Donnelly J. Hill Building in Memphis;
(e) Old Supreme Court Building in Knoxville;
(f) Henley Street State Office Building in Knoxville.

Two buildings do not have outstanding general obligation bonds. The buildings are:

(a) Central Services Building in Nashville;
(b) Tennessee Regulatory Authority Building in Nashville.

Subject to the disposition of the state office buildings with outstanding debt, the appropriations shall be expended pursuant to a defeasement plan approved by the State Funding Board.

30. Department of Transportation

There is hereby appropriated for the use of the Department of Transportation such receipts of highway revenues as are now provided by law, or may hereafter be so provided, to accrue to that department during the fiscal year, beginning July 1, 2013, to be expended by the Commissioner of Transportation, all according to the following schedule:

			2013-2014
1.	Headquarters	$	99,966,700.00
2.	Bureau of Administration		49,899,000.00
3.	Bureau of Operations		252,115,600.00
4.	Bureau of Engineering		78,479,800.00
5.	Field Engineering		92,216,000.00
6.	Bureau of Environment and Planning		67,111,000.00
7.	Field Construction		107,008,600.00
8.	Field Maintenance Operations		68,003,300.00

Total Title III-30	$	814,800,000.00
Grand Total	$	13,553,673,300.00

Said funds so appropriated shall be obligated and expended under the provisions of Tennessee Code Annotated, Title 4, Chapter 3, Part 10 and Title 9, Chapter 4, Part 51. There is further appropriated to the Department of Transportation such departmental revenue, expressly including federal matching funds, as may accrue to the department.

The "Proposed Highway Program for Fiscal Year 2013-2014", prepared by the Department of Transportation as a supplement to and as "Supporting Data for the Budget Request," is hereby incorporated into and made a part of the Appropriations Act.

Whenever a determination is made that one or more of the projects in the approved program cannot be proceeded with, the Commissioner of Transportation shall furnish, in written form as prescribed by the Chairs of the Finance, Ways and Means Committees of the Senate and House and the Chairs of the Transportation Committees of the Senate and House, the reasons for such proposed cancellation or rescheduling of said project, together with a recommendation for a substitute project. The notice of cancellation or rescheduling of said project shall be submitted to the Speaker of the Senate, the Speaker of the House of Representatives, the Chairs of the Finance, Ways and Means Committees of the Senate and House, the Chairs of the Transportation Committees of the Senate and House and to the individual Senator and Representative in whose districts the canceled project or proposed substitution is located.

From the funds appropriated above in Item 5, Field Engineering, the sum of $9,540,000 is allocated for the purpose of funding the state's eighty percent (80%) share of the project cost of the 1990 Bridge Grant Program. For the fiscal 2013-2014 budget, the state shall fund an eighty percent (80%) share of this program and local governments shall be responsible for funding the remaining twenty percent (20%), as set forth in Tennessee Code Annotated, Title 54, Chapter 4, Part 5.

For the fiscal year beginning July 1, 2013, the Commissioner of Transportation shall distribute this money among the ninety-five (95) county geographical areas of the state according to the following formula:

One-half of the funds shall be distributed equally, and one-half shall be distributed on the basis of structural needs. Structural needs shall be determined by calculating the ratio of linear feet of bridges with a load rating of less than ten tons, in each county geographical area, located on public roads other than those on a federal-aid system or the state system of highways, to the total linear feet of like bridges in the state.

31. State Funding Board

There is hereby appropriated to the State Funding Board for interest and reduction of the state debt, for debt service expense and interest on proposed bond authorization:

			2013-2014
1.	Interest on State Debt	$	71,244,000.00
2.	Retirement of Bonds		133,780,000.00
3.	Debt Service Expense		1,000,000.00
4.	Amortization of Authorized and Unissued Construction Bonds		93,700,000.00
5.	Amortization of Authorized and Unissued Highway Bonds		131,600,000.00
6.	Amortization of Bonds Issued – November 2012		11,000,000.00
	Total Title III-31	$	442,324,000.00

The appropriation made under Section 1, Title III-31, Items 1, 2, 3, 4, 5, and 6, is made under the provisions of Tennessee Code Annotated, Title 9, Chapter 9, and may be increased to such amounts as will be necessary to carry out such provisions.

32. Capital Outlay

There is hereby appropriated to each of the departments and agencies enumerated herein, funds for major maintenance, equipment, construction and acquisition of land, and for expansion, improvement, betterments and repairs to existing structures. The Commissioner of Finance and Administration is hereby authorized to transfer the amounts herein appropriated to the Capital Projects Fund for the use of the said departments and agencies.

1.	Department of Children's Services	$	1,210,000.00
2.	Department of Commerce and Insurance		450,000.00
3.	Department of Education		10,250,000.00
4.	Department of Environment and Conservation		5,460,000.00
5.	Department of Finance and Administration		2,400,000.00
6.	Department of General Services		15,552,000.00
7.	Department of Intellectual and Developmental Disabilities		4,340,000.00
8.	Historical Commission		1,303,000.00
9.	Department of Human Services		310,000.00
10.	Department of Military		3,070,000.00
11.	Tennessee Rehabilitative Initiative in Correction		990,000.00
12.	Department of Veterans Affairs		950,000.00
13.	Secretary of State		2,600,000.00
14.	Tennessee Board of Regents		67,510,000.00
15.	University of Tennessee		48,600,000.00
	Total Title III-32	$	164,995,000.00

Said funds herein appropriated shall be used solely for improvements, betterments, and additions to state structures and for the acquisition of additional land and space, including the purchase of existing structures and grants, as described or referred to above and as approved by the State Building Commission; provided, further, that such funds as are appropriated herein shall be utilized to finance only those projects, improvements, betterments, or additions which are presented in the State of Tennessee's 2013-2014 Budget Document, as amended by any changes or additional projects contained in the Appropriations Act as passed on third and final consideration; provided, further, that all funds appropriated in this act or other general acts of this session for capital outlay shall be subject to the provisions of Tennessee Code Annotated, Title 4, Chapter 15, Part 1, and further expressly providing for the making of grants to governmental entities and/or to certain not-for-profit organizations listed herein, and for the purposes identified on pages A-155 through A-158 and pages A-163 through A-175 of the 2013-2014 Budget Document or otherwise identified in this act, and such grants so identified and approved are determined to be for a public purpose: (a) Country Music Foundation, Inc., located in Davidson County; (b) Ladies' Hermitage Association, located in Davidson County; (c) Knoxville Botanical Gardens and Arboretum, located in Knox County; (d) Chattanooga History Center, located in Hamilton County; (e) Tennessee Performing Arts Center Management Corporation, located in Davidson County; (f) Lorraine Civil Rights Museum Foundation, located in Shelby County; (g) Watkins College of Art, Design, and Film, located in Davidson County.

33. Capital Outlay - Sinking Fund

There is hereby appropriated for the fiscal year beginning July 1, 2013, to the Sinking Fund from the receipts of the tax levied by Tennessee Code Annotated, Title 67, Chapter 4, Part 20, "The Excise Tax Law", an amount to be determined by the State Funding Board.

SECTION 2. Capital Outlay and Major Maintenance

Item 1. Any funds appropriated by this General Assembly for capital outlay, capital maintenance, major maintenance, and Department of General Services state-facilities pre-planning shall not revert to the general fund but shall remain available until expended. It is the intent of the General Assembly that funds of capital outlay nature shall remain available until expended for the purpose for which the appropriations were made.

In the fiscal years ending June 30, 2013, and June 30, 2014, the carry-forward and reappropriation of unexpended appropriations for major maintenance and Department of General Services state facilities pre-planning shall be subject to approval by the Commissioner of Finance and Administration based upon the availability of revenues and reserves in the general fund at June 30, 2013, and June 30, 2014.

Item 2. Any unexpended capital outlay or capital maintenance funds appropriated by previous General Assemblies for completed or discontinued projects shall be accumulated in a capital account to be administered by the Department of Finance and Administration. Expenditure of these funds is subject to approval by the State Building Commission upon recommendation of the University of Tennessee, State Board of Regents, or Department of General Services, as applicable, and certification of available funds by the Commissioner of Finance and Administration.

Item 3. From the appropriations made to the State Funding Board in Section 1, Title III-31, the Funding Board is hereby authorized to allocate and provide to the Capital Projects Fund such funds not required for debt service during fiscal year 2013-2014 for projects duly authorized and approved by the General Assembly; provided, however, that when the Funding Board allocates funds under this provision, any other appropriation or bond authorization for said purpose is hereby reduced accordingly.

Item 4. From the funds appropriated for capital outlay in this act and other acts of the legislature, the Commissioner of Finance and Administration, with the approval of the State Building Commission, is authorized to charge the administrative costs of the construction programs to the capital outlay appropriations or to transfer from the Capital Projects Fund to the general fund an amount sufficient to cover those costs. Such expenditures shall be from non-bond proceeds.

Item 5. From the funds appropriated for capital outlay in this act and other acts of the legislature, the Commissioner of Finance and Administration is authorized to establish and charge the costs of design and engineering positions to the capital outlay appropriations or to transfer from the Capital Projects Fund to the general fund an amount sufficient to cover these costs. This item is subject to approval by the State Building Commission.

Item 6. From the funds appropriated for capital outlay in this act and other acts of the legislature, the Commissioner of Finance and Administration, with the approval of the State Building Commission, is authorized to transfer the appropriations for capital outlay to the Department of Finance and Administration to provide for the centralized administration of capital outlay. It is further the legislative intent to allow for centralized administration of any project recommended by the Commissioner of Finance and Administration and approved by the State Building Commission.

Item 7. To the extent that the accumulated yearly interest and earnings of the Natural Resources Trust Fund are available through June 30, 2013, said funds are hereby appropriated to the Department of Environment and Conservation to be available for projects which are reviewed and evaluated under procedures established by the authority of Tennessee Code Annotated, Section 11-14-308.

Item 8. There is hereby appropriated to the Department of Mental Health and Substance Abuse Services the proceeds from the sale of any real property and facilities being used by the department. The appropriation shall be available to fund the department's master plan for facilities subject to approval by the State Building Commission.

This appropriation is made notwithstanding the provisions of Section 20 of this act and the provisions of Tennessee Code Annotated, Title 54, Chapter 2, Part 2, to the contrary.

Item 9. There is hereby appropriated to the Department of Military the proceeds from the sale of any real property and facilities being used by the department. The appropriation shall be available to fund replacement facilities for the department subject to approval by the State Building Commission.

This appropriation is made notwithstanding the provisions of Section 20 of this act and the provisions of Tennessee Code Annotated, Title 54, Chapter 2, Part 2, to the contrary.

Item 10. There is hereby appropriated to the Department of Intellectual and Developmental Disabilities the proceeds from the sale of any real property and facilities being used by the department. The appropriation shall be available to fund replacement facilities for the department subject to approval by the State Building Commission.

This appropriation is made notwithstanding the provisions of Section 20 of this act and the provisions of Tennessee Code Annotated, Title 54, Chapter 2, Part 2, to the contrary.

Item 11. Other provisions of the law to the contrary notwithstanding, any proceeds from the sale of surplus land and real property in Davidson County are hereby reappropriated to the Department of Finance and Administration to provide for the state's office space and support facilities requirements in Davidson County.

This appropriation is made notwithstanding the provisions of Section 20 of this act and the provisions of Tennessee Code Annotated, Title 54, Chapter 2, Part 2, to the contrary. Any reappropriation made pursuant to the provisions of this item is subject to the approval of the State Building Commission.

Item 12. The appropriation in Section 1, Title III-7, and the appropriation reduction in Section 38 to the Department of Correction, Sentencing Act of 1985, are made pursuant to TCA, Section 9-4-210.

(a) The appropriation in Section 1, Title III-7 reflects a base appropriation reduction of $9,573,400, and the appropriation reduction in Section 38 reflects a fiscal year 2012-2013 reduction of $928,800, which recognize the increased recurring operating costs at the Southeastern Tennessee State Regional Correctional Facility in fiscal years 2012-2013 and 2013-2014.

(b) The appropriation in the amount of $17,714,600 is hereby reappropriated to the department for major maintenance and capital outlay purposes.

(c) From the balance of the reserve fund carried forward at June 30, 2013, there is hereby appropriated the sum of $33,585,400 to the department for major maintenance and capital outlay purposes in the 2013-2014 fiscal year.

(d) From any remaining reserve fund balance carried forward at June 30, 2013, there is hereby appropriated a sum sufficient to the department for major maintenance and capital outlay purposes.

(e) Other appropriations made under this act to the Department of Correction, Sentencing Act of 1985, are hereby reappropriated to the department for major maintenance and capital outlay purposes.

(f) The capital outlay projects for the Department of Correction, identified on page A-155 of the 2013-2014 Budget Document, include an amount of $10,000,000 of capital projects fund residual funds which were from the Sentencing Act of 1985 appropriation source for a previous capital improvement project expanding the Southeastern Tennessee State Regional Correctional Facility. Such residual funds hereby are reappropriated in the year beginning July 1, 2013, for the purpose of funding the Bledsoe Correctional Complex Expansion project listed on page A-155.

(g) On or before October 1, 2013, the Commissioner of Finance and Administration shall submit a detailed financial report to the Chairs of the Finance, Ways and Means Committees of the Senate and House of Representatives and to the Chairs of the State and Local Government Committee of the Senate and State Government Committee of the House of Representatives concerning all activities of the Sentencing Act of 1985 reserve account (established and maintained pursuant to TCA, § 9-4-210) during fiscal year 2012-2013. The report shall indicate the account balance on July 1, 2012, and shall itemize all funds deposited into the reserve account as well as all funds allocated from the reserve account. For each such allocation from the reserve account, the report shall describe the purpose, amount and location of the allocation as well as any other information deemed to be informative by the Commissioner.

Item 13. From the appropriation made to the Department of Economic and Community Development for capital outlay grants to the Wacker Chemie AG Plant project in Section 1, Title III-32 of Chapter 554, Public Acts of 2009, the Commissioner of Finance and Administration is authorized to approve transfers to the FastTrack Infrastructure and Job Training Assistance program in the general fund.

Item 14. Capital improvement projects recommended for higher education institutions in the 2013-2014 Budget Document on page A-156 include funding partially from institutional sources. It is the legislative intent that such projects include an institutional matching component, applicable to the first $75 million of project costs, at the following rates by type of institution: (a) universities, 25 percent; (b) community colleges, 10 percent; (c) non-formula units, 10 percent; and (d) technology centers, 5 percent. Matching funds may include gifts, grants, institutional funds, student fees, and other non-state sources. The provisions of this item shall not apply to the project identified as Nissan Education and Training Facility in the Board of Regents projects and the UTK Steam Plant Conversion to Natural Gas at the University of Tennessee Knoxville campus.

The provisions of this paragraph are effective immediately, the public welfare requiring it. It is further the legislative intent that institutions of higher education be authorized to proceed with capital improvement projects funded in the 2012-2013 and 2013-2014 enacted capital outlay budgets by using Tennessee State School Bond Authority bonds as bridge funding for the institutional matching component, under guidelines of and subject to approval of projects by the authority, and that such bonds as may be authorized be canceled as the matching funds are raised.

Item 15. From the funds appropriated in Public Acts of 2012, Chapter 1028, Section 1, Title III-32, Capital Outlay, to the Department of Safety for the interoperable communication system upgrade, and in Section 71(b), Item 6(B) of Chapter 1108, Public Acts of 2010, to the Department of Safety for the highway patrol communication system capital outlay project, the Commissioner of Finance and Administration is authorized to transfer sums sufficient from the capital outlay fund to the general fund or systems development fund as required.

Item 16. From the appropriation made in Section 1, Title III-32, Item 4, of Chapter 1108, Public Acts of 2010, to the Department of Intellectual and Developmental Disabilities, to provide alternative residential settings for clients and plan for the future, the Commissioner of Finance and Administration is authorized to transfer sums sufficient to the general fund to provide for other transitional costs.

SECTION 3.

Item 1. Appropriations made under Section 1, Titles III-11 and III-16, for the operation of the state regulatory boards, shall be subject to allotment by the Commissioner of Finance and Administration, and no expenditure shall be made by any said boards out of fees collected by them unless and until such allotments have been made by the Commissioner of Finance and Administration. Such allotments for the operation of said respective boards as are made by the Commissioner of Finance and Administration shall be disbursed under the provisions of Tennessee Code Annotated, Title 4, Chapter 3, Part 10 and Title 9, Chapter 4, Part 51.

The allotment hereinabove provided shall be subject to the condition that no money shall be paid therefrom for the salary of any employee of said boards unless and until such salary has been approved by the Commissioner of Human Resources. The appointment of all employees of said boards shall likewise be approved by the Commissioner of Human Resources.

Notwithstanding any provision of law to the contrary, no member of any board or commission established by law or pursuant to law, which receives an appropriation under this act, regardless of the source of funding, shall receive any compensation, whether denominated per diem or by whatever name called, except for days in which such member actually works four (4) or more hours performing duties directly relating to that board's or commission's activities, or for time or days spent attending meetings of that board or commission. The chair or head of each board or commission, the department head to which such board or commission is attached administratively, and the Commissioner of Finance and Administration, shall prescribe procedures to contain, as a minimum, a certification of time worked by each member claiming compensation.

Item 2. Except as otherwise provided in this section, the appropriations to the Wildlife Resources Agency under Section 1, Title III-6, shall be paid out of the special fund established under Tennessee Code Annotated, Title 70, Chapter 1, Part 4 and Section 69-9-203. Such appropriations shall be expended under the provisions of Tennessee Code Annotated, Title 4, Chapter 3, Part 10 and Title 9, Chapter 4, Part 51, and shall be used only for the expenses of the Wildlife Resources Agency pursuant to Tennessee Code Annotated, Title 70 and Title 69, Chapter 9, Part 2, and no part of the unexpended fund left at the end of the fiscal year shall be used for any other purpose but shall be carried over in said fund and may be expended during the next year, and all of said fees and revenues provided by Tennessee Code Annotated, Title 70 and Title 69, Chapter 9, Part 2, are herein specifically apportioned and appropriated to the use and for the benefit of the Wildlife Resources Agency to be expended under the provisions of Tennessee Code Annotated, Title 4, Chapter 3, Part 10 and Title 9, Chapter 4, Part 51. Nothing in this item shall be construed as relieving the Wildlife Resources Agency of the duty of policing littering of lakes and streams.

Item 3. The appropriation to the State Board of Law Examiners in Section 1, Title II, Item 17, shall be from funds generated by fees collected by the board under the provisions of Tennessee Code Annotated, Title 23, Chapter 1.

In case the appropriation to the board shall prove inadequate to allow the board to function efficiently, the Commissioner of Finance and Administration may make an additional allotment thereto from the general fund, the total of all allotments to the board not to exceed the revenues paid into the treasury by the board.

Item 4. The appropriation to the Department of Financial Institutions in Section 1, Title III-12, shall be derived from banking fees assessed pursuant to Tennessee Code Annotated, Title 45, Chapter 1, Part 1. No part of the unexpended fees left at the end of the fiscal year shall revert to the general fund.

DEPARTMENTAL REVENUES

SECTION 4. All departmental revenues of every kind, as hereinafter defined, collected by any department, institution, office, or agency, in the course of its operations, for its own use, are hereby appropriated to it in addition to the specific appropriations made by this act, unless otherwise provided in this act or other provision of law. Federal aid funds granted to the state for the use of or to be administered by any department, institution, or agency, are likewise appropriated. For the purpose of this section "departmental revenues" are defined as (1) earnings or charges for goods or services; (2) donations, contributions or participation by political subdivisions, foundations, corporations, firms or persons. State revenues, in contradistinction to departmental revenues, are the proceeds of taxes, licenses, fees, fines, forfeiture or other imposts laid specifically by law.

Notwithstanding any provision of the previous paragraph, the Department of Health shall deposit all funds generated by fees or taxes collected by such entity in the general fund of the state. Any appropriations for the operation of such entity shall be subject to allotment by the Commissioner of Finance and Administration, and no expenditure shall be made by any such entity out of fees or taxes collected by it, unless and until such allotments have been made by the Commissioner of Finance and Administration. Such allotments for the operation of such entity as are made by the Commissioner of Finance and Administration shall be disbursed under the provisions of Tennessee Code Annotated, Title 4, Chapter 3, Part 10 and Title 9, Chapter 4, Part 51.

The departmental revenues and federal aid funds appropriated under this act shall include the amounts hereinafter set out:

	I. LEGISLATIVE		2013-2014
1.	Legislative Administration Services	$	17,000.00
2.	House of Representatives		28,500.00
3.	State Senate		22,000.00
4.	General Assembly Support Services		70,000.00
	Total Legislature	$	137,500.00
	Total Title I	$	137,500.00
	II. JUDICIAL		
1.	Appellate and Trial Courts	$	27,300.00
2.	Supreme Court Buildings		613,000.00
3.	Child Support Referees		1,648,200.00
4.	Indigent Defendants' Counsel		5,000.00
5.	Council of Juvenile and Family Court Judges		67,000.00
6.	Judicial Conference		40,000.00
7.	Judicial Programs and Commissions		498,200.00
8.	Administrative Office of the Courts		1,283,700.00
9.	Appellate Court Clerks		1,627,100.00
	Total Title II	$	5,809,500.00
	III. EXECUTIVE		
	1. Constitutional and Quasi-Judicial Offices		
1.	Attorney General and Reporter		
	1.1 Attorney General and Reporter	$	11,282,500.00
	1.2 Special Litigation		788,800.00
	Total Attorney General and Reporter	$	12,071,300.00
2.	District Attorneys General Conference		
	2.1 District Attorneys General	$	7,712,500.00
	2.2 District Attorneys General Conference		161,000.00
	2.3 Executive Director		1,273,700.00
	2.4 IV-D Child Support Enforcement		20,065,700.00
	Total District Attorneys General Conference	$	29,212,900.00
3.	Secretary of State		
	3.1 Secretary of State	$	7,183,300.00
	3.2 Records Management		1,130,000.00
	3.3 State Library and Archives		3,634,300.00
	3.4 Regional Library System		822,500.00

PUBLIC CHAPTER NO. 453 (cont'd)

	3.5 Bureau of Ethics and Campaign Finance		515,100.00
	3.6 Charitable Solicitations and Charitable Gaming		1,680,500.00
	3.7 Help America Vote Act		27,500,000.00
	Total Secretary of State	$	42,465,700.00
4.	District Public Defenders Conference		
	4.1 District Public Defenders	$	1,832,600.00
	Total District Public Defenders Conference	$	1,832,600.00
5.	Comptroller of the Treasury		
	5.1 Division of Administration	$	109,400.00
	5.2 Office of Management Services		272,500.00
	5.3 Division of State Audit		4,610,400.00
	5.4 Division of Local Government Audit		1,348,200.00
	5.5 Investigations		120,000.00
	5.6 Office of State and Local Finance		561,100.00
	5.7 Office of Local Government		100,000.00
	5.8 Division of Property Assessments		1,719,500.00
	5.9 State Board of Equalization		107,500.00
	5.10 Offices of Research and Education Accountability		100,000.00
	5.11 Office of State Assessed Properties		125,000.00
	Total Comptroller of the Treasury	$	9,173,600.00
6.	Treasury Department		
	6.1 Treasury Department	$	28,914,200.00
	6.2 Small and Minority-Owned Business Assistance Program		250,000.00
	6.3 Baccalaureate Education System Trust		125,100.00
	6.4 Interlock Assistance Fund		411,700.00
	Total Treasury Department	$	29,701,000.00
7.	Claims and Compensation		
	7.1 Criminal Injuries Compensation	$	4,930,000.00
	7.2 Unclaimed Property		31,750,000.00
	7.3 Risk Management Fund		57,680,100.00
	Total Claims and Compensation	$	94,360,100.00
	Total Title III-1	$	218,817,200.00

2. Executive Offices

1.	Commissions		
	1.1 Commission on Children and Youth	$	1,823,200.00
	1.2 Commission on Aging and Disability		29,112,000.00
	1.3 Alcoholic Beverage Commission		6,201,100.00
	1.4 Human Rights Commission		774,300.00
	1.5 Advisory Commission on Intergovernmental Relations		2,743,800.00
	1.6 Tennessee Housing Development Agency		247,532,700.00
	1.7 Arts Commission		1,582,000.00
	1.8 Tennessee Regulatory Authority		581,800.00
	1.9 Tennessee Rehabilitative Initiative in Correction		38,648,900.00
	1.10 State Museum		5,000.00
	Total Commissions	$	329,004,800.00
2.	Department of Finance and Administration		
	2.1 Division of Administration	$	7,946,300.00
	2.2 Office for Information Resources		144,382,000.00
	2.3 Benefits Administration		10,864,100.00
	2.4 Division of Accounts		14,350,600.00
	2.5 Criminal Justice Programs		21,079,300.00
	2.6 Volunteer Tennessee		4,286,800.00
	2.7 Office of Inspector General		4,773,000.00
	2.8 Enterprise Resource Planning		24,975,000.00
	2.9 Shared Services Solutions		859,300.00
	2.10 Business Solutions Delivery		841,200.00
	Total Department of Finance and Administration	$	234,357,600.00
3.	Department of Human Resources		
	3.1 Executive Administration	$	2,582,400.00

	3.2	Human Resource Development		2,018,400.00
	3.3	Technical Services		5,209,100.00
	3.4	Employee Relations		1,358,000.00
		Total Department of Human Resources	$	11,167,900.00
4.		Department of General Services		
	4.1	Administration	$	5,403,000.00
	4.2	Postal Services		21,058,000.00
	4.3	Motor Vehicle Management		34,725,000.00
	4.4	Real Estate Asset Management		17,019,300.00
	4.5	Printing and Media Services		4,676,200.00
	4.6	Procurement Office		5,844,800.00
	4.7	Office of Information Technology Services (OITS)		2,177,100.00
	4.8	Warehousing and Distribution		4,904,800.00
	4.9	State Facilities Pre-Planning		8,000,000.00
		Total Department of General Services	$	103,808,200.00
5.		Department of Veterans Affairs	$	1,019,700.00
		Total Title III-2	$	679,358,200.00

3. Department of Agriculture

1.	Administration and Grants	$	5,509,700.00
2.	Regulatory Services		7,762,700.00
3.	Market Development		343,400.00
4.	Forestry Operations		7,934,200.00
5.	Grain Indemnity Fund		126,700.00
6.	Agricultural Regulatory Fund		120,000.00
	Total Title III-3	$	21,796,700.00

4. Department of Tourist Development

1.	Administration and Marketing	$	1,047,200.00
2.	Welcome Centers		7,731,000.00
	Total Title III-4	$	8,778,200.00

5. Department of Environment and Conservation

1.	Administrative Services	$	11,877,500.00
2.	Recreation Educational Services		4,475,800.00
3.	Land and Water Conservation Fund		750,000.00
4.	Archaeology		60,500.00
5.	Geology		647,600.00
6.	Tennessee State Parks		37,081,600.00
7.	State Parks Maintenance		479,600.00
8.	Historical Commission		549,600.00
9.	West Tennessee River Basin Authority		395,100.00
10.	Environment Administration		3,101,500.00
11.	Air Pollution Control		16,763,100.00
12.	Radiological Health		5,356,500.00
13.	Water Pollution Control		13,192,800.00
14.	Solid Waste Management		10,691,100.00
15.	DOE Oversight		6,506,500.00
16.	Hazardous Waste Remedial Action Fund		10,657,600.00
17.	Water Supply		6,151,400.00
18.	Groundwater Protection		4,563,800.00
19.	Underground Storage Tanks		2,077,300.00
20.	Clean Water and Drinking Water State Revolving Fund		44,615,300.00
21.	Used Oil Collection Program		1,000.00
22.	Fleming Training Center		918,800.00
23.	Office of Sustainable Practices		492,400.00
24.	Office of Energy Programs		4,078,500.00
25.	Energy Loan Programs		5,200,000.00
26.	Tennessee Heritage Conservation Trust Fund		1,000,000.00

	Total Title III-5	$	191,684,900.00
	6. Tennessee Wildlife Resources Agency		
1.	Wildlife Resources Agency	$	32,980,200.00
2.	Boating Safety		4,152,400.00
3.	Wetlands Acquisition Fund		15,000.00
	Total Title III-6	$	37,147,600.00
	7. Department of Correction		
1.	Administration	$	4,856,900.00
2.	Correction Academy		64,900.00
3.	Probation and Parole Field Supervision		1,969,500.00
4.	Sex Offender Treatment Program		60,000.00
5.	State Prosecutions		800,000.00
6.	Tennessee Prison for Women		843,100.00
7.	Turney Center Industrial Complex		1,327,000.00
8.	Mark Luttrell Correctional Facility		542,000.00
9.	Charles B. Bass Correctional Complex		1,131,800.00
10.	Southeastern Tennessee State Regional Correctional Facility		2,220,800.00
11.	West Tennessee State Penitentiary		1,320,200.00
12.	Riverbend Maximum Security Institution		426,900.00
13.	Northeast Correctional Complex		1,316,500.00
14.	Northwest Correctional Complex		1,732,400.00
15.	Morgan County Correctional Complex		1,654,400.00
16.	Lois M. DeBerry Special Needs Facility		397,400.00
17.	Hardeman County Incarceration Agreement		18,900.00
18.	Hardeman County Agreement – Whiteville		18,700.00
19.	South Central Correctional Center		18,700.00
20.	Sentencing Act of 1985		7,500.00
	Total Title III-7	$	20,727,600.00
	8. Department of Economic and Community Development		
1.	Administrative Services	$	858,900.00
2.	Business Development		577,400.00
3.	Innovation Programs		125,000.00
4.	Tennessee Job Skills Program		5,285,200.00
5.	Policy and Federal Programs		25,039,200.00
6.	FastTrack Infrastructure and Job Training Assistance		340,500.00
7.	Film and Television Incentive Fund		48,600.00
8.	Community and Rural Development		262,800.00
	Total Title III-8	$	32,537,600.00
	9. Department of Education		
1.	Administration	$	1,556,400.00
2.	ESEA No Child Left Behind		372,816,900.00
3.	Technology, Infrastructure, and Support Systems		200,000.00
4.	Training and Professional Development		3,000.00
5.	Curriculum and Instruction		1,247,600.00
6.	Improving Schools Program		27,144,700.00
7.	Accountability and Assessment		5,435,300.00
8.	After-School Programs Special Account		400,000.00
9.	Early Childhood Education		1,374,500.00
10.	Energy Efficient Schools Initiative		15,422,800.00
11.	School Nutrition Program		356,355,700.00
12.	Special Education Services		266,039,100.00
13.	Career and Technical Education Programs		24,617,900.00
14.	Alvin C. York Institute		1,054,900.00
15.	Tennessee School for the Blind		913,000.00
16.	Tennessee School for the Deaf		543,400.00
17.	West Tennessee School for the Deaf		222,700.00
18.	Tennessee Early Intervention Services		23,306,600.00
19.	Race to the Top		129,377,700.00

20.	Achievement School District		71,574,000.00
21.	Major Maintenance		90,000.00
	Total Title III-9	$	1,299,696,200.00

10. Higher Education

1.	Tennessee Higher Education Commission	$	17,503,800.00
2.	Tennessee Student Assistance Awards		6,800,000.00
3.	Federal Family Education Loan Program (FFELP)		190,001,900.00
4.	Tennessee Student Assistance Corporation		24,271,900.00
5.	Academic Scholars Program		378,700.00
6.	Loan/Scholarship Programs		2,374,100.00
7.	THEC Grants		1,856,900.00
	Total Title III-10	$	243,187,300.00

11. Department of Commerce and Insurance

1.	Administration	$	6,083,700.00
2.	Insurance		13,334,600.00
3.	Securities		2,216,600.00
4.	Consumer Affairs		82,000.00
5.	TennCare Oversight		2,276,100.00
6.	Fire Prevention		20,743,200.00
7.	Fire Service and Codes Enforcement Academy		953,000.00
8.	Peace Officer Standards and Training (POST) Commission		43,300.00
9.	Tennessee Law Enforcement Training Academy		1,381,900.00
10.	911 Emergency Communications Fund		5,810,500.00
11.	Regulatory Boards		598,700.00
12.	Corrections Institute		60,000.00
	Total Title III-11	$	53,583,600.00

12.	Department of Financial Institutions	$	8,316,000.00
	Total Title III-12	$	8,316,000.00

13. Department of Labor and Workforce Development

1.	Administration	$	7,144,700.00
2.	Tennessee Occupational Safety and Health Administration (TOSHA)		4,437,800.00
3.	Mines		191,300.00
4.	Boilers and Elevators		61,800.00
5.	Labor Standards		197,000.00
6.	Workers' Compensation		183,900.00
7.	Second Injury Fund		275,000.00
8.	Workforce Development		68,422,600.00
9.	Adult Basic Education		11,701,600.00
10.	Employment Security		81,424,500.00
	Total Title III-13	$	174,040,200.00

14. Department of Mental Health and Substance Abuse Services

1.	Administrative Services Division	$	5,093,900.00
2.	Mental Health Services		
	2.1 Community Mental Health Services		18,907,300.00
	2.2 Middle Tennessee Mental Health Institute		14,873,000.00
	2.3 Western Mental Health Institute		13,765,100.00
	2.4 Moccasin Bend Mental Health Institute		11,459,000.00
	2.5 Memphis Mental Health Institute		3,974,700.00
3.	Community Substance Abuse Services		35,540,700.00
	Total Title III-14	$	103,613,700.00

15. Department of Military

1.	Administration	$	962,700.00
2.	Army National Guard		6,008,300.00
3.	Air National Guard		12,554,800.00
4.	Tennessee Emergency Management Agency		10,044,800.00
5.	TEMA Disaster Relief Grants		10,000,000.00
6.	Homeland Security Grants		33,022,800.00
7.	Armories Utilities		4,263,000.00
8.	Armories Maintenance		7,190,200.00
	Total Title III-15	$	84,046,600.00

16. Department of Health

1.	Administration		
	1.1 Executive Administration	$	4,115,900.00
	1.2 Policy Planning and Assessment		7,197,900.00
2.	Manpower Resources and Facilities		
	2.1 Bureau of Health Licensure and Regulation		8,561,000.00
	2.2 Emergency Medical Services		1,430,500.00
	2.3 Laboratory Services		12,447,600.00
	2.4 Health Related Boards		129,000.00
3.	Community Health Services		
	3.1 General Environmental Health		178,600.00
	3.2 Maternal and Child Health		23,441,800.00
	3.3 Communicable and Environmental Disease Services		52,422,100.00
	3.4 Community and Medical Services		10,258,500.00
	3.5 Women, Infants, and Children (WIC)		137,814,700.00
4.	Local Health Services		138,119,700.00
	Total Title III-16	$	396,117,300.00

17. Department of Human Services

1.	Administration		
	1.1 Administration	$	47,250,600.00
	1.2 Field Operations		11,674,400.00
	1.3 County Rentals		11,066,800.00
	1.4 Appeals and Hearings		8,967,700.00
	1.5 Organizational Performance Management		4,057,800.00
2.	Family Assistance Services		
	2.1 Child Support		54,938,700.00
	2.2 Child Care Benefits		178,128,000.00
	2.3 Temporary Cash Assistance		100,841,500.00
	2.4 Food Stamp Benefits		2,043,156,300.00
	2.5 Family Assistance Services		114,372,900.00
3.	Community Services		146,575,900.00
4.	Rehabilitative Services		
	4.1 Vocational Rehabilitation		66,698,500.00
	4.2 Disability Determination		69,389,200.00
	Total Title III-17	$	2,857,118,300.00

18. Department of Revenue

1.	Administration Division	$	2,933,400.00
2.	Tax Enforcement Division		2,976,800.00
3.	Information Technology Resources Division		6,704,200.00
4.	Taxpayer and Vehicle Services Division		3,084,600.00
5.	Processing Division		3,067,800.00
6.	Audit Division		9,504,800.00

	Total Title III-18	$	28,271,600.00
19.	Tennessee Bureau of Investigation	$	29,567,200.00
	Total Title III-19	$	29,567,200.00
20.	Department of Safety		
1.	Administration	$	546,000.00
2.	Driver License Issuance		33,597,800.00
3.	Highway Patrol		13,124,900.00
4.	Auto Theft Investigations		350,000.00
5.	Office of Homeland Security		3,661,300.00
6.	Technical Services		6,912,900.00
	Total Title III-20	$	58,192,900.00
21.	Department of Finance and Administration, Strategic Health-Care Programs		
1.	CoverTN	$	13,982,900.00
2.	CoverKids		176,815,400.00
3.	CoverRX		400,000.00
4.	Health-Care Planning and Innovation		2,716,500.00
	Total Title III-21	$	193,914,800.00
22.	Department of Children's Services		
1.	Administration	$	20,762,300.00
2.	Family Support Services		10,119,800.00
3.	Custody Services		136,686,600.00
4.	Adoption Services		39,761,500.00
5.	Child and Family Management		135,836,100.00
6.	John S. Wilder Youth Development Center		364,500.00
7.	Woodland Hills Youth Development Center		428,100.00
8.	Mountain View Youth Development Center		347,400.00
9.	New Visions Youth Development Center		36,700.00
10.	Major Maintenance		15,000.00
	Total Title III-22	$	344,358,000.00
23.	Department of Intellectual and Developmental Disabilities		
1.	Intellectual Disabilities Services Administration	$	16,599,700.00
2.	Developmental Disabilities Council		1,861,600.00
3.	Community Intellectual Disabilities Services		6,149,400.00
4.	Quality Assurance Program		8,753,600.00
5.	Clover Bottom Developmental Center		14,792,500.00
6.	Greene Valley Developmental Center		49,524,000.00
7.	Harold Jordan Center		2,873,800.00
8.	West Tennessee Regional Office		11,916,100.00
9.	Middle Tennessee Regional Office		9,143,700.00
10.	East Tennessee Regional Office		9,088,900.00
11.	West Tennessee Resource Center		1,455,100.00
12.	Middle Tennessee Resource Center		404,500.00
13.	East Tennessee Resource Center		770,600.00
14.	West Tennessee Community Homes		18,038,900.00
15.	Middle Tennessee Community Homes		2,415,000.00
16.	East Tennessee Community Homes		15,086,200.00
17.	Major Maintenance		30,000.00
	Total Title III-23	$	168,903,600.00
24.	Department of Finance and Administration, Bureau of TennCare		
1.	TennCare Administration	$	146,080,000.00
2.	TennCare Medical Services		5,013,835,900.00

3.	Supplemental Payments		661,919,600.00
4.	Intellectual Disabilities Services		571,298,300.00
5.	Medicare Services		284,706,400.00
	Total Title III-24	$	6,677,840,200.00

25. Department of Transportation

1.	Headquarters	$	68,792,200.00
2.	Bureau of Administration		15,435,000.00
3.	Bureau of Operations		316,800,100.00
4.	Bureau of Engineering		101,023,700.00
5.	Field Engineering		94,668,400.00
6.	Bureau of Environment and Planning		89,574,500.00
7.	Field Construction		312,833,800.00
8.	Field Maintenance Operations		3,963,500.00
	Total Title III-25	$	1,003,091,200.00

26. Facilities Revolving Fund

1.	Facilities Operations	$	53,349,400.00
2.	Facilities Maintenance		4,000,000.00
3.	Leases and Space Planning		49,059,600.00
4.	FRF Capital Projects		930,000.00
5.	FRF Debt Service		23,900,000.00
	Total Title III-26	$	131,239,000.00

27. State Building Commission

1.	Major Maintenance and Equipment	$	150,000.00
	Total Title III-27	$	150,000.00
	Grand Total	$	15,072,042,700.00

REFUND OF RECEIPTS

SECTION 5.

Item 1. There is hereby appropriated the necessary and sufficient sums to refund any collection or part thereof made erroneously or illegally for the use or benefit of the state or any of its departments, institutions, offices or agencies. Such refunds shall be made in accordance with existing law as applicable in any particular case. In case revenues are not adequate to meet in full all appropriations made, the appropriations made for Sinking Fund Debt Service and the amounts necessary to cover the salary and wage obligations of the state shall have preferential payment.

Item 2. With respect to any revenues or receipts collected by any department or agency with the exception of those collected by the Department of Revenue, notwithstanding any provisions of the law to the contrary, such amounts as are determined to have been erroneously paid may be refunded by such procedure as may be approved by the Commissioner of Finance and Administration and the Comptroller of the Treasury.

SECTION 6. In addition to the appropriations made to the State Funding Board in Section 1, Title III-31, of this act, there is appropriated the following items:

Item 1. There is hereby appropriated a sum sufficient from the internal service funds available to the Department of Finance and Administration, Office of Information Resources, to provide the debt service on general obligation bond and note issues authorized in the following amounts:

(1) Chapter 952, Public Acts of 1996	$	20,000,000.00
(2) Chapter 962, Public Acts of 2006	$	26,279,930.67

Item 2.

(a) From the funds appropriated in Section 1, Title III-31, Item 5, Amortization of Authorized and Unissued Highway Bonds, the sum of $76,000,000.00 is appropriated in lieu of issuing highway bonds under the provisions of Chapter 501, Public Acts of 2005; and the sum of $1,000,000 is appropriated in lieu of issuing bonds under the provisions of Chapter 1024, Public Acts of 2012; and the sum of $27,600,000.00 is appropriated in lieu of issuing bonds under the provisions of Chapter 1193, Public Acts of 2008 (State Route 840 bonds). The State Funding Board shall take the necessary action to cancel the unissued bonds.

(b) Chapter 552, Public Acts of 2009, authorized bonds in the amount of $87,500,000 for implementation of Phase I of the Tennessee transportation infrastructure improvement bond program of 2009 to be expended for the construction of bridges and highways. To the extent that bridge projects are converted to federal financing in the fiscal year ending June 30, 2014, the State Funding Board shall take the necessary action to cancel the unissued bridge bonds in an amount equal to the conversion to federal funding.

Item 3. For the purpose of defraying the costs of issuance of debt and the administration of authorized programs of the Tennessee Local Development Authority, there is hereby appropriated to the Tennessee Local Development Authority an amount not to exceed $25,000.00 from the State Loan Program Fund. Such amounts shall be determined as necessary by the State Funding Board and the Tennessee Local Development Authority.

Item 4. From the appropriation made in Section 1, Title III-31, of this act to the State Funding Board, a sum not to exceed $3,900,000 is earmarked to pay debt service on general obligation bonds issued under the authority of Chapter 582, Public Acts of 1996, for the purpose of making a grant to the Metropolitan Government of Nashville and Davidson County for the construction of a sports stadium. It is the legislative intent that said appropriations shall be funded first from the sales tax revenues allocated under the provisions of Tennessee Code Annotated, Section 67-6-103(d)(1), and any revenues in excess of debt service requirements shall be reserved at June 30 and not revert to the fund balance and that said appropriations, to the extent required, shall be funded second from revenues and reserves available to the debt service fund.

Item 5. To provide the debt service on the general obligation bonds authorized under Chapter 313, Public Acts of 2003, there is hereby appropriated a sum sufficient from the funds available to the State Funding Board pursuant to agreements entered into thereunder.

Item 6. From the funds appropriated in Section 1 and Section 4 of this act to the Tennessee Board of Regents for defraying operating expenses in this act and other acts of legislature, with the approval of the State Building Commission a sum sufficient is appropriated to be used for payments to the State Funding Board as required for any debt issued under the authorization of Chapter 313, Public Acts of 2003.

Item 7. From the funds appropriated in Section 1 and Section 4 of this act to the Tennessee Board of Regents for defraying operating expenses in this act and other acts of the legislature for the state technology centers, with the approval of the State Building Commission a sum sufficient is appropriated to be used for payments to the State Funding Board as required for any debt issued in an amount not to exceed $34,000,000 under the authorization of Chapter 470, Public Acts of 2011.

Item 8. From the funds appropriated in Section 1 and Section 4 of this act to the Tennessee Board of Regents for defraying operating expenses in this act and other acts of legislature, with the approval of the State Building Commission a sum sufficient is appropriated to be used for payments to the State Funding Board as required for any debt issued in an amount not to exceed $10,700,000 under the authorization of Chapter 591, Public Acts of 2007.

Item 9. In addition to the appropriations made in Section 1, Title III-31, of this act to the State Funding Board, and to the extent that the board issues any tax revenue anticipation notes pursuant to the provisions of Tennessee Code Annotated, Section 9-10-101, there is hereby appropriated a sum sufficient from subsequently available funds of the state to pay debt service on such notes within the fiscal year of issuance.

Item 10. There is hereby appropriated to the Tennessee State School Bond Authority a sum sufficient in the amount of payments allowable to the Authority from the federal government pursuant to the qualified school construction bond program or similar programs, for purposes of debt service on such bonds.

PUBLIC CHAPTER NO. 453 (cont'd)

Item 11. The provisions of this item shall be effective immediately, the public welfare requiring it. The funding of the appropriations for interest on state debt and retirement of bonds made in Section 1, Title III-31 of this act and in Section 1, Title III-31 of Chapter 1029, Public Acts of 2012, includes an allocation of motor vehicle title fees to the debt service fund in the amount of $2,700,000. The allocation is made from the sum generated by the $1.50 motor vehicle title fee imposed under the provisions of Tennessee Code Annotated, Section 55-6-101(a)(1).

It is the legislative intent to recognize that the revenue generated from the $1.50 fee is earmarked for the purpose of paying the principal and interest on bonds authorized in the amount of $5,000,000.00 and issued pursuant to the provisions of Chapter 1028, Public Acts of 1992. Any funds in excess of the amount so required are earmarked for the purpose of paying the principal and interest on general obligation bonds authorized to fund capital projects at state parks in the following amounts:

(1) Chapter 528, Public Acts of 1993	$20,000,000.00
(2) Chapter 850, Public Acts of 1994	$34,415,000.00
(3) Chapter 945, Public Acts of 1996	$14,000,000.00
(4) Chapter 952, Public Acts of 1996	$10,100,000.00
(5) Chapter 990, Public Acts of 1996	$16,000,000.00

Item 12. From the funds appropriated in Section 1, Title III-31, Item 4, of this act, for Amortization of Authorized and Unissued Construction Bonds, the sum of $7,000,000.00 is appropriated in lieu of issuing bonds for the interoperable communication system upgrade under the provisions of Chapter 1024, Public Acts of 2012. The State Funding Board shall take the necessary action to cancel unissued bonds.

Item 13. There is hereby appropriated a sum sufficient from general fund interest earnings for the purpose of funding the State of Tennessee's liability under IRS regulations for arbitrage interest earnings on proceeds from general obligation debt.

Item 14. For the purpose of defraying administrative costs of authorized programs of the Tennessee Local Development Authority, there is hereby appropriated to the Tennessee Local Development Authority an amount not to exceed $700,000 from loan repayment amounts attributable to community provider loans. Such amounts shall be determined as necessary by the State Funding Board and the Tennessee Local Development Authority.

SECTION 7.

The appropriations made by this act under Sections 1 and 4 shall be subject to the following provisions, limitations, or restrictions. From the funds appropriated to the:

Item 1. It is the legislative intent that annual dues assessed by the Council of State Governments (CSG), the National Conference of State Legislatures (NCSL), and the National Conference of Insurance Legislators be paid timely from the funds appropriated in Section 1, Title III-22, Item 17, for Intergovernmental Conference Dues in the following amounts: (a) CSG, $166,318; (b) NCSL, $207,918; and National Conference of Insurance Legislators, $10,000.

Item 2. The appropriation made in Section 1, Title II, Item 6, of this act, for Civil Legal Representation shall be adjusted to an amount equal to the revenue collected in the fiscal year ending June 30, 2013, from the earmarked litigation tax levied pursuant to Tennessee Code Annotated, Section 67-4-602(g) and Section 16-3-808.

In addition to the preceding appropriation, there is hereby appropriated a sum sufficient not to exceed the revenue collected in the fiscal year ending June 30, 2013, from the earmarked bail bond tax levied pursuant to Tennessee Code Annotated, Section 67-4-806, for the purpose of developing and providing continuing education for professional Bail Bonding Agents and providing civil legal representation to low-income Tennesseans.

Item 3. From the appropriation made for the State Election Commission under Section 1, Title III-1, Item 3.2, there is hereby appropriated funds for expenses of the State Election Commission, including the printing of election laws, the office of the Coordinator of Elections, and other expenses of administering election laws. The salary of each member of the State Election Commission shall be six thousand eight hundred fifty-seven dollars and fourteen cents ($6,857.14) annually. The Secretary of State is hereby authorized to make all necessary purchases of election supplies from funds appropriated for such purpose in accordance with state purchasing procedures. The provisions of this item relative to the salary of State Election Commission members shall be effective immediately, the public welfare requiring it, and notwithstanding the contrary provisions of Public Acts of 2012, Chapter 1028, Section 7, Item 2.

Item 4. From the funds appropriated to the Office of the Comptroller of the Treasury and the Department of Finance and Administration, there is hereby authorized to be allocated an amount not to exceed $45,000.00 for the purpose of meeting the State of Tennessee's participation in the cost of supporting the National Council on Governmental Accounting or a governmental accounting standards board in the establishment of governmental accounting standards and principles.

Item 5. Department of Treasury, Criminal Injuries Compensation Fund, there is appropriated a sum not to exceed $256,100 from the Criminal Injuries Compensation Fund for grants to the District Attorneys General for domestic violence prevention and drug enforcement activities authorized under Tennessee Code Annotated, Section 29-13-116.

Item 6. Maintenance of the Tennessee Residence in the amount of sixty thousand dollars ($60,000.00) per year, and travel expenses as certified by the Governor, shall be paid by the Commissioner of Finance and Administration from the appropriations made under Section 1, Title III-2, Item 1.1, for the Governor's Office, it being the legislative intent that the residence should be maintained and operated as the official residence and office of the Chief Executive of Tennessee in a manner required of the Office of Governor.

Item 7. Arts Commission in Section 1, Title III-2, Item 2.8, the sum of $80,000.00 is hereby appropriated for the purpose of making a grant to Fisk University for the necessary staff, services and other costs associated with maintaining and showing the Stieglitz Collection at Fisk University. It is the legislative intent that this appropriation is a direct appropriation grant and that it be processed accordingly by the Commissioner of Finance and Administration. This appropriation is made under the provisions of Tennessee Code Annotated, Section 4-20-202.

Item 8. From the appropriation to the Arts Commission in Section 1, Title III-2, Item 2.8, an amount of $100,000 is for the purpose of a grant to the Tennessee Performing Arts Center Management Corporation for educational activities.

Item 9. From the appropriation to the Arts Commission in Section 1, Title III-2, Item 2.8, an amount of $45,000 is for the purpose of a grant to Africa in April Cultural Awareness Festival, Inc., to support the Africa in April Cultural Awareness Festival.

Item 10. Department of Finance and Administration in Section 1, Title III-2, Item 3.5, there is hereby earmarked a sum sufficient from the proceeds of the $15.00 privilege tax on marriage licenses for purposes of funding family violence shelters and shelter services. This appropriation is made under the provisions of Tennessee Code Annotated, Section 67-4-411.

Item 11. From the appropriations to the Environmental Protection Fund in Section 1, Title III-5, the sum of $5,280,000 is from revenues available to the Environmental Protection Fund pursuant to Tennessee Code Annotated, Title 68, Chapter 203, from funds paid by the Tennessee Valley Authority (TVA) pursuant to a Consent Decree regarding air emissions in Tennessee. Departmental revenues shall be adjusted accordingly. These funds shall be exempt from and shall not be considered in the calculations required by § 68-203-104(b), (c), or (d). These funds shall be available for the purpose of funding energy conservation, alternative energy and/or pollution prevention projects and any other projects authorized by the Consent Decree.

Item 12. Department of Correction in Section 1, Title III-7, Item 5, the department is authorized to make a grant of up to $182,000 to "Project Return."

Item 13. Department of Correction in Section 1, Title III-7, Item 5, the sum of $136,500 is for the sole purpose of making a grant in such amount to DISMAS, Inc., to be used for assisting with their programs in the State of Tennessee, and for no other purpose. From the funds appropriated to DISMAS, Inc., there is earmarked the sum of $25,000 to Chattanooga Endeavors (formerly DISMAS House of Chattanooga) and $8,000 to Better Decisions (formerly DECISIONS, a program of the DISMAS, Inc., home office) for the sole purpose of maintaining operations at their former level.

Item 14. The appropriation to the Department of Correction, Sex Offender Treatment Program in Section 1, Title III-7, Item 6, is made pursuant to Tennessee Code Annotated, Section 39-13-709.

Item 15. Department of Economic and Community Development, Innovation Programs, in Section 1, Title III-8, Item 3, the amount of $100,000.00 is to be paid to the Nashville Minority Business Center and the amount of $100,000.00 is to be paid to the Minority Enterprise Development as direct appropriation grants.

Item 16. Commission on Fire Fighting Personnel Standards and Education in Section 1, Title III-11, Item 6, funds are earmarked for payment to eligible units of local government to pay bonus supplements to firefighters who successfully complete during calendar year 2013 an in-service training program appropriate to such firefighter's rank and responsibility and the size and location of the department of at least forty (40) hours duration at a school established or certified by such commission. The funds appropriated by this item shall be disbursed in accordance with the provisions of Tennessee Code Annotated, Title 4, Chapter 24 and Section 56-4-205(c), and no supplement to any person shall exceed six hundred dollars ($600.00).

Item 17. Peace Officer Standards and Training (POST) Commission in Section 1, Title III-11, Item 7, funds are earmarked for payment to eligible units of local government which have required all police officers to complete during calendar year 2013 an in-service training course appropriate to each officer's rank and responsibility commensurate with the size and location of the department of at least forty (40) hours duration at a school certified or recognized by the POST Commission. The funds appropriated by this item shall be disbursed in accordance with the provisions of Tennessee Code Annotated, Title 38, Chapter 8, Part 1, and no recipient shall be eligible to receive a supplement of more than six hundred dollars ($600.00).

Item 18. Department of Health in Section 1, Title III-16, Item 3.4, the amount of $113,700 is to be paid to St. Jude Hospital in Memphis to defray, in whole or in part, the expenses of patients and their families who are citizens and residents of Tennessee in traveling to and from St. Jude Hospital. Such payments shall be administered by the hospital and shall be made on the basis of need. Such patients, or their families, requesting assistance from these funds shall supply such documents supporting need and travel expenses as the hospital may require.

Item 19. In the fiscal year ending June 30, 2014, it is the legislative intent that the sum of two million dollars ($2,000,000) be credited to the Health Access Incentive Account pursuant to Tennessee Code Annotated, Section 66-29-121, and that $1,000,000 of the appropriation made in Section 4, Title III-16, of this act be funded from the program's reserve balance.

Item 20. From the appropriation to the Department of Health in Section 1, Title III-16 of this act, there is appropriated the sum of $50,000 for the sole purpose of contracting with a nonprofit organization for promotion of health awareness among Tennessee males. Such nonprofit organization must have been established prior to January 1, 2004; must have received a contract administered through the Tennessee Department of Health; must have received funding through the vitamin supplement settlement of June 2003, administered by the Tennessee attorney general's office; and must possess substantial experience with general health outreach and education activities for males in Tennessee, including activities for the general population and the underserved living in Tennessee.

Item 21. The appropriations made in Section 1, Title III-22, Items 18 and 19, of this act to the UT Center for Business and Economic Research are reimbursement for research assistance to the Department of Finance and Administration ($159,200) and for services delivered under the state data contract with the U.S. Census Bureau ($278,000).

Item 22. From the appropriation in Section 1, Title III-27, for the Emergency and Contingency Fund, there is hereby appropriated an amount not to exceed three hundred nineteen thousand three hundred dollars ($319,300.00) for the following purposes: (1) forest fire control in the Division of Forestry, (2) payment of indemnities for destruction of livestock and extraordinary veterinary payrolls for cattle market fluctuations by the Department of Agriculture, (3) payment of extraordinary expenditures for insect and pest control efforts by the Department of Agriculture, and (4) the cost of personnel and equipment needed to restore law and order in instances arising out of civil disorders.

SECTION 8. In addition to the appropriations made in Section 1 of this act and subject to the provisions of Tennessee Code Annotated, Title 4, Chapter 3, Part 10 and Title 9, Chapter 4, Part 51, there is hereby appropriated a sum sufficient:

Item 1. To pay all lawful claims due from the state to any of the several counties thereof on account of unpaid court costs, unpaid allotments of taxes distributable by the state to the counties and such other sums as may be due from the state to the counties, but none of such funds shall be distributed to the counties of the state until after the validity of the claims has been investigated and approved by the State Comptroller and the Governor. Provided, however, that such funds shall not include funds due to counties and cities for the state share of costs to cities and counties as required by Section 24, Article II, of the Constitution of Tennessee.

Item 2. From the appropriations in Sections 1 and 4 of this act, for state agencies to pay the professional privilege tax levied in Tennessee Code Annotated, Title 67, Chapter 4, Part 17, on behalf of full-time state employees who are subject to the tax; and who use the certification in their job duties. The payment is subject to approval by the department or agency head in accordance with the provisions of Tennessee Code Annotated, Section 67-4-1709.

Item 3. For the purpose of implementing an employee maintenance policy by the Department of Finance and Administration. It is the legislative intent to hold harmless, employees affected by the maintenance policy who were employed as of June 30, 1998. The Commissioner of Finance and Administration is authorized to allocate the appropriation to the appropriate organizational units and programs of state government and to adjust federal aid and departmental revenue allotments accordingly.

Item 4. Settlement and Judgment Awards and Similar Awards. To affected state agencies, such sums as are received by the Attorney General and Reporter or other state officials and agencies in settlements and judgments and similar awards for the purposes received, as determined by the Attorney General and Reporter in accordance with such settlements and judgments. The Commissioner of Finance and Administration shall classify such funds as are received in accordance with generally accepted accounting principles and, as advised by the Attorney General and Reporter, is authorized to allot such funds for expenditure by the appropriate departments and organizational units of state government. This appropriation shall not include any amounts of a settlement, judgment, or award not required to be set-aside or expended for a specific purpose, nor any amounts intended to reimburse or benefit the general fund, and such revenue hereby expressly is not appropriated. The Attorney General and Reporter shall file a written quarterly report with the Speaker of the Senate, the Speaker of the House of Representatives and the Office of Legislative Budget Analysis upon receipt of any settlement or judgment in excess of $1,000,000; such report shall specify the nature of the settlement or judgment, the amount of the settlement or judgment and the purposes for which any such settlement or judgment funds are received.

Item 5. From general fund interest earnings for the purpose of funding the state's liability for the exchange of interest with the federal government as provided for in the Cash Management Act of 1990.

Item 6. From earmarked and/or dedicated agency revenues and reserves to provide for the costs of implementing the state's Underground Storage Tanks Program. The Commissioner of Finance and Administration shall allocate the costs to the individual agencies and establish the appropriations required from revenues and reserves available to the individual agencies.

Item 7. To the Tennessee Code Commission for the following purposes: (1) to purchase pocket supplements for the state-owned sets of Tennessee Code Annotated; (2) to purchase replacement volumes for state-owned sets of Tennessee Code Annotated; (3) to purchase replacement sets of Tennessee Code Annotated; (4) to purchase sets of Tennessee Code Annotated for judges of new courts created during the 2013 Session of the General Assembly; (5) to purchase pocket supplements for the state-owned sets of the Index to the Private Acts of Tennessee; and (6) to pay for proofreading and other expenses involved in preparing supplements and replacement volumes for Tennessee Code Annotated.

Item 8. To pay the salaries and travel expenses of all persons appointed to sit as Special Judges, Special District Attorneys General and/or Special Prosecutors under statutes relating to the state judicial system.

Item 9. To provide for indigent defendants counsel in capital cases.

Item 10. To pay fees of special counsel who may be employed by the Governor on recommendation of the Attorney General, in accordance with Tennessee Code Annotated, Section 8-6-106, and to pay other expenses in special cases of litigation involving the state. In matters involving the Tennessee Regulatory Authority, Housing Development Agency,

PUBLIC CHAPTER NO. 453 (cont'd)

Wildlife Resources Agency, Department of Financial Institutions, regulatory boards and other programs and agencies funded by earmarked or dedicated revenues, the sum sufficient appropriation shall be provided from said earmarked or dedicated revenues. In matters involving departments, agencies and/or programs funded in whole or in part with federal aid and/or departmental revenues and reserves, the sum sufficient appropriation may be provided in whole or in part from said revenues and reserves.

Item 11. To the Administrative Office of the Courts from revenues and reserves available to the following programs:

(a) "Divorcing Parent Education and Mediation Fund" and the "Marriage License Tax" pursuant to Tennessee Code Annotated, Section 36-6-413(b)(2).

(b) Tennessee Judicial Information System Fund pursuant to Tennessee Code Annotated, Section 16-3-807.

(c) Board of Professional Responsibility, Tennessee Lawyers Assistance Programs, Continuing Legal Education and Client Protection Fund. Additional positions as required are authorized to be established.

(d) Municipal Court Judges and Municipal Court Clerks Training and Continuing Legal Education pursuant to Tennessee Code Annotated, Section 16-18-304.

(e) General Sessions Judges' Conference pursuant to Tennessee Code Annotated, Section 16-15-5007 and Section 67-4-606(a)(9), to defray expenses of serving the general sessions courts.

(f) Board of Court Reporting pursuant to Tennessee Code Annotated, Section 20-9-616.

(g) Judicial Commissioner Continuing Education Account pursuant to Tennessee Code Annotated, Section 67-4-602(k)(5).

Item 12. To the Attorney General and Reporter from the revenues and reserves available to the following programs:

(a) False Claims Act Fund established pursuant to Tennessee Code Annotated, Section 4-18-104(j). The Commissioner of Finance and Administration is authorized to adjust the appropriation made under Section 1, Title III-1, Item 1.1, of this act to recognize any reimbursement for expenses already provided.

(b) Reserve for Attorney General Litigation Settlement. The Commissioner of Finance and Administration is authorized to establish positions as may be required.

Item 13. To the District Attorneys General Conference from the revenues and reserves of the district attorneys expunction fund created by Tennessee Code Annotated, Section 40-32-101(g)(11), for the purposes therein specified.

Item 14. To the District Public Defenders Conference from the revenues and reserves of the public defenders expunction fund created by Tennessee Code Annotated, Section 40-32-101(g)(12), for the purposes therein specified.

Item 15. To provide for payment of administrative law judge services. The Commissioner of Finance and Administration is authorized to allocate the funds to the appropriate organizational units, adjust departmental revenues accordingly, and establish authorized positions.

Item 16. To the Comptroller of the Treasury from the Telecommunications Ad Valorem Tax Reduction Fund to provide for the administration of the program and payments from the fund as provided by law. The Commissioner of Finance and Administration is authorized to reduce the appropriation made in Section 1, Title III-1, Item 5.13 to the amount of taxes apportioned for this purpose, if the apportionment is less than the appropriation.

Item 17. To the Tennessee Local Development Authority a sum sufficient from the Underground Storage Tank Fund for the purpose of paying debt service and expenses in connection with any debt issued pursuant to the provisions of Chapter 444, Public Acts of 1997, relative to underground storage tanks.

Item 18. To the Treasury Department, Small and Minority-Owned Business Assistance Program, from funds allocated to the program pursuant to Tennessee Code Annotated, Section 65-5-113.

Item. 19. To Claims and Compensation, in Section 1, Title I-1, Item 8.2, Unclaimed Property for payment of an audit settlement fee. The appropriation may be increased or decreased to reflect the actual fee to be paid.

Item 20. To the Tennessee Advisory Commission on Intergovernmental Relations (TACIR) from the TACIR reserves authorized by Tennessee Code Annotated, Section 4-10-107. The Commissioner of Finance and Administration is authorized to adjust departmental revenues accordingly, and establish authorized positions as needed.

Item 21. To the Office for Information Resources from the general obligation bonds/notes authorized under Chapter 952, Public Acts of 1996, for data processing services and telecommunications services; and from the general obligation bonds/notes authorized under Chapter 962, Public Acts of 2006, for the purpose of acquisition and implementation of enterprise resource planning software.

Item 22. From revenues collected from accounts receivable, to provide for a consultant's services in review of accounts receivable management for the State of Tennessee and for the implementation of those recommendations to the extent the recommendations are approved by the Commissioner of Finance and Administration. The Commissioner of Finance and Administration may establish such positions as may be required to cost-effectively implement such recommendation. The Commissioner also is authorized to allocate a portion of the revenues collected to the appropriate organizational units and programs of state government and to adjust federal aid and other departmental revenue accordingly. Each allocation shall be a one-time incentive to maximize accounts receivable collections and shall be used to fund non-recurring items only.

Item 23. To the Department of Finance and Administration to reimburse the federal government for arbitrage on the state's general obligation debt.

Item 24. To the Department of Finance and Administration from revenues and reserves available to the following programs:

(a) To provide funding for the additional sexual assault program services pursuant to Tennessee Code Annotated, Title 71, Chapter 6, Part 3. Any unexpended funds shall not revert to the general fund balance at June 30 and are hereby reappropriated in the subsequent fiscal year.

(b) To provide funding for family violence shelters and shelter services pursuant to Tennessee Code Annotated, Section 39-13-101. Any unexpended funds shall not revert to the general fund at June 30 and are hereby reappropriated in the subsequent fiscal year.

(c) To provide funding from the revenues apportioned to the Domestic Violence Community Education Fund pursuant to Tennessee Code Annotated, Section 36-3-616.

(d) To provide funding from the litigation tax apportioned to fund grants to local governments to purchase and maintain electronic fingerprint imaging systems pursuant to Tennessee Code Annotated, Section 67-4-602.

(e) To provide funding for grant awards to local law enforcement agencies for purposes of obtaining and maintaining equipment and personnel needed in the enforcement of alcohol related traffic offenses and for the purpose of funding grant awards to halfway houses whose primary focus is to assist drug and alcohol offenders pursuant to Tennessee Code Annotated, Section 55-10-403(t)(3)(D) and (F). Any unexpended funds shall not revert to the general fund at June 30 and are hereby reappropriated in the subsequent fiscal year.

Item 25. To the Department of Agriculture from revenues and reserves available to the following programs:

(a) Agricultural Resources Conservation Fund pursuant to Tennessee Code Annotated, Section 67-4-409(l).

(b) Agricultural Regulatory Fund pursuant to Tennessee Code Annotated, Title 43, Chapter 1, Part 7.

(c) Certified Cotton Growers' Organization Fund pursuant to Tennessee Code Annotated, Title 43, Chapter 6, Part 4.

(d) Tennessee Grain Indemnity Fund pursuant to Tennessee Code Annotated, Title 43, Chapter 32, Part 2.

(e) Market Development, Agricultural Development Fund pursuant to Tennessee Code Annotated, Section 55-4-267.

(f) Division of Forestry, from the proceeds of revenue allocated pursuant to Tennessee Code Annotated, Section 11-14-305(b)(3), pertaining to the sale and replacement of real property.

(g) Division of Regulatory Services a sum sufficient pursuant to Tennessee Code Annotated, Section 47-18-1311, pertaining to kerosene and motor fuels quality inspection.

(h) Beef Promotion Board pursuant to Tennessee Code Annotated, Sections 43-29-109 and 43-29-118.

Item 26. To the Department of Environment and Conservation from revenues and reserves available to the following programs:

(a) Local Park Land Acquisition Fund, State Lands Acquisition Fund, and State Lands Compensation Fund pursuant to Tennessee Code Annotated, Sections 67-4-409(i) and 67-4-409(j).

(b) Heritage Conservation Trust Fund pursuant to Tennessee Code Annotated, Section 11-7-103.

(c) State parks program from revenues derived from nonprofit support groups pursuant to Tennessee Code Annotated, Title 11, Chapter 3, Part 2.

(d) State Park Fund pursuant to Tennessee Code Annotated, Title 11, Chapter 3, Part 3.

(e) From revenues derived from the sale of Tennessee Elk River Development Agency lands. This appropriation is subject to approval by the Commissioner of Finance and Administration.

(f) Environmental Protection Fund pursuant to Tennessee Code Annotated, Title 68, Chapter 203, Part 1. Departmental revenues shall be adjusted accordingly.

(g) Radiation Reclamation Trust Fund and the Perpetual Care Trust Fund pursuant to Tennessee Code Annotated, Section 68-202-405.

(h) Solid Waste Assistance program from revenues received pursuant to Tennessee Code Annotated, Title 67, Chapter 4, Part 16 and Title 68, Chapter 211, Part 8.

(i) Used Oil Collection Fund pursuant to Tennessee Code Annotated, Section 68-211-1004.

(j) Hazardous Waste Remedial Action Fund pursuant to Tennessee Code Annotated, Title 68, Chapter 212, Part 2.

(k) Petroleum Underground Storage Tank Fund pursuant to Tennessee Code Annotated, Title 68, Chapter 215, Part 1.

(l) Drycleaner Environmental Response Fund pursuant to Tennessee Code Annotated, Title 68, Chapter 217, Part 1.

(m) Solid Waste Disposal Site Restoration Fund pursuant to Tennessee Code Annotated, Section 68-211-116.

(n) Hazardous Waste Trust Fund pursuant to Tennessee Code Annotated, Section 68-212-108.

Item 27. To the Wildlife Resources Agency from revenues available to the Wetlands Acquisition Fund and the Wetlands Compensation Fund pursuant to Tennessee Code Annotated, Section 67-4-409(g).

Item 28. To the Wildlife Resources Agency from the general fund for any difference between the actual charges to the agency under the indirect cost allocation plan and the amount the TWRA can justify and continue to receive federal funds.

Item 29. To the Wildlife Resources Agency from its own revenues to implement the programs, activities and projects approved by the Wildlife Resources Agency Commission. The Commissioner of Finance and Administration is authorized to adjust departmental revenue accordingly and to establish positions as may be required.

Item 30. To the Department of Correction from the reserves for parole and probation supervision and rehabilitation fees pursuant to Tennessee Code Annotated, Section 40-28-203(c).

Item 31. To the Department of Correction from revenues and reserves available for the following programs:

(a) Sex Offender Treatment Program pursuant to Tennessee Code Annotated, Section 39-13-709.

(b) Supervision and rehabilitation fees pursuant to Tennessee Code Annotated, Section 40-28-203(c).

Item 32. To the Department of Economic and Community Development, in addition to the appropriation in Section 1, Title III-8, Item 4, for the headquarters relocation assistance program pursuant to Tennessee Code Annotated, Section 67-4-2109(g)(2).

Item 33. In the fiscal years ending June 30, 2013 and 2014, there are hereby appropriated sums sufficient from the unexpended balances of prior year accrued liabilities for the Special Schools and Tennessee Early Intervention Services. The Commissioner of Finance and Administration shall determine the amounts of appropriations to be established pursuant to the requirements of Tennessee Code Annotated, Section 49-50-1002(b)(2). These appropriations are in addition to appropriations made to the Department of Education in Section 1, Title III-9 of the 2012 Appropriations Act and elsewhere in this act. The provisions of this item shall be effective immediately, the public welfare requiring it.

Item 34. In the fiscal years ending June 30, 2013 and 2014, there are hereby appropriated sums sufficient in amounts equal to the unexpended balances of prior year accrued liabilities in the following education programs: (a) Safe Schools Act of 1998; (b) State testing programs; and (c) Governor's Schools. These appropriations are in addition to the appropriations made to the Department of Education in Section 1, Title III-9 of the 2012 Appropriations Act and elsewhere in this act. The provisions of this item shall be effective immediately, the public welfare requiring it.

Item 35. To the Department of Commerce and Insurance, Division of Regulatory Boards, from revenues and reserves available for the following purposes:

(a) To purchase examinations for regulatory boards. This appropriation is contingent upon the fees collected for giving examinations being in excess of the budgeted estimates.

(b) To fund data processing systems development and implementation. Said appropriations are made pursuant to Tennessee Code Annotated, Section 4-3-1011.

(c) To the Real Estate Education and Recovery Fund, to provide for court-ordered payments and to print and distribute to all licensees a manual of laws and rules and regulations.

(d) To the Auctioneer Education and Recovery Fund, to provide for court-ordered payments.

(e) To the Cemetery Consumer Protection Fund pursuant to Tennessee Code Annotated, Section 46-1-105.

(f) To the Pre-Need Funeral Consumer Protection Fund pursuant to Tennessee Code Annotated, Section 62-5-414. The Commissioner of Finance and Administration is authorized to make transfers from the Pre-Need Funeral Consumer Protection Fund to the Burial Services program in the Division of Regulatory Boards.

Item 36. To the Department of Commerce and Insurance, 911 Emergency Communications Fund, from the revenues collected pursuant to Tennessee Code Annotated, Title 7, Chapter 86, Part 3.

Item 37. To the Department of Labor and Workforce Development from revenues and reserves available to the following programs:

(a) Uninsured Employers Fund program pursuant to Tennessee Code Annotated, Section 50-6-801.

(b) Tennessee Occupational Safety and Health Administration (TOSHA) program pursuant to Tennessee Code Annotated, Title 50, Chapter 6, Part 4.

(c) Boilers and Elevators pursuant to Tennessee Code Annotated, Section 68-121-108, Section 68-121-117 and Section 68-122-205. Appropriations established under this authority shall be in lieu of the departmental revenue appropriation in Section 4, Title III-13, Item 4, of this act.

(d) Lawful Employment Enforcement Fund pursuant to Tennessee Code Annotated, Section 50-1-708.

(e) Workers' Compensation Employee Misclassification and Enforcement Fund pursuant to Tennessee Code Annotated, Section 50-6-913.

(f) Unemployment Compensation Administration Fund pursuant to Tennessee Code Annotated, Section 50-7-502.

Item 38. To the Department of Mental Health and Substance Abuse Services from the revenues and reserves available to the following programs:

(a) Alcohol and Drug Addiction Treatment Fund pursuant to Tennessee Code Annotated, Section 40-33-211(c)(2).

(b) Drug Court Treatment Program Resources Fund to provide funding to establish drug courts pursuant to Tennessee Code Annotated, Title 16, Chapter 22, Part 1.

Item 39. To the Department of Military to provide for the cost of personnel and equipment needed to maintain law and order in instances arising out of civil disorders.

Item 40. To the Department of Military, Disaster Relief Grants, for the purpose of matching federal funds and to the Department of Military to pay the administrative costs of the Disaster Relief Program. Said appropriations shall be made first from the Reserve for Disaster Relief, and they are in addition to the appropriation made in Section 1, Title III-15, Item 5, of this act. Federal aid and other departmental revenue may be adjusted accordingly.

Any unexpended funds remaining in the Reserve for Disaster Relief or from the appropriation made in Section 1, Title III-15, Item 5, of this act, other acts of this General Assembly or acts by previous General Assemblies shall not revert to the general fund balance at June 30.

Item 41. To the Department of Health from revenues and reserves available to the following programs:

(a) Nursing Home Resident Protection Trust Fund pursuant to Tennessee Code Annotated, Section 68-11-827.

(b) Health Access Incentive Account, pursuant to Tennessee Code Annotated, Sections 66-29-121 and 66-29-151.

(c) Child Safety Fund pursuant to Tennessee Code Annotated, Section 55-9-602(f)(7).

(d) Medicaid Nursing Home Trust Fund pursuant to Federal Regulations, Chapter 42, Section 488.442.

(e) Traumatic Brain Injury Fund to allow for the provision of enhanced and/or new services which benefit traumatic brain injury persons and their families as authorized in Tennessee Code Annotated, Title 68, Chapter 55, Part 4. Any additional appropriations provided under this item are non-recurring from carry-forward funds which exist in the Traumatic Brain Injury Fund and are subject to approval of the Commissioner of Finance and Administration.

(f) Health Related Boards, for data processing systems development and implementation costs and for the cost of investigations and subsequent prosecution of licensees in violation of their practice acts. Said appropriations are made pursuant to Tennessee Code Annotated, Section 4-3-1011.

(g) Commercial Breeder Act pursuant to Tennessee Code Annotated, Title 44, Chapter 17, Part 7.

Item 42. To the Department of Health to provide funding from the reserve for the State Health Planning Division, pursuant to Tennessee Code Annotated, Section 68-11-1625.

Item 43. To the Department of Revenue to pay interest, attorney fees and other costs which are due with certain taxpayer refund payments.

Item 44. To the Department of Revenue from the C.I.D. Anti-Theft reserve fund pursuant to Tennessee Code Annotated, Section 55-3-208.

Item 45. To the Department of Revenue, Administration Division, from proceeds resulting from investigation and enforcement of state tobacco laws.

Item 46. To the Department of Revenue for sales tax disaster relief payments made pursuant to Tennessee Code Annotated, Section 67-6-396. Said appropriations shall be made first from the Department of Revenue unencumbered balance reserve for sales tax disaster relief, and they are in addition to the appropriation made in Section 1, Title III-18, Item 8, of this act. The provisions of this item shall be effective immediately, the public welfare requiring it.

Item 47. To the Department of Revenue, in addition to the appropriation in Section 1, Title III-18, Item 9, Tax Refund Interest Expense, for interest due to taxpayers on tax refunds pursuant to Tennessee Code Annotated, Section 67-1-801(b)(1).

Item 48. To the Tennessee Bureau of Investigation from revenues and reserves available to the following programs:

(a) For the purpose of maintaining the expunged criminal offender and pretrial diversion database and other systems pursuant to Tennessee Code Annotated, Section 40-32-101(d)(2).

(b) From annual revenues collected pursuant to Tennessee Code Annotated, Section 40-32-101(g)(10) to defray the costs incurred from the additional expunction petitions filed and granted as the result of the provisions of Tennessee Code Annotated, Section 40-32-101(g); provided, however, that pursuant to the law, these revenues are not reserved.

(c) TBI Toxicology Unit Intoxicant Testing Fund pursuant to Tennessee Code Annotated, Section 55-10-419.

Item 49. To the Department of Safety from revenues and reserves available to the following programs:

(a) Motorcycle Rider Safety reserve fund pursuant to Tennessee Code Annotated, Section 55-51-104.

(b) Driver Education reserve fund pursuant to Tennessee Code Annotated, Section 67-4-606(a)(2)(B).

Item 50. To the Department of Transportation for payments to the Risk Management Fund. Said appropriation shall be made from the highway fund balance.

Item 51. To the Department of Transportation, for the Air, Water and Rail Transportation program, from the Transportation Equity Fund. This appropriation is subject to the availability of revenue in the fund.

Item 52. To the Department of Transportation, in addition to the appropriations made in Section 1, Title III-30, for highway maintenance and state highway construction such amount as the Commissioner of Finance and Administration shall determine is available from tax revenues allocated to the highway fund and from the highway fund balance.

Item 53. From the revenues and reserves of the interlock assistance fund created pursuant to Tennessee Code Annotated, Section 55-10-403, in the amounts allocated to the departments of Finance and Administration, Mental Health and Substance Abuse Services, and Safety, as follows:

(a) To the Department of Finance and Administration, Office of Criminal Justice Programs, for grants to local law enforcement agencies for obtaining and maintaining equipment and personnel for alcohol-related offenses;

(b) To the Department of Mental Health and Substance Abuse Services, Community Substance Abuse Services, for the alcohol and drug addiction treatment fund; and

(c) To the Department of Safety from its revenues pursuant to the cited law, to defray its expense of administering the program.

The provisions of this item shall take effect upon becoming law, the public welfare requiring it.

SECTION 9. In addition to the appropriations made in Section 4 of this act and subject to the provisions of Tennessee Code Annotated, Title 4, Chapter 3, Part 10 and Title 9, Chapter 4, Part 51, there is hereby appropriated a sum sufficient:

Item 1. To the Attorney General and Reporter, if the appropriation made in Section 4, Title III-1, Item 1.1, shall prove inadequate to allow the Attorney General and Reporter to represent the state agencies and officials before the Claims Commission, or state agencies and officials in other cases of litigation or other legal matters. The Commissioner of Finance and Administration, upon the request of the Attorney General and Reporter, is hereby authorized to increase the departmental revenue estimate by an amount sufficient to provide for such representation and to establish positions as may be required.

Item 2. To the Attorney General and Reporter a sum sufficient from the Risk Management Fund for the purposes of implementing the provisions of Tennessee Code Annotated, Title 8, Chapter 42, relative to legal representation for state employees. The Commissioner of Finance and Administration, upon the request of the Attorney General and Reporter, is authorized to establish positions as may be required to implement the provisions of Tennessee Code Annotated, Title 8, Chapter 42, Part 1.

Item 3. To the Bureau of Ethics and Campaign Finance from fees collected by the agency.

Item 4. To the Secretary of State, Help America Vote Act program, in Section 4, Title III-1, Item 3.7, from the state reserve for the Help America Vote Act for the purpose of matching federal funds.

Item 5. To the Office of the District Public Defenders Conference pursuant to Tennessee Code Annotated, Section 40-14-210. Additional positions as required are authorized to be established.

Item 6. To the State Treasurer, with the concurrence of the Speaker of the Senate and the Speaker of the House of Representatives, for the purpose of developing and implementing programs designed to enhance investment and pensions administration performance, including programs designed to recruit, hire, and retain qualified investment and administrative staff. The State Treasurer, with approval from the Commissioner of Finance and Administration, is further authorized to establish additional positions and funding for such positions needed to effectuate the purposes of this section.

Item 7. To the State Treasurer, Unclaimed Property, for payment of claims and claims administrative expense.

PUBLIC CHAPTER NO. 453 (cont'd)

Item 8. To the State Treasurer from the revolving account created pursuant to Tennessee Code Annotated, Section 9-4-603(g).

Item 9. To the Treasury Department from revenues and reserves available to the Financial Literacy Program pursuant to Tennessee Code Annotated, Section 49-6-1706.

Item 10. To the Department of Treasury from the earnings of the funds of the Tennessee Consolidated Retirement System for implementation of project CONCORD as authorized in TCA 8-34-321; provided, however, that said sum sufficient shall be subject to the approval of the Commissioner of Finance and Administration. The State Treasurer shall file a request to establish such sum sufficient with the Commissioner of Finance and Administration and the Chair and Vice Chair of the Council on Pensions and Insurance. The Commissioner of Finance and Administration shall not act upon such request until in receipt of a letter from the Chair and Vice Chair of the Council on Pensions and Insurance acknowledging receipt of the State Treasurer's request. Within the appropriation approved pursuant to this item, the State Treasurer, with the approval of the Speaker of the Senate and the Speaker of the House of Representatives, is authorized to establish positions and funding needed to effectuate TCA 8-34-321.

Item 11. From the fund created in Tennessee Code Annotated, Section 65-5-113, to the State Treasurer for purposes of conducting a purchasing disparity study. It is the legislative intent that such study include the University of Tennessee system and the state university and community college system; provided, however, the costs of such study shall not exceed amounts previously set aside therefor. Should available funds be insufficient to conduct a valid purchasing disparity study, funds appropriated by this item may be used to conduct a review to determine best practices related to increasing purchasing opportunities with small and minority-owned businesses and to implement recommendations arising from the study.

Item 12. From federal funds available to the Tennessee Housing Development Agency, there is hereby appropriated a sum sufficient to meet obligations incurred by the agency, pursuant to the federal Section 8 program and the Hardest Hit Fund (HHF) Program.

Item 13. To the Tennessee Housing Development Agency from the sale or rental of housing and other property rehabilitated by the Neighborhood Stabilization Program.

Item 14. To Tennessee Rehabilitative Initiative in Correction Board (TRICOR), in an amount equal to the balance in the revolving fund, for benefit of the program.

Item 15. To the Tennessee State Museum from (a) deferred revenue and departmental revenues available to the museum to be used for the purchase of artifacts, and (b) donations made to the State Museum. Any unexpended revenues shall not revert to the general fund balance at June 30 and such revenues shall be carried forward in a reserve at June 30 and are hereby reappropriated in the subsequent fiscal year.

Item 16. The Commissioner of Finance and Administration is authorized to adjust departmental revenues related to inter-agency agreements with the Electronic Health Initiative for the purpose of implementing federal electronic health initiatives.

Item 17. To the Department of General Services for equipment and supplies ordered but not delivered at June 30, 2013.

Item 18. To the Department of General Services, Warehousing and Distribution program, from available revenues and reserves.

Item 19. To the Department of Tourist Development from revenues received from communities, businesses, non-state organizations, federal funds, and other sources of departmental revenue to be used for marketing programs of the department. Any unexpended balances at June 30 shall be carried forward in a reserve and are hereby reappropriated in the subsequent fiscal year.

Item 20. To the Department of Environment and Conservation, West Tennessee River Basin Authority, from funds provided by the counties within the authority area.

Item 21. To the Department of Environment and Conservation, Tennessee State Parks, from revenues collected by the parks system.

Item 22. To the Department of Correction all monies collected as contraband from the inmate population at any of the facilities operated by or under authority of the department. Any unexpended revenue shall not revert to the state general fund balance pursuant to Tennessee Code Annotated, Section 4-6-147.

Item 23. To the Department of Economic and Community Development from revenues received from communities, businesses, non-state organizations, federal funds, and other sources of departmental revenue to be used for marketing programs of the department. Any unexpended balances at June 30 shall be carried forward in a reserve and are hereby reappropriated in the subsequent fiscal year.

Item 24. To the Department of Economic and Community Development:

(a) To meet community development block grant expenditure requirements. This appropriation shall be from federal aid funds.

(b) From monies received from conferences, trade missions, trade shows and other activities which reimburse the state for expenses.

(c) From interest earnings allocated to the FastTrack Program; Job Skills Fund; and Small Cities Community Development Block Grant (CDBG).

(d) From revenues and reserves of the Small Business Energy Loan Program, Local Government Energy Loan Program, and Tennessee Energy Loan Program.

Item 25. To the Tennessee Film, Entertainment and Music Commission from departmental revenues received by the Commission. This appropriation is subject to approval by the Commissioner of Finance and Administration.

Item 26. To the Tennessee Industrial Finance Corporation from any revenues available to the organization to be expended pursuant to Tennessee Code Annotated, Title 4, Chapter 17, Part 4.

Item 27. To the Department of Education, Achievement School District program, from donations made to the program.

Item 28. To the Department of Commerce and Insurance:

(a) Division of Insurance, from revenue and reserves of the Insurance Education Fund.

(b) Division of Securities, from the revenues and reserves of the Securities Enforcement and Legal Training reserve and the Securities Education Fund.

(c) Consumer Affairs, from departmental revenues and reserves for consumer education purposes.

(d) Division of Fire Prevention, for payment of electrical inspections. This appropriation is contingent upon the fees collected for making electrical inspections being in excess of the budgeted estimate.

Item 29. To the Department of Labor and Workforce Development from federal aid funds and other departmental revenues. Subject to this appropriation, authorized positions may be increased up to one hundred (100) positions.

Item 30. To the Department of Labor and Workforce Development from federal National Emergency Grant funds.

Item 31. To the Department of Mental Health and Substance Abuse Services from revenue received from behavioral health organizations and other non-state organizations for inpatient mental health services provided for publicly funded or potentially publicly funded persons.

Item 32. To the Department of Military, TEMA and Disaster Relief Grants, from federal aid disaster relief funds.

Item 33. To the Department of Military from station commander's upkeep and maintenance fund created pursuant to Tennessee Code Annotated, Section 58-1-512, to be used for purposes specified therein. The provisions of this item shall be effective immediately, the public welfare requiring it.

Item 34. To the Department of Human Services, subject to the financial reporting requirement that the value of federal food stamps be recognized in the state's accounting system, there is hereby appropriated a sum sufficient from federal funds to recognize the value of food stamps.

Item 35. To the Tennessee Bureau of Investigation from revenues and reserves available to the following programs:

(a) To conduct records and background checks for handgun carry permits pursuant to Tennessee Code Annotated, Section 39-17-1351.

(b) To conduct criminal history records checks on purchasers of firearms (Tennessee Instant Check System – TICS) pursuant to Tennessee Code Annotated, Section 39-17-1316.

(c) To conduct criminal history checks for employment requirements pursuant to TCA, Sections 33-2-1201; 37-5-502; 49-5-400; 68-11-233; 68-11-234; and 71-2-403.

(d) To certify endorsement of transporting hazardous material on commercial driver licenses pursuant to Federal Register Part IV, 49 CFR Part 1572.

(e) To provide criminal history information through the Tennessee Online Records Information System (TORIS) pursuant to TCA 38-6-120.

Item 36. To the Department of Safety, Driver License Issuance, from revenues and reserves available to defray expenses of handgun carry permit program pursuant to Tennessee Code Annotated, Section 39-17-1351.

Item 37. To the Department of Safety, the Department of Revenue, the Tennessee Bureau of Investigation, the Tennessee National Guard and the Alcoholic Beverage Commission from the proceeds of property seized and forfeited under federal procedures which are shared with the departments or the commission.

Item 38. To the Department of Transportation from local government funds, federal aid and other departmental revenues.

Item 39. To the Comptroller of the Treasury, Division of Property Assessments, from revenues and reserves derived from the annual assessor's training session. The provisions of this item shall be effective upon becoming law, the public welfare requiring it.

Item 40. To the Department of Safety from any donations received from any non-profit organization created pursuant to Tennessee Code Annotated, Section 4-3-2017. The provisions of this item shall be effective upon becoming law, the public welfare requiring it.

SECTION 10. The appropriations made by this act under Sections 1 and 4 shall be subject to the following provisions, limitations, or restrictions:

Item 1. Notwithstanding any provision of the law to the contrary, any institution which receives state funds appropriated by the provisions of this act shall be subject to audit by the Comptroller of the Treasury as to the expenditure and obligation of such funds.

Item 2. Any personal services, professional services or consultant services contracts concerning management services of all types, management studies, planning services, public relations, evaluations, systems designs, data processing, auditing or accounting services entered into by an executive department or agency of state government shall be executed by the head of such department or agency and shall be subject to approval by the Commissioner of Finance and Administration. No funds appropriated under this act to a department or agency shall be used for such contracts unless such approval is received or is otherwise authorized by the approving Commissioner of Finance and Administration.

Item 3. No funds appropriated by this act shall be obligated and/or expended for any newsletter, periodical, or other material which is to be distributed to all, or substantially all, state employees (excluding higher education) until the agency head proposing to make such distribution contacts the two Speakers and makes available equal space for legislative information in such newsletter, periodical, or other material. This item shall not apply to policy and/or procedural directives.

Item 4. From the funds appropriated to the TennCare program, the state shall comply with applicable federal law.

Item 5. During fiscal year 2013-2014 it is the legislative intent to encourage that all conferences, workshops, meetings, seminars, programs, and similar endeavors conducted for officials and/or employees of the legislative, executive, or judicial branch of state government be conducted in state facilities whenever practicable.

Item 6. From the appropriation for travel expenses of Justices of the Supreme Court and for the members of the Court of Appeals and the Court of Criminal Appeals, each member of said Courts shall be reimbursed for necessary traveling expenses incurred by them during their absence from the counties of their residence on official business; provided, however, that such travel expenses shall be limited to board and lodging and mileage each way necessary to travel on official business. Any judge seeking reimbursement for official expense under this section shall file with the Director of the Administrative Office of the Courts, or other official upon whom this duty may be lodged by law, a statement of such amounts necessarily expended in the discharge of such official duties and upon receipt of this verified statement, warrant for reimbursement for such expenses shall be issued.

Item 7. The Supreme Court shall fix the salaries of the marshals for the Eastern, Middle, and Western Divisions, which salary shall be payable out of the appropriations for Appellate Court Clerks.

Item 8. The commission in charge of the Supreme Court Building in Nashville, established by Tennessee Code Annotated, Section 16-3-701, is authorized to employ an experienced Engineer-Superintendent to supervise the air-conditioning and heating of the Supreme Court Building at Nashville and to employ the necessary assistants to keep and maintain the building. Payment for said services shall be paid out of the appropriations made by this act.

Light, heat and water for the Supreme Court Building in Nashville and for the Supreme Court Building in Knoxville is to be provided by the Department of General Services out of the appropriation herein made for it.

Item 9. Employees of the office of the Executive Secretary to the District Public Defenders Conference, District Public Defenders and employees of a District Public Defenders Office, as created pursuant to Tennessee Code Annotated, Title 8, Chapter 14, shall only travel and shall be reimbursed for travel expenses in accordance with the provisions of the comprehensive travel regulations promulgated by the Department of Finance and Administration and approved by the Attorney General.

Item 10. The appropriation made in Section 1, Title III-1, Item 5.9, for the Tax Relief Program, is made for the purpose of providing tax relief for elderly low-income homeowners, disabled homeowners, and disabled veteran homeowners, as provided by law. The income eligibility limit for elderly low-income homeowners and for homeowners totally and permanently disabled shall be adjusted for the fiscal year 2013-2014 under the provisions of Tennessee Code Annotated, Sections 67-5-702 and 67-5-703.

Item 11. Notwithstanding any provision of the law to the contrary, from the appropriations made for the Department of the Treasury, there is hereby appropriated funds sufficient to defray the cost of administering, on behalf of state employees compensated on the centralized state payroll system, Tennessee Code Annotated, Title 8, Chapter 25, Part 1, the same being the "Government Employees' Deferred Compensation Plan Act", and Tennessee Code Annotated, Title 8, Chapter 25, Part 3, the same being the "Profit Sharing or Salary Reduction Plans for State Employees", and Tennessee Code Annotated, Section 8-25-501, the same being a "Cafeteria Benefits Plan" for state employees.

Item 12. From the funds appropriated for the Criminal Injuries Compensation Fund, pursuant to § 40-38-405 there is earmarked the sum of $100,000 for the sole purpose of making a grant in such amount to the Tennessee Coalition Against Domestic and Sexual Violence to support the activities of the Tommy Burks Victim Assistance Academy.

Item 13. Subject to the concurrence of the Commissioner of Finance and Administration, the Commissioner of Human Resources is authorized to develop and implement a system whereby the cost of the Board of Appeals created by Tennessee Code Annotated, Section 8-30-108, and of services rendered to the Department of Human

Resources by the Administrative Procedures Division of the Department of State is recovered from those departments, boards and commissions to whom services are rendered.

Item 14. The funds appropriated in Section 4, Title III-3, Item 4, to Forestry Operations, shall include the proceeds from timber sales conducted by the Department of Agriculture. It is the legislative intent that said proceeds shall be accounted for as departmental revenue.

Item 15. From the appropriation in Section 1, Title III-3, Item 3, Department of Agriculture, Market Development, the following amounts are earmarked:

(a) Non-recurring grants of $250,000 to the Future Farmers of America (FFA) and $250,000 to the 4-H Foundation.

Item 16. From the appropriation made in Section 1, Title III-3, Item 5, to the Department of Agriculture, Forestry Operations, the sum of $3,457,100 is intended to fund the depreciation cost to replace bulldozers and associated equipment. Unexpended funds for this purpose may be carried forward and held in reserve until such a time as replacement is deemed necessary.

Item 17. From the appropriation made for the Department of Tourist Development, there is hereby appropriated a sum not to exceed twelve thousand five hundred dollars ($12,500.00), sufficient to defray the cost of advertising and other expenses in connection with special events in which Tennessee is represented and/or events within the state for which Tennessee will act as official host. Any allotment of funds made under the authority of this section shall be made only on the approval of the Commissioner of Finance and Administration.

Item 18. From the appropriations made in this act, there shall be paid expenses incurred by the Department of Economic and Community Development and the Department of Tourist Development, representing the state in its official capacity; provided, however, that nothing herein shall authorize the expenditure by each agency for such purposes in excess of five thousand dollars ($5,000.00) per annum. The amount and purposes of such expenses are subject to approval by the Commissioner of Finance and Administration.

Item 19. From the appropriation made to State Prosecutions in Section 1, Title III-7, Item 7, payments to reimburse counties for housing state prisoners shall not exceed $37.00 per inmate per day. Provided, however, the $37.00 per inmate per day limitation on reimbursement payments shall be inapplicable to the extent the state is obligated by the specific terms of a written contract to provide reimbursement at a rate in excess of $37.00 per inmate per day, but only to the extent of that contractual obligation.

Item 20. Notwithstanding any provision of the law to the contrary, where a judicial proceeding is transferred from one jurisdiction to another for trial on a defendant's motion for change of venue, the limitation of one thousand dollars ($1,000.00) for the board and lodging of the jury shall not apply, provided the Comptroller of the Treasury on the advice of the State Attorney General, determines that additional funds for boarding and lodging the jury are necessary.

Item 21. No funds appropriated by the provisions of this act to the Department of Economic and Community Development shall be used to contract for services, or to renew any contract for services, with any individual or entity if such individual or entity's position presents an actual or apparent conflict of interest between duties owed to the State of Tennessee under such contract and duties owed to any third party. It is the legislative intent that work performed under service contracts shall be performed in-house by the department to the extent possible.

Item 22.

(a) From funds previously appropriated for such purpose, it is the intent of the General Assembly that there is established the Jimmy Naifeh Center for Effective Leadership at the University of Tennessee to prepare elected and appointed officials for the challenges of serving the public; to provide leadership and management programming for government officials from across the state and the nation; and to provide studies and research in public service on any and all matters relating to the development of professional skills to enhance effectiveness as representatives of the people.

PUBLIC CHAPTER NO. 453 (cont'd)

(b) It is the intent of the General Assembly that in addition to or as part of the services provided pursuant to subsection (a), the Center shall administer the Tennessee Government Executive Institute, the Tennessee Government Management Institute, and the Local Government Leadership Program as well as other such programs or initiatives that promote leadership development and public service.

Item 23. The Department of Mental Health and Substance Abuse Services is authorized to expend up to one hundred fifty thousand dollars ($150,000) in available funds for the purpose of implementing the provisions of Tennessee Code Annotated, Section 12-4-330, and such funds are specifically appropriated for that purpose.

Item 24. The appropriation to the Department of Health, Trauma System Fund, in Section 1, Title III-16, Item 2.5, is made pursuant to Tennessee Code Annotated, Title 68, Chapter 59, "Tennessee Trauma Center Funding Law of 2007." Subject to approval by the Commissioner of Finance and Administration there is hereby appropriated a sum sufficient from the Trauma System Fund reserve and the appropriation may be increased or decreased as collections from the tax established pursuant to Tennessee Code Annotated, Section 67-4-1025(e) justify.

Item 25. Within the amount appropriated in Section 1, Title III-17, and in Section 4, Title III-17, for Temporary Assistance to Needy Families, the Commissioner of Human Services shall establish by rule or regulation, pursuant to the provisions of Tennessee Code Annotated, Section 71-3-155, to be effective July 1, 2013, the standard of need for each family size in the Families First program; provided, the maximum grant for each family size will remain at the Fiscal Year 2013-2014 established level; and, provided further, that the Commissioner of Human Services, in consultation with the Commissioner of Finance and Administration, may by rule to be effective on July 1, 2013, establish certain categories of Families First recipients to whom an additional grant differential for the family size up to a maximum of fifty dollars ($50.00) per family may be paid.

Item 26. The appropriations to the Department of Revenue under Section 1, Title III-18, provide for all the activities of the department and include amounts in lieu of percentages allowed by law on collection of certain taxes and revenues; such percentage shall be covered into and made a part of the general fund. Appropriations also include amounts for motor vehicle registration and any other activities which may be administered by the Department of Revenue.

Item 27. No funds appropriated by the provisions of this act for any cultural, specialty earmarked, new specialty earmarked, and collegiate license plate shall be allocated by the Department of Finance and Administration to the Department of Revenue until such plate has met all statutory requirements for issuance, as provided in Tennessee Code Annotated, Title 55, Chapter 4.

Item 28. The appropriation to the Tennessee Association of Rescue Squads in Section 1, Title III-22, Item 8, is for the sole purpose of maintaining a state headquarters of the association and to pay the salary of an executive director of the association and other expenses appurtenant thereto.

Item 29. Notwithstanding any provision of the law to the contrary, the Department of Transportation shall not release or make available information which reveals the amount of funding available for any project.

Item 30. From the funds appropriated by this act, the State Funding Board is directed to conduct a study of the budgeted contingency costs of capital outlay projects compared to the actual costs of such capital outlay projects to increase efficiency in state government. Such study shall examine the methodologies and reporting requirements of entities completing such capital outlay projects and the use of such contingency funds to develop best practices for managing the public debt of the state. It is the legislative intent that all entities eligible to receive state bond proceeds participate in such study by providing timely information and other services as requested by the State Funding Board.

Item 31. The General Assembly recognizes that demands on available state revenue are such that it may be necessary to establish priorities among state services and programs and to revise the methods of allocating state resources. Therefore, it is the legislative intent that local governments should consider in undertaking long-term obligations based on state payments, specifically state per diem payments for housing state inmates in local jails, that existing payments may be reduced or eliminated in the future and such not be regarded as the principal source of funding for debt repayment obligations.

Item 32. The appropriation made in Section 1, Title III-22, Item 30, for Tobacco MSA diligent enforcement systems development is for the purpose of developing an information system or systems for the Attorney General and Reporter and the Department of Revenue, and includes a recurring amount of $240,700 for system operational costs, which shall remain in the general fund allotments, including $24,100 for the Attorney General and Reporter and $216,600 for the Department of Revenue; and the recurring funds shall be transferred to the operating allotments of the agencies at the time the Commissioner of Finance and Administration determines for system operating purposes. The non-recurring amount of $962,400 may be transferred to the systems development fund, and the non-recurring amount of $532,900 shall be available for the Attorney General and Reporter systems development requirements and $429,500 for the Department of Revenue systems development requirements. The Commissioner of Finance and Administration is authorized to make transfers between the two non-recurring accounts, with the agreement of the Attorney General and Reporter and the Commissioner of Revenue, or to consolidate the amounts into a single project account for development of a single system serving both agencies, if deemed appropriate by the two commissioners and the Attorney General and Reporter.

Item 33. The contingency appropriation in Section 1, Title III-22, Item 34, for a grant to Knox County in lieu of tax is for the purpose of providing a grant in lieu of estimated intangible property tax funds that the county will not collect if a moratorium is placed upon the collection of the tax from certain domestic mutual insurance companies. The grant of funds to Knox County is contingent upon Senate Bill No. 885/House Bill No. 574 or a similar bill becoming a law and placing a moratorium upon collection of such tax. Payment shall be made timely upon receipt of a bill from Knox County at the time the tax would otherwise be collected during the year ending June 30, 2014. The grant shall not exceed the amount appropriated.

SECTION 11. The appropriations made by this act under Sections 1 and 4 to the Department of Education shall be subject to the following provisions, limitations, or restrictions:

Item 1. The appropriation made in Section 1, Title III-9, Item 2.1c, for the Basic Education Program (BEP), shall be administered pursuant to the provisions of the Education Improvement Act (Public Chapter No. 535 of the Public Acts of 1992) and Public Chapter No. 369 of the Public Acts of 2007. The BEP formula shall be calculated for the fiscal year using the following criteria:

(a) The state shall provide seventy percent (70%) of the funds generated for the instructional positions component;

(b) The dollar value of the BEP instructional positions component shall be forty thousand four hundred forty-seven dollars ($40,447);

(c) The formula shall provide one hundred percent (100%) funding for at-risk students in grades K-12;

(d) The formula shall provide funding for English language learners at a ratio of one to thirty (1:30) and one to three hundred (1:300) for teachers to students and translators to students, respectively;

(e) Each local education agency (LEA) shall receive no less than a twenty-five percent (25%) state share in the non-classroom components;

(f) The cost differential factor shall be applied at a level of fifty percent (50%); and

(g) Local fiscal capacity shall be calculated by applying a weight of fifty percent (50%) of the current multiple regression analysis model and fifty percent (50%) of the model based on local jurisdictions' ability to raise revenue for education from local option sales tax and property tax as provided in Public Chapter 369 of 2007.

Item 2. From the appropriations made to the Department of Education under Section 1, Title III-9, of this act, the Department of Education is authorized to pay through disbursements to local education agencies (LEAs), the following amounts based on the Basic Education Program (BEP) formula, of participation in the basic accident and medical expense insurance plan, authorized by Tennessee Code Annotated, Title 8, Chapter 27, Part 3, by eligible employees of local education agencies:

(a) For the benefit of eligible local education instructional employees and their dependents, an amount not to exceed forty-five percent (45%) of the total statewide cost;

(b) For the benefit of eligible local education support staff employees and their dependents, an amount not to exceed thirty percent (30%) of the total statewide cost.

Furthermore, local education agencies are required to contribute a portion of the premium for participation in the basic accident and medical expense insurance plan at the following levels:

(1) Pursuant to Tennessee Code Annotated, Section 8-27-303(j)(1), each local education agency shall pay on behalf of each instructional employee participating in the health insurance coverage authorized by Tennessee Code Annotated, Sections 8-27-302 and 303 a minimum of forty-five percent (45%) of the monthly premium for the coverage elected by the instructional employee.

(2) Pursuant to Tennessee Code Annotated, Section 8-27-303(j)(2), each local education agency shall pay on behalf of each support staff employee participating in the health insurance coverage authorized by Tennessee Code Annotated, Sections 8-27-302 and 303 a minimum of ten percent (10%) of the monthly premium for the coverage elected by the support staff employee.

The Local Education Insurance Committee shall determine a calendar year 2014 plan of benefits, related services, and monthly premiums for each of the health care options offered through the "basic plan" it authorizes pursuant to Section 8-27-302, Tennessee Code Annotated, which results, with reasonable certainty, in the provision of sufficient revenues to pay plan expenses and to provide for the funding of reserves for estimated incurred but unreported claims. The aggregate amount of funds obligated through the determination of the plans of benefits and the monthly premiums by the Local Education Insurance Committee shall not exceed the amount appropriated to the Department of Education, Basic Education Program's insurance component in this act. The monthly premiums shall be subject to the approval of the Commissioner of Finance and Administration pursuant to Section 4-3-1006, Tennessee Code Annotated.

For purposes of these appropriations, "base premium" means the lowest premium offered by the Local Education Insurance Plan, without regard to any surcharges added to the premium for participation in the standard plan, a higher-cost network, or other premium adjustments that incent cost-savings to the plan.

The Local Education Insurance Committee shall recognize the annualized rate and benefits adjustments intended to be effective on January 1, 2014, which are required so that the plan of benefits, on an annualized basis, shall not exceed the recurring amount appropriated to the Department of Education.

Item 3. From the appropriation made to the Department of Education under Section 1, Title III-9, of this act, for technology programs, there is hereby earmarked a sum sufficient for the expenditures of the Web Project.

Item 4. From the appropriation made in Section 1, Title III-9, Item 2.1c, Basic Education Program, an amount of $27,500,000 is appropriated for the purpose of providing additional BEP funding for student enrollment growth on a current-year student basis, and such funds shall be distributed pursuant to Tennessee Code Annotated, Section 49-3-351(d), to the extent available.

Item 5. Under the provisions of Tennessee Code Annotated, Sections 49-3-357 and 49-3-358, pertaining to interest accruing on investments and deposits to the Education Trust Fund and the Basic Education Program, it is the legislative intent that only interest earnings be recognized and that no interest expense be charged to the fund and the program.

Item 6. The Department of Education shall submit to the Office of Legislative Budget Analysis the revised BEP funding formula for the ensuing fiscal year no later than February 1 of each year.

Item 7. Local education agencies are required to report average daily membership (ADM) to the Department of Education on a scheduled basis. To the extent a local education agency fails to report accurate and timely ADM information to the department, the BEP payments for the subsequent fiscal year shall be based on the second prior year ADM figure, unless the late-reported ADM figures are lower than the second prior year.

Item 8. In the year ending June 30, 2013, from funds appropriated in Public Acts of 2012, Chapter 1029, Section I, Title III-9, Item 2.1(c), Basic Education Program (BEP), any funds withheld pursuant to Tennessee Code Annotated, Section 49-3-353, including an amount of $3,374,933 withheld from Davidson County, hereby are authorized to be distributed by the Commissioner of Education to local education agencies (LEAs) in amounts that represent each LEA's share of the BEP relative to statewide BEP funding. Such distribution shall exclude any LEA in violation of Section 49-3-353. Such funds as may be distributed as provided in this item hereby are appropriated for such purpose. The provisions of this item shall be effective immediately, the public welfare requiring it.

Item 9. The appropriation in Section 1, Title III-9, Item 4.1, Alvin C. York Institute, includes a non-recurring appropriation of $2,294,400, and 16 full-time positions are funded from the non-recurring source. It is the legislative intent that the Commissioner of Education provide to the Governor by December 1, 2013, a transition plan approved by the commissioner and the local education agency in Fentress County relative to transition of the Alvin C. York Institute to the local education agency by July 1, 2015. If such plan is not approved by the commissioner and the local education agency, the commissioner on December 1, 2013, shall provide to the Commissioner of Finance and Administration an estimate of the state appropriation requirement and local funding requirement and the Basic Education Program-generated positions if the school were to be funded and staffed in fiscal year 2014-2015 in amounts estimated through the Basic Education Program funding formula. Failing a commitment from the local education agency to provide the local share, it is the legislative intent that the appropriation to the institute and authorized positions be reduced in the 2014-2015 budget to the amounts that can be funded by the state share of the formula estimate and other departmental revenues available to the institute.

SECTION 12.

Item 1. There is hereby appropriated the sum of three million dollars ($3,000,000.00) to the Department of Human Services, which sum shall be in addition to all other appropriations made to the Department of Human Services and which sum shall be used for the sole purpose of increasing the amount available to social service contractors, as provided for in Tennessee Code Annotated, Title 71, Chapter 1, Part 2.

Item 2. It is the intent of the General Assembly that the Commissioner of Finance and Administration shall have the authority to promulgate, as emergency rules pursuant to Tennessee Code Annotated, Section 4-5-208, those rules and regulations which concern the Medicaid/TennCare program, including Medicare Crossover payments, and which require promulgation in order for the state to fiscally function (i) within the appropriations provided for the Medicaid/TennCare program or (ii) within the availability of revenues received for the Medicaid/TennCare program.

Item 3. In addition to any other funds appropriated by the provisions of this act, there is hereby appropriated to the Department of Finance and Administration for distribution to the appropriate entities a sum sufficient to fund any bill on which the fiscal note indicates that the cost of implementation of the bill as enacted is not significant. It is the legislative intent that if funding is earmarked for implementation in such bills that the funds appropriated in this item be reduced accordingly. It is the legislative intent to recognize a revenue loss from bills that result in no expenditure increase but forgo revenue which has not been collected previously.

Item 4. In addition to any other funds appropriated by the provisions of this act, if the fiscal note on any bill states that state revenues would be increased in an amount equal to or greater than state expenditures as a result of the enactment of such bill, then there is appropriated a sum sufficient from such increased revenue to the appropriate entity, as determined by the Commissioner of Finance and Administration, to implement such bill.

Item 5. The provisions of this item shall take effect upon becoming law, the public welfare requiring it. From the appropriations made in this act, there hereby is appropriated a sum sufficient for implementation of any legislation cited or otherwise described by category in this act or in the Budget Document transmitted by the Governor that has an effective date prior to July 1 of the current calendar year, provided that such legislation is funded in the Budget Document as submitted by the Governor or in the final legislative balancing schedules summarizing enacted amendments incorporated into this act or other appropriations acts of this legislative session and that the fiscal impact of implementing the legislation, as indicated in the final cumulative fiscal note of the Fiscal Review Committee on enacted legislation, is less than or equal to the amounts indicated in the Budget Document or the amendment balancing schedules. The final legislative balancing schedules may incorporate in summary form the amounts included in the amendment(s) submitted by the Governor, to the extent adopted, as indicated on the balancing schedule accompanying the Governor's recommended amendment(s).

SECTION 13. The provisions of this section shall take effect upon becoming a law, the public welfare requiring it.

Item 1. The Commissioner of Finance and Administration is authorized to reallocate appropriations for Board of Claims premiums and property insurance premiums among state agencies and programs, based on the actuarial study provided by the State Treasurer, and to adjust federal and other departmental revenues accordingly. There is further appropriated for this purpose sums sufficient from dedicated and earmarked revenues to provide for the allocation of appropriations to those agencies and programs funded by dedicated and earmarked revenues. The Commissioner of Finance and Administration also shall reduce appropriations from the general fund and from dedicated and earmarked revenues where necessary, to reflect the allocations of the actuarial study.

Item 2. From the appropriation made in Section 4, Title III-1, Item 7.3, Risk Management Fund, funds may be expended for purposes outlined in TCA 9-8-109(d), including, but not limited to, contracting with a third party for claims management services.

SECTION 14. The appropriations made by this act and all other appropriations, including appropriations of departmental revenues as set forth in Section 4 of this act, except such as may be made for the expenses of the Legislative Branch, and the appropriations made for the Judiciary, including the Attorney General and Reporter, District Attorneys General, Public Defenders, and the Office of the Post-Conviction Defender, the Secretary of State, Comptroller of the Treasury and State Treasurer, shall be obligated and expended under the provisions of Tennessee Code Annotated, Title 4, Chapter 3, Part 10 and Title 9, Chapter 4, Part 51, which shall remain in full force and effect; and in case of conflict with any other law, the provisions of such laws shall prevail, except as otherwise herein specifically provided. All appropriations except those made by acts authorizing bond issues and expenditures thereof and those excepted from obligations and expenditure hereinabove, though made by other statutes, shall likewise be obligated and expended under the provisions of Tennessee Code Annotated, Title 4, Chapter 3, Part 10 and Title 9, Chapter 4, Part 51.

SECTION 15.

Item 1. No part of the fund appropriated to any department, office, instrumentality, or agency of the state government shall be expended in any other such entity, but if the head of any department, office, commission or instrumentality of the state government finds that there is a surplus in any classification, division, or unit under such entity, and a deficiency in any other division, unit or classification, then in that event the head of such department, office, commission or instrumentality of the state government may transfer such portion of such funds as may be necessary for the one division, unit or classification where the surplus exists to the other, except as otherwise provided herein, provided such transfer is approved by the Commissioner of Finance and Administration. Such transfer of funds pursuant to this item shall be subject to the approval of a majority of a committee comprised of the Speaker of the Senate, the Speaker of the House and the Comptroller of the Treasury.

Item 2. The Commissioner of Finance and Administration may establish in any department, office, commission or instrumentality of the state government a clearing account through which all salaries and wages, including the state's portion of retirement, insurance, Social Security, etc., may be disbursed. In the event such accounts are established, department records shall be maintained showing the distribution of such amounts among the various appropriation codes, and any financial reports shall present expenditures as if such expenditures had been made through the individual appropriation accounts.

Item 3. The Commissioner of Finance and Administration shall have power and authority to refuse, with the approval of the Governor, to approve or honor any and all requisitions for purchases, except requisitions for purchases authorized by the Legislative Branch, including the Secretary of State, Comptroller of the Treasury and State Treasurer, and the Judiciary, including the Attorney General and Reporter. In case any division or function of government for which an appropriation is provided in this act or otherwise, shall be transferred from an existing department, to any other department, such transfer shall automatically result in the appropriation for such transferred division or function becoming available to the department to which such transfer is made for the purposes of such transferred division or function.

PUBLIC CHAPTER NO. 453 (cont'd)

Item 4. From the appropriations made to the various state departments and agencies under this act, and other general acts appropriating money, there may be paid any expenses incurred by said departments and agencies for the purpose of conducting and serving as host for regional or national conferences of which such departments or agencies may be members. Before any funds shall be expended under this authorization, the amount and purpose of the proposed expenditure shall be approved by the Commissioner of Finance and Administration.

Item 5. Notwithstanding any provision of law to the contrary, no state department or agency in the Executive Branch of state government is authorized to make organizational changes within such department or agency without the prior approval of the Commissioner of Finance and Administration. Where such organizational changes require a transfer of funds between organizational accounts and are contrary to the manner in which appropriations have been made herein, approval of said transfers is subject to approval by the Commissioner of Finance and Administration and by a majority of a committee comprised of the Speaker of the Senate, the Speaker of the House and the Comptroller of the Treasury.

Item 6. The Commissioner of Finance and Administration is authorized to draw down disputed federal funds and to reserve the funds to prevent their expenditure until the dispute is settled; and the Commissioner of Finance and Administration in consultation with the State Treasurer is authorized to allocate interest earnings on the draw-down of disputed federal funds and to pay interest earnings to the federal government in those instances when expenditures are ultimately disallowed.

Item 7. The Commissioner of General Services is authorized to impose a reasonable real estate transaction fee on all real estate transactions when the transaction is processed through the Department of General Services. Said fee structure shall be subject to approval by the State Building Commission.

Subject to the approval of the State Building Commission, there is hereby appropriated a sum sufficient to replace any real estate transaction fees that are waived.

Item 8. The Commissioner of Finance and Administration shall maintain a policy to recover state funds and the state's costs associated with checks, warrants, drafts, and electronic funds transfers deposited to a state account that are subsequently returned unpaid by the drawer's bank.

Item 9. The Commissioner of Finance and Administration is authorized to maintain an indirect cost recovery plan to recognize overhead costs associated with the operations of the Tennessee Regulatory Authority, Wildlife Resources Agency, Department of Financial Institutions, Housing Development Agency and the regulatory boards and commissions not under the administration of the Department of Commerce and Insurance or the Department of Health. The Commissioner is further authorized to charge the departments and agencies covered by the indirect cost recovery plan for their individual overhead costs.

Item 10. The state regulatory fee shall be assessed at the rate of $5.00 for one year and $10.00 for two years. The fee shall be in lieu of any allocation of indirect costs which would otherwise be allocated to the regulatory boards covered by the provisions of Tennessee Code Annotated, Section 4-3-1011(b)(2).

Item 11. If any appropriation in this act fails to designate a department or agency of state government to be responsible for the administration of the appropriation, then the Commissioner of Finance and Administration is hereby directed to designate the state department or agency to administer the appropriation.

Unless otherwise directed by language in this act, appropriation grants to agencies outside of state government shall be administered in such manner as the Commissioner of Finance and Administration shall determine. Direct appropriation grants for the benefit of agencies outside of state government may be administered by the Department of Finance and Administration.

Item 12. For the purposes of this item, the term "chief fiscal officer" shall mean the position within a state agency that has overall daily responsibility for the oversight of the fiscal operation for that agency. The Commissioner of Human Resources in consultation with the Commissioner of Finance and Administration shall designate and classify position(s) within each agency of the Executive Branch of state government as chief fiscal officer(s) for that agency. Qualifications and appointments to fill existing or future vacancies shall be in accordance with procedures established by the Commissioner of Human Resources with the approval of the Commissioner of Finance and Administration.

Item 13. From the appropriations made in this act to pay the salaries of state employees who are hired on or after July 1, 2013, the Commissioner of Finance and Administration is authorized to require that those salaries be paid through direct-deposit procedures.

Item 14. The Commissioner of Finance and Administration is hereby authorized to adjust departmental revenue and reserve estimates and related expenditures: (a) for internal service funds and enterprise funds to record fees received for services provided to departments, agencies, boards, and commissions, and (b) to record payment for services provided to state agencies by another state agency.

Item 15. The Commissioner of Finance and Administration is hereby authorized to adjust departmental revenue and related expenditures to recognize (a) the carry-over of federal funds and other departmental revenues that were budgeted and allotted but unexpended or unobligated at June 30; (b) an increase in the federal rate of reimbursement or match in federal programs so that there is less state expense or the additional federal funds are available to meet increasing costs without improving programs; and (c) an unexpected increase in federal grant funds so that there is less state expense or the additional federal funds are available to meet increasing costs without improving programs.

Item 16. The Commissioner of Finance and Administration is hereby authorized to adjust the estimates of federal block grant funds and other federal grant-in-aid funds estimated in Section 4 and Section 31 of this act to reflect the actual allocations of federal revenues made available to the State of Tennessee by the federal government.

Item 17. From the appropriation made in Section 4, Title III-2, Item 4.4, to General Services, Real Estate Asset Management, the Commissioner of Finance and Administration is authorized to establish new positions for property management for new buildings the state maintains.

Item 18. Financial Systems Billings. From the funds appropriated in this act, the Commissioner of Finance and Administration is authorized to approve adjustments in rates charged by the Department of Finance and Administration for enterprise resource planning (ERP, or Edison) and the Division of Accounts, the Department of Human Resources, and the Department of General Services; to reserve any funds needed to rebate savings to the federal government; and to reallocate state appropriations between departments and reduce appropriations, and adjust federal aid and other departmental revenue accordingly.

Item 19. From the appropriations made for accounting functions and other fiscal activities in this act and other acts of the legislature, the Commissioner of Finance and Administration is authorized to establish and charge the costs of accounting positions and other fiscal positions to said appropriations. The Commissioner of Finance and Administration is further authorized to transfer between departments and agencies existing accounting positions, other fiscal positions and the funding provided in this act for transferred positions.

SECTION 16.

Item 1. Each department, division or agency for the benefit of which an appropriation is made herein and which participates in the Consolidated Retirement System, shall pay from such appropriation monthly such sums as may be due such Consolidated Retirement System as the state's contribution from such department, division or agency.

SECTION 17.

Item 1. From the appropriations made herein, the various departments, agencies, boards and commissions of state government shall pay on behalf of each participating employee within the respective departments, agencies, boards and commissions, not less than eighty percent (80%) of the cost of each individual's participation in the basic group medical insurance program and one hundred percent (100%) of the cost of twenty thousand dollars ($20,000.00) of basic term life insurance coverage and forty thousand dollars ($40,000.00) of basic special accident insurance coverage for each participating employee; such basic medical, life and accident insurance program to be established pursuant to Tennessee Code Annotated, Title 8, Chapter 27, Part 2.

The employer contribution amounts established by the State Insurance Committee for eligible participating employees shall not exceed, in the aggregate, the amounts appropriated in this act. The State Insurance Committee shall determine a calendar year 2014 plan of benefits, related services, and monthly premiums for each of the health care options it authorizes pursuant to Section 8-27-201, Tennessee Code Annotated, which result, with reasonable certainty, in the provision of sufficient revenues to pay plan expenses and to provide for the funding of reserves for estimated incurred but unreported claims. The monthly premiums and the employer contribution amounts shall be subject to the approval of the Commissioner of Finance and Administration pursuant to Section 4-3-1006, Tennessee Code Annotated.

The State Insurance Committee shall recognize the annualized rate and benefits adjustments intended to be effective on January 1, 2014, which are required so that the plan of benefits, on an annualized basis, shall not exceed the recurring revenues to pay plan expenses.

Item 2. From the appropriations made herein the Department of Military is hereby authorized to pay, on behalf of each participating national guardsman called up to state active duty, the cost of each individual's participation in the state-approved Group Life Insurance Plan for national guardsmen called up to state active duty. The provisions of Tennessee Code Annotated, Title 8, Chapter 27, Part 2, shall apply.

Item 3. The State Insurance Committee shall establish and maintain, within the appropriations made in this act for supplemental medical insurance for retired state employees and retired teachers and in accordance with Tennessee Code Annotated, Section 8-27-702, the respective contribution levels to be made by the state on behalf of the eligible participating retirees. The annualized contribution rate established by the Committee for the eligible participating employees shall not exceed the amount appropriated in this act, and the rate established is subject to approval by the Commissioner of Finance and Administration.

Item 4. It is the legislative intent that the State Insurance Committee establish a schedule of premium payments for retirees participating in the group insurance plan under the provisions of Tennessee Code Annotated, Section 8-27-205(b).

Item 5. The Commissioner of Finance and Administration is hereby authorized to establish positions and make appropriate adjustments to the Benefits Administration budget to reflect changes in the contractual arrangements for medical and other insurance coverage provided to state insurance plan participants. The establishment of additional positions and the allotment of additional departmental revenue are subject to approval by the State Insurance Committee.

SECTION 18. From the appropriations made by this act, claims for official travel expenses of state employees and members of boards and commissions, notwithstanding any provision of the law to the contrary, shall be subject to the provisions of comprehensive travel regulations as approved by the Attorney General and the Commissioner of Finance and Administration under the provisions of Tennessee Code Annotated, Section 4-3-1008.

SECTION 19. Whenever similar or duplicate appropriations are made in this act to those carried in any other act, such appropriation herein shall not be deemed as a supplemental appropriation, it being the legislative intent that there shall be no overlapping appropriations for equivalent amounts; but if this act simply supplements the appropriations made by the other act, then such supplemental appropriation shall be valid. The same shall apply to similar or duplicate appropriations made solely within this act.

SECTION 20. Notwithstanding the provisions of Tennessee Code Annotated, Title 54, Chapter 2, Part 2, to the contrary, whenever the State of Tennessee has any surplus lands or other surplus real properties which are sold or conveyed during the fiscal year ending June 30, 2014, the proceeds from the sale of such lands or other real property shall be subject to the provisions of Tennessee Code Annotated, Section 12-2-112.

SECTION 21. The State Procurement Commission may, if it considers such action in the interest of the state, authorize the Chief Procurement Officer to negotiate for the purchase of computer programs and associated software systems without following the procedures set out in Tennessee Code Annotated, Title 12, Chapter 3, relative to requisitioning and the receipt of bids. Such purchases shall be made at and for the best possible price, and each such purchase shall be confirmed by the State Procurement Commission before becoming effective. This exception shall not apply to the purchase of computer equipment machinery or associated hardware, but the same shall continue to be acquired in accordance with the procedures set out in Tennessee Code Annotated, Title 12, Chapter 3.

SECTION 22. Notwithstanding the provisions of Tennessee Code Annotated, Title 66, Chapter 29, warrants, drafts, and checks drawn on the State Treasury that have not been redeemed within 12 months of issue date shall be cancelled and written off the state's books with the funds reverting to the fund of issue. Subsequent claims by the payee of said instruments shall be honored upon receipt of documentation to substantiate the claim. The Commissioner of Finance and Administration and the State Treasurer shall ensure the state's compliance with the unclaimed property law.

SECTION 23.

Item 1. Budget and Authorized Positions Reconciliation and Reporting; Allotments. It is hereby declared to be the legislative intent that the Commissioner of Finance and Administration revise the funding recommendations and personnel summaries contained in the Budget Document to conform with this act, other general acts of this Session and any other actions which affect the level of departmental or other such revenue; it is the legislative intent that the commissioner make all necessary adjustments to revenues, appropriations, authorized positions, and totals to effectuate the provisions of this act as amended by the General Assembly. Said revised summaries shall be provided to the Office of Legislative Budget Analysis, Finance, Ways and Means Committees of the Senate and House of Representatives and to the Office of the Comptroller of the Treasury and Fiscal Review Committee.

In establishing allotments from the appropriations herein made, the Commissioner of Finance and Administration may establish total spending authorizations in the amount of the specific appropriation from state revenues herein made, plus the federal and departmental revenues estimated to be available as presented in the revised funding summaries cited above. In the event federal and departmental revenues for any particular program, appropriation code, or other classification are less than the amount estimated to be available under the allotments then and to that extent the spending authorizations are hereby reduced; to the extent that federal or departmental revenues in excess of the amounts allotted are realized, such excess shall not constitute increased spending authorizations, except under the conditions herein specified.

In establishing the allotments herein authorized, the Commissioner of Finance and Administration shall divide the total spending authorizations by allotment code, into two subdivisions, as follows:

1. Personal Services and Benefits
2. Other Operating Expenses

Item 2. Program Expansion Reports (Federal and Other Departmental Revenue). No state revenues shall be expended by any state agency unless such revenues are appropriated by the General Assembly, as reflected in the provisions of this act and the revised summaries cited above. No state agency shall establish any new programs or expand any existing programs, beyond the scope of those already established, recognized and approved by the General Assembly, as reflected in this act and the revised summaries cited above, unless each such new or expanded program is funded entirely from unanticipated or excess departmental revenues or federal revenues. However, no such expenditure of unanticipated or excess departmental revenues or federal revenues shall occur until written notice of the program and the availability of unanticipated or excess departmental revenues or federal revenues is submitted by the Commissioner of Finance and Administration to the Chairs of the Finance, Ways and Means Committees of the Senate and House of Representatives and until said committee chairs have acknowledged in writing receipt of such written notice; provided, however, that capital outlay program projects, whether capital improvements or capital maintenance, shall be submitted to the State Building Commission to be acknowledged. When submitted, a copy of operational budget expansion reports shall be provided to the Fiscal Review Committee executive director and the Office of Legislative Budget Analysis director for information purposes. For the purposes of this paragraph, the term "departmental revenues" means earnings or charges for goods or services; or donations, contributions or participation by political subdivisions, foundations, corporations, firms or persons; and the term "state revenues" means the proceeds of taxes, licenses, fees, fines, forfeiture or other imposts laid specifically by state law.

An expansion report shall not be acknowledged by the Chairs of the Finance, Ways and Means committees during a time that the General Assembly is in regular, annual session until each Finance, Ways and Means Committee has held a hearing on the proposed program expansion, or the committees have held a joint hearing.

State fiscal stabilization funds available under U.S. Public Law 111-5, American Recovery and Reinvestment Act, and any subsequent revenue-sharing relief to the states in excess of the amounts specifically appropriated or identified in this act shall not be used to expand programs until specifically appropriated by the General Assembly.

Item 3. Reporting on Certain Federal Grant Applications. Each state agency shall report to the Chairs of the Finance, Ways and Means committees of the Senate and the House of Representatives and to the Office of Legislative Budget Analysis when the agency applies for a federal grant of more than $100,000.

Item 4. Time-Limited Federal Criminal Justice Grant-Funded Positions. The Commissioner of Finance and Administration shall report to the Chairs of the Senate and House Finance, Ways and Means Committees on positions funded by federal criminal justice grants that are time-limited. The report shall include the number of positions and costs by federal program and by state agency and program, the period of the grant, the outlook for federal continuation of the grant beyond the expiration date, and any conditions of the grant indicating a state obligation upon expiration of the grant. A copy of the report also shall be provided to the Office of Legislative Budget Analysis director and the Fiscal Review Committee executive director.

Item 5. Non-recurring Grants Notification. The Department of Finance and Administration, under guidelines it shall issue, shall direct state agencies to notify in writing by November 1 each entity (other than state agencies or individuals) receiving a grant under this act which is from a non-recurring appropriation that such funding has been identified in the Budget or appropriations act to expire at the end of the fiscal year, and that such entity is advised to seek alternative non-state funding for future fiscal years or to reduce its budget.

Item 6. Capital Outlay Projects Change Reporting. The Commissioner of Finance and Administration shall provide a written quarterly report to the director of the Office of Legislative Budget Analysis and to the executive director of the Fiscal Review Committee identifying additions, deletions or other modifications of capital improvement and capital maintenance projects occurring subsequent to enactment of the annual budget through the appropriations and bond authorization acts.

Item 7. Overlapped Positions Reports. The Commissioner of Human Resources shall submit a monthly report to the Office of Legislative Budget Analysis regarding positions that have been overlapped for ninety (90) days or more. In addition, the budget as introduced shall indicate the number of positions overlapped for ninety (90) days or more at a time no more than thirty (30) days before transmittal of the budget.

SECTION 24.

Item 1. Notwithstanding any provision of the law to the contrary, the heads of the respective departments for which appropriations are made in Section 1, Titles I, II, III-1, Items 1, 3, 5, and 7, are authorized to revise their respective budgets and personnel authorizations within the appropriations made in Sections 1 and 4 of this act and to submit those revised summaries to the Commissioner of Finance and Administration, who shall incorporate them into the revised funding recommendations and personnel summaries and allotments and spending authorizations required by Section 23 of this act.

Item 2. All funds appropriated in Section 1, Title III-1, Items 3, 5 and 7 and in Section 4, Title III-1, Items 3, 5 and 6, shall be administered in a ministerial capacity by the Department of Finance and Administration in accordance with budgets and any revisions thereto of the respective entities for which such appropriations are made. Such budgets and any revisions thereto shall be subject to the concurrence of the Speaker of the Senate and Speaker of the House of Representatives.

SECTION 25. Except where sovereign immunity has been or shall hereafter be expressly waived by the General Assembly, all appropriations of state revenues and departmental revenues made in this act and in prior acts to the state, its departments, agencies, boards, educational institutions, instrumentalities, and incorporated entities performing the state's governmental functions shall be state funds and shall be protected by the state's sovereign immunity from every court's judgment, decree, attachment, or other legal process; provided, however, that any statutory or other provision authorizing an agency, board, or entity to sue and be sued shall not constitute a waiver of sovereign immunity.

SECTION 26. From the appropriation made for the General Assembly under Section 1, Title I, payment shall be made for, but not limited to, the following items:

1. Any lawful expenses of the One Hundred Eighth General Assembly, for which funds have not been obligated on June 30, 2013, such funds herein appropriated as are required may be made available during the fiscal year ending June 30, 2013.

2. The lawful expenses of the One Hundred Eighth General Assembly.

3. The cost of staffing, maintaining and operating the offices of the Speaker of the Senate and the Speaker of the House of Representatives, including necessary travel and other expenses incident to said offices, not covered by Title I, Items 1.2 and 1.3, of this act.

4. Such expenses as may be incurred for maintaining legislative facilities including the maintenance and staffing and such other expenses as may be necessary to provide offices and other services to members of the General Assembly and their staff in state facilities in Nashville.

5. Expenses and travel pay to legislators for each day when attending conferences, workshops, and other official meetings, both within and without the State of Tennessee, when said travel is approved by the Speaker of the Senate and/or the Speaker of the House of Representatives. Payments shall be at the same rate provided for members of the standing committees of the General Assembly when meeting between sessions. Provided, further, that reimbursement may be made to legislators for registration fees incurred while attending conferences and meetings as may be approved by the Speaker of the Senate and/or the Speaker of the House of Representatives.

6. Expenses and travel pay allowed to members of the Joint Legislative Services Committee at the same rates and in the same manner provided by Tennessee Code Annotated, Section 3-1-106, and to members of the Fiscal Review Committee, as authorized under Tennessee Code Annotated, Section 3-7-102.

7. The Speakers may transfer to the Office of Legal Services for the General Assembly and to the Fiscal Review Committee sufficient funds to enable them to complete all studies assigned to them by the One Hundred Eighth General Assembly, and to furnish such help as may be required by standing, select and joint committees of the General Assembly.

8. Membership dues to the National Conference of State Legislatures, similar service organizations, and such other conferences as may be approved by the Speaker of the Senate and the Speaker of the House of Representatives.

9. Any expenditures for legislative purposes called for by resolutions or joint resolutions properly adopted by either or both Houses of the General Assembly.

10. Payment of expenses to any member, as provided by law, for attendance at any meeting of any standing, special, or select committee of the General Assembly, whether such meeting occurs during or between sessions of the General Assembly. Such expenses for meetings held between sessions shall be paid at the same rate as provided in the general law for meetings held while the General Assembly is in session.

11. In addition to appropriations made under Section 1, Title I, there is hereby appropriated a sum sufficient to cover any increase automatically occurring under mandate of law in any compensation, benefits, or expenses funded under Section 1, Title I.

12. From funds available to the General Assembly, there is earmarked a sum sufficient for the sole purpose of funding expenses of members of the General Assembly for meetings of study committees of the General Assembly on which they serve; provided, that such expense payment is subject to approval by the Speaker of the House of Representatives and the Speaker of the Senate in accordance with Tennessee Code Annotated, Section 3-1-106.

All items listed above, together with any other expenses for the General Assembly, upon the approval of the Speaker of the Senate and/or the Speaker of the House of Representatives, shall be paid through the Office of Legislative Administration, who shall also be authorized to make arrangements for, and incur obligations incident to, any convening of the One Hundred Eighth General Assembly.

Provided, further, that during any period when the Offices of the Speaker of the Senate or the Speaker of the House of Representatives are vacant, or otherwise upon authority of the Speakers, the Director of the Office of Legislative Administration is hereby authorized to do any act which the Speaker might do under the provisions of this section.

The provisions of the section shall not be construed to countermand any general act passed by the One Hundred Eighth General Assembly.

SECTION 27. The Speaker of each House of the General Assembly shall be paid from funds appropriated to the General Assembly the following sums:

Seven hundred fifty dollars ($750.00) for their ex-officio services during any session of the General Assembly; plus the sum of five thousand seven hundred dollars ($5,700.00) annually for local office expenses in their county of residence which will be in addition to the cost of maintaining and operating offices in the State Capitol. In addition, each Speaker shall be allowed the same amount for expenses and travel pay as that provided for members of the standing committees of the General Assembly when meeting between sessions, for attending meetings of standing, select, or joint committees of the General Assembly or when absent from their county of residence on official duty as Speaker.

The allowance for ex-officio duties authorized by this section shall be paid at the request of each Speaker at any time after adjournment of a session. The amount authorized hereby for local office expenses shall be paid annually on or after November 1st of each year at the request of each Speaker. Requests for payments shall be addressed to the Director of the Office of Legislative Administration and need not be accompanied by a list of expenditures for which allowances the reimbursements are claimed. Payments for attending meetings between sessions or when absent from county of residence shall be paid from time to time on request of each Speaker.

SECTION 28. In order to prevent duplication of effort and to establish professional standards, audits to be performed by internal audit staffs or grantees of departmental activities funded from appropriations made in this act shall be coordinated with the Office of the Comptroller of the Treasury, and such reports as may be issued shall be prepared in accordance with standards established as required by law by the Comptroller of the Treasury. No department, agency, institution, board, or commission shall cause internal auditing to be performed by persons who do not meet the job specifications for internal auditors established by the Commissioner of Human Resources and approved by the Commissioner of Finance and Administration and the Comptroller of the Treasury, pursuant to Tennessee Code Annotated, Section 4-3-304.

SECTION 29. The appropriations to public institutions of higher education set forth in Section 1 of this act shall be subject to the conditions and limitations set forth in this section, and shall not be subject to other provisions of this act except as otherwise expressly stated.

Item 1. Salaries to be paid from the appropriations made to educational institutions shall be fixed as follows:

The President and the staff of the University of Tennessee, by the Board of Trustees; the Presidents and staffs of the institutions within, and the Chancellor and staff of, the State University and Community College System of Tennessee, by the Board of Regents; and the Directors and staffs of the technology centers by the Board of Regents; all of which shall be within the appropriations provided and available for said purposes.

Item 2. Each higher education institution, including technology centers, shall report to the Commissioner of Finance and Administration, the Tennessee Higher Education Commission, and the Office of Legislative Budget Analysis, the actual amount of expenditures for maintenance and operation of the physical plant, exclusive of utilities, for the fiscal year, and any deviation in these expenditures from the amounts recommended in the funding formula for these purposes, prorated to reflect actual funding levels appropriated in this act.

Item 3. All institutional revenues of any kind collected by the institutions in the course of their operations for their own use are hereby appropriated to the institutions in addition to the specific appropriations made by this act.

Item 4. It is the intent of the General Assembly that the fee charges among the public institutions of higher education of the state, be subject to the nature and scope of the institutions, and that the State Board of Regents and the Board of Trustees of the University of Tennessee shall consult with the Higher Education Commission before establishing the fee schedules for the universities, community colleges and technology centers.

Item 5. The appropriations herein for higher education and appropriations of all higher education departmental and institutional revenue are subject to the provisions of Tennessee Code Annotated, Title 9, Chapter 4, and subsections (4) and (5) of Tennessee Code Annotated, Section 4-3-1006. Within the general requirements of these provisions, the Commissioner of Finance and Administration, in consultation with the Comptroller of the Treasury and the Higher Education Commission, shall specify the content and procedures for submitting operating budgets and revisions thereto. The operating budgets shall be submitted to the Higher Education Commission by the respective governing boards. The Higher Education Commission shall then submit such operating budgets with their comments to the Department of Finance and Administration for approval. In addition, the appropriations in this act to institutions of higher education shall be subject to the requirements, restrictions and controls of the State Board of Claims and the State Building Commission in the same manner as other agencies of the state. The governing boards shall submit to the Office of Legislative Budget Analysis both the original and revised operating budgets proposed. The Tennessee Higher Education Commission shall submit to the Office of Legislative Budget Analysis the revised higher education funding formula for the ensuing fiscal year no later than December 1 of each year.

Item 6. From the appropriations made herein, institutions of higher education are hereby authorized to pay, on behalf of each participating employee, a percentage amount equal to the amount paid by other agencies of the state of the cost of each employee's participation in the state-approved Group Insurance Plan for state employees.

Item 7. Except where sovereign immunity has been or shall hereafter be expressly waived by the General Assembly, all appropriations of state funds and institutional revenues made in this act and prior acts to institutions of higher education shall be state funds and shall be protected by the state's sovereign immunity from any court's judgment, decree, attachment, or other legal process, provided, that any statutory or other provision authorizing any entity to sue and be sued shall not constitute a waiver of sovereign immunity.

Item 8. From the appropriations made in this act and other appropriations acts, the budgetary units in higher education shall pay to the Tennessee Consolidated Retirement System the employer's share of retirement and shall pay to the Social Security Administration the Social Security costs including the additional benefit costs associated with pay, pay raises funded from fees, revenues, payroll savings or any other funding source.

Item 9. The appropriations in this act for Centers of Excellence and Campus Centers of Emphasis are subject to allocation by the Higher Education Commission and the Commissioner of Finance and Administration. In allocating the appropriation for Centers of Excellence, a consideration shall be planned reductions to existing expenditures to supplement funding for the centers.

Item 10. There is hereby appropriated a sum sufficient to pay insurance claims filed by lending institutions under the provisions of the Federal Family Education Loan Program and the costs associated with administering that program. Provided, however, such payments shall be made and such costs shall be paid from funds and reserves received and maintained by the Tennessee Student Assistance Corporation for the Federal Family Education Loan Program and the State of Tennessee shall in no way be liable for such claims.

Item 11. In addition to any other funds appropriated by the provisions of this act, there is appropriated to the Student Assistance Corporation all reserve balances now held by the Corporation for the Student Loan Program authorized by Tennessee Code Annotated, Title 49, Chapter 4, Part 5. It being the legislative intent that these reserves may be used to cover any expenditures resulting from over-awards of assistance to students enrolled during the 2013-2014 academic year under the Student Assistance Program and may use that portion of earnings from the Student Loan Program reserves to conduct the training, administration and default management for students, schools and lenders in the Federal Family Education Loan Program, Part 4 and the Student Loan Program, Part 5. The allotment of funds appropriated by this item shall be subject to the provisions of Tennessee Code Annotated, Title 4, Chapter 3, Part 10 and Title 9, Chapter 4, Part 51.

Item 12. In the Tennessee Student Assistance Awards Program any prior year appropriations recovered from prior recipients by June 30, 2014, shall not revert to the fund balance but shall be added to the reserve balances now held by the Student Assistance Corporation for the Student Loan Program authorized by Tennessee Code Annotated, Title 49, Chapter 4, Part 5.

Item 13. Proceeds collected from prior recipients of the teacher loan/scholarship programs authorized by Tennessee Code Annotated, Title 49, Chapter 4, Part 2, shall not revert to the fund balance but shall be deferred and added to the funds appropriated in the succeeding year for expenditure as awards in the Teaching Scholars Program (Tennessee Code Annotated, Section 49-4-212).

Item 14. Proceeds collected from prior recipients of the Minority Teaching Fellows Program authorized by Tennessee Code Annotated, Title 49, Chapter 4, Part 7, shall not revert to the fund balance but shall be deferred and added to the funds appropriated in the succeeding year for expenditure as awards in the Minority Teaching Fellows Program (Tennessee Code Annotated, Section 49-4-706).

Item 15. There is hereby appropriated a sum sufficient to the Tennessee Student Assistance Corporation from accumulated interest earnings in the Academic Scholars Program (Tennessee Code Annotated, Section 49-4-203) and in the Christa McAuliffe Scholarships Program (Tennessee Code Annotated, Section 49-4-705).

Item 16. In the fiscal year ending June 30, 2014, there is appropriated a sum sufficient to the Tennessee Student Assistance Corporation from revenues received pursuant to TCA 49-4-702(c) for the loan-scholarship program for graduate students in professional nursing. Said funds shall not revert to the general fund, but shall be carried forward for future student awards.

Item 17. There is hereby appropriated a sum sufficient to the Baccalaureate Education System Trust Board of Directors from fees and other charges for participation in the prepayment tuition program operated by the board under the provisions of Tennessee Code Annotated, Title 49, Chapter 7, Part 8.

Item 18. It is hereby declared to be the legislative intent that the Tennessee Higher Education Commission shall, as part of the budget recommendation to the Governor each year, provide estimates of likely increases in student fees at various levels of state appropriations varying from zero increase in state appropriations to full funding of the Commission's recommendations. It is further the intent of the General Assembly that the Commission include within its recommendations the total revenues expected to be available to each higher education institution for educational and general purposes (including state appropriations, student fees and any other available funds), compared to total educational and general revenues recommended for each institution under the Commission's formula at full funding.

Item 19. State appropriations to higher education institutions will be budgeted and expended in a manner that advances the priorities and goals of the approved higher education master plan.

Item 20. From non-recurring funds appropriated in this act to the Community College System of the Tennessee Board of Regents for purposes of implementing the phase-in of the outcome-based formula, the board is authorized to reserve a portion of such funds to: (a) supplement future funding of such formula phase-in for the community college system; or (b) fulfill the requirements of Tennessee Code Annotated, Section 49-8-101(c) regarding the operation of the Tennessee community college system as a unified system. The Tennessee Board of Regents shall file a written report with the Commissioner of Finance and Administration and the chairs of the Education Committees of the Senate and House of Representatives concerning the provisions of this item.

Item 21. To the Tennessee Higher Education Commission the unexpended balance of the Gates Foundation grant carried forward in the amount of $425,616.68 at the prior June 30 pursuant to Public Acts of 2011, Chapter 473, Section 23, Item 1, and 2011-2012 Program Expansion Report number 7.

Item 22. From the appropriation to UT Martin in Section 1, Title III-10, the sum of $200,000 is for the purpose of making a grant to the Parsons-Decatur County Higher Education Foundation for the Parsons Center. It is the intent of the General Assembly that such funds shall not be distributed by means of the higher education formula.

Item 23. It is the legislative intent that the appropriation in Section 1, Title III-10, Item 4.6, Equipment for Community Colleges and Technology Centers, be used solely to meet the workforce training and educational needs of Tennesseans by only investing the funds in up-to-date equipment for hands-on student training. No part of the funds shall be used for any other purpose. Before drawing any portion of this appropriation from the state's accounts, the Chancellor of the State University and Community College System shall report in writing the allocations by institution and intended uses to the Governor, the Speaker of the Senate, the Speaker of the House of Representatives, the Chairs of the Education Committees of the Senate and House of Representatives, and the Office of Legislative Budget Analysis, and the Commissioner of Finance and Administration shall not allot the appropriation until the allocation plan is approved by the Governor. Allotments may be made in multiple portions, to the extent that allocations and intended uses are approved in multiple phases.

Item 24. The appropriation in Section 1, Title III-10, Item 3.1(g), UT Research Initiatives, includes a non-recurring amount of $5,000,000 to match a National Science

PUBLIC CHAPTER NO. 453 (cont'd)

Foundation (NSF) grant and University of Tennessee funds for development of an advanced supercomputing center, and such grant is to be made by NSF on a competitive basis. The General Assembly recognizes that it is the Governor's intent to recommend and provide a total of $20,000,000 over a four-year period beginning on July 1, 2013, to match the NSF funds. It is the legislative intent that, if such grant award is not made by the NSF to develop the Tennessee center, the amount appropriated be returned to the state.

Item 25. The capital outlay projects listed in the 2013-2014 Budget Document and which are identified with the heading "Proposed Capital Projects from School Bonds and Other Sources, Fiscal Year 2013-2014," are presented for informational purposes only. The projects are subject to recommendation and approval procedures involving the higher education institutions and their governing boards, the Tennessee Higher Education Commission, Finance and Administration, the Tennessee State School Bond Authority, the State Funding Board and the State Building Commission.

The following proposed capital outlay projects, to be funded from school bonds, institutional/auxiliary and other funds, are in addition to those projects listed on pages A-160 through A-162 in the 2013-2014 Budget Document:

State University and Community College System (Tennessee Board of Regents):

East Tennessee State University:		
College of Medicine Building 60 Renovations	$	12,930,000
D.P. Culp and Stone Hall Renovations		15,000,000
Millennium Center Renovation		1,500,000
New Data Center		1,500,000
New Football Stadium		18,000,000
Total ETSU	$	48,930,000
Middle Tennessee State University:		
Andrew W. Miller Center Renovations	$	6,000,000
Bus Maintenance Facility		1,750,000
Campus Demolitions and Site Improvements		2,750,000
College Heights Renovation		830,000
Flight Simulator Building Construction		700,000
Recreational Fields Lighting		350,000
ROTC Training Tower Construction		160,000
Warehouse Building Renovations		530,000
Women's Softball Batting Enclosure		100,000
Total MTSU	$	13,170,000
Tennessee State University:		
Center for Health and Research Building Upgrades	$	200,000
Hale Stadium Renovations and Site Improvements		1,000,000
Total TSU	$	1,200,000
Tennessee Technological University:		
Athletics Facilities Improvements	$	32,000,000
Athletics Maintenance & Storage Facility Construction		370,000
Capitol Quad Steam Line Replacement		1,640,000
Craft Center Sewage Treatment Plant Replacement		320,000
Hyder-Burks Equestrian Facility Construction		1,000,000
Outdoor Tennis Courts Replacement		1,240,000
Residence Halls Mechanical Upgrades		21,500,000
Residence Halls Roof Replacements		750,000
Tech Village Apartments Renovations		1,450,000
Total TTU	$	60,270,000
University of Memphis:		
Basketball Training Center Construction	$	25,000,000
Indoor Football Practice Facility		14,000,000
Lambuth Campus Improvements		1,200,000
Research Facilities Upgrades		1,500,000

Soccer Field Improvements		3,000,000
Total UoM	$	44,700,000
Dyersburg State Community College:		
Baseball and Softball Field Lighting	$	490,000
Softball Multipurpose Building		330,000
Total DSCC	$	820,000
Jackson State Community College:		
Campus-wide Restroom Renovations		250,000
Nashville State Community College:		
Clarksville Campus Renovations	$	6,690,000
New Academic Building Parking		370,000
Total NASCC	$	7,060,000
Pellissippi State Community College:		
Strawberry Plains Renovation		5,700,000
Roane State Community College:		
Campus-wide Paving	$	460,000
Gym Seating Upgrades		190,000
New Maintenance Equipment Building		100,000
Total RSCC	$	750,000
Southwest Tennessee Community College:		
Macon Cove Campus Industrial Readiness Facility	$	3,500,000
Whitehaven Center Renovations		5,600,000
Total STCC	$	9,100,000
Volunteer State Community College:		
Livingston Campus Site and Building Improvements	$	5,000,000
New Satellite Teaching Facility		3,650,000
Total VSCC	$	8,650,000
Total Tennessee Board of Regents	**$**	**200,600,000**
University of Tennessee:		
UT Martin:		
Football Press Box Improvements	$	6,400,000
Administration Building Renovations		500,000
Total UTM	$	6,900,000
Total University of Tennessee	**$**	**6,900,000**
Grand Total	**$**	**207,500,000**

The requests for ETSU D.P. Culp Center Renovation in the amount of $3,500,000; ETSU Stone Hall Renovations in the amount of $3,500,000; and the VSCC New Robertson County Academic Building in the amount of $3,650,000, as identified on pages A-160 and A-161 of the 2013-2014 Budget Document are to be canceled.

SECTION 30. Salaries provided under the appropriations made in Sections 1 and 4 of this act to the respective departments, institutions, offices and agencies shall be fixed as under the provisions of Tennessee Code Annotated, Title 8, Chapter 23.

Within the appropriations made for the Office of the Attorney General and Reporter under this act, the salaries of the attorneys, legal and clerical staff and other employees shall be fixed by the Attorney General. The expenditures provided for herein shall not exceed the amount of the appropriation to the Office of the Attorney General and Reporter.

The salaries of all employees of the Judicial Branch, except those whose salaries are set by law, shall be fixed by the Director of the Administrative Office of the Courts with the approval of the

Chief Justice of the Supreme Court. The compensation of the judges, chancellors, and justices of the state's trial and appellate courts shall be set in accordance with Tennessee Code Annotated, Section 8-23-103.

Within the appropriations herein made, the salaries of the subordinates and employees of the Treasurer, Comptroller, Secretary of State, and the Fiscal Review Committee shall be fixed by the heads thereof, respectively, and the salaries of the employees and subordinates of the Joint Legislative Services Committee shall be fixed by such committee in accordance with the provisions of Tennessee Code Annotated, Title 3, Chapters 10 through 14, inclusive; all other salaries and wages in departments, institutions, offices and agencies shall be approved by the Commissioner of Human Resources, provided, however, that the establishment of salary ranges within such departments, institutions, offices and agencies shall be subject to the approval of the Commissioner of Finance and Administration. To the extent that additional funds are appropriated or are generated within a department or agency by abolishing vacant and funded positions, subject to review and approval of the Commissioner of Finance and Administration and the Commissioner of Human Resources, salary increases may be granted from such funds.

Employee promotions shall be reported to the General Assembly under the provisions of Tennessee Code Annotated, Section 8-30-211(b).

SECTION 31. The provisions of this section shall take effect upon becoming a law, the public welfare requiring it. Under the provisions of Section 4 and Section 23 of this act, it is the legislative intent to appropriate the proceeds of federal block grant programs, as assumed by the State of Tennessee, in the following manner:

1. Social Services block grant in the amount of $15,872,600 to the Department of Human Services and in the amount of $21,210,500 to the Department of Children's Services.

2. Mental Health Services block grant in the amount of $8,422,200 to the Department of Mental Health and Substance Abuse Services.

3. Child Care Development Funds block grant in the amount of $146,223,500 to the Department of Human Services.

4. Maternal and Child Health block grant in the amount of $14,688,900 to the Department of Health.

5. Preventive Health block grant in the amount of $992,100 to the Department of Health.

6. Community Services block grant in the amount of $10,741,800 to the Department of Human Services.

7. Low-Income Energy Assistance block grant in the amount of $23,404,800 to the Department of Human Services.

8. Substance Abuse Prevention and Treatment block grant in the amount of $29,522,700 to the Department of Mental Health and Substance Abuse Services.

9. Temporary Assistance to Needy Families (TANF) block grant in the amount of $213,560,600 to the Department of Human Services.

10. Small Cities Community Development block grant in the amount of $48,938,500 to the Department of Economic and Community Development. Said sum being the estimated allocation of funds for the fiscal years 2012-2013 and 2013-2014 combined.

Provided, however, that all expenditures of any community development block grant funds in addition to those appropriated and enumerated in this section shall be subject to the following limitations and restrictions:

The Housing and Community Development Act of 1981 made it possible for states to assume administration of the Small Cities Community Development Block Grant (CDBG) previously administered by the U.S. Department of Housing and Urban Development (HUD). In Tennessee, the CDBG Program shall be administered by the Department of Economic and Community Development (ECD).

There shall be appropriated by the General Assembly to ECD such funds as may be allocated to Tennessee by the federal government for the CDBG Program. The state-administered

CDBG Program shall be developed within the parameters of the CDBG legislation, applicable federal regulations, and consultation with citizens and elected officials in Tennessee.

The CDBG goals shall be three-fold: (1) target on areas of economic distress; (2) stimulate the growth of jobs and income in these areas; and (3) maximize the number of grantees. Additionally, all CDBG projects must meet one of the three national objectives of (1) principally benefiting persons of low and moderate income; (2) elimination or prevention of slums and blight; or (3) elimination of conditions detrimental to health, safety or public welfare. ECD shall be authorized to make grants and/or loans of CDBG monies to eligible city and county governments in Tennessee to achieve these goals. Loan payments and interest shall be reserved for reappropriation and shall not revert to the general fund balance at year end.

Eligible applicants shall be all city and county governments in Tennessee except those cities of and counties designated by HUD as CDBG entitlement areas. Cities excluded from the state-administered CDBG Program include Memphis and Shelby County, Nashville (Davidson County), Chattanooga, Knoxville and Knox County, Clarksville, Bristol, Johnson City, Oak Ridge, Murfreesboro, Kingsport, Hendersonville, Morristown, Cleveland, Franklin, and Jackson. These cities and counties will receive their CDBG funds directly from HUD.

Based upon anticipated CDBG allocations of $24,449,900 in fiscal year 2012-2013 and of $24,488,600 in fiscal year 2013-2014, the following target funding levels shall be established:

	2012-2013	2013-2014
Administrative Costs ....$	589,000	$ 589,800
Industrial Location/Expansions/Retentions...	500,000	500,000
Community Livability..................................	1,976,900	2,238,600
Water/Sewer/Solid Waste	17,526,900	18,000,000
Housing and Neighborhood Revitalization....	2,857,100	1,960,200
Commercial Façade Improvements.............	0	200,000
Set-Aside	1,000,000	1,000,000

A fifty percent (50%) reduction in any category will be permitted to facilitate proper program management and allow administrative flexibility. The funds so reduced shall be allocated to other categories with priority given to water/sewer/solid waste projects.

Selection criteria for project approvals shall be uniform within categories, objective and quantitative, and shall be based on project need, project feasibility, project impact, community need, the percent of project beneficiaries that have family incomes below the low and moderate income (LMI) levels, and, for community livability projects, essentialness.

Project application materials will be supplemented, as appropriate, by site visits and by informed opinions of state agencies knowledgeable about particular projects.

The level of CDBG assistance for individual projects shall be determined by the following factors: (1) a maximum grant of $500,000.00 and/or a maximum loan of $750,000.00 for individual projects ($300,000.00 for community livability projects); (2) a maximum grant and/or loan to any applicant of $750,000.00 in two successive years; and (3) the grantee's ability to pay. Higher grant levels (up to $1,000,000.00) may be approved for regional projects.

If modifications in the expenditure plan for the CDBG Program are required, said modifications shall be accomplished in the following manner: (1) if the General Assembly is in session such modifications shall be approved by the General Assembly, or (2) if the General Assembly is not in session, the Governor may, (a) submit such modifications to the State Funding Board for approval or, (b) call a special session of the General Assembly for approval.

The Housing and Economic Recovery Act of 2008, U.S. Public Law 110-289, authorizes additional funding for the Small Cities Neighborhood Stabilization Community Development block grant. It is the legislative intent to appropriate the proceeds, as assumed by the State of Tennessee, in fiscal year 2012-2013 in the amount of $11,225,700 to the Tennessee Housing Development Agency. Any unexpended funds at June 30, 2013, are hereby reappropriated in the 2013-2014 fiscal year.

SECTION 32. The appropriations made in Section 1, Title III-8, Item 8, to the Department of Economic and Community Development for the FastTrack Infrastructure and Job Training Assistance Programs shall be expended pursuant to Tennessee Code Annotated, Sections 4-3-716 and 4-3-717. The Commissioner of Finance and Administration is authorized to transfer sums sufficient from the appropriation for FastTrack Infrastructure and Job Training Assistance to Community and Rural Development, Business Development and Innovation Programs for economic development projects. The Commissioner of Economic and Community Development is authorized to transfer sums sufficient from the appropriation for FastTrack Infrastructure and Job Training Assistance to Tennessee Jobs Skills Program, subject to the approval of the Commissioner of Finance and Administration. There is hereby reappropriated sums sufficient from any amounts carried forward in the FastTrack fund at the end of each fiscal year pursuant to Tennessee Code Annotated, Section 4-3-716(d).

SECTION 33. On or before January 31 of each calendar year, the Center for Business and Economic Research of the University of Tennessee shall cause to be published a comprehensive report on the state's economy. Said report shall be based on projections from the Tennessee Econometric Model and such other information as the Center may deem appropriate. The report shall contain projections for ten years (beginning with the calendar year preceding the year in which the report is due) of the annual economic activity (level and percent change over prior year) for each of the state's major economic sectors; shall include ten-year projections of selected economic indicators, as specified by the State Funding Board; and shall also include a narrative description of the short-term and long-term prospects for economic and business activity in the state based on these indicators. Quarterly projections shall also be published if available.

Said report shall be distributed to the Governor and the other members of the State Funding Board. The State Funding Board shall report to the General Assembly as provided in Tennessee Code Annotated, Section 9-4-5202.

SECTION 34. The provisions of this section shall take effect upon becoming law, the public welfare requiring it. From the appropriations made in Chapter 1029, Public Acts of 2012, the Commissioner of Finance and Administration is authorized to make transfers from the appropriations made:

Item 1. To the District Attorneys General in Section 1, Title III-1, Item 2.

Item 2. To the Department of Finance and Administration in Section 1, Title III-2, Item 3, and to adjust federal aid and other departmental revenue accordingly.

Item 3. To the Department of Agriculture in Section 1, Title III-3, and to adjust federal aid and other departmental revenue accordingly.

Item 4. To the Department of Environment and Conservation in Section 1, Title III-5, and to adjust federal aid and other departmental revenue accordingly.

Item 5. To the Department of Economic and Community Development in Section 1, Title III-8.

Item 6. To the Department of Education in Section 1, Title III-9, and to adjust federal aid and other departmental revenue accordingly.

Item 7. To the administration and support services programs in Section 1, Title III-10, Items 1.1 through 1.7, which are administered by the Tennessee Higher Education Commission or the Tennessee Student Assistance Corporation, and may include transfers to, but not from, the Foreign Language Institute.

Item 8. To the Department of Safety in Section 1, Title III-20, and to adjust federal aid and other departmental revenue accordingly.

Item 9. From the unexpended balance of the appropriation in Section 1, Title III-22, Miscellaneous Appropriations, a sum sufficient is authorized to be transferred for the purpose of reimbursing the Tennessee Consolidated Retirement System for payments made relative to Item 2.1 of the cited title.

SECTION 35. The Commissioner of Finance and Administration is authorized to make the following transfers from the appropriations made in this act:

Item 1. To the Judicial Branch in Section 1, Title II, but excluding the appropriations for Board of Law Examiners, Board of Professional Responsibility, Tennessee Lawyers Assistance Program, Continuing Legal Education and Client Protection Fund. Transfer of appropriations to or between Guardian ad Litem, Indigent Defendants' Counsel, Civil Legal Representation, Court Interpreter Services, and Verbatim Transcripts are sanctioned, but transfers from these programs to other programs are excluded.

Item 2. In Section 1 for the IV-D Child Support Program, a reallocation of funds between the District Attorneys General and the Department of Human Services is authorized.

The Commissioner of Finance and Administration is further authorized to adjust federal aid and other departmental revenues, and to establish positions as may be required.

Item 3. To the Department of General Services, Division of Motor Vehicle Management Internal Service Fund, from the funds appropriated to state agencies and programs by this act, a sum sufficient for the acquisition of motor vehicles.

Item 4. From the funds appropriated in Section 1, Title III-3, to the Department of Agriculture for the agricultural enhancement program.

Item 5. To the Department of Environment and Conservation in Section 1, Title III-5, to recognize administrative reorganizations and to adjust authorized positions, federal aid and other departmental revenue accordingly.

Item 6. To the Department of Correction in Section 1, Title III-7, and to adjust the number of authorized positions within the department's authorized level.

Item 7. To the Department of Economic and Community Development, in Section 1, Title III-8, from Community and Rural Development and Policy and Federal Programs to Economic Development District Grants to comply with the requirements of Chapter 521, Public Acts of 2007.

Item 8. To the Department of Economic and Community Development in Section 1, Title III-8, to recognize administrative reorganizations. The Commissioner of Finance and Administration is authorized to adjust authorized positions, federal aid, and other departmental revenue accordingly.

Item 9. In Section 1 for Targeted Case Management Services, a reallocation of funds between the Department of Education and the Department of Children's Services is authorized. The Commissioner of Finance and Administration is further authorized to adjust departmental revenues as may be required.

Item 10. To the Department of Education in Section 1, Title III-9, to recognize administrative reorganizations addressing the management of the federal Race to the Top grant program and implementation of Public Acts of 2010 (E.S.), Public Chapter 2, the Tennessee First to the Top Act of 2010, and to adjust authorized positions, federal aid and other departmental revenue accordingly. To implement the Achievement School District program, the Commissioner of Finance and Administration is further authorized to increase authorized positions in the Department of Education and to adjust federal aid and other departmental revenue accordingly.

Item 11. To the Department of Labor and Workforce Development in Section 1, Title III-13, and to adjust federal aid and other departmental revenue accordingly.

Item 12. To the Department of Mental Health and Substance Abuse Services in Section 1, Title III-14, and to adjust federal aid and other departmental revenue accordingly.

Item 13. To the Department of Military, but excluding Disaster Relief Grants, in Section 1, Title III-15, and to adjust federal aid and other departmental revenue accordingly.

Item 14. To the Department of Health in Section 1, Title III-16, and to adjust federal aid and other departmental revenue accordingly.

Item 15. From the appropriations made to the Department of Human Services and the TennCare program in Section 1, for eligibility determination for the Medicaid Program and various federal family assistance programs, the Commissioner of Finance and Administration is authorized to reallocate appropriations between the department and program, and to adjust federal and departmental revenue estimates accordingly, in order to reflect actual costs of eligibility determination services and Medicaid case management services.

Item 16. To the Department of Human Services in Section 1, Title III-17, and to adjust federal aid and other departmental revenue accordingly.

Item 17. To the Department of Revenue in Section 1, Title III-18, and to adjust departmental revenue accordingly.

Item 18. To the Department of Finance and Administration, Strategic Health-Care Programs in Section 1, Title III-21, and to adjust federal aid and other departmental revenues accordingly.

Item 19. The appropriations made in Section 1, Title III-22, Miscellaneous Appropriations, are authorized to be allocated and transferred to the appropriate organizational units and programs of state government by the Commissioner of Finance and Administration. For each appropriation so allocated and transferred, there is further appropriated sums sufficient from dedicated and earmarked revenues to provide for the comparable allocation of appropriations to those agencies and programs funded by dedicated and earmarked revenues. The appropriation for the Homeland Security Emergency Fund is subject to approval by the Director of Homeland Security.

In addition to the appropriations made in Section 4 of this act, there is hereby appropriated to the organizational units and programs of state government all federal aid funds and departmental revenue earnings associated with the allocation and transfer of Miscellaneous Appropriations authorized under the preceding paragraph in this item.

Item 20. To the Department of Children's Services in Section 1, Title III-23, and to adjust federal aid and other departmental revenue accordingly.

Item 21. To the Department of Intellectual and Developmental Disabilities in Section 1, Title III-25, and to adjust federal aid and other departmental revenue accordingly.

Item 22. To the Department of Finance and Administration, TennCare program in Section 1, Title III-26, and to adjust federal aid and other departmental revenue accordingly.

Item 23. To the Department of Transportation in Section 1, Title III-30, to provide additional funds for resurfacing as determined by the Commissioner of Transportation.

Item 24. To the Department of Transportation in Section 1, Title III-30, to recognize administrative reorganizations and to adjust authorized positions, federal aid and other departmental revenue accordingly.

The Commissioner of Transportation, with the approval of the Commissioner of Finance and Administration, is authorized to reorganize programs within the Department of Transportation for better accounting and personnel management practices made possible by implementation of the enterprise resource planning system.

Item 25. From the appropriations to the Department of Environment and Conservation in Section 1, Title III-5, and Section 4, Title III-5, and other sections of this act, subject to approval of the Commissioner of Finance and Administration, the Department of Environment and Conservation is authorized to consolidate the following programs at July 1, 2013: Water Pollution Control, Water Supply, and Groundwater Protection. The appropriation to the Environmental Protection Fund and authorized positions of the three consolidated programs may be reduced, and the Commissioner of Finance and Administration shall adjust departmental revenues and authorized positions of the restructured programs accordingly. It is the legislative intent that no appropriation of general fund revenue to the programs and no authorized positions be diverted to other functions of the department as a result of the consolidation.

SECTION 36. The provisions of this section shall take effect upon becoming a law, the public welfare requiring it. Subject to the availability of funding at June 30, 2013, any unexpended balances of appropriations made under Chapter 1029, Public Acts of 2012, other acts of this General Assembly or acts by previous General Assemblies, listed in this section are hereby reappropriated to be expended in the 2013-2014 fiscal year and such appropriations shall be carried forward in a reserve into the fiscal year beginning July 1, 2013. The reappropriation and carry-forward of these funds is subject to approval by the Commissioner of Finance and Administration. Unless otherwise noted, the unexpended balances reappropriated are authorized under Chapter 1029, Public Acts of 2012, and they are the appropriations made:

Item 1. For data processing services, systems development, data processing equipment purchases and leases and telecommunication systems purchases and leases. The Commissioner of Finance and Administration is authorized to transfer from the amounts carried forward sums sufficient for the Computer Equipment Replacement Fund and to the Systems Development Fund.

Item 2. Settlement and Judgment Awards and Similar Awards. From the appropriations in this act and previous appropriations acts, from funds received by the

Attorney General and Reporter or other state officials and agencies in settlements and judgments and similar awards, the unexpended balance of such funds shall be reserved and carried forward until expended for the intended purposes; and such funds as are carried forward hereby are appropriated for the intended purposes. The provisions of this item shall not require the reserving of such funds in cases in which the settlement or judgment does not require the set-aside or expenditure of funds for a specific purpose or in amounts that are intended to benefit the general fund, provided, however, that funds designated for the Attorney General and Reporter shall be reserved in the Attorney General Litigation Settlement Reserve.

Item 3. Notwithstanding any provision of law to the contrary, all funds appropriated to the Legislative Branch which remain unobligated and unexpended at the end of any fiscal year, shall not revert to the general fund but shall be carried forward in a reserve to be expended in accordance with the approval of the Speaker of the House of Representatives and the Speaker of the Senate. This item shall not be subject to the approval of the Commissioner of Finance and Administration.

Item 4. To the Judicial Branch in Section 1, Title II, but excluding the appropriations for Guardian ad Litem, Indigent Defendants' Counsel, Civil Legal Representation, Court Interpreter Services, Verbatim Transcripts, Council of Juvenile and Family Court Judges, Board of Law Examiners, Board of Professional Responsibility, Tennessee Lawyers Assistance Program, Continuing Legal Education, and Client Protection Fund. The reappropriated funds shall be expended for the integrated computer system for the Tennessee Court System under the provisions of Tennessee Code Annotated, Section 16-3-807. This item shall not be subject to the approval of the Commissioner of Finance and Administration.

Item 5. To the Judicial Branch, Administrative Office of the Courts in Section 1, Title II, Item 13, to defray expenses of serving the General Sessions Courts and the General Sessions Judges' Conference pursuant to Tennessee Code Annotated, Section 16-15-5007 and Section 67-4-606(a)(9).

Item 6. To the Administrative Office of the Courts from the unexpended balance of revenue from the gift received to benefit the Hillman Taylor Library in Memphis.

Item 7. To the Judicial Branch, Board of Law Examiners in Section 1, Title II, Item 16. The carry-forward amount shall be the difference between expenditures and revenues, including any reserve balance.

Item 8. To the Judicial Branch, Council of Juvenile and Family Court Judges in Section 36, Item 7, and in Section 65, Item 6, of Chapter 554, Public Acts of 2009, the non-recurring appropriation to provide for juvenile mental health evaluations.

Item 9. To the Attorney General and Reporter, from the non-recurring appropriation of $1,500,000 made in the fiscal year ending June 30, 2009, from Tobacco Master Settlement Agreement (MSA) payments received in February 2009 that were previously withheld by tobacco companies. The appropriation is for the purpose of funding costs related to impending diligent enforcement arbitration proceedings and shall remain available until expended.

Item 10. To the District Attorneys General from revenues earned from the Department of Human Services for food stamp fraud prosecution activities, the unexpended balance of such funds, not to exceed $100,000.

Item 11. To the Secretary of State for publication of the Blue Book pursuant to Section 1, Title III-1, Item 3.3 and Section 36, Item 9.

Item 12. To the Secretary of State, Charitable Solicitations and Charitable Gaming, in Section 36, Item 10, and in Section 4, Title III-1, Item 3.5. The unexpended balances of departmental revenue are hereby reappropriated to fund a charitable solicitations systems development project.

Item 13. To the Secretary of State, Library Construction, the remaining funds from the $1,000,000 appropriated in Section 41, Item 3, of Chapter 1029, Public Acts of 2012, and in Chapter 963, Section 1, Title III-1, Item 3.9, of the Public Acts of 2006 for library construction. The Secretary of State is authorized to reallocate remaining funds from projects that have not developed to other unspecified locations and counties where future library construction projects may develop.

PUBLIC CHAPTER NO. 453 (cont'd)

Item 14. To the Treasury Department for college savings incentive initiatives and a college savings plan in Public Acts of 2010, Chapter 1108, Section 1, Title III-1, Item 7.3, and Section 35, Item 3; and Public Acts of 2011, Chapter 473, Section 1, Title III-1, Item 7.3, and Section 72, Item 3, and Section 36, Item 60; and Public Acts of 2012, Chapter 1029, Section 1, Title III-1, Item 7.3, and Section 36, Item 56.

Item 15. To the Alcoholic Beverage Commission from the unexpended balance of departmental revenues of the Alcohol Server Responsibility and Training Program authorized by Tennessee Code Annotated, Title 57, Chapter 3, Part 7.

Item 16. To the Human Rights Commission in Section 1, Title III-2, Item 2.4, an amount not to exceed $200,000.

Item 17. To the Health Services and Development Agency in Section 1, Title III-2, Item 2.5, in an amount not to exceed $300,000 for the purpose of paying audit costs.

Item 18. To the Department of Finance and Administration, Strategic Health-Care Programs, in Section 36, Item 14, and in Section 1, Title III-2, Item 3.10 of Chapter 1108, Public Acts of 2010, for Health Information Technology, in an amount not to exceed $5,275,000, to provide non-recurring funds to advance the appropriate use of health information technology and to improve quality of care. The Commissioner of Finance and Administration is authorized to transfer sums sufficient to the information systems fund and to other appropriate organizational units of state government. The appropriation was transferred to Cover Tennessee Health Care Programs, Health Care Planning and Innovation effective July 1, 2011.

Item 19. To the Department of Finance and Administration, Strategic Health-Care Programs, from the appropriation made in Section 36, Item 15, and in Section 1, Title III-2, Item 3.8 of Chapter 603, Public Acts of 2007, for State Health Planning Division, for the decision support system, in a non-recurring amount not to exceed $975,005.90. The appropriation was transferred to Strategic Health-Care Programs, Health-Care Planning and Innovation, effective July 1, 2011.

Item 20. To the Department of Finance and Administration in Section 36, Item 17, and in Section 1, Title III-22, Miscellaneous Appropriations, Item 33.4, of Chapter 603, Public Acts of 2007, for the use of Nashville MTA bus services for state employees, in an amount not to exceed $200,000.

Item 21. To the Department of General Services any unexpended real estate fees collected by the Real Estate Asset Management Division.

Item 22. To the Department of General Services, Real Estate Asset Management Division, the proceeds from the sale of surplus personal property assigned to the division.

Item 23. To the Department of Veterans Affairs in Section 36, Item 18, and in Section 1, Title III-2, Item 6, of Chapter 503, Public Acts of 2005, the unexpended balance of the $300,000 appropriation for Memphis cemetery headstones realignment, which is hereby reappropriated for that purpose and for other non-recurring costs at the veterans cemeteries.

Item 24. To the Department of Veterans Affairs in Section 4, Title III-2, Item 5, the greater of $500,000 or the total of unexpended burial fees and federal burial grant funds shall not revert to the general fund.

Item 25. To the Department of Agriculture the unexpended balance of revenues from timber sales at state forests and state parks.

Item 26. To the Department of Agriculture for the agricultural enhancement program in Section 36, Item 22, and in Section 1, Title III-3, Items 1, 2, 3, and 5.

Item 27. To the Department of Environment and Conservation, Water Pollution Control, for land reclamation, in Section 1, Title III-5, Item 15.

Item 28. To the Department of Environment and Conservation for the Biofuels Project in Section 36, Item 26, and in Section 57, Item 21, of Chapter 963, Public Acts of 2006.

Item 29. To the Tennessee Historical Commission in Section 1, Title III-5, Items 3 and 8, for the Tennessee Wars Commission.

Item 30. To the Tennessee Historical Commission the unexpended funds from any prior appropriations for publications, historical markers and other historical activities.

Item 31. To the Tennessee Historical Commission the unexpended balance of the $35,000 appropriation in Section 74, Item 37, for an audit of war memorials and development of a plan to remedy any problems discovered with the memorials. Such amount as is reserved may also be used for printing a report of the audit and the plan, and such funds as are reserved are hereby reappropriated for the purpose originally appropriated and for this purpose.

Item 32. To the Department of Correction, Community Corrections, in Section 1, Title III-7, Item 23, and Section 36, Item 47, pursuant to Tennessee Code Annotated, Section 40-36-304(c)(1).

Item 33. To the Department of Economic and Community Development in Section 36, Item 29, and from the appropriations made in Section 1, Title III-8, to support the Three-Star community program, the Main Street program, and other community development programs.

Item 34. To the Department of Economic and Community Development for non-FastTrack economic development project grants made in the Business Development program.

Item 35. To the Department of Economic and Community Development, Tennessee Film and Television Incentive Fund, pursuant to T.C.A., Section 4-3-4903(e), the Commissioner of Finance and Administration is authorized to carry forward unexpended balances of any appropriations made for the incentive fund.

Item 36. To the Department of Economic and Community Development in Section 36, Item 32, and in Section 12, Item 24, of Chapter 554, Public Acts of 2009, for rural assistance grants, and to the Secretary of State in an amount not to exceed $1,030,000 provided by a grant from Economic and Community Development.

Item 37. To the Department of Economic and Community Development, the unexpended balances of appropriations made in Section 41, Item 27, of Chapter 1029, Public Acts of 2012, and in Chapter 554, Public Acts of 2009, in Section 65, Item 3, for an advanced manufacturing technology center, and Item 4, to the Energy Efficiency and Clean Energy Technology Initiatives. The appropriation in sub-item (c)(ii) of Item 4 is further reappropriated, as follows: For participation in a multi-state initiative with the U.S. Department of Energy to demonstrate electric vehicle technologies, the sum of $2,500,000 for a grant and the sum of $2,500,000 for rebates to purchase electric vehicles that are eligible under the multi-state initiative.

Item 38. To the Department of Economic and Community Development from the unexpended balances of appropriations made in Section 41, Item 34, for the headquarters relocation assistance program pursuant to Tennessee Code Annotated, Section 67-4-2109(g)(2).

Item 39. To the Department of Economic and Community Development, TNInvestco Tax Credits program, in Section 38, Item 9.2, of this act.

Item 40. All funds appropriated to the Department of Education for the purposes of the state testing programs which remain unobligated and unexpended at the end of any fiscal year shall not revert to the general fund but shall be carried forward in a reserve to be expended for the purposes of such programs.

Item 41. To the Department of Education in Section 36, Item 35, and in Section 1, Title III-9, Item 2.1e, of Chapter 603, Public Acts of 2007, in a non-recurring amount of $2,000,000 for the Teach Tennessee Program.

Item 42. To the Department of Education in Section 36, Item 36, and in Section 1, Title III-9, Item 2.1e, of Chapter 503, Public Acts of 2005, in a non-recurring amount of $5,000,000 to fund a professional development, leadership, and training initiative program.

Item 43. To the Department of Education in Section 36, Item 37, and in Section 1, Title III-9, Item 2.1a, for the Governor's Schools Program.

Item 44. To the Department of Education, the unexpended balance of appropriations for the Safe Schools Act of 1998, in Section 8, Item 34, of this act and Public Acts of 2012,

Chapter 1029, Section 1, Title III-9, Item 2.2(a) and Section 41, Item 19, pursuant to Tennessee Code Annotated, Section 49-6-4302(c)(2)(D).

Item 45. To the Department of Education, any unexpended state appropriations, not to exceed ten percent (10%) of the total appropriated funds for the Tennessee Early Intervention Services program in both the Department of Education and the Department of Children's Services. Said reserve is subject to the approval of the Commissioner of Finance and Administration.

Item 46. To the Department of Education, Achievement School District, the unexpended balance of allocations made to the district from the Basic Education Program formula.

Item 47. To the Department of Education, Achievement School District program, from donations made to the program.

Item 48. To the Department of Education the unexpended balance of grants received from non-state entities for the provision of program services.

Item 49. To the Department of Education, Career and Technical Education Program, from the unexpended balance of an $185,000 transfer to the program at June 30, 2012, for the purpose of funding activities of the cooperative innovative education consortium and the office of postsecondary coordination and alignment, pursuant to Tennessee Code Annotated, Title 49, Chapter 15. The unexpended balance at June 30, 2012, of the appropriation in Public Acts of 2012, Section 36, Item 38, and Public Acts of 2007, Chapter 603, Section 12, Item 54, to the State Board of Education was transferred to the Department of Education, Career and Technical Education Program, pursuant to Tennessee Code Annotated, Section 49-15-104(e).

Item 50. To the Department of Labor and Workforce Development in Section 36, Item 39, and in Section 1, Title III-13, Item 7, for the Second Injury Fund.

Item 51. To the Department of Mental Health and Substance Abuse Services in Section 1, Title III-14, Item 2.5, and Section 36, Item 40, for housing initiatives for the seriously and persistently mentally ill.

Item 52. To the Department of Military in Section 1, Title III-15, Item 1 and Item 3, and Section 36, Item 41, for tuition assistance.

Item 53. To the Department of Human Services for the purpose of Child Support Enforcement which remain unobligated and unexpended may be carried forward in reserve.

Item 54. To the Department of Human Services for the purpose of Vocational Rehabilitation services to clients which remain unobligated and unexpended may be carried forward in reserve.

Item 55. To the Department of Revenue for the production of license plates.

Item 56. To the Department of Revenue, Administration Division, from proceeds resulting from investigation and enforcement of state tobacco laws.

Item 57. To the Department of Revenue in Section 64, Item 1(16) for sales tax disaster relief pursuant to Tennessee Code Annotated, Section 67-6-396.

Item 58. To the Tennessee Bureau of Investigation in Section 36, Item 57, and Section 41, Item 35, of Public Acts of 2012, Chapter 1029, in an amount not to exceed $750,000, to provide funds to local governments for costs related to methamphetamine clean-up.

Item 59. To the Tennessee Bureau of Investigation in Section 66, Item 8, drug enforcement funds, the unexpended balance of the non-recurring appropriation of $603,800.

Item 60. To the Department of Safety and the Tennessee Bureau of Investigation from the handgun carry permit fees paid pursuant to Tennessee Code Annotated, Section 39-17-1351.

Item 61. To Miscellaneous Appropriations in Section 1, Title III-22, Item 27; Section 36, Items 48 and 49; and Section 41, Item 40, to fund a severance benefit plan for the voluntary buyout program in calendar year 2008 and reduction-in-force separations which have occurred or will occur as a result of budget legislation in the 2008 through 2013 legislative sessions and in accordance with the severance benefit plan in the applicable general appropriations act. The funds hereby are reappropriated to provide for such costs in the fiscal year ending June 30, 2014, and the Commissioner of Finance and Administration is authorized to reduce the amount carried forward to an amount estimated to be required.

Item 62. To Miscellaneous Appropriations in Section 36, Item 51, to fund a severance benefit plan for the reduction-in-force separations which have occurred or will occur at Clover Bottom Developmental Center as a result of the budget reduction in the 2010 and subsequent legislative sessions and in accordance with the benefit plan in the Public Acts of 2010, Chapter 1108, Section 61. The funds hereby are reappropriated to provide for such costs in the fiscal year ending June 30, 2014, and the Commissioner of Finance and Administration is authorized to reduce the amount carried forward to an amount estimated to be required. At each subsequent fiscal year-end, the required amount shall be carried forward until such time as all severance-benefit obligations, under the terms of the 2010 act, to the employees of the center who were employed before July 1, 2010, are satisfied. An amount required for employees of the center who were employed after June 30, 2010, also shall be carried forward until such time as all severance-benefit obligations to the employees are satisfied under the terms of the subsequent and applicable appropriations act.

Item 63. To the Department of Children's Services in Section 1, Title III-23. Subject to the availability of revenue, the Commissioner of Finance and Administration is authorized to carry forward funds to provide for a statewide needs assessment of child welfare services.

Item 64. To the Department of Transportation in Section 1, Title III-30, Item 8, for equipment purchases.

Item 65. To the Department of Transportation for any appropriations which are reserved at June 30, 2013.

Item 66. National Mortgage Servicers Consent Judgment. To the affected agencies, the unexpended balances of the following appropriations made in Public Acts of 2012, Chapter 1029, Section 65, pursuant to the National Mortgage Servicers Consent Judgment, including:

(a) To the Tennessee Housing Development Agency, $34,500,000 to be used for its Keep My Tennessee Home financial assistance program and for foreclosure counseling.

(b) To the Department of Commerce and Insurance, Division of Consumer Affairs, for the Consumer Education Fund, $250,000.

(c) To the Department of Financial Institutions, $1,000,000 from the Conference of State Bank Supervisors to be allocated as follows and used for: (i) $350,000 for examiner training; (ii) $350,000 for information technology support and equipment; (iii) $125,000 for a financial literacy grant to the Tennessee Financial Literacy Commission; and (iv) $175,000 for consumer education efforts by the consumer resources section of the Department of Financial Institutions. The Commissioner of Financial Institutions is authorized to reallocate amounts among these purposes.

Item 67. To the Department of Treasury, Unclaimed Property, in Section 38, Item 2.1, of this act for payment of the audit settlement fee, if the fee has not been paid by June 30, 2013. The amount carried forward may be adjusted to reflect the amount of the required fee payment for the audit settlement revenue collected or recognized in the year ending June 30, 2013.

Item 68. To the Department of Finance and Administration, Bureau of TennCare, Intellectual Disabilities Services, in Section 38, Item 4.1, of this act for the Arlington lawsuit exit plan.

Item 69. To the Department of General Services, Real Estate Asset Management, in Section 38, Item 5.1, of this act for real estate transaction fees, which restores to the program fees which reverted to the general fund at June 30, 2012.

Item 70. To the Department of Tourist Development, in Section 38, Item 6.1, of this act for tourism marketing.

Item 71. To the Department of Mental Health and Substance Abuse Services, in Section 38, Item 10.1, Community Mental Health Services, and Item 10.2, Lakeshore Mental Health Institute (MHI), of this act for transition costs, including build-out costs and other closure costs, incurred because of the closure of the institute, to the extent that such costs remain but are not expensed entirely at June 30, 2013. It is the legislative intent that these funds be carried forward in the general fund reserve for unencumbered balance and that at June 30, 2013, the general fund reserve for mental health trust fund be reduced in the amount of Lakeshore MHI transition costs, including severance benefits, build-out costs and other closure costs, expensed in the fiscal year ending June 30, 2013, and in the amount carried forward in the reserve for unencumbered balance at June 30, 2013. At June 30, 2014, or at the close of any fiscal year in which all transition costs have been finally recorded, whichever is later, it is the legislative intent that any unexpended balance of the amount carried forward pursuant to this item be transferred to the mental health trust fund.

Item 72. To the Miscellaneous Appropriations, in Section 38, Item 12.1, of this act to support future Tobacco MSA revenue estimates (diligent-enforcement arbitration settlement), in the amount of the appropriation established pursuant to Section 38.

Item 73. To the Miscellaneous Appropriations, in Section 38, Item 12.2, of this act for innovation fund.

Item 74. The Comptroller of the Treasury, Division of Property Assessments is authorized to carry forward unexpended revenue derived from the annual assessor's training session.

Item 75. To the Department of Economic and Community Development, in Section 38, Item 9.2, TNInvestco Tax Credits.

Item 76. To the Department of Education, Career and Technical Education Program, from the unexpended balance of the non-recurring appropriation of $300,000 in Section 64, Item 1.17, which pursuant to Public Acts of 2012, Chapter 967, was allotted to the Department of Education, relative to the cooperative innovative education consortium and dual credit course pilot projects. Such funds as may be carried forward hereby are reappropriated for the purposes of the program set forth in Tennessee Code Annotated, Title 49, Chapter 15, Part 1.

Item 77. The Department of Safety is authorized to carry forward the unexpended balance of any donation from any non-profit organization created pursuant to Tennessee Code Annotated, Section 4-3-2017.

SECTION 37. The provisions of this section shall take effect upon becoming a law, the public welfare requiring it. Subject to the availability of revenue at June 30, 2013, any unexpended balances of appropriations made under Chapter 1029, Public Acts of 2012, other acts of this General Assembly or acts by previous General Assemblies for benefit of an agency of local government or a third-party nonprofit organization for which there is a grant agreement/contract approved by the Commissioner of Finance and Administration are hereby reappropriated to be expended in the 2013-2014 fiscal year and such appropriations shall be carried forward in a reserve into the fiscal year beginning July 1, 2013. The Commissioner of Finance and Administration shall provide a list of any unexpended balances carried forward to the Director of Accounts and to the Division of State Audit. The reappropriation and carry-forward of these funds is subject to approval by the Commissioner of Finance and Administration, and expenditure and reporting requirements are adjusted accordingly to the fiscal year in which the funds are received by the grant recipient, notwithstanding any provision in the grant agreement to the contrary.

SECTION 38. The provisions of this section shall take effect upon becoming a law, the public welfare requiring it. There is hereby appropriated the following amounts which shall be in addition to the appropriations provided under Chapter 1029, Public Acts of 2012:

1. Comptroller of the Treasury
   1.1 Property Tax Relief .... $ 2,500,000.00

2. Claims and Compensation
   2.1 Unclaimed Property - Audit Settlement Fee 2,890,500.00

3. Finance and Administration
   3.1 Office for Information Resources - Next Generation Information Technology Initiative 2,500,000.00

4. Finance and Administration, Bureau of TennCare

PUBLIC CHAPTER NO. 453 (cont'd)

	4.1	Intellectual Disabilities Services – Arlington Lawsuit Exit Plan Implementation	300,000.00
5.		General Services	
	5.1	Real Estate Asset Management – Real Estate Transaction Fees – 2011-2012 Closing Correction	1,565,000.00
6.		Tourist Development	
	6.1	Administration and Marketing – Tourism Marketing	250,000.00
7.		Environment and Conservation	
	7.1	State Parks - Operating Costs and Revenue Undercollection	$ 2,550,000.00
	7.2	Groundwater Protection – Revenue Undercollection	1,000,000.00
		Total Department of Environment and Conservation	$ 3,550,000.00
8.		Correction	
	8.1	State Prosecutions - State Inmates in Local Jails	$ 41,778,400.00
	8.2	Prisons - Medical Contract:	
		a. Tennessee Prison for Women	$ 489,000.00
		b. Turney Center Industrial Complex	431,900.00
		c. Mark Luttrell Correctional Facility	189,800.00
		d. Charles B. Bass Correctional Complex	361,300.00
		e. Southeastern Tennessee State Regional Correctional Facility	260,000.00
		f. West Tennessee State Penitentiary	391,500.00
		g. Riverbend Maximum Security Institution	288,500.00
		h. Northeast Correctional Complex	277,300.00
		i. Northwest Correctional Complex	340,600.00
		j. Morgan County Correctional Complex	585,900.00
		k. Lois M. DeBerry Special Needs Facility	796,700.00
		l. Hardeman County Incarceration Agreement	33,900.00
		m. Hardeman County Agreement — Whiteville	25,700.00
		n. South Central Correctional Center	27,900.00
		Sub-Total Prisons — Medical Contract	$ 4,500,000.00
	8.3	Southeastern TN Regional State Regional Correctional Facility – Bledsoe Prison Expansion – Payroll Reconciliation	928,800.00
	8.4	Sentencing Act of 1985 – Bledsoe Prison Expansion – Payroll Reconciliation – Reduce Appropriation	(928,800.00)
		Total Department of Correction	$ 46,278,400.00
9.		Economic and Community Development	
	9.1	FastTrack Infrastructure and Job Training Assistance	$ 35,000,000.00
	9.2	TNInvestco Tax Credits	31,100,000.00
		Total Economic and Community Development	$ 66,100,000.00
10.		Mental Health and Substance Abuse Services	
	10.1	Community Mental Health Services – Lakeshore MHI Closure Transition Costs	$ 1,700,000.00
	10.2	Lakeshore Mental Health Institute – Closure – Build-out Costs	1,000,000.00
		Total Mental Health and Substance Abuse Services	$ 2,700,000.00
11.		Safety	
	11.1	Driver License Issuance – Reinstatement Revenue Loss (2011 Legislation Revenue Estimate Correction)	7,645,000.00
12.		Miscellaneous Appropriations	
	12.1	Contingency Appropriation – Reserve for Future Tobacco MSA Revenue Estimates (Arbitration Settlement)	$ 5,300,000.00
	12.2	Innovation Fund	250,000.00
	12.3	Retirees Health Insurance (Medicare Supplement)	1,300,000.00
	12.4	Postage Rate Increase	500,000.00

	12.5 Risk Management - Closed Facilities	727,500.00
	Total Miscellaneous Appropriations	$ 8,077,500.00
	Total General Fund..	$144,356,400.00
13.	Facilities Revolving Fund	
	13.1 Leases and Space Planning – Holdover Leases and Relocation Costs..	$ 4,300,000.00
	13.2 FRF Capital Projects – Office Modernization – Cabling................	1,000,000.00
	Total Facilities Revolving Fund	$ 5,300,000.00
	GRAND TOTAL	$149,656,400.00

The appropriation in this section to Claims and Compensation, Item 2.1, Unclaimed Property – Audit Settlement Fee, in the amount of $2,890,500.00 may be increased or decreased to reflect the actual fee to be paid, and for such purpose, there hereby is appropriated a sum sufficient for payment of the audit settlement fee.

As provided in this section, in Item 8.4, Sentencing Act of 1985, the appropriation made in Public Acts of 2012, Chapter 1029, Section 1, Title III-7, Item 18, Sentencing Act of 1985, is reduced in the amount of $928,800.00 to reflect the additional operating cost at Southeastern Tennessee State Regional Correctional Facility for the Bledsoe County state prison expansion.

The appropriations in Item 10 of this section to Mental Health and Substance Abuse Services are funded from revenues and reserves available to the Mental Health Trust Fund pursuant to Tennessee Code Annotated, Section 12-2-117, for the purpose of transition costs, including build-out and other closure costs at Lakeshore Mental Health Institute.

The appropriation in Item 12.1 of this section for future Tobacco Master Settlement Agreement (MSA) revenue estimates is contingent upon receiving revenue from the Tobacco MSA diligent-enforcement arbitration settlement agreement, and the amount of the appropriation may be decreased to the amount of arbitration settlement revenue received, if the arbitration settlement revenue recognized at June 30, 2013, is less than $5,300,000.00. If such arbitration settlement agreement revenue is recognized instead in the year beginning July 1, 2013, then the appropriation for future Tobacco MSA revenue estimates shall be established in the year beginning July 1, 2013, and such funds hereby are appropriated.

The Commissioner of Finance and Administration is authorized to allot and transfer these appropriations to the appropriate expenditure account within each department, agency or branch of government and to adjust authorized positions accordingly. The Commissioner of Finance and Administration is further authorized to adjust federal aid and departmental revenues accordingly.

SECTION 39. Program Expansions from Federal and Other Departmental Revenue. The provisions of this section shall take effect upon becoming law, the public welfare requiring it. At June 30, 2013, any unexpended balances of departmental revenues and federal aid funds appropriated in this section are hereby reappropriated in the fiscal year beginning July 1, 2013.

There is hereby appropriated from departmental revenues and federal aid funds the amounts hereinafter set out:

	2012-2013	2013-2014
Comptroller of the Treasury		
1. Division of Property Assessments	$ 0	$ 30,000
TennCare		
1. TennCare Medical Services	50,000,000	100,000,000
General Services		
1. Real Estate Asset Management	119,900	479,400
Agriculture		
1. Forestry Operations	0	319,400
Environment and Conservation		
1. Office of Sustainable Practices	0	180,000

Education (K-12)		
1. Technology, Infrastructure, and Support Systems	$ 43,400	$ 111,300
2. Curriculum and Instruction	0	500,000
Sub-Total Education (K-12)	$ 43,400	$ 611,300
Mental Health and Substance Abuse Services		
1. Community Alcohol and Drug Abuse Services	$ 1,000,000	$ 1,000,000
2. Community Mental Health Services	1,000,000	1,000,000
Sub-Total Mental Health and Substance Abuse Services	$ 2,000,000	$ 2,000,000
Health		
1. Bureau of Health Licensure and Regulation	80,400	642,900
Total	**$ 52,243,700**	**$ 104,263,000**

The Commissioner of Finance and Administration is authorized to establish fifteen (15) full-time positions and to allocate them to the appropriate organizational units, including eight (8) positions in the District Attorneys General Conference, two (2) in the Department of General Services, and five (5) in the Department of Agriculture.

SECTION 40. There is hereby appropriated a sum sufficient to recognize any accrued liability of the state and any obligations between state agencies at June 30, 2014, and federal aid and departmental revenues may be adjusted accordingly. This appropriation is subject to certification of the accrued liability and obligations between state agencies by the Commissioner of Finance and Administration to the State Comptroller. The commissioner shall provide a copy of the certification to the Office of Legislative Budget Analysis.

SECTION 41. The provisions of this section shall take effect upon becoming a law, the public welfare requiring it.

Item 1.

(1) From the appropriations made in Sections 1 and 4 of this act, there are appropriated sums sufficient to fund the following programs:

(a) An amount sufficient to implement and pay the cost of administering the Section 125 cafeteria plan established for state employees is hereby appropriated for that purpose. From the appropriation made in this item and any annual forfeited contributions, the State Treasurer, with the approval of the Commissioner of Finance and Administration, is authorized to establish positions and funding for such positions in the Department of Treasury to fund recurring and non-recurring costs of administering the cafeteria plan established for such employees. There is hereby appropriated a sum sufficient to pay additional costs of administering the State Employee Cafeteria Plan as a result of increased participation in the plan by state employees; and

(b) An amount up to but not exceeding $600,000 for the wellness program or other state employee insurance programs administered by the Department of Finance and Administration; and

(c) An amount up to but not exceeding $10,000 for the daycare program for children of state employees as administered by the Department of Human Services, provided, that allotment of funds under this sub-item is subject to approval of the Commissioner of Finance and Administration; and

(d) An amount up to but not exceeding $154,500 to fund the administrative costs of the state employee sick leave bank administered by the Department of Human Resources; and

(e) An amount to provide for the employer match to the state's 401(k) plan for state employees compensated on the centralized state payroll system pursuant to TCA, Title 8, Chapter 25.

(2) There is hereby appropriated in Section 1, Title III-22, Item 16, of this act the sum of $9,197,000 for the fifty dollar ($50) match for state employees compensated on the centralized state payroll system if the amount appropriated in Sections 1 and 4 is insufficient.

(3) There is hereby appropriated a sum sufficient from employer FICA tax savings from the Section 125 cafeteria plan maintained by the University of Tennessee to provide for the employer match to the state's 401(k) plan for employees of institutions under the University of Tennessee system pursuant to TCA, Title 8, Chapter 25. Should this be insufficient to provide for the fifty dollar ($50) match, there is appropriated in Section 1, Title III-10, of this act, the sum of $2,838,100 to supplement funding for such match.

(4) There is hereby appropriated a sum sufficient from employer FICA tax savings from the Section 125 cafeteria plan maintained by the Board of Regents system to provide for the employer match to the state's 401(k) plan for employees of institutions under the Board of Regents system pursuant to TCA, Title 8, Chapter 25. Should this be insufficient to provide for the fifty dollar ($50) match, there is appropriated in Section 1, Title III-10, of this act, the sum of $4,328,500 to supplement funding for such match.

(5) The State Treasurer shall have the authority to contract with the optional retirement plan vendors to provide investment products to optional retirement plan participants under the state's 401(k) program.

Item 2. From the appropriations made in Section 1, Titles III-2 through III-30 and in Section 4, Titles III-2 through III-27, to the Executive Branch departments and agencies, the Commissioner of Finance and Administration is authorized to transfer amounts budgeted for contract services to payroll and to increase the number of authorized positions to replace contractors with state employees.

Item 3. The Commissioner of Finance and Administration is hereby authorized to establish a reserve account for Community Services Agency (CSA). If any CSA ceases to operate, any fund balances may be deposited to this account. There is hereby appropriated a sum sufficient from the reserve account to provide for outstanding obligations of any CSA or the ongoing operational cost of any CSA. Disbursement from this fund is subject to the approval of the Commissioner of Finance and Administration.

Item 4. FastTrack Infrastructure and Job Training Assistance Program and Business Development Program. The Commissioner of Finance and Administration is authorized to transfer from the general fund to the capital projects fund available appropriations made in this act and previous appropriations acts to the Department of Economic and Community Development for economic development projects, including amounts allotted to the FastTrack Infrastructure and Job Training Assistance program and Business Development program. A transfer may not be made if it would result in a deficiency in available funds for any FastTrack or Business Development project for which a contractual agreement has been made, unless such agreement has been amended to reduce the amount required to be expended in the amount to be transferred or unless appropriations are available otherwise.

Transfers also may be made from the capital projects fund to the two operating budget programs from available funds appropriated to the Department of Economic and Community Development for economic development capital outlay projects. Transfers are authorized only from available current funds in the capital projects fund and may not include any amounts from bond authorizations. Before transfers from the capital projects fund may occur, the Commissioner of Finance and Administration shall determine that the current funds are available, that any associated grant agreement for the capital outlay project has been amended to reduce the capital outlay grant in the amount to be transferred or that an agreement has not been made for the capital outlay grant, and that the State Building Commission has approved the capital outlay project current-funds reduction. Such transfers may not be made if they would result in a deficiency in available funds for any capital outlay project previously funded.

Transfers authorized in this item are subject to the approval of the Commissioner of Finance and Administration.

Item 5. The Commissioner of Finance and Administration is authorized to establish state appropriations and reduce appropriations of departmental revenue made in Section 4 and other sections of this act to the extent required to reflect proper accounting of state revenues under generally accepted accounting principles. To the extent that state appropriations are established, departmental revenue estimates shall be reduced. In no instance shall the adjustments made under this provision result in a greater allotment of funds than is otherwise provided by this act.

Item 6. The Commissioner of Finance and Administration is authorized to transfer information systems printing services and associated position authorizations from the Department of Finance and Administration, Office for Information Resources, to the Department of General Services, Printing and Media Services. Departmental revenue estimates of the two programs shall be adjusted accordingly.

Item 7. The Commissioner of Finance and Administration is authorized to transfer procurement positions from departments and agencies funded by this act to the central procurement office attached to the Department of General Services, upon the request of the chief procurement officer, and to adjust departmental revenue estimates and authorized positions accordingly. The plan for centralization of such procurement functions is subject to approval of the Commissioner of Finance and Administration.

Item 8. The appropriation in Section 1, Title III-14, Item 2.4, to Memphis Mental Health Institute reflects a recurring base reduction of $2,042,000 and in Title III-14, Item 2.5, to Community Mental Health Services a recurring base increase of $2,042,000. The appropriation in Item 2.4 to Memphis Mental Health Institute also includes a non-recurring amount of $455,700, which is intended to provide for transition costs, including the payment of severance benefits to employees who are terminated, as provided in Section 59 of this act, and for other transition purposes. The Commissioner of Finance and Administration shall reduce the number of authorized full-time positions at the institute by an estimated 48, but may make position adjustments as necessary within the amount of the appropriation to the institute.

Item 9. The appropriations in Section 1 and Section 68, Item 1, of this act to the Department of General Services, State Facilities Pre-Planning program, are for the purpose of properly preparing capital outlay projects for funding consideration. Work of the program includes project scope development, project budget development, risk analysis, business case studies, design services through the construction-document phase (full planning), schedule development, and other services related to pre-construction project services. The provisions of this item do not waive the requirements of law and State Building Commission policy concerning approval of capital outlay project planning.

Item 10. In the fiscal year ending June 30, 2014, the Commissioner of Finance and Administration is authorized to carry forward unexpended balances of appropriations made to Miscellaneous Appropriations in Section 1, Title III-22, Item 32, of this act for the completion of a weighted caseload study by the Comptroller of the Treasury to analyze the distribution of judicial, district attorney general and public defender positions throughout the state. It is the legislative intent that such funds as are carried forward be reappropriated to be expended in the 2014-2015 fiscal year.

SECTION 42.

(a) Notwithstanding any provision of the law to the contrary, no law of general application which imposes increased expenditure requirements on cities and counties in excess of one million dollars ($1,000,000.00) shall take effect unless the state share of the cost of such law is specifically appropriated by the provisions of this act.

(b) From the growth in state-shared taxes apportioned to cities and counties and from the increase in local revenue generated from passage of any general law during the 2013 annual session of the 108th General Assembly not otherwise appropriated pursuant to this act, a sum sufficient hereby is appropriated to fund the state share of the cost of any law of general application which requires, without local discretion, that incorporated municipalities or county governments increase expenditures as a direct consequence of passage of any general law.

SECTION 43. The provisions of this section shall take effect upon becoming a law, the public welfare requiring it.

Item 1. It is the legislative intent to recognize over-appropriation reversion savings in the general fund in the following amounts:

(a) In fiscal year 2012-2013 to recognize an over-appropriation of $123,100,000, including a base recurring over-appropriation of $86,700,000 and a non-recurring over-appropriation of $36,400,000.

PUBLIC CHAPTER NO. 453 (cont'd)

(b) In fiscal year 2013-2014 to recognize an over-appropriation of $70,400,000, including a base recurring over-appropriation of $72,300,000 and a non-recurring over-appropriation adjustment of negative $1,900,000.

(c) From the amounts in paragraph (b) of this item, a recurring amount of $400,000 shall be achieved by reducing the appropriations made in Section 1 to recognize savings achieved by mileage reimbursement reductions resulting from the motor vehicle management program, and the over-appropriation shall be reduced accordingly.

(d) From the amounts in paragraph (b) of this item, a recurring amount of $3,900,000 shall be achieved by reducing the appropriations made in Section 1 to recognize savings achieved by space reductions resulting from the office modernization project, and the over-appropriation shall be reduced accordingly; and a non-recurring allotment of $1,900,000 will be made to the line-items of the budget, and the negative non-recurring over-appropriation shall be increased accordingly to zero dollars.

(e) With the adjustments in items (c) and (d), the 2013-2014 over-appropriation becomes $68,000,000, including a base recurring over-appropriation of $68,000,000 and a non-recurring over-appropriation adjustment of zero dollars.

(f) It is the legislative intent that any reversion from higher education appropriations to the general fund balance at June 30, 2014, be drawn from the unexpended balance in the Tennessee Higher Education Commission and the Tennessee Student Assistance Corporation, but not from Tennessee Student Assistance Awards.

Item 2. In the fiscal year ending June 30, 2013, there shall be reserved or designated a sum in the general fund balance to provide for non-recurring appropriations and other appropriations intended to be funded in the 2013-2014 fiscal year from the general fund balance at June 30, 2013. The Commissioner of Finance and Administration shall determine the amount to be reserved or designated.

Item 3. Under the provisions of Tennessee Code Annotated, Section 55-6-107(a), the sum of $4,100,000 shall be allocated to the general fund for the cost of issuing motor vehicle registration plates in the fiscal year ending June 30, 2013.

Item 4. Unexpended appropriations in an amount to be determined by the Commissioner of Finance and Administration shall be transferred from the debt service fund to the general fund in the fiscal year ending June 30, 2013

Item 5. In the fiscal year ending June 30, 2013, tax revenues allocated to the debt service fund, including motor vehicle title fees, in excess of $402,200,000 shall be transferred to the general fund. If said allocation to the debt service fund is less than $402,200,000, then the allocation of excise tax revenues to the debt service fund shall be increased in an amount to provide the allocation of $402,200,000 to the debt service fund.

Item 6. In the fiscal year ending June 30, 2013, the allocation of motor vehicle title fees to the debt service fund shall be the sum generated by the $1.50 fee under the provisions of Tennessee Code Annotated, Section 55-6-101(a)(1).

Item 7. In the fiscal year ending June 30, 2013, the appropriations made in Section 1, Title III-17 of the 2012 Appropriations Act to the Department of Human Services to fund programs or services for temporary assistance shall be reduced in an amount equal to the unexpended and unobligated balances of the appropriations. The reductions shall be made to recognize over-appropriation savings in programs or services for temporary assistance in the fiscal year ending June 30, 2013.

Item 8. Pursuant to Tennessee Code Annotated, Section 67-6-103(k), there is apportioned from the general fund share of the sales and use tax into cities and counties state shared taxes for the County Revenue Partnership Fund the sum of $1,000,000 in the fiscal year ending June 30, 2013, and the sum of $1,000,000 in the fiscal year ending June 30, 2014. These apportionments recognize the state share of certain laws imposing costs on local governments, to include: (a) Public Acts of 2009, Chapter 531, Section 30, relative to commitment of children to state custody at a rate above 300 percent of the average commitment rate from counties, in the amount of $400,000; and (b) Public Acts of 2012, Chapter 987, relative to domestic assault, in the amount of $600,000.

SECTION 44.

Item 1. There is hereby appropriated a sum sufficient from the State Office Buildings and Support Facilities Revolving Fund to provide for expenditures authorized under Title 9, Chapter 4, Part 9, of the Tennessee Code Annotated. There is appropriated a sum sufficient to the revolving fund in recognition of the lease cost of space for which recovery is not in the state's best interest. The Commissioner of Finance and Administration is authorized to allot, from the amount carried forward under Tennessee Code Annotated, Title 9, Chapter 4, Part 9, to provide funding for state office buildings and support facilities, and is further authorized to make appropriation transfers between the revolving fund and state departments and agencies.

Item 2. Funds herein appropriated for capital outlay of the state office building and support facilities revolving fund shall be used solely for improvements, betterments, and additions to state structures and for the acquisition of additional land and space, including the purchase of existing structures, as approved by the State Building Commission; provided, further, that such funds as are appropriated herein shall be utilized to finance only those projects, improvements, betterments, or additions which are presented in the State of Tennessee's 2013-2014 Budget Document, as amended by any changes or additional projects contained in the Appropriations Act as passed on third and final consideration; provided, further, that all funds appropriated in this act or other general acts of this session for capital outlay of the state office buildings and support facilities revolving fund shall be subject to the provisions of Tennessee Code Annotated, Title 4, Chapter 15, Part 1.

Item 3. The appropriation made to the state office building and support facilities revolving fund pursuant to Public Acts of 2009, Chapter 554, Section 68, Item 8(b), for purposes authorized by Public Acts of 2009, Chapter 529, "The Tennessee Clean Energy Act of 2009," and reappropriated in Public Acts of 2012, Chapter 1029, Section 41, Item 28, is hereby reappropriated for the same purpose.

SECTION 45. The provisions of this section shall take effect upon becoming a law, the public welfare requiring it.

Item 1. There is hereby created a Capital Projects Account in the Office for Information Resources for the administration of the Information Systems Capital Projects Budget.

This account is established to provide for:

(a) Implementation of the statewide Management Information Systems (MIS) Plan;

(b) Ability to separate the operational budget of the Office for Information Resources and the system development projects contained in the MIS Plan; and

(c) Financial control of the system development projects, including equipment replacement for the various agencies of state government.

Item 2. There is hereby authorized the transfer of those sums appropriated for Information Systems Capital Projects in Sections 1 and 4 and in Section 36, Item 1, of this act. Federal aid funds and other departmental revenues shall be adjusted accordingly to reflect the transfer of state appropriations.

Item 3. The Commissioner of Finance and Administration is authorized to transfer to the Capital Projects Account any appropriations made in Sections 1 and 4 of this act resulting from operating savings derived from implementation of information systems funded through this section.

Item 4. From the appropriations made for systems development and other data processing activities in this act and other acts of the legislature, the Commissioner of Finance and Administration is authorized to establish and charge the costs of information systems analyst positions, workstation support positions, and other data processing positions to said appropriations. The Commissioner of Finance and Administration is further authorized to transfer between departments and agencies existing information systems analyst positions, workstation support positions, and other data processing positions and the funding provided in this act for transferred positions.

Item 5. Expenditure of any funds, subject to the jurisdiction of the Information Systems Council, appropriated for systems development, the purchase of computer software or the purchase of computer hardware shall be subject to the policies of such Council.

Item 6. From the appropriations made for information systems activities in this act and other acts of the legislature, the Commissioner of Finance and Administration is authorized to transfer from professional services to payroll amounts budgeted for contractors. Additionally, the Commissioner of Finance and Administration is authorized to increase authorized positions in order to replace contractors with state employees.

Item 7. The Commissioner of Finance and Administration is authorized to approve an adjustment in rates charged by the Office for Information Resources and to reserve any funds needed to rebate savings to the federal government and to reallocate state appropriations between departments and to adjust federal aid and other departmental revenue accordingly. Any adjustment of rates or reserve of funds pursuant to the provisions of this act shall be reported to the Information Systems Council.

Item 8. The Commissioner of Finance and Administration shall have the authority to allocate savings generated from rate reductions from the Office for Information Resources Services to support modifications needed to be made to existing applications resulting from technology obsolescence or product nonperformance to extend the life of a system.

Item 9. From the funds appropriated in Section 1, Titles III-2 through III-30 and in Section 4, Titles III-2 through III-27 of this act, the Commissioner of Finance and Administration is authorized to establish positions and to transfer positions to provide staff for the Enterprise Resource Planning (ERP) systems development project.

SECTION 46.

Item 1. The revenues allocated under the provisions of Tennessee Code Annotated, Title 55, Chapter 4, Part 2 – Special License Plates, are hereby appropriated in a sum sufficient amount as provided in Part 2.

Item 2. From the motor vehicle registration fees imposed pursuant to Tennessee Code Annotated, Section 55-4-132, there is hereby appropriated a sum sufficient in the fiscal year ending June 30, 2014, to be used solely for the development, acquisition, and updating of a computerized titling and registration system, and for the operation of the titling and registration system. The Commissioner of Finance and Administration is authorized to allocate the funds to implement the intent of the act.

SECTION 47. The provisions of this section shall take effect upon becoming a law, the public welfare requiring it.

Item 1. From state revenues and other funds available to the general fund in excess of requirements for the fiscal year ending June 30, 2013, the Commissioner of Finance and Administration shall establish the Revenue Fluctuation Reserve in such amount as may be available under the provisions of Tennessee Code Annotated, Section 9-4-211. Provided, it is the legislative intent that the Revenue Fluctuation Reserve be set at a level of not less than $356,000,000 on June 30, 2013.

Item 2. From state revenues and other funds available to the general fund in excess of requirements for the fiscal year ending June 30, 2014, the Commissioner of Finance and Administration shall establish the Revenue Fluctuation Reserve in such amount as may be available under the provisions of Tennessee Code Annotated, Section 9-4-211. Provided, it is the legislative intent that the Revenue Fluctuation Reserve be set at a level of not less than $456,000,000 on June 30, 2014.

Item 3. It is the legislative intent that at June 30, 2013, any surplus general fund revenue, after fulfilling the requirements of Public Acts of 2012, Chapter 1029, and of this act, including all requirements of the closing of accounts at June 30, 2013, be deposited in a reserve for future requirements.

Item 4. At June 30, 2013, the Commissioner of Finance and Administration is authorized to transfer an amount of $123,700,000 to the TennCare reserve, it being the legislative intent to restore to the reserve the amounts appropriated from the reserve for the shortfall in the pharmacy program and the Medicare crossover program in fiscal years 2011-2012 and 2012-2013.

Item 5. At June 30, 2013, the Commissioner of Finance and Administration is authorized to transfer from the reserve for mental health trust fund to the general fund an amount of $1,923,100 in order to recognize the fiscal year 2011-2012 transition costs for the closure of Lakehore Mental Health Institute, which were funded by an appropriation from the mental health trust fund in Public Acts of 2012, Chapter 1029, Section 38. The provisions of this item are intended to correct an error in the calculation of the mental health trust fund reserve balance at June 30, 2012.

Item 6. At June 30, 2013, the Commissioner of Finance and Administration is authorized to transfer from the reserve for mental health trust fund to the general fund an amount of $2,700,000, relative to the appropriation in Section 38 of this act for the costs associated with the closure of Lakeshore Mental Health Institute.

Item 7. At June 30, 2013, the Commissioner of Finance and Administration is authorized to transfer from the Department of General Services motor vehicle management reserve the amount of $3,000,000 to recognize dispatch vehicle savings.

Item 8. In the year beginning July 1, 2013, the Commissioner of Finance and Administration is authorized to transfer from the systems development fund to the general fund an amount of $600,000, relative to a previous appropriation for federal Real ID compliance, and for the purpose of funding the appropriation to the Department of Safety in Section 68, Item 2, relative to an image verification system.

Item 9. The estimate of revenue from the Tobacco Master Settlement Agreement (MSA) arbitration settlement is estimated to be $72,400,000 in the year ending June 30, 2013. At June 30, 2013, and June 30, 2014, an amount of $23,100,000, or any such sum as may be received in excess of $49,300,000 in revenue collected and available from the settlement, shall be reserved for future health and wellness requirements. It is the legislative intent that such funds be available to fund non-recurring health and wellness appropriations in fiscal year 2014-2015.

SECTION 48. The provisions of this section shall take effect upon becoming a law, the public welfare requiring it.

Item 1. The Commissioner of Finance and Administration is authorized to transfer all federal and state health care funds, except those funds appropriated to support the State Group Insurance Program, the Local Education Insurance Program and the Local Government Health Insurance Program, to the TennCare Program for the purpose of implementing any program approved by waiver, state plan amendment and/or state and federal legislation pursuant to the provisions of health care services to Tennesseans designated as eligible by TennCare. In addition, any premiums collected by the TennCare Program are explicitly authorized to be appropriated to the program for the purpose of carrying out the provisions of TennCare.

The Commissioner of Finance and Administration is further authorized to transfer state funds and positions, as required, between TennCare and Mental Health Services; Intellectual and Developmental Disabilities; other Health Services; Children's Services; Human Services, Strategic Health-Care Programs; and Commerce and Insurance, Division of TennCare Oversight.

Item 2. For fiscal year 2013-2014, in addition to all other appropriations to the TennCare Program, the Commissioner of Finance and Administration is authorized to use certified public expenditures and/or intergovernmental transfers from all government-related TennCare service providers and local governments for the purpose of matching funds under federal law for the TennCare Program. The use of the certified public expenditures and/or intergovernmental transfers shall be in accordance with federal law and regulations.

Item 3. Subject to the availability of funding at June 30, 2013, the Commissioner of Finance and Administration is authorized to carry forward into the fiscal year beginning July 1, 2013, any unexpended balances of appropriations made under Chapter 1029, Public Acts of 2012, for TennCare and such funds as are carried forward are hereby reappropriated to be expended in the 2013-2014 fiscal year.

Item 4. The Commissioner of Finance and Administration is hereby authorized to expend or lend from the funds appropriated such sums as the Commissioner deems appropriate to assist TennCare HMO(s) in their operations and obtain services from contractors, consultants, and other third parties to give such assistance, such being determined by the General Assembly to be for a public purpose. The Commissioner shall provide prompt notification to the Speakers of the Senate and House of Representatives and to the Chairs of the Finance, Ways and Means Committees regarding any such expenditure or loan with complete details of the amounts and recipients involved in such transactions.

Item 5. The Commissioner of Finance and Administration is hereby authorized to adjust revenue estimates and related expenditures in Section 4, Title III-24, related to premiums and drug rebates for the purpose of carrying out the provisions of TennCare.

Item 6. The Commissioner of Finance and Administration is authorized to impose service limitations, to reduce optional eligibility categories, mandate standardized reimbursement levels, and/or reduce, or limit, optional benefits in the TennCare Program as necessary to control program expenditures in the fiscal years ending June 30, 2013, and June 30, 2014.

Item 7. In the fiscal year ending June 30, 2014, the Commissioner of Finance and Administration is authorized to transfer a sum sufficient, not to exceed $8,969,100, from the TennCare reserve to the Department of Intellectual and Developmental Disabilities for systems development purposes.

Item 8. From the appropriations made to the TennCare Program in this act in Section 1, Title III-26 and Section 4, Title III-24, for the Program Integrity Unit, the Commissioner of Finance and Administration is authorized to transfer positions from TennCare to the Attorney General and Reporter and to adjust departmental revenue estimates accordingly.

Item 9. Subject to the availability of funding at June 30, 2013, the Commissioner of Finance and Administration is authorized to carry forward into the fiscal year beginning July 1, 2013, any unexpended balances of appropriations made under Chapter 1108, Public Acts of 2010, Section 67, Item 1, for planning of additional PACE (Program of All-Inclusive Care for the Elderly) programs. Further, the Commissioner of Finance and Administration is authorized to adjust federal aid and other departmental revenues accordingly.

SECTION 49.

Item 1. From the appropriation made in Section 1, Title III-22, Item 13, for a state employee salary increase, it is the legislative intent to provide a 1.5 percent across-the-board salary increase effective July 1, 2013, for each state employee and to adjust the appropriate salary ranges in a like manner. The salary increase is not applicable to employees in positions which come under the provisions of a statutorily mandated pay plan; provided, however, that employees who come under the provision of a statutorily mandated plan shall be paid in accordance with the provisions of such plan.

Item 2.

(a) It is the legislative intent to provide funding for a 1.5 percent salary increase for the survey portion of the commissioned officer pay plan in the Department of Safety and the Tennessee Law Enforcement Training Academy as referenced in Tennessee Code Annotated, Section 4-7-205, effective July 1, 2013.

(b) It is the legislative intent to provide funding for a 1.5 percent salary increase for the survey portion of the Tennessee Wildlife Resources Agency pay plan effective July 1, 2013.

Item 3. The appropriations made in Section 1, Title III-10, for Higher Education include $18,600,000 to fund a 1.5 percent salary increase for higher education employees effective July 1, 2013.

Item 4. From the appropriation made in Section 1, Title III-22, Item 14.2, Salary Market Adjustment at 7/1/2013 – Additional Funds, in the amount of $27,900,000, which includes amounts of $27,500,000 from the general fund and $400,000 from dedicated funds, it is the legislative intent to provide funds for a salary market adjustment for state employees, effective July 1, 2013. Adjustments for this purpose from dedicated funds in excess of $400,000 and from departmental revenues hereby are appropriated.

From the $27,500,000 general fund appropriation, it is the legislative intent to earmark for non-executive agencies the following amounts in fiscal year 2013-2014:

Legislature	$	466,900.00
Fiscal Review Committee		23,300.00
Court System..		447,900.00
Attorney General and Reporter.......................................		320,600.00

Secretary of State		408,400.00
Comptroller of the Treasury		701,400.00
Treasury Department		3,400.00
Total Non-Executive Agencies	$	2,371,900.00

Item 5. Public Acts of 2012, Chapter 1029, at Section 49, Item 4, provided for a salary market adjustment effective January 1, 2013, for state employees from a $15,000,000 general fund appropriation, reflecting a six-month cost, in Section 1, Title III-22, Item 14.1, of that act. The recurring annualized appropriation of $30,000,000 is included in the line-item appropriations in Section 1 of this act, including an amount of $26,668,000 in Section 1, Title III-22, Item 14.1, Salary Market Adjustment at 7/1/2013, of this act. The salary market study for employees of the executive branch is on-going. In the year ending June 30, 2013, the appropriation in Public Acts of 2012, Section 1, Title III-22, Item 14.1, Salary Market Adjustment, hereby is reduced in the amount of $13,334,000. Notwithstanding the provisions of Public Acts of 2012, Chapter 1029, Section 49, Item 4, it is the legislative intent that such market adjustments to employee salaries in selected position classifications be made on July 1, 2013, except for adjustments for employees covered by the provisions of Item 6 of this section. The provisions of this item shall be effective immediately, the public welfare requiring it.

Item 6. Salary market adjustments during fiscal years 2012-2013 and 2013-2014 in the following agencies shall be made in accordance with law applying to such agencies: Legislature, Fiscal Review Committee, Court System, Office of the Attorney General and Reporter, Secretary of State, Comptroller of the Treasury, and Treasury Department. The appropriations earmarked in the amount of $1,666,000 in Public Acts of 2012, Chapter 1029, Section 49, Item 4, for certain non-executive agencies remain available for expenditure in year ending June 30, 2013. The provisions of this item shall be effective immediately, the public welfare requiring it.

Item 7.

(a) From the funds appropriated for the Salary Market Adjustment, there is earmarked the sum of $1,700,000 to provide funding for an additional three percent (3%) salary increase for the survey portion of the commissioned officer pay plan in the Department of Safety and the Tennessee Law Enforcement Training Academy as referenced in Tennessee Code Annotated, Section 4-7-205, effective July 1, 2013. It is the legislative intent that such increase be in addition to the increase provided in Item 2 of this Section.

(b) In addition to the funds appropriated in Section 1, Title III-6, to the Wildlife Resources Agency, there is appropriated from its revenues a sum sufficient to provide an additional three percent (3%) salary increase for the survey portion of the Tennessee Wildlife Resources Agency pay plan effective July 1, 2013. It is the legislative intent that such increase be in addition to the increase provided in Item 2 of this Section.

SECTION 50. From the appropriation in Section 1, Title III-11, Item 10, Regulatory Boards, an amount of $300,000 is earmarked from the Board of Architectural and Engineering Examiners revenues or reserve funds for disbursement to accredited interior design programs, accredited architectural programs, accredited engineering programs and accredited landscape architectural programs of any college or university in the state of Tennessee, after application to and subject to approval by the Board of Architectural and Engineering Examiners. The Board will develop guidelines for application, award and disbursement of the funds appropriated herein.

SECTION 51. From the appropriations made in Section 1 and Section 4 of this act, the Commissioner of Finance and Administration is authorized to transfer appropriation savings resulting from energy management projects to the major maintenance accounts of the departments and agencies. These funds may be used to pay debt service on associated bonds, to reimburse the general fund for appropriations made for energy management capital projects, to pay energy management fees, and to fund energy projects approved by the State Building Commission.

SECTION 52.

Item 1. From the Lottery for Education Account, the After-School Programs Special Account, and other accounts and sub-accounts established pursuant to Tennessee Code Annotated, Title 4, Chapter 51, the Tennessee Education Lottery Implementation Law, sums sufficient hereby are appropriated for the higher education scholarship programs and other education programs authorized by that law and by Title 49, Chapter 4, Part 9, relative to higher education scholarships; Title 49, Chapter 6, Part 7, relative to after-school educational programs. The appropriation from these sources for after-school programs pursuant to Title 49, Chapter 6, Part 7, shall not exceed the balance available in the After-School Programs Special Account at June 30, 2013, and such balance hereby is appropriated for expenditure in the fiscal year beginning July 1, 2013; provided, that the appropriation is contingent upon the availability of funds in the proper account and upon the availability of excess funds from net lottery proceeds, after the funding of higher education scholarships. The availability of excess funds shall be determined by the Commissioner of Finance and Administration prior to the distribution of any excess funds. A copy of such determination shall be filed with the Chairs of the Education committees of the Senate and House of Representatives and the Office of Legislative Budget Analysis.

Item 2.

(a) For students who first received the Tennessee HOPE scholarship, Tennessee HOPE access grant or Tennessee HOPE scholarship for nontraditional students before the fall semester of 2009, award amounts for the 2013-2014 academic year (two semesters) shall be:

(1) $4,000 for an eligible student under the HOPE scholarship award or HOPE nontraditional scholarship award pursuant to § 49-4-914(a);

(2) $2,000 for an eligible student under the HOPE scholarship award pursuant to § 49-4-914(b);

(3) $1,500 for an eligible student under the ASPIRE need-based supplemental award pursuant to § 49-4-915; and

(4) $1,000 for an eligible student under the General Assembly Merit Scholar supplemental award pursuant to § 49-4-916;

(b) For students who first received the Tennessee HOPE scholarship, Tennessee HOPE access grant or Tennessee HOPE scholarship for nontraditional students beginning the fall semester of 2009 or thereafter, award amounts for the 2013-2014 academic year shall be:

(1) $2,000 per semester for an eligible student under the HOPE scholarship award or HOPE nontraditional scholarship award pursuant to § 49-4-914(a);

(2) $1,000 per semester for an eligible student under the HOPE scholarship award pursuant to § 49-4-914(b);

(3) $750 per semester for an eligible student under the ASPIRE need-based supplemental award pursuant to § 49-4-915;

(4) $500 per semester for an eligible student under the General Assembly Merit Scholar supplemental award pursuant to § 49-4-916; and

(5) Pursuant to the provisions of § 49-4-920, the award amount for an eligible student under the Tennessee HOPE access grant shall be $1,375 per semester at four-year schools and $875 per semester at two-year schools;

(c) The 2013-2014 award amount for an eligible student under the Wilder-Naifeh Technical Skills Grant pursuant to § 49-4-921 shall be $2,000;

(d) The 2013-2014 award amount for an eligible student under the Tennessee HOPE foster child tuition grant shall be determined under the provisions of § 49-4-933;

(e) The 2013-2014 award amount shall be $1,000 per semester for successful completion of twelve (12) or more semester hours for an eligible student under the Helping Heroes Grant pursuant to § 49-4-938; provided, however, that the total amount expended for Helping Heroes Grants shall not exceed $750,000;

(f) The 2013-2014 award amount shall be determined pursuant to the provisions of § 49-4-939 for an eligible student under the Tennessee Rural Health scholarship; provided, however, that the total amount expended for Tennessee Rural Health scholarships shall not exceed $300,000; and

(g) The 2013-2014 award amount shall be determined by the Tennessee Student Assistance Corporation in accordance with § 49-4-930 for an eligible student under the dual enrollment grant.

Item 3. A sum sufficient, not to exceed the available balance in the Lottery for Education After-School Programs Grant Fund (LEAP Grant Fund), is appropriated from the fund for the purpose of awarding 3-year grants in accordance with the provisions of Tennessee Code Annotated, Title 49, Chapter 6, Part 7.

Item 4. A sum sufficient, not to exceed the available balance in the Energy Efficient Schools Council Fund, is appropriated from the fund for the purpose of the Energy Efficient Schools Initiative in accordance with the provisions of Tennessee Code Annotated, Title 49, Chapter 17.

Item 5. From the appropriations in Sections 1 and 4 of this act, the sum of $6,800,000 from the Lottery for Education Account is appropriated to the Tennessee Student Assistance Corporation for the sole purpose of supplementing Tennessee Student Assistance Awards.

Item 6. From the Lottery for Education Account, there is earmarked the sum of $54,000 for the sole purpose of implementing Senate Bill No. 538/House Bill No. 1055, relative to the classification of home schooled students for purposes of the Tennessee HOPE scholarship, if such bill becomes a law.

Item 7. From the Lottery for Education Account, there is earmarked the sum of $192,000 for the sole purpose of implementing Senate Bill No. 36/House Bill No. 21, relative to postsecondary financial assistance for students with intellectual disabilities, if such bill becomes a law.

Item 8. From the Lottery for Education Account, there is earmarked the sum of $12,000 for the sole purpose of implementing Senate Bill No. 719/House Bill No. 862, relative to allowing dependent children of certain workers to be eligible for the Tennessee HOPE lottery scholarship, if such bill becomes a law.

SECTION 53. From the appropriation made in Section 4 of this act, to the Department of Commerce and Insurance, Division of Insurance, it is the legislative intent to recognize base level funding of $7,479,700 in the fiscal year ending June 30, 2014. It is further the legislative intent that expenditures in excess of the $7,479,700 base level shall be funded from the increase in revenues generated by Chapter 333, Public Acts of 2001, which established funding appropriated to the Division of Insurance in the fiscal year ending June 30, 2001, as the base level.

SECTION 54. There are appropriated all tax revenues which are allocated by statute in accordance with the provisions of such statutes. The provisions of this section shall apply to all statutes becoming a law prior to July 1, 2014.

SECTION 55. Notwithstanding any provision of this act to the contrary, a direct appropriation to a non-governmental agency or entity shall not be disbursed until the recipient has filed with the head of the agency through which such disbursement is being made a plan specifying the proposed use of such funds and the benefits anticipated to be derived therefrom. As a prerequisite to the receipt of such direct appropriation, the recipient shall agree to provide to the agency head, within ninety (90) days of the close of the fiscal year within which such direct appropriation was received, an accounting of the actual expenditure of such funds including a notarized statement that the report is true and correct in all material respects; provided, however, that the head of the agency through which such disbursement is being made may require, in lieu of the accounting as provided above, an audited financial statement of the non-governmental agency or entity. A copy of such accounting or audit, as the case may be, shall be filed with the Office of the Comptroller of the Treasury.

SECTION 56.

Item 1. The provisions of this item shall take effect upon becoming law, the public welfare requiring it.

(a) In the fiscal years ending June 30, 2013, and June 30, 2014, the unexpended balances of health care safety net appropriations, including Project Diabetes, in Public Acts of 2005, Chapter 503, and in Public Acts of 2006, Chapter 963, and in Public Acts of 2007, Chapter 603, and in the Public Acts of 2008, Chapter 1203, and in Public Acts of 2009, Chapter 554, and in Public Acts of 2010, Chapter 1108, and in Public Acts of 2011, Chapter 473, and in Public Acts of 2012, Chapter 1029, and in this act may be carried forward and hereby are reappropriated for expenditure in the succeeding fiscal year, subject to approval of the Commissioner of

PUBLIC CHAPTER NO. 453 (cont'd)

Finance and Administration. Provided, however, that payroll savings from Department of Health positions established for the health care safety net shall revert to the general fund.

(b) From the health care safety net reserves carried forward at June 30, 2013, the Commissioner of Finance and Administration is authorized to transfer funds between health care safety net programs and to Cover Tennessee Health-Care Programs.

Item 2. All appropriations in this act for the AccessTN may be used for matching federal funds available, through waiver or otherwise, for expanding premium assistance, subject to the approval of the Commissioner of Finance and Administration.

Item 3. In addition to the appropriations elsewhere in this act, sums sufficient hereby are appropriated to the appropriate programs from the revenues and reserves of CoverTN, AccessTN, CoverRx, CoverKids, Project Diabetes, and health care safety net programs.

SECTION 57.

Item 1. The departmental revenues appropriated in this act from federal Homeland Security grant programs are subject to the following provisions:

(a) The allotment of these funds is subject to approval of the Commissioner of Finance and Administration, and the distribution among state and local agencies shall be subject to approval of or under procedures of the state Homeland Security Council.

(b) The Commissioner of Finance and Administration is hereby authorized to reallocate appropriations within the affected state agencies and to reallocate homeland security appropriations among the affected agencies for the purpose of providing the required state match to these and other federal homeland security and bioterrorism grants; to adjust position authorizations among affected departments, offices, and programs for that purpose; and to adjust federal and other departmental revenue estimates accordingly. The commissioner shall file any such reallocations or adjustments with the Fiscal Review Committee and the Office of Legislative Budget Analysis.

Item 2. There are appropriated sums sufficient to the Department of Safety, Office of Homeland Security, from federal grant funds and to other agencies of state government receiving homeland security federal grant funds.

Item 3. In the fiscal year ending June 30, 2013, the unexpended balance of the state appropriation to the Department of Safety in Public Acts of 2012, Chapter 1029, Section 1, Title III-20, Item 7, Office of Homeland Security, and in Public Acts of 2011, Chapter 473, Section 57, Item 3, may be reserved to be carried forward into the next fiscal year, and such amounts as may be carried forward hereby are appropriated. Said reserve is subject to the availability of revenue and to the approval of the Commissioner of Finance and Administration. The provisions of this item shall be effective immediately, the public welfare requiring it.

Item 4. In the fiscal year ending June 30, 2013, the unexpended balance of the state appropriation to the Miscellaneous Appropriations in Public Acts of 2012, Chapter 1029, Section 1, Title III-22, Item 6, Homeland Security Emergency Fund, and in Public Acts of 2011, Chapter 473, Section 57, Item 4, may be reserved to be carried forward into the next fiscal year, and such amounts as may be carried forward hereby are appropriated. Said reserve is subject to the availability of revenue and to the approval of the Commissioner of Finance and Administration. The provisions of this item shall be effective immediately, the public welfare requiring it.

SECTION 58. The provisions of this section shall take effect upon becoming a law, the public welfare requiring it. In the fiscal year ending June 30, 2013, any unexpended appropriations of U.S. Economic Recovery Act Funds made in this act or in earlier appropriations acts are hereby reappropriated to be expended in the 2013-2014 fiscal year and such appropriations shall be carried in a reserve into the fiscal year beginning July 1, 2013. This appropriation and carry-forward is subject to approval by the Commissioner of Finance and Administration.

SECTION 59. The provisions of this section shall take effect upon becoming a law, the public welfare requiring it. From the appropriations in Public Acts of 2008, Chapter 1203; in Public Acts of 2009, Chapter 554; in Public Acts of 2010, Chapter 1108, in Section 1, Title III-22, Item 25; in Public

Acts of 2011, Chapter 473, in Section 1, Title III-22, Item 27; in Public Acts of 2012, Chapter 1029, in Section 1, Title III-22, Item 27, and Section 41, Item 40; and in Section 1, Title III-22, Item 23, of this act, a sum sufficient is appropriated to fund a severance plan to be used in conjunction with the base budget personnel reductions required by this act. Provided, however, that severance benefits shall not be considered to have been due to any terminated employee who is re-employed by the state within sixty days of termination, and any such employee shall reimburse the state on a pro-rata basis in such circumstance. Any such repayment shall be made in accordance with applicable payroll and accounting policies and procedures so that the repayment amount is paid by the end of the calendar year.

The severance benefit plan shall consist of:

(1) A base payment of $3,200.

(2) College tuition assistance for 2 years to be capped at the average of the highest four-year public Tennessee college undergraduate level; provided, however, that such assistance shall only be provided for periods of actual attendance within a period of time to be determined by the Commissioner of Finance and Administration.

SECTION 60. From the appropriations in Section 1, Title III-26, the following non-recurring amounts are appropriated to the TennCare Program in order to restore in the fiscal year beginning July 1, 2013, certain recurring reductions made in fiscal year 2009-2010 and fiscal year 2010-2011, referenced on pages A-47 and A-48 of the 2013-2014 Budget Document and for other purposes identified in this section. The reductions restored are identified by reference to reduction items stated in Volume 2, Base Budget Reductions, of the 2009-2010 and 2010-2011 Budget Documents.

Item 1.

(a) If Senate Bill No. 441/House Bill No. 544, the annual coverage assessment act, becomes a law, there hereby is appropriated from the appropriations in Section 1, Title III-26, of this act, the sum of $449,800,000 (non-recurring) to the TennCare Program for the following purposes, and the Commissioner of Finance and Administration is authorized to adjust federal and other departmental revenue accordingly; provided, however, that if the federal government disallows the coverage assessment as a valid source to match federal Medicaid funds, the appropriations in this Item 1(a) shall be null and void, and the appropriations in Section 1, Title III-26 shall be reduced accordingly. If the cited bill does not become a law, the appropriations in Section 1, Title III-26 of this act, are hereby reduced in the amount of $449,800,000.

Reduction Number	Description		Amount
(i) FY 2009-2010 Base Reductions Restored:			
12	Essential Access Hospital Payments	$	34,500,000
13	Graduate Medical Education		17,250,000
15	Critical Access Hospital Payments		3,450,000
20	Medicare Part A Reimbursement		12,264,900
23	Provider Reimbursement and Co-Pay		61,308,200
	Subtotal	$	128,773,100
(ii) FY 2010-2011 Base Reductions Restored:			
10	Hospital Reimbursement Ceiling	$	35,200,200
16	In-Patient Services		37,906,300
17	Lab and X-Ray Procedures		19,393,200
18	Therapies		4,220,700
19	Out-Patient Services		15,637,600
24	Office Visits		17,741,000
	Subtotal	$	130,099,000
(iii) Other Appropriations:			
	Disproportionate Share Hospital Payments	$	27,952,900
	Add'l Cost-Based Reimbursement for Critical Access		6,000,000
	Hospital Payments – Unreimbursed Costs		156,975,000
	Subtotal	$	190,927,900
	Total	$	449,800,000

(b) There is further appropriated to the TennCare Program, in addition to the appropriation in this item in (a)(iii), Other Appropriations, Hospital Payments – Unreimbursed Costs, a sum sufficient from any amount in excess of $449,800,000 collected from the coverage assessment for the purpose of hospital payments for unreimbursed costs.

(c) To the extent that revenue collected from the coverage assessment is less than $449,800,000, the appropriation in this item in (a)(iii), Other Appropriations, Hospital Payments – Unreimbursed Costs, hereby is reduced in the amount of the under-collection.

(d) From the funds available in TennCare maintenance of coverage trust fund at June 30, 2013, there hereby is appropriated to the TennCare program a sum sufficient for the purposes authorized in law. The Commissioner of Finance and Administration is authorized to adjust federal and other departmental revenue accordingly. The allotment of funds under this item is subject to approval of the Commissioner of Finance and Administration.

SECTION 61. From appropriations in Public Acts of 2011, Chapter 473, Section 72, Item 20; in Public Acts of 2012, Chapter 1029, Section 1, Title III-32, Item 7; and in Section 1, Title III-32, Item 6, of this act, it is the legislative intent that the Commissioner of Finance and Administration, in consultation with a task force that he shall appoint, develop a comprehensive, statewide capital improvements master plan that encompasses the needs of state facilities and programs throughout Tennessee, including facilities managed in the state office buildings and support facilities revolving fund, other state facilities and properties, and the facilities and properties of the University of Tennessee and the State University and Community College System. The plan should assess current facilities, including capital maintenance and renovation; the need for additional or expanded facilities to accommodate state programs and service delivery; efficiencies that may be achieved by consolidation of facilities; and the potential use or disposition of any properties that may be surplus or available to the state. The plan should include site and facilities analysis, review of existing space uses, and future needs. In the recommendations, the plan also shall include a timetable of priority listings of capital improvement and capital maintenance projects for fiscal year 2014-2015 and for the four (4) subsequent fiscal years and priority listings for capital improvements and capital maintenance for the longer range. The plan should explain the general bases of facilities assessment and for setting of priorities.

The higher education component of the master plan shall be developed by the Tennessee Higher Education Commission, in consultation with the University of Tennessee and the State University and Community College System and shall be integrated into the comprehensive, statewide master plan by the task force and the commissioner. The commissioner shall submit to the Governor and the State Building Commission by June 30, 2014, the comprehensive capital improvements master plan.

The commissioner, or in his absence his designee, shall chair the task force. The commissioner, in consultation with affected department heads, may appoint such task force members as he deems appropriate, including staff of the Department of Finance and Administration, Department of General Services, and other departments and agencies that maintain, manage, or operate numerous facilities or real property; and, in consultation with the President of the University of Tennessee, the Chancellor of the State University and Community College System, and the Executive Director of the Tennessee Higher Education Commission (THEC), staff representing each of the higher education systems and THEC; and such other persons as the Commissioner of Finance and Administration deems appropriate, including private sector representatives.

From the appropriation in this item, the commissioner may expend funds for consulting services, task force expenses, and reimbursement of travel and lodging expenses of private-sector representatives under the provisions of the state comprehensive travel regulations, provided, however, that state agency and higher education personnel shall be reimbursed for travel expenses by their own agencies.

SECTION 62. Contingency Appropriations from Tobacco MSA Arbitration Settlement.

Item 1. Appropriations in Sections 1 and 38 of this act totaling $49,300,000 are contingent upon the state's receiving revenue from the Tobacco Master Settlement Agreement (MSA) diligent-enforcement arbitration settlement and such revenue being available funds. The estimate of such revenue is $72,400,000, which is estimated to be collected in the year ending June 30, 2013, but the appropriation also is effective if the revenue is collected in the year ending June 30, 2014. The appropriations, listed in priority order of funding, are:

(1) An amount of $5,300,000 in Section 38, Item 12.1, Contingency Appropriation – Reserve for Future Tobacco MSA Revenue Estimates (Arbitration Settlement). It is the legislative intent that this amount be used to support continuing Tobacco MSA revenue collections, as the other Tobacco MSA revenue is expected to decline by a total of $5,300,000 during fiscal years 2013-2014 through 2016-2017, before increasing as a result of the settlement in fiscal year 2017-2018.

(2) An amount of $24,000,000 in Section 1, Title III-32, Capital Outlay, Item 15, University of Tennessee, for UTK Steam Plant Conversion to Natural Gas, as described on pages A-156 and A-168 of the 2013-2014 Budget Document. Full funding of this appropriation is contingent upon the state's receiving $29,300,000 or more of revenue from the arbitration settlement. If a lesser amount is received, but more than $5,300,000, such lesser amount hereby is appropriated for this capital outlay project.

(3) An amount of $20,000,000 in Section 1, Title III-22, Miscellaneous Appropriations, Item 29, Contingency Appropriation – Health and Wellness Initiatives (Tobacco MSA Source). This appropriation is contingent upon the state's receiving more than $29,300,000 from the arbitration settlement, and the appropriation for this purpose hereby is made in such amount as may be received above the level of $29,300,000 from the Tobacco MSA arbitration settlement, but not to exceed $20,000,000.

Item 2. Health and Wellness Initiatives. From the contingency appropriation for Health and Wellness Initiatives, it is the legislative intent to provide emphasis on prevention and long-term medical cost savings across the entire state in order to accomplish the following goals enunciated by the Tennessee Department of Health: (1) prevent child and adolescent tobacco use, reducing the long-term cost and burden of heart disease, diabetes, chronic lung disease, asthma, and cancer; (2) reduce exposure to second-hand smoke, which reduces childhood ear infections and asthma; (3) eliminate smoking during pregnancy, which reduces low birth-weight baby hospitalization costs; (4) cessation of smoking by adults, which reduces health-care costs for individuals, families, and employers and improves community labor pools. The plan for use of these funds includes both primary prevention, which is to help persons not to begin using tobacco products, and secondary prevention, which is to help tobacco users to cease tobacco use.

It is the legislative intent that the unexpended balance of this appropriation be carried forward each June 30 until expended for the purposes stated in this item, and such funds shall not revert to the general fund at June 30, 2014.

These funds shall be allocated in such appropriated amounts as may be available in the following priority order:

Priority 1 – For the Governor's Health and Wellness Initiative, an amount not to exceed $5,000,000. This initiative is intended to evaluate and promote adoption of health and wellness programs and to promote sustained local initiatives; leverage private contributions and foundation support to develop sustained local initiatives; and perform research, education, awareness, measurement, and reporting on the initiative.

Priority 2 – For a 95-County Distribution, an amount not to exceed $15,000,000. The distribution of these funds shall be made by the Department of Health to local programs over a three-year period beginning with a distribution in fiscal year 2013-2014. The state distribution plan shall recognize health disparities in places and populations of this state; regional funding will be allocated using a formula that recognizes a 20 percent base amount, 40 percent based on population, and 40 percent based on need, as indicated by prevalence of tobacco use and tobacco-related health conditions. Upon development of allocation plans approved by the Tennessee Department of Health, the distribution is to be made to regional and county health councils, which are facilitated by local health departments and are engaged in community health assessments. The annual regional allocation plans for use of these funds must set priorities for primary and secondary prevention strategies and target health-disparity populations. Health councils shall be responsible for allocating funds to projects and partners, while applying continuous improvement methods and evaluation to measure results.

First-year distribution to any region is contingent upon approval by the Tennessee Department of Health of a regional plan documenting tobacco use and tobacco-related health conditions. It is the legislative intent that second- and third-year distribution to any region be contingent upon approval by the department of a revised regional plan and regional reporting of results of program evaluation, using the Plan-Do-Study-Act quality cycle to continuously improve effectiveness.

Item 3. Reserve for Health and Wellness Initiatives. An amount of $23,100,000, or any sum as may exceed $49,300,000 in revenue collected and available from the settlement, shall be reserved for future health and wellness non-recurring requirements as provided in Section 47, Item 9, of this act.

SECTION 63. Other 2012-2013 Supplemental Appropriations. The provisions of this section shall take effect upon becoming law, the public welfare requiring it. There is hereby appropriated the following amounts, which shall be in addition to the appropriations provided in Public Acts of 2012, Chapter 1029, and in Section 38 of this act, and 26 full-time (FT) positions are authorized to be established, as indicated in the table below:

			2012-2013
	From General Fund State Revenue:		
1.	Labor - 2012 Public Chapter 682 - Unemployment Compensation - Spouses in Military Transfers	$	130,000
2.	Mental Health - Moccasin Bend MHI - Accreditation (26 FT)		350,000
3.	Capital Outlay - Montgomery County Veterans Home		4,300,000
	Sub-Total From General Fund State Revenue	**$**	**4,780,000**
	From Dedicated State Revenue:		
1.	Agriculture - Beef Promotion Board		110,000
	Total	**$**	**4,890,000**

SECTION 64. Restore 2013-2014 Base Reductions – Intellectual and Developmental Disabilities. In addition to the amounts appropriated in Sections 1 and 4 of this act, the following amounts are appropriated, and the Commissioner of Finance and Administration is authorized to adjust federal aid and other departmental revenues and position authorizations accordingly. Such federal aid and other departmental revenue adjustments and full-time (FT) and part-time (PT) position authorizations are estimated in the text of the following line items. These appropriations restore to the Department of Intellectual and Developmental Disabilities 19 full-time positions that had been identified for abolishment in the 2013-2014 Budget Document, Vol. 2, Base Budget Reductions, pages 46-48.

		Recurring Appropriation		Departmental Revenue	
I.	**TennCare -** Intellectual Disabilities Services	$	436,700	$	688,400
II.	**Dept. of Intellectual and Developmental Disabilities (DIDD):**				
1.	Intellectual Disabilities Services Administration (3 FT)	$	18,900	$	170,500
2.	Greene Valley Developmental Center (12 FT)		0		812,000
3.	West Tenn. Regional Office (2 FT)		15,800		142,600
4.	West Tenn. Resource Center (2 FT)		191,000		0
	Sub-Total DIDD	$	225,700	$	1,125,100
	Total (19 FT)	**$**	**662,400**	**$**	**1,813,500**

SECTION 65. Core Services Restored. In addition to the amounts appropriated in Section 1 of this act, the following amounts are appropriated from the general fund and education fund, as applicable, for the purpose of restoring certain core services identified in the 2013-2014 Budget Document on page A-50, and, for the Arts Academy, in the 2009-2010 Budget Document, Vol. 2, Base Budget Reductions, page 6, and identified as a core service in the 2011-2012 Budget Document, Vol. 2, Base Budget Reductions, page 91. The Commissioner of Finance and Administration is authorized to adjust federal aid and other departmental revenues accordingly. Provided, however, that the negative amounts in line items of this section are appropriation reductions or deletions and the positive amounts are appropriation increases.

		Recurring		Non-Recurring	
1.	Education - Arts Academy - Teacher Professional Development	$	0	$	200,000
2.	Education - Science Alliance Museums		750,000		(750,000)
3.	Mental Health - Peer Support Centers		1,377,300		(1,377,300)

PUBLIC CHAPTER NO. 453 (cont'd)

4. Intellectual and Developmental Disabilities - Family Support Program	2,681,500	(2,681,500)
5. Human Services – Human Resource Agencies and Community Action Agencies - Operating Subsidy	0	1,415,600
Total	**$ 4,808,800**	**$ (3,193,200)**

SECTION 66. Legislation. In addition to the appropriations in Sections 1 and 4 of this act, the following amounts hereby are appropriated for the purpose of implementing the cited bills, and such additional or lesser amounts indicated in the final fiscal note on the bills as enacted hereby are appropriated. The Commissioner of Finance and Administration is authorized to allocate the appropriations to the appropriate organizational units and to adjust federal aid and other departmental revenues and authorized positions accordingly. Federal and other departmental revenue adjustments may be made in reconciliation to said fiscal notes and to available federal aid and other departmental revenue. Adjustments to the number of authorized positions indicated in the line items as full-time (FT), part-time (PT), and seasonal shall be reconciled to the fiscal notes. The negative amounts in line items of this section are appropriation reductions, and the positive amounts are appropriation increases. The appropriation in each item of this section is subject to the bill cited in that item becoming a law, except as otherwise provided.

Item 1. General Fund and Education Fund Appropriations. The following appropriations are from the general fund and education fund, as applicable.

	Recurring	**Non-Recurring**
1. SB 200 / HB 194 - Labor - Workers Compensation Reform - Fiscal Note Reconciliation (6 FT)	$ (396,800)	$ (606,900)
2. SB 202 / HB 196 - Correction - Gang Enhanced Sentencing - Fiscal Note Reconciliation @ $25,500	(3,200)	0
3. SB 501 / HB 506 - Budget Implementation General Law Changes - Sum Sufficient Estimated @ $0	0	0
4. SB 675 / HB 531 - Correction - Lynn's Law Caretaker Abuse or Neglect of Adult - Incarceration	14,200	0
5. SB 830 / HB 702 - State Charter School Panel (2 FT)	239,000	0
Total	**$ (146,800)**	**$ (606,900)**

Item 2. Dedicated Source and Earmarked Appropriations. The following appropriations are from dedicated state revenue sources and departmental revenues.

	Appropriation	**Departmental Revenue**
1. SB 148 / HB 161 - C&I - Collection Service Board - Managers at Collection Offices	$ (30,600)	$ 0
2. SB 169 / HB 163 - Financial Institutions - Electronic Payments Authorization	8,200	0
3. SB 194 / HB 188 - TSAC - Need-Based Education Grants @ 2-Year Schools - Transfer $50 M from TSAC Reserve	1,250,000	0
4. SB 197 / HB 191 - Tennessee Regulatory Authority	(523,000)	0
5. SB 833 / HB 551 - Labor – Workers Compensation Employee Misclassification Fund (6 FT)	370,000	0
6. Health - Electronic Licensure Application - Bill Not Filed - Delete Appropriation	(745,000)	0
Total	**$ 329,600**	**$ 0**

If Senate Bill No. 194/House Bill No. 188, relative to need-based education grants at two-year schools, becomes a law, the Commissioner of Finance and Administration is authorized to transfer from the Tennessee Student Assistance Corporation (TSAC) operating fund of the Federal Family Education Loan Program referenced in U.S. Code Annotated, Title 20, Section 1072b, the sum of $50,000,000 to the need-based educational fund created by the state legislation for the purpose of using interest earnings for the need-based grants. The commissioner, upon advice of the executive director of TSAC, may adjust the amount to be transferred based upon the balance required for the TSAC operating fund and may make transfers from the operating fund at any time an excess in the operating fund justifies. If the bill becomes a law by June 30, 2013, such transfers may begin in the fiscal year ending on June 30, 2013. The provisions of this paragraph shall be effective upon becoming law, the public welfare requiring it.

SECTION 67. TennCare Eligibility Determination. In addition to the amounts appropriated in Sections 1 and 4 of this act, the following amounts are appropriated for the purpose of establishing an eligibility determination process in the TennCare Bureau. The Commissioner of Finance and Administration is authorized to allocate the appropriations to the appropriate organizational units and to adjust federal aid and other departmental revenues and authorized positions accordingly. Provided, however, that the negative amounts in line items of this section are appropriation reductions or deletions and the positive amounts are appropriation increases.

	Recurring Appropriation	Departmental Revenue
1. TennCare Administration – Eligibility Determination Staff and Operational	$ 16,800,000	$ 16,800,000
2. TennCare Administration - Human Services Eligibility System Reduction	(4,000,000)	(4,000,000)
3. Human Services - Administration – Eligibility System Reduction	0	(8,000,000)
Total	**$ 12,800,000**	**$ 4,800,000**

The Bureau of TennCare is authorized to overlap up to 256 employees in existing authorized positions during the transition of the TennCare eligibility determination process, and the Commissioner of Finance and Administration is authorized to establish up to 256 positions in the TennCare Bureau as eligibility determination positions are abolished in the Department of Human Services. The number of additional positions established in the TennCare Bureau for this purpose shall not at any time exceed the number of eligibility determination positions abolished in the Department of Human Services, except as may be approved by the commissioner under the provisions of Section 23, Item 2, of this act. As the positions are established in the TennCare Bureau, the overlap of employees shall be reduced accordingly.

SECTION 68. Other Additions to Budget. In addition to the amounts appropriated in Sections 1 and 4 of this act, the following amounts are appropriated, and the Commissioner of Finance and Administration is authorized to allocate the appropriations to the appropriate organizational units and to adjust federal aid and other departmental revenues and position authorizations accordingly. Full-time (FT) and part-time (PT) position authorizations are estimated in the text of the following line items.

Item 1. General Fund and Education Fund Appropriations. The following appropriations are from the general fund and education fund, as applicable.

	Recurring	Non-Recurring
1. Legislature - Information Technology and On-Line Services	$ 500,000	$ 0
2. Legislature - National Black Caucus of State Legislators - Memphis Meeting	0	100,000
3. Public Defender - Shelby County Public Defender - Juvenile Cases	1,010,400	0
4. F&A - Criminal Justice Office - Family Violence Services	250,000	0
5. TennCare - Intellectual Disabilities Services - Accreditation Fee	87,300	0
6. Intellectual and Developmental Disabilities - Accreditation Fee	19,400	0
7. General Services - State Facilities Pre-Planning	1,000,000	0
8. Environment and Conservation – Chickasaw Basin Authority	0	100,000

PUBLIC CHAPTER NO. 453 (cont'd)

9.	Historical Commission – Civil War Site Preservation Fund (SB 642 / HB 301) – Grants for Acquisition	0	482,000
10.	Historical Commission – Wars Commission Publication	0	18,000
11.	Economic and Community Development (E&CD) - FastTrack Infrastructure and Job Training Assistance - Projects	0	44,600,000
12.	E&CD - Carroll Co. Lake - Grant to Carroll County Watershed Authority – Refinancing	0	5,000,000
13.	E&CD - Legacy Parks Foundation in Knoxville - Economic Development Grant - Match City and County funds	0	30,000
14.	Education - 2012 PC 967 - Dual Credit Articulation	0	300,000
15.	Education - Advance Placement Access	0	200,000
16.	Higher Education - Non-Formula Units:		
	Research and Public Service:		
	UT Agriculture Experiment Station	$ 608,600	$ 0
	UT Agriculture Extension Service	735,800	0
	TSU McMinnville Center	13,600	0
	TSU Institute of Ag. and Environmental Research	55,200	0
	TSU Cooperative Education	75,300	0
	TSU McIntire-Stennis Forestry Research	4,400	0
	UT Space Institute	190,100	0
	UT Institute for Public Service	113,500	0
	UT County Technical Assistance Service	41,200	0
	UT Municipal Technical Advisory Service	68,300	0
	Other Specialized Units:		
	Loan/Scholarships Program	29,800	0
	TN Foreign Language Institute	9,500	0
	Contract Education	54,500	0
	Program Initiatives:		
	Centers of Excellence	438,500	0
	Campus Centers of Emphasis	31,600	0
	Academic Scholars Program	10,000	0
	UT Access and Diversity Initiative	138,800	0
	TBR Access and Diversity Initiative	245,100	0
	THEC Grants	58,000	0
	UT Research Initiatives	139,900	0
	Sub-Total Higher Education - Non-Formula Units	$ 3,061,700	$ 0
17.	Higher Education - Board of Regents - Chairs of Excellence	0	400,000
18.	Labor - 2012 Public Chapter 682 - Unemployment Compensation - Spouses in Military Transfers	150,000	0
19.	Labor - Adult Basic Education - GED Exam Cost	675,000	0
20.	Mental Health - Moccasin Bend MHI - Accreditation (26 FT)	1,564,800	0
21.	Mental Health - Residential Adolescent Substance Treatment	0	500,000
22.	Revenue Dept. - Tobacco MSA Diligent Enforcement - Audit Staff (6 FT)	392,900	29,700
	Total	**$ 8,711,500**	**$ 51,759,700**

From the appropriation in this item to the Department of Economic and Community Development relative to Carroll County Lake, the department shall make a grant to the Carroll County Watershed Authority for the purpose of the authority's refinancing its existing outstanding debt associated with the lake project. The authority shall submit a plan to the department on the details of the intended use of the funds to pay off $5,000,000 of the existing debt incurred in the construction and improvement of the Carroll County Lake project, and the plan is subject to the approval of the department. The terms and conditions of the grant agreement shall include a provision requiring the authority to submit to the department, as soon as practical, but no later than June 30, 2014, an accounting of the actual expenditure of the grant to pay off existing indebtedness and a provision obligating the authority to reimburse the grant funds to the state, if the authority does not comply with the conditions of the approved plan and the grant agreement. The terms and conditions of the grant agreement shall be subject to approval of the Commissioner of Finance and Administration and the State Funding Board. Any reimbursement to the state of granted funds shall be deposited by the department to the general fund, as may be directed by the Department of Finance and Administration, Division of Accounts.

The appropriation in this item to the Department of Education for Advanced Placement Access is for the purpose of implementing Senate Bill No. 634/House Bill No. 705, establishing a pilot program to explore ways to expand access and offerings of advanced placement tests in Tennessee, if such bill becomes a law. If such bill does not become a law, the appropriation in this item to the Department of Education for Advanced Placement Access is for the purpose of a pilot program to explore ways to expand access and offerings of advanced placement tests in Tennessee.

The appropriation in this item to the Board of Regents for the Chairs of Excellence program is for the purpose of matching $600,000 available in the Board of Regents system and a $1,000,000 gift. The appropriation shall be transferred to the chairs of excellence endowment fund, Board of Regents general account, created pursuant to Tennessee Code Annotated, Section 49-7-501.

Item 2. Dedicated Source Appropriations. The following appropriations are from dedicated state revenue sources and departmental revenue.

	Appropriation	Departmental Revenue
1. Court System - Board of Professional Responsibility (1 FT)	$ 31,000	$ 0
2. TennCare - Alternative Payment Method Modeling (from Maintenance of Coverage Trust Fund)	5,000,000	756,000
3. Agriculture - Beef Promotion Board	145,000	0
4. Financial Institutions - Bank Examination Staffing – Adjustment to Recommendation	85,600	0
5. Health - Health Related Boards - Pharmacy Investigators (3 FT)	511,900	0
6. Safety - Driver License Issuance - Image Verification System for Real ID - Transfer from Systems Development Fund	600,000	0
Total	**$ 6,373,500**	**$ 756,000**

The appropriation in Item 2.2 to the TennCare Bureau for alternative payment method modeling is from the maintenance of coverage trust fund and federal funds and shall be used to develop alternative payment methodologies as allowed under law. The appropriation hereby is declared to be a sum sufficient not to exceed $5,000,000. A sum sufficient of this appropriation may be allotted in the fiscal year ending June 30, 2013, and the balance in the year beginning July 1, 2013. The provisions of this paragraph shall take effect upon becoming law, the public welfare requiring it.

SECTION 69. Reorganizations. In addition to the amounts appropriated in Sections 1 and 4 of this act, the following amounts are appropriated, and the Commissioner of Finance and Administration is authorized to allocate the appropriations to the appropriate organizational units and to adjust federal aid and other departmental revenues and authorized positions accordingly. Provided, however, that the negative amounts in line items of this section are appropriation reductions or deletions and the positive amounts are appropriation increases. Full-time (FT) and part-time (PT) position authorizations are estimated in the text of the following line items.

	Recurring Appropriation	Departmental Revenue
I. **TennCare** - Intellectual Disabilities Services - DIDD Arlington Exit Plan	$ (400,000)	$ (400,000)

II. **Health -** Health Licensure and Regulation - DIDD Arlington Exit Plan		200,000		600,000
III. **Agriculture:**				
1. Administration - Base Reduction #3, Position Abolishments (Abolish 2 FT statistical analysts)	$	(97,800)	$	0
2. Forestry Operations - Base Reduction #3, Position Abolishments (Restore 2 FT support)		80,900		0
Sub-Total Agriculture	**$**	**(16,900)**	**$**	**0**
IV. **Safety:**				
1. Highway Patrol - Base Reduction #2, Administrative Support Staff (-3 FT)	$	(198,400)	$	0
2. Administration - Base Reduction #2, Administrative Support Staff (+3 FT)		198,400		0
Sub-Total Safety	**$**	**0**	**$**	**0**
Total	**$**	**(216,900)**	**$**	**200,000**

SECTION 70. Capital Outlay Additional Provisions. The following provisions are in addition to other provisions of this act concerning the capital outlay budget and the facilities revolving fund capital outlay budget.

Item 1. In addition to the Facilities Revolving Fund capital maintenance projects listed on page A-181 of the 2013-2014 Budget Document, the following are funded in the appropriations in Section 1, Title III-29, of this act:

(a) Department of General Services – State Capitol Renovation Phase 3 in the amount of $1,400,000, and cupola restoration in the amount of $700,000 from the general fund.

(b) Department of Agriculture – Ellington Agricultural Center rewiring and cable for new telephone and computer systems, in the amount of $820,000 from reserves of the state office buildings and support facilities revolving fund.

Item 2. In addition to the capital outlay projects listed on pages A-155 through A-158 of the 2013-2014 Budget Document, the following are funded in the appropriations in Section 1, Title III-32, of this act:

(a) Department of Environment and Conservation – Rocky Fork State Park road and utilities infrastructure in the amount of $1,260,000.

(b) Department of Finance and Administration – Design, modeling, signs, and way finding in the amount of $800,000.

(c) Department of Finance and Administration – Memorials master planning for the Capitol complex in the amount of $100,000.

(d) Department of General Services – New State Museum planning in the amount of $475,000. It is the legislative intent that this appropriation be used by the task force to be established by the Governor and called the Governor's New State Museum Task Force, comprised of at least three members appointed by the Governor, one of whom he shall designate as chair of the task force, and the chair of the Douglas Henry State Museum Commission. The task force is to be charged with developing a new master plan that will include a conceptual program, site and location analysis and recommendation, an operating plan, and a capital funding plan that requires at least 25 percent of the funding to come from private sources. This appropriation for planning can be used for professional services, including a project manager, architectural and engineering consultants, museum consultants, fund-raising consultants, and other necessary expenses.

(e) Historical Commission – Historic Sites acquisition, improvements, maintenance, and interpretation in the amount of $500,000.

PUBLIC CHAPTER NO. 453 (cont'd)

(f) Department of Veterans Affairs – West Tennessee Cemetery at Memphis materials storage shed in the amount of $310,000.

(g) Department of Veterans Affairs – A new West Tennessee veterans cemetery, for land acquisition and planning of a site in the Parkers Crossroads vicinity in the amount of $350,000.

(h) Veterans Homes Board – Montgomery County Veterans Home Additional Funds – The project, listed on page A-156 of the 2013-2014 Budget Document, is deleted and not included in Section 1, Title III-32, of this act, but a 2012-2013 supplemental appropriation of $4,300,000 is made in Section 63 of this act for the same project, for the purposes described in the Budget Document on pages A-156 and A-166.

(i) Secretary of State – New State Library and Archives Planning in the amount of $2,600,000. From this appropriation three alternative plans shall be developed for total project costs in the amounts of $65,000,000; $80,000,000; and $95,000,000; and such alternative plans shall be presented to the Governor for his consideration in developing a future budget recommendation that he may transmit to the General Assembly.

In addition to the appropriation in Section 1, Title III-32, of this act, there is further appropriated, from a previous appropriation in the amount of $1,600,000 to the facilities revolving fund in Public Acts of 2012, Section 1, Title III-29, Item 4, and identified in the 2012-2013 Budget Document on page A-170, for interior renovation of the existing State Library and Archives, a sum sufficient from any unexpended balance of the $1,600,000 appropriation, to be used for the capital outlay needs of the State Library and Archives, including for the new State Library and Archives project, and for such purpose, the unexpended balance of said appropriation hereby is reappropriated. Expenditure of the reappropriated funds for this purpose is subject to approval of the State Building Commission, upon recommendation of the Secretary of State and the Commissioner of General Services and upon certification of availability of funds by the Commissioner of Finance and Administration. Any amount of the reappropriated funds approved by the State Building Commission for use in the new State Library and Archives project shall be reduced from the interior renovation project, and such amount shall be transferred from the facilities revolving fund to the capital projects fund.

(j) Tennessee Board of Regents – University of Memphis Community Facility. The appropriation in Section 1, Title III-32, reflects a state appropriation reduction in the amount of $300,000, and an amount of $300,000 from institutional sources shall be provided to correct the institutional match requirement for this project. The total project cost on page A-156 of the 2013-2014 Budget Document is not affected by this adjustment.

(k) University of Tennessee – UT Martin – Grant to Parsons-Decatur County Higher Education Foundation for the nursing building expansion in the amount of $1,000,000, matching donated funds.

Item 3. The capital outlay appropriation recommendations in the 2013-2014 Budget Document hereby are amended, as follows:

(a) The Tennessee Wildlife Resources Agency project from dedicated sources, described on page A-159 of the Budget Document as Nashville Central Office Mechanical/Electrical Upgrades, is amended to delete the federal aid amount of $2,570,000, and there hereby is appropriated an additional amount of $2,570,000 from the wildlife resources fund revenues, making the total appropriation from wildlife resources fund revenues $3,430,000.

(b) The higher education capital improvement project in the State University and Community College System, described on page A-156 as Northeast State Community College Technical Education Complex, is amended to increase the total cost by $1,210,000, funded from institutional sources, and correcting the total project cost to $34,440,000 and the institutional match requirement to $2,710,000.

Item 4. Two capital outlay projects identified in the 2013-2014 Budget Document, page A-156, hereby are renamed, without change in intent of the projects:

(a) Austin Peay State University – Trahern Building Addition and Renovation is renamed as Fine Arts Improvements.

(b) Tennessee Technological University – New Chemistry Building and Infrastructure is renamed as Laboratory Science Building and Infrastructure.

Item 5. From the unexpended balance of the capital outlay appropriation of $12,000,000 to the Department of Intellectual and Developmental Disabilities for construction of group homes for clients of Clover Bottom Developmental Center in Public Acts of 2010, Chapter 1108, Section 10, Item 38, the department may use available funds to construct state-owned homes for behavioral respite and intensive behavioral residential programs in any region of the state. Expenditure of these reappropriated funds is subject to approval of the State Building Commission, upon recommendation by the Commissioner of Intellectual and Developmental Disabilities that adequate funds are available, from the capital outlay appropriation in the 2010 act or other available capital outlay appropriations to the department, to provide for the Clover Bottom clients and upon certification of availability of funds by the Commissioner of Finance and Administration.

SECTION 71. If Senate Bill No. 170/House Bill No. 164, relative to procurement, does not become a law, then any contract for services enumerated in Section 10, Item 2, relative to executive departments and agencies of state government, shall be subject to the approval of the Comptroller of the Treasury; and such contracts entered into by the legislative or judicial branches shall be subject to the approval of the Comptroller of the Treasury.

SECTION 72. Program Adjustments Funded by Departmental Revenue. The appropriations of departmental revenue in Section 4 to the following programs shall be adjusted for the stated purposes:

Item 1. To the TennCare Bureau, Intellectual Disabilities Services, an amount of $11,400,000 from federal aid hereby is appropriated to correct the revenue estimate reduction that was overstated in the 2013-2014 Budget Document, Volume 2, Base Budget Reductions, page 32, item 14, TennCare Share of Intellectual and Developmental Disabilities Base Reductions.

Item 2. The Department of Education, Achievement School District, hereby is reduced by $16,567,700 from departmental revenue sources, and full-time authorized positions reduced by 82, to reflect a corrected estimate of the schools and students in the district.

SECTION 73. Federal Program Reductions. The General Assembly recognizes that reductions in federal grants-in-aid resulting from the sequester of federal programs by the United States government will require extraordinary actions by the Commissioner of Finance and Administration to manage the state budget within available resources and without detrimental effect on state finances. It is the legislative intent that the reduced programs not be maintained at their former level by substituting state funds for the reduced federal aid.

Item 1. Accordingly, the Commissioner of Finance and Administration shall reduce the federal and other departmental revenue estimates and reduce the allotment of funds in an amount equal to the revenue reductions, in accordance with Section 23, Item 1, it being the legislative intent that such withdrawal of federal aid necessitates a reduction of spending authorization in order to protect the state finances.

Item 2. The commissioner also shall reduce the number of authorized positions of each program affected by the federal aid reductions, to the extent positions were funded by the federal aid being reduced, and any employees terminated as a result of such action shall be provided severance benefits as provided in Section 59 of this act.

Item 3. State funds appropriated to match federal aid that has been reduced shall be set aside in an allotment reserve of the affected program and shall not be expended except to the extent necessary to provide for severance benefits and other actions necessary to reduce programs; provided, however, that the allotment of state funds shall be authorized to the extent necessary to fulfill state maintenance-of-effort (MOE) requirements under federal law. To the extent that state MOE requirements are reduced by the federal programs, state funds in the amount of the allowable MOE reduction also shall be reserved and not expended, except as provided above in this item. The provisions of this item shall not operate to require the reserving of state funds that have been appropriated in excess of the previous level of required state match or MOE in order to enhance the affected joint federal-state program.

Item 4. It is the legislative intent that the state matching funds held in allotment reserve as a result of these actions revert to the appropriate fund balance at June 30, 2014, in addition to the amounts estimated in the over-appropriation in Section 43 of this act, and that such funds as may be estimated at mid-year, when the 2014-2015 Budget is transmitted, be available for the Governor's budget recommendations for the maintenance of any priority program services, if approved in the 2014 appropriations bill enacted by the General Assembly.

Item 5. The Commissioner of Finance and Administration, by December 31, 2013, shall report to the Senate and House Finance, Ways and Means committees on the reductions made by department and by state program, including the amounts of federal and other departmental revenue and allotments reduced, the matching state appropriations held in reserve and not allotted, the number of positions reduced, and a general summary of the impact on program services. After the report date, the commissioner shall provide any updated information in a fiscal year-end report encompassing the same categories of information, if the program reductions have changed from the earlier report.

SECTION 74.

Item 1. From the appropriation to the FastTrack Infrastructure and Job Training Assistance program in Section 1, Title III-8, Item 8, an amount of $3,000,000 that is included in the recurring amount identified on page B-352 of the 2013-2014 Budget Document is hereby designated as a non-recurring appropriation.

Item 2. It is the legislative intent that at June 30, 2013, an amount of $8,000,000 shall revert to the general fund balance from the amount carried forward at June 30, 2012, in the Department of Finance and Administration, Strategic Health-Care Programs, Health-Care Planning and Innovation, for health information technology pursuant to Section 36, Item 14 of Chapter 1029 of the Public Acts of 2012. The provisions of this item shall take effect upon becoming law, the public welfare requiring it.

SECTION 75.

Item 1.

(a) From the funds appropriated to the Department of Transportation, there is earmarked a sum sufficient for the sole purpose of funding any general bill or resolution, that becomes law, designating an interstate, United States highway or state highway as a memorial highway or as a memorial bridge for certain individuals killed in the line of duty, pursuant to § 54-1-133, that is not otherwise funded in this act.

(b) From the funds appropriated to the Department of Transportation, there is earmarked a sum sufficient for the sole purpose of implementing state-funded signage erected pursuant to Senate Bill No. 64/House Bill No. 1030, if such bill becomes law.

(c) This item shall take effect upon becoming a law, the public welfare requiring it.

Item 2. From funds available to any department, commission, board, agency, or other entity of state government, there is earmarked a sum sufficient to fund any bill or resolution, that becomes law, on which the fiscal note indicates that the cost of implementation of the bill or resolution will be funded within existing appropriations of the entity, within the availability of revenues received by the entity, or within other existing budgetary resources. It is the legislative intent that such funding be earmarked for implementation of any such bills or resolutions in the fiscal year ending June 30, 2013, and in subsequent fiscal years. This item shall take effect upon becoming law, the public welfare requiring it.

Item 3. From the federal funds available to the Administrative Office of the Courts, there is earmarked the sum of $200,000 (non-recurring) for the sole purpose of establishing specialized veteran's courts in accordance with the purposes described in Chapter 943 of the Public Acts of 2012. This appropriation shall be contingent upon sufficient federal funds being available in fiscal year 2013-2014 as determined by the Commissioner of Finance and Administration in consultation with the Director of the Administrative Office of the Courts by November 1, 2013.

Item 4. From the improvement funds appropriated to the Department of Tourist Development, there is earmarked the sum of $157,500 (non-recurring) to be used for the purposes of website development, marketing, advertising and other support services for the Tennessee Sesquicentennial Commission.

Item 5. The appropriation made to the Department of General Services in Section 1, Title III-32, of this act is reduced by the sum of $500,000. Such funding reduction is for the purpose of eliminating funding for the Tennessee Aquarium Ecology Lab grant.

Item 6. The appropriation made to the Department of General Services in Section 1, Title III-32, of this act is reduced by the sum of $500,000. Such funding reduction is for the purpose of eliminating funding for the Jonesborough Jackson Theatre grant.

Item 7. From the funds appropriated to Tennessee Board of Regents, there is earmarked the sum of $50,300 for the sole purpose of implementing Senate Bill No. 643/House Bill No. 236, relative to renaming technology centers, if such bill becomes a law.

Item 8. From the Interlock Assistance Fund, there is appropriated the sum of $175,300 for the sole purpose of implementing Senate Bill No. 670/House Bill No. 353, relative to expanded use of ignition interlock devices, if such bill becomes a law.

Item 9. From the funds appropriated to the Secretary of State, there is earmarked the sum of $4,000 (non-recurring) for the sole purpose of implementing HJR 51, relative to an online Blue Book curriculum, if such resolution is adopted.

SECTION 76.

Item 1. In addition to any other funds appropriated by the provisions of this act, there is appropriated a sum sufficient to implement all bills and resolutions having an estimated first year's cost of $50,000 or less which become law. It is the legislative intent that if such bills and resolutions are otherwise funded by the provisions of this act, then the funds appropriated in this item shall be reduced accordingly.

Item 2. In addition to any other funds appropriated by the provisions of this act, there is hereby appropriated a sum sufficient to cities and counties for the sole purpose of funding the state share of the mandated local cost of implementing the provisions of any bill imposing a mandatory cost on local governments in excess of $1,000,000, not otherwise funded in this act. The state share shall be an amount equal to ten percent (10%) of the mandated local cost of implementing each such bill.

Item 3. In addition to any other funds appropriated by the provisions of this act, there is appropriated the sum of $100,000 (recurring) to the Department of Health for the sole purpose of making a grant in such amount to the Crumley House located in Washington County, to be used for the provision of programs and services on behalf of persons suffering from traumatic brain injuries.

Item 4. In addition to any other funds appropriated by the provisions of this act, there is appropriated the sum of $400,000 (recurring) to the Department of Mental Health and Substance Abuse Services for the sole purpose of funding professional counseling services provided by Not Alone, Inc., in three (3) additional regions of Tennessee for veterans and their families who suffer from post-traumatic stress disorder (PTSD).

Item 5. In addition to any other funds appropriated by the provisions of this act, there is appropriated the sum of $1,862,500 (non-recurring) to the Department of Mental Health and Substance Abuse Services for the sole purpose of making grants in the amount of $372,500 each to five (5) community alcohol and drug services providers of adolescent residential treatment services.

Item 6. In addition to any other funds appropriated by the provisions of this act, there is appropriated the sum of $1,000,000 (non-recurring) to the Department of General Services for the sole purpose of making grants in the amount of $200,000 each to the four (4) accredited Tennessee zoos and the Tennessee Aquarium, to be used for capital improvement projects.

Item 7. In addition to any other funds appropriated by the provisions of this act, there is appropriated the sum of $400,000 (non-recurring) to Austin Peay State University to match private and public funds of approximately $400,000 to be used toward completion of an Animal Science Facility on the APSU Agriculture and Environmental Education Center (AEEC) Farm.

Item 8. In addition to any other funds appropriated by the provisions of this act, there is appropriated the sum of $100,000 (recurring) to the Comptroller of the Treasury for the purpose of higher education policy evaluation. The Comptroller is authorized to establish one (1) full-time position.

Item 9.

(a) In addition to any other funds appropriated by the provisions of this act, there is appropriated the sum of $52,800 (recurring) to the Tennessee higher education commission for the sole purpose of restoring the base budget reduction in that amount to the commission's budget.

(b) In addition to any other funds appropriated by the provisions of this act, there is appropriated the sum of $28,800 (recurring) to the Tennessee higher education commission for the sole purpose of restoring the base budget reduction in that amount to the Tennessee student assistance corporation's budget.

Item 10. In addition to any other funds appropriated by the provisions of this act, there is appropriated the sum of $500,000 (non-recurring) to the Department of Finance and Administration for the sole purpose of making a grant in such amount to Meharry Medical College, to be used in support of the Meharry HBCU Wellness Project.

Item 11. In addition to any other funds appropriated by the provisions of this act, there is appropriated from the general fund the sum of $50,000 (non-recurring) to the Administrative Office of the Courts for the sole purpose of establishing specialized veteran's courts in accordance with the purposes described in Chapter 943 of the Public Acts of 2012.

Item 12. In addition to any other funds appropriated by the provisions of this act, there is appropriated the sum of $150,000 (non-recurring) to the Department of Finance and Administration for the sole purpose of making a grant in such amount to the James K. Polk Memorial Association, to be used for renovation and improvement of the James K. Polk Home and surrounding property that has been conveyed to the association.

Item 13. In addition to any other funds appropriated by the provisions of this act, there is appropriated the sum of $250,000 (non-recurring) to the Department of Health for the sole purpose of the vaccine billables project.

Item 14. In addition to any other funds appropriated by the provisions of this act, there is appropriated the sum of $125,000 (non-recurring) to the Department of Education for the sole purpose of allocating such sum as grants in equal amounts to each Tennessee public television station, to be used for equipment, programs and operational expenses.

Item 15. In addition to any other funds appropriated by the provisions of this act, there is appropriated the sum of $829,620, including $529,500 (recurring) and $300,120 (non-recurring), to the Tennessee Bureau of Investigation for the sole purpose of additional agents, equipment and associated expenses. The TBI is authorized to establish six (6) full-time positions; it is the legislative intent that two (2) positions be assigned to each grand division.

Item 16. In addition to any other funds appropriated by the provisions of this act, there is appropriated the sum of $603,800 (non-recurring) to the Tennessee Bureau of Investigation for the sole purpose of restoring confidential fund money for drug enforcement and investigation operations.

Item 17. In addition to any other funds appropriated by the provisions of this act, there is appropriated the sum of $750,000 (non-recurring) to the Tennessee Bureau of Investigation (TBI) for the sole purpose of equipment and operational expenses associated with the bureau's methamphetamine task force. Any funds appropriated by this item shall not revert to the general fund but shall remain available to the TBI until expended for the purpose of methamphetamine clean-up.

Item 18. In addition to any other funds appropriated by the provisions of this act, there is appropriated the sum of $44,200 (of which amount $37,500 is non-recurring) to the Tennessee Holocaust Commission to be expended as follows:

$6,700 (recurring) to restore a base funding reduction;

$12,000 (non-recurring) to print 1,000 additional copies of "Living On", a book and DVD set which chronicles the story of Holocaust survivors and U.S. Army liberators living in Tennessee; and

$25,500 (non-recurring) to create a new class of teaching fellows to serve as community liaisons.

PUBLIC CHAPTER NO. 453 (cont'd)

Item 19. In addition to any other funds appropriated by the provisions of this act, there is appropriated the sum of $10,000 (non-recurring) to the Department of Finance and Administration for the sole purpose of making a grant in such amount to Diggs-Kraus Sickle Cell Center at the Regional Medical Center at Memphis (The MED), to be used for research and services.

Item 20. In addition to any other funds appropriated by the provisions of this act, there is appropriated the sum of $2,000,000 (recurring) to the Department of Intellectual and Developmental Disabilities, to be used for increasing the rate of reimbursement paid to community providers of services for individuals with intellectual and developmental disabilities.

Item 21. In addition to any other funds appropriated by the provisions of this act, there is appropriated the sum of $64,000 (recurring) to the Department of Children's Services for the sole purpose of making grants in amounts of $2,000 each to the thirty-two (32) Tennessee Child Advocacy Centers, which coordinate local and state services in the investigation and prosecution of child-abuse cases.

Item 22. In addition to any other funds appropriated by the provisions of this act, there is appropriated the sum of $91,000 (recurring) to the Commission on Children and Youth for the sole purpose of making grants, as follows:

$1,500 each to the forty-four (44) Court Appointed Special Advocates (CASA) programs located across the state, to be used for program and operational expenses;

$25,000 to the Tennessee Court Appointed Special Advocates (CASA) Association to maintain current staffing levels.

Item 23. In addition to any other funds appropriated by the provisions of this act, there is appropriated from the general fund the sum of $875,000 (non-recurring) to the Department of Transportation, to be used to conduct a study concerning the forecasted growth, movement, and heavy volume of freight on all transportation modes in this state, including, but not limited to, the latest data and projections for growth trends in freight movement. The department shall report its findings and recommendations to the Transportation and Safety Committee of the Senate and the Transportation Committee of the House of Representatives no later than October 1, 2014.

Item 24. In addition to any other funds appropriated by the provisions of this act, there is appropriated the sum of $500,000 (recurring) to the University of Tennessee Institute for Public Service - Law Enforcement Innovation Center to support technology transfer, management best practices and training for law enforcement agencies.

Item 25. In addition to any other funds appropriated by the provisions of this act, there is appropriated the sum of $225,000 (recurring) to the Comptroller of the Treasury for the sole purpose of restoring three (3) positions for the State Board of Equalization.

Item 26. In addition to any other funds appropriated by the provisions of this act, there is appropriated the sum of $500,000 (non-recurring) to the Department of Human Services for the sole purpose of making a grant in such amount to the Second Harvest Food Bank of Middle Tennessee, to be used for the purpose of purchasing, handling, and transporting food for hunger relief. The Second Harvest Food Bank of Middle Tennessee shall distribute the funds to the five (5) food banks across the state, as follows:

35% to Second Harvest Food Bank of Middle Tennessee;
25% to Memphis Food Bank;
20% to Second Harvest Food Bank of East Tennessee;
10% to Chattanooga Area Food Bank;
10% to Second Harvest Food Bank of Northeast Tennessee.

Item 27. In addition to any other funds appropriated by the provisions of this act, there is appropriated the sum of $50,000 (non-recurring) to the Department of Veterans Affairs for the sole purpose of making a grant in such amount to West Tennessee Veterans Home, Inc., to facilitate the opening of a retirement and nursing home for veterans in West Tennessee.

Item 28. In addition to any other funds appropriated by the provisions of this act, there is appropriated the sum of $125,000 (non-recurring) to the Department of Education for the sole purpose of statewide implementation of career and technical education programming through the Tennessee Alliance of Boys & Girls Clubs.

Item 29. In addition to any other funds appropriated by the provisions of this act, there is appropriated the sum of $150,000 (recurring) to the Department of Health for the sole purpose of making a grant in such amount to St. Jude Hospital in Memphis, to defray, in whole or in part, the expenses of patients and their families who are citizens and residents of Tennessee in traveling to and from St. Jude Hospital. Such payments shall be administered by the hospital and shall be made on the basis of need. Such patients, or their families, requesting assistance from these funds shall supply such documents supporting need and travel expenses as the hospital may require.

Item 30. In addition to any other funds appropriated by the provisions of this act, there is appropriated the sum of $49,000 (recurring) to the Department of Finance and Administration for the sole purpose of making a grant in such amount to A Secret Safe Place for Newborns of Tennessee, Inc., to be used for operational expenses.

Item 31. In addition to any other funds appropriated by the provisions of this act, there is appropriated the sum of $107,500 (recurring) to the Department of Health for the sole purpose of restoring funding for child health and development (CHAD) services.

Item 32. In addition to any other funds appropriated by the provisions of this act, there is appropriated the sum of $392,500 (recurring) to the Department of Health for the sole purpose of restoring healthy start services.

Item 33. In addition to any other funds appropriated by the provisions of this act, there is appropriated the sum of $150,000 (recurring) to the State Museum for the sole purpose of operational expenses.

Item 34. In addition to any other funds appropriated by the provisions of this act, there is appropriated the sum of $100,000 (recurring) to the Department of Finance and Administration for the sole purpose of making a grant in such amount to Tennessee History for Kids, Inc., to be used for programs, services, and operational expenses.

Item 35. In addition to any other funds appropriated by the provisions of this act, there is appropriated the sum of $95,000 (non-recurring) to the Department of Finance and Administration for the sole purpose of making a grant in such amount to the Academy for Youth Empowerment in Shelby County, to be used for programs, services and operational expenses in support of the organization's regional activities.

Item 36. In addition to any other funds appropriated by the provisions of this act, there is appropriated the sum of $100,000 (non-recurring) to the Tennessee Historical Commission for the sole purpose of making a grant in such amount to the Stax Museum in Memphis, to be used for defrayal of operational costs.

Item 37. In addition to any other funds appropriated by the provisions of this act, there is appropriated the sum of $75,000 (non-recurring) to the Department of Finance and Administration for the sole purpose of making a grant in such amount to a Tennessee nonprofit fund supporting services to communities of greatest need to be used for enterprise development week youth economic summits in Nashville, Chattanooga, Knoxville and Memphis.

Item 38. In addition to any other funds appropriated by the provisions of this act, there is appropriated the sum of $62,500 (recurring) to the Department of Veterans Affairs for the sole purpose of establishing and funding one (1) veteran support position.

Item 39. In addition to any other funds appropriated by the provisions of this act, there is appropriated the sum of $248,500 (non-recurring) to the Department of Military for the sole purpose of restoring base funding for the tuition assistance program available to Air Guard personnel.

Item 40. In addition to any other funds appropriated by the provisions of this act, there is appropriated the sum of $450,000 (non-recurring) to the Department of Economic and Community Development for the sole purpose of local planning transition grants. It is the intent of the General Assembly that each of the nine (9) development districts receive $50,000.

Item 41. In addition to any other funds appropriated by the provisions of this act, there is appropriated the sum of $20,000 (non-recurring) to the Department of Finance and Administration for the sole purpose of making grants in equal amounts of $5,000 each to the four (4) Tennessee National Coalition of 100 Black Women chapters located in Memphis, Nashville, Chattanooga and Knoxville, to be used for programs and services.

Item 42. In addition to any other funds appropriated by the provisions of this act, there is appropriated the sum of $48,000 (non-recurring) to the Department of Finance and Administration for the sole purpose of making a grant in such amount to the YMCA, to be used for the YMCA Community Action Project (Y-CAP) to provide mentoring, tutoring and counseling for at-risk and troubled youth across Tennessee. It is the legislative intent that the department make grants in equal amounts from the sum provided to the YMCA organizations in Memphis, Nashville, Knoxville and Chattanooga.

Item 43. In addition to any other funds appropriated by the provisions of this act, there is appropriated the sum of $50,000 (non-recurring) to the Tennessee Historical Commission for the sole purpose of making a grant in such amount to the Alex Haley House and Museum for programs and operational expenses.

Item 44. In addition to any other funds appropriated by the provisions of this act, there is appropriated the sum of $350,000 (non-recurring) to the Department of General Services for the sole purpose of making a grant in such amount to the Lorraine Civil Rights Museum Foundation to be used for structural improvements at the National Civil Rights Museum.

Item 45. In addition to any other funds appropriated by the provisions of this act, there is appropriated the sum of $30,000 (recurring) to the Tennessee Historical Commission for the sole purpose of supplementing funding available for Historic Sites acquisition, improvements, maintenance, and interpretation.

SECTION 77.

Item 1. From the funds appropriated to the University of Tennessee System by the provisions of this act, no later than September 1, 2013, the Chancellor of the University of Tennessee at the Knoxville campus is directed to report to the Chairs of the Finance, Ways and Means Committees of the Senate and the House of Representatives concerning the planned allocation of student activity fees and other fees collected from students (excluding fees received for housing, meals, and tuition) for the fall semester. No later than January 15, 2014, the Chancellor shall file a similar report concerning the planned allocation of such fees for the spring semester.

Item 2. From the appropriations made in this act, the State Architect is directed to examine the capital projects that have expended funds on planning, construction plans or both in the ten (10) years immediately preceding the effective date of this act. The examination shall be limited to those projects that have not been canceled or determined to be unnecessary as of the effective date of this act. The State Architect shall compile a list of such projects and submit the list, and any findings and recommendations, to the Chairs of the Finance, Ways and Means Committees of the Senate and House of Representatives no later than October 1, 2013. The Building Commission is directed to prioritize the list of projects and submit the list to the Governor and Chairs of the Finance, Ways and Means Committees of the Senate and House of Representatives no later than January 1, 2014.

SECTION 78. The Tennessee Code Commission is requested to place an appropriate, permanent note following the codification of any public act which is codified and which has not received constitutionally required first year's funding through the provisions of this act

SECTION 79. The Commissioner of Finance and Administration is requested to make all necessary adjustments to revenues, authorized positions and totals as necessary to effectuate the provisions of this act as amended by the General Assembly.

SECTION 80. If any provisions of this act or the application thereof to any person or circumstance is held invalid, such invalidity shall not affect other provisions or applications of this act which can be given effect without the invalid provision or application, and to that end the provisions of this act are declared to be severable.

SECTION 81. No expenditure of public funds pursuant to this act shall be made in violation of the provisions of Title VI of the Civil Rights Act of 1964, as codified in 42 United States Code, 2000(d).

Effective date 7/1/2013

SECTION 82. This act shall take effect July 1, 2013, the public welfare requiring it; provided, however, that any provision of this act which authorizes prior or immediate expenditures and any section or item which specifies an immediate effective date shall take effect upon becoming a law, the public welfare requiring it.

PUBLIC CHAPTER NO. 454

PUBLIC CHAPTER NO. 454

SENATE BILL NO. 501

By Norris

Substituted for: House Bill No. 506

By Sargent, McCormick

AN ACT to amend Tennessee Code Annotated, Title 4; Title 5; Title 6; Title 8; Title 9; Title 10; Title 11; Title 12; Title 13; Title 16; Title 17; Title 18; Title 29; Title 33; Title 36; Title 37; Title 38; Title 39; Title 40; Title 41; Title 43; Title 45; Title 47; Title 48; Title 49; Title 50; Title 53; Title 54; Title 55; Title 56; Title 57; Title 58; Title 59; Title 60; Title 62; Title 63; Title 64; Title 65; Title 66; Title 67; Title 68; Title 69; Title 70 and Title 71, relative to statutory revisions required for implementation of the annual appropriations act.

BE IT ENACTED BY THE GENERAL ASSEMBLY OF THE STATE OF TENNESSEE:

49-3-351 SECTION 1. Tennessee Code Annotated, Section 49-3-351(a), is amended by deleting subdivision (4) in its entirety.

12-4-320 SECTION 2. Tennessee Code Annotated, Section 12-4-320, is amended by deleting the section in its entirety.

4-32-101, 4-32-103 SECTION 3. Tennessee Code Annotated, Title 4, is amended by deleting Chapter 32 in its entirety.

4-29-234, 41-52-101—41-52-104 SECTION 4. Tennessee Code Annotated, Title 41, Chapter 52, Part 1, is hereby deleted in its entirety.

12-2-117 SECTION 5. Tennessee Code Annotated, Section 12-2-117(b), is amended by adding the following subdivisions:

(3) Notwithstanding the provisions of subdivision (b)(2), on June 30, 2013, the commissioner of finance and administration shall transfer from the special trust fund to the general fund an amount of $1,923,100 in order to recognize the fiscal year 2011-2012 transition costs related to the closure of Lakeshore mental health institute, which were funded by an appropriation from the special trust fund in Public Acts of 2012, Chapter 1029, Section 38, and, if the 2013 general appropriations bill provides for such additional transfer, an amount not to exceed $2,700,000, relative to an appropriation in the 2013 general appropriations act from the special trust fund for additional transition costs which may be incurred in fiscal years 2012-2013 and 2013-2014. The commissioner of finance and administration shall determine the amount of the additional transfer in accordance with provisions stated in the 2013 general appropriations act.

(4) If the 2014 or future general appropriations acts provide for funding of additional transition costs related to the closure of Lakeshore mental health institute, then the commissioner of finance and administration is authorized to transfer from the special trust fund to the general fund such additional amounts as may be specified in the general appropriations act.

(5) The general assembly expressly declares that the transition costs addressed in subdivisions (b)(3) and (b)(4) may include, without limitation, severance benefits, terminal leave, other pay and benefits costs, build-out costs, transition to community services costs, and other costs of closure of the institute.

71-3-106 SECTION 6. Tennessee Code Annotated, Section 71-3-106, is amended by deleting the section in its entirety.

9-4-5501—9-4-5503 SECTION 7. Tennessee Code Annotated, Title 9, Chapter 4, is amended by deleting Part 55 in its entirety.

54-2-201—54-2-209 SECTION 8. Tennessee Code Annotated, Title 54, Chapter 2, is amended by deleting Part 2 in its entirety.

12-2-119—12-2-121 SECTION 9. Tennessee Code Annotated, Title 12, Chapter 2, Part 1, is amended by adding the following sections:

12-2-119. Notwithstanding any provision of law to the contrary, proceeds from the sale and conveyance of surplus real property or improvements managed as state office buildings and support facilities revolving fund property shall be deposited in the state office buildings and support facilities revolving fund, created by § 9-4-901, to be used for capital outlay.

12-2-120. Notwithstanding any provision of law to the contrary, proceeds from the sale and conveyance of surplus real property or improvements used for operation of state prisons, if not managed as state office buildings and support facilities revolving fund property, shall be deposited in the Sentencing Act of 1985 reserve, created pursuant to § 9-4-210, to be used for purposes authorized by that section.

12-2-121. Notwithstanding any provision of law to the contrary, proceeds from the sale and conveyance of surplus real property or improvements used for state armories or other operations of the department of military, if not managed as state office buildings and support facilities revolving fund property, shall be deposited in a reserve for military facilities, which hereby is created in the general fund, to be used for capital outlay for replacement facilities of the department and other capital outlay of the department.

4-3-1011 SECTION 10. Tennessee Code Annotated, Section 4-3-1011(a), is amended by deleting the subsection in its entirety and by substituting instead the following:

(a) Notwithstanding any provision of the law to the contrary, upon receiving from the commissioner of finance and administration the approved work program, as provided in § 9-4-5110, for the department of commerce and insurance, division of regulatory boards, and department of health, division of health-related boards, the commissioners of those departments shall certify by October 31 to the commissioner of finance and administration and, as applicable, to the director of the division of regulatory boards, as defined in § 4-3-1304, and to the director of the division of health-related boards, as defined in § 63-1-131, the total amount of board fee revenue required by each board for the current fiscal year, based on the approved work program. The commissioners of commerce and insurance and of health shall include the direct costs allocated to each board for the then-current fiscal year and shall reduce the certified amount by the amount of any excess fees from the immediately preceding two-year period, it being the legislative intent that fees and expenditures should be equal over a two-year period for each board, as provided in § 4-29-121. Such certification shall not preclude the retention of any board fee revenue estimated to be required for support of each board's operation for the then-current two-year period.

4-3-1011 SECTION 11. Tennessee Code Annotated, Section 4-3-1011(c)(1), is amended by deleting the word "commissioner's".

4-3-1011 SECTION 12. Tennessee Code Annotated, Section 4-3-1011(c)(1) and (2), is amended by inserting after the word "commissioner" the words "of finance and administration".

9-4-5117 SECTION 13. The language of Tennessee Code Annotated, Section 4-3-1011, as amended by this act, shall be transferred in its entirety to Title 9, Chapter 4, Part 51, and shall be redesignated as § 9-4-5117.

68-203-104 SECTION 14. Tennessee Code Annotated, Section 68-203-104(a)(1), is amended by deleting the subdivision in its entirety and by substituting instead the following:

(1) Notwithstanding any provision of the law to the contrary, upon receiving from the commissioner of finance and administration the approved work program allotments, as provided in § 9-4-5110, for the department of environment and conservation, the commissioner of environment and conservation shall certify to the commissioner of finance and administration and to the promulgating authorities the amount of fees required by each program for the current fiscal year, based on the approved work program. Upon receipt of such certification, all such fee schedules shall be reviewed by the promulgating authority.

68-203-104 SECTION 15. Tennessee Code Annotated, Section 68-203-104(a)(4), is amended by deleting the words "commissioner of finance and administration's certification" and by substituting instead the word "certification".

9-4-5106 SECTION 16. Tennessee Code Annotated, Section 9-4-5106(a)(4), is amended by deleting from the final sentence the language "at the time the budget is submitted" and by substituting instead the language "no later than fourteen (14) days after the budget document is transmitted or by the general bill cut-off date in the respective houses, whichever is later".

9-4-611 SECTION 17. Tennessee Code Annotated, Title 9, Chapter 4, Part 6, is amended by adding the following section:

9-4-611. Notwithstanding any provision of law to the contrary, no member of any state board or commission established by law or pursuant to law, which receives an appropriation, regardless of the source of funding, shall receive any compensation, whether denominated per diem or by whatever name called, except for days in which such member actually works four (4) or more hours performing duties directly relating to that board's or commission's activities or for time or days spent attending meetings of that board or commission. The provisions of this section shall not preclude payment of salaries which are set by law in annual or monthly amounts. The chair or head of each board or commission, the department head to which such board or commission is attached administratively, and the commissioner of finance and administration shall prescribe procedures to contain, as a minimum, a certification of time worked by each member claiming compensation.

67-4-1709 SECTION 18. Tennessee Code Annotated, Section 67-4-1709, is amended by designating the existing language as subsection "(a)" and by adding the following subsection:

(b) State agencies, including without limitation the university of Tennessee and the state university and community college system, are authorized to pay the privilege tax levied in this part on behalf of full-time state employees who are subject to the tax and who use the certification in their job duties, if an appropriation for such purpose is made in the general appropriations act. The payment by a state department or agency is subject to approval by the department or agency head and to the provisions of this part.

8-25-309 SECTION 19. Tennessee Code Annotated, Title 8, Chapter 25, Part 3, is amended by adding the following section:

8-25-309. The state treasurer may assess the costs associated with administering this program to the participating employees in order that such plan shall operate without administrative cost to or contribution from this state.

8-25-501 SECTION 20. Tennessee Code Annotated, Section 8-25-501, is amended by adding the following subsection:

(d) With concurrence of the state insurance committee, the state treasurer may credit plan savings and assess the costs associated with administering these programs to the state agencies of participating employees, it being the intent that state agency payroll savings deriving from the plan be the funding source for administration.

8-26-116 SECTION 21. Tennessee Code Annotated, Title 8, Chapter 26, is amended by adding the following section:

8-26-116. Notwithstanding any provision of law to the contrary, claims for official travel expenses of state employees and members of boards and commissions shall be subject to the provisions of the uniform travel rules and regulations issued by the commissioner of finance and administration pursuant to § 4-3-1008, except for employees and members of boards and commissions attached to the court system and the general assembly, who shall be subject to travel rules and regulations under law applying to them and approved by the head of those departments.

8-26-101 SECTION 22. Tennessee Code Annotated, Section 8-26-101(1), is amended by designating the existing language as subdivision "(A)" and by adding the following subdivision:

(B) From the appropriation made in the appropriations act for the operation of such courts, the justices, judges, and chancellors shall be reimbursed for necessary travel expenses incurred by them during their absence from the counties of their residence on official business; provided, however, that such travel expenses shall be limited to board and lodging and mileage or conveyance expense each way necessary to travel on official business. Any justice, judge, or chancellor seeking reimbursement for official expense under this section shall file with the director of the administrative office of the courts, or other official upon whom this duty may be lodged by law, a statement of such amounts necessarily expended in the discharge of such official duties, and upon receipt of this verified statement, warrant for reimbursement for such expenses shall be issued.

40-18-107 SECTION 23. Tennessee Code Annotated, Section 40-18-107, is amended by designating the existing language as subsection "(a)" and by adding the following subsection:

(b) Notwithstanding the provisions of subsection (a), if a judicial proceeding is transferred from one jurisdiction to another for trial on a defendant's motion for change of venue, then the limitation of one thousand dollars ($1,000) for the board and lodging of the jury shall not apply, provided that the comptroller of the treasury, on the advice of the attorney general and reporter, determines that additional funds for boarding and lodging of the jury are necessary.

9-4-5113 SECTION 24. Tennessee Code Annotated, Section 9-4-5113, is amended by designating the existing language as subsection "(a)" and by adding the following subsections:

(b) The provisions of subsection (a) shall not apply to the general assembly, state court system, district attorneys general, district public defenders, office of the post-conviction defender, secretary of state, comptroller of the treasury, and the state treasurer; provided, however, that the chief administrative officer for each of these agencies shall ensure, before entering into any contract, agreement, or obligation involving the expenditure of money, that there is a balance in the appropriation from which such obligation is required to be paid that is not otherwise encumbered to pay obligations previously incurred.

(c) All funds appropriated to the secretary of state, comptroller of the treasury, and state treasurer shall be administered in a ministerial capacity by the department of finance and administration in accordance with budgets and any revisions thereto of the respective entities for which such appropriations are made.

4-3-1006 SECTION 25. Tennessee Code Annotated, Section 4-3-1006, is amended by adding the following subdivision:

(8) Examine all requisitions for purchases as the department may deem necessary, with power and authority to refuse to approve or honor any and all requisitions for purchases, except requisitions for purchases of the general assembly, state court system, attorney general and reporter, secretary of state, comptroller of the treasury, and state treasurer.

4-3-1105 SECTION 26. Tennessee Code Annotated, Section 4-3-1105, is amended by adding the following subdivision:

(22) Impose a reasonable real estate transaction fee on all real estate transactions when the transaction is processed through the department of general services and to grant a fee waiver when deemed appropriate by the department. Said fee structure and waivers shall be subject to approval by the state building commission.

8-30-104 SECTION 27. Tennessee Code Annotated, Section 8-30-104(a), is amended by inserting the following language as subdivision "(16)" and by renumbering subsequent subdivisions accordingly:

(16) In consultation with the commissioner of finance and administration, to designate a position or positions of appropriate classification within each executive branch agency of state government as chief fiscal officer or officers for that agency. Qualifications and appointments to fill any such position that, from time to time, may be vacant shall be in accordance with procedures established by the commissioner of human resources, with the approval of the commissioner of finance and administration. For the purposes of this subdivision, the term "chief fiscal officer" shall mean the position within a state agency that has overall daily responsibility for oversight of the agency fiscal operation;

8-23-202 SECTION 28. Tennessee Code Annotated, Section 8-23-202, is amended by adding the following subsection:

(c) The commissioner of finance and administration is authorized to require that salaries of state employees be paid through direct-deposit procedures in accordance with policies established by the commissioner.

4-3-1006 SECTION 29. Tennessee Code Annotated, Section 4-3-1006, is amended by adding the following subdivision:

(9) Review and approve or refuse to approve any personal services, professional services, or consultant services contract concerning management services of all types, management studies, planning services, public relations, evaluations, systems designs, data processing, auditing, or accounting services entered into by an executive branch department or agency of state government.

9-4-601 SECTION 30. Tennessee Code Annotated, Section 9-4-601(a), is amended by designating the existing language as subdivision "(1)" and by adding the following subdivision:

(2) Notwithstanding the provisions of title 66, chapter 29, warrants, drafts, and checks drawn on the state treasury that have not been redeemed within twelve (12) months of issue date shall be cancelled and written off the state's books, with the funds reverting to the fund of issue. Subsequent claims by the payee of said instruments shall be honored upon receipt

of documentation to substantiate the claim. The commissioner of finance and administration and the state treasurer shall ensure the state's compliance with the unclaimed property law.

9-1-103 SECTION 31. Tennessee Code Annotated, Title 9, Chapter 1, is amended by adding the following section:

9-1-120.

(a) Except to the extent that sovereign immunity is expressly waived by the general assembly, all appropriations of state revenues and departmental revenues previously and hereafter made to the state, its departments, agencies, boards, educational institutions, instrumentalities, and incorporated entities performing the state's governmental functions shall be state funds and shall be protected by the state's sovereign immunity from every court's judgment, decree, attachment, or other legal process.

(b) Except to the extent that sovereign immunity is expressly waived by the general assembly, all appropriations of state funds and institutional and program revenues previously and hereafter made to institutions and programs of higher education shall be state funds and shall be protected by the state's sovereign immunity from any court's judgment, decree, attachment, or other legal process.

4-4-101 SECTION 32. Tennessee Code Annotated, Section 4-4-101, is amended by designating the existing language as subsection "(a)" and by adding the following subsection:

(b) Notwithstanding the provisions of subsection (a), no state department or agency in the executive branch of state government shall make organizational changes within such department or agency without the prior approval of the commissioner of finance and administration. If such organizational changes require a transfer of funds between organizational accounts and are contrary to the manner in which appropriations have been made in the appropriations act, then such transfer of funds is subject to approval by the commissioner of finance and administration and by a majority of a committee comprised of the speaker of the senate, the speaker of the house of representatives, and the comptroller of the treasury; provided, however, if the transfer of funds is merely a change in the organizational account to which the appropriation is allocated and does not constitute a change in the purpose of the appropriation, then the approval of the committee shall not be required, provided further, however, the approval of the commissioner of finance and administration shall be required.

9-4-5110 SECTION 33. Tennessee Code Annotated, Section 9-4-5110, is amended by designating the existing language as subsection "(a)" and by adding the following subsection:

(b) Notwithstanding the provisions of subsection (a), the speakers of the senate and the house of representatives or, by joint delegation, their director of legislative administration; the chief justice or, by delegation, the administrative director of the courts; the attorney general and reporter; the secretary of state; the comptroller of the treasury; and state treasurer are authorized to revise their respective budgets and personnel authorizations within the appropriations made in the appropriations act and to submit those revised summaries to the commissioner of finance and administration, who shall approve the work program of those agencies, if within the amounts appropriated.

9-4-5112 SECTION 34. Tennessee Code Annotated, Section 9-4-5112, is amended by designating the existing language as subsection "(a)" and by adding the following subsection:

(b) Revisions to the work programs of the secretary of state, comptroller of the treasury, and state treasurer shall be approved by the commissioner of finance and administration if submitted in accordance with the provisions of the appropriations act, if within the amounts appropriated, and if submitted with the concurrence of the speaker of the senate and the speaker of the house of representatives.

12-2-102 SECTION 35. Tennessee Code Annotated, Section 12-2-102, is amended by deleting the language "finance and administration" and by substituting instead the language "general services"; and is further amended by deleting the language "one (1) with the state planning office,".

12-2-103, 12-2-104, 12-2-105, 12-2-106, 12-2-108, 12-2-109, 12-2-111, 12-2-112, 12-2-114, 12-2-116 SECTION 36. Tennessee Code Annotated, Sections 12-2-103, 12-2-104, 12-2-105, 12-2-106, 12-2-108, 12-2-109, 12-2-111, 12-2-112, 12-2-114, and 12-2-116, are amended by deleting the language "finance and administration" and by substituting instead the language "general services".

12-2-112 SECTION 37. Tennessee Code Annotated, Section 12-2-112(a)(7), is amended by deleting the first sentence and by substituting instead the following:

PUBLIC CHAPTER NO. 454 (cont'd)

The funds so collected from the sale and conveyance of such property not otherwise specified shall be paid into the general fund of the state; provided that all expenses incurred during such sale shall be paid from the proceeds and the balance of such proceeds shall be deposited into the general fund, except where otherwise provided by law. In instances in which other law specifies that the proceeds be deposited into a fund other than the general fund or into a special account in the general fund, the expenses of such sale or conveyance shall be paid from such other fund or special account.

9-4-904 SECTION 38. Tennessee Code Annotated, Section 9-4-904, is amended by deleting the words "finance and administration" and by substituting instead the words "general services".

9-4-907 SECTION 39. Tennessee Code Annotated, Section 9-4-907, is amended by deleting the words "finance and administration" and by substituting instead the words "general services"; and is further amended by adding the following language to the end of the first sentence:

provided, however, that until such time as a policy shall be issued by the commissioner of general services and approved by the state building commission, the policy formerly issued by the commissioner of finance and administration and approved by the state building commission shall remain effective.

9-4-5106, 9-4-5115 SECTION 40. Tennessee Code Annotated, Title 9, Chapter 4, Part 51, is amended by deleting § 9-4-5115 in its entirety; by designating the existing language of § 9-4-5106(a)(1) as subdivision "(A)", and by adding the following subdivision to § 9-4-5106(a)(1):

(B) Part 1 also shall include a schedule on tax exemptions, identifying, to the extent practicable, all exemptions from state taxes and estimating the amount of revenue which would be collected by the state in the ensuing fiscal year if the exemptions were not to exist. The schedule shall include an estimate for each such exemption. The estimates of such exemptions shall be based upon the revenue estimates included in the budget document.

4-3-1003 SECTION 41. Tennessee Code Annotated, Section 4-3-1003(c), is amended by deleting the subsection in its entirety.

4-3-5301—4-3-5305 SECTION 42. Tennessee Code Annotated, Title 4, Chapter 3, is amended by deleting Part 53 in its entirety.

SECTION 43. If any provision of this act or the application thereof to any person or circumstance is held invalid, such invalidity shall not affect other provisions or applications of this act which can be given effect without the invalid provision or application, and to that end the provisions of this act are declared to be severable.

Effective date 5/16/2013 SECTION 44. Sections 1 through 4 of this act shall take effect on July 1, 2013, and all other sections shall take effect upon becoming a law, the public welfare requiring it.

PUBLIC CHAPTER NO. 455

PUBLIC CHAPTER NO. 455

SENATE BILL NO. 1392

By Kelsey

Substituted for: House Bill No. 1049

By Coley

AN ACT to amend Tennessee Code Annotated, Title 71, Chapter 4, Part 21, relative to the council for the deaf and hard of hearing.

BE IT ENACTED BY THE GENERAL ASSEMBLY OF THE STATE OF TENNESSEE:

4-29-236
71-4-2101 —
71-4-2109

SECTION 1. Tennessee Code Annotated, Title 71, Chapter 4, Part 21, is amended by deleting the part in its entirety and substituting instead the following:

71-4-2101.

(1) A "deaf person" is defined as one whose hearing is totally impaired or one whose hearing, with or without amplification, is so seriously impaired that the primary means of receiving spoken language is through visual input such as, but not limited to, speechreading, sign language, finger spelling, or writing.

(2) A "Deaf-Blind person" means the same as an "individual who is deaf-blind" and both mean any individual:

(A)(i) Who has a central visual acuity of 20/200 or less in the better eye with corrective lenses, or a field defect such that the peripheral diameter of visual field subtends an angular distance no greater than 20 degrees, or a progressive visual loss having a prognosis leading to one or both these conditions;

(ii) Who has a chronic hearing impairment so severe that most speech cannot be understood with optimum amplification, or a progressive hearing loss having a prognosis leading to this condition; and

(iii) For whom the combination of impairments described in clauses (i) and (ii) cause extreme difficulty in attaining independence in daily life activities, achieving psychosocial adjustment, or obtaining a vocation;

(B) Who despite the inability to be measured accurately for hearing and vision loss due to cognitive or behavioral constraints, or both, can be determined through functional and performance assessment to have severe hearing and visual disabilities that cause extreme difficulty in attaining independence in daily life activities, achieving psychosocial adjustment, or obtaining vocational objectives; or

(C) Meets such other requirements as the Secretary may prescribe by regulation; and

(3) "Secretary" means the United States Secretary of Education.

71-4-2102.

(a) Effective July 1, 2013, there is hereby created the Tennessee Council for the Deaf, Deaf-Blind, and Hard of Hearing, which has the duty to:

(1) Advocate services affecting people who are deaf, deaf-blind, and hard of hearing in the areas of public services, health care, education, vocational training, employment opportunity, emergency services, resource sharing and communication;

(2) Act as a bureau of information for people who are deaf, deaf-blind, and hard of hearing to state agencies and public institutions providing health care, employment, vocational, educational services, resource sharing, and

emergency services to the Deaf, Deaf-Blind, and Hard of Hearing, and to local agencies and programs;

(3) Collect facts and statistics and other special studies of conditions affecting the health and welfare of people who are Deaf, Deaf-Blind, and Hard of Hearing in this state;

(4) Provide for a mutual exchange of ideas and information on the national, state, and local levels;

(5) Encourage and assist local governments and agencies in the development of programs for people who are deaf, deaf-blind, and hard of hearing;

(6) Cooperate with public and private agencies and units of local, state, and federal governments in promoting coordination in programs for the deaf, deaf-blind, and hard of hearing;

(7) Authorize the executive director to prepare an annual report and needs assessment to the council that reviews the status of state services for the deaf, deaf-blind, and hard of hearing. The council shall submit the approved report and needs assessment to the Governor, Lt. Governor, and Speaker of the House of Representatives and make this report available to organizations serving the deaf, deaf-blind, and hard of hearing; and

(8) Make recommendations for needed improvements and to serve as an advisory body in regard to new legislation affecting the deaf, deaf-blind, and hard of hearing.

71-4-2103.

(a) The council for the deaf, deaf-blind, and hard of hearing shall consist of eighteen (18) members and shall be composed as follows: the commissioners of education, human services, health, mental health and substance abuse, and safety or their designees, the assistant commissioner of rehabilitation services or the assistant commissioner's designee, a representative of the Tennessee Regulatory Authority, a representative of the Tennessee Emergency Management Agency, the President of the Tennessee Association of the Deaf, two (2) deaf consumer representatives appointed by the governor, one (1) President of a Hearing Loss Association of America Chapter, two (2) hard of hearing consumer representatives appointed by the governor, the President of the Tennessee Registry of Interpreters for the Deaf, the President of the Tennessee Hands & Voices, one (1) deaf-blind representative who may be appointed by the governor from lists of qualified persons submitted by interested deaf-blind groups including, but not limited to, the Tennessee Organization of the Deaf-Blind and the TN Deaf-Blind Association, and one (1) minority representative who may be appointed by the governor from lists of qualified persons submitted by interested minority deaf advocate groups including, but not limited to chapters of the Tennessee Black Deaf Advocates. In appointing the deaf-blind representative and the minority representative to the council as provided in this subsection, the governor shall consult with interested deaf-blind and minority deaf advocate groups to determine qualified persons to fill the positions.

(b) The deaf, deaf-blind and hard of hearing representatives shall serve terms of three (3) years, except that to ensure staggered terms, the Governor shall designate that two (2) of the six (6) members initially appointed to serve a one (1) year term, two (2) to serve two (2) year terms, and two (2) to serve three (3) year terms. Any position that becomes vacant prior to the expiration of a full term shall be filled only for the period of the unexpired term. In making appointments to the council for the deaf, deaf-blind, and hard of hearing, the Governor shall strive to ensure that at least one (1) person appointed to serve on the council is sixty (60) years of age or older.

(c) The commissioner of education shall call the first meeting of the council, at which time, and annually thereafter, the members shall elect a chair. Thereafter, the council shall meet at the call of the chair, but at least quarterly.

(d) Members of the council shall receive no compensation for their services other than reimbursement for traveling and other expenses incurred in the performance of their official duties. All reimbursement for travel expenses shall be in accordance with the comprehensive travel regulations as promulgated by the department of finance and administration and approved by the attorney general and reporter.

71-4-2104.

(a) The council for the deaf, deaf-blind, and hard of hearing shall recommend to the Governor an executive director and shall fix the executive director's duties and responsibilities. The executive director shall serve as executive officer and secretary to the council and shall be a full-time employee of the council. Compensation for the executive director shall be established by the council with the approval of the commissioner of human resources. All reimbursement for travel expenses shall be in accordance with the comprehensive travel regulations as promulgated by the department of finance and administration and approved by the attorney general and reporter.

(b) The executive director, with the advice and consent of the council, may, to the extent of available funds, plan and oversee the establishment of service centers for the deaf, deaf-blind, and hard of hearing, as well as, or in addition to, support and coordinate the activities of the existing centers in cooperation with the local board of directors.

(c) The executive director, with the advice and consent of the council, shall:

(1) Promote accessibility of all governmental services to deaf, deaf-blind, and hard of hearing citizens in Tennessee;

(2) Identify agencies, both public and private that provide community services, evaluate the extent to which they make services available to Deaf, Deaf-Blind, and Hard of Hearing people, and cooperate with the agencies in coordinating and extending these services;

(3) Encourage the mutual exchange of ideas and information on services for deaf, deaf-blind, and hard of hearing people between federal, state and local governmental agencies, and private organizations and individuals;

(4) Survey the needs of people who are deaf, deaf-blind, and hard of hearing in Tennessee, and assist the council in the preparation of its report to the Governor, Lt. Governor, and Speaker of the House of Representatives;

(5) Develop a strategy to create minimum standards for all sign language interpreters in Tennessee and make recommendations on how to implement these strategies to appropriate state departments, the Governor, Lt. Governor, Speaker of the House of Representatives and General Assembly;

(6) Promote the training of interpreters for the deaf, deaf-blind, and hard of hearing; and

(7) Perform such other duties as may be required by law.

(d) In selecting an executive director, the council shall select an individual who is fluent in the American sign language of the deaf and otherwise qualified.

(e) The executive director is authorized to arrange for such clerical or other assistance as may be required and as approved by the council.

71-4-2105.

The council for the deaf, deaf-blind, and hard of hearing may request and shall receive from any department, division, board, bureau, commission, or agency of the state or of any political subdivision of the state such data as might be needed to enable it to properly carry out its activities under this part.

71-4-2106.

The council shall ensure that long range planning is conducted, which shall include a description of the locations and geographic service areas for community service centers, as well as a determination of personnel needs and strategies for coordinating service providers at state and local levels.

71-4-2107.

The purposes of community service centers for the deaf, deaf-blind, and hard of hearing shall be to:

(1) Inform deaf, deaf-blind, and hard of hearing persons and their families of their rights to services offered locally and to coordinate their referral to the appropriate organization;

(2) Coordinate communication between deaf, deaf-blind, and hard of hearing persons and the desired agency or organization, and promote the accessibility of community services to deaf, deaf-blind, and hard of hearing persons;

(3) Coordinate the provision of instruction in sign language to persons in community agencies;

(4) Inform interested staff of community and professional organizations about the nature of deafness, deaf-blindness and hearing loss and the capabilities of people experiencing it;

(5) Provide services as outlined by this part to employers of deaf, deaf-blind, and hard of hearing persons and related members of the family that may be involved;

(6) Provide the specified services to the deaf, deaf-blind, and hard of hearing persons qualified under this part without cost;

(7) Serve as an advocate for the rights and needs of people who are deaf, deaf-blind, and hard of hearing; and

(8) Help deaf, deaf-blind, and hard of hearing citizens to become self-sufficient in meeting their needs in the community.

71-4-2108.

The council for the deaf, deaf-blind, and hard of hearing is authorized to pursue and receive monies from any source, including appropriate federal funds, gifts, grants, and bequests, which shall be expended for the purposes designated in this part.

71-4-2109.

The Governor is authorized to designate existing departments of state government, or divisions of state government, to provide statewide services to the deaf, deaf-blind, and hard of hearing as specified in this part.

Effective date 7/1/2013

SECTION 2. For purposes of making appointments to the council for the deaf, deaf-blind, and hard of hearing, this act shall take effect upon becoming a law, the public welfare requiring it. For all other purposes, this act shall take effect on July 1, 2013, the public welfare requiring it.

PUBLIC CHAPTER NO. 456

PUBLIC CHAPTER NO. 456

SENATE BILL NO. 1380

By Bowling

Substituted for: House Bill No. 1259

By Butt, Fitzhugh, Cooper

AN ACT to amend Tennessee Code Annotated, Title 13, relative to property owners and the land use planning process.

BE IT ENACTED BY THE GENERAL ASSEMBLY OF THE STATE OF TENNESSEE:

13-14-111 SECTION 1. Tennessee Code Annotated, Section 13-14-111(a), is amended by deleting the language "according to the following schedule:" from the last sentence and by substituting instead the language "according to subdivision (c)(3)."

13-14-111 SECTION 2. Tennessee Code Annotated, Section 13-14-111(b), is amended by deleting the language "twenty cents (20¢)" and by substituting instead the language "twenty-one cents (21¢)".

13-14-111 SECTION 3. Tennessee Code Annotated, Section 13-14-111(c)(3), is amended by deleting all of the language before the punctuation ":" and by substituting instead the following:

> The amount of state funding to each development district shall be based upon the per capita assessment established by the individual development district boards. The per capita assessment and corresponding state funding levels for the nine (9) development districts are as follows

13-3-101 SECTION 4. Tennessee Code Annotated, Section 13-3-101(j)(1), is amended by adding the following sentence at the end of the subdivision:

> At least one (1) hour of the annual education requirement shall concentrate on the rights of private property owners and the relationship of those rights to the public planning process.

Effective date 5/20/2013 SECTION 5. This act shall take effect upon becoming a law, the public welfare requiring it.

PUBLIC CHAPTER NO. 457

PUBLIC CHAPTER NO. 457

SENATE BILL NO. 1349

By Yager, Bowling, Niceley, Finney, Ketron

Substituted for: House Bill No. 877

By McDaniel, Harrison, Sargent, Matlock, Hawk, Ramsey, Weaver, Fitzhugh, Keisling, Kent Williams

AN ACT to amend Tennessee Code Annotated, Title 67 and Title 68, relative to tires.

BE IT ENACTED BY THE GENERAL ASSEMBLY OF THE STATE OF TENNESSEE:

67-4-1610 SECTION 1. Tennessee Code Annotated, Section 67-4-1610, is amended by designating the existing language as subsection (a) and by adding the following new subsection (b):

(b) Notwithstanding Chapter 994 of the Public Acts of 2000, or any other provision of law to the contrary, the remaining amount of the fee levied by § 67-4-1603 that is not retained by the dealer pursuant to subsection (a) shall be allocated as follows:

(1) If a county does not have a tire grant contract with the department of environment and conservation pursuant to the tire grant program administered under § 68-211-867, one dollar ($1.00) per tire sold in that county shall be sent directly by the commissioner of revenue to such county to be used for beneficial end use of waste tires in accordance with § 68-211-867 and not used for any other purposes. The remaining balance of the fee shall be allocated to the solid waste management fund established by § 68-211-821. The county shall include in its annual progress report to the department of environment and conservation pursuant to § 68-211-814(a) data on how many waste tires it manages and what is done with them; or

(2) If a county has a tire grant contract with the department of environment and conservation pursuant to the tire grant program administered under § 68-211-867, or had such a tire grant contract that was in effect at the time the fee was imposed, the remainder of the fee per tire sold in that county shall be allocated to the solid waste management fund established by § 68-211-821. The department of environment and conservation shall return a minimum of one dollar ($1.00) per tire sold in such counties to the county under its grant contract. If the grant contract either does not allow the department of environment and conservation to return a minimum of one dollar ($1.00) per tire sold in a county to such county, or would require repayment of any such funds, the department of environment and conservation shall return a minimum of one dollar ($1.00) per tire sold in such county to the county through additional grants, unrelated to the tire grant contract, for beneficial end use of waste tires in accordance with § 68-211-867 and not used for any other purposes. Such counties are not required to submit any additional workplan, budget, or other similar document. Any such additional grants shall be based on one dollar ($1.00) per tire sold in the county minus any amounts returned under the tire grant contract. The county shall include in its annual progress report to the department of environment and conservation pursuant to § 68-211-814(a) data on how many waste tires it manages and what is done with them.

67-4-1610 SECTION 2. It is the purpose of this act to require that a minimum of one dollar ($1.00) of the one dollar and thirty-five cents ($1.35) per tire pre-disposal fee be returned to the county in which the fee was imposed regardless of whether the county has a tire grant contract with the department of environment and conservation.

Effective date 7/1/2014 SECTION 3. This act shall take effect on July 1, 2014, the public welfare requiring it, and shall apply to any pre-disposal fee received by the commissioner of revenue or the department of environment and conservation after such effective date regardless of when the fee was imposed.

PUBLIC CHAPTER NO. 459

SENATE BILL NO. 1345

By Yager

Substituted for: House Bill No. 413

By Armstrong

AN ACT to amend Tennessee Code Annotated, Title 57, relative to intoxicating liquors.

BE IT ENACTED BY THE GENERAL ASSEMBLY OF THE STATE OF TENNESSEE:

57-4-102 SECTION 1. Tennessee Code Annotated, Section 57-4-102(20)(A), is amended by deleting the language "fifty (50) or more rooms" in the first sentence and substituting instead the language "twenty (20) or more rooms".

57-4-102 SECTION 2. Tennessee Code Annotated, Section 57-4-102(26), is amended by adding the following as a new subdivision thereto:

(__) A commercially operated facility open to the public for persons ages twenty-one (21) years of age or older that has all of the following characteristics:

(i) Is located within three (3) miles of Dale Hollow Lake;

(ii) Has a kitchen that serves food to customers;

(iii) Is licensed to sell beer;

(iv) Is located in an A frame building built in 1968;

(v) Has a deck of more than one thousand square feet (1,000 sq. ft); and

(vi) Is located in any county having a population of not less than seven thousand eight hundred fifty-one (7,851) nor more than seven thousand eight hundred sixty-five (7,865) according to the 2010 federal census or any subsequent federal census.

Effective date 5/20/2013 SECTION 3. This act shall take effect upon becoming a law, the public welfare requiring it.

PUBLIC CHAPTER NO. 459

PUBLIC CHAPTER NO. 459

SENATE BILL NO. 1140

By Overbey, Massey

Substituted for: House Bill No. 1287

By Dennis, Rich, Stewart, Armstrong, Mark White, Moody

AN ACT to amend Tennessee Code Annotated, Title 39, relative to criminal offenses.

BE IT ENACTED BY THE GENERAL ASSEMBLY OF THE STATE OF TENNESSEE:

39-17-907 SECTION 1. Tennessee Code Annotated, Section 39-17-907, is amended by deleting subsection (b) in its entirety and substituting instead the following:

> (b) No minor under the age of eighteen (18) years old may be admitted to a movie theatre if the movie has been found to be "harmful to minors" pursuant to § 39-17-901. It is a deceptive practice under title 47, chapter 18, part 1, to advertise or promote a motion picture as having a rating other than the rating that has been assigned to it.

Effective date 5/20/2013 SECTION 2. This act shall take effect upon becoming a law, the public welfare requiring it.

PUBLIC CHAPTER NO. 460

PUBLIC CHAPTER NO. 460

SENATE BILL NO. 1080

By Johnson, Ketron, Watson, Gardenhire, Kelsey, Haile, Beavers, Bowling, Campfield

Substituted for: House Bill No. 1098

By Durham, Sargent, Casada, Rich, Lynn, Sparks, Joe Carr, Lamberth, Littleton, Rogers, Dawn White, Womick, Dean

AN ACT to amend Tennessee Code Annotated, Title 55, Chapter 4, Part 1 and Title 68, relative to motor vehicle inspection requirements.

BE IT ENACTED BY THE GENERAL ASSEMBLY OF THE STATE OF TENNESSEE:

SECTION 1. (a) The commissioner of the department of environment and conservation shall develop a proposal for a revised state implementation plan that eliminates motor vehicle inspection testing requirements mandated pursuant to title 55, and title 68, chapter 201 for all motor vehicles in this state that are three (3) or less model-years old.

(b) No later than January 1, 2014, the commissioner shall report to the speakers of the senate and house of representatives, the senate transportation and safety committee, the house of representatives agriculture and natural resources committee, and the senate commerce and labor committee the details of the proposed revised state implementation plan, including but not limited to:

(1) A description of the specific controls or alternatives for specific controls that would be placed on other activities, businesses, industries, vehicles or individuals in any county in this state in order to replace the removal of tons of emissions or pollutants that may be added by eliminating motor vehicle emissions testing requirements mandated pursuant to title 55 and title 68, chapter 201 for all motor vehicles in this state that are three (3) or less model-years old; and

(2) An identification of Tennessee statutes that would need to be amended to implement the proposal developed pursuant to subsection (a).

Effective date 5/20/2013

SECTION 2. This act shall take effect upon becoming a law, the public welfare requiring it.

PUBLIC CHAPTER NO. 461

PUBLIC CHAPTER NO. 461

SENATE BILL NO. 1064

By Burks

Substituted for: House Bill No. 1041

By Watson, Sexton, Shipley, Rich, Lamberth, Weaver, Hardaway, Parkinson, Faison, Lundberg, Curtis Johnson, Mark White, Shepard, Kevin Brooks, McCormick, Calfee, Roach, Carter, Hawk, Fitzhugh, Armstrong, Evans, Womick, Ryan Williams, Eldridge, Rogers

AN ACT to amend Tennessee Code Annotated, Titles 39 and 40, relative to criminal offenses and criminal procedure.

BE IT ENACTED BY THE GENERAL ASSEMBLY OF THE STATE OF TENNESSEE:

SECTION 1. Subdivisions (a)(1)(A)(ii) and (a)(1)(B)(ii) of Section 2 shall be known and may be cited as "Boomer's Law".

39-13-102 SECTION 2. Tennessee Code Annotated, Section 39-13-102, is amended by deleting subdivision (a)(1) and substituting instead the following:

(a)(1) A person commits aggravated assault who:

(A) Intentionally or knowingly commits an assault as defined in § 39-13-101, and the assault:

(i) Results in serious bodily injury to another;

(ii) Results in the death of another;

(iii) Involved the use or display of a deadly weapon; or

(iv) Was intended to cause bodily injury to another by strangulation or bodily injury by strangulation was attempted; or

(B) Recklessly commits an assault as defined in § 39-13-101(a)(1), and the assault:

(i) Results in serious bodily injury to another;

(ii) Results in the death of another; or

(iii) Involved the use or display of a deadly weapon.

39-13-102 SECTION 3. Tennessee Code Annotated, Section 39-13-102, is amended by deleting subdivision (e)(1) and substituting instead the following:

(e)(1)(A) Aggravated assault under:

(i) Subsection (d) is a Class A misdemeanor;

(ii) Subdivision (a)(1)(A)(i), (iii), or (iv) is a Class C felony;

(iii) Subdivision (a)(1)(A)(ii) is a Class C felony;

(iv) Subdivision (b) or (c) is a Class C felony;

(v) Subdivision (a)(1)(B)(i) or (iii) is a Class D felony;

(vi) Subdivision (a)(1)(B)(ii) is a Class D felony.

(B) However, the maximum fine shall be fifteen thousand dollars ($15,000) for an offense under subdivision (a)(1)(A), subdivision (a)(1)(B), subsection (c), or subsection (d) committed against any of the following persons who are discharging or attempting to discharge their official duties:

(A) Law enforcement officer:

(B) Firefighter;

(C) Medical fire responder;

(D) Paramedic;

(E) Emergency medical technician;

(F) Health care provider; or

(G) Any other first responder.

40-35-501 SECTION 4. Tennessee Code Annotated, Section 40-35-501, is amended by creating the following new subdivision to subsection (k) to be appropriately designated:

(k)( ) There shall be no release eligibility for a person committing aggravated assault as defined in § 39-13-102, that results in death of another, on or after July 1, 2013, until the person has served seventy-five percent (75%) of the sentence imposed by the court less sentence credits earned and retained. However, no sentence reduction credits authorized by § 41-21-236, or any other provision of law, shall operate to reduce below sixty percent (60%) the percentage of sentence imposed by the court such person must serve before becoming release eligible.

Effective date 7/1/2013 SECTION 5. This act shall take effect July 1, 2013, the public welfare requiring it and shall apply to all offenses committed on or after such date.

PUBLIC CHAPTER NO. 462

PUBLIC CHAPTER NO. 462

SENATE BILL NO. 1054

By Kelsey

Substituted for: House Bill No. 1263

By Dale Carr

AN ACT to amend Tennessee Code Annotated, Title 6, Chapter 51, Part 1; Title 6, Chapter 58 and Title 67, Chapter 5, Part 5, relative to municipal annexation.

BE IT ENACTED BY THE GENERAL ASSEMBLY OF THE STATE OF TENNESSEE:

6-51-108 SECTION 1. Tennessee Code Annotated, Section 6-51-108, is amended by adding the following as a new subsection (b) and redesignating the present subsection (b) and remaining subsections accordingly:

(b)(1) This subsection shall apply to any municipality whose annexation ordinance becomes effective by court order pursuant to § 6-51-103(d).

(2) Within ten (10) days after the date on which a court order is entered sustaining the validity of a proposed annexation, any annexing municipality to which this subsection applies shall submit written notification, meeting the requirements of subdivision (b)(3), to each person owning real property in the territory that the territory will become a part of the municipality. In the event an appeal is taken from the court order, the annexing municipality shall notify the property owners in writing of the pending appeal. If on appeal the court affirms the validity of the proposed annexation, the municipality shall submit written notification, meeting the requirements of subdivision (b)(3), to the property owners within ten (10) days of entry of judgment of the appellate court.

(3) The advance written notification shall include the date on which the annexed territory becomes a part of the municipality, a detailed description of the annexed territory, and the reasons for the annexation. The notification shall be sent by first class mail to the last known address listed in the office of the property assessor for each property owner of record within the annexed territory.

(4) A person with personal knowledge of the mailing of the notification shall submit a notarized affidavit to the presiding officer of the annexing municipality attesting that the notifications were mailed in accordance with subdivision (b)(3).

67-5-504 SECTION 2. Tennessee Code Annotated, Section 67-5-504, is amended by adding the following as a new subsection (c):

(c) Any annexing municipality that makes assessments of taxes shall only assess the tax on real property within the annexed territory if the annexation takes effect prior to January 1 of the year in which the assessment is made.

6-51-103 SECTION 3. Tennessee Code Annotated, Section 6-51-103(d), is amended by designating the present language as subdivision (1), and by deleting the word "therefrom" at the end of the subsection and substituting instead the following:

from the judgment, or unless the presiding court grants the municipality's petition to defer the effective date pursuant to subdivision (d)(2).

6-51-103 SECTION 4. Tennessee Code Annotated, Section 6-51-103(d), is further amended by adding the following language as a new subdivision (2):

(2) Upon petition of the municipality, the presiding court may, as part of the judgment sustaining the validity of the annexation ordinance, order that the effective date of the ordinance be fixed as December 31 following the date of entry of the judgment or determination of appeal. In making any order under this subdivision (d)(2), the court shall consider the necessity of the deferred effective date to render municipal services to the annexed territory within a reasonable time. The petition shall be filed by the municipality in the presiding court where the annexation ordinance is being contested in a quo warranto proceeding as provided in this section.

Effective date 5/20/2013

SECTION 5. This act shall take effect upon becoming a law, the public welfare requiring it, and Section 2 of this act shall apply to assessments made on or after January 1, 2012.

PUBLIC CHAPTER NO. 463

PUBLIC CHAPTER NO. 463

SENATE BILL NO. 1040

By Kelsey

Substituted for: House Bill No. 256

By Hardaway, John Deberry, Stewart, Towns, Parkinson

AN ACT to amend Tennessee Code Annotated, Title 29, Chapter 3, relative to abatement of nuisances.

BE IT ENACTED BY THE GENERAL ASSEMBLY OF THE STATE OF TENNESSEE:

29-3-110 SECTION 1. Tennessee Code Annotated, Section 29-3-110, is amended by adding the following language as a new, appropriately designated subsection:

(c) In the order of abatement, the court may also assess costs of public services required to abate or manage the nuisance, including, but not limited to, law enforcement costs, if any, caused by the public nuisance. The governmental entity shall submit evidence of such costs to the court.

Effective date 5/20/2013 SECTION 2. This act shall take effect upon becoming a law, the public welfare requiring it.

PUBLIC CHAPTER NO. 464

PUBLIC CHAPTER NO. 464

SENATE BILL NO. 1036

By Kelsey, Crowe, Harper, Yager, Overbey

Substituted for: House Bill No. 919

By Moody, Rogers, Littleton, Weaver, Camper, Parkinson, Coley, Gilmore, Hardaway, Dawn White, Eldridge, Womick

AN ACT to amend Tennessee Code Annotated, Title 4, Chapter 3; Title 38 and Title 71, Chapter 1, relative to human trafficking task force.

BE IT ENACTED BY THE GENERAL ASSEMBLY OF THE STATE OF TENNESSEE:

4-3-3001 — 4-3-3005

SECTION 1. Tennessee Code Annotated, Title 4, Chapter 3, is amended by adding the following as a new part:

4-3-3001.

The governor shall establish a human trafficking task force to develop and implement a state plan for the prevention of human trafficking.

4-3-3002.

The human trafficking task force shall meet at least biannually and is authorized to address all aspects of human trafficking, including, but not limited to, sex trafficking and labor trafficking of both United States citizens and foreign nationals.

4-3-3003.

(a) The human trafficking task force shall be comprised of the following members:

(1) A human trafficking task force chairperson, to be appointed by the governor;

(2) One (1) representative from each of the following:

(A) Tennessee bureau of investigation;

(B) Office of the attorney general and reporter;

(C) Department of labor and workforce development;

(D) Tennessee Association of Chiefs of Police;

(E) Tennessee Sheriffs' Association;

(F) Department of safety;

(G) District attorneys general conference;

(H) District public defenders conference;

(I) Department of health;

(J) Department of children's services; and

(K) Department of human services;

(3) At least one (1) representative from each of the following entities, associations, or categories, to be appointed by the governor:

(A) Non-governmental organization specializing in human trafficking;

(B) Member of a community or group disproportionately affected by human trafficking;

(C) Agency or group specializing in child services and runaway services;

(D) Academic researcher specializing in human trafficking; and

(E) Survivor or victim of human trafficking; and

(4) One (1) member of the house of representatives to be appointed by the speaker of the house of representatives and one (1) member of the senate to be appointed by the speaker of the senate.

(b) The governor may invite representatives of the following to be members of the human trafficking task force:

(1) United States attorney's offices; and

(2) Federal law enforcement agencies, including, but not limited to, the federal bureau of investigation and United States immigration and customs enforcement.

(c) The task force shall serve without compensation, and members of the task force shall not be reimbursed for necessary expenses in attending such meetings, unless otherwise required by law.

4-3-3004.

The human trafficking task force, directly or through one or more of its constituent agencies, shall:

(1) Develop the state plan for the prevention of human trafficking;

(2) Coordinate the collection and sharing of human trafficking data regarding victims, while ensuring their privacy, among government agencies;

(3) Coordinate the sharing of information regarding detection of criminal groups involved in human trafficking among government agencies;

(4) Consider establishing policies regarding time limits for the issuance of law enforcement agency endorsements described in 8 CFR 214.11(f)(1);

(5) Establish policies to improve cooperation between state government agencies and non-governmental organizations and other advocacy groups to prevent human trafficking and provide assistance to victims;

(6) Review the effectiveness of existing services and facilities regarding victims of human trafficking;

(7) Make recommendations regarding a system to coordinate services for victims of human trafficking, including, but not limited to, the following services:

(A) Health services, including mental health;

(B) Housing;

(C) Education and job training;

(D) English as a second language classes;

(E) Language interpretation services;

(F) Legal services; and

(G) Victim compensation; and

PUBLIC CHAPTER NO. 464 (cont'd)

(8) Evaluate approaches used by other state and local governments to increase public awareness for human trafficking and its victims.

4-3-3005.

The human trafficking task force shall submit an annual report to the governor or the governor's designee by December 31 of each year. Such report shall include detailed information on the findings and recommendations of the human trafficking task force.

Effective date 7/1/2013

SECTION 2. For the purpose of making appointments to the human trafficking task force, this act shall take effect upon becoming a law, the public welfare requiring it. For all other purposes, this act shall take effect July 1, 2013, the public welfare requiring it.

PUBLIC CHAPTER NO. 465

PUBLIC CHAPTER NO. 465

SENATE BILL NO. 1033

By Kelsey, Ford, Crowe, Overbey, Yager

Substituted for: House Bill No. 130

By Coley, Hardaway, Rogers, Littleton, Moody, Weaver, Camper, Parkinson, Jones, Todd, Eldridge, Butt, Haynes, Mark White, Joe Carr, Kane, Evans, Womick, McManus, Towns, Keisling, Sparks

AN ACT to amend Tennessee Code Annotated, Title 39 and Title 40, relative to sex crimes.

BE IT ENACTED BY THE GENERAL ASSEMBLY OF THE STATE OF TENNESSEE:

39-13-533 SECTION 1. Tennessee Code Annotated, Title 39, Chapter 13, Part 5, is amended by adding the following as a new section:

39-13-533.

(a) A person commits the offense of promoting travel for prostitution if the person sells or offers to sell travel services that the person knows to include travel for the purpose of engaging in what would be prostitution if occurring in the state.

(b) "Travel services" means, but is not limited to, transportation by air, sea, road or rail, related ground transportation, hotel accommodations, or package tours, whether offered on a wholesale or retail basis.

(c) Promoting travel for prostitution is a Class D felony.

(d) Nothing in this section shall be construed to prohibit prosecution under any other law.

39-13-309 SECTION 2. Tennessee Code Annotated, Section 39-13-309(a)(2), is amended by deleting the subdivision in its entirety and substituting instead the following:

(2) Recruits, entices, harbors, transports, provides, purchases, or obtains by any other means, another person for the purpose of providing a commercial sex act.

39-13-301 SECTION 3. Tennessee Code Annotated, Section 39-13-301, is amended by deleting from subdivision (15) the language ""Sexual servitude" means", substituting instead the language ""Commercial sex act" means", and deleting subdivision (4) in its entirety.

Effective date 7/1/2013 SECTION 4. This act shall take effect July 1, 2013, the public welfare requiring it.

PUBLIC CHAPTER NO. 466

PUBLIC CHAPTER NO. 466

SENATE BILL NO. 948

By Campfield

Substituted for: House Bill No. 456

By Hardaway, Rogers

AN ACT to amend Tennessee Code Annotated, Title 71, relative to public assistance benefits.

BE IT ENACTED BY THE GENERAL ASSEMBLY OF THE STATE OF TENNESSEE:

SECTION 1. The commissioner of human services shall study issues, within existing resources, related to the issuance of a photo identification card to each eligible household in the food stamp and temporary assistance to needy families programs. The study shall identify the benefits and practical implementation concerns associated with requiring the issuance and use of such identification. The commissioner shall make such report to the health committee of the house of representatives and the health and welfare committee of the senate on or before January 15, 2014.

Effective date 5/20/2013

SECTION 2. This act shall take effect upon becoming a law, the public welfare requiring it.

PUBLIC CHAPTER NO. 467

PUBLIC CHAPTER NO. 467

SENATE BILL NO. 875

By Henry, Johnson

Substituted for: House Bill No. 724

By Stewart, Powell, Sargent

AN ACT to amend Tennessee Code Annotated, Title 9, Chapter 21, relative to the definition of "certain unfunded pension obligations" for which local governments may issue bonds.

WHEREAS, pension liabilities for local governments are increasing and becoming a growing financial burden for local governments in this state; and

WHEREAS, it would be in the public interest for local governments to have additional means by which to fund their increasing pension liabilities; and

WHEREAS, state law currently permits local governments to issue their general obligation bonds and revenue bonds for "certain unfunded pension obligations," as such term is defined in the Tennessee Code Annotated; and

WHEREAS, the current historically low interest-rate environment presents local governments with a unique opportunity to borrow monies at a rate cheaper than the rate on which they would earn on the investment of such funds; and

WHEREAS, the issuance of bonds by local governments and the subsequent investment of such bond proceeds at a rate higher than the rate at which they were borrowed would provide local governments with profit earnings with which to fund their pension liabilities; and

WHEREAS, to permit the greatest number of local governments to take advantage of the opportunities presented by this interest-rate environment to fund their pension liabilities, it is necessary to expand the definition of "certain unfunded pension obligations" for which local governments may issue their bonds; and

WHEREAS, the State Funding Board and the Comptroller of the Treasury shall retain their ability under Tennessee Code Annotated, Section 9-21-127, to reject any proposed issuance of bonds by local governments to fund their pension obligations; and

WHEREAS, to provide local governments with additional means by which to fund their increasing pension liabilities, the Tennessee General Assembly desires to expand the definition of "certain unfunded pension obligations" in Tennessee Code Annotated, Section 9-21-105, for which local governments may issue their bonds; now, therefore,

BE IT ENACTED BY THE GENERAL ASSEMBLY OF THE STATE OF TENNESSEE:

9-21-105 SECTION 1. Tennessee Code Annotated, Section 9-21-105(4)(A), is amended by inserting the following as a new subdivision:

(iv) Pension benefits for past service of employees of a local government which is either (A) a metropolitan government with a general obligation rating of at least Aa1 (or its equivalent) from one or more nationally recognized rating agencies or (B) a municipality with a general obligation rating of Aaa (or its equivalent) from one or more nationally recognized rating agencies that is located within a county with a general obligation rating of Aaa (or its equivalent) from one or more nationally recognized rating agencies and, in either case, whose pension benefits arise from a defined benefit plan administered by the local government;

9-21-105 SECTION 2. Tennessee Code Annotated, Section 9-21-105(4)(A)(ii), is amended by deleting the language "or" after the semi-colon at the end of the subdivision.

9-21-105 SECTION 3. Tennessee Code Annotated, Section 9-21-105(4)(A)(iii), is amended by adding the language "or" after the semi-colon at the end of the subdivision.

9-21-105 SECTION 4. Tennessee Code Annotated, Section 9-21-105(4), is amended by inserting the following as a new subdivision:

(D) Subdivision (4)(A)(iv) shall cease to be effective on July 1, 2015; provided, that no bonds issued pursuant to this subdivision (4) prior to July 1, 2015, shall be rendered ineffectual;

9-21-127 SECTION 5. Tennessee Code Annotated, Section 9-21-127, is amended by inserting the following after the first sentence:

A local government that issues bonds for certain unfunded pension obligations pursuant to § 9-21-105(4)(A)(iv) shall not be required to receive a recommendation by the comptroller of the treasury or the comptroller's designee or the approval of the state funding board if (A) the principal amount of the bonds is amortized over the term of the bonds such that the bonds are not balloon indebtedness (as defined below) and (B) the local government has (i) adopted a debt management policy in compliance with guidelines promulgated by the state funding board; (ii) available for public inspection its financial statements prepared in compliance with generally accepted accounting principles for state and local governments with an unqualified auditor's opinion for the two most recent fiscal years; (iii) presented to its governing body at a public hearing an explanation of the risk exposure associated with such bonds, economic and demographic assumptions used in the funding assumptions, alternative funding options considered, issuance costs associated with the proposed bonds and any conflicts of interest among the professionals involved (if disclosing such conflicts would not violate any rules of professional conduct); (iv) engaged or will engage a financial advisor, bond counsel and actuarial consultant in connection with the issuance of such bonds; (v) a full-time finance staff of at least three (3) persons; and (vi) an audit committee. As used herein, the term "balloon indebtedness" shall mean any bond (A) twenty percent (20%) or more of the principal amount of which is payable during any twelve month period or (B) fifty percent (50%) or more of the principal amount of which is payable in the aggregate twenty (20) years or more after the date of issuance.

Effective date 5/20/2013

SECTION 6. This act shall take effect upon becoming law, the public welfare requiring it.

PUBLIC CHAPTER NO. 468

PUBLIC CHAPTER NO. 468

SENATE BILL NO. 856

By Tate, Ford

Substituted for: House Bill No. 1170

By Towns, Todd

AN ACT to amend Tennessee Code Annotated, Title 68, Chapter 115, relative to the Tennessee Athletic Commission Act of 2008.

BE IT ENACTED BY THE GENERAL ASSEMBLY OF THE STATE OF TENNESSEE:

68-115-211 SECTION 1. Tennessee Code Annotated, Section 68-115-211, is amended by deleting the section and substituting instead the following language:

> Every promoter of a professional contest of unarmed combat shall provide proof of medical insurance coverage for medical, surgical, and hospital care to cover injuries sustained by a combatant while engaged in professional contests of unarmed combat, in an amount not less than twenty-five thousand dollars ($25,000).

Effective date 5/20/2013 SECTION 2. This act shall take effect upon becoming a law, the public welfare requiring it.

PUBLIC CHAPTER NO. 469

PUBLIC CHAPTER NO. 469

SENATE BILL NO. 835

By Ketron

Substituted for: House Bill No. 328

By Curtiss, Hardaway

AN ACT to amend Tennessee Code Annotated, Title 62 and Title 66, relative to the construction industry.

BE IT ENACTED BY THE GENERAL ASSEMBLY OF THE STATE OF TENNESSEE:

62-6-103 SECTION 1. Tennessee Code Annotated, Section 62-6-103(a)(1), is amended by deleting the subdivision in its entirety and substituting instead the following:

(a)(1) Any person, firm or corporation engaged in contracting in this state shall be required to submit evidence of qualification to engage in contracting, and shall be licensed as provided in this part. It is unlawful for any person, firm, or corporation to engage in or offer to engage in contracting for any project in this state, unless, at the time of such engagement or offer to engage, the person, firm, or corporation has been duly licensed with a monetary limitation sufficient to allow the person, firm, or corporation to engage in or offer to engage in such contracting project under this chapter. The board for licensing contractors shall have the authority to grant or allow an exception, in an amount not to exceed ten percent (10%), to the monetary limitation of such license provided in subdivision (a)(1). Any person, firm, or corporation engaged in contracting, including a person, firm, or corporation that engages in the construction of residences or dwellings constructed on private property for the purpose of resale, lease, rent, or any other similar purpose, shall be required to submit evidence of qualification to engage in contracting and shall be licensed. It is unlawful for any person, firm, or corporation to engage in, or offer to engage in, contracting as described in subdivision (a)(1) unless the person, firm, or corporation has been duly licensed under this part.

62-6-103 SECTION 2. Tennessee Code Annotated, Section 62-6-103, is amended by adding the following new subsection thereto:

(c) Notwithstanding any law to the contrary, no lien otherwise authorized pursuant to title 66, chapter 11 shall be available to any person, firm, or corporation engaged in construction in violation of this chapter.

66-11-102 SECTION 3. Tennessee Code Annotated, Section 66-11-102(a), is amended by deleting the subsection in its entirety and substituting instead the following:

(a) There shall be a lien on any lot or tract of real property upon which an improvement has been made by a prime contractor or any remote contractor; provided, that the lienor has complied with title 62, chapter 6. If the lienor has not fully complied with title 62, chapter 6, no lien is established by this chapter. The lien shall secure the contract price.

66-11-101 SECTION 4. Tennessee Code Annotated, Section 66-11-101(16), is amended by deleting the language "underground".

66-11-104 SECTION 5. Tennessee Code Annotated, Section 66-11-104(a), is hereby amended by deleting the word "underground".

Effective date 7/1/2013 SECTION 6. This act shall take effect July 1, 2013, the public welfare requiring it, and shall apply to contracts entered into or renewed on or after the effective date and to liens filed for construction performed on or after the effective date.

PUBLIC CHAPTER NO. 470

PUBLIC CHAPTER NO. 470

SENATE BILL NO. 796

By Beavers, Gardenhire, Kelsey, Bell, Crowe, Niceley

Substituted for: House Bill No. 591

By Van Huss, Carter, Stewart, Holt, Hall, Matheny

AN ACT to amend Tennessee Code Annotated, Title 29 and Title 39, relative to surveillance.

BE IT ENACTED BY THE GENERAL ASSEMBLY OF THE STATE OF TENNESSEE:

39-13-609 SECTION 1. Tennessee Code Annotated, Title 39, Chapter 13, Part 6, is amended by adding the following language as a new section:

(a) This section shall be known and may be cited as the "Freedom from Unwarranted Surveillance Act".

(b) As used in this section:

(1) "Drone" means a powered, aerial vehicle that:

(A) Does not carry a human operator and is operated without the possibility of direct human intervention from within or on the aircraft;

(B) Uses aerodynamic forces to provide vehicle lift;

(C) Can fly autonomously or be piloted remotely; and

(D) Can be expendable or recoverable;

(2) "Law enforcement agency" means a lawfully established state or local public agency that is responsible for the prevention and detection of crime, local government code enforcement, and the enforcement of penal, traffic, regulatory, game, or controlled substance laws.

(c) Except as provided in subsection (d), no law enforcement agency shall use a drone to gather evidence or other information.

(d) This section shall not prohibit the use of a drone:

(1) To counter a high risk of a terrorist attack by a specific individual or organization if the United States secretary of homeland security determines that credible intelligence indicates that there is such a risk;

(2) If the law enforcement agency first obtains a search warrant signed by a judge authorizing the use of a drone;

(3) If the law enforcement agency possesses reasonable suspicion that, under particular circumstances, swift action is needed to prevent imminent danger to life;

(4) To provide continuous aerial coverage when law enforcement is searching for a fugitive or escapee or is monitoring a hostage situation; or

(5) To provide more expansive aerial coverage when deployed for the purpose of searching for a missing person.

(e) An aggrieved party may initiate a civil action against a law enforcement agency to obtain all appropriate relief, as determined by the court, in order to prevent or remedy a violation of this section.

(f) No data collected on an individual, home, or areas other than the target that justified deployment may be used, copied or disclosed for any purpose. Such data must be deleted as soon as possible, and in no event later than twenty-four (24) hours after collection.

(g)(1) The use of a drone to gather evidence or information shall constitute a search. Any law enforcement agency that uses a drone, or other substantially similar device to gather evidence or obtain information, shall comply in all respects with the fourth amendment to the Constitution of the United States and article I, § 7, of the Constitution of Tennessee.

(2) Absent exigent circumstances or another authorized exception to the warrant requirement, evidence obtained or collected in violation of this section shall not be admissible as evidence in a criminal prosecution in any court of law in this state.

Effective date 5/20/2013

SECTION 2. This act shall take effect July 1, 2013, the public welfare requiring it.

PUBLIC CHAPTER NO. 471

PUBLIC CHAPTER NO. 471

SENATE BILL NO. 657

By Tracy, Ford

Substituted for: House Bill No. 515

By Dean, Rogers

AN ACT to amend Tennessee Code Annotated, Title 54 and Title 55, relative to transportation.

BE IT ENACTED BY THE GENERAL ASSEMBLY OF THE STATE OF TENNESSEE:

54-5-1103 SECTION 1. Tennessee Code Annotated, Section 54-5-1103(c), is amended by deleting the subsection in its entirety and by substituting instead the following:

(c) Notwithstanding § 12-4-109(a)(2), any contract to perform administrative services shall be awarded to the contractor whose proposal offers the best value for the state rather than the least cost to the retail user of the signs. In determining the best value for the state, the department may consider:

(1) The quality of service offered;

(2) The contractor's overall qualifications to partner with the department. This includes determining fair market value of advertising space and establishing a fee structure that provides a combination of revenue to the department and fair pricing to the advertisers;

(3) The contractor's financial resources and ability to perform;

(4) The percentage of revenue sharing provided to the department by the contractor; and

(5) Any other factor the department considers relevant.

54-5-1104 SECTION 2. Tennessee Code Annotated, Section 54-5-1104, is amended by deleting the section in its entirety.

54-5-1106 SECTION 3. Tennessee Code Annotated, Section 54-5-1106, is amended by deleting the section in its entirety and by substituting instead the following:

54-5-1106. No lease payments, royalty payments, or funds of any type received by the state pursuant to this part shall be used for the purchase of nonconforming billboards or used as payment for the taking or removal of nonconforming billboards.

54-5-1110 SECTION 4. Tennessee Code Annotated, Section 54-5-1110, is amended by deleting the section in its entirety and by substituting instead the following:

(a) Those food service businesses qualified under this program as of July 1, 2001, and that continue thereafter to be qualified and pay all fees required, shall not be replaced by any business that becomes qualified after July 1, 2001.

(b) Notwithstanding subsection (a), if the department elects to award advertising space based on a competitive selection process, the food service businesses qualified under the program as of July 1, 2001, will need to compete in such a competitive selection process and may be replaced by any business that submits a more competitive proposal under such a process.

54-5-1103 SECTION 5. Tennessee Code Annotated, Section 54-5-1103(a)(2), is amended by deleting the first sentence in its entirety, which reads as follows:

Contracts for administrative services shall be subject to §§ 12-4-109--12-4-111.

Effective date 5/20/2013 SECTION 6. This act shall take effect upon becoming a law, the public welfare requiring it.

PUBLIC CHAPTER NO. 472

PUBLIC CHAPTER NO. 472

SENATE BILL NO. 653

By Tracy

Substituted for: House Bill No. 511

By Dean

AN ACT to amend Tennessee Code Annotated, Title 54, relative to transportation.

BE IT ENACTED BY THE GENERAL ASSEMBLY OF THE STATE OF TENNESSEE:

54-1-134 SECTION 1. Tennessee Code Annotated, Section 54-1-134(a), is amended by deleting the subsection in its entirety and by substituting instead the following:

(a)(1) As used in this subsection (a), "state highway structure" includes any state highway facility; building; bridge; overpass; tunnel; barricade; fence; wall; traffic control device; right-of-way; sign or marker of any nature whatsoever erected upon or maintained within or adjacent to a state highway or the state highway right-of-way by any authorized source or under the authority of the department; and letters or figures of any nature whatsoever on any sign, marker, barricade or fence.

(2) It is an offense for any person who is not authorized to construct or repair a state highway structure to knowingly carve upon, write, paint or otherwise mark upon, deface, rearrange, or alter any state highway structure.

(3) It is an offense for any person who is not authorized to construct or repair a state highway structure to knowingly, in any manner, destroy, damage, knock down, mutilate, mar, steal or remove any state highway structure.

(4) A violation of subdivision (a)(2) or (a)(3) is a Class A misdemeanor.

(5) Whenever any state highway structure described in this subsection (a) is damaged knowingly or negligently by any person, firm or corporation, the person, firm or corporation shall be liable for the damage to the state highway structure, to be recovered by a civil action in the name of the state. The civil action shall be instituted by the attorney general and reporter, whose duty it shall be to represent the state in the action.

54-5-701 SECTION 2. Tennessee Code Annotated, Title 54, Chapter 5, Part 7, is amended by deleting
54-5-702 Sections 54-5-701 and 54-5-702 in their entirety.

54-7-201 SECTION 3. Tennessee Code Annotated, Section 54-7-201, is amended by deleting subsection (d) in its entirety and by redesignating the remaining subsection accordingly.

54-7-207 SECTION 4. Tennessee Code Annotated, Title 54, Chapter 7, Part 2, is amended by adding the following as a new, appropriately designated section:

54-7-20_.

(a)(1) As used in this subsection (a), "county highway structure" includes any county highway; highway facility; building; bridge; overpass; tunnel; barricade; fence; wall; traffic control device; right-of-way; sign or marker of any nature whatsoever erected upon or maintained within or adjacent to a county highway or the county highway right-of-way.

(2) It is an offense for any person who is not authorized to construct or repair a county highway structure to knowingly carve upon, write, paint or otherwise mark upon, deface, rearrange, or alter any county highway structure.

(3) It is an offense for any person who is not authorized to construct or repair a county highway structure to knowingly, in any manner, destroy, damage, knock down, mutilate, mar, steal or remove any county highway structure.

(4) A violation of subdivision (a)(2) or (a)(3) is a Class A misdemeanor.

(5) In addition to any criminal penalty provided by law for a violation of subdivision (a)(2) or (a)(3), there is created a separate civil cause of action for the cost of any damage resulting from such prohibited action.

(6) There is created a civil cause of action for the cost of any damage done whenever a person negligently damages any county highway structure.

(7) Criminal actions prosecuted pursuant to this subsection shall be brought by the district attorney general of the judicial district in which the damage occurred. Civil actions instituted pursuant to this subsection shall be brought by the county attorney or an attorney employed by the chief administrative officer of the county highway department.

(b)(1) Any person who reports information to a law enforcement officer that leads to the apprehension and conviction of a person for a violation of this section shall receive a reward of two hundred fifty dollars ($250). The county where the conviction occurs shall provide the reward money from the proceeds of the fines collected under this section.

(2) The proceeds from the fines imposed for violations of this section shall be collected by the respective court clerks and then deposited in a dedicated county fund. The fund shall not revert to the county general fund at the end of a fiscal year but shall remain for the vandalism enforcement rewards established in subdivision (b)(1).

(3) Each county shall expend the funds generated by the fines provided for in this section by appropriation for the vandalism enforcement rewards. Excess funds, if any, may be expended for litter control programs on adoption of an appropriate resolution by the county legislative body.

(c) Notwithstanding any law to the contrary, this section shall apply to all counties.

Effective date 7/1/2013

SECTION 5. This act shall take effect July 1, 2013, the public welfare requiring it.

PUBLIC CHAPTER NO. 473

PUBLIC CHAPTER NO. 473

SENATE BILL NO. 643

By Tracy, Bowling, Ketron, Burks, Beavers, Bell, Campfield, Crowe, Dickerson, Finney, Ford, Gardenhire, Green, Gresham, Haile, Harper, Henry, Hensley, Johnson, Kelsey, Kyle, Massey, McNally, Niceley, Norris, Overbey, Southerland, Stevens, Summerville, Tate, Watson, Yager, Mr. Speaker Ramsey

Substituted for: House Bill No. 236

By Harry Brooks, Pitts, Ragan, Calfee, Windle, Keisling, Goins, Kane, Shaw, Moody, Littleton, Camper, Miller, Sparks, Powell, Butt, Mark White, Fitzhugh, Favors, Weaver, Floyd, Eldridge

AN ACT to amend Tennessee Code Annotated, Section 4-3-1405; Section 8-50-114; Section 39-13-114; Title 49; Section 54-5-708 and Section 67-6-329, relative to technology centers.

BE IT ENACTED BY THE GENERAL ASSEMBLY OF THE STATE OF TENNESSEE:

49-11-401 — 49-11-408 SECTION 1. Tennessee Code Annotated, Title 49, Chapter 11, Part 4, is amended by deleting the words "state technology centers" wherever they appear and substituting instead the words "state colleges of applied technology" and by deleting the words "state technology center" wherever they appear and substituting instead the words "state college of applied technology".

49-11-401 SECTION 2. Tennessee Code Annotated, Section 49-11-401(b), is amended by deleting the subsection in its entirety and substituting instead the following:

(b) The individual colleges of applied technology established by this part shall be known as "Tennessee College of Applied Technology – " followed by the name of the city, town or place in which or near which the college is located.

49-11-402 SECTION 3. Tennessee Code Annotated, Section 49-11-402(a)(2), is amended by deleting the words "or centers" and substituting instead the words "or colleges" and by deleting the words "of less than college grade" and substituting instead the words "of less than university or community college grade".

49-11-402 SECTION 4. Tennessee Code Annotated, Section 49-11-402(a)(3), is amended by deleting the words "two-year terminal training center" and substituting instead the words "two-year terminal training college".

49-11-402 SECTION 5. Tennessee Code Annotated, Section 49-11-402(c), is amended by deleting the word "centers" wherever it appears and substituting instead the words "colleges of applied technology".

49-11-104 SECTION 6. Tennessee Code Annotated, Section 49-11-104(c), is amended by deleting the words "state technology centers" and substituting instead the words "state colleges of applied technology".

49-8-101 SECTION 7. Tennessee Code Annotated, Section 49-8-101, is amended by deleting the words "technology centers" wherever they appear and substituting instead the words "colleges of applied technology".

4-3-1405 SECTION 8. Tennessee Code Annotated, Section 4-3-1405(e), is amended by deleting the words "technology centers" and substituting instead the words "colleges of applied technology".

8-50-114 SECTION 9. Tennessee Code Annotated, Section 8-50-114, is amended by deleting the words "technology center" wherever they appear and substituting instead the words "college of applied technology".

39-13-114 SECTION 10. Tennessee Code Annotated, Section 39-13-114(a)(2), is amended by deleting the words "Technology center" and substituting instead the words "College of applied technology".

49-2-116 SECTION 11. Tennessee Code Annotated, Section 49-2-116(b)(1), is amended by deleting the words "state technology center" and substituting instead the words "state college of applied technology".

49-3-318 SECTION 12. Tennessee Code Annotated, Section 49-3-318(c), is amended by deleting the words "state technology centers" and substituting instead the words "state colleges of applied technology".

PUBLIC CHAPTER NO. 473 (cont'd)

49-4-902
49-4-921
49-4-937 SECTION 13. Tennessee Code Annotated, Title 49, Chapter 4, Part 9, is amended by deleting the words "Tennessee technology centers" wherever they appear and substituting instead the words "Tennessee colleges of applied technology" and by deleting the words "Tennessee technology center" wherever they appear and substituting instead the words "Tennessee college of applied technology".

49-7-102 SECTION 14. Tennessee Code Annotated, Section 49-7-102(c)(6), is amended by deleting the words "of the state university, community college and area technology center system".

49-7-116 SECTION 15. Tennessee Code Annotated, Section 49-7-116(a), is amended by deleting the words "state technology center" and substituting instead the words "state college of applied technology".

49-7-155 SECTION 16. Tennessee Code Annotated, Section 49-7-155(a)(3), is amended by deleting the words "Tennessee technology center" wherever they appear and substituting instead the words "Tennessee college of applied technology".

49-7-202 SECTION 17. Tennessee Code Annotated, Section 49-7-202, is amended by deleting the words "technology centers" wherever they appear and substituting instead the words "colleges of applied technology".

49-7-2004 SECTION 18. Tennessee Code Annotated, Section 49-7-2004(a)(5), is amended by deleting the words "technology centers" wherever they appear and substituting instead the words "colleges of applied technology" and by deleting the words "technology center" and substituting instead the words "college of applied technology".

49-7-2202 SECTION 19. Tennessee Code Annotated, Section 49-7-2202(1), is amended by deleting the words "technology centers" and substituting instead the words "colleges of applied technology".

49-8-109 SECTION 20. Tennessee Code Annotated, Section 49-8-109(a), is amended by deleting the words "technology centers" and substituting instead the words "colleges of applied technology".

49-8-201 SECTION 21. Tennessee Code Annotated, Section 49-8-201, is amended by deleting the words "technology center" wherever they appear and substituting instead the words "college of applied technology" and by deleting the words "technology centers" wherever they appear and substituting instead the words "colleges of applied technology".

49-8-401 SECTION 22. Tennessee Code Annotated, Section 49-8-401(c), is amended by deleting the words "technology centers" and substituting instead the words "colleges of applied technology".

49-15-101 SECTION 23. Tennessee Code Annotated, Section 49-15-101(a), is amended by deleting the words "technology centers" and substituting instead the words "colleges of applied technology".

49-15-105 SECTION 24. Tennessee Code Annotated, Section 49-15-105(b)(3), is amended by deleting the words "technology center" wherever they appear and substituting instead the words "college of applied technology".

54-5-708 SECTION 25. Tennessee Code Annotated, Section 54-5-708, is amended by deleting the words "technology centers" wherever they appear and substituting instead the words "colleges of applied technology".

67-6-329 SECTION 26. Tennessee Code Annotated, Section 67-6-329(a)(7), is amended by deleting the words "technology centers" wherever they appear and substituting instead the words "colleges of applied technology".

SECTION 27. The Tennessee Code Commission is requested to revise appropriate references from "Tennessee technology center", "Tennessee technology centers", "technology center" or "technology centers" wherever located within Tennessee Code Annotated to "Tennessee college of applied technology", "Tennessee colleges of applied technology", "college of applied technology" or "colleges of applied technology" respectively as sections are amended or volumes are replaced.

Effective
date
7/1/2013 SECTION 28. This act shall take effect July 1, 2013, the public welfare requiring it.

PUBLIC CHAPTER NO. 474

PUBLIC CHAPTER NO. 474

SENATE BILL NO. 608

By Yager

Substituted for: House Bill No. 479

By Powers

AN ACT to amend Tennessee Code Annotated, Title 64, Chapter 10, to create the Cumberland Regional Business and Agribusiness Marketing Authority.

BE IT ENACTED BY THE GENERAL ASSEMBLY OF THE STATE OF TENNESSEE:

64-10-201 — 64-10-222 SECTION 1. Tennessee Code Annotated, Title 64, Chapter 10, is amended by adding the following as a new part:

64-10-201.

(a) The Cumberland regional business and agribusiness marketing authority is hereby created as a public body corporate and politic, referred to as the authority in this part. The authority is a public and governmental body acting as an agent and instrumentality of the counties with respect to which the authority is organized. As such, all property of the authority, both real and personal, is exempt from all local, state and federal taxation.

(b) The acquisition, operating and financing of the authority and related purposes are hereby declared to be for public and governmental purposes and a matter of public necessity to further the economy and growth of the business and agricultural industry of the region.

(c) The purposes of the Cumberland regional business and agribusiness marketing authority are to:

(1) Create a business support process that accelerates the successful development of start-up and fledgling companies by providing entrepreneurs with an array of targeted resources and services;

(2) Have the authority to establish and operate a market for agricultural products of the region through a food distribution center, to provide farmers of the region with a ready market for agricultural products, and to provide the citizens of the region and other buyers a convenient place to purchase these products; and

(3) Further the economy and growth of the region served by the authority by planning, acquiring, constructing, improving, extending, furnishing, equipping, financing, owning, operating and maintaining support for small business incubators for the region.

64-10-202. As used in this part, unless the context otherwise requires:

(1) "Agribusiness" means a business dealing with agricultural products or engaged in providing products or services to farmers;

(2) "Authority" means the Cumberland regional business and agribusiness marketing authority;

(3) "Board" means the board of directors of the Cumberland regional business and agribusiness marketing authority;

(4) "Business" means any start-up or existing business;

(5) "Center" means the regional food distribution center established by the authority;

(6) "Department" means the department of agriculture;

(7) "Region" means the area consisting of the counties of Anderson, Campbell, Cumberland, Fentress, Loudon, Morgan, Roane, Scott and any other county in the eastern grand division that becomes a member of the authority in accordance with the provisions of § 64-10-215; and

64-10-203.

(a)(1) Subject to the provisions of subsection (b), the authority shall be governed by a board of directors consisting of the county mayor of each county, or the county mayor's designee, that is a member of the authority. Subject to the provisions of § 64-10-215, the following counties shall comprise the authority: Anderson; Campbell; Cumberland; Fentress; Loudon; Morgan; Roane; and Scott.

(2) The term of any designee shall expire with the term of the county mayor who appointed such designee. The initial terms of designees, if any, shall be as follows:

(A) The initial terms of the designees from Anderson and Cumberland counties shall be one (1) year;

(B) The initial terms of the designees from Loudon, Morgan and Fentress counties shall be two (2) years; and

(C) The initial terms of the designees from Campbell, Roane and Scott counties shall be three (3) years.

(3) Following the initial terms of service, the term of office for each designee shall be three (3) years.

(4) The board shall also have two (2) nonvoting members as follows:

(A) The president of Roane State Community College, or the president's designee; and

(B) One (1) member elected by the board.

(5) The board shall, at its first meeting of each calendar year, elect from its voting membership a chair, a vice chair, a secretary and a treasurer, each to serve terms of one (1) year and until a successor is elected.

(6) The term of office of the county mayor serving on the board shall be coterminous with such official's elective term of office.

(b) Should a board member who is a designee attend less than fifty percent (50%) of the called meetings during a calendar year, the board is authorized to declare a vacancy on the board for that position. The board shall then notify the county mayor who appointed such designee of the vacancy and, if the county mayor fails to appoint a new designee within thirty (30) days, then the board shall, by majority vote, replace the member with a knowledgeable person from the county for which a vacancy was declared by the board.

(c) The board shall meet at least quarterly. More frequent meetings may be called at the discretion of the board.

64-10-204.

The board shall establish an executive committee consisting of the chair, vice chair, secretary, treasurer and the president of Roane State Community College or the president's designee, as an ex officio member. The executive committee is authorized to act on behalf of the board in the day-to-day operations of the authority. The executive committee shall meet at least monthly, either in person or by telephone conference, and make a full report to the board at its regular meetings.

64-10-205.

(a) The board may appoint an advisory committee consisting of one (1) member from each county that is a member of the authority.

(b) If appointed by the board, it shall be the duty of the advisory committee to consult with and advise the board regarding the operation and financial management of the authority.

64-10-206.

(a) The authority has the following powers:

(1) Perpetual succession in corporate name;

(2) Sue and be sued in its name;

(3) Adopt, use and alter a corporate seal, which shall be judicially noticed;

(4) Enter into such contracts and cooperative agreements with federal, state and local governments, with agencies of such governments, with private individuals, corporations, associations and other organizations as the board may deem necessary or convenient to enable it to carry out the purposes of this part;

(5) Adopt, amend and repeal bylaws;

(6) Appoint such managers, officers, employees, attorneys and agents as the board deems necessary for the transaction of its business, fix their compensation, define their duties and require bonds of such of them as the board may determine. The salaries of any such employees may be paid out of such funds as may be available to the authority; and

(7) Accept the transfer of grants, funds, assets and liabilities of the authority upon the termination of the interlocal government cooperative agreement establishing the authority, in accordance with the provisions of § 64-10-217.

(b) The board shall:

(1) Approve an annual budget for the authority;

(2) Adopt a purchasing policy and a personnel policy consistent with state and federal law; and

(3) Adopt policies and procedures for fiscal control and accounting.

(c) The board may do all other things that are necessary or appropriate for carrying out this part that are not prohibited by law or this part.

64-10-207.

(a)(1) The authority is authorized and empowered to issue its bonds, notes or other obligations from time to time for the purpose of paying in whole or in part the cost of acquiring necessary lands and interests therein, and of constructing and acquiring constructed facilities and improvements necessary to further the economy and growth of the agriculture industry of the region, and the expenses incidental thereto. Prior to the adoption of any resolution of the board authorizing the sale of bonds, notes or other obligations, or entering into any contract or other arrangement in the planning or preparation for the sale of bonds, notes or other obligations, the authority shall review such plans with the comptroller of the treasury or the comptroller's designee. The state funding board established by § 9-9-101 is authorized to contract or to make other arrangements as it may deem necessary to provide for the issuance of such bonds, notes or other obligations of the authority or, in the state funding board's discretion, the authority may enter into such contracts or other arrangements. Any contract or arrangement entered into for the purpose of the issuance of any bonds, notes or other obligations shall be subject to the approval of the state funding board.

(2) Any resolution of the board authorizing the sale of bonds, notes or other obligations shall be submitted to the state funding board, and such resolution shall only become effective upon receiving the approval of the state funding board. The state funding board, upon rejecting any resolution of the

board authorizing the issuance of bonds, notes or other obligations, shall state in writing the reasons for its action.

(b)(1) Except as otherwise expressly provided in this subsection (b), all bonds, including notes or other obligations of the authority, issued by the authority, are payable solely out of the revenues and receipts derived from the authority's projects or of any revenues of the authority as may be designated in the proceedings of the board under which the bonds are authorized to be issued; provided, that notes issued in anticipation of the issuance of bonds may be retired out of the proceeds of such bonds. Such bonds may be executed and delivered by the authority at any time and from time to time, may be in such form and denominations and of such terms and maturities, may be in registered or bearer form either as to principal or interest or both, may be payable in such installments and at such time or times not exceeding forty (40) years from the date thereof, may be payable at such place or places whether within or without Tennessee, may bear interest at such rate or rates payable at such time or times and at such place or places and evidenced in such manner, may be executed by such officers of the authority and may contain such provisions not inconsistent herewith, all as shall be provided in the proceedings of the board whereunder the bonds shall be authorized to be issued.

(2) If deemed advisable by the board, there may be retained in the proceedings under which any bonds of the authority are authorized to be issued an option to redeem all or any part thereof as may be specified in such proceedings, at such price or prices and after such notice or notices and on such terms and conditions as may be set forth in such proceedings and as may be briefly recited on the face of the bonds, however nothing contained in this subsection (b) shall be construed to confer on the authority any right or option to redeem any bonds except as may be provided in the proceedings under which they shall be issued.

(3) Any bonds of the authority may be sold at public or private sale in such manner, at such price and from time to time as may be determined by the board to be most advantageous, and the authority may pay all expenses, premiums and commissions that its board may deem necessary or advantageous in connection with the issuance thereof. Issuance by the board of one (1) or more series of bonds for one (1) or more purposes shall not preclude it from issuing other bonds in connection with the same project or any other project, but the proceedings whereunder any subsequent bonds may be issued shall recognize and protect any prior pledge or mortgage made for any prior issue of bonds.

(4) Proceeds of bonds issued by the authority may be used for the purpose of constructing, acquiring, reconstructing, improving, equipping, furnishing, bettering or extending any project or projects, including the payment of interest on the bonds during construction of any such project and for two (2) years after the estimated date of completion, for payment of engineering, fiscal, architectural and legal expenses incurred in connection with such project and the issuance of the bonds, and for the establishment of a reasonable reserve fund for the payment of principal of and interest on such bonds in the event of a deficiency in the revenues and receipts available for such payment.

(c) Subject to the approvals required in subsection (a), any bonds or notes of the authority at any time outstanding may, at any time and from time to time, be refunded by the authority by the issuance of its refunding bonds in such amount as the board may deem necessary, but not exceeding the sum of the following:

(1) The principal amount of the obligations being refinanced;

(2) Applicable redemption premiums thereon;

(3) Unpaid interest on such obligations to the date of delivery or exchange of the refunding bonds;

(4) In the event the proceeds from the sale of the refunding bonds are to be deposited in trust as provided in this section, the amount of interest to accrue on such obligations from the date of delivery to the first or any subsequent available redemption date or dates selected, in its discretion, by

the board or to the date or dates of maturity, whichever shall be determined by the board to be most advantageous or necessary to the authority;

(5) A reasonable reserve for the payment of principal of and interest on such bonds or a renewal and replacement reserve;

(6) If the project to be constructed from the proceeds of the obligations being refinanced has not been completed, an amount sufficient to meet the interest charges on the refunding bonds during the construction of such project and for two (2) years after the estimated date of completion, but only to the extent that interest charges have not been capitalized from the proceeds of the obligations being refinanced; and

(7) Expenses, premiums and commissions of the authority, including bonds discount, deemed by the board to be necessary for the issuance of the refunding bonds. A determination by the board that any refinancing is advantageous or necessary to the authority, or that any of the amounts provided in this subdivision should be included in such refinancing or that any of the obligations to be refinanced should be called for redemption on the first or any subsequent available redemption date permitted to remain outstanding until their respective dates of maturity, shall be conclusive.

(d) Any such refunding may be effected whether the obligations to be refunded have then matured or thereafter mature, either by the exchange or the refunding bonds for the obligations to be refunded thereby with the consent of the holders of the obligations so to be refunded, or by sale of the refunding bonds, and the application of the proceeds thereof to the payment of the obligations to be refunded thereby, and regardless of whether or not the obligations proposed to be refunded are payable on the same date or different dates or are due serially or otherwise.

(e) Prior to the issuance of the refunding bonds, the board shall cause notice of its intention to issue the refunding bonds, identifying the obligations proposed to be refunded and setting forth the estimated date of delivery of the refunding bonds, to be given to the holders of the outstanding obligations by mail to each registered holder and, if the outstanding bonds or coupons are not registered securities, by publication of an appropriate notice one (1) time each in a newspaper having general circulation in the area of the project and in a financial newspaper published in New York, New York, having national circulation. As soon as practicable after the delivery of the refunding bonds, and whether or not any of the obligations to be refunded are to be called for redemption, the board shall cause notice of the issuance of the refunding bonds to be given in the manner provided in this subsection (e).

(f) If any of the obligations to be refunded are to be called for redemption, the board shall cause notice of redemption to be given in the manner required by the proceedings authorizing such outstanding obligations.

(g) The principal proceeds from the sale of any refunding bonds shall be applied only as follows:

(1) To the immediate payment and retirement of the obligations being refunded; or

(2) To the extent not required for the immediate payment of the obligations being refunded, then such proceeds shall be deposited in trust to provide for the payment and retirement of the obligations being refunded; but provision may be made for the pledging and disposition of any surplus, including, without limitation, provision for the pledging of any such surplus to the payment of the principal of and interest on any issue or series of refunding bonds. Money in any such trust fund may be invested in direct obligations of the United States government, or obligations the principal of and interest on which are guaranteed by the United States government, or obligations of any authority or instrumentality of the United States government or in certificates of deposit issued by a bank or trust company located in this state, if such certificates are secured by a pledge of any of such obligations having any aggregate market value, exclusive of accrued interest, equal at least to the principal amount of the certificates so secured. Nothing in this subsection shall be construed as a limitation on the duration of any deposit in trust for the retirement of obligations being refunded but that have not matured and that

are not presently redeemable or, if presently redeemable, have not been called for redemption.

(h) All such bonds, refunding bonds and the interest coupons applicable thereto are hereby made and shall be construed to be negotiable instruments.

(i) The principal of and interest on any bonds issued by the authority may be secured by a pledge of the revenues and receipts out of which the same shall be made payable and may be secured by a mortgage or deed of trust covering all or any part of the projects from which the revenues or receipts so pledged may be derived, including any enlargements of and additions to any such projects thereafter made, or by an assignment and pledge of all or any part of the authority's interest in and rights under the leases, sale contracts or loan agreements relating to such projects, or any part thereof. The resolution under which the bonds are authorized to be issued and any such mortgage or deed of trust may contain any agreements and provisions respecting the maintenance of the projects covered thereby, the fixing and collection of rents or payments with respect to any projects or portions thereof covered by such resolution, mortgage or deed of trust, the creation and maintenance of special funds from such revenues and from the proceeds of such bonds and the rights and remedies available in the event of default, all as the board deems advisable and not in conflict with the provisions hereof. Each pledge, agreement, mortgage and deed of trust made for the benefit or security of any of the bonds of the authority shall continue to be effective until the principal of and interest on the bonds for the benefit of which the same were made have been fully paid. In the event of default in such payment or in any agreements of the authority made as a part of the contract under which the bonds were issued, whether contained in the proceedings authorizing the bonds or in any mortgage and deed of trust executed as security for the bonds, such payment or agreement may be enforced by suit, mandamus, the appointment of a receiver in equity or by foreclosure of any such mortgage and deed of trust, or any one (1) or more of the remedies listed in this part.

64-10-208.

The board is authorized to appoint an executive director and staff whose salaries shall be paid out of the revenues generated by the authority.

64-10-209.

(a) The board shall establish the time, date and place for its regular meetings. The chair or a majority of the voting members of the board, by petition, may call special meetings of the board.

(b) A majority of the entire voting membership of the board and not simply a majority of those members present shall be necessary to conduct business.

(c) The members of the board, executive committee or advisory committee, if an advisory committee is appointed, shall serve without compensation, but may be allowed necessary travel and other expenses while engaged in the business of the authority. All reimbursement for travel expenses shall be in accordance with the provisions of the comprehensive travel regulations as promulgated by the department of finance and administration and approved by the attorney general and reporter.

64-10-210. The counties that are members of the authority are hereby authorized and empowered to:

(1) Appropriate sufficient funds for the use of the authority amounts of money that their respective governing bodies, acting in their sole discretion, shall approve to be paid from the general fund of the respective county. County legislative bodies are empowered to levy and collect ad valorem taxes for such purposes, which are hereby declared to be for county public purposes; and

(2) Issue their bonds as provided in title 9, chapter 21, to obtain funds for the financing of public works by the authority pursuant to cooperative agreements with the authority.

64-10-211. In addition to the provisions of § 64-10-210, the authority may receive grants, appropriations, other contributions of funds, and real or personal property, from the state of Tennessee, the federal government, any other governmental entity or any nonprofit organization, individuals, companies, or corporations.

64-10-212. The financial affairs of the authority shall be conducted in accordance with state law and the procedures established by the comptroller of the treasury. The board may establish such bank accounts for the authority as the board deems appropriate and consistent with state law. The authority is authorized to invest any funds of the authority in any investment that would be an eligible investment of a county.

64-10-213.

(a) The board of directors of the authority shall cause an annual audit to be made of the books and records of the authority. Within thirty (30) days after receipt by the authority, a copy of the annual audit shall be filed with the board, and if the department of audit has not prepared the audit, with the comptroller of the treasury or comptroller's designee. The comptroller of the treasury, through the department of audit, shall be responsible for determining that such audits are prepared in accordance with generally accepted governmental auditing standards and that such audits meet the minimum standards prescribed by the comptroller of the treasury. The comptroller of the treasury shall promulgate such rules and regulations as are required to assure that the books and records are kept in accordance with generally accepted accounting principles and that audit standards prescribed by the comptroller of the treasury are met.

(b) These audits shall be prepared by either certified public accountants, public accountants, or by the department of audit. In the event the governing body of the authority shall fail or refuse to have the audit prepared, then the comptroller of the treasury may appoint a certified public accountant, or public accountant or direct the department of audit to prepare the audit, the cost of such audit to be paid by the authority.

(c) The comptroller of the treasury is authorized to modify the requirements for an audit as set out in this section when the activity, in the comptroller of the treasury's judgment, is not sufficient to justify the expenses of a complete audit. Furthermore, the comptroller of the treasury is authorized to direct the department of audit to make an audit or financial review of the books and records of the authority.

(d) The current operating financial statements of the authority, and any other pertinent information as required by the comptroller, or the comptroller's designee, shall be submitted annually with the copy of the annual audit, or upon request, to the comptroller, or the comptroller's designee.

64-10-214. The board may direct the disposal of the authority's obsolete or surplus property, except for land purchased under the provisions of the state's grant agreement, contract number 100/005-01-91, executed May 23, 1991, and any improvements thereon, which shall immediately be offered, at no cost, to the state. Any disposal of interest in land or improvements to real property purchased pursuant to the abovementioned grant agreement shall receive prior approval of the state building commission. Such disposal shall comply with the general law applicable to counties' sound business practices.

64-10-215.

(a) Any county in the eastern grand division not a member of the authority may become a member by:

(1) Notifying the board of its desire to become a member;

(2) Adopting a resolution by a two-thirds (2/3) vote of the county legislative body; and

(3) Contributing funds in an amount to be determined by the board, which shall not exceed the highest contribution by any county already a member as adjusted for inflation or deflation by the consumer price index, all cities average, published by the United States department of labor.

(b) Upon approval by the board and the county legislative body of the county seeking to become a member, the county shall become a member of the authority when the authority receives the necessary contribution. When a county is added as a member of the authority, the board shall cause the resolution of the county legislative body providing for addition of the county as a member of the authority to be filed with the secretary of state as an addendum. New members shall be entitled to membership on the board. The county mayor of any such county, or the county mayor's designee, shall become a member of the board for an initial term of office to be established by the board.

64-10-216. The board of directors of the authority shall report annually to the governing bodies of the various counties of the area. Such reports shall include a summary of all activities and accomplishments for the period, a copy of the annual audit prepared in accordance with § 64-10-213, and the proposed plans for the next year.

64-10-217. Upon the dissolution of the corporation, after all creditors of the corporation have been paid, its assets shall be distributed to one (1) or more organizations that qualify as exempt organizations under Section 501(c)(3) of the internal revenue code of 1986, or corresponding section of any future federal tax code, or shall be distributed to the federal government, or to a state or local government or an institution of the board of regents system for exclusively public purposes.

64-10-218.

The authority, its properties at any time owned by it and the income and revenues derived from such properties shall be exempt from all state, county and municipal taxation. All bonds, notes and other obligations issued by the authority and the income from such bonds, notes, and other obligations shall be exempt from all state, county and municipal taxation, except inheritance, transfer and estate taxes or except as otherwise provided by state law. Bonds issued by the authority shall be deemed to be securities issued by a public instrumentality or a political subdivision of the state.

64-10-219.

(a) Any county, city or utility district may take all actions under this part by resolution of its governing body. Any county, city or utility district shall have all powers necessary in order to further the purposes of this part.

(b) Any county, city or utility district may enter into agreements with the authority for the orderly transfer of all or any part of its system and to enter into an agreement for the authority to assume, to pay or to refund bonds, notes or other obligations issued by a county, city or utility district entered into by the county, city or utility district to acquire, construct or equip all or any part of a system.

(c) Any county, city or utility district is authorized to advance, donate or lend money to the authority and to provide that funds available to it for a system shall be paid to the authority.

(d) Any county, city or utility district shall have the same right to enter into any agreement with the authority that the wastewater board deems necessary to carry out the purposes of this part as a county, city or utility district has to enter into similar agreements with wastewater treatment authorities as provided by title 68, chapter 221, part 6.

64-10-220. Nothing contained in this part shall be construed as a restriction or a limitation upon any powers that a county, city or utility district might otherwise have under any laws of this state, but shall be construed as cumulative of and supplemental to any such powers. No proceedings, notice or approval shall be required with respect to the issuance of bonds, notes or other obligations of the authority or any instrument as security for the bonds, notes or other obligations except as provided in this part, any law to the contrary notwithstanding; provided, that nothing in this section shall be construed to deprive the state and its governmental subdivisions of their respective police powers or to impair any power of any official or agency of the state and its governmental subdivisions that may be otherwise provided by law.

64-10-221. For the purposes of this part and title 4, chapter 31, the authority shall be deemed to be a local government unit and shall be eligible for the same grants, loans, and other assistance, and subject to the same obligations and requirements imposed by law related to such grants, loans, and assistance as any other local government unit.

64-10-222. This part is remedial in nature and shall be liberally construed to effect its purpose and the powers granted in this part may be exercised without regard to requirements, restrictions or procedural provisions contained in any other law or charter except as expressly provided in this part.

SECTION 2. If any provision of this act or the application thereof to any person or circumstance is held invalid, such invalidity shall not affect other provisions or applications of the act which can be given effect without the invalid provision or application, and to that end the provisions of this act are declared to be severable.

Effective date 5/20/2013

SECTION 3. This act shall take effect upon becoming a law, the public welfare requiring it.

PUBLIC CHAPTER NO. 475

PUBLIC CHAPTER NO. 475

SENATE BILL NO. 595

By Johnson, Tracy, Ketron, Yager, Bell, Bowling, Crowe, Dickerson, Green, Haile, Kelsey, Norris, Stevens, Watson, Mr. Speaker Ramsey

Substituted for: House Bill No. 500

By Casada, Durham, Rich, Tidwell, Weaver, Rogers, Butt, Alexander, Dean, Halford, Ryan Williams, Dale Carr, Lollar, Timothy Hill, John Deberry, Ragan, Powers, Lundberg, Sexton, McManus, McDaniel, Eldridge, Sparks, Coley, Womick, Hawk, Shipley, Swann, Doss, Forgety, Lamberth, Travis, Marsh, Mark White, Calfee, Keisling, Spivey, Faison, Littleton, Floyd, Carter, Dunn, Goins, Holt, Hall, Evans

AN ACT to amend Tennessee Code Annotated, Title 8, Chapter 3, relative to creating the office of the repealer.

BE IT ENACTED BY THE GENERAL ASSEMBLY OF THE STATE OF TENNESSEE:

3-12-109 SECTION 1. (a) There is created the office of the repealer within the office of legal services created pursuant to § 3-12-101. The director of legal services shall serve as the administrator of the office of the repealer. The research analysts of the house of representatives and of the senate shall assist the office of legal services in performing the functions of the office of the repealer.

(b) In order to assist the chairs of the standing committees, and other members of the general assembly, it shall be the duty of the office of the repealer to:

(1) Solicit and receive suggestions and supporting information concerning state statutes, uncodified public acts, or rules that may be anachronistic, obsolete, defective, duplicative, contradictory, unnecessary or incomprehensible;

(2) Review and evaluate systematically such suggestions and supporting information;

(3) Identify specific state statutes, uncodified public acts, or rules that may, in fact, be anachronistic, obsolete, defective, duplicative, contradictory, unnecessary or incomprehensible and that may, therefore, be appropriate for legislative consideration of repeal, modification or revision; and

(4) Report findings and recommendations annually, beginning December 1, 2014, to the speaker of the senate, the speaker of the house of representatives, and the chairs of the standing committees.

(c) In consultation with the director of legislative information systems, the office of the repealer shall establish an online capability to solicit and receive suggestions and supporting information pursuant to subdivision (b)(1) above.

Effective date 7/1/2013

SECTION 2. For purposes of implementing Section 1(c), this act shall take effect upon becoming law, the public welfare requiring it. For all other purposes, this act shall take effect on July 1, 2013.

PUBLIC CHAPTER NO. 476

PUBLIC CHAPTER NO. 476

SENATE BILL NO. 519

By Burks, Bowling, Stevens

Substituted for: House Bill No. 549

By Curtiss, Eldridge, Faison

AN ACT to amend Tennessee Code Annotated, Title 50, Chapter 6, relative to workers' compensation exemptions.

BE IT ENACTED BY THE GENERAL ASSEMBLY OF THE STATE OF TENNESSEE:

50-6-903 SECTION 1. Tennessee Code Annotated, Section 50-6-903, is amended by adding the following language as a new, appropriately designated subsection:

(c)(1) A construction services provider who is an individual and who does not meet the criteria established in subsection (a), but who is a member of a recognized religious sect or division and is an adherent of established tenets or teachers of such sect or division by reason of which such construction services provider is conscientiously opposed to acceptance of the benefits provided by this chapter may apply for an exemption from § 50-6-902(a); provided, however, that no more than five (5) individuals associated with one business entity may be exempt from § 50-6-902(a).

(2) Any applicant applying for an exemption from § 50-6-902(a) pursuant to subdivision (c)(1) shall provide an affidavit from the leader of the recognized religious sect or division stating that the individual filing the application for an exemption is a member of the recognized religious sect or division and is exempt, as evidenced by the Internal Revenue Service Form 4029, or similar form used by the internal revenue service. The leader of the recognized religious sect or division shall notify the secretary of state and department, in writing, if the member of the recognized religious sect or division who obtains an exemption from § 50-6-902(a) leaves or withdraws membership from the recognized religious sect or division.

(3) Each individual employee of a construction services provider who meets the religious exemption requirements pursuant to this subsection (c) shall pay the fees set out in § 50-6-912(a)(1) and (a)(2). Any collected fees shall be deposited into the employee misclassification education and enforcement fund, pursuant to § 50-6-913.

50-6-904 SECTION 2. Tennessee Code Annotated, Section 50-6-904(a)(F), is amended by deleting the subdivision in its entirety and substituting instead the following:

(F) The federal employer identification number issued to the applicant if a sole proprietor or a business entity for which the applicant is an officer, member, partner or owner seeking exemption pursuant to § 50-6-903, and the last four (4) digits of the applicant's social security number; provided, however, if an applicant seeks an exemption pursuant to § 50-6-903(c), the applicant may provide the last four (4) digits of a control number issued to the applicant by the social security administration instead of the last four (4) digits of the applicant's social security number;

50-6-904 SECTION 3. Tennessee Code Annotated, Section 50-6-904(a)(2), is amended by adding the following new subdivision thereto:

(J) If the construction services provider is applying for an exemption pursuant to the criteria set out in § 50-6-903(c), the provider shall submit a copy of an approved Internal Revenue Service Form 4029 or similar form used by the internal revenue service, to show that an application for exemption from social security and Medicare taxes and waiver of benefits has been approved for such provider applying for an exemption pursuant to this part.

Effective date 1/1/2014 SECTION 4. For purposes of promulgating rules and regulations, this act shall take effect upon becoming a law, the public welfare requiring it. For all other purposes, this act shall take effect January 1, 2014.

PUBLIC CHAPTER NO. 477

PUBLIC CHAPTER NO. 477

SENATE BILL NO. 491

By Campfield, Ford

Substituted for: House Bill No. 412

By Armstrong, Fitzhugh, Dunn, Gloria Johnson

AN ACT to amend Tennessee Code Annotated, Title 62, Chapter 4, Part 1, relative to manicurists.

BE IT ENACTED BY THE GENERAL ASSEMBLY OF THE STATE OF TENNESSEE:

62-4-125 SECTION 1. Tennessee Code Annotated, Section 62-4-125, is amended by adding the following language as a new subsection:

(e) A manicurist may provide manicuring services to an ill, disabled or homebound individual, or to such individual's caregiver, custodian or guardian, in the individual's residence.

Effective date 5/20/2013 SECTION 2. This act shall take effect upon becoming a law, the public welfare requiring it.

PUBLIC CHAPTER NO. 478

PUBLIC CHAPTER NO. 478

SENATE BILL NO. 439

By Henry, Overbey

Substituted for: House Bill No. 209

By Sargent, McDaniel

AN ACT to amend Tennessee Code Annotated, Section 4-20-301, relative to the Douglas Henry state museum commission.

BE IT ENACTED BY THE GENERAL ASSEMBLY OF THE STATE OF TENNESSEE:

4-20-301 SECTION 1. Tennessee Code Annotated, Section 4-20-301(b), is amended by deleting the subsection in its entirety and by substituting instead the following:

(b)(1) Two (2) members of the commission shall be appointed by the speaker of the house of representatives. These members shall serve four-year terms.

(2) Two (2) members of the commission shall be appointed by the speaker of the senate. These members shall serve four-year terms.

Effective date 5/20/2013 SECTION 2. This act shall take effect upon becoming a law, the public welfare requiring it.

PUBLIC CHAPTER NO. 479

PUBLIC CHAPTER NO. 479

SENATE BILL NO. 251

By Green

Substituted for: House Bill No. 431

By Pitts, Evans

AN ACT to amend Tennessee Code Annotated, Title 40; Title 55, Chapter 10 and Title 55, Chapter 12, relative to noncompliance with the Tennessee Financial Responsibility Law of 1977.

BE IT ENACTED BY THE GENERAL ASSEMBLY OF THE STATE OF TENNESSEE:

55-12-139 SECTION 1. Tennessee Code Annotated, Section 55-12-139, is amended by deleting subsection (c) and substituting the following:

(c)(1) It is an offense to fail to provide evidence of financial responsibility pursuant to this section.

(2) Except as provided in subdivision (c)(3), a violation of subdivision (c)(1) is a Class C misdemeanor punishable only by a fine of not more than one hundred dollars ($100).

(3)(A) A violation of subdivision (c)(1) is a Class A misdemeanor, if a person is not in compliance with the financial responsibility requirements of this chapter at the time of an accident resulting in bodily injury or death and such person was at fault for the accident.

(B) For purposes of subdivision (3)(A), a person is at fault for an accident if the person acted with criminal negligence, as defined in § 39-11-106, in the operation of such person's motor vehicle.

Effective date 7/1/2013 SECTION 2. This act shall take effect July 1, 2013, the public welfare requiring it.

PUBLIC CHAPTER NO. 480

PUBLIC CHAPTER NO. 480

SENATE BILL NO. 182

By Norris

Substituted for: House Bill No. 176

By McCormick

6-51-115; 67-4-2301 – 2308; 67-4-2401 – 2410; 67-4-2501 – 2508; 67-4-2701 – 2712; 67-6-102, 103, 201, 202, 203, 205, 206, 209, 217, 219, 221, 226, 227, 313, 322, 329, 349, 385, 386, 407, 408, 504, 528, 536, 539, 601, 702, 704, 706, 710, 712, 714, 715, 716, 901, 902, 904, 905, 906, 907

AN ACT to amend Tennessee Code Annotated, Title 67, and Chapter 602 of the Public Acts of 2007 and Chapter 530 of the Public Acts of 2009 and Chapter 72 of the Public Acts of 2011, relative to taxation.

BE IT ENACTED BY THE GENERAL ASSEMBLY OF THE STATE OF TENNESSEE:

SECTION 1. Section 187 of Chapter 602 of the Public Acts of 2007, as amended by Chapter 530 of the Public Acts of 2009, and as further amended by Chapter 72 of the Public Acts of 2011, is amended by deleting the language:

> Sections 127 through 178 of this act shall take effect on July 1, 2013, the public welfare requiring it.

and by substituting instead the language:

> Sections 127 through 178 of this act shall take effect on July 1, 2015, the public welfare requiring it.

67-2-110

SECTION 2. Tennessee Code Annotated, Section 67-2-110(a), is amended by adding at the end of the subsection the following new sentence:

> Additionally, the trustee of a trust, which is treated under 26 U.S.C. §§ 671-678 as owned by one grantor or one other person and which does not obtain a taxpayer identification number, as permitted under the Internal Revenue Code and accompanying regulations, shall not be required to file returns under this chapter nor to pay the tax, but shall report the total amount of income received by the trustee to the resident grantor or other person, who shall file the return and pay the tax levied by this chapter.

Effective date 5/20/2013

SECTION 3. This act shall take effect upon becoming a law, the public welfare requiring it.

PUBLIC CHAPTER NO. 481

PUBLIC CHAPTER NO. 481

SENATE BILL NO. 69

By Burks, Massey

Substituted for: House Bill No. 30

By Sexton

AN ACT to amend Tennessee Code Annotated, Title 39; Title 40; Title 54; Title 55 and Title 62, relative to motor vehicles.

BE IT ENACTED BY THE GENERAL ASSEMBLY OF THE STATE OF TENNESSEE:

55-5-131 SECTION 1. Tennessee Code Annotated, Title 55, Chapter 5, Part 1, is amended by adding the following language as a new, appropriately designated section:

55-5-1__.

(a) There is created the accurate vehicle identification number (VIN) reporting advisory committee, to be composed of twelve (12) members as follows:

(1) One (1) member of the senate to be appointed by the speaker of the senate;

(2) One (1) member of the house of representatives to be appointed by the speaker of the house of representatives;

(3) The executive director of the Tennessee Association of Chiefs of Police or the director's designee;

(4) The executive director of the Tennessee Sheriffs' Association or the director's designee;

(5) The executive director of the district attorneys general conference or the director's designee;

(6) The commissioner of the department of revenue or the commissioner's designee;

(7) The commissioner of the department of safety or the commissioner's designee;

(8) The president of the Tennessee Scrap Recyclers Association or the president's designee;

(9) A representative from an automobile dismantler's company, to be appointed by the speaker of the house of representatives;

(10) A representative from the automobile auction industry, to be appointed by the speaker of the senate;

(11) The executive director of the Tennessee Automotive Association or the director's designee; and

(12) The executive director of the Tennessee Independent Automobile Dealers Association or the director's designee.

(b) The accurate vehicle identification number (VIN) reporting advisory committee shall make recommendations regarding the creation of an automated, real-time system to assist private industries, law enforcement agencies, and the state in verifying the accuracy of VINs of motor vehicles that are purchased for parts, dismantling or scrap. The committee shall also study the cost and feasibility of making a system available for access and use to motor vehicle dismantlers, recyclers, scrap metal processors, state and local law enforcement agencies, the department of safety, and the department of revenue.

(c) The committee shall be convened by the member with the most years of continuous service in the general assembly, and at its first meeting shall elect a chair, vice chair, and other officers as the committee deems necessary.

(d) The committee shall only meet on days when the house of representatives and the senate are otherwise meeting in committee.

(e) The members of the committee shall serve without compensation and travel expenses.

(f) The committee shall report its findings and recommendations to the governor, speaker of the senate, speaker of the house of representatives, and comptroller of the treasury no later than April 1, 2014, at which time the committee shall cease to exist.

Effective date 5/20/2013

SECTION 2. This act shall take effect upon becoming a law, the public welfare requiring it.

PUBLIC CHAPTER NO. 482

PUBLIC CHAPTER NO. 482

SENATE BILL NO. 64

By Tracy

Substituted for: House Bill No. 1030

By Dean

AN ACT to amend Tennessee Code Annotated, Title 54, relative to transportation infrastructures.

BE IT ENACTED BY THE GENERAL ASSEMBLY OF THE STATE OF TENNESSEE:

SECTION 1.

(a)(1) Notwithstanding any provision of law to the contrary, the bridge on U.S. Highway 70 in Cumberland County is hereby designated as the "Sgt. Morgan W. Strader Memorial Bridge" in recognition of the life of valor and death in combat of Sgt. Morgan W. Strader, United States Marine Corps, who made the ultimate sacrifice on November 12, 2004, while serving his country in Fallujah, Iraq.

(2) The department of transportation is directed to erect suitable signs or affix suitable markers designating the bridge described in subdivision (a)(1) as the "Sgt. Morgan W. Strader Memorial Bridge." The cost of such signage shall be funded in accordance with Tennessee Code Annotated, Section 54-1-133.

(3) The erection of signs shall be within the guidelines prescribed by the Manual on Uniform Traffic Control Devices.

(4) This subsection shall become operative only if the federal highway administrator advises the commissioner of transportation in writing that the provisions of this subsection shall not render Tennessee in violation of federal laws and regulations and subject to penalties prescribed therein.

(b)(1) Notwithstanding any provision of law to the contrary, the segment of U.S. Highway 45 in Chester County from Estes Church of Christ at Montezuma Road northward to the corporate limits of the City of Henderson is hereby designated the "Dan Cole Memorial Highway" in recognition of the life of valor of Chief Warrant Officer 4 Daniel Cole, United States Army, one of Tennessee's finest citizens.

(2) The department of transportation is directed to erect suitable signs or to affix suitable markers designating the segment of U.S. Highway 45 described in subdivision (b)(1) as the "Dan Cole Memorial Highway". The cost of such signage shall be funded in accordance with Tennessee Code Annotated, Section 54-1-133.

(3) The erection of such signs shall be within the guidelines prescribed by the Manual on Uniform Traffic Control Devices.

(4) This subsection shall become operative only if the federal highway administrator advises the commissioner of transportation in writing that the provisions of this subsection shall not render Tennessee in violation of federal laws and regulations and subject to penalties prescribed therein.

(5) The appellation "Dan Cole Memorial Highway" provided for in this subsection is for honorary purposes only and nothing contained herein shall be construed as requiring the alteration of any address, or the governmental system for assigning addresses, in any county, municipality, or other governmental entity affected by this subsection.

(6) Nothing contained in this subsection shall be construed as requiring the alteration of any previously named segments of U.S. Highway 45 described in subdivision (b)(1).

PUBLIC CHAPTER NO. 482 (cont'd)

(c)(1) Notwithstanding any provision of law to the contrary, the parallel bridges (Bridge No. 94-SR397-0015 and Bridge No. 94-SR397-0016) that span the Harpeth River on State Route 397 (Mack Hatcher Memorial Parkway) at mile marker 6.82 and east of U.S. Highway 431/State Route 106 (Hillsboro Road) in Williamson County are hereby jointly designated as the "Matthew James Bergman Bridge" to honor the memory of PO2 Cryptologic Technician Interpretive Matthew James Bergman, United States Navy, a remarkable young man and one of Tennessee's most heroic citizens.

(2) The department of transportation is directed to erect suitable signs or to affix suitable markers designating the parallel bridges described in subdivision (c)(1) as the "Matthew James Bergman Bridge". The cost of such signage shall be funded in accordance with Tennessee Code Annotated, Section 54-1-133.

(3) The erection of such signs shall be within the guidelines prescribed by the Manual on Uniform Traffic Control Devices.

(4) This subsection shall become operative only if the federal highway administrator advises the commissioner of transportation in writing that the provisions of this subsection shall not render Tennessee in violation of federal laws and regulations and subject to penalties prescribed therein.

(d)(1) Notwithstanding any provision of law to the contrary, the bridge spanning the Harpeth River on U.S. Highway 431/State Route 106 (Hillsboro Road) north of State Route 397 (Mack Hatcher Memorial Parkway) and near Fulton Greer Lane is hereby designated the "Robert Douglas Marlin Memorial Bridge" in recognition of the life of valor and death in combat of Private First Class Robert Douglas Marlin, United States Marine Corps, one of Tennessee's most heroic citizens.

(2) The department of transportation is directed to erect suitable signs or to affix suitable markers designating the bridge described in subdivision (d)(1) as the "Robert Douglas Marlin Memorial Bridge". The cost of such signage shall be funded in accordance with Tennessee Code Annotated, Section 54-1-133.

(3) The erection of such signs shall be within the guidelines prescribed by the Manual on Uniform Traffic Control Devices.

(4) This subsection shall become operative only if the federal highway administrator advises the commissioner of transportation in writing that the provisions of this subsection shall not render Tennessee in violation of federal laws and regulations and subject to penalties prescribed therein.

(e)(1) Notwithstanding any provision of law to the contrary, the bridge spanning Flat Creek on Rutledge Pike (U.S. Highway 11W/State Route 1) in Knox County is hereby designated the "Sgt. Jesse J. Coffey Memorial Bridge" in recognition of the life of valor and death in combat of Sergeant Jesse J. Coffey, United States Army, one of Tennessee's most heroic citizens.

(2) The department of transportation is directed to erect suitable signs or to affix suitable markers designating the bridge described in subdivision (e)(1) as the "Sgt. Jesse J. Coffey Memorial Bridge". The cost of such signage shall be funded in accordance with Tennessee Code Annotated, Section 54-1-133.

(3) The erection of such signs shall be within the guidelines prescribed by the Manual on Uniform Traffic Control Devices.

(4) This subsection shall become operative only if the federal highway administrator advises the commissioner of transportation in writing that the provisions of this subsection shall not render Tennessee in violation of federal laws and regulations and subject to penalties prescribed therein.

(f)(1) Notwithstanding any provision of law to the contrary, the segment of State Route 58 (which is commonly referred to as Highway 58) in Hamilton County, Tennessee, from such route's intersection with Harrison Bay Road northward to such route's intersection with Mahan Gap Road is hereby designated the "Shane M. Daughetee Memorial Highway" as a lasting tribute to Shane M. Daughetee, who served with distinction as a member of the Highway 58 Volunteer Fire Department in Hamilton County, before losing his life on January 26, 2007, while responding to a fire call.

(2) The department of transportation is directed to erect suitable signs or to affix suitable markers designating the segment of State Route 58 described in subdivision (f)(1) as the "Shane M. Daughetee Memorial Highway". Such signs or markers shall be erected so as to be visible to motorists in the northbound and southbound lanes of State Route 58. The cost of such signage shall be funded in accordance with Tennessee Code Annotated, Section 54-1-133.

(3) The erection of such signs shall be within the guidelines prescribed by the Manual on Uniform Traffic Control Devices.

(4) This subsection shall become operative only if the federal highway administrator advises the commissioner of transportation in writing that the provisions of this subsection shall not render Tennessee in violation of federal laws and regulations and subject to penalties prescribed therein.

(5) The appellation "Shane M. Daughetee Memorial Highway" provided for in this subsection is for honorary purposes only and nothing contained herein shall be construed as requiring the alteration of any address, or the governmental system for assigning addresses, in any county, municipality, or other governmental entity affected by this subsection.

(6) Nothing in this subsection shall be construed as requiring the alteration of any previously named segments of State Route 58 described in subdivision (f)(1).

(g)(1) Notwithstanding any provision of law to the contrary, the segment of James White Parkway from the South Knoxville Bridge that spans the Tennessee River to Moody Avenue is hereby designated the "Capt. Marcus Ray Alford, Sr. Memorial Highway" in recognition of the life of valor and death in combat of Captain Marcus Ray Alford, Sr., United States Army, who lost his life on February 21, 2010, in a helicopter crash while serving his country in Iraq.

(2) The department of transportation is directed to erect suitable signs or to affix suitable markers designating the segment described in subdivision (g)(1) as the "Capt. Marcus Ray Alford, Sr. Memorial Highway". The cost of such signage shall be funded in accordance with Tennessee Code Annotated, Section 54-1-133.

(3) The erection of such signs shall be within the guidelines prescribed by the Manual on Uniform Traffic Control Devices.

(4) This subsection shall become operative only if the federal highway administrator advises the commissioner of transportation in writing that the provisions of this subsection shall not render Tennessee in violation of federal laws and regulations and subject to penalties prescribed therein.

(5) The appellation "Capt. Marcus Ray Alford, Sr. Memorial Highway" provided for in this subsection is for honorary purposes only and nothing contained herein shall be construed as requiring the alteration of any address, or the governmental system for assigning addresses, in any county, municipality, or other governmental entity affected by this subsection.

(6) Nothing in this subsection shall be construed as requiring the alteration of any previously named segments of James White Parkway described in subdivision (g)(1).

(h)(1) Notwithstanding any provision of law to the contrary, the bridge spanning the Tennessee River on Interstate 75 in Loudon County, Tennessee, is hereby designated the "Sgt. Mitchell W. Stout Memorial Bridge" in recognition of the life of valor and death in combat of Sgt. Mitchell W. Stout, United States Army, who made the ultimate sacrifice on March 12, 1970, while courageously protecting his fellow soldiers from a grenade blast at Khe Gio Bridge during the Vietnam War.

(2) The department of transportation is directed to erect suitable signs or to affix suitable markers designating the bridge described in subdivision (h)(1) as the "Sgt. Mitchell W. Stout Memorial Bridge". The cost of such signage shall be funded in accordance with Tennessee Code Annotated, Section 54-1-133.

(3) The erection of such signs shall be within the guidelines prescribed by the Manual on Uniform Traffic Control Devices.

(4) This subsection shall become operative only if the federal highway administrator advises the commissioner of transportation in writing that the provisions of this subsection shall not render Tennessee in violation of federal laws and regulations and subject to penalties prescribed therein.

(i)(1) Notwithstanding any provision of law to the contrary, the bridge spanning Goose Creek on State Route 67 in Mountain City, Tennessee, located west of such route's intersection with U.S. Highway 421 is hereby designated the "Spc. Frederick Green Memorial Bridge" to honor the memory of a remarkable young man who lost his life in the tragedy at Fort Hood, Texas, on November 5, 2009.

(2) The department of transportation is directed to erect suitable signs or to affix suitable markers designating the bridge described in subdivision (i)(1) as the "Spc. Frederick Green Memorial Bridge." The cost of such signage shall be funded in accordance with Tennessee Code Annotated, Section 54-1-133.

(3) The erection of such signs shall be within the guidelines prescribed by the Manual on Uniform Traffic Control Devices.

(4) This subsection shall become operative only if the federal highway administrator advises the commissioner of transportation in writing that the provisions of this subsection shall not render Tennessee in violation of federal laws and regulations and subject to penalties prescribed therein.

(j)(1) Notwithstanding any provision of law to the contrary, the segment of the highway commonly known as Amnicola Highway (which highway includes segments of State Route 58) in Chattanooga, Tennessee, from Curtain Pole Road to Crutchfield Street is hereby designated the "Officer Richard Alexander Memorial Highway" as a lasting tribute to the late Richard Alexander, who served as a police officer with the Chattanooga Police Department for twenty-two years before losing his life on October 5, 2000, while on duty.

(2) The department of transportation is directed to erect suitable signs or to affix suitable markers designating the segment of Amnicola Highway described in subdivision (j)(1) as the "Officer Richard Alexander Memorial Highway". The cost of such signage shall be funded in accordance with Tennessee Code Annotated, Section 54-1-133.

(3) The erection of such signs shall be within the guidelines prescribed by the Manual on Uniform Traffic Control Devices.

(4) This subsection shall become operative only if the federal highway administrator advises the commissioner of transportation in writing that the provisions of this subsection shall not render Tennessee in violation of federal laws and regulations and subject to penalties prescribed therein.

(5) The appellation "Officer Richard Alexander Memorial Highway" provided for in this subsection is for honorary purposes only and nothing contained herein shall be construed as requiring the alteration of any address, or the governmental system for assigning addresses, in any county, municipality, or other governmental entity affected by this subsection.

(6) Nothing in this subsection shall be construed as requiring the alteration of any previously named segments of Amnicola Highway described in subdivision (j)(1).

(k)(1) Notwithstanding any provision of law to the contrary, the segment of Interstate 40 in Henderson County, Tennessee, from mile marker 101 to mile marker 104 is hereby designated the "Thomas Birthel Wilson Memorial Highway" to honor the memory of this beloved resident of Henderson County who courageously served his country during World War II and who ably served his fellow citizens as an employee of the Tennessee Department of Transportation before losing his life while working on a project on this interstate.

(2) The department of transportation is directed to erect suitable signs or to affix suitable markers designating the segment of Interstate 40 described in subdivision (k)(1) as the "Thomas Birthel Wilson Memorial Highway."

(3) The erection of such signs shall be within the guidelines prescribed by the Manual on Uniform Traffic Control Devices.

(4) This subsection shall become operative only if the federal highway administrator advises the commissioner of transportation in writing that the provisions of this subsection shall not render Tennessee in violation of federal laws and regulations and subject to penalties prescribed therein.

(5) The appellation "Thomas Birthel Wilson Memorial Highway" provided for in this subsection is for honorary purposes only and nothing contained herein shall be construed as requiring the alteration of any address, or the governmental system for assigning addresses, in any county, municipality, or other governmental entity affected by this subsection.

(l)(1) Notwithstanding any provision of law to the contrary, the segment of U.S. Highway 25/State Route 63 (Cougar Lane) in Campbell County that lies entirely within the school zone in front of Campbell County Comprehensive High School is hereby designated the "Ken Bruce Memorial Highway" as a lasting tribute to this beloved resident of Campbell County, who ably served his fellow citizens as vice principal of the high school and who lost his life in the tragic shooting at the high school on November 8, 2005.

(2) The department of transportation is directed to erect suitable signs or to affix suitable markers designating the segment of U.S. Highway 25/State Route 63 described in subdivision (l)(1) as the "Ken Bruce Memorial Highway".

(3) The erection of such signs shall be within the guidelines prescribed by the Manual on Uniform Traffic Control Devices.

(4) This subsection shall become operative only if the federal highway administrator advises the commissioner of transportation in writing that the provisions of this subsection shall not render Tennessee in violation of federal laws and regulations and subject to penalties prescribed therein.

(5) The appellation "Ken Bruce Memorial Highway" provided for in this subsection is for honorary purposes only and nothing contained herein shall be construed as requiring the alteration of any address, or the governmental system for assigning addresses, in any county, municipality, or other governmental entity affected by this subsection.

(m)(1) Notwithstanding any provision of law to the contrary, the segment of Pellissippi Parkway (which parkway includes segments of State Scenic Route 162 and Interstate 140) in Knox County, Tennessee, from the Solway Road Exit to the South Northshore Drive Exit is hereby designated the "Maria Compere Memorial Highway" to honor the memory of this beloved resident of Knoxville, Tennessee, whose boundless dedication to the city's beautification led her to found the Knoxville Green Association, which organized the planting of more than 1 million daffodils along Pellissippi Parkway for over two decades.

(2) The department of transportation is directed to erect suitable signs or to affix suitable markers designating the segment described in subdivision (m)(1) as the "Maria Compere Memorial Highway".

(3) The erection of such signs shall be within the guidelines prescribed by the Manual on Uniform Traffic Control Devices.

(4) This subsection shall become operative only if the federal highway administrator advises the commissioner of transportation in writing that the provisions of this subsection shall not render Tennessee in violation of federal laws and regulations and subject to penalties prescribed therein.

(5) The appellation "Maria Compere Memorial Highway" provided for in this subsection is for honorary purposes only and nothing contained herein shall be construed as requiring the alteration of any address, or the governmental system for assigning addresses, in any county, municipality, or other governmental entity affected by this subsection.

SECTION 2. (a) Notwithstanding any provision of law to the contrary, the bridge currently under construction on State Route 30 (College Street), in the City of Spencer, which will serve as an overpass for the expansion of State Route 111, is hereby designated the "Veterans Memorial Bridge" in honor of the many brave sons and daughters of Tennessee who have served this great country in the United States Armed Forces.

(b) The department of transportation is directed to erect suitable signs or to affix suitable markers designating the bridge currently under construction on State Route 30 (College Street) in the City of Spencer described in subsection (a) as the "Veterans Memorial Bridge".

(c) The erection of such signs shall be within the guidelines prescribed by the Manual on Uniform Traffic Control Devices.

(d) This section shall become operative only if the federal highway administrator advises the commissioner of transportation in writing that the provisions of this section shall not render Tennessee in violation of federal laws and regulations and subject to penalties prescribed therein.

(e) This section shall become operative only if the cost of the manufacture and installation of such signs is paid to the department of transportation from non-state funds within one (1) year of the effective date of this act. Such payment shall be made prior to any expenditure by the state for the manufacture or installation of such signs. The department shall return any unused portion of the estimated cost to the person or entity paying for such signs within thirty (30) days of the erection of such signs. If the actual cost exceeds the estimated cost, an amount equal to the difference in such costs shall be remitted to the department in non-state funds within thirty (30) days of the sponsoring person or entity receiving an itemized invoice of the actual cost from the department.

SECTION 3. (a) Notwithstanding any provision of law to the contrary, the bridge spanning the Elk River on U.S. Highway 321/State Route 159 that is near mile marker 7 and the intersection of such route with Poga Road in Elk Mills, Tennessee, is hereby designated as the "E.C. Miller Bridge" to honor the memory of this talented banjo player and beloved resident of Carter County.

(b) The department of transportation is directed to erect suitable signs or affix suitable markers designating the bridge described in subsection (a) as the "E.C. Miller Bridge".

(c) The erection of signs shall be within the guidelines prescribed by the Manual on Uniform Traffic Control Devices.

(d) This section shall become operative only if the federal highway administrator advises the commissioner of transportation in writing that the provisions of this section shall not render Tennessee in violation of federal laws and regulations and subject to penalties prescribed therein.

(e) This section shall become operative only if the cost of the manufacture and installation of such signs is paid to the department of transportation from non-state funds within one (1) year of the effective date of this act. Such payment shall be made prior to any expenditure by the state for the manufacture or installation of such signs. The department shall return any unused portion of the estimated cost to the person or entity paying for such signs within thirty (30) days of the erection of such signs. If the actual cost exceeds the estimated cost, an amount equal to the difference in such costs shall be remitted to the department in non-state funds within thirty (30) days of the sponsoring person or entity receiving an itemized invoice of the actual cost from the department.

SECTION 4. (a) Notwithstanding any provision of law to the contrary, the bridge spanning Dyers Creek on U.S. Highway 79 located near Stewart County High School between Robertson Hill Road and Durwachter Road in Dover, Tennessee, is hereby designated the "Dr. Robert Henry Lee Bridge" in appreciation of one of the City of Dover's distinctive citizens and an even more accomplished human being.

(b) The department of transportation is directed to erect suitable signs or to affix suitable markers designating the bridge described in subsection (a) as the "Dr. Robert Henry Lee Bridge".

(c) The erection of such signs shall be within the guidelines prescribed by the Manual on Uniform Traffic Control Devices.

(d) This section shall become operative only if the federal highway administrator advises the commissioner of transportation in writing that the provisions of this section shall not render Tennessee in violation of federal laws and regulations and subject to penalties prescribed therein.

(e) This section shall become operative only if the cost of the manufacture and installation of such signs is paid to the department of transportation from non-state funds

within one (1) year of the effective date of this act. Such payment shall be made prior to any expenditure by the state for the manufacture or installation of such signs. The department shall return any unused portion of the estimated cost to the person or entity paying for such signs within thirty (30) days of the erection of such signs. If the actual cost exceeds the estimated cost, an amount equal to the difference in such costs shall be remitted to the department in non-state funds within thirty (30) days of the sponsoring person or entity receiving an itemized invoice of the actual cost from the department.

SECTION 5. (a) Notwithstanding any provision of law to the contrary, the segment of State Route 79 from the Dover Bridge to Joiner Hollow Road in Stewart County, Tennessee, is hereby designated the "Van Lewis Riggins, Sr. Memorial Highway" to honor the memory of this exemplary resident of Stewart County, who made significant contributions to education in the county and statewide as a high school teacher and principal, and superintendent of schools.

(b) The department of transportation is directed to erect suitable signs or to affix suitable markers designating the segment described in subsection (a) as the "Van Lewis Riggins, Sr. Memorial Highway".

(c) The erection of such signs shall be within the guidelines prescribed by the Manual on Uniform Traffic Control Devices.

(d) This section shall become operative only if the federal highway administrator advises the commissioner of transportation in writing that the provisions of this section shall not render Tennessee in violation of federal laws and regulations and subject to penalties prescribed therein.

(e) This section shall become operative only if the cost of the manufacture and installation of such signs is paid to the department of transportation from non-state funds within one (1) year of the effective date of this act. Such payment shall be made prior to any expenditure by the state for the manufacture or installation of such signs. The department shall return any unused portion of the estimated cost to the person or entity paying for such signs within thirty (30) days of the erection of such signs. If the actual cost exceeds the estimated cost, an amount equal to the difference in such costs shall be remitted to the department in non-state funds within thirty (30) days of the sponsoring person or entity receiving an itemized invoice of the actual cost from the department.

(f) The appellation "Van Lewis Riggins, Sr. Memorial Highway" provided for in this section is for honorary purposes only and nothing contained in this section shall be construed as requiring the alteration of any address, or the governmental system for assigning addresses, in any county, municipality, or other governmental entity affected by this section.

(g) Nothing in this section shall be construed as requiring the alteration of any previously named segments of State Route 79 described in subsection (a).

SECTION 6. (a) Notwithstanding any other provision of law to the contrary, the bridge located on State Route 57, approximately two (2) miles east of U.S. Highway 45, in McNairy County is hereby designated the "Buford 'Peck' White Memorial Bridge" in recognition of the life of Buford "Peck" White, who was a beloved husband and father of seven children before losing his life on June 7, 1948, while working on the construction crew that built the bridge.

(b) The department of transportation is directed to erect suitable signs or to affix suitable markers designating the bridge described in subsection (a) as the "Buford 'Peck' White Memorial Bridge".

(c) The erection of such directional signs shall be within the guidelines prescribed by the Manual on Uniform Traffic Control Devices.

(d) This section shall become operative only if the federal highway administrator advises the commissioner of transportation in writing that the provisions of this section shall not render Tennessee in violation of federal laws and regulations and subject to penalties prescribed therein.

(e) This section shall become operative only if the cost of the manufacture and installation of such signs is paid to the department of transportation from non-state funds within one (1) year of the effective date of this act. Such payment shall be made prior to any expenditure by the state for the manufacture or installation of such signs. The department shall return any unused portion of the estimated cost to the person or entity paying for such signs within thirty (30) days of the erection of such signs. If the actual cost exceeds the estimated cost, an amount equal to the difference in such costs shall be remitted to the department in non-state funds within thirty (30) days of the sponsoring person or entity receiving an itemized invoice of the actual cost from the department.

SECTION 7. (a) Notwithstanding any provision of law to the contrary, the bridge located on State Route 59 between Mt. Sinai Baptist Church and the intersection of Interstate 40 in Fayette County is hereby designated as the "Cullen L. Waddell, Sr. Bridge" in honor of this influential member of the Longtown community and one of Fayette County's most illustrious citizens.

(b) The department of transportation is directed to erect suitable signs or affix suitable markers designating the bridge described in subsection (a) as the "Cullen L. Waddell, Sr. Bridge."

(c) The erection of signs shall be within the guidelines prescribed by the Manual on Uniform Traffic Control Devices.

(d) This section shall become operative only if the federal highway administrator advises the commissioner of transportation in writing that the provisions of this section shall not render Tennessee in violation of federal laws and regulations and subject to penalties prescribed therein.

(e) This section shall become operative only if the cost of the manufacture and installation of such signs is paid to the department of transportation from non-state funds within one (1) year of the effective date of this act. Such payment shall be made prior to any expenditure by the state for the manufacture or installation of such signs. The department shall return any unused portion of the estimated cost to the person or entity paying for such signs within thirty (30) days of the erection of such signs. If the actual cost exceeds the estimated cost, an amount equal to the difference in such costs shall be remitted to the department in non-state funds within thirty (30) days of the sponsoring person or entity receiving an itemized invoice of the actual cost from the department.

SECTION 8. (a) Notwithstanding any provision of law to the contrary, the bridge spanning Short Creek on State Route 196 (Chulahoma Road) approximately two (2) miles south of such route's intersection with Raleigh-LaGrange Road in Fayette County is hereby designated as the "Charlie and Laura Edenton Memorial Bridge" in memory of these two remarkable human beings.

(b) The department of transportation is directed to erect suitable signs or affix suitable markers designating the bridge described in subsection (a) as the "Charlie and Laura Edenton Memorial Bridge."

(c) The erection of signs shall be within the guidelines prescribed by the Manual on Uniform Traffic Control Devices.

(d) This section shall become operative only if the federal highway administrator advises the commissioner of transportation in writing that the provisions of this section shall not render Tennessee in violation of federal laws and regulations and subject to penalties prescribed therein.

(e) This section shall become operative only if the cost of the manufacture and installation of such signs is paid to the department of transportation from non-state funds within one (1) year of the effective date of this act. Such payment shall be made prior to any expenditure by the state for the manufacture or installation of such signs. The department shall return any unused portion of the estimated cost to the person or entity paying for such signs within thirty (30) days of the erection of such signs. If the actual cost exceeds the estimated cost, an amount equal to the difference in such costs shall be remitted to the department in non-state funds within thirty (30) days of the sponsoring person or entity receiving an itemized invoice of the actual cost from the department.

SECTION 9. (a) Notwithstanding any other provision of law to the contrary, the segment of U.S. Highway 64 in Hardeman County between the municipalities of Bolivar and Hornsby is hereby designated the "Scotty Plunk Memorial Highway" as a lasting tribute to a singular public servant and even more accomplished human being.

(b) The department of transportation is directed to erect suitable signs or to affix suitable markers designating the segment of U.S. Highway 64 described in subsection (a) as the "Scotty Plunk Memorial Highway".

(c) The erection of such directional signs shall be within the guidelines prescribed by the Manual on Uniform Traffic Control Devices.

(d) This section shall become operative only if the federal highway administrator advises the commissioner of transportation in writing that the provisions of this section shall not render Tennessee in violation of federal laws and regulations and subject to penalties prescribed therein.

(e) This section shall become operative only if the cost of the manufacture and installation of such signs is paid to the department of transportation from non-state funds within one (1) year of the effective date of this act. Such payment shall be made prior to any expenditure by the state for the manufacture or installation of such signs. The department shall return any unused portion of the estimated cost to the person or entity paying for such signs within thirty (30) days of the erection of such signs. If the actual cost exceeds the estimated cost, an amount equal to the difference in such costs shall be remitted to the department in non-state funds within thirty (30) days of the sponsoring person or entity receiving an itemized invoice of the actual cost from the department.

(f) The appellation "Scotty Plunk Memorial Highway" provided for in this section is for honorary purposes only and nothing contained herein shall be construed as requiring the alteration of any address, or the governmental system for assigning addresses, in any county, municipality, or other governmental entity affected by this section.

(g) Nothing in this section shall be construed as requiring the alteration of any previously named segments of U.S. Highway 64 described in subsection (a).

SECTION 10. (a) Notwithstanding any provision of law to the contrary, the segment of State Route 76 in Fayette County from South Watkins Drive to Liberty Road is hereby designated the "Chief J.A. 'Tony' Pace Law Enforcement Highway" as a lasting tribute to the late J.A. "Tony" Pace, who served with distinction as Chief of Police of the City of Moscow for thirteen years before his retirement in 2010.

(b) The department of transportation is directed to erect suitable signs or to affix suitable markers designating the segment of State Route 76 described in subsection (a) as the "Chief J.A. 'Tony' Pace Law Enforcement Highway".

(c) The erection of such signs shall be within the guidelines prescribed by the Manual on Uniform Traffic Control Devices.

(d) This section shall become operative only if the federal highway administrator advises the commissioner of transportation in writing that the provisions of this section shall not render Tennessee in violation of federal laws and regulations and subject to penalties prescribed therein.

(e) This section shall become operative only if the cost of the manufacture and installation of such signs is paid to the department of transportation from non-state funds within one (1) year of the effective date of this act. Such payment shall be made prior to any expenditure by the state for the manufacture or installation of such signs. The department shall return any unused portion of the estimated cost to the person or entity paying for such signs within thirty (30) days of the erection of such signs. If the actual cost exceeds the estimated cost, an amount equal to the difference in such costs shall be remitted to the department in non-state funds within thirty (30) days of the sponsoring person or entity receiving an itemized invoice of the actual cost from the department.

(f) The appellation "Chief J.A. 'Tony' Pace Law Enforcement Highway" provided for in this section is for honorary purposes only and nothing contained herein shall be construed as requiring the alteration of any address, or the governmental system for assigning addresses, in any county, municipality, or other governmental entity affected by this section.

(g) Nothing in this section shall be construed as requiring the alteration of any previously named segments of State Route 76 described in subsection (a).

SECTION 11. (a) Notwithstanding any provision of law to the contrary, the segment of State Route 59 in Fayette County from State Route 222 to Wilson Road is hereby designated the "Col. Will Rhea Winfrey Memorial Highway" as a lasting tribute to one of the most distinguished military officers and public servants this state has ever produced.

(b) The department of transportation is directed to erect suitable signs or to affix suitable markers designating the segment of State Route 76 described in subsection (a) as the "Col. Will Rhea Winfrey Memorial Highway."

(c) The erection of such signs shall be within the guidelines prescribed by the Manual on Uniform Traffic Control Devices.

(d) This section shall become operative only if the federal highway administrator advises the commissioner of transportation in writing that the provisions of this section shall not render Tennessee in violation of federal laws and regulations and subject to penalties prescribed therein.

(e) This section shall become operative only if the cost of the manufacture and installation of such signs is paid to the department of transportation from non-state funds within one (1) year of the effective date of this act. Such payment shall be made prior to any expenditure by the state for the manufacture or installation of such signs. The department shall return any unused portion of the estimated cost to the person or entity paying for such signs within thirty (30) days of the erection of such signs. If the actual cost exceeds the estimated cost, an amount equal to the difference in such costs shall be remitted to the department in non-state funds within thirty (30) days of the sponsoring person or entity receiving an itemized invoice of the actual cost from the department.

(f) The appellation "Col. Will Rhea Winfrey Memorial Highway" provided for in this section is for honorary purposes only and nothing contained herein shall be construed as requiring the alteration of any address, or the governmental system for assigning addresses, in any county, municipality, or other governmental entity affected by this section.

(g) Nothing in this section shall be construed as requiring the alteration of any previously named segments of State Route 59 described in subsection (a).

SECTION 12. (a) Notwithstanding any provision of law to the contrary, the 3.2 mile segment of U.S. Highway 64 in McNairy County from the intersection of such highway and Sulphur Springs Road westward to the intersection of such highway and Rose Creek Road is hereby designated the "Larron King Memorial Highway" in a lasting tribute to this accomplished resident of Selmer, Tennessee.

(b) The department of transportation is directed to erect suitable signs or to affix suitable markers designating the segment of U.S. Highway 64 described in subsection (a) as the "Larron King Memorial Highway."

(c) The erection of such signs shall be within the guidelines prescribed by the Manual on Uniform Traffic Control Devices.

(d) This section shall become operative only if the federal highway administrator advises the commissioner of transportation in writing that the provisions of this section shall not render Tennessee in violation of federal laws and regulations and subject to penalties prescribed therein.

(e) This section shall become operative only if the cost of the manufacture and installation of such signs is paid to the department of transportation from non-state funds within one (1) year of the effective date of this act. Such payment shall be made prior to any expenditure by the state for the manufacture or installation of such signs. The department shall return any unused portion of the estimated cost to the person or entity paying for such signs within thirty (30) days of the erection of such signs. If the actual cost exceeds the estimated cost, an amount equal to the difference in such costs shall be remitted to the department in non-state funds within thirty (30) days of the sponsoring person or entity receiving an itemized invoice of the actual cost from the department.

(f) The appellation "Larron King Memorial Highway" provided for in this section is for honorary purposes only and nothing contained herein shall be construed as requiring the alteration of any address, or the governmental system for assigning addresses, in any county, municipality, or other governmental entity affected by this section.

(g) Nothing in this section shall be construed as requiring the alteration of any previously named segments of U.S. Highway 64 described in subsection (a).

SECTION 13. (a) Notwithstanding any provision of law to the contrary, the new bridge spanning the Cumberland River on State Route 109 south of Gallatin in Sumner County is hereby designated the "Walter T. Durham Bridge" in honor of a gentleman who has proven his love of and loyalty to the State of Tennessee during his tenure as State Historian.

(b) The department of transportation is directed to erect suitable signs or to affix suitable markers designating the bridge described in subsection (a) as the "Walter T. Durham Bridge".

(c) The erection of such signs shall be within the guidelines prescribed by the Manual on Uniform Traffic Control Devices.

(d) This section shall become operative only if the federal highway administrator advises the commissioner of transportation in writing that the provisions of this section shall not render Tennessee in violation of federal laws and regulations and subject to penalties prescribed therein.

(e) This section shall become operative only if the cost of the manufacture and installation of such signs is paid to the department of transportation from non-state funds within one (1) year of the effective date of this act. Such payment shall be made prior to any expenditure by the state for the manufacture or installation of such signs. The department shall return any unused portion of the estimated cost to the person or entity paying for such signs within thirty (30) days of the erection of such signs. If the actual cost exceeds the estimated cost, an amount equal to the difference in such costs shall be remitted to the department in non-state funds within thirty (30) days of the sponsoring person or entity receiving an itemized invoice of the actual cost from the department.

SECTION 14. (a) Notwithstanding any provision of law to the contrary, the segment of U.S. Highway 31W contained within the corporate limits of the City of Millersville, Sumner County, is hereby designated the "John W. Reynolds, Sr. Memorial Highway".

(b) The department of transportation is directed to erect suitable signs or to affix suitable markers designating the segment of U.S. Highway 31W described in subsection (a) as the "John W. Reynolds, Sr. Memorial Highway".

(c) The erection of such signs shall be within the guidelines prescribed by the Manual on Uniform Traffic Control Devices.

(d) This section shall become operative only if the federal highway administrator advises the commissioner of transportation in writing that the provisions of this section shall not render Tennessee in violation of federal laws and regulations and subject to penalties prescribed therein.

(e) This section shall become operative only if the cost of the manufacture and installation of such signs is paid to the department of transportation from non-state funds within one (1) year of the effective date of this act. Such payment shall be made prior to any expenditure by the state for the manufacture or installation of such signs. The department shall return any unused portion of the estimated cost to the person or entity paying for such signs within thirty (30) days of the erection of such signs. If the actual cost exceeds the estimated cost, an amount equal to the difference in such costs shall be remitted to the department in non-state funds within thirty (30) days of the sponsoring person or entity receiving an itemized invoice of the actual cost from the department.

(f) The appellation "John W. Reynolds, Sr. Memorial Highway" provided for in this section is for honorary purposes only and nothing contained herein shall be construed as requiring the alteration of any address, or the governmental system for assigning addresses, in any county, municipality, or other governmental entity affected by this section.

(g) Nothing contained in this section shall be construed as requiring the alteration of any previously named segment or segments of any highway described in subsection (a) as the "John W. Reynolds, Sr. Memorial Highway".

SECTION 15. (a) Notwithstanding any provision of law to the contrary, the segment of U.S. Highway 43 that lies between the two (2) junctions of such highway with Shelton Drive in Lawrence County, Tennessee, is hereby designated the "Thomas 'Tom' Todd Memorial Highway" in memory of Samuel Thomas Todd, a beloved resident of Saint Joseph, Tennessee, and devoted husband and father.

(b) The department of transportation is directed to erect suitable signs or to affix suitable markers designating the segment of U.S. Highway 43 described in subsection (a) as the "Thomas 'Tom' Todd Memorial Highway".

(c) The erection of such signs shall be within the guidelines prescribed by the Manual on Uniform Traffic Control Devices.

(d) This section shall become operative only if the federal highway administrator advises the commissioner of transportation in writing that the provisions of this section shall not render Tennessee in violation of federal laws and regulations and subject to penalties prescribed therein.

(e) This section shall become operative only if the cost of the manufacture and installation of such signs is paid to the department of transportation from non-state funds

within one (1) year of the effective date of this act. Such payment shall be made prior to any expenditure by the state for the manufacture or installation of such signs. The department shall return any unused portion of the estimated cost to the person or entity paying for such signs within thirty (30) days of the erection of such signs. If the actual cost exceeds the estimated cost, an amount equal to the difference in such costs shall be remitted to the department in non-state funds within thirty (30) days of the sponsoring person or entity receiving an itemized invoice of the actual cost from the department.

(f) The appellation "Thomas 'Tom' Todd Memorial Highway" provided for in this section is for honorary purposes only and nothing contained herein shall be construed as requiring the alteration of any address, or the governmental system for assigning addresses, in any county, municipality, or other governmental entity affected by this section.

(g) Nothing in this section shall be construed as requiring the alteration of any previously named segments of U.S. Highway 43 described in subsection (a).

SECTION 16. (a) Notwithstanding any provision of law to the contrary, the bridge spanning Shoal Creek on U.S. Highway 64/State Route 242 (W. Gaines Street) in Lawrence County, Tennessee, is hereby designated the "Ivan Johnston Bridge" to honor the memory of the late Ivan Johnston, an outstanding public servant for the people of the City of Lawrenceburg, who served as the city's Mayor for twenty-five years.

(b) The department of transportation is directed to erect suitable signs or to affix suitable markers designating the bridge described in subsection (a) as the "Ivan Johnston Bridge".

(c) The erection of such signs shall be within the guidelines prescribed by the Manual on Uniform Traffic Control Devices.

(d) This section shall become operative only if the federal highway administrator advises the commissioner of transportation in writing that the provisions of this section shall not render Tennessee in violation of federal laws and regulations and subject to penalties prescribed therein.

(e) This section shall become operative only if the cost of the manufacture and installation of such signs is paid to the department of transportation from non-state funds within one (1) year of the effective date of this act. Such payment shall be made prior to any expenditure by the state for the manufacture or installation of such signs. The department shall return any unused portion of the estimated cost to the person or entity paying for such signs within thirty (30) days of the erection of such signs. If the actual cost exceeds the estimated cost, an amount equal to the difference in such costs shall be remitted to the department in non-state funds within thirty (30) days of the sponsoring person or entity receiving an itemized invoice of the actual cost from the department.

SECTION 17. (a) Notwithstanding any provision of law to the contrary, the bridge spanning Factory Creek on State Route 242 (West Point Road) in Lawrence County, Tennessee, is hereby designated the "Ted Kimbrell Memorial Bridge" to honor the memory of one of the City of Westpoint's distinctive citizens.

(b) The department of transportation is directed to erect suitable signs or to affix suitable markers designating the bridge described in subsection (a) as the "Ted Kimbrell Memorial Bridge".

(c) The erection of such signs shall be within the guidelines prescribed by the Manual on Uniform Traffic Control Devices.

(d) This section shall become operative only if the federal highway administrator advises the commissioner of transportation in writing that the provisions of this section shall not render Tennessee in violation of federal laws and regulations and subject to penalties prescribed therein.

(e) This section shall become operative only if the cost of the manufacture and installation of such signs is paid to the department of transportation from non-state funds within one (1) year of the effective date of this act. Such payment shall be made prior to any expenditure by the state for the manufacture or installation of such signs. The department shall return any unused portion of the estimated cost to the person or entity paying for such signs within thirty (30) days of the erection of such signs. If the actual cost exceeds the estimated cost, an amount equal to the difference in such costs shall be remitted to the department in non-state funds within thirty (30) days of the sponsoring person or entity receiving an itemized invoice of the actual cost from the department.

SECTION 18. (a) The general assembly finds that:

(1) From time to time, the members of this general assembly have seen fit to name certain highways and bridges to honor the memory of those exemplary Tennesseans who, during their lifetime, contributed significantly to the growth and prosperity of their respective communities;

(2) Rod Brasfield was a gifted comedian who was prominently featured on the Grand Ole Opry from 1947 until his death in 1958; he was posthumously inducted into the Country Music Hall of Fame in 1987;

(3) With his trademark baggy suit, battered hat, and rubbery face, Mr. Brasfield was an audience favorite and soon became the primary comic on *The Prince Albert Show*;

(4) A comedian of Renaissance talents, Mr. Brasfield also performed double comedy routines with the legendary Minnie Pearl, appeared with Elvis Presley at Atlanta's Fox Theatre, and played Andy Griffith's sidekick in the movie, *A Face in the Crowd*; his ventriloquist dummy, Bocephus, provided the inspiration for Hank Williams bestowing that nickname upon his then infant son, Hank, Jr.;

(5) After marrying a Hohenwald school teacher, Eleanor Humphrey, Rod Brasfield began residing in Hohenwald himself and often referred to himself as the Hohenwald Flash;

(6) In his comedy routines, he often mentioned the Hohenwald restaurant, Snip-Snap-and-Bite, which he had once owned, and thus both Hohenwald and the restaurant became renowned throughout the WSM Radio listening area; and

(7) For these and many other reasons, the Lewis County Board of Commissioners has petitioned this body to name a segment of State Route 48 in such county in honor of this talented comedian who helped put Hohenwald on the map.

(b) Notwithstanding any provision of law to the contrary, and for the reasons described in subsection (a), the segment of State Route 48 in Lewis County from the northern corporate limits of the City of Hohenwald to a point two (2) miles north of such corporate limits is hereby designated the "Rod Brasfield Memorial Highway" to honor the memory of this gifted comedian who contributed significantly to the growth and prosperity of the Hohenwald community and the state of Tennessee.

(c) The department of transportation is directed to erect suitable signs or to affix suitable markers designating the segment of State Route 48 described in subsection (b) as the "Rod Brasfield Memorial Highway".

(d) The erection of such signs shall be within the guidelines prescribed by the Manual on Uniform Traffic Control Devices.

(e) This section shall become operative only if the federal highway administrator advises the commissioner of transportation in writing that the provisions of this section shall not render Tennessee in violation of federal laws and regulations and subject to penalties prescribed therein.

(f) This section shall become operative only if the cost of the manufacture and installation of such signs is paid to the department of transportation from non-state funds within one (1) year of the effective date of this act. Such payment shall be made prior to any expenditure by the state for the manufacture or installation of such signs. The department shall return any unused portion of the estimated cost to the person or entity paying for such signs within thirty (30) days of the erection of such signs. If the actual cost exceeds the estimated cost, an amount equal to the difference in such costs shall be remitted to the department in non-state funds within thirty (30) days of the sponsoring person or entity receiving an itemized invoice of the actual cost from the department.

(g) The appellation "Rod Brasfield Memorial Highway" provided for in this section is for honorary purposes only and nothing contained herein shall be construed as requiring the alteration of any address, or the governmental system for assigning addresses, in any county, municipality, or other governmental entity affected by this section.

(h) Nothing contained in this section shall be construed as requiring the alteration of any previously named segments of State Route 48 described in subsection (b).

PUBLIC CHAPTER NO. 482 (cont'd)

SECTION 19. (a) Notwithstanding any provision of law to the contrary, the bridge spanning North Choate Creek on U.S. Highway 64 West/State Route 15 (Lawrenceburg Highway) in Giles County, Tennessee, is hereby designated the "Flenoy Johnson Memorial Bridge" to honor the memory of this beloved resident of Giles County.

(b) The department of transportation is directed to erect suitable signs or to affix suitable markers designating the bridge described in subsection (a) as the "Flenoy Johnson Memorial Bridge".

(c) The erection of such signs shall be within the guidelines prescribed by the Manual on Uniform Traffic Control Devices.

(d) This section shall become operative only if the federal highway administrator advises the commissioner of transportation in writing that the provisions of this section shall not render Tennessee in violation of federal laws and regulations and subject to penalties prescribed therein.

(e) This section shall become operative only if the cost of the manufacture and installation of such signs is paid to the department of transportation from non-state funds within one (1) year of the effective date of this act. Such payment shall be made prior to any expenditure by the state for the manufacture or installation of such signs. The department shall return any unused portion of the estimated cost to the person or entity paying for such signs within thirty (30) days of the erection of such signs. If the actual cost exceeds the estimated cost, an amount equal to the difference in such costs shall be remitted to the department in non-state funds within thirty (30) days of the sponsoring person or entity receiving an itemized invoice of the actual cost from the department.

SECTION 20. (a) Notwithstanding any provision of law to the contrary, the segment of U.S. Highway 412 East (East Main Street) in Hohenwald, Tennessee, from such highway's intersection with Brewer Drive to Ponderosa Drive is hereby designated the "Guy J. Nicholson Highway" as a lasting tribute to this exemplary public servant, who honorably served his fellow citizens as the Mayor of Hohenwald for twenty-three years.

(b) The department of transportation is directed to erect suitable signs or to affix suitable markers designating the segment of U.S. Highway 412 East described in subsection (a) as the "Guy J. Nicholson Highway".

(c) The erection of such signs shall be within the guidelines prescribed by the Manual on Uniform Traffic Control Devices.

(d) This section shall become operative only if the federal highway administrator advises the commissioner of transportation in writing that the provisions of this section shall not render Tennessee in violation of federal laws and regulations and subject to penalties prescribed therein.

(e) This section shall become operative only if the cost of the manufacture and installation of such signs is paid to the department of transportation from non-state funds within one (1) year of the effective date of this act. Such payment shall be made prior to any expenditure by the state for the manufacture or installation of such signs. The department shall return any unused portion of the estimated cost to the person or entity paying for such signs within thirty (30) days of the erection of such signs. If the actual cost exceeds the estimated cost, an amount equal to the difference in such costs shall be remitted to the department in non-state funds within thirty (30) days of the sponsoring person or entity receiving an itemized invoice of the actual cost from the department.

(f) The appellation "Guy J. Nicholson Highway" provided for in this section is for honorary purposes only and nothing contained herein shall be construed as requiring the alteration of any address, or the governmental system for assigning addresses, in any county, municipality, or other governmental entity affected by this section.

(g) Nothing contained in this section shall be construed as requiring the alteration of any previously named segments of U.S. Highway 412 described in subsection (a).

SECTION 21. (a) Notwithstanding any provision of law to the contrary, State Bridge No. 60-SR106-2.94 on U.S. Highway 431 (State Route 106) in Maury County is hereby designated the "Casey Grant Heithcock Memorial Bridge" as a lasting tribute to an outstanding young man and patriot.

(b) The department of transportation is directed to erect suitable signs or to affix suitable markers designating the bridge described in subsection (a) as the "Casey Grant Heithcock Memorial Bridge".

(c) The erection of such signs shall be within the guidelines prescribed by the Manual on Uniform Traffic Control Devices.

(d) This section shall become operative only if the federal highway administrator advises the commissioner of transportation in writing that the provisions of this section shall not render Tennessee in violation of federal laws and regulations and subject to penalties prescribed therein.

(e) This section shall become operative only if the cost of the manufacture and installation of such signs is paid to the department of transportation from non-state funds within one (1) year of the effective date of this act. Such payment shall be made prior to any expenditure by the state for the manufacture or installation of such signs. The department shall return any unused portion of the estimated cost to the person or entity paying for such signs within thirty (30) days of the erection of such signs. If the actual cost exceeds the estimated cost, an amount equal to the difference in such costs shall be remitted to the department in non-state funds within thirty (30) days of the sponsoring person or entity receiving an itemized invoice of the actual cost from the department.

SECTION 22. (a) Notwithstanding any other provision of law to the contrary, the bridge which spans the Tennessee River on U.S. Highway 129 (State Route 115) in Knoxville is hereby redesignated as the "J.E. 'Buck' Karnes Bridge - Medal of Honor Recipient".

(b) The department of transportation is directed to erect suitable signs or to affix suitable markers designating the bridge described in subsection (a) as the "J.E. 'Buck' Karnes Bridge - Medal of Honor Recipient".

(c) The erection of such signs shall be within the guidelines prescribed by the Manual on Uniform Traffic Control Devices.

(d) This section shall become operative only if the federal highway administrator advises the commissioner of transportation in writing that the provisions of this section shall not render Tennessee in violation of federal laws and regulations and subject to penalties prescribed therein.

(e) This section shall become operative only if the cost of the manufacture and installation of such signs is paid to the department of transportation from non-state funds within one (1) year of the effective date of this act. Such payment shall be made prior to any expenditure by the state for the manufacture or installation of such signs. The department shall return any unused portion of the estimated cost to the person or entity paying for such signs within thirty (30) days of the erection of such signs. If the actual cost exceeds the estimated cost, an amount equal to the difference in such costs shall be remitted to the department in non-state funds within thirty (30) days of the sponsoring person or entity receiving an itemized invoice of the actual cost from the department.

SECTION 23. (a) Notwithstanding any provision of law to the contrary, the bridge located in the Springdale community of Claiborne County on U.S. Highway 25E is hereby designated the "Katie Johnson and William West Memorial Bridge" in memory of two fine citizens who lost their lives in an automobile accident on such bridge.

(b) The department of transportation is directed to erect suitable signs or to affix suitable markers designating the bridge described in subsection (a) as the "Katie Johnson and William West Memorial Bridge".

(c) The erection of such signs shall be within the guidelines prescribed by the Manual on Uniform Traffic Control Devices.

(d) This section shall become operative only if the federal highway administrator advises the commissioner of transportation in writing that the provisions of this section shall not render Tennessee in violation of federal laws and regulations and subject to penalties prescribed therein.

(e) This section shall become operative only if the cost of the manufacture and installation of such signs is paid to the department of transportation from non-state funds within one (1) year of the effective date of this act. Such payment shall be made prior to any expenditure by the state for the manufacture or installation of such signs. The department shall return any unused portion of the estimated cost to the person or entity paying for such

PUBLIC CHAPTER NO. 482 (cont'd)

signs within thirty (30) days of the erection of such signs. If the actual cost exceeds the estimated cost, an amount equal to the difference in such costs shall be remitted to the department in non-state funds within thirty (30) days of the sponsoring person or entity receiving an itemized invoice of the actual cost from the department.

SECTION 24. (a) Notwithstanding any provision of law to the contrary, the segment of U.S. Highway 25E within Hamblen County is hereby designated the "Medal of Honor Highway".

(b) The department of transportation is directed to erect suitable signs or to affix suitable markers designating the segment of U.S. Highway 25E described in subsection (a) as the "Medal of Honor Highway".

(c) The erection of such signs shall be within the guidelines prescribed by the Manual on Uniform Traffic Control Devices.

(d) This section shall become operative only if the federal highway administrator advises the commissioner of transportation in writing that the provisions of this section shall not render Tennessee in violation of federal laws and regulations and subject to penalties prescribed therein.

(e) This section shall become operative only if the cost of the manufacture and installation of such signs is paid to the department of transportation from non-state funds within one (1) year of the effective date of this act. Such payment shall be made prior to any expenditure by the state for the manufacture or installation of such signs. The department shall return any unused portion of the estimated cost to the person or entity paying for such signs within thirty (30) days of the erection of such signs. If the actual cost exceeds the estimated cost, an amount equal to the difference in such costs shall be remitted to the department in non-state funds within thirty (30) days of the sponsoring person or entity receiving an itemized invoice of the actual cost from the department.

(f) The appellation "Medal of Honor Highway" provided for in this section is for honorary purposes only and nothing contained herein shall be construed as requiring the alteration of any address, or the governmental system for assigning addresses, in any county, municipality, or other governmental entity affected by this section.

(g) Nothing contained in this section shall be construed as requiring the alteration of any previously named segment or segments of any highway described in subsection (a) as the "Medal of Honor Highway".

SECTION 25. (a) Notwithstanding any provision of law to the contrary, the bridge presently under construction on U.S. Highway 25E at or near 475 S. Davy Crockett Parkway, Morristown in Hamblen County is hereby designated the "Pvt. Calvin John Ward Memorial Bridge".

(b) The department of transportation is directed to erect suitable signs or to affix suitable markers designating the bridge described in subsection (a) as the "Pvt. Calvin John Ward Memorial Bridge".

(c) The erection of such signs shall be within the guidelines prescribed by the Manual on Uniform Traffic Control Devices.

(d) This section shall become operative only if the federal highway administrator advises the commissioner of transportation in writing that the provisions of this section shall not render Tennessee in violation of federal laws and regulations and subject to penalties prescribed therein.

(e) This section shall become operative only if the cost of the manufacture and installation of such signs is paid to the department of transportation from non-state funds within one (1) year of the effective date of this act. Such payment shall be made prior to any expenditure by the state for the manufacture or installation of such signs. The department shall return any unused portion of the estimated cost to the person or entity paying for such signs within thirty (30) days of the erection of such signs. If the actual cost exceeds the estimated cost, an amount equal to the difference in such costs shall be remitted to the department in non-state funds within thirty (30) days of the sponsoring person or entity receiving an itemized invoice of the actual cost from the department.

SECTION 26. (a) Notwithstanding any provision of law to the contrary, the bridge on U.S. Highway 25E in Hamblen County that spans U.S. Highway 11E is hereby designated the "Sgt. Edward R. Talley Memorial Bridge".

(b) The department of transportation is directed to erect suitable signs or to affix suitable markers designating the bridge described in subsection (a) as the "Sgt. Edward R. Talley Memorial Bridge".

(c) The erection of such signs shall be within the guidelines prescribed by the Manual on Uniform Traffic Control Devices.

(d) This section shall become operative only if the federal highway administrator advises the commissioner of transportation in writing that the provisions of this section shall not render Tennessee in violation of federal laws and regulations and subject to penalties prescribed therein.

(e) This section shall become operative only if the cost of the manufacture and installation of such signs is paid to the department of transportation from non-state funds within one (1) year of the effective date of this act. Such payment shall be made prior to any expenditure by the state for the manufacture or installation of such signs. The department shall return any unused portion of the estimated cost to the person or entity paying for such signs within thirty (30) days of the erection of such signs. If the actual cost exceeds the estimated cost, an amount equal to the difference in such costs shall be remitted to the department in non-state funds within thirty (30) days of the sponsoring person or entity receiving an itemized invoice of the actual cost from the department.

SECTION 27. (a) Notwithstanding any provision of law to the contrary, the bridge on State Route 129 (Ostella Road) located in the southern part of Marshall County, Tennessee, is hereby designated the "Robert M. Burgess Memorial Bridge" to honor the memory of this beloved resident of Marshall County, Tennessee, who ably served his fellow citizens through his community involvement.

(b) The department of transportation is directed to erect suitable signs or to affix suitable markers designating the bridge described in subsection (a) as the "Robert M. Burgess Memorial Bridge".

(c) The erection of such signs shall be within the guidelines prescribed by the Manual on Uniform Traffic Control Devices.

(d) This section shall become operative only if the federal highway administrator advises the commissioner of transportation in writing that the provisions of this section shall not render Tennessee in violation of federal laws and regulations and subject to penalties prescribed therein.

(e) This section shall become operative only if the cost of the manufacture and installation of such signs is paid to the department of transportation from non-state funds within one (1) year of the effective date of this act. Such payment shall be made prior to any expenditure by the state for the manufacture or installation of such signs. The department shall return any unused portion of the estimated cost to the person or entity paying for such signs within thirty (30) days of the erection of such signs. If the actual cost exceeds the estimated cost, an amount equal to the difference in such costs shall be remitted to the department in non-state funds within thirty (30) days of the sponsoring person or entity receiving an itemized invoice of the actual cost from the department.

SECTION 28. (a) Notwithstanding any provision of law to the contrary, the bridge spanning Rock Creek on State Route 11/U.S. Highway 31-A (Nashville Highway) in Marshall County, Tennessee, is hereby designated the "Bob Smartt Memorial Bridge" to honor the memory of this beloved resident of Marshall County, Tennessee, who ably served his fellow citizens through his community involvement and civic leadership.

(b) The department of transportation is directed to erect suitable signs or to affix suitable markers designating the bridge described in subsection (a) as the "Bob Smartt Memorial Bridge".

(c) The erection of such signs shall be within the guidelines prescribed by the Manual on Uniform Traffic Control Devices.

(d) This section shall become operative only if the federal highway administrator advises the commissioner of transportation in writing that the provisions of this section shall not render Tennessee in violation of federal laws and regulations and subject to penalties prescribed therein.

(e) This section shall become operative only if the cost of the manufacture and installation of such signs is paid to the department of transportation from non-state funds

within one (1) year of the effective date of this act. Such payment shall be made prior to any expenditure by the state for the manufacture or installation of such signs. The department shall return any unused portion of the estimated cost to the person or entity paying for such signs within thirty (30) days of the erection of such signs. If the actual cost exceeds the estimated cost, an amount equal to the difference in such costs shall be remitted to the department in non-state funds within thirty (30) days of the sponsoring person or entity receiving an itemized invoice of the actual cost from the department.

SECTION 29. (a) Notwithstanding any provision of law to the contrary, the bridge spanning Collins Creek on State Route 106 (South Ellington Parkway) in Marshall County, Tennessee, is hereby designated the "Captain Bobby G. Walker Bridge" as a lasting tribute to the late Bobby G. Walker, who served with distinction as Captain of the Lewisburg Police Department from 1981 through 1995.

(b) The department of transportation is directed to erect suitable signs or to affix suitable markers designating the bridge described in subsection (a) as the "Captain Bobby G. Walker Bridge".

(c) The erection of such signs shall be within the guidelines prescribed by the Manual on Uniform Traffic Control Devices.

(d) This section shall become operative only if the federal highway administrator advises the commissioner of transportation in writing that the provisions of this section shall not render Tennessee in violation of federal laws and regulations and subject to penalties prescribed therein.

(e) This section shall become operative only if the cost of the manufacture and installation of such signs is paid to the department of transportation from non-state funds within one (1) year of the effective date of this act. Such payment shall be made prior to any expenditure by the state for the manufacture or installation of such signs. The department shall return any unused portion of the estimated cost to the person or entity paying for such signs within thirty (30) days of the erection of such signs. If the actual cost exceeds the estimated cost, an amount equal to the difference in such costs shall be remitted to the department in non-state funds within thirty (30) days of the sponsoring person or entity receiving an itemized invoice of the actual cost from the department.

SECTION 30. (a) Notwithstanding any provision of law to the contrary, Bridge No. 59-11-3.71 on U.S. Highway 31-A (Sam Davis Highway) in Cornersville, Tennessee, is hereby designated the "Col. Jerry Cashion Memorial Bridge" to honor the memory of Col. Jerry Cashion, who courageously served his country during the Persian Gulf War in Operation Iraqi Freedom and who received the Legion of Merit award.

(b) The department of transportation is directed to erect suitable signs or to affix suitable markers designating the bridge described in subsection (a) as the "Col. Jerry Cashion Memorial Bridge".

(c) The erection of such signs shall be within the guidelines prescribed by the Manual on Uniform Traffic Control Devices.

(d) This section shall become operative only if the federal highway administrator advises the commissioner of transportation in writing that the provisions of this section shall not render Tennessee in violation of federal laws and regulations and subject to penalties prescribed therein.

(e) This section shall become operative only if the cost of the manufacture and installation of such signs is paid to the department of transportation from non-state funds within one (1) year of the effective date of this act. Such payment shall be made prior to any expenditure by the state for the manufacture or installation of such signs. The department shall return any unused portion of the estimated cost to the person or entity paying for such signs within thirty (30) days of the erection of such signs. If the actual cost exceeds the estimated cost, an amount equal to the difference in such costs shall be remitted to the department in non-state funds within thirty (30) days of the sponsoring person or entity receiving an itemized invoice of the actual cost from the department.

SECTION 31. (a) Notwithstanding any provision of law to the contrary, the department of transportation is directed to erect suitable signs or to affix suitable markers that include the language "In Honor of Cecil & Frances Langford" at the location of the Mill Creek Bridge, which is the first bridge on State Route 52 going westward upon exiting Overton County, Tennessee, into Clay County, Tennessee.

PUBLIC CHAPTER NO. 482 (cont'd)

(b) The erection of such signs shall be within the guidelines prescribed by the Manual on Uniform Traffic Control Devices.

(c) This section shall become operative only if the federal highway administrator advises the commissioner of transportation in writing that the provisions of this section shall not render Tennessee in violation of federal laws and regulations and subject to penalties prescribed therein.

(d) This section shall become operative only if the cost of the manufacture and installation of such signs is paid to the department of transportation from non-state funds within one (1) year of the effective date of this act. Such payment shall be made prior to any expenditure by the state for the manufacture or installation of such signs. The department shall return any unused portion of the estimated cost to the person or entity paying for such signs within thirty (30) days of the erection of such signs. If the actual cost exceeds the estimated cost, an amount equal to the difference in such costs shall be remitted to the department in non-state funds within thirty (30) days of the sponsoring person or entity receiving an itemized invoice of the actual cost from the department.

SECTION 32. (a) Notwithstanding any provision of law to the contrary, the segment of State Route 111 in Pickett County, Tennessee, from the bridge on such route southward to mile marker 12 is hereby designated the "Earl G. Pemberton Memorial Highway" to honor the memory of one of Pickett County's distinctive citizens.

(b) The department of transportation is directed to erect suitable signs or to affix suitable markers designating the segment of State Route 111 described in subsection (a) as the "Earl G. Pemberton Memorial Highway". Such signs shall be erected or affixed so as to be visible to both northbound and southbound motorists on State Route 111.

(c) The erection of such signs shall be within the guidelines prescribed by the Manual on Uniform Traffic Control Devices.

(d) This section shall become operative only if the federal highway administrator advises the commissioner of transportation in writing that the provisions of this section shall not render Tennessee in violation of federal laws and regulations and subject to penalties prescribed therein.

(e) This section shall become operative only if the cost of the manufacture and installation of such signs is paid to the department of transportation from non-state funds within one (1) year of the effective date of this act. Such payment shall be made prior to any expenditure by the state for the manufacture or installation of such signs. The department shall return any unused portion of the estimated cost to the person or entity paying for such signs within thirty (30) days of the erection of such signs. If the actual cost exceeds the estimated cost, an amount equal to the difference in such costs shall be remitted to the department in non-state funds within thirty (30) days of the sponsoring person or entity receiving an itemized invoice of the actual cost from the department.

(f) The appellation "Earl G. Pemberton Memorial Highway" provided for in this section is for honorary purposes only and nothing contained herein shall be construed as requiring the alteration of any address, or the governmental system for assigning addresses, in any county, municipality, or other governmental entity affected by this section.

(g) Nothing in this section shall be construed as requiring the alteration of any previously named segments of State Route 111 described in subsection (a).

SECTION 33. (a) The segment of U.S. Highway 27 within Rhea County that is not otherwise named pursuant to Chapter 607 of the Public Acts of 2012, or any other law, is hereby designated the "Veterans Memorial Highway" in honor of the many brave sons and daughters who have served this great country in the United States Armed Forces.

(b) The department of transportation is directed to erect suitable signs or to affix suitable markers designating the segment of U.S. Highway 27 described in subsection (a) as the "Veterans Memorial Highway".

(c) The erection of such signs shall be within the guidelines prescribed by the Manual on Uniform Traffic Control Devices.

(d) This section shall become operative only if the federal highway administrator advises the commissioner of transportation in writing that the provisions of this section shall not render Tennessee in violation of federal laws and regulations and subject to penalties prescribed therein.

(e) This section shall become operative only if the cost of the manufacture and installation of such signs is paid to the department of transportation from non-state funds within one (1) year of the effective date of this act. Such payment shall be made prior to any expenditure by the state for the manufacture or installation of such signs. The department shall return any unused portion of the estimated cost to the person or entity paying for such signs within thirty (30) days of the erection of such signs. If the actual cost exceeds the estimated cost, an amount equal to the difference in such costs shall be remitted to the department in non-state funds within thirty (30) days of the sponsoring person or entity receiving an itemized invoice of the actual cost from the department.

(f) The appellation "Veterans Memorial Highway" provided for in this section is for honorary purposes only and nothing contained herein shall be construed as requiring the alteration of any address, or the governmental system for assigning addresses, in any county, municipality or other governmental entity affected by this section.

(g) Nothing contained in this section shall be construed as requiring the alteration of any previously named segment or segments of any highway described in subsection (a) as the "Veterans Memorial Highway".

SECTION 34. (a) Notwithstanding any provision of law to the contrary, the bridge spanning Emory River on U.S. Highway 27/State Route 29 in Morgan County is hereby designated the "J.C. Barnes Memorial Bridge" in recognition of the life of beloved husband and father J.C. Barnes, a WWII veteran of the United States Army and a recipient of the Silver Star, Bronze Star and Purple Heart.

(b) The department of transportation is directed to erect suitable signs or to affix suitable markers designating the bridge described in subsection (a) as the "J.C. Barnes Memorial Bridge".

(c) The erection of such signs shall be within the guidelines prescribed by the Manual on Uniform Traffic Control Devices.

(d) This section shall become operative only if the federal highway administrator advises the commissioner of transportation in writing that the provisions of this section shall not render Tennessee in violation of federal laws and regulations and subject to penalties prescribed therein.

(e) This section shall become operative only if the cost of the manufacture and installation of such signs is paid to the department of transportation from non-state funds within one (1) year of the effective date of this act. Such payment shall be made prior to any expenditure by the state for the manufacture or installation of such signs. The department shall return any unused portion of the estimated cost to the person or entity paying for such signs within thirty (30) days of the erection of such signs. If the actual cost exceeds the estimated cost, an amount equal to the difference in such costs shall be remitted to the department in non-state funds within thirty (30) days of the sponsoring person or entity receiving an itemized invoice of the actual cost from the department.

SECTION 35. (a) Notwithstanding any provision of law to the contrary, both spans of the bridge (72SR0290003 and 72SR0290004) spanning Richland Creek at mile 5.58 on State Route 29 (U.S. Highway 27 Bypass) in the City of Dayton, Rhea County, is hereby designated the "James William 'Bill' Pope, Jr. Bridge".

(b) The department of transportation is directed to erect suitable signs or to affix suitable markers designating the bridge described in subsection (a) as the "James William 'Bill' Pope, Jr. Bridge".

(c) The erection of such signs shall be within the guidelines prescribed by the Manual on Uniform Traffic Control Devices.

(d) This section shall become operative only if the federal highway administrator advises the commissioner of transportation in writing that the provisions of this section shall not render Tennessee in violation of federal laws and regulations and subject to penalties prescribed therein.

(e) This section shall become operative only if the cost of the manufacture and installation of such signs is paid to the department of transportation from non-state funds within one (1) year of the effective date of this act. Such payment shall be made prior to any expenditure by the state for the manufacture or installation of such signs. The department shall return any unused portion of the estimated cost to the person or entity paying for such signs within thirty (30) days of the erection of such signs. If the actual cost exceeds the estimated cost, an amount equal to the difference in such costs shall be remitted to the department in non-state funds within thirty (30) days of the sponsoring person or entity receiving an itemized invoice of the actual cost from the department.

SECTION 36. (a) Notwithstanding any provision of law to the contrary, the bridge spanning Sugar Creek on State Route 147 located at log mile .27 in Big Sandy, Tennessee, is hereby designated the "Joe Wilson Memorial Bridge" to honor the memory of this beloved resident of Big Sandy, Tennessee, who ably served his fellow citizens as the owner of Wilson's Grocery for over sixty years.

(b) The department of transportation is directed to erect suitable signs or to affix suitable markers designating the bridge described in subsection (a) as the "Joe Wilson Memorial Bridge".

(c) The erection of such signs shall be within the guidelines prescribed by the Manual on Uniform Traffic Control Devices.

(d) This section shall become operative only if the federal highway administrator advises the commissioner of transportation in writing that the provisions of this section shall not render Tennessee in violation of federal laws and regulations and subject to penalties prescribed therein.

(e) This section shall become operative only if the cost of the manufacture and installation of such signs is paid to the department of transportation from non-state funds within one (1) year of the effective date of this act. Such payment shall be made prior to any expenditure by the state for the manufacture or installation of such signs. The department shall return any unused portion of the estimated cost to the person or entity paying for such signs within thirty (30) days of the erection of such signs. If the actual cost exceeds the estimated cost, an amount equal to the difference in such costs shall be remitted to the department in non-state funds within thirty (30) days of the sponsoring person or entity receiving an itemized invoice of the actual cost from the department.

SECTION 37. (a) Notwithstanding any provision of law to the contrary, the U.S. Highway 70 bypass at the intersection of such highway with State Route 191 (Forrest Avenue) in Camden, Tennessee, is hereby designated the "Matthew Draper Memorial Bypass" to honor the memory of this beloved resident of the City of Camden, Tennessee.

(b) The department of transportation is directed to erect suitable signs or to affix suitable markers designating the bypass described in subsection (a) as the "Matthew Draper Memorial Bypass". Such signs shall be erected or affixed on the right of way of the bypass so as to be visible to motorists entering the intersection of State Route 191 (Forrest Avenue) and U.S. Highway 70 (East Main Street).

(c) The erection of such signs shall be within the guidelines prescribed by the Manual on Uniform Traffic Control Devices.

(d) This section shall become operative only if the federal highway administrator advises the commissioner of transportation in writing that the provisions of this section shall not render Tennessee in violation of federal laws and regulations and subject to penalties prescribed therein.

(e) This section shall become operative only if the cost of the manufacture and installation of such signs is paid to the department of transportation from non-state funds within one (1) year of the effective date of this act. Such payment shall be made prior to any expenditure by the state for the manufacture or installation of such signs. The department shall return any unused portion of the estimated cost to the person or entity paying for such signs within thirty (30) days of the erection of such signs. If the actual cost exceeds the estimated cost, an amount equal to the difference in such costs shall be remitted to the department in non-state funds within thirty (30) days of the sponsoring person or entity receiving an itemized invoice of the actual cost from the department.

(f) The appellation "Matthew Draper Memorial Bypass" provided for in this section is for honorary purposes only and nothing contained herein shall be construed as requiring the alteration of any address, or the governmental system for assigning addresses, in any county, municipality, or other governmental entity affected by this section.

SECTION 38. (a) Notwithstanding any provision of law to the contrary, the segment of State Route 184 in Obion County from mile marker 4.00 to mile marker 8.85 is hereby designated the "Dr. E.W. Youngblood Memorial Highway" to honor the memory of this exemplary public servant who courageously served his country in the historic Battle of Iwo Jima.

(b) The department of transportation is directed to erect suitable signs or to affix suitable markers designating the segment of State Route 184 described in subsection (a) as the "Dr. E.W. Youngblood Memorial Highway."

(c) The erection of such signs shall be within the guidelines prescribed by the Manual on Uniform Traffic Control Devices.

(d) This section shall become operative only if the federal highway administrator advises the commissioner of transportation in writing that the provisions of this section shall not render Tennessee in violation of federal laws and regulations and subject to penalties prescribed therein.

(e) This section shall become operative only if the cost of the manufacture and installation of such signs is paid to the department of transportation from non-state funds within one (1) year of the effective date of this act. Such payment shall be made prior to any expenditure by the state for the manufacture or installation of such signs. The department shall return any unused portion of the estimated cost to the person or entity paying for such signs within thirty (30) days of the erection of such signs. If the actual cost exceeds the estimated cost, an amount equal to the difference in such costs shall be remitted to the department in non-state funds within thirty (30) days of the sponsoring person or entity receiving an itemized invoice of the actual cost from the department.

(f) The appellation "Dr. E.W. Youngblood Memorial Highway" provided for in this section is for honorary purposes only and nothing contained herein shall be construed as requiring the alteration of any address, or the governmental system for assigning addresses, in any county, municipality, or other governmental entity affected by this section.

(g) Nothing contained in this section shall be construed as requiring the alteration of any previously named segments of State Route 184 described in subsection (a).

SECTION 39. (a) Notwithstanding any provision of law to the contrary, the segment of State Route 58 between its intersection with State Route 68N and the Meigs/Roane county line is hereby designated the "Herman Woody Memorial Highway", to honor the memory of Herman Woody, who was a teacher and principal in the Meigs County School System for 33 years, a World War II veteran, and a remarkable resident of Meigs County.

(b) The department of transportation is directed to erect suitable signs or to affix suitable markers designating the segment of State Route 58 described in subsection (a) as the "Herman Woody Memorial Highway".

(c) The erection of such signs shall be within the guidelines prescribed by the Manual on Uniform Traffic Control Devices.

(d) This section shall become operative only if the federal highway administrator advises the commissioner of transportation in writing that the provisions of this section shall not render Tennessee in violation of federal laws and regulations and subject to penalties prescribed therein.

(e) This section shall become operative only if the cost of the manufacture and installation of such signs is paid to the department of transportation from non-state funds within one (1) year of the effective date of this act. Such payment shall be made prior to any expenditure by the state for the manufacture or installation of such signs. The department shall return any unused portion of the estimated cost to the person or entity paying for such signs within thirty (30) days of the erection of such signs. If the actual cost exceeds the estimated cost, an amount equal to the difference in such costs shall be remitted to the department in non-state funds within thirty (30) days of the sponsoring person or entity receiving an itemized invoice of the actual cost from the department.

(f) The appellation "Herman Woody Memorial Highway" provided for in this section is for honorary purposes only and nothing contained herein shall be construed as requiring the alteration of any address, or the governmental system for assigning addresses, in any county, municipality, or other governmental entity affected by this section.

(g) Nothing contained in this section shall be construed as requiring the alteration of any previously named segment or segments of any highway described in subsection (a) as the "Herman Woody Memorial Highway".

SECTION 40. (a) Notwithstanding any provision of law to the contrary, State Bridge No. 78-SR449-4.32 on State Route 449 (Veterans Boulevard) in the City of Sevierville, Sevier County, is hereby designated the "Michael L. Rawlings Memorial Bridge" to honor the memory of the late Michael L. Rawlings, who served with distinction as Fire Chief of Sevierville from 1994 until his untimely death in 2011.

(b) The department of transportation is directed to erect suitable signs or to affix suitable markers designating the bridge described in subsection (a) as the "Michael L. Rawlings Memorial Bridge".

(c) The erection of such signs shall be within the guidelines prescribed by the Manual on Uniform Traffic Control Devices.

(d) This section shall become operative only if the federal highway administrator advises the commissioner of transportation in writing that the provisions of this section shall not render Tennessee in violation of federal laws and regulations and subject to penalties prescribed therein.

(e) This section shall become operative only if the cost of the manufacture and installation of such signs is paid to the department of transportation from non-state funds within one (1) year of the effective date of this act. Such payment shall be made prior to any expenditure by the state for the manufacture or installation of such signs. The department shall return any unused portion of the estimated cost to the person or entity paying for such signs within thirty (30) days of the erection of such signs. If the actual cost exceeds the estimated cost, an amount equal to the difference in such costs shall be remitted to the department in non-state funds within thirty (30) days of the sponsoring person or entity receiving an itemized invoice of the actual cost from the department.

SECTION 41. (a) Notwithstanding any provision of law to the contrary, the segment of Interstate 75 in Knox County from Exit 108 (Merchants Drive) to Exit 110 (Callahan Drive) is hereby designated the "IBEW 760 Training Center Highway".

(b) The department of transportation is directed to erect suitable signs or to affix suitable markers designating the segment of Interstate 75 described in subsection (a) as the "IBEW 760 Training Center Highway".

(c) The erection of such signs shall be within the guidelines prescribed by the Manual on Uniform Traffic Control Devices.

(d) This section shall become operative only if the federal highway administrator advises the commissioner of transportation in writing that the provisions of this section shall not render Tennessee in violation of federal laws and regulations and subject to penalties prescribed therein.

(e) This section shall become operative only if the cost of the manufacture and installation of such signs is paid to the department of transportation from non-state funds within one (1) year of the effective date of this act. Such payment shall be made prior to any expenditure by the state for the manufacture or installation of such signs. The department shall return any unused portion of the estimated cost to the person or entity paying for such signs within thirty (30) days of the erection of such signs. If the actual cost exceeds the estimated cost, an amount equal to the difference in such costs shall be remitted to the department in non-state funds within thirty (30) days of the sponsoring person or entity receiving an itemized invoice of the actual cost from the department.

(f) The appellation "IBEW 760 Training Center Highway" provided for in this section is for honorary purposes only and nothing contained herein shall be construed as requiring the alteration of any address, or the governmental system for assigning addresses, in any county, municipality, or other governmental entity affected by this section.

(g) Nothing in this section shall be construed as requiring the alteration of any previously named segments of Interstate 75 described in subsection (a).

SECTION 42. (a) Notwithstanding any provision of law to the contrary, the bridge on State Route 143 in the Roan Mountain State Park in Carter County, Tennessee, is hereby designated the "Carroll Boone Bridge" in honor of one of Carter County's distinctive citizens.

(b) The department of transportation is directed to erect suitable signs or to affix suitable markers designating the bridge described in subsection (a) as the "Carroll Boone Bridge".

(c) The erection of such signs shall be within the guidelines prescribed by the Manual on Uniform Traffic Control Devices.

(d) This section shall become operative only if the federal highway administrator advises the commissioner of transportation in writing that the provisions of this section shall not render Tennessee in violation of federal laws and regulations and subject to penalties prescribed therein.

(e) This section shall become operative only if the cost of the manufacture and installation of such signs is paid to the department of transportation from non-state funds within one (1) year of the effective date of this act. Such payment shall be made prior to any expenditure by the state for the manufacture or installation of such signs. The department shall return any unused portion of the estimated cost to the person or entity paying for such signs within thirty (30) days of the erection of such signs. If the actual cost exceeds the estimated cost, an amount equal to the difference in such costs shall be remitted to the department in non-state funds within thirty (30) days of the sponsoring person or entity receiving an itemized invoice of the actual cost from the department.

SECTION 43. (a) Notwithstanding any provision of law to the contrary, the segment of State Route 143 in Carter County from the end of Sen. Robert 'Bob' Burleson Parkway to the top of Roan Mountain in front of Jack's Grocery is hereby designated the "Jack Barnett Parkway" in appreciation of one of Carter County's distinctive citizens.

(b) The department of transportation is directed to erect suitable signs or to affix suitable markers designating the segment of State Route 143 described in subsection (a) as the "Jack Barnett Parkway".

(c) The erection of such signs shall be within the guidelines prescribed by the Manual on Uniform Traffic Control Devices.

(d) This section shall become operative only if the federal highway administrator advises the commissioner of transportation in writing that the provisions of this section shall not render Tennessee in violation of federal laws and regulations and subject to penalties prescribed therein.

(e) This section shall become operative only if the cost of the manufacture and installation of such signs is paid to the department of transportation from non-state funds within one (1) year of the effective date of this act. Such payment shall be made prior to any expenditure by the state for the manufacture or installation of such signs. The department shall return any unused portion of the estimated cost to the person or entity paying for such signs within thirty (30) days of the erection of such signs. If the actual cost exceeds the estimated cost, an amount equal to the difference in such costs shall be remitted to the department in non-state funds within thirty (30) days of the sponsoring person or entity receiving an itemized invoice of the actual cost from the department.

(f) The appellation "Jack Barnett Parkway" provided for in this section is for honorary purposes only and nothing contained herein shall be construed as requiring the alteration of any address, or the governmental system for assigning addresses, in any county, municipality, or other governmental entity affected by this section.

(g) Nothing in this section shall be construed as requiring the alteration of any previously named segments of State Route 143 described in subsection (a).

SECTION 44. (a) Notwithstanding any provision of law to the contrary, the segment of State Route 295 in Pickett County, Tennessee, from such route's intersection with North Main Street to such route's intersection with Harlan Lee Road is hereby designated the "Jonathan David Cook Memorial Highway" to honor the memory of this beloved resident of Byrdstown, Tennessee.

(b) The department of transportation is directed to erect suitable signs or to affix suitable markers designating the segment of State Route 295 described in subsection (a) as the "Jonathan David Cook Memorial Highway". Such signs shall be erected or affixed so as to be visible to both eastbound and westbound motorists on State Route 295.

(c) The erection of such signs shall be within the guidelines prescribed by the Manual on Uniform Traffic Control Devices.

(d) This section shall become operative only if the federal highway administrator advises the commissioner of transportation in writing that the provisions of this section shall not render Tennessee in violation of federal laws and regulations and subject to penalties prescribed therein.

(e) This section shall become operative only if the cost of the manufacture and installation of such signs is paid to the department of transportation from non-state funds within one (1) year of the effective date of this act. Such payment shall be made prior to any expenditure by the state for the manufacture or installation of such signs. The department shall return any unused portion of the estimated cost to the person or entity paying for such signs within thirty (30) days of the erection of such signs. If the actual cost exceeds the estimated cost, an amount equal to the difference in such costs shall be remitted to the department in non-state funds within thirty (30) days of the sponsoring person or entity receiving an itemized invoice of the actual cost from the department.

(f) The appellation "Jonathan David Cook Memorial Highway" provided for in this section is for honorary purposes only and nothing contained herein shall be construed as requiring the alteration of any address, or the governmental system for assigning addresses, in any county, municipality, or other governmental entity affected by this section.

(g) Nothing in this section shall be construed as requiring the alteration of any previously named segments of State Route 295 described in subsection (a).

SECTION 45.

(a)(1) Notwithstanding any provision of law to the contrary, the eastern span of the bridge spanning the Holston River on State Route 75 in Sullivan County is hereby designated the "Joseph Julian Henry Memorial Bridge".

(2) Notwithstanding any provision of law to the contrary, the western span of the bridge spanning the Holston River on State Route 75 in Sullivan County is hereby designated the "Orville Depew 'Dick' Kitzmiller and Riley Lee Milhorn Memorial Bridge".

(b) The department of transportation is directed to erect suitable signs or to affix suitable markers designating such bridge as described in subsection (a).

(c) The erection of such signs shall be within the guidelines prescribed by the Manual on Uniform Traffic Control Devices.

(d) This section shall become operative only if the federal highway administrator advises the commissioner of transportation in writing that the provisions of this section shall not render Tennessee in violation of federal laws and regulations and subject to penalties prescribed therein.

(e) This section shall become operative only if the cost of the manufacture and installation of such signs is paid to the department of transportation from non-state funds within one (1) year of the effective date of this act. Such payment shall be made prior to any expenditure by the state for the manufacture or installation of such signs. The department shall return any unused portion of the estimated cost to the person or entity paying for such signs within thirty (30) days of the erection of such signs. If the actual cost exceeds the estimated cost, an amount equal to the difference in such costs shall be remitted to the department in non-state funds within thirty (30) days of the sponsoring person or entity receiving an itemized invoice of the actual cost from the department.

SECTION 46. (a) Notwithstanding any provision of law to the contrary, the bridge spanning Duck River on State Route 41 near the northern corporate boundary of Manchester, Tennessee, is hereby designated the "Veterans Memorial Bridge" in honor of the many brave sons and daughters of Tennessee who have served this great country in the United States Armed Forces.

(b) The department of transportation is directed to erect suitable signs or to affix suitable markers designating the bridge described in subsection (a) as the "Veterans Memorial Bridge".

(c) The erection of such signs shall be within the guidelines prescribed by the Manual on Uniform Traffic Control Devices.

(d) This section shall become operative only if the federal highway administrator advises the commissioner of transportation in writing that the provisions of this section shall not render Tennessee in violation of federal laws and regulations and subject to penalties prescribed therein.

(e) This section shall become operative only if the cost of the manufacture and installation of such signs is paid to the department of transportation from non-state funds

within one (1) year of the effective date of this act. Such payment shall be made prior to any expenditure by the state for the manufacture or installation of such signs. The department shall return any unused portion of the estimated cost to the person or entity paying for such signs within thirty (30) days of the erection of such signs. If the actual cost exceeds the estimated cost, an amount equal to the difference in such costs shall be remitted to the department in non-state funds within thirty (30) days of the sponsoring person or entity receiving an itemized invoice of the actual cost from the department.

SECTION 47. (a) Notwithstanding any provision of law to the contrary, the segment of State Route 297 (Newcomb Pike) in Campbell County from the intersection of such route's intersection with Old Oswego Road/Newcomb Park/Old Wooldridge Pike to such route's intersection with Whistle Creek Road is hereby designated the "Everett Douglas Straight" to honor the memory of this beloved resident of Newcomb, Tennessee.

(b) The department of transportation is directed to erect suitable signs or to affix suitable markers designating the segment of State Route 297 described in subsection (a) as the "Everett Douglas Straight".

(c) The erection of such signs shall be within the guidelines prescribed by the Manual on Uniform Traffic Control Devices.

(d) This section shall become operative only if the federal highway administrator advises the commissioner of transportation in writing that the provisions of this section shall not render Tennessee in violation of federal laws and regulations and subject to penalties prescribed therein.

(e) This section shall become operative only if the cost of the manufacture and installation of such signs is paid to the department of transportation from non-state funds within one (1) year of the effective date of this act. Such payment shall be made prior to any expenditure by the state for the manufacture or installation of such signs. The department shall return any unused portion of the estimated cost to the person or entity paying for such signs within thirty (30) days of the erection of such signs. If the actual cost exceeds the estimated cost, an amount equal to the difference in such costs shall be remitted to the department in non-state funds within thirty (30) days of the sponsoring person or entity receiving an itemized invoice of the actual cost from the department.

(f) The appellation "Everett Douglas Straight" provided for in this section is for honorary purposes only and nothing contained herein shall be construed as requiring the alteration of any address, or the governmental system for assigning addresses, in any county, municipality, or other governmental entity affected by this section.

SECTION 48. (a) Notwithstanding any provision of law to the contrary, the bridge spanning Swan Creek located at mile marker 20.63 on State Route 50 in Hickman County is hereby designated as the "J.W. Alderson and Thomas James Parham Memorial Bridge" to honor the memory of two distinguished residents of Hickman County who ably served their fellow citizens.

(b) The department of transportation is directed to erect suitable signs or affix suitable markers designating the bridge described in subsection (a) as the "J.W. Alderson and Thomas James Parham Memorial Bridge."

(c) The erection of signs shall be within the guidelines prescribed by the Manual on Uniform Traffic Control Devices.

(d) This section shall become operative only if the federal highway administrator advises the commissioner of transportation in writing that the provisions of this section shall not render Tennessee in violation of federal laws and regulations and subject to penalties prescribed therein.

(e) This section shall become operative only if the cost of the manufacture and installation of such signs is paid to the department of transportation from non-state funds within one (1) year of the effective date of this act. Such payment shall be made prior to any expenditure by the state for the manufacture or installation of such signs. The department shall return any unused portion of the estimated cost to the person or entity paying for such signs within thirty (30) days of the erection of such signs. If the actual cost exceeds the estimated cost, an amount equal to the difference in such costs shall be remitted to the department in non-state funds within thirty (30) days of the sponsoring person or entity receiving an itemized invoice of the actual cost from the department.

SECTION 49. (a) Notwithstanding any provision of law to the contrary, the segment of U.S. Highway 231/State Route 10 in Walter Hill, Tennessee, that lies in front of the Walter Hill School is hereby designated the "Chase Donnell Memorial Highway" to honor the memory of this beloved resident of the Walter Hill community and an energetic, tender-hearted young boy who passed away on March 10, 2008, after a courageous fight against cancer.

(b) The department of transportation is directed to erect suitable signs or to affix suitable markers designating the segment of U.S. Highway 231 described in subsection (a) as the "Chase Donnell Memorial Highway."

(c) The erection of such signs shall be within the guidelines prescribed by the Manual on Uniform Traffic Control Devices.

(d) This section shall become operative only if the federal highway administrator advises the commissioner of transportation in writing that the provisions of this section shall not render Tennessee in violation of federal laws and regulations and subject to penalties prescribed therein.

(e) This section shall become operative only if the cost of the manufacture and installation of such signs is paid to the department of transportation from non-state funds within one (1) year of the effective date of this act. Such payment shall be made prior to any expenditure by the state for the manufacture or installation of such signs. The department shall return any unused portion of the estimated cost to the person or entity paying for such signs within thirty (30) days of the erection of such signs. If the actual cost exceeds the estimated cost, an amount equal to the difference in such costs shall be remitted to the department in non-state funds within thirty (30) days of the sponsoring person or entity receiving an itemized invoice of the actual cost from the department.

(f) The appellation "Chase Donnell Memorial Highway" provided for in this section is for honorary purposes only and nothing contained herein shall be construed as requiring the alteration of any address, or the governmental system for assigning addresses, in any county, municipality, or other governmental entity affected by this section.

(g) Nothing in this section shall be construed as requiring the alteration of any previously named segments of U.S. Highway 231 described in subsection (a).

SECTION 50. (a) Notwithstanding any provision of law to the contrary, the segment of State Route 266 (Sam Ridley Parkway West) in Smyrna, Tennessee, from the interchange of Interstate 24 eastward to such route's intersection with Needham Drive is hereby designated the "Bob Spivey Highway" in honor of Bob Spivey, who ably served his fellow citizens as the Mayor of Smyrna from 2001 to 2009 and whose leadership was instrumental in Smyrna's continued population growth and retail development.

(b) The department of transportation is directed to erect suitable signs or to affix suitable markers designating the segment of State Route 266 described in subsection (a) as the "Bob Spivey Highway". Such signs or markers shall be erected so as to be visible to motorists in the eastbound and westbound lanes of State Route 266.

(c) The erection of such signs shall be within the guidelines prescribed by the Manual on Uniform Traffic Control Devices.

(d) This section shall become operative only if the federal highway administrator advises the commissioner of transportation in writing that the provisions of this section shall not render Tennessee in violation of federal laws and regulations and subject to penalties prescribed therein.

(e) This section shall become operative only if the cost of the manufacture and installation of such signs is paid to the department of transportation from non-state funds within one (1) year of the effective date of this act. Such payment shall be made prior to any expenditure by the state for the manufacture or installation of such signs. The department shall return any unused portion of the estimated cost to the person or entity paying for such signs within thirty (30) days of the erection of such signs. If the actual cost exceeds the estimated cost, an amount equal to the difference in such costs shall be remitted to the department in non-state funds within thirty (30) days of the sponsoring person or entity receiving an itemized invoice of the actual cost from the department.

(f) The appellation "Bob Spivey Highway" provided for in this section is for honorary purposes only and nothing contained herein shall be construed as requiring the alteration of any address, or the governmental system for assigning addresses, in any county, municipality, or other governmental entity affected by this section.

SECTION 51. (a) Notwithstanding any provision of law to the contrary, the segment of U.S. Highway 41/State Route 1 (South Lowry Street/New Nashville Highway) in Smyrna, Tennessee, from the interchange of State Route 840 to the northwestern edge of the Omni Hut restaurant is hereby designated the "Major James Walls Memorial Highway" as a lasting tribute to the late James Walls, who ably served his fellow residents of Smyrna, Tennessee, as the founder of the Omni Hut, a popular Polynesian restaurant that opened in 1960, and who courageously served his country during World War II.

(b) The department of transportation is directed to erect suitable signs or to affix suitable markers designating the segment of U.S. Highway 41 described in subsection (a) as the "Major James Walls Memorial Highway".

(c) The erection of such signs shall be within the guidelines prescribed by the Manual on Uniform Traffic Control Devices.

(d) This section shall become operative only if the federal highway administrator advises the commissioner of transportation in writing that the provisions of this section shall not render Tennessee in violation of federal laws and regulations and subject to penalties prescribed therein.

(e) This section shall become operative only if the cost of the manufacture and installation of such signs is paid to the department of transportation from non-state funds within one (1) year of the effective date of this act. Such payment shall be made prior to any expenditure by the state for the manufacture or installation of such signs. The department shall return any unused portion of the estimated cost to the person or entity paying for such signs within thirty (30) days of the erection of such signs. If the actual cost exceeds the estimated cost, an amount equal to the difference in such costs shall be remitted to the department in non-state funds within thirty (30) days of the sponsoring person or entity receiving an itemized invoice of the actual cost from the department.

(f) The appellation "Major James Walls Memorial Highway" provided for in this section is for honorary purposes only and nothing contained herein shall be construed as requiring the alteration of any address, or the governmental system for assigning addresses, in any county, municipality, or other governmental entity affected by this section.

(g) Nothing in this section shall be construed as requiring the alteration of any previously named segments of U.S. Highway 41 described in subsection (a).

SECTION 52. (a) Notwithstanding any provision of law to the contrary, the segment of State Route 266 (Jefferson Pike) in Smyrna, Tennessee, from such route's intersection with Gills Street eastward to the eastern edge of the property located at 7931 West Jefferson Pike is hereby designated the "Ernie Johns Highway" in appreciation of this accomplished resident of Smyrna, Tennessee, who ably served his fellow citizens as Rutherford County Historian since 1982 and who currently serves as Rutherford County Historian Emeritus.

(b) The department of transportation is directed to erect suitable signs or to affix suitable markers designating the segment of State Route 266 described in subsection (a) as the "Ernie Johns Highway".

(c) The erection of such signs shall be within the guidelines prescribed by the Manual on Uniform Traffic Control Devices.

(d) This section shall become operative only if the federal highway administrator advises the commissioner of transportation in writing that the provisions of this section shall not render Tennessee in violation of federal laws and regulations and subject to penalties prescribed therein.

(e) This section shall become operative only if the cost of the manufacture and installation of such signs is paid to the department of transportation from non-state funds within one (1) year of the effective date of this act. Such payment shall be made prior to any expenditure by the state for the manufacture or installation of such signs. The department shall return any unused portion of the estimated cost to the person or entity paying for such signs within thirty (30) days of the erection of such signs. If the actual cost exceeds the estimated cost, an amount equal to the difference in such costs shall be remitted to the department in non-state funds within thirty (30) days of the sponsoring person or entity receiving an itemized invoice of the actual cost from the department.

(f) The appellation "Ernie Johns Highway" provided for in this section is for honorary purposes only and nothing contained herein shall be construed as requiring the alteration of any address, or the governmental system for assigning addresses, in any county, municipality, or other governmental entity affected by this section.

(g) Nothing in this section shall be construed as requiring the alteration of any previously named segments of State Route 266 described in subsection (a).

SECTION 53. (a) Notwithstanding any provision of law to the contrary, the bridge on State Route 102 near Smyrna High School in Smyrna, Tennessee, is hereby designated the "Mark David Fields Memorial Bridge" to honor the memory of this beloved resident of Smyrna.

(b) The department of transportation is directed to erect suitable signs or to affix suitable markers designating the bridge described in subsection (a) as the "Mark David Fields Memorial Bridge".

(c) The erection of such signs shall be within the guidelines prescribed by the Manual on Uniform Traffic Control Devices.

(d) This section shall become operative only if the federal highway administrator advises the commissioner of transportation in writing that the provisions of this section shall not render Tennessee in violation of federal laws and regulations and subject to penalties prescribed therein.

(e) This section shall become operative only if the cost of the manufacture and installation of such signs is paid to the department of transportation from non-state funds within one (1) year of the effective date of this act. Such payment shall be made prior to any expenditure by the state for the manufacture or installation of such signs. The department shall return any unused portion of the estimated cost to the person or entity paying for such signs within thirty (30) days of the erection of such signs. If the actual cost exceeds the estimated cost, an amount equal to the difference in such costs shall be remitted to the department in non-state funds within thirty (30) days of the sponsoring person or entity receiving an itemized invoice of the actual cost from the department.

SECTION 54. (a) Notwithstanding any provision of law to the contrary, the bridge on State Route 101 between mile marker 6 and 7 in Bledsoe County is hereby designated the "Leo Smith Bridge" in honor of one of Bledsoe County's best assets.

(b) The department of transportation is directed to erect suitable signs or to affix suitable markers designating the bridge described in subsection (a) as the "Leo Smith Bridge".

(c) The erection of such signs shall be within the guidelines prescribed by the Manual on Uniform Traffic Control Devices.

(d) This section shall become operative only if the federal highway administrator advises the commissioner of transportation in writing that the provisions of this section shall not render Tennessee in violation of federal laws and regulations and subject to penalties prescribed therein.

(e) This section shall become operative only if the cost of the manufacture and installation of such signs is paid to the department of transportation from non-state funds within one (1) year of the effective date of this act. Such payment shall be made prior to any expenditure by the state for the manufacture or installation of such signs. The department shall return any unused portion of the estimated cost to the person or entity paying for such signs within thirty (30) days of the erection of such signs. If the actual cost exceeds the estimated cost, an amount equal to the difference in such costs shall be remitted to the department in non-state funds within thirty (30) days of the sponsoring person or entity receiving an itemized invoice of the actual cost from the department.

SECTION 55. (a) Notwithstanding any provision of law to the contrary, the bridge spanning White Oak Creek in the town of Sunbright, Tennessee, is hereby designated the "Dudley Freels Memorial Bridge" to honor the memory of Dudley Freels, who served the Sunbright community with distinction as the Fire Chief of the Sunbright Volunteer Fire Department and who was a dedicated public servant for Morgan County as a county commissioner.

(b) The department of transportation is directed to erect suitable signs or to affix suitable markers designating the bridge described in subsection (a) as the "Dudley Freels Memorial Bridge".

(c) The erection of such signs shall be within the guidelines prescribed by the Manual on Uniform Traffic Control Devices.

(d) This section shall become operative only if the federal highway administrator advises the commissioner of transportation in writing that the provisions of this section shall not render Tennessee in violation of federal laws and regulations and subject to penalties prescribed therein.

(e) This section shall become operative only if the cost of the manufacture and installation of such signs is paid to the department of transportation from non-state funds within one (1) year of the effective date of this act. Such payment shall be made prior to any expenditure by the state for the manufacture or installation of such signs. The department shall return any unused portion of the estimated cost to the person or entity paying for such signs within thirty (30) days of the erection of such signs. If the actual cost exceeds the estimated cost, an amount equal to the difference in such costs shall be remitted to the department in non-state funds within thirty (30) days of the sponsoring person or entity receiving an itemized invoice of the actual cost from the department.

SECTION 56. (a) Notwithstanding any provision of law to the contrary, the bridge on State Route 96 (Lascassas Pike) between Greystone Drive and Browns Mill Road in Rutherford County is hereby designated the "PFC William H. Martin, Jr. Bridge" in honor of William H. Martin, Jr., one of Rutherford County's best assets who courageously served his country during World War II.

(b) The department of transportation is directed to erect and maintain two (2) signs designating the bridge described in subsection (a). Such signs shall be erected and placed vertically. The top sign shall bear the language "Martin Branch". The bottom sign shall bear the following language in substantially the same format:

PFC William H. Martin, Jr. Bridge

World War II

(c) The erection of such signs shall be within the guidelines prescribed by the Manual on Uniform Traffic Control Devices.

(d) This section shall become operative only if the federal highway administrator advises the commissioner of transportation in writing that the provisions of this section shall not render Tennessee in violation of federal laws and regulations and subject to penalties prescribed therein.

(e) This section shall become operative only if the cost of the manufacture and installation of such signs is paid to the department of transportation from non-state funds within one (1) year of the effective date of this act. Such payment shall be made prior to any expenditure by the state for the manufacture or installation of such signs. The department shall return any unused portion of the estimated cost to the person or entity paying for such signs within thirty (30) days of the erection of such signs. If the actual cost exceeds the estimated cost, an amount equal to the difference in such costs shall be remitted to the department in non-state funds within thirty (30) days of the sponsoring person or entity receiving an itemized invoice of the actual cost from the department.

SECTION 57. A presentation copy or copies of this act, or pertinent sections thereof, shall be made available to members of the general assembly upon their request to the appropriate clerk's office.

Effective date 5/20/2013

SECTION 58. This act shall take effect upon becoming a law, the public welfare requiring it.

PUBLIC CHAPTER NO. 483

PUBLIC CHAPTER NO. 483

SENATE BILL NO. 36

By Overbey, Finney, Bowling, Crowe, Green, Dickerson, Massey, Burks, Harper, Ketron, Norris, Tate

Substituted for: House Bill No. 21

By Ramsey, Jernigan, Casada, Harry Brooks, Pitts, Mark White, Moody, Kane, Hardaway, Eldridge, Kevin Brooks, Evans

AN ACT to amend Tennessee Code Annotated, Title 49, Chapter 4, Part 9, relative to postsecondary financial assistance from net lottery proceeds for students with intellectual disabilities.

BE IT ENACTED BY THE GENERAL ASSEMBLY OF THE STATE OF TENNESSEE:

49-4-942 SECTION 1. Tennessee Code Annotated, Title 49, Chapter 4, Part 9, is amended by adding the following language as a new, appropriately designated section:

49-4-9__.

(a) As used in this section, an "eligible postsecondary program" means a postsecondary program recognized by the Postsecondary Educational Alliance and offered by an eligible postsecondary institution that assists students with intellectual disabilities, as defined in § 33-1-101, who have completed high school, but who need a strong system of education supports and services to access and obtain postsecondary education. To be an eligible postsecondary program, a program shall consist of a two-year individualized program of study designed to provide meaningful postsecondary activities, including academic, career development and exploration and independent living skills, on the postsecondary campus.

(b) To be eligible for a Tennessee STEP UP scholarship, a student with a documented intellectual disability shall:

(1) Not be ineligible for the scholarship under § 49-4-904;

(2) Have been a Tennessee resident, as defined by regulations promulgated by the board of regents under § 49-8-104, for one (1) year immediately preceding the date of application for a scholarship or the renewal of a scholarship;

(3) Complete high school in a Tennessee high school in accordance with the requirements of the student's individualized education program (IEP) and receive a high school diploma or certificate, a special education diploma, a transition certificate or an IEP certificate;

(4) Be admitted to and enroll in an eligible postsecondary institution in an eligible postsecondary program no later than sixteen (16) months after completing high school; and

(5) Apply for a Tennessee STEP UP scholarship.

(c)(1) To continue to be eligible for a Tennessee STEP UP scholarship, a student shall:

(A) Maintain continual enrollment in the eligible postsecondary program as defined by the eligible postsecondary institution; and

(B) Make satisfactory academic progress in the student's program of study as determined by the eligible postsecondary institution.

(2) If a student ceases to be eligible for the Tennessee STEP UP scholarship at any time for any reason, then the student shall not be able to regain the scholarship.

(d)(1) A student may receive a Tennessee STEP UP scholarship under this section until the first of the following events:

(A) The student receives a credential signifying completion of the eligible postsecondary program; or

(B) Two (2) years have passed from the date of the student's initial enrollment in the eligible postsecondary program.

(2) A Tennessee STEP UP scholarship student who has an approved medical or personal leave of absence from an eligible postsecondary program may continue to receive the scholarship upon resuming the student's education in the eligible postsecondary program; provided, that the student continues to meet all applicable eligibility requirements. A student who takes an approved leave of absence shall be eligible for the scholarship until the first of the following events:

(A) The student has received a credential signifying completion of the eligible postsecondary program; or

(B) The sum of the number of years that the student attended the eligible postsecondary program prior to the leave of absence and the number of years of attendance after the leave of absence equals two (2) years.

(e) Subject to the amounts appropriated by the general assembly and any law relating to a shortfall in funds available for postsecondary financial assistance from the net proceeds of the state lottery, the amount of a Tennessee STEP UP scholarship shall be the same as the amount of a Tennessee HOPE scholarship awarded under § 49-4-914(a) to students attending eligible four-year postsecondary institutions.

(f) If the sum of all financial aid, including a Tennessee STEP UP scholarship, for which a student qualifies exceeds the institutionally defined total cost of education at the eligible postsecondary institution the scholarship recipient is attending, then the student's Tennessee STEP UP scholarship shall be reduced so that the financial aid actually received by the student does not exceed the institutionally defined total cost of education.

Effective date 5/20/2013

SECTION 2. This act shall take effect upon becoming law, the public welfare requiring it, and shall apply to students initially entering eligible postsecondary programs in the 2013-2014 academic year and academic years thereafter.

PUBLIC CHAPTER NO. 484

PUBLIC CHAPTER NO. 484

SENATE BILL NO. 23

By Tracy, Beavers

Substituted for: House Bill No. 1029

By Dean, Hardaway

AN ACT to amend Tennessee Code Annotated, Title 55, Chapter 4, relative to special license plates.

BE IT ENACTED BY THE GENERAL ASSEMBLY OF THE STATE OF TENNESSEE:

55-4-202 SECTION 1. Tennessee Code Annotated, Section 55-4-202(c)(7), is amended by adding the following as a new, appropriately designated subdivision:

( ) Concerned Motorcyclists of Tennessee/American Bikers Active Towards Education;

55-4-246 SECTION 2. Tennessee Code Annotated, Title 55, Chapter 4, Part 2, is amended by adding the following as a new, appropriately designated section:

(a) An owner or lessee of a motor vehicle who is a resident of this state upon complying with state motor vehicle laws relating to registration and licensing of motor vehicles and paying the regular fee applicable to the motor vehicle and the fee provided in § 55-4-203, shall be issued a Concerned Motorcyclists of Tennessee/American Bikers Active Towards Education new specialty earmarked license plate for a motor vehicle authorized by § 55-4-210(c).

(b) The new specialty earmarked license plates shall contain the official Concerned Motorcyclists of Tennessee/American Bikers Active Towards Education, Inc., ("C.M.T./A.B.A.T.E.") logo "dyin 2b seen" or other appropriate design representative of C.M.T./A.B.A.T.E. and shall be designed in consultation with C.M.T./A.B.A.T.E.

(c) The funds produced from the sale of the Concerned Motorcyclists of Tennessee/American Bikers Towards Education new specialty earmarked license plates shall be allocated to C.M.T./A.B.A.T.E., in accordance with § 55-4-215. The funds shall be used to assist motorcyclists involved in accidents caused by uninsured motorists with cost of living expenses while the motorcyclists are unable to work. The Board of Trustees of C.M.T./A.B.A.T.E., as appointed by the board of directors, shall administer the collection and disposition of the funds allocated pursuant to this section.

(d) Subject to the requirements of § 55-4-201, the commissioner is authorized and shall issue a license plate to an owner or lessee of a motorcycle who is otherwise eligible for a Concerned Motorcyclists of Tennessee/American Bikers Towards Education plate under this section; provided, however, that the owner or lessee shall comply with the state motor vehicle laws relating to registration and licensing of motorcycles and shall pay the regular fee applicable to motorcycles and the applicable fee specified in § 55-4-203 prior to the issuance of the plate. The motorcycle plates authorized by this subsection shall be substantially the same in design and configuration, allowing for variations due to size restrictions, as the regular motor vehicle registration plates authorized by § 55-4-202(c)(7), as applicable.

(e) For the purposes of § 55-4-201(h)(1), all license plates authorized or issued pursuant to subsections (a) and (d) shall be included jointly in any determinations for initial issuance and continuation of issuance.

55-4-202 SECTION 3. Tennessee Code Annotated, Section 55-4-202(c)(7), is amended by adding the following as a new, appropriately designated subdivision:

( ) Tennessee Tech University;

55-4-254 SECTION 4. Tennessee Code Annotated, Title 55, Chapter 4, is amended by adding the following as a new, appropriately designated section:

55-4-___.

(a) An owner or lessee of a motor vehicle who is a resident of this state, upon complying with state motor vehicle laws relating to registration and licensing of motor vehicles and paying the regular fee applicable to the motor vehicle and the fee provided for in § 55-4-203, shall be issued a Tennessee Tech University new specialty earmarked license plate for a motor vehicle authorized by § 55-4-210(c).

(b) The new specialty earmarked plates provided for in this section shall contain the official colors and Athletic Eagle Head logo of Tennessee Tech University and shall include language referencing the university's Centennial Celebration in an appropriate design. Such plates shall be designed in consultation with a representative from Tennessee Tech University's Creative Services division.

(c) The funds produced from the sale of such new specialty earmarked license plates shall be allocated to the Tennessee Tech University Foundation in accordance with § 55-4-215 to be used to support initiatives that directly relate to the goals established by the Complete College Act of 2010.

55-4-202 SECTION 5. Tennessee Code Annotated, Section 55-4-202(c)(7), is amended by adding the following as a new, appropriately designated subdivision:

( ) Alpha Eta Rho International Aviation Fraternity;

55-4-282 SECTION 6. Tennessee Code Annotated, Title 55, Chapter 4, is amended by adding the following as a new, appropriately designated section:

55-4-___.

(a) An owner or lessee of a motor vehicle who is a resident of this state and who is certified as a member or alumni member of the Alpha Eta Rho International Aviation Fraternity, upon complying with state motor vehicle laws relating to registration and licensing of motor vehicles and paying the regular fee applicable to the motor vehicle and the fee provided for in § 55-4-203, shall be issued an Alpha Eta Rho International Aviation Fraternity new specialty earmarked license plate for a motor vehicle authorized by § 55-4-210(c).

(b) The application for these license plates shall be accompanied by proof satisfactory to the commissioner, certifying the applicant to be a member or alumni member of the fraternity pursuant to subsection (a).

(c) The new specialty earmarked license plates provided for in this section shall contain an appropriate logo or other design representative of the Alpha Eta Rho International Aviation Fraternity. The plates shall be designed in consultation with the board of directors of the Alpha Eta Rho Foundation.

(d) The funds produced from the sale of Alpha Eta Rho International Aviation Fraternity new specialty earmarked license plates shall be allocated to the Alpha Eta Rho Foundation pursuant to § 55-4-215, for distribution to the Tennessee chapters of the fraternity. The funds shall be used to further the fraternity's educational goals for the future of collegiate aviation in Tennessee, including supporting educational and scholarship programs.

55-4-202 SECTION 7. Tennessee Code Annotated, Section 55-4-202(c)(7), is amended by adding the following as a new, appropriately designated subdivision:

( ) Vanderbilt University Athletic Department;

55-4-283 SECTION 8. Tennessee Code Annotated, Title 55, Chapter 4, is amended by adding the following as a new, appropriately designated section:

55-4-___.

(a) An owner or lessee of a motor vehicle who is a resident of Tennessee, upon complying with state motor vehicle laws relating to registration and licensing of motor vehicles and paying the regular fee applicable to the motor vehicle and the fee provided for in § 55-4-203, shall be issued a Vanderbilt University Athletic Department new specialty earmarked license plate for a motor vehicle authorized by § 55-4-210(c).

(b) The new specialty earmarked license plates provided for in this section shall be designed in consultation with the Vanderbilt University Board of Trust.

(c) The funds produced from the sale of Vanderbilt University Athletic Department new specialty earmarked license plates shall be allocated to the Vanderbilt University Board of Trust, in accordance with § 55-4-215, for distribution to the Vanderbilt University Athletic Department. The funds shall be used exclusively to fund scholarships for student athletes at Vanderbilt University.

55-4-202 SECTION 9. Tennessee Code Annotated, Section 55-4-202(c)(7), is amended by adding the following as a new, appropriately designated subdivision:

( ) Northwest Tennessee Disaster Services;

55-4-284 SECTION 10. Tennessee Code Annotated, Title 55, Chapter 4, is amended by adding the following as a new, appropriately designated section:

55-4-___.

(a) Owners or lessees of motor vehicles who are residents of Tennessee, upon complying with state motor vehicle laws relating to registration and licensing of motor vehicles and paying the regular fee applicable to the motor vehicle and the fee provided for in § 55-4-203, shall be issued a Northwest Tennessee Disaster Services new specialty earmarked license plate for a motor vehicle authorized by § 55-4-210(c).

(b) The new specialty earmarked license plates provided for in this section shall be designed with the assistance of Northwest Tennessee Disaster Services.

(c) The funds produced from the sale of Northwest Tennessee Disaster Services new specialty earmarked license plates pursuant to § 55-4-215 shall be allocated to Northwest Tennessee Disaster Services for the sole purpose of disaster relief efforts.

55-4-248 SECTION 11. Tennessee Code Annotated, Section 55-4-248, is amended by adding the following as a new subsection (f):

(f) Upon the death of the spouse who was entitled to receive the Masons new specialty earmarked license plate, the widow shall be entitled to receive a Masons new specialty earmarked license plate for a motor vehicle owned or leased by such widow, upon complying with state motor vehicle laws relating to registration and licensing of motor vehicles and paying the regular fee applicable to the motor vehicle and the fee provided for in § 55-4-203. The application shall be accompanied by a copy of the death certificate.

55-4-202 SECTION 12. Tennessee Code Annotated, Section 55-4-202(c)(7), is amended by adding the following as a new, appropriately designated subdivision:

( ) Suicide Prevention;

55-4-285 SECTION 13. Tennessee Code Annotated, Title 55, Chapter 4, is amended by adding the following as a new, appropriately designated section:

55-4-___.

(a) Owners or lessees of motor vehicles who are residents of Tennessee, upon complying with state motor vehicle laws relating to registration and licensing of motor vehicles and paying the regular fee applicable to the motor vehicle and the fee provided for in § 55-4-203, shall be issued a Suicide Prevention new specialty earmarked license plate for a motor vehicle authorized by § 55-4-210(c).

(b) The new specialty earmarked license plates provided for in this section shall contain an appropriate logo or other design representative of the Tennessee Suicide Prevention Network (TSPN) and the Jason Foundation. The plates shall be designed in consultation with the executive director of the Tennessee Suicide Prevention Network (TSPN) and the president of the Jason Foundation.

(c) The funds produced from the sale of Suicide Prevention new specialty earmarked license plates pursuant to § 55-4-215 shall be allocated to the Tennessee Suicide Prevention Network (TSPN) for the sole purpose of promoting the cause of suicide prevention in this state. The funds shall be used to further TSPN's awareness and education efforts in this state, including, but not limited to, local suicide prevention training sessions, support groups, debriefing sessions, and statewide awareness campaigns.

55-4-202 SECTION 14. Tennessee Code Annotated, Section 55-4-202(c)(7), is amended by adding the following as a new, appropriately designated subdivision:

( ) Safe Schools;

55-4-289 SECTION 15. Tennessee Code Annotated, Title 55, Chapter 4, is amended by adding the following as a new, appropriately designated section:

55-4-___.

(a) An owner or lessee of a motor vehicle who is a resident of this state, upon complying with state motor vehicle laws relating to registration and licensing of motor vehicles and paying the regular fee applicable to the motor vehicle and the fee provided for in § 55-4-203, shall be issued a Safe Schools new specialty earmarked license plate for a motor vehicle authorized by § 55-4-210(c).

(b) The new specialty earmarked license plates provided for in this section shall contain the logo "Safe Schools" and shall be designed in consultation with the department of education.

(c) There is created a special account within the general fund to be known as the "school safety account," referred to in this section as the "account". The funds produced from the sale of Safe Schools new specialty earmarked license plates shall be allocated to the department of education and deposited in the account. Amounts remaining in the account at the end of each fiscal year shall not revert to the general fund. Money in the account shall be invested by the state treasurer pursuant to title 9, chapter 4, part 6 for the sole benefit of the account. All earnings attributable to such investments shall be credited to the account.

(d) The owners or lessees of motor vehicles who obtain new specialty earmarked license plates pursuant to this section may designate that the proceeds from the fees shall be allocated to a particular named school. The department of education shall remit the proceeds to the local education agency operating the named school, and the local school board shall allocate the proceeds for the benefit of the named school, and shall make the funds available to the school. Any undesignated proceeds from the fees shall be distributed to the local education agency according to the average daily attendance of schools which serve the counties in which the proceeds were generated.

(e) The funds shall be used solely for implementing safety upgrades at schools, hiring school resource officers, improving school security, and providing resources for school safety plans and teams.

55-4-202 SECTION 16. Tennessee Code Annotated, Section 55-4-202(c)(7), is amended by adding the following as a new, appropriately designated subdivision:

( ) Harpeth River Watershed Association;

55-4-297 SECTION 17. Tennessee Code Annotated, Title 55, Chapter 4, Part 2, is amended by adding the following as a new, appropriately designated section:

(a) An owner or lessee of a motor vehicle who is a resident of this state upon complying with state motor vehicle laws relating to registration and licensing of motor vehicles and paying the regular fee applicable to the motor vehicle and the fee provided in § 55-4-203, shall be issued a Harpeth River Watershed Association new specialty earmarked license plate for a motor vehicle authorized by § 55-4-210(c).

(b) The new specialty earmarked license plates shall be of an appropriate design representative of the Harpeth River Watershed Association. The plates shall be designed in consultation with the Harpeth River Watershed Association.

(c) The funds produced from the sale of the Harpeth River Watershed Association new specialty earmarked license plates shall be allocated to the Harpeth River Watershed Association, in accordance with § 55-4-215. The funds shall be used for restoring and protecting the ecological health of the Harpeth River and clean water in Tennessee.

(d) Notwithstanding § 55-4-201(h)(1), the Harpeth River Watershed Association new specialty earmarked license plates authorized by this section shall have two (2) years from the effective date of this act or until July 1, 2015, whichever is later, to meet applicable initial issuance requirements of § 55-4-201(h)(1).

(e) Section 55-4-201(f) shall not apply to the new specialty earmarked license plate authorized by this section.

55-4-301 SECTION 18. Tennessee Code Annotated, Title 55, Chapter 4, Part 2, is amended by adding the following as a new, appropriately designated section:

(a) An owner or lessee of a motor vehicle who is a resident of this state, upon complying with state motor vehicle laws relating to registration and licensing of motor vehicles and paying the regular fee applicable to the motor vehicle and the fee provided for in § 55-4-203, shall be issued a Juvenile Diabetes Research Foundation new specialty earmarked license plate for a motor vehicle authorized by § 55-4-210(c).

(b) The new specialty earmarked license plates shall contain the logo or other appropriate design representative of the Juvenile Diabetes Research Foundation. The plates shall be designed in consultation with the executive officers of the Juvenile Diabetes Research Foundation.

(c) In accordance with § 55-4-215, the funds produced from the sale of the Juvenile Diabetes Research Foundation new specialty earmarked license plates shall be allocated to the Juvenile Diabetes Research Foundation, a leading global organization focused on type 1 diabetes research.

55-4-202 SECTION 20. Tennessee Code Annotated, Section 55-4-202(c)(7), is amended by adding the following as a new, appropriately designated subdivision:

( ) Tennessee Theatre;

55-4-303 SECTION 21. Tennessee Code Annotated, Title 55, Chapter 4, Part 2, is amended by adding the following as a new, appropriately designated section:

(a) An owner or lessee of a motor vehicle who is a resident of this state upon complying with state motor vehicle laws relating to registration and licensing of motor vehicles and paying the regular fee applicable to the motor vehicle and the fee provided in § 55-4-203, shall be issued a Tennessee Theatre new specialty earmarked license plate for a motor vehicle authorized by § 55-4-210(c).

(b) The new specialty earmarked license plates shall be of an appropriate design representative of the Tennessee Theatre. The plates shall be designed in consultation with the Tennessee Theatre.

(c) The funds produced from the sale of the Tennessee Theatre new specialty earmarked license plates shall be allocated to the Tennessee Theatre, in accordance with § 55-4-215. Such funds shall be used exclusively to benefit and further the goals of the Tennessee Theatre.

55-4-202 SECTION 22. Tennessee Code Annotated, Section 55-4-202(c)(7), is amended by adding the following as a new, appropriately designated subdivision:

( ) Adoption;

55-4-304 SECTION 23. Tennessee Code Annotated, Title 55, Chapter 4, Part 2, is amended by adding the following as a new, appropriately designated section:

(a) An owner or lessee of a motor vehicle who is a resident of Tennessee, upon complying with state motor vehicle laws relating to registration and licensing of motor vehicles and paying the regular fee applicable to the motor vehicle and the fee provided for in § 55-4-203, shall be issued a new specialty earmarked license plate for a motor vehicle authorized by § 55-4-210(c), to recognize and encourage the compassionate practice of adoption.

(b) The new specialty earmarked license plates provided for in this section shall be designed to recognize the benevolent aspects of adoption. Such plates shall be designed in consultation with distinguished adoption entities.

(c) The funds produced from the sale of such new specialty earmarked license plates shall be allocated equally to the Adoption Foundation of Tennessee, Inc., and Harmony Adoptions of Tennessee, Inc., in accordance with § 55-4-215. Such funds shall be used exclusively to facilitate adoption in Tennessee.

(d) Section 55-4-201(f) shall not apply to the new specialty earmarked license plate authorized by this section.

55-4-202 SECTION 24. Tennessee Code Annotated, Section 55-4-202(c)(7), is amended by adding the following as a new, appropriately designated subdivision:

( ) Sons of the American Revolution;

55-4-305 SECTION 25. Tennessee Code Annotated, Title 55, Chapter 4, Part 2, is amended by adding the following as a new, appropriately designated section:

(a) An owner or lessee of a motor vehicle who is a resident of this state, upon complying with state motor vehicle laws relating to registration and licensing of motor vehicles and paying the regular fee applicable to the motor vehicle and the fee provided in § 55-4-203, shall be issued a Sons of the American Revolution new specialty earmarked license plate for a motor vehicle authorized by § 55-4-210(c).

(b) The new specialty earmarked license plates shall be of an appropriate design representative of the Gadsden flag, and shall include the language "Don't Tread on Me." Such plates shall be designed in consultation with the executive officers of the Tennessee Society of the Sons of the American Revolution.

(c) The funds produced from the sale of Sons of the American Revolution new specialty earmarked license plates shall be allocated to the Tennessee Society of the Sons of the American Revolution, in accordance with § 55-4-215. The funds shall be used to promote the activities of the Tennessee Society of the Sons of the American Revolution, to include youth programs and patriot grave identification, location, documentation and marking.

55-4-306 SECTION 26. Tennessee Code Annotated, Section 55-4-306, is amended by deleting subsections (c) and (d) in their entirety and by substituting instead the following:

(c) The funds produced from the sale of Choose Life new specialty earmarked license plates shall be allocated to New Life Resources in accordance with § 55-4-215. New Life Resources is a 501(c)(3) nonprofit organization incorporated in 1995 to provide resources for women and families facing difficult or unexpected pregnancies. The funds shall be used exclusively for counseling and financial assistance, including food, clothing, and medical assistance for pregnant women in Tennessee; coordinating statewide awareness campaigns and a toll-free helpline; and reimbursing social service providers who prepare adoptions throughout the state for services and programs targeting at-risk women and families.

55-4-253 SECTION 27. Tennessee Code Annotated, Section 55-4-253, is amended by deleting subsections (a) and (b) in their entirety and by substituting instead the following language:

(a) An owner or lessee of a motor vehicle who is a resident of this state and who is an honorably discharged veteran of the United States armed forces, or a civilian veteran of the United States army corps of engineers, upon complying with state motor vehicle laws relating to registration and licensing of motor vehicles and upon paying the regular fee applicable to the motor vehicle and the fee provided in § 55-4-203, shall be issued an honorably discharged veteran registration plate for a motor vehicle authorized by § 55-4-210(c). A surviving spouse of such a deceased honorably discharged veteran, upon complying with state motor vehicle laws relating to registration and licensing of motor vehicles, upon paying the regular fee applicable to the vehicle and the fee prescribed by § 55-4-203, and upon providing a copy of the death certificate of the deceased honorably discharged veteran, shall be issued a registration plate pursuant to this section, until the surviving spouse remarries.

(b) All applications pursuant to this section shall be accompanied by orders or a statement of discharge from the appropriate branch of the United States armed forces classifying the applicant as an honorably discharged veteran, or by orders or official documentation from the United States army corps of engineers classifying the applicant as a civilian veteran; provided, that, notwithstanding any law to the contrary, an honorably discharged veteran of the United States armed forces or a surviving spouse of an honorably discharged veteran of the United States armed forces shall be required to submit the required documentation only when initially applying for registration plates under this section and subsequent registration plates under this section shall be issued to that person without the repeated presentation of the required documentation. This subsection (b) shall not apply in the case of an application by a surviving spouse in which the deceased honorably discharged veteran had been issued a license plate or license plates under this section.

55-4-374 SECTION 28. Tennessee Code Annotated, Section 55-4-374, is amended by adding the following new subsection:

(d) Notwithstanding § 55-4-201(h)(1), the Tennessee Federation of Garden Clubs new specialty earmarked license plates authorized pursuant to this section shall have one (1) year from the effective date of this act or until July 1, 2014, whichever is later, to meet the applicable minimum issuance requirements of § 55-4-201(h)(1).

55-4-365 SECTION 29. Tennessee Code Annotated, Section 55-4-365, is amended by adding the following language as a new, appropriately designated subsection:

( ) Notwithstanding § 55-4-201(h)(1), the Autism Awareness new specialty earmarked license plates authorized pursuant to this section shall have one (1) year from the effective date of this act or until July 1, 2014, whichever is later, to meet the applicable minimum issuance requirements of § 55-4-201(h)(1).

55-4-368 SECTION 30. Tennessee Code Annotated, Section 55-4-368, is amended by adding the following language as a new, appropriately designated subsection:

( ) Notwithstanding § 55-4-201(h)(1), the "I RECYCLE" new specialty earmarked license plates authorized pursuant to this section shall have one (1) year from the effective date of this act or until July 1, 2014, whichever is later, to meet the applicable minimum issuance requirements of § 55-4-201(h)(1).

55-4-361 SECTION 31. Tennessee Code Annotated, Section 55-4-361, is amended by adding the following language as a new subsection (d):

(d) Notwithstanding the time limitations of § 55-4-201(h)(1), the Almost Home Animal Rescue new specialty earmarked license plates authorized by this section shall have until July 1, 2014, to meet the applicable minimum issuance requirements of § 55-4-201(h)(1).

55-4-358 SECTION 32. Tennessee Code Annotated, Section 55-4-358, is amended by adding the following language as a new subsection (d):

(d) Notwithstanding § 55-4-201(h)(1), the Tennessee Tennis new specialty earmarked license plate for a motor vehicle authorized by this section shall have one (1) year from the effective date of this act or until July 1, 2014, whichever is later, to meet the applicable minimum issuance requirements of § 55-4-201(h)(1).

55-4-360 SECTION 33. Tennessee Code Annotated, Section 55-4-360, is amended by adding the following language as a new, appropriately designated subsection:

( ) Notwithstanding § 55-4-201(h)(1), the East Tennessee Children's Hospital new specialty earmarked license plates authorized pursuant to this section shall have one (1) year from the effective date of this act or until July 1, 2014, whichever is later, to meet the applicable minimum issuance requirements of § 55-4-201(h)(1).

55-4-313 SECTION 34. Tennessee Code Annotated, Section 55-4-313(f), is amended by deleting the language "July 1, 2013," and by substituting instead the language "July 1, 2014,".

55-4-347 SECTION 35. Tennessee Code Annotated, Section 55-4-347, is amended by deleting subsection (d) in its entirety and by substituting instead the following language:

(d) Notwithstanding § 55-4-201(h)(1), the Historic Collierville new specialty earmarked license plates authorized pursuant to this section shall have one (1) year from the effective date of this act or until July 1, 2014, whichever is later, to meet the applicable minimum issuance requirements of § 55-4-201(h)(1).

55-4-347 SECTION 36. If any provision of this act or the application thereof to any person or circumstance is held invalid, such invalidity shall not affect other provisions or applications of the act which can be given effect without the invalid provision or application, and to that end the provisions of this act are declared to be severable.

Effective date 7/1/2013 SECTION 37. Sections 28 through 35 of this act shall take effect upon becoming a law, the public welfare requiring it. All remaining sections of this act shall take effect July 1, 2013, the public welfare requiring it.

PUBLIC CHAPTER NO. 485

PUBLIC CHAPTER NO. 485

SENATE BILL NO. 1032

By Kelsey, Ford, Crowe, Beavers, Burks

Substituted for: House Bill No. 520

By Watson, Coley, Hardaway, Parkinson, Rogers, Littleton, Moody, Weaver, Camper, Jones, Lamberth

AN ACT to amend Tennessee Code Annotated, Title 39 and Title 40, relative to commercial sex acts.

BE IT ENACTED BY THE GENERAL ASSEMBLY OF THE STATE OF TENNESSEE:

39-13-515 SECTION 1. Tennessee Code Annotated, Section 39-13-515, is amended by deleting the section in its entirety and by substituting instead the following:

(a) A person commits an offense under this section who promotes prostitution.

(b) Except as provided in subsection (c), promoting prostitution is a Class E felony.

(c) Promoting prostitution of a minor is punishable as trafficking for a commercial sex act under § 39-13-309.

Effective date 7/1/2013 SECTION 2. This act shall take effect July 1, 2013, the public welfare requiring it.

Index

B

F

I

J

K

M

S

T

Y